Real-Time Data Analysis Exercises

Up-to-date macro data is a great way to engage in and understand the usefulness of macro variables and their impact on the economy. Real-Time Data Analysis exercises communicate directly with the Federal Reserve Bank of St. Louis's FRED® site, so every time FRED posts new data, students see new data.

End-of-chapter exercises accompanied by the Real-Time Data Analysis icon  include Real-Time Data versions in **MyEconLab**.

Select in-text figures labeled **MyEconLab** Real-Time Data update in the electronic version of the text using FRED data.

Current News Exercises

Posted weekly, we find the latest microeconomic and macroeconomic news stories, post them, and write auto-graded multi-part exercises that illustrate the economic way of thinking about the news.

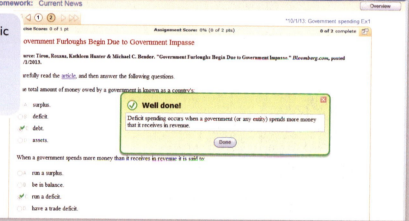

Interactive Homework Exercises

Participate in a fun and engaging activity that helps promote active learning and mastery of important economic concepts.

Pearson's experiments program is flexible and easy for instructors and students to use. For a complete list of available experiments, visit *www.myeconlab.com*.

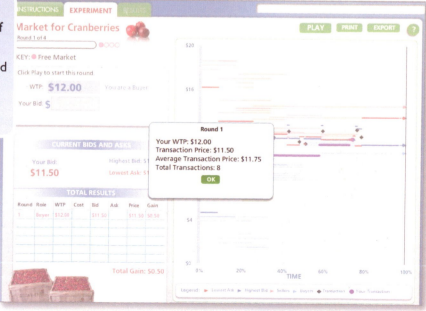

MICROECONOMICS

SEVENTH EDITION

THE PEARSON SERIES IN ECONOMICS

Abel/Bernanke/Croushore
Macroeconomics*

Bade/Parkin
Foundations of Economics*

Berck/Helfand
The Economics of the Environment

Bierman/Fernandez
Game Theory with Economic Applications

Blanchard
Macroeconomics*

Blau/Ferber/Winkler
The Economics of Women, Men, and Work

Boardman/Greenberg/Vining/Weimer
Cost-Benefit Analysis

Boyer
Principles of Transportation Economics

Branson
Macroeconomic Theory and Policy

Bruce
Public Finance and the American Economy

Carlton/Perloff
Modern Industrial Organization

Case/Fair/Oster
Principles of Economics*

Chapman
Environmental Economics: Theory, Application, and Policy

Cooter/Ulen
Law & Economics

Daniels/VanHoose
International Monetary & Financial Economics

Downs
An Economic Theory of Democracy

Ehrenberg/Smith
Modern Labor Economics

Farnham
Economics for Managers

Folland/Goodman/Stano
The Economics of Health and Health Care

Fort
Sports Economics

Froyen
Macroeconomics

Fusfeld
The Age of the Economist

Gerber
International Economics*

González-Rivera
Forecasting for Economics and Business

Gordon
Macroeconomics*

Greene
Econometric Analysis

Gregory
Essentials of Economics

Gregory/Stuart
Russian and Soviet Economic Performance and Structure

Hartwick/Olewiler
The Economics of Natural Resource Use

Heilbroner/Milberg
The Making of the Economic Society

Heyne/Boettke/Prychitko
The Economic Way of Thinking

Holt
Markets, Games, and Strategic Behavior

Hubbard/O'Brien
Economics*

Money, Banking, and the Financial System*

Hubbard/O'Brien/Rafferty
Macroeconomics*

Hughes/Cain
American Economic History

Husted/Melvin
International Economics

Jehle/Reny
Advanced Microeconomic Theory

Johnson-Lans
A Health Economics Primer

Keat/Young/Erfle
Managerial Economics

Klein
Mathematical Methods for Economics

Krugman/Obstfeld/Melitz
International Economics: Theory & Policy*

Laidler
The Demand for Money

Leeds/von Allmen
The Economics of Sports

Leeds/von Allmen/Schiming
Economics*

Lynn
Economic Development: Theory and Practice for a Divided World

Miller
Economics Today*

Understanding Modern Economics

Miller/Benjamin
The Economics of Macro Issues

Miller/Benjamin/North
The Economics of Public Issues

Mills/Hamilton
Urban Economics

Mishkin
The Economics of Money, Banking, and Financial Markets*

The Economics of Money, Banking, and Financial Markets, Business School Edition*

Macroeconomics: Policy and Practice*

Murray
Econometrics: A Modern Introduction

O'Sullivan/Sheffrin/Perez
Economics: Principles, Applications, and Tools*

Parkin
Economics*

Perloff
Microeconomics*

Microeconomics: Theory and Applications with Calculus*

Perloff/Brander
Managerial Economics and Strategy*

Phelps
Health Economics

Pindyck/Rubinfeld
Microeconomics*

Riddell/Shackelford/Stamos/Schneider
Economics: A Tool for Critically Understanding Society

Roberts
The Choice: A Fable of Free Trade and Protection

Rohlf
Introduction to Economic Reasoning

Roland
Development Economics

Scherer
Industry Structure, Strategy, and Public Policy

Schiller
The Economics of Poverty and Discrimination

Sherman
Market Regulation

Stock/Watson
Introduction to Econometrics

Studenmund
Using Econometrics: A Practical Guide

Tietenberg/Lewis
Environmental and Natural Resource Economics

Environmental Economics and Policy

Todaro/Smith
Economic Development

Waldman/Jensen
Industrial Organization: Theory and Practice

Walters/Walters/Appel/Callahan/Centanni/Maex/O'Neill
Econversations: Today's Students Discuss Today's Issues

Weil
Economic Growth

Williamson
Macroeconomics

*denotes MyEconLab titles   Visit www.myeconlab.com to learn more.

MICROECONOMICS

SEVENTH EDITION

JEFFREY M. PERLOFF

University of California, Berkeley

PEARSON

Boston   Columbus   Indianapolis   New York   San Francisco   Upper Saddle River
Amsterdam   Cape Town   Dubai   London   Madrid   Milan   Munich   Paris   Montreal   Toronto
Delhi   Mexico City   Sao Paulo   Sydney   Hong Kong   Seoul   Singapore   Taipei   Tokyo

For Alexx, Gregg, Laura, and Spenser

Editor in Chief: Donna Battista
Executive Acquisitions Editor: Adrienne D'Ambrosio
Digital Publisher: Denise Clinton
Editorial Project Manager: Sarah Dumouchelle
Editorial Assistant: Patrick Henning
Executive Marketing Manager: Lori DeShazo
Managing Editor: Jeff Holcomb
Senior Production Project Manager: Meredith Gertz
Senior Manufacturing Buyer: Carol Melville
Art Director and Cover Designer: Jonathan Boylan
Cover Photo: Pearson Education, Inc.
Image Manager: Rachel Youdelman
Photo Research: Integra Software Services, Ltd.
Associate Project Manager—Text Permissions:
  Samantha Blair Graham

Text Permissions Research: Electronic Publishing
  Services
Director of Media: Susan Schoenberg
Executive Media Producer: Melissa Honig
MyEconLab Content Lead: Courtney Kamauf
Full-Service Project Management and Text Design:
  Gillian Hall, The Aardvark Group
Copyeditor: Rebecca Greenberg
Proofreader: Holly McLean-Aldis
Indexer: John Lewis
Composition and Illustrations: Laserwords Maine
Printer/Binder: RR Donnelley, Willard
Cover Printer: Lehigh Phoenix
Text Font: Sabon

Credits and acknowledgments borrowed from other sources and reproduced, with permission, in this textbook appear on appropriate page within the text and on page A-96.

Many of the designations by manufacturers and seller to distinguish their products are claimed as trademarks. Where those designations appear in this book, and the publisher was aware of a trademark claim, the designations have been printed in initial caps or all caps.

Library of Congress Cataloging-in-Publication Data

Perloff, Jeffrey M.
  Microeconomics / Jeffrey Perloff.—7th edition.
    p. cm.
  Includes bibliographical references and index.
  ISBN 978-0-13-345691-2
  1. Microeconomics. I. Title.
  HB172.P39 2015
  338.5–dc22

                          2013050602

10 9 8 7 6 5 4 3

www.pearsonhighered.com

ISBN-13: 978-0-13-345691-2
ISBN-10: 0-13-345691-9

Brief Contents

Contents

Preface

When I was a student, I fell in love with microeconomics because it cleared up many mysteries about the world and provided the means to answer new questions. I wrote this book to illustrate that economic theory has practical, problem-solving uses and is not an empty academic exercise.

This book shows how individuals, policy makers, lawyers and judges, and firms can use microeconomic tools to analyze and resolve problems. For example, students learn that

- individuals can draw on microeconomic theories when deciding about issues such as whether to invest and whether to sign a contract that pegs prices to the government's measure of inflation;
- policy makers (and voters) can employ microeconomics to predict the impact of taxes, regulations, and other measures before they are enacted;
- lawyers and judges use microeconomics in antitrust, discrimination, and contract cases; and
- firms apply microeconomic principles to produce at minimum cost and maximize profit, select strategies, decide whether to buy from a market or to produce internally, and write contracts to provide optimal incentives for employees.

My experience in teaching microeconomics for the departments of economics at MIT; the University of Pennsylvania; and the University of California, Berkeley; the Department of Agricultural and Resource Economics at Berkeley; and the Wharton Business School has convinced me that students prefer this emphasis on real-world issues.

Features

This book differs from other microeconomics texts in three main ways:

- It places greater emphasis than other texts on *modern theories*—such as industrial organization theories, game theory, transaction cost theory, information theory, contract theory, and behavioral economics—that are useful in analyzing actual markets.
- It uses *real-world economic examples* to present the basic theory and offers extensive Applications to a variety of real-world situations.
- It employs step-by-step *problem-based learning* to demonstrate how to use microeconomic theory to solve business problems and analyze policy issues.

Modern Theories

This book has all of the standard economic theory, of course. However, what sets it apart is its emphasis on modern theories that are particularly useful for understanding how firms behave and the effects of public policy.

Industrial Organization. How do firms differentiate their products to increase their profits? When does market outcome depend on whether firms set prices or quantities? What effects do government price regulations have on firms' behavior? These and many other questions are addressed by industrial organization theories.

Game Theory. What's the optimal way to bid in an auction? How do firms set prices to prevent entry of rival firms? What strategy should parents use when their college-graduate child moves back in with them? Game theory provides a way of thinking about strategies and it provides methods to choose optimal strategies.

Contract Theory. What kind of a contract should a firm offer a worker to induce the employee to work hard? How do people avoid being exploited by others who have superior information? Modern contract theory shows how to write contracts to avoid or minimize such problems.

Behavioral Economics. Should a firm allow workers to opt in or opt out of a retirement system? How should people respond to ultimatums? We address questions such as these using behavioral economics—one of the hottest new areas of economic theory—which uses psychological research and theory to explain why people deviate from rational behavior.

Real-World Economics

This book demonstrates that economics is practical and provides a useful way to understand actual markets and firms' and consumers' decisions in two ways. First, it presents the basic theory using models estimated with real-world data. Second, it uses the theory to analyze hundreds of real-world applications.

Using Estimated Models to Illustrate Theory. The basic theory is presented using estimated demand curves, supply curves, production functions, and cost functions in most chapters. For example, students see how imported oil limits pricing by U.S. oil producers using estimated supply and demand curves, derive a Japanese beer manufacturer's cost curve based on an estimated production function, examine regulation of natural gas monopolies using estimated demand and cost curves, and analyze oligopoly firms' strategies using estimated demand curves and cost and profit data from the real-world rivalries between United Airlines and American Airlines and between Coke and Pepsi.

Applications. Applications use economic theory to predict the price effect of allowing drilling in the Arctic National Wildlife Refuge based on estimated demand and supply curves, demonstrate how iTunes price increases affect music downloads using survey data, explain why some top-end designers limit the number of designer bags customers can buy, measure the value of using the Internet, and analyze how a tariff on chickens affects the importation of cars.

Problem-Based Learning

People, firms, and policy makers have to solve economic problems daily. This book uses a problem-solving approach to demonstrate how economic theory can help them make good decisions.

Solved Problems. After the introductory chapter, each chapter provides an average of over five Solved Problems. Each Solved Problem poses a qualitative or quantitative question and then uses a step-by-step approach to model good problem-solving techniques. These issues range from whether Peter Guber and Joe Lacob should have bought the Golden State Warriors, how to determine Intel's and AMD's profit-maximizing quantities and prices using their estimated demand curves and marginal costs, and how regulating a monopoly's price affects consumers and firms.

Challenges. Starting with Chapter 2, each chapter begins with a Challenge that presents information about an important, current real-world issue and concludes with a series of questions about that material. At the end of the chapter, a Challenge Solution answers these questions using methods presented in that chapter. That is, the Challenge combines the approaches of Applications and Solved Problems to motivate the material in the chapter. The issues covered include the effects from introducing genetically modified foods, why Americans buy more e-books than do Germans, comparing rationing water to raising its price during droughts, whether higher salaries for star athletes raise ticket prices, whether it pays to go to college, and how Heinz can use sales to increase its profit on ketchup.

End-of-Chapter Questions. Starting with Chapter 2, each chapter ends with an extensive set of questions, many of which are based on real-world problems. Each Solved Problem and Challenge has at least one associated end-of-chapter question that references them and asks students to extend or reapply their analyses. Many of the questions are related to the Applications. Answers to selected end-of-chapter questions appear at the end of the book, and all of the end-of-chapter questions are available in MyEconLab for self-assessment, homework, or testing.

What's New in the Seventh Edition

The Seventh Edition is substantially updated and modified based on the extremely helpful suggestions of faculty and students who used the first six editions. Four major changes run throughout the book:

- All chapters are revised, and all but two are substantially revised.
- All the Challenges and almost all the examples and Applications throughout the book are updated or new.
- The book has a significant number of new Solved Problems.
- The end-of-chapter questions are arranged by subject headings, new questions have been added, and many others updated.

Challenges, Solved Problems, and Questions

All of the Challenges are new or updated. Because many users requested more Solved Problems, I increased the number of Solved Problems in this edition to 106 from 94 in the previous edition. In addition, many other Solved Problems are new or substantially updated and revised. Starting in this edition, every Solved Problem has at least one associated Question at the end of the chapter.

About 40% of these Solved Problems are tied to real-world events. Many of these are associated with an adjacent Application or examples in the text. In addition to the Challenges, examples of a paired Application and Solved Problem include an investigation into whether farmers benefit from a major drought, the effect of oil drilling in the Arctic National Wildlife Refuge on prices, the opportunity cost of getting an MBA, the social cost of a natural gas price ceiling, Apple's iPad pricing, and the price effects of reselling textbooks bought abroad in the United States.

Starting with Chapter 2, the end of each chapter has an average of over 40 verbal, graphical, and mathematical Questions. This edition has 769 Questions, 61 more than in the previous edition. Over 27% of the Questions are new or updated. Many of these Questions are based on recent real-life events and issues drawn from newspapers, journal articles, and other sources.

Applications

The Seventh Edition has 131 Applications, 5 more than in the previous edition. Of these, 46% are new and 45% are updated, so that 91% are new or updated. The vast majority of the Applications cover events in 2012 and 2013, a few deal with historical events, and the remaining ones examine timeless material.

To make room for the new Applications, 27 older Applications from the Sixth Edition were moved to MyEconLab. Also, several new ones have been added to the hundreds of Applications and other materials in MyEconLab.

Behavioral Economics

The Seventh Edition has a revised treatment of behavioral economics in the chapters on consumer choice, monopoly, interest rates, and uncertainty. It also adds a new behavioral economics section in the game theory chapter.

New and Revised Material in Chapters

Every chapter is revised—including most sections. Virtually every chapter has updated examples and statistics. Some of the larger changes include:

- Chapters 2 and 3 use two new empirical studies (avocados and corn) to illustrate the basic supply and demand model. They have four new and a number of revised Solved Problems.
- Chapters 4 and 5 have three new Solved Problems and extensive updating of data. Chapter 5 has a new section on compensating and equivalent variations.
- Chapter 6 adds many new estimated production functions and a new discussion of returns to scale as a function of firm size.
- Chapter 7 has substantially revised sections on effects of taxes on costs, long-run costs, and learning by doing. It uses a new Japanese beer empirical example to illustrate the theory, and has a new Solved Problem.
- Chapter 8 has new statistics and a new Solved Problem. Several sections are substantially revised, including an extended treatment of the shutdown decision.
- Chapter 9 updates many statistics and has substantially revised sections on rents, price effects on consumer surplus, and trade, and the Challenge Solution. The trade section uses a new empirical oil example.
- Chapter 10 has a revised Challenge Solution and a new Solved Problem.
- Chapter 11 is reorganized, revised, and updated, particularly the sections on market failure and the causes of monopoly. The chapter has three new Solved Problems, two of which now address the iPad.
- Chapter 12 is completely reorganized and rewritten, particularly the group discrimination section and the nonlinear pricing section, which is expanded. It has a new Challenge.
- Chapter 13 is reorganized. Revised sections include cartel, antitrust laws, mergers, Cournot differentiated products, and Bertrand vs. Cournot.

- Chapter 14's revision removes the discussion of iterative dominance (relying on dominant strategy and best-response approaches), divides the treatment of dynamic games into sections on repeated and sequential games, expands the repeated game material, and adds a new behavioral game theory section.
- Chapter 17's major revision includes new section heads and significant revisions to the sections on probability, attitudes toward risk, and behavioral economics. The material on uncertainty and discounting is now on MyEconLab.
- Chapter 18 updates the pollution data, has a new subsection on the benefits versus costs from controlling pollution, and a new Solved Problem.
- Chapter 19 is extensively revised and reorganized, with new material on insurance markets and a rewritten section on reducing adverse selection.
- Chapter 20 is fundamentally rewritten and has four new Solved Problems. The first half of the chapter is entirely new.

Alternative Organizations

Because instructors differ as to the order in which they cover material, this text has been designed for maximum flexibility. The most common approach to teaching microeconomics is to follow the sequence of the chapters in the first half of this book: supply and demand (Chapters 2 and 3), consumer theory (Chapters 4 and 5), the theory of the firm (Chapters 6 and 7), and the competitive model (Chapters 8 and 9). Many instructors then cover monopoly (Chapter 11), price discrimination (Chapter 12), oligopoly (Chapters 13 and 14), input markets (Chapter 15), uncertainty (Chapter 17), and externalities (Chapter 18).

A common variant is to present uncertainty (Sections 17.1 through 17.3) immediately after consumer theory. Many instructors like to take up welfare issues between discussions of the competitive model and noncompetitive models, as Chapter 10, on general equilibrium and economic welfare, does. Alternatively, that chapter may be covered at the end of the course. Faculty can assign material on factor markets earlier (Section 15.1 could follow the chapters on competition, and the remaining sections could follow Chapter 11). The material in Chapters 14–20 can be presented in a variety of orders, though Chapter 20 should follow Chapter 19 if both are covered, and Section 17.4 should follow Chapter 16.

Many business school courses skip consumer theory (and possibly some aspects of supply and demand, such as Chapter 3) to allow more time for consideration of the topics covered in the second half of this book. Business school faculty may want to place particular emphasis on game and theory strategies (Chapter 14), capital markets (Chapter 16), and modern contract theory (Chapters 19 and 20).

Optional, technically demanding sections are marked with a star (★). Subsequent sections and chapters can be understood even if these sections are skipped.

MyEconLab

MyEconLab's powerful assessment and tutorial system works hand-in-hand with this book.

Features for Students

MyEconLab puts students in control of their learning through a collection of testing, practice, and study tools. Students can study on their own, or they can complete assignments created by their instructor. In MyEconLab's structured environment, students practice what they learn, test their understanding, and pursue a personalized study plan generated from their performance on sample tests and quizzes. In Homework or Study Plan mode, students have access to a wealth of tutorial features, including the following:

- Instant feedback on exercises taken directly from the text helps students understand and apply the concepts.
- Links to the eText version of this textbook allow the student to quickly revisit a concept or an explanation.
- Enhanced Pearson eText, available within the online course materials and offline via an iPad/Android app, allows instructors and students to highlight, bookmark, and take notes.
- Learning aids help students analyze a problem in small steps, much the same way an instructor would do during office hours.
- Temporary Access for students who are awaiting financial aid provides a grace period of temporary access.

Experiments in MyEconLab

Experiments are a fun and engaging way to promote active learning and mastery of important economic concepts. Pearson's Experiment program is flexible and easy for instructors and students to use.

- Single-player experiments, which can be assigned for homework, allow students to play against virtual players from anywhere at any time they have an Internet connection.
- Multiplayer experiments allow instructors to assign and manage a real-time experiment with their classes.
- Pre- and post-questions for each experiment are available for assignment in MyEconLab.

For a complete list of available experiments, visit **www.myeconlab.com**.

Features for Instructors

MyEconLab includes comprehensive homework, quiz, text, and tutorial options, where instructors can manage all assessment needs in one program.

- All of the end-of-chapter questions are available for assignment and auto-grading.
- All of the Solved Problems are available for assignment and auto-grading.
- Test Bank questions are available for assignment or testing.
- The Custom Exercise Builder allows instructors the flexibility of creating their own problems for assignments.
- The powerful Gradebook records each student's performance and time spent on the tests, study plan, and homework and can generate reports by student, class, or chapter.
- Advanced Communication Tools enable students and instructors to communicate through email, discussion board, chat, and ClassLive.
- Customization options provide new and enhanced ways to share documents, add content, and rename menu items.
- A prebuilt course option provides a turn-key method for instructors to create a MyEconLab course that includes assignments by chapter.

Supplements

A full range of supplementary materials to support teaching and learning accompanies this book.

- The *Online Instructor's Manual* revised by Jennifer Steele has many useful and creative teaching ideas. It also offers a chapter outline, additional discussion questions, additional questions and problems, and solutions for all additional questions and problems.
- The *Online Solutions Manual* provides solutions for all the end-of-chapter questions in the text.
- The *Online Test Bank* by Shana McDermott of the University of New Mexico, James Swanson of the University of Central Missouri, and Lourenço Paz of Syracuse University features problems of varying levels of complexity, suitable for homework assignments and exams. Many of these multiple-choice questions draw on current events.
- The *Computerized Test Bank* reproduces the Test Bank material in the TestGen software, which is available for Windows and Macintosh. With TestGen, instructors can easily edit existing questions, add questions, generate tests, and print the tests in a variety of formats.
- The *Online PowerPoint Presentation* by Ting Levy of Florida Atlantic University contains text figures and tables, as well as lecture notes. These slides allow instructors to walk through examples from the text during in-class presentations.

These teaching resources are available online for download at the Instructor Resource Center, **www.pearsonhighered.com/perloff**, and on the catalog page for *Microeconomics*.

Acknowledgments

My greatest debt is to my students. My students at MIT, the University of Pennsylvania, and the University of California, Berkeley, patiently dealt with my various approaches to teaching them microeconomics and made useful (and generally polite) suggestions.

The various editions have benefited from the early work by the two best development editors in the business, Jane Tufts and Sylvia Mallory. Jane Tufts reviewed drafts of the first edition of this book for content and presentation. By showing me how to present the material as clearly, orderly, and thoroughly as possible, she greatly strengthened this text. Sylvia Mallory worked valiantly to improve my writing style and helped to shape and improve every aspect of the book's contents and appearance in each of the first four editions.

I am extremely grateful to Adrienne D'Ambrosio, Executive Acquisitions Editor, and Sarah Dumouchelle, Editorial Project Manager, at Pearson, who helped me plan this revision and made very valuable suggestions at each stage of the process. Adrienne, as usual, skillfully handled all aspects of planning, writing, and producing this textbook. In addition, Sarah made sure that the new material in this edition is clear, editing all the chapters, and assisted in arranging the supplements program.

Over the years, many excellent research assistants—Hayley Chouinard, R. Scott Hacker, Guojun He, Nancy McCarthy, Enrico Moretti, Lisa Perloff, Asa Sajise, Hugo Salgado, Gautam Sethi, Edward Shen, Klaas van 't Veld, and Ximing Wu—worked hard to collect facts, develop examples and figures, and check material.

Many people were very generous in providing me with data, models, and examples, including among others: Thomas Bauer (University of Bochum), Peter Berck (University of California, Berkeley), James Brander (University of British Columbia), Leemore Dafny (Northwestern University), Lucas Davis (University of California, Berkeley), James Dearden (Lehigh University), Farid Gasmi (Université des Sciences Sociales), Avi Goldfarb (University of Toronto), Claudia Goldin (Harvard University), Rachel Goodhue (University of California, Davis), William Greene (New York University), Nile Hatch (University of Illinois), Larry Karp (University of California, Berkeley), Ryan Kellogg (University of Michigan), Arthur Kennickell (Federal Reserve, Washington), Fahad Khalil (University of Washington), Lutz Kilian (University of Michigan), Christopher Knittel (University of California, Davis), Jean-Jacques Laffont (deceased), Ulrike Malmendier (University of California, Berkeley), Karl D. Meilke (University of Guelph), Eric Muehlegger (Harvard University), Giancarlo Moschini (Iowa State University), Michael Roberts (North Carolina State University), Wolfram Schlenker (Columbia University), Junichi Suzuki (University of Toronto), Catherine Tucker (MIT), Harald Uhlig (University of Chicago), Quang Vuong (Université des Sciences Sociales, Toulouse, and University of Southern California), and Joel Waldfogel (University of Minnesota).

Writing a textbook is hard work for everyone involved. I am grateful to the many teachers of microeconomics who spent untold hours reading and commenting on proposals and chapters. Many of the best ideas in this book are due to them.

I am particularly grateful to Jim Brander of the University of British Columbia who provided material for Chapters 13 and 14, has given me many deep and insightful comments on many editions of this book, and with whom I wrote another, related book. Much of the new material in this edition was jointly written with him. My other biggest debt is to James Dearden, Lehigh University, who has made extremely insightful comments on all prior editions and wrote some of the end-of-chapter questions.

In earlier editions, Peter Berck made major contributions to Chapter 16. Charles F. Mason made particularly helpful comments on many chapters. Larry Karp helped me to develop two of the sections and carefully reviewed the content of several others. Robert Whaples, Wake Forest University, read many chapters in earlier editions and offered particularly useful comments. He also wrote the first draft of one of my favorite Applications.

I am grateful to the following people who reviewed the book or sent me valuable suggestions at various stages:

M. Shahid Alam, Northeastern University
Anne Alexander, University of Wyoming
Samson Alva, Boston College
Richard K. Anderson, Texas A & M University
Niels Anthonisen, University of Western Ontario
Wilma Anton, University of Central Florida
Emrah Arbak, State University of New York at Albany
Scott E. Atkinson, University of Georgia
Talia Bar, Cornell University
Raymond G. Batina, Washington State University
Anthony Becker, St. Olaf College
Robert A. Berman, American University
Gary Biglaiser, University of North Carolina, Chapel Hill
S. Brock Blomberg, Wellesley College
Hein Bogaard, George Washington University
Vic Brajer, California State University, Fullerton

Jurgen Brauer, Augusta State University
Bruce Brown, Cal Polytech Pomona and UCLA
Cory S. Capps, University of Illinois, Urbana-Champaign
John Cawley, Cornell University
Indranil Chakraborty, University of Oklahoma
Leo Chan, University of Kansas
Joni S. Charles, Southwest Texas State University
Kwang Soo Cheong, University of Hawaii at Manoa
Joy L. Clark, Auburn University, Montgomery
Dean Croushore, Federal Reserve Bank of Philadelphia
Douglas Dalenberg, University of Montana
Andrew Daughety, Vanderbilt University
Carl Davidson, Michigan State University
Ronald Deiter, Iowa State University
Manfred Dix, Tulane University
John Edgren, Eastern Michigan University

Patrick Emerson, University of Colorado, Denver
Xin Fang, Hawai'i Pacific University
Bernard Fortin, Université Laval
Tom Friedland, Rutgers University
Roy Gardner, Indiana University
Rod Garratt, University of California, Santa Barbara
Wei Ge, Bucknell University
Lisa Giddings, University of Wisconsin, La Crosse
J. Fred Giertz, University of Illinois, Urbana-Champaign
Haynes Goddard, University of Cincinnati
Steven Goldman, University of California, Berkeley
Julie Gonzalez, University of California, Santa Cruz
Rachel Goodhue, University of California, Davis
Srihari Govindan, University of Western Ontario
Gareth Green, Seattle University
Thomas A. Gresik, Pennsylvania State University
Jonathan Gruber, MIT
Steffan Habermalz, University of Nebraska, Kearney
Claire Hammond, Wake Forest University
John A. Hansen, State University of New York, Fredonia
Philip S. Heap, James Madison University
L. Dean Hiebert, Illinois State University
Kathryn Ierulli, University of Illinois, Chicago
Mike Ingham, University of Salford, U.K.
Samia Islam, Boise State University
D. Gale Johnson, University of Chicago
Erik Jonasson, Lund University, Sweden
Charles Kahn, University of Illinois, Urbana-Champaign
Vibha Kapuria-Foreman, Colorado College
Paula M. Kazi, Bucknell University
Carrie Kerekes, Florida Gulf Coast University
Alan Kessler, Providence College
Kristin Kiesel, California State University, Sacramento
Kate Krause, University of New Mexico
Robert Lemke, Lake Forest College
Jing Li, University of Pennsylvania
Qihong Liu, University of Oklahoma
Zhou Lu, City College of New York
Fred Luk, University of California, Los Angeles
Robert Main, Butler University
David Malueg, Tulane University
Steve Margolis, North Carolina State University
Kate Matraves, Michigan State University
James Meehan, Colby College
Claudio Mezzetti, University of North Carolina, Chapel Hill
Chun-Hui Miao, University of South Carolina
Janet Mitchell, Cornell University
Felix Munoz-Garcia, Washington State University
Babu Nahata, University of Louisville
Kathryn Nantz, Fairfield University
Jawwad Noor, Boston University
Yuka Ohno, Rice University
Patrick B. O'Neil, University of North Dakota
John Palmer, University of Western Ontario
Christos Papahristodoulou, Uppsala University

Silve Parviainen, University of Illinois, Urbana-Champaign
Sharon Pearson, University of Alberta
Anita Alves Pena, Colorado State University
Ingrid Peters-Fransen, Wilfrid Laurier University
Jaishankar Raman, Valparaiso University
Sunder Ramaswamy, Middlebury College
Lee Redding, University of Michigan, Dearborn
David Reitman, Department of Justice
Luca Rigotti, Tillburg University
S. Abu Turab Rizvi, University of Vermont
Bee Yan Aw Roberts, Pennsylvania State University
Richard Rogers, Ashland University
Nancy Rose, Sloan School of Business, MIT
Joshua Rosenbloom, University of Kansas
Roy Ruffin, University of Houston
Matthew Rutledge, Boston College
Alfonso Sanchez-Penalver, University of Massachusetts, Boston
George Santopietro, Radford College
David Sappington, University of Florida
Rich Sexton, University of California, Davis
Quazi Shahriar, San Diego State University
Jacques Siegers, Utrecht University, The Netherlands
Alasdair Smith, University of Sussex
William Doyle Smith, University of Texas at El Paso
Philip Sorenson, Florida State University
Peter Soule, Park College
Robert Stearns, University of Maryland
Jennifer Lynn Steele, Washington State University
Shankar Subramanian, Cornell University
Albert J. Sumell, Youngstown State University
Beck A. Taylor, Baylor University
Scott Templeton, Clemson University
Mark L. Tendall, Stanford University
Justin Tevie, University of New Mexico
Wade Thomas, State University of New York, Oneonta
Judith Thornton, University of Washington
Vitor Trindade, Syracuse University
Nora Underwood, University of California, Davis
Burcin Unel, University of Florida
Kay Unger, University of Montana
Alan van der Hilst, University of Washington
Bas van der Klaauw, Free University Amsterdam and Tinbergen Institute
Andrew Vassallo, Rutgers University
Jacob L. Vigdor, Duke University
Peter von Allmen, Moravian College
Eleanor T. von Ende, Texas Tech University
Curt Wells, Lund University
Lawrence J. White, New York University
John Whitehead, East Carolina University
Colin Wright, Claremont McKenna College
Bruce Wydick, University of San Francisco
Peter Zaleski, Villanova University
Artie Zillante, Florida State University
Mark Zupan, University of Arizona

In addition, I thank Bob Solow, the world's finest economics teacher, who showed me how to simplify models without losing their essence. I've also learned a great deal over the years about economics and writing from my coauthors on other projects, especially Dennis Carlton (my coauthor on *Modern Industrial Organization*), Jackie Persons, Steve Salop, Michael Wachter, Larry Karp, Peter Berck, Amos Golan, and Dan Rubinfeld (whom I thank for still talking to me despite my decision to write this book).

It was a pleasure to work with the good people at Pearson, who were incredibly helpful in producing this book. Marjorie Williams and Barbara Rifkin signed me to write it. I would like to thank Donna Battista, Editor-in-Chief for Business Publishing, and Denise Clinton, Publisher for MyEconLab, who were instrumental in making the entire process work. Meredith Gertz did her usual outstanding job of supervising the production process, assembling the extended publishing team, and managing the design of the handsome interior. She makes the entire process as smooth as possible.

I thank Jonathan Boylan for the cover design. I also want to acknowledge, with appreciation, the efforts of Melissa Honig, Noel Lotz, and Courtney Kamauf in developing MyEconLab, the online assessment and tutorial system for the book.

Gillian Hall and the rest of the team at The Aardvark Group Publishing Services have my sincere gratitude for designing the book and keeping the project on track and on schedule. As always, I'm particularly thankful to work with Gillian, who is wonderfully flexible and committed to producing the best book possible. Rebecca Greenberg did a superior copyediting for this edition—and made many important contributions to the content.

Finally, and most importantly, I thank my wife, Jackie Persons, and daughter, Lisa Perloff, for their great patience and support during the nearly endless writing process. And I apologize for misusing their names—and those of my other relatives and friends—in the book!

J. M. P.

Introduction

1

An Economist's Theory of Reincarnation: If you're good, you come back on a higher level. Cats come back as dogs, dogs come back as horses, and people— if they've been really good like George Washington—come back as money.

If each of us could get all the food, clothing, and toys we wanted without working, no one would study economics. Unfortunately, most of the good things in life are scarce—we can't all have as much as we want. Thus, scarcity is the mother of economics.

Microeconomics is the study of how individuals and firms make themselves as well off as possible in a world of scarcity and the consequences of those individual decisions for markets and the entire economy. In studying microeconomics, we examine how individual consumers and firms make decisions and how the interaction of many individual decisions affects markets and the entire economy.

Microeconomics is often called *price theory* to emphasize the important role that prices play. Microeconomics explains how the actions of all buyers and sellers determine prices and how prices influence the decisions and actions of individual buyers and sellers.

> **microeconomics**
> the study of how individuals and firms make themselves as well off as possible in a world of scarcity and the consequences of those individual decisions for markets and the entire economy

---

1. **Microeconomics: The Allocation of Scarce Resources.** Microeconomics is the study of the allocation of scarce resources.

2. **Models.** Economists use models to make testable predictions.

3. **Uses of Microeconomic Models.** Individuals, governments, and firms use microeconomic models and predictions in decision making.

> In this chapter, we examine three main topics

1.1 Microeconomics: The Allocation of Scarce Resources

Individuals and firms allocate their limited resources to make themselves as well off as possible. Consumers pick the mix of goods and services that makes them as happy as possible given their limited wealth. Firms decide which goods to produce, where to produce them, how much to produce to maximize their profits, and how to produce those levels of output at the lowest cost by using more or less of various inputs such as labor, capital, materials, and energy. The owners of a depletable natural resource such as oil decide when to use it. Government decision makers—to benefit consumers, firms, or government bureaucrats—decide which goods and services the government produces and whether to subsidize, tax, or regulate industries and consumers.

Trade-Offs

People make trade-offs because they can't have everything. A society faces three key trade-offs:

- **Which goods and services to produce:** If a society produces more cars, it must produce fewer of other goods and services, because there are only so many *resources*—workers, raw materials, capital, and energy—available to produce goods.
- **How to produce:** To produce a given level of output, a firm must use more of one input if it uses less of another input. For example, cracker and cookie manufacturers switch between palm oil and coconut oil, depending on which is less expensive.
- **Who gets the goods and services:** The more of society's goods and services you get, the less someone else gets.

Who Makes the Decisions

These three allocation decisions may be made explicitly by the government or may reflect the interaction of independent decisions by many individual consumers and firms. In the former Soviet Union, the government told manufacturers how many cars of each type to make and which inputs to use to make them. The government also decided which consumers would get a car.

In most other countries, how many cars of each type are produced and who gets them are determined by how much it costs to make cars of a particular quality in the least expensive way and how much consumers are willing to pay for them. More consumers would own a handmade Rolls-Royce and fewer would buy a mass-produced Ford Taurus if a Rolls were not 13 times more expensive than a Taurus.

Prices Determine Allocations

Prices link the decisions about *which goods and services to produce, how to produce them,* and *who gets them.* Prices influence the decisions of individual consumers and firms, and the interactions of these decisions by consumers, firms, and the government determine price.

market
an exchange mechanism that allows buyers to trade with sellers

Interactions between consumers and firms take place in a **market,** which is an exchange mechanism that allows buyers to trade with sellers. A market may be a town square where people go to trade food and clothing, or it may be an international telecommunications network over which people buy and sell financial securities. Typically, when we talk about a single market, we refer to trade in a single good or group of goods that are closely related, such as soft drinks, movies, novels, or automobiles.

Most of this book concerns how prices are determined within a market. We show that the *number of buyers and sellers* in a market and the amount of *information* they have help determine whether the price equals the cost of production. We also show that if there is no market—and hence no market price—serious problems, such as high levels of pollution, result.

1.2 Models

Everything should be made as simple as possible, but not simpler.
—Albert Einstein

model
a description of the relationship between two or more economic variables

To *explain* how individuals and firms allocate resources and how market prices are determined, economists use a **model**: a description of the relationship between two or more economic variables. Economists also use models to *predict* how a change in one variable will affect another.

Application

Income Threshold Model and China

According to an *income threshold model*, no one who has an income level below a particular threshold buys a particular consumer durable, such as a refrigerator or car. The theory also holds that almost everyone whose income is above that threshold buys the product.

If this theory is correct, we predict that, as most people's incomes rise above the threshold in emergent economies, consumer durable purchases will increase from near zero to large numbers virtually overnight. This prediction is consistent with evidence from Malaysia, where the income threshold for buying a car is about $4,000.

In China, incomes have risen rapidly and now exceed the threshold levels for many types of durable goods. As a result, many experts correctly predicted that the greatest consumer durable goods sales boom in history would take place there. Anticipating this boom, many companies have greatly increased their investments in durable goods manufacturing plants in China. Annual foreign direct investments have gone from $916 million a year in 1983 to $116 billion in 2011. In expectation of this growth potential, even traditional political opponents of the People's Republic—Taiwan, South Korea, and Russia—are investing in China.

One of the most desirable durable goods is a car. Li Rifu, a 46-year-old Chinese farmer and watch repairman, thought that buying a car would improve the odds that his 22- and 24-year-old sons would find girlfriends, marry, and produce grandchildren. Soon after Mr. Li purchased his Geely King Kong for the equivalent of $9,000, both sons met girlfriends, and his older son got married. Four-fifths of all new cars sold in China are bought by first-time customers. An influx of first-time buyers was responsible for China's ninefold increase in car sales from 2000 to 2009. By 2010, China became the second largest producer of automobiles in the world, trailing only Germany. In addition, foreign automobile companies built Chinese plants. For example, Ford invested $600 million in its Chongqing factory in 2012.[1]

Simplifications by Assumption

We stated the income threshold model in words, but we could have presented it using graphs or mathematics. Regardless of how the model is described, an economic model is a simplification of reality that contains only its most important features. Without simplifications, it is difficult to make predictions because the real world is too complex to analyze fully.

By analogy, if the manual accompanying your new TiVo recorder has a diagram showing the relationships between all the parts in the TiVo, the diagram will be overwhelming and useless. In contrast, if it shows a photo of the lights on the front

[1]The sources for Applications are available at the back of this book.

of the machine with labels describing the significance of each light, the manual is useful and informative.

Economists make many *assumptions* to simplify their models.[2] When using the income threshold model to explain car purchasing behavior in China, we *assume* that factors other than income, such as the color of cars, are irrelevant to the decision to buy cars. Therefore, we ignore the color of cars that are sold in China in describing the relationship between average income and the number of cars consumers want. If this assumption is correct, by ignoring color, we make our analysis of the auto market simpler without losing important details. If we're wrong and these ignored issues are important, our predictions may be inaccurate.

Throughout this book, we start with strong assumptions to simplify our models. Later, we add complexities. For example, in most of the book, we assume that consumers know the price each firm charges. In many markets, such as the New York Stock Exchange, this assumption is realistic. It is not realistic in other markets, such as the market for used automobiles, in which consumers do not know the prices each firm charges. To devise an accurate model for markets in which consumers have limited information, we add consumer uncertainty about price into the model in Chapter 19.

Testing Theories

Blore's Razor: When given a choice between two theories, take the one that is funnier.

Economic *theory* is the development and use of a model to test *hypotheses*, which are predictions about cause and effect. We are interested in models that make clear, testable predictions, such as "If the price rises, the quantity demanded falls." A theory that said "People's behavior depends on their tastes, and their tastes change randomly at random intervals" is not very useful because it does not lead to testable predictions.

Economists test theories by checking whether predictions are correct. If a prediction does not come true, they may reject the theory.[3] Economists use a model until it is refuted by evidence or until a better model is developed.

A good model makes sharp, clear predictions that are consistent with reality. Some very simple models make sharp predictions that are incorrect, and other more complex models make ambiguous predictions—any outcome is possible—which are untestable. The skill in model building is to chart a middle ground.

The purpose of this book is to teach you how to think like an economist in the sense that you can build testable theories using economic models or apply existing models to new situations. Although economists think alike in that they develop and use testable models, they often disagree. One may present a logically consistent argument that prices will go up next quarter. Another, using a different but equally logical theory, may contend that prices will fall. If the economists are reasonable, they agree that pure logic alone cannot resolve their dispute. Indeed, they agree that they'll have to use empirical evidence—facts about the real world—to find out which prediction is correct.

---

[2]An economist, an engineer, and a physicist are stranded on a desert island with a can of beans but no can opener. How should they open the can? The engineer proposes hitting the can with a rock. The physicist suggests building a fire under it to build up pressure and burst the can open. The economist thinks for a while and then says, "*Assume* that we have a can opener. . . ."

[3]We can use evidence on whether a theory's predictions are correct to *refute* the theory but not to *prove* it. If a model's prediction is inconsistent with what actually happened, the model must be wrong, so we reject it. Even if the model's prediction is consistent with reality, however, the model's prediction may be correct for the wrong reason. Hence we cannot prove that the model is correct—we can only fail to reject it.

Although one economist's model may differ from another's, a key assumption in most microeconomic models is that individuals allocate their scarce resources so as to make themselves as well off as possible. Of all affordable combinations of goods, consumers pick the bundle of goods that gives them the most possible enjoyment. Firms try to maximize their profits given limited resources and existing technology. That resources are limited plays a crucial role in these models. Were it not for scarcity, people could consume unlimited amounts of goods and services, and sellers could become rich beyond limit.

As we show throughout this book, the maximizing behavior of individuals and firms determines society's three main allocation decisions: which goods are produced, how they are produced, and who gets them. For example, diamond-studded pocket combs will be sold only if firms find it profitable to sell them. The firms will make and sell these combs only if consumers value the combs at least as much as it costs the firm to produce them. Consumers will buy the combs only if they get more pleasure from the combs than they would from the other goods they could buy with the same resources.

Positive Versus Normative

The use of models of maximizing behavior sometimes leads to predictions that seem harsh or heartless. For instance, a World Bank economist predicted that if an African government used price controls to keep the price of food low during a drought, food shortages would occur and people would starve. The predicted outcome is awful, but the economist was not heartless. The economist was only making a scientific prediction about the relationship between cause and effect: Price controls (cause) lead to food shortages and starvation (effect).

positive statement
a testable hypothesis about cause and effect

Such a scientific prediction is known as a **positive statement**: a testable hypothesis about cause and effect. "Positive" does not mean that we are certain about the truth of our statement—it only indicates that we can test the truth of the statement.

If the World Bank economist is correct, should the government control prices? If the government believes the economist's predictions, it knows that the low prices help those consumers who are lucky enough to be able to buy as much food as they want while hurting both the firms that sell food and the people who are unable to buy as much food as they want, some of whom may die. As a result, the government's decision whether to use price controls turns on whether the government cares more about the winners or the losers. In other words, to decide on its policy, the government makes a value judgment.

Instead of first making a prediction and testing it before making a value judgment to decide whether to use price controls, the government could make a value judgment directly. The value judgment could be based on the belief that "because people *should* have prepared for the drought, the government *should not* try to help them by keeping food prices low." Alternatively, the judgment could be based on the view that "people *should* be protected against price gouging during a drought, so the government *should* use price controls."

normative statement
a conclusion as to whether something is good or bad

These two statements are *not* scientific predictions. Each is a value judgment or **normative statement**: a conclusion as to whether something is good or bad. A normative statement cannot be tested because a value judgment cannot be refuted by evidence. It is a prescription rather than a prediction. A normative statement concerns what somebody believes *should* happen; a positive statement concerns what *will* happen.

Although a normative conclusion can be drawn without first conducting a positive analysis, a policy debate will be more informed if positive analyses are conducted first.[4] For instance, if your normative belief is that the government should help the poor, should you vote for a candidate who advocates a higher minimum wage (a law that requires that firms pay wages at or above a specified level)? One who believes in a European-style welfare system (guaranteeing health care, housing, and other basic goods and services)? A politician who wants an end to our current welfare system? Someone who wants to implement a negative income tax (in which the less income a person has, the more the government gives that person)? Or a candidate who favors job training programs? Positive economic analysis can be used to predict whether these programs will benefit poor people but not whether they are good or bad. Using these predictions and your value judgment, you can decide for whom to vote.

Economists' emphasis on positive analysis has implications for what we study and even our use of language. For example, many economists stress that they study people's *wants* rather than their *needs*. Although people need certain minimum levels of food, shelter, and clothing to survive, most people in developed economies have enough money to buy goods well in excess of the minimum levels necessary to maintain life. Consequently, in wealthy countries, calling something a "need" is often a value judgment. You almost certainly have been told by some elder that "you *need* a college education." That person was probably making a value judgment—"you *should* go to college"—rather than a scientific prediction that you will suffer terrible economic deprivation if you do not go to college. We can't test such value judgments, but we can test a hypothesis such as "One-third of the college-age population *wants* to go to college at current prices."

1.3 Uses of Microeconomic Models

Because microeconomic models *explain* why economic decisions are made and allow us to make *predictions*, they can be very useful for individuals, governments, and firms in making decisions. Throughout this book, we consider examples of how microeconomics aids in actual decision making.

Individuals can use microeconomics to make purchasing and other decisions (Chapters 4 and 5). Consumers' purchasing and investing decisions are affected by inflation and cost of living adjustments (Chapter 5). Whether it pays financially to go to college depends, in part, on interest rates (Chapter 16). Consumers decide for whom to vote based on candidates' views on economic issues.

Firms must decide which production methods to use to minimize cost (Chapter 7) and maximize profit (starting with Chapter 8). They may choose a complex pricing scheme or advertise to raise profits (Chapter 12). They select strategies to maximize profit when competing with a small number of other firms (Chapters 13 and 14). Some firms reduce consumer information to raise profits (Chapter 19). Firms use economic principles to structure contracts with other firms (Chapter 20).

Your government's elected and appointed officials use (or could use) economic models in many ways. Recent administrations have placed increased emphasis on economic analysis. Today, economic and environmental impact studies are required before many projects can commence. The President's Council of Economic Advisers and other federal economists analyze and advise national government agencies on the likely economic effects of all major policies.

---

[4]Some economists draw the normative conclusion that, as social scientists, economists *should* restrict ourselves to positive analyses. Others argue that we shouldn't give up our right to make value judgments just like the next person (who happens to be biased, prejudiced, and pigheaded, unlike us).

One major use of microeconomic models by governments is to predict the probable impact of a policy before it is adopted. For example, economists predict the likely impact of a tax on the prices consumers pay and on the tax revenues raised (Chapter 3), whether a price control will create a shortage (Chapter 2), the differential effects of tariffs and quotas on trade (Chapter 9), and the effects of regulation on monopoly price and the quantity sold (Chapter 11).

Summary

1. **Microeconomics: The Allocation of Scarce Resources.** Microeconomics is the study of the allocation of scarce resources. Consumers, firms, and governments must make allocation decisions. The three key trade-offs a society faces are which goods and services to produce, how to produce them, and who gets them. These decisions are interrelated and depend on the prices that consumers and firms face and on government actions. Market prices affect the decisions of individual consumers and firms, and the interaction of the decisions of individual consumers and firms determines market prices. The organization of the market, especially the number of firms in the market and the information consumers and firms have, plays an important role in determining whether the market price is equal to or higher than marginal cost.

2. **Models.** Models based on economic theories are used to predict the future or to answer questions about how some change, such as a tax increase, affects various sectors of the economy. A good theory is simple to use and makes clear, testable predictions that are not refuted by evidence. Most microeconomic models are based on maximizing behavior. Economists use models to construct *positive* hypotheses concerning how a cause leads to an effect. These positive questions can be tested. In contrast, *normative* statements, which are value judgments, cannot be tested.

3. **Uses of Microeconomic Models.** Individuals, governments, and firms use microeconomic models and predictions to make decisions. For example, to maximize its profits, a firm needs to know consumers' decision-making criteria, the trade-offs between various ways of producing and marketing its product, government regulations, and other factors. For large companies, beliefs about how a firm's rivals will react to its actions play a critical role in how it forms its business strategies.

2 Supply and Demand

Talk is cheap because supply exceeds demand.

Countries around the globe are debating whether to permit firms to grow or sell genetically modified (GM) foods, which have their DNA altered through genetic engineering rather than through conventional breeding.[1] The introduction of GM techniques can affect both the quantity of a crop farmer's supply and whether consumers want to buy that crop.

The first commercial GM food was Calgene's Flavr Savr tomato, which the company claimed resisted rotting and could stay on the vine longer to ripen to full flavor. It was first marketed in 1994 without any special labeling. Other common GM crops include canola, corn, cotton, rice, soybean, and sugar cane. Using GM techniques, farmers can produce more output at a given cost.

As of 2012, GM food crops, which are mostly insect-resistant, herbicide-tolerant, or stacked gene (has several traits) varieties of corn, soybean, and canola oilseed, were grown in 29 countries, but over 40% of the acreage was in the United States. In the United States in 2012, the share of crops that were GM was 88% for corn, 93% for soybean, and 94% for cotton.

Some scientists and consumer groups have raised safety concerns about GM crops. In some countries, certain GM foods have been banned. In 2008, the European

Union (EU) was forced to end its de facto ban on GM crop imports when the World Trade Organization ruled that the ban lacked scientific merit and hence violated international trade rules. As of 2013, most of the EU still banned planting most GM crops. In the EU, Australia, and several other countries, governments have required that GM products be labeled. Although Japan has not approved the cultivation of GM crops, it is the nation with the greatest GM food consumption and does not require labeling.

According to some polls, 70% of consumers in Europe object to GM foods. Fears cause some consumers to refuse to buy a GM crop (or the entire crop if GM products cannot be distinguished). Consumers in other countries, such as the United States, are less concerned about GM foods.

Whether a country approves GM crops turns on questions of safety and of economics. Will the use of GM seeds lead to lower prices and more food sold? What happens to prices and quantities sold if many consumers refuse to buy GM crops? (We will return to these questions at the end of this chapter.)

---

[1]Sources for Challenges, which appear at the beginning of chapters, and Applications, which appear throughout the chapters, are listed at the end of the book.

To analyze questions concerning the price and quantity responses from introducing new products or technologies, imposing government regulations or taxes, or other events, economists may use the *supply-and-demand model*. When asked, "What is the most important thing you know about economics?" a common reply is, "Supply equals demand." This statement is a shorthand description of one of the simplest yet most powerful models of economics. The supply-and-demand model describes how consumers and suppliers interact to determine the quantity of a good or service sold in a market and the price at which it is sold. To use the model, you need to determine three things: buyers' behavior, sellers' behavior, and how they interact.

After reading this chapter, you should be adept enough at using the supply-and-demand model to analyze some of the most important policy questions facing your country today, such as those concerning international trade, minimum wages, and price controls on health care.

After reading that grandiose claim, you may ask, "Is that all there is to economics? Can I become an expert economist that fast?" The answer to both these questions is no, of course. In addition, you need to learn the limits of this model and what other models to use when this one does not apply. (You must also learn the economists' secret handshake.)

Even with its limitations, the supply-and-demand model is the most widely used economic model. It provides a good description of how competitive markets function. *Competitive markets* are those with many buyers and sellers, such as most agriculture markets, labor markets, and stock and commodity markets. Like all good theories, the supply-and-demand model can be tested—and possibly shown to be false. But in competitive markets, where it works well, it allows us to make accurate predictions easily.

In this chapter, we examine six main topics

1. **Demand.** The quantity of a good or service that consumers demand depends on price and other factors such as consumers' incomes and the price of related goods.

2. **Supply.** The quantity of a good or service that firms supply depends on price and other factors such as the cost of inputs firms use to produce the good or service.

3. **Market Equilibrium.** The interaction between consumers' demand and firms' supply determines the market price and quantity of a good or service that is bought and sold.

4. **Shocking the Equilibrium.** Changes in a factor that affect demand (such as consumers' incomes), supply (such as a rise in the price of inputs), or a new government policy (such as a new tax) alter the market price and quantity of a good.

5. **Equilibrium Effects of Government Interventions.** Government policies may alter the equilibrium and cause the quantity supplied to differ from the quantity demanded.

6. **When to Use the Supply-and-Demand Model.** The supply-and-demand model applies only to competitive markets.

2.1 Demand

Potential consumers decide how much of a good or service to buy on the basis of its price and many other factors, including their own tastes, information, prices of other goods, income, and government actions. Before concentrating on the role of price in determining demand, let's look briefly at some of the other factors.

Consumers' *tastes* determine what they buy. Consumers do not purchase foods they dislike, artwork they hate, or clothes they view as unfashionable or uncomfortable. Advertising may influence people's tastes.

Similarly, *information* (or misinformation) about the uses of a good affects consumers' decisions. A few years ago when many consumers were convinced that oatmeal could lower their cholesterol level, they rushed to grocery stores and bought large quantities of oatmeal. (They even ate some of it until they remembered that they couldn't stand how it tastes.)

The *prices of other goods* also affect consumers' purchase decisions. Before deciding to buy Levi's jeans, you might check the prices of other brands. If the price of a close *substitute*—a product that you view as similar or identical to the one you are considering purchasing—is much lower than the price of Levi's jeans, you may buy that brand instead. Similarly, the price of a *complement*—a good that you like to consume at the same time as the product you are considering buying—may affect your decision. If you eat pie only with ice cream, the higher the price of ice cream, the less likely you are to buy pie.

Income plays a major role in determining what and how much to purchase. People who suddenly inherit great wealth may purchase a Rolls-Royce or other luxury items and would probably no longer buy do-it-yourself repair kits.

Government rules and regulations affect purchase decisions. Sales taxes increase the price that a consumer must spend for a good, and government-imposed limits on the use of a good may affect demand. In the nineteenth century, one could buy Bayer heroin, a variety of products containing cocaine, and other drug-related products that are now banned in most countries. When a city's government bans the use of skateboards on its streets, skateboard sales fall.[2]

Other factors may also affect the demand for specific goods. Consumers are more likely to use a particular smart phone app (application) if their friends use that one. The demand for small, dead evergreen trees is substantially higher in December than in other months.

Although many factors influence demand, economists usually concentrate on how price affects the quantity demanded. The relationship between price and quantity demanded plays a critical role in determining the market price and quantity in a supply-and-demand analysis. To determine how a change in price affects the quantity demanded, economists must hold constant other factors such as income and tastes that affect demand.

The Demand Curve

quantity demanded
the amount of a good that consumers are willing to buy at a given price, holding constant the other factors that influence purchases

demand curve
the *quantity demanded* at each possible price, holding constant the other factors that influence purchases

The amount of a good that consumers are *willing* to buy at a given price, holding constant the other factors that influence purchases, is the **quantity demanded**. The quantity demanded of a good or service can exceed the quantity *actually* sold. For example, as a promotion, a local store might sell DVDs for $1 each today only. At that low price, you might want to buy 25 DVDs, but because the store ran out of stock, you can buy only 10 DVDs. The quantity you demand is 25—it's the amount you *want*, even though the amount you *actually buy* is only 10.

We can show the relationship between price and the quantity demanded graphically. A **demand curve** shows the quantity demanded at each possible price, holding constant the other factors that influence purchases. Figure 2.1 shows the estimated

---

[2]When a Mississippi woman attempted to sell her granddaughter for $2,000 and a car, state legislators were horrified to discover that they had no law on the books prohibiting the sale of children and quickly passed such a law. (Mac Gordon, "Legislators Make Child-Selling Illegal," *Jackson Free Press*, March 16, 2009.)

Figure 2.1 A Demand Curve

The estimated demand curve, D^1, for avocados shows the relationship between the quantity demanded per month and the price per lb. The downward slope of this demand curve shows that, holding other factors that influence demand constant, consumers demand fewer avocados when the price rises and more when the price falls. That is, a change in price causes a *movement along the demand curve.*

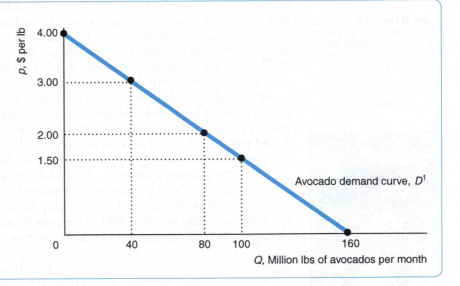

monthly demand curve, D^1, for avocados in the United States.[3] Although this demand curve is a straight line, demand curves may also be smooth curves or wavy lines. By convention, the vertical axis of the graph measures the price, p, per unit of the good. Here the price of avocados is measured in dollars per pound (abbreviated "lb"). The horizontal axis measures the quantity, Q, of the good, which is usually expressed in some *physical measure per time period.* Here, the quantity of avocados is measured in millions of pounds (lbs) per month.

The demand curve hits the vertical axis at $4, indicating that no quantity is demanded when the price is $4 per lb or higher. The demand curve hits the horizontal quantity axis at 160 million lbs per month, the quantity of avocados that consumers would want if the price were zero. To find out what quantity is demanded at a price between zero and $4, we pick that price—say, $2—on the vertical axis, draw a horizontal line across until we hit the demand curve, and then draw a vertical line down to the horizontal quantity axis. As the figure shows, the quantity demanded at a price of $2 per lb is 80 million lbs per month.

One of the most important things to know about the graph of a demand curve is what is *not* shown. All relevant economic variables that are not explicitly included in the demand curve graph—income, prices of other goods (such as other fruits or vegetables), tastes, information, and so on—are held constant. Thus, the demand curve shows how quantity varies with price but not how quantity varies with income, the price of substitute goods, tastes, information, or other variables.[4]

---

[3]To obtain our estimated supply and demand curves, we used estimates from Carman (2006), which we updated with more recent (2012) data from the California Avocado Commission and supplemented with information from other sources. The numbers have been rounded so that the figures use whole numbers.

[4]Because prices, quantities, and other factors change simultaneously over time, economists use statistical techniques to hold the effects of factors other than the price of the good constant so that they can determine how price affects the quantity demanded (see Appendix 2A at the back of the book). As with any estimate, the demand curve estimates are probably more accurate in the observed range of prices than at very high or very low prices.

Effect of Prices on the Quantity Demanded   Many economists claim that the most important *empirical* finding in economics is the **Law of Demand**: Consumers demand more of a good the lower its price, holding constant tastes, the prices of other goods, and other factors that influence the amount they consume. According to the Law of Demand, *demand curves slope downward*, as in Figure 2.1.[5]

A downward-sloping demand curve illustrates that consumers demand a larger quantity of this good when its price is lowered and a smaller quantity when its price is raised. What happens to the quantity of avocados demanded if the price of avocados drops and all other variables remain constant? If the price of avocados falls from $2.00 per lb to $1.50 per lb in Figure 2.1, the quantity consumers want to buy increases from 80 million lbs to 100 million lbs.[6] Similarly, if the price increases from $2 to $3, the quantity consumers demand decreases from 80 to 40.

These changes in the quantity demanded in response to changes in price are *movements along the demand curve*. Thus, the demand curve concisely summarizes the answers to the question "What happens to the quantity demanded as the price changes, when all other factors are held constant?"

Effects of Other Factors on Demand   If a demand curve measures the effects of price changes when all other factors that affect demand are held constant, how can we use demand curves to show the effects of a change in one of these other factors, such as the price of tomatoes? One solution is to draw the demand curve in a three-dimensional diagram with the price of avocados on one axis, the price of tomatoes on a second axis, and the quantity of avocados on the third axis. But what would you do if the demand curve depended on one more factor?

Economists use a simpler approach to show the effect on demand of a change in a factor that affects demand other than the price of the good. A change in any factor other than the price of the good itself causes a *shift of the demand curve* rather than a *movement along the demand curve*.

The price of substitute goods affects the quantity of avocados demanded. Many consumers view tomatoes as a substitute for avocados. The original, estimated avocado demand curve in Figure 2.1 is based on an average price of tomatoes of $0.80 per lb. Figure 2.2 shows how the avocado demand curve shifts *outward* or *to the right* from the original demand curve D^1 to a new demand curve D^2 if the price of tomatoes increases by 55¢. On D^2, more avocados are demanded at any given price than on D^1 because tomatoes, a substitute good, have become more expensive. At a price of $2 per lb, the quantity of avocados demanded goes from 80 million lbs on D^1, before the increase in the price of tomatoes, to 91 million lbs on D^2, after the increase.

Similarly, consumers tend to buy more avocados as their incomes rise. Thus, if income rises, the demand curve for avocados shifts to the right, indicating that consumers demand more avocados at any given price.

Other factors may also affect the demand curve for various goods. For example, if cigarettes become more addictive, the demand curve of existing smokers would

---

[5]Theoretically, a demand curve could slope upward (Chapter 5); however, available empirical evidence strongly supports the Law of Demand.

[6]Economists typically do not state the relevant physical and time period measures unless they are particularly useful. They refer to *quantity* rather than something useful such as "metric tons per year" and *price* rather than "cents per pound." I'll generally follow this convention, usually referring to the price as $2 (with the "per lb" understood) and the quantity as 80 (with the "million lbs per month" understood).

Law of Demand
consumers demand more of a good the lower its price, holding constant tastes, the prices of other goods, and other factors that influence consumption

Figure 2.2 A Shift of the Demand Curve

The demand curve for avocados shifts to the right from D^1 to D^2 as the price of tomatoes, a substitute, increases by 55¢ per lb. As a result of the increase in the price of tomatoes, more avocados are demanded at any given price.

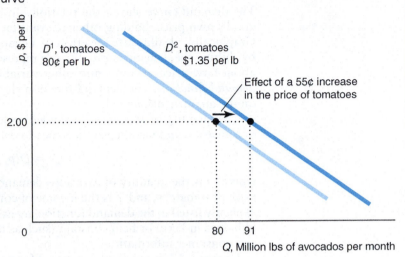

shift to the right.[7] Similarly, information can shift a demand curve. Reinstein and Snyder (2005) found that favorable movie reviews shifted the opening weekend demand curve to the right by 25% for a drama, but favorable reviews did not significantly shift the demand curve for an action film or a comedy.

To properly analyze the effects of a change in some variable on the quantity demanded, we must distinguish between a *movement along a demand curve* and a *shift of a demand curve*. A change in the *price of a good* causes a *movement along a demand curve*. A change in *any other factor besides the price of the good* causes a *shift of the demand curve*.

Application

Calorie Counting at Starbucks

New York City started requiring mandatory posting of calories on menus in chain restaurants in mid-2008. Bollinger, Leslie, and Sorensen (2011) found that New York City's mandatory calorie posting caused average calories per transaction at Starbucks to fall by 6% due to reduced consumption of high-calorie foods. They found larger responses to information among wealthier and better-educated consumers and among those who prior to the law consumed relatively more calories.

Some states have since passed similar laws. Although a 2010 U.S. health care law required that the Food and Drug Administration (FDA) write rules requiring chain restaurants and other firms to post calories on menus and in vending machines, the FDA had not written the rules by June 2013. Nonetheless, some firms have started posting such information. McDonald's announced in 2012 that it would start posting calorie information on its menus, and Coca-Cola announced in 2013 that it would put calorie information on the front of its products.

---

[7]A Harvard School of Public Health study concluded that cigarette manufacturers raised nicotine levels in cigarettes by 11% from 1998 to 2005 to make them more addictive. Gardiner Harris, "Study Showing Boosted Nicotine Levels Spurs Calls for Controls," *San Francisco Chronicle*, January 19, 2007, A-4.

The Demand Function

The demand curve shows the relationship between the quantity demanded and a good's own price, holding other relevant factors constant at some particular levels. Graphically, we illustrate the effect of a change in one of these other relevant factors by shifting the demand curve. We can represent the same information—information about how price, income, and other variables affect quantity demanded—using a *demand function*. The demand function shows the effect of *all* the relevant factors on the quantity demanded.

The quantity of avocados demanded varies with the price of avocados, the price of tomatoes, and income, so the avocado demand function, D, is

$$Q = D(p, p_t, Y) \tag{2.1}$$

where Q is the quantity of avocados demanded, p is the price of avocados, p_t is the price of tomatoes, and Y is the income of consumers. Any other factors that are not explicitly listed in the demand function are assumed to be irrelevant (such as the price of llamas in Peru) or held constant (such as the prices of other related goods, tastes, and consumer information).

Equation 2.1 is a general functional form—it does not specify exactly how Q varies with the explanatory variables, p, p_t, and Y. The estimated demand function that corresponds to the demand curve D^1 in Figures 2.1 and 2.2 has a specific (linear) form. If we measure quantity in millions of lbs per month, avocado and tomato prices in dollars per lb, and average monthly income in dollars, the demand function is

$$Q = 104 - 40p + 20p_t + 0.01Y. \tag{2.2}$$

When we draw the demand curve D^1 in Figures 2.1 and 2.2, we hold p_t and Y at specific values. The price per lb for tomatoes is $0.80, and average income is $4,000 per month. If we substitute these values for p_t and Y in Equation 2.2, we can rewrite the quantity demanded as a function of only the price of avocados:

$$
\begin{aligned}
Q &= 104 - 40p + 20p_t + 0.01Y \\
&= 104 - 40p + (20 \times 0.80) + (0.01 \times 4{,}000) \\
&= 160 - 40p. \tag{2.3}
\end{aligned}
$$

The linear demand function in Equation 2.3 corresponds to the straight-line demand curve D^1 in Figure 2.1 with particular given values for the price of tomatoes and for income. The constant term, 160, in Equation 2.3 is the quantity demanded (in millions of lbs per month) if the price is zero. Setting the price equal to zero in Equation 2.3, we find that the quantity demanded is $Q = 160 - (40 \times 0) = 160$. Figure 2.1 shows that $Q = 160$ where D^1 hits the quantity axis—where price is zero.

We can use Equation 2.3 to determine how the quantity demanded varies with a change in price: a movement *along* the demand curve. If the price falls from p_1 to p_2, the change in price, Δp, equals $p_2 - p_1$. (The Δ symbol, the Greek letter delta, means "change in" the variable following the delta, so Δp means "change in price.") If the price of avocados falls from $p_1 = \$2$ to $p_2 = \$1.50$, then $\Delta p = \$1.50 - \$2 = -\$0.50$. The quantity demanded changes from $Q_1 = 80$ at a price of $2 to $Q_2 = 100$ at a price of $1.50, so

$\Delta Q = Q_2 - Q_1 = 100 - 80 = 20$ million lbs per month. That is, as price falls by 50¢ per pound, the quantity rises by 20 million lbs per month.

More generally, the quantity demanded at p_1 is $Q_1 = D(p_1)$, and the quantity demanded at p_2 is $Q_2 = D(p_2)$. The change in the quantity demanded, $\Delta Q = Q_2 - Q_1$, in response to the price change (using Equation 2.3) is

$$
\begin{aligned}
\Delta Q &= Q_2 - Q_1 \\
&= D(p_2) - D(p_1) \\
&= (160 - 40p_2) - (160 - 40p_1) \\
&= -40(p_2 - p_1) \\
&= -40\Delta p.
\end{aligned}
$$

Thus, the change in the quantity demanded, ΔQ, is -40 times the change in the price, Δp. For example, if $\Delta p = -\$0.50$, then $\Delta Q = -40\Delta p = -40(-0.50) = 20$ million lbs.

This effect is consistent with the Law of Demand. A 50¢ decrease in price causes a 20 million lb per month increase in quantity demanded. Similarly, raising the price would cause the quantity demanded to fall.

The slope of a demand curve is $\Delta p / \Delta Q$, the "rise" (Δp, the change along the vertical axis) divided by the "run" (ΔQ, the change along the horizontal axis). The slope of demand curve D^1 in Figures 2.1 and 2.2 is

$$
\text{Slope} = \frac{\text{rise}}{\text{run}} = \frac{\Delta p}{\Delta Q} = \frac{\$1 \text{ per lb}}{-40 \text{ million lbs per month}}
$$

$$
= -\$0.025 \text{ per million lbs per month.}
$$

The negative sign of this slope is consistent with the Law of Demand. The slope says that the price rises by \$1 per lb as the quantity demanded falls by 40 million lbs per month.

Thus, we can use the demand curve to answer questions about how a change in price affects the quantity demanded and how a change in the quantity demanded affects price. We can also answer these questions using demand functions.

Solved Problem 2.1	How much would the price have to fall for consumers to be willing to buy 1 million more lbs of avocados per month?

Answer

1. *Express the price that consumers are willing to pay as a function of quantity.* We use algebra to rewrite the demand function as an *inverse demand function*, where price depends on the quantity demanded. Subtracting Q from both sides of Equation 2.3 and adding $40p$ to both sides, we find that $40p = 160 - Q$. Dividing both sides of the equation by 40, we obtain the inverse demand function:

$$
p = 40 - 0.025Q \tag{2.4}
$$

2. *Use the inverse demand curve to determine how much the price must change for consumers to buy 1 million more lbs of avocados per year.* We want the new quantity, Q_2, to equal the original quantity, Q_1, plus one: $Q_2 = Q_1 + 1$. Using

the inverse demand function, Equation 2.4, we can determine by how much the price must change:

$$\Delta p = p_2 - p_1$$
$$= (40 - 0.025Q_2) - (40 - 0.025Q_1)$$
$$= -0.025(Q_2 - Q_1)$$
$$= -0.025\Delta Q.$$

The change in quantity is $\Delta Q = Q_2 - Q_1 = (Q_1 + 1) - Q_1 = 1$, so the change in price is $\Delta p = -0.025$. That is, for consumers to demand 1 million more lbs of avocados per month, the price must fall by 2.5¢ per pound, which is a *movement along the demand curve.*

Summing Demand Curves

If we know the demand curve for each of two consumers, how do we determine the total demand curve for the two consumers combined? The total quantity demanded *at a given price* is the sum of the quantity each consumer demands at that price.

We can use the demand functions to determine the total demand of several consumers. Suppose that the demand function for Consumer 1 is

$$Q_1 = D^1(p)$$

and the demand function for Consumer 2 is

$$Q_2 = D^2(p).$$

At price p, Consumer 1 demands Q_1 units, Consumer 2 demands Q_2 units, and the total demand of both consumers is the sum of the quantities each demands separately:

$$Q = Q_1 + Q_2 = D^1(p) + D^2(p).$$

We can generalize this approach to look at the total demand for three or more consumers.

It makes sense to add the quantities demanded only when all consumers face the same price. Adding the quantity Consumer 1 demands at one price to the quantity Consumer 2 demands at another price would be like adding apples and oranges.

Application

Aggregating Corn Demand Curves

We illustrate how to combine individual demand curves to get an aggregate demand curve graphically using estimated demand curves for corn (McPhail and Babcock, 2012). The figure shows the U.S. feed demand (the use of corn to feed animals) curve, the U.S. food demand curve, and the aggregate demand curve from these two sources.[8]

To derive the sum of the quantity demanded for these two uses at a given price, we add the quantities from the individual demand curves at that price. That is, we add the demand curves horizontally. At the 2012 average price for corn, $7.40, the quantity demanded for food is 1.3 billion bushels per year and the quantity demanded for feed is 4.6 billion bushels. Thus, the total quantity demanded at that price is $Q = 1.3 + 4.6 = 5.9$.

---

[8]For graphical simplicity, we do not show the other major U.S. demand curves for export, storage, and use in biofuels (ethanol). Thus, this aggregate demand curve is not the total demand curve for corn.

When the price of corn exceeds $27.56 per bushel, farmers stop using corn for animal feed, so the quantity demanded for this use equals zero. Thus, the total demand curve is the same as the food demand curve at prices above $27.56.

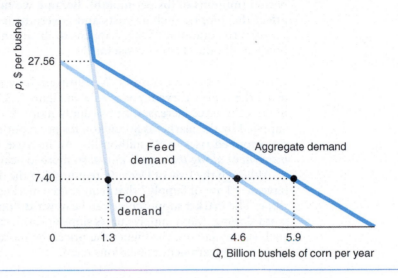

2.2 Supply

Knowing how much consumers want is not enough by itself for us to determine the market price and quantity. We also need to know how much firms want to supply at any given price.

Firms determine how much of a good to supply based on the price of that good and other factors, including the costs of production and government rules and regulations. Usually, we expect firms to supply more at a higher price. Before concentrating on the role of price in determining supply, we'll briefly describe the role of some of the other factors.

Costs of production affect how much firms want to sell of a good. As a firm's cost falls, it is willing to supply more, all else the same. If the firm's cost exceeds what it can earn from selling the good, the firm sells nothing. Thus, factors that affect costs also affect supply. A technological advance that allows a firm to produce a good at lower cost leads the firm to supply more of that good, all else the same.

Government rules and regulations affect how much firms want to sell or are allowed to sell. Taxes and many government regulations—such as those covering pollution, sanitation, and health insurance—alter the costs of production. Other regulations affect when and how the product can be sold. In some countries, retailers may not sell most goods and services on days of particular religious significance. In the United States, the sale of cigarettes and liquor to children is prohibited. Many cities around the world restrict the number of taxicabs.

quantity supplied
the amount of a good that firms *want* to sell at a given price, holding constant other factors that influence firms' supply decisions, such as costs and government actions

supply curve
the *quantity supplied* at each possible price, holding constant the other factors that influence firms' supply decisions

The Supply Curve

The **quantity supplied** is the amount of a good that firms *want* to sell at a given price, holding constant other factors that influence firms' supply decisions, such as costs and government actions. We can show the relationship between price and the quantity supplied graphically. A **supply curve** shows the quantity supplied at each possible price, holding constant the other factors that influence firms' supply decisions.

Figure 2.3 shows the estimated supply curve, S^1, for avocados. As with the demand curve, the price on the vertical axis is measured in dollars per physical unit (dollars per lb), and the quantity on the horizontal axis is measured in physical units per time period (millions of lbs per month). Because we hold fixed other variables that may affect the supply, such as costs and government rules, the supply curve concisely answers the question "What happens to the quantity supplied as the price changes, holding all other factors constant?"

Effects of Price on Supply We illustrate how price affects the quantity supplied using the supply curve for avocados in Figure 2.3. The supply curve is upward sloping. As the price increases, firms supply more. If the price is $2 per lb, the quantity supplied by the market is 80 million lbs per month. If the price rises to $3, the quantity supplied rises to 95 million lbs. An increase in the price of avocados causes a *movement along the supply curve*, so more avocados are supplied.

Although the Law of Demand requires that the demand curve slope downward, we have *no* "Law of Supply" that requires the market supply curve to have a particular slope. The market supply curve can be upward sloping, vertical, horizontal, or downward sloping. Many supply curves slope upward, such as the one for avocados. Along such supply curves, the higher the price, the more firms are willing to sell, holding costs and government regulations fixed.

Effects of Other Variables on Supply A change in a relevant variable other than the good's own price causes the entire *supply curve to shift*. Suppose the price of fertilizer used to produce avocados increases by 55¢ from 40¢ to 95¢ per lb. This increase in the price of a key factor of production causes the cost of avocado production to rise. Because it is now more expensive to produce avocados, the supply curve shifts *inward* or *to the left*, from S^1 to S^2 in Figure 2.4.[9] That is, firms want to supply fewer avocados at any given price than before the fertilizer-based cost increase. At a price of $2 per lb for avocados, the quantity supplied falls from 80 million lbs on S^1 to 69 million on S^2 (after the cost increase).

Figure 2.3 A Supply Curve

The estimated supply curve, S^1, for avocados shows the relationship between the quantity supplied per month and the price per lb, holding constant cost and other factors that influence supply. The upward slope of this supply curve indicates that firms supply more of this good when its price is high and less when the price is low. An increase in the price of avocados causes firms to supply a larger quantity of avocados; any change in price results in a movement *along the supply curve*.

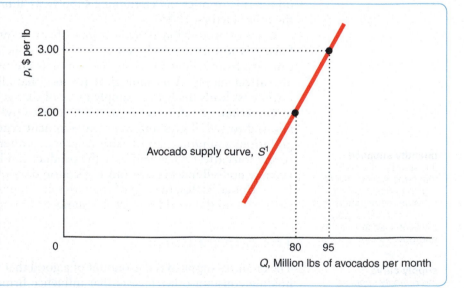

[9]Alternatively, we may say that the supply curve shifts *up* because firms' costs of production have increased, so that firms will supply a given quantity only at a higher price.

Again, it is important to distinguish between a *movement along a supply curve* and a *shift of the supply curve*. When the price of avocados changes, the change in the quantity supplied reflects a *movement along the supply curve*. When costs, government rules, or other variables that affect supply change, the entire *supply curve shifts*.

The Supply Function

We can write the relationship between the quantity supplied and price and other factors as a mathematical relationship called the *supply function*. Using a general functional form, we can write the avocado supply function, S, as

$$Q = S(p, p_f), \qquad (2.5)$$

where Q is the quantity of avocados supplied, p is the price of avocados, and p_f is the price of fertilizer. The supply function, Equation 2.5, might also incorporate other factors such as wages, transportation costs, and the state of technology, but by leaving them out, we are implicitly holding them constant.

Our estimated supply function for avocados is

$$Q = 58 + 15p - 20p_f, \qquad (2.6)$$

where Q is the quantity in millions of lbs per month, p is the price of avocados in dollars per lb, and p_f is the price of fertilizer in dollars per lb. If we fix the fertilizer price at 40¢ per lb, we can rewrite the supply function in Equation 2.6 as solely a function of the avocado price. Substituting $p_f = \$0.40$ into Equation 2.5, we find that

$$Q = 58 + 15p - (20 \times 0.40) = 50 + 15p. \qquad (2.7)$$

What happens to the quantity supplied if the price of avocados increases by $\Delta p = p_2 - p_1$? As the price increases from p_1 to p_2, the quantity supplied goes from Q_1 to Q_2, so the change in quantity supplied is

$$\Delta Q = Q_2 - Q_1 = (50 + 15p_2) - (50 + 15p_1) = 15(p_2 - p_1) = 15\Delta p.$$

Thus, a \$1 increase in price ($\Delta p = 1$) causes the quantity supplied to increase by $\Delta Q = 15$ million lbs per month. This change in the quantity of avocados supplied as p increases is a *movement along the supply curve*.

Figure 2.4 A Shift of a Supply Curve

A 55¢ per lb increase in the price of fertilizer, which is used to produce avocados, causes the supply curve for avocados to shift left from S^1 to S^2. At the price of avocados at \$2 per lb, the quantity supplied falls from 80 on S^1 to 69 on S^2.

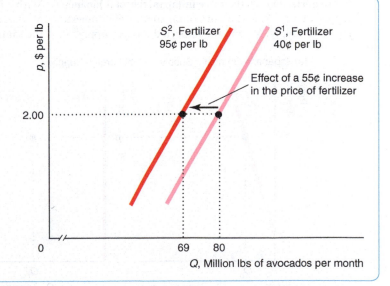

Summing Supply Curves

The total supply curve shows the total quantity produced by all suppliers at each possible price. For example, the total supply of rice in Japan is the sum of the domestic and foreign supply curves of rice.

Suppose that the domestic supply curve (panel a) and foreign supply curve (panel b) of rice in Japan are as Figure 2.5 shows. The total supply curve, S in panel c, is the horizontal sum of the Japanese *domestic* supply curve, S^d, and the *foreign* supply curve, S^f. In the figure, the Japanese and foreign supplies are zero at any price equal to or less than $\underline{p}$, so the total supply is zero. At prices above $\underline{p}$, the Japanese and foreign supplies are positive, so the total supply is positive. For example, when price is p^*, the quantity supplied by Japanese firms is Q_d^* (panel a), the quantity supplied by foreign firms is Q_f^* (panel b), and the total quantity supplied is $Q^* = Q_d^* + Q_f^*$ (panel c). Because the total supply curve is the horizontal sum of the domestic and foreign supply curves, the total supply curve is flatter than the other two supply curves.

Effects of Government Import Policies on Supply Curves

We can use this approach for deriving the total supply curve to analyze the effect of government policies on the total supply curve. Japan banned the importation of foreign rice until 1994 and even today severely restricts imports. We want to determine how much less was supplied at any given price to the Japanese market because of this ban.

Without a ban, the foreign supply curve is S^f in panel b of Figure 2.5. A ban on imports eliminates the foreign supply, so the foreign supply curve after the ban is imposed, $\overline{S}^f$, is a vertical line at $Q_f = 0$. The import ban had no effect on the domestic supply curve, S^d, so the supply curve remains the same as in panel a.

Because the foreign supply with a ban, $\overline{S}^f$, is zero at every price, the total supply with a ban, $\overline{S}$, in panel c is the same as the Japanese domestic supply, S^d, at any given price. The total supply curve under the ban lies to the left of the total supply curve without a ban, S. Thus, the effect of the import ban is to rotate the total supply curve toward the vertical axis.

Figure 2.5 Total Supply: The Sum of Domestic and Foreign Supply

If foreigners may sell their rice in Japan, the total Japanese supply of rice, S, is the horizontal sum of the domestic Japanese supply, S^d, and the imported foreign supply, S^f.

With a ban on foreign imports, the foreign supply curve, $\overline{S}^f$, is zero at every price, so the total supply curve, $\overline{S}$, is the same as the domestic supply curve, S^d.

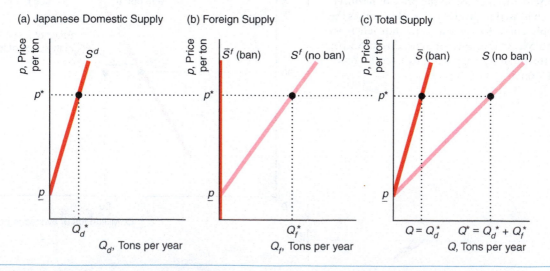

quota

the limit that a government sets on the quantity of a foreign-produced good that may be imported

The limit that a government sets on the quantity of a foreign-produced good that may be imported is called a **quota**. By absolutely banning the importation of rice, the Japanese government set a quota of zero on rice imports. Sometimes governments set positive quotas, $\overline{Q} > 0$. The foreign firms may supply as much as they want, Q_f, as long as they supply no more than the quota: $Q_f \leq \overline{Q}$.

We investigate the effect of such a quota in Solved Problem 2.2. In most of the solved problems in this book, you are asked to determine how a *change* in a variable or policy *affects* one or more variables. In this problem, the policy *changes* from no quota to a quota, which *affects* the total supply curve.

Solved Problem 2.2

How does the quota set by the United States on foreign sugar imports of $\overline{Q}$ affect the total American supply curve for sugar given the domestic supply curve, S^d in panel a of the graph, and the foreign supply curve, S^f in panel b?

Answer

1. *Determine the American supply curve without the quota.* The *no-quota* total supply curve, S in panel c, is the horizontal sum of the U.S. domestic supply curve, S^d, and the no-quota foreign supply curve, S^f.

2. *Show the effect of the quota on foreign supply.* At prices less than $\overline{p}$, foreign suppliers want to supply quantities less than the quota, $\overline{Q}$. As a result, the foreign supply curve under the quota, $\overline{S}^f$, is the same as the no-quota foreign supply curve, S^f, for prices less than $\overline{p}$. At prices above $\overline{p}$, foreign suppliers want to supply more but are limited to $\overline{Q}$. Thus the foreign supply curve with a quota, $\overline{S}^f$, is vertical at $\overline{Q}$ for prices above $\overline{p}$.

3. *Determine the American total supply curve with the quota.* The total supply curve with the quota, $\overline{S}$, is the horizontal sum of S^d and $\overline{S}^f$. At any price above $\overline{p}$, the total supply equals the quota plus the domestic supply. For example, at p^*, the domestic supply is Q_d^* and the foreign supply is $\overline{Q}_f$, so the total supply is $Q_d^* + \overline{Q}_f$. Above $\overline{p}$, $\overline{S}$ is the domestic supply curve shifted $\overline{Q}$ units to the right. As a result, the portion of $\overline{S}$ above $\overline{p}$ has the same slope as S^d.

4. *Compare the American total supply curves with and without the quota.* At prices less than or equal to $\overline{p}$, the same quantity is supplied with and without the quota, so $\overline{S}$ is the same as S. At prices above $\overline{p}$, less is supplied with the quota than without one, so $\overline{S}$ is steeper than S, indicating that a given increase in price raises the quantity supplied by less with a quota than without one.

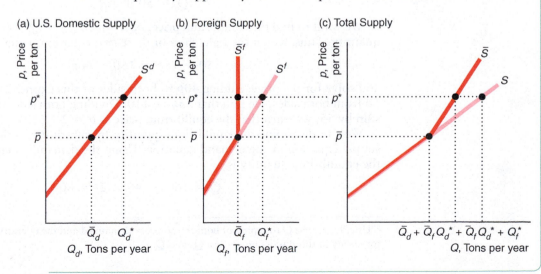

(a) U.S. Domestic Supply   (b) Foreign Supply   (c) Total Supply

2.3 Market Equilibrium

The supply and demand curves determine the price and quantity at which goods and services are bought and sold. The demand curve shows the quantities consumers want to buy at various prices, and the supply curve shows the quantities firms want to sell at various prices. Unless the price is set so that consumers want to buy exactly the same amount that suppliers want to sell, either some buyers cannot buy as much as they want or some sellers cannot sell as much as they want.

When all traders are able to buy or sell as much as they want, we say that the market is in **equilibrium**: a situation in which no one wants to change his or her behavior. A price at which consumers can buy as much as they want and sellers can sell as much as they want is called an *equilibrium price*. The quantity that is bought and sold at the equilibrium price is called the *equilibrium quantity*.

equilibrium
a situation in which no one wants to change his or her behavior

Using a Graph to Determine the Equilibrium

To illustrate how supply and demand curves determine the equilibrium price and quantity, we use our old friend, the avocado example. Figure 2.6 shows the supply, S, and demand, D, curves for avocados. The supply and demand curves intersect at point e, the market equilibrium. The equilibrium price is $2 per lb, and the equilibrium quantity is 80 million lbs per month, which is the quantity firms want to sell at that price *and* the quantity consumers want to buy at that price.

Using Math to Determine the Equilibrium

We can determine the equilibrium mathematically, using algebraic representations of the supply and demand curves. We use these two equations to solve for the equilibrium price at which the quantity demanded equals the quantity supplied (the equilibrium quantity). The demand curve, Equation 2.3, shows the relationship between the quantity demanded, Q_d, and the price:[10]

$$Q_d = 160 - 40p.$$

The supply curve, Equation 2.7, tells us the relationship between the quantity supplied, Q_s, and the price:

$$Q_s = 50 + 15p.$$

We want to find the equilibrium price, p, at which $Q_d = Q_s = Q$, the equilibrium quantity. Thus, we set the right sides of these two equations equal,

$$50 + 15p = 160 - 40p,$$

and solve for the price. Adding $40p$ to both sides of this expression and subtracting 50 from both sides, we find that $55p = 110$. Dividing both sides of this last expression by 55, we learn that the equilibrium price is $p = 2$.

We can determine the equilibrium quantity by substituting this p into either the supply equation or the demand equation. Using the demand equation, we find that the equilibrium quantity is

$$Q = 160 - (40 \times 2) = 80$$

---

[10]Usually, we use Q to represent both the quantity demanded and the quantity supplied. However, for clarity in this discussion, we use Q_d and Q_s.

Figure 2.6 Market Equilibrium

The intersection of the supply curve, S, and the demand curve, D, for avocados determines the market equilibrium point, e, where $p = \$2$ per lb and $Q = 80$ million lbs per month. At the lower price of $p = \$1.60$, the quantity supplied, 74, is less than the quantity demanded, 96, which results in excess demand of 22. At $p = \$2.40$, a price higher than the equilibrium price, the excess supply is 22 because the quantity demanded, 64, is less than the quantity supplied, 86. With either excess demand or excess supply, market forces drive the price back to the equilibrium price of $2.

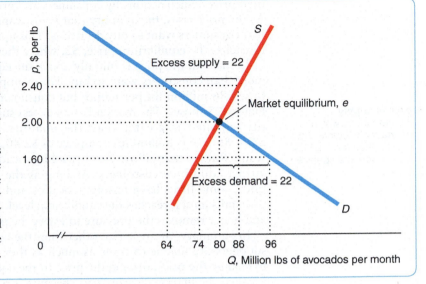

million lbs per month. We obtain the same quantity by using the supply curve equation: $Q = 50 + (15 \times 2) = 80$.

Forces That Drive the Market to Equilibrium

A market equilibrium is not just an abstract concept or a theoretical possibility. We can observe markets in equilibrium. Indirect evidence that a market is in equilibrium is that you can buy as much as you want of the good at the market price. You can almost always buy as much as you want of such common goods as milk and ballpoint pens.

Amazingly, a market equilibrium occurs without any explicit coordination between consumers and firms. In a competitive market such as that for agricultural goods, millions of consumers and thousands of firms make their buying and selling decisions independently. Yet each firm can sell as much as it wants; each consumer can buy as much as he or she wants. It is as though an unseen market force, like an *invisible hand*, directs people to coordinate their activities to achieve a market equilibrium.

What really causes the market to move to an equilibrium? If the price is not at the equilibrium level, consumers or firms have an incentive to change their behavior in a way that will drive the price to the equilibrium level, as we now illustrate.

If the price were initially lower than the equilibrium price, consumers would want to buy more than suppliers want to sell. If the price of avocados is $1.60 in Figure 2.5, firms are willing to supply 74 million lbs per month but consumers demand 96 million lbs. At this price, the market is in *disequilibrium*: the quantity demanded is not equal to the quantity supplied. The market has **excess demand**: the amount by which the quantity demanded exceeds the quantity supplied at a specified price. At a price of $1.60 per lb, the excess demand is 22 ($= 96 - 74$) million lbs per month.

Some consumers are lucky enough to buy the avocados at $1.60 per lb. Other consumers cannot find anyone who is willing to sell them avocados at that price. What can they do? Some frustrated consumers may offer to pay suppliers more than $1.60 per lb. Alternatively, suppliers, noticing these disappointed consumers, might raise

excess demand
the amount by which the *quantity demanded* exceeds the *quantity supplied* at a specified price

their prices. Such actions by consumers and producers cause the market price to rise. As the price rises, the quantity that firms want to supply increases and the quantity that consumers want to buy decreases. This upward pressure on price continues until it reaches the equilibrium price, $2, where the excess demand is eliminated.

If, instead, the price is initially above the equilibrium level, suppliers want to sell more than consumers want to buy. For example, at a price of $2.40, suppliers want to sell 86 million lbs per month but consumers want to buy only 64 million lbs, as Figure 2.5 shows. The market has an **excess supply**—the amount by which the quantity supplied is greater than the quantity demanded at a specified price—of 22(= 86 − 64) million lbs at a price of $2.40. Not all firms can sell as much as they want. Rather than allow their unsold avocados to spoil, firms lower the price to attract additional customers. As long as the price remains above the equilibrium price, some firms have unsold avocados and want to lower the price further. The price falls until it reaches the equilibrium level, $2, which eliminates the excess supply and hence removes the pressure to lower the price further.[11]

In summary, at any price other than the equilibrium price, either consumers or suppliers are unable to trade as much as they want. These disappointed people act to change the price, driving the price to the equilibrium level. The equilibrium price is called the *market clearing price* because it removes from the market all frustrated buyers and sellers: The market has no excess demand or excess supply at the equilibrium price.

excess supply
the amount by which the *quantity supplied* is greater than the *quantity demanded* at a specified price

2.4 Shocking the Equilibrium

Once an equilibrium is achieved, it can persist indefinitely because no one applies pressure to change the price. The equilibrium changes only if a shock occurs that shifts the demand curve or the supply curve. These curves shift if one of the variables we were holding constant changes. If tastes, income, government policies, or costs of production change, the demand curve or the supply curve or both shift, and the equilibrium changes.

Effects of a Shift in the Demand Curve

Suppose that the price of fresh tomatoes increases by 55¢ per lb, so consumers substitute avocados for tomatoes. As a result, the demand curve for avocados shifts outward from D^1 to D^2 in panel a of Figure 2.7. At any given price, consumers want more avocados than they did before the price of tomatoes rose. In particular, at the original equilibrium price of avocados of $2, consumers now want to buy 91 million lbs of avocados per month. At that price, however, suppliers still want to sell only 80 million lbs. As a result, excess demand is 11 million lbs. Market pressures drive the price up until it reaches a new equilibrium at $2.20. At that price, firms want to sell 83 million lbs and consumers want to buy 83 million lbs, the new equilibrium quantity. Thus, the equilibrium moves from e_1 to e_2 as a result of the increase in the price

---

[11]Not all markets reach equilibrium through the independent actions of many buyers or sellers. In institutionalized or formal markets, such as the Chicago Mercantile Exchange—where agricultural commodities, financial instruments, energy, and metals are traded—buyers and sellers meet at a single location (or on a single Web site). In these markets, certain individuals or firms, sometimes referred to as *market makers*, act to adjust the price and bring the market into equilibrium very quickly.

> **Figure 2.7** Equilibrium Effects of a Shift of a Demand or Supply Curve
>
> (a) A 55¢ per lb increase in the price of tomatoes causes the demand curve for avocados to shift outward from D^1 to D^2. At the original equilibrium (e_1) price of $2, excess demand is 11 million lbs per month. Market pressures drive the price up until it reaches $2.20 at the new equilibrium, e_2. (b) An increase in the price of fertilizer by 55¢ per lb causes producers' costs to rise, so they supply fewer avocados at every price. The supply curve for avocados shifts to the left from S^1 to S^2, driving the market equilibrium from e_1 to e_2, where the new equilibrium price is $2.20.
>
> (a) Effect of a 55¢ Increase in the Price of Tomatoes
>
>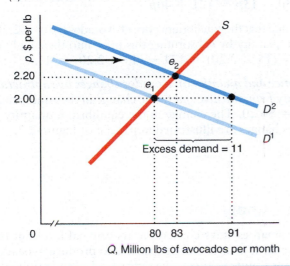
>
> (b) Effect of a 55¢ Increase in the Price of Fertilizer
>
>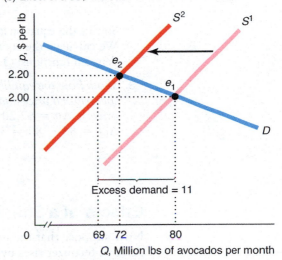

of tomatoes. Both the equilibrium price and the equilibrium quantity of avocados rise as a result of the outward shift of the avocado demand curve. Here the increase in the price of tomatoes causes a *shift of the demand curve*, which in turn causes a *movement along the supply curve*.

Solved Problem 2.3

Using algebra, determine how the equilibrium price and quantity of avocados change from the initial levels, $p = \$2$ and $Q = 80$, if the price of fresh tomatoes increases from its original price of $p_t = 80¢$ by 55¢ to $1.35.

Answer

1. *Show how the demand and supply functions change due to the increase in the price of tomatoes.* In the demand function, Equation 2.2, the quantity demanded depends on the price of tomatoes, p_t, and income, Y. We set income at its original value, 4,000 to obtain:

    $$Q = 104 - 40p + 20p_t + 0.01Y$$
    $$= 104 - 40p + 20p_t + (0.01 \times 4{,}000)$$
    $$= 144 - 40p + 20p_t.$$

(As a check of this equation, when we substitute the original $p_t = \$0.80$ into this equation we get $Q = 160 - 40p$, which is the original demand function, Equation 2.3, that depends on only the price of avocados.) Inserting the new price of tomatoes, $1.35, into this equation, we obtain the new demand equation

$$Q = 144 - 40p + (20 \times 1.35) = 171 - 40p.$$

Thus, an increase in the price of tomatoes shifts the intercept of the demand curve, causing the demand curve to shift to the right by 11(= 171 − 160) million lbs per month. The supply function does not depend on the price of tomatoes, so the supply function remains the same as in Equation 2.7:

$$Q = 50 + 15p.$$

2. *Equate the supply and demand functions to determine the new equilibrium.* The equilibrium price is determined by equating the right sides of these supply and demand equations:

$$50 + 15p = 171 − 40p.$$

Solving this equation for p, we find that the equilibrium price of avocados is $p = \$2.20$. We calculate the equilibrium quantity by substituting this price into the supply or demand functions: $Q = 50 + (15 \times 2.20) = 171 − (40 \times 2.20) = 83$.

3. *Show how the equilibrium price and quantity of avocados changes by subtracting the original price and quantity from the new ones.* The change in the equilibrium price is $\Delta p = \$2.20 − \$2 = \$0.20$. The change in the equilibrium quantity is $\Delta Q = 83 − 80 = 3$. These changes are illustrated in panel a of Figure 2.7.

Effects of a Shift in the Supply Curve

Now suppose that the price of tomatoes stays constant at its original level but the price of fertilizer rises by 55¢ per lb. It is now more expensive to produce avocados because the price of an important input, fertilizer, has increased. As a result, the supply curve for avocados shifts to the left from S^1 to S^2 in panel b of Figure 2.7. At any given price, producers want to supply fewer avocados than they did before the price of fertilizer increased. At the original equilibrium price for avocados of $2 per lb, consumers still want 80 million lbs, but producers are now willing to supply only 69 million lbs, so excess demand is 11 million lbs. Market pressure forces the price of avocados up until it reaches a new equilibrium at e_2, where the equilibrium price is $2.20 and the equilibrium quantity is 72. The increase in the price of fertilizer causes the equilibrium price to rise but the equilibrium quantity to fall. Here a *shift of the supply curve* results in a *movement along the demand curve*.

In summary, a change in an underlying factor, such as the price of a substitute or the price of an input, shifts the demand curve or the supply curve. As a result of a shift in the demand or supply curve, the equilibrium changes. To describe the effect of this change, we compare the original equilibrium price and quantity to the new equilibrium values.

2.5 Equilibrium Effects of Government Interventions

A government can affect a market equilibrium in many ways. Sometimes government actions cause a shift in the supply curve, the demand curve, or both curves, which causes the equilibrium to change. Some government interventions, however, cause the quantity demanded to differ from the quantity supplied.

Policies That Shift Supply Curves

Governments employ a variety of policies that shift supply curves. Two common policies are licensing laws and quotas.

Licensing Laws A government *licensing law* limits the number of firms that may sell goods in a market. For example, many local governments around the world limit the number of taxicabs (see Chapter 9). Governments use zoning laws to limit the number of bars, bookstores, hotel chains, as well as firms in many other markets. In developed countries, licenses are distributed to early entrants or exams are used to determine who is licensed. In developing countries, licenses often go to relatives of government officials or to whomever offers those officials the largest bribe.

Application

Occupational Licensing

Many occupations are licensed in the United States. In those occupations, working without a license is illegal. More than 800 occupations are licensed at the local, state, or federal level, including animal trainers, dietitians and nutritionists, doctors, electricians, embalmers, funeral directors, hair dressers, librarians, nurses, psychologists, real estate brokers, respiratory therapists, salespeople, teachers, and tree trimmers (but not economists).

During the early 1950s, fewer than 5% of U.S. workers were in occupations covered by licensing laws at the state level. Since then, the share of licensed workers has grown, reaching nearly 18% by the 1980s, at least 20% in 2000, and 29% in 2008. Licensing is more common in occupations that require extensive education: More than 40% of workers with post-college education are required to have a license compared to only 15% of those with less than a high school education.

In some occupations to get licensed one must pass a test, which is frequently designed by licensed members of the occupation. By making the exam difficult, current workers can limit entry. For example, only 42% of people taking the California State Bar Examination in 2011 and 2012 passed it, although all of them had law degrees. (The national rate for lawyers passing state bar exams in 2012 was higher, but still only 67%.)

To the degree that testing is objective, licensing may raise the average quality of the workforce. However, its primary effect is to restrict the number of workers in an occupation. To analyze the effects of licensing, one can use a graph similar to panel b of Figure 2.7, where the wage is on the vertical axis and the number of workers per year is on the horizontal axis. Licensing shifts the occupational supply curve to the left, reducing the equilibrium quantity of workers and raising the wage. Kleiner and Krueger (2013) found that licensing raises occupational wages by 18%.

Quotas Quotas typically limit the amount of a good that can be sold (rather than the number of firms that sell it). Quotas are commonly used to limit imports. As we saw earlier, quotas on imports affect the supply curve. We illustrate the effect of quotas on market equilibrium.

The Japanese government's ban (the quota was set to zero) on rice imports raised the price of rice in Japan substantially. Figure 2.8 shows the Japanese demand curve for rice, D, and the total supply curve without a ban, S. The intersection of S and D determines the equilibrium, e_1, if rice imports are allowed.

Figure 2.8 A Ban on Rice Imports Raises the Price in Japan

A ban on rice imports shifts the total supply of rice in Japan without a ban, S, to $\bar{S}$, which equals the domestic supply alone. As a result, the equilibrium changes from e_1 to e_2. The ban causes the price to rise from p_1 to p_2 and the equilibrium quantity to fall to Q_1 from Q_2.

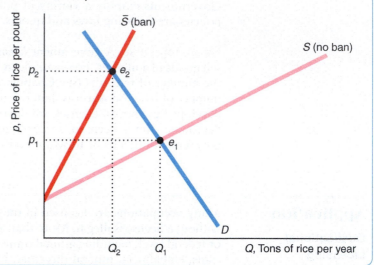

What is the effect of a ban on foreign rice on Japanese supply and demand? The ban has no effect on demand if Japanese consumers do not care whether they eat domestic or foreign rice. The ban causes the total supply curve to rotate toward the origin from S (total supply is the horizontal sum of domestic and foreign supply) to $\bar{S}$ (total supply equals the domestic supply).

The intersection of $\bar{S}$ and D determines the new equilibrium, e_2, which lies above and to the left of e_1. The ban caused a shift of the supply curve and a movement along the demand curve. It led to a fall in the equilibrium quantity from Q_1 to Q_2 and a rise in the equilibrium price from p_1 to p_2. Because of the Japanese nearly total ban on imported rice, the price of rice in Japan was 10.5 times higher than the price in the rest of the world in 2001, but is only about 50% higher today.

A quota of $\bar{Q}$ may have a similar effect to an outright ban; however, a quota may have no effect on the equilibrium if the quota is set so high that it does not limit imports. We investigate this possibility in Solved Problem 2.4.

Solved Problem 2.4

What is the effect of a United States quota on sugar of $\bar{Q}$ on the equilibrium in the U.S. sugar market? *Hint:* The answer depends on whether the quota binds (is low enough to affect the equilibrium).

Answer

1. *Show how a quota, $\bar{Q}$, affects the total supply of sugar in the United States.* The graph reproduces the no-quota total American supply curve of sugar, S, and the total supply curve under the quota, $\bar{S}$ (which we derived in Solved Problem 2.2). At a price below $\bar{p}$, the two supply curves are identical because the quota is not binding: It is greater than the quantity foreign firms want to supply. Above $\bar{p}$, $\bar{S}$ lies to the left of S.

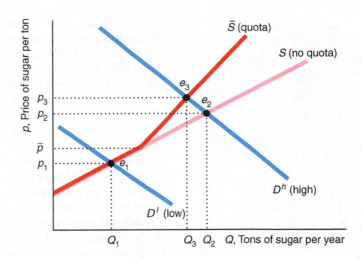

2. *Show the effect of the quota if the original equilibrium quantity is less than the quota so that the quota does not bind.* Suppose that the American demand is relatively *low* at any given price so that the demand curve, D^l, intersects both the supply curves at a price below $\bar{p}$. The equilibria both before and after the quota is imposed are at e_1, where the equilibrium price, p_1, is less than $\bar{p}$. Thus if the demand curve lies near enough to the origin that the quota is not binding, the quota has no effect on the equilibrium.

3. *Show the effect of the quota if the quota binds.* With a relatively *high* demand curve, D^h, the quota affects the equilibrium. The no-quota equilibrium is e_2, where D^h intersects the no-quota total supply curve, S. After the quota is imposed, the equilibrium is e_3, where D^h intersects the total supply curve with the quota, $\bar{S}$. The quota raises the price of sugar in the United States from p_2 to p_3 and reduces the quantity from Q_2 to Q_3.

Comment: Currently, 70% of the sugar Americans consume is produced domestically, while the rest is imported from about 40 countries under a quota system.[12] Due to the quota, the 2012 U.S. wholesale price of sugar was 60% higher than the price in the rest of the world. (This increase in price is applauded by nutritionists who deplore the amount of sugar consumed in the typical U.S. diet.)

Policies That Cause Demand to Differ from Supply

Some government policies do more than merely shift the supply or demand curve. For example, governments may control prices directly, a policy that leads to either excess supply or excess demand if the price the government sets differs from the equilibrium price. We illustrate this result with two types of price control programs: price ceilings and price floors. When the government sets a *price ceiling* at $\bar{p}$, the price at which goods are sold may be no higher than $\bar{p}$. When the government sets a *price floor* at $\underline{p}$, the price at which goods are sold may not fall below $\underline{p}$.

---

[12]Mark J. Perry, **www.aei-ideas.org/2012/02/u-s-sugar-policy-cost-american-consumers-almost-4-billion-last-year**, February 14, 2012. The United States also imports sugar from Mexico, which is not covered by a quota due to a free-trade treaty.

Price Ceilings Price ceilings have no effect if they are set above the equilibrium price that would be observed in the absence of the price controls. If the government says that firms may charge no more than $\bar{p} = \$5$ per gallon of gas and firms are actually charging $p = \$1$, the government's price control policy is irrelevant. However, if the equilibrium price, p, was above the price ceiling $\bar{p}$, the price actually observed in the market would be the price ceiling.

The United States used price controls during both world wars, the Korean War, and in 1971–1973 during the Nixon administration, among other times. The U.S. experience with gasoline illustrates the effects of price controls. In the 1970s, the Organization of Petroleum Exporting Countries (OPEC) reduced supplies of oil (which is converted into gasoline) to Western countries. As a result, the total supply curve for gasoline in the United States—the horizontal sum of domestic and OPEC supply curves—shifted to the left from S^1 to S^2 in Figure 2.9. Because of this shift, the equilibrium price of gasoline would have risen substantially, from p_1 to p_2. In an attempt to protect consumers by keeping gasoline prices from rising, the U.S. government set price ceilings on gasoline in 1973 and 1979.

The government told gas stations that they could charge no more than $\bar{p} = p_1$. Figure 2.9 shows the price ceiling as a solid horizontal line extending from the price axis at $\bar{p}$. The price control is binding because $p_2 > \bar{p}$. The observed price is the price ceiling. At $\bar{p}$, consumers *want* to buy $Q_d = Q_1$ gallons of gasoline, which is the equilibrium quantity they bought before OPEC acted. However, firms supply only Q_s gallons, which is determined by the intersection of the price control line with S^2. As a result of the binding price control, excess demand is $Q_d - Q_s$.

Were it not for the price controls, market forces would drive up the market price to p_2, where the excess demand would be eliminated. The government price ceiling prevents this adjustment from occurring. As a result, an enforced price ceiling causes a **shortage**: a persistent excess demand.

shortage
a persistent excess demand

At the time of the controls, some government officials argued that the shortages were caused by OPEC's cutting off its supply of oil to the United States, but that's

---

Figure 2.9 Price Ceiling on Gasoline

After a shock, the supply curve shifts from S^1 to S^2. Under the government's price control program, gasoline stations may not charge a price above the price ceiling, $\bar{p} = p_1$. At that price, producers are willing to supply only Q_s, which is less than the amount $Q_1 = Q_d$ that consumers want to buy. The result is excessive demand, or a shortage of $Q_d - Q_s$.

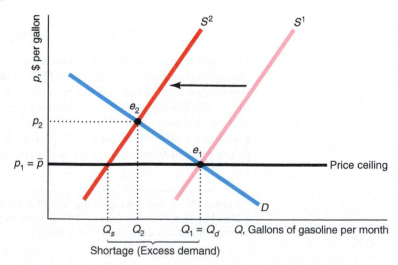

not true. Without the price controls, the new equilibrium would be e_2. In this equilibrium, the price, p_2, is much higher than before, p_1; however, no shortage results. Moreover, without controls, the quantity sold, Q_2, is greater than the quantity sold under the control program, Q_s.

With a binding price ceiling, the supply-and-demand model predicts an *equilibrium with a shortage*. In this equilibrium, the quantity demanded does not equal the quantity supplied. The reason that we call this situation an equilibrium, even though a shortage exists, is that no consumers or firms want to act differently, given the law. Without the price controls, consumers facing a shortage would try to get more output by offering to pay more, or firms would raise prices. With effective government price controls, they know that they can't drive up the price, so they live with the shortage.

What happens? Some lucky consumers get to buy Q_s units at the low price of $\bar{p}$. Other potential customers are disappointed: They would like to buy at that price, but they cannot find anyone willing to sell gas to them.

What determines which consumers are lucky enough to find goods to buy at the low price when a price control is imposed? With enforced price controls, sellers use criteria other than price to allocate the scarce commodity. Firms may supply their friends, long-term customers, or people of a certain race, gender, age, or religion. They may sell their goods on a first-come, first-served basis. Or they may limit everyone to only a few gallons.

Another possibility is for firms and customers to evade the price controls. A consumer could go to a gas station owner and say, "Let's not tell anyone, but I'll pay you twice the price the government sets if you'll sell me as much gas as I want." If enough customers and gas station owners behaved that way, no shortage would occur. A study of 92 major U.S. cities during the 1973 gasoline price controls found no gasoline lines in 52 of them. However, in cities such as Chicago, Hartford, New York, Portland, and Tucson, potential customers waited in line at the pump for an hour or more.[13] Deacon and Sonstelie (1989) calculated that for every dollar consumers saved during the 1980 gasoline price controls, they lost $1.16 in waiting time and other factors.

This experience dissuaded most U.S. jurisdictions from imposing gasoline price controls, even when gasoline prices spiked following Hurricane Katrina in the summer of 2008. The one exception was Hawaii, which imposed price controls on the wholesale price of gasoline starting in September 2005, but suspended the controls indefinitely in early 2006 due to the public's unhappiness with the law. However, many other countries have imposed price controls on gasoline more recently, such as Argentina in 2013.

Application	Robert G. Mugabe, who has ruled Zimbabwe with an iron fist for a third of a century, has used price controls to try to stay in power by currying favor among the poor.[14] In 2001, he imposed price controls on many basic commodities, including food, soap, and cement, which led to shortages of these goods, and a thriving *black*, or *parallel, market* developed in which the controls were ignored. Prices on the black market were two or three times higher than the controlled prices.
Price Controls Kill	

He imposed more extreme controls in 2007. A government edict cut the prices of 26 essential items by up to 70%, and a subsequent edict imposed price controls on a

---

[13]See MyEconLab, Chapter 2, "Gas Lines," for a discussion of the effects of the 1973 and 1979 gasoline price controls.

[14]Mr. Mugabe justified price controls as a means to deal with profiteering businesses that he said were part of a Western conspiracy to reimpose colonial rule. Actually, they were a vain attempt to slow the hyperinflation that resulted from his printing Zimbabwean money rapidly. Prices increased 500 billion times from 2000 to 2007, and the government printed currency with a face value of 100 trillion Zimbabwe dollars.

much wider range of goods. Gangs of price inspectors patrolled shops and factories, imposing arbitrary price reductions. State-run newspapers exhorted citizens to turn in store owners whose prices exceeded the limits.

The Zimbabwean police reported that they arrested at least 4,000 businesspeople for not complying with the price controls. The government took over the nation's slaughterhouses after meat disappeared from stores, but in a typical week, butchers killed and dressed only 32 cows for the entire city of Bulawayo, which consists of 676,000 people.

Citizens initially greeted the price cuts with euphoria because they had been unable to buy even basic necessities because of hyperinflation and past price controls. Yet most ordinary citizens were unable to obtain much food because most of the cut-rate merchandise was snapped up by the police, soldiers, and members of Mr. Mugabe's governing party, who were tipped off prior to the price inspectors' rounds.

Manufacturing slowed to a crawl because firms could not buy raw materials and because the prices firms received were less than their costs of production. Businesses laid off workers or reduced their hours, impoverishing the 15% or 20% of adult Zimbabweans who still had jobs. The 2007 price controls on manufacturing crippled this sector, forcing manufacturers to sell goods at roughly half of what it cost to produce them. By mid-2008, the output by Zimbabwe's manufacturing sector had fallen 27% compared to the previous year. As a consequence, Zimbabweans died from starvation. Although we have no exact figures, according to the World Food Program, over five million Zimbabweans faced starvation in 2008.

Aid shipped into the country from international relief agencies and the two million Zimbabweans who had fled abroad helped keep some people alive. In 2008, the World Food Program made an urgent appeal for $140 million in donations to feed Zimbabweans, stating that drought and political upheaval would soon exhaust the organization's stockpiles. The economy shrank by 40% percent between 2000 and 2007. Thankfully, the price controls were lifted in 2009.

Price Floors   Governments also commonly use price floors. One of the most important examples of a price floor is a minimum wage in a labor market. A minimum wage law forbids employers from paying less than the minimum wage, $\underline{w}$.

Minimum wage laws date from 1894 in New Zealand, 1909 in the United Kingdom, and 1912 in Massachusetts. The Fair Labor Standards Act of 1938 set a federal U.S. minimum wage of 25¢ per hour. The U.S. federal minimum hourly wage rose to $7.25 in 2009 and remained at that level through mid-2013, but 19 states have higher state minimum wages. The minimum wage in Canada differs across provinces, ranging from C$9.50 to C$11.00 (where C$ stands for Canadian dollars, which roughly equal U.S. dollars) in 2013. The U.K. minimum wage for adults is £6.31 ($9.81) as of October 2013. If the minimum wage is *binding*—that is, if it exceeds the equilibrium wage, w^*—it creates *unemployment*: a persistent excess supply of labor.[15] The original 1938 U.S. minimum wage law caused massive unemployment in Puerto Rico.[16]

---

[15]Where the minimum wage applies to only a few labor markets (Chapter 10) or where only a single firm hires all the workers in a market (Chapter 15), a minimum wage may not cause unemployment (see Card and Krueger, 1995, for empirical evidence). The U.S. Department of Labor maintains at its Web site (**www.dol.gov**) an extensive history of the minimum wage law, labor markets, state minimum wage laws, and other information. For European countries, see **epp.eurostat.ec.europa .eu/statistics_explained/index.php/Minimum_wage_statistics**.

[16]See MyEconLab, Chapter 2, "Minimum Wage Law in Puerto Rico."

Solved Problem 2.5

Suppose everyone is paid the same wage in a labor market. If a binding minimum wage, $\underline{w}$, is imposed, what happens to the equilibrium in this market?

Answer

1. *Show the initial equilibrium before the minimum wage is imposed.* The figure shows the supply and demand curves for labor services (hours worked). Firms buy hours of labor service—they hire workers. The quantity measue on the horizontal axis is hours worked per year, and the price measure on the vertical axis is the wage per hour. With no government intervention, the intersection of the supply and demand curves determine the market equilibrium at e, where the wage is w^* and the number of hours worked is L^*.

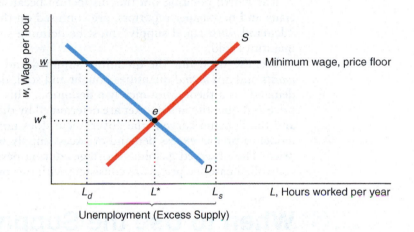

2. *Draw a horizontal line at the minimum wage, and show how the market equilibrium changes.* The minimum wage creates a price floor, a horizontal line, at $\underline{w}$. At that wage, the quantity demanded falls to L_d and the quantity supplied rises to L_s. As a result, excess supply or unemployment is $L_s - L_d$. The minimum wage prevents market forces from eliminating this excess supply, so it leads to an equilibrium with unemployment.

Comment: It is ironic that a law designed to help workers by raising their wages may harm some of them by causing them to become unemployed. A minimum wage law benefits only those who remain employed.[17]

Why Supply Need Not Equal Demand

The price ceiling and price floor examples show that the quantity supplied does not necessarily equal the quantity demanded in a supply-and-demand model. The quantity supplied need not equal the quantity demanded because of the way we defined these two concepts. We defined the quantity supplied as the amount firms *want to sell* at a given price, holding other factors that affect supply, such as the price of inputs, constant. The quantity demanded is the quantity that consumers *want to buy* at a given price, if other factors that affect demand are held constant. The quantity that

---

[17]The minimum wage could raise the wage enough that total wage payments, wL, rise despite the fall in demand for labor services. If the workers could share the unemployment—everybody works fewer hours than he or she wants—all workers could benefit from the minimum wage.

firms want to sell and the quantity that consumers want to buy at a given price need not equal the *actual* quantity that is bought and sold.

When the government imposes a binding price ceiling of $\overline{p}$ on gasoline, the quantity demanded is greater than the quantity supplied. Despite the lack of equality between the quantity supplied and the quantity demanded, the supply-and-demand model is useful in analyzing this market because it predicts the excess demand that is actually observed.

We could have defined the quantity supplied and the quantity demanded so that they must be equal. If we were to define the quantity supplied as the amount firms *actually* sell at a given price and the quantity demanded as the amount consumers *actually* buy, supply must equal demand in all markets because the quantity demanded and the quantity supplied are *defined* to be the same quantity.

It is worth pointing out this distinction because many people, including politicians and newspaper reporters, are confused on this point. Someone insisting that "demand *must* equal supply" must be defining supply and demand as the *actual* quantities sold.

Because we define the quantities supplied and demanded in terms of people's *wants* and not *actual* quantities bought and sold, the statement that "supply equals demand" is a theory, not merely a definition. This theory says that the equilibrium price and quantity in a market are determined by the intersection of the supply curve and the demand curve if the government does not intervene. Further, we use the model to predict excess demand or excess supply when a government does control price. The observed gasoline shortages during periods when the U.S. government controlled gasoline prices are consistent with this prediction.

2.6 When to Use the Supply-and-Demand Model

As we've seen, supply-and-demand theory can help us to understand and predict real-world events in many markets. Through Chapter 10, we discuss competitive markets in which the supply-and-demand model is a powerful tool for predicting what will happen to market equilibrium if underlying conditions—tastes, incomes, and prices of inputs—change. The types of markets for which the supply-and-demand model is useful are described at length in these chapters, particularly in Chapters 8 and 9. Briefly, this model is applicable in markets in which:

- **Everyone is a price taker.** Because no consumer or firm is a very large part of the market, no one can affect the market price. Easy entry of firms into the market, which leads to a large number of firms, is usually necessary to ensure that firms are price takers.
- **Firms sell identical products.** Consumers do not prefer one firm's good to another.
- **Everyone has full information about the price and quality of goods.** Consumers know if a firm is charging a price higher than the price others set, and they know if a firm tries to sell them inferior-quality goods.
- **Costs of trading are low.** It is not time-consuming, difficult, or expensive for a buyer to find a seller and make a trade or for a seller to find and trade with a buyer.

Markets with these properties are called *perfectly competitive markets*.

In a market with many firms and consumers, no single firm or consumer is a large enough part of the market to affect the price. If you stop buying bread or if one of the many thousands of wheat farmers stops selling the wheat used to make the bread, the price of bread will not change. Consumers and firms are *price takers*: They cannot affect the market price.

In contrast, if a market has only one seller of a good or service—a *monopoly* (see Chapter 11)—that seller is a *price setter* and can affect the market price. Because demand curves slope downward, a monopoly can increase the price it receives by reducing the amount of a good it supplies. Firms are also price setters in an *oligopoly*—a market with only a small number of firms—or in markets where they sell differentiated products so that a consumer prefers one product to another (see Chapter 13). In markets with price setters, the market price is usually higher than that predicted by the supply-and-demand model. That doesn't make the model generally wrong. It means only that the supply-and-demand model does not apply to markets with a small number of sellers or buyers. In such markets, we use other models.

If consumers have less information than a firm, the firm can take advantage of consumers by selling them inferior-quality goods or by charging a much higher price than that charged by other firms. In such a market, the observed price is usually higher than that predicted by the supply-and-demand model, the market may not exist at all (consumers and firms cannot reach agreements), or different firms may charge different prices for the same good (see Chapter 19).

The supply-and-demand model is also not entirely appropriate in markets in which it is costly to trade with others because the cost of a buyer finding a seller or of a seller finding a buyer is high. **Transaction costs** are the expenses of finding a trading partner and making a trade for a good or service other than the price paid for that good or service. These costs include the time and money spent to find someone with whom to trade. For example, you may have to pay to place a newspaper advertisement to sell your gray 1999 Honda with 137,000 miles on it. Or you may have to go to many stores to find one that sells a shirt in exactly the color you want, so your transaction costs include transportation costs and your time. The labor cost of filling out a form to place an order is a transaction cost. Other transaction costs include the costs of writing and enforcing a contract, such as the cost of a lawyer's time. Where transaction costs are high, no trades may occur, or if they do occur, individual trades may occur at a variety of prices (see Chapters 12 and 19).

Thus, the supply-and-demand model is not appropriate in markets with only one or a few firms (such as electricity), differentiated products (movies), consumers who know less than sellers about quality or price (used cars), or high transaction costs (nuclear turbine engines). Markets in which the supply-and-demand model has proved useful include agriculture, finance, labor, construction, services, wholesale, and retail.

transaction costs
the expenses of finding a trading partner and making a trade for a good or service beyond the price paid for that good or service

Challenge Solution

Quantities and Prices of Genetically Modified Foods

We conclude this chapter by returning to the challenge posed at its beginning where we asked about the effects on the price and quantity of a crop, such as corn, from the introduction of GM seeds. The supply curve shifts to the right because GM seeds produce more output than traditional seeds, holding all else constant. If consumers fear GM products, the demand curve for corn shifts to the left. We want to determine how the after-GM equilibrium compares to the before-GM equilibrium. When an event shifts both curves, then the qualitative effect on the equilibrium price and quantity may be difficult to predict, even if we know the direction in which each curve shifts. Changes in the equilibrium price and quantity depend on exactly how much the curves shift. In our analysis, we want to take account of the possibility that the demand curve may shift only slightly in some countries where consumers don't mind GM products but substantially in others where many consumers fear GM products.

In the figure, the original, before-GM equilibrium, e_1, is determined by the intersection of the before-GM supply curve, S^1, and the before-GM demand curve, D^1, at price p_1 and quantity Q_1. Both panels a and b of the figure show this same equilibrium. After GM seeds are introduced, the supply curve, S^2, shifts to the right of the original supply curve, S^1 in both panels.

Panel a shows the situation if consumers have little concern about GM crops, so that the new demand curve, D^2, lies only slightly to the left of the original demand curve, D^1. In panel b, where consumers are greatly concerned about GM crops, the new demand curve D^3 lies substantially to the left of D^1.

In panel a, the new equilibrium e_2 is determined by the intersection of S^2 and D^2. In panel b, the new equilibrium e_3 reflects the intersection of S^2 and D^3. The equilibrium price falls from p_1 to p_2 in panel a and to p_3 in panel b. However, the equilibrium quantity rises from Q_1 to Q_2 in panel a, but falls to Q_3 in panel b. That is, the price falls in both cases, but the quantity may rise or fall depending on how much the demand curve shifts. Thus, whether growers in a country decide to adopt GM seeds turns crucially on consumer resistance to these new products.

(a) Little Consumer Concern

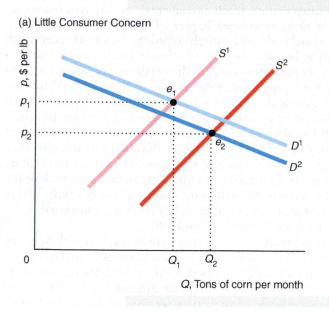

(b) Substantial Consumer Concern

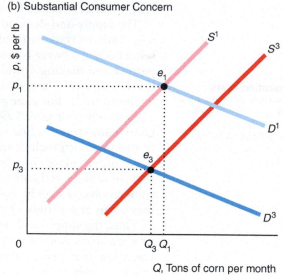

Q, Tons of corn per month

Summary

1. **Demand.** The quantity of a good or service demanded by consumers depends on their tastes, the price of a good, the price of goods that are substitutes and complements, their income, information, government regulations, and other factors. The *Law of Demand*—which is based on observation—says that *demand curves slope downward.* The higher the price, the less of the good is demanded, holding constant other factors that affect demand. A change in price causes a *movement along the demand curve.* A change in income, tastes, or another factor that affects demand other than price causes a *shift of the demand curve.* To get a total demand curve, we horizontally sum the demand curves of individuals or types of consumers or countries. That is, we add the quantities demanded by each individual at a given price to get the total demanded.

2. **Supply.** The quantity of a good or service supplied by firms depends on the price, costs, government regulations, and other factors. The market supply curve need not slope upward but usually does. A change in price causes a *movement along the supply curve.* A change in a government regulation or the price of an input causes a *shift of the supply curve.* The total supply curve is the horizontal sum of the supply curves for individual firms.

3. **Market Equilibrium.** The intersection of the demand curve and the supply curve determines the equilibrium price and quantity in a market. Market forces—actions of consumers and firms—drive the price and quantity to the equilibrium levels if they are initially too low or too high.

4. **Shocking the Equilibrium.** A change in an underlying factor other than price causes a shift of the supply curve or the demand curve, which alters the equilibrium. For example, if the price of tomatoes rises, the demand curve for avocados shifts outward, causing a movement along the supply curve and leading to a new equilibrium at a higher price and quantity. If changes in these underlying factors follow one after the other, a market that adjusts slowly may stay out of equilibrium for an extended period.

5. **Equilibrium Effects of Government Intervention.** Some government policies—such as a ban on imports—cause a shift in the supply or demand curves, thereby altering the equilibrium. Other government policies—such as price controls or a minimum wage—cause the quantity supplied to be greater or less than the quantity demanded, leading to persistent excesses or shortages.

6. **When to Use the Supply-and-Demand Model.** The supply-and-demand model is a powerful tool to explain what happens in a market or to make predictions about what will happen if an underlying factor in a market changes. This model, however, is applicable only in markets with many buyers and sellers; identical goods; certainty and full information about price, quantity, quality, incomes, costs, and other market characteristics; and low transaction costs.

Questions

All questions are available on MyEconLab; * = *answer appears at the back of this book;* **A** = *algebra problem.*

1. Demand

*1.1 The estimated demand function (Moschini and Meilke, 1992) for Canadian processed pork is $Q = 171 - 20p + 20p_b + 3p_c + 2Y$, where Q is the quantity in million kilograms (kg) of pork per year, p is the dollar price per kg (all prices cited are in Canadian dollars), p_b is the price of beef per kg, p_c is the price of chicken in dollars per kg, and Y is average income in thousands of dollars. What is the demand function if we hold p_b, p_c, and Y at their typical values during the period studied: $p_b = 4$, $p_c = 3\frac{1}{3}$, and $Y = 12.5$? **A**

*1.2 Using the estimated demand function for processed pork from Question 1.1, show how the quantity demanded at a given price changes as per capita income, Y, increases by $100 a year. **A**

1.3 Using the estimated demand function for processed pork from Question 1.1, suppose that the price of beef, p_b, rises from $4 to $5.20. In what direction and by how much does the demand curve for processed pork shift? **A**

1.4 Given the inverse demand function for pork (Question 1.1) is $p = 14.30 - 0.05Q$, how much would the price have to rise for consumers to want to buy 2 million fewer kg of pork per year? (*Hint*: See Solved Problem 2.1.) **A**

1.5 Given the estimated demand function Equation 2.2 for avocados, $Q = 104 - 40p + 20p_t + 0.01Y$, show how the demand curve shifts as per capita income, Y, increases by $1,000 a year. Illustrate this shift in a diagram. **A**

1.6 The food and feed demand curves used in the Application "Summing the Corn Demand Curves" were estimated by McPhail and Babcock (2012) to be $Q_{food} = 1,487 - 22.1p$ and $Q_{feed} = 6,247.5 - 226.7p$, respectively. Mathematically derive the total demand curve, which the Application's figure illustrates. (*Hint*: Remember that the demand curve for feed is zero at prices above $27.56.) **A**

*1.7 Suppose that the inverse demand function for movies is $p = 120 - Q_1$ for college students and $p = 120 - 2Q_2$ for other town residents. What is the town's total demand function ($Q = Q_1 + Q_2$ as a function of p)? Use a diagram to illustrate your answer. (*Hint*: See the Application "Summing the Corn Demand Curves.") **A**

1.8 Duffy-Deno (2003) estimated the demand functions for broadband service are $Q_s = 15.6p^{-0.563}$ for small firms and $Q_l = 16.0p^{-0.296}$ for larger ones, where price is in cents per kilobyte per second and quantity is in millions of kilobytes per second (Kbps). What is the total demand function for all firms? (*Hint*: See the Application "Summing the Corn Demand Curves.") **A**

2. Supply

*2.1 The estimated supply function (Moschini and Meilke, 1992) for processed pork in Canada is $Q = 178 + 40p - 60p_h$, where quantity is in millions of kg per year and the prices are in

Canadian dollars per kg. How does the supply function change if the price of hogs doubles from $1.50 to $3 per kg? **A**

2.2 Use Equation 2.6, the estimated supply function for avocados, $Q = 58 + 15p - 20p_f$, to determine how much the supply curve for avocados shifts if the price of fertilizer rises by $1.10 per lb. Illustrate this shift in a diagram.

2.3 If the supply of rice from the United States is $Q_a = a + bp$, and the supply from the rest of the world is $Q_r = c + ep$, what is the world supply? **A**

2.4 How would the shape of the total supply curve in Solved Problem 2.2 change if the U.S. domestic supply curve hit the vertical axis at a price above $\bar{p}$?

3. Market Equilibrium

*3.1 Use a supply-and-demand diagram to explain the statement "Talk is cheap because supply exceeds demand." At what price is this comparison being made?

3.2 Every house in a small town has a well that provides water at no cost. However, if the town wants more than 10,000 gallons a day, it has to buy the extra water from firms located outside of the town. The town currently consumes 9,000 gallons per day.

  a. Draw the linear demand curve.

  b. The firms' supply curve is linear and starts at the origin. Draw the market supply curve, which includes the supply from the town's wells.

  c. Show the equilibrium. What is the equilibrium quantity? What is the equilibrium price? Explain.

3.3 A large number of firms are capable of producing chocolate-covered cockroaches. The linear, upward-sloping supply curve starts on the price axis at $6 per box. A few hardy consumers are willing to buy this product (possibly to use as gag gifts). Their linear, downward-sloping demand curve hits the price axis at $4 per box. Draw the supply and demand curves. Does this market have an equilibrium at a positive price and quantity? Explain your answer.

3.4 The estimated Canadian processed pork demand function (Moschini and Meilke, 1992) is $Q = 171 - 20p + 20p_b + 3p_c + 2Y$ (see Question 1.1), and the supply function is $Q = 178 + 40p - 60p_h$ (see Question 2.1). Solve for the equilibrium price and quantity in terms of the price of hogs, p_h; the price of beef, p_b; the price of chicken, p_c; and income, Y. If $p_h = 1.5$ (dollars per kg), $p_b = 4$ (dollars per kg), $p_c = 3\frac{1}{3}$ (dollars per kg), and $Y = 12.5$ (thousands of dollars), what are the equilibrium price and quantity?

*3.5 The demand function for a good is $Q = a - bp$, and the supply function is $Q = c + ep$, where a, b, c, and e are positive constants. Solve for the equilibrium price and quantity in terms of these four constants. **A**

*3.6 Green et al. (2005) estimated the supply and demand curves for California processing tomatoes. The supply function is $\ln(Q) = 0.2 + 0.55 \ln(p)$, where Q is the quantity of processing tomatoes in millions of tons per year and p is the price in dollars per ton. The demand function is $\ln(Q) = 2.6 - 0.2 \ln(p) + 0.15 \ln(p_t)$, where p_t is the price of tomato paste (which is what processing tomatoes are used to produce) in dollars per ton. In 2002, $p_t = 110$. What is the demand function for processing tomatoes, where the quantity is solely a function of the price of processing tomatoes? Solve for the equilibrium price and quantity of processing tomatoes (explain your calculations, and round to two digits after the decimal point). Draw the supply and demand curves (note that they are not straight lines), and label the equilibrium and axes appropriately. **A**

4. Shocking the Equilibrium

4.1 The United States is increasingly *outsourcing* jobs to India: having the work done in India rather than in the United States. For example, the Indian firm Tata Consultancy Services, which provides information technology services, increased its workforce by 70,000 workers in 2010 and expected to add 60,000 more in 2011 ("Outsourcing Firm Hiring 60,000 Workers in India," *San Francisco Chronicle*, June 16, 2011). As a result of increased outsourcing, wages of some groups of Indian skilled workers have increased substantially over the years. Use a supply-and-demand diagram to explain this outcome.

4.2 The major BP oil spill in the Gulf of Mexico substantially reduced the harvest of shrimp and other seafood in the Gulf, but had limited impact on the prices that U.S. consumers paid in 2010 (Emmeline Zhao, "Impact on Seafood Prices Is Limited," *Wall Street Journal*, June 20, 2010). The reason was that the United States imports about 83% of its seafood and only 2% of domestic supplies come from the Gulf. Use a supply-and-demand diagram to illustrate what happened.

4.3 The U.S. supply of frozen orange juice comes from Florida and Brazil. What is the effect of a freeze that damages oranges in Florida on the price of frozen orange juice in the United States and on the quantities of orange juice sold by Floridian and Brazilian firms?

4.4 Use supply-and-demand diagrams to illustrate the qualitative effect of the following possible shocks on the U.S. avocado market.

a. A new study shows significant health benefits from eating avocados.

b. Trade barriers that restricted avocado imports from Mexico are eliminated ("Free Trade Party Dip," *Los Angeles Times*, February 6, 2007).

c. A recession causes a decline in per capita income.

d. Genetically modified avocado plants that allow for much greater output or yield without increasing cost are introduced into the market.

4.5 Increasingly, instead of advertising in newspapers, individuals and firms use Web sites that offer free or inexpensive classified ads, such as **ClassifiedAds.com, Craigslist.org, Realtor.com, Jobs.com, Monster.com,** and portals like **Google** and **Yahoo.** Using a supply-and-demand model, explain what will happen to the equilibrium levels of newspaper advertising as the use of the Internet grows. Will the growth of the Internet affect the supply curve, the demand curve, or both? Why?

4.6 Ethanol, a fuel, is made from corn. Ethanol production increased 5.5 times from 2000 to 2008 and another 34% from 2008 to February 2013 (**www.ethanolrfa.org**). Show the effect of this increased use of corn for producing ethanol on the price of corn and the consumption of corn as food using a supply-and-demand diagram.

4.7 The demand function for roses is $Q = a - bp$, and the supply function is $Q = c + ep + ft$, where a, b, c, e, and f are positive constants and t is the average temperature in a month. Show how the equilibrium quantity and price vary with temperature. (*Hint*: See Solved Problem 2.3.) **A**

4.8 Using the information in Question 3.6, determine how the equilibrium price and quantity of processing tomatoes change if the price of tomato paste falls by 10%. (*Hint*: See Solved Problem 2.3.) **A**

4.9 Use the demand and supply functions for avocado, Equations 2.2 and 2.6, to derive the new equilibria in Figure 2.7.

5. Equilibrium Effects of Government Interventions

5.1 The Application "Occupational Licensing" analyzed the effect of exams in licensed occupations given that their only purpose was to shift the supply curve to the left. How would the analysis change if the exam also raised the average quality of people in that occupation, thereby also affecting demand?

*5.2 Is it possible that an outright ban on foreign imports will have no effect on the equilibrium price? (*Hint*: Suppose that imports occur only at relatively high prices.)

5.3 In 2002, the U.S. Fish and Wildlife Service proposed banning imports of beluga caviar to protect the beluga sturgeon in the Caspian and Black seas, whose sturgeon populations had fallen 90% in the last two decades. The United States imports 60% of the world's beluga caviar. On the world's legal wholesale market, a kilogram of caviar costs an average of $500, and about $100 million worth is sold per year. What effect would the U.S. ban have on world prices and quantities? Would such a ban help protect the beluga sturgeon? (In 2005, the service decided not to ban imports.) (*Hint*: See Solved Problem 2.4.)

5.4 What is the effect of a quota $\overline{Q} > 0$ on equilibrium price and quantity? (*Hint*: Carefully show how the total supply curve changes. See Solved Problem 2.4.)

5.5 A group of American doctors have called for a limit on the number of foreign-trained physicians permitted to practice in the United States. What effect would such a limit have on the equilibrium quantity and price of doctors' services in the United States? How are American-trained doctors and consumers affected? (*Hint*: See Solved Problem 2.4.)

5.6 Usury laws place a ceiling on interest rates that lenders such as banks can charge borrowers. Low-income households in states with usury laws have significantly lower levels of consumer credit (loans) than comparable households in states without usury laws. Why? (*Hint*: The interest rate is the price of a loan, and the amount of the loan is the quantity measure.)

5.7 The Thai government actively intervenes in markets (Nophakhun Limsamarnphun, "Govt Imposes Price Controls in Response to Complaints," *The Nation*, May 12, 2012).

a. The government increased the daily minimum wage by 40% to Bt300 (300 bahts ≈ $9.63). Show the effect of a higher minimum wage on the number of workers demanded, the supply of workers, and unemployment if the law is applied to the entire labor market.

b. Show how the increase in the minimum wage and higher rental fees at major shopping malls and retail outlets affected the supply curve of ready-to-eat meals. Explain why the equilibrium price of a meal rose to Bt40 from Bt30.

c. In response to complaints from citizens about higher prices of meals, the government imposed price controls on ten popular meals. Show the effect of these price controls in the market for meals.

d. What is the likely effect of the price controls on meals on the labor market?

5.8 Some cities impose rent control laws, which are price controls or limits on the price of rental accommodations (apartments, houses, and mobile homes). As of 2012, New York City alone had approximately one million apartments under rent control. In a supply-and-demand diagram, show the effect of the rent control law on the equilibrium rental price and quantity of New York City apartments, and show the amount of excess demand.

*5.9 After a major disaster such as the Los Angeles earthquake and hurricanes such as Katrina, retailers often raise the price of milk, gasoline, and other staples because supplies have fallen. In some states, the government forbids such price increases. What is the likely effect of such a law?

5.10 Suppose that the government imposes a price support (price floor) on processing tomatoes at $65 per ton. The government will buy as much as farmers want to sell at that price. Thus, processing firms pay $65. Use the information in Question 3.6 to determine how many tons of tomatoes firms buy and how many tons the government buys. Illustrate your answer in a supply-and-demand diagram. (*Hint*: See Solved Problem 2.5.) **A**

6. When to Use the Supply-and-Demand Model

6.1 Are predictions using the supply-and-demand model likely to be reliable in each of the following markets? Why or why not?

a. Apples.

b. Convenience stores.

c. Electronic games (a market with three major firms).

d. Used cars.

7. Challenge

*7.1 Humans who consume beef products made from diseased animal parts can develop mad cow disease (bovine spongiform encephalopathy, or BSE, a new variant of Creutzfeldt-Jakob disease), a deadly affliction that slowly eats holes in sufferers' brains. The first U.S. case, in a cow imported from Canada, was reported in December 2003. As soon as the United States revealed the discovery of the single diseased cow, more than 40 countries slapped an embargo on U.S. beef, causing beef supply curves to shift to the left in those importing countries, and at least initially a few U.S. consumers stopped eating beef. (Schlenker and Villas-Boas, 2009, found that U.S. consumers regained confidence and resumed their earlier levels of beef buying within three months.) In the first few weeks after the U.S. ban, the quantity of beef sold in Japan fell substantially, and the price rose. In contrast,

in January 2004, three weeks after the first discovery, the U.S. price fell by about 15% and the quantity sold increased by 43% over the last week in October 2003. Use supply-and-demand diagrams to explain why these events occurred.

7.2 In the previous question, you were asked to illustrate why the mad cow disease announcement initially caused the U.S. equilibrium price of beef to fall and the quantity to rise. Show that if the supply and demand curves had shifted in the same directions as above but to greater or lesser degrees, the equilibrium quantity might have fallen. Could the equilibrium price have risen?

7.3 Due to fear about mad cow disease, Japan stopped importing animal feed from Britain in 1996, beef imports and processed beef products from 18 countries including EU members starting in 2001, and similar imports from Canada and the United States in 2003. After U.S. beef imports were banned, McDonald's Japan and other Japanese importers replaced much of the banned U.S. beef with Australian beef, causing an export boom for Australia ("China Bans U.S. Beef," **cnn.com**, December 24, 2003; "Beef Producers Are on the Lookout for Extra Demand," **abc.net.au**, June 13, 2005). Use supply and demand curves to show the impact of these events on the domestic Australian beef market.

7.4 When he was the top American administrator in Iraq, L. Paul Bremer III set a rule that upheld Iraqi law: anyone 25 years and older with a "good reputation and character" could own one firearm, including an AK-47 assault rifle. Iraqi citizens quickly began arming themselves. Akram Abdulzahra has a revolver handy at his job in an Internet cafe. Haidar Hussein, a Baghdad bookseller, has a new fully automatic assault rifle. After the bombing of a sacred Shiite shrine in Samarra at the end of February 2006 and the subsequent rise in sectarian violence, the demand for guns increased, resulting in higher prices. The average price of a legal, Russian-made Kalashnikov AK-47 assault rifle jumped from $112 to $290 from February to March 2006, and the price of bullets shot up from 24¢ to 33¢ each (Jeffrey Gettleman, "Sectarian Suspicion in Baghdad Fuels a Seller's Market for Guns," *New York Times*, April 3, 2006). This increase occurred despite the hundreds of thousands of firearms and millions of rounds of ammunition that American troops had been providing to Iraqi security forces, some of which eventually ended up in the hands of private citizens. Use a graph to illustrate why prices rose. Did the price have to rise, or did the rise have to do with the shapes of and relative shifts in the demand and supply curves?

7.5 The prices received by soybean farmers in Brazil, the world's second-largest soybean producer and exporter, tumbled 30%, in part because of China's decision to cut back on imports and in part because of a bumper soybean crop in the United States, the world's leading exporter (Todd Benson, "A Harvest at Peril," *New York Times*, January 6, 2005, C6). In addition, Asian soy rust, a deadly crop fungus, is destroying large quantities of the Brazilian crops.

a. Use a supply-and-demand diagram to illustrate why Brazilian farmers are receiving lower prices.

b. If you knew only the *direction* of the shifts in both the supply and the demand curves, could you predict that prices would fall? Why or why not?

3 Applying the Supply-and-Demand Model

New Jersey's decision to eliminate the tax on Botox has users elated. At least I think they're elated.
—I can't really tell.

Challenge

Who Pays the Gasoline Tax?

U.S. consumers and politicians debate endlessly about whether to increase or decrease gasoline taxes, even though U.S. gasoline taxes are very low relative to those in most other industrialized nations. The typical American paid a tax of 49¢ per gallon of gasoline in 2013, which included the federal tax of 18.4¢ and the average state gasoline tax of 30.6¢ per gallon. The comparable tax was $1.48 in Canada, $4.38 in France, $4.50 in Germany, and $4.68 in the United Kingdom.

Regularly at international climate meetings—such as the one in Bonn in 2013—government officials, environmentalists, and economists from around the world argue strongly for an increase in the tax on gasoline and other fuels (or, equivalently, on carbon) to retard global warming and improve the air we breathe.

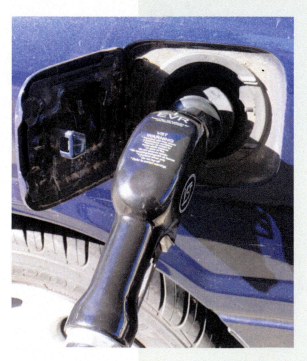

However, whenever gas prices rise suddenly, other politicians call for removing gasoline taxes, at least temporarily. Illinois and Indiana suspended their taxes during an oil price spike in 2000, as did Alaska in 2008. While running for president, Senators John McCain and Hillary Clinton called for a summer gas tax holiday during the summer of 2008. They wanted Congress to suspend the 18.4¢ per gallon federal gas tax during the traditional high-price summer months to lower gasoline prices. Then-Senator Barack Obama chided them for "pandering," arguing in part that such a suspension would primarily benefit oil firms rather than consumers. A similar debate took place in Britain in 2008. In 2011, the New Hampshire legislature debated a state tax holiday, and Representative Heath Shuler proposed a 45-day federal gasoline tax holiday. In 2013, the Indiana House minority leader proposed a tax holiday.

A critical issue in these debates concerns who pays the tax. Do firms pass the gasoline tax on to consumers in the form of higher prices or absorb the tax themselves? Is the ability of firms to pass a gas tax on to consumers different in the short run (such as during the summer months) than in the long run?

We can use a supply-and-demand analysis to answer such questions. When an underlying factor that affects the demand or supply curve—such as a tax—changes, the equilibrium price and quantity also change. Chapter 2 showed that you can predict the direction of the change—the *qualitative* change—in equilibrium price and quantity even without knowing the exact shape of the supply and demand curves. In most of the examples in Chapter 2, all you needed to know to give a qualitative answer was the direction in which the supply curve or demand curve shifted when an underlying factor changed.

To determine the exact amount the equilibrium quantity and price change—the *quantitative* change—you can use estimated equations for the supply and demand functions, as we demonstrated using the avocado example in Chapter 2. This chapter shows how to use a single number to describe how sensitive the quantity demanded or supplied is to a change in price and how to use these summary numbers to obtain quantitative answers to what-if questions, such as the effects of a tax on the price that consumers pay.

<table>
<tr>
<td>In this chapter, we examine four main topics</td>
<td>

1. **How Shapes of Supply and Demand Curves Matter.** The effect of a shock (such as a new tax or an increase in the price of an input) on market equilibrium depends on the shape of supply and demand curves.

2. **Sensitivity of the Quantity Demanded to Price.** The sensitivity of the quantity demanded to price is summarized by a single measure called the *price elasticity of demand*.

3. **Sensitivity of the Quantity Supplied to Price.** The sensitivity of the quantity supplied to price is summarized by a single measure called the *price elasticity of supply*.

4. **Effects of a Sales Tax.** How a sales tax increase affects the equilibrium price and quantity of a good and whether the tax falls more heavily on consumers or suppliers depends on the shape of the supply and demand curves.

</td>
</tr>
</table>

3.1 How Shapes of Supply and Demand Curves Matter

Well, there goes the price of lobsters!

The shapes of the supply and demand curves determine by how much a shock affects the equilibrium price and quantity. We illustrate the importance of the shape of the demand curve using the estimated avocado demand and supply curves (Chapter 2). The supply of avocados depends on the price of avocados and the price of fertilizer, a major input in producing avocados. A 55¢ per pound increase in the price of fertilizer causes the avocado supply curve to shift to the left from S^1 to S^2 in panel a of Figure 3.1. The *shift of the supply curve* causes a *movement along the demand curve, D^1*, which is downward sloping. The equilibrium quantity falls from 80 to 72 million pounds (lbs) per month, and the equilibrium price rises 20¢ from $2.00 to $2.20 per lb, hurting consumers.

A supply shock would have different effects if the demand curve had a different shape. Suppose that the quantity demanded was not sensitive to a change in the price, so the same amount is demanded no matter what the price is, as in vertical demand curve

Figure 3.1 How the Effect of a Supply Shock Depends on the Shape of the Demand Curve

A 55¢ increase in the price of fertilizer shifts the avocado supply curve to the left from S^1 to S^2. (a) Given the actual, estimated downward-sloping linear demand curve, D^1, the equilibrium price rises from $2.00 to $2.20 and the equilibrium quantity falls from 80 to 72. (b) If the demand curve were vertical, D^2, the supply shock would cause price to rise to $2.73 while quantity would remain unchanged. (c) If the demand curve were horizontal, D^3, the supply shock would not affect price but would cause quantity to fall to 69.

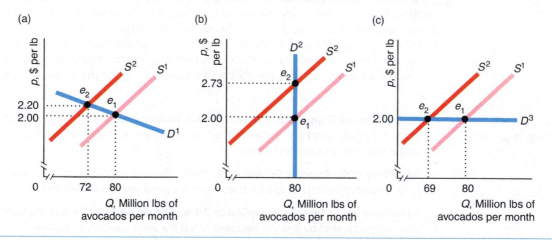

D^2 in panel b. A 55¢ increase in the price of fertilizer again shifts the supply curve from S^1 to S^2. Equilibrium quantity does not change, but the price consumers pay rises by 73¢ to $2.73. Thus, the amount consumers spend rises by more when the demand curve is vertical instead of downward sloping.

Now suppose that consumers are very sensitive to price, as in the horizontal demand curve, D^3, in panel c. Consumers will buy virtually unlimited quantities of avocados at $2 per lb (or less), but, if the price rises even slightly, they stop buying avocados. Here an increase in the price of fertilizer has *no* effect on the price consumers pay; however, the equilibrium quantity drops to 69 million lbs per month. Thus, how much the equilibrium quantity falls and how much the equilibrium price of avocados rises when the price of fertilizer increases depends on the shape of the demand curve.

3.2 Sensitivity of the Quantity Demanded to Price

Knowing how much quantity demanded falls as the price increases, holding all else constant, is therefore important in predicting the effect of a shock in a supply-and-demand model. We can determine how much quantity demanded falls as the price rises using an accurate drawing of the demand curve or the demand function (the equation that describes the demand curve). It is convenient, however, to be able to summarize the relevant information to answer what-if questions without having to write out an equation or draw a graph. Armed with such a summary statistic, a firm can predict the effect on the price of its product and its revenue—price times quantity sold—from a shift in the market supply curve.

In this section, we discuss a summary statistic that describes how much the quantity demanded changes in response to an increase in price at a given point. In the next section, we discuss a similar statistic for the supply curve. Then, we show how the government can use these summary measures for supply and demand to predict the effect of a new sales tax on the equilibrium price, firms' revenues, and tax receipts.

The most commonly used measure of the sensitivity of one variable, such as the quantity demanded, to a change in another variable, such as price, is an **elasticity**, which is the percentage change in one variable in response to a given percentage change in another variable.

elasticity
the percentage change in a variable in response to a given percentage change in another variable

Price Elasticity of Demand

price elasticity of demand
(or *elasticity of demand*, ε) the percentage change in the *quantity demanded* in response to a given percentage change in the price

The **price elasticity of demand** (or in common use, the *elasticity of demand*) is the percentage change in the quantity demanded, Q, in response to a given percentage change in the price, p, at a particular point on the demand curve. The price elasticity of demand (represented by ε, the Greek letter epsilon) is

$$\varepsilon = \frac{\text{percentage change in quantity demanded}}{\text{percentage change in price}} = \frac{\Delta Q/Q}{\Delta p/p}, \qquad (3.1)$$

where the symbol Δ (the Greek letter delta) indicates a change, so ΔQ is the change in the quantity demanded; $\Delta Q/Q$ is the percentage change in the quantity demanded; Δp is the change in price; and $\Delta p/p$ is the percentage change in price.[1] For example, if a 1% increase in the price results in a 3% decrease in the quantity demanded, the elasticity of demand is $\varepsilon = -3\%/1\% = -3$.[2] Thus, the elasticity of demand is a pure number (it has no units of measure).

A negative sign on the elasticity of demand illustrates the Law of Demand: Less quantity is demanded as the price rises. The elasticity of demand concisely answers the question, "How much does quantity demanded fall in response to a 1% increase in price?" A 1% increase in price leads to an ε% change in the quantity demanded.

It is often more convenient to calculate the elasticity of demand using an equivalent expression,

$$\varepsilon = \frac{\Delta Q/Q}{\Delta p/p} = \frac{\Delta Q}{\Delta p} \frac{p}{Q}, \qquad (3.2)$$

where $\Delta Q/\Delta p$ is the ratio of the change in quantity to the change in price (the inverse of the demand curve's slope).

We can use Equation 3.2 to calculate the elasticity of demand for a linear demand curve, which has a demand function (holding fixed other variables that affect demand) of

$$Q = a - bp. \qquad (3.3)$$

---

[1]When we use calculus, we use infinitesimally small changes in price (Δp approaches zero), so we write the elasticity as $(dQ/dp)(p/Q)$. When discussing elasticities, we assume that the change in price is small.

[2]Because demand curves slope downward according to the Law of Demand, the elasticity of demand is a negative number. Realizing that, some economists ignore the negative sign when reporting a demand elasticity. Instead of saying the demand elasticity is -3, they would say that the elasticity is 3 (with the negative sign understood).

In Equation 3.3, a is the quantity demanded when price is zero, $Q = a - (b \times 0) = a$, and $-b$ is the ratio of the fall in quantity to the rise in price, $\Delta Q/\Delta p$.[3] Thus, for a linear demand curve, the elasticity of demand is

$$\varepsilon = \frac{\Delta Q}{\Delta p} \frac{p}{Q} = -b\frac{p}{Q}. \tag{3.4}$$

Solved Problem 3.1

The estimated equation for the linear U.S. corn demand curve is[4]

$$Q = 15.6 - 0.5p, \tag{3.5}$$

where p is the price in dollars per bushel and Q is the quantity demanded in billion bushels per year. What is the elasticity of demand at the point on the demand curve where the price is $p = \$7.20$ per bushel (the price in early 2013)?

Answer

Substitute the slope coefficient b, the price, and the quantity values into Equation 3.4. Equation 3.5 is a special case of the general demand function Equation 3.3 ($Q = a - bp$), where $a = 15.6$ and $b = 0.5$. Evaluating Equation 3.5 at $p = \$7.20$, we find that the quantity demanded is $Q = 15.6 - (0.5 \times 7.20) = 12$ billion bushels per year. Substituting $b = 0.5$, $p = \$7.20$, and $Q = 12$ into Equation 3.4, we learn that the elasticity of demand at this point on the demand curve is

$$\varepsilon = -b\frac{p}{Q} = -0.5 \times \frac{7.20}{12} = -0.3.$$

Comment: At this point on the demand curve, a 1% increase in the price of corn leads to a -0.3% fall in the quantity of corn demanded. That is, a price increase causes a less than proportionate fall in the quantity of corn demanded.

Elasticity Along the Demand Curve

The elasticity of demand varies along most demand curves. The elasticity of demand is different at every point along a downward-sloping linear demand curve, but the elasticities are constant along horizontal and vertical linear demand curves.

Downward-Sloping Linear Demand Curve On strictly downward-sloping linear demand curves—those that are neither vertical nor horizontal—the elasticity of demand, $\varepsilon = -b(p/Q)$, b is constant along the line, but the ratio of p/Q varies, so the elasticity also varies. The elasticity is a more negative number the higher the price is. A 1% increase in price causes a larger percentage fall in quantity near the top (left) of the demand curve than near the bottom (right).

This pattern is illustrated in Figure 3.2, which shows the linear corn demand curve given by Equation 3.5. Where the demand curve hits the quantity axis ($p = 0$ and $Q = a = 15.6$ billion bushels per year), the elasticity of demand is $\varepsilon = -b(0/a) = 0$, according to Equation 3.4. Where the price is zero, a 1% increase

---

[3]As the price increases from p_1 to p_2, the quantity demanded goes from Q_1 to Q_2, so the change in quantity demanded is $\Delta Q = Q_2 - Q_1 = (a - bp_2) - (a - bp_1) = -b(p_2 - p_1) = -b\Delta p$. Thus, $\Delta Q/\Delta p = -b$. (The slope of the demand curve is $\Delta p/\Delta Q = -1/b$.)

[4]This demand curve is a linearized version of the estimated demand curve in Roberts and Schlenker (forthcoming). I have rounded their estimated elasticities slightly for algebraic simplicity.

Figure 3.2 Elasticity Along the Corn Demand Curve

With a linear demand curve, such as the corn demand curve, the higher the price, the more elastic the demand curve (ε is larger in absolute value—a larger negative number). The demand curve is perfectly inelastic ($\varepsilon = 0$) where the demand curve hits the horizontal axis, is perfectly elastic where the demand curve hits the vertical axis, and has unitary elasticity ($\varepsilon = -1$) at the midpoint of the demand curve.

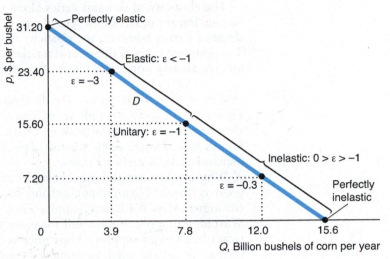

in price does not raise the price, so quantity does not change. At a point where the elasticity of demand is zero, the demand curve is said to be *perfectly inelastic*. As a physical analogy, if you try to stretch an inelastic steel rod, the length does not change. The change in the price is the force pulling at demand; if the quantity demanded does not change in response to this pulling, it is perfectly inelastic.

For quantities between the midpoint of the linear demand curve and the lower end where $Q = a$, the demand elasticity lies between 0 and -1; that is, $0 > \varepsilon > -1$. A point along the demand curve where the elasticity is between 0 and -1 is *inelastic* (but not perfectly inelastic). Where the demand curve is inelastic, a 1% increase in price leads to a fall in quantity of less than 1%. For example, as we saw in Solved Problem 3.1, at the point where $p = \$7.20$ and $Q = 12$, $\varepsilon = -0.3$, so a 1% increase in price causes quantity to fall by -0.3%. A physical analogy is a piece of rope that does not stretch much—is inelastic—when you pull on it: Changing price has relatively little effect on quantity.

At the midpoint of the linear demand curve, $p = a/(2b) = \$15.60$ and $Q = a/2 = 7.8$, so $\varepsilon = -bp/Q = -b(a/[2b])/(a/2) = -1$. Such an elasticity of demand is called a *unitary elasticity*: A 1% increase in price causes a 1% fall in quantity.

At prices higher than at the midpoint of the demand curve, the elasticity of demand is less than negative one, $\varepsilon < -1$. In this range, the demand curve is called *elastic*. A physical analogy is a rubber band that stretches substantially when you pull on it. A 1% increase in price causes quantity to fall by more than 1%. Figure 3.2 shows that the elasticity is -3 where $p = \$23.40$ and $Q = 3.9$: A 1% increase in price causes a 3% drop in quantity.

As the price rises, the elasticity gets more and more negative, approaching negative infinity. Where the demand curve hits the price axis, it is *perfectly elastic*.[5] At the

---

[5]The demand curve hits the price axis at $p = a/b$ and $Q = 0$, so the elasticity is $-bp/0$. As the quantity approaches 0, the elasticity approaches negative infinity, $-\infty$. An intuition for this convention is provided by looking at a sequence, where -1 divided by $1/10$ is -10, -1 divided by $1/100$ is -100, and so on. The smaller the number we divide by, the more negative is the result, which goes to $-\infty$ in the limit.

price $a/b = \$31.20$ where $Q = 0$, a 1% decrease in p causes the quantity demanded to become positive, which is an infinite increase in quantity.

The elasticity of demand varies along most demand curves, not just downward-sloping linear ones. Along a special type of demand curve, called a *constant elasticity demand curve*, however, the elasticity is the same at every point along the curve.[6] Two extreme cases of these constant-elasticity demand curves are the strictly vertical and the strictly horizontal linear demand curves.

Horizontal Demand Curve   The demand curve that is horizontal at p^* in panel a of Figure 3.3 shows that people are willing to buy as much as firms sell at any price less than or equal to p^*. If the price increases even slightly above p^*, however, demand falls to zero. Thus, a small increase in price causes an infinite drop in quantity, so the demand curve is perfectly elastic.

Why would a demand curve be horizontal? One reason is that consumers view this good as identical to another good and do not care which one they buy. Suppose that consumers view Washington apples and Oregon apples as identical. They won't buy Washington apples if these sell for more than apples from Oregon. Similarly, they won't buy Oregon apples if their price is higher than that of Washington apples. If the two prices are equal, consumers do not care which type of apple they buy. Thus, the demand curve for Oregon apples is horizontal at the price of Washington apples.

Vertical Demand Curve   A vertical demand curve, panel b in Figure 3.3, is perfectly inelastic everywhere. Such a demand curve is an extreme case of the linear demand curve with an infinite (vertical) slope. If the price goes up, the quantity demanded is unchanged ($\Delta Q/\Delta p = 0$), so the elasticity of demand must be zero: $(\Delta Q/\Delta p)(p/Q) = 0(p/Q) = 0$.

A demand curve is vertical for *essential goods*—goods that people feel they must have and will pay anything to get. Because Jerry is a diabetic, his demand curve

---

Figure 3.3   Vertical and Horizontal Demand Curves

(a) A horizontal demand curve is perfectly elastic at p^*.
(b) A vertical demand curve is perfectly inelastic at every price. (c) A diabetic's demand curve for insulin is perfectly inelastic below p^* and perfectly elastic at p^*, which is the maximum price the individual can afford to pay.

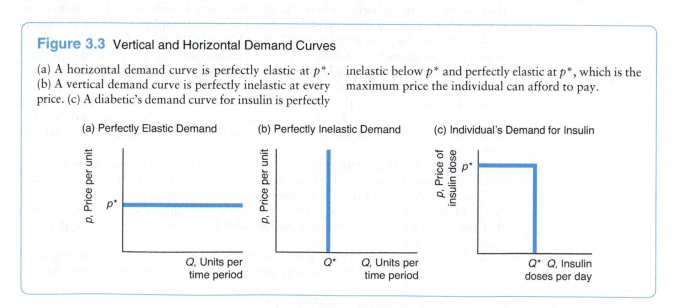

---

[6]Constant-elasticity demand curves all have the form $Q = Ap^\varepsilon$, where A is a positive constant and ε, a negative constant, is the demand elasticity at every point along these demand curves. See Question 2.6.

for insulin could be vertical at a day's dose, Q^*. More realistically, he may have a demand curve (panel c of Figure 3.3) that is perfectly inelastic only at prices below p^*, the maximum price he can afford to pay. Because he cannot afford to pay more than p^*, he buys nothing at higher prices. As a result, his demand curve is perfectly elastic up to Q^* units at a price of p^*.

Demand Elasticity and Revenue

Any shock that causes the equilibrium price to change affects the industry's *revenue*, which is the price times the market quantity sold. At the initial price p_1 in Figure 3.4, consumers buy Q_1 units at point e_1 on the demand curve D. Thus, the revenue is $R_1 = p_1 \times Q_1$. The revenue equals the area of the rectangle with a height of p_1 and a length of Q_1. At price p_1, the area of the revenue rectangle equals areas $A + B$. If the equilibrium price rises to p_2, so that the quantity demanded falls to Q_2, the new revenue is $R_2 = p_2 \times Q_2$, or area $A + C$. The change in the revenue due to the increase in price is $R_2 - R_1 = (A + C) - (A + B) = C - B$. Whether the revenue rises or falls when the price increases depends on the elasticity of demand, as the next Solved Problem shows.

Figure 3.4 Effect of a Price Change on Revenue

When the price is p_1, consumers buy Q_1 units at e_1 on the demand curve D, so revenue is $R_1 = p_1 \times Q_1$, which is area $A + B$. If the price increases to p_2, the consumers buy Q_2 units at e_2, so the revenue is $R_2 = p_2 \times Q_2$, which is area $A + C$. Thus, the change in revenue is $R_2 - R_1 = (A + C) - (A + B) = C - B$.

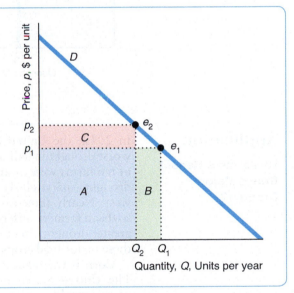

Solved Problem 3.2

Does an increase in price cause revenue to increase or decrease if the demand curve is inelastic at the initial price? How does it change if the demand curve is elastic?

Answer

1. *Consider the extreme case where the demand curve is perfectly inelastic and then generalize to the inelastic case.* In panel a of the figure, the demand curve D^1 is vertical and hence perfectly inelastic. As a consequence, as the price rises from p_1 to p_2, the quantity demanded does not change, so this figure does not have an area B, unlike Figure 3.4. Revenue increases by area $C = (p_2 - p_1)Q_2$. If the demand curve were inelastic (but not perfectly inelastic) at the initial price, a price increase would cause a less than proportional decrease in quantity. Because price rises by more than the quantity falls, revenue rises: Area B in Figure 3.4 would be relatively thin and have little area, so $C > B$.

2. *Show that if the demand curve is elastic at the initial price, then area C is relatively small.* Panel b of the figure shows a relatively flat demand curve, D^2, which is elastic at the initial price. A small percentage increase in price causes a greater percentage drop in quantity, so that area *B* is large and area *C* is small. With such a demand curve, an increase in price causes revenue to fall.[7]

(a) Perfectly Inelastic

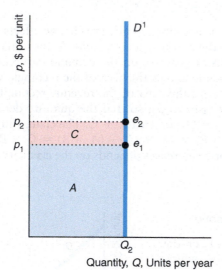

(b) Relatively Elastic

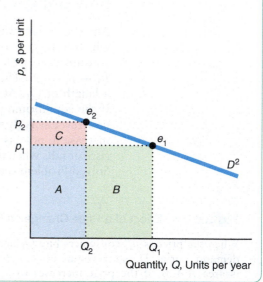

Application

Do Farmers Benefit from a Major Drought?

In 2012, the United States suffered its worst drought in half a century. Eight out of ten farms were in areas affected by the drought—particularly those in the Midwest. Nearly three-quarters of corn and soybean farmers suffered from a severe or greater drought, decimating production of these major field crops.

Corn is the highest valued U.S. crop. The United States produces one-third of the world's corn and is the leading exporter of corn. In 2012, although corn farmers planted 5.6% more land than in the previous year, total production fell 13% due to the drought.[8]

Does it follow that farmers' revenues fell substantially? Farmers whose crops were largely destroyed suffered major losses of revenue. However, total revenue rose 3.8% from 2011 to 2012. Revenue increased because the price of corn rose by more,

---

[7]This result is discussed in greater detail using mathematics in Chapter 11.

[8]The actual change in the quantity sold in the United States was less, as producers drew down inventories and corn exports fell.

19%, than quantity fell, 13%. As Solved Problem 3.2 shows, given that the demand curve for corn is inelastic, an increase in price (or equivalently, a decrease in quantity) causes corn revenue to rise.

Of course, the flip side of this coin is that bumper crops can be a disaster for farmers. The gigantic 2013 crop resulted in an August price that was 21% below that of 2012.

Demand Elasticities over Time

The shape of the demand curve depends on the relevant time period. Consequently, a short-run elasticity may differ substantially from a long-run elasticity. The duration of the *short run* depends on how long it takes consumers or firms to adjust for a particular good.

Two factors that determine whether short-run demand elasticities are larger or smaller than long-run elasticities are ease of substitution and storage opportunities. Often one can substitute between products in the long run but not in the short run.

When oil prices nearly doubled in 2008, most Western consumers did not greatly alter the amount of gasoline that they demanded in the short run. Someone who drove 27 miles to and from work every day in a 1998 Ford truck could not easily reduce the amount of gasoline purchased. However, in the long run, this person could buy a small car, get a job closer to home, join a car pool, or in other ways reduce the amount of gasoline purchased.

A survey of hundreds of estimates of gasoline demand elasticities across many countries (Graham and Glaister, 2004) found that the average estimate of the short-run elasticity was −0.21, and the long-run elasticity was −0.55. Thus, a 1% increase in price lowers the quantity demanded by only 0.21% in the short run but by more than twice as much, 0.55%, in the long run. Similarly, Grossman and Chaloupka (1998) estimated that the long-run elasticity of demand from a rise in the street price of cocaine, −1.35, is more elastic than the short-run elasticity, −0.96, for young adults (aged 17–29).

For goods that can be stored easily, short-run demand curves may be more elastic than long-run curves. Prince (2008) estimated that the demand curve for computers is more elastic in the short run, −2.74, than in the long run, −2.17. If frozen orange juice goes on sale this week at your local supermarket, you may buy large quantities and store the extra in your freezer. As a result, you may respond more to a short-run price change for frozen orange juice than to a comparable long-run price change.

Because demand elasticities differ over time, the effect of a price increase on revenue may also differ over time. For example, because the demand curve for gasoline is more inelastic in the short run than in the long run, a given increase in price raises revenue by more in the short run than in the long run.

Other Demand Elasticities

We refer to the price elasticity of demand as *the* elasticity of demand. However, other types of demand elasticities show how the quantity demanded changes in response to changes in variables other than price that affect the quantity demanded. Two such demand elasticities are the income elasticity of demand and the cross-price elasticity of demand.

Income Elasticity As income increases, the demand curve shifts. If the demand curve shifts to the right, a larger quantity is demanded at any given price. If instead the demand curve shifts to the left, a smaller quantity is demanded at any given price.

We can measure how sensitive the quantity demanded at a given price is to income by using an elasticity. The **income elasticity of demand** (or *income elasticity*) is the percentage change in the quantity demanded in response to a given percentage change in income, Y. The income elasticity of demand may be calculated as

income elasticity of demand
(or *income elasticity*) the percentage change in the *quantity demanded* in response to a given percentage change in income

$$\xi = \frac{\text{percentage change in quantity demanded}}{\text{percentage change in income}} = \frac{\Delta Q/Q}{\Delta Y/Y} = \frac{\Delta Q}{\Delta Y}\frac{Y}{Q},$$

where ξ is the Greek letter xi. If quantity demanded increases as income rises, the income elasticity of demand is positive. If the quantity does not change as income rises, the income elasticity is zero. Finally, if the quantity demanded falls as income rises, the income elasticity is negative.

We can calculate the income elasticity for avocados using the estimated demand function, Equation 2.2:

$$Q = 104 - 40p + 20p_t + 0.01Y, \tag{3.6}$$

where we measure quantity in millions of lbs per month, avocado and tomato prices in dollars per lb, and average monthly income in dollars. Because the change in quantity as income changes is $\Delta Q/\Delta Y = 0.01,$[9] we can write the income elasticity as

$$\xi = \frac{\Delta Q}{\Delta Y}\frac{Y}{Q} = 0.01\frac{Y}{Q}.$$

At the competitive equilibrium, quantity is $Q = 50$ and income is $Y = 4,000$, so the income elasticity is $\xi = 0.01 \times (4,000/50) = 0.8$. The positive income elasticity shows that an increase in income causes the avocado demand curve to shift to the right. Holding the price of avocados constant at \$2 per lb, a 1% increase in income causes the demand curve for avocados to shift to the right by $0.4 (= \xi \times 50 \times 0.01)$ million lbs, which is about 0.8% of the equilibrium quantity.

Income elasticities play an important role in our analysis of consumer behavior in Chapter 5. Typically, goods that society views as necessities, such as food, have income elasticities between zero and one. Goods that society considers to be luxuries generally have income elasticities greater than one.

cross-price elasticity of demand
the percentage change in the *quantity demanded* in response to a given percentage change in the price of another good

Cross-Price Elasticity The **cross-price elasticity of demand** is the percentage change in the quantity demanded in response to a given percentage change in the price of another good, p_o. The cross-price elasticity may be calculated as

$$\frac{\text{percentage change in quantity demanded}}{\text{percentage change in price of another good}} = \frac{\Delta Q/Q}{\Delta p_o/p_o} = \frac{\Delta Q}{\Delta p_o}\frac{p_o}{Q}.$$

When the cross-price elasticity is negative, the goods are *complements* (Chapter 2). If the cross-price elasticity is negative, people buy less of the good when the price of the other good increases: The demand curve for this good shifts to the left. For example, if people like cream in their coffee, as the price of cream rises, they consume less coffee, so the cross-price elasticity of the quantity of coffee with respect to the price of cream is negative.

---

[9]At income Y_1, the quantity demanded is $Q_1 = 104 - 40p + 20p_t + 0.01Y_1$. At income Y_2, $Q_2 = 104 - 40p + 20p_t + 0.01Y_2$. Thus, $\Delta Q = Q_2 - Q_1 = 0.01(Y_2 - Y_1) = 0.01(\Delta Y)$, so $\Delta Q/\Delta Y = 0.01$.

If the cross-price elasticity is positive, the goods are *substitutes* (Chapter 2). As the price of the other good increases, people buy more of this good. For example, the quantity demanded of avocados increases when the price of tomatoes, p_t, rises. From Equation 3.6, we know that $\Delta Q/\Delta p_t = 20$. As a result, the cross-price elasticity between the price of tomatoes and the quantity of avocados is

$$\frac{\Delta Q}{\Delta p_t} \frac{p_t}{Q} = 20 \frac{p_t}{Q}.$$

At the equilibrium where $p = \$2$ per lb, $Q = 50$ million lbs per year, and $p_t = \$0.80$ per lb, the cross-price elasticity is $20 \times (0.8/50) = 0.32$. As the price of tomatoes rises by 1%, the quantity of avocados demanded rises by about one-third of 1%.

Taking account of cross-price elasticities is important in making business and policy decisions. For example, General Motors wants to know how much a change in the price of a Toyota affects the demand for its Chevy. Society wants to know if taxing soft drinks will substantially increase the demand for milk.

3.3 Sensitivity of the Quantity Supplied to Price

To answer many what-if questions, we need information about the sensitivity of the quantity supplied to changes in price. For example, to determine how a sales tax will affect market price, a government needs to know the sensitivity to price of both the quantity supplied and the quantity demanded.

Elasticity of Supply

price elasticity of supply
(or *elasticity of supply,* η)
the percentage change
in the *quantity supplied*
in response to a given
percentage change in the
price

Just as we can use the elasticity of demand to summarize information about the shape of a demand curve, we can use the elasticity of supply to summarize information about the supply curve. The **price elasticity of supply** (or *elasticity of supply*) is the percentage change in the quantity supplied in response to a given percentage change in the price. The price elasticity of supply (represented by η, the Greek letter eta) is

$$\eta = \frac{\text{percentage change in quantity supplied}}{\text{percentage change in price}} = \frac{\Delta Q/Q}{\Delta p/p} = \frac{\Delta Q}{\Delta p} \frac{p}{Q}, \quad (3.7)$$

where Q is the *quantity supplied*. If $\eta = 2$, a 1% increase in price leads to a 2% increase in the quantity supplied.

The definition of the elasticity of supply, Equation 3.7, is very similar to the definition of the elasticity of demand, Equation 3.1. The key distinction is that the elasticity of supply describes the movement along the *supply* curve as price changes, whereas the elasticity of demand describes the movement along the *demand* curve as price changes. That is, in the numerator, supply elasticity depends on the percentage change in the *quantity supplied*, whereas demand elasticity depends on the percentage change in the *quantity demanded*.

If the supply curve is upward sloping, $\Delta p/\Delta Q > 0$, the supply elasticity is positive: $\eta > 0$. If the supply curve slopes downward, the supply elasticity is negative: $\eta < 0$.

We use the terms *inelastic* and *elastic* to describe *upward-sloping* supply curves, just as we did for demand curves. If $\eta = 0$, we say that the supply curve is *perfectly inelastic*: The supply does not change as price rises. If $0 < \eta < 1$, the supply curve is *inelastic* (but not perfectly inelastic): A 1% increase in price causes a less than 1% rise in the quantity supplied. If $\eta = 1$, the supply curve has a *unitary elasticity*: A 1% increase in price causes a 1% increase in quantity. If $\eta > 1$, the supply curve is *elastic*. If η is infinite, the supply curve is *perfectly elastic*.

The supply function of a linear supply curve is

$$Q = g + hp, \tag{3.8}$$

where g and h are constants. By the same reasoning as before, $\Delta Q = h\Delta p$, so $h = \Delta Q/\Delta p$ shows the change in the quantity supplied as price changes. Thus, the elasticity of supply for a linear supply function is

$$\eta = \frac{\Delta Q}{\Delta p}\frac{p}{Q} = h\frac{p}{Q}. \tag{3.9}$$

We can illustrate this calculation using the U.S. supply function for corn (based on Roberts and Schlenker, forthcoming),

$$Q = 10.2 + 0.25p, \tag{3.10}$$

where Q is the quantity of corn supplied in billion bushels per year and p is the price of corn in dollars per bushel. Equation 3.10 is a special case of the general supply function Equation 3.8, $Q = g + hp$, where $g = 10.2$ and $h = 0.25$.

Thus, if the price is $7.20 per bushel and the quantity is 12 billion bushels per year, we substitute $h = 0.25$, $p = 7.20$, and $Q = 12$ into Equation 3.9 to find the elasticity of supply at this point on the supply curve:

$$\eta = h\frac{p}{Q} = 0.25 \times \frac{7.20}{12} = 0.15.$$

At this point on the supply curve, a 1% increase in the price of corn leads to a 0.15% rise in the quantity of corn demanded, which is only about a seventh as much. That is, the supply curve is inelastic at this point.

Elasticity Along the Supply Curve

The elasticity of supply varies along most linear supply curves. Only *constant elasticity of supply curves* have the same elasticity at every point along the curve.[10] Two extreme examples of both constant elasticity of supply curves and linear supply curves are the vertical and horizontal supply curves.

The elasticity of supply for a linear supply function is $\eta = h(p/Q)$, Equation 3.9. If $h > 0$, as the ratio p/Q rises, the supply elasticity rises. As the corn supply function in Equation 3.10 shows, $h = 0.25$ is positive for corn, so the elasticity of supply, $\eta = 0.25(p/Q)$, increases as p/Q rises. The corn supply curve, Figure 3.5, is inelastic at each point shown. It is 0.125 at $p = \$5.60$, 0.15 at $p = \$7.20$, and about 0.164 at $p = \$8$.

A supply curve that is vertical at a quantity, Q^*, is perfectly inelastic. Regardless of the price, firms supply Q^*. An example of inelastic supply is a perishable item such as fresh fruit. If the perishable good is not sold, it quickly becomes worthless. Thus, the seller accepts any market price for the good.

A supply curve that is horizontal at a price, p^*, is perfectly elastic. Firms supply as much as the market wants—a potentially unlimited amount—if the price is p^* or above. Firms supply nothing at a price below p^*, which does not cover their cost of production.

---

[10]Constant elasticity of supply curves are of the form $Q = Bp^{\eta}$, where B is a constant and η is the constant elasticity of supply at every point along the curve.

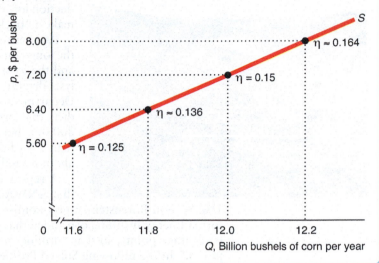

Figure 3.5 Elasticity Along the Corn Supply Curve

The elasticity of supply, η, varies along the corn supply curve. The higher the price, the larger is the supply elasticity.

Supply Elasticities over Time

Supply curves may have different elasticities in the short run than in the long run. If a manufacturing firm wants to increase production in the short run, it can do so by hiring workers to use its machines around the clock, but how much it can expand its output is limited by the fixed size of its manufacturing plant and the number of machines it has. In the long run, however, the firm can build another plant and buy or build more equipment. Thus, we would expect this firm's long-run supply elasticity to be greater than its short-run elasticity.

For example, Clemens and Gottlieb (2013) estimate that the health care supply elasticity is 0.7 in the short run and 1.4 in the long run. That is, supply is twice as elastic in the long run.

Application

Oil Drilling in the Arctic National Wildlife Refuge

We can use information about supply and demand elasticities to answer an important public policy question: Would selling oil from the Arctic National Wildlife Refuge (ANWR) substantially affect the price of oil? ANWR, established in 1980, is the largest of Alaska's 16 national wildlife refuges, covers 20 million acres, and is believed to contain large deposits of petroleum (about the amount consumed in the United States in 2005). For decades, a debate has raged over whether the owners of ANWR—the citizens of the United States—should keep it undeveloped or permit oil drilling.[11]

In the simplest form of this complex debate, President Barack Obama has sided with environmentalists who stress that drilling would harm the wildlife refuge and pollute the environment. On the other side, the Republican Governors Association (in 2012), former President George W. Bush, and other drilling proponents argue that extracting this oil would substantially reduce the price of petroleum as well as decrease U.S. dependence on foreign oil. Recent large increases and drops in the price of gasoline and unrest in the Middle East have heightened this intense debate.

[11]I am grateful to Robert Whaples, who wrote an earlier version of this analysis. In the following discussion, we assume for simplicity that the oil market is competitive, and use current values of price and quantities even though drilling in ANWR could not take place for at least a decade.

The effect of selling ANWR oil on the world price of oil is a key element of this dispute. We can combine oil production information with supply and demand elasticities to make a "back of the envelope" estimate of the price effects.

Baumeister and Peersman (forthcoming) estimate that the long-run elasticity of demand, ε, for oil is about -0.25 and the long-run supply elasticity, η, is about 0.25. Analysts dispute how much ANWR oil will be produced. The Department of Energy's Energy Information Service predicts that production from ANWR would average about 800,000 barrels per day. That production would be less than 1% of the worldwide oil production, which averaged about 89 million barrels per day in 2012.

A report by the U.S. Department of Energy predicted that ANWR drilling could lower the price of oil by about 1%. Severin Borenstein, an economist who is the director of the University of California Energy Institute, concluded that ANWR might reduce oil prices by up to a few percentage points, so that "drilling in ANWR will never noticeably affect gasoline prices." In the following Solved Problem, we can make our own calculations of the price effect of drilling in ANWR.

Solved Problem 3.3

What would be the effect of ANWR production on the world price of oil given that $\varepsilon = -0.25$, $\eta = 0.25$ (Baumeister and Peersman, forthcoming), the pre-ANWR daily world production of oil is $Q_1 = 90$ million barrels per day, the pre-ANWR world price is $p_1 = \$100$ per barrel, and daily ANWR production would be 0.8 million barrels per day?[12] For simplicity, assume that the supply and demand curves are linear and that the introduction of ANWR oil would cause a parallel shift in the world supply curve to the right by 0.8 million barrels per day.

Answer

1. *Determine the long-run linear demand function that is consistent with pre-ANWR world output and price.* Equation 3.4 gives the general formula for a linear demand curve: $Q = a - bp$, where a is the quantity when $p = 0$ (where the demand curve hits the horizontal axis) and $b = \Delta Q/\Delta p$. At the original equilibrium, e_1 in the figure, $p_1 = \$100$ and $Q_1 = 90$ million barrels per day, so the elasticity of demand is $\varepsilon = (\Delta Q/\Delta p)(p_1/Q_1) = -b(100/90) = -0.25$. Using algebra, we find that $b = -0.25(90/100) = -0.225$, so the demand function is $Q = a - 0.225p$. At e_1, the quantity demanded is $Q = 90 = a - (0.225 \times 100)$. Using algebra, we find that $a = 90 + (0.225 \times 100) = 112.5$. Thus, the demand function is $Q = 112.5 - 0.225p$.

2. *Determine the long-run linear supply function that is consistent with pre-ANWR world output and price.* The general formula for a linear supply curve is $Q = c + dp$, where c is the quantity where $p = 0$ and $d = \Delta Q/\Delta p$. Where S^1 intercepts D at the original equilibrium, e_1, the elasticity of supply is $\eta = (\Delta Q/\Delta p)(p_1/Q_1) = d(100/90) = 0.25$. Solving this equation, we find

---

[12]From 2011 through mid-2013, the price of a barrel of oil fluctuated between about $80 and $120 per barrel, and was slightly less than $100 over the first half of 2013. The calculated percentage change in the price in this Solved Problem is not sensitive to the choice of the initial price of oil.

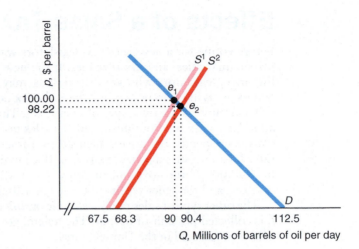

that $d = 0.25(90/100) = 0.225$, so the supply function is $Q = c + 0.225p$. Evaluating this equation at e_1, $Q = 90 = b + (0.225 \times 100)$. Solving for b, we find that $b = 90 - (0.225 \times 100) = 67.5$. Thus, the supply function is $Q = 67.5 + 0.225p$.

3. *Determine the post-ANWR long-run linear supply function.* The oil pumped from ANWR would cause a parallel shift in the supply curve, moving S^1 to the right by 0.8 to S^2. That is, the slope remains the same, but the intercept on the quantity axis increases by 0.8. Thus, the supply function for S^2 is $Q = 68.3 + 0.225p$.

4. *Use the demand curve and the post-ANWR supply function to calculate the new equilibrium price and quantity.* The new equilibrium, e_2, occurs where S^2 intersects D. Setting the right side of the demand function equal to the right side of the post-ANWR supply function, we obtain an expression for the post-ANWR price, p_2:

$$112.5 - 0.225p_2 = 68.3 + 0.225p_2.$$

We can solve this expression for the new equilibrium price: $p_2 \approx \$98.22$. That is, the price drops about \$1.78, or approximately 1.78%. If we substitute this new price into either the demand curve or the post-ANWR supply curve, we find that the new equilibrium quantity is 90.40 million barrels per day. That is, equilibrium output rises by 0.40 million barrels per day (0.44%), which is only a little more than half of the predicted daily ANWR supply, because other suppliers will decrease their output slightly in response to the lower price.

Comment: Our conclusion that selling ANWR oil causes only a small drop in the world oil price would not change substantially if our estimates of the elasticities of supply and demand were moderately larger or smaller. The main reason for this result is that the ANWR output would be a very small portion of worldwide supply—the new supply curve is only slightly to the right of the initial supply curve.

Thus, drilling in ANWR cannot insulate the U.S. market from international events that roil the oil market. A new war in the Persian Gulf could easily shift the worldwide supply curve to the left by up to 24 million barrels per day (the amount of oil produced in the Persian Gulf), or 30 times ANWR's production. Such a shock would cause the price of oil to shoot up substantially whether or not we drill in ANWR.

3.4 Effects of a Sales Tax

Before voting for a new sales tax, legislators want to predict the effect of the tax on prices, quantities, and tax revenues. If the new tax will produce a large increase in the price, legislators who vote for the tax may lose their jobs in the next election. Voters' ire is likely to be even greater if the tax does not raise significant tax revenues.

Governments use two types of sales taxes. The most common sales tax is called an *ad valorem* tax by economists and *the* sales tax by real people. For every dollar the consumer spends, the government keeps a fraction, α, which is the ad valorem tax rate. Japan's national sales tax is 5%. If a Japanese consumer buys a Nintendo Wii for ¥20,000,[13] the government collects α × ¥20,000 = 5% × ¥20,000 = ¥1,000 in taxes, and the seller receives (1 − α) × ¥20,000 = ¥19,000.[14]

The other type of sales tax is a *specific* or *unit* tax, where a specified dollar amount, t, is collected per unit of output. The federal government collects t = 18.4¢ on each gallon of gas sold in the United States.

In this section, we examine four questions about the effects of a sales tax:

1. What effect does a specific sales tax have on equilibrium prices and quantity as well as on tax revenue?
2. Do the equilibrium price and quantity depend on whether the specific tax is collected from suppliers or their customers?
3. Is it true, as many people claim, that taxes assessed on producers are *passed along* to customers? That is, do consumers pay for the entire tax?
4. Do comparable ad valorem and specific taxes have the same effects on equilibrium prices and quantities and on tax revenue?

How much a tax affects the equilibrium price and quantity and how much of the tax falls on consumers depends on the shape of the supply and demand curves, which is summarized by the elasticities. Knowing only the elasticities of supply and demand, we can make accurate predictions about the effects of a new tax and determine how much of the tax falls on consumers.

Equilibrium Effects of a Specific Tax

We illustrate the answer to the first question about the equilibrium effects of a specific tax using our estimated corn supply and demand curves. We start by assuming that a new specific tax of t = \$2.40 per bushel on corn is collected from firms (farmers). If a customer pays a price of p to a firm, the government takes t so the firm keeps $p − t$.

Thus, at every possible price paid by customers, firms are willing to supply less than when they received the full amount customers paid. Before the tax, firms were willing to supply 11.6 billion bushels of corn per year at a price of \$5.60 per bushel, as the pre-tax supply curve S^1 in panel a of Figure 3.6 shows. After the tax, if customers pay \$5.60, firms receive only \$3.20 (=\$5.60 − \$2.40), so they are not willing to supply 11.6 billion bushels. For firms to be willing to supply that quantity, consumers

---

[13]The symbol for Japan's currency, the yen, is ¥. Roughly, ¥100 = \$1.

[14]For specificity, we assume that the price firms receive is $p = (1 − α)p^*$, where p^* is the price consumers pay and α is the ad valorem tax rate on the price consumers pay. Many governments, however, set the ad valorem sales tax, β, as an amount added to the price sellers charge, so consumers pay $p^* = (1 + β)p$. By setting α and β appropriately, the taxes are equivalent. Here $p = p^*/(1 + β)$, so $(1 − α) = 1/(1 + β)$. For example, if $β = \frac{1}{3}$, then $α = \frac{1}{4}$.

Figure 3.6 Equilibrium Effects of a Specific Tax

(a) The specific tax of $t = \$2.40$ per bushel of corn collected from producers shifts the pre-tax corn supply curve, S^1, up to the post-tax supply curve, S^2. The tax causes the equilibrium to shift from e_1 (determined by the intersection of S^1 and D^1) to e_2 (intersection of S^2 with D^1). The equilibrium price—the price consumers pay—increases

from $p_1 = \$7.20$ to $p_2 = \$8.00$. The government collects tax revenues of $T = tQ_2 = \$27.84$ billion per year. (b) The specific tax collected from customers shifts the demand curve down by $t = \$2.40$ from D^1 to D^2. The new equilibrium is the same as when the tax is applied to suppliers in panel a.

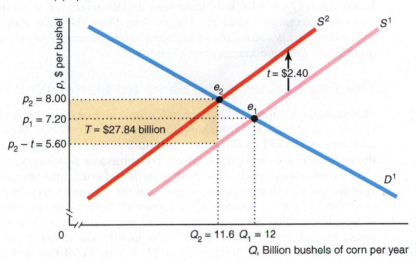

(a) Specific Tax Collected from Producers

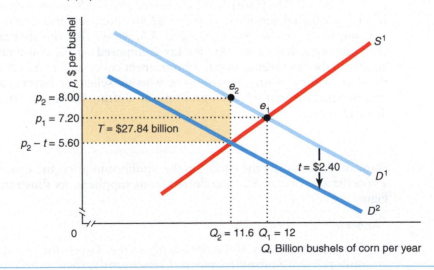

(b) Specific Tax Collected from Customers

must pay $\$8.00$ so that firms receive $\$5.60 (=\$8.00 - \$2.40)$ after the tax. By this reasoning, the after-tax supply curve, S^2, is $t = \$2.40$ above the original supply curve S^1 at every quantity.

We can compare the pre-tax and post-tax equilibria to identify the effect of the tax. The intersection of the pre-tax corn supply curve, S^1, and the corn demand curve D^1

in panel a determines the pre-tax equilibrium, e_1. The equilibrium price is $p_1 = \$7.20$, and the equilibrium quantity is $Q_1 = 12$.

The tax shifts the supply curve to S^2, so the after-tax equilibrium is e_2, where customers pay $p_2 = \$8$, farmers receive $p_2 - \$2.40 = \$5.60$, and $Q_2 = 11.6$. Thus, the tax causes the equilibrium price that customers pay to increase ($\Delta p = p_2 - p_1 = \$8 - \$7.20 = 80\cent$) and the equilibrium quantity to fall ($\Delta Q = Q_2 - Q_1 = 11.6 - 12 = -0.4$).

Although the customers and producers are worse off because of the tax, the government acquires new tax revenue of $T = tQ = \$2.40$ per bushel $\times$ 11.6 billion bushels per year $= \$27.84$ billion per year. The length of the shaded rectangle in Figure 3.6 is $Q_2 = 11.6$ billion per year, and its height is $t = \$2.40$ per bushel, so the area of the rectangle equals the tax revenue. Thus, the answer to our first question is that *a specific tax causes the equilibrium price customers pay to rise, the equilibrium quantity to fall, and tax revenue to rise.*

The Equilibrium Is the Same No Matter Who Is Taxed

Our second question is, "Do the equilibrium price or quantity depend on whether the specific tax is collected from suppliers or their customers?" We can use our supply-and-demand model to show that the equilibrium is the same regardless of whether the government collects the tax from consumers or producers.

If a customer pays the firm p for a bushel of corn, and the government collects a specific tax t from the customer, the total the customer pays is $p + t$. Suppose that customers bought a quantity Q at a price p^* before the tax. After the tax, they are willing to continue to buy Q only if the price falls to $p^* - t$, so that the after-tax price, $p^* - t + t$, remains at p^*. Consequently, the demand curve as seen by firms shifts down by $t = \$2.40$ from D^1 to D^2 in panel b of Figure 3.6.

The intersection of D^2 and the supply curve S^1 determines the after-tax equilibrium quantity $Q_2 = 11.6$. At that quantity, the price received by producers is $p_2 - t = \$5.60$. The price paid by consumers, $p_2 = \$8$ (on the original demand curve D^1 at Q_2, which determines e_2), is $t = \$2.40$ above the price received by producers.

Comparing the two panels in Figure 3.6, we see that the after-tax equilibrium is the same regardless of whether the tax is imposed on the consumers or the sellers. Similarly, the tax revenue that the government collects, $T = \$27.84$ billion, remains the same. Consequently, regardless of whether sellers or buyers pay the tax to the government, you can solve tax problems by shifting the supply curve or shifting the demand curve.

Solved Problem 3.4

Show mathematically the effects on the equilibrium price and quantity of corn from a specific tax of $t = \$2.40$ collected from suppliers, as illustrated in panel a of Figure 3.6.

Answer

1. *Show how the tax shifts the supply curve.* Given the tax t, farmers receive only $p - t$ if consumers pay p. Consequently, their supply function changes from Equation 3.10, $Q = 10.2 + 0.25p$, to $Q = 10.2 + 0.25(p - t)$ $= 10.2 + 0.25(p - 2.4) = 9.6 + 0.25p$. As panel a of Figure 3.6 shows, the after-tax supply curve, S^2, shifts up from S^1 by t as a result.

2. *Determine the after-tax equilibrium price by equating the after-tax supply function and the original demand function.* Because the tax does not affect the

demand function Equation 3.5, $Q = 15.6 - 0.5p$, we equate the right side of the demand function and the after-tax supply function: $15.6 - 0.5p = 9.6 + 0.25p$. Solving for the equilibrium price, we learn that $p = 8$.

3. *Determine the after-tax equilibrium quantity by substituting the equilibrium price in either the demand function or the after-tax supply function.* Using the demand function, we find that the equilibrium quantity is $Q = 15.6 - (0.5 \times 8) = 11.6$.

Firms and Customers Share the Burden of the Tax

Our third question concerns whether firms can raise their price enough that their customers bear the entire tax. We first discuss the amount passed along to consumers and then show how that amount depends on the elasticities of supply and demand.

Tax Incidence If the government sets a new specific tax of t, it changes the tax from 0 to t: $\Delta t = t - 0 = t$. The **incidence of a tax on consumers** is the share of the tax that falls on consumers. The incidence of the tax that falls on consumers is $\Delta p / \Delta t$, the amount by which the price to consumers rises as a fraction of the amount the tax increases.

In the corn example in Figure 3.6, a $\Delta t = \$2.40$ increase in the specific tax causes customers to pay $\Delta p = 80¢$ more per bushel than they would if no tax were assessed. Thus, customers bear one-third of the incidence of the corn tax:

$$\frac{\Delta p}{\Delta t} = \frac{\$0.80}{\$2.40} = \frac{1}{3}.$$

The change in the price that firms receive is $(p_2 - t) - p_1 = (8 - \$2.40) - \$7.20 = \$5.60 - \$7.20 = -\$1.60$. That is, they receive $1.60 less per bushel than they would in the absence of the tax. The incidence of the tax on farmers—the amount by which the price to them falls, divided by the tax—is $\$1.60/\$2.40 = \frac{2}{3}$. The sum of the share of the tax on customers, $\frac{1}{3}$, and that on firms, $\frac{2}{3}$, equals the entire tax effect, 1. Equivalently, the increase in price to customers minus the drop in price to farmers equals the tax: $\$0.80 - (-\$1.60) = \$2.40 = t$.

Tax Effects Depend on Elasticities The tax incidence on customers depends on the elasticities of supply and demand. In response to a change in the tax of Δt, the price customers pay increases by

$$\Delta p = \left(\frac{\eta}{\eta - \varepsilon}\right)\Delta t, \tag{3.11}$$

where ε is the demand elasticity and η is the supply elasticity at the equilibrium (this equation is derived in Appendix 3A). The demand elasticity for corn is $\varepsilon = -0.3$, and the supply elasticity is $\eta = 0.15$, so a change in the tax of $\Delta t = \$2.40$ causes the price customers pay to rise by

$$\Delta p = \left(\frac{\eta}{\eta - \varepsilon}\right)\Delta t = \frac{0.15}{0.15 - [-0.3]} \times \$2.40 = 80¢,$$

as Figure 3.6 shows.

By dividing both sides of Equation 3.11 by Δt, we learn that the incidence of the tax that falls on consumers is

$$\frac{\Delta p}{\Delta t} = \frac{\eta}{\eta - \varepsilon}. \tag{3.12}$$

incidence of a tax on consumers
the share of the tax that falls on consumers

Thus, the incidence of the corn tax that falls on consumers is

$$\frac{0.15}{0.15 - (-0.3)} = \frac{1}{3}.$$

For a given supply elasticity, the more elastic demand is, the less the equilibrium price rises when a tax is imposed. For example, if the corn supply elasticity remains 0.15, but the demand elasticity doubles to -0.6 (that is, the linear demand curve had a less steep slope through the original equilibrium point), the incidence on consumers would fall to $0.15/(0.15 - [-0.6]) = 0.2$, and the price customers pay would rise by only $[0.15/(0.15 - [-0.6])] \times \$2.40 = 48¢$ instead of $80¢$.

Similarly, for a given demand elasticity, the greater the supply elasticity, the larger the increase in the equilibrium price customers pay when a tax is imposed. In the corn example, if the demand elasticity remains -0.3 but the supply elasticity doubles to 0.3, the incidence would rise to $0.3/(0.3 - [-0.3]) = 0.5$, and the price to customers would increase by $[0.3/(0.3 - [-0.3])] \times \$2.40 = \$1.20$ instead of $80¢$.

Application

Taxes to Prevent Obesity

Many governments use taxes to discourage people from buying "sin" goods, such as cigarettes and alcohol. Recently, many governments have added sugar and fat to this list of sin goods. They have started to tax sugar and fats to slow the worldwide rise in obesity rates.

For example, in 2011, Hungary imposed a tax (initially nicknamed the "hamburger tax" and then the "chip tax") on fatty foods as well as higher tariffs on soda and alcohol, with the proceeds going to health care. This tax generated about $75 million in revenue in 2012. By 2013, Denmark, Finland, France, Ireland, Romania, and the United Kingdom have either taxed sugary sodas, fatty cheeses, salty chips, and other foods or debated doing so. In the United States, at least 25 states have "Twinkie taxes" that differentially tax soft drinks, candy, chewing gum, and snack foods such as potato chips.

A number of nutritionists have argued that cheap corn is a major cause of obesity. Corn is used for animal feed, so cheap corn lowers the price of meat and encourages greater meat (and fat) consumption. Corn is also used to produce high-fructose corn syrup, the main sweetener in soft drinks, fruit drinks, and many foods, such as peanut butter and spaghetti sauce. To discourage the consumption of meat, soft drinks, and other fattening foods, a number of nutritionists and others have called for a tax on corn or corn syrup.[15]

Would a tax on corn significantly lower the consumption of corn? The answer depends on how elastic the corn demand curve is and on how much of the tax is passed on to consumers.

In Figure 3.6, we consider a gigantic specific tax of $2.40 per bushel, which is one-third of the equilibrium price. However, this large tax only reduces the equilibrium quantity from 12 to 11.6 billion bushels per year, or $3\frac{1}{3}\%$.

Why would a corn tax have such a small effect on quantity? Given the supply and demand elasticities, only a third of the tax, $80¢$, is passed on to customers, which is one-ninth of the equilibrium price. Even if the entire tax were passed through to consumers, it would not greatly change the quantity demanded because the demand curve is inelastic at the equilibrium, $\varepsilon = -0.3$.

---

[15]Corn farmers receive large subsidies, which are negative taxes. Thus, rather than taxing corn, the government could reduce these subsidies to achieve the same end.

Solved Problem 3.5

If the supply curve is perfectly elastic and demand is linear and downward sloping, what is the effect of a $1 specific tax collected from producers on equilibrium price and quantity, and what is the incidence on consumers? Why?

Answer

1. *Determine the equilibrium in the absence of a tax.* Before the tax, the perfectly elastic supply curve, S^1 in the graph, is horizontal at p_1. The downward-sloping linear demand curve, D, intersects S^1 at the pre-tax equilibrium, e_1, where the price is p_1 and the quantity is Q_1.

2. *Show how the tax shifts the supply curve and determine the new equilibrium.* A specific tax of $1 shifts the pre-tax supply curve, S^1, upward by $1 to S^2, which is horizontal at $p_1 + 1$. The intersection of D and S^2 determines the after-tax equilibrium, e_2, where the price consumers pay is $p_2 = p_1 + 1$, the price firms receive is $p_2 - 1 = p_1$, and the quantity is Q_2.

3. *Compare the before- and after-tax equilibria.* The specific tax causes the equilibrium quantity to fall from Q_1 to Q_2, the price firms receive to remain at p_1, and the equilibrium price consumers pay to rise from p_1 to $p_2 = p_1 + 1$. The entire incidence of the tax falls on consumers:

$$\frac{\Delta p}{\Delta t} = \frac{p_2 - p_1}{\Delta t} = \frac{\$1}{\$1} = 1.$$

4. *Explain why.* Consumers must absorb the entire tax because firms will not supply the good at a price that is any lower than they received before the tax, p_1. Thus, the price must rise enough that the price suppliers receive after the tax is unchanged. As customers do not want to consume as much at a higher price, the equilibrium quantity falls.

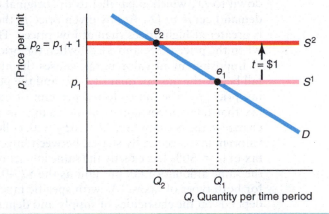

Ad Valorem and Specific Taxes Have Similar Effects

Our fourth question asks whether an ad valorem tax has the same effects on equilibrium prices and quantities as a comparable specific tax. In contrast to specific sales taxes, governments levy ad valorem taxes on a wide variety of goods. Most states apply an ad valorem sales tax to almost all goods and services, exempting only a few staples such as food and medicine.

Suppose that the government imposes an ad valorem tax of α, instead of a specific tax, on the price that consumers pay for corn. We already know that the equilibrium

Figure 3.7 Comparison of an Ad Valorem and a Specific Tax

Without a tax, the demand curve is D and the supply curve is S. An ad valorem tax of $\alpha = 30\%$ shifts the demand curve facing firms to D^a. The gap between D and D^a, the per-unit tax, is larger at higher prices. In contrast, the demand curve facing firms given a specific tax of $2.40 per bushel, D^s, is parallel to D. The after-tax equilibrium, e_2, and the tax revenue, T, are the same with both of these taxes.

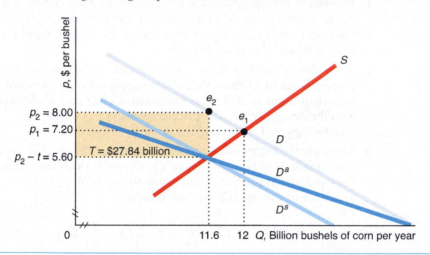

price is $8 with a specific tax of $2.40 per bushel. At that price, an ad valorem tax of $\alpha = \$2.40/\$8 = 30\%$ raises the same amount of tax per unit as a $2.40 specific tax.

It is usually easiest to analyze the effects of an ad valorem tax by shifting the demand curve. Figure 3.7 shows how a specific tax and an ad valorem tax shift the corn demand curve. The specific tax shifts the original, pre-tax demand curve, D, down to D^s, which is parallel to the original curve. The ad valorem tax rotates the demand curve to D^a. At any given price p, the gap between D and D^a is αp, which is greater at high prices than at low prices. The gap is $2.40 (= 0.3 \times \$8$) per unit when the price is $8, and $1.20 when the price is $4.

Imposing an ad valorem tax causes the after-tax equilibrium quantity, 11.6, to fall below the pre-tax quantity, 12, and the post-tax price, p_2, to rise above the pre-tax price, p_1. The tax collected per unit of output is $t = \alpha p_2$. The incidence of the tax that falls on consumers is the change in price, $\Delta p = (p_2 - p_1)$, divided by the change in the per-unit tax, $\Delta t = \alpha p_2 - 0$, collected: $\Delta p/(\alpha p_2)$. The incidence of an ad valorem tax is generally shared between buyers and sellers. Because the ad valorem tax of $\alpha = 30\%$ has exactly the same impact on the equilibrium corn price and raises the same amount of tax per unit as the $2.40 specific tax, the incidence is the same for both types of taxes. (As with specific taxes, the incidence of the ad valorem tax depends on the elasticities of supply and demand, but we'll spare you going through that in detail.)

Solved Problem 3.6

If the short-run supply curve for fresh fruit is perfectly inelastic and the demand curve is a downward-sloping straight line, what is the effect of an ad valorem tax on equilibrium price and quantity, and what is the incidence on consumers? Why?

Answer

1. *Determine the before-tax equilibrium.* The perfectly inelastic supply curve, S, is vertical at Q^* in the graph. The pre-tax demand curve, D^1, intersects S at e_1,

where the equilibrium price to both consumers and producers is p^* and the equilibrium quantity is Q^*.

2. *Show how the tax shifts the demand curve, and determine the after-tax equilibrium.* When the government imposes an ad valorem tax with a rate of α, the demand curve as seen by the firms rotates down to D^2, where the gap between the two demand curves is αp^*. The intersection of S and D^2 determines the after-tax equilibrium, e_2. The equilibrium quantity remains unchanged at Q^*. Consumers continue to pay p^*. The government collects αp^* per unit, so firms receive less, $(1 - \alpha)p^*$, than the p^* they received before the tax.

3. *Determine the incidence of the tax on consumers.* The consumers continue to pay the same price, so $\Delta p = 0$ when the tax increases by αp^* (from 0), and the incidence of the tax that falls on consumers is $0/(\alpha p^*) = 0$.

4. *Explain why the incidence of the tax falls entirely on firms.* Firms absorb the entire tax because they supply the same amount of fruit, Q^*, no matter what tax the government sets. If firms were to raise the price, consumers would buy less fruit and suppliers would be stuck with the essentially worthless excess quantity, which would spoil quickly. Thus, because suppliers prefer to sell their produce at a positive price rather than a zero price, they absorb any tax-induced drop in price.

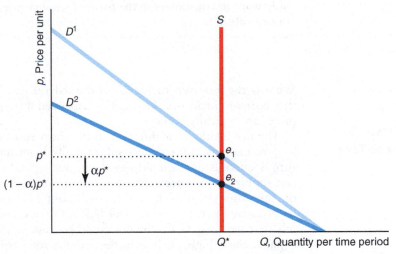

Subsidies

A *subsidy* is a negative tax. The government takes money from firms or consumers using a tax, but gives money using a subsidy. Governments often give subsidies to firms to encourage the production of specific goods and services such as certain crops, health care, motion pictures, and clean energy.

Our analysis of the effects of taxes also applies to subsidies. Because a subsidy is a negative tax, a subsidy has the opposite effect on the equilibrium as does a tax.

For example, suppose that in the corn market the original supply curve in panel a of Figure 3.6 was S^2 and that the original equilibrium was e_2. A specific subsidy of \$2.40 per bushel would shift the supply curve down to S^1, so that the post-subsidy equilibrium would be e_1. Thus, the subsidy would *lower* the equilibrium price and *increase* the quantity.

Application

The Ethanol Subsidy

For thirty years, the U.S. government subsidized ethanol directly and indirectly with the goal of replacing 15% of U.S. gasoline use with this biofuel.[16] The explicit ethanol subsidy ended in 2012. (However, as of 2013, the government continues to subsidize corn, the main input, and requires that ethanol be combined with gasoline, which greatly increases the demand for ethanol.)

In 2011, the last year of the ethanol subsidy, the subsidy cost the government $6 billion. According to a 2010 Rice University study, the government spent $4 billion in 2008 to replace about 2% of the U.S. gasoline supply with ethanol, at a cost of about $1.95 per gallon on top of the gasoline retail price. The combined ethanol and corn subsidies amounted to about $2.59 per gallon of ethanol.

What was the subsidy's incidence on ethanol consumers? That is, how much of the subsidy went to purchasers of ethanol? Because a subsidy is a negative tax, we can use the same consumer incidence formula, Equation 3.12, for a subsidy as for a tax.

According to McPhail and Babcock (2012), the supply elasticity of ethanol, η, is about 0.13, and the demand elasticity is about -2.1. Thus, at the equilibrium, the supply curve is relatively inelastic (nearly the opposite of the situation in Solved Problem 3.5, where the supply curve was perfectly elastic), and the demand curve is relatively elastic. Using Equation 3.12, the consumer incidence was $\eta/(\eta - \varepsilon) = 0.13/(0.13 - [-2.1]) \approx 0.06$. In other words, almost none of the subsidy went to consumers in the form of a lower price—producers captured almost the entire subsidy.

Challenge Solution

Who Pays the Gasoline Tax?

What is the long-run incidence of the federal gasoline tax on consumers? What is the short-run incidence if the tax is suspended during summer months when gasoline prices are typically higher?

The tax incidence is different in the short run than in the long run, because the long-run supply curve differs substantially from the short-run curve. The long-run supply curve is upward sloping, as in our typical figure. However, the U.S. short-run supply curve is very close to vertical. The U.S. refinery capacity has fallen over the last three decades. In 2012, only about 17.3 million barrels of crude oil could be processed per day by the 144 U.S. refineries, compared to the 18.6 million barrels that the then 324 refineries could process in 1981. When demand for gasoline is particularly high, such as in the summer for family vacations and car trips, these refineries operate at full capacity, so they cannot increase output in the short run. Consequently, at the quantity corresponding to maximum capacity, the supply curve for gasoline is nearly vertical.

In the long run, the U.S. federal 18.4¢ per gallon specific tax on gasoline is shared roughly equally between gasoline companies and consumers (Chouinard and Perloff, 2007). However, because the short-run supply curve is less elastic than the long-run supply curve, more of the tax will fall on gasoline firms in the short run (see Solved Problem 3.6). By the same reasoning, if the tax is suspended in the short run, more of the benefit will go to the firms than in the long run.

We contrast the long-run and short-run effects of a gasoline tax in the figure. In both panels, the specific gasoline tax, t, collected from consumers (for simplicity) causes the before-tax demand curve D^1 to shift down by t to the after-tax demand curve D^2.

---

[16]Henry Ford designed the first Model T in 1908 to run on ethanol, gasoline, or a combination.

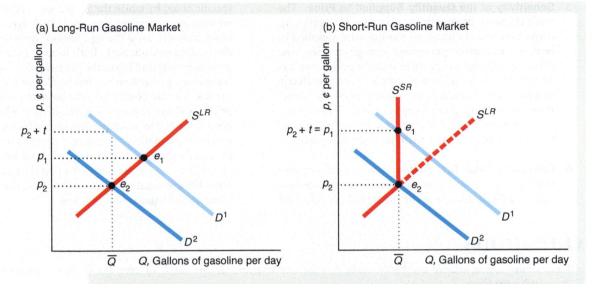

(a) Long-Run Gasoline Market

(b) Short-Run Gasoline Market

In the long run in panel a, imposing the tax causes the equilibrium to shift from e_1 (intersection of D^1 and S^{LR}) to e_2 (intersection of D^2 with S^{LR}). The price that firms receive falls from p_1 to p_2, and the consumers' price goes from p_1 to $p_2 + t$. Given the upward-sloping long-run supply curve, the incidence of the tax is roughly half, so the tax is equally shared by consumers and firms.

In contrast, the short-run supply curve in panel b is vertical at full capacity, $\overline{Q}$. The short-run equilibrium shifts from e_1 (intersection of D^1 and S^{SR}) to e_2 (intersection of D^2 with S^{SR}), so the price that consumers pay is the same before the tax, p_1, and after the tax, $p_2 + t$. The price that gasoline firms receive falls by the full amount of the tax. Thus, the gasoline firms absorb the tax in the short run but share half of it with consumers in the long run. As a result, then-Senator Obama's prediction that temporarily suspending the gas tax during the summer would primarily benefit firms and not consumers was correct.

Summary

1. **How Shapes of Supply and Demand Curves Matter.** The degree to which a shock (such as a price increase of a factor) shifts the supply curve and affects the equilibrium price and quantity depends on the shape of the demand curve. Similarly, the degree to which a shock (such as a price increase of a substitute) shifts the demand curve and affects the equilibrium depends on the shape of the supply curve.

2. **Sensitivity of the Quantity Demanded to Price.** The price elasticity of demand (or elasticity of demand), ε, summarizes the shape of a demand curve at a particular point. The elasticity of demand is the percentage change in the quantity demanded in response to a given percentage change in price. For example, a 1% increase in price causes the quantity demanded to fall by ε%. Because demand curves slope downward according to the Law of Demand, the elasticity of demand is always negative.

The demand curve is perfectly inelastic if $\varepsilon = 0$, inelastic if $0 > \varepsilon > -1$, unitary elastic if $\varepsilon = -1$, elastic if $\varepsilon < -1$, and perfectly elastic when ε approaches negative infinity. A vertical demand curve is perfectly inelastic at every price. A horizontal demand curve is perfectly elastic.

The income elasticity of demand is the percentage change in the quantity demanded in response to a given percentage change in income. The cross-price elasticity of demand is the percentage change in the quantity demanded of one good when the price of a related good increases by a given percentage.

Where consumers can substitute between goods more readily in the long run, long-run demand curves are more elastic than short-run demand curves. However, if goods can be stored easily, short-run demand curves are more elastic than long-run curves.

3. **Sensitivity of the Quantity Supplied to Price.** The price elasticity of supply (or elasticity of supply), η, is the percentage change in the quantity supplied in response to a given percentage change in price. The elasticity of supply is positive if the supply curve has an upward slope. A vertical supply curve is perfectly inelastic. A horizontal supply curve is perfectly elastic. If producers can increase output at lower extra cost in the long run than in the short run, the long-run elasticity of supply is greater than the short-run elasticity.

4. **Effects of a Sales Tax.** The two common types of sales taxes are ad valorem taxes, by which the government collects a fixed percent of the price paid per unit, and specific taxes, by which the government collects a fixed amount of money per unit sold. Both types of sales taxes typically raise the equilibrium price and lower the equilibrium quantity. Both usually raise the price consumers pay and lower the price suppliers receive, so consumers do not bear the full burden or incidence of the tax. The effect of a tax on equilibrium quantities, prices, and tax revenue is unaffected by whether the tax is collected from consumers or producers. The tax incidence that falls on consumers depends on the supply and demand elasticities. Equivalent ad valorem and specific taxes have the same effect on the equilibrium. Subsidies are negative taxes, so they have the opposite effect on the equilibrium of taxes.

Questions

All questions are available on MyEconLab; * = *answer appears at the back of this book*; **A** = *algebra problem*; **C** = *calculus problem*.

1. How Shapes of Supply and Demand Curves Matter

1.1 Using graphs similar to those in Figure 3.1, illustrate how the effect of a demand shock depends on the shape of the supply curve. Consider supply curves that are horizontal, linear upward sloping, linear downward sloping, and vertical.

1.2 During football weekends, many people travel to South Bend, Indiana, to see a Notre Dame football game. Hotel prices are much higher on football weekends than during the other 341 days of the year—particularly in years when Notre Dame is expected to have a winning season. Use a supply-and-demand diagram to illustrate why, when the demand curve shifts to the right, the prices of hotel rooms shoot up. (*Hint*: Carefully explain the shape of the supply curve, taking into account what happens when capacity is reached, such as occurs when all hotel rooms are filled.)

1.3 Six out of ten teens no longer use watches to tell time—they've turned to cell phones and iPods. Sales of inexpensive watches dropped 12% from 2004 to 2005, and sales of teen favorite, Fossil, Inc., fell 19%. Sales dropped 9% in 2009, during the Great Recession. However, sales rose by 9% in both 2010 and 2011 and by 4% in 2012. During all of these ups and downs, the price of inexpensive watches has not changed substantially. What can you conclude about the shape of the supply curve? Illustrate these events using a graph.

1.4 After a major freeze destroyed many Californian crops, the price of celery increased several hundred percent. What can you conclude about the shape of its supply curve? The price increase was more moderate for avocados because they can be imported from other countries. Use a graph to explain why the ability to import avocados moderated the price increase.

2. Sensitivity of the Quantity Demanded to Price

2.1 In a commentary piece on the rising cost of health insurance ("Healthy, Wealthy, and Wise," *Wall Street Journal*, May 4, 2004, A20), economists John Cogan, Glenn Hubbard, and Daniel Kessler state, "Each percentage-point rise in health-insurance costs increases the number of uninsured by 300,000 people." Assuming that their claim is correct, demonstrate that the price elasticity of demand for health insurance depends on the number of people who are insured. What is the price elasticity if 200 million people are insured? What is the price elasticity if 220 million people are insured? (*Hint*: See Solved Problem 3.1.) **A**

*2.2 According to Duffy-Deno (2003), when the price of broadband access capacity (the amount of information one can send over an Internet connection) increases 10%, commercial customers buy about 3.8% less capacity. What is the elasticity of demand for broadband access capacity for firms? Is demand at the current price inelastic? **A**

2.3 Gillen and Hasheminia (2013) estimate that the elasticity of demand for air travel is −0.17 for people traveling alone and −3.09 for couples. Are these demand elasticities elastic or inelastic? For which type of traveler is demand more elastic? Why do you think these elasticities differ in this way?

2.4 Cranfield (2012) estimated that the demand elasticities were −0.83, −0.61, and −0.76 for Canadian beef, chicken, and pork respectively. Are these demand elasticities elastic or inelastic? Which product is the least elastic?

2.5 What section of a straight-line demand curve is elastic?

*2.6 Use calculus to prove that the elasticity of demand is a constant ε everywhere along the demand curve whose demand function is $Q = Ap^ε$. **C**

2.7 Duffy-Deno (2003) estimated that the demand function for broadband service was $Q_s = 15.6p^{-0.563}$ for small firms and $Q_l = 16.0p^{-0.296}$ for larger ones. These two demand functions cross. What can you say about the elasticities of demand on the two demand curves at the point where they cross? What can you say about the elasticities of demand more generally (at other prices)? (*Hint*: The question about the crossing point may be a red herring. Explain why.) **C**

2.8 Suppose that the demand curve for wheat in each country is inelastic up to some "choke" price p^*—a price so high that nothing is bought—so that the demand curve is vertical at Q^* at prices below p^* and horizontal at p^*. If p^* and Q^* vary across countries, what does the world's demand curve look like? Discuss how the elasticity of demand varies with price along the world's demand curve.

2.9 Nataraj (2007) found that a 100% increase in the price of water for heavy users in Santa Cruz, California, caused the quantity of water they demanded to fall by an average of 20%. (Before the increase, heavy users initially paid $1.55 per unit, but afterward they paid $3.14 per unit.) In percentage terms, how much did their water expenditure (price times quantity)—which is the water company's revenue—change? (*Hint*: See Solved Problem 3.2.)

2.10 Illustrate the revenue effects in the Application "Do Farmers Benefit from a Major Drought?" (*Hint*: See Solved Problem 3.2.)

2.11 If the demand elasticity is −1 at the initial equilibrium and price increases by 1%, by how much does revenue change? (*Hint*: See Solved Problem 3.2.)

2.12 Traditionally, the perfectly round, white saltwater pearls from oysters have been prized above small, irregularly shaped, and strangely colored freshwater pearls from mussels. Scientists in China (where 99% of freshwater pearls originate) perfected a means of creating bigger, rounder, and whiter freshwater pearls. These superior mussel pearls now sell well at Tiffany's and other prestigious jewelry stores (though at slightly lower prices than saltwater pearls). What is the likely effect of this innovation on the cross-elasticity of demand for saltwater pearls given a change in the price of freshwater pearls?

2.13 The coconut oil demand function (Buschena and Perloff, 1991) is

$$Q = 1{,}200 - 9.5p + 16.2p_p + 0.2Y,$$

where Q is the quantity of coconut oil demanded in thousands of metric tons per year, p is the price of coconut oil in cents per pound, p_p is the price of palm oil in cents per pound, and Y is the income of consumers. Assume that p is initially 45¢ per pound, p_p is 31¢ per pound, and Q is 1,275 thousand metric tons per year. Calculate the income elasticity of demand for coconut oil. (If you do not have all the numbers necessary to calculate numerical answers, write your answers in terms of variables.) **A**

*2.14 Using the coconut oil demand function from Question 2.13, calculate the price and cross-price elasticities of demand for coconut oil. **A**

3. Sensitivity of the Quantity Supplied to Price

*3.1 The linear supply function is Equation 3.8, $Q = g + hp$. Derive a formula for the elasticity of supply in terms of p (and not Q). Now give one entirely in terms of Q. **A**

3.2 Use calculus to derive the elasticity of supply if the supply function is $Q = Bp^{0.5}$. **C**

*3.3 When the U.S. government announced that a domestic mad cow was found in December 2003, analysts estimated that domestic supplies would increase in the short run by 10.4% as many other countries barred U.S. beef. An estimate of the price elasticity of beef demand is −1.6 (Henderson, 2003). Assuming that only the domestic supply curve shifted, how much would you expect the price to change? **A**

3.4 Will Mexico stop producing tequila? Because of record-low industry prices for the agave azul plant, from which tequila is distilled, farmers in Jalisco and other Mexican states are switching to more lucrative plants like corn (Kyle Arnold, "No Mas Tequila," *The Monitor*, September 17, 2007). Planting of agave rose substantially from 2000 through 2004, and then started to plummet as the price of inexpensive tequila fell. The number of agave planted went from 60 million in 2000, to 93 million in 2002, to 12.8 million in 2006, and the downward trend continued in 2007. It takes seven years for an agave plant to be ready for harvesting. The price of inexpensive tequila has dropped 35% to 40% in recent years, but the price of high-end tequilas, which have been growing in popularity, has remained stable. Discuss the relative sizes of the short-run and long-run supply elasticities of tequila. What do you think the supply elasticity of high-quality tequila is? Why? If the demand curve for inexpensive tequila has remained relatively unchanged, is the demand curve relatively elastic or inelastic at the equilibrium? Why?

3.5 According to Borjas (2003), immigration into the United States increased the labor supply of working men by 11.0% from 1980 to 2000 and reduced the wage of the average native worker by 3.2%. From these results, can we make any inferences about the elasticity of supply or demand? Which curve (or curves) changed, and why? Draw a supply-and-demand diagram and label the axes to illustrate what happened.

3.6 Cranfield (2012) estimated that the elasticity of demand for Canadian beef was −0.83. If the supply curve of beef is nearly inelastic in the short run and a change in the law causes the supply curve to shift to the left by 10%, how much will the price rise?

3.7 Solved Problem 3.3 claims that a new war in the Persian Gulf could shift the world supply curve to the left by up to 24 million barrels per day, causing the world price of oil to soar regardless of whether we drill in ANWR. Use the same type of analysis as in the Solved Problem to calculate how much such a shock would cause the price to rise with and without the ANWR production. **A**

3.8 In 2012, the governors of several livestock producing states asked the U.S. Environmental Protection Agency (EPA) to suspend federal ethanol mandates due to a major drought (Amanda Peterka, "EPA Denies Waiver of Corn-based Fuel Requirements," *Greenwire*, November 16, 2012). The mandates require that gasoline be mixed with a specified amount of ethanol, which is produced from corn. Over 30% of the corn crop is used to make ethanol. The governors wanted more corn used for feeding livestock and humans. The EPA rejected the requests because it was "highly unlikely" that waiving the volume requirements for ethanol would affect corn, food, and fuel prices. Use the estimated demand and supply functions, Equations 3.5 and 3.10, to estimate how much a shift of the demand curve to the left by 30% would affect the price of corn. (*Hint*: See Solved Problem 3.3.)

4. Effects of a Sales Tax

4.1 Dan has a much higher elasticity of demand for fish than most other people. Is the incidence of a tax on fish, which is sold in a competitive market, greater for him than for other people?

4.2 An empirical study by Callison and Kaestner (2012) suggests that a 100% cigarette tax would be required to decrease adult smoking by as much as 5%. What does this result imply about the shapes of the supply and demand curves (assuming that the cigarette market is competitive)?

4.3 Governments often use a sales tax to raise *tax revenue*, which is the tax per unit times the quantity sold. All else the same, will a specific tax raise more tax revenue if the demand curve is inelastic or elastic at the original price?

4.4 In early 2010, the U.S. government offered an $8,000 subsidy to new homebuyers. What effect does a per-house subsidy have on the equilibrium price and quantity of the housing market? What is the incidence of the subsidy on buyers? (*Hints*: A subsidy is a negative tax. See the Application "The Ethanol Subsidy.")

4.5 Quebec, Canada, offers a per-child subsidy on day care for young children that lowers the price to $7 per child as of 2011 (at a cost of about $10,000 per child per year). (*Hint*: A subsidy is a negative tax.)

a. What is the effect of this subsidy on the equilibrium price and quantity?

b. Show the incidence of the subsidy on day care providers and parents using a supply-and-demand diagram.

*4.6 Use math to show that, as the supply curve at the equilibrium becomes nearly perfectly elastic, the entire incidence of the tax falls on consumers. **A**

4.7 Given the 2013 federal tax of $1.01 per pack of cigarettes and an estimated elasticity of demand for the U.S. population of −0.3, what is the effect of a 10¢ increase in the federal tax? How would your answer change if the state tax does not change? **A**

4.8 Green et al. (2005) estimate that the demand elasticity is −0.47 and the long-run supply elasticity is 12.0 for almonds. The corresponding elasticities are −0.68 and 0.73 for cotton and −0.26 and 0.64 for processing tomatoes. If the government were to apply a specific tax to each of these commodities, what incidence would fall on consumers? **A**

4.9 A constant elasticity supply curve, $Q = Bp^\eta$, intersects a constant elasticity demand curve, $Q = Ap^\varepsilon$, where A, B, η, and ε are constants. What is the incidence of a $1 specific tax? Does your answer depend on where the supply curve intersects the demand curve? Why? **A**

4.10 The United Kingdom has a drinking problem. British per-capita consumption of alcohol rose 19% between 1980 and 2007, compared with a 13%

decline in other developed countries. Worried about excessive drinking among young people, the British government increased the tax on beer by 42% from 2008 to 2012. Under what conditions will this specific tax substantially reduce the equilibrium quantity of alcohol? Answer in terms of the elasticities of the demand and supply curves.

4.11 What is the effect of a $1 specific tax on equilibrium price and quantity if demand is perfectly inelastic? What is the incidence on consumers? Explain. (*Hint*: See Solved Problems 3.5 and 3.6.)

4.12 What is the effect of a $1 specific tax on equilibrium price and quantity if demand is perfectly elastic? What is the incidence on consumers? Explain. (*Hint*: See Solved Problems 3.5 and 3.6.)

4.13 What is the effect of a $1 specific tax on equilibrium price and quantity if supply is perfectly inelastic? What is the incidence on consumers? Explain. (*Hint*: See Solved Problems 3.5 and 3.6.)

4.14 What is the effect of a $1 specific tax on equilibrium price and quantity if demand is perfectly elastic and supply is perfectly inelastic? What is the incidence on consumers? Explain. (*Hint*: See Solved Problems 3.5 and 3.6.)

*4.15 Do you care whether a 15¢ tax per gallon of milk is collected from milk producers or from consumers at the store? Why?

4.16 If the inverse demand function is $p = a - bQ$ and the inverse supply function is $p = c + dQ$, show that the incidence of a specific tax of t per unit falling on consumers is $b/(b + d) = \eta/(\eta - \varepsilon)$. **A**

4.17 Algebraically solve for the after-tax equilibrium price and quantity in the corn market if a specific tax of $t = \$2.40$ is applied to customers, as panel b of Figure 3.6 illustrates. (*Hint*: See Solved Problem 3.4.) **A**

4.18 On July 1, 1965, the federal ad valorem taxes on many goods and services were eliminated. By comparing the prices from before and after this change, we can determine how much the price fell in response to the tax's elimination. When the tax was in place, the tax per unit on a good that sold for p was αp. If the price fell by αp when the tax was eliminated, consumers must have been bearing the full incidence of the tax. The entire amount of the tax cut was passed on to consumers for all commodities and services Brownlee and Perry (1967) studied.

Taxes had been collected at the retail level (except for motion picture admissions and club dues) and excise taxes had been imposed at the manufacturer level for most commodities, including face powder, sterling silverware, wristwatches, and handbags. List the conditions (in terms of the elasticities or shapes of supply or demand curves) that are consistent with consumers bearing the full incidence of the taxes. Use graphs to illustrate your answer.

*4.19 Essentially none of the savings from removing the federal ad valorem tax were passed on to consumers for motion picture admissions and club dues (Brownlee and Perry, 1967; see Question 4.18). List the conditions (in terms of the elasticities or shapes of supply or demand curves) that are consistent with the incidence of the taxes falling entirely on firms. Use graphs to illustrate your answer.

4.20 For a tax on sugar or fat to reduce the consumption of fattening foods and drinks by a very large amount, what elasticities should the demand and supply curves have? (*Hint*: See the Application "Taxes to Prevent Obesity.")

5. Challenge

5.1 The Challenge Solution says that a gas tax is roughly equally shared by consumers and firms in the long run. If so, what can you say about the elasticities of supply and demand? If in the short run the supply curve is nearly vertical, what (if anything) can you infer about the demand elasticity from observing the effect of a tax on the change in price and quantity?

5.2 Ten million tourists visited New Orleans in 2004. However, in 2005, Hurricane Katrina damaged many parts of New Orleans and disrupted the tourist business in the years thereafter. Only 3.7 million tourists visited New Orleans in 2006 and 7.1 million in 2007. Subsequent hurricanes also discouraged tourist visits, but the number of tourists slowly grew back to the pre-Katrina level by 2013 (www.crt.state.la.us). Use a supply-and-demand diagram to show the likely effects on price and quantity of the hurricanes' effect on the demand curve. Indicate the magnitude of the likely equilibrium price and quantity effects. Show how the answer depends on the shapes of the supply and demand curves. (*Hint*: What is the shape of the supply curve of hotel rooms when the city is at full capacity?)

4 Consumer Choice

If this is coffee, please bring me some tea; but if this is tea, please bring me some coffee.
—Abraham Lincoln

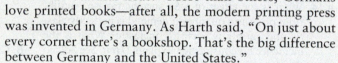

Challenge

Why Americans Buy More E-Books Than Do Germans

Are you reading this text electronically? E-books are appearing everywhere in the English-speaking world. Thanks to the popularity of the Kindle, iPad, and other e-book readers, in 2012, e-books accounted for 25% of U.S. trade books, 33% of U.S. fiction books, and 13% of U.K. trade books. E-books sold well in Australia and Canada as well. In contrast, in Germany, only about 1% of books are e-books.

Why are e-books more successful in the United States than in Germany? Jürgen Harth of the German Publishers and Booksellers Association attributed the difference to tastes, or what he called a "cultural issue." More than others, Germans love printed books—after all, the modern printing press was invented in Germany. As Harth said, "On just about every corner there's a bookshop. That's the big difference between Germany and the United States."

An alternative explanation concerns government regulations and taxes that affect prices in Germany. Even if Germans and Americans have the same tastes, Americans are more likely to buy e-books because they are less expensive than printed books in the United States. However, e-books are more expensive than printed books in Germany. Unlike in the United States, where publishers and booksellers are free to set prices, Germany regulates book prices. To protect small booksellers, its fixed-price system requires all booksellers to charge the same price for new printed books. In addition, although e-books can sell for slightly lower prices, they are subject to a 19% tax rather than to the 7% tax that applies to printed books.[1] So do differences in tastes account for why Germans and Americans read different types of books, or can taxes and price differences explain their behavior?

Microeconomics provides powerful insights into the myriad questions and choices facing consumers. In addition to the e-book question, we can address questions such as: How can we use information about consumers' allocations of their budgets across various goods in the past to predict how a price change will affect their demands for goods today? Are consumers better off receiving cash or a comparable amount in food stamps? Why do young people buy relatively more alcohol and less marijuana when they turn 21?

---

[1]The United Kingdom has a similar difference in tax rates.

To answer questions about individual decision making, we need a model of individual behavior. Our model of consumer behavior is based on the following premises:

- Individual *tastes* or *preferences* determine the amount of pleasure people derive from the goods and services they consume.
- Consumers face *constraints* or limits on their choices.
- Consumers *maximize* their well-being or pleasure from consumption, subject to the constraints they face.

Consumers spend their money on the bundle of products that give them the most pleasure. If you like music and don't have much of a sweet tooth, you spend a lot of your money on concerts and iTune songs and relatively little on candy.[2] By contrast, your chocoholic friend with a tin ear may spend a great deal on Hershey's Kisses and very little on music.

All consumers must choose which goods to buy because limits on wealth prevent them from buying everything that catches their fancy. In addition, government rules restrict what they may buy: Young consumers can't buy alcohol or cigarettes legally, and people of all ages are prohibited from buying crack and other "recreational" drugs. Therefore, consumers buy the goods that give them the most pleasure, subject to the constraints that they cannot spend more money than they have and that they cannot spend it in ways that the government prevents.

In economic analyses designed to explain behavior (positive analysis—see Chapter 1) rather than judge it (normative statements), economists assume that *the consumer is the boss*. If your brother gets pleasure from smoking, economists don't argue with him that it is bad for him any more than they'd tell your sister, who likes reading Stephen King, that she should read Adam Smith's *The Wealth of Nations* instead.[3] Accepting each consumer's tastes is not the same as condoning the resulting behaviors. Economists want to predict behavior. They want to know, for example, whether your brother will smoke more next year if the price of cigarettes decreases 10%. The prediction is unlikely to be correct if economists say, "He shouldn't smoke; therefore, we predict he'll stop smoking next year." A prediction based on your brother's actual tastes is more likely to be correct: "Given that he likes cigarettes, he is likely to smoke more of them next year if the price falls."

<table>
<tr><td rowspan="5">In this chapter, we examine five main topics</td><td>1. **Preferences.** We use three properties of preferences to predict which combinations, or *bundle*, of goods an individual prefers to other combinations.</td></tr>
<tr><td>2. **Utility.** Economists summarize a consumer's preferences using a *utility* function, which assigns a numerical value to each possible bundle of goods, reflecting the consumer's relative ranking of these bundles.</td></tr>
<tr><td>3. **Budget Constraint.** Prices, income, and government restrictions limit a consumer's ability to make purchases by determining the rate at which a consumer can trade one good for another.</td></tr>
<tr><td>4. **Constrained Consumer Choice.** Consumers maximize their pleasure from consuming various possible bundles of goods given their income, which limits the amount of goods they can purchase.</td></tr>
<tr><td>5. **Behavioral Economics.** Experiments indicate that people sometimes deviate from rational, maximizing behavior.</td></tr>
</table>

---

[2]Remember that microeconomics is the study of trade-offs: Should you save your money or buy that Superman *Action Comics* Number 1 you've always wanted? Indeed, an anagram for *microeconomics* is *income or comics*.

[3]As the ancient Romans put it, "De gustibus non est disputandum"—there is no disputing about (accounting for) tastes. Or, as Joan Crawford's character said in the movie *Grand Hotel* (1932), "Have caviar if you like, but it tastes like herring to me."

4.1   Preferences

I have forced myself to contradict myself in order to avoid conforming to my own taste.   —Marcel Duchamp, Dada artist

We start our analysis of consumer behavior by examining consumer preferences. Using three basic assumptions, we can make many predictions about preferences. Once we know about consumers' preferences, we can add information about the constraints consumers face so that we can answer many questions, such as the one posed in the Challenge at the beginning of this chapter, or derive demand curves, as is done in the next chapter.

As a consumer, you choose among many goods. Should you have ice cream or cake for dessert? Should you spend most of your money on a large apartment or rent a single room and use the savings to pay for trips and concerts? In short, you must allocate your money to buy a *bundle* (*market basket* or combination) of goods.

How do consumers choose the bundles of goods they buy? One possibility is that consumers behave randomly and blindly choose one good or another without any thought. However, consumers appear to make systematic choices. For example, most consumers buy very similar items each time they visit a grocery store.

To explain consumer behavior, economists *assume* that consumers have a set of tastes or preferences that they use to guide them in choosing between goods. These tastes may differ substantially among individuals. Let's start by specifying the underlying assumptions in the economist's model of consumer behavior.

Properties of Consumer Preferences

Do not unto others as you would that they would do unto you. Their tastes may not be the same.   —George Bernard Shaw

A consumer chooses between bundles of goods by ranking them as to the pleasure the consumer gets from consuming each. We summarize a consumer's ranking with *preference relation* symbols: weakly prefers, $\succsim$, strictly prefers, $\succ$, and indifferent between, $\sim$. If the consumer likes Bundle a at least as much as Bundle b, we say that the consumer *weakly prefers a to b*, which we write as $a \succsim b$

Given this weak preference relation, we can derive two other relations. If the consumer weakly prefers Bundle a to b, $a \succsim b$, but the consumer does not weakly prefer b to a, then we say that the consumer *strictly prefers a to b*—would definitely choose a rather than b if given a choice—which we write as $a \succ b$.

If the consumer weakly prefers a to b and weakly prefers b to a—that is $a \succsim b$ and $b \succsim a$—then we say that the consumer is *indifferent* between the bundles, or likes the two bundles equally, which we write as $a \sim b$

We make three assumptions about the properties of consumers' preferences. For brevity, we refer to these properties as *completeness*, *transitivity*, and *more is better*.

Completeness   The completeness property holds that, when facing a choice between any two bundles of goods, Bundles a and b, a consumer can rank them so that one and only one of the following relationships is true: $a \succsim b$, $b \succsim a$ or both relationships hold so that $a \sim b$ This property rules out the possibility that the consumer cannot decide which bundle is preferable.

Transitivity   It would be very difficult to predict behavior if consumers' rankings of bundles were not logically consistent. The transitivity property eliminates the possibility of certain types of illogical behavior. According to this property, a consumer's preferences over bundles is consistent in the sense that, if the consumer *weakly prefers a to b, a $\succsim$ b*, and weakly prefers *b to c, b $\succsim$ c* then the consumer also weakly prefers *a to c, a $\succsim$ c*

If your sister told you that she preferred a scoop of ice cream to a piece of cake, a piece of cake to a candy bar, and a candy bar to a scoop of ice cream, you'd probably think she'd lost her mind. At the very least, you wouldn't know which dessert to serve her.

If completeness and transitivity hold, then the preference relation $\succsim$ is said to be *rational*. That is, the consumer has well-defined preferences between any pair of alternatives.

More Is Better The more-is-better property states that, all else the same, more of a commodity is better than less of it.[4] Indeed, economists define a **good** as a commodity for which more is preferred to less, at least at some levels of consumption. In contrast, a **bad** is something for which less is preferred to more, such as pollution. We now concentrate on goods (except in Chapter 18).

good
a commodity for which more is preferred to less, at least at some levels of consumption

bad
something for which less is preferred to more, such as pollution

Although the completeness and transitivity properties are crucial to the analysis that follows, the more-is-better property is included to simplify the analysis—our most important results would follow even without this property.

So why do economists assume that the more-is-better property holds? The most compelling reason is that it appears to be true for most people.[5] Another reason is that if consumers can freely dispose of excess goods, a consumer can be no worse off with extra goods. (We examine a third reason later in the chapter: Consumers buy goods only when this condition is met.)

Application

You Can't Have Too Much Money

Percentage of Americans who say they would have cosmetic surgery if they could afford it: 69.   —*Harper's* Index, 2010

As we might expect, studies of people in many nations find that richer people are happier on average than poorer people (Helliwell et al., 2012). But, do people become satiated? Can people be so rich that they can buy everything they want and additional income does not increase their feelings of well-being? Using data from many countries, Stevenson and Wolfers (2013) found no evidence of a satiation point beyond which wealthier countries or wealthier individuals have no further increases in subjective well-being. Moreover, they found a clear positive relationship between average levels of self-reported feelings of happiness or satisfaction and income per capita within and across countries.

Less scientific, but perhaps more compelling, is a 2005 survey of wealthy U.S. citizens who were asked, "How much wealth do you need to live comfortably?"

---

[4]*Jargon alert*: Economists call this property *nonsatiation* or *monotonicity*.

[5]When teaching microeconomics to Wharton MBAs, I told them about a cousin of mine who had just joined a commune in Oregon. His worldly possessions consisted of a tent, a Franklin stove, enough food to live on, and a few clothes. He said that he didn't need any other goods—that he was *satiated*. A few years later, one of these students bumped into me on the street and said, "Professor, I don't remember your name or much of anything you taught me in your course, but I can't stop thinking about your cousin. Is it really true that he doesn't want *anything* else? His very existence is a repudiation of my whole way of life." Actually, my cousin had given up his ascetic life and was engaged in telemarketing, but I, for noble pedagogical reasons, responded, "Of course he still lives that way—you can't expect everyone to have the tastes of an MBA."

On average, those with a net worth of over $1 million said that they needed $2.4 million to live comfortably, those with at least $5 million in net worth said that they need $10.4 million, and those with at least $10 million wanted $18.1 million. Apparently, most people never have enough.

Preference Maps

Surprisingly enough, with just these three properties, we can tell a lot about a consumer's preferences. One of the simplest ways to summarize information about a consumer's preferences is to create a graphical interpretation—a map—of them. For graphical simplicity, we concentrate throughout this chapter on choices between only two goods, but the model can be generalized to handle any number of goods.

Each semester, Lisa, who lives for fast food, decides how many pizzas and burritos to eat. Panel a of Figure 4.1 shows the various bundles of pizzas and burritos she might consume, with (individual-size) pizzas per semester on the horizontal axis and burritos per semester on the vertical axis.

At Bundle e, for example, Lisa consumes 25 pizzas and 15 burritos per semester. By the more-is-better property, Lisa prefers all the bundles that lie above and to the right (area A) to Bundle e because they contain at least as much or more of both pizzas and burritos as Bundle e. Thus, she prefers Bundle f (30 pizzas and 20 burritos) in that region.

By using the more-is-better property, Lisa prefers e to all the bundles that lie in area B, below and to the left of e, such as Bundle d (15 pizzas and 10 burritos). All the bundles in area B contain fewer pizzas or fewer burritos, or fewer of both, than does Bundle e.

From panel a, we do not know whether Lisa prefers Bundle e to bundles such as b (30 pizzas and 10 burritos) in area D, which is the region below and to the right of e, or c (15 pizzas and 25 burritos) in area C, which is the region above and to the

Figure 4.1 Bundles of Pizzas and Burritos Lisa Might Consume

Pizzas per semester are on the horizontal axis, and burritos per semester are on the vertical axis. (a) Lisa prefers more to less, so she prefers Bundle e to any bundle in area B, including d. Similarly, she prefers any bundle in area A, including f, to e. (b) The indifference curve, I^1, shows a set of bundles (including c, e, and a) among which she is indifferent. (c) The three indifference curves, I^1, I^2, and I^3, are part of Lisa's preference map, which summarizes her preferences.

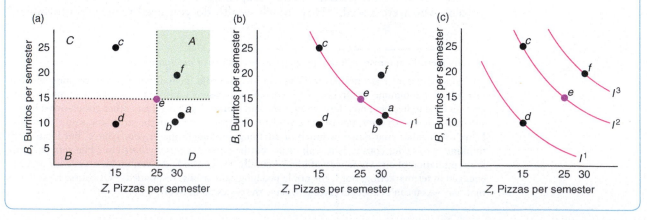

left of Bundle *e*. We can't use the more-is-better property to determine which bundle is preferred because each of these bundles contains more of one good and less of the other than *e* does. To be able to state with certainty whether Lisa prefers particular bundles in areas *C* or *D* to Bundle *e*, we have to know more about her tastes for pizza and burritos.

indifference curve
the set of all bundles of goods that a consumer views as being equally desirable

Indifference Curves Suppose we asked Lisa to identify all the bundles that gave her the same amount of pleasure as consuming Bundle *e*. Using her answers, we draw curve *I* in panel b of Figure 4.1 through all bundles she likes as much as *e*. Curve *I* is an **indifference curve**: the set of all bundles of goods that a consumer views as being equally desirable.

Indifference curve *I* includes Bundles *c*, *e*, and *a*, so Lisa is indifferent about consuming Bundles *c*, *e*, and *a*. From this indifference curve, we also know that Lisa prefers *e* (25 pizzas and 15 burritos) to *b* (30 pizzas and 10 burritos). How do we know that? Bundle *b* lies below and to the left of Bundle *a*, so Lisa strictly prefers Bundle *a* to Bundle *b*, $a \succ b$, by the more-is-better property. Both Bundle *a* and Bundle *e* are on indifference curve *I*, so Lisa is indifferent between Bundle *e* and Bundle *a*, $e \sim a$. Because Lisa is indifferent between *e* and *a* and she prefers *a* to *b*, she must prefer *e* to *b*, $e \succ b$, by transitivity.

indifference map
(or *preference map*) a complete set of indifference curves that summarize a consumer's tastes or preferences

If we asked Lisa many, many questions, we could, in principle, draw an entire set of indifference curves through every possible bundle of burritos and pizzas. Lisa's preferences are summarized in an **indifference map** or *preference map*, which is a complete set of indifference curves that summarize a consumer's tastes. It is referred to as a "map" because it uses the same principle as a topographical or contour map, in which each line shows all points with the same height or elevation. With an indifference map, each line shows points (combinations of goods) with the same utility or well-being. Panel c of Figure 4.1 shows three of Lisa's indifference curves: I^1, I^2, and I^3.

We assume that indifference curves are continuous—have no gaps—as the figure shows. The indifference curves are parallel in the figure, but they need not be. We can demonstrate that all indifference curve maps must have the following four properties:

1. Bundles on indifference curves farther from the origin are preferred to those on indifference curves closer to the origin.
2. An indifference curve goes through every possible bundle.
3. Indifference curves cannot cross.
4. Indifference curves slope downward.

First, we show that bundles on indifference curves farther from the origin are preferred to those on indifference curves closer to the origin. By the more-is-better property, Lisa prefers Bundle *f* to Bundle *e* in panel c of Figure 4.1. She is indifferent among Bundle *f* and all the other bundles on indifference curve I^3, just as she is indifferent among all the bundles on indifference curve I^2, such as Bundles *c* and *e*. By the transitivity property, she prefers Bundle *f* to Bundle *e*, which she likes as much as Bundle *c*, so she also prefers Bundle *f* to Bundle *c*. By this type of reasoning, she prefers all bundles on I^3 to all bundles on I^2.

Second, we show that an indifference curve goes through every possible bundle as a consequence of the completeness property: The consumer can compare any bundle to another. Compared to a given bundle, some bundles are preferred, some are enjoyed equally, and some are inferior. Connecting the bundles that give the same pleasure produces an indifference curve that includes the given bundle.

Third, we show that indifference curves cannot cross: A given bundle cannot be on two indifference curves. Suppose that two indifference curves crossed at Bundle *e* as in panel a of Figure 4.2. Because Bundles *e* and *a* lie on the same indifference curve

Figure 4.2 Impossible Indifference Curves

(a) Suppose that the indifference curves cross at Bundle *e*. Lisa is indifferent between *e* and *a* on indifference curve I^0 and between *e* and *b* on I^1. If Lisa is indifferent between *e* and *a* and she is indifferent between *e* and *b*, she must be indifferent between *a* and *b* by transitivity. But *b* has more of both pizzas and burritos than *a*, so she *must* prefer *a* to *b*. Because of this contradiction, indifference curves cannot cross. (b) Suppose that indifference curve *I* slopes upward. The consumer is indifferent between *b* and *a* because they lie on *I* but prefers *b* to *a* by the more-is-better assumption. Because of this contradiction, indifference curves cannot be upward sloping. (c) Suppose that indifference curve *I* is thick enough to contain both *a* and *b*. The consumer is indifferent between *a* and *b* because both are on *I* but prefers *b* to *a* by the more-is-better assumption because *b* lies above and to the right of *a*. Because of this contradiction, indifference curves cannot be thick.

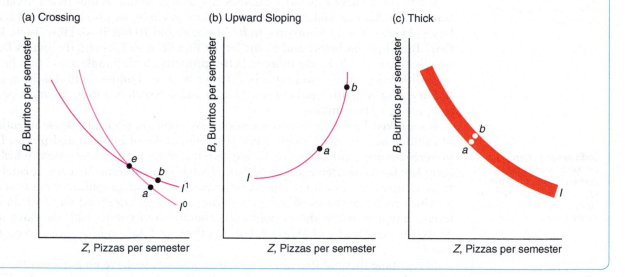

(a) Crossing

(b) Upward Sloping

(c) Thick

I^0, Lisa is indifferent between *e* and *a*. Similarly, she is indifferent between *e* and *b* because both are on I^1. By transitivity, if Lisa is indifferent between *e* and *a* and she is indifferent between *e* and *b*, she must be indifferent between *a* and *b*. But that's impossible! Bundle *b* is above and to the right of Bundle *a*, so Lisa *must* prefer *b* to *a* by the more-is-better property. Thus, because preferences are transitive and more is better than less, indifference curves cannot cross.

Fourth, we show that indifference curves must be downward sloping. Suppose to the contrary that an indifference curve sloped upward, as in panel b of Figure 4.2. The consumer is indifferent between Bundles *a* and *b* because both lie on the same indifference curve, *I*. But the consumer prefers *b* to *a* by the more-is-better property: Bundle *a* lies below and to the left of Bundle *b*. Because of this contradiction—the consumer cannot both be indifferent between *a* and *b* and strictly prefer *b* to *a*—indifference curves cannot be upward sloping. For example, if Lisa views pizza and burritos as goods, she can't be indifferent between a bundle of one pizza and one burrito and another bundle with six of each.

Solved Problem
4.1

Can indifference curves be thick?

Answer

Draw an indifference curve that is at least two bundles thick, and show that a preference property is violated. Panel c of Figure 4.2 shows a thick indifference curve, *I*, with two bundles, *a* and *b*, identified. Bundle *b* lies above and to the right of *a*: Bundle

b has more of both burritos and pizza. Thus, by the more-is-better property, Bundle b must be strictly preferred to Bundle a, $b \succ a$. But the consumer must be indifferent between a and b, $a \sim b$, because both bundles are on the same indifference curve. Because both relationships between a and b cannot be true, we have a contradiction. Consequently, indifference curves cannot be thick.

Comment: We illustrate this point by drawing indifference curves with very thin lines in our figures.

We are out of tickets for Swan Lake.
Do you want tickets for Wrestlemania?

Willingness to Substitute Between Goods Lisa is willing to make some trades between goods. The downward slope of her indifference curves shows that Lisa is willing to give up some burritos for more pizza or vice versa. She is indifferent between Bundles a and b on her indifference curve I in panel a of Figure 4.3. If she initially has Bundle a (eight burritos and three pizzas), she could get to Bundle b (five burritos and four pizzas) by trading three burritos for one more pizza. She is indifferent whether she makes this trade or not.

Lisa's willingness to trade one good for another is measured by her **marginal rate of substitution** (*MRS*): the maximum amount of one good a consumer will sacrifice to obtain one more unit of another good. The marginal rate of substitution refers to the trade-off (rate of substitution) of burritos for a marginal (small additional or incremental) change in the number of pizzas. Lisa's marginal rate of substitution of burritos for pizza is

$$MRS = \frac{\Delta B}{\Delta Z},$$

marginal rate of substitution (*MRS*) the maximum amount of one good a consumer will sacrifice to obtain one more unit of another good

where ΔZ is the number of pizzas Lisa will give up to get ΔB, more burritos, or vice versa, and pizza (Z) is on the horizontal axis. *The marginal rate of substitution is the slope of the indifference curve.*[6]

Moving from Bundle a to Bundle b in panel a of Figure 4.3, Lisa will give up three burritos, $\Delta B = -3$, to obtain one more pizza, $\Delta Z = 1$, so her marginal rate of substitution is $-3/1 = -3$. That is, the slope of the indifference curve is -3. The negative sign shows that Lisa is willing to give up some of one good to get more of the other: Her indifference curve slopes downward.

Curvature of Indifference Curves Must an indifference curve, such as I in panel a of Figure 4.3, be *convex* to the origin (that is, must the middle of the curve be closer to the origin than if the indifference curve were a straight line)? An indifference curve doesn't have to be convex, but casual observation suggests that most people's indifference curves are convex. When people have a lot of one good, they are willing to give up a relatively large amount of it to get a good of which they have relatively little. However, after that first trade, they are willing to give up less of the first good to get the same amount more of the second good.

---

[6]The *slope* is *the rise over the run*: how much we move along the vertical axis (rise) as we move along the horizontal axis (run). Technically, by the marginal rate of substitution, we mean the slope at a particular bundle. That is, we want to know what the slope is as ΔZ gets very small. In calculus terms, the relevant slope is a derivative. See Appendix 4A.

Figure 4.3 Marginal Rate of Substitution

(a) At Bundle *a*, Lisa is willing to give up three burritos for one more pizza; at *b*, she is willing to give up only two burritos to obtain another pizza. That is, the relatively more burritos she has, the more she is willing to trade for another pizza. (b) An indifference curve of this shape is unlikely to be observed. Lisa would be willing to give up more burritos to get one more pizza, the fewer the burritos she has. Moving from Bundle *c* to *b*, she will trade one pizza for three burritos, whereas moving from *b* to *a*, she will trade one pizza for two burritos, even though she now has relatively more burritos to pizzas.

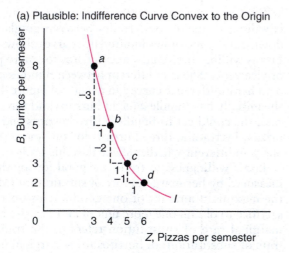

(a) Plausible: Indifference Curve Convex to the Origin

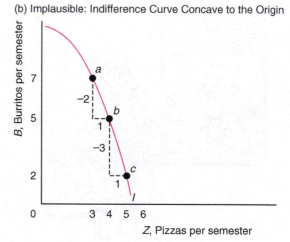

(b) Implausible: Indifference Curve Concave to the Origin

Lisa is willing to give up three burritos to obtain one more pizza when she is at *a* in panel a of Figure 4.3. At *b*, she is willing to trade only two burritos for a pizza. At *c*, she is even less willing to trade; she will give up only one burrito for another pizza. This willingness to trade fewer burritos for one more pizza as we move down and to the right along the indifference curve reflects a *diminishing marginal rate of substitution*: The marginal rate of substitution approaches zero as we move down and to the right along an indifference curve. That is, the indifference curve becomes flatter (less sloped) as we move down and to the right.

It is hard to imagine that Lisa's indifference curves are *concave*, as in panel b of Figure 4.3, rather than *convex*, as in panel a. If her indifference curve is concave, Lisa would be willing to give up more burritos to get one more pizza, the fewer the burritos she has. In panel b, she trades one pizza for three burritos moving from Bundle *c* to *b*, and she trades one pizza for only two burritos moving from *b* to *a*, even though her ratio of burritos to pizza is greater. Though it is difficult to imagine concave indifference curves, two extreme versions of downward-sloping, convex indifference curves are plausible: straight-line or right-angle indifference curves.

perfect substitutes
goods that a consumer is completely indifferent as to which to consume

One extreme case is **perfect substitutes**: goods that a consumer is completely indifferent as to which to consume. Because Bill cannot taste any difference between Coca-Cola and Pepsi-Cola, he views them as perfect substitutes: He is indifferent between one additional can of Coke and one additional can of Pepsi. His indifference curves for these two goods are straight, parallel lines with a slope of −1 everywhere along the curve, as in panel a of Figure 4.4. Thus, Bill's marginal rate of substitution is −1 at every point along these indifference curves. The slope of indifference curves of perfect substitutes need not always be −1; it can be any constant rate. For example, Chris knows from reading the labels that Clorox bleach is twice as strong as a generic brand. As a result, Chris is indifferent between one cup of Clorox and two cups of the generic bleach. The slope of his indifference curve is $-\frac{1}{2}$, where the generic bleach is on the horizontal axis.[7]

perfect complements
goods that a consumer is interested in consuming only in fixed proportions

The other extreme case is **perfect complements**: goods that a consumer is interested in consuming only in fixed proportions. Maureen doesn't like pie by itself or ice cream by itself but loves pie à la mode: a slice of pie with a scoop of vanilla ice cream on top. Her indifference curves have right angles in panel b of Figure 4.4. If she has only one piece of pie, she gets as much pleasure from it and one scoop of ice cream, Bundle *a*, as from it and two scoops, Bundle *d*, or as from it and three scoops, Bundle *e*. That is, she won't eat the extra scoops because she does not have pieces of pie to go with the ice cream. Therefore, she consumes only bundles like *a*, *b*, and *c* in which pie and ice cream are in equal proportions.

With a bundle like *a*, *b*, or *c*, she will not substitute a piece of pie for an extra scoop of ice cream. For example, if she were at *b*, she would be unwilling to give up an extra slice of pie to get, say, two extra scoops of ice cream, as at point *e*. Indeed, she wouldn't give up the slice of pie for a virtually unlimited amount of extra ice cream because the extra ice cream is worthless to her.

The standard-shaped, convex indifference curve in panel c of Figure 4.4 lies between these two extreme examples. Convex indifference curves show that a consumer views two goods as imperfect substitutes.

Figure 4.4 Perfect Substitutes, Perfect Complements, Imperfect Substitutes

(a) Bill views Coke and Pepsi as perfect substitutes. His indifference curves are straight, parallel lines with a marginal rate of substitution (slope) of −1. Bill is willing to exchange one can of Coke for one can of Pepsi. (b) Maureen likes pie à la mode but does not like pie or ice cream by itself: She views ice cream and pie as perfect complements. She will not substitute between the two; she consumes them only in equal quantities. (c) Lisa views burritos and pizza as imperfect substitutes. Her indifference curve lies between the extreme cases of perfect substitutes and perfect complements.

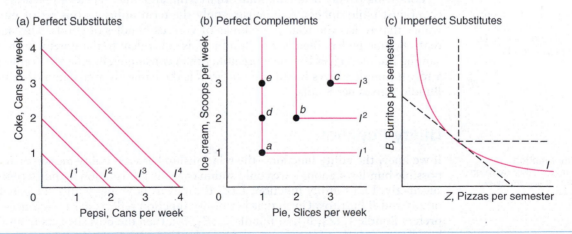

---

[7]Sometimes it is difficult to guess which goods are close substitutes. According to *Harper's* Index 1994, flowers, perfume, and fire extinguishers rank 1, 2, and 3 among Mother's Day gifts that Americans consider "very appropriate."

Application

Indifference Curves Between Food and Clothing

The figure shows estimated indifference curves of the average U.S. consumer between food consumed at home and clothing. The food and clothing measures are weighted averages of various goods. At relatively low quantities of food and clothing, the indifference curves, such as I^1, are nearly right angles: perfect complements. As we move away from the origin, the indifference curves become flatter: closer to perfect substitutes.

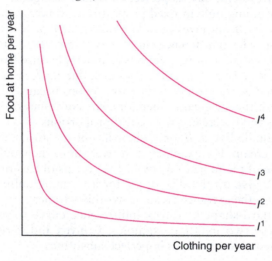

One interpretation of these indifference curves is that minimum levels of food and clothing are necessary to support life. The consumer cannot trade one good for the other if it means having less than these critical levels. As the consumer obtains more of both goods, however, the consumer is increasingly willing to trade between the two goods. According to these estimates, food and clothing are perfect complements when the consumer has little of either good and perfect substitutes when the consumer has large quantities of both goods.

4.2 Utility

Underlying our model of consumer behavior is the belief that consumers can compare various bundles of goods and decide which gives them the greatest pleasure. We can summarize a consumer's preferences by assigning a numerical value to each possible bundle to reflect the consumer's relative ranking of these bundles.

Following Jeremy Bentham, John Stuart Mill, and other nineteenth-century British economist-philosophers, economists apply the term **utility** to this set of numerical values that reflect the relative rankings of various bundles of goods. The statement that "Bonnie prefers Bundle x to Bundle y" is equivalent to the statement that "consuming Bundle x gives Bonnie more utility than consuming Bundle y." Bonnie prefers x to y if Bundle x gives Bonnie 10 *utils* (*util* is the name given to a unit of utility) and Bundle y gives her 8 utils.

utility a set of numerical values that reflect the relative rankings of various bundles of goods

Utility Function

If we knew the **utility function**—the relationship between utility measures and every possible bundle of goods—we could summarize the information in indifference maps succinctly. Lisa's utility function, $U(Z, B)$, tells us how many utils she gets from Z pizzas and B burritos. Given that her utility function reflects her preferences, if Lisa prefers Bundle 1, (Z_1, B_1), to Bundle 2, (Z_2, B_2), then the utils she gets from the first bundle exceeds that from the second bundle: $U(Z_1, B_1) > U(Z_2, B_2)$.

For example, suppose that the utility, U, that Lisa gets from burritos and pizzas is

$$U(Z, B) = \sqrt{ZB}. \qquad (4.1)$$

From Equation 4.1, we know that the more she consumes of either good, the greater the utility that Lisa receives. Using this function, we can determine whether she would be happier if she had Bundle x with 16 pizzas and 9 burritos or Bundle y with

utility function the relationship between *utility* values and every possible bundle of goods

13 of each. The utility she gets from x is 12 (= $\sqrt{16 \times 9}$) utils. The utility she gets from y is 13 (= $\sqrt{13 \times 13}$) utils. Therefore, she prefers y to x.

The utility function is a concept that economists use to help them think about consumer behavior; utility functions do not exist in any fundamental sense. If you asked your mother what her utility function is, she would be puzzled—unless, of course, she is an economist. But if you asked her enough questions about choices of bundles of goods, you could construct a function that accurately summarizes her preferences. For example, by questioning people, Rousseas and Hart (1951) constructed indifference curves between eggs and bacon, and MacCrimmon and Toda (1969) constructed indifference curves between French pastries and money (which can be used to buy all other goods).

Typically, consumers can easily answer questions about whether they prefer one bundle to another, such as "Do you prefer a bundle with one scoop of ice cream and two pieces of cake to another bundle with two scoops of ice cream and one piece of cake?" But they have difficulty answering questions about how much more they prefer one bundle to another because they don't have a measure to describe how their pleasure from two goods or bundles differs. Therefore, we may know a consumer's rank-ordering of bundles, but we are unlikely to know by how much more that consumer prefers one bundle to another.

Ordinal Preferences

If we know only consumers' relative rankings of bundles, our measure of pleasure is *ordinal* rather than *cardinal*. An ordinal measure is one that tells us the relative ranking of two things but not how much more one rank is than another.

If a professor assigns only letter grades to an exam, we know that a student who receives a grade of A did better than a student who received a B, but we can't say how much better from that ordinal scale. Nor can we tell whether the difference in performance between an A student and a B student is greater or less than the difference between a B student and a C student.

A cardinal measure is one by which absolute comparisons between ranks may be made. Money is a cardinal measure. If you have \$100 and your brother has \$50, we know not only that you have more money than your brother but also that you have exactly twice as much money as he does.

Because utility is an ordinal measure, we should not put any weight on the absolute differences between the utility associated with one bundle and another.[8] We care only about the relative utility or ranking of the two bundles.

Utility and Indifference Curves

An indifference curve consists of all those bundles that correspond to a particular level of utility, say $\overline{U}$. If Lisa's utility function is $U(Z, B)$, then the expression for one of her indifference curves is

$$\overline{U} = U(Z, B). \tag{4.2}$$

---

[8]Let $U(Z, B)$ be the original utility function and $V(Z, B)$ be the new utility function after we have applied a *positive monotonic transformation*: a change that increases the value of the function at every point. These two utility functions give the same ordinal ranking to any bundle of goods. (Economists often express this idea by saying that a *utility function is unique only up to a positive monotonic transformation*.) Suppose that $V(Z, B) = \alpha + \beta U(Z, B)$, where $\beta > 0$. The rank ordering is the same for these utility functions because $V(Z, B) = \alpha + \beta U(Z, B) > V(Z^*, B^*) = \alpha + \beta U(Z^*, B^*)$ if and only if $U(Z, B) > U(Z^*, B^*)$.

This expression determines all those bundles of Z and B that give her $\overline{U}$ utils of pleasure. For example, if her utility function is Equation 4.1, $U = \sqrt{ZB}$, then the indifference curve $4 = \overline{U} = \sqrt{ZB}$ includes any (Z, B) bundles such that $ZB = 16$, including the bundles (4, 4), (2, 8), (8, 2), (1, 16), and (16, 1).

The three-dimensional diagram in Figure 4.5 shows how Lisa's utility varies with the amounts of pizza, Z, and burritos, B, that she consumes. Panel a shows this relationship from a frontal view, while panel b shows the same relationship looking at it from one side. The figure measures Z on one axis on the "floor" of the diagram, B on the other axis on the floor of the diagram, and U(Z, B) on the vertical axis. For example, in the figure, Bundle a lies on the floor of the diagram and contains two pizzas and two burritos. Directly above it on the utility surface, or *hill of happiness*, is a point labeled U(2, 2). The vertical height of this point shows how much utility Lisa gets from consuming Bundle a. In the figure, $U(Z, B) = \sqrt{ZB}$, so this height is $U(2, 2) = \sqrt{2 \times 2} = 2$. Because she prefers more to less, her utility rises as Z increases, B increases, or both goods increase. That is, Lisa's hill of happiness rises as she consumes more of either or both goods.

What is the relationship between Lisa's utility function and one of her indifference curves—those combinations of Z and B that give Lisa a particular level of utility? Imagine that the hill of happiness is made of clay. If you cut the hill at a particular level of utility, the height corresponding to Bundle a, U(2, 2) = 2, you get a smaller hill above the cut. The bottom edge of this hill—the edge where you cut—is the curve I*. Now, suppose that you lower that smaller hill straight down onto the floor and trace the outside edge of this smaller hill. The outer edge of the hill on the two-dimensional

Figure 4.5 The Relationship Between the Utility Function and Indifference Curves

Panels a and b show Lisa's utility, U(Z, B), from different angles as a function of the amount of pizza, Z, and burritos, B, that she consumes. Each panel measures Z along one axis on the floor of the diagram, and B along the other axis on the floor. Utility is measured on the vertical axis. As Z, B, or both increase, she has more utility: She is on a higher point on the diagram. If we project all the points on the curve I* that are at a given height—a given level of utility—on the utility surface onto the floor of the diagram, we obtain the indifference curve I.

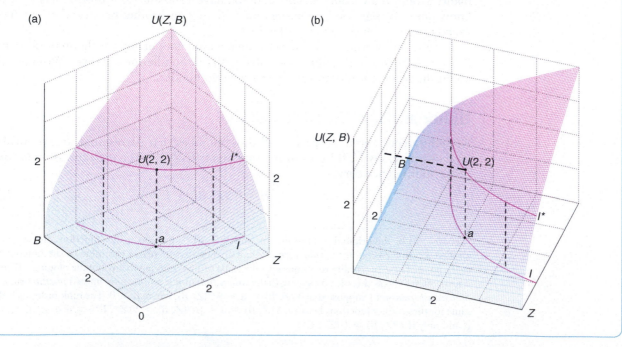

floor is indifference curve *I*. Making other parallel cuts in the hill of happiness, placing the smaller hills on the floor, and tracing their outside edges, you can obtain a map of indifference curves on which each indifference curve reflects a different level of utility.

Marginal Utility

Using Lisa's utility function for burritos and pizza, we can show how her utility changes if she gets to consume more of one of the goods. We now suppose that Lisa has the utility function in panel a of Figure 4.6. The curve shows how Lisa's utility rises as she consumes more pizzas while we hold her consumption of burritos fixed at 10. Because pizza is a *good*, Lisa's utility rises as she consumes more pizza.

If her consumption of pizzas increases from $Z = 4$ to 5, $\Delta Z = 5 - 4 = 1$, her utility increases from $U = 230$ to 250, $\Delta U = 250 - 230 = 20$. The extra utility ($\Delta U$) that she gets from consuming the last unit of a good ($\Delta Z = 1$) is the **marginal utility** from that good. Thus, marginal utility is the slope of the utility function as we hold the quantity of the other good constant (see Appendix 4A for a calculus derivation):

marginal utility
the extra utility that a consumer gets from consuming the last unit of a good

$$MU_Z = \frac{\Delta U}{\Delta Z}.$$

Figure 4.6 Utility and Marginal Utility

As Lisa consumes more pizza, holding her consumption of burritos constant at 10, her total utility, U, increases and her marginal utility of pizza, MU_Z, decreases (though it remains positive).

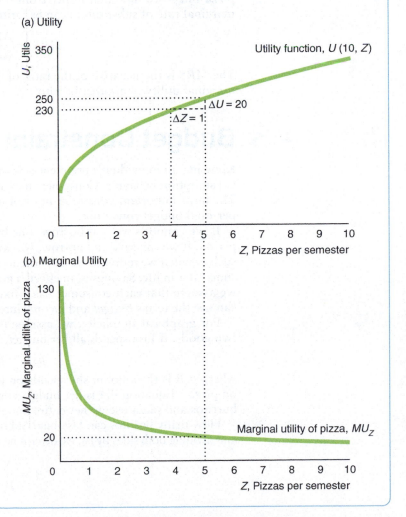

Lisa's marginal utility from increasing her consumption of pizza from 4 to 5 is

$$MU_Z = \frac{\Delta U}{\Delta Z} = \frac{20}{1} = 20.$$

Panel b in Figure 4.6 shows that Lisa's marginal utility from consuming one more pizza varies with the number of pizzas she consumes, holding her consumption of burritos constant. Her marginal utility of pizza curve falls as her consumption of pizza increases, but the marginal utility remains positive: Each extra pizza gives Lisa pleasure, but it gives her less pleasure than the previous pizza relative to other goods.

Utility and Marginal Rates of Substitution

Earlier we learned that the marginal rate of substitution (*MRS*) is the slope of the indifference curve. The marginal rate of substitution can also be expressed in terms of marginal utilities. If Lisa has 10 burritos and 4 pizzas in a semester and gets one more pizza, her utility rises. That extra utility is the marginal utility from the last pizza, MU_Z. Similarly, if she received one extra burrito instead, her marginal utility from the last burrito is MU_B.

Suppose that Lisa trades from one bundle on an indifference curve to another by giving up some burritos to gain more pizza. She gains marginal utility from the extra pizza but loses marginal utility from fewer burritos. As Appendix 4A shows, the marginal rate of substitution can be written as

$$MRS = \frac{\Delta B}{\Delta Z} = -\frac{MU_Z}{MU_B}. \tag{4.3}$$

The *MRS* is the negative of the ratio of the marginal utility of another pizza to the marginal utility of another burrito.

4.3 Budget Constraint

Knowing an individual's preferences is only the first step in analyzing that person's consumption behavior. Consumers maximize their well-being subject to constraints. The most important constraint most of us face in deciding what to consume is our personal budget constraint.

If we cannot save and borrow, our budget is the income we receive in a given period. If we can save and borrow, we can save money early in life to consume later, such as when we retire; or we can borrow money when we are young and repay those sums later in life. Savings is, in effect, a good that consumers can buy. For simplicity, we assume that each consumer has a fixed amount of money to spend now, so we can use the terms *budget* and *income* interchangeably.

For graphical simplicity, we assume that consumers spend their money on only two goods. If Lisa spends all her budget, Y, on pizza and burritos, then

$$p_B B + p_Z Z = Y, \tag{4.4}$$

where $p_B B$ is the amount she spends on burritos and $p_Z Z$ is the amount she spends on pizzas. Equation 4.4 is her budget constraint. It shows that her expenditures on burritos and pizza use up her entire budget.

How many burritos can Lisa buy? Subtracting $p_Z Z$ from both sides of Equation 4.4 and dividing both sides by p_B, we determine the number of burritos she can purchase to be

$$B = \frac{Y}{p_B} - \frac{p_Z}{p_B} Z. \tag{4.5}$$

According to Equation 4.5, she can buy more burritos if her income increases, if the prices of burritos or pizzas fall, or if she buys fewer pizzas.[9] For example, if she has one more dollar of income (Y), she can buy $1/p_B$ more burritos.

If $p_Z = \$1$, $p_B = \$2$, and $Y = \$50$, Equation 4.5 is

$$B = \frac{\$50}{\$2} - \frac{\$1}{\$2}Z = 25 - \tfrac{1}{2}Z. \tag{4.6}$$

As Equation 4.6 shows, every two pizzas cost Lisa one burrito. How many burritos can she buy if she spends all her money on burritos? By setting $Z = 0$ in Equation 4.5, we find that $B = Y/p_B = \$50/\$2 = 25$. Similarly, if she spends all her money on pizza, $B = 0$ and $Z = Y/p_Z = \$50/\$1 = 50$.

Instead of spending all her money on pizza or all on burritos, she can buy some of each. Table 4.1 shows four possible bundles she could buy. For example, she can buy 20 burritos and 10 pizzas with $50.

Equation 4.6 is plotted in Figure 4.7. This line is called a **budget line** or *budget constraint*: the bundles of goods that can be bought if the entire budget is spent on those goods at given prices. This budget line shows the combinations of burritos and pizzas that Lisa can buy if she spends all of her $50 on these two goods. The four bundles in Table 4.1 are labeled on this line.

Lisa could, of course, buy any bundle that costs less than $50. The **opportunity set** is all the bundles a consumer can buy, including all the bundles inside the budget constraint and

budget line
(or *budget constraint*) the bundles of goods that can be bought if the entire budget is spent on those goods at given prices

opportunity set
all the bundles a consumer can buy, including all the bundles inside the budget constraint and on the budget constraint

---

Figure 4.7 Budget Constraint

Lisa's budget line L^1 hits the vertical, burritos axis at 25 and the horizontal, pizza axis at 50 if $Y = \$50$, $p_Z = \$1$, and $p_B = \$2$. Lisa can buy any bundle in the opportunity set, the shaded area, including points on L^1. The formula for the budget line is $B = Y/p_B - (p_Z/p_B)Z = \$50/\$2 - (\$1/\$2)Z$. If Lisa buys one more unit of Z, she must reduce her consumption of B by $-(p_Z/p_B) = -\tfrac{1}{2}$ to stay within her budget. Thus the slope, $\Delta B/\Delta Z$, of her budget line, which is also called the marginal rate of transformation (MRT), is $-(p_Z/p_B) = -\tfrac{1}{2}$.

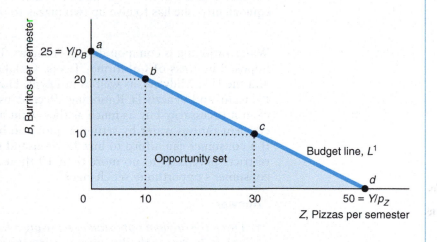

Table 4.1 Allocations of a $50 Budget Between Burritos and Pizza

Bundle	Burritos	Pizza
a	25	0
b	20	10
c	10	30
d	0	50

---

[9]Using calculus, we find that $dB/dY = 1/p_B > 0$, $dB/dZ = -p_Z/p_B < 0$, $dB/dp_Z = -Z/p_B < 0$, and $dB/dp_B = -(Y - p_Z Z)/(p_B)^2 = -B/p_B < 0$.

on the budget constraint (all those bundles of positive Z and B such that $p_B B + p_Z Z \leq Y$). Lisa's opportunity set is the shaded area in Figure 4.7. She could buy 10 burritos and 15 pieces of pizza for $35, which falls inside the budget constraint. Unless she wants to spend the other $15 on some other good, though, she might as well spend all of it on the food she loves and pick a bundle on the budget constraint rather than inside it.

Slope of the Budget Constraint

The slope of the budget line is determined by the relative prices of the two goods. Given that the budget line, Equation 4.5, is $B = Y/p_B - (p_Z/p_B)Z$, every extra unit of Z that Lisa purchases reduces B by $-p_Z/p_B$. That is, the slope of the budget line is $\Delta B/\Delta Z = -p_Z/p_B$.[10] Thus, the slope of the budget line depends on only the relative prices.

Lisa faces prices of $p_Z = \$1$ and $p_B = \$2$, so the slope of her budget line is $-p_Z/p_B = -\$1/\$2 = -\frac{1}{2}$. For example, if we reduce the number of pizzas from 10 at point b in Figure 4.7 to 0 at point a, the number of burritos that Lisa can buy rises from 20 at point b to 25 at point a, so $\Delta B/\Delta Z = (25 - 20)/(0 - 10) = 5/(-10) = -\frac{1}{2}$.[11]

marginal rate of transformation (*MRT*) the trade-off the market imposes on the consumer in terms of the amount of one good the consumer must give up to obtain more of the other good

The slope of the budget line is called the **marginal rate of transformation** (*MRT*): the trade-off the market imposes on the consumer in terms of the amount of one good the consumer must give up to purchase more of the other good:

$$MRT = \frac{\Delta B}{\Delta Z} = -\frac{p_Z}{p_B}. \tag{4.7}$$

Because Lisa's $MRT = -\frac{1}{2}$, she can "trade" an extra pizza for half a burrito; or, equivalently, she has to give up two pizzas to obtain an extra burrito.

Solved Problem 4.2

Water rationing is common during droughts. From 2010–2013, water quotas were imposed in areas of California, Texas, Oklahoma, Florida, the U.S. Great Plains, and the U.S. Midwest, as well as in Egypt, Honduras, India, Kenya, New Zealand, Pakistan, and Venezuela. Rationing affects consumers' opportunity sets because they cannot necessarily buy as much as they want at market prices. Suppose that a government rations water by setting a quota on how much a consumer can purchase. If a consumer can afford to buy 12 thousand gallons a month but the government restricts purchases to no more than 10 thousand gallons a month, how does the consumer's opportunity set change?

Answer

1. *Draw the original opportunity set using a budget line between water and all other goods.* In the graph, the consumer can afford to buy up to 12 thousand gallons of water a week if not constrained. The opportunity set, areas A and B, is bounded by the axes and the budget line.

2. *Add a line to the figure showing the quota, and determine the new opportunity set.* A vertical line at 10 thousand gallons on the water axis indicates the quota.

---

[10]As the budget line hits the horizontal axis at Y/p_Z and the vertical axis at Y/p_B, we can use the "rise over run" method to determine that the slope of the budget line is $-(Y/p_B)/(Y/p_Z) = -p_Z/p_B$. Alternatively, we can determine the slope by differentiating the budget constraint, Equation 4.5, with respect to Z: $dB/dZ = -p_Z/p_B$.

[11]The budget constraint in Figure 4.7 is a smooth, continuous line, which implies that Lisa can buy fractional numbers of burritos and pizzas. That's plausible because Lisa can buy a burrito at a *rate* of one-half per time period, by buying one burrito every other week.

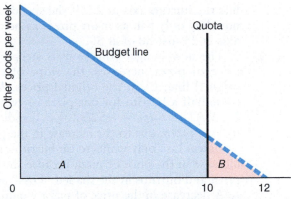

The new opportunity set, area *A*, is bounded by the axes, the budget line, and the quota line.

3. *Compare the two opportunity sets*. Because of the rationing, the consumer loses part of the original opportunity set: the triangle *B* to the right of the 10 thousand gallons line. The consumer has fewer opportunities because of rationing.

Effect of a Change in Price on the Opportunity Set

If the price of pizza doubles but the price of burritos is unchanged, the budget constraint swings in toward the origin in panel a of Figure 4.8. If Lisa spends all her money on burritos, she can buy as many burritos as before, so the budget line still

Figure 4.8 Changes in the Budget Constraint

(a) If the price of pizza increases from $1 to $2 a slice while the price of a burrito remains $2, Lisa's budget constraint rotates from L^1 to L^2 around the intercept on the burrito axis. The slope, or *MRT*, of the original budget line, L^1, is $-\frac{1}{2}$, while the *MRT* of the new budget line, L^2, is -1. The shaded area shows the combinations of pizza and burritos that Lisa can no longer afford. (b) If Lisa's income increases by $50 and prices don't change, her new budget constraint moves from L^1 to L^3. This shift is parallel: Both budget lines have the same slope (*MRT*) of $-\frac{1}{2}$. The new opportunity set is larger by the shaded area.

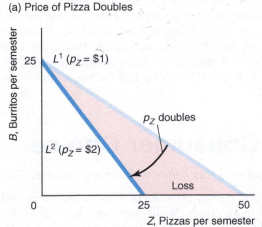

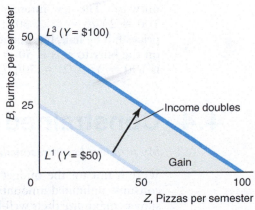

hits the burrito axis at 25. If she spends all her money on pizza, however, she can now buy only half as many pizzas as before, so the budget line intercepts the pizza axis at 25 instead of at 50.

The new budget constraint is steeper and lies inside the original one. As the price of pizza increases, the slope of the budget line, *MRT*, changes. On the original line, L^1, at the original prices, $MRT = -\frac{1}{2}$, which shows that Lisa could trade half a burrito for one pizza or two pizzas for one burrito. On the new line, L^2, $MRT = p_Z/p_B = -\$2/\$2 = -1$, indicating that she can now trade one burrito for one pizza, due to the increase in the price of pizza.

Unless Lisa only wants to eat burritos, she is unambiguously worse off due to this increase in the price of pizza because she can no longer afford the combinations of pizza and burritos in the shaded "Loss" area.

A decrease in the price of pizza would have the opposite effect: The budget line would rotate outward around the intercept of the line and the burrito axis. As a result, the opportunity set would increase.

Effect of a Change in Income on the Opportunity Set

If the consumer's income increases, the consumer can buy more of all goods. Suppose that Lisa's income increases by \$50 per semester to $Y = \$100$. Her budget constraint shifts outward—away from the origin—and is parallel to the original constraint in panel b of Figure 4.8. Why is the new constraint parallel to the original one? The intercept of the budget line on the burrito axis is Y/p_B, and the intercept on the pizza axis is Y/p_Z. Thus, holding prices constant, the intercepts shift outward in proportion to the change in income. Originally, if she spent all her money on pizza, Lisa could buy $50 = \$50/\$1$ pizzas; now she can buy $100 = \$100/\$1$. Similarly, the burrito axis intercept goes from $25 = \$50/\$2$ to $50 = \$100/\$2$. A change in income affects the position but not the slope of the budget line, because the slope is determined solely by the relative prices of pizza and burritos. A decrease in the prices of both pizza and burritos has the same effect as an increase in income, as the next Solved Problem shows.

Solved Problem 4.3

Is Lisa better off if her income doubles or if the prices of both the goods she buys fall by half?

Answer

Show that her budget line and her opportunity set are the same with either change. As panel b of Figure 4.8 shows, if her income doubles, her budget line has a parallel shift outward. The new intercepts at $50 = 2Y/p_B = (2 \times 50)/2$ on the burrito axis and $100 = 2Y/p_Z = (2 \times 50)/1$ on the pizza axis are double the original values. If the prices fall by half, her budget line is the same as if her income doubles. The intercept on the burrito axis is $50 = Y/(p_B/2) = 50/(2/2)$, and the intercept on the pizza axis is $100 = Y/(p_Z/2) = 50/(1/2)$.

4.4 Constrained Consumer Choice

My problem lies in reconciling my gross habits with my net income. —Errol Flynn

Were it not for the budget constraint, consumers who prefer more to less would consume unlimited amounts of all goods. Well, they can't have it all! Instead, consumers maximize their well-being subject to their budget constraints. Now, we determine the bundle of goods that maximizes well-being subject to the budget constraint.

The Consumer's Optimal Bundle

Veni, vidi, Visa. (We came, we saw, we went shopping.) —Jan Barrett

Given information about Lisa's preferences (as summarized by her indifference curves) and how much she can spend (as summarized by her budget constraint), we can determine Lisa's optimal bundle. Her optimal bundle is the bundle out of all the bundles that she can afford that gives her the most pleasure.[12]

We first show that Lisa's optimal bundle must be on the budget constraint in Figure 4.9. Bundles that lie on indifference curves above the constraint, such as those on I^3, are not in the opportunity set. So even though Lisa prefers f on indifference curve I^3 to e on I^2, f is too expensive and she can't purchase it. Although Lisa could buy a bundle inside the budget constraint, she does not want to do so, because more is better than less: For any bundle inside the constraint (such as d on I^1), another bundle on the constraint has more of at least one of the two goods, and hence she prefers the bundle on the constraint. Therefore, the optimal bundle must lie on the budget constraint.

We can also show that bundles that lie on indifference curves that cross the budget constraint (such as I^1, which crosses the constraint at a and c) are less desirable than certain other bundles on the constraint. Only some of the bundles on indifference curve I^1 lie within the opportunity set: Bundles a and c and all the points on I^1 between them, such as d, can be purchased. Because I^1 crosses the budget constraint, the bundles between a and c on I^1 lie strictly inside the constraint, so some bundles in the opportunity set (area A + area B) are preferable to these bundles on I^1 and are affordable. By the more-is-better property, Lisa prefers e to d because e has more of both pizza and burritos than d. By transitivity, e is preferred to a, c, and all the other points on I^1—even those, like g, that Lisa can't afford. Because indifference curve I^1 crosses the budget constraint, area B contains at least one bundle that is preferred to—lies above and to the right of—at least one bundle on the indifference curve.

Figure 4.9 Consumer Maximization, Interior Solution

Lisa's optimal bundle is e (10 burritos and 30 pizzas) on indifference curve I^2. Indifference curve I^2 is tangent to her budget line at e. Bundle e is the bundle on the highest indifference curve (highest utility) that she can afford. Any bundle that is preferred to e (such as points on indifference curve I^3) lies outside of her opportunity set, so she cannot afford them. Bundles inside the opportunity set, such as d, are less desirable than e because they represent less of one or both goods.

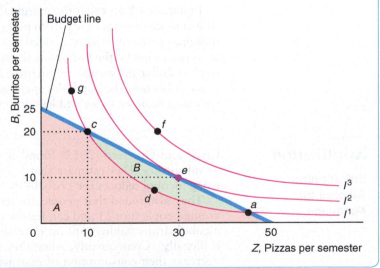

---

[12]Appendix 4B uses calculus to determine the bundle that maximizes utility subject to the budget constraint. In this section, we use graphical techniques.

Thus, the optimal bundle—the *consumer's optimum*—must lie on the budget constraint and be on an indifference curve that does not cross it. If Lisa is consuming this bundle, she has no incentive to change her behavior by substituting one good for another.

So far we've shown that the optimal bundle must lie on an indifference curve that touches the budget constraint but does not cross it. We can reach this outcome in two ways. The first is an *interior solution*, in which the optimal bundle has positive quantities of both goods and lies between the ends of the budget line. The other possibility, called a *corner solution*, occurs when the optimal bundle is at one end of the budget line, where the budget line forms a corner with one of the axes.

Interior Solution In Figure 4.9, Bundle *e* on indifference curve I^2 is the optimum bundle. It is in the interior of the budget line away from the corners. Lisa prefers consuming a balanced diet, *e*, of 10 burritos and 30 pizzas, to eating only one type of food or the other.

For the indifference curve I^2 to touch the budget constraint but not cross it, it must be *tangent* to the budget constraint: The budget constraint and the indifference curve have the same slope at the point *e* where they touch. The slope of the indifference curve, the marginal rate of substitution, measures the rate at which Lisa is *willing* to trade burritos for pizza: $MRS = -MU_Z/MU_B$, Equation 4.3. The slope of the budget line, the marginal rate of transformation, measures the rate at which Lisa *can* trade her money for burritos or pizza in the market: $MRT = -p_Z/p_B$, Equation 4.7. Thus, Lisa's utility is maximized at the bundle where the rate at which she is willing to trade burritos for pizza equals the rate at which she can trade:

$$MRS = -\frac{MU_Z}{MU_B} = -\frac{p_Z}{p_B} = MRT.$$

Rearranging terms, this condition is equivalent to

$$\frac{MU_Z}{p_Z} = \frac{MU_B}{p_B}. \tag{4.8}$$

Equation 4.8 says that the marginal utility of pizza divided by the price of a pizza (the amount of extra utility from pizza per dollar spent on pizza), MU_Z/p_Z, equals the marginal utility of burritos divided by the price of a burrito, MU_B/p_B. Thus, Lisa's utility is maximized if the last dollar she spends on pizza gets her as much extra utility as the last dollar she spends on burritos. If the last dollar spent on pizza gave Lisa more extra utility than the last dollar spent on burritos, Lisa could increase her happiness by spending more on pizza and less on burritos. Her cousin Spenser is a different story.

Application

Substituting Alcohol for Marijuana

Crost and Guerrero (2012) found that young people view alcohol and marijuana as substitutes. They estimate that a 1 percentage point increase in the probability of using alcohol reduces the probability of using marijuana by 0.2 percentage points.

They also found that people are sensitive to changes in the relative prices. When young people turn 21 and can legally drink in the United States, their cost of buying alcohol drops (taking into account their time and the risk of being caught buying it illegally). Consequently, when they turn 21, they drink more alcohol and sharply decrease their consumption of marijuana. This effect is stronger for women, whose consumption of marijuana falls by 17%, than for men, whose consumption drops by 6%. Apparently, one unintended consequence of barring teenagers from legally drinking is that they are more likely to consume marijuana.

Figure 4.10 Consumer Maximization, Corner Solution

Spenser's indifference curves are flatter than Lisa's indifference curves in Figure 4.9. That is, he is willing to give up more pizzas for one more burrito than is Lisa. Spenser's optimal bundle occurs at a corner of the opportunity set at Bundle *e*: 25 burritos and 0 pizzas.

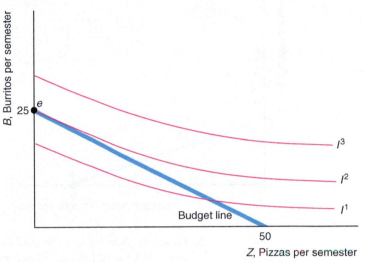

Corner Solution Some consumers choose to buy only one of the two goods: a *corner solution*. They so prefer one good to another that they only purchase the preferred good.

Spenser's indifference curves in Figure 4.10 are flatter than Lisa's in Figure 4.9. His optimal bundle, *e*, where he buys 25 burritos and no pizza, lies on an indifference curve that touches the budget line only once, at the upper-left corner.

Bundle *e* is the optimal bundle because the indifference curve does not cross the constraint into the opportunity set. If it did, another bundle would give Spenser more pleasure.

Spenser's indifference curve is not tangent to his budget line. It would cross the budget line if both the indifference curve and the budget line were continued into the "negative pizza" region of the diagram, on the other side of the burrito axis.

Solved Problem 4.4

The concentration of the active ingredient, sodium hypochlorite, in Clorox is twice that of the generic brand. Consequently, Chris views one cup of Clorox to be a perfect substitute for two cups of the generic. If Clorox costs $3 gallon, the generic costs $1, and Chris allocates $Y = \$6$ per year, what bundle does Chris buy? If the price of Clorox falls to $2, how does Chris's behavior change?

Answer

1. *Draw representative indifference curves.* Chris's indifference curves are straight lines with a slope of $-\frac{1}{2}$. For example, indifference curve I^2 hits the generic axis at 6 and the Clorox axis at 3 in both panels of the figure.

2. *Draw the initial budget line and show the bundle Chris chooses.* The initial budget line is L^1 in panel a of the figure. Chris can purchase 6($= \$6/\$1$) gallons of generic bleach, 2($= \$6/\$3$) gallons of Clorox, or any linear combination of generic and Clorox bleach that costs $6. The highest indifference curve that touches L^1 is I^2, which hits L^1 at Bundle *e* at the generic bleach axis. Because Clorox is only twice as strong as the generic but costs three times as much, Chris buys 6 gallons of the generic and no Clorox. Thus, Chris is at a corner solution.

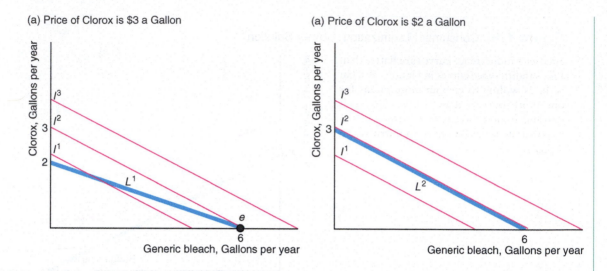

(a) Price of Clorox is $3 a Gallon

(a) Price of Clorox is $2 a Gallon

3. *Draw the new budget line and describe how Chris's behavior changes*. When the price of Clorox falls to $2 per gallon, the budget line is L^2 in panel b. Now the budget line L^2 and the indifference curve I^2 lie one on top of each other. Chris is indifferent between buying any bundle on I^2 including 6 gallons of the generic, 3 gallons of Clorox, 2 gallons of Clorox and 2 gallons of generic, 1 gallon of Clorox and 4 gallons of generic, and so forth. That is, Chris might buy a bundle at either corner or in the interior.

★ Optimal Bundles on Convex Sections of Indifference Curves[13]

Earlier we argued, on the basis of introspection, that most indifference curves are convex to the origin. Now that we know how to determine a consumer's optimal bundle, we can give a more compelling explanation about why we assume that indifference curves are convex. We can show that if indifference curves are smooth, optimal bundles lie either on convex sections of indifference curves or at the point where the budget constraint hits an axis.

Suppose that indifference curves were strictly concave to the origin, as in panel a of Figure 4.11. Indifference curve I^1 is tangent to the budget line at d, but that bundle is not optimal. Bundle e on the corner between the budget constraint and the burrito axis is on a higher indifference curve, I^2, than d is. Thus, if a consumer had strictly concave indifference curves, the consumer would buy only one good—here, burritos. Similarly, as we saw in Solved Problem 4.4, consumers with straight-line indifference curves buy only the least expensive good. Because we do not see consumers buying only one good, indifference curves must have convex sections.

If indifference curves have both concave and convex sections as in panel b of Figure 4.11, the optimal bundle lies in a convex section or at a corner. Bundle d, where a concave section of indifference curve I^1 is tangent to the budget line, cannot be an optimal bundle. Here, e is the optimal bundle and is tangent to the budget constraint in the convex portion of the higher indifference curve I^2. *If a consumer*

---

[13]Starred sections are optional.

Figure 4.11 Optimal Bundles on Convex Sections of Indifference Curves

(a) Indifference curve I^1 is tangent to the budget line at Bundle d, but Bundle e is superior because it lies on a higher indifference curve, I^2. If indifference curves are strictly concave to the origin, the optimal bundle, e, is at a corner. (b) If indifference curves have both concave and convex sections, a bundle such as d, which is tangent to the budget line in the concave portion of indifference curve I^1, cannot be an optimal bundle because there must be a preferable bundle in the convex portion of a higher indifference curve, e on I^2 (or at a corner).

(a) Strictly Concave Indifference Curves

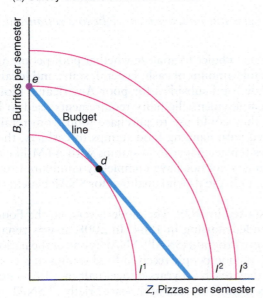

(b) Concave and Convex Indifference Curves

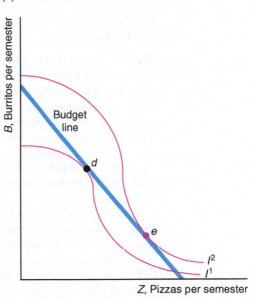

buys positive quantities of two goods, the indifference curve is convex and tangent to the budget line at that optimal bundle.

Buying Where More Is Better

Whoever said money can't buy happiness didn't know where to shop.

A key assumption in our analysis of consumer behavior is that more is preferred to less: Consumers are not satiated. We now show that if both goods are consumed in positive quantities and their prices are positive, more of either good must be preferred to less. Suppose that the opposite were true and that Lisa prefers fewer burritos to more. Because burritos cost her money, she could increase her well-being by reducing the amount of burritos she consumes until she consumes no burritos—a scenario that violates our assumption that she consumes positive quantities of both goods.[14]

---

[14]Similarly, at her optimal bundle, Lisa cannot be *satiated*—indifferent between consuming more or fewer burritos. Suppose that her budget is obtained by working and that Lisa does not like working at the margin. Were it not for the goods she can buy with what she earns, she would not work as many hours as she does. Thus, if she were satiated and did not care if she consumed fewer burritos, she would reduce the number of hours she worked, thereby lowering her income, until her optimal bundle occurred at a point where more was preferred to less or she consumed none.

Though it is possible that consumers prefer less to more at some large quantities, we do not observe consumers making purchases where that occurs.

In summary, we do not observe consumer optima at bundles where indifference curves are concave or consumers are satiated. Thus, we can safely assume that indifference curves are convex and that consumers prefer more to less in the ranges of goods that we actually observe.

Food Stamps

I've known what it is to be hungry, but I always went right to a restaurant.
—Ring Lardner

We can use the theory of consumer choice to analyze whether poor people are better off receiving food or a comparable amount of cash. Federal, state, and local governments work together to provide food subsidies for poor Americans. Households that meet income, asset, and employment eligibility requirements used to be given coupons—food stamps—that they could use to purchase food from retail stores. To reduce the stigma associated with handing food stamps to cashiers, the federal government required that states replace paper food stamps with ATM-like cards by June 2009. However, this change may not have completely eliminated the stigma problem: Only three-quarters of individuals who qualified for SNAP benefits received them in fiscal year 2010.

The U.S. Food Stamp Plan started in 1939. The modern version, the Food Stamp Program, was permanently funded starting in 1964. In 2008, it was renamed the Supplemental Nutrition Assistance Program (SNAP). SNAP is one of the nation's largest social welfare programs: 47 million people received food stamps at a cost of $81 billion in 2012.[15] By the time they reach 20 years of age, half of all Americans and 90% of black children have received food stamps at least briefly.[16] SNAP provided the average recipient about $133.41 a month ($4.45 a day) in 2012.

Since the Food Stamp Program started in 1964, economists, nutritionists, and policymakers have debated "cashing out" food stamps by providing checks or cash instead of coupons that can be spent only on food. Legally, food stamps may not be sold, though a black market for them exists. Would a switch to a comparable cash subsidy increase the well-being of food stamp recipients? Would the recipients spend less on food and more on other goods?

Poor people who receive cash have more choices than those who receive a comparable amount of food stamps. With food stamps, only extra food can be obtained. With cash, either food or other goods can be purchased. As a result, a cash grant raises a recipient's opportunity set by more than food stamps of the same value do, as we now show.

In Figure 4.12, the price of a unit of food and the price of all other goods are both $1, with an appropriate choice of units. A person with a monthly income of Y has a budget line that hits both axes at Y: The person can buy Y units of food

---

[15]In January 2013, 15% of all U.S. residents received food stamps. To learn the share in your county, go to **www.slate.com/articles/news_and_politics/map_of_the_week/2013/04/food_stamp_recipients_by_county_an_interactive_tool_showing_local_snap_data.html**.

[16]According to Professor Mark Rank as cited in Jason DeParle and Robert Gebeloff, "The Safety Net: Food Stamp Use Soars, and Stigma Fades," *New York Times*, November 29, 2009.

Figure 4.12 Food Stamps Versus Cash

The lighter line shows the original budget line of an individual with Y income per month. The heavier line shows the budget constraint with $100 worth of food stamps. The budget constraint with a grant of $100 in cash is a line between $Y + 100$ on both axes. The opportunity set increases by area B with food stamps but by $B + C$ with cash. An individual with these indifference curves consumes Bundle d (with less than 100 units of food) with no subsidy, e (Y units of all other goods and 100 units of food) with food stamps, and f (more than Y units of all other goods and less than 100 units of food) with a cash subsidy. This individual's utility is greater with a cash subsidy than with food stamps.

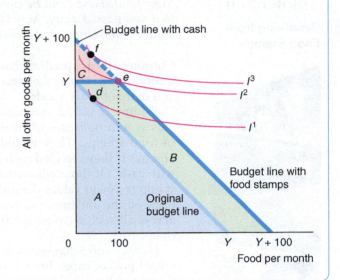

per month, Y units of all other goods, or any linear combination. The opportunity set is area A.

If that person receives a subsidy of $100 in cash per month, the person's new monthly income is $Y + \$100$. The budget constraint with cash hits both axes at $Y + 100$ and is parallel to the original budget constraint. The opportunity set increases by $B + C$ to $A + B + C$.

If the person receives $100 worth of food stamps, the food stamp budget constraint has a kink. Because the food stamps can be spent only on food, the budget constraint shifts 100 units to the right for any quantity of other goods up to Y units. For example, if the recipient buys only food, now $Y + 100$ units of food can be purchased. If the recipient buys only other goods with the original Y income, that person can get Y units of other goods plus 100 units of food. However, the food stamps cannot be turned into other goods, so the recipient can't buy $Y + 100$ units of other goods, as can be done under the cash transfer program. The food stamps opportunity set is areas $A + B$, which is larger than the presubsidy opportunity set by B. The opportunity set with food stamps is smaller than that with the cash transfer program by C.

A recipient benefits as much from cash or an equivalent amount of food stamps if the recipient would have spent at least $100 on food if given cash. In other words, the individual is indifferent between cash and food stamps if that person's indifference curve is tangent to the downward-sloping section of the food stamp budget constraint.

Conversely, if the recipient would not spend at least $100 on food if given cash, the recipient prefers receiving cash to food stamps. Figure 4.12 shows the indifference curves of an individual who prefers cash to food stamps. This person chooses Bundle e (Y units of all other goods and 100 units of food) if given food stamps but Bundle f (more than Y units of all other goods and less than 100 units of food) if given cash. This individual is on a higher indifference curve, I^2 rather than I^1, if given cash rather than food stamps.

Application

Benefiting from Food Stamps

Your food stamps will be stopped effective March 1992 because we received notice that you passed away. May God bless you. You may reapply if there is a change in your circumstances.   —Department of Social Services, Greeneville, South Carolina

Consumer theory predicts that if food stamp recipients were instead given cash, their utility would remain the same or rise and some recipients would consume less food and more of other goods.

Whitmore (2002) estimated that between 20% and 30% of food stamp recipients would be better off if they were given cash instead of an equivalent value in food stamps. They would spend less on food than their food stamp benefit amount if they received cash instead of stamps, and therefore would be better off with cash. Of those who would trade their food stamps for cash, the average food stamp recipient values the stamps at 80% of their face value (although the average price on the underground economy is only 65%). Thus, Whitmore estimated that across all such recipients, $500 million was wasted by giving food stamps rather than cash.

Hoynes and Schanzenbach (2009) found that food stamps result in a decrease in out-of-pocket expenditures on food and an increase in overall food expenditures. For those households that would prefer cash to food stamps—those that spend relatively little of their income on food—food stamps cause them to increase their food consumption by about 22%, compared to 15% for other recipients, and 18% overall.

However, a more recent study, Beatty and Tuttle (2012), concluded that households spend more on food out of extra food stamps than out of extra cash. They found that recipients spent 36% of additional food stamp benefits on food.

4.5   Behavioral Economics

behavioral economics
by adding insights from psychology and empirical research on human cognition and emotional biases to the rational economic model, economists try to better predict economic decision making

So far, we have assumed that consumers are rational, maximizing individuals. A new field of study, **behavioral economics**, adds insights from psychology and empirical research on human cognition and emotional biases to the rational economic model to better predict economic decision making.[17] We discuss three applications of behavioral economics in this section: tests of transitivity, the endowment effect, and salience and bounded rationality. Later in the book, we examine whether a consumer is influenced by the purchasing behavior of others (Chapter 11), why many people lack self-control (Chapter 16), and the psychology of decision making under uncertainty (Chapter 17).

Tests of Transitivity

In our presentation of the basic consumer choice model at the beginning of this chapter, we assumed that consumers make transitive choices. But do they actually make transitive choices?

A number of studies of both humans and animals show that preferences usually are transitive. Weinstein (1968) used an experiment to determine how frequently people

---

[17]The introductory chapter of Camerer et al. (2004) and DellaVigna (2009) are excellent surveys of the major papers in this field and heavily influenced the following discussion.

give intransitive responses. None of the subjects knew the purpose of the experiment. They were given choices between ten goods, offered in pairs, in every possible combination. To ensure that monetary value would not affect their calculations, they were told that all of the goods had a value of $3. Weinstein found that 93.5% of the responses of adults—people over 18 years old—were transitive. However, only 79.2% of children aged 9–12 gave transitive responses.

Psychologists have also tested for transitivity using preferences for colors, photos of faces, and so forth. Bradbury and Ross (1990) found that, given a choice of three colors, nearly half of 4–5 year olds are intransitive, compared to 15% for 11–13 year olds, and 5% for adults. Bradbury and Ross showed that novelty (a preference for a new color) is responsible for most intransitive responses, and that this effect is especially strong in children.

Based on these results, one might conclude that it is appropriate to assume that adults exhibit transitivity for most economic decisions. On the other hand, one might modify the theory when applying it to children or when novel goods are introduced.

Economists normally argue that rational people should be allowed to make their own consumption choices so as to maximize their well-being. However, some might conclude that children's lack of transitivity or rationality provides a justification for political and economic restrictions and protections placed on young people.

Endowment Effect

Experiments show that people have a tendency to stick with the bundle of goods that they currently possess. One important reason for this tendency is called the **endowment effect,** which occurs when people place a higher value on a good if they own it than they do if they are considering buying it.

endowment effect
people place a higher value on a good if they own it than they do if they are considering buying it

We normally assume that an individual can buy or sell goods at the market price. Rather than rely on income to buy some mix of two goods, an individual who was *endowed* with several units of one good could sell some and use that money to buy units of another good.

We assume that a consumer's endowment does not affect the indifference curve map. In a classic buying and selling experiment, Kahneman et al. (1990) challenged this assumption. In an undergraduate law and economics class at Cornell University, 44 students were divided randomly into two groups. Members of one group were given coffee mugs that were available at the student store for $6. Those students *endowed* with a mug were told that they could sell it and were asked the minimum price that they would accept for the mug. The subjects in the other group, who did not receive a mug, were asked how much they would pay to buy the mug. Given the standard assumptions of our model and that the subjects were chosen randomly, we would expect no difference between the selling and buying prices. However, the median selling price was $5.75 and the median buying price was $2.25, so sellers wanted more than twice what buyers would pay. This type of experiment has been repeated with many variations and typically an endowment effect is found.

However, some economists believe that this result has to do with the experimental design. Plott and Zeiler (2005) argued that if you take adequate care to train the subjects in the procedures and make sure they understand them, we no longer find this result. List (2003) examined the actual behavior of sports memorabilia collectors and found that amateurs who do not trade frequently exhibited an endowment effect, unlike professionals and amateurs who traded a lot. Thus, experience may minimize or eliminate the endowment effect, and people who buy goods for resale may be less likely to become attached to these goods.

Others accept the results and have considered how to modify the standard model to reflect the endowment effect (Knetsch, 1992). One implication of these experimental results is that people will only trade away from their endowments if prices change substantially. This resistance to trade could be captured by having a kink in the indifference curve at the endowment bundle. (We showed indifference curves with a kink at a 90° angle in panel b of Figure 4.4.) These indifference curves could have an angle greater than 90°, and the indifference curve could be curved at points other than at the kink. If the indifference curve has a kink, the consumer does not shift to a new bundle in response to a small price change, but may shift if the price change is large.

Application **Opt In Versus Opt Out**	One practical implication of the endowment effect is that consumers' behavior may differ depending on how a choice is posed. Many workers are offered the choice of enrolling in their firm's voluntary tax-deferred retirement (pension) plan, called a 401(k) plan. The firm can pose the choice in two ways: It can automatically sign up employees for the program and let them opt out if they want, or it can tell employees that to participate in the program they must sign up (opt in) to participate. These two approaches might seem identical, but the behaviors they lead to are not. Madrian and Shea (2001, 2002) found that well over twice as many workers participate if they are automatically enrolled (but may opt out) than if they must opt in: 86% versus 37%. In short, inertia matters. Because of this type of evidence, federal law was changed in 2006 and 2007 to make it easier for employers to enroll their employees in their 401(k) plans automatically. According to Aon Hewitt, the share of large firms that automatically enroll new hires in 401(k) plans was 67% in 2012, up from 58% in 2007. According to the U.S. Bureau of Labor Statistics, participation in defined-contribution retirement plans in firms with over 500 employees rose from 45% in 2008 to 61% in 2012, due to the increased use of automatic enrollment.

Salience and Bounded Rationality

Up to now in this chapter, we have assumed that consumers know their own income or endowment, the relevant prices, and their own tastes, and hence they make informed decisions. Those assumptions are not always valid. Behavioral economists and psychologists have demonstrated that people are more likely to consider information if it is presented in a way that grabs their attention or if it takes relatively little thought or calculation to understand. Economists use the term *salience*, in the sense of *striking* or *obvious*, to describe this idea.

For example, *tax salience* is awareness of a tax. If the posted price in a store does not include the tax, some consumers may not take the tax into account in making decisions. Tax salience has important implications for tax policy. In Chapter 3, where we assumed that consumers pay attention to prices and taxes, we showed that the tax incidence on consumers is the same regardless of whether the tax is collected from consumers or sellers. However, if consumers are inattentive to taxes, they're more likely to bear the tax burden if they're taxed. If a tax on consumers rises and consumers don't notice, their demand for the good becomes relatively inelastic, causing consumers to bear more of the tax incidence (see Equation 3.11). In contrast, if the tax is placed on sellers and the sellers want to pass at least some of the tax on to consumers, they raise their price, which consumers observe.

bounded rationality
people have a limited capacity to anticipate, solve complex problems, or enumerate all options

An alternative explanation for ignoring taxes is **bounded rationality**: people have a limited capacity to anticipate, solve complex problems, or enumerate all options. To avoid having to perform hundreds of calculations when making purchasing decisions at a grocery store, many people chose not to calculate the tax-inclusive price. However, when that post-tax price information is easily available to them, consumers make use of it.

One way to modify the standard model is to assume that people incur a cost when making calculations—such as the time taken or the mental strain—and that deciding whether to incur this cost is part of their rational decision-making process. People incur this calculation cost only if they think the gain from a better choice of goods exceeds the cost. More people pay attention to a tax when the tax rate is high or when their demand for the good is elastic (they are sensitive to price). Similarly, some people are more likely to pay attention to taxes when making large, one-time purchases—such as for a computer or car—rather than small, repeated purchases—such as for a bar of soap.

Application **Unaware of Taxes**	If a grocery store's posted price includes the sales tax, consumers observe a change in the price as the tax rises. On the other hand, if a store posts the pre-tax price and collects the tax at the cash register, consumers are less likely to note that the post-tax price has increased when the tax rate increases. Chetty et al. (2009) compared consumers' response to a rise in an ad valorem sales tax on beer (called an *excise tax*), which is included in the posted price of beer, to an increase in a general ad valorem sales tax, which is collected at the cash register but not included in the posted price. An increase in either tax has the same effect on the final price, so an increase in either tax should have the same effect on purchases if consumers pay attention to both taxes.[18]

< Chetty et al. found that a 10% increase in the posted price, which includes the excise tax, reduces beer consumption by 9%, while a 10% increase in the price due to a rise in the sales tax that is not posted reduces consumption by only 2%. They also conducted an experiment where they posted tax-inclusive prices for 750 products in a grocery store and found that demand for these products fell by about 8% relative to control products in that store and comparable products at nearby stores.

Some consumers may ignore the tax because they forgot about it—salience—while others may not know that a tax applies at all. In grocery stores in some states, taxes may apply to alcohol and toiletries but not to food. Consequently, someone buying toothpaste may not realize that it is taxed. Zheng et al. (2013) used the finding by Chetty et al. that 20% of shoppers mistakenly think there is no sales tax on toothpaste to calculate that the information effect explains 31% of the sales drop in the Chetty et al. study when taxes were included in the posted price.

Goldin and Homonoff (2013) found that all customers respond to changes in cigarettes' posted price, but that only low-income consumers respond to taxes levied at the register. Thus, a tax collected at the register is less effective in discouraging smoking than if everyone paid attention to the tax. However, such a tax is progressive, falling more heavily on rich people who are more likely to ignore it.

Challenge Solution **Why Americans Buy More E-Books Than Do Germans**	Why do Germans largely ignore e-books, while many Americans are quickly switching to this technology? While it's possible that this difference is due to different tastes in the two countries, there's evidence that attitudes toward e-books is similar in the two countries. For example, according to surveys, 59% of Americans and 56% of Germans report that they have no interest in e-books. Price differences provide a better explanation.

---

[18]The final price consumers pay is $p^* = p(1 + \beta)(1 + \alpha)$, where p is the pre-tax price, α is the general sales tax, and β is the excise tax on beer.

Suppose that Max, a German, and Bob, a Yank, are avid readers with identical incomes and tastes. Each is indifferent between reading a novel in a traditional book and using an e-reader so that their indifference curves have a slope of -1, as the red line in the figure illustrates. We can use an indifference curve–budget line analysis to explain why Max buys printed books while Bob chooses electronic ones.

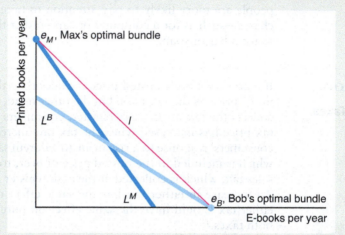

In both countries, the pre-tax price of e-books is lower than that of printed books. In the United States, the after-tax price of e-books remains lower, so Bob's budget line L^B is flatter than his indifference curve. However, because the German tax system sets a lower rate for printed books than for e-books, the after-tax price of e-books is higher in Germany, so Max's budget line L^M is steeper than his indifference curve. Thus, as the figure shows, Bob maximizes his utility by spending his entire book budget on e-books. He chooses the Bundle e_B, where his indifference curve I hits his budget line L^B on the e-book axis. In contrast, Max spends his entire book budget on printed books, at point e_M.

If Bob and Max viewed the two types of books as imperfect substitutes and had the usual convex indifference curves, they would each buy a mix of e-books and printed books. However, because of the relatively lower price of e-books in the United States, Bob would buy relatively more e-books.

Summary

Consumers maximize their utility (well-being) subject to constraints based on their income and the prices of goods.

1. **Preferences.** To predict consumers' responses to changes in constraints, economists use a theory about individuals' preferences. One way of summarizing consumers' preferences is with a family of indifference curves. An indifference curve consists of all bundles of goods that give the consumer a particular level of utility. Based on observations of consumers' behavior, economists assume that consumers' preferences have three properties: completeness, transitivity, and more is better. Given these three assumptions, indifference curves have the following properties:

   ■ Consumers get more pleasure from bundles on indifference curves the farther from the origin the curves are.

   ■ An indifference curve goes through any given bundle.

   ■ Indifference curves cannot cross.

   ■ Indifference curves slope downward.

   ■ Indifference curves are thin.

2. **Utility.** Economists call the set of numerical values that reflect the relative rankings of bundles of goods *utility*. Utility is an ordinal measure: By comparing the utility a consumer gets from each of two bundles, we know that the consumer prefers the bundle with the higher utility, but we can't tell by how much the consumer prefers that bundle. The marginal utility from a good is the extra utility a person gets from consuming one more unit of that good, holding the consumption of all other goods constant. The rate at which a

consumer is willing to substitute Good 1 for Good 2, the marginal rate of substitution, *MRS*, depends on the relative amounts of marginal utility the consumer gets from each of the two goods.

3. **Budget Constraint.** The amount of goods consumers can buy at given prices is limited by their income. As a result, the greater their income and the lower the prices of goods, the better off they are. The rate at which they can exchange Good 1 for Good 2 in the market, the marginal rate of transformation, *MRT*, depends on the relative prices of the two goods.

4. **Constrained Consumer Choice.** Each person picks an affordable bundle of goods to consume so as to maximize his or her pleasure. If an individual consumes both Good 1 and Good 2 (an interior solution), the individual's utility is maximized when the following four equivalent conditions hold:

   ■ The indifference curve between the two goods is tangent to the budget constraint.

   ■ The consumer buys the bundle of goods that is on the highest obtainable indifference curve.

   ■ The consumer's marginal rate of substitution (the slope of the indifference curve) equals the marginal rate of transformation (the slope of the budget line).

   ■ The last dollar spent on Good 1 gives the consumer as much extra utility as the last dollar spent on Good 2.

However, consumers do not buy some of all possible goods (corner solutions). The last dollar spent on a good that is actually purchased gives more extra utility than would a dollar's worth of a good the consumer chose not to buy.

5. **Behavioral Economics.** Using insights from psychology and empirical research on human cognition and emotional biases, economists are starting to modify the rational economic model to better predict economic decision making. While adults tend to make transitive choices, children are less likely to do so, especially when novelty is involved. Consequently, some would argue that children's ability to make economic choices should be limited. If consumers have an endowment effect, such that they place a higher value on a good if they own it than they do if they are considering buying it, they are less sensitive to price changes and hence less likely to trade than would be predicted by the standard economic model. Many consumers ignore sales taxes and do not take them into account when making decisions.

Questions

All questions are available on MyEconLab; * = *answer appears at the back of this book;* **A** = *algebra problem;* **C** = *calculus problem.*

1. Preferences

1.1 Give as many reasons as you can why we believe that economists assume that the more-is-better property holds and describe how these explanations relate to the results in the Application "You Can't Have Too Much Money."

1.2 Can an indifference curve be downward sloping in one section, but then bend backward so that it forms a "hook" at the end of the indifference curve? (*Hint:* See Solved Problem 4.1.)

1.3 Give as many reasons as you can why we believe that indifference curves are convex and explain.

1.4 Don is altruistic. Show the possible shape of his indifference curves between charity and all other goods.

*1.5 Arthur spends his income on bread and chocolate. He views chocolate as a good but is neutral about bread, in that he doesn't care if he consumes it or not. Draw his indifference curve map.

1.6 Miguel considers tickets to the Houston Grand Opera and to Houston Astros baseball games to be perfect substitutes. Show his preference map. What is his utility function?

*1.7 Sofia will consume hot dogs only with whipped cream. Show her preference map. What is her utility function?

1.8 Which of the following pairs of goods are complements and which are substitutes? Are the goods that are substitutes likely to be perfect substitutes for some or all consumers?

   a. A popular novel and a gossip magazine

   b. A razor and a blade

   c. A gun and a stick of butter

   d. A Panasonic DVD player and a JVC DVD player

2. Utility

2.1 Does the utility function $V(Z, B) = \alpha + [U(Z, B)]^2$ give the same ordering over bundles as does $U(Z, B)$? **A**

2.2 Fiona requires a minimum level of consumption, a *threshold*, to derive additional utility: $U(X, Z)$

is 0 if $X + Z \leq 5$ and is $X + Z$ otherwise. Draw Fiona's indifference curves. Which of our usual assumptions are violated by this example?

2.3 If Joe views two candy bars and one piece of cake as perfect substitutes, what is his marginal rate of substitution between candy bars and cake?

2.4 Julia consumes cans of anchovies, A, and boxes of biscuits, B. Each of her indifference curves reflects strictly diminishing marginal rates of substitution. Where $A = 2$ and $B = 2$, her marginal rate of substitution between cans of anchovies and boxes of biscuits equals $-1 (= MU_A/MU_B)$. Will she prefer a bundle with three cans of anchovies and a box of biscuits to a bundle with two of each? Why? **A**

*2.5 José Maria's utility function is $U(B, Z) = AB^\alpha Z^\beta$. What is his marginal utility of B? What is his marginal utility of Z? What is his marginal rate of substitution between B and Z? **C**

3. Budget Constraint

3.1 Suppose Gregg consumes chocolate candy bars and oranges. He is given four candy bars and three oranges. He can buy or sell a candy bar for $2 each. Similarly, he can buy or sell an orange for $1. If he has no other source of income, draw his budget constraint and write the equation. What is the most he can spend, Y, on these goods?

3.2 What happens to the budget line if the government applies a specific tax of $1 per gallon on gasoline but does not tax other goods? What happens to the budget line if the tax applies only to purchases of gasoline in excess of 10 gallons per week?

3.3 What is the effect of a quota of 13 thousand gallons of water per month on the opportunity set of the consumer in Solved Problem 4.2?

*3.4 What is the effect of a 50% income tax on Dale's budget line and opportunity set?

3.5 Change Solved Problem 4.3 so that Lisa's budget and the price of pizza double, but the price of burritos remains constant. Show how her budget constraint and opportunity set changes. Is Lisa necessarily better off than before these changes? (*Hint*: What happens to the intercepts of the budget line?)

4. Constrained Consumer Choice

4.1 What happens to a consumer's optimum if all prices and income double? (*Hint*: What happens to the intercepts of the budget line?)

4.2 Some of the largest import tariffs, the tax on imported goods, are on shoes. Strangely, the cheaper the shoes, the higher the tariff. The highest U.S. tariff, 67%, is on a pair of $3 canvas sneakers, while the tariff on $12 sneakers is 37%, and that on $300 Italian leather imports is 12% (Blake W. Krueger, "A Shoe Tariff With a Big Footprint," *Wall Street Journal*, November 22, 2012). Laura buys either inexpensive, canvas sneakers ($3 before the tariff) or more expensive gym shoes ($12 before the tariff) for her many children. Use an indifference curve–budget line analysis to show how imposing these unequal tariffs affects the bundle of shoes that she buys compared to what she would have bought in the absence of tariffs. Can you confidently predict whether she'll buy relatively more expensive gym shoes after the tariff? Why or why not?

4.3 Suppose that Boston consumers pay twice as much for avocados as for tangerines, whereas San Diego consumers pay half as much for avocados as for tangerines. Assuming that consumers maximize their utility, which city's consumers have a higher marginal rate of substitution of avocados for tangerines? Explain your answer.

4.4 Ralph usually buys one pizza and two colas from the local pizzeria. The pizzeria announces a special: All pizzas after the first one are half-price. Show the original and new budget constraint. What can you say about the bundle Ralph will choose when faced with the new constraint?

*4.5 Andy purchases only two goods, apples (a) and kumquats (k). He has an income of $40 and can buy apples at $2 per pound and kumquats at $4 per pound. His utility function is $U(a, k) = 3a + 5k$. That is, his (constant) marginal utility for apples is 3 and his marginal utility for kumquats is 5. What bundle of apples and kumquats should he purchase to maximize his utility? Why? **A**

*4.6 David's utility function is $U = B + 2Z$, so $MU_B = 1$ and $MU_Z = 2$. Describe the location of his optimal bundle (if possible) in terms of the relative prices of B and Z. **A**

4.7 Linda loves buying shoes and going out to dance. Her utility function for pairs of shoes, S, and the number of times she goes dancing per month, T, is $U(S, T) = 2ST$, so $MU_S = 2T$ and $MU_T = 2S$. It costs Linda $50 to buy a new pair of shoes or to spend an evening out dancing. Assume that she has $500 to spend on clothing and dancing.

   a. What is the equation for her budget line? Draw it (with T on the vertical axis), and label the slope and intercepts.

b. What is Linda's marginal rate of substitution? Explain.

c. Solve mathematically for her optimal bundle. Show how to determine this bundle in a diagram using indifference curves and a budget line. **A**

4.8 Vasco's utility function is $U = 10X^2Z$. The price of X is $p_X = \$10$, the price of Z is $p_z = \$5$, and his income is $Y = \$150$. What is his optimal consumption bundle? (*Hint*: See Appendix 4B.) Show this bundle in a graph. **C**

*4.9 Diogo has a utility function $U(B, Z) = AB^\alpha Z^\beta$, where A, α, and β are constants, B is burritos, and Z is pizzas. If the price of burritos, p_B, is $2 and the price of pizzas, p_Z, is $1, and Y is $100, what is Diogo's optimal bundle? **C**

4.10 Felix chooses between water and all other goods. If he spends all his money on water, he can buy 12 thousand gallons per week. At current prices, his optimal bundle is e_1. Show e_1 in a diagram. During a drought, the government limits the number of gallons per week that he may purchase to 10 thousand. Using diagrams, discuss under which conditions his new optimal bundle, e_2, will be the same as e_1. If the two bundles differ, can you state where e_2 must be located?

4.11 Salvo and Huse (forthcoming) found that roughly one-fifth of flexible-fuel (cars that can run on a mix of ethanol and gasoline) car owners choose gasoline when the price of gas is 20% above that of ethanol (in energy-adjusted terms) and, similarly, one-fifth of motorists choose ethanol when ethanol is 20% more expensive than gasoline. What can you say about these people's tastes?

4.12 According to **towerswatson.com**, at large employers, 48% of employees earning between $10,000 and $24,999 a year participated in a voluntary retirement savings program, compared to 91% who earned more than $100,000. We can view savings as a good. In a figure, plot savings versus all other goods. Show why a person is more likely to "buy" some savings (put money in a retirement account) as the person's income rises.

4.13 Maureen only drinks a cup of coffee with one teaspoon of sugar. In an indifference curve–budget line diagram, show the bundle of coffee and sugar that gives her the most pleasure. Are her indifference curve and the budget line tangent at that bundle?

4.14 A poor person who has an income of $1,000 receives $100 worth of food stamps. Draw the

budget constraint if the food stamp recipient can sell these coupons on the black market for less than their face value.

4.15 Show how much an individual's opportunity set increases if the government gives food stamps rather than sells them at subsidized rates.

4.16 Since 1979, recipients have been given food stamps. Before 1979, people bought food stamps at a subsidized rate. For example, to get $1 worth of food stamps, a household paid about 15¢ (the exact amount varied by household characteristics and other factors). What is the budget constraint facing an individual if that individual may buy up to $100 per month in food stamps at 15¢ per each $1 coupon?

4.17 Is a poor person more likely to benefit from $100 a month worth of food stamps (that can be used only to buy food) or $100 a month worth of clothing stamps (that can be used only to buy clothing)? Why?

*4.18 Is a wealthy person more likely than a poor person to prefer to receive a government payment of $100 in cash to $100 worth of food stamps? Why or why not?

4.19 Federal housing and food stamp subsidy programs are two of the largest in-kind transfer programs for the poor. President Barack Obama's 2011 budget allocated the Housing Choice Voucher Program $19.6 billion. Many poor people are eligible for both programs: 30% of housing assistance recipients also used food stamps, and 38% of food stamp program participants also received housing assistance (Harkness and Newman, 2003). Suppose Jill's income is $500 a month, which she spends on food and housing. The price of food and housing is each $1 per unit. Draw her budget line. If she receives $100 in food stamps and $200 in a housing subsidy (which she can spend only on housing), how do her budget line and opportunity set change?

4.20 The local swimming pool charges nonmembers $10 per visit. If you join the pool, you can swim for $5 per visit but you have to pay an annual fee of F. Use an indifference curve diagram to find the value of F such that you are indifferent between joining and not joining. Suppose that the pool charged you exactly that F. Would you go to the pool more or fewer times than if you did not join? For simplicity, assume that the price of all other goods is $1.

4.21 In Solved Problem 4.4, if the generic bleach increases its strength to equal that of Clorox without changing its price, what bundles will Chris buy if the price of Clorox is $3 or $2?

5. Behavioral Economics

5.1 Illustrate the logic of the endowment effect using a kinked indifference curve. Let the angle be greater than 90°. Suppose that the prices change, so the slope of the budget line through the endowment changes. Use the diagram to explain why an individual whose endowment point is at the kink will only trade from the endowment point if the price change is substantial.

*5.2 Why would a consumer's demand for a supermarket product change when the product price is quoted inclusive of taxes rather than before tax? Is the same effect as likely for people buying a car? (*Hint*: See the Application "Unaware of Taxes.")

6. Challenge

6.1 Suppose the Challenge Solution were changed so that Max and Bob have identical tastes, with the usual-shaped indifference curves. Use a figure to discuss how the different slopes of their budget lines affect the bundles of printed books and e-books that each chooses. Can you make any unambiguous statements about how their bundles differ? Can you make an unambiguous statement if you know that Bob's budget line goes through Max's optimal bundle?

*6.2 West Virginians who live near the border with other states can shop on either side of the border. If they buy food in West Virginia, their total cost is the price of the food plus the tax. If they buy across the border in states that do not tax food, the total cost is the price plus the cost due to the extra travel. Tosun and Skidmore (2007) found that West Virginian food sales dropped 8% in border counties when a 6% sales tax on food was imposed. Explain why. (*Hint*: See the Challenge Solution and Solved Problem 4.4.)

6.3 Einav et al. (2012) found that people who live in high sales tax locations are much more likely than other consumers to purchase goods over the Internet because Internet purchases are generally exempt from the sales tax if the firm is located in another state. They found that a 1% increase in a state's sales tax increases online purchases by that state's residents by just under 2%. Is the explanation for this result similar to that in the Challenge Solution? Why or why not?

6.4 Until 2012, California, Pennsylvania, and Texas required firms to collect sales taxes for online sales if the chain had a physical presence (a "brick" store as opposed to a "click" store) in those states. Thus, those states collected taxes on Best Buy's online sales, because it had stores in each of those states, but they did not collect taxes from **Amazon.com** because it did not have physical locations in those states. Starting in 2012, Amazon had to pay taxes in these states. After the tax was imposed on Amazon, Best Buy had a 4% to 6% increase in its online sales in those states relative to the rest of the chain (**www.bizjournals.com/twincities/ news/2013/01/11/best-buys-online-sales-up-in-states.html**). Use an indifference curve–budget line diagram to show why Best Buy's sales rose after taxes were imposed on Amazon. (*Hint*: Start by drawing a typical consumer's indifference curve between buying a good from Amazon or from Best Buy.)

Applying Consumer Theory

5

The IRS = Theirs.

Childcare subsidies are common throughout the world. According to an Organization for Economic Cooperation and Development report in 2012, childcare spending as a percentage of gross domestic product was 0.9% in Sweden and Norway, 0.5% in the United Kingdom, 0.4% in France, 0.3% in Japan, and 0.1% in Germany and the United States.

Challenge

Per-Hour Versus Lump-Sum Childcare Subsidies

The increased employment of mothers outside the home has led to a steep rise in childcare over the past several decades. In the United States today, nearly seven out of ten mothers work outside the home—more than twice the rate in 1970. Eight out of ten employed mothers with children under age six are likely to have some form of nonparental childcare arrangement. Six out of ten children under the age of six are in childcare, as are 45% of children under age one.

Childcare is a major burden for the poor, and the expense may prevent poor mothers from working. Paying for childcare for children under the age of five absorbed 25% of the earnings for families with annual incomes under $14,400, but only 6% for families with incomes of $54,000 or more. Government childcare subsidies increase the probability that a single mother will work at a standard job by 7% (Tekin, 2007). As one would expect, the subsidies have larger impacts on welfare recipients than on wealthier mothers.

In large part to help poor families obtain childcare so that the parents can work, the U.S. Child Care and Development Fund (CCDF) provided $5.7 billion to states in 2013. Childcare programs vary substantially across states in their generosity and in the form of the subsidy.[1] Most states provide an *ad valorem* or a specific subsidy (see Chapter 3) to lower the hourly rate that a poor family pays for childcare.

Rather than subsidizing the price of childcare, the government could provide an unrestricted lump-sum payment that could be spent on childcare or on all other goods, such as food and housing. Canada provides such lump-sum payments.

For a given government expenditure, does a per-hour subsidy or a lump-sum subsidy provide greater benefit to recipients? Which option increases the demand for childcare services by more? Which one inflicts less cost on other consumers of childcare?

---

[1]For example, in 2009, for a family with two children to be eligible for a subsidy, the family's maximum income was $4,515 in California and $2,863 in Louisiana. The maximum subsidy for a toddler was $254 per week in California and $92.50 per week in Louisiana. The family's fee for childcare ranged between 20% and 60% of the cost of care in Louisiana, between 2% and 10% in Maine, and between $0 and $495 per month in Minnesota.

We can answer these questions using consumer theory. We can also use consumer theory to derive demand curves, to analyze the effects of providing cost-of-living adjustments to deal with inflation, and to derive labor supply curves.

We start by using consumer theory to show how to determine the shape of a demand curve for a good by varying the price of a good, holding other prices and income constant. Firms use information about the shape of demand curves when setting prices. Governments apply this information in predicting the impact of policies such as taxes and price controls.

We then use consumer theory to show how an increase in income causes the demand curve to shift. Firms use information about the relationship between income and demand to predict which less-developed countries will substantially increase their demand for the firms' products.

Next, we show that an increase in the price of a good has two effects on demand. First, consumers would buy less of the now relatively more expensive good even if they were compensated with cash for the price increase. Second, consumers' incomes can't buy as much as before because of the higher price, so consumers buy less of at least some goods.

We use this analysis of these two demand effects of a price increase to show why the government's measure of inflation, the Consumer Price Index (CPI), overestimates the amount of inflation. Because of this bias in the CPI, some people gain and some lose from contracts that adjust payment based on the government's inflation index. If you signed a long-term lease for an apartment in which your rent payments increase over time in proportion to the change in the CPI, you lose and your landlord gains from this bias.

Finally, we show how we can use the consumer theory of demand to determine an individual's labor *supply* curve. Knowing the shape of workers' labor supply curves is important in analyzing the effect of income tax rates on work and on tax collections. Many politicians, including Presidents John F. Kennedy, Ronald Reagan, and George W. Bush, have argued that if the income tax rates were cut, workers would work so many more hours that tax revenues would increase. If so, everyone could be made better off by a tax cut. If not, the deficit could grow to record levels. Economists use empirical studies based on consumer theory to predict the effect of the tax rate cut on tax collections, as we discuss at the end of this chapter.

In this chapter, we examine five main topics

1. **Deriving Demand Curves.** We use consumer theory to derive demand curves, showing how a change in price causes a shift along a demand curve.

2. **How Changes in Income Shift Demand Curves.** We use consumer theory to determine how a demand curve shifts because of a change in income.

3. **Effects of a Price Change.** A change in price has two effects on demand, one having to do with a change in relative prices and the other concerning a change in the consumer's opportunities.

4. **Cost-of-Living Adjustments.** Using an analysis of the two effects of price changes, we show that the CPI overestimates the rate of inflation.

5. **Deriving Labor Supply Curves.** Using consumer theory to derive the demand curve for leisure, we can derive workers' labor supply curves and use them to determine how a reduction in the income tax rate affects labor supply and tax revenues.

5.1 Deriving Demand Curves

We use consumer theory to show by how much the quantity demanded of a good falls as its price rises. An individual chooses an optimal bundle of goods by picking the point on the highest indifference curve that touches the budget line (Chapter 4). When a price changes, the budget constraint the consumer faces shifts, so the consumer chooses a new optimal bundle. By varying one price and holding other prices and income constant, we determine how the quantity demanded changes as the price changes, which is the information we need to draw the demand curve. After deriving an individual's demand curve, we show the relationship between consumer tastes and the shape of the demand curve, which is summarized by the elasticity of demand (Chapter 3).

Indifference Curves and a Rotating Budget Line

We derive a demand curve using the information about tastes from indifference curves (see Appendix 4B for a mathematical approach). To illustrate how to construct a demand curve, we estimated a set of indifference curves between wine and beer, using data for U.S. consumers. Panel a of Figure 5.1 shows three estimated

Figure 5.1 Deriving an Individual's Demand Curve

If the price of beer falls, holding the price of wine, the budget, and tastes constant, the typical American consumer buys more beer, according to our estimates. (a) At the actual budget line, L^1, where the price of beer is $12 per unit and the price of wine is $35 per unit, the average consumer's indifference curve, I^1, is tangent at Bundle e_1, 26.7 gallons of beer per year and 2.8 gallons of wine per year. If the price of beer falls to $6 per unit, the new budget constraint is L^2, and the average consumer buys 44.5 gallons of beer per year and 4.3 gallons of wine per year. (b) By varying the price of beer, we trace out the individual's demand curve, D^1. The beer price-quantity combinations E_1, E_2, and E_3 on the demand curve for beer in panel b correspond to optimal Bundles e_1, e_2, and e_3 in panel a.

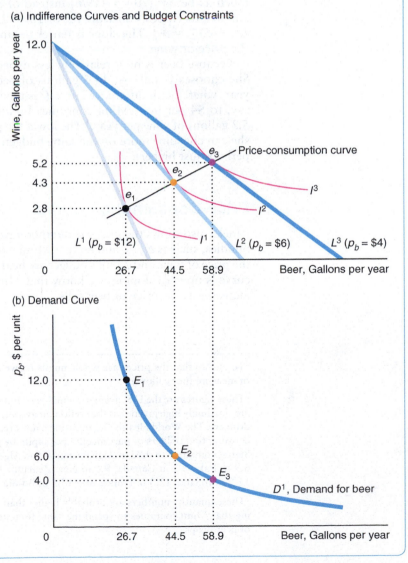

indifference curves for a typical U.S. consumer, whom we call Mimi. These indifference curves are convex to the origin: Mimi views beer and wine as imperfect substitutes (Chapter 4). We can construct Mimi's demand curve for beer by holding her budget, her tastes, and the price of wine constant at their initial levels and varying the price of beer.

The vertical axis in panel a measures the number of gallons of wine Mimi consumes each year, and the horizontal axis measures how many gallons of beer she drinks per year. Mimi spends $Y = \$419$ per year on beer and wine. The price of beer, p_b, is $12 per unit, and the price of wine, p_w, is $35 per unit.[2] The slope of her budget line, L^1, is $-p_b/p_w = -12/35 \approx \frac{1}{3}$. At those prices, Mimi consumes Bundle e_1, 26.7 gallons of beer per year and 2.8 gallons of wine per year, a combination that is determined by the tangency of indifference curve I^1 and budget line L^1.[3]

If the price of beer falls in half to $6 per unit while the price of wine and her budget remain constant, Mimi's budget line rotates outward to L^2. If she were to spend all her money on wine, she could buy the same 12 ($\approx 419/35$) gallons of wine per year as before, so the intercept on the vertical axis of L^2 is the same as for L^1. However, if Mimi were to spend all her money on beer, she could buy twice as much as before (70 [$\approx 419/6$] instead of 35 gallons of beer), so L^2 hits the horizontal axis twice as far from the origin as L^1. As a result, L^2 has a flatter slope than L^1, $-6/35 \approx -\frac{1}{6}$. The slope is flatter because the price of beer has fallen relative to the price of wine.

Because beer is now relatively less expensive, Mimi drinks relatively more beer. She chooses Bundle e_2, 44.5 gallons of beer per year and 4.3 gallons of wine per year, where her indifference curve I^2 is tangent to L^2. If the price of beer falls again, say, to $4 per unit, Mimi consumes Bundle e_3, 58.9 gallons of beer per year and 5.2 gallons of wine per year.[4] The lower the price of beer, the happier Mimi is because she can consume more on the same budget: She is on a higher indifference curve (or perhaps just higher).

Price-Consumption Curve

Panel a also shows the *price-consumption curve*, which is the line through the optimal bundles, such as e_1, e_2, and e_3, that Mimi would consume at each price of beer, when the price of wine and Mimi's budget are held constant. Because the price-consumption curve is upward sloping, we know that Mimi's consumption of both beer and wine increases as the price of beer falls.

---

[2]To ensure that the prices are whole numbers, we state the prices with respect to an unusual unit of measure (not gallons).

[3]These figures are the U.S. average annual per capita consumption of wine and beer. These numbers are startlingly high given that they reflect an average that includes teetotalers and (apparently heavy) drinkers. The World Health Organization's most recent statistics for each country as of 2013 for the consumption of liters of pure alcohol per capita by people 15 years and older was 8.6 in the United States, compared to 0.02 in Afghanistan, 0.5 in Algeria, 2.4 in Israel, 5.5 in Mexico, 6.7 in Norway, 6.9 in Italy, 8.2 in Canada, 9.6 in New Zealand, 10.3 in the United Kingdom, 10.4 in Australia, 11.9 in Ireland, 12.3 in France, and 13.5 in Bosnia and Herzegovina.

[4]These quantity numbers are probably higher than they would be in reality because we are assuming that Mimi continues to spend the same total amount of money on beer and wine as the price of beer drops.

With different tastes—different shaped indifference curves—the price-consumption curve could be flat or downward sloping. If it were flat, then as the price of beer fell, the consumer would continue to purchase the same amount of wine and consume more beer. If the price-consumption curve were downward sloping, the individual would consume more beer and less wine as the price of beer fell.

Application **Smoking Versus Eating and Phoning**	Tobacco use, one of the biggest public health threats the world has ever faced, killed 100 million people in the twentieth century. In 2013, the U.S. Centers for Disease Control and Prevention (CDC) reported that cigarette smoking and secondhand smoke are responsible for one in every five deaths each year in the United States. Half of all smokers die of tobacco-related causes. Worldwide, tobacco kills 5.4 million people a year: one in ten adult deaths.

Of the more than one billion smokers in the world, over 80% live in low- and middle-income countries. One way to get people—particularly poor people—to quit smoking is to raise the price of tobacco relative to the prices of other goods (thereby changing the slope of the budget constraints that individuals face). In poorer countries, smokers are giving up cigarettes to buy cell phones. As cell phones have recently become affordable in many poorer countries, the price ratio of cell phones to tobacco has fallen substantially.

According to Labonne and Chase (2011), in 2003, before cell phones were common, 42% of households in the Philippine villages they studied used tobacco, and 2% of total village income was spent on tobacco. After the price of cell phones fell, ownership of the phones quadrupled from 2003 to 2006. As consumers spent more on mobile phones, tobacco use fell by one-third in households in which at least one member had smoked (so that consumption fell by one-fifth for the entire population). That is, if we put cell phones on the horizontal axis and tobacco on the vertical axis and lower the price of cell phones, the price-consumption curve is downward sloping (unlike that in panel a of Figure 5.1).

Cigarette taxes are often used to increase the price of cigarettes relative to other goods. At least 163 countries tax cigarettes to raise tax revenue and to discourage smoking. Lower-income and younger populations are more likely than others to quit smoking if the price increases. Nikaj and Chaloupka (2013) estimated the demand elasticity for cigarettes on youth smoking in 38 countries to be -1.5. However, in the relatively poor countries, the elasticity was -2.2. When the after-tax price of cigarettes in Canada increased 158% from 1979 to 1991 (after adjusting for inflation), teenage smoking dropped by 61% and overall smoking fell by 38%.

But what happens to those who continue to smoke heavily? To pay for their now more expensive habit, they have to reduce their expenditures on other goods, such as housing and food. Busch et al. (2004) found that a 10% increase in the price of cigarettes causes poor, smoking families to cut back on cigarettes by 9%, alcohol and transportation by 11%, food by 17%, and health care by 12%. These smoking families allocate 36% of their expenditures to housing compared to 40% for nonsmokers. Thus, to continue to smoke, these people cut back on many basic goods. If we put tobacco on the horizontal axis and all other goods on the vertical axis, the price-consumption curve is upward sloping, so that as the price of tobacco rises, the consumer buys less of both tobacco and all other goods.

The Demand Curve Corresponds to the Price-Consumption Curve

We can use the same information in the price-consumption curve to draw Mimi's demand curve for beer, D^1, in panel b of Figure 5.1. Corresponding to each possible price of beer on the vertical axis of panel b, we record on the horizontal axis the quantity of beer demanded by Mimi from the price-consumption curve.

Points E_1, E_2, and E_3 on the demand curve in panel b correspond to Bundles e_1, e_2, and e_3 on the price-consumption curve in panel a. Both e_1 and E_1 show that when the price of beer is \$12, Mimi demands 26.7 gallons of beer per year. When the price falls to \$6 per unit, Mimi increases her consumption to 44.5 gallons of beer, point E_2. The demand curve, D^1, is downward sloping as predicted by the Law of Demand.

Solved Problem 5.1

Mahdu views Coke, q, and Pepsi as perfect substitutes: He is indifferent as to which one he drinks. The price of a 12-ounce can of Coke is p, the price of a 12-ounce can of Pepsi is p^*, and his weekly cola budget is Y. Derive Mahdu's demand curve for Coke using the method illustrated in Figure 5.1. (*Hint*: See Solved Problem 4.4.)

Answer

1. *Use indifference curves to derive Mahdu's equilibrium choice.* Panel a of the figure shows that his indifference curves I^1 and I^2 have a slope of −1 because Mahdu is indifferent as to which good he buys (see Chapter 4). We keep the price of Pepsi, p^*, fixed and vary the price of Coke, p. Initially, the budget line L^1 is steeper than the indifference curves because the price of Coke is greater than that of Pepsi, $p_1 > p^*$. Mahdu maximizes his utility by choosing Bundle e_1, where he purchases only Pepsi (a corner solution, see Chapter 4). If the price of Coke is $p_2 < p^*$, the budget line L^2 is flatter than the indifference curves. Mahdu maximizes his utility at e_2, where he spends his cola budget on Coke, buying as many cans of Coke as he can afford, $q_2 = Y/p_2$, and he consumes no Pepsi. If the price of Coke is $p_3 = p^*$, his budget line would have the same slope as his indifference curves, and one indifference curve would lie on top of the budget line. Consequently, he would be indifferent between buying any quantity of q between 0 and $Y/p_3 = Y/p^*$ (and his total purchases of Coke and Pepsi would add to $Y/p_3 = Y/p^*$).

2. *Use the information in panel a to draw his Coke demand curve.* Panel b shows Mahdu's demand curve for Coke, q, for a given price of Pepsi, p^*, and Y. When the price of Coke is above p^*, his demand curve lies on the vertical axis, where he demands zero units of Coke, such as point E_1 in panel b, which corresponds to e_1 in panel a. If the prices are equal, he buys any amount of Coke up to a maximum of $Y/p_3 = Y/p^*$. If the price of Coke is $p_2 < p^*$, he buys Y/p_2 units at point E_2, which corresponds to e_2 in panel a. When the price of Coke is less than that of Pepsi, the Coke demand curve asymptotically approaches the horizontal axis as the price of Coke approaches zero.

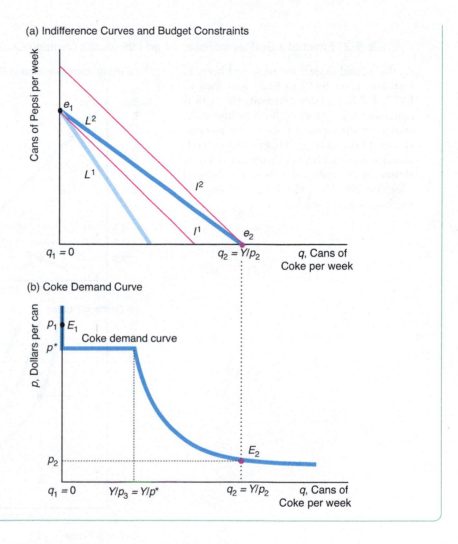

(a) Indifference Curves and Budget Constraints

(b) Coke Demand Curve

5.2 How Changes in Income Shift Demand Curves

To trace out the demand curve, we looked at how an increase in the good's price—holding income, tastes, and other prices constant—causes a downward *movement along the demand curve*. Now we examine how an increase in income, when all prices are held constant, causes a *shift of the demand curve*.

Businesses routinely use information on the relationship between income and the quantity demanded. For example, in deciding where to market its products, Whirlpool wants to know which countries are likely to spend a relatively large percentage of any extra income on refrigerators and washing machines.

Effects of a Rise in Income

We illustrate the relationship between the quantity demanded and income by examining how Mimi's behavior changes when her income rises while the prices of beer and wine remain constant. Figure 5.2 shows three ways of looking at the relationship

As the annual budget for wine and beer, Y, increases from \$419 to \$628 and then to \$837, holding prices constant, the typical consumer buys more of both products, as shown by the upward slope of the income-consumption curve (a). That the typical consumer buys more beer as income increases is shown by the outward shift of the demand curve for beer (b) and the upward slope of the Engel curve for beer (c).

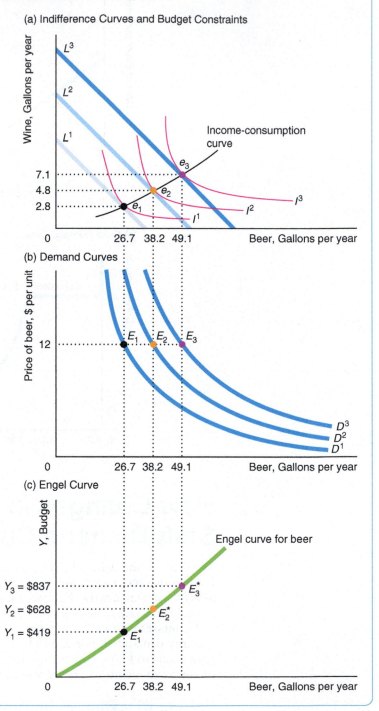

Figure 5.2 Effect of a Budget Increase on an Individual's Demand Curve

(a) Indifference Curves and Budget Constraints

(b) Demand Curves

(c) Engel Curve

between income and the quantity demanded. All three diagrams have the same horizontal axis: the quantity of beer consumed per year. In the consumer theory diagram, panel a, the vertical axis is the quantity of wine consumed per year. In the demand curve diagram, panel b, the vertical axis is the price of beer per unit. Finally, in panel c, which shows the relationship between income and quantity directly, the vertical axis is Mimi's budget, Y.

A rise in Mimi's income causes the budget constraint to shift outward in panel a, which increases Mimi's opportunities. Her budget constraint L^1 at her original income, $Y = \$419$, is tangent to her indifference curve I^1 at e_1.

As before, Mimi's demand curve for beer is D^1 in panel b. Point E_1 on D^1, which corresponds to point e_1 in panel a, shows how much beer—26.7 gallons per year—Mimi consumes when the price of beer is \$12 per unit (and the price of wine is \$35 per unit).

Now suppose that Mimi's beer and wine budget, Y, increases by roughly 50% to \$628 per year. Her new budget line, L^2 in panel a, is farther from the origin but parallel to her original budget constraint, L^1, because the prices of beer and wine are unchanged. Given this larger budget, Mimi chooses Bundle e_2. The increase in her income causes her demand curve to shift to D^2 in panel b. Holding Y at \$628, we can derive D^2 by varying the price of beer, in the same way as we derived D^1 in Figure 5.1. When the price of beer is \$12 per unit, she buys 38.2 gallons of beer per year, E_2 on D^2. Similarly, if Mimi's income increases to \$837 per year, her demand curve shifts to D^3.

The *income-consumption curve* through Bundles e_1, e_2, and e_3 in panel a shows how Mimi's consumption of beer and wine increases as her income rises. As Mimi's income goes up, her consumption of both wine and beer increases.

We can show the relationship between the quantity demanded and income directly rather than by shifting demand curves to illustrate the effect. In panel c, we plot an **Engel curve**, which shows the relationship between the quantity demanded of a single good and income, holding prices constant. Income is on the vertical axis, and the quantity of beer demanded is on the horizontal axis. On Mimi's Engel curve for beer, points E_1^*, E_2^*, and E_3^* correspond to points E_1, E_2, and E_3 in panel b and to e_1, e_2, and e_3 in panel a.

Engel curve
the relationship between the quantity demanded of a single good and income, holding prices constant

---

Solved Problem 5.2

Mahdu views Coke and Pepsi as perfect substitutes. The price of a 12-ounce can of Coke, p, is less than the price of a 12-ounce can of Pepsi, p^*. What does Mahdu's Engel curve for Coke look like? How much does his weekly cola budget have to rise for Mahdu to buy one more can of Coke per week?

Answer

1. *Use indifference curves to derive Mahdu's optimal choice.* Because Mahdu views the two brands as perfect substitutes, his indifference curves, such as I^1 and I^2 in panel a of the graphs, are straight lines with a slope of –1. When his income is Y_1, his budget line hits the Pepsi axis at Y_1/p^* and the Coke axis at Y_1/p. Mahdu maximizes his utility by consuming Y_1/p cans of the less expensive Coke and no Pepsi (a corner solution). As his income rises, say, to Y_2, his budget line shifts outward and is parallel to the original one, with the same slope of $-p/p^*$. Thus, at each income level, his budget lines are flatter than his indifference curves, so his equilibria lie along the Coke axis.

2. *Use the first figure to derive his Engel curve.* Because his entire budget, Y, goes to buying Coke, Mahdu buys $q = Y/p$ cans of Coke. This expression, which shows the relationship between his income and the quantity of Coke he buys, is Mahdu's

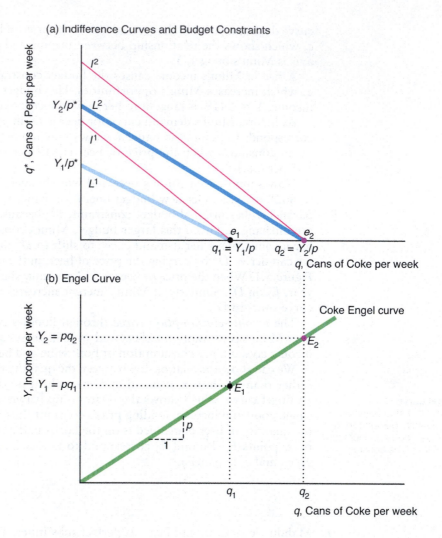

(a) Indifference Curves and Budget Constraints

(b) Engel Curve

Engel curve for Coke. The points E_1 and E_2 on the Engel curve in panel b correspond to e_1 and e_2 in panel a. We can rewrite this expression for his Engel curve as $Y = pq$. This relationship is drawn in panel b as a straight line with a slope of p. As q increases by one can ("run"), Y increases by p ("rise"). Because all of his cola budget goes to buying Coke, Mahdu's income needs to rise by only p for him to buy one more can of Coke per week.

Consumer Theory and Income Elasticities

Income elasticities tell us how much the quantity demanded changes as income increases. We can use income elasticities to summarize the shape of the Engel curve, the shape of the income-consumption curve, or the movement of the demand curves when income increases. For example, firms use income elasticities to predict the impact of income taxes on consumption. We first discuss the definition of income elasticities and then show how they are related to the income-consumption curve.

Income Elasticities   We defined the income elasticity of demand in Chapter 3 as

$$\xi = \frac{\text{percentage change in quantity demanded}}{\text{percentage change in income}} = \frac{\Delta Q/Q}{\Delta Y/Y},$$

where ξ is the Greek letter xi. Mimi's income elasticity of beer, ξ_b, is 0.88, and that of wine, ξ_w, is 1.38 (based on our estimates for the average U.S. consumer). When her income goes up by 1%, she consumes 0.88% more beer and 1.38% more wine. Thus, according to these estimates, as income falls, consumption of beer and wine by the average American falls—contrary to frequent (unsubstantiated) claims in the media that people drink more as their incomes fall during recessions.

Most goods, like beer and wine, have positive income elasticities. A good is called a **normal good** if as much or more of it is demanded as income rises. Thus, a good is a normal good if its income elasticity is greater than or equal to zero: $\xi \geq 0$.

Some goods, however, have negative income elasticities: $\xi < 0$. A good is called an **inferior good** if less of it is demanded as income rises. No value judgment is intended by the use of the term *inferior*. An inferior good need not be defective or of low quality. Some of the better-known examples of inferior goods are foods such as potatoes and cassava that very poor people typically eat in large quantities. Some economists—apparently seriously—claim that human meat is an inferior good: Only when the price of other foods is very high and people are starving will they turn to cannibalism. Bezmen and Depken (2006) estimate that pirated goods are inferior: a 1% increase in per-capita income leads to a 0.25% reduction in piracy.

Another strange example concerns treating children as a consumption good. Even though people can't buy children in a market, people can decide how many children to have. Guinnane (2011) surveyed the literature and reported that most studies find that the income elasticity for the number of children in a family is negative but close to zero. Thus, the number of children demanded is not very sensitive to income.

Income-Consumption Curves and Income Elasticities The shape of the income-consumption curve for two goods tells us the sign of the income elasticities: whether the income elasticities for those goods are positive or negative. We know that Mimi's income elasticities of beer and wine are positive because the income-consumption curve in panel a of Figure 5.2 is upward sloping. As income rises, the budget line shifts outward and hits the upward-sloping income-consumption line at higher levels of both goods. Thus, as her income rises, Mimi demands more beer and wine, so her income elasticities for beer and wine are positive. Because the income elasticity for beer is positive, the demand curve for beer shifts to the right in panel b of Figure 5.2 as income increases.

To illustrate the relationship between the slope of the income-consumption curve and the sign of income elasticities, we examine Peter's choices of food and housing. Peter purchases Bundle e in Figure 5.3 when his budget constraint is L^1. When his income increases, so that his budget constraint is L^2, he selects a bundle on L^2. Which bundle he buys depends on his tastes—his indifference curves.

The horizontal and vertical dotted lines through e divide the new budget line, L^2, into three sections. In which of these three sections the new optimal bundle is located determines Peter's income elasticities of food and clothing.

Suppose that Peter's indifference curve is tangent to L^2 at a point in the upper-left section of L^2 (to the left of the vertical dotted line that goes through e), such as Bundle a. If Peter's income-consumption curve is ICC^1, which goes from e through a, he buys more housing and less food as his income rises. (We draw the possible ICC curves as straight lines for simplicity. In general, they may curve.) Here, housing is a normal good and food an inferior good.

If instead the new optimal bundle is located in the middle section of L^2 (above the horizontal dotted line and to the right of the vertical dotted line), such as at b, his income-consumption curve ICC^2 through e and b is upward sloping. He buys more of both goods as his income rises, so both food and housing are normal goods.

normal good
a commodity of which as much or more is demanded as income rises

inferior good
a commodity of which less is demanded as income rises

Figure 5.3 Income-Consumption Curves and Income Elasticities

At the initial income, the budget constraint is L^1 and the optimal bundle is e. After income rises, the new constraint is L^2. With an upward-sloping income-consumption curve such as ICC^2, both goods are normal. With an income-consumption curve such as ICC^1 that goes through the upper-left section of L^2 (to the left of the vertical dotted line through e), housing is normal and food is inferior. With an income-consumption curve such as ICC^3 that cuts L^2 in the lower-right section (below the horizontal dotted line through e), food is normal and housing is inferior.

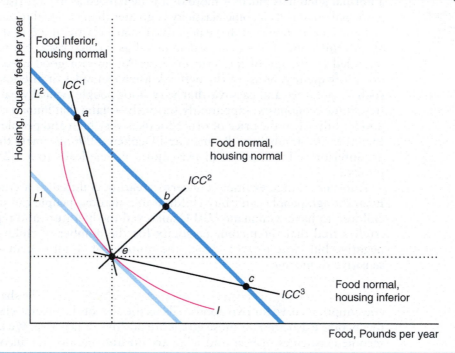

Now suppose that his new optimal bundle is in the bottom-right segment of L^2 (below the horizontal dotted line). If his new optimal bundle is c, his income-consumption curve ICC^3 slopes downward from e through c. As his income rises, Peter consumes more food and less housing, so food is a normal good and housing is an inferior good.

Some Goods Must Be Normal It is impossible for all goods to be inferior. We illustrate this point using Figure 5.3. At his original income, Peter faced budget constraint L^1 and bought the combination of food and housing e. When his income goes up, his budget constraint shifts outward to L^2. Depending on his tastes (the shape of his indifference curves), he may buy more housing and less food, such as Bundle a; more of both, such as b; or more food and less housing, such as c. Therefore, either both goods are normal or one good is normal and the other is inferior.

If both goods were inferior, Peter would buy less of both goods as his income rises—which makes no sense. Were he to buy less of both, he would be buying a bundle that lies inside his original budget constraint L^1. Even at his original, relatively low income, he could have purchased that bundle but chose not to, buying e instead. By the more-is-better assumption of Chapter 4, for any given bundle inside the constraint, a bundle on the budget constraint gives Peter more utility.

Even if an individual does not buy more of the usual goods and services, that person may put the extra money into savings. Empirical studies find that savings is a normal good.

Application

Fast-Food Engel Curve

Is a meal at a fast-food restaurant a normal or inferior good? This question is important because, as incomes have risen over the last quarter century, Americans have spent a larger share of their income on fast food, which has been blamed for increased obesity. However, a number of studies find that obesity falls with income, which suggests that a fast-food meal may be an inferior good, at least at high incomes.

Kim and Leigh (2011) estimated the demand for fast-food restaurant visits as a function of prices, income, and various socioeconomic variables such as age, family size, and whether the family received food stamps (which lowers the price of supermarket food relative to restaurant food). They find that fast-food restaurant visits increase with income up to $60,000, and then decrease as income rises more.[5]

The figure derives the Engel curve for Gail, a typical consumer, based on their estimates. Panel a shows that Gail spends her money on fast-food meals (horizontal axis, where Y is measured in thousands) and all other goods (vertical axis). As Gail's income increases from $30,000 to $60,000, her budget line shifts outward, from L^1 to L^2. As a result, she eats more restaurant meals: Her new optimal bundle, e_2, lies to the right of e_1. Thus, a fast-food meal is a normal good in this range.

As her income increases further to $90,000, her budget line shifts outward to L^3, and she reduces her consumption of hamburgers: Bundle e_3 lies to the left of e_2. Thus, at higher incomes, Gail views a fast-food meal as an inferior good.

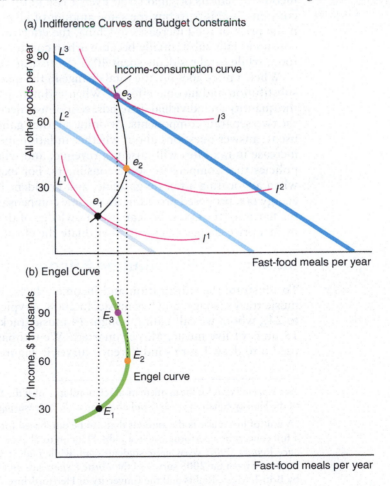

(a) Indifference Curves and Budget Constraints

(b) Engel Curve

---

[5]In contrast, they found that full-service restaurant visits increase with income up to $95,000.

Panel b shows her corresponding Engel curve for fast food. As her income rises from $30,000 to $60,000, she moves up and to the right from E_1 (which corresponds to e_1 in panel a) to E_2. Her Engel curve is upward sloping in this range, indicating that she buys more fast-food meals as her income rises. As her income rises further, her Engel curve is backward bending.

5.3 Effects of a Price Change

substitution effect
the change in the quantity of a good that a consumer demands when the good's price changes, holding other prices and the consumer's utility constant

income effect
the change in the quantity of a good a consumer demands because of a change in income, holding prices constant

Holding tastes, other prices, and income constant, an increase in a price of a good has two effects on an individual's demand. One is the **substitution effect**: the change in a good's quantity that a consumer demands when the good's price rises, holding other prices and the consumer's utility constant. If utility is held constant, as the price of the good increases, consumers *substitute* other now relatively cheaper goods for that one.

The other effect is the **income effect**: the change in a good's quantity a consumer demands because of a change in income, holding prices constant. An increase in price reduces a consumer's buying power, effectively reducing the consumer's *income* or opportunity set and causing the consumer to buy less of at least some goods. A doubling of the price of all the goods the consumer buys is equivalent to a drop in income to half its original level. Even a rise in the price of only one good reduces a consumer's ability to buy the same amount of all goods as previously. For example, if the price of food increases in China, the effective purchasing power of a Chinese consumer falls substantially because urban consumers spent 36% of their income on food, while rural residents spent 40% (*Statistical Yearbook of China*, 2012).

When a price goes up, the total change in the quantity purchased is the sum of the substitution and income effects.[6] When estimating the effects of a price change on the quantity an individual demands, economists decompose this combined effect into the two separate components. By doing so, they gain extra information that they can use to answer questions about whether inflation measures are accurate, whether an increase in tax rates will raise tax revenue, and what the effects are of government policies that compensate some consumers. For example, President Jimmy Carter, when advocating a tax on gasoline, and President Bill Clinton, when calling for an energy tax, proposed providing an income compensation for poor consumers to offset the harms of the taxes. We can use knowledge of the substitution and income effects from a price change of energy to evaluate the effect of these policies.

Income and Substitution Effects with a Normal Good

To illustrate the substitution and income effects, we examine the choice between music tracks (songs) and live music. In 2008, a typical British young person (ages 14 to 24), whom we call Laura, bought 24 music tracks, T, per quarter and consumed 18 units of live music, M, per quarter.[7] We estimated Laura's utility function and used it to draw Laura's indifference curves in Figure 5.4.[8]

---

[6]See Appendix 5A for the mathematical relationship, called the *Slutsky equation*. See also the discussion of the Slutsky equation at MyEconLab, Chapter 5, "Measuring the Substitution and Income Effects."

[7]A unit of live music is the amount that can be purchased for £1 (that is, it does not correspond to a full concert or a performance in a pub). Data on total expenditures are from *The Student Experience Report, 2007*, **www.unite-students.com**, while budget allocations between live and recorded music are from the 2008 survey of the *Music Experience and Behaviour in Young People* produced by British Music Rights and the University of Hertfordshire.

[8]Laura's estimated utility function is $U = T^{0.4}M^{0.6}$, which is a Cobb-Douglas utility function (Appendix 4A).

Figure 5.4 Substitution and Income Effects with Normal Goods

A doubling of the price of music tracks from £0.5 to £1 causes Laura's budget line to rotate from L^1 to L^2. The imaginary budget line L^* has the same slope as L^2 and is tangent to indifference curve I^1. The shift of the optimal bundle from e_1 to e_2 is the *total effect* of the price change. The total effect can be decomposed into the *substitution effect*—the movement from e_1 to e^*—and the *income effect*—the movement from e^* to e_2.

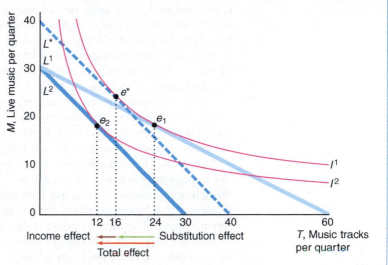

Because Laura's entertainment budget for the quarter is $Y = £30$, the price of a music track from Amazon.com or its major competitors is £0.5, and the price for a unit of live music is £1 (where we pick the unit appropriately), her original budget constraint is L^1 in Figure 5.4. She can afford to buy 60 music tracks and no live music, 30 units of live music and no music tracks, or any combination between these extremes.

Given her estimated utility function, Laura's demand functions are $T = 0.4Y/p_T$ music tracks and $M = 0.6Y/p_M$. At the original prices and with an entertainment budget of $Y = £30$ per quarter, Laura chooses Bundle e_1, $T = 0.4 \times £30/£0.5 = 24$ music tracks and $M = 0.6 \times £30/£1 = 18$ units of live music per quarter, where her indifference curve I^1 is tangent to her budget constraint L^1.

Now suppose that the price of a music track doubles to £1, causing Laura's budget constraint to rotate inward from L^1 to L^2 in Figure 5.4. The new budget constraint, L^2, is twice as steep, $-p_T/p_M = -1/1 = -1$, as is L^1, $-p_T/p_M = -0.5/1 = -0.5$, because music tracks are now twice as expensive. Laura's opportunity set is smaller, so she can choose between fewer music track–live music bundles than she could at the lower music track price. The area between the two budget constraints reflects the decrease in her opportunity set owing to the price increase of music tracks. At this higher price for music tracks, Laura's new optimal bundle is e_2 (where she buys $T = 0.4 \times 30/1 = 12$ music tracks), which occurs where her indifference curve I^2 is tangent to L^2.

The movement from e_1 to e_2 is the total change in her consumption owing to the price rise of music tracks. In particular, the *total effect* on Laura's consumption of music tracks from the price increase of tracks is that she now buys 12 (= 24 − 12) fewer tracks per quarter. In the figure, the red arrow pointing to the left and labeled "Total effect" shows this decrease. We can break the total effect into a substitution effect and an income effect.

As the price of music tracks increases, Laura's opportunity set shrinks even though her income is unchanged. If, as a thought experiment, we compensate her for this loss by giving her extra income, we can determine her substitution effect. The *substitution effect* is the change in the quantity demanded from a *compensated change in the price* of music tracks, which occurs when we increase Laura's income by enough to offset the rise in the price of music tracks so that her utility stays constant. To determine the substitution effect, we draw an imaginary budget constraint, L^*, that is parallel to L^2 and tangent to Laura's original indifference curve, I^1. This imaginary budget constraint, L^*, has the same slope, -1, as L^2, because both curves are based on the new, higher price of music tracks. For L^* to be tangent to I^1, we need to increase Laura's budget from £30 to £40 to offset the harm from the higher price of music tracks (reduced utility). If Laura's budget constraint were L^*, she would choose Bundle e^*, where she buys $T = 0.4 \times 40/1 = 16$ tracks.

Thus, if the price of tracks rises relative to that of live music and we hold Laura's utility constant by raising her income, Laura's optimal bundle shifts from e_1 to e^*, which is the substitution effect. She buys 8 (= 24 − 16) fewer tracks per quarter, as the green arrow pointing to the left labeled "Substitution effect" shows.

Laura also faces an income effect because the price increase of tracks shrinks her opportunity set, so she must buy a bundle on a lower indifference curve. As a thought experiment, we can ask how much we would have to lower Laura's income while holding prices constant for her to choose a bundle on this new, lower indifference curve. The *income effect* is the change in the quantity of a good a consumer demands because of a change in income, holding prices constant. The parallel shift of the budget constraint from L^* to L^2 captures this effective decrease in income. The movement from e^* to e_2 is the income effect, as the brown arrow pointing to the left labeled "Income effect" shows. As her budget decreases from £40 to £30, Laura consumes 4 (= 16 − 12) fewer tracks per year.

The *total effect* from the price change is the *sum of the substitution and income effects*, as the arrows show. Laura's total effect in music tracks per year from a rise in the price of music tracks is

$$\text{Total effect} = \text{substitution effect} + \text{income effect}$$
$$-12 = -8 + (-4).$$

Because indifference curves are convex to the origin, *the substitution effect is unambiguous*: Less of a good is consumed when its price rises. A consumer always substitutes a less expensive good for a more expensive one, holding utility constant. The substitution effect causes a *movement along an indifference curve*.

The income effect causes a shift to another indifference curve due to a change in the consumer's opportunity set. The direction of the income effect depends on the income elasticity. Because a music track is a normal good for Laura, her income effect is negative. Thus, both Laura's substitution effect and her income effect go in the same direction, so the total effect of the price rise must be negative.

Solved Problem 5.3

Kathy loves apple pie à la mode (a slice of pie with a scoop of vanilla ice cream on top) but she doesn't like apple pie by itself or vanilla ice cream by itself. That is, she views apple pie and vanilla ice cream as perfect complements. At the initial prices, she consumed two pieces of pie per week. After the price of pie rises, she chooses to consume only one piece of pie. In a graph similar to Figure 5.4, show the substitution, income, and total effects of the price change.

Answer

1. *Show that the price increase causes the budget line to rotate at the intersection on the ice cream axis and that her optimal bundle shifts from two units of pie and ice cream to one unit.* In the figure, her initial budget line is L^1 and her optimal bundle

is e_1, where her indifference curve I^1 touches L^1. When the price of pie increases, her new budget line is L^2 and her new optimal bundle is e_2.

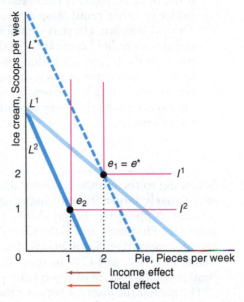

2. *Draw a line, L^*, that is parallel to L^2 and that touches her original indifference curve, I^1, and show the relationship between the new tangency point, e^*, and her original one, e^1.* The indifference curve I^1 touches L^* at e^*, which is the same point as e_1.

3. *Discuss the substitution, income, and total effects.* No substitution effect occurs because Kathy is unwilling to substitute between pie and ice cream. The brown arrow shows the income effect of the price increase is a decrease from two pieces of pie per week to one. The red arrow shows that the total effect is identical to the income effect.

Solved Problem 5.4

Next to its plant, a manufacturer of dinner plates has an outlet store that sells plates of both first quality (perfect plates) and second quality (plates with slight blemishes). The outlet store sells a relatively large share of seconds. At its regular stores elsewhere, the firm sells many more first-quality plates than second-quality plates. Why? (Assume that consumers' tastes with respect to plates are the same everywhere and the cost of shipping each plate from the factory to the firm's other stores is s.)

Answer

1. *Determine how the relative prices of plates differ between the two types of stores.* The slope of the budget line consumers face at the factory outlet store is $-p_1/p_2$, where p_1 is the price of first-quality plates and p_2 is the price of the seconds. It costs the same to ship, s, a first-quality plate as a second because they weigh the same and have to be handled in the same way. At all other stores, the firm adds the cost of shipping to the price it charges at its factory outlet store, so the price of a first-quality plate is $p_1 + s$ and the price of a second is $p_2 + s$. As a result, the slope of the budget line consumers face at the other retail stores is $-(p_1 + s)/(p_2 + s)$. The seconds are relatively less expensive at the factory outlet than at other stores. For example, if $p_1 = \$2$, $p_2 = \$1$, and $s = \$1$ per plate, the slope of the budget line is -2 at the outlet store and $-3/2$ elsewhere. Thus, the first-quality plate costs twice as much as a second at the outlet store but only 1.5 times as much elsewhere.

2. *Use the relative price difference to explain why relatively more seconds are bought at the factory outlet.* Holding a consumer's income and tastes fixed, if the price of seconds rises relative to that of firsts (as we go from the factory outlet to other retail shops), most consumers will buy relatively more firsts. The substitution effect is unambiguous: Were they compensated so that their utilities were held constant, consumers would unambiguously substitute firsts for seconds. It is possible that the income effect could go in the other direction; however, as most consumers spend relatively little of their total budget on plates, the income effect is presumably small relative to the substitution effect. Thus, we expect relatively fewer seconds to be bought at the retail stores than at the factory outlet.

Application

Shipping the Good Stuff Away

According to the economic theory discussed in Solved Problem 5.4, we expect that the relatively larger share of higher-quality goods will be shipped, the greater the per-unit shipping fee. Is this theory true, and is the effect large? To answer these questions, Hummels and Skiba (2004) examined shipments between 6,000 country pairs for more than 5,000 goods. They found that doubling per-unit shipping costs results in a 70% to 143% increase in the average price (excluding the cost of shipping) as a larger share of top-quality products are shipped.

The greater the distance between the trading countries, the higher the cost of shipping. Hummels and Skiba speculate that the relatively high quality of Japanese goods is due to that country's relatively great distance to major importers.

Income and Substitution Effects with an Inferior Good

If a good is inferior, the income effect and the substitution effect move in opposite directions. For most inferior goods, the income effect is smaller than the substitution effect. As a result, the total effect moves in the same direction as the substitution effect, but the total effect is smaller. However, if the income effect more than offsets the substitution effect, we have a **Giffen good**, for which a decrease in its price causes the quantity demanded to fall.[9]

Giffen good
a commodity for which a decrease in its price causes the quantity demanded to fall

Jensen and Miller (2008) found that rice is a Giffen good in Hunan, China. Ximing, a typical inhabitant of Hunan, views rice as a Giffen good. A fall in the rice price saves him money that he spends on other goods. Indeed, he decides to increase his spending on other goods even further by buying less rice. Thus, his demand curve for this Giffen good has an *upward* slope.

However, the Law of Demand (Chapter 2) says that demand curves slope downward. You're no doubt wondering how I'm going to worm my way out of this apparent contradiction. The answer is that I claimed that the Law of Demand was an empirical regularity, not a theoretical necessity. Although it is theoretically possible for a demand curve to slope upward, other than rice consumption in Hunan, China, economists have found few real-world examples of Giffen goods.[10]

---

[9]Robert Giffen, a nineteenth-century British economist, argued that poor people in Ireland increased their consumption of potatoes when the price rose because of a blight. However, more recent studies of the Irish potato famine dispute this observation.

[10]However, Battalio, Kagel, and Kogut (1991) conducted an experiment that showed that quinine water is a Giffen good for lab rats!

Solved Problem 5.5

Ximing spends his money on rice, a Giffen good, and all other goods. Show that when the price of rice falls, Ximing buys less rice. Decompose this total effect of a price change on his rice consumption into a substitution effect and an income effect.

Answer

1. *Determine Ximing's original optimal bundle, e_1, using the tangency between his original budget line and one of his indifference curves.* In the figure, his original budget line, L^1, is tangent to his indifference curve I^1 at e_1.

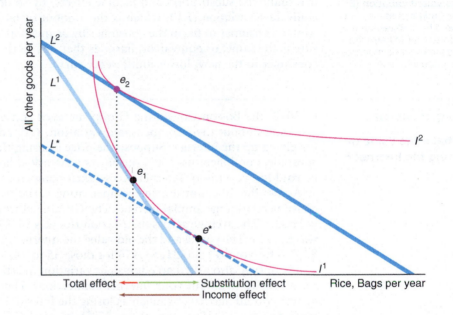

2. *Show how the optimal bundle changes from a drop in the price of rice.* As the price of rice drops, his new budget line, L^2, becomes flatter, rotating around the original budget line's intercept on the vertical axis. The tangency between L^2 and indifference curve I^2 occurs at e_2, where Ximing consumes less rice than before because rice is a Giffen good.

3. *Draw a new, hypothetical budget line L^* based on the new price but that keeps Ximing on the original indifference curve.* Ximing's opportunity set grows when the rice price falls. To keep him on his original indifference curve, his income would have to fall by enough so that his new budget line, L^2, shifts down to L^*, which is tangent to his original indifference curve I^1 at e^*.

4. *Identify the substitution and income effects.* The substitution effect is the change in q_1 from the movement from e_1 to e^*: Ximing buys more rice when the price of rice drops but he remains on his original indifference curve. The movement from e^* to e_2 determines the income effect: Ximing buys less rice as his income increases, holding prices constant. The total effect, the movement from e_1 to e_2, is the sum of the positive substitution effect and the negative income effect. Ximing buys less rice because the income effect is larger than the substitution effect.

★ Compensating Variation and Equivalent Variation

compensating variation (CV)
the amount of money one would have to give a consumer to offset completely the harm from a price increase

In Figure 5.4 and in Solved Problem 5.5's figure, we determined the substitution and income effects using an imaginary budget constraint, L^*, that was parallel to the new budget constraint, L^2, and tangent to the original indifference curve, I^1. We were calculating the **compensating variation** (CV), which is the amount of money one would have to give a consumer to offset completely the harm from a price increase—to keep the consumer on the original indifference curve. This measure of the harm from a price increase is called the compensating variation because we give money to the consumer to fully compensate the consumer.

equivalent variation (EV)
the amount of money one would have to take from a consumer to harm the consumer by as much as the price increase

Alternatively, we could draw L^* so that it was parallel to L^1 and tangent to I^2 to determine the substitution and income effects. By so doing, we would calculate the **equivalent variation** (EV), which is the amount of money one would have to take from a consumer to harm the consumer by as much as the price increase. This measure is the same, or equivalent, harm as that due to the price increase: It moves the consumer to the new, lower indifference curve.

Application

What's the Value of Using the Internet?

In 2012, the Boston Consulting Group surveyed consumers in the 20 major world economies about their compensated variation, CV, and equivalent variation, EV, for giving up the Internet. Suppose the price of using the Internet rose so much that consumers no longer used it. Consumers were asked how much they would have to be paid to live without Internet access: their compensating variation.

Across the 20 countries, the compensating variation was between 3% to 6% of consumers' average annual income. The CV ranged from $323 in Turkey to $4,453 in France. The average across the 20 countries was $1,430, while the average U.S. CV was $2,528. The young and the old value the Internet more than others. The CV was $2,926 for youths 18 to 21, $1,456 for those 35 to 44, and $3,506 for those over 55.

The survey also asked an equivalent variation question: What would you give up for a year to maintain your Internet connection? That is, giving up what good or activity would hurt you as much as losing the Internet? Most U.S. consumers would trade fast food (83%), chocolate (77%), alcohol (73%), or coffee (69%) for the Internet. Nearly half would forgo exercise (43%). Some were desperate enough to give up their car (10%) or showers (7%). Indeed, over a fifth (21%) would skip sex.[11]

Some economists question whether such answers to survey questions are plausible and reliable. For this reason, economists typically calculate conjectural variation and equivalent variation using statistical methods based on observed behavior.

5.4 Cost-of-Living Adjustments

By knowing both the substitution and income effects, we can answer questions that we couldn't if we knew only the total effect. For example, if firms have an estimate of the income effect, they can predict the impact of a negative income tax (a gift of money from the government) on the consumption of their products. Similarly, if we know the size of both effects, we can determine how accurately the government measures inflation.

---

[11]Most of these percentages are similar in the United Kingdom and France, where 21% of Brits would give up cars, 17% showers, and 25% sex; while 23% of French consumers would give up cars, 5% showers, and 16% sex.

Many long-term contracts and government programs include *cost-of-living adjustments (COLAs)*, which raise prices or incomes in proportion to an index of inflation. Not only business contracts but also rental contracts, alimony payments, salaries, pensions, and Social Security payments are frequently adjusted in this manner over time. We will use consumer theory to show that a cost-of-living measure that governments commonly use overestimates how the true cost of living changes over time. Because of this overestimate, you overpay your landlord if the rent on your apartment rises with this measure.

Inflation Indexes

The prices of most goods rise over time. We call the increase in the overall price level *inflation*.

Real Versus Nominal Prices   The actual price of a good is called the *nominal price*. The price adjusted for inflation is the *real price*.

Because the overall level of prices rises over time, nominal prices usually increase more rapidly than real prices. For example, the nominal price of a McDonald's hamburger rose from 15¢ in 1955 to 89¢ in 2013, which is nearly a sixfold increase. However, the real price of a burger fell because the prices of other goods rose more rapidly than that of a burger.

How do we adjust for inflation to calculate the real price? Governments measure the cost of a standard bundle of goods for use in comparing prices over time using the Consumer Price Index (CPI). Each month, the government reports how much it costs to buy the bundle of goods that an average consumer purchased in a *base* year (with the base year changing every few years).

By comparing the cost of buying this bundle over time, we can determine how much the overall price level has increased. In the United States, the CPI was 26.8 in 1955 and 231.5 in April 2013.[12] The cost of buying the bundle of goods increased 864% ($\approx 231.5/26.8$) from 1955 to 2013.

We can use the CPI to calculate the real price of a hamburger over time. In terms of 2013 dollars, the real price of a hamburger in 1955 was

$$\frac{\text{CPI for 2013}}{\text{CPI for 1955}} \times \text{price of a burger} = \frac{231.5}{26.8} \times 15¢ \approx 1.30.$$

That is, if you could have purchased the hamburger in 1955 with 2013 dollars—which are worth less than 1955 dollars—the hamburger would have cost $1.30. The real price in 2013 dollars (and the nominal price) of a hamburger in 2013 was only 89¢. Thus, the real price of a hamburger fell by nearly one-third. If we compared the real prices in both years using 1955 dollars, we would reach the same conclusion that the real price of hamburgers fell by about one-third.

Calculating Inflation Indexes   The government collects data on the quantities and prices of 364 individual goods and services, such as housing, dental services, watch and jewelry repairs, college tuition fees, taxi fares, women's hairpieces and wigs, hearing aids, slipcovers and decorative pillows, bananas, pork sausage, and funeral expenses. These prices rise at different rates. If the government merely reported all

---

[12]The number 231.5 is not an actual dollar amount. Rather, it is the actual dollar cost of buying the bundle divided by a constant that was chosen so that the average expenditure in the period 1982–1984 was 100.

these price increases separately, most of us would find this information overwhelming. It is much more convenient to use a single summary statistic, the CPI, which tells us how prices rose *on average*.

We can use an example with only two goods, clothing and food, to show how the CPI is calculated. In the first year, consumers buy C_1 units of clothing and F_1 units of food at prices p_C^1 and p_F^1. We use this bundle of goods, C_1 and F_1, as our base bundle for comparison. In the second year, consumers buy C_2 and F_2 units at prices p_C^2 and p_F^2.

The government knows from its survey of prices each year that the price of clothing in the second year is p_C^2/p_C^1 times as large as the price the previous year and the price of food is p_F^2/p_F^1 times as large. If the price of clothing was $1 in the first year and $2 in the second year, the price of clothing in the second year is $\frac{2}{1} = 2$ times, or 100%, larger than in the first year.

One way we can average the price increases of each good is to weight them equally. But do we really want to do that? Do we want to give as much weight to the price increase for skateboards as to the price increase for automobiles? An alternative approach is to give a larger weight to the price change of a good as we spend more of our income on that good—its budget share. The CPI takes this approach to weighting, using budget shares.[13]

The CPI for the first year is the amount of income it takes to buy the market basket actually purchased that year:

$$Y_1 = p_C^1 C_1 + p_F^1 F_1. \tag{5.1}$$

The cost of buying the first year's bundle in the second year is

$$Y_2 = p_C^2 C_1 + p_F^2 F_1. \tag{5.2}$$

To calculate the rate of inflation, we determine how much more income it would take to buy the first year's bundle in the second year, which is the ratio of Equation 5.1 to Equation 5.2:

$$\frac{Y_2}{Y_1} = \frac{p_C^2 C_1 + p_F^2 F_1}{p_C^1 C_1 + p_F^1 F_1}.$$

For example, from April 2012 to April 2013, the U.S. CPI rose from $Y_1 = 230.1$ to $Y_2 = 232.5$, so $Y_2/Y_1 \approx 1.01$. Thus, it cost 1% more in 2012 than in 2013 to buy the same bundle of goods.

The ratio Y_2/Y_1 reflects how much prices rise on average. By multiplying and dividing the first term in the numerator by p_C^1 and multiplying and dividing the second term by p_F^1, we find that this index is equivalent to

$$\frac{Y_2}{Y_1} = \frac{\left(\dfrac{p_C^2}{p_C^1}\right) p_C^1 C_1 + \left(\dfrac{p_F^2}{p_F^1}\right) p_F^1 F_1}{Y_1} = \left(\frac{p_C^2}{p_C^1}\right) \theta_C + \left(\frac{p_F^2}{p_F^1}\right) \theta_F,$$

where $\theta_C = p_C^1 C_1/Y_1$ and $\theta_F = p_F^1 F_1/Y_1$ are the budget shares of clothing and food in the first or base year. The CPI is a *weighted average* of the price increase for each good, p_C^2/p_C^1 and p_F^2/p_F^1, where the weights are each good's budget share in the base year, θ_C and θ_F.

---

[13] This discussion of the CPI is simplified in a number of ways. Sophisticated adjustments are made to the CPI that are ignored here, including repeated updating of the base year (chaining).

Effects of Inflation Adjustments

A CPI adjustment of prices in a long-term contract overcompensates for inflation. We use an example involving an employment contract to illustrate the difference between using the CPI to adjust a long-term contract and using a true cost-of-living adjustment, which holds utility constant.

CPI Adjustment   Klaas signed a long-term contract when he was hired. According to the COLA clause in his contract, his employer increases his salary each year by the same percentage as that by which the CPI increases. If the CPI this year is 5% higher than the CPI last year, Klaas' salary rises automatically by 5% over last year's.

Klaas spends all his money on clothing and food. His budget constraint in the first year is $Y_1 = p_C^1 C + p_F^1 F$, which we rewrite as

$$C = \frac{Y_1}{p_C^1} - \frac{p_F^1}{p_C^1} F.$$

The intercept of the budget constraint, L^1, on the vertical (clothing) axis in Figure 5.5 is Y_1/p_C^1, and the slope of the constraint is $-p_F^1/p_C^1$. The tangency of his indifference curve I^1 and the budget constraint L^1 determine his optimal consumption bundle in the first year, e_1, where he purchases C_1 and F_1.

In the second year, his salary rises with the CPI to Y_2, so his budget constraint, L^2, in that year is

$$C = \frac{Y_2}{p_C^2} - \frac{p_F^2}{p_C^2} F.$$

The new constraint, L^2, has a flatter slope, $-p_F^2/p_C^2$, than L^1 because the price of clothing rose more than the price of food. The new constraint goes through the original optimal bundle, e_1, because, by increasing his salary using the CPI, the firm ensures that Klaas can buy the same bundle of goods in the second year that he chose in the first year.

He *can* buy the same bundle, but *does* he? The answer is no. His optimal bundle in the second year is e_2, where indifference curve I^2 is tangent to his new budget constraint, L^2. The movement from e_1 to e_2 is the *total effect* from the changes in the real prices of clothing and food. *This adjustment to his income does not keep him on his original indifference curve, I^1.*

Indeed, Klaas is better off in the second year than in the first. The CPI adjustment *overcompensates* for the change in inflation in the sense that his utility increases.

Klaas is better off because the prices of clothing and food did not increase by the same amount. Suppose that the price of clothing and food had both increased by *exactly* the same amount. After a CPI adjustment, Klaas' budget constraint in the second year, L^2, would be exactly the same as in the first year, L^1, so he would choose exactly the same bundle, e_1, in the second year as in the first year.

Because the price of food rose by less than the price of clothing, L^2 is not the same as L^1. Food became cheaper relative to clothing, so by consuming more food and less clothing Klaas has higher utility in the second year.

Had clothing become relatively less expensive, Klaas would have raised his utility in the second year by consuming relatively more clothing. Thus, it doesn't matter which good becomes relatively less expensive over time—it's only necessary for one of them to become a relative bargain for Klaas to benefit from the CPI compensation.

Figure 5.5 The Consumer Price Index

In the first year, when Klaas has an income of Y_1, his optimal bundle is e_1, where indifference curve I^1 is tangent to his budget constraint, L^1. In the second year, the price of clothing rises more than the price of food. Because his salary increases in proportion to the CPI, his second-year budget constraint, L^2, goes through e_1, so he can buy the same bundle as in the first year. His new optimal bundle, however, is e_2, where I^2 is tangent to L^2. The CPI adjustment overcompensates him for the increase in prices: Klaas is better off in the second year because his utility is greater on I^2 than on I^1. With a smaller true cost-of-living adjustment, Klaas' budget constraint, L^*, is tangent to I^1 at e^*.

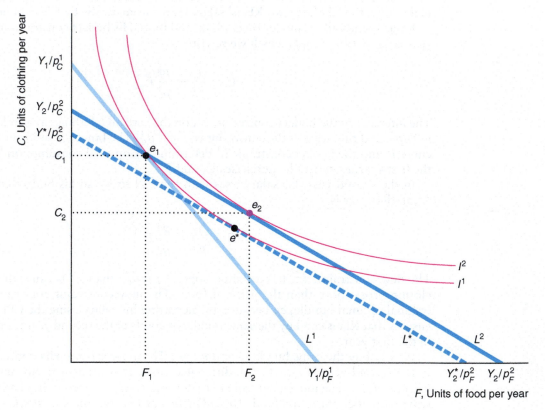

Application

Paying Employees to Relocate

International firms are increasingly relocating workers throughout their home countries and internationally. According to Mercer's worldwide survey of corporations, 53% of corporations increased long-term foreign assignments for its workers in 2011–2012, and 55% expected to increase assignments in 2013–2014.

As you might expect, some workers are not enthusiastic about being relocated. In a survey by Runzheimer International, 79% of relocation managers responded that they confronted resistance from employees who were asked to relocate to high-cost locations.

One possible approach to enticing employees to relocate is for the firm to assess the goods and services consumed by employees in the original location and then pay those employees enough to allow them to consume essentially the same items in the new location. According to a survey by Mercer, 79% of international firms reported that they provided their workers with enough income abroad to maintain their home lifestyle based on CPI-type indexes.

If employees are indifferent about where they live as long as they can buy the goods they want, then these firms are overcompensating them. We can show this result using Figure 5.5. In the figure, L^1 is a worker's budget constraint in the home country, and e_1 is the worker's optimal bundle. The firm's compensation allows the worker to buy the same bundle, e_1, on the new budget line, L^2, in the new country. The worker is better off at e_2 than at e_1. A smaller compensation that would shift the budget line from L^1 to L^* would be sufficient to induce the worker to move.

★ **True Cost-of-Living Adjustment** We now know that a CPI adjustment overcompensates for inflation. What we want is a *true cost-of-living index*: an inflation index that holds utility constant over time.

How big an increase in Klaas' salary would leave him exactly as well off in the second year as in the first? We can answer this question by applying the same technique we use to identify the substitution and income effects. We draw an imaginary budget line, L^* in Figure 5.5, that is tangent to I^1, so that Klaas' utility remains constant but has the same slope as L^2. The income, Y^*, corresponding to that imaginary budget constraint, is the amount that leaves Klaas' utility constant. Had Klaas received Y^* in the second year instead of Y_2, he would have chosen Bundle e^* instead of e_2. Because e^* is on the same indifference curve, I^1, as e_1, Klaas' utility would be the same in both years.

The COLA example in Table 5.1 illustrates how the CPI overcompensates Klaas.[14] Suppose that p_C^1 is $1, p_C^2 is $2, p_F^1 is $4, and p_F^2 is $5. In the first year, Klaas spends his income, Y_1, of $400 on $C_1 = 200$ units of clothing and $F_1 = 50$ units of food and has a utility of 2,000, which is the level of utility on I^1. If his income did not increase in the second year, he would substitute toward the relatively inexpensive food, cutting his consumption of clothing in half but reducing his consumption of food by only a fifth. His utility would fall to 1,265.

If his second-year income increases in proportion to the CPI, he can buy the same bundle, e_1, in the second year as in the first. His second-year income is $Y_2 = \$650 \ (= p_C^2 C_1 + p_F^2 F_1 = [\$2 \times 200] + [\$5 \times 50])$. Klaas is better off if his budget increases to Y_2. He substitutes toward the relatively inexpensive food, buying less clothing than in the first year but more food, e_2. His utility rises from 2,000 to approximately 2,055 (the level of utility on I^2).

Table 5.1 Cost-of-Living Adjustments

	p_C	p_F	Income, Y	Clothing	Food	Utility, U
First year	$1	$4	$Y_1 = \$400$	200	50	2,000
Second year	$2	$5				
No adjustment			$Y_1 = \$400$	100	40	≈ 1,265
CPI adjustment			$Y_2 = \$650$	162.5	65	≈ 2,055
True COLA			$Y^* \approx \$632.50$	≈ 158.1	≈ 63.2	2,000

---

[14]In Table 5.1 and Figure 5.7, we assume that Klaas has a utility function $U = 20\sqrt{CF}$.

How much would his income have to rise to leave him only as well off as he was in the first year? If his second-year income is $Y^* \approx \$632.50$, by appropriate substitution toward food, e^*, he can achieve the same level of utility, 2,000, as in the first year.

We can use the income that just compensates Klaas, Y^*, to construct a true cost-of-living index. In this example, the true cost-of-living index rose 58.1% ($\approx [632.50 - 400]/400$), while the CPI rose 62.5% ($= [650 - 400]/400$).

Size of the CPI Substitution Bias We have just demonstrated that the CPI has an *upward bias*: an individual's utility rises if we increase that person's income by the same percentage as the CPI rises. If we make the CPI adjustment, we are implicitly assuming—incorrectly—that consumers do not substitute toward relatively inexpensive goods when prices change but keep buying the same bundle of goods over time. We call this overcompensation a *substitution bias*.

The CPI calculates the increase in prices as Y_2/Y_1. We can rewrite this expression as

$$\frac{Y_2}{Y_1} = \frac{Y^*}{Y_1} \frac{Y_2}{Y^*}.$$

The first term to the right of the equal sign, Y^*/Y_1, is the increase in the true cost of living. The second term, Y_2/Y^*, reflects the substitution bias in the CPI. It is greater than one because $Y_2 > Y^*$. In the example in Table 5.1, $Y_2/Y^* = 650/632.50 \approx 1.028$, so the CPI overestimates the increase in the cost of living by about 2.8%. A number of studies estimate that the U.S. substitution bias is at least 0.5%.

No substitution bias occurs if all prices increase at the same rate so that relative prices remain constant. The faster some prices rise relative to others, the more pronounced is the upward bias caused by substitution to now less expensive goods.

5.5 Deriving Labor Supply Curves

The human race is faced with a cruel choice: work or daytime television.

Throughout this chapter, we've used consumer theory to examine consumers' *demand* behavior. Perhaps surprisingly, we can also use the consumer theory model to derive the *supply curve* of labor. We are going to do that by deriving a demand curve for time spent *not* working and then using that demand curve to determine the supply curve of hours spent working.

Labor-Leisure Choice

People choose between working to earn money to buy goods and services and consuming *leisure*: all time spent not working. In addition to sleeping, eating, and playing, leisure includes time spent cooking meals and fixing things around the house. The number of hours worked per day, H, equals 24 minus the hours of leisure or nonwork, N, in a day:

$$H = 24 - N.$$

Using consumer theory, we can determine the demand curve for leisure once we know the price of leisure. What does it cost you to watch TV or go to school or do

If I get less than 8 hours sleep, I stay awake for more than 16 hours.

anything for an hour other than work? It costs you the wage, w, you could have earned from an hour's work: The price of leisure is forgone earnings. The higher your wage, the more an hour of leisure costs you. For this reason, taking an afternoon off costs a lawyer who earns $250 an hour much more than it costs someone who earns the minimum wage.

We use an example to show how the number of hours of leisure and work depends on the wage, unearned income (such as inheritances and gifts from parents), and tastes. Jackie spends her total income, Y, on various goods. For simplicity, we assume that the price of these goods is $1 per unit, so she buys Y goods. Her utility, U, depends on how many goods and how much leisure she consumes:

$$U = U(Y, N).$$

Initially, we assume that Jackie can choose to work as many or as few hours as she wants for an hourly wage of w. Jackie's earned income equals her wage times the number of hours she works, wH. Her total income, Y, is her earned income plus her unearned income, Y^*:

$$Y = wH + Y^*.$$

Panel a of Figure 5.6 shows Jackie's choice between leisure and goods. The vertical axis shows how many goods, Y, Jackie buys. The horizontal axis shows both hours of leisure, N, which are measured from left to right, and hours of work, H, which are measured from right to left. Jackie maximizes her utility given the *two* constraints she faces. First, she faces a time constraint, which is a vertical line at 24 hours of leisure. The number of hours in a day is fixed at 24, so all the money in the world won't buy her more hours in a day. Second, Jackie faces a budget constraint. Because Jackie has no unearned income, her initial budget constraint, L^1, is $Y = w_1 H = w_1(24 - N)$. The slope of her budget constraint is $-w_1$, because each extra hour of leisure she consumes costs her w_1 goods.

Jackie picks her optimal hours of leisure, $N_1 = 16$, so that she is on the highest indifference curve, I^1, that touches her budget constraint. She works $H_1 = 24 - N_1 = 8$ hours per day and earns an income of $Y_1 = w_1 H_1 = 8w_1$.

We derive Jackie's demand curve for leisure using the same method that we used to derive Mimi's demand curve for beer. We raise the price of leisure—the wage—in panel a of Figure 5.6 to trace out Jackie's demand curve for leisure in panel b. As the wage increases from w_1 to w_2, leisure becomes more expensive, and Jackie demands less of it.

By subtracting her demand for leisure at each wage—her demand curve for leisure in panel a of Figure 5.7—from 24, we construct her labor supply curve—the hours she is willing to work as a function of the wage—in panel b.[15] Her supply curve for hours worked is the mirror image of the demand curve for leisure: For every extra hour of leisure that Jackie consumes, she works one hour less.

---

[15]Appendix 5B shows how to derive the labor supply curve using calculus.

Figure 5.6 Demand for Leisure

(a) Jackie chooses between leisure, N, and other goods, Y, subject to a time constraint (vertical line at 24 hours) and a budget constraint, L^1, which is $Y = w_1 H = w_1(24 - N)$, with a slope of $-w_1$. The tangency of her indifference curve, I^1, with her budget constraint, L^1, determines her optimal bundle, e_1, where she has $N_1 = 16$ hours of leisure and works $H_1 = 24 - N_1 = 8$ hours. If her wage rises from w_1 to w_2, Jackie shifts from optimal bundle e_1 to e_2. (b) Bundles e_1 and e_2 correspond to E_1 and E_2 on her leisure demand curve.

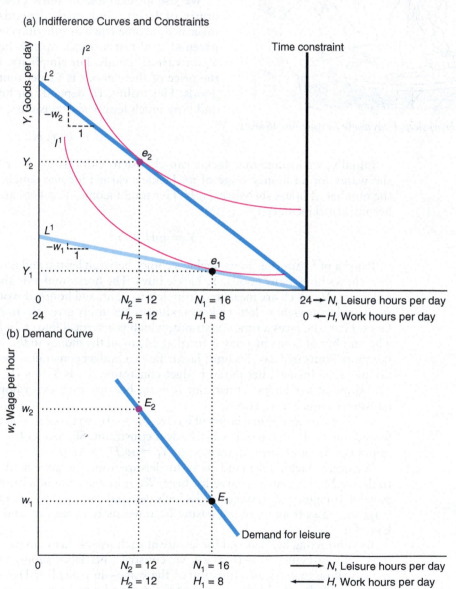

Figure 5.7 Supply Curve of Labor

(a) Jackie's demand for leisure is downward sloping. (b) At any given wage, the number of hours that Jackie works, H, and the number of hours of leisure, N, that she consumes add to 24. Thus, her supply curve for hours worked, which equals 24 hours minus the number of hours of leisure she demands, is upward sloping.

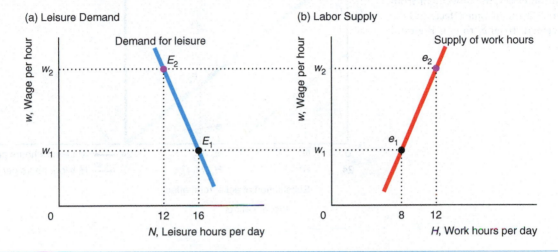

Income and Substitution Effects

An increase in the wage causes both income and substitution effects, which alter an individual's demand for leisure and supply of hours worked. The *total effect* of an increase in Jackie's wage from w_1 to w_2 is the movement from e_1 to e_2 in Figure 5.8. Jackie works $H_2 - H_1$ fewer hours and consumes $N_2 - N_1$ more hours of leisure.

By drawing an imaginary budget constraint, L^*, that is tangent to her original indifference curve with the slope of the new wage, we can divide the total effect into substitution and income effects. The *substitution effect*, the movement from e_1 to e^*, must be negative: A compensated wage increase causes Jackie to consume fewer hours of leisure, N^*, and work more hours, H^*.

As the wage rises, if Jackie works the same number of hours as before, she has a higher income. The *income effect* is the movement from e^* to e_2. Because leisure is a normal good for Jackie, as her income rises, she consumes more leisure. When leisure is a normal good, the substitution and income effects work in opposite directions, so whether leisure demand increases or not depends on which effect is larger. Jackie's income effect dominates the substitution effect, so the total effect for leisure is positive: $N_2 > N_1$. Jackie works fewer hours as the wage rises, so her labor supply curve is backward bending.

If leisure is an inferior good, both the substitution effect and the income effect work in the same direction, and hours of leisure definitely fall. As a result, if leisure is an inferior good, a wage increase unambiguously causes the hours worked to rise.

Figure 5.8 Income and Substitution Effects of a Wage Change

A wage change causes both a substitution and an income effect. The movement from e_1 to e^* is the substitution effect, the movement from e^* to e_2 is the income effect, and the movement from e_1 to e_2 is the total effect.

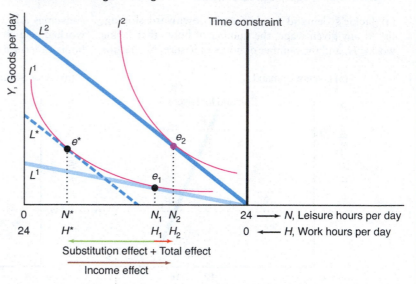

Solved Problem 5.6

Enrico receives a no-strings-attached scholarship that pays him an extra Y^* per day. How does this scholarship affect the number of hours he wants to work? Does his utility increase?

Answer

1. *Show his consumer optimum without unearned income.* When Enrico had no unearned income, his budget constraint, L^1 in the graphs, hit the hours-leisure axis at 0 hours and had a slope of $-w$.

2. *Show how the unearned income affects his budget constraint.* The extra income causes a parallel upward shift of his budget constraint by Y^*. His new budget constraint, L^2, has the same slope as before because his wage does not change. The extra income cannot buy Enrico more time, of course, so L^2 cannot extend to the right of the time constraint. As a result, at 0 hours, L^2 shifts up vertically to Y^*: His income is Y^* if he works no hours. Above Y^*, L^2 slants toward the goods axis with a slope of $-w$.

3. *Show that the relative position of the new to the original optimum depends on his tastes.* The change in the number of hours he works depends on Enrico's tastes. Panels a and b show two possible sets of indifference curves. In both diagrams, when facing budget constraint L^1, Enrico chooses to work H_1 hours. In panel a, leisure is a normal good, so as his income rises, Enrico consumes more leisure than originally: He moves from Bundle e_1 to Bundle e_2. In panel b, he views leisure as an inferior good and consumes fewer hours of leisure than originally: He moves from e_1 to e_3. (Another possibility is that the number of hours he works is unaffected by the extra unearned income.)

4. *Discuss how his utility changes.* Regardless of his tastes, Enrico has more income in the new optimum and is on a higher indifference curve after receiving the scholarship. In short, he believes that more money is better than less.

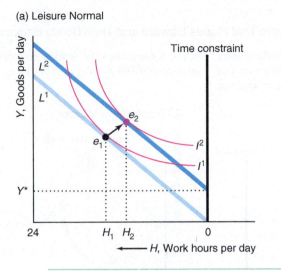

(a) Leisure Normal

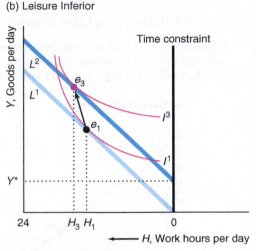

(b) Leisure Inferior

Shape of the Labor Supply Curve

Whether the labor supply curve slopes upward, bends backward, or has sections with both properties depends on the income elasticity of leisure. Suppose that a worker views leisure as an inferior good at low wages and as a normal good at high wages. As the wage increases, the worker's demand for leisure first falls and then rises. Consequently, as the wage rises, the hours supplied to the market first rise and then fall. (Alternatively, the labor supply curve may slope upward and then backward even if leisure is normal at all wages: At low wages, the substitution effect—work more hours—dominates the income effect—work fewer hours—while the opposite occurs at higher wages.)

The budget line rotates upward from L^1 to L^2 as the wage rises in panel a of Figure 5.9. Because leisure is an inferior good at low incomes, in the new optimal bundle, e_2, this worker consumes less leisure and more goods than at the original bundle, e_1.

At higher incomes, however, leisure is a normal good. At an even higher wage, the new optimum is e_3, on budget line L^3, where the quantity of leisure demanded is higher and the number of hours worked is lower. Thus, the corresponding supply curve for labor slopes upward at low wages and bends backward at higher wages in panel b.

Do labor supply curves slope upward or backward? Economic theory alone cannot answer this question: Both forward-sloping and backward-bending supply curves are *theoretically* possible. Empirical research is necessary to resolve this question.

Most studies (see the survey in Keane, 2011) find that the labor supply curves for British and American men are relatively vertical because the income and substitution effects are offsetting or both small. Similar results are found in other countries such as Japan (Kuroda and Yamamoto, 2008) and the Netherlands (Evers et al., 2008). Keane's average across all studies of males' pure substitution wage elasticity is about 0.31 (although most of the estimates are below 0.15). Most studies in Keane's survey find that females' labor supply curves are less elastic at the equilibrium, with most long-run wage elasticity estimates ranging from 1.25 to 5.6.

Figure 5.9 Deriving a Labor Supply Curve That Slopes Upward and Then Bends Backward

At low incomes, an increase in the wage causes the worker to work more: the movement from e_1 to e_2 in panel a or from E_1 to E_2 in panel b. At higher incomes, an increase in the wage causes the worker to work fewer hours: the movement from e_2 to e_3 or from E_2 to E_3.

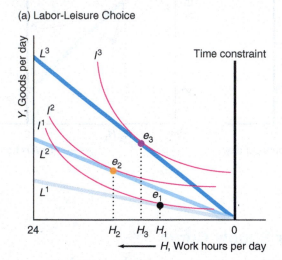

(a) Labor-Leisure Choice

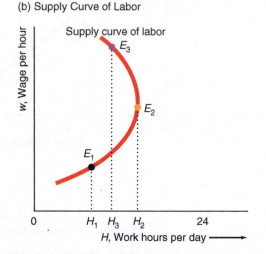

(b) Supply Curve of Labor

Application

Working After Winning the Lottery

Would you stop working if you won a lottery or inherited a large sum? Economists want to know how unearned income affects the amount of labor people are willing to supply because this question plays a crucial role in many government debates on taxes and welfare. For example, some legislators oppose negative income tax and welfare programs because they claim that giving money to poor people will stop them from working. Is that assertion true?

We could clearly answer this question if we could observe the behavior of a large group of people, only some of whom were randomly selected to receive varying but large amounts of unearned income each year for decades. Luckily for us, governments conduct such experiments by running lotteries.

Imbens et al. (2001) compared the winners of major prizes to others who played the Massachusetts Megabucks lottery. Major prizes ranged from $22,000 to $9.7 million, with an average of $1.1 million, and were paid in yearly installments over two decades.

The average winner received $55,200 in prize money per year and chose to work slightly fewer hours so that his or her labor earnings fell by $1,877 per year. That is, winners increased their consumption and savings but did not substantially decrease how much they worked.

For every dollar of unearned income, winners reduced their work effort and hence their labor earnings by 11¢ an hour on average. Men and women, big and very big prize winners, and people of all education levels behaved the same way. However, the behavior of winners differed by age and by income groups. People ages 55 to 65 reduced their labor efforts by about a third more than younger people did, presumably because they decided to retire early. (Hedenus, 2012, found similar results in Sweden for smaller prizes.) Most striking, people with no earnings in the year before winning the lottery tended to increase their labor earnings after winning.

Kuhn et al. (2011) examined the Dutch Postcode Lottery, in which prizes are awarded weekly to lottery participants living in randomly selected postal codes. On average, the prizes are equal to about eight months of income. Household heads who received prizes did not change how many hours they worked.[16]

Income Tax Rates and Labor Supply

Why do we care about the shape of labor supply curves? One reason is that we can tell from the shape of the labor supply curve whether an increase in the income tax rate—a percent of earnings—will cause a substantial reduction in the hours of work.[17] Taxes on earnings are an unattractive way of collecting money for the government if supply curves are upward sloping because the taxes cause people to work fewer hours, reducing the amount of goods society produces and raising less tax revenue than if the supply curve were vertical or backward bending. On the other hand, if supply curves are backward bending, a small increase in the tax rate increases tax revenue *and* boosts total production (but reduces leisure).

Although unwilling to emulate Lady Godiva's tax-fighting technique—allegedly, her husband, Leofric, the Earl of Mercia, agreed to eliminate taxes if she rode naked through the Coventry marketplace—various U.S. presidents have advocated tax cuts. Presidents John F. Kennedy, Ronald Reagan, and George W. Bush argued that cutting the marginal tax rate (the percentage of the last dollar earned that the government takes in taxes) would stimulate people to work longer and produce more, both desirable effects. President Reagan claimed that tax receipts would increase due to the additional work.

Because tax rates have changed substantially over time, we have a natural experiment to test this hypothesis. The Kennedy tax cuts lowered the top federal personal marginal tax rate from 91% to 70%. Due to the Reagan tax cuts, the maximum rate fell to 50% in 1982–1986, 38.5% in 1987, and 28% in 1988–1990. The rate rose to 31% in 1991–1992 and to 39.6% in 1993–2000. The Bush tax cuts reduced this rate to 38.6% for 2001–2003, 37.6% for 2004–2005, and 35% in 2006. It stayed at that rate until rising to 39.6% in 2013.

Many other countries' central governments have also lowered their top marginal tax rates in recent years. The top U.K. rate fell sharply during the Thatcher administration from 83% to 60% in 1979 and to 40% in 1988. It rose to 50% in 2010, and fell to 45% in April 2013. Japan's top rate fell from 75% in 1983 to 60% in 1987, to 50% in 1988, and to 37% in 1999, but rose to 40% in 2007. In 1988, Canada raised the marginal tax rates for the two lowest income groups and lowered them for those falling into the top nine brackets.

Of more concern to individuals than the federal marginal tax rate is the tax rate that includes taxes collected by all levels of government. According to the Organization for Economic Cooperation and Development (OECD), the top all-inclusive marginal tax rate in 2011 was 15.0% in the Czech Republic, 30.0% in Mexico, 33.0% in New Zealand, 41.92% in the United States (on average across the states), 46.4%

---

[16]These results of small reductions in work by people who actually won a lottery are in striking contrast to what people say they would do if they won a lottery. According to Highhouse et al. (2010), only 68% of surveyed U.S. working males said they would continue to work if they won a large lottery.

[17]Although taxes are ancient, the income tax is a relatively recent invention. William Pitt the Younger introduced the British income tax (10% on annual incomes above £60) in 1798 to finance the war with Napoleon. The U.S. Congress followed suit in 1861, using the income taxes (3% on annual incomes over $800) to pay for the Civil War.

in Canada, 46.5% in Australia, 50.0% in Japan and the United Kingdom, 52.2% in Denmark, 53.7% in Belgium, and 56.6% in Sweden.

If the tax does not affect the pre-tax wage, the effect of imposing a marginal tax rate of $\alpha = 28\% = 0.28$ is to reduce the effective wage from w to $(1 - \alpha)w = 0.72w$.[18] The tax reduces the after-tax wage by 28%, so a worker's budget constraint rotates downward, similar to rotating the budget constraint downward from L^3 to L^2 or from L^2 to L^1, in Figure 5.9.

As that figure indicates, if the budget constraint rotates downward, the hours of work may increase or decrease, depending on whether leisure is a normal or an inferior good. The worker in panel b has a labor supply curve that at first slopes upward and then bends backward. If the worker's wage is very high, the worker is in the backward-bending section of the labor supply curve.

If so, the relationship between the marginal tax rate, α, and tax revenue, αwH, is bell-shaped, as in Figure 5.10. This figure is the estimated U.S. tax revenue curve (Trabandt and Uhlig, 2011). At the marginal rate for the typical person, $\alpha = 28\%$, the government collects 100% of the amount of tax revenue that it is currently collecting. At a zero tax rate, a small increase in the tax rate *must* increase the tax revenue because no revenue was collected when the tax rate was zero. However, if the tax rate rises a little more, the tax revenue collected must rise even higher, for two reasons: First, the government collects a larger percentage of every dollar earned because the

Figure 5.10 The Relationship of U.S. Tax Revenue to the Marginal Tax Rate

This curve shows how U.S. income tax revenue varies with the marginal income tax rate, α, according to Trabandt and Uhlig (2009). The typical person pays $\alpha = 28\%$, which corresponds to 100% of the current tax revenue that the government collects. The tax revenue would be maximized at 130% of its current level if the marginal rate were set at $\alpha^* = 63\%$. For rates below α^*, an increase in the marginal rate raises larger tax revenue. However, at rates above α^*, an increase in the marginal rate decreases tax revenue.

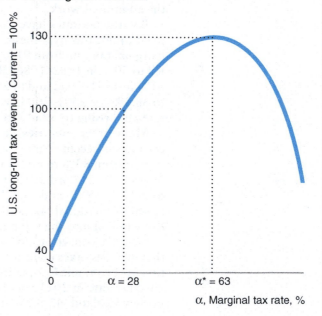

[18]Under a progressive income tax system, the marginal tax rate increases with income, and the marginal tax rate is greater than the average tax rate. Suppose that the marginal tax rate is 20% on the first $10,000 earned and 30% on the second $10,000. Someone who earns $20,000 pays a tax of $2,000 (= 0.2 × $10,000) on the first $10,000 of earnings and $3,000 on the next $10,000. That taxpayer's average tax rate is 25% (= [$2,000 + $3,000]/$20,000). In 2012, the U.S. marginal tax rate on a single person with a taxable income of $50,000 was 25%, while the average rate was 17.06%. For simplicity, in the following analysis, we assume that the marginal tax rate is a constant, α, so the average tax rate is also α.

tax rate is higher. Second, employees work more hours as the tax rate rises because workers are in the backward-bending sections of their labor supply curves.

As the marginal rate increases, tax revenue rises until the marginal rate reaches $\alpha^* = 63\%$, where the U.S. tax revenue would be 130% of its current level.[19] If the marginal tax rate increases more, workers are in the upward-sloping sections of their labor supply curves, so an increase in the tax rate reduces the number of hours worked. When the tax rate rises high enough, the reduction in hours worked more than offsets the gain from the higher rate, so the tax revenue falls.

It makes little sense for a government to operate at very high marginal tax rates in the downward-sloping portion of this bell-shaped curve. The government could get more output *and* more tax revenue by cutting the marginal tax rate.

Challenge Solution	We now return to the questions raised at the beginning of the chapter: For a given government expenditure, does a childcare per-hour subsidy or a lump-sum subsidy provide greater benefit to recipients? Which option increases the demand for childcare services by more? Which one inflicts less cost on other consumers of childcare?
Per-Hour Versus Lump-Sum Childcare Subsidies	To determine which program benefits recipients more, we employ a model of consumer choice. The figure shows a poor family that chooses between *hours of childcare per day* (Q) and *all other goods per day*. Given that the price of all other goods is $1 per unit, the expenditure on all other goods is the income, Y, not spent on childcare. The family's initial budget constraint is L^o. The family chooses Bundle e_1 on indifference curve I^1, where the family consumes Q_1 hours of childcare services.

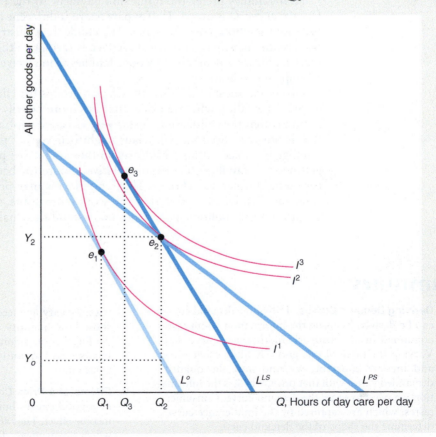

---

[19]On average for 14 European Union countries, α is also less than α^*, but raising the rate to α^* would raise European tax revenue by only 8% (Trabandt and Uhlig, 2011).

If the government gives a childcare price subsidy, the new budget line, L^{PS}, rotates out along the childcare axis. Now the family consumes Bundle e_2 on (higher) indifference curve I^2. The family consumes more hours of childcare, Q_2, because childcare is now less expensive and it is a normal good.

One way to measure the value of the subsidy the family receives is to calculate how many *other goods* the family could buy before and after the subsidy. If the family consumes Q_2 hours of childcare, the family could have consumed Y_o other goods with the original budget constraint and Y_2 with the price-subsidy budget constraint. Given that Y_2 is the family's remaining income after paying for childcare, the family buys Y_2 units of all other goods. Thus, the value to the family of the childcare price subsidy is $Y_2 - Y_o$.

If, instead of receiving a childcare price subsidy, the family were to receive a lump-sum payment of $Y_2 - Y_o$, taxpayers' costs for the two programs would be the same. The family's budget constraint after receiving a lump-sum payment, L^{LS}, has the same slope as the original one, L^o, because the relative prices of childcare and all other goods are the same as originally (see Section 4.3). This budget constraint must go through e_2 because the family has just enough money to buy that bundle. However, given this budget constraint, the family would be better off if it buys Bundle e_3 on indifference curve I^3 (the reasoning is the same as that in the Consumer Price Index analysis in Figure 5.5). The family consumes less childcare with the lump-sum subsidy: Q_3 rather than Q_2.

Poor families prefer the lump-sum payment to the price subsidy because indifference curve I^3 is above I^2. Taxpayers are indifferent between the two programs because they both cost the same. The childcare industry prefers the price subsidy because the demand curve for its service is farther to the right: At any given price, more childcare is demanded by poor families who receive a price subsidy rather than a lump-sum subsidy.

Given that most of the directly affected groups benefit from lump-sum payments to price subsidies, why are price subsidies more heavily used? One possible explanation is that the childcare industry very effectively lobbied for price subsidies, but that is not true. Second, politicians might believe that poor families will not make intelligent choices about childcare, so they might see price subsidies as a way of getting such families to consume relatively more (or better-quality) childcare than they would otherwise choose. Third, politicians may prefer that poor people consume more childcare so that they can work more hours, thereby increasing society's wealth. Fourth, politicians may not understand this analysis.

Summary

1. **Deriving Demand Curves.** Individual demand curves can be derived by using the information about tastes contained in a consumer's indifference curve map. Varying the price of one good, holding other prices and income constant, we find how the quantity demanded varies with that price, which is the information we need to draw the demand curve. Consumers' tastes, which are captured by the indifference curves, determine the shape of the demand curve.

2. **How Changes in Income Shift Demand Curves.** The entire demand curve shifts as a consumer's income

rises. By varying income, holding prices constant, we show how quantity demanded shifts with income. An Engel curve summarizes the relationship between income and quantity demanded, holding prices constant.

3. **Effects of a Price Change.** An increase in the price of a good causes both a substitution effect and an income effect. The *substitution effect* is the amount by which a consumer's demand for the good changes as a result of a price increase when we compensate the consumer for the price increase by raising the individual's

income by enough that his or her utility does not change. The substitution effect is unambiguous: A compensated rise in a good's price *always* causes consumers to buy less of that good. The *income effect* shows how a consumer's demand for a good changes as the consumer's income falls. The price rise lowers the consumer's opportunities, because the consumer can buy less than before with the same income. The income effect can be positive or negative. If a good is normal (income elasticity is positive), the income effect is negative.

4. **Cost-of-Living Adjustments.** The government's major index of inflation, the Consumer Price Index, overestimates inflation by ignoring the substitution effect. Though on average small, the substitution bias may be substantial for particular individuals or firms.

5. **Deriving Labor Supply Curves.** Using consumer theory, we can derive the daily demand curve for leisure, which is time spent on activities other than work. By subtracting the demand curve for leisure from 24 hours, we obtain the labor supply curve, which shows how the number of hours worked varies with the wage. Depending on whether leisure is an inferior good or a normal good, the supply curve of labor may be upward sloping or backward bending. The shape of the supply curve for labor determines the effect of a tax cut. Empirical evidence based on this theory shows why tax cuts did not always increase the tax revenue of individuals as predicted by various administrations.

Questions

All questions are available on MyEconLab; * = *answer appears at the back of this book;* **A** = *algebra problem;* **C** = *calculus problem.*

1. Deriving Demand Curves

1.1 Draw diagrams similar to Figure 5.1 showing that the price-consumption curve can be horizontal or downward sloping.

*1.2 In Figure 5.1, how does Mimi's utility at E_1 on D^1 compare to that at E_2?

As we move down from the highest point on an individual's downward-sloping demand curve, must the individual's utility rise?

1.3 Derive and plot Olivia's demand curve for pie if she eats pie only à la mode and does not eat either pie or ice cream alone (pie and ice cream are perfect complements). (*Hint*: See Solved Problem 5.1.)

1.4 Manufactured diamonds have become as big and virtually indistinguishable from the best natural diamonds. In 2013, manufactured diamonds retailed for between 20% and 30% less than mined diamonds. Suppose consumers change from believing that manufactured diamonds, M, were imperfect substitutes for natural diamonds, N, to perfect substitutes, so that their utility function becomes $U(M, N) = M + N$. What effect will that have on the demand for manufactured diamonds? Derive the new demand curve for manufactured diamonds and draw it. **A**

1.5 How would your answer to Question 1.4 change if $U = \ln(M + N)$, so that consumers have diminishing marginal utility of diamonds? **A**

1.6 Illustrate the effect of cheaper phones in the Philippines that is described in the Application "Smoking Versus Eating and Phoning" using a figure similar to Figure 5.1.

1.7 Derive the demand curve for pizza, Z, if Lisa's utility function is $U = Z^{0.25}B^{0.75}$, where B is burritos. **C**

2. How Changes in Income Shift Demand Curves

2.1 Derive and plot Olivia's Engel curve for pie if she eats pie only à la mode and does not eat either pie or ice cream alone (pie and ice cream are perfect complements). (*Hint*: See Solved Problem 5.2.)

2.2 Have your folks given you cash or promised to leave you money after they're gone? If so, your parents may think of such gifts as a good. They must decide whether to spend their money on fun, food, drink, cars, or on transfers to you. Hmmm. Altonji and Villanueva (2007) estimated that, for every extra dollar of expected lifetime resources, parents give their adult offspring between 2¢ and 3¢ in bequests and about 3¢ in transfers. Those gifts are about one-fifth of what they give their children under 18 and spend on college. Illustrate how an increase in your parents' income affects their allocations between bequests to you and all other goods ("fun") in two related graphs, where you show an income-consumption curve in one and an Engel curve for bequests in the other. (*Hint*: See Solved Problem 5.2.)

2.3 Hugo views donuts and coffee as perfect complements: He always eats one donut with a cup of coffee and will not eat a donut without coffee or drink coffee without a donut. Derive and plot Hugo's Engel curve for donuts. How much does his weekly budget have to rise for Hugo to buy one more donut per week? (*Hint*: See Solved Problem 5.2.) **A**

*2.4 Don spends his money on food and on operas. Food is an inferior good for Don. Does he view an opera performance as an inferior or a normal good? Why? In a diagram, show a possible income-consumption curve for Don.

*2.5 Using calculus, show that not all goods can be inferior. (*Hint*: Start with the identity that $y = p_1q_1 + p_2q_2 + \ldots + p_nq_n$.) **C**

2.6 Could an individual's Engel curve be the mirror image of the one in the Application "Fast-Food Engel Curve" (quantity is first decreasing and then increasing with income)? Show in a figure. Can you think of a good where such a figure would apply?

3. Effects of a Price Change

3.1 Michelle spends all her money on food and clothing. When the price of clothing decreases, she buys more clothing.

    a. Does the substitution effect cause her to buy more or less clothing? Explain. (If the direction of the effect is ambiguous, say so.)

    b. Does the income effect cause her to buy more or less clothing? Explain. (If the direction of the effect is ambiguous, say so.)

3.2 Steve's utility function is $U = BC$, where $B =$ veggie burgers per week and $C =$ packs of cigarettes per week. Here, $MU_B = C$ and $MU_C = B$. What is his marginal rate of substitution if veggie burgers are on the vertical axis and cigarettes are on the horizontal axis? Steve's income is $120, the price of a veggie burger is $2, and that of a pack of cigarettes is $1. How many burgers and how many packs of cigarettes does Steve consume to maximize his utility? When a new tax raises the price of a burger to $3, what is his new optimal bundle? Illustrate your answers in a graph. In a related graph, show his demand curve for burgers with after-tax price on the vertical axis and show the points on the demand curve corresponding to the before- and after-tax equilibria. (*Hint*: See Appendix 4B.) **C**

3.3 Cori eats eggs and toast for breakfast and insists on having three pieces of toast for every two eggs she eats. What is her utility function? If the price of eggs increases but we compensate Cori to make

her just as "happy" as she was before the price change, what happens to her consumption of eggs? Draw a graph and explain your diagram. Does the change in her consumption reflect a substitution or an income effect? **A**

3.4 Under what conditions does the income effect reinforce the substitution effect? Under what conditions does it have an offsetting effect? If the income effect more than offsets the substitution effect for a good, what do we call that good?

3.5 Using a figure similar to Figure 5.4 or that in Solved Problem 5.3, discuss the substitution, income, and total effects of a price change for Coke for Mahdu who views Coke and Pepsi as perfect substitutes. (*Hint*: See Solved Problem 5.1.)

3.6 Relatively more high-quality navel oranges are sold in California than in New York. Why? (*Hint*: See Solved Problem 5.4.)

*3.7 Draw a figure to illustrate the answer given in Solved Problem 5.4. Use math and a figure to show how adding an ad valorem tax changes the analysis. (See the Application "Shipping the Good Stuff Away.")

3.8 Remy views ice cream and fudge sauce as perfect complements. Is it possible that either of these goods or both of them are Giffen goods? (*Hint*: See Solved Problem 5.5.)

3.9 Redraw Figure 5.4 using an equivalent variation rather than a compensating variation approach.

4. Cost-of-Living Adjustments

4.1 The *Economist* magazine publishes the Big Mac Index for various countries, based on the price of a Big Mac at McDonald's over time. Under what circumstances would people find this index to be as useful as or more useful than the Consumer Price Index in measuring how their true cost of living changes over time?

4.2 During his first year at school, Ximing buys eight new college textbooks at a cost of $50 each. Used books cost $30 each. When the bookstore announces a 20% price increase in new texts and a 10% increase in used texts for the next year, Ximing's father offers him $80 extra. Is Ximing better off, the same, or worse off after the price change? Why?

4.3 Ann's only income is her annual college scholarship, which she spends exclusively on gallons of ice cream and books. Last year when ice cream cost $10 and used books cost $20, Ann spent her

$250 scholarship on five gallons of ice cream and ten books. This year, the price of ice cream rose to $15 and the price of books increased to $25. So that Ann can afford the same bundle of ice cream and books that she bought last year, her college raised her scholarship to $325. Ann has the usual-shaped indifference curves. Will Ann change the amount of ice cream and books that she buys this year? If so, explain how and why. Will Ann be better off, as well off, or worse off this year than last year? Why?

*4.4 Alix views coffee and cream as perfect complements. In the first period, Alix picks an optimal bundle of coffee and cream, e_1. In the second period, inflation occurs, the prices of coffee and cream change by different amounts, and Alix receives a cost-of-living adjustment (COLA) based on the Consumer Price Index (CPI) for these two goods. After the price changes and she receives the COLA, her new optimal bundle is e_2. Show the two equilibria in a figure. Is she better off, worse off, or equally well off at e_2 compared to e_1? Explain why. By how much will a CPI for these two goods differ from the true cost-of-living index?

4.5 Change Figure 5.5 so that L^2 is steeper than L^1 (but still goes through e_1); that is, food increases by more than clothing in the second year. Show the conclusion that Klaas is still better off after receiving a CPI adjustment. Explain the logic behind the following statement: "The analysis holds as long as the relative prices differ in the two years. Whether both prices, one price, or neither price is higher than in the second year is irrelevant to the analysis."

5. Deriving Labor Supply Curves

5.1 Using calculus, show the effect of a change in the wage on the amount of leisure an individual wants to consume. (*Hint:* See Appendix 5B.) **C**

5.2 If an individual's labor supply curve slopes upward at low wages and bends backward at high wages, is leisure a Giffen good? If so, at high or low wage rates? (*Hint:* See Solved Problems 5.5 and 5.6.)

5.3 Bessie, who can currently work as many hours as she wants at a wage of w, chooses to work ten hours a day. Her boss decides to limit the number of hours that she can work to eight hours per day. Show how her budget constraint and choice of hours change. Is she unambiguously worse off as a result of this change? Why? (*Hint:* See Solved Problem 5.6.)

5.4 Suppose that Roy could choose how many hours to work at a wage of w and chose to work seven hours a day. The employer now offers him time-and-a-half wages ($1.5w$) for every hour he works beyond a minimum of eight hours per day. Show how his budget constraint changes. Will he choose to work more than seven hours a day? (*Hint:* See Solved Problem 5.6.)

5.5 Jerome moonlights: He holds down two jobs. The higher-paying job pays w, but he can work at most eight hours. The other job pays w^*, but he can work as many hours as he wants. Show how Jerome determines how many hours to work. (*Hint:* See Solved Problem 5.6.)

5.6 Suppose that the job in Question 5.5 that had no restriction on hours was the higher-paying job. How do Jerome's budget constraint and behavior change? (*Hint:* See Solved Problem 5.6.)

5.7 Suppose that Bill's wage varies with the hours he works: $w(H) = \alpha H$, $\alpha > 0$. Show how the number of hours he chooses to work depends on his tastes.

5.8 Joe won $365,000 a year for life in the state lottery. Use a labor-leisure choice analysis to answer the following questions:

a. Show how Joe's lottery winnings affect the position of his budget line.

b. After winning the lottery, Joe continues to work the same number of hours each day (see the Application "Working After Winning the Lottery"). What is the income effect from Joe's lottery gains?

c. Suppose Joe's employer the same week increases Joe's hourly wage rate. Use the income effect you derived in part b as well as the substitution effect to analyze whether Joe chooses to work more hours per week. (*Hint:* See Solved Problem 5.6.)

5.9 Taxes during the fourteenth century were very progressive. The 1377 poll tax on the Duke of Lancaster was 520 times the tax on a peasant. A poll tax is a lump-sum (fixed amount) tax per person, which does not vary with the number of hours a person works or how much that person earns. Use a graph to show the effect of a poll tax on the labor-leisure decision. Does knowing that the tax was progressive tell us whether a nobleman or a peasant—assuming they have identical tastes—worked more hours?

5.10 Today most developed countries have progressive income taxes where rich people pay a higher marginal tax rate than poor people. Under such a taxation program, is the marginal tax higher than, equal to, or lower than the average tax? **A**

5.11 Several political leaders, including some recent candidates for the U.S. presidency, have proposed a flat income tax, where the marginal tax rate is constant.

   a. Show that if each person is allowed a "personal deduction" where the first $10,000 is untaxed, the flat tax can be a progressive tax.

   b. Proponents of the flat tax claim that it will stimulate production (relative to the current progressive income tax where marginal rates increase with income). Discuss the merits of their claim.

5.12 Under a welfare plan, poor people are given a lump-sum payment of $L. If they accept this welfare payment, they must pay a high tax, $t = \frac{1}{2}$, on anything they earn. If they do not accept the welfare payment, they do not have to pay a tax on their earnings. Show that whether an individual accepts welfare depends on the individual's tastes.

5.13 Inheritance taxes are older than income taxes. Caesar Augustus instituted a 5% tax on all inheritances (except gifts to children and spouses) to provide retirement funds for the military. During the George W. Bush administration, congressional Republicans and Democrats vociferously debated the wisdom of cutting income taxes and inheritance taxes (which the Republicans call the "death tax") to stimulate the economy by inducing people to work harder. Presumably the government cares about a tax's effect on work effort and tax revenues.

   a. Suppose George views leisure as a normal good. He works at a job that pays w an hour. Use a labor-leisure analysis to compare the effects on the hours he works from a marginal tax rate on his wage, t, or a lump-sum tax (a tax collected regardless of the number of hours he works), T. If the per-hour tax is used, he works 10 hours and earns $10w(1 - t)$. The government sets $T = 10wt$, so that it earns the same from either tax.

   b. Now suppose that the government wants to raise a given amount of revenue through taxation with either an inheritance tax or an income (wage) tax. Which is likely to reduce George's hours of work more, and why?

*5.14 Prescott (2004) argues that U.S. employees work 50% more than do German, French, and Italian employees because they face lower marginal tax rates. Assuming that workers in all four countries have the same tastes toward leisure and goods, must it necessarily be true that U.S. employees will work longer hours? Use graphs to illustrate your answer, and explain why. Does Prescott's evidence indicate anything about the relative sizes of the substitution and income effects? Why or why not?

6. Challenge

6.1 The U.S. Supreme Court ruled in 2002 that school-voucher programs do not violate the Establishment Clause of the First Amendment, provided that parents, not the state, direct where the money goes. Education vouchers are increasingly used in various parts of the United States. Suppose that the government offers poor people a $5,000 education voucher, which can be used only to pay for education. Doreen would be better off with $5,000 in cash than with the education voucher. In a graph, determine the cash value, V, Doreen places on the education voucher (that is, the amount of cash that would leave her as well off as with the education voucher). Show how much education and "all other goods" she would consume with the education voucher or with a cash payment of V.

*6.2 How could the government set a smaller lump-sum subsidy than in the figure in the Challenge Solution that would make poor parents as well off as the price subsidy yet cost less? Given the tastes shown in the figure, what would be the effect on the number of hours of childcare service that these parents buy?

*6.3 How do parents who do not receive childcare subsidies feel about the two programs discussed and illustrated in the Challenge Solution? (*Hint*: Use a supply-and-demand analysis from Chapters 2 and 3.)

Firms and Production

6

Progress was all right. Only it went on too long. —James Thurber

Why does a measure of labor productivity—the output produced per worker—rise for many firms during recessions? During the boom years period of 2005 through November 2007, the annual average output per worker was lower in U.S. manufacturing than during the Great Recession of 2007–2009 as well during the relatively low-demand years since then through 2013.

Challenge

Labor Productivity During Recessions

Firms produce less output during recessions as demand for their products falls. Consequently, firms typically lay off workers during recessions. Thus, whether output per worker rises or falls depends on whether output or employment falls by more. The labor productivity pattern over the business cycle differs across industries. If we know about a firm's production process, can we predict whether output produced per worker will rise or fall with each additional layoff?

This chapter looks at the types of decisions that the owners of firms have to make. First, a decision must be made as to how a firm is owned and managed. American Licorice Co., for example, is a corporation—it is not owned by an individual or partners—and is run by professional managers. Second, the firm must decide how to produce. American Licorice Co. now uses relatively more machines and robots and fewer workers than in the past. Third, if a firm wants to expand output, it must decide how to do that in both the short run and the long run. In the short run, American Licorice Co. can expand output by extending the workweek to six or seven days and using extra materials. To expand output more, American Licorice Co. would have to install more equipment (such as extra robotic arms), hire more workers, and eventually build a new plant, all of which take time. Fourth, given its ability to change its output level, a firm must determine how large to grow. American Licorice Co. determines its current investments on the basis of its beliefs about demand and costs in the future.

In this chapter, we examine the nature of a firm and how a firm chooses its inputs so as to produce efficiently. In Chapter 7, we examine how the firm chooses the least costly among all possible efficient production processes. In Chapter 8, we combine this information about costs with information about revenues to determine how a firm picks the output level that maximizes profit.

The main lesson of this chapter and the following chapters is that firms are not black boxes that mysteriously transform inputs (such as labor, capital, and material) into outputs. Economic theory explains how firms make decisions about production processes, types of inputs to use, and the volume of output to produce.

In this chapter, we examine six main topics

1. **The Ownership and Management of Firms.** How businesses are organized affects who makes decisions and the firm's objective, such as whether it tries to maximize profit.

2. **Production Function.** A production function summarizes how a firm converts inputs into outputs using one of the available technologies.

3. **Short-Run Production.** In the short run, only some inputs can be varied, so the firm changes its output by adjusting its variable inputs.

4. **Long-Run Production.** The firm has more flexibility in how it produces and how it changes its output level in the long run when all factors can be varied.

5. **Returns to Scale.** How the ratio of output to input varies with the size of the firm is an important factor in determining the size of a firm.

6. **Productivity and Technical Change.** The amount of output that can be produced with a given amount of inputs varies across firms and over time.

6.1 The Ownership and Management of Firms

firm
an organization that converts inputs such as labor, materials, energy, and capital into outputs, the goods and services that it sells

A **firm** is an organization that converts *inputs* such as labor, materials, and capital into *outputs*, the goods and services that it sells. U.S. Steel combines iron ore, machinery, and labor to create steel. A local restaurant buys raw food, cooks it, and serves it. A landscape designer hires gardeners and rents machines, buys trees and shrubs, transports them to a customer's home, and supervises the project.

Private, Public, and Nonprofit Firms

Atheism is a non-prophet organization.   —George Carlin

Firms operate in the private, public, or nonprofit sectors. The *private sector*, sometimes referred to as the *for-profit private sector*, consists of firms owned by individuals or other nongovernmental entities whose owners try to earn a profit. Throughout this book, we concentrate on these firms. In almost every country, this sector contributes the most to the gross domestic product (GDP, a measure of a country's total output).

The *public sector* consists of firms and organizations that are owned by governments or government agencies. For example, the National Railroad Passenger Corporation (Amtrak) is owned primarily by the U.S. government. The armed forces and the court system are also part of the public sector, as are most schools, colleges, and universities.

The *nonprofit* or *not-for-profit sector* consists of organizations that are neither government-owned nor intended to earn a profit. Organizations in this sector typically pursue social or public interest objectives. Well-known examples include Greenpeace, Alcoholics Anonymous, and the Salvation Army, along with many other charitable, educational, health, and religious organizations. According to the 2012 *U.S. Statistical Abstract*, the private sector created 75% of the U.S. gross domestic product, the government sector was responsible for 12%, and nonprofits and households produced the remaining 13%.

Sometimes all three sectors play an important role in the same industry. For example, in the United States, the United Kingdom, Canada, and in many other countries, for-profit, nonprofit, and government-owned hospitals coexist. A single enterprise may be partially owned by a government and partially owned by private interests. For example, during the 2007–2009 Great Recession, the U.S. government took a partial ownership position in many firms in the financial and automobile industries.

Application

Chinese State-Owned Enterprises

For years, China's communist economy was dominated by firms owned by the government, which are called state-owned enterprises (SOEs). Recently, however, China has started transitioning to a market-based economy, emphasizing privately owned firms. It has reduced the number of SOEs but has kept the largest ones.

Chinese SOEs have always been large relative to private firms. In 1999, SOEs were 36% of Chinese industrial firms and controlled nearly 68% of industrial assets (capital). Since then, the Chinese government has allowed many small SOEs to become private or go bankrupt, while it continues to subsidize large SOEs. By 2011, only 5% of these firms were SOEs, but they held 42% of industrial assets.

The Ownership of For-Profit Firms

The legal structure of a firm determines who is liable for its debts. Firms in the private sector have three primary legal forms of organization: a sole proprietorship, a general partnership, or a corporation.

Sole proprietorships are firms owned by a single individual.

Partnerships are businesses jointly owned and controlled by two or more people operating under a partnership agreement.

Corporations are owned by *shareholders*, who own the firm's *shares* (also called *stock*). Each share (or unit of stock) is a unit of ownership in the firm. Therefore, shareholders own the firm in proportion to the number of shares they hold. The shareholders elect a board of directors to represent them. In turn, the board of directors usually hires managers who manage the firm's operations. Some corporations are very small and have a single shareholder. Others are very large and have thousands of shareholders. The legal name of a corporation often includes the term Incorporated (Inc.) or Limited (Ltd) to indicate its corporate status.

limited liability
condition whereby the personal assets of the owners of the corporation cannot be taken to pay a corporation's debts if it goes into bankruptcy

A fundamental characteristic of corporations is that the owners are not personally liable for the firm's debts; they have **limited liability**: The personal assets of corporate owners cannot be taken to pay a corporation's debts even if it goes into bankruptcy. Because corporations have limited liability, the most that shareholders can lose is the amount they paid for their stock, which typically becomes worthless if the corporation declares bankruptcy.[1]

---

[1]The United States since 1996, the United Kingdom since 2000, and other countries allow any sole proprietorship, partnership, or corporation to register as a *limited liability company* (LLC). Thus, all firms—not just corporations—can now obtain limited liability. Adopting the LLC form has some costs that many firms are not willing to incur, including registration fees, and firms in some industries are not eligible. Therefore, traditional sole proprietorships and partnerships with unlimited personal liability for the owners remain very common.

The purpose of limiting liability was to allow firms to raise funds and grow beyond what was possible when owners risked personal assets on any firm in which they invested. According to the 2012 *U.S. Statistical Abstract*, U.S. corporations are responsible for 81% of business receipts and 58% of net business income even though they are only 18% of all nonfarm firms. Nonfarm sole proprietorships are 72% of firms but make only 4% of the sales revenue and earn 15% of net income. Partnerships are 10% of firms, account for 15% of revenue, and make 27% of net income.

Eighty-one percent of all corporations earn less than $1 million a year, and they account for only 3% of corporative revenue (*U.S. Statistical Abstract*, 2012). In contrast, less than 1% of all corporations earn over $50 million, but they make 77% of total corporate revenue. In 2012, Exxon-Mobil was the U.S. corporation with the largest worldwide revenue. Its revenue of $434 billion exceeded the annual GDP of fairly large countries, such as Austria ($301 billion) and Greece ($216 billion).[2]

As these statistics illustrate, larger firms tend to be corporations and smaller firms are often sole proprietorships. This pattern reflects a natural evolution in the life cycle of the firm, as an entrepreneur may start a small business as a sole proprietorship and then incorporate as the firm's operations expand. Indeed, successful corporations typically expand, and a relatively small number of corporations account for most of the revenue and income in the U.S. economy.

The Management of Firms

In a small firm, the owner usually manages the firm's operations. In larger firms, typically corporations and larger partnerships, a manager or a management team usually runs the company. In such firms, owners, managers, and lower-level supervisors are all decision makers.

Various decision makers may have conflicting objectives. What is in the best interest of the owners may not be in the best interest of managers or other employees. For example, a manager may want a fancy office, a company car, a corporate jet, and other perks, but an owner would likely oppose those drains on profit.

The owner replaces the manager if the manager pursues personal objectives rather than the firm's objectives. In a corporation, the board of directors is responsible for ensuring that the manager stays on track. If the manager and the board of directors are ineffective, the shareholders can fire both or change certain policies through votes at the corporation's annual shareholders' meeting. Until Chapter 20, we'll ignore the potential conflict between managers and owners and assume that the owner *is* the manager of the firm and makes all the decisions.

What Owners Want

profit (π)
the difference between revenue *R*, and cost *C*: $\pi = R - C$

Economists usually assume that a firm's owners try to maximize profit. Presumably, most people invest in a firm to make money—lots of money, they hope. They want the firm to earn a positive profit rather than make a loss (a negative profit). A firm's **profit**, π, is the difference between its revenue, *R*, which is what it earns from selling a good, and its cost, *C*, which is what it pays for labor, materials, and other inputs:

$$\pi = R - C.$$

Typically, revenue is *p*, the price, times *q*, the firm's quantity: $R = pq$.

---

[2]*Fortune Magazine* annually provides a list of the largest corporations: **www.forbes.com/sites/scottdecarlo/2012/04/18/the-worlds-biggest-companies**. GDP data are from the IMF for 2011.

In reality, some owners have other objectives, such as running as large a firm as possible, owning a fancy building, or keeping risks low. However, Chapter 8 shows that a firm in a highly competitive market is likely to be driven out of business if it doesn't maximize its profit.

To maximize profits, a firm must produce as efficiently as possible, as we will consider in this chapter. A firm engages in **efficient production** (achieves *technological efficiency*) if it cannot produce its current level of output with fewer inputs, given existing knowledge about technology and the organization of production. Equivalently, the firm produces efficiently if, given the quantity of inputs used, no more output could be produced using existing knowledge.

efficient production
the current level of output cannot be produced with fewer inputs, given existing knowledge about technology and the organization of production

If the firm does not produce efficiently, it cannot be profit maximizing—so efficient production is a *necessary condition* for profit maximization. Even if a firm produces a given level of output efficiently, it is not maximizing profit if that output level is too high or too low or if it is using excessively expensive inputs. Thus, efficient production alone is not a *sufficient condition* to ensure that a firm's profit is maximized.

A firm may use engineers and other experts to determine the most efficient ways to produce using a known method or technology. However, this knowledge does not indicate which of the many technologies, each of which uses different combinations of inputs, allows for production at the lowest cost or with the highest possible profit. How to produce at the lowest cost is an economic decision typically made by the firm's manager (see Chapter 7).

6.2 Production Function

A firm uses a *technology* or *production process* to transform *inputs* or *factors of production* into *outputs*. Firms use many types of inputs. Most of these inputs can be grouped into three broad categories:

- **Capital** (K). Long-lived inputs such as land, buildings (factories, stores), and equipment (machines, trucks)
- **Labor** (L). Human services such as those provided by managers, skilled workers (architects, economists, engineers, plumbers), and less-skilled workers (custodians, construction laborers, assembly-line workers)
- **Materials** (M). Raw goods (oil, water, wheat) and processed products (aluminum, plastic, paper, steel)

The output can be a *service*, such as an automobile tune-up by a mechanic, or a *physical product*, such as a computer chip or a potato chip.

Firms can transform inputs into outputs in many different ways. Candy-manufacturing companies differ in the skills of their workforce and the amount of equipment they use. While all employ a chef, a manager, and relatively unskilled workers, some candy firms also use skilled technicians and modern equipment. In small candy companies, the relatively unskilled workers shape the candy, decorate it, package it, and box it by hand. In slightly larger firms, the relatively unskilled workers use conveyor belts and other equipment that was invented decades ago. In modern, large-scale plants, the relatively unskilled laborers work with robots and other state-of-the-art machines, which are maintained by skilled technicians. Before deciding which production process to use, a firm needs to consider its various options.

production function
the relationship between the quantities of inputs used and the maximum quantity of output that can be produced, given current knowledge about technology and organization

The various ways inputs can be transformed into output are summarized in the **production function**: the relationship between the quantities of inputs used and the *maximum* quantity of output that can be produced, given current knowledge about technology and organization. The production function for a firm that uses only labor and capital is

$$q = f(L, K), \tag{6.1}$$

where q units of output (wrapped candy bars) are produced using L units of labor services (days of work by relatively unskilled assembly-line workers) and K units of capital (the number of conveyor belts).

The production function shows only the *maximum* amount of output that can be produced from given levels of labor and capital, because *the production function includes only efficient production processes*. A profit-maximizing firm is not interested in production processes that are inefficient and waste inputs: Firms do not want to use two workers to do a job that can be done as efficiently by one worker.

A firm can more easily adjust its inputs in the long run than in the short run. Typically, a firm can vary the amount of materials and of relatively unskilled labor it uses comparatively quickly. However, it needs more time to find and hire skilled workers, order new equipment, or build a new manufacturing plant.

The more time a firm has to adjust its inputs, the more factors of production it can alter. The **short run** is a period of time so brief that at least one factor of production cannot be varied practically. A factor that cannot be varied practically in the short run is called a **fixed input**. In contrast, a **variable input** is a factor of production whose quantity can be changed readily by the firm during the relevant time period. The **long run** is a lengthy enough period of time that all inputs can be varied. In the long run, all factors of productions are variable inputs. The firm has no fixed inputs in the long run.

Suppose that a painting company's customers all want the paint job on their homes to be finished by the end of the day. The firm could complete these projects on time if it had one fewer job. To complete all the jobs, it needs to use more inputs. The firm does not have time to buy or rent an extra truck and buy another compressor to run a power sprayer; these inputs are fixed in the short run. To get the work done that afternoon, the firm uses the company's one truck to pick up and drop off temporary workers, each equipped with only a brush and paint, at the last job. However, in the long run, the firm can adjust all its inputs. If the firm wants to paint more houses every day, it hires more full-time workers, gets a second truck, purchases more compressors to run the power sprayers, and uses a computer to keep track of all its projects.

How long it takes for all inputs to be variable depends on the factors a firm uses. For a janitorial service whose only major input is workers, the short run is a very brief period of time. In contrast, an automobile manufacturer may need many years to build a new manufacturing plant or to design and construct a new type of machine. A pistachio farmer needs the better part of a decade before newly planted trees yield a substantial crop of nuts.

For many firms, materials and often labor are variable inputs over a month. However, labor is not always a variable input. Finding additional highly skilled workers may take substantial time. Similarly, capital may be a variable or fixed input. A firm can rent some capital assets (such as trucks, furniture, and office equipment) quickly, but it may take the firm years to obtain larger capital assets (buildings and large, specialized pieces of equipment).

To illustrate the greater flexibility that a firm has in the long run than in the short run, we examine the production function in Equation 6.1, in which output is a function of only labor and capital. We look at first the short-run and then the long-run production processes.

short run
a period of time so brief that at least one factor of production cannot be varied practically

fixed input
a factor of production that cannot be varied practically in the short run

variable input
a factor of production whose quantity can be changed readily by the firm during the relevant time period

long run
a lengthy enough period of time that all inputs can be varied

6.3 Short-Run Production

The short run is a period in which at least one input is fixed. We consider a production process with only two inputs in which capital is a fixed input and labor is a variable input. The firm can increase output only by increasing the amount of labor it uses. In the short run, the firm's production function is

$$q = f(L, \overline{K}), \qquad (6.2)$$

where q is output, L is the amount of labor, and $\overline{K}$ is the fixed number of units of capital.

To illustrate the short-run production process, we consider a firm that assembles computers for a manufacturing firm that supplies it with the necessary parts, such as computer chips and disk drives. The assembly firm cannot increase its capital—eight workbenches fully equipped with tools, electronic probes, and other equipment for testing computers—in the short run, but it can hire extra workers or pay current workers extra to work overtime so as to increase production.

Total Product

The exact relationship between *output* or *total product* and *labor* can be illustrated by using a particular function, Equation 6.2, a table, or a figure. Table 6.1 shows the relationship between output and labor when capital is fixed for a firm. The first column lists the fixed amount of capital: eight fully equipped workbenches. As the number of workers (the amount of labor, second column) increases, total output (the number of computers assembled in a day, third column) first increases and then decreases.

Table 6.1 Total Product, Marginal Product, and Average Product of Labor with Fixed Capital

Capital, $\overline{K}$	Labor, L	Output, Total Product, q	Marginal Product of Labor, $MP_L = \Delta q/\Delta L$	Average Product of Labor, $AP_L = q/L$
8	0	0		
8	1	5	5	5
8	2	18	13	9
8	3	36	18	12
8	4	56	20	14
8	5	75	19	15
8	6	90	15	15
8	7	98	8	14
8	8	104	6	13
8	9	108	4	12
8	10	110	2	11
8	11	110	0	10
8	12	108	−2	9
8	13	104	−4	8

With zero workers, no computers are assembled. One worker with access to the firm's equipment assembles five computers in a day. As the number of workers increases, so does output: 1 worker assembles 5 computers in a day, 2 workers assemble 18, 3 workers assemble 36, and so forth. However, the maximum number of computers that can be assembled with the capital on hand is limited to 110 per day. That maximum can be produced with 10 or 11 workers. Adding extra workers beyond 11 lowers production as workers get in each other's way. The dashed line in the table indicates that a firm would not use 11 or more workers, because doing so would be inefficient. That is, the production function—which only includes efficient production—involves fewer than 11 workers.

Marginal Product of Labor

We can show how extra workers affect the total product by using two additional concepts: the marginal product of labor and the average product of labor. Before deciding whether to hire one more worker, a manager wants to determine how much this extra worker, $\Delta L = 1$, will increase output, Δq. That is, the manager wants to know the **marginal product of labor** (MP_L): the change in total output resulting from using an extra unit of labor, holding other factors (capital) constant. If output changes by Δq when the number of workers increases by ΔL, the change in output per worker is[3]

marginal product of labor (MP_L)
the change in total output, Δq, resulting from using an extra unit of labor, ΔL, holding other factors constant: $MP_L = \Delta q/\Delta L$

$$MP_L = \frac{\Delta q}{\Delta L}.$$

As Table 6.1 shows, if the number of workers increases from 1 to 2, $\Delta L = 1$, output rises by $\Delta q = 13 = 18 - 5$, so the marginal product of labor is 13.

Solved Problem 6.1

For a linear production function $q = f(L, K) = 2L + K$, what is the short-run production function given that capital is fixed at $\overline{K} = 100$? What is the marginal product of labor?

Answer

1. *Obtain the short-run production functions by setting* $\overline{K} = 100$. The short-run production function is $q = 2L + 100$.

2. *Determine the marginal product of labor by showing how q changes as L is increased by* ΔL *units.* The output at $L + \Delta L$ is $q = 2(L + \Delta L) + 100$. Taking the difference between this output and the output with L units of labor, $q = 2L + 100$, we find that $\Delta q = (2[L + \Delta L] + 100) - (2L + 100) = 2\Delta L$. Thus, the marginal product of labor is $MP_L = \Delta q/\Delta L = 2$.[4]

---

[3]With the long-run production function $q = f(L, K)$, the calculus definition of the marginal product of labor is $MP_L = \partial q/\partial L = \partial f(L, K)/\partial L$, where capital is held constant at K. In the short run with capital fixed at $\overline{K}$, we can write the production function as solely a function of labor $q = f(L, \overline{K}) = \hat{f}(L)$. Thus, in the short run, $MP_L = dq/dL = d\hat{f}(L)/dL$.

[4]Using calculus, we can derive the same result by differentiating the short-run production function with respect to labor: $MP_L = d(2L + 100)/dL = 2$.

Average Product of Labor

average product of labor (AP_L)
the ratio of output, q, to the number of workers, L, used to produce that output: $AP_L = q/L$

Before hiring extra workers, a manager may also want to know whether output will rise in proportion to this extra labor. To answer this question, the firm determines how extra workers affect the **average product of labor** (AP_L): the ratio of output to the number of workers used to produce that output,

$$AP_L = \frac{q}{L}.$$

Table 6.1 shows that 9 workers can assemble 108 computers a day, so the average product of labor for 9 workers is 12 (= 108/9) computers a day. Ten workers can assemble 110 computers in a day, so the average product of labor for 10 workers is 11 (= 110/10) computers. Thus, increasing the labor force from 9 to 10 workers lowers the average product per worker.

Graphing the Product Curves

Figure 6.1 and Table 6.1 show how output, the average product of labor, and the marginal product of labor vary with the number of workers. (The figures are smooth curves because the firm can hire a "fraction of a worker" by employing a worker for

Figure 6.1 Production Relationships with Variable Labor

(a) The total product curve shows how many computers, q, can be assembled with eight fully equipped workbenches and a varying number of workers, L, who work an eight-hour day (see columns 2 and 3 in Table 6.1). Where extra workers reduce the number of computers assembled, the total product curve is a dashed line, which indicates that such production is inefficient production and not part of the production function. The slope of the line from the origin to point A is the average product of labor for six workers. (b) The marginal product of labor ($MP_L = \Delta q/\Delta L$, column 4 of Table 6.1) equals the average product of labor ($AP_L = q/L$, column 5 of Table 6.1) at the peak of the average product curve.

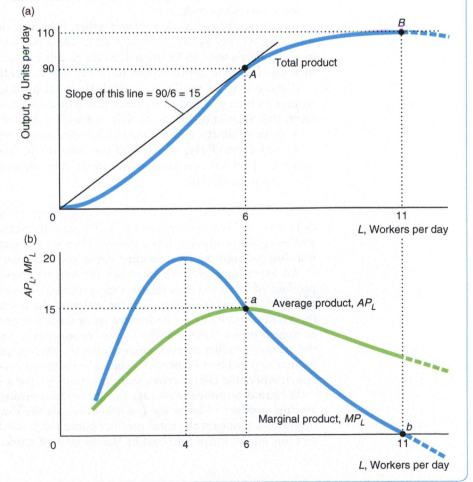

a fraction of a day.) The curve in panel a of Figure 6.1 shows how a change in labor affects the *total product*, which is the amount of output (or *total product*) that can be produced by a given amount of labor. Output rises with labor until it reaches its maximum of 110 computers at 11 workers, point *B*; with extra workers, the number of computers assembled falls.

Panel b of the figure shows how the average product of labor and marginal product of labor vary with the number of workers. We can line up the figures in panels a and b vertically because the units along the horizontal axes of both figures, the number of workers per day, are the same. The vertical axes differ, however. The vertical axis is total product in panel a and the average or marginal product of labor—a measure of output per unit of labor—in panel b.

Effect of Extra Labor In most production processes, the average product of labor first rises and then falls as labor increases. One reason the AP_L curve initially rises in Figure 6.1 is that it helps to have more than two hands when assembling a computer. One worker holds a part in place while another one bolts it down. As a result, output increases more than in proportion to labor, so the average product of labor rises. Doubling the number of workers from one to two more than doubles the output from 5 to 18 and causes the average product of labor to rise from 5 to 9, as Table 6.1 shows.

Similarly, output may initially rise more than in proportion to labor because of greater specialization of activities. With greater specialization, workers are assigned to tasks at which they are particularly adept, and time is saved by not having workers move from task to task.

As the number of workers rises further, however, output may not increase by as much per worker as they have to wait to use a particular piece of equipment or get in each other's way. In Figure 6.1, as the number of workers exceeds 6, total output increases less than in proportion to labor, so the average product falls.

If more than 11 workers are used, the total product curve falls with each extra worker as the crowding of workers gets worse. Because that much labor is not efficient, that section of the curve is drawn with a dashed line to indicate that it is not part of the production function, which includes only efficient combinations of labor and capital. Similarly, the dashed portions of the average and marginal product curves are irrelevant because no firm would hire additional workers if doing so meant that output would fall.

Relationship of the Product Curves The three curves in Figure 6.1 are geometrically related. First we use panel b to illustrate the relationship between the average and marginal product of labor curves. Then we use panels a and b to show the relationship between the total product curve and the other two curves.

An extra hour of work increases the average product of labor if the marginal product of labor exceeds the average product. Similarly, if an extra hour of work generates less extra output than the average, the average product falls. Therefore, the average product rises with extra labor if the marginal product curve is above the average product curve, and the average product falls if the marginal product is below the average product curve. Consequently, the average product curve reaches its peak, point *a* in panel b of Figure 6.1, where the marginal product and average product are equal: where the curves cross. (See Appendix 6A for a mathematical proof.)

We can determine the average product of labor using the total product curve. The average product of labor for *L* workers equals the slope of a straight line from the origin to a point on the total product curve for *L* workers in panel a. The slope of this line equals output divided by the number of workers, which is the definition of the average product of labor. For example, the slope of the straight line drawn from the origin to point A ($L = 6$, $q = 90$) is 15, which equals the *rise* of $q = 90$ divided by the *run* of $L = 6$. As panel b shows, the average product of labor for 6 workers at point a is 15.

The marginal product of labor also has a geometric interpretation in terms of the total product curve. The slope of the total product curve at a given point, $\Delta q/\Delta L$, equals the marginal product of labor. That is, the marginal product of labor equals the slope of a straight line that is tangent to the total output curve at a given point. For example, at point B in panel a where the firm uses 11 workers, the line tangent to the total product curve is flat, so the marginal product of labor is zero: A little extra labor has no effect on output. The total product curve is upward sloping when the firm uses fewer than 11 workers, so the marginal product of labor is positive. If the firm is foolish enough to hire more than 11 workers, the total product curve slopes downward (dashed line), so the MP_L is negative: Extra workers lower output. Again, this portion of the MP_L curve is not part of the production function.

With 6 workers, the average product of labor equals the marginal product of labor, at the peak of the AP_L curve. The reason is that the line from the origin to point A in panel a is tangent to the total product curve, so the slope of that line, 15, is the marginal product of labor and the average product of labor at point a in panel b.

Law of Diminishing Marginal Returns

Next to "supply equals demand," probably the most commonly used phrase of economic jargon is the "law of diminishing marginal returns." This law determines the shapes of the total product and marginal product of labor curves as the firm uses more and more labor.

The *law of diminishing marginal returns* (or *diminishing marginal product*) holds that if a firm keeps increasing an input, holding all other inputs and technology constant, the corresponding increases in output will become smaller eventually. That is, if only one input is increased, *the marginal product of that input will diminish eventually*.

In Table 6.1, if the firm goes from 1 to 2 workers, the marginal product of labor is 13. If 1 or 2 more workers are used, the marginal product rises: The marginal product for 3 workers is 18, and the marginal product for 4 workers is 20. However, if the firm increases the number of workers beyond 4, the marginal product falls: The marginal product of 5 workers is 19, and that for 6 workers is 15. Beyond 4 workers, each extra worker adds less and less extra output, so the total product curve rises by smaller increments. At 11 workers, the marginal product is zero. In short, the law of diminishing marginal returns says that if a firm keeps adding one more unit of an input, the extra output it gets grows smaller and smaller. This diminishing return to extra labor may be due to too many workers sharing too few machines or to crowding, as workers get in each other's way. Thus, as the amount of labor used grows large enough, the marginal product curve approaches zero and the corresponding total product curve becomes nearly flat.

Unfortunately, many people, when attempting to cite this empirical regularity, overstate it. Instead of talking about the law of *diminishing marginal returns*, they talk about *diminishing returns*—leaving out the word *marginal*. The two phrases have different meanings. If as labor increases the marginal returns fall but remain positive, the total return rises. In panel b of Figure 6.1, marginal returns start to diminish when the labor input exceeds 4 but total returns rise, as panel a shows, until the labor input exceeds 11, where the marginal returns become negative. With *diminishing returns*, extra labor causes *output* to fall. The production process has diminishing (total) returns for more than 11 workers—a dashed line in panel a.

Thus, saying that the production process has diminishing returns is much stronger than saying that it has diminishing *marginal* returns. We often observe firms producing where the marginal returns to labor are diminishing, but no well-run firm operates where total returns diminish. Such a firm could produce more output by using fewer inputs.

A second common misinterpretation of this law is to claim that marginal products must fall as we increase an input without requiring that technology and other inputs stay constant. If we increase labor while simultaneously increasing other factors or adopting superior technologies, the marginal product of labor may rise indefinitely. Thomas Malthus provided the most famous example of this fallacy.

Application

Malthus and the Green Revolution

In 1798, Thomas Malthus—a clergyman and professor of modern history and political economy—predicted that population (if unchecked) would grow more rapidly than food production because the quantity of land was fixed. The problem, he believed, was that the fixed amount of land would lead to a diminishing marginal product of labor, so output would rise less than in proportion to the increase in farm workers. Malthus grimly concluded that mass starvation would result. Brander and Taylor (1998) argue that such a disaster may have occurred on Easter Island around 500 years ago.

Today, the earth supports a population almost seven times as great as it was when Malthus made his predictions. Why haven't most of us starved to death? The simple explanation is that fewer workers using less land can produce much more food today than was possible when Malthus was alive. The output of a U.S. farm worker today is more than double that of an average worker just 50 years ago. We do not see diminishing marginal returns to labor because the production function has changed due to substantial technological progress in agriculture and because farmers make greater use of other inputs such as fertilizers, capital, and superior seeds.

Two hundred years ago, most of the population had to work in agriculture to feed themselves. Today, less than 1% of the U.S. population works in agriculture. Over the last century, food production grew substantially faster than the population in most developed countries. For example, since World War II, the U.S. population doubled but U.S. food production tripled.

In 1850 in the United States, it took more than 80 hours of labor to produce 100 bushels of corn. Introducing mechanical power cut the required labor in half. Labor hours were again cut in half by the introduction of hybrid seed and chemical fertilizers, and then in half again by the advent of herbicides and pesticides. Biotechnology, with the introduction of herbicide-tolerant and insect-resistant crops, has reduced the labor required to produce 100 bushels of corn to about two hours—2.5% of the hours of work it took in 1850. Over the past 60 years, the output per work has more than doubled, and the corn yield per acre has increased by 6.2 times.

Of course, the risk of starvation is more severe in developing countries. Nearly all (98%) of the world's hungry people live in developing countries. Luckily, one man decided to defeat the threat of Malthusian disaster personally. Do you know anyone who saved a life? A hundred lives? Do you know the name of the man who probably saved the most lives in history? According to some estimates, during the second half of the twentieth century, Norman Borlaug and his fellow scientists prevented a *billion deaths* with their *Green Revolution*, which included development of drought- and insect-resistant crop varieties, improved irrigation, better use of fertilizer and pesticides, and improved equipment.

However, as Dr. Borlaug noted in his 1970 Nobel Prize speech, superior science is not the complete answer to preventing starvation. A sound economic system and a stable political environment are also needed.

Economic and political failures such as the breakdown of economic production and distribution systems due to wars have caused per capita food production to fall, resulting in about 27% of the population in sub-Saharan Africa in 2012 suffering from significant undernourishment. If these economic and political problems cannot be solved, Malthus' prediction may prove to be right for the wrong reason.

6.4 Long-Run Production

We started our analysis of production functions by looking at a short-run production function in which one input, capital, was fixed, and the other, labor, was variable. In the long run, however, both of these inputs are variable. With both factors variable, a firm can usually produce a given level of output by using a great deal of labor and very little capital, a great deal of capital and very little labor, or moderate amounts of both. That is, the firm can substitute one input for another while continuing to produce the same level of output, in much the same way that a consumer can maintain a given level of utility by substituting one good for another.

Typically, a firm can produce in a number of different ways, some of which require more labor than others. For example, a lumberyard can produce 200 planks an hour with 10 workers using hand saws, with 4 workers using handheld power saws, or with 2 workers using bench power saws.

We illustrate a firm's ability to substitute between inputs in Table 6.2, which shows the amount of output per day the firm produces with various combinations of labor per day and capital per day. The labor inputs (L) are along the top of the table, and the capital inputs (K) are in the first column. The table shows four combinations

Table 6.2 Output Produced with Two Variable Inputs

Capital, K	Labor, L					
	1	2	3	4	5	6
1	10	14	17	20	22	24
2	14	20	24	28	32	35
3	17	24	30	35	39	42
4	20	28	35	40	45	49
5	22	32	39	45	50	55
6	24	35	42	49	55	60

of labor and capital that the firm can use to produce 24 units of output: The firm may employ (a) 1 worker and 6 units of capital, (b) 2 workers and 3 units of capital, (c) 3 workers and 2 units of capital, or (d) 6 workers and 1 unit of capital.

Isoquants

isoquant

a curve that shows the efficient combinations of labor and capital that can produce a single (*iso*) level of output (*quantity*)

These four combinations of labor and capital are labeled *a*, *b*, *c*, and *d* on the "*q* = 24" curve in Figure 6.2. We call such a curve an **isoquant**, which is a curve that shows the efficient combinations of labor and capital that can produce a single (*iso*) level of output (*quantity*). If the production function is $q = f(L, K)$, then the equation for an isoquant where output is held constant at $\bar{q}$ is

$$\bar{q} = f(L, K).$$

An isoquant shows the flexibility that a firm has in producing a given level of output. Figure 6.2 shows three isoquants corresponding to three levels of output. These isoquants are smooth curves because the firm can use fractional units of each input.

We can use these isoquants to illustrate what happens in the short run when capital is fixed and only labor varies. As Table 6.2 shows, if capital is constant at 2 units, 1 worker produces 14 units of output (point *e* in Figure 6.2), 3 workers produce 24 units (point *c*), and 6 workers produce 35 units (point *f*). Thus, if the firm holds one factor constant and varies another factor, it moves from one isoquant to another. In contrast, if the firm increases one input while lowering the other appropriately, the firm stays on a single isoquant.

Properties of Isoquants   Isoquants have most of the same properties as indifference curves. The biggest difference between indifference curves and isoquants is that an isoquant holds quantity constant, whereas an indifference curve holds utility

Figure 6.2 Family of Isoquants

These isoquants show the combinations of labor and capital that produce various levels of output. Isoquants farther from the origin correspond to higher levels of output. Points *a*, *b*, *c*, and *d* are various combinations of labor and capital the firm can use to produce *q* = 24 units of output. If the firm holds capital constant at 2 and increases labor from 1 (point *e*) to 3 (*c*) to 6 (*f*), it shifts from the *q* = 14 isoquant to the *q* = 24 isoquant and then to the *q* = 35 isoquant.

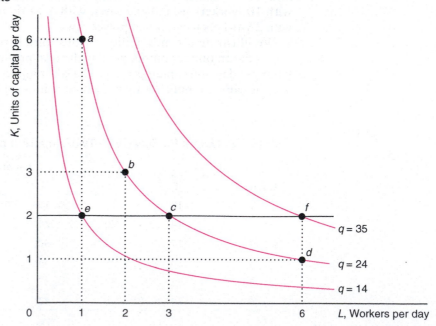

constant. We now discuss three major properties of isoquants. Most of these properties result from firms producing efficiently.

First, *the farther an isoquant is from the origin, the greater the level of output*. That is, the more inputs a firm uses, the more output it gets if it produces efficiently. At point *e* in Figure 6.2, the firm is producing 14 units of output with 1 worker and 2 units of capital. If the firm holds capital constant and adds 2 more workers, it produces at point *c*. Point *c* must be on an isoquant with a higher level of output—here, 24 units—if the firm is producing efficiently and not wasting the extra labor.

Second, *isoquants do not cross*. Such intersections are inconsistent with the requirement that the firm always produces efficiently. For example, if the $q = 15$ and $q = 20$ isoquants crossed, the firm could produce at either output level with the same combination of labor and capital. The firm must be producing inefficiently if it produces $q = 15$ when it could produce $q = 20$. So that labor-capital combination should not lie on the $q = 15$ isoquant, which should include only efficient combinations of inputs. Thus, efficiency requires that isoquants do not cross.

Third, *isoquants slope downward*. If an isoquant sloped upward, the firm could produce the same level of output with relatively few inputs or relatively many inputs. Producing with relatively many inputs would be inefficient. Consequently, because isoquants show only efficient production, an upward-sloping isoquant is impossible. Virtually the same argument can be used to show that isoquants must be thin.

Shape of Isoquants The curvature of an isoquant shows how readily a firm can substitute one input for another. The two extreme cases are production processes in which inputs are perfect substitutes or in which they cannot be substituted for each other.

If the inputs are perfect substitutes, each isoquant is a straight line. Suppose either potatoes from Maine, *x*, or potatoes from Idaho, *y*, both of which are measured in pounds per day, can be used to produce potato salad, *q*, measured in pounds. The production function is

$$q = x + y.$$

One pound of potato salad can be produced by using 1 pound of Idaho potatoes and no Maine potatoes, 1 pound of Maine potatoes and no Idahoes, or $\frac{1}{2}$ pound of each type of potato. Panel a of Figure 6.3 shows the $q = 1, 2,$ and 3 isoquants. These isoquants are straight lines with a slope of -1 because we need to use an extra pound of Maine potatoes for every pound fewer of Idaho potatoes used.[5]

Sometimes it is impossible to substitute one input for the other: Inputs must be used in fixed proportions. Such a production function is called a *fixed-proportions production function*. For example, the inputs to produce a 12-ounce box of cereal, *q*, are cereal (in 12-ounce units per day) and cardboard boxes (boxes per day). If the firm has one unit of cereal and one box, it can produce one box of cereal. If it has one unit of cereal and two boxes, it can still make only one box of cereal. Thus, in panel b, the only efficient points of production are the large dots along the 45° line.[6] Dashed lines show that the isoquants would be right angles if isoquants could include inefficient production processes.

---

[5]The isoquant for $\overline{q} = 1$ pound of potato salad is $1 = x + y$, or $y = 1 - x$. This equation shows that the isoquant is a straight line with a slope of -1.

[6]This fixed-proportions production function is $q = \min(g, b)$, where *g* is the number of 12-ounce measures of cereal, *b* is the number of boxes used in a day, and the min function means "the minimum number of *g* or *b*." For example, if *g* is 4 and *b* is 3, *q* is 3.

Figure 6.3 Substitutability of Inputs

(a) If the inputs are perfect substitutes, each isoquant is a straight line. (b) If the inputs cannot be substituted at all, the isoquants are right angles (the dashed lines show that the isoquants would be right angles if we included inefficient production). (c) Typical isoquants lie between the extreme cases of straight lines and right angles. Along a curved isoquant, the ability to substitute one input for another varies.

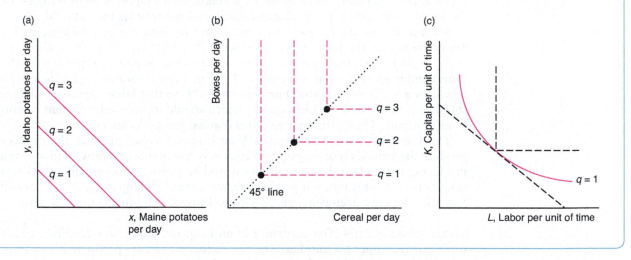

Other production processes allow imperfect substitution between inputs. The isoquants are convex (so the middle of the isoquant is closer to the origin than it would be if the isoquant were a straight line). They do not have the same slope at every point, unlike the straight-line isoquants. Most isoquants are smooth, slope downward, curve away from the origin, and lie between the extreme cases of straight lines (perfect substitutes) and right angles (nonsubstitutes), as panel c illustrates.

Application

A Semiconductor Integrated Circuit Isoquant

We can show why isoquants curve away from the origin by deriving an isoquant for semiconductor integrated circuits (ICs, or "chips")—the "brains" of computers and other electronic devices. Semiconductor manufacturers buy silicon wafers and then use labor and capital to produce the chips.

A chip consists of multiple layers of silicon wafers. A key step in the production process is to line up these layers. Three alternative alignment technologies are available, using different combinations of labor and capital. In the least capital-intensive technology, employees use machines called *aligners*, which require workers to look through microscopes and line up the layers by hand. To produce 200 ten-layer chips per day takes 8 workers using 8 aligners.

A second, more capital-intensive technology uses machines called *steppers*. The stepper aligns the layers automatically. This technology requires less labor: To produce 200 ten-layer chips per day requires 3 workers and 6 steppers.

A third, even more capital-intensive technology combines steppers with wafer-handling equipment, which further reduces the amount of labor needed. One worker using 4 steppers with wafer-handling capabilities can manufacture 200 ten-layer chips per day.

In the diagram, the vertical axis measures the amount of capital used. An aligner represents less capital than a basic stepper, which in turn is less capital than a stepper with wafer-handling capabilities. All three technologies use labor and capital in fixed proportions. The diagram shows the three right-angle isoquants corresponding to each of these three technologies.

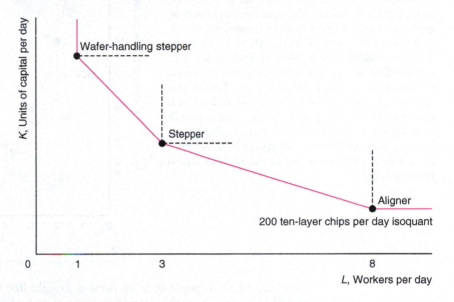

Some plants employ a combination of these technologies, so that some workers use one type of machine while others use different types. By doing so, the plant can produce using intermediate combinations of labor and capital, as the solid-line, kinked isoquant illustrates. The firm does *not* use a combination of the aligner and the wafer-handling stepper technologies because those combinations are less efficient than using the basic stepper: The line connecting the aligner and wafer-handling stepper technologies is farther from the origin than the lines between those technologies and the basic stepper technology.

New processes are constantly being invented. As they are introduced, the isoquant will have more and more kinks (one for each new process) and will begin to resemble the smooth, convex isoquants we've been drawing.

Substituting Inputs

The slope of an isoquant shows a firm's ability to replace one input with another while holding output constant. Figure 6.4 illustrates this substitution using an estimated isoquant for a service firm, which uses labor, L, and capital, K, to produce q units of service.[7] The isoquant shows various combinations of L and K that the firm can use to produce 10 units of output.

The firm can produce 10 units of output using the combination of inputs at a or b. At point a, the firm uses 2 workers and 16 units of capital. The firm could produce the same amount of output using $\Delta K = -6$ fewer units of capital if it used one more

---

[7]This isoquant for $q = 10$ is based on the estimated "personal and other service" (such as gardening, hairdressers, laundry) production function $q = 2.35L^{0.5}K^{0.4}$ (Devine et al., 2012), where a unit of labor, L, is a worker-day. Because capital, K, includes various types of machines, and output, q, reflects different types of service, their units cannot be described by any common terms.

Figure 6.4 How the Marginal Rate of Technical Substitution Varies Along an Isoquant

Moving from point *a* to *b*, a service firm (Devine et al., 2012) can produce the same amount of output, $q = 10$, using six fewer units of capital, $\Delta K = -6$, if it uses one more worker, $\Delta L = 1$. Thus, its $MRTS = \Delta K/\Delta L = -6$. Moving from point *b* to *c*, its $MRTS$ is -3. If it adds yet another worker, moving from *c* to *d*, its $MRTS$ is -2. Finally, if it moves from *d* to *e*, its $MRTS$ is -1. Thus, because it curves away from the origin, this isoquant exhibits a diminishing marginal rate of technical substitution. That is, each extra worker allows the firm to reduce capital by a smaller amount as the ratio of capital to labor falls.

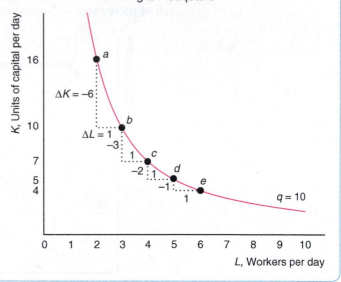

worker, $\Delta L = 1$, point *b*. If we drew a straight line from *a* to *b*, its slope would be $\Delta K/\Delta L = -6$. Thus, this slope tells us how many fewer units of capital (6) the firm can use if it hires one more worker.[8]

The slope of an isoquant is called the *marginal rate of technical substitution* (*MRTS*):

$$MRTS = \frac{\text{change in capital}}{\text{change in labor}} = \frac{\Delta K}{\Delta L}.$$

marginal rate of technical substitution (MRTS) the number of extra units of one input needed to replace one unit of another input that enables a firm to keep the amount of output it produces constant

The **marginal rate of technical substitution** tells us how many units of capital the firm can replace with an extra unit of labor while holding output constant. Because isoquants slope downward, the *MRTS* is negative. That is, the firm can produce a given level of output by substituting more capital for less labor (or vice versa).

Substitutability of Inputs Varies Along an Isoquant The marginal rate of technical substitution varies along a curved isoquant, as in Figure 6.4 for the service firm. If the firm is initially at point *a* and it hires one more worker, the firm gives up 6 units of capital and yet remains on the same isoquant at point *b*, so the *MRTS* is -6. If the firm hires another worker, the firm can reduce its capital by 3 units and yet stay on the same isoquant, moving from point *b* to *c*, so the *MRTS* is -3. If the firm moves from point *c* to *d*, the *MRTS* is -2; and if it moves from point *d* to *e*, the *MRTS* is -1. This decline in the *MRTS* (in absolute value) along an isoquant as the firm increases labor illustrates *diminishing marginal rates of technical substitution*. The more labor and less capital the firm has, the harder it is to replace remaining capital with labor and the flatter the isoquant becomes.

In the special case in which isoquants are straight lines, isoquants do not exhibit diminishing marginal rates of technical substitution because neither input becomes more valuable in the production process: The inputs remain perfect substitutes. Solved Problem 6.2 illustrates this result.

---

[8]The slope of the isoquant at a point equals the slope of a straight line that is tangent to the isoquant at that point. Thus, the straight line between two nearby points on an isoquant has nearly the same slope as that of the isoquant.

Solved Problem 6.2

Does the marginal rate of technical substitution vary along the isoquant for the firm that produced potato salad using Idaho and Maine potatoes? What is the *MRTS* at each point along the isoquant?

Answer

1. *Determine the shape of the isoquant.* As panel a of Figure 6.3 illustrates, the potato salad isoquants are straight lines because the two types of potatoes are perfect substitutes.

2. *On the basis of the shape, conclude whether the MRTS is constant along the isoquant.* Because the isoquant is a straight line, the slope is the same at every point, so the *MRTS* is constant.

3. *Determine the MRTS at each point.* Earlier, we showed that the slope of this isoquant was −1, so the MRTS is −1 at each point along the isoquant. That is, because the two inputs are perfect substitutes, 1 pound of Idaho potatoes can be replaced by 1 pound of Maine potatoes.

Substitutability of Inputs and Marginal Products   The marginal rate of technical substitution is equal to the negative of the ratio of marginal products, as we now show.[9] The marginal rate of technical substitution tells us how much a firm can increase one input and lower the other while still staying on the same isoquant. Knowing the marginal products of labor and capital, we can determine how much one input must increase to offset a reduction in the other.

Because the marginal product of labor, $MP_L = \Delta q/\Delta L$, is the increase in output per extra unit of labor, if the firm hires ΔL more workers, its output increases by $MP_L \times \Delta L$. For example, if the MP_L is 2 and the firm hires one extra worker, its output rises by 2 units.

A decrease in capital alone causes output to fall by $MP_K \times \Delta K$, where $MP_K = \Delta q/\Delta K$ is the marginal product of capital—the output the firm loses from decreasing capital by one unit, holding all other factors fixed. To keep output constant, $\Delta q = 0$, this fall in output from reducing capital must exactly equal the increase in output from increasing labor:

$$(MP_L \times \Delta L) + (MP_K \times \Delta K) = 0.$$

Rearranging these terms, we find that

$$-\frac{MP_L}{MP_K} = \frac{\Delta K}{\Delta L} = MRTS. \tag{6.3}$$

Thus, the negative of the ratio of the marginal products equals the *MRTS*.

We can use Equation 6.3 to explain why marginal rates of technical substitution diminish as we move to the right along the isoquant in Figure 6.4. The fewer pieces of capital per worker, the more valuable is each piece of capital, so the marginal product of capital rises. Similarly, the more workers per piece of capital, the lower is the marginal product of labor. As we replace capital with labor—move downward and to the right along the isoquant—the marginal product of capital increases and the marginal product of labor falls. Thus, the $MRTS = -MP_L/MP_K$ falls in absolute value as we move down and to the right along the isoquant.

---

[9]See Appendix 6B for a derivation using calculus.

Cobb-Douglas Production Function We can illustrate how to determine the *MRTS* for a particular production function, the Cobb-Douglas production function:[10]

$$q = AL^{\alpha}K^{\beta}, \tag{6.4}$$

where A, α, and β are all positive constants.

In empirical studies, economists have found that the production processes in a very large number of industries can be accurately summarized by the Cobb-Douglas production function. For the estimated production function of a service firm in Figure 6.4 (Devine et al., 2012), the Cobb-Douglas production function is $q = 2.35L^{0.5}K^{0.4}$, so $A = 2.35$, $\alpha = 0.5$, and $\beta = 0.4$.

The constants α and β determine the relationships between the marginal and average products of labor and capital (see Appendix 6C). The marginal product of labor is α times the average product of labor, $AP_L = q/L$:

$$MP_L = \alpha q/L = \alpha AP_L. \tag{6.5}$$

Similarly, the marginal product of capital is

$$MP_K = \beta q/K = \beta AP_K. \tag{6.6}$$

For a Cobb-Douglas production function, the marginal rate of technical substitution along an isoquant that holds output fixed at $\overline{q}$ is

$$MRTS = -\frac{MP_L}{MP_K} = -\frac{\alpha\overline{q}/L}{\beta\overline{q}/K} = -\frac{\alpha}{\beta}\frac{K}{L}. \tag{6.7}$$

For example, for the service firm, the $MRTS = -(0.5/0.4)K/L = -1.25K/L$. As we move down and to the right along the isoquant, the capital/labor ratio, K/L, falls, so the *MRTS* approaches zero.

6.5 Returns to Scale

So far, we have examined the effects of increasing one input while holding the other input constant (shifting from one isoquant to another) or decreasing the other input by an offsetting amount (the movement along a single isoquant). We now turn to the question of *how much output changes if a firm increases all its inputs proportionately*. The answer helps a firm determine its *scale* or size in the long run.

In the long run, a firm can increase its output by building a second plant and staffing it with the same number of workers as in the first one. Whether the firm chooses to do so depends in part on whether its output increases less than in proportion, in proportion, or more than in proportion to its inputs.

Constant, Increasing, and Decreasing Returns to Scale

constant returns to scale (CRS)
property of a production function whereby when all inputs are increased by a certain percentage, output increases by that same percentage

If, when all inputs are increased by a certain percentage and output increases by that same percentage, the production function is said to exhibit **constant returns to scale** (*CRS*). A firm's production process, $q = f(L, K)$, has constant returns to scale if, when the firm doubles its inputs—by, for example, building an identical second plant and using the same amount of labor and equipment as in the first plant—it doubles its output:

$$f(2L, 2K) = 2f(L, K) = 2q.$$

---

[10]This production function is named after its discoverers, Charles W. Cobb, a mathematician, and Paul H. Douglas, an economist and U.S. Senator.

We can check whether the potato salad production function has constant returns to scale. If a firm uses x_1 pounds of Idaho potatoes and y_1 pounds of Maine potatoes, it produces $q_1 = x_1 + y_1$ pounds of potato salad. If it doubles both inputs, using $x_2 = 2x_1$ Idaho and $y_2 = 2y_1$ Maine potatoes, it doubles its output:

$$q_2 = x_2 + y_2 = 2x_1 + 2y_1 = 2q_1.$$

Thus, the potato salad production function exhibits constant returns to scale.

If output rises more than in proportion to an equal percentage increase in all inputs, the production function is said to exhibit **increasing returns to scale** (*IRS*). A technology exhibits increasing returns to scale if doubling inputs more than doubles the output:

$$f(2L, 2K) > 2f(L, K) = 2q.$$

Why might a production function have increasing returns to scale? One reason is that, although it could duplicate a small factory and double its output, the firm might be able to more than double its output by building a single large plant, thereby allowing for greater specialization of labor or capital. In the two smaller plants, workers have to perform many unrelated tasks such as operating, maintaining, and fixing the machines they use. In the large plant, some workers may specialize in maintaining and fixing machines, thereby increasing efficiency. Similarly, a firm may use specialized equipment in a large plant but not in a small one.

If output rises less than in proportion to an equal percentage increase in all inputs, the production function exhibits **decreasing returns to scale** (*DRS*). A technology exhibits decreasing returns to scale if doubling inputs causes output to rise less than in proportion:

$$f(2L, 2K) < 2f(L, K) = 2q.$$

One reason for decreasing returns to scale is that the difficulty of organizing, coordinating, and integrating activities increases with firm size. An owner may be able to manage one plant well but may have trouble running two plants. In some sense, the owner's difficulties in running a larger firm may reflect our failure to take into account some factor such as management in our production function. When the firm increases the various inputs, it does not increase the management input in proportion. If so, the "decreasing returns to scale" is really due to a fixed input. Another reason is that large teams of workers may not function as well as small teams, in which each individual takes greater personal responsibility.

This'll save a lot of time!

increasing returns to scale (IRS) property of a production function whereby output rises more than in proportion to an equal increase in all inputs

decreasing returns to scale (DRS) property of a production function whereby output increases less than in proportion to an equal percentage increase in all inputs

---

Solved Problem 6.3

Under what conditions does a Cobb-Douglas production function (Equation 6.4, $q = AL^\alpha K^\beta$) exhibit decreasing, constant, or increasing returns to scale?

Answer

1. *Show how output changes if both inputs are doubled.* If the firm initially uses L and K amounts of inputs, it produces $q_1 = AL^\alpha K^\beta$. After the firm doubles the amount of both labor and capital it uses, it produces

$$q_2 = A(2L)^\alpha(2K)^\beta = 2^{\alpha+\beta}AL^\alpha K^\beta = 2^{\alpha+\beta}q_1. \tag{6.8}$$

That is, q_2 is $2^{\alpha+\beta}$ times q_1. If we define $\gamma = \alpha + \beta$, then Equation 6.8 tells us that

$$q_2 = 2^{\gamma}q_1. \tag{6.9}$$

Thus, if the inputs double, output increases by 2^{γ}.

2. *Give a rule for determining the returns to scale.* If $\gamma = 1$, we know from Equation 6.9 that $q_2 = 2^1 q_1 = 2q_1$. That is, output doubles when the inputs double, so the Cobb-Douglas production function has constant returns to scale. If $\gamma < 1$, then $q_2 = 2^{\gamma}q_1 < 2q_1$ because $2^{\gamma} < 2$. That is, when inputs double, output increases less than in proportion, so this Cobb-Douglas production function exhibits decreasing returns to scale. For example, if $\gamma = 0.8$, then $q_2 = 2^{0.8}q_1 \approx 1.74q_1$, so doubling inputs increases output by only 1.74 times. Finally, the Cobb-Douglas production function has increasing returns to scale if $\gamma > 1$, so that $q_2 > 2q_1$. For example, if $\gamma = 1.2$, then $q_2 = 2^{1.2}q_1 \approx 2.3q_1$. Thus, the rule for determining returns to scale for a Cobb-Douglas production function is that the returns to scale are decreasing if $\gamma < 1$, constant if $\gamma = 1$, and increasing if $\gamma > 1$.

Comment: One interpretation of γ is that it is the elasticity of output with respect to all inputs. When all inputs increase by 1%, output increases by γ%. For example, if $\gamma = 1$, a 1% increase in all inputs increases output by 1%, so the elasticity equals one.

Application

Returns to Scale in Various Industries

Increasing, constant, and decreasing returns to scale are commonly observed. The table shows estimates of Cobb-Douglas production functions and returns to scale in various industries.

	Labor, α	Capital, β	Scale, $\gamma = \alpha + \beta$
Decreasing Returns to Scale			
U.S. tobacco products[a]	0.18	0.33	0.51
Bangladesh glass[b]	0.27	0.45	0.72
Danish food and beverages[c]	0.69	0.18	0.87
Chinese high technology[d]	0.28	0.66	0.94
Constant Returns to Scale			
Japanese synthetic rubber[e]	0.50	0.50	1.00
Japanese beer[e]	0.60	0.40	1.00
New Zealand wholesale trade[f]	0.60	0.42	1.02
Danish publish and printing[c]	0.89	0.14	1.03
Increasing Returns to Scale			
New Zealand mining[f]	0.69	0.45	1.14
Bangladesh leather products[b]	0.86	0.27	1.13
Bangladesh fabricated metal[b]	0.98	0.28	1.26

[a]Hsieh (1995); [b]Hossain et al. (2012); [c]Fox and Smeets (2011); [d]Zhang et al. (2012); [e]Flath (2011); [f]Devine et al. (2012).

The accompanying graphs use isoquants to illustrate the returns to scale for three firms: a Japanese beer firm, a U.S. tobacco firm, and a Bangladesh fabricated metal firm. We measure the units of labor, capital, and output so that, for all three firms, 100 units of labor and 100 units of capital produce 100 units of output on the $q = 100$ isoquant in the three panels. These graphs illustrate that the spacing of the isoquant reflects the returns to scale. The closer together the $q = 100$ and $q = 200$ isoquants, the greater the returns to scale.

In panel a, the beer firm has constant returns to scale because $\gamma = 1$: A 1% increase in the inputs causes output to rise by 1%. If both its labor and capital are doubled from 100 to 200 units, output doubles to 200 ($= 100 \times 2^1$, multiplying the original output by the rate of increase using Equation 6.9).

In panel b, the tobacco firm has decreasing returns to scale because $\gamma = 0.51$. The same doubling of inputs causes output to rise to only 142 ($\approx 100 \times 2^{0.51}$) for the tobacco firm: output rises less than in proportion to inputs.

In panel c, the fabricated metal firm exhibits increasing returns to scale because $\gamma = 1.26$. If it doubles its inputs, its output more than doubles, to 239 ($\approx 100 \times 2^{1.26}$), so the production function has increasing returns to scale.

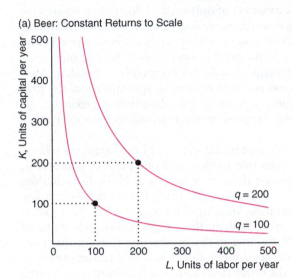

(a) Beer: Constant Returns to Scale

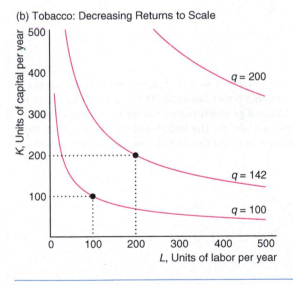

(b) Tobacco: Decreasing Returns to Scale

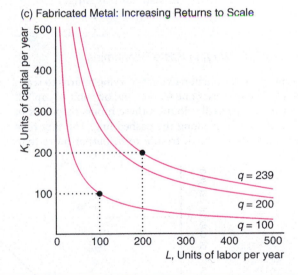

(c) Fabricated Metal: Increasing Returns to Scale

Varying Returns to Scale

When the production function is a Cobb-Douglas, the returns to scale are the same at all levels of output. However, in other industries, a production function's returns to scale may vary as the output level changes. A firm might, for example, have increasing returns to scale at low levels of output, constant returns to scale for some range of output, and decreasing returns to scale at higher levels of output.

Sato and Söderbom (2012) found that the returns to scale fell with firm size for Swedish firms. The returns to scale were 1.156 for micro firms (fewer than 10 employees), 1.081 for small firms (10 to 49 employees), 1.010 for medium-sized firms (50 to 249 employees), and 0.934 for large firms.

Many production functions have increasing returns to scale for small amounts of output, constant returns for moderate amounts of output, and decreasing returns for large amounts of output. When a firm is small, increasing labor and capital allows for gains from cooperation between workers and greater specialization of workers and equipment—*returns to specialization*—so the production function exhibits increasing returns to scale. As the firm grows, returns to scale are eventually exhausted. After the firm grows to the point where it has no more returns to specialization, the production process exhibits constant returns to scale. If the firm continues to grow, the owner starts having difficulty managing everyone, so the firm suffers from decreasing returns to scale.

We show such a pattern in Figure 6.5. Again, the spacing of the isoquants reflects the returns to scale. Initially, the firm has one worker and one piece of equipment, point *a*, and produces 1 unit of output on the $q = 1$ isoquant. If the firm doubles its inputs, it produces at *b*, where $L = 2$ and $K = 2$, which lies on the dashed line through the origin and point *a*. Output more than doubles to $q = 3$, so the production function exhibits increasing returns to scale in this range. Another doubling of inputs to *c* causes output to double to 6 units, so the production function has constant returns to scale in this range. Another doubling of inputs to *d* causes output to increase by only a third, to $q = 8$, so the production function has decreasing returns to scale in this range.

Figure 6.5 Varying Scale Economies

This production function exhibits varying returns to scale. Initially, the firm uses one worker and one unit of capital, point *a*. It repeatedly doubles these inputs to points *b*, *c*, and *d*, which lie along the dashed line. The first time the inputs are doubled, from *a* to *b*, output more than doubles from $q = 1$ to $q = 3$, so the production function has increasing returns to scale. The next doubling, from *b* to *c*, causes a proportionate increase in output, constant returns to scale. At the last doubling, from *c* to *d*, the production function exhibits decreasing returns to scale.

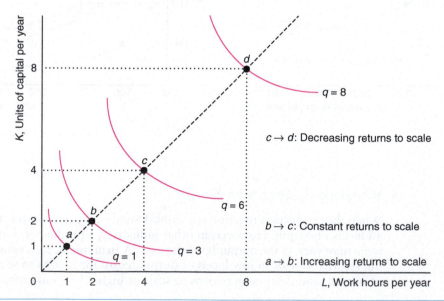

6.6 Productivity and Technical Change

Because firms may use different technologies and different methods of organizing production, the amount of output that one firm produces from a given amount of inputs may differ from that produced by another firm. Further, after a technical or managerial innovation, a firm can produce more today from a given amount of inputs than it could in the past.

Relative Productivity

This chapter has assumed that firms produce efficiently. A firm must produce efficiently to maximize its profit. However, even if each firm in a market produces as efficiently as possible, firms may not be equally *productive*—one firm may be able to produce more than another from a given amount of inputs.

A firm may be more productive than another if its management knows a better way to organize production or if it has access to a new invention. Union-mandated work rules, racial or gender discrimination, government regulations, or other institutional restrictions that affect only certain firms may lower the relative productivity of those firms.

Differences in productivity across markets may be due to differences in the degree of competition. In competitive markets, where many firms can enter and exit easily, less productive firms lose money and are driven out of business, so the firms that continue to produce are equally productive (see Chapter 8). In a less competitive market with few firms and no possibility of entry by new ones, a less productive firm may be able to survive, so firms with varying levels of productivity are observed.[11]

Application **A Good Boss Raises Productivity**	Does a good supervisor make workers more productive? To answer this question, Lazear et al. (2012) looked at a large service-oriented company. Supervisor quality varied substantially as measured by the boss effect on worker productivity. Replacing one of the 10% worst bosses with one of the 10% best ones raised a team's output by about the same amount as would adding one worker to a nine-member team. Thus, differences in managers can cause one firm to be more productive than another.

Innovations

In its production process, a firm tries to use the best available technological and managerial knowledge. An advance in knowledge that allows more output to be produced with the same level of inputs is called **technical progress**. The invention of new products is a form of technical innovation. The use of robotic arms increases the number of automobiles produced with a given amount of labor and raw materials. Better *management* or *organization of the production process* similarly allows the firm to produce more output from given levels of inputs.

technical progress an advance in knowledge that allows more output to be produced with the same level of inputs

---

[11]See MyEconLab, Chapter 6, "German Versus British Productivity" and "U.S. Electric Generation Efficiency."

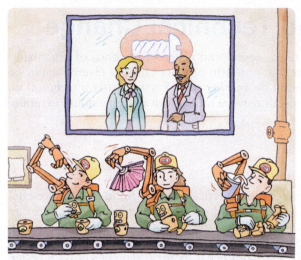

Surprisingly, those robo-arms increase productivity substantially.

Technical Progress   A technological innovation changes the production process. Last year a firm produced

$$q_1 = f(L, K)$$

units of output using L units of labor services and K units of capital service. Due to a new invention that the firm uses, this year's production function differs from last year's, so the firm produces 10% more output with the same inputs:

$$q_2 = 1.1 f(L, K).$$

Flath (2011) estimated the annual rate of technical innovation in Japanese manufacturing firms to be 0.91% for electric copper, 0.87% for medicine, 0.33% for steel pipes and tubes, 0.19% for cement, and 0.08% for beer. Chou et al. (2012) estimated that the annual average productivity growth rate was 10.2% in information technology (IT) goods and service industries for 19 developed countries.

This type of technological progress reflects *neutral technical change*, in which a firm can produce more output using the same ratio of inputs. For example, a technical innovation in the form of a new printing press may allow more output to be produced using the same ratio of inputs as before: one worker to one printing press. In our neutral technical change example, the firm's rate of growth of output was $10\% = \Delta q/q_1 = [1.1f(L, K) - f(L, K)]/f(L, K)$ in one year due to the technical change.

Neutral technical progress leaves the shapes of the isoquants unchanged. However, each isoquant is now associated with more output. For example, in Figure 6.5, if neutral technical progress occurred that doubled output for any combination of inputs, we would relabel the isoquants from lowest to highest as $q = 2$, $q = 6$, $q = 12$, and $q = 16$.

Nonneutral technical changes are innovations that alter the proportion in which inputs are used. If a printing press that required two people to operate is replaced by one that can be run by a single worker, the technical change is *labor saving*. Basker (2012) found that the introduction of barcode scanners in grocery stores increased the average product of labor by 4.5% on average across stores. Amazon bought Kiva Systems in 2012 with the intention of using its robots to move items in Amazon's warehouses, partially replacing workers. Other robots help doctors perform surgery quicker and reduce patients' recovery times. Here, technical progress changes the shapes of isoquants.

Organizational Change   Organizational change may also alter the production function and increase the amount of output produced by a given amount of inputs. In the early 1900s, Henry Ford revolutionized mass production through two organizational innovations. First, he introduced interchangeable parts, which cut the time required to install parts because workers no longer had to file or machine individually made parts to get them to fit.

Second, Ford introduced a conveyor belt and an assembly line to his production process. Before this innovation, workers walked around the car, and each worker performed many assembly activities. In Ford's plant, each worker specialized in a single activity such as attaching the right rear fender to the chassis. A conveyor belt moved the car at a constant speed from worker to worker along the assembly line. Because his workers gained proficiency from specializing in only a few activities, and because the conveyor belts reduced the number of movements workers had to make,

Ford could produce more automobiles with the same number of workers. These innovations reduced the ratio of labor to capital used. In 1908, the Ford Model T sold for $850, when rival vehicles sold for $2,000. By the early 1920s, Ford had increased production from fewer than a thousand cars per year to two million cars per year.

Application

Tata Nano's Technical and Organizational Innovations

In 2009, the automotive world was stunned when India's Tata Motors introduced the Nano, its tiny, fuel-efficient four-passenger car. With a base price of less than $2,500, it was by far the world's least expensive car. The next cheapest car in India, the Maruti 800, sold for about $4,800.

The Nano's dramatically lower price was not the result of amazing new inventions, but rather due to organizational innovations that led to simplifications and the use of less expensive materials and procedures. Although Tata Motors filed for 34 patents related to the design of the Nano (compared to the roughly 280 patents awarded to General Motors annually), most of these patents were for mundane items such as the two-cylinder engine's balance shaft and the configuration of the transmission gears.

Instead of relying on innovations, Tata reorganized both production and distribution to lower costs. It reduced manufacturing costs at every stage of the process with a no-frills design, decreased vehicle weight, and made other major production improvements.

The Nano has a single windshield wiper, one side-view mirror, no power steering, a simplified door-opening lever, three nuts on the wheels instead of the customary four, and a trunk that does not open from the outside—it is accessed by folding down the rear seats. The Nano has smaller overall dimensions than the Maruti, but about 20% more seating capacity because of design decisions, such as putting the wheels at the extreme edges of the car. The Nano is much lighter than comparable models due to the reduced amount of steel, the use of lightweight steel, and the use of aluminum in the engine. The ribbed roof structure is not only a style element but also a strength structure, which is necessary because the design uses thin-gauge sheet metal. Because the engine is in the rear, the driveshaft doesn't need complex joints as in a front-engine car with front-wheel drive. To cut costs further, the company reduced the number of tools needed to make the components and thereby increased the life of the dies used by three times the norm. In consultation with their suppliers, Tata's engineers determined how many useful parts the design required, which helped them identify functions that could be integrated in parts.

Tata's plant can produce 250,000 Nanos per year and benefits from economies of scale. However, Tata's major organizational innovation was its open distribution and remote assembly. The Nano's modular design enables an experienced mechanic to assemble the car in a workshop. Therefore, Tata Motors can distribute a complete knock-down kit to be assembled and serviced by local assembly hubs and entrepreneurs closer to consumers. The cost of transporting these kits, produced at a central manufacturing plant, is charged directly to the customer. This approach is expected to speed up the distribution process, particularly in the more remote locations of India. The car has been a great success. By 2013, Tata was the nation's largest car company and was selling the Nano in other countries, such as Jamaica.

Challenge Solution

Labor Productivity During Recessions

We can use what we've learned to answer the question posed at the beginning of the chapter about how labor productivity, as measured by the average product of labor, changes during a recession when a firm reduces its output by reducing the number of workers it employs. How much will the output produced per worker rise or fall with each additional layoff?

In the short run when the firm holds its capital constant, layoffs have the positive effect of freeing up machines to be used by the remaining workers. However, if layoffs mean that the remaining workers might have to "multitask" to replace departed colleagues, the firm will lose the benefits from specialization. When a firm has many workers, the advantage of freeing up machines is important and increased multitasking is unlikely to be a problem. With only a few workers, freeing up more machines does not help much—some machines might stand idle part of the time—while multitasking becomes a more serious problem. As a result, laying off a worker might raise the average product of labor if the firm has many workers relative to the available capital, but might reduce average product if it has only a few workers.

For example, in panel b of Figure 6.1, the average product of labor rises with the number of workers up to six workers and then falls as the number of workers increases. As a result, the average product of labor falls if the firm initially has two to six workers and lays one off, but rises if the firm initially has more seven or more workers and lays off a worker.

However, for some production functions, layoffs always raise labor productivity because the AP_L curve is downward sloping everywhere. For such a production function, the positive effect of freeing up capital always dominates any negative effect of layoffs on the average product of labor.

Consider a Cobb-Douglas production function, $q = AL^\alpha K^\beta$, where $AP_L = q/L = q = AL^{\alpha-1}K^\beta$. As Appendix 6C shows, if we increase labor slightly the change in the AP_L is $(\alpha - 1)AL^{\alpha-2}K^\beta$. Thus, if $(\alpha - 1)$ is negative (that is, $\alpha < 1$), the AP_L falls with extra labor. This condition holds for all of the estimated Cobb-Douglas production functions listed in the Application "Returns to Scale in Various Industries" (though not necessarily in all industries).

For example, for the beer firm's estimated Cobb-Douglas production function (Flath, 2011), $q = AL^{0.6}K^{0.4}$, $\alpha = 0.6$ is less than 1, so the AP_L curve slopes downward at every quantity. We can illustrate how much the AP_L rises with a layoff for this particular production function. If $A = 1$ and $L = K = 10$ initially, then the firm's output is $q = 10^{0.6} \times 10^{0.4} = 10$, and its average product of labor is $AP_L = q/L = 10/10 = 1$. If the number of workers is reduced by one, then output falls to $q = 9^{0.6} \times 10^{0.4} \approx 9.39$, and the average product of labor rises to $AP_L \approx 9.39/9 \approx 1.04$. That is, a 10% reduction in labor causes output to *fall* by 6.1%, but causes the average product of labor to *rise* by 4%. The firm's output falls less than 10% because each remaining worker is more productive.

This increase in labor productivity in many industries reduces the impact of the recession on output in the United States. However, this increase in labor productivity is not always observed in other countries that are less likely to lay off workers during a downturn. Until recently, most large Japanese firms did not lay off workers during recessions. Thus, in contrast to U.S. firms, their average product of labor decreased substantially during recessions because their output fell while labor remained constant.

Similarly, European firms show 30% less employment volatility over time than do U.S. firms, at least in part because European firms that fire workers are subject to a tax (Veracierto, 2008).[12] Consequently, with other factors held constant in the short run, recessions might be more damaging to the profit and output of a Japanese or European firm than to the profit and output of a comparable U.S. firm. However, retaining good workers over short-run downturns might be a good long-run policy for the firm as well as for workers.

---

[12]Severance payments for blue-collar workers with ten years of experience may exceed one year of wages in some European countries, unlike in the United States.

Summary

1. **The Ownership and Management of Firms.** The three types of firms are private, public, and nonprofit. Private firms may be sole proprietorships, partnerships, or corporations. In small firms (particularly sole proprietorships and partnerships), the owners usually run the company. In large firms (such as most corporations), the owners hire a manager to run the company. Owners want to maximize profits. If managers have different objectives than owners, owners must keep a close watch over managers to ensure that profits are maximized.

2. **Production Function.** A production function summarizes how a firm combines inputs such as labor, capital, and materials to produce output using the current state of knowledge about technology and management. A production function shows how much output can be produced efficiently from various levels of inputs. A firm produces efficiently if it cannot produce its current level of output with less of any one input, holding other inputs constant.

3. **Short-Run Production.** In the short run, a firm cannot adjust the quantity of some inputs, such as capital. The firm varies its output by adjusting its variable inputs, such as labor. If all factors are fixed except labor, and a firm that was using very little labor increases its use of labor, its output may rise more than in proportion to the increase in labor because of greater specialization of workers. Eventually, however, as more workers are hired, the workers get in each other's way or wait to share equipment, so output increases by smaller and smaller amounts. This latter phenomenon is described by the law of diminishing marginal returns: The marginal product of an input—the extra output from the last unit of input—eventually decreases as more of that input is used, holding other inputs fixed.

4. **Long-Run Production.** In the long run, when all inputs are variable, firms can substitute between inputs. An isoquant shows the combinations of inputs that can produce a given level of output. The marginal rate of technical substitution is the absolute value of the slope of the isoquant and indicates how easily the firm can substitute one factor of production for another. Usually, the more of one input the firm uses, the more difficult it is to substitute that input for another input, so the marginal rates of technical substitution decreases.

5. **Returns to Scale.** If, when a firm increases all inputs in proportion, its output increases by the same proportion, the production process is said to exhibit constant returns to scale. If output increases less than in proportion to inputs, the production process has decreasing returns to scale; if it increases more than in proportion to inputs, it has increasing returns to scale. All three types of returns to scale are commonly seen in actual industries. Many production processes exhibit first increasing, then constant, and finally decreasing returns to scale as the size of the firm increases.

6. **Productivity and Technical Change.** Although all firms in an industry produce efficiently, given what they know and the institutional and other constraints they face, some firms may be more productive than others: They can produce more output from a given bundle of inputs. Technological progress allows a firm to produce a given level of output using fewer inputs than it did previously. Technological progress changes the production function.

Questions

All questions are available on MyEconLab; * = *answer appears at the back of this book;* **A** = *algebra problem;* **C** = *calculus problem.*

1. The Ownership and Management of Firms

1.1 Are firms with limited liability likely to be larger than other firms? Why?

1.2 What types of firms would not normally maximize profit?

1.3 What types of organization allow owners of a firm to obtain the advantages of limited liability?

2. Production Function

2.1 With respect to production functions, how long is the *short run*?

2.2 Consider Boeing (a producer of jet aircraft), General Mills (a producer of breakfast cereals), and Wacky Jack's (which claims to be the largest U.S. provider of singing telegrams). For which of these firms is the *short run* the longest period of time? For which is the long run the shortest? Explain.

*2.3 Suppose that for the production function $q = f(L, K)$, if $L = 3$ and $K = 5$ then $q = 10$. Is it possible that $L = 3$ and $K = 6$ also produces $q = 10$ for this production function? Why or why not?

3. Short-Run Production

*3.1 If each extra worker produces an extra unit of output, how do the total product, average product of labor, and marginal product of labor vary with labor?

3.2 If the production function is $q = f(L, K) = 3L + 2K$, and capital is fixed at $\overline{K} = 50$, what is the short-run production function? What is the marginal product of labor? (*Hint*: See Solved Problem 6.1.)

*3.3. Suppose that the production function is $q = L^{0.75}K^{0.25}$.

   a. What is the average product of labor, holding capital fixed at $\overline{K}$? **A**

   b. What is the marginal product of labor? (*Hints*: See Solved Problem 6.1. Calculate how much q changes as L increases by 1 unit for a particular pair of K and L, use calculus, or see Appendix 6C.) **C**

3.4 Each extra worker produces an extra unit of output up to six workers. After six, no additional output is produced. Draw the total product, average product of labor, and marginal product of labor curves.

3.5 Why do we expect the law of diminishing marginal returns to hold?

3.6 Ben swims 50,000 yards per week in his practices. Given this amount of training, he will swim the 100-yard butterfly in 52.6 seconds and place tenth in a big upcoming meet. Ben's coach calculates that if Ben increases his practice to 60,000 yards per week, his time will decrease to 50.7 seconds and he will place eighth in the meet. If Ben practices 70,000 yards per week, his time will be 49.9 and he will win the meet.

   a. In terms of Ben's *time* in the big meet, what is his marginal productivity of the number of yards he practices? Does the marginal product diminish as the practice yards increase?

   b. In terms of Ben's *place* in the big meet, what is his marginal productivity of the number of yards he practices? Does the marginal product diminish as the practice yards increase?

   c. Does Ben's marginal productivity of the number of yards he practices depend on how he measures his productivity, either place or time, in the big meet?

3.7 In the short run, a firm cannot vary its capital, $K = 2$, but can vary its labor, L. It produces output q. Explain why the firm will or will not experience diminishing marginal returns to labor in the short run if its production function is

   a. $q = 10L + K$.

   b. $q = L^{0.5}K^{0.5}$. **C**

3.8 Based on the information in the Application "Malthus and the Green Revolution," how did the average product of labor in corn production change over time?

4. Long-Run Production

4.1 Draw a circle in a diagram with labor services on one axis and capital services on the other. This circle represents all the combinations of labor and capital that produce 100 units of output. Now, draw the isoquant for 100 units of output. (*Hint*: Remember that the isoquant includes only the efficient combinations of labor and capital.)

4.2 What is the difference between an isoquant and an indifference curve?

4.3 Why must isoquants be thin? (*Hint*: See the explanation of why indifference in Chapter 4.)

4.4 Suppose that a firm has a fixed-proportions production function, in which one unit of output is produced using one worker and two units of capital. If the firm has an extra worker and no more capital, it still can produce only one unit of output. Similarly, one more unit of capital does the firm no good.

   a. Draw the isoquants for this production function.

   b. Draw the total product, average product, and marginal product of labor curves (you will probably want to use two diagrams) for this production function.

4.5 According to Card (2009), (a) workers with less than a high school education are perfect substitutes for those with a high school education, (b) "high school equivalent" and "college equivalent" workers are imperfect substitutes, and (c) within education groups, immigrants and natives are imperfect substitutes. For each of these comparisons, draw the isoquants for a production function that uses two types of workers. For example, in part (a), production is a function of workers with a high school diploma and workers with less education.

4.6 What is the production function if L and K are perfect substitutes and each unit of q requires 1 unit of L or 1 unit of K (or a combination of these inputs that adds up to 1)?

*4.7 At $L = 4$ and $K = 4$, the marginal product of labor is 2 and the marginal product of capital is 3. What is the marginal rate of technical substitution? **A**

*4.8 Mark launders his white clothes using the production function $q = B + 0.5G$, where B is the number of cups of Clorox bleach and G is the number of cups of generic bleach that is half as potent. Draw an isoquant. What are the marginal products of B and G? If B is on the vertical axis, what is the marginal rate of technical substitution at each point on an isoquant? (*Hint*: See Solved Problem 6.2.)

*4.9 To produce a recorded CD, $q = 1$, a firm uses one blank disk, $D = 1$, and the services of a recording machine, $M = 1$, for one hour. Draw an isoquant for this production process. Explain the reason for its shape.

4.10 The production function at Ginko's Copy Shop is $q = 1,000 \times \min(L, 3K)$, where q is the number of copies per hour, L is the number of workers, and K is the number of copy machines. As an example, if $L = 4$ and $K = 1$, then $\min(L, 3K) = 3$, and $q = 3,000$.

  a. Draw the isoquants for this production function.

  b. Draw the total product, average product, and marginal product of labor curves for this production function for some fixed level of capital.

4.11 Using the figure in the Application "A Semiconductor Integrated Circuit Isoquant," show that as the firm employs additional fixed-proportion technologies, the firm's overall isoquant approaches a smooth curve.

4.12 By studying, Will can produce a higher grade, G_W, on an upcoming economics exam. His production function depends on the number of hours he studies marginal analysis problems, A, and the number of hours he studies supply-and-demand problems, R. Specifically, $G_W = 2.5A^{0.36}R^{0.64}$. His roommate David's grade-production function is

$$G_D = 2.5A^{0.25}R^{0.75}.$$

  a. What is Will's marginal product of studying supply-and-demand problems? What is David's? (*Hint*: See Appendix 6C.)

  b. What is Will's marginal rate of technical substitution between studying the two types of problems? What is David's?

  c. Is it possible that Will and David have different marginal productivity functions but the same marginal rate of technical substitution functions? Explain. (*Hint*: See the section "Cobb-Douglas Production Function.") **C**

5. Returns to Scale

5.1 To speed relief to isolated South Asian communities that were devastated by the December 2004 tsunami, the U.S. government doubled the number of helicopters from 45 to 90 in early 2005. Navy admiral Thomas Fargo, head of the U.S. Pacific Command, was asked if doubling the number of helicopters would "produce twice as much [relief]." He predicted, "Maybe pretty close to twice as much." (Vicky O'Hara, *All Things Considered*, National Public Radio, January 4, 2005, **www.npr.org/dmg/dmg.php?prgCode=ATC&showDate=04-Jan-2005&segNum=10&NPRMediaPref=WM&getAd=1**). Identify the outputs and inputs and describe the production process. Is the admiral discussing a production process with nearly constant returns to scale, or is he referring to another property of the production process?

5.2 Michelle's business produces ceramic cups using labor, clay, and a kiln. She can manufacture 25 cups a day with one worker and 35 with two workers. Does her production process necessarily illustrate *decreasing returns to scale* or *diminishing marginal returns to labor*? What is the likely explanation for why output doesn't increase proportionately with the number of workers?

5.3 Show in a diagram that a production function can have diminishing marginal returns to a factor and constant returns to scale.

5.4 Under what conditions do the following production functions exhibit decreasing, constant, or increasing returns to scale?

  a. $q = L + K$

  b. $q = L^\alpha K^\beta$

  c. $q = L + L^\alpha K^\beta + K$
  (*Hint*: See Solved Problem 6.3.) **A**

*5.5 Haskel and Sadun (2012) estimate the production function for U.K. supermarkets is $Q = L^{0.23}K^{0.10}M^{0.66}$, where L is labor, K is capital, and M is materials. What kind of returns to scale do these production functions exhibit? (*Hint*: See Solved Problem 6.3.) **A**

5.6 A production function is said to be homogeneous of degree γ if $f(xL, xK) = x^\gamma f(L, K)$, where x is a positive constant. That is, the production function has the same returns to scale for every combination of inputs. For such a production function, show that the marginal product of labor and marginal product of capital functions are homogeneous of degree if $\gamma - 1$. **C**

5.7 Is it possible that a firm's production function exhibits increasing returns to scale while exhibiting diminishing marginal productivity of each of its inputs? To answer this question, calculate the marginal productivities of capital and labor for U.S. tobacco products, Japanese beer, and Bangladesh fabricated metal firms using the information listed in the Application "Returns to Scale in Various Industries." (*Hint*: See Appendix 6C.) **A**

6. Productivity and Technical Change

6.1. Does it follow that because we observe that the average product of labor is higher for Firm 1 than for Firm 2, Firm 1 is more productive in the sense that it can produce more output from a given amount of inputs? Why?

*6.2 Firm 1 and Firm 2 use the same type of production function, but Firm 1 is only 90% as productive as Firm 2. That is, the production function of Firm 2 is $q_2 = f(L, K)$, and the production function of Firm 1 is $q_1 = 0.9f(L, K)$. At a particular level of inputs, how does the marginal product of labor differ between the firms? **C**

6.3 Until the mid-eighteenth century when spinning became mechanized, cotton was an expensive and relatively unimportant textile (Virginia Postrel, "What Separates Rich Nations from Poor Nations?" *New York Times*, January 1, 2004). Where it used to take an Indian hand-spinner 50,000 hours to hand-spin 100 pounds of cotton, an operator of a 1760s-era hand-operated cotton mule-spinning machine could produce 100 pounds of stronger thread in 300 hours. When the self-acting mule spinner automated the process after 1825, the time dropped to 135 hours, and cotton became an inexpensive, common cloth. Was this technological progress neutral? In a figure, show how these technological changes affected isoquants.

6.4 In a manufacturing plant, workers use a specialized machine to produce belts. A new machine is invented that is laborsaving. With the new machine, the firm can use fewer workers and still produce the same number of belts as it did using the old machine. In the long run, both labor and capital (the machine) are variable. From what you know, what is the effect of this invention on the AP_L, MP_L, and returns to scale? If you require more information to answer this question, specify what you need to know.

7. Challenge

7.1 How would the answer to the Challenge Solution change if we used the marginal product of labor rather than the average product of labor as our measure of labor productivity?

*7.2 During recessions, U.S. firms lay off a larger proportion of their workers than Japanese firms do. (It has been claimed that Japanese firms continue to produce at high levels and store the output or sell it at relatively low prices during the recession.) Assuming that the production function remains unchanged over a period that is long enough to include many recessions and expansions, would you expect the average product of labor to be higher in Japan or the United States? Why?

Costs

An economist is a person who, when invited to give a talk at a banquet, tells the audience there's no such thing as a free lunch.

The manager of a semiconductor manufacturing firm, who can choose from many different production technologies, must determine whether the firm should use the same technology in its foreign plant that it uses in its domestic plant. U.S. semiconductor manufacturing firms have been moving much of their production abroad since 1961, when Fairchild Semiconductor built a plant in Hong Kong. According to the Semiconductor Industry Association, worldwide semiconductor sales from the Americas dropped from 66% in 1976, to 34% in 1998, and to 18% in April 2013.

Semiconductor firms are moving their production abroad because of lower taxes, lower labor costs, and capital grant benefits. Capital grants are funds provided by a foreign government to a firm to induce them to produce in that country. Such grants can reduce the cost of owning and operating an overseas semiconductor fabrication facility by as much as 25% compared to the costs of a U.S.-based plant.

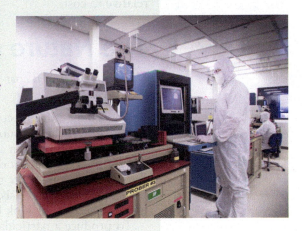

The semiconductor manufacturer can produce a chip using sophisticated equipment and relatively few workers or many workers and less complex equipment. In the United States, firms use a relatively capital-intensive technology, because doing so minimizes their cost of producing a given level of output. Will that same technology be cost minimizing if they move their production abroad?

A firm uses a two-step procedure in determining how to produce a certain amount of output efficiently. It first determines which production processes are *technologically efficient* so that it can produce the desired level of output with the least amount of inputs. As we saw in Chapter 6, the firm uses engineering and other information to determine its production function, which summarizes the many technologically efficient production processes available.

The firm's second step is to pick from these technologically efficient production processes the one that is also **economically efficient**, minimizing the cost of producing a specified amount of output. To determine which process minimizes its cost of production, the firm uses information about the production function and the cost of inputs.

economically efficient minimizing the cost of producing a specified amount of output

By reducing its cost of producing a given level of output, a firm can increase its profit. Any profit-maximizing competitive, monopolistic, or oligopolistic firm minimizes its cost of production.

| In this chapter, we examine five main topics | 1. **The Nature of Costs.** When considering the cost of a proposed action, a good manager of a firm takes account of forgone alternative opportunities. |

2. **Short-Run Costs.** To minimize its costs in the short run, a firm adjusts its variable factors (such as labor), but it cannot adjust its fixed factors (such as capital).

3. **Long-Run Costs.** In the long run, a firm adjusts all its inputs because usually all inputs are variable.

4. **Lower Costs in the Long Run.** Long-run cost is as low as or lower than short-run cost because the firm has more flexibility in the long run, technological progress occurs, and workers and managers learn from experience.

5. **Cost of Producing Multiple Goods.** If the firm produces several goods simultaneously, the cost of each may depend on the quantity of all the goods produced.

Businesspeople and economists need to understand the relationship between costs of inputs and production to determine the least costly way to produce. Economists have an additional reason for wanting to know about costs. As we'll see in later chapters, the relationship between output and costs plays an important role in determining the nature of a market—how many firms are in the market and how high price is relative to cost.

7.1 The Nature of Costs

How much would it cost you to stand at the wrong end of a shooting gallery?
—S. J. Perelman

To show how a firm's cost varies with its output, we first have to measure costs. Businesspeople and economists often measure costs differently. Economists include all relevant costs. To run a firm profitably, a manager should think like an economist and consider all relevant costs. Although a skilled manager acknowledges this point, the manager may direct the firm's accountant or bookkeeper to measure costs in ways that are more consistent with tax laws and other laws so as to make the firm's financial statements look better to stockholders or minimize the firm's taxes.

To produce a particular amount of output, a firm incurs costs for the required inputs such as labor, capital, energy, and materials. A firm's manager (or accountant) determines the cost of labor, energy, and materials by multiplying the factor's price by the number of units used. If workers earn $20 per hour and work a total of 100 hours per day, then the firm's cost of labor is $20 \times 100 = $2,000$ per day. The manager can easily calculate these *explicit costs*, which are its direct, out-of-pocket payments for inputs to its production process within a given time period. While calculating explicit costs is straightforward, some costs are *implicit* in that they reflect only a forgone opportunity rather than an explicit, current expenditure. Properly taking account of forgone opportunities requires particularly careful attention when dealing with durable capital goods, as past expenditures for an input may be irrelevant to current cost calculations if that input has no current, alternative use.

Opportunity Costs

economic cost or opportunity cost
the value of the best alternative use of a resource

The **economic cost** or **opportunity cost** is the value of the best alternative use of a resource. The economic or opportunity cost includes both explicit and implicit costs. If a firm purchases and uses an input immediately, that input's opportunity cost is the amount the firm pays for it. However, if the firm does not use the input in its production process, its best alternative would be to sell it to someone else at the market price. The concept of an opportunity cost becomes particularly useful when the firm uses an input that is not available for purchase in a market or that it purchased in a market in the past.

A key example of such an opportunity cost is the value of a manager's time. For instance, Maoyong owns and manages a firm. He pays himself only a small monthly salary of $1,000 because he also receives the firm's profit. However, Maoyong could work for another firm and earn $11,000 a month. Thus, the opportunity cost of his time is $11,000—from his best alternative use of his time—not the $1,000 he actually pays himself.

The classic example of an implicit opportunity cost is captured in the phrase "There's no such thing as a free lunch." Suppose that your parents offer to take you to lunch tomorrow. You know that they'll pay for the meal, but you also know that this lunch is not truly free. Your opportunity cost for the lunch is the best alternative use of your time. Presumably, the best alternative use of your time is studying this textbook, but other possible alternatives include earning money working or watching television. Often such an opportunity cost is substantial.[1] (What are you giving up to study opportunity costs?)

| Application | During major economic downturns, do applications to MBA programs fall, hold steady, or take off like tech stocks during the first Internet bubble? Knowledge of opportunity costs helps us answer this question. |

Application

The Opportunity Cost of an MBA

During major economic downturns, do applications to MBA programs fall, hold steady, or take off like tech stocks during the first Internet bubble? Knowledge of opportunity costs helps us answer this question.

The biggest cost of attending an MBA program is often the opportunity cost of giving up a well-paying job. Someone who leaves a job paying $6,000 per month to attend an MBA program is, in effect, incurring a $6,000 per month opportunity cost, in addition to the tuition and cost of textbooks (though this one is well worth the money).

Thus, it is not surprising that MBA applications rise in bad economic times when outside opportunities decline. People thinking of going back to school face a reduced opportunity cost of entering an MBA program if they think they might be laid off or might not be promoted during an economic downturn. As Stacey Kole, deputy dean for the MBA program at the University of Chicago's Graduate School of Business, observed, "When there's a go-go economy, fewer people decide to go back to school. When things go south, the opportunity cost of leaving work is lower."

In 2008, when U.S. unemployment rose sharply and the economy was in poor shape, the number of people seeking admission to MBA programs rose sharply. The number of applicants to MBA programs for the class of 2008–2009 increased over the previous year by 79% in the United States, 77% in the United Kingdom, and 69% in other European programs. Applicants increased substantially for 2009–2010 as well in Canada and Europe. However, as economic conditions improved, global applications fell in 2011 and were slightly down in 2012.

Solved Problem 7.1

Meredith's firm sends her to a conference for managers and has paid her registration fee. Included in the registration fee is free admission to a class on how to price derivative securities such as options. She is considering attending, but her most attractive

---

[1]See MyEconLab, Chapter 7, "Waiting for the Doctor."

alternative opportunity is to attend a talk by Warren Buffett about his investment strategies, which is scheduled at the same time. Although she would be willing to pay $100 to hear his talk, the cost of a ticket is only $40. Given she incurs no other costs to attend either event, what is Meredith's opportunity cost of attending the derivatives talk?

Answer

To calculate her opportunity cost, determine the benefit that Meredith would forgo by attending the derivatives class. Because she incurs no additional fee to attend the derivatives talk, Meredith's opportunity cost is the forgone benefit of hearing the Buffett speech. Because she values hearing the Buffett speech at $100, but only has to pay $40, her net benefit from hearing that talk is $60 = $100 − $40). Thus, her opportunity cost of attending the derivatives talk is $60.

Costs of Durable Inputs

durable good
a product that is usable for years

Determining the opportunity cost of capital, such as land or equipment, requires special considerations. Capital is a **durable good**: a product that is usable for years. Two problems may arise in measuring the cost of capital. The first is how to allocate the initial purchase cost over time. The second is what to do if the value of the capital changes over time.

We can avoid these two measurement problems if capital is rented instead of purchased. For example, suppose a firm can rent a small pick-up truck for $400 a month or buy it outright for $20,000. If the firm rents the truck, the rental payment is the relevant opportunity cost per month. The truck is rented month to month, so the firm does not have to worry about how to allocate the purchase cost of a truck over time. Moreover, the rental rate will adjust if the cost of trucks changes over time. Thus, if the firm can rent capital for short periods of time, it calculates the cost of this capital in the same way that it calculates the cost of nondurable inputs such as labor services or materials.

The firm faces a more complex problem in determining the opportunity cost of the truck if they purchase it. The firm's accountant may *expense* the truck's purchase price by treating the full $20,000 as a cost at the time that the truck is purchased. Another option is the accountant may *amortize* the cost by spreading the $20,000 over the life of the truck, following rules set by an accounting organization or by a relevant government authority such as the Internal Revenue Service (IRS).

A manager who wants to make sound decisions does not expense or amortize the truck using such rules. The true opportunity cost of using a truck that the firm owns is the amount that the firm could earn if it rented the truck to others. That is, regardless of whether the firm rents or buys the truck, the manager views the opportunity cost of this capital good as the rental rate for a given period of time. If the value of an older truck is less than that of a newer one, the rental rate for the truck falls over time.

But what if the firm cannot find anyone to rent trucks? It is still important to determine an appropriate opportunity cost. Suppose that the firm has two choices: It can choose not to buy the truck and keep the truck's purchase price of $20,000, or it can use the truck for a year and sell it for $17,000 at the end of the year. If the firm does not purchase the truck, it will deposit the $20,000 in a bank account that pays 5% per year, so the firm will have $21,000 at the end of the year. Thus, the opportunity cost of capital of using the truck for a year is $21,000 − $17,000 = $4,000.[2] This $4,000 opportunity cost equals the $3,000 depreciation of the truck (= $20,000 − $17,000) plus the $1,000 in forgone interest that the firm could have earned over the year if the firm had invested the $20,000.

Because the values of trucks, machines, and other equipment decline over time, their rental rates fall, so the firm's opportunity costs decline. In contrast, the value of some land, buildings, and other forms of capital may rise over time. To maximize profit, a firm must properly measure the opportunity cost of a piece of capital even if its value rises over time. If a beauty parlor buys a building when similar buildings in the area rent for $1,000 per month, the opportunity cost of using the building is $1,000 a month. If property values increase so that rents in the area rise to $2,000 per month, the beauty parlor's opportunity cost of its building rises to $2,000 per month.

Sunk Costs

sunk cost
a past expenditure that cannot be recovered

An opportunity cost is not always easy to observe but should always be taken into account when deciding how much to produce. In contrast, a **sunk cost**—a past expenditure that cannot be recovered—though easily observed, is not relevant to a firm when deciding how much to produce now. If an expenditure is sunk, it is not an opportunity cost.

If a firm buys a forklift for $25,000 and can resell it for the same price, it is not a sunk expenditure, and the opportunity cost of the forklift is $25,000. If instead the firm buys a specialized piece of equipment for $25,000 and cannot resell it, then the original expenditure is a sunk cost. Because this equipment has no alternative use and cannot be resold, its opportunity cost is zero, and it should not be included in the firm's current cost calculations. If the specialized equipment that originally cost $25,000 can be resold for $10,000, then only $15,000 of the original expenditure is a sunk cost, and the opportunity cost is $10,000.

To illustrate why a sunk cost should not influence a manager's current decisions, consider a firm that paid $300,000 for a piece of land for which the market value has fallen to $200,000. Now, the land's true opportunity cost is $200,000. The $100,000 difference between the $300,000 purchase price and the current market value of $200,000 is a sunk cost that has already been incurred and cannot be recovered. The land is worth $240,000 to the firm if it builds a plant on this parcel. Is it worth carrying out production on this land or should the land be sold for its market value of $200,000? If the firm uses the original purchase price in its decision-making process, the firm will falsely conclude that using the land for production will result in a $60,000 loss: the $240,000 value of using the land minus the purchase price of $300,000. Instead, the firm should use the land because it is worth $40,000 more as a production facility than if the firm sells the land for $200,000, its next best alternative. Thus, the firm should use the land's opportunity cost to make its decisions and ignore the land's sunk cost. In short, "There's no use crying over spilt milk."

7.2 Short-Run Costs

To make profit-maximizing decisions, a firm needs to know how its cost varies with output. A firm's cost rises as it increases its output. A firm cannot vary some of its inputs, such as capital, in the short run (Chapter 6). As a result, it is usually more

---

[2]The firm would also pay for gasoline, insurance, licensing fees, and other operating costs, but these items would all be expensed as operating costs and would not appear in the firm's accounts as capital costs.

costly for a firm to increase output in the short run than in the long run, when all inputs can be varied. In this section, we look at the cost of increasing output in the short run.

Short-Run Cost Measures

We start by using a numerical example to illustrate the basic cost concepts. We then examine the graphic relationship between these concepts.

Fixed

Variable

fixed cost (F)
a production expense that does not vary with output

variable cost (VC)
a production expense that changes with the quantity of output produced

cost (total cost, C)
the sum of a firm's variable cost and fixed cost:
$C = VC + F$

marginal cost (MC)
the amount by which a firm's cost changes if the firm produces one more unit of output

Fixed Cost, Variable Cost, and Total Cost   To produce a given level of output in the short run, a firm incurs costs for both its fixed and variable inputs. A firm's **fixed cost** (F) is its production expense that does not vary with output. The fixed cost includes the cost of inputs that the firm cannot practically adjust in the short run, such as land, a plant, large machines, and other capital goods. The fixed cost for a capital good a firm owns and uses is the opportunity cost of not renting it to someone else. The fixed cost is $48 per day for the firm in Table 7.1.

A firm's **variable cost** (VC) is the production expense that changes with the quantity of output produced. The variable cost is the cost of the variable inputs—the inputs the firm can adjust to alter its output level, such as labor and materials. Table 7.1 shows that the firm's variable cost changes with output. Variable cost goes from $25 a day when 1 unit is produced to $46 a day when 2 units are produced.

A firm's **cost** (or **total cost**, C) is the sum of a firm's variable cost and fixed cost:

$$C = VC + F.$$

The firm's total cost of producing 2 units of output is $94 per day, which is the sum of the fixed cost, $48, and the variable cost, $46. Because variable cost changes with the level of output, total cost also varies with the level of output, as the table illustrates.

To decide how much to produce, a firm uses several measures of how its cost varies with the level of output. Table 7.1 shows four such measures that we derive using the fixed cost, the variable cost, and the total cost.

Marginal Cost   A firm's **marginal cost** (MC) is the amount by which a firm's cost changes if the firm produces one more unit of output. The marginal cost is[3]

$$MC = \frac{\Delta C}{\Delta q},$$

where ΔC is the change in cost when output changes by Δq. Table 7.1 shows that, if the firm increases its output from 2 to 3 units, $\Delta q = 1$, its total cost rises from $94 to $114, $\Delta C = $20, so its marginal cost is $20 = \Delta C/\Delta q$.

---

[3]If we use calculus, the marginal cost is $MC = dC(q)/dq$, where $C(q)$ is the cost function that shows how cost varies with output. The calculus definition says how cost changes for an infinitesimal change in output. To illustrate the idea, however, we use larger changes in the table.

Table 7.1 Variation of Short-Run Cost with Output

Output, q	Fixed Cost, F	Variable Cost, VC	Total Cost, C	Marginal Cost, MC	Average Fixed Cost, $AFC = F/q$	Average Variable Cost, $AVC = VC/q$	Average Cost, $AC = C/q$
0	48	0	48				
1	48	25	73	25	48	25	73
2	48	46	94	21	24	23	47
3	48	66	114	20	16	22	38
4	48	82	130	16	12	20.5	32.5
5	48	100	148	18	9.6	20	29.6
6	48	120	168	20	8	20	28
7	48	141	189	21	6.9	20.1	27
8	48	168	216	27	6	21	27
9	48	198	246	30	5.3	22	27.3
10	48	230	278	32	4.8	23	27.8
11	48	272	320	42	4.4	24.7	29.1
12	48	321	369	49	4.0	26.8	30.8

Because only variable cost changes with output, we can also define marginal cost as the change in variable cost from a one-unit increase in output:

$$MC = \frac{\Delta VC}{\Delta q}.$$

As the firm increases output from 2 to 3 units, its variable cost increases by $\Delta VC = \$20 = \$66 - \$46$, so its marginal cost is $MC = \Delta VC/\Delta q = \$20$. A firm uses marginal cost in deciding whether it pays to change its output level.

average fixed cost (AFC)
the fixed cost divided by the units of output produced: $AFC = F/q$

average variable cost (AVC)
the variable cost divided by the units of output produced: $AVC = VC/q$

average cost (AC)
the total cost divided by the units of output produced: $AC = C/q$

Average Costs Firms use three average cost measures. The **average fixed cost** (AFC) is the fixed cost divided by the units of output produced: $AFC = F/q$. The average fixed cost falls as output rises because the fixed cost is spread over more units. The average fixed cost falls from $48 for 1 unit of output to $4 for 12 units of output in Table 7.1.

The **average variable cost** (AVC) is the variable cost divided by the units of output produced: $AVC = VC/q$. Because the variable cost increases with output, the average variable cost may either increase or decrease as output rises. The average variable cost is $25 at 1 unit, falls until it reaches a minimum of $20 at 6 units, and then rises. As we show in Chapter 8, a firm uses the average variable cost to determine whether to shut down operations when demand is low.

The **average cost** (AC)—or *average total cost*—is the total cost divided by the units of output produced: $AC = C/q$. The average cost is the sum of the average fixed cost and the average variable cost:[4]

$$AC = AFC + AVC.$$

In Table 7.1, as output increases, average cost falls until output is 8 units and then rises. The firm makes a profit if its average cost is below its price, which is the firm's average revenue.

---

[4]Because $C = VC + F$, if we divide both sides of the equation by q, we obtain $AC = C/q = F/q + VC/q = AFC + AVC$.

Short-Run Cost Curves

We illustrate the relationship between output and the various cost measures using curves in Figure 7.1. Panel a shows the variable cost, fixed cost, and total cost curves that correspond to Table 7.1. The fixed cost, which does not vary with output, is a horizontal line at $48. The variable cost curve is zero at zero units of output and rises with output. The total cost curve, which is the vertical sum of the variable cost curve and the fixed cost line, is $48 higher than the variable cost curve at every output level, so the variable cost and total cost curves are parallel.

Panel b shows the average fixed cost, average variable cost, average cost, and marginal cost curves. The average fixed cost curve falls as output increases. It approaches

Figure 7.1 Short-Run Cost Curves

(a) Because the total cost differs from the variable cost by the fixed cost, *F*, of $48, the total cost curve, *C*, is parallel to the variable cost curve, *VC*. (b) The marginal cost curve, *MC*, cuts the average variable cost, *AVC*, and average cost, *AC*, curves at their minimums. The height of the *AC* curve at point *a* equals the slope of the line from the origin to the cost curve at *A*. The height of the *AVC* at *b* equals the slope of the line from the origin to the variable cost curve at *B*. The height of the marginal cost is the slope of either the *C* or *VC* curve at that quantity.

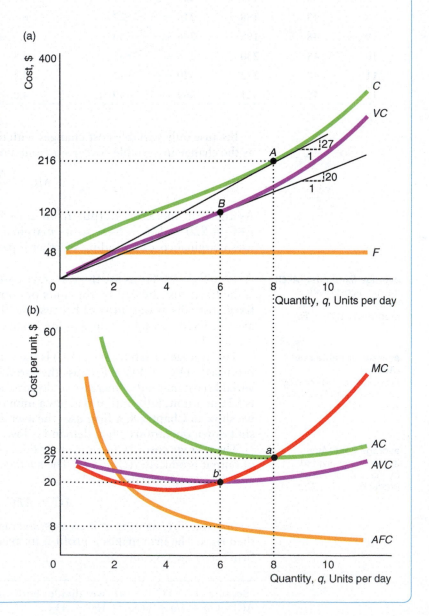

zero as output gets large because the fixed cost is spread over many units of output. The average cost curve is the vertical sum of the average fixed cost and average variable cost curves. For example, at 6 units of output, the average variable cost is 20 and the average fixed cost is 8, so the average cost is 28.

The relationships between the average and marginal curves to the total curves are similar to those between the total product, marginal product, and average product curves, which we discussed in Chapter 6. The average cost at a particular output level is the slope of a line from the origin to the corresponding point on the cost curve. The slope of that line is the rise—the cost at that output level—divided by the run—the output level—which is the definition of the average cost. In panel a, the slope of the line from the origin to point A is the average cost for 8 units of output. The height of the cost curve at A is 216, so the slope is 216/8 = 27, which is the height of the average cost curve at the corresponding point *a* in panel b.

Similarly, the average variable cost is the slope of a line from the origin to a point on the variable cost curve. The slope of the line from the origin to B in panel a is 20—the height of the variable cost curve, 120, divided by the number of units of output, 6—which is the height of the average variable cost at 6 units of output, point *b* in panel b.

The marginal cost is the slope of either the cost curve or the variable cost curve at a given output level. As the cost and variable cost curves are parallel, they have the same slope at any given output. The difference between cost and variable cost is fixed cost, which does not affect marginal cost.

Panel a of Figure 7.1 shows a line from the origin that is tangent to the cost curve at A. Thus, the slope of this line equals both the average cost and the marginal cost at 8 units of output. This equality occurs at the corresponding point *a* in panel b, where the marginal cost curve intersects the average cost. (See Appendix 7A for a mathematical proof.)

Where the marginal cost curve is below the average cost, the average cost curve declines with output. Because the average cost of 47 for 2 units is greater than the marginal cost of the third unit, 20, the average cost for 3 units falls to 38. Where the marginal cost is above the average cost, the average cost curve rises with output. At 8 units, the marginal cost equals the average cost, so the average is unchanging, which is the minimum point, *a*, of the average cost curve.

We can show the same results using the graph. Because the line from the origin is tangent to the variable cost curve at B in panel a, the marginal cost equals the average variable cost at the corresponding point *b* in panel b. Again, where marginal cost is above average variable cost, the average variable cost curve rises with output; where marginal cost is below average variable cost, the average variable cost curve falls with output. Because the average cost curve is above the average variable cost curve everywhere and the marginal cost curve is rising where it crosses both average curves, the minimum of the average variable cost curve, *b*, is at a lower output level than the minimum of the average cost curve, *a*.

Production Functions and the Shape of Cost Curves

The production function determines the shape of a firm's cost curves. The production function shows the amount of inputs needed to produce a given level of output. The firm calculates its cost by multiplying the quantity of each input by its price and summing the costs of the inputs.

If a firm produces output using capital and labor, and its capital is fixed in the short run, the firm's variable cost is its cost of labor. Its labor cost is the wage per hour, w, times the number of hours of labor, L, employed by the firm: $VC = wL$.

In the short run, when the firm's capital is fixed, the only way the firm can increase its output is to use more labor. If the firm increases its labor enough, it reaches the point of *diminishing marginal return to labor*, at which each extra worker increases output by a smaller amount. We can use this information about the relationship between labor and output—the production function—to determine the shape of the variable cost curve and its related curves.

Shape of the Variable Cost Curve   If input prices are constant, the production function determines the shape of the variable cost curve. We illustrate this relationship for the firm in Figure 7.2. The firm faces a constant input price for labor, the wage, of $10 per hour.

The total product of labor curve in Figure 7.2 shows the firm's short-run production function relationship between output and labor when capital is held fixed. At point *a*, the firm uses 5 hours of labor to produce 1 unit of output. At point *b*, it takes 20 hours of labor to produce 5 units of output. Here, output increases more than in proportion to labor: Output rises 5 times when labor increases 4 times. In contrast, as the firm moves from *b* to *c*, output increases less than in proportion. Output doubles to 10 as result of increasing labor from 20 to 46—an increase of 2.3 times. The movement from *c* to *d* results in even a smaller increase in output relative to labor. This flattening of the total product curve at higher levels of labor reflects diminishing marginal returns to labor.

This curve shows both the production relation of output to labor and the variable cost relation of output to cost. Because each hour of work costs the firm $10, we can use an alternative measure for the horizontal axis in Figure 7.2: the firm's variable

Figure 7.2 Variable Cost and Total Product of Labor

The firm's short-run variable cost curve and its total product of labor curve have the same shape. The total product of labor curve uses the horizontal axis measuring hours of work. The variable cost curve uses the horizontal axis measuring labor cost, which is the only variable cost.

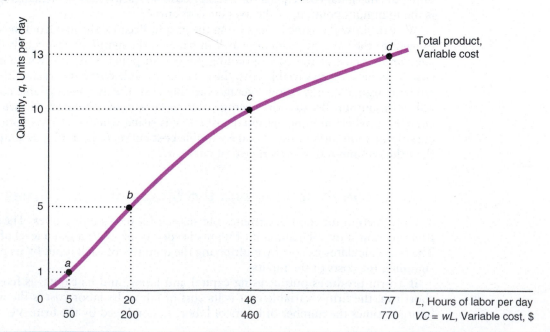

cost, which is its cost of labor. To produce 5 units of output takes 20 hours of labor, so the firm's variable cost is $200. By using the variable cost labels on the horizontal axis, the total product of labor curve becomes the variable cost curve.

As output increases, the variable cost increases more than proportionally due to the diminishing marginal returns. Because the production function determines the shape of the variable cost curve, it also determines the shape of the marginal, average variable, and average cost curves. We now examine the shape of each of these cost curves in detail, because when making decisions, managers rely more on these per-unit cost measures than on total variable cost.

Shape of the Marginal Cost Curve The marginal cost is the change in variable cost as output increases by one unit: $MC = \Delta VC/\Delta q$. In the short run, capital is fixed, so the only way the firm can produce more output is to use extra labor. The extra labor required to produce one more unit of output is $\Delta L/\Delta q$. The extra labor costs the firm w per unit, so the firm's cost rises by $w(\Delta L/\Delta q)$. As a result, the firm's marginal cost is

$$MC = \frac{\Delta VC}{\Delta q} = w\frac{\Delta L}{\Delta q}.$$

The marginal cost equals the wage times the extra labor necessary to produce one more unit of output. To increase output by one unit from 5 to 6 units takes 4 extra workers in Figure 7.2. If the wage is $5 per hour, the marginal cost is $20.

How do we know how much extra labor we need to produce one more unit of output? That information comes from the production function. The marginal product of labor—the amount of extra output produced by another unit of labor, holding other inputs fixed—is $MP_L = \Delta q/\Delta L$. Thus, the extra labor we need to produce one more unit of output, $\Delta L/\Delta q$, is $1/MP_L$, so the firm's marginal cost is

$$MC = \frac{w}{MP_L}. \tag{7.1}$$

Equation 7.1 says that the marginal cost equals the wage divided by the marginal product of labor. If the firm is producing 5 units of output, it takes 4 extra hours of labor to produce 1 more unit of output in Figure 7.2, so the marginal product of an hour of labor is $\frac{1}{4}$. Given a wage of $5 an hour, the marginal cost of the sixth unit is $5 divided by $\frac{1}{4}$, or $20, as panel b of Figure 7.1 shows.

Equation 7.1 shows that the marginal cost moves in the opposite direction of the marginal product of labor. At low levels of labor, the marginal product of labor commonly rises with additional labor because extra workers help the original workers and they can collectively make better use of the firm's equipment (Chapter 6). As the marginal product of labor rises, the marginal cost falls.

Eventually, however, as the number of workers increases, workers must share the fixed amount of equipment and may get in each other's way, so the marginal cost curve slopes upward because of diminishing marginal returns to labor. Thus, the marginal cost first falls and then rises, as panel b of Figure 7.1 illustrates.

Shape of the Average Cost Curves Diminishing marginal returns to labor, which determine the shape of the variable cost curve, also determine the shape of the average variable cost curve. The average variable cost is the variable cost divided by output: $AVC = VC/q$. For the firm we've been examining, whose only variable input is labor, variable cost is wL, so average variable cost is

$$AVC = \frac{VC}{q} = \frac{wL}{q}.$$

Because the average product of labor is q/L, average variable cost is the wage divided by the average product of labor:

$$AVC = \frac{w}{AP_L}. \tag{7.2}$$

In Figure 7.2, at 5 units of output, the average product of labor is $\frac{1}{4}$ $(= q/L = 5/20)$, so the average variable cost is $40, which is the wage, $10, divided by the average product of labor, $\frac{1}{4}$.

With a constant wage, the average variable cost moves in the opposite direction of the average product of labor in Equation 7.2. As we discussed in Chapter 6, the average product of labor tends to rise and then fall, so the average cost tends to fall and then rise, as in panel b of Figure 7.1.

The average cost curve is the vertical sum of the average variable cost curve and the average fixed cost curve, as in panel b. If the average variable cost curve is U-shaped, adding the strictly falling average fixed cost makes the average cost fall more steeply than the average variable cost curve at low output levels. At high output levels, the average cost and average variable cost curves differ by ever smaller amounts, as the average fixed cost, F/q, approaches zero. Thus, the average cost curve is also U-shaped.

Application

Short-Run Cost Curves for a Beer Manufacturer

The short-run average cost curve for a Japanese beer manufacturer is U-shaped, even though its average variable cost is strictly upward sloping. The graph (based on the estimates of Flath, 2011) shows the firm's various short-run cost curves, where the firm's capital is fixed at $\overline{K} = 100$. Appendix 7B derives the firm's short-run cost curves mathematically.

The firm's average fixed cost (AFC) falls as output increases. The firm's average variable cost curve is strictly increasing. The average cost (AC) curve is the vertical sum of the average variable cost (AVC) and average fixed cost curves. Because the average fixed cost curve falls with output and the average variable cost curve rises with output, the average cost curve is U-shaped. The firm's marginal cost (MC) lies above the rising average variable cost curve for all positive quantities of output and cuts the average cost curve at its minimum.

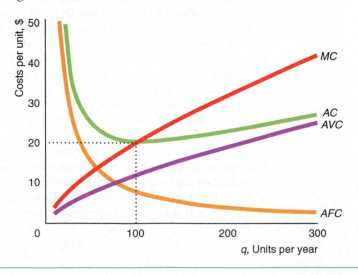

Effects of Taxes on Costs

Taxes applied to a firm shift some or all of the marginal and average cost curves. For example, suppose that the government collects a specific tax of $10 per unit of output from the firm. This tax, which varies with output, affects the firm's variable cost but not its fixed cost. As a result, it affects the firm's average cost, average variable cost, and marginal cost curves but not its average fixed cost curve.

At every quantity, the average variable cost, average cost, and marginal cost rise by the full amount of the tax. In the example in Table 7.1, the firm's average variable cost before the tax, AVC^b, is $21 if it produces 8 units of output. After the tax, the firm must pay the government $10 per unit, so the firm's after-tax average variable cost rises to $31. More generally, the firm's after-tax average variable cost, AVC^a, is its average variable cost of production—the before-tax average variable cost—plus the tax per unit, $10: $AVC^a = AVC^b + \$10$.

The average cost equals the average variable cost plus the average fixed cost. Because the tax increases average variable cost by $10 and does not affect the average fixed cost, the tax increases average cost from $AC^b = \$27$ to $AC^a = \$37$.

The tax also increases the firm's marginal cost. For example, in Table 7.1, its before-tax marginal cost, MC^b is $27 at 8 units of output. To produce this last unit of output, the cost to the firm is the before-tax marginal cost of producing the extra unit, $MC^b = \$27$, plus $10, so its after-tax marginal cost is $MC^a = MC^b + \$10 = \$37$.

Figure 7.3 shows that the $10 specific tax shifts the firm's average cost and marginal cost curves up by the amount of the tax. The after-tax marginal cost intersects the after-tax average cost at its minimum. Because both the marginal and average cost curves shift upward by exactly the same amount, both the before-tax and after-tax average cost curves reach their minimums at 8 units of output, as Figure 7.3 shows. So even though a specific tax increases a firm's average cost, it does not affect the output at which average cost is minimized.

Figure 7.3 Effect of a Specific Tax on Cost Curves

A specific tax of $10 per unit shifts both the marginal cost and average cost curves upward by $10. Because of the parallel upward shift of the average cost curve, the minimum of both the before-tax average cost curve, AC^b, and the after-tax average cost curve, AC^a, occurs at the same output, 8 units.

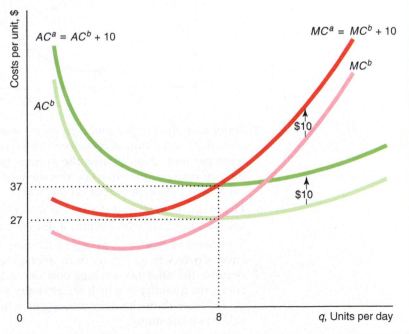

Similarly, we can analyze the effect of a franchise tax on costs. A *franchise tax*— also called a *business license fee*—is a lump sum that a firm pays for the right to operate a business. For example, a four-year license to sell hot dogs from a cart outside the former Tavern on the Green restaurant in New York City's Central Park cost $1.39 million in 2012. These taxes do not vary with output, so they affect firms' fixed costs only—not their variable costs.

Solved Problem 7.2

What is the effect of a lump-sum franchise tax $\mathscr{L}$ on the quantity at which a firm's after-tax average cost curve reaches its minimum? (Assume that the firm's before-tax average cost curve is U-shaped.)

Answer

1. *Determine the average tax per unit of output.* Because the franchise tax is a lump-sum payment that does not vary with output, the more the firm produces, the less tax it pays per unit. The tax per unit is $\mathscr{L}/q$. If the firm sells only 1 unit, its cost is $\mathscr{L}$; however, if it sells 100 units, its tax payment per unit is only $\mathscr{L}/100$.

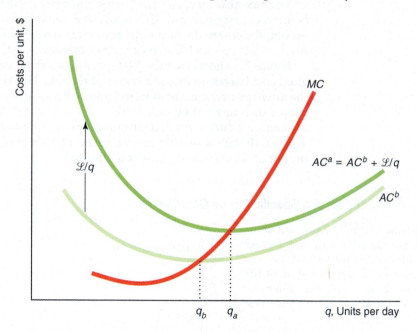

2. *Show how the tax per unit affects the average cost.* The firm's after-tax average cost, AC^a, is the sum of its before-tax average cost, AC^b, and its average tax payment per unit, $\mathscr{L}/q$. Because the average tax payment per unit falls with output, the gap between the after-tax average cost curve and the before-tax average cost curve also falls with output on the graph.

3. *Determine the effect of the tax on the marginal cost curve.* Because the franchise tax does not vary with output, it does not affect the marginal cost curve.

4. *Compare the minimum points of the two average cost curves.* The marginal cost curve crosses from below both average cost curves at their minimum points. Because the after-tax average cost curve lies above the before-tax average cost curve, the quantity at which the after-tax average cost curve reaches its minimum, q_a, is larger than the quantity, q_b, at which the before-tax average cost curve achieves a minimum.

Short-Run Cost Summary

We discussed three cost-level curves—total cost, fixed cost, and variable cost—and four cost-per-unit curves—average cost, average fixed cost, average variable cost, and marginal cost. Understanding the shapes of these curves and the relationships between them is crucial to understanding the analysis of firm behavior in the rest of this book. Fortunately, we can derive most of what we need to know about the shapes of and the relationships between the curves using four basic concepts:

- In the short run, the cost associated with inputs that cannot be adjusted is fixed, while the cost from inputs that can be adjusted is variable.
- Given that input prices are constant, the shapes of the variable cost and cost curves are determined by the production function.
- Where a variable input exhibits diminishing marginal returns, the variable cost and cost curves become relatively steep as output increases, so the average cost, average variable cost, and marginal cost curves rise with output.
- Because of the relationship between a marginal and an average, both the average cost and average variable cost curves fall when marginal cost is below them and rise when marginal cost is above them. Thus, the marginal cost curve cuts both these average cost curves at their minimum points.

7.3 Long-Run Costs

In the long run, the firm adjusts all its inputs so that its cost of production is as low as possible. The firm can change its plant size, design and build new machines, and otherwise adjust inputs that were fixed in the short run.

All Costs Are Avoidable in the Long Run

Although firms may incur fixed costs in the long run, these fixed costs are *avoidable* (rather than *sunk*, as in the short run). The rent of F per month that a restaurant pays is a fixed cost because it does not vary with the number of meals (output) served. In the short run, this fixed cost is sunk: The firm must pay F even if the restaurant does not operate. In the long run, this fixed cost is avoidable: The firm does not have to pay this rent if it shuts down. The long run is determined by the length of the rental contract during which time the firm is obligated to pay rent.

In the examples throughout this chapter, we assume that all inputs can be varied in the long run so that the firm has no long-run fixed costs ($F = 0$). As a result, the long-run total cost equals the long-run variable cost: $C = VC$. Thus, our firm is concerned about only three cost concepts in the long run—total cost, average cost, and marginal cost—instead of the seven cost concepts that it considers in the short run.

Minimizing Cost

To produce a given quantity of output at minimum cost, our firm uses information about the production function and the price of labor and capital. The firm chooses how much labor and capital to use in the long run, whereas the firm chooses only how much labor to use in the short run when capital is fixed. As a consequence, the firm's long-run cost is lower than its short-run cost of production if it has to use the "wrong" level of capital in the short run. In this section, we show how a firm picks the cost-minimizing combinations of inputs in the long run.

A firm can produce a given level of output using many different *technologically efficient* combinations of inputs, as summarized by an isoquant (Chapter 6). From among the technologically efficient combinations of inputs, a firm wants to choose the particular bundle with the lowest cost of production, which is the *economically efficient* combination of inputs. To do so, the firm combines information about technology from the isoquant with information about the cost of labor and capital.

We now show how information about cost can be summarized in an *isocost line*. Then we show how a firm can combine the information in an isoquant and isocost lines to pick the economically efficient combination of inputs.

Isocost Line

The cost of producing a given level of output depends on the price of labor and capital. The firm hires L hours of labor services at a wage of w per hour, so its labor cost is wL. The firm rents K hours of machine services at a rental rate of r per hour, so its capital cost is rK. (If the firm owns the capital, r is the implicit rental rate.) The firm's total cost is the sum of its labor and capital costs:

$$C = wL + rK. \tag{7.3}$$

The firm can hire as much labor and capital as it wants at these constant input prices.

The firm can use many combinations of labor and capital that cost the same amount. Suppose that the wage rate, w, is $10 an hour and the rental rate of capital, r, is $20. Five of the many combinations of labor and capital that the firm can use that cost $200 are listed in Table 7.2. These combinations of labor and capital are plotted on an **isocost line**, which is all the combinations of inputs that require the same (*iso*) total expenditure (*cost*). Figure 7.4 shows three isocost lines. The $200 isocost line represents all the combinations of labor and capital that the firm can buy for $200, including the combinations *a* through *e* in Table 7.2.

Along an isocost line, cost is fixed at a particular level, $\overline{C}$, so by setting cost at $\overline{C}$ in Equation 7.3, we can write the equation for the $\overline{C}$ isocost line as

$$\overline{C} = wL + rK.$$

Using algebra, we can rewrite this equation to show how much capital the firm can buy if it spends a total of $\overline{C}$ and purchases L units of labor:

$$K = \frac{\overline{C}}{r} - \frac{w}{r}L. \tag{7.4}$$

By substituting $\overline{C} = \$200$, $w = \$10$, and $r = \$20$ in Equation 7.4, we find that the $200 isocost line is $K = 10 - \frac{1}{2}L$. We can use Equation 7.4 to derive three properties of isocost lines.

isocost line
all the combinations of inputs that require the same (*iso*) total expenditure (*cost*)

Table 7.2 Bundles of Labor and Capital That Cost the Firm $200

Bundle	Labor, L	Capital, K	Labor Cost, $wL = \$10L$	Capital Cost, $rK = \$20K$	Total Cost, $wL + rK$
a	20	0	$200	$0	$200
b	14	3	$140	$60	$200
c	10	5	$100	$100	$200
d	6	7	$60	$140	$200
e	0	10	$0	$200	$200

Figure 7.4 A Family of Isocost Lines

An isocost line shows all the combinations of labor and capital that cost the firm the same amount. The greater the total cost, the farther from the origin the isocost lies. All the isocosts have the same slope, $-w/r = -\frac{1}{2}$. The slope shows the rate at which the firm can substitute capital for labor holding total cost constant: For each extra unit of capital it uses, the firm must use two fewer units of labor to hold its cost constant.

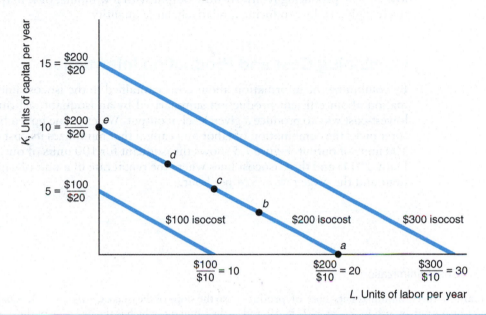

First, where the isocost lines hit the capital and labor axes depends on the firm's cost, $\overline{C}$, and on the input prices. The $\overline{C}$ isocost line intersects the capital axis where the firm is using only capital. Setting $L = 0$ in Equation 7.4, we find that the firm buys $K = \overline{C}/r$ units of capital. In the figure, the $200 isocost line intersects the capital axis at $200/$20 = 10 units of capital. Similarly, the intersection of the isocost line with the labor axis is at $\overline{C}/w$, which is the amount of labor the firm hires if it uses only labor. In the figure, the intersection of the $200 isocost with the labor axis occurs at $L = 20$, where $K = 10 - \frac{1}{2} \times 20 = 0$.

Second, isocosts that are farther from the origin have higher costs than those that are closer to the origin. Because the isocost lines intersect the capital axis at $\overline{C}/r$ and the labor axis at $\overline{C}/w$, an increase in the cost shifts these intersections with the axes proportionately outward. The $100 isocost line hits the capital axis at 5 and the labor axis at 10, whereas the $200 isocost line intersects at 10 and 20.

Third, the slope of each isocost line is the same. From Equation 7.4, if the firm increases labor by ΔL, it must decrease capital by

$$\Delta K = -\frac{w}{r}\Delta L.$$

Dividing both sides of this expression by ΔL, we find that the slope of an isocost line, $\Delta K/\Delta L$, is $-w/r$. Thus, the slope of the isocost line depends on the relative prices of the inputs. The slope of the isocost lines in the figure is $-w/r = -\$5/\$10 = -\frac{1}{2}$. If the firm uses two more units of labor, $\Delta L = 2$, it must reduce capital by one unit, $\Delta K = -\frac{1}{2}\Delta L = -1$, to keep its total cost constant. Because all isocost lines are based on the same relative prices, they all have the same slope, so they are parallel.

The isocost line plays a similar role in the firm's decision making as the budget line does in consumer decision making. Both an isocost line and a budget line are straight lines whose slopes depend on relative prices. However, the isocost and budget lines have an important difference. The consumer has a single budget line determined by the consumer's income. The firm faces many isocost lines, each of which corresponds to a different level of expenditures the firm might make. A firm may incur a relatively low cost by producing relatively little output with few inputs, or it may incur a relatively high cost by producing a relatively large quantity.

Combining Cost and Production Information

By combining the information about costs contained in the isocost lines with information about efficient production summarized by an isoquant, a firm chooses the lowest-cost way to produce a given level of output. We examine how a beer manufacturer picks the combination of labor and capital that minimizes its cost of producing 100 units of output. Figure 7.5 shows the isoquant for 100 units of output (based on Flath, 2011) and three isocost lines where the rental rate of a unit of capital is $8 per hour and the wage rate is $24 per hour.

Figure 7.5 Cost Minimization

The beer manufacturer minimizes its cost of producing 100 units of output by producing at x ($L = 50$ and $K = 100$). This cost-minimizing combination of inputs is determined by the tangency between the $q = 100$ isoquant and the lowest isocost line, $2,000, that touches that isoquant. At x, the isocost is tangent to the isoquant, so the slope of the isocost, $-w/r = -3$, equals the slope of the isoquant, which is the negative of the marginal rate of technical substitution. That is, the rate at which the firm can trade capital for labor in the input markets equals the rate at which it can substitute capital for labor in the production process.

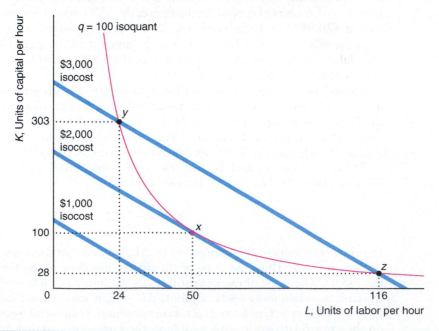

The firm can choose any of three equivalent approaches to minimize its cost:

- **Lowest-isocost rule.** Pick the bundle of inputs where the lowest isocost line touches the isoquant.
- **Tangency rule.** Pick the bundle of inputs where the isoquant is tangent to the isocost line.
- **Last-dollar rule.** Pick the bundle of inputs where the last dollar spent on one input gives as much extra output as the last dollar spent on any other input.

Lowest-Isocost Rule Using the *lowest-isocost rule*, the firm minimizes its cost by using the combination of inputs on the isoquant that is on the lowest isocost line that touches the 100 unit isoquant. In Figure 7.5, the $2,000 isocost line touches the isoquant at the bundle of inputs x, where the firm uses $L = 50$ workers and $K = 100$ units of capital. We want to show that Bundle x is the least costly way to produce 100 units of output. We need to demonstrate that other practical combinations of input produce less than 100 units or produce 100 units at greater cost.

Because the $2,000 isocost line just touches the isoquant, any lower isocost line, such as the $1,000 isocost line, does not touch the isoquant. Each combination of inputs on the $1,000 isocost line lies below the isoquant, so the firm cannot produce 100 units of output for $1,000.

The firm can produce 100 units of output using other combinations of inputs beside x; however, using these other bundles of inputs is more expensive. For example, the firm can produce 100 units of output using the combinations y ($L = 24$, $K = 303$) or z ($L = 116$, $K = 28$). However, both these combinations lie on the $3,000 isocost, so producing 100 units of output with these bundles costs more than using Bundle x.

Tangency Rule If an isocost line crosses the isoquant twice, as the $3,000 isocost line does, another lower isocost line must also touch the isoquant. The lowest possible isocost line that touches the isoquant, the $2,000 isocost line, is tangent to the isoquant at a single bundle, x. As a consequence, the firm can identify the low-cost bundle using the *tangency rule*: The firm chooses the input bundle where the relevant isoquant is tangent to an isocost line to produce a given level of output at the lowest cost.

At the point of tangency, the slope of the isoquant equals the slope of the isocost line. As we showed in Chapter 6, the slope of the isoquant is the marginal rate of technical substitution ($MRTS$). The isocost's slope is the negative of the ratio of the wage to the cost of capital, $-w/r$. Thus, to minimize its cost of producing a given level of output, a firm chooses its inputs so that the marginal rate of technical substitution equals the negative of the relative input prices:[5]

$$MRTS = -\frac{w}{r}. \tag{7.5}$$

The firm picks inputs so that the rate at which it can substitute capital for labor in the production process, the $MRTS$, exactly equals the rate at which it can trade capital for labor in input markets, $-w/r$.

In Figure 7.5, the slope of the isocost line is $-w/r = -24/8 = -3$. At Bundle x, the slope of the isoquant line, its $MRTS$, is also -3. In contrast, at y, the $MRTS$ is -18.9375, which is steeper than the isocost's slope of $-w/r = -3$. Because the slopes are not equal at y, the firm can produce 100 units of output at lower cost.

---

[5]Appendix 7C derives Equation 7.5 using calculus.

Solved Problem 7.3

Use the tangency rule to determine the cost-minimizing bundles of labor and capital for a general Cobb-Douglas production function, $q = AL^\alpha K^\beta$, and for the specific beer production function that underlies Figure 7.5, $q = 1.516L^{0.6}K^{0.4}$, where $w = 24$ and $r = 8$.

Answer

1. *Use the general Cobb-Douglas production function and Equation 7.5 to determine the tangency condition for the general Cobb-Douglas.* According to Equation 6.7, the slope of a Cobb-Douglas isoquant is $MRTS = -(\alpha/\beta)(K/L)$. According to Equation 7.5, cost is minimized if the $MRTS$ equals the slope of the isocost, $-w/r$:

$$-\frac{\alpha}{\beta}\frac{K}{L} = -\frac{w}{r}.$$

Rearranging this expression, we find that, at the cost-minimizing bundle,

$$K = \frac{w\beta}{r\alpha}L. \tag{7.6}$$

2. *Substitute the specific values for our beer example into Equation 7.6.* For the beer production function, $\alpha = 0.6$ and $\beta = 0.4$. Substituting those values and $w = 24$ and $r = 8$ into Equation 7.6, we find that

$$K = \frac{24 \times 0.4}{8 \times 0.6}L = 2L. \tag{7.7}$$

That is, at a cost-minimizing input bundle, the firm uses twice as many units of K as of L.

Last-Dollar Rule We can interpret the tangency rule, Equation 7.5, in another way. We showed in Chapter 6, Equation 6.3, that the marginal rate of technical substitution equals the negative of the ratio of the marginal product of labor to that of capital: $MRTS = -MP_L/MP_K$. Thus, the cost-minimizing condition in Equation 7.5 is equivalent to $-MP_L/MP_K = -w/r$. This expression may be rewritten as

$$\frac{MP_L}{w} = \frac{MP_K}{r}. \tag{7.8}$$

Equation 7.8 is the *last-dollar rule*: Cost is minimized if inputs are chosen so that the last dollar spent on labor adds as much extra output, MP_L/w, as the last dollar spent on capital, MP_K/r.

Using Equations 6.5 and 6.6, we know that the beer firm's marginal product of labor is $MP_L = 0.6q/L$ and its marginal product of capital is $MP_K = 0.4q/K$ At $x(L = 50, K = 100)$, where $q = 100$, the beer firm's marginal product of labor is $1.2 (= 0.6 \times 100/50)$ and its marginal product of capital is $0.4 (= 0.4 \times 100/100)$. The last dollar spent on labor produces

$$\frac{MP_L}{w} = \frac{1.2}{24} = 0.05$$

more units of output. The last dollar spent on capital leads to

$$\frac{MP_K}{r} = \frac{0.4}{8} = 0.05$$

extra output. Thus, spending one more dollar on labor at x gets the firm as much extra output as spending the same amount on capital. Equation 7.6 holds, so the firm is minimizing its cost of producing 100 units of output.

If instead the firm produced at y ($L = 24$, $K = 303$), where it is using more capital and less labor, its MP_L is 2.5 (= 0.6 × 100/24) and the MP_K is approximately 0.13 (≈ 0.4 × 100/303). As a result, the last dollar spent on labor generates $MP_L/w ≈ 0.1$ more units of output, whereas the last dollar spent on capital gets only a fourth as much extra output, $MP_K/r ≈ 0.017$. At y, if the firm shifts one dollar from capital to labor, output falls by 0.017 because of the reduced capital, but increases by 0.1 because of the extra labor, so the firm has a net gain of 0.083 more output at the same cost. The firm should shift even more resources from capital to labor—which increases the marginal product of capital and decreases the marginal product of labor—until Equation 7.6 holds with equality at x.

To summarize, a firm has three equivalent rules that it can use to pick the lowest-cost combination of inputs to produce a given level of output when isoquants are smooth: the lowest-isocost rule, the tangency rule (Equations 7.5 and 7.6), and the last-dollar rule (Equation 7.8). If the isoquant is not smooth, the lowest-cost method of production cannot be determined by using the tangency rule or the last-dollar rule. The lowest-isocost rule always works—even when isoquants are not smooth (as in Chapter 6's Application "A Semiconductor Integrated Circuit Isoquant").

Factor Price Changes

Once the beer manufacturer determines the lowest-cost combination of inputs to produce a given level of output, it uses that method as long as the input prices remain constant. How should the firm change its behavior if the cost of one of the factors changes? Suppose that the wage falls from $24 to $8 but the rental rate of capital stays constant at $8.

The firm minimizes its new cost by substituting away from the now relatively more expensive input, capital, toward the now relatively less expensive input, labor. The change in the wage does not affect technological efficiency, so it does not affect the isoquant in Figure 7.6. Because of the wage decrease, the new isocost lines have a flatter slope, $-w/r = -8/8 = 1$, than the original isocost lines, $-w/r = -24/8 = -3$.

The relatively steep original isocost line is tangent to the 100-unit isoquant at Bundle x ($L = 50$, $K = 100$). The new, flatter isocost line is tangent to the isoquant at Bundle v ($L = 77$, $K = 52$). Thus, the firm uses more labor and less capital as labor becomes relatively less expensive. Moreover, the firm's cost of producing 100 units falls from $2,000 to $1,032 because of the decrease in the wage. This example illustrates that a change in the relative prices of inputs affects the mix of inputs that a firm uses.

Solved Problem 7.4

If a firm manufactures in its home country, it faces input prices for labor and capital of $\hat{w}$ and $\hat{r}$ and produces $\hat{q}$ units of output using $\hat{L}$ units of labor and $\hat{K}$ units of capital. Abroad, the wage and cost of capital are half as much as at home. If the firm manufactures abroad, will it change the amount of labor and capital it uses to produce $\hat{q}$? What happens to its cost of producing $\hat{q}$?

Answer

1. *Determine whether the change in factor prices affects the slopes of the isoquant or the isocost lines.* The change in input prices does not affect the isoquant, which depends only on technology (the production function). Moreover, cutting all the input prices in half does not affect the slope of the isocost lines. The original slope was $-\hat{w}/\hat{r}$, and the new slope is $-(\hat{w}/2)/(\hat{r}/2) = -\hat{w}/\hat{r}$.

2. *Using a rule for cost minimization, determine whether the firm changes its input mix.* A firm minimizes its cost by producing where its isoquant is tangent to the lowest possible isocost line. That is, the firm produces where the slope of its isoquant, *MRTS*, equals the slope of its isocost line, $-w/r$. Because the slopes of the isoquant and the isocost lines are unchanged after input prices are cut in half, the firm continues to produce $\hat{q}$ using the same amount of labor, $\hat{L}$, and capital, $\hat{K}$, as originally.

3. *Calculate the original cost and the new cost and compare them.* The firm's original cost of producing $\hat{q}$ units of output was $\hat{w}\hat{L} + \hat{r}\hat{K} = \hat{C}$. Its new cost of producing the same amount of output is $(\hat{w}/2)\hat{L} + (\hat{r}/2)\hat{K} = \hat{C}/2$. Thus, its cost of producing $\hat{q}$ falls by half when the input prices are halved. The isocost lines have the same slope as before, but the cost associated with each isocost line is halved.

Figure 7.6 Change in Factor Price

Originally, the wage was $24 and the rental rate of capital was $8, so the lowest isocost line ($2,000) was tangent to the $q = 100$ isoquant at x ($L = 50, K = 100$). When the wage fell to $8, the isocost lines became flatter: Labor became relatively less expensive than capital. The slope of the isocost lines falls from $-w/r = -24/8 = -3$ to $-8/8 = -1$. The new lowest isocost line ($1,032) is tangent at v ($L = 77, K = 52$). Thus, when the wage falls, the firm uses more labor and less capital to produce a given level of output, and the cost of production falls from $2,000 to $1,032.

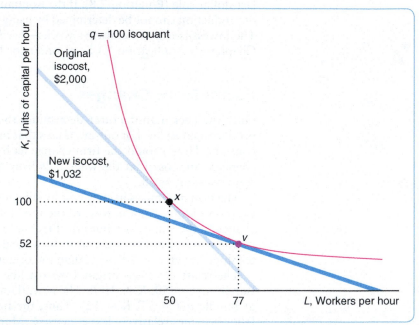

The Long-Run Expansion Path and the Long-Run Cost Function

We now know how a firm determines the cost-minimizing output for any given level of output. By repeating this analysis for different output levels, the firm determines how its cost varies with output.

Panel a of Figure 7.7 shows the relationship between the lowest-cost factor combinations and various levels of output for the beer manufacturer when input prices are held constant at $w = $24 and $r = $8. The curve through the tangency points is the

Figure 7.7 Expansion Path and Long-Run Cost Curve

(a) The curve through the tangency points between isocost lines and isoquants, such as x, y, and z, is called the expansion path. The points on the expansion path are the cost-minimizing combinations of labor and capital for each output level. The beer manufacturer's expansion path is a straight line. (b) The beer manufacturer's expansion path shows the same relationship between long-run cost and output as the long-run cost curve.

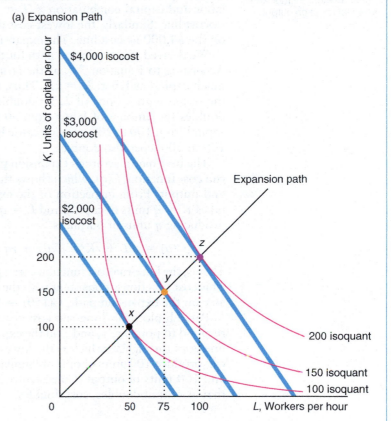

(a) Expansion Path

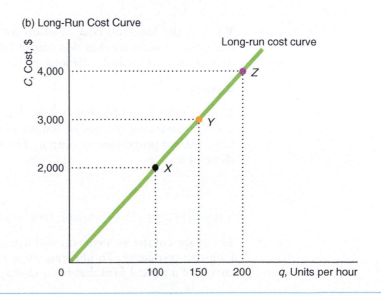

(b) Long-Run Cost Curve

expansion path
the cost-minimizing
combination of labor and
capital for each output
level

long-run **expansion path**: the cost-minimizing combination of labor and capital for each output level. The lowest-cost way to produce 100 units of output is to use the labor and capital combination x ($L = 50$ and $K = 100$), which lies on the $2,000 isocost line. Similarly, the lowest-cost way to produce 200 units is to use z, which is on the $4,000 isocost line. The expansion path goes through x and z.

We derived this expansion path for the beer manufacturer in Solved Problem 7.3. According to Equation 7.7, at the cost-minimizing bundles, the firm uses twice as much capital as labor: $K = 2L$. Thus, the expansion path is a straight line through the origin with a slope of 2. To double its output from 100 to 200 units, the firm doubles the amount of labor from 50 to 100 workers and doubles the amount of capital from 100 to 200 units. Because both inputs double when output doubles from 100 to 200, cost also doubles.

The beer manufacturer's expansion path contains the same information as its long-run cost function, $C(q)$, which shows the relationship between the cost of production and output. From inspection of the expansion path, to produce q units of output takes $K = q$ units of capital and $L = q/2$ units of labor.[6] Thus, the long-run cost of producing q units of output is

$$C(q) = wL + rK = wq/2 + rq = (w/2 + r)q = (24/2 + 8)q = 20q.$$

That is, the long-run cost function corresponding to this expansion path is $C(q) = 20q$. This cost function is consistent with the expansion path in panel a: $C(100) = \$2,000$ at x on the expansion path, $C(150) = \$3,000$ at y, and $C(200) = \$4,000$ at z.

Panel b plots this long-run cost curve. Points X, Y, and Z on the cost curve correspond to points x, y, and z on the expansion path. For example, the $2,000 isocost line goes through x, which is the lowest-cost combination of labor and capital that can produce 100 units of output. Similarly, X on the long-run cost curve is at $2,000 and 100 units of output. Consistent with the expansion path, the cost curve shows that as output doubles, cost doubles.

**Solved Problem
7.5**

What is the long-run cost function for a fixed-proportions production function (Chapter 6) when it takes one unit of labor and one unit of capital to produce one unit of output? Describe the long-run cost curve.

Answer

Multiply the inputs by their prices, and sum to determine total cost. The long-run cost of producing q units of output is $C(q) = wL + rK = wq + rq = (w + r)q$. Cost rises in proportion to output. The long-run cost curve is a straight line with a slope of $w + r$.

The Shape of Long-Run Cost Curves

The shapes of the average cost and marginal cost curves depend on the shape of the long-run cost curve. To illustrate these relationships, we examine the long-run cost curves of a typical firm that has a U-shaped long-run average cost curve.

---

[6]We can derive this result formally. As the expansion path shows, cost is minimized when $2L = K$. Substituting this expression into the production function, $q = 1.516L^{0.6}K^{0.4}$, we find that $q = 1.516L^{0.6}(2L)^{0.4} = 1.516 \times 2^{0.4}L = 2L$, or $L = q/2$. Thus, $K = 2L = q$.

The long-run cost curve in panel a of Figure 7.8 corresponds to the long-run average and marginal cost curves in panel b. Unlike the straight-line long-run cost curves of the beer firm in Figure 7.7 and the firm with fixed-proportions production in Solved Problem 7.5, the long-run cost curve of this firm rises less than in proportion to output at outputs below q^* and then rises more rapidly.

We can apply the same type of analysis that we used to study short-run curves to look at the geometric relationship between long-run total, average, and marginal curves. A line from the origin is tangent to the long-run cost curve at q^*, where the marginal cost curve crosses the average cost curve, because the slope of that line equals the marginal and average costs at that output. The long-run average cost curve falls when the long-run marginal cost curve is below it and rises when the long-run marginal cost curve is above it. Thus, the marginal cost curve crosses the average cost curve at the lowest point on the average cost curve.

Figure 7.8 Long-Run Cost Curves

(a) The long-run cost curve rises less rapidly than output at output levels below q^* and more rapidly at higher output levels. (b) As a consequence, the marginal cost and average cost curves are U-shaped. The marginal cost curve crosses the average cost curve at its minimum at q^*.

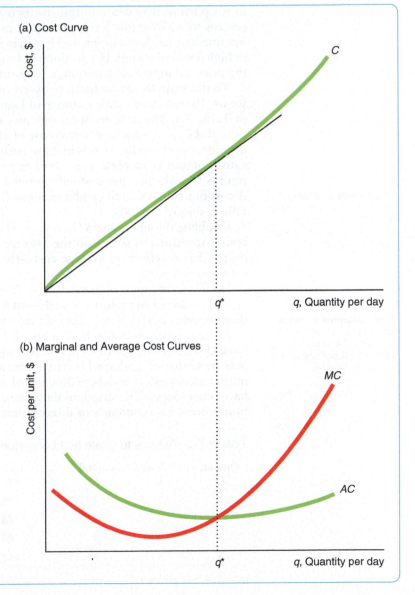

Why does the average cost curve first fall and then rise, as in panel b? The explanation differs from those given for why short-run average cost curves are U-shaped.

A key reason why the short-run average cost curve is initially downward sloping is that the average fixed cost curve is downward sloping: Spreading the fixed cost over more units of output lowers the average fixed cost per unit. Because a firm has no fixed costs in the long run, the initial downward slope of the long-run average cost curve is not due to fixed costs.

A major reason why the short-run average cost curve slopes upward at higher levels of output is diminishing marginal returns. In the long run, however, all factors can be varied, so diminishing marginal returns do not explain the upward slope of a long-run average cost curve.

Ultimately, as with the short-run curves, the shape of the long-run curves is determined by the production function relationship between output and inputs. In the long run, returns to scale play a major role in determining the shape of the average cost curve and other cost curves. As we discussed in Chapter 6, increasing all inputs in proportion may cause output to increase more than in proportion (increasing returns to scale) at low levels of output, in proportion (constant returns to scale) at intermediate levels of output, and less than in proportion (decreasing returns to scale) at high levels of output. If a production function has this returns-to-scale pattern and the prices of inputs are constant, a long-run average cost curve must be U-shaped.

To illustrate the relationship between returns to scale and long-run average cost, we use the returns-to-scale example of Figure 6.5, the data for which are reproduced in Table 7.3. The firm produces one unit of output using a unit each of labor and capital. Given a wage and rental cost of capital of $12 per unit, the total cost and average cost of producing this unit are both $24. Doubling both inputs ($L = K = 2$) causes output to increase more than in proportion to 3 units, reflecting increasing returns to scale. Because cost only doubles and output triples, the average cost falls. A cost function is said to exhibit **economies of scale** if the average cost of production falls as output expands.

economies of scale
property of a cost function whereby the average cost of production falls as output expands

Doubling the inputs again ($L = K = 4$) causes output to double ($q = 6$) as well—constant returns to scale—so the average cost remains constant. If an increase in output has no effect on average cost—the average cost curve is flat—there are *no economies of scale*.

Doubling the inputs once more ($L = K = 8$) causes only a small increase in output ($q = 8$)—decreasing returns to scale—so average cost increases. A firm suffers from **diseconomies of scale** if average cost rises when output increases.

diseconomies of scale
property of a cost function whereby the average cost of production rises when output increases

Average cost curves can have many different shapes. Competitive firms typically have U-shaped average cost curves. Average cost curves in noncompetitive markets may be U-shaped, L-shaped (average cost at first falls rapidly and then levels off as output increases), everywhere downward sloping, or everywhere upward sloping or have other shapes. The shapes of the average cost curves indicate whether the production process has economies or diseconomies of scale.

Table 7.3 Returns to Scale and Long-Run Costs

Output, Q	Labor, L	Capital, K	Cost, $C = wL + rK$	Average Cost, $AC = C/q$	Returns to Scale
1	1	1	24	24	
3	2	2	48	16	Increasing
6	4	4	96	16	Constant
8	8	8	192	24	Decreasing

$w = r = \$12$ per unit.

Table 7.4 Shape of Average Cost Curves in Canadian Manufacturing

Scale Economies		Share of Manufacturing Industries, %
Economies of scale: Initially downward-sloping *AC*	57	
Everywhere downward-sloping *AC*		18
L-shaped *AC* (downward-sloping, then flat)		31
U-shaped *AC*		8
No economies of scale: Flat *AC*	23	
Diseconomies of scale: Upward-sloping *AC*	14	

Source: Robidoux and Lester (1992).

Table 7.4 summarizes the shapes of average cost curves of firms in various Canadian manufacturing industries (as estimated by Robidoux and Lester, 1992). The table shows that U-shaped average cost curves are the exception rather than the rule in Canadian manufacturing and that nearly one-third of these average cost curves are L-shaped. Some of these apparently L-shaped average cost curves may be part of a U-shaped curve with long, flat bottoms, where we don't observe any firm producing enough to exhibit diseconomies of scale.

Application

Economies of Scale in Nuclear Power Plants

Economies of scale can be achieved across an entire company through more efficient management. Over the last decade and a half, the industry consolidated substantially as many U.S. nuclear power plants switched from operating in a regulated to an unregulated market. In the 1970s and 1980s, the typical independent nuclear firm operated a single nuclear power plant. By the late 1990s, the average was three plants. However, the average jumped to six plants in 2000 and is now about nine plants. Indeed, the three largest companies—Entergy, Exelon, and NextEra—operate about one third of all the nuclear capacity in the United States.

This consolidation improves operating efficiency in several ways. Rather than have a single plant use contract employees to perform infrequent tasks, such as refueling outages, which occur every 18 months on average, a consolidated nuclear company can hire highly skilled employees and train them to appreciate the idiosyncrasies of the company's reactors. In addition, consolidated firms may have employees and managers share best practices across plants. Gary Leidich, the president of FirstEnergy Nuclear, said that when the company acquired three nuclear plants they went from three separate facilities, "each pretty much doing their own thing" to a corporate organization where managers work together. For example, all the plant operators have a daily 7:30 A.M. conference call to discuss potential problems, and managers at FirstEnergy travel from plant to plant.

These economies of scale due to consolidation result in more efficient plants with substantially fewer outages. Consolidation decreases plant outages from, on average, 21 days per year to 15 days per year. Although this change may not seem substantial, a typical 2,000-megawatt nuclear power plant produces about $100,000 worth of power every hour, so 6 days of extra production increases revenues by over $14 million a year.

According to the estimates of Davis and Wolfram (2012), consolidation increases efficiency (net energy generation relative to plant capacity) and thereby reduces cost per unit of energy produced. According to their estimates, a firm with 16 extra plants would increase efficiency by 7.7 percentage points.

Estimating Cost Curves Versus Introspection

Economists use statistical methods to estimate a cost function. Sometimes, however, we can infer the shape by casual observation and deductive reasoning.

For example, in the good old days, the Good Humor company sent out fleets of ice-cream trucks to purvey its products. It seems likely that the company's production process had fixed proportions and constant returns to scale: If it wanted to sell more, Good Humor dispatched one more truck and one more driver. Drivers and trucks are almost certainly nonsubstitutable inputs (the isoquants are right angles). If the cost of a driver is w per day, the rental cost is r per day, and q quantity of ice cream is sold in a day, then the cost function is $C = (w + r)q$.

Such deductive reasoning can lead one astray, as I once discovered. A water heater manufacturing firm provided me with many years of data on the inputs it used and the amount of output it produced. I also talked to the company's engineers about the production process and toured the plant (which resembled a scene from Dante's *Inferno*, with staggering noise levels and flames everywhere).

A water heater consists of an outside cylinder of metal, a liner, an electronic control unit, hundreds of tiny parts (screws, washers, etc.), and a couple of rods that slow corrosion. Workers cut out the metal for the cylinder, weld it together, and add the other parts. "Okay," I said to myself, "this production process must be one of fixed proportions because the firm needs one of everything to produce a water heater. How could you substitute a cylinder for an electronic control unit? Or how can you substitute labor for metal?"

I then used statistical techniques to estimate the production and cost functions. Following the usual procedure, however, I did not assume that I knew the exact form of the functions. Rather, I allowed the data to "tell" me the type of production and cost functions. To my surprise, the estimates indicated that the production process was not one of fixed proportions. Rather, the firm could readily substitute between labor and capital.

"Surely I've made a mistake," I said to the plant manager after describing these results. "No," he said, "that's correct. There's a great deal of substitutability between labor and metal."

"How can they be substitutes?"

"Easy," he said. "We can use a lot of labor and waste very little metal by cutting out exactly what we want and being very careful. Or we can use relatively little labor, cut quickly, and waste more metal. When the cost of labor is relatively high, we waste more metal. When the cost of metal is relatively high, we cut more carefully." This practice minimizes the firm's cost.

7.4 Lower Costs in the Long Run

In its long-run planning, a firm chooses a plant size and makes other investments so as to minimize its long-run cost on the basis of how many units it produces. Once it chooses its plant size and equipment, these inputs are fixed in the short run. Thus, the firm's long-run decision determines its short-run cost. Because the firm cannot vary its capital in the short run but can vary it in the long run, short-run cost is at least as high as long-run cost and is higher if the "wrong" level of capital is used in the short run.

Long-Run Average Cost as the Envelope of Short-Run Average Cost Curves

As a result, the long-run average cost is always equal to or below the short-run average cost. Suppose, initially, that the firm in Figure 7.9 has only three possible plant sizes. The firm's short-run average cost curve is $SRAC^1$ for the smallest possible plant. The average cost of producing q_1 units of output using this plant, point a on $SRAC^1$, is $10. If instead the plant used the next larger plant size, its cost of producing q_1 units of output, point b on $SRAC^2$, would be $12. Thus, if the firm knows that it will produce only q_1 units of output, it minimizes its average cost by using the smaller plant size. If it expects to be producing q_2, its average cost is lower on the $SRAC^2$ curve, point e, than on the $SRAC^1$ curve, point d.

In the long run, the firm chooses the plant size that minimizes its cost of production, so it picks the plant size that has the lowest average cost for each possible output level. At q_1, it opts for the small plant size, whereas at q_2, it uses the medium plant size. Thus, the long-run average cost curve is the solid, scalloped section of the three short-run cost curves.

If a firm may choose any plant size it wants, the long-run average curve, $LRAC$, is smooth and U-shaped. The $LRAC$ is tangent at one point to each possible short-run average cost curve, making it the *envelope* of the short-run curves. These tangency points are not necessarily the minimum points on the short-run curves. For example, the $LRAC$ includes a on $SRAC^1$ and not its minimum point, c. A small plant operating at minimum average cost cannot produce at as low an average cost as a slightly larger plant that is taking advantage of economies of scale.

Figure 7.9 Long-Run Average Cost as the Envelope of Short-Run Average Cost Curves

If there are only three possible plant sizes, with short-run average costs $SRAC^1$, $SRAC^2$, and $SRAC^3$, the long-run average cost curve is the solid, scalloped portion of the three short-run curves. $LRAC$ is the smooth and U-shaped long-run average cost curve if there are many possible short-run average cost curves.

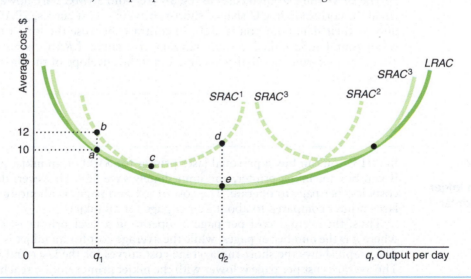

Application

Long-Run Cost Curves in Beer Manufacturing

The graph shows the relationship between short-run and long-run average cost curves for the Japanese beer manufacturer (based on the estimates of Flath, 2011). Because this production function has constant returns to scale, doubling both inputs doubles output, so the long-run average cost, *LRAC*, is constant. If capital is fixed at 200 units, the firm's short-run average cost curve is $SRAC^1$. If the firm produces 200 units of output, its short-run and long-run average costs are equal. At any other output, its short-run cost is higher than its long-run cost.

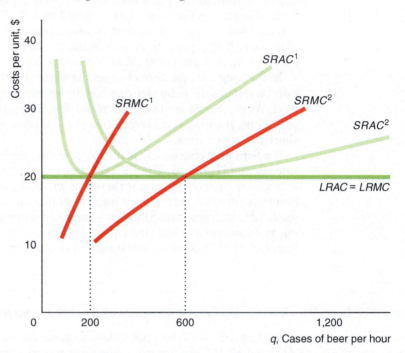

The short-run marginal cost curves, $SRMC^1$ and $SRMC^2$, are upward sloping and equal the corresponding U-shaped short-run average cost curves, $SRAC^1$ and $SRAC^2$, only at their minimum points, $20. In contrast, because the long-run average cost is horizontal at $20, the long-run marginal cost curve, *LRMC*, is horizontal at $20. Thus, the long-run marginal cost curve is *not* the envelope of the short-run marginal cost curves.

Application

Choosing an Inkjet or a Laser Printer

In 2013, you can buy a personal laser printer for $100 or an inkjet printer for $31. If you buy the inkjet printer, you immediately save $69. However, the laser printer costs less per page to operate. The cost of ink and paper is about 4¢ per page for a laser printer compared to about 7¢ per page for an inkjet.

Thus, the average cost per page of operating a laser printer is $100/q + 0.04$, where q is the number of pages, while the average cost for an inkjet is $31/q + 0.07$. The graph shows the short-run average cost curves for the laser and inkjet printers. The average cost per page is lower with the inkjet printer until q reaches 2,300 pages where the average cost of both is about 8.3¢ per page. For larger quantities, the laser is less expensive per page.

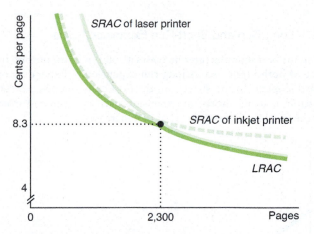

So, should you buy the laser printer? If you'll print more than 2,300 pages over its lifetime, the laser printer is less expensive to operate than the inkjet. If the printers last two years and you print 23 or more pages per week, then the laser printer has a lower average cost.

Short-Run and Long-Run Expansion Paths

Long-run cost is lower than short-run cost because the firm has more flexibility in the long run. To show the advantage of flexibility, we can compare the short-run and long-run expansion paths, which correspond to the short-run and long-run cost curves.

The beer manufacturer has greater flexibility in the long run. The tangency of the firm's isoquants and isocost lines determines the long-run expansion path in Figure 7.10. The firm expands output by increasing both its labor and its capital, so its long-run expansion path is upward sloping. To increase its output from 100 to 200 units (move from x to z), it doubles its capital from 100 to 200 units and its labor from 50 to 100 workers. Its cost increases from $2,000 to $4,000.

In the short run, the firm cannot increase its capital, which is fixed at 100 units. The firm can increase its output only by using more labor, so its short-run expansion path is horizontal at $K = 100$. To expand its output from 100 to 200 units (move from x to y), the firm must increase its labor from 50 to 159 workers, and its cost rises from $2,000 to $4,616. Doubling output increases long-run cost by a factor of 2 and short-run cost by approximately 2.3.

The Learning Curve

What we have to learn to do, we learn by doing. —Aristotle

A firm's average cost may fall over time for three reasons. First, operating at a larger scale in the long run may lower average cost due to increasing returns to scale (IRS). Second, technological progress (see Chapter 6) may increase productivity and thereby lower average cost. Third, a firm may benefit from **learning by doing**: the productive skills and knowledge that workers and managers gain from experience.

Workers given a new task may perform it slowly the first few times they try, but their speed increases with practice. Managers may learn how to organize production more efficiently, discover which workers to assign to which tasks, and determine where more inventories are needed and where they can be reduced. Engineers may

learning by doing
the productive skills and knowledge that workers and managers gain from experience

Figure 7.10 Long-Run and Short-Run Expansion Paths

In the long run, the beer manufacturer increases its output by using more of both inputs, so its long-run expansion path is upward sloping. In the short run, the firm cannot vary its capital, so its short-run expansion path is horizontal at the fixed level of output. That is, it increases its output by increasing the amount of labor it uses. Expanding output from 100 to 200 raises the beer firm's long-run cost from $2,000 to $4,000 but raises its short-run cost from $2,000 to $4,616.

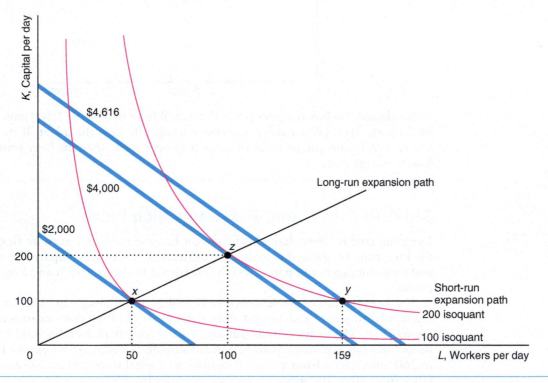

optimize product designs by experimenting with various production methods. For these and other reasons, the average cost of production tends to fall over time, and the effect is particularly strong with new products.

In some firms, learning by doing is a function of the time elapsed since the start of production of a particular product. However, more commonly, learning is a function of *cumulative output*: the total number of units of output produced since the product was introduced.

learning curve
the relationship between average costs and cumulative output

The **learning curve** is the relationship between average costs and cumulative output. The learning curve for Intel central processing units (CPUs) in panel a of Figure 7.11 shows that Intel's average cost fell very rapidly with the first few million units of cumulative output, but then dropped relatively slowly with additional units (Salgado, 2008).

If a firm is operating in the economies of scale section of its average cost curve, expanding output lowers its cost for two reasons. Its average cost falls today because of economies of scale, and for any given level of output, its average cost is lower in the next period due to learning by doing.

In panel b of Figure 7.11, the firm is producing q_1 units of output at point A on average cost curve AC^1 in the first period. We assume that each period is long enough that the firm can vary all factors of production. If the firm expands its output to q_2 in

Figure 7.11 Learning by Doing

(a) As Intel produced more cumulative CPUs, the average cost of production fell (Salgado, 2008). (b) In the short run, extra production reduces a firm's average cost owing to economies of scale: because $q_1 < q_2 < q_3$, A is higher than B, which is higher than C. In the long run, extra production reduces average cost because of learning by doing. To produce q_2 this period costs B on AC^1, but to produce that same output in the next period would cost

only b on AC^2. If the firm produces q_3 instead of q_2 in this period, its average cost in the next period is AC^3 instead of AC^2 because of additional learning by doing. Thus, extra output in this period lowers the firm's cost in two ways: It lowers average cost in this period due to economies of scale and lowers average cost for any given output level in the next period due to learning by doing.

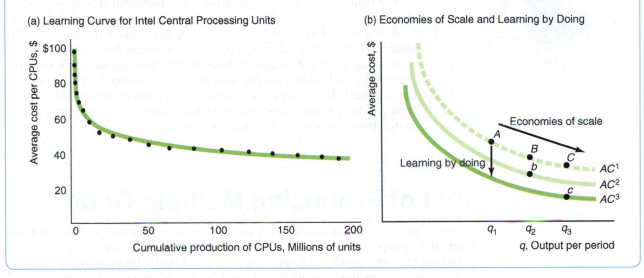

(a) Learning Curve for Intel Central Processing Units

(b) Economies of Scale and Learning by Doing

Period 1, its average cost falls in this period to B because of economies of scale. The learning by doing in this period results in a lower average cost, AC^2, in Period 2. If the firm continues to produce q_2 units of output in the next period, its average cost falls to b on AC^2.

If instead of expanding output to q_2 in Period 1, the firm expands to q_3, its average cost is even lower in Period 1 (C on AC^1) due to even more economies of scale. Moreover, its average cost in the Period 2, AC^3, is even lower due to the extra experience producing more output in Period 1. If the firm continues to produce q_3 in Period 2, its average cost is c on AC^3. Thus, all else being the same, if learning by doing depends on cumulative output, firms have an incentive to produce more in any one period than they otherwise would to lower their costs in the future.

Application

Learning by Drilling

Learning by doing can substantially reduce the cost of drilling oil wells. Two types of firms work together to drill oil wells. Oil production companies such as Exxon-Mobil and Chevron perform the technical design and planning of wells to be drilled. The actual drilling is performed by drilling companies that own and staff drilling rigs. The time it takes to drill a well varies across fields, which differ in terms of the types of rock covering the oil and the depth of the oil.

Kellogg (2011) found that the more experience—the cumulative number of wells that the oil production firm drilled in the field over the past two years—the less time it takes the firm to drill another well. His estimated learning curve shows that drilling time decreases rapidly at first, falling by about 15% after the first 25 wells

have been drilled, but that drilling time does not fall much more with additional experience.

This decrease in drilling time is the sum of the benefits from two types of experience. The time it takes to drill a well falls as the production company drills (1) more wells in the field and (2) more wells in that field with a particular drilling company. The second effect occurs because the two firms learn to work better together in a particular field. Because neither firm can apply its learning with a particular partner to its work with another partner, production companies prefer to continue to work with the same drilling rig firms over time.

The reduction in drilling time from a production firm's average stand-alone experience over the past two years is 6.4% or 1.5 fewer days to drill a well. This time savings reduces the cost of drilling a well by about $16,300. The relationship-specific learning from experience due to working with a drilling company for the average duration over two years reduces drilling time per well by 3.8%, or about $9,700 per well. On average, the reduction in drilling time from working with one rig crew regularly is twice as much as from working with rigs that frequently switch from one production firm to another.

7.5 Cost of Producing Multiple Goods

Few firms produce only a single good, but we discuss single-output firms for simplicity. If a firm produces two or more goods, the cost of one good may depend on the output level of the other. Outputs are linked if a single input is used to produce both of them. For example, mutton and wool both come from sheep, cattle provide beef and hides, and oil supplies both heating fuel and gasoline. It is less expensive to produce beef and hides together than separately. If the goods are produced together, a single steer yields one unit of beef and one hide. If beef and hides are produced separately (throwing away the unused good), the same amount of output requires two steers and more labor.

economies of scope
situation in which it is less expensive to produce goods jointly than separately

More generally, we refer to **economies of scope** if it is less expensive to produce goods jointly than separately (Panzar and Willig, 1977, 1981). A measure of the degree of economies of scope (SC) is

$$SC = \frac{C(q_1, 0) + C(0, q_2) - C(q_1, q_2)}{C(q_1, q_2)},$$

where $C(q_1, 0)$ is the cost of producing q_1 units of the first good by itself, $C(0, q_2)$ is the cost of producing q_2 units of the second good, and $C(q_1, q_2)$ is the cost of producing both goods together. If the cost of producing the two goods separately, $C(q_1, 0) + C(0, q_2)$, is the same as producing them together, $C(q_1, q_2)$, then SC is zero. If it is cheaper to produce the goods jointly, SC is positive. If SC is negative, the diseconomies of scope imply that it is cheaper to produce the goods separately.

production possibility frontier
the maximum amount of outputs that can be produced from a fixed amount of input

To illustrate this idea, suppose that Laura spends one day collecting mushrooms and wild strawberries in the woods. Her **production possibility frontier**—the maximum amounts of outputs (mushrooms and strawberries) that can be produced from a fixed amount of input (Laura's effort during one day)—is PPF^1 in Figure 7.12. The production possibility frontier summarizes the trade-off Laura faces: She picks fewer mushrooms if she collects more strawberries in a day.

Figure 7.12 Joint Production

If there are economies of scope, the production possibility frontier is bowed away from the origin, PPF^1. If instead the production possibility frontier is a straight line, PPF^2, the cost of producing both goods does not fall if they are produced together.

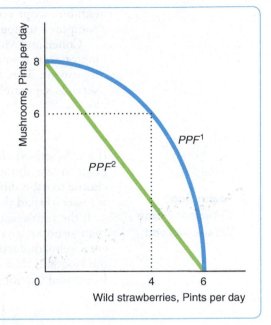

If Laura spends all day collecting only mushrooms, she picks 8 pints; if she spends all day picking strawberries, she collects 6 pints. If she picks some of each, however, she can harvest more total pints: 6 pints of mushrooms and 4 pints of strawberries. The product possibility frontier is concave (the middle of the curve is farther from the origin than it would be if it were a straight line) because of the diminishing marginal returns from collecting only one of the two goods. If she collects only mushrooms, she must walk past wild strawberries without picking them. As a result, she has to walk farther if she collects only mushrooms than if she picks both. Thus, she benefits from economies of scope in jointly collecting mushrooms and strawberries.

If instead the production possibility frontier were a straight line, the cost of producing the two goods jointly would not be lower. Suppose, for example, that mushrooms grow in one section of the woods and strawberries in another section. In that case, Laura can collect only mushrooms without passing any strawberries. That production possibility frontier is a straight line, PPF^2 in Figure 7.12. By allocating her time between the two sections of the woods, Laura can collect any combination of mushrooms and strawberries by spending part of her day in one section of the woods and part in the other.

Application

Economies of Scope

Empirical studies show that some processes have economies of scope, others have none, and some have diseconomies of scope. Producing and transmitting electricity has substantial economies of scope, $SC = 0.2$, in Japan (Ida and Kuwahara, 2004). The scope economies are almost the same in the United States, where separating production from transmitting and distributing electricity would increase average cost by 19% to 26% ($CS = 0.19$ to 0.26) depending on the firm's size (Meyer, 2012).

Gonçalves and Barros (2013) examined whether providing auxiliary clinical services in Portuguese hospitals is cost effective. They did not find economies of scope between clinical chemistry service and other medical services, so outsourcing that service would not raise costs. However, in medical imaging, computed tomography exhibits scope economies with most other services, which suggests that outsourcing computed tomography would raise the costs of producing those other outputs.

Cohen and Morrison Paul (2011) investigated whether it is cost effective for Washington state hospitals to provide both inpatient and outpatient services for drug abuse treatment. They found large diseconomies of scale, so it is cheaper to provide these services separately.

Challenge Solution

Technology Choice at Home Versus Abroad

If a U.S. semiconductor manufacturing firm shifts production from the firm's home plant to one abroad, should it use the same mix of inputs as at home? The firm may choose to use a different technology because the firm's cost of labor relative to capital is lower abroad than in the United States.

If the firm's isoquant is smooth, the firm uses a different bundle of inputs abroad than at home, given that the relative factor prices differ as Figure 7.6 shows. However, semiconductor manufacturers may have kinked isoquants. The figure shows the isoquant that we examined in Chapter 6 in the Application "A Semiconductor Integrated Circuit Isoquant."

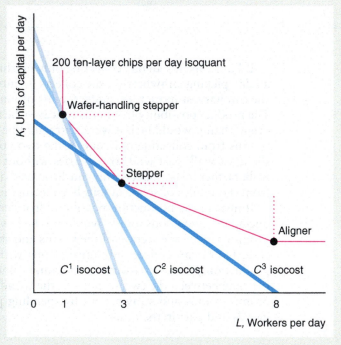

In its U.S. plant, the semiconductor manufacturing firm uses a wafer-handling stepper technology because the C^1 isocost line, which is the lowest isocost line that touches the isoquant, hits the isoquant at that technology.

The firm's cost of both inputs is less abroad than in the United States, and its cost of labor is relatively less than the cost of capital at its foreign plant than at its U.S. plant. The slope of its isocost line is $-w/r$, where w is the wage and r is the rental cost of the manufacturing equipment. The smaller w is relative to r, the less steeply sloped is its isocost curve. Thus, the firm's foreign isocost line is flatter than its domestic C^1 isocost line.

If the firm's isoquant were smooth, the firm would certainly use a different technology at its foreign plant than in its home plant. However, its isoquant has kinks, so a small change in the relative input prices does not necessarily lead to a change in production technology. The firm could face either the C^2 or C^3 isocost curves, both of which are flatter than the C^1 isocost. If the firm faces the C^2 isocost line, which is only slightly flatter than the C^1 isocost, the firm still uses the capital-intensive wafer-handling stepper technology in its foreign plant. However, if the firm faces the much flatter C^3 isocost line, which hits the isoquant at the stepper technology, it switches technologies. (If the isocost line were even flatter, it could hit the isoquant at the aligner technology.)

Even if the wage change is small so that the firm's isocost is C^2 and the firm does not switch technologies abroad, the firm's cost will be lower abroad with the same technology because C^2 is less than C^1. However, if the wage is low enough that it can shift to a more labor-intensive technology, its costs will be even lower: C^3 is less than C^2.

Thus, whether the firm uses a different technology in its foreign plant than in its domestic plant turns on the relative factor prices in the two locations and whether the firm's isoquant is smooth. If the isoquant is smooth, even a slight difference in relative factor prices will induce the firm to shift along the isoquant and use a different technology with a different capital-labor ratio. However, if the isoquant has kinks, the firm will use a different technology only if the relative factor prices differ substantially.

Summary

From all technologically efficient production processes, a firm chooses the one that is economically efficient. The economically efficient production process is the technologically efficient process for which the cost of producing a given quantity of output is lowest, or the one that produces the most output for a given cost.

1. **The Nature of Costs.** In making decisions about production, managers need to take into account the opportunity cost of an input, which is the value of the input's best alternative use. For example, if the manager is the owner of the company and does not receive a salary, the amount that the owner could have earned elsewhere—the forgone earnings—is the opportunity cost of the manager's time and is relevant in deciding whether the firm should produce or not. A durable good's opportunity cost depends on its current alternative use. If the past expenditure for a durable good is sunk—that is, it cannot be recovered—then that input has no opportunity cost and hence should not influence current production decisions.

2. **Short-Run Costs.** In the short run, the firm can vary the costs of the factors that it can adjust, but the costs of other factors are fixed. The firm's average fixed cost falls as its output rises. If a firm has a short-run average cost curve that is U-shaped, its marginal cost

curve is below the average cost curve when average cost is falling and above the average cost when it is rising, so the marginal cost curve cuts the average cost curve at its minimum.

3. **Long-Run Costs.** In the long run, all factors can be varied, so all costs are variable. As a result, average cost and average variable cost are identical. The firm chooses the combination of inputs it uses to minimize its cost. To produce a given output level, it chooses the lowest isocost line that touches the relevant isoquant, which is tangent to the isoquant. Equivalently, to minimize cost, the firm adjusts inputs until the last dollar spent on any input increases output by as much as the last dollar spent on any other input. If the firm calculates the cost of producing every possible output level given current input prices, it knows its cost function: Cost is a function of the input prices and the output level. If the firm's average cost falls as output expands, it has economies of scale. If its average cost rises as output expands, there are diseconomies of scale.

4. **Lower Costs in the Long Run.** The firm can always do in the long run what it does in the short run, so its long-run cost can never be greater than its short-run cost. Because some factors are fixed in the short run, to expand output, the firm must greatly increase its

use of other factors, which is relatively costly. In the long run, the firm can adjust all factors, a process that keeps its cost down. Long-run cost may also be lower than short-run cost due to technological progress or learning by doing.

5. **Cost of Producing Multiple Goods.** For some goods, it is less expensive to produce two goods jointly rather than separately due to economies of scope. For other goods, diseconomies of scope make it is less expensive to produce the goods separately.

Questions

All questions are available on MyEconLab; * = *answer appears at the back of this book;* **A** = *algebra problem;* **C** = *calculus problem.*

1. The Nature of Costs

1.1 Executives at Leonesse Cellars, a premium winery in Southern California, were surprised to learn that shipping wine by sea to some cities in Asia was less expensive than sending it to the East Coast of the United States, so they started shipping to Asia (David Armstrong, "Discount Cargo Rates Ripe for the Taking," *San Francisco Chronicle*, August 28, 2005). Because of the large U.S. trade imbalance with major Asian nations, cargo ships arrive at West Coast seaports fully loaded but return to Asia half to completely empty. Use the concept of opportunity cost to help explain the differential shipping rates.

1.2 You have a ticket to go to a concert by one of your favorite groups, the Hives, which you cannot resell. However, you can buy a ticket for $30 to attend a talk by Steven Colbert, which is at the same time as the concert. You are willing to pay up to $90 to hear Colbert. Given that there are no other costs involved in attending either event, what is your opportunity cost of attending the Hives concert? (*Hint*: See Solved Problem 7.1.)

*1.3 "'There are certain fixed costs when you own a plane,' [Andre] Agassi explained during a break in the action at the Volvo/San Francisco tennis tournament, 'so the more you fly it, the more economic sense it makes. . . . The first flight after I bought it, I took some friends to Palm Springs for lunch.'" (Scott Ostler, "Andre Even Flies Like a Champ," *San Francisco Chronicle*, February 8, 1993, C1.) Discuss whether Agassi's statement is reasonable.

*1.4 A firm purchased copper pipes a few years ago at $10 per pipe and stored them, using them only as the need arises. The firm could sell its remaining pipes in the market at the current price of $9. What is the opportunity cost of each pipe and what is the sunk cost?

2. Short-Run Costs

2.1 Many corporations allow CEOs to use the firm's corporate jet for personal travel. The Internal Revenue Service (IRS) requires that the firm report personal use of its corporate jet as taxable executive income, and the Securities and Exchange Commission (SEC) requires that publicly traded corporations report the value of this benefit to shareholders. An important issue is the determination of the value of this benefit. The IRS values a CEO's personal flight at or below the price of a first-class ticket. The SEC values the flight at the "incremental" cost of the flight: the additional costs to the corporation of the flight. The third alternative is the market value of chartering an aircraft. Of the three methods, the first-class ticket is least expensive and the chartered flight is most expensive.

a. What factors (such as fuel) determine the marginal explicit cost to a corporation of an executive's personal flight? Does any one of the three valuation methods correctly determine the marginal explicit cost?

b. What is the marginal opportunity cost to the corporation of an executive's personal flight?

2.2 In the twentieth century, department stores and supermarkets largely replaced smaller specialty stores, as consumers found it more efficient to go to one store rather than many stores. Consumers incur a transaction or search cost to shop, primarily the opportunity cost of their time. This transaction cost consists of a fixed cost of traveling to and from the store and a variable cost that rises with the number of different types of items the consumer tries to find on the shelves. By going to a supermarket that carries meat, fruits and vegetables, and other items, consumers can avoid some of the fixed transaction costs of traveling to a separate butcher shop, produce mart, and so forth. Use math or figures to explain why a shopper's average costs are lower when buying at a single supermarket than from many stores. (*Hint*: Define the goods as the items purchased and brought home.)

2.3 Using the information in Table 7.1, construct another table showing how a lump-sum franchise tax of $30 affects the various average cost curves of the firm.

2.4 In 1796, Gottfried Christoph Härtel, a German music publisher, calculated the cost of printing music using an engraved plate technology and used these estimated cost functions to make production decisions. Härtel figured that the fixed cost of printing a musical page—the cost of engraving the plates—was 900 pfennings. The marginal cost of each additional copy of the page was 5 pfennings (Scherer, 2001).

   a. Graph the total cost, average total cost, average variable cost, and marginal cost functions.

   b. Is there a cost advantage to having only one music publisher print a given composition? Why?

   c. Härtel used his data to do the following type of analysis. Suppose he expected to sell exactly 300 copies of a composition at 15 pfennings per page of the composition. What was the greatest amount the publisher would be willing to pay the composer per page of the composition?

2.5 The only variable input a janitorial service firm uses to clean offices is workers who are paid a wage, w, of $8 an hour. Each worker can clean four offices in an hour. Use math to determine the variable cost, the average variable cost, and the marginal cost of cleaning one more office. Draw a diagram like Figure 7.1 to show the variable cost, average variable cost, and marginal cost curves. **A**

2.6 Give the formulas for and plot AFC, MC, AVC, and AC if the cost function is

   a. $C = 10 + 10q$

   b. $C = 10 + q^2$

   c. $C = 10 + 10q - 4q^2 + q^3$ **A**

2.7 Gail works in a flower shop, where she produces ten floral arrangements per hour. She is paid $10 an hour for the first eight hours she works and $15 an hour for each additional hour she works. If Gail's wage is the firm's only variable cost, what is the firm's cost function? What are its AC, AVC, and MC functions? Draw the AC, AVC, and MC curves. **A**

2.8 A firm's cost curve is $C = F + 10q - bq^2 + q^3$, where $b > 0$.

   a. For what values of b are cost, average cost, and average variable cost positive? (From now on, assume that all these measures of cost are positive at every output level.)

   b. What is the shape of the AC curve? At what output level is the AC minimized?

   c. At what output levels does the MC curve cross the AC and the AVC curves? **C**

2.9 A firm has two plants that produce identical output. The cost functions are $C_1 = 10q - 4q^2 + q^3$ and $C_2 = 10q - 2q^2 + q^3$.

   a. At what output levels does the average cost curve of each plant reach its minimum?

   b. If the firm wants to produce four units of output, how much should it produce in each plant? **C**

*2.10 A firm builds wooden shipping crates. How does the cost of producing a 1-cubic-foot crate (each side is 1-foot square) compare to the cost of building an 8-cubic-foot crate if wood costs $1 a square foot and the firm has no labor or other costs? More generally, how does cost vary with volume?

2.11 A Chinese high technology manufacturing firm has a production function of $q = 10L^{0.28}K^{0.64}$ (based on Zhang et al., 2012). It faces factor prices of $w = 10$ and $r = 20$. What are its short-run marginal cost and average variable cost curves? (*Hint:* See Appendix 7B.) **A**

2.12 Suppose in Solved Problem 7.2 that the government charges the firm a franchise tax each year (instead of only once). Describe the effect of this tax on the marginal cost, average variable cost, short-run average cost, and long-run average cost curves.

2.13 In the Application "Short-Run Cost Curves for a Beer Manufacturer," the short-run variable cost function for Japanese beer is $VC = 0.55q^{1.67}$. If the fixed cost is 600 and the firm produces 550 units, determine the C, VC, MC, AFC, and AVC. What happens to these costs if the firm increases its output to 600? **A**

3. Long-Run Costs

3.1 Initially a firm's wage is $w = 10$ and its rental cost of capital is $r = 10$. After its wage rate doubles, how do its isocost lines change?

*3.2 You have 60 minutes to take an exam with 2 questions. You want to maximize your score. Toward the end of the exam, the more time you spend on either question, the fewer extra points per minute you get for that question. How should you allocate your time between the two questions? (*Hint:* Think about producing an output of a score on the exam using inputs of time spent on each of the problems. Then use Equation 7.8.)

*3.3 A bottling company uses two inputs to produce bottles of the soft drink Sludge: bottling machines (K) and workers (L). The isoquants have the usual smooth shape. The machine costs $1,000 per day to run. The workers earn $200 per day. At the current level of production, the marginal product of the machine is an additional 200 bottles per day, and the marginal product of labor is 50 more bottles per day. Is this firm producing at minimum cost? If it is minimizing cost, explain why. If it is not minimizing cost, explain how the firm should change the ratio of inputs it uses to lower its cost. (*Hint*: Examine the conditions for minimizing cost: Equations 7.5 or 7.8. See Solved Problem 7.3.)

3.4 Use the tangency rule to determine the cost-minimizing bundles of labor and capital for a Japanese synthetic rubber firm's production function $q = L^{0.5}K^{0.5}$ (Flath, 2011) where $w = 10$ and $r = 10$. How does your answer change if $w = 20$ and $r = 10$? (*Hint*: See Solved Problem 7.3.)

3.5 A U.S. electronics firm is considering moving its production abroad. Its production function is $q = L^{0.5}K^{0.5}$ (based on Hsieh, 1995), so its $MP_L = \frac{1}{2}K^{0.5}/L^{0.5}$ and its $MP_K = \frac{1}{2}L^{0.5}/K^{0.5}$ (as Appendix 6C shows). The U.S. factor prices are $w = r = 10$. In Mexico, the wage is half that in the United States but the firm faces the same cost of capital: $w^* = 5$ and $r^* = r = 10$. What are L and K, and what is the cost of producing $q = 100$ units in both countries? (*Hint*: See Solved Problem 7.3.) **A**

*3.6 A U.S. apparel manufacturer is considering moving its production abroad. Its production function is $q = L^{0.7}K^{0.3}$ (based on Hsieh, 1995), so its $MP_L = 0.7q/L$ and its $MP_K = 0.3q/K$. In the United States, $w = 7$ and $r = 3$. At its Asian plant, the firm will pay a 10% lower wage and a 10% higher cost of capital: $w = 7/1.1$ and $r = 3 \times 1.1$. What are L and K, and what is the cost of producing $q = 100$ units in both countries? What would the cost of production be in Asia if the firm had to use the same factor quantities as in the United States? (*Hint*: See Solved Problem 7.4.) **A**

*3.7 The all-American baseball is made using cork from Portugal, rubber from Malaysia, yarn from Australia, and leather from France, and it is stitched (108 stitches exactly) by workers in Costa Rica. To assemble a baseball takes one unit each of these inputs. Ultimately, the finished product must be shipped to its final destination—say, Cooperstown, New York. The materials used cost the same anywhere. Labor costs are lower in Costa Rica than in a possible alternative manufacturing site in Georgia, but shipping costs from Costa Rica are higher. What production function is used? What is the cost function? What can you conclude about shipping costs if it is less expensive to produce baseballs in Costa Rica than in Georgia? (*Hint*: See Solved Problem 7.4.)

3.8 Suppose that the government subsidizes the cost of workers by paying for 25% of the wage (the rate offered by the U.S. government in the late 1970s under the New Jobs Tax Credit program). What effect will this subsidy have on the firm's choice of labor and capital to produce a given level of output? (*Hint*: See Solved Problem 7.4.)

3.9 California's State Board of Equalization imposed a higher tax on "alcopops," flavored beers containing more than 0.5% alcohol-based flavorings, such as vanilla extract. Such beers are taxed as distilled spirits at $3.30 a gallon rather than as beer at 20¢ a gallon. In response, manufacturers reformulated their beverages so as to avoid the tax. By early 2009, instead of collecting a predicted $38 million a year in new taxes, the state collected only about $9,000 (Guy L. Smith, "On Regulation of 'Alcopops,'" *San Francisco Chronicle*, April 10, 2009). Use an isocost-isoquant diagram to explain the firms' response. (*Hint*: Alcohol-based flavors and other flavors may be close to perfect substitutes.)

3.10 The Bouncing Ball Ping Pong Co. sells table tennis sets that consist of two paddles and one net. What is the firm's long-run expansion path if it incurs no costs other than what it pays for paddles and nets, which it buys at market prices? How does its expansion path depend on the relative prices of paddles and nets? (*Hint*: See Solved Problem 7.5.)

3.11 Boxes of cereal are produced by using a fixed-proportion production function: One box and one unit (12 ounces) of cereal produce one box of cereal. What is the expansion path? What is the cost function? (*Hint*: See Solved Problem 7.5.)

*3.12 What is the long-run cost function if the production function is $q = L + K$?

3.13 Suppose that your firm's production function has constant returns to scale. What is the expansion path? (*Hint*: See Solved Problem 7.5.)

3.14 A U.S. glass manufacturer's production function is $q = 10L^{0.5}K^{0.5}$ (based on Hsieh, 1995). Its marginal product functions are $MP_L = 5K^{0.5}/L^{0.5} = 0.5q/L$ and $MP_K = 5L^{0.5}/K^{0.5} = 0.5q/K$. Suppose that its wage, w, is $1 per hour and the rental cost of capital, r, is $4.

a. Draw an accurate figure showing how the glass firm minimizes its cost of production. (*Hint*: See Solved Problem 7.4.)

b. What is the equation of the (long-run) expansion path for the glass firm? Illustrate this path in a graph.

c. Derive the long-run total cost curve equation as a function of q. **A**

3.15 According to Haskel and Sadun (2012), the United Kingdom started regulating the size of grocery stores in the early 1990s, and today the average size of a typical U.K. grocery store is roughly half the size of a typical U.S. store and two-thirds the size of a typical French store. What implications would such a restriction on size have on a store's average costs? Discuss in terms of economies of scale and scope.

4. Lower Costs in the Long Run

4.1 A U-shaped long-run average cost curve is the envelope of U-shaped short-run average cost curves. On what part of the short-run curve (downward sloping, flat, or upward sloping) does the short-run curve touch the long-run curve? (*Hint*: Your answer should depend on where on the long-run curve the two curves touch.)

*4.2 A firm's average cost is $AC = \alpha q^{\beta}$, where $\alpha > 0$. How can you interpret α? (*Hint*: Suppose that $q = 1$.) What sign must β have if there is learning by doing? What happens to average cost as q gets larger? Draw the average cost curve as a function of output for a particular set of α and β. **A**

4.3 In what types of industry would you expect to see substantial learning by doing? Why?

*4.4 A firm's learning curve, which shows the relationship between average cost and cumulative output (the sum of its output since the firm started producing), is $AC = a + bN^{-r}$; where AC is its average cost; N is its cumulative output; a, b, and r are positive constants; and $0 < r < 1$.

   a. What is the firm's AC if $r = 0$? What can you say about the firm's ability to learn by doing?

   b. If r exceeds zero, what can you say about the firm's ability to learn by doing? What happens to its AC as its cumulative output, N, gets extremely large? Given this result, what is your interpretation of a? **A**

5. Cost of Producing Multiple Goods

5.1 What can you say about Laura's economies of scope if her time is valued at $5 an hour and her production possibility frontier is PPF^1 in Figure 7.12?

*5.2 A refiner produces heating fuel and gasoline from crude oil in virtually fixed proportions. What can you say about economies of scope for such a firm? What is the sign of its measure of economies of scope, SC?

6. Challenge

*6.1 In the figure in the Challenge Solution, show that there are wage and cost of capital services such that the firm is indifferent between using the wafer-handling stepper technology and the stepper technology. How does this wage/cost of capital ratio compare to those in the C^2 and C^3 isocosts?

6.2 Rosenberg (2004) reported the invention of a new machine that serves as a mobile station for receiving and accumulating packed flats of strawberries close to where they are picked, reducing workers' time and the burden of carrying full flats of strawberries. A machine-assisted crew of 15 pickers produces as much output, q^*, as that of an unaided crew of 25 workers. In a 6-day, 50-hour workweek, the machine replaces 500 worker hours. At an hourly wage cost of $10, a machine saves $5,000 per week in labor costs, or $130,000 over a 26-week harvesting season. The cost of machine operation and maintenance expressed as a daily rental is $200, or $1,200 for a 6-day week. Thus, the net savings equal $3,800 per week, or $98,800 for 26 weeks.

   a. Draw the q^* isoquant assuming that only two technologies are available (pure labor and labor-machine). Label the isoquant and axes as thoroughly as possible.

   b. Add an isocost line to show which technology the firm chooses. (Be sure to measure wage and rental costs on a comparable time basis.)

   c. Draw the corresponding cost curves (with and without the machine), assuming constant returns to scale, and label the curves and the axes as thoroughly as possible.

8 Competitive Firms and Markets

Competition produces the best markets and the worst humans.

Challenge

The Rising Cost of Keeping On Truckin'

Businesses complain constantly about the costs and red tape that government regulations impose on them. U.S. truckers and trucking firms have a particular beef. In recent years, federal and state fees have increased substantially and truckers have had to adhere to many new regulations.

The Federal Motor Carrier Safety Administration (FMCSA) along with state transportation agencies in 41 states administer interstate trucking licenses through the Unified Carrier Registration Agreement. According to FMCSA's Web site in 2013, it has 27 types of driver regulations, 16 types of vehicle regulations, 42 types of company regulations, 4 types of hazardous materials regulations, and 14 types of other regulatory guidance. (Of course, they may have added some additional rules while I wrote this last sentence.[1]) A trucker must also maintain minimum insurance coverage, pay registration fees, and follow policies that differ across states before the FMCSA will issue the actual authorities (grant permission to operate). The registration process is so complex and time-consuming that firms pay substantial amounts to brokers who expedite the application process and take care of state licensing requirements.

For a large truck, the annual federal interstate registration fee can exceed $8,000. To operate, truckers and firms must pay for many additional fees and costly regulations. These largely lump-sum costs—which are not related to the number of miles driven—have increased substantially in recent years. During the 2007–2009 financial crisis, many states raised their annual fee from a few hundred to several thousand dollars per truck. Before going into the interstate trucking business, a firm must participate in the New Entrant Safety Assurance Process, which raised the standard of compliance for passing the new entrant safety audit starting in 2009. As of 2012, each truck must add an electronic onboard recorder, which documents travel time and distance and costs $1,500. What effect do these new fixed costs have on the trucking industry's market price and quantity? Are individual firms providing more or fewer trucking services? Does the number of firms in the market rise or fall? (As we'll discuss at the end of the chapter, the answer to one of these questions is surprising.)

---

[1]Indeed, the first time I checked after writing that sentence, I found that they had added a new rule forbidding truckers from texting while driving. (Of course, many of these rules and regulations help protect society and truckers in particular.)

One of the major questions a trucking or other firm faces is "How much should we produce?" To pick a level of output that maximizes its profit, a firm must consider its cost function and how much it can sell at a given price. The amount the firm thinks it can sell depends in turn on the market demand of consumers and its beliefs about how other firms in the market will behave. The behavior of firms depends on the **market structure**: the number of firms in the market, the ease with which firms can enter and leave the market, and the ability of firms to differentiate their products from those of their rivals.

market structure
the number of firms in the market, the ease with which firms can enter and leave the market, and the ability of firms to differentiate their products from those of their rivals

In this chapter, we look at a *competitive market structure*, one in which many firms produce identical products and firms can easily enter and exit the market. Because each firm produces a small share of the total market output and its output is identical to that of other firms, each firm is a *price taker* that cannot raise its price above the market price. If it were to try to do so, this firm would be unable to sell any of its output because consumers would buy the good at a lower price from the other firms in the market. The market price summarizes all a firm needs to know about the demand of consumers *and* the behavior of its rivals. Thus, a competitive firm can ignore the specific behavior of individual rivals in deciding how much to produce.[2]

In this chapter, we examine four main topics

1. **Perfect Competition.** A competitive firm is a price taker, and as such, it faces a horizontal demand curve.

2. **Profit Maximization.** To maximize profit, any firm must make two decisions: how much to produce and whether to produce at all.

3. **Competition in the Short Run.** Variable costs determine a profit-maximizing, competitive firm's supply curve and market supply curve, and with the market demand curve, the competitive equilibrium in the short run.

4. **Competition in the Long Run.** Firm supply, market supply, and competitive equilibrium are different in the long run than in the short run because firms can vary inputs that were fixed in the short run.

8.1 Perfect Competition

Competition is a common market structure that has very desirable properties, so it is useful to compare other market structures to competition. In this section, we describe the properties of competitive firms and markets.

Price Taking

When most people talk about "competitive firms," they mean firms that are rivals for the same customers. By this interpretation, any market with more than one firm is competitive. However, to an economist, only some of these multifirm markets are competitive.

Economists say that a market is *competitive* if each firm in the market is a *price taker*: a firm that cannot significantly affect the market price for its output or the prices at which it buys inputs. Why would a competitive firm be a price taker?

---

[2]In contrast, each oligopolistic firm must consider the behavior of each of its small number of rivals, as we discuss in Chapter 13.

Because it has no choice. The firm *has* to be a price taker if it faces a demand curve that is horizontal at the market price. If the demand curve is horizontal at the market price, the firm can sell as much as it wants at that price, so it has no incentive to lower its price. Similarly, the firm cannot increase the price at which it sells by restricting its output because it faces an infinitely elastic demand (see Chapter 3): A small increase in price results in its demand falling to zero.

Why the Firm's Demand Curve Is Horizontal

Perfectly competitive markets have five characteristics that force firms to be price takers:

1. The market consists of many small buyers and sellers.
2. All firms produce identical products.
3. All market participants have full information about price and product characteristics.
4. Transaction costs are negligible.
5. Firms can easily enter and exit the market.

Large Number of Buyers and Sellers   If the sellers in a market are small and numerous, no single firm can raise or lower the market price. The more firms in a market, the less any one firm's output affects the market output and hence the market price.

For example, the 107,000 U.S. soybean farmers are price takers. If a typical grower were to drop out of the market, market supply would fall by only $1/107,000 = 0.00093\%$, so the market price would not be noticeably affected. Each soybean farm can sell as much output as it can produce at the prevailing market equilibrium price, so each farm faces a demand curve that is a horizontal line at the market price.

Similarly, perfect competition requires that buyers be price takers as well. For example, if firms sell to only a single buyer—such as producers of weapons that are allowed to sell to only the government—then the buyer can set the price and the market is not perfectly competitive.

Identical Products   Firms in a perfectly competitive market sell *identical* or *homogeneous* products. Consumers do not ask which farm grew a Granny Smith apple because they view all Granny Smith apples as essentially identical. If the products of all firms are identical, it is difficult for a single firm to raise its price above the going price charged by other firms.

In contrast, in the automobile market—which is not perfectly competitive—the characteristics of a BMW 5 Series and a Honda Civic differ substantially. These products are *differentiated* or *heterogeneous*. Competition from Civics would not be very effective in preventing BMW from raising its price.

Full Information   If buyers know that different firms are producing identical products and they know the prices charged by all firms, no single firm can unilaterally raise its price above the market equilibrium price. If it tried to do so, consumers would buy the identical product from another firm. However, if consumers are unaware that products are identical or they don't know the prices charged by other firms, a single firm may be able to raise its price and still make sales.

Negligible Transaction Costs   Perfectly competitive markets have very low transaction costs. Buyers and sellers do not have to spend much time and money finding each other or hiring lawyers to write contracts to execute a trade.[3] If transaction costs are low, it is easy for a customer to buy from a rival firm if the customer's usual supplier raises its price.

In contrast, if transaction costs are high, customers might absorb a price increase from a traditional supplier. For example, because some consumers prefer to buy milk at a local convenience store rather than travel several miles to a supermarket, the convenience store can charge slightly more than the supermarket without losing all its customers.

In some perfectly competitive markets, many buyers and sellers are brought together in a single room, so transaction costs are virtually zero. For example, transaction costs are very low at FloraHolland's daily flower auctions in the Netherlands, which attract 7,000 suppliers and 4,500 buyers from around the world. It has 125,000 auction transactions every day, with 12 billion cut flowers and 1.3 billion plants trading in a year.

Free Entry and Exit   The ability of firms to enter and exit a market freely leads to a large number of firms in a market and promotes price taking. Suppose a firm can raise its price and increase its profit. If other firms are not able to enter the market, the firm will not be a price taker. However, if other firms can quickly and easily enter the market, the higher profit encourages entry by new firms until the price is driven back to the original level. Free exit is also important: If firms can freely enter a market but cannot exit easily if prices decline, they are reluctant to enter the market in response to a possibly temporary profit opportunity.[4]

Perfect Competition in the Chicago Mercantile Exchange   The Chicago Mercantile Exchange, where buyers and sellers can trade wheat and other commodities, has the various characteristics of perfect competition including thousands of buyers and sellers who are price takers. Anyone can be a buyer or a seller. Indeed, a trader might buy wheat in the morning and sell it in the afternoon. They trade virtually *identical products*. Buyers and sellers have *full information* about products and prices, which are posted for everyone to see. Market participants waste no time finding someone who wants to trade and they can easily place buy or sell orders in person, over the telephone, or electronically without paperwork, so *transaction costs are negligible*. Finally, *buyers and sellers can easily enter this market and trade wheat*. These characteristics lead to an abundance of buyers and sellers and to price-taking behavior by these market participants.

Deviations from Perfect Competition

Many markets possess some but not all the characteristics of perfect competition, but they are still highly competitive so that buyers and sellers are, for all practical purposes, price takers. For example, a government may limit entry into a market, but if the market has many buyers and sellers, they may still be price takers. Many cities use zoning laws to limit the number of certain types of stores or motels, yet these cities still have a large number of these firms. Other cities impose moderately large transaction costs on entrants by requiring them to buy licenses, post bonds, and deal with

---

[3]Average number of hours per week that an American and a Chinese person, respectively, spend shopping: 4, 10.—*Harper's Index*, 2008.

[4]For example, many governments require that firms give workers six months' warning before they exit a market or pay them a severance fee.

a slow moving city bureaucracy, yet a significant number of firms enter the market. Similarly, even if only some customers have full information, that may be sufficient to prevent firms from deviating significantly from price taking. For example, tourists do not know the prices at various stores, but locals do and use their knowledge to prevent one store from charging unusually high prices.

Economists use the terms *competition* and *competitive* more restrictively than do others. To an economist, a competitive firm is a price taker. In contrast, when most people talk about competitive firms, they mean that firms are rivals for the same customers. Even in a market with only a few firms, the firms compete for the same customers so they are competitive in this broader sense. From now on, we will use the terms *competition* and *competitive* to refer to all markets in which no buyer or seller can significantly affect the market price—they are price takers—even if the market is not perfectly competitive.

Derivation of a Competitive Firm's Demand Curve

Are the demand curves faced by individual competitive firms actually flat? To answer this question, we use a modified supply-and-demand diagram to derive the demand curve for an individual firm.

residual demand curve
the market demand that is
not met by other sellers at
any given price

An individual firm faces a **residual demand curve**: the market demand that is not met by other sellers at any given price. The firm's residual demand function, $D^r(p)$, shows the quantity demanded from the firm at price p. A firm sells only to people who have not already purchased the good from another seller. We can determine how much demand is left for a particular firm at each possible price using the market demand curve and the supply curve for all *other* firms in the market. The quantity the market demands is a function of the price: $Q = D(p)$. The supply curve of the other firms is $S^o(p)$. The residual demand function equals the market demand function, $D(p)$, minus the supply function of all other firms:

$$D^r(p) = D(p) - S^o(p). \tag{8.1}$$

At prices so high that the amount supplied by other firms, $S^o(p)$, is greater than the quantity demanded by the market, $D(p)$, the residual quantity demanded, $D^r(p)$, is zero.

In Figure 8.1 we derive the residual demand for a Canadian manufacturing firm that produces metal chairs. Panel b shows the market demand curve, D, and the supply of all but one manufacturing firm, S^o.[5] At $p = \$66$ per chair, the supply of other firms, 500 units (where one unit is 1,000 metal chairs) per year, exactly equals the market demand (panel b), so the residual quantity demanded of the remaining firm (panel a) is zero.

At prices below $66, the other chair manufacturers are not willing to supply as much as the market demands. At $p = \$63$, for example, the market demand is 527 units, but other firms want to supply only 434 units. As a result, the residual quantity demanded from the individual firm at $p = \$63$ is 93 ($= 527 - 434$) units. Thus, the residual demand curve at any given price is the horizontal difference between the market demand curve and the supply curve of the other firms.

---

[5]The figure uses constant elasticity demand and supply curves. The elasticity of supply, $\eta = 3.1$, is based on the estimated cost function from Robidoux and Lester (1988) for Canadian office furniture manufacturers. I estimate that the elasticity of demand is $\varepsilon = -1.1$ using data from Statistics Canada, *Office Furniture Manufacturers*.

Figure 8.1 Residual Demand Curve

The residual demand curve, $D^r(p)$, that a single office furniture manufacturing firm faces is the market demand, $D(p)$, minus the supply of the other firms in the market, $S^o(p)$. The residual demand curve is much flatter than the market demand curve.

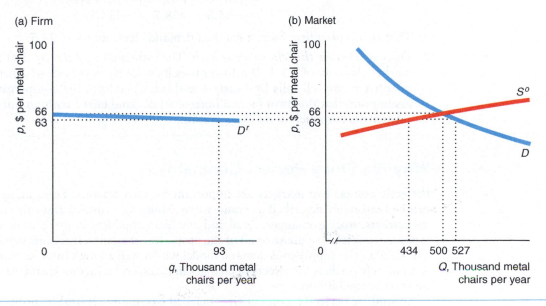

(a) Firm   (b) Market

The residual demand curve the firm faces in panel a is much flatter than the market demand curve in panel b. As a result, the elasticity of the residual demand curve is much higher than the market elasticity.

If the market has n identical firms, the elasticity of demand, ε_i, facing Firm i is

$$\varepsilon_i = n\varepsilon - (n - 1)\eta_o, \tag{8.2}$$

where ε is the market elasticity of demand (a negative number), η_o is the elasticity of supply of each of the other firms (typically a positive number), and $n - 1$ is the number of other firms (see Appendix 8A for the derivation).

As Equation 8.2 shows, a firm's residual demand curve is more elastic the more firms, n, are in the market, the more elastic the market demand, ε, and the larger the elasticity of supply of the other firms, η_o. The residual demand elasticity, ε_i, must be at least as elastic as $n\varepsilon$ if the supply curve slopes up so that the second term makes the estimate more elastic. Thus, using $n\varepsilon$ as an approximation is conservative. For example, even though the estimated market elasticity of demand for soybeans is very inelastic at about $\varepsilon = -0.2$, because $n = 107{,}000$, the residual demand facing a single soybean farm must be at least $n\varepsilon = 107{,}000 \times (-0.2) = -21{,}400$, which is extremely elastic.

Solved Problem 8.1

The Canadian metal chair manufacturing market has $n = 78$ firms. The estimated elasticity of supply is $\eta = 3.1$, and the estimated elasticity of demand is $\varepsilon = -1.1$. Assuming that the firms are identical, calculate the elasticity of demand facing a single firm. Is its residual demand curve highly elastic?

Answer

1. *Use Equation 8.2 and the estimated elasticities to calculate the residual demand elasticity facing a firm.* Substituting the elasticities into Equation 8.2, we find that

$$\varepsilon_i = n\varepsilon - (n - 1)\eta_o$$
$$= [78 \times (-1.1)] - [77 \times 3.1]$$
$$= -85.8 - 238.7 = -324.5.$$

That is, a typical firm faces a residual demand elasticity of -324.5.

2. *Discuss whether this elasticity is high.* The estimated ε_i is nearly 300 times the market elasticity of -1.1. If a firm raises its price by one-tenth of a percent, the quantity it can sell falls by nearly one-third. Therefore, the competitive model assumption that this firm faces a horizontal demand curve with an infinite price elasticity is not much of an exaggeration.

Why We Study Perfect Competition

Perfectly competitive markets are important for two reasons. First, many markets can be reasonably described as competitive. Many agricultural and other commodity markets, stock exchanges, retail and wholesale, building construction, and other types of markets have many or all of the properties of a perfectly competitive market. The competitive supply-and-demand model works well enough in these markets that it accurately predicts the effects of changes in taxes, costs, incomes, and other factors on market equilibrium.

Second, a perfectly competitive market has many desirable properties (see Chapter 9). Economists use the perfectly competitive model as the ideal against which real-world markets are compared. Throughout the rest of this book, we consider that society as a whole is worse off if the properties of the perfectly competitive market fail to hold. From this point on, for brevity, we use the phrase *competitive market* to mean a *perfectly competitive market* unless we explicitly note an imperfection.

8.2 Profit Maximization

"Too caustic?" To hell with the cost. If it's a good picture, we'll make it.
—Samuel Goldwyn

Economists usually assume that *all* firms—not just competitive firms—want to maximize their profits. One reason is that many businesspeople say that their objective is to maximize profits. A second reason is that a firm—especially a competitive firm—that does not maximize profit is likely to lose money and be driven out of business.

In this section, we examine how any type of firm—not just a competitive firm—maximizes its profit. We then examine how a competitive firm in particular maximizes profit.

Profit

A firm's *profit*, π, is the difference between a firm's revenues, R, and its cost, C:

$$\pi = R - C.$$

If profit is negative, $\pi < 0$, the firm makes a *loss*.

Measuring a firm's revenue sales is straightforward: revenue is price times quantity. Measuring cost is more challenging. For an economist, the correct measure of cost is the *opportunity cost* or *economic cost*: the value of the best alternative use of any input the firm employs. As discussed in Chapter 7, the full opportunity cost of inputs used might exceed the explicit or out-of-pocket costs recorded in financial accounting statements. This distinction is important because a firm may make a serious mistake if it incorrectly measures profit by ignoring some relevant opportunity costs.

economic profit
revenue minus opportunity cost

We always refer to profit or **economic profit** as revenue minus opportunity (economic) cost. For tax or other reasons, *business profit* may differ. For example, if a firm uses only explicit cost, then its reported profit may be larger than its economic profit.

A couple of examples illustrate the difference in the two profit measures and the importance of this distinction. Suppose that you start your own firm.[6] You have to pay explicit costs such as workers' wages and the price of materials. Like many owners, you do not pay yourself a salary. Instead, you take home a business profit of $20,000 per year.

Economists (well-known spoilsports) argue that your profit is less than $20,000. Economic profit equals your business profit minus any additional opportunity cost. Suppose that instead of running your own business, you could have earned $25,000 a year working for someone else. The opportunity cost of your time working for your business is $25,000—your forgone salary. So even though your firm made a business profit of $20,000, your economic loss (negative economic profit) is $5,000. Put another way, the price of being your own boss is $5,000.

By looking at only the business profit and ignoring opportunity cost, you conclude that running your business is profitable. However, if you consider economic profit, you realize that working for others maximizes your income.

Similarly, when a firm decides whether to invest in a new venture, it must consider its next best alternative use of its funds. A firm that is considering setting up a new branch in Tucson must consider all the alternatives—placing the branch in Santa Fe, putting the money that the branch would cost in the bank and earning interest, and so on. If the best alternative use of the money is to put it in the bank and earn $10,000 per year in interest, the firm should build the new branch in Tucson only if it expects to make $10,000 or more per year in business profits. That is, the firm should create a Tucson branch only if its economic profit from the new branch is zero or positive. If its economic profit is zero, then it is earning the same return on its investment as it would from putting the money in its next best alternative, the bank. From this point on, when we use the term *profit*, we mean economic profit unless we specifically refer to business profit.

Two Steps to Maximizing Profit

A firm's profit varies with its output level. The firm's profit function is

$$\pi(q) = R(q) - C(q).$$

---

[6]Michael Dell started a mail-order computer company while he was in college. Today, his company is one of the world's largest personal computer companies. *Forbes* estimated Mr. Dell's wealth at $15.3 billion as of March 2013.

A firm decides how much output to sell to maximize its profit. To maximize its profit, any firm (not just competitive, price-taking firms) must answer two questions:

- **Output decision.** If the firm produces, what output level, q^*, maximizes its profit or minimizes its loss?
- **Shutdown decision.** Is it more profitable to produce q^* or to shut down and produce no output?

The profit curve in Figure 8.2 illustrates these two basic decisions. This firm makes losses at very low and very high output levels and positive profits at moderate output levels. The profit curve first rises and then falls, reaching a maximum profit of π^* when its output is q^*. Because the firm makes a positive profit at that output, it chooses to produce q^* units of output.

Output Rules   A firm can use one of three equivalent rules to choose how much output to produce. All types of firms maximize profit using the same rules. The most straightforward rule is

Output Rule 1: The firm sets its output where its profit is maximized.

The profit curve in Figure 8.2 is maximized at π^* when output is q^*. If the firm knows its entire profit curve, it can immediately set its output to maximize its profit.

Even if the firm does not know the exact shape of its profit curve, it may be able to find the maximum by experimenting. The firm slightly increases its output. If profit increases, the firm increases the output more. The firm keeps increasing output until profit does not change. At that output, the firm is at the peak of the profit curve. If profit falls when the firm first increases its output, the firm tries decreasing its output. It keeps decreasing its output until it reaches the peak of the profit curve.

marginal profit
the change in profit a firm gets from selling one more unit of output

What the firm is doing is experimentally determining the slope of the profit curve. The slope of the profit curve is the firm's **marginal profit**: the change in the profit the firm gets from selling one more unit of output, $\Delta\pi/\Delta q$.[7] In the figure, the marginal

---

Figure 8.2 Maximizing Profit

By setting its output at q^*, the firm maximizes its profit at π^*.

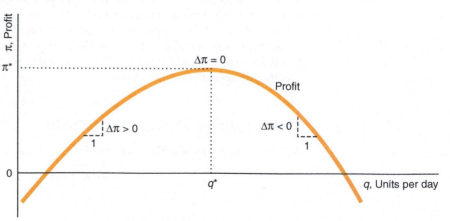

---

[7]The marginal profit is the derivative of the profit function, $\pi(q)$, with respect to quantity, $d\pi(q)/dq$.

profit or slope is positive when output is less than q^*, zero when output is q^*, and negative when output is greater than q^*. Thus, the second, equivalent rule is

Output Rule 2: A firm sets its output where its marginal profit is zero.

A third way to express this profit-maximizing output rule is in terms of cost and revenue. The marginal profit depends on a firm's *marginal cost* and *marginal revenue*. A firm's *marginal cost* (MC) is the amount by which a firm's cost changes if it produces one more unit of output (Chapter 7): $MC = \Delta C/\Delta q$, where ΔC is the change in cost when output changes by Δq. Similarly, a firm's **marginal revenue**, MR, is the change in revenue it gets from selling one more unit of output: $\Delta R/\Delta q$, where ΔR is the change in revenue.[8] If a firm that was selling q units of output sells one more unit of output, the extra revenue, $MR(q)$, raises its profit, but the extra cost, $MC(q)$, lowers its profit. The change in the firm's profit from producing one more unit is the difference between the marginal revenue and the marginal cost:[9]

marginal revenue (MR) the change in revenue a firm gets from selling one more unit of output

$$\text{Marginal profit}(q) = MR(q) - MC(q).$$

Does it pay for a firm to produce one more unit of output? If the marginal revenue from this last unit of output exceeds its marginal cost, $MR(q) > MC(q)$, the firm's marginal profit is positive, $MR(q) - MC(q) > 0$, so it pays to increase output. The firm keeps increasing its output until its marginal profit $= MR(q) - MC(q) = 0$. There, its marginal revenue equals its marginal cost: $MR(q) = MC(q)$. If the firm produces more output where its marginal cost exceeds its marginal revenue, $MR(q) < MC(q)$, the extra output reduces the firm's profit. Thus, a third, equivalent rule is (Appendix 8B):

Output Rule 3: A firm sets its output where its marginal revenue equals its marginal cost:

$$MR(q) = MC(q).$$

Shutdown Rule The firm chooses to produce if it can make a profit. If the firm is making a loss, however, does it shut down? The answer, surprisingly, is "It depends." The rule for whether a firm should shut down can be expressed in two equivalent ways. The first way to state the rule is

Shutdown Rule 1: The firm shuts down only if it can reduce its loss by doing so.

In the short run, the firm has variable costs, such as from labor and materials, and fixed costs, such as plant and equipment (Chapter 7). If the fixed cost is *sunk*, this expense cannot be avoided by stopping operations—the firm pays this cost whether it shuts down or not. Thus, the sunk fixed cost is irrelevant to the shutdown decision. By shutting down, the firm stops receiving revenue and stops paying the avoidable costs, but it is still stuck with its fixed cost. Thus, it pays for the firm to shut down only if its revenue is less than its avoidable cost.

Suppose that the weekly firm's revenue is $R = \$2,000$, its variable cost is $VC = \$1,000$, and its fixed cost is $F = \$3,000$, which is the price it paid for a

---

[8]The marginal revenue is the derivative of the revenue function with respect to quantity: $MR(q) = dR(q)/dq$.

[9]Because profit is $\pi(q) = R(q) - C(q)$, marginal profit is the difference between marginal revenue and marginal cost:

$$\frac{d\pi(q)}{dq} = \frac{dR(q)}{dq} - \frac{dC(q)}{dq} = MR - MC.$$

machine that it cannot resell or use for any other purpose. This firm is making a short-run loss:

$$\pi = R - VC - F = \$2,000 - \$1,000 - \$3,000 = -\$2,000.$$

If the firm shuts down, it loses its fixed cost, $3,000, so it is better off operating. Its revenue more than covers its avoidable, variable cost and offsets some of the fixed cost.

However, if its revenue is only $500, its loss is $3,500, which is greater than the loss from the fixed cost alone of $3,000. Because its revenue is less than its avoidable, variable cost, the firm reduces its loss by shutting down.

In conclusion, the firm compares its revenue to its variable cost only when deciding whether to stop operating. Because the fixed cost is sunk, the firm pays this cost whether it shuts down or not. The sunk fixed cost is irrelevant to the shutdown decision.[10]

In the long run, all costs are avoidable because the firm can eliminate them all by shutting down. Thus, in the long run, where the firm can avoid all losses by not operating, it pays to shut down if the firm faces any loss at all. As a result, we can restate the shutdown rule as:

Shutdown Rule 2: The firm shuts down only if its revenue is less than its avoidable cost.

Both versions of the shutdown rule hold for all types of firms in both the short run and the long run.

8.3 Competition in the Short Run

Having considered how firms maximize profit in general, we now examine the profit-maximizing behavior of competitive firms, derive their supply curves, and then determine the competitive equilibrium in the short run. In the next section, we examine competitive firms and competitive markets in the long run.

The *short run* is a period short enough that at least one input cannot be varied (Chapter 6). Because a firm cannot quickly build a new plant or make other large capital expenditures, a new firm cannot enter a market in the short run. Similarly, a firm cannot fully exit in the short run. It can choose not to produce—to shut down—but it is stuck with some fixed inputs such as a plant or other capital that it cannot quickly sell or assign to other uses. In the long run, all inputs can be varied so firms can enter and fully exit the industry.

We treat the short run and the long run separately for two reasons. First, profit-maximizing firms may choose to operate at a loss in the short run, whereas they do not do so in the long run. Second, a firm's long-run supply curve typically differs from its short-run supply curve.

In both the short run and the long run, a competitive firm, like other firms, first determines the output at which it maximizes its profit (or minimizes its loss). Second, it decides whether to produce or to shut down.

---

[10]We usually assume that fixed cost is sunk. However, if a firm can sell its capital for as much as it paid, its fixed cost is avoidable and should be taken into account when the firm is considering whether to shut down. A firm with a fully avoidable fixed cost always shuts down if it makes a short-run loss. If a firm buys a specialized piece of machinery for $1,000 that can be used only in its business but can be sold for scrap metal for $100, then $100 of the fixed cost is avoidable and $900 is sunk. Only the avoidable portion of fixed cost is relevant for the shutdown decision.

Short-Run Output Decision

We've already seen that *any* firm maximizes its profit at the output where its marginal profit is zero or, equivalently, where its marginal cost equals its marginal revenue. Because it faces a horizontal demand curve, a competitive firm can sell as many units of output as it wants at the market price, p. Thus, a competitive firm's revenue, $R = pq$, increases by p if it sells one more unit of output, so its marginal revenue is p.[11] For example, if the firm faces a market price of $2 per unit, its revenue is $10 if it sells 5 units and $12 if it sells 6 units, so its marginal revenue for the sixth unit is $2 = \$12 - \$10$ (the market price). Because a competitive firm's marginal revenue equals the market price, *a profit-maximizing competitive firm produces the amount of output at which its marginal cost equals the market price*:

$$MC(q) = p. \tag{8.3}$$

To illustrate how a competitive firm maximizes its profit, we examine a representative firm in the highly competitive Canadian lime manufacturing industry. Lime is a nonmetallic mineral used in mortars, plasters, cements, bleaching powders, steel, paper, glass, and other products. The lime plant's estimated average cost curve, AC, first falls and then rises in panel a of Figure 8.3.[12] As always, the marginal cost curve, MC, intersects the average cost curve at its minimum point.

If the market price of lime is $p = \$8$ per metric ton, the competitive firm faces a horizontal demand curve (marginal revenue curve) at $8. The MC curve crosses the firm's demand curve (or price or marginal revenue curve) at point e, where the firm's output is 284 units (where a unit is a thousand metric tons).

Thus at a market price of $8, the competitive firm maximizes its profit by producing 284 units. If the firm produced fewer than 284 units, the market price would be above its marginal cost. As a result, the firm could increase its profit by expanding output because the firm earns more on the next ton, $p = \$8$, than it costs to produce it, $MC < \$8$. If the firm were to produce more than 284 units, the market price would be below its marginal cost, $MC > \$8$, and the firm could increase its profit by reducing its output. Thus, the competitive firm maximizes its profit by producing that output at which its marginal cost equals its marginal revenue, which is the market price.[13]

At that 284 units, the firm's profit is $\pi = \$426,000$, which is the shaded rectangle in panel a. The length of the rectangle is the number of units sold, $q = 284,000$ (or 284 units). The height of the rectangle is the firm's average profit per unit. Because the firm's profit is its revenue, $R(q) = pq$, minus its cost, $\pi(q) = R(q) - C(q)$, its average profit per unit is the difference between

---

[11]We can derive this result using calculus. Because $R(q) = pq$, $MR = dR(q)/dq = d(pq)/dq = p$.

[12]The figure is based on Robidoux and Lester's (1988) estimated variable cost function. In the figure, we assume that the minimum of the average variable cost curve is $5 at 50,000 metric tons of output. Based on information from Statistics Canada, we set the fixed cost so that the average cost is $6 at 140,000 tons.

[13]The firm chooses its output level to maximize its *total profit* rather than its *average profit* per ton. If the firm were to produce 140 units, where its average cost is minimized at $6, the firm would maximize its average profit at $2, but its total profit would be only $280,000. Although the firm gives up 50¢ in profit per ton when it produces 284 units instead of 140 units, it more than makes up for that lost profit per ton by selling an extra 144 units. At $1.50 profit per ton, the firm's total profit is $426,000, $146,000 higher than it is at 140 units.

Figure 8.3 How a Competitive Firm Maximizes Profit

(a) A competitive lime manufacturing firm maximizes its profit at $\pi^* = \$426{,}000$, where its marginal revenue, MR, which is the market price, $p = \$8$, equals its marginal cost, MC. (b) The corresponding profit curve reaches its peak at 284 units of lime. Estimated cost curves are based on Robidoux and Lester (1988).

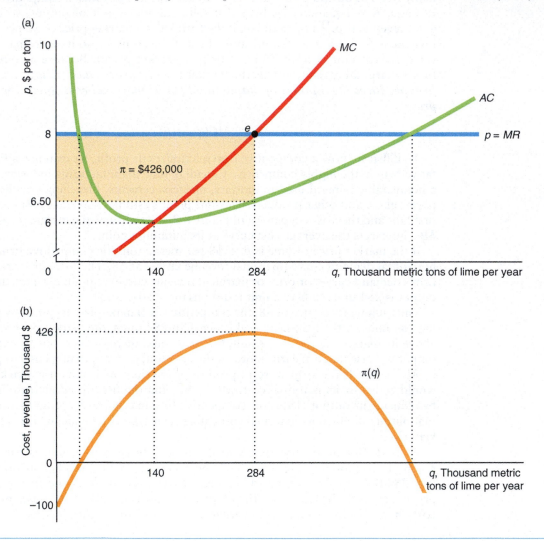

the market price (or average revenue), $p = R(q)/q = pq/q$, and its average cost, $AC = C(q)/q$:

$$\frac{\pi(q)}{q} = \frac{R(q) - C(q)}{q} = \frac{R(q)}{q} - \frac{C(q)}{q} = p - AC. \qquad (8.4)$$

At 284 units, the lime firm's average profit per unit is $\$1.50 = p - AC(284) = \$8 - \$6.50$, and the firm's profit is $\pi = \$1.50 \times 284{,}000 = \$426{,}000$. Panel b shows that this profit is the maximum possible profit because it is the peak of the profit curve.

Solved Problem 8.2

If a competitive firm's cost increases due to an increase in the price of a factor of production or a tax, the firm's manager can quickly determine by how much to adjust output by calculating how the firm's marginal cost has changed and applying the profit-maximization rule. Suppose that the Canadian province of Manitoba imposes a specific (per-unit) tax of t per ton of lime produced in the province. Manitoba has only one lime-producing firm, so the tax affects only that firm and hence has virtually no effect on the market price. If the tax is imposed, how should the Manitoba firm change its output level to maximize its profit, and how does its maximum profit change?

Answer

1. *Show how the tax shifts the marginal cost and average cost curves.* The firm's before-tax marginal cost curve is MC^1 and its before-tax average cost curve is AC^1. Because the specific tax adds t to the per-unit cost, it shifts the after-tax marginal cost curve up to $MC^2 = MC^1 + t$ and the after-tax average cost curve to $AC^2 = AC^1 + t$ (see Chapter 7).

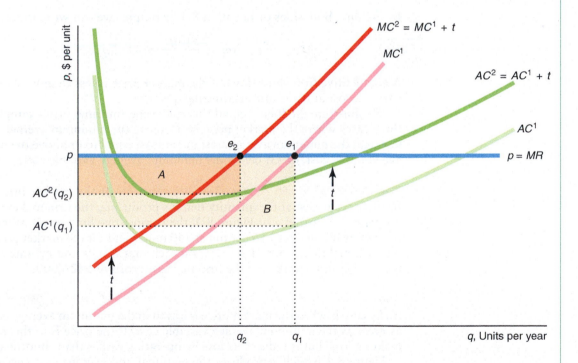

2. *Determine the before-tax and after-tax equilibria and the amount by which the firm adjusts its output.* Where the before-tax marginal cost curve, MC^1, hits the horizontal demand curve, p, at e_1, the profit-maximizing quantity is q_1. The after-tax marginal cost curve, MC^2, intersects the demand curve, p, at e_2 where the profit-maximizing quantity is q_2. Thus, in response to the tax, the firm produces $q_1 - q_2$ fewer units of output.

3. *Show how the profit changes after the tax.* Because the market price is constant but the firm's average cost curve shifts upward, the firm's profit at every output level falls. The firm sells fewer units (because of the increase in MC)

and makes less profit per unit (because of the increase in AC). The after-tax profit is area $A = \pi_2 = [p - AC^2(q_2)]q_2$, and the before-tax profit is area $A + B = \pi_1 = [p - AC^1(q_1)]q_1$, so profit falls by area B due to the tax.[14]

Short-Run Shutdown Decision

Once a firm determines the output level that maximizes its profit or minimizes its loss, it must decide whether to produce that output level or to shut down and produce nothing. This decision is easy for the lime firm in Figure 8.3 because, at the output that maximizes its profit, it makes a positive economic profit. However, the question remains whether a firm should shut down if it is making a loss in the short run.

All firms—not just competitive firms—use the same shutdown rule: The firm shuts down only if it can reduce its loss by doing so. The firm shuts down only if its revenue is less than its avoidable variable cost: $R(q) < VC(q)$. For a competitive firm, this rule is

$$pq < VC(q). \tag{8.5}$$

By dividing both sides of Equation 8.5 by output, we can write this condition as

$$p < \frac{VC(q)}{q} = AVC(q).$$

A competitive firm shuts down if the market price is less than its short-run average variable cost at the profit-maximizing quantity.

We illustrate the logic behind this rule using our lime firm example. We look at three cases where the market price is (1) above the minimum average cost (AC), (2) less than the minimum average cost but at least equal to or above the minimum average variable cost, or (3) below the minimum average variable cost.

The Market Price Is Above the Minimum *AC* If the market price is above the firm's average cost at the quantity that it's producing, the firm makes a profit and so it operates. In panel a of Figure 8.3, the competitive lime firm's average cost curve reaches its minimum of $6 per ton at 140 units. Thus, if the market price is above $6, the firm makes a profit of $p - AC$ on each unit it sells and operates. In the figure, the market price is $8, and the firm makes a profit of $426,000.

The Market Price Is Between the Minimum *AC* and the Minimum *AVC* The tricky case is when the market price is less than the minimum average cost but at least as great as the minimum average variable cost. If the price is in this range, the firm makes a loss, but it reduces its loss by operating rather than shutting down.

Figure 8.4 (which reproduces the marginal and average cost curves for the lime firm from panel a of Figure 8.3 and adds the average variable cost curve) illustrates

---

[14]We can solve this problem using calculus. The firm's profit is $\pi = pq - [C(q) + tq]$, where $C(q)$ is the firm's before-tax cost and $C(q) + tq$ is its after-tax cost. We obtain the necessary condition for the firm to maximize its after-tax profit by taking the first derivative of profit with respect to quantity and setting it equal to zero:

$$\frac{d\pi}{dq} = \frac{d(pq)}{dq} - \frac{d[C(q) + tq]}{dq} = p - \left[\frac{dC(q)}{dq} + t\right] = p - [MC + t] = 0.$$

Thus, the firm produces where $p = MC + t$.

Figure 8.4 The Short-Run Shutdown Decision

The competitive lime manufacturing plant operates if price is above the minimum of the average variable cost curve, point *a*, at $5. With a market price of $5.50, the firm produces 100 units because that price is above $AVC(100) = \$5.14$, so the firm more than covers its out-of-pocket, variable costs. At that price, the firm makes a loss of area $A = \$62,000$ because the price is less than the average cost of $6.12. If it shuts down, its loss is its fixed cost, area $A + B = \$98,000$. Thus, the firm does not shut down.

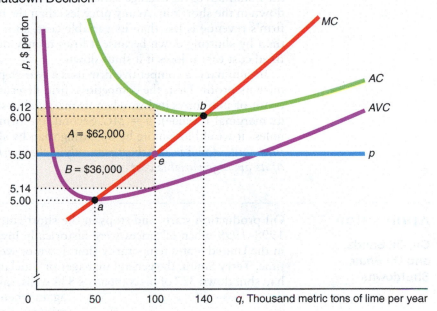

this case for the lime firm. The lime firm's average cost curve reaches a minimum of $6 at 140 units, while its average variable cost curve hits its minimum of $5 at 50 units. If the market price is between $5 and $6, the lime firm loses money (its profit is negative) because the price is less than its AC, but the firm does not shut down.

For example, if the market price is $5.50, the firm minimizes its loss by producing 100 units where the marginal cost curve crosses the price line. At 100 units, the average cost is $6.12, so the firm's loss is $-62¢ = p - AC(100) = \$5.50 - \$6.12$ on each unit that it sells.

Why does the firm produce given that it is making a loss? The reason is that the firm reduces its loss by operating rather than shutting down because its revenue exceeds its variable cost—or equivalently, the market price exceeds its average variable cost.

If the firm shuts down in the short run it incurs a loss equal to its fixed cost of $98,000, which is the sum of rectangles A and B.[15] If the firm operates and produces $q = 100$ units, its average variable cost is $AVC = \$5.14$, which is less than the market price of $p = \$5.50$ per ton. It makes $36¢ = p - AVC = \$5.50 - \$5.14$ more on each ton than its average variable cost. The difference between the firm's revenue and its variable cost, $R - VC$, is the rectangle $B = \$36,000$, which has a length of 100 thousand tons and a height of 36¢. Thus, if the firm operates, it loses only $62,000 (rectangle A), which is less than its loss if it shuts down, $98,000. The firm makes a smaller loss by operating than by shutting down because its revenue more than covers its variable cost and hence helps to reduce the loss from the fixed cost.

[15]The average cost is the sum of the average variable cost and the average fixed cost, $AC = AVC + F/q$ (Chapter 7). Thus, the gap between the average cost and the average variable cost curves at any given output is $AC - AVC = F/q$. Consequently, the height of the rectangle $A + B$ is $AC(100) - AVC(100) = F/100$, and the length of the rectangle is 100 units, so the area of the rectangle is F, or $98,000 = \$62,000 + \$36,000$.

The Market Price Is Less than the Minimum *AVC* If the market price dips below the minimum of the average variable cost, $5 in Figure 8.4, then the firm should shut down in the short run. At any price less than the minimum average variable cost, the firm's revenue is less than its variable cost, so it makes a greater loss by operating than by shutting down because it loses money on each unit sold in addition to the fixed cost that it loses if it shuts down.

In summary, a competitive firm uses a two-step decision-making process to maximize its profit. First, the competitive firm determines the output that maximizes its profit or minimizes its loss when its marginal cost equals the market price (which is its marginal revenue): $p = MC$. Second, the firm chooses to produce that quantity unless it would lose more by operating than by shutting down. Thus, *a competitive firm shuts down in the short run only if the market price is less than the minimum of its average variable cost curve.*

Application

Oil, Oil Sands, and Oil Shale Shutdowns

Oil production starts and stops in the short run as the market price fluctuates. In 1998–1999 when oil prices were historically low, 74,000 of the 136,000 oil wells in the United States temporarily shut down or were permanently abandoned. At the time, Terry Smith, the general manager of Tidelands Oil Production Company, who had shut down 327 of his company's 834 wells, said that he would operate these wells again when price rose above $10 a barrel—his minimum average variable cost.

Getting oil from oil wells is relatively easy. It is harder and more costly to obtain oil from other sources, so firms that use those alternative sources have a higher minimum average variable cost—higher shutdown points—and hence shut down at higher price than companies that pump oil from wells.

It might surprise you to know that Canada has the third-largest known oil reserves in the world, 174 billion barrels (estimated as of 2012), trailing only Saudi Arabia and Venezuela and far exceeding Iran in fourth place. Yet you rarely hear about Canada's vast oil reserves, which cover an area the size of Florida, because 97% of those reserves are in oil sands.

Oil sands are a mixture of heavy petroleum (bitumen), water, and sandstone. Extracting oil from oil sands is expensive and causes significant pollution in the production process. To liberate four barrels of crude oil from the sands, a processor must burn the equivalent of a fifth barrel. With the technology currently available, two tons of oil sands yielded only a single barrel (42 gallons) of oil.

The first large oil sands mining began in the 1960s, but because oil prices were often less than the $25-per-barrel average variable cost of recovering oil from the sands at that time, production was frequently shut down. However, in recent years, technological improvements in the production process have lowered the average variable cost to $18 a barrel. That, coupled with higher oil prices, has led to continuous oil sands production without shutdowns. As of 2013, more than 50 oil companies had operations in the Canadian oil sands, including major international producers such as Exxon-Mobile, BP (formerly British Petroleum), and Royal Dutch Shell, major Canadian producers such as Suncor and Husky, and companies from China, Japan, and South Korea.

The huge amounts of oil hidden in oil sands may be dwarfed by those found in oil shale, which is sedimentary rock containing oil. According to current estimates, oil shale deposits in Colorado and neighboring areas in Utah and Wyoming contain 800 billion recoverable barrels, the equivalent of 40 years of U.S. oil consumption. The United States has between 1 and 2 trillion recoverable barrels from oil shale, which is at least four times Saudi Arabia's proven reserves of crude oil, which are in underground pools.

A federal task force report concluded that the United States will be able to produce 3 million barrels of oil a day from oil shale and sands by 2035. Shell Oil reports that its average variable cost of extracting oil from shale is $30 a barrel in Colorado. In recent years, the lowest price for world oil was $39 a barrel on December 12, 2008. Since then prices have risen significantly, reaching $100 per barrel in early 2011 and remaining close to or above that level through mid-2013. Therefore, oil shale production has become profitable and extraction is occurring.

Solved Problem 8.3

A competitive firm's bookkeeper, upon reviewing the firm's books, finds that the firm spent twice as much on its plant, a fixed cost, as the firm's manager had previously thought. Should the manager change the output level because of this new information? How does this new information affect profit?

Answer

1. *Show that a change in fixed costs does not affect the firm's decisions.* How much the firm produces and whether it shuts down in the short run depend only on the firm's variable costs. (The firm picks its output level so that its marginal cost—which depends only on variable costs—equals the market price, and it shuts down only if market price is less than its minimum average variable cost.) Learning that the amount spent on the plant was greater than previously believed should not change the output level that the manager chooses.

2. *Show that the change in how the bookkeeper measures fixed costs does not affect economic profit.* The change in the bookkeeper's valuation of the historical amount spent on the plant may affect the firm's short-run business profit but does not affect the firm's true economic profit. The economic profit is based on opportunity costs—the amount for which the firm could rent the plant to someone else—and not on historical payments.

Short-Run Firm Supply Curve

We just demonstrated how a competitive firm chooses its output for a given market price in a way that maximizes its profit or minimizes its losses. By repeating this analysis at different possible market prices, we can show how the amount the competitive firm supplies varies with the market price.

As the market price increases from $p_1 = \$5$ to $p_2 = \$6$ to $p_3 = \$7$ to $p_4 = \$8$, the lime firm increases its output from 50 to 140 to 215 to 285 units per year, as Figure 8.5 shows. The profit-maximizing output at each market price is determined by the intersection of the relevant demand curve—market price line—and the firm's

Figure 8.5 How the Profit-Maximizing Quantity Varies with Price

As the market price increases, the lime manufacturing firm produces more output. The change in the price traces out the marginal cost (*MC*) curve of the firm. The firm's short-run supply (*S*) curve is the *MC* curve above the minimum of its *AVC* curve (at e_1).

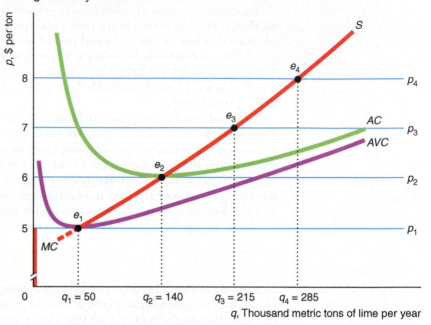

marginal cost curve, as equilibria e_1 through e_4 illustrate. That is, as the market price increases, the equilibria trace out the marginal cost curve. However, if the price falls below the firm's minimum average variable cost at $5, the firm shuts down. Thus, the competitive firm's short-run supply curve is its marginal cost curve above its minimum average variable cost.

The firm's short-run supply curve, *S*, is a solid red line in the figure. At prices above $5, the short-run supply curve is the same as the marginal cost curve. The supply is zero when price is less than the minimum of the *AVC* curve of $5. (From now on, to keep the graphs as simple as possible, we will not show the supply curve at prices below the minimum *AVC*.)

Short-Run Market Supply Curve

The market supply curve is the horizontal sum of the supply curves of all the individual firms in the market (Chapter 2). In the short run, the maximum number of firms in a market, *n*, is fixed because new firms need time to enter the market. If all the firms in a competitive market are identical, each firm's supply curve is identical, so the market supply at any price is *n* times the supply of an individual firm. Where firms have different shutdown prices, the market supply reflects a different number of firms at various prices even in the short run. We examine competitive markets first with firms that have identical costs and then with firms that have different costs.

Short-Run Market Supply with Identical Firms   To illustrate how to construct a short-run market supply curve, we suppose that the lime manufacturing market has *n* = 5 competitive firms with identical cost curves. Panel a of Figure 8.6 plots the short-run supply curve, S^1, of a typical firm—the *MC* curve above the minimum *AVC*—where the horizontal axis shows the firm's output, *q*, per year.

Figure 8.6 Short-Run Market Supply with Five Identical Lime Firms

(a) The short-run supply curve, S^1, for a typical lime manufacturing firm is its MC above the minimum of its AVC. (b) The market supply curve, S^5, is the horizontal sum of the supply curves of each of the five identical firms. The curve S^4 shows what the market supply curve would be with only four firms in the market.

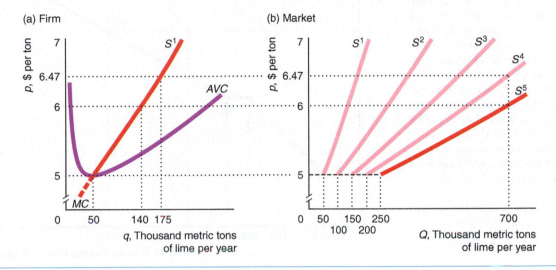

Panel b illustrates the competitive market supply curve, the dark line S^5, where the horizontal axis is market output, Q, per year. The price axis is the same in the two panels.

If the market price is less than $5 per ton, no firm supplies any output, so the market supply is zero. At $5, each firm is willing to supply $q = 50$ units, as in panel a. Consequently, the market supply is $Q = 5q = 250$ units in panel b. At $6 per ton, each firm supplies 140 units, so the market supply is 700 ($= 5 \times 140$) units.

Suppose, however, that the market has fewer than five firms in the short run. The light-color lines in panel b show the market supply curves for various other numbers of firms. The market supply curve is S^1 with one price-taking firm, S^2 with two firms, S^3 with three firms, and S^4 with four firms. The market supply curve flattens as the number of firms in the market increases because the market supply curve is the horizontal sum of more and more upward-sloping firm supply curves. As the number of firms grows very large, the market supply curve approaches a horizontal line at $5. Thus, *the more identical firms producing at a given price, the flatter (more elastic) the short-run market supply curve at that price.* As a result, the more firms in the market, the less the price has to increase for the short-run market supply to increase substantially. Consumers pay $6 per ton to obtain 700 units of lime with five firms but must pay $6.47 per ton to obtain that much with only four firms.

Short-Run Market Supply with Firms That Differ If the firms in a competitive market have different minimum average variable costs, not all firms produce at every price. These varying shutdown points affect the shape of the short-run market supply curve. Suppose that the only two firms in the lime market are our typical lime firm with a supply curve of S^1 and another firm with a higher marginal and minimum average cost with the supply curve of S^2 in Figure 8.7. The first firm produces if the market price is at least $5, whereas the second firm does not produce unless the price is $6 or more. At $5, the first firm produces 50 units, so

Figure 8.7 Short-Run Market Supply with Two Different Lime Firms

The supply curve S^1 is the same as for the typical lime firm in Figure 8.6. A second firm has an *MC* that lies to the left of the original firm's cost curve and a higher minimum of its *AVC*. Thus, its supply curve, S^2, lies above and to the left of the original firm's supply curve, S^1. The market supply curve, S, is the horizontal sum of the two supply curves. When the price is $6 or higher, both firms produce, and the market supply curve is flatter than the supply curve of either individual firm.

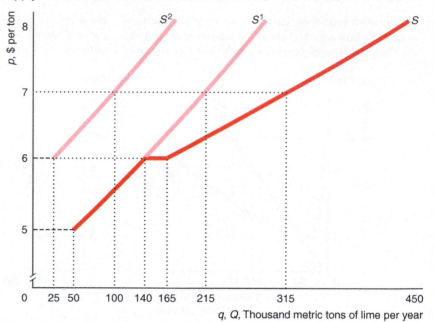

the quantity on the market supply curve, S, is 50 units. Between $5 and $6, only the first firm produces, so the market supply, S, is the same as the first firm's supply, S^1. At and above $6, both firms produce, so the market supply curve is the horizontal summation of their two individual supply curves. For example, at $7, the first firm produces 215 units, and the second firm supplies 100 units, so the market supply is 315 units.

As with the identical firms, where both firms are producing, the market supply curve is flatter than that of either firm. Because the second firm does not produce at as low a price as the first firm, the short-run market supply curve has a steeper slope (less elastic supply) at relatively low prices than it would if the firms were identical.

Where firms differ, only the low-cost firm supplies goods at relatively low prices. As the price rises, the other, higher-cost firm starts supplying, creating a stair-like market supply curve. The more suppliers with differing costs, the more steps in the market supply curve. As price rises and more firms are supplying goods, the market supply curve flattens, so it takes a smaller increase in price to increase supply by a given amount. Stated the other way, the more firms differ in costs, the steeper the market supply curve at low prices. Differences in costs are one explanation for why some market supply curves are upward sloping.

Short-Run Competitive Equilibrium

By combining the short-run market supply curve and the market demand curve, we can determine the short-run competitive equilibrium. We first show how to determine the equilibrium in the lime market, and we then examine how the equilibrium changes when firms are taxed.

Suppose that the lime market has five identical firms in the short-run equilibrium. Panel a of Figure 8.8 shows the short-run cost curves and the supply curve, S^1, for a typical firm, and panel b shows the corresponding short-run competitive market supply curve, S.

In panel b, the initial demand curve, D^1, intersects the market supply curve at E_1, the market equilibrium. The equilibrium quantity is $Q_1 = 1,075$ units of lime per year, and the equilibrium market price is $7.

Each competitive firm faces a horizontal demand curve at the equilibrium price of $7. Each price-taking firm chooses its output where its marginal cost curve intersects the horizontal demand curve at e_1 in panel a. Because each firm is maximizing its profit at e_1, no firm wants to change its behavior, so e_1 is the firm's equilibrium. Each firm makes a short-run profit of area $A + B = \$172,000$, which is the average profit per ton, $p - AC = \$7 - \$6.20 = 80$¢, times the firm's output, $q_1 = 215$ units. The equilibrium market output, Q_1, is the number of firms, n, times the equilibrium output of each firm: $Q_1 = nq_1 = 5 \times 215$ units $= 1,075$ units (panel b).

Now suppose that the demand curve shifts to D^2. The new market equilibrium is E_2, where the price is only $5. At that price, each firm produces $q = 50$ units, and market output is $Q = 250$ units. In panel a, each firm loses $98,500, area $A + C$, because it makes an average per ton of $(p - AC) = (\$5 - \$6.97) = -\$1.97$ and it sells $q_2 = 50$ units. However, such a firm does not shut down because price equals the firm's average variable cost, so the firm is covering its out-of-pocket expenses.

Figure 8.8 Short-Run Competitive Equilibrium in the Lime Market

(a) The short-run supply curve is the marginal cost above minimum average variable cost of $5. If the price is $5, each firm makes a short-run loss of $(p - AC)q = (\$5 - \$6.97) \times 50,000 = -\$98,500$, area $A + C$. At a price of $7, the short-run profit of a typical lime firm is $(p - AC)q = (\$7 - \$6.20) \times 215,000 = \$172,000$, area $A + B$. (b) If the lime market has only five firms in the short run, the market supply is S, and the market demand curve is D^1, then the short-run equilibrium is E_1, the market price is $7, and market output is $Q_1 = 1,075$ units. If the demand curve shifts to D^2, the market equilibrium is $p = \$5$ and $Q_2 = 250$ units.

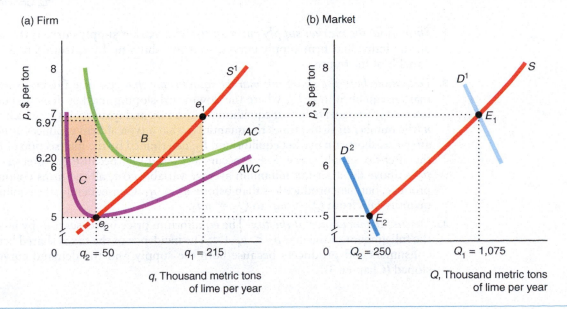

**Solved Problem
8.4**

What is the effect on the short-run equilibrium of a specific tax of t per unit that is collected from all n firms in a market? What is the incidence of the tax?

Answer

1. *Show how the tax shifts a typical firm's marginal cost and average cost curves and hence its supply curve.* In Solved Problem 8.2, we showed that such a tax causes the marginal cost curve, the average cost curve, and (hence) the minimum average cost of the firm to shift up by t, as illustrated in panel a of the figure. As a result, the short-run supply curve of the firm, labeled $S^1 + t$, shifts up by t from the pre-tax supply curve, S^1.

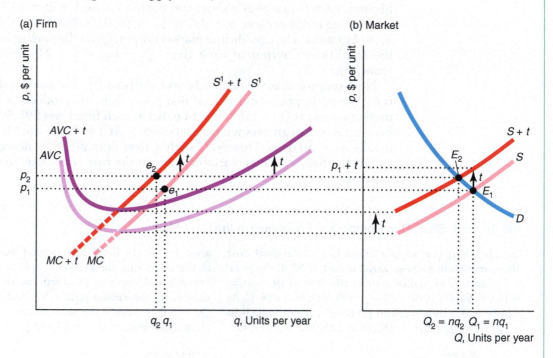

2. *Show how the market supply curve shifts.* The market supply curve is the sum of all the individual firm supply curves, so it too shifts up by t, from S to $S + t$ in panel b of the figure.

3. *Determine how the short-run market equilibrium changes.* The pre-tax, short-run market equilibrium is E_1, where the downward-sloping market demand curve D intersects S in panel b. In that equilibrium, price is p_1 and quantity is Q_1, which equals n (the number of firms) times the quantity q_1 that a typical firm produces at p_1. The after-tax, short-run market equilibrium, E_2, determined by the intersection of D and the after-tax supply curve, $S + t$, occurs at p_2 and Q_2. Because the after-tax price p_2 is above the after-tax minimum average variable cost, all the firms continue to produce, but they produce less than before: $q_2 < q_1$. Consequently, the equilibrium quantity falls from $Q_1 = nq_1$ to $Q_2 = nq_2$.

4. *Discuss the incidence of the tax.* The equilibrium price increases, but by less than the full amount of the tax: $p_2 < p_1 + t$. The incidence of the tax is shared between consumers and producers because both the supply and the demand curves are sloped (Chapter 3).

8.4 Competition in the Long Run

I think there is a world market for about five computers.
—Thomas J. Watson, IBM chairman, 1943

In the long run, competitive firms can vary inputs that were fixed in the short run, so the long-run firm and market supply curves differ from the short-run curves. After briefly looking at how a firm determines its long-run supply curve so as to maximize its profit, we examine the relationship between short-run and long-run market supply curves and competitive equilibria.

Long-Run Competitive Profit Maximization

The firm's two profit-maximizing decisions—how much to produce and whether to produce at all—are simpler in the long run than in the short run. In the long run, typically all costs are variable, so the firm does not have to consider whether fixed costs are sunk or avoidable.

The firm chooses the quantity that maximizes its profit using the same rules as in the short run. The firm picks the quantity that maximizes long-run profit, the difference between revenue and long-run cost. Equivalently, it operates where long-run marginal profit is zero and where marginal revenue equals long-run marginal cost.

After determining the output level, q^*, that maximizes its profit or minimizes its loss, the firm decides whether to produce or shut down. As always, the firm shuts down if its revenue is less than its avoidable or variable cost. Because all costs are variable in the long run, the firm shuts down in the long run if it would make an economic loss by operating.

Long-Run Firm Supply Curve

A firm's long-run supply curve is its long-run marginal cost curve above the minimum of its long-run average cost curve (because all costs are variable in the long run). The firm is free to choose its capital in the long run, so the firm's long-run supply curve may differ substantially from its short-run supply curve.

The firm chooses a plant size to maximize its long-run economic profit in light of its beliefs about the future. If its forecast is wrong, it may be stuck with a plant that is too small or too large for its level of production in the short run. The firm acts to correct this mistake in plant size in the long run.

The firm in Figure 8.9 has different short- and long-run cost curves. In the short run, the firm uses a plant that is smaller than the optimal long-run size if the price is $35. (Having a short-run plant size that is too large is also possible.) The firm produces 50 units of output per year in the short run, where its short-run marginal cost, $SRMC$, equals the price, and makes a short-run profit equal to area A. The firm's short-run supply curve, S^{SR}, is its short-run marginal cost above the minimum, $20, of its short-run average variable cost, $SRAVC$.

If the firm expects the price to remain at $35, it builds a larger plant in the long run. Using the larger plant, the firm produces 110 units per year, where its long-run marginal cost, $LRMC$, equals the market price. It expects to make a long-run profit, area $A + B$, which is greater than its short-run profit by area B because it sells 60 more units and its equilibrium long-run average cost, $LRAC = \$25$, is lower than its short-run average cost in equilibrium, $28.

Figure 8.9 The Short-Run and Long-Run Supply Curves

The firm's long-run supply curve, S^{LR}, is zero below its minimum average cost of $24 and equals the long-run marginal cost, *LRMC*, at higher prices. The firm produces more in the long run than in the short run, 110 units instead of 50 units, and earns a higher profit, area *A* + *B* instead of just area *A*.

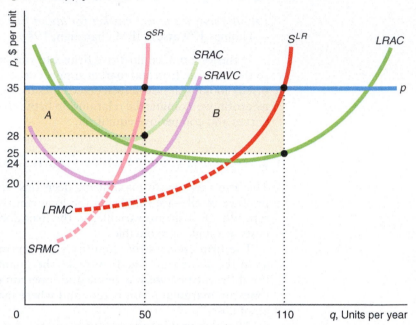

The firm does not operate at a loss in the long run when all inputs are variable. It shuts down if the market price falls below the firm's minimum long-run average cost of $24. Thus, the competitive firm's long-run supply curve is its long-run marginal cost curve above $24.

Application

The Size of Ethanol Processing Plants

When a large number of firms initially built ethanol processing plants, they built relatively small ones. When the ethanol market took off in the first half decade of the twenty-first century, with the price reaching a peak of $4.23 a gallon in June 2006, many firms built larger plants or greatly increased their plant size. The average plant capacity nearly doubled from 1999 to 2012.

However, with the more recent collapse of that market—the price fell below $3 and often below $1.50 from 2007 through mid-2013—many firms either closed their plants or reduced their size. As of December 2012 the United States had 211 ethanol plants, of which at least 20 were shut down. The capacity of plants under construction or expansion went from 3,644 million gallons per year in 2005 to 5,635 in 2007, but since then the size fell to 1,432 in 2010, 522 in 2011, and 158 in 2013.

Long-Run Market Supply Curve

The competitive market supply curve is the horizontal sum of the supply curves of the individual firms in both the short run and the long run. Because the maximum number of firms in the market is fixed in the short run (it takes time to build a new plant, buy equipment, and hire workers), we add the supply curves of a known number of firms to obtain the short-run market supply curve. The only way for the market to supply more output in the short run is for existing firms to produce more.

However, in the long run, firms can enter the market. Thus, before we can add all the relevant firm supply curves to obtain the long-run market supply curve, we need to determine how many firms are in the market at each possible market price. We now look in detail at how market entry and exit affect the long-run market supply curve.

Entry and Exit The number of firms in a market in the long run is determined by the *entry* and *exit* of firms. In the long run, each firm decides whether to enter or exit depending on whether it can make a long-run profit.

Even in the long run, entry is limited in some markets because firms face significant costs to enter, such as large start-up costs, or barriers to entry, such as a government restriction. For example, many city governments limit the number of cabs, creating an insurmountable barrier that prevents additional taxis from entering. Similarly, patent protection prevents new firms from producing the patented product until the patent expires.

However, in unregulated, perfectly competitive markets, firms can enter and exit freely in the long run. For example, many construction firms that provide only labor services enter and exit a market several times a year. In the United States in the fourth quarter of 2011, an estimated 202,000 new small firms entered the market and 191,000 firms exited.[16] The annual rates of entry and exit of such firms are both about 10% of the total number of firms per year.

In such markets, a shift of the market demand curve to the right attracts firms to enter. For example, if there were no government regulations, the market for taxicabs would have free entry and exit. Car owners could enter or exit the market quickly. If the demand curve for cab rides shifted to the right, the market price would rise, and existing cab drivers would make unusually high profits in the short run. Seeing these profits, other car owners would enter the market, causing the market supply curve to shift to the right and the market price to fall. Entry would continue until the last firm to enter—the *marginal firm*—makes zero long-run profit.

Similarly, if the demand curve shifts to the left so that the market price drops, firms suffer losses. Firms with minimum average costs above the new, lower market price exit the market. Firms continue to leave the market until the next firm considering leaving, the marginal firm, is again earning a zero long-run profit.

Thus, in a market with free entry and exit:

- A firm enters the market if it can make a long-run profit, $\pi > 0$.
- A firm exits the market to avoid a long-run loss, $\pi < 0$.

If firms in a market are making zero long-run profit, they are indifferent between staying in the market and exiting. We presume that if they are already in the market, they stay in the market when they are making zero long-run profit.

Application

Fast-Food Firms' Entry in Russia

American fast-food restaurants are flooding into Russia. When McDonald's opened its first restaurant in Pushkin Square in 1990, workers greeted gigantic lines of customers. As of 2013, McDonald's has 357 restaurants in 85 Russian cities and plans to open another 150 over the next three years. For years, McDonald's faced little western competition, despite the popularity of western fast food. The average bill at a Russian fast-food outlet is $8.92 compared to $6.50 in the United States (even though Russian incomes are about one-sixth U.S. incomes).

---

[16]www.sba.gov/sites/default/files/files/SBQB_2013q1.pdf, first quarter, 2013.

Belatedly recognizing the profit opportunities, other chains are flooding into Russia. Subway entered Russia in 1994 and has more than 400 restaurants as of 2013. It says that it will have 1,000 shops by 2015. Burger King opened 22 restaurants in just two years and now has 70 restaurants. Wendy's had 2 restaurants and plans to have 180 throughout Russia by 2020. Yum Brands (which owns KFC, Pizza Hut, and Taco Bell) announced plans to nearly double the number of its restaurants in Russia and former Soviet countries to around 400 by 2015, with the goal of earning $1 billion in annual revenue.

Moscow is particularly ripe for entry by pizza restaurants. With a population of 13 million, it has only about 300 pizza restaurants. In contrast, Manhattan, with a population only about a tenth as large (1.6 million) has 4,000 pizza joints.

Christopher Wynne, an American who is fluent in Russian and gained Russian expertise researching arms proliferation, left his original career to open pizza restaurants in Russia. He bought 51% of the Papa John's Russian franchise. Although he competes with the U.S. chains Sbarro and Domino's and a Russian chain, Pizza Fabrika, among others, he says, "I could succeed in my sleep there is so much opportunity here." In 2011, Mr. Wynne opened his twenty-fifth Papa John's outlet in Russia, doubling the number from the previous year. Nineteen are in Moscow. He expects to have 50 restaurants in Moscow and the surrounding area by 2013.

Each restaurant costs about $400,000 to open, but a restaurant can start earning an operating profit in three months. Mr. Wynne will continue opening outlets until the marginal restaurant earns zero economic profit.

Long-Run Market Supply with Identical Firms and Free Entry The *long-run market supply curve is flat* at the minimum long-run average cost *if firms can freely enter and exit* the market, an unlimited number of *firms have identical costs*, and *input prices are constant*. This result follows from our reasoning about the short-run supply curve, in which we showed that the market supply was flatter, the more firms in the market. With many firms in the market in the long run, the market supply curve is effectively flat. ("Many" is 10 firms in the vegetable oil market.)

The long-run supply curve of a typical vegetable oil mill, S^1 in panel a of Figure 8.10, is the long-run marginal cost curve above a minimum long-run average cost of $10. Because each firm shuts down if the market price is below $10, the long-run market supply curve is zero at a price below $10. If the price rises above $10, firms are making positive profits, so new firms enter, expanding market output until profits are driven to zero, where price is again $10. The long-run market supply curve in panel b is a horizontal line at the minimum long-run average cost of the typical firm, $10. At a price of $10, each firm produces $q = 150$ units (where one unit equals 100 metric tons). Thus, the total output produced by n firms in the market is $Q = nq = n \times 150$ units. Extra market output is obtained by new firms entering the market.

In summary, the long-run market supply curve is horizontal if the market has free entry and exit, an unlimited number of firms have identical costs, and input prices are constant. We next examine four reasons why a long-run market supply curve is not flat: limited entry, differences in cost functions across firms, input prices rise (or fall) when output increases, or a country demands a large share of a good from the world's market.

Long-Run Market Supply When Entry Is Limited First, if the number of firms in a market is limited in the long run, the market supply curve slopes upward. The number of firms is limited if the government restricts that number, if firms need a

Figure 8.10 Long-Run Firm and Market Supply with Identical Vegetable Oil Firms

(a) The long-run supply curve of a typical vegetable oil mill, S^1, is the long-run marginal cost curve above the minimum average cost of $10. (b) The long-run market supply curve is

horizontal at the minimum of the long-run minimum average cost of a typical firm. Each firm produces 150 units, so market output is $150n$, where n is the number of firms.

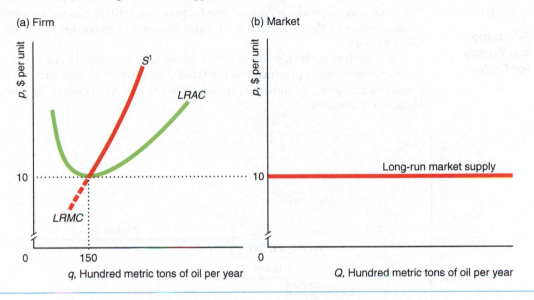

scarce resource, or if entry is costly. An example of a scarce resource is the limited number of lots on which a luxury beachfront hotel can be built in Miami Beach. High entry costs restrict the number of firms in a market because firms enter only if the long-run economic profit is greater than the cost of entering.

The only way to get more output if the number of firms is limited is for existing firms to produce more. Because individual firms' supply curves slope upward, the long-run market supply curve is also upward sloping. The reasoning is the same as in the short run, as panel b of Figure 8.6 illustrates, given that no more than five firms can enter. The market supply curve is the upward-sloping S^5 curve, which is the horizontal sum of the five firms' upward-sloping marginal cost curves above minimum average cost.

Long-Run Market Supply When Firms Differ A second reason why some long-run market supply curves slope upward is that firms differ. Firms with relatively low minimum long-run average costs are willing to enter the market at lower prices than others, resulting in an upward-sloping long-run market supply curve (similar to the short-run example in Figure 8.7).

Many markets have a number of low-cost firms and other higher-cost firms.[17] If lower-cost firms can produce as much output as the market wants, only low-cost firms produce, and the long-run market supply curve is horizontal at the minimum of the low-cost firm's average cost curve. The long-run supply curve is upward

---

[17]Syverson (2004) estimated that, in the typical 4-digit (narrowly defined) U.S. manufacturing industry, the 90th percentile plant produces 90% more output from the same input as the 10th percentile plant. Atalay (2012) found that 7% of the standard deviation (a measure of variation) of these plant-level productivities is due to differences in the price of materials that plants face. Thus, these markets have substantial variations in costs.

sloping *only* if lower-cost firms cannot produce as much output as the market demands because each of these firms has a limited capacity and the number of these firms is limited.

Application

Upward-Sloping Long-Run Supply Curve for Cotton

Many countries produce cotton. Production costs differ among countries because of differences in the quality of land, rainfall, costs of irrigation, costs of labor, and other factors.

The length of each step-like segment of the long-run supply curve of cotton in the graph is the quantity produced by the labeled country. The amount that the low-cost countries can produce must be limited, or we would not observe production by the higher-cost countries.

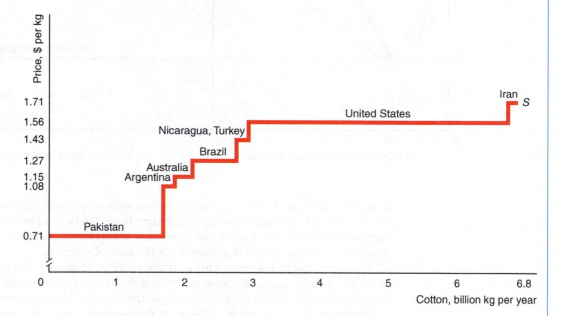

The height of each segment of the supply curve is the typical minimum average cost of production in that country. The average cost of production in Pakistan is less than half that in Iran. The supply curve has a step-like appearance because we are using an average of the estimated average cost in each country, which is a single number. If we knew the individual firms' supply curves in each of these countries, the market supply curve would have a smoother shape.

As the market price rises, the number of countries producing rises. At market prices below $1.08 per kilogram, only Pakistan produces. If the market price is below $1.50, the United States and Iran do not produce. If the price increases to $1.56, the United States supplies a large amount of cotton. In this range of the supply curve, supply is very elastic. For Iran to produce, the price has to rise to $1.71. Price increases in that range result in only a relatively small increase in supply. Thus, the supply curve is relatively inelastic at prices above $1.56.

Long-Run Market Supply When Input Prices Vary with Output   A third reason why market supply curves may slope is nonconstant input prices. In markets in which factor prices rise or fall when output increases, the long-run supply curve slopes even if firms have identical costs and can freely enter and exit.

If the market buys a relatively small share of the total amount of a factor of production that is sold, then, as market output expands, the price of the factor is unlikely to be affected. For example, dentists do not hire enough receptionists to affect the market wage for receptionists.

In contrast, if the market buys most of the total sales of a factor, the price of that input is more likely to vary with market output. As wine manufacturers expand and buy more wine grapes, the price of these grapes may rise because the wine manufacturers are the main purchaser of these grapes and the amount of grape growing land is limited.

To produce more goods, firms must use more inputs. If the prices of some or all inputs rise when more inputs are purchased, the cost of producing the final good also rises. We call a market in which input prices rise with output an *increasing-cost market*. Few steelworkers lack a fear of heights and are willing to construct tall buildings, so their supply curve is steeply upward sloping. As more skyscrapers are built at one time, the demand for these workers shifts to the right, driving up their wage.

We assume that all firms in a market have the same cost curves and that input prices rise as market output expands. We use the cost curves of a representative firm in panel a of Figure 8.11 to derive the upward-sloping market supply curve in panel b.

When input prices are relatively low, each identical firm has the same long-run marginal cost curve, MC^1, and average cost curve, AC^1, in panel a. A typical firm produces at minimum average cost, e_1, and sells q_1 units of output. The market supply is Q_1 in panel b when the market price is p_1. The n_1 firms collectively sell $Q_1 = n_1 q_1$ units of output, which is point E_1 on the market supply curve in panel b.

Figure 8.11 Long-Run Firm and Market Supply in an Increasing-Cost Market

(a) At a relatively low market output, Q_1 (in panel b), the firm's long-run marginal and average cost curves are MC^1 and AC^1. At the higher market quantity Q_2, the cost curves shift upward to MC^2 and AC^2 because of the higher input prices. Given identical firms, each firm produces at minimum average cost, such as points e_1 and e_2. (b) Long-run market supply, S, is upward sloping.

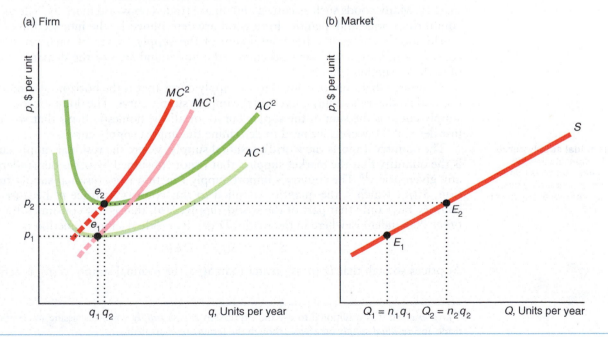

If the market demand curve shifts outward, the market price rises to p_2, new firms enter, and market output rises to Q_2, causing input prices to rise. As a result, the marginal cost curve shifts from MC^1 to MC^2, and the average cost curve rises from AC^1 to AC^2. The typical firm produces at a higher minimum average cost, e_2. At this higher price, n_2 firms operate in the market, so market output is $Q_2 = n_2q_2$ at point E_2 on the market supply curve.

Thus, in both an increasing-cost market and a constant-cost market—in which input prices remain constant as output increases—firms produce at minimum average cost in the long run. The difference is that the minimum average cost rises as market output increases in an increasing-cost market, whereas minimum average cost is constant in a constant-cost market. In conclusion, *the long-run supply curve is upward sloping in an increasing-cost market and flat in a constant-cost market.*

In decreasing-cost markets, as market output rises, at least some factor prices fall. As a result, *in a decreasing-cost market, the long-run market supply curve is downward sloping.*

Increasing returns to scale may cause factor prices to fall. For example, when the personal computer market was young, the demand for hard drives was lower than today. As a result, those drives were partially assembled by hand at relatively high cost. As demand for these drives increased, it became practical to automate more of the production process so that drives could be produced at a lower per-unit cost. The decrease in the price of these drives lowers the cost of personal computers.

Thus, theory tells us that competitive long-run market supply curves may be flat, upward sloping, or downward sloping. If all firms are identical in a market in which firms can freely enter and input prices are constant, the long-run market supply curve is flat. If entry is limited, firms differ in costs, or input prices rise with output, the long-run supply curve is upward sloping. Finally, if input prices fall with market output, the long-run supply curve may be downward sloping.

Long-Run Market Supply Curve with Trade   A fourth reason why a market supply curve may slope is that a country demands a large share of a good sold on a world market. Many goods such as cotton and oil are traded on world markets. The world equilibrium price and quantity for a good are determined by the intersection of the world supply curve—the horizontal sum of the supply curves of each producing country—and the world demand curve—the horizontal sum of the demand curves of each consuming country.

A country that imports a good has a supply curve that is the horizontal sum of its domestic industry's supply curve and the import supply curve. The domestic long-run supply curve is the sum of the supply curves of all the domestic firms that we have just derived. However, we need to determine the import supply curve.

residual supply curve
the quantity that the market supplies that is not consumed by other demanders at any given price

The country imports the world's residual supply, where the **residual supply curve** is the quantity that the market supplies that is not consumed by other demanders at any given price.[18] The country's import supply function is its residual supply function, $S^r(p)$, which is the quantity supplied to this country at price p. Because the country buys only that part of the world supply, $S(p)$, that is not consumed by any *other* demander elsewhere in the world, $D^o(p)$, its residual supply function is

$$S^r(p) = S(p) - D^o(p). \qquad (8.6)$$

At prices so high that $D^o(p)$ is greater than $S(p)$, the residual supply, $S^r(p)$, is zero.

---

[18]*Jargon alert*: It is traditional to use the expression *excess supply* when discussing international trade and *residual supply* otherwise, though the terms are equivalent.

In Figure 8.12, we derive Japan's residual supply curve for cotton in panel a using the world supply curve, S, and the demand curve of the rest of the world, D^o, in panel b. The scales differ for the quantity axes in the two panels. At a price of $850 per metric ton, the demand in other countries exhausts world supply (D^o intersects S at 32 million metric tons per year), so Japan has no residual supply. At a much higher price, $935, Japan's excess supply, 4 million metric tons, is the difference between the world supply, 34 million tons, and the quantity demanded elsewhere, 30 million tons. As the figure illustrates, the residual supply curve facing Japan is much closer to horizontal than is the world supply curve.

The elasticity of residual supply, η_r, facing a given country is (by a similar argument to that in Appendix 8A)

$$\eta_r = \frac{\eta}{\theta} - \frac{1-\theta}{\theta}\varepsilon_o, \tag{8.7}$$

where η is the market supply elasticity, ε_o is the demand elasticity of the other countries, and $\theta = Q_r/Q$ is the importing country's share of the world's output.

If a country imports a small fraction of the world's supply, we expect it to face a nearly perfectly elastic, horizontal residual supply curve. On the other hand, a relatively large consumer of the good might face an upward-sloping residual supply curve.

We can illustrate this difference for cotton, where $\eta = 0.5$ and $\varepsilon = -0.7$ (Green et al., 2005), which is virtually equal to ε_o. The United States imports $\theta = 0.1\%$ of the world's cotton, so its residual supply elasticity is

$$\eta_r = \frac{\eta}{0.001} - \frac{0.999}{0.001}\varepsilon_o$$
$$= 1{,}000\eta - 999\varepsilon_o$$
$$= (1{,}000 \times 0.5) - (999 \times [-0.7]) = 1{,}199.3,$$

which is 2,398.6 times more elastic than the world's supply elasticity. Canada's import share is 10 times larger, $\theta = 1\%$, so its residual supply elasticity is "only" 119.3.

Figure 8.12 Excess or Residual Supply Curve

Japan's excess supply curve, S^r, for cotton is the horizontal difference between the world's supply curve, S, and the demand curve of the other countries in the world, D^o.

(a) Japan's Excess Supply Curve

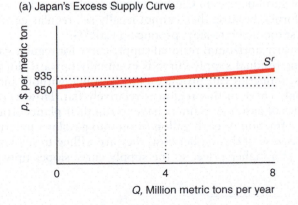

(b) World Supply and Rest of World Demand

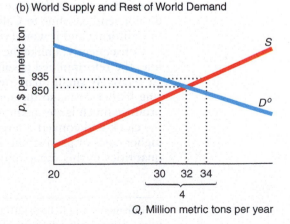

Nonetheless, its residual supply curve is nearly horizontal: A 1% increase in its price would induce imports to more than double, rising by 119.3%. Even Japan's $\theta = 2.5\%$ leads to a relatively elastic $\eta_r = 46.4$. In contrast, China imports 18.5% of the world's cotton, so its residual supply elasticity is 5.8. Even though its residual supply elasticity is more than 11 times larger than the world's elasticity, it is still small enough that its excess supply curve is upward sloping.

Thus, if a country imports a small share of the world's output, then it faces a horizontal import supply curve at the world equilibrium price. If its domestic supply curve is everywhere above the world price, then it only imports and faces a horizontal supply curve. If some portion of its upward-sloping domestic supply curve is below the world price, then its total supply curve is the upward-sloping domestic supply curve up to the world price, and then is horizontal at the world price (Chapter 9 shows such a supply curve for oil).

This analysis of trade applies to trade within a country too. The following Application shows that it can be used to look at trade across geographic areas or jurisdictions such as states.

Application

Reformulated Gasoline Supply Curves

You can't buy the gasoline sold in Milwaukee in other parts of Wisconsin. Houston gas isn't the same as western Texas gas. California, Minnesota, Nevada, and most of America's biggest cities use one or more of at least 46 specialized blends (sometimes referred to as *boutique fuels*), while much of the rest of the country uses regular gas. Because special blends are often designed to cut air pollution, they are more likely to be required by the U.S. Clean Air Act Amendments, state laws, or local ordinances in areas with serious pollution problems. For example, the objective of the federal Reformulated Fuels Program (RFG) is to reduce ground-level ozone-forming pollutants. It specifies both content criteria (such as benzene content limits) and emissions-based performance standards for refiners.

In states in which regular gasoline is used, wholesalers in one state ship gasoline across state lines in response to slightly higher prices in neighboring states. Consequently, the residual supply curve for regular gasoline for a given state is close to horizontal.

In contrast, gasoline is usually not imported into jurisdictions that require special blends. Few refiners produce any given special blend. Only 13 California refineries can produce California's special low-polluting blend of gasoline, California Reformulated Gasoline (CaRFG).[19] Because refineries require expensive upgrades to produce a new kind of gas, they generally do not switch from producing one type of gas to another type. Thus, even if the price of gasoline rises in California, wholesalers in other states do not send gasoline to California, because they cannot legally sell regular gasoline in California and it would cost too much to start producing CaRFG.

Consequently, unlike the nearly horizontal residual supply curve for regular gasoline, the reformulated gasoline residual supply curve is eventually upward sloping. At relatively small quantities, refineries can produce more gasoline without incurring higher costs, so the supply curve in this region is relatively flat. However, to produce much larger quantities of gasoline, refiners have to run their plants around the clock and convert a larger fraction of each gallon of oil into gasoline, incurring higher costs of production. Because of this higher cost, they are willing to sell larger quantities in this range only at a higher price, so the supply curve slopes upward.

---

[19]Auffhammer and Kellogg (2011) showed that California's regulation helps to reduce ground-level ozone, significantly improving air quality, but that current federal regulations are not effective.

When the refineries reach capacity, no matter how high the price gets, firms cannot produce more gasoline (at least until new refineries go online), so the supply curve becomes vertical.

California normally operates in the steeply upward-sloping section of its supply curve. At the end of the summer of 2009, when gas prices fell in the rest of the nation, California's gas price jumped an extra 30¢ per gallon relative to the average national price due to a series of production problems at its refineries.

Brown et al. (2008) found that when the federal RFG was first imposed, prices in regulated metropolitan areas increased by an average of 3¢ per gallon relative to unregulated areas. However, the jump was over 7¢ in some cities such as Chicago as the demand curve went from intersecting the supply curve in the flat section to intersecting it in the upward-sloping section.

Solved Problem 8.5

In the short run, what happens to the competitive market price of gasoline if the demand curve in a state shifts to the right as more people move to the state or start driving gas-hogging SUVs? In your answer, distinguish between areas in which regular gasoline is sold and jurisdictions that require special blends.

Answer

1. *Show the effect of a shift of the demand curve in areas that use regular gasoline.* In an area that uses regular gasoline, the supply curve in panel a of the figure is horizontal because firms in neighboring states will supply as much gasoline as desired at the market price. Thus, as the demand curve shifts to the right from D^1 to D^2, the equilibrium shifts along the supply curve from e_1 to e_2 and the price remains at p_1.

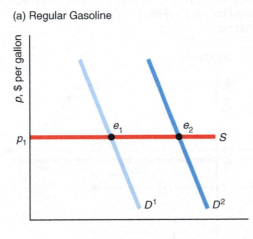

(a) Regular Gasoline

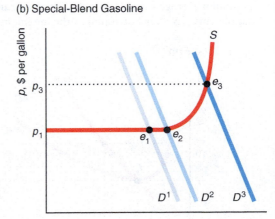

(b) Special-Blend Gasoline

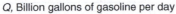

Q, Billion gallons of gasoline per day   *Q*, Billion gallons of gasoline per day

2. *Show the effect of both a small and a large shift of the demand curve in a jurisdiction that uses a special blend.* The supply curve in panel b is drawn as described in the Application. If the demand curve shifts slightly to the right from D^1 to D^2, the price remains unchanged at p_1 because the new demand curve intersects the

supply curve in the flat region at e_2. However, if the demand curve shifts farther to the right to D^3, then the new point of intersection, e_3, is in the upward-sloping section of the supply curve and the price increases to p_3. Consequently, unforeseen "jumps" in demand are more likely to cause a *price spike*—a large increase in price—in jurisdictions that use special blends.[20]

Long-Run Competitive Equilibrium

The intersection of the long-run market supply and demand curves determines the long-run competitive equilibrium. With identical firms, constant input prices, and free entry and exit, the long-run competitive market supply is horizontal at minimum long-run average cost, so the equilibrium price equals long-run average cost. A shift in the demand curve affects only the equilibrium quantity and not the equilibrium price, which remains constant at minimum long-run average cost.

The market supply curve is different in the short run than in the long run, so the long-run competitive equilibrium differs from the short-run equilibrium. The relationship between the short- and long-run equilibria depends on where the market demand curve crosses the short- and long-run market supply curves. Figure 8.13 illustrates this point using the short- and long-run supply curves for the vegetable oil mill market.

Figure 8.13   The Short-Run and Long-Run Equilibria for Vegetable Oil

(a) A typical vegetable oil mill produces where price equals its *MC*, so it is willing to produce 150 units of oil at a price of $10, or 165 units at $11. (b) The short-run market supply curve, S^{SR}, is the horizontal sum of 20 individual firms' short-run marginal cost curves above minimum average variable cost, $7. The long-run market supply curve, S^{LR}, is horizontal at the minimum average cost, $10. If the demand curve is D^1, in the short-run equilibrium, F_1, 20 firms sell 2,000 units of oil at $7. In the long-run equilibrium, E_1, 10 firms sell 1,500 units at $10. If demand is D^2, the short-run equilibrium is F_2 ($11, 3,300 units, 20 firms) and the long-run equilibrium is E_2 ($10, 3,600 units, 24 firms).

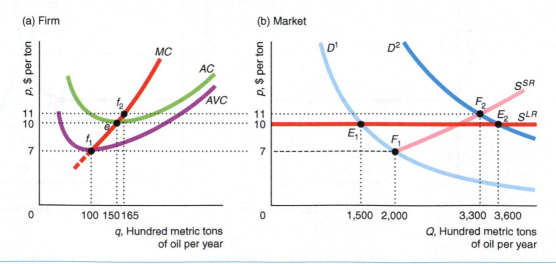

The short-run supply curve for a typical firm in panel a is the marginal cost above the minimum of the average variable cost, $7. At a price of $7, each firm produces 100 units, so the 20 firms in the market in the short run collectively supply 2,000 ($= 20 \times 100$) units of oil in panel b. At higher prices, the short-run market supply curve slopes upward because it is the horizontal summation of the firm's upward-sloping marginal cost curves.

We assume that the firms use the same size plant in the short and long run so that the minimum average cost is $10 in both the short and long run. Because all firms have the same costs and can enter freely, the long-run market supply curve is flat at the minimum average cost, $10, in panel b. At prices between $7 and $10, firms supply goods at a loss in the short run but not in the long run.

If the market demand curve is D^1, the short-run market equilibrium, F_1, is below and to the right of the long-run market equilibrium, E_1. This relationship is reversed if the market demand curve is D^2.[21]

In the short run, if the demand is as low as D^1, the market price in the short-run equilibrium, F_1, is $7. At that price, each of the 20 firms produces 100 units, at f_1 in panel a. The firms lose money because the price of $7 is below average cost at 100 units. These losses drive some of the firms out of the market in the long run, so market output falls and the market price rises. In the long-run equilibrium, E_1, price is $10, and each firm produces 150 units, e, and breaks even. As the market demands only 1,500 units, only 10 ($= 1,500/150$) firms produce, so half the firms that produced in the short run exit the market.[22] Thus, with the D^1 demand curve, price rises and output falls in the long run.

If demand expands to D^2, in the short run, each of the 20 firms expands its output to 165 units, f_2, and the price rises to $11, where the firms make profits: The price of $11 is above the average cost at 165 units. These profits attract entry in the long run, and the price falls. In the long-run equilibrium, each firm produces 150 units, e, and 3,600 units are sold by the market, E_2, by 24 ($= 3,600/150$) firms. Thus, with the D^2 demand curve, price falls and output rises in the long run.

Challenge Solution **The Rising Cost of Keeping On Truckin'**	We return to the Challenge questions about the effects of higher annual fees and other lump-sum costs on the trucking market price and quantity, the output of individual firms, and the number of trucking firms (assuming that the demand curve remains constant). Because firms may enter and exit this industry in the long run, such higher lump-sum costs can have a counterintuitive effect on the competitive equilibrium. All trucks of a certain size are essentially identical, and trucks can easily enter and exit the industry (government regulations aside). A typical firm's cost curves are shown in panel a and the market equilibrium in panel b of the figure.

---

[21]Using data from Statistics Canada, I estimate that the elasticity of demand for vegetable oil is $\varepsilon = -0.8$. Both D^1 and D^2 are constant elasticity demand curves, but the quantity demanded at any price on D^2 is 2.4 times that on D^1.

[22]How do we know which firms leave? If the firms are identical, the theory says nothing about which ones leave and which ones stay. The firms that leave make zero economic profit, and those that stay make zero economic profit, so firms are indifferent as to whether they stay or exit.

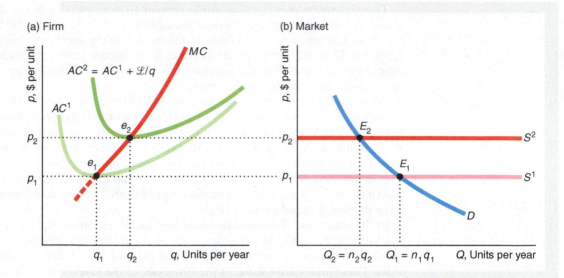

(a) Firm

(b) Market

The new, higher fees and other lump-sum costs raise the fixed cost of operating by $\mathscr{L}$. In panel a, a lump-sum, franchise tax shifts the typical firm's average cost curve upward from AC^1 to $AC^2 = AC^1 + \mathscr{L}/q$ but does not affect the marginal cost (see the answer to Solved Problem 7.2). As a result, the minimum average cost rises from e_1 to e_2.

Given that an unlimited number of identical truckers are willing to operate in this market, the long-run market supply curve is horizontal at the minimum average cost. Thus, the market supply curve shifts upward in panel b by the same amount as the minimum average cost increases. Given a downward-sloping market demand curve D, the new equilibrium, E_2, has a lower quantity, $Q_2 < Q_1$, and higher price, $p_2 > p_1$, than the original equilibrium, E_1.

As the market price rises, the quantity that a firm produces rises from q_1 to q_2 in panel a. Because the marginal cost curve is upward sloping at the original equilibrium, when the average cost curve shifts up due to the higher fixed cost, the new minimum point on the average cost curve corresponds to a larger output than in the original equilibrium. Thus, any trucking firm still operating in the market produces at a larger volume.

Because the market quantity falls but each firm remaining in the market produces more, the number of firms in the market must fall. At the initial equilibrium, the number of firms was $n_1 = Q_1/q_1$. The new equilibrium number of firms, $n_2 = Q_2/q_2$, must be smaller than n_1 because $Q_2 < Q_1$ and $q_2 > q_1$. Therefore, an increase in fixed cost causes the market price and quantity to rise and the number of trucking firms to fall, as most people would have expected, but it has the surprising effect that it causes producing firms to increase the amount of services that they provide.

Summary

1. **Perfect Competition.** Perfect competition is a market structure in which buyers and sellers are price takers. Each firm faces a horizontal demand curve. A firm's demand curve is horizontal because perfectly competitive markets have five characteristics: there are a very large number of small buyers and sellers, firms produce identical (homogeneous) products, buyers have full information about product prices and characteristics, transaction costs are negligible, and there is free entry and exit in the long run. Many markets are highly competitive—firms are very close to being price takers—even if they do not strictly possess all five of the characteristics associated with perfect competition.

2. **Profit Maximization.** Most firms maximize economic profit, which is revenue minus economic cost (explicit and implicit cost). Because business profit, which is revenue minus only explicit cost, does not include implicit cost, economic profit tends to be less than business profit. A firm earning zero economic profit is making as much as it could if its resources were devoted to their best alternative uses. To maximize profit, all firms (not just competitive firms) must make two decisions. First, the firm determines the quantity at which its profit is highest. Profit is maximized when marginal profit is zero or, equivalently, when marginal revenue equals marginal cost. Second, the firm decides whether to produce at all.

3. **Competition in the Short Run.** To maximize its profit, a competitive firm (like a firm in any other market structure) chooses its output level where marginal revenue equals marginal cost. Because a competitive firm is a price taker, its marginal revenue equals the market price, so it sets its output so that price equals marginal cost. New firms cannot enter in the short run. In addition, firms that are in the industry have some fixed inputs that cannot be changed and whose costs cannot be avoided. In this sense firms cannot exit the industry in the short run. However, a profit-maximizing firm shuts down and produces no output if the market price is less than its minimum average variable cost. Thus, a competitive firm's short-run supply curve is its marginal cost curve above its minimum average variable cost. The short-run market supply curve is the sum of the supply curves of the fixed number of firms producing in the short run. The short-run competitive equilibrium is determined by the intersection of the market demand curve and the short-run market supply curve.

4. **Competition in the Long Run.** In the long run, a competitive firm sets its output where the market price equals its long-run marginal cost. It shuts down if the market price is less than the minimum of its average long-run cost, because all costs are variable in the long run. Consequently, the competitive firm's supply curve is its long-run marginal cost above its minimum long-run average cost. The long-run supply curve of a firm may have a different slope than the short-run curve because it can vary its fixed factors in the long run. The long-run market supply curve is the horizontal sum of the supply curves of all the firms in the market. If all firms are identical, entry and exit are easy, and input prices are constant, the long-run market supply curve is flat at minimum average cost. If firms differ, entry is difficult or costly, input prices vary with output, or a country demands a large share of a good on a world market, the long-run market supply curve has a slope. The long-run market equilibrium price and quantity are different from the short-run equilibrium price and quantity.

Questions

All questions are available on MyEconLab; * = *answer appears at the back of this book;* **A** = *algebra problem;* **C** = *calculus problem.*

1. Perfect Competition

1.1 A competitive firm faces a relatively horizontal residual demand curve. Do the following conditions make the demand curve flatter (and why)?

   a. Ease of entry.

   b. A large number of firms in the market.

   c. The market demand curve is relatively elastic at the equilibrium.

   d. The supply curves of other firms are relatively elastic.

1.2 Why would high transaction costs or imperfect information tend to prevent price-taking behavior?

1.3 Based on Roberts and Schlenker (forthcoming), the corn demand elasticity is $\varepsilon = -0.3$, and the supply elasticity is $\eta = 0.15$. According to the 2007 Census of Agriculture, the United States has 347,760 corn farms. Assuming that the farms are of roughly equal size, what is the elasticity of demand facing a single farm? (*Hint:* See Solved Problem 8.1.)

1.4 Based on Equation 8.2, by how much does the residual elasticity of demand facing a firm increase as the number of firms increases by one firm? (*Hint:* See Solved Problem 8.1.) **A or C**

2. Profit Maximization

2.1 Should a firm shut down (and why) if its revenue is $R = \$1,000$ per week,

   a. its variable cost is $VC = \$500$, and its sunk fixed cost is $F = \$600$?

   b. its variable cost is $VC = \$1,001$, and its sunk fixed cost $F = \$500$?

2.2 Should a firm shut down if its weekly revenue is $1,000, its variable cost is $500, and its fixed cost is $800, of which $600 is avoidable if it shuts down? Why?

2.3 Should a competitive firm ever produce when it is losing money (making a negative economic profit)? Why or why not?

2.4 The producers of "Spider-Man: Turn Off the Dark" spent $75 million bringing their musical to Broadway (Kevin Flynn and Patrick Healy, "How the Numbers Add Up [Way Up] for 'Spider-Man,'" *New York Times*, June 23, 2011). They spent $9 million alone on sets, costumes, and shoes. Their operating expenses were $1.2 million a week as of January 2011. Since then, they revamped the show and lowered their operating costs to about $1 million a week. The show is selling out but bringing in between $1.2 million and $1.3 million a week. The producers acknowledge that at the show's current earning level, "Spider-Man" would need to run more than seven years to pay back the investors. Only 18 Broadway shows have ever run for seven years or longer. Should "Spider-Man" shut down or keep operating? Why?

*2.5 A firm's profit function is $\pi(q) = R(q) - C(q) = 120q - (200 + 40q + 10q^2)$. What is the positive output level that maximizes the firm's profit (or minimizes its loss)? What are the firm's revenue, variable cost, and profit? Should it operate or shut down in the short run? **C**

3. Competition in the Short Run

*3.1 A marginal cost curve may be U-shaped. As a result, the *MC* curve may hit the firm's demand curve or price line at two output levels. Which is the profit-maximizing output? Why?

3.2 If the cost function for John's Shoe Repair is $C(q) = 100 + 10q - q^2 + \frac{1}{3}q^3$, and its marginal cost function is $MC = 10 - 2q + q^2$, what is its profit-maximizing condition given that the market price is p? **A**

*3.3 If a competitive firm's cost function is $C(q) = a + bq + cq^2 + dq^3$, where a, b, c, and d are constants, what is the firm's marginal cost function? What is the firm's profit-maximizing condition? **C**

3.4 The cost function for Acme Laundry is $C(q) = 10 + 10q + q^2$, so its marginal cost function is $MC = 10 + 2q$, where q is tons of laundry cleaned. Derive the firm's average cost and average variable cost curves. What q should the firm choose so as to maximize its profit if the market price is p? How much does it produce if the competitive market price is $p = 50$? **A**

3.5 If a specific subsidy (negative tax) of s is given to only one competitive firm, how should that firm

change its output level to maximize its profit, and how does its maximum profit change? (*Hint*: See Solved Problem 8.2.)

3.6 How would the answer to Solved Problem 8.2 change if, instead of a specific tax, Manitoba imposes an ad valorem tax (see Chapter 3) of α percent on lime produced in that province? (*Hints*: See Solved Problem 8.2. What role does the market price play in the analyses of the two types of tax?)

3.7 Beta Laundry's pre-tax cost function is $C(q) = 30 + 20q + q^2$, so its marginal cost function is $MC = 20 + 2q$.

   a. What quantity maximizes the firm's profit if the market price is p? How much does it produce if $p = 60$?

   b. If the government imposes a specific tax of $t = 2$, what quantity maximizes its after-tax profit? Does it operate or shut down? (*Hint*: See Solved Problem 8.2.) **A**

3.8 If the pre-tax cost function for John's Shoe Repair is $C(q) = 100 + 10q - q^2 + \frac{1}{3}q^3$, and it faces a specific tax of $t = 10$, what is its profit-maximizing condition if the market price is p? Can you solve for a single, profit-maximizing q in terms of p? (*Hint*: See Solved Problem 8.2.) **C**

3.9 Initially, the market price was $p = 20$, and the competitive firm's minimum average variable cost was 18, while its minimum average cost was 21. Should it shut down? Why? Now this firm's average variable cost increases by 3 at every quantity, while other firms in the market are unaffected. What happens to its average cost? Should this firm shut down? Why?

3.10 In radio ads, Mercedes-Benz of San Francisco says that it has been owned and operated by the same family in the same location for 51 years (as of 2013). It then makes two claims: first, that because it has owned this land for so long, it has lower overhead than other nearby auto dealers, and second, because of its lower overhead, it has lower costs that allows it to charge a lower price on its cars. Discuss the logic of these claims. (*Hint*: See Solved Problem 8.3.)

3.11 According to the "Oil, Oil Sands, and Oil Shale Shutdowns" Application, the minimum average variable cost of processing oil sands dropped from $25 a barrel in the 1960s to $18 due to technological advances. In a figure, show how this change affects the supply curve of a typical competitive firm and the supply curve of all the firms producing oil from oil sands.

3.12 The last of California's operating gold mines closed after World War II because mining had become unprofitable when the price of gold was $34.71 an ounce (about $446 in current dollars). However, in 2012, the price of gold approached historic highs, hovering around $1,700 an ounce. As a consequence, the first large-scale hard rock gold mining operation in more than half a century reopened, and several others were posed to reopen in 2013 (Don Thompson, "Gold Mining is Back in the Sierra Foothills," *Appeal-Democrat*, December 17, 2012; **www.macrotrends.net/1333/ gold-and-silver-prices-100-year-historical-chart**, viewed June 22, 2013).

    a. Show in a figure what this information implies about the shape of the gold extraction cost function.

    b. Use the cost function you drew in part a to show how an increase in the market price of gold affects the amount of gold that a competitive firm extracts. Show the change in the firm's equilibrium profit.

3.13 In the summer of 2012, due to plentiful lobsters, the price of lobster in Maine fell to $1.25 a pound, which was 70% below normal and nearly a 30-year low. According to Bill Adler, head of the Massachusetts Lobstermen's Association, "Anything under $4 [a pound], lobstermen can't make any money" (Jerry A. Dicolo and Nicole Friedman, "Lobster Glut Slams Prices," *Wall Street Journal*, July 16, 2012). At least 30 boats announced that they would stay in port until the price rose. However, Canadian and other U.S. fishers continued to harvest lobsters. Why did some lobster boats stop fishing while others continued?

*3.14 For Red Delicious apple farmers in Washington, 2001 was a terrible year (Linda Ashton, "Bumper Crop a Bummer for Struggling Apple Farmers," *San Francisco Chronicle*, January 9, 2001). The average price for Red Delicious was $10.61 per box, well below the shutdown level of $13.23. Many farmers did not pick the apples off their trees. Other farmers bulldozed their trees, getting out of the Red Delicious business for good, taking 25,000 acres out of production. Why did some farms choose not to pick apples, and others to bulldoze their trees? (*Hint*: Consider the average variable cost and expectations about future prices.)

3.15 In 2009, the voters of Oakland, California, passed a measure to tax medical cannabis (marijuana), effectively legalizing it. In 2010, the City Council adopted regulations permitting industrial-scale marijuana farms with no size limits but requiring each to pay a $211,000 per year fee (Matthai Kuruvila, "Oakland Allows Industrial-Scale Marijuana Farms," *San Francisco Chronicle*, July 21, 2010; Malia Wollan, "Oakland, Seeking Financial Lift, Approves Giant Marijuana Farms," *New York Times*, July 21, 2010). One proposal calls for a 100,000-square-feet farm, the size of two football fields. Prior to this legalization, only individuals could grow marijuana. These small farmers complained bitterly, arguing that the large firms would drive them out of the industry they helped to build due to economies of scale. Draw a figure to illustrate the situation. Under what conditions (such as relative costs, position of the demand curve, number of low-cost firms) will the smaller, higher-cost growers be driven out of business? (In 2012, the federal government brought an end to this business in Oakland. However, Colorado and Washington passed laws permitting marijuana sales as of 2013.)

3.16 The African country Lesotho gains most of its export earnings—90% in 2004—from its garment and textile factories. Your t-shirts from Walmart and fleece sweats from JCPenney probably were made there. In 2005, the demand curve for Lesotho products shifted down precipitously due to the end of textile quotas on China, the resulting increase in Chinese exports, and the plunge of the U.S. dollar exchange rate against its currency. Lesotho's garment factories had to sell roughly $55 worth of clothing in the United States to cover a factory worker's monthly wage in 2002, but they had to sell an average of $109 to $115 in 2005. Consequently, in the first quarter of 2005, 6 of Lesotho's 50 clothes factories shut down, as the world price plummeted below their minimum average variable cost. These shutdowns eliminated 5,800 of the 50,000 garment jobs. Layoffs at other factories have eliminated another 6,000. Since 2002, Lesotho has lost an estimated 30,000 textile jobs.

    a. What is the shape of the demand curve facing Lesotho textile factories, and why? (*Hint*: They are price takers in the world market.)

    b. Use figures to show how the increase in Chinese exports affected the demand curve the Lesotho factories face.

    c. Discuss how the change in the exchange rate affected their demand curve, and explain why.

    d. Use figures to explain why the factories have temporarily or permanently shut down. How does a factory decide whether to shut down temporarily or permanently?

3.17 The Internet is affecting holiday shipping. In years past, the busiest shipping period was Thanksgiving week. Now as people have become comfortable with e-commerce, they purchase later in the year and are more likely to have gifts shipped (rather than purchasing locally). FedEx, along with Amazon and other e-commerce firms, hires extra workers during this period, and many regular workers log substantial overtime hours.

a. Are a firm's marginal and average costs likely to rise or fall with this extra business? (Discuss economies of scale and the slopes of marginal and average cost curves.)

b. Use side-by-side firm-market diagrams to show the effects on the number of firms, equilibrium price and output, and profits of such a seasonal shift in demand for e-retailers in both the short run and the long run. Explain your reasoning.

3.18 Navel oranges are grown in California and Arizona. If Arizona starts collecting a specific tax per orange from its firms, what happens to the long-run market supply curve? (*Hints*: Assume that all firms initially have the same costs. Your answer may depend on whether unlimited entry occurs. See Solved Problem 8.4.)

3.19 What is the effect on the short-run equilibrium of a specific subsidy of s per unit that is given to all n firms in a market? What is the incidence of the subsidy? (*Hint*: See Solved Problem 8.4.)

3.20 As of 2013, customers at California grocery and drug stores must pay an extra 10¢ for each paper bag that the store provides (the store keeps this fee). Does such a charge affect the marginal cost of any particular good? If so, by how much? Is this fee likely to affect the overall amount that consumers pay for groceries?

3.21 Each of the 10 firms in a competitive market has a cost function of $C = 25 + q^2$, so its marginal cost is $MC = 2q$. The market demand function is $Q = 120 - p$. Determine the equilibrium price, quantity per firm, and market quantity. **A**

3.22 A shock causes the demand curve to shift to the right. What properties of the market are likely to lead to a large increase in the equilibrium price? (*Hint*: See the discussion of the shape of the market supply curve and Solved Problem 8.5.)

4. Competition in the Long Run

4.1 In June 2005, Eastman Kodak announced that it no longer would produce black-and-white

photographic paper—the type used to develop photographs by a traditional darkroom process. Kodak based its decision on the substitution of digital photography for traditional photography. In making its exit decision, did Kodak compare the price of its paper and average variable cost (at its optimal output)? Alternatively, did Kodak compare the price of its paper and average total cost (again at its optimal output)?

4.2 Redraw Figure 8.9 showing a situation in which the short-run plant size is too large relative to the optimal long-run plant size.

*4.3 What is the effect on firm and market equilibrium of the U.S. law requiring a firm to give its workers six months' notice before it can shut down its plant?

4.4 Each firm in a competitive market has a cost function of $C = q^2$, so its marginal cost function is $MC = 2q$. The market demand function is $Q = 24 - p$. Determine the long-run equilibrium price, quantity per firm, market quantity, and number of firms. **A**

4.5 Cheap handheld video cameras have revolutionized the hard-core pornography market. Previously, making movies required expensive equipment and some technical expertise. Today, anyone with a couple hundred dollars and a moderately steady hand can buy and use a video camera to make a movie. Consequently, many new firms have entered the market, and the supply curve of porn movies has slithered substantially to the right. Whereas only 1,000 to 2,000 video porn titles were released annually in the United States from 1986 to 1991, that number grew to 10,300 in 1999 and to 13,588 by 2005.[23] Use a side-by-side diagram to illustrate how this technological innovation affected the long-run supply curve and the equilibrium in this market.

4.6 The "Upward-Sloping Long-Run Supply Curve for Cotton" Application shows a supply curve for cotton. Discuss the equilibrium if the world demand curve crosses this supply curve in either (a) a flat section labeled Brazil or (b) the following vertical section. What do farms in the United States do?

4.7 Redraw Figure 8.11 to show what happens if factor costs fall as the industry's quantity increases.

*4.8 Derive Equation 8.7. (*Hint*: Use a method similar to that used in Appendix 8A.) **C**

[23]"Branded Flesh," *Economist*, August 14, 1999: 56; **internet-filter-review.toptenreviews.com/internet-pornography-statistics-pg9.html**.

*4.9 As of 2013, the federal specific tax on gasoline is 18.4¢ per gallon, and state specific taxes ranges from 8¢ in Alaska to 43¢ in California. A statistical study (Chouinard and Perloff, 2004) found that the incidence (Chapter 3) of the federal specific tax on consumers is substantially lower than that from state specific taxes. When the federal specific tax increases by 1¢, the retail price rises by about 0.5¢: Retail consumers bear half the tax incidence. In contrast, when a state that uses regular gasoline increases its specific tax by 1¢, the incidence of the tax falls almost entirely on consumers: The retail price rises by nearly 1¢.

a. What are the incidences of the federal and state specific gasoline taxes on firms?

b. Explain why the incidence on consumers differs between a federal and a state specific gasoline tax assuming that the market is competitive. (*Hint*: Consider the residual supply curve facing a state compared to the supply curve facing the nation.)

c. Using the residual supply equation (Equation 8.6), estimate how much more elastic is the residual supply elasticity to one state than is the national supply elasticity. For simplicity, assume that all 50 states are identical. **A**

4.10 The 2010 oil spill in the Gulf of Mexico caused the oil firm BP and the U.S. government to greatly increase purchases of boat services, various oil-absorbing materials, and other goods and services to minimize damage from the spill. Use side-by-side firm and market diagrams to show the effects (number of firms, price, output, profits) of such a shift in demand in one such industry in both the short run and the long run. Explain how your answer depends on whether the shift in demand is expected to be temporary or permanent.

4.11 Before the late 1990s, people bought air tickets from a travel agent. When airline deregulation in the late 1970s led U.S. air travel to more than triple between 1975 and 2000, the number of travel agents grew from 45,000 to 124,000. In the late 1990s, Internet travel sites such as Travelocity, Expedia, Priceline, and Orbitz entered the market. As a result, travel agents began to disappear. Of those travel agents working in 2000, 10% left in 2001, another 6% in 2002, and 43% by 2010 (Waldfogel, 2012). Use figures to explain what happened in the market for travel agents.

5. Challenge

5.1 In the Challenge Solution, would it make a difference to the analysis whether the lump-sum costs such as registration fees are collected annually or only once when the firm starts operation? How would each of these franchise taxes affect the firm's long-run supply curve? Explain your answer.

5.2 Change the answer given in the Challenge Solution for the short run rather than for the long run. (*Hint*: The answer depends on where the demand curve intersects the original short-run supply curve.)

5.3 The 1995 North American Free Trade Agreement provides for two-way, long-haul trucking across the U.S.-Mexican border. U.S. truckers have objected, arguing that the Mexican trucks don't have to meet the same environmental and safety standards as U.S. trucks. They are concerned that the combination of these lower fixed costs and lower Mexican wages will result in Mexican drivers taking business from them. Their complaints have delayed implementation of this agreement (except for a small pilot program during the Bush administration, which was ended during the Obama administration). What would be the short-run and long-run effects of allowing entry of Mexican drivers on market price and quantity and the number of U.S. truckers?

*5.4 Abortion clinics operate in a nearly perfectly competitive market, close to their break-even point. Medoff (2007) estimated that the price elasticity of demand for abortions is −1.071 and the income elasticity is 1.24. The average real price of abortions has remained relatively constant over the last 25 years, which suggests that the supply curve is horizontal.

a. By how much would the market price of abortions and the number of abortions change if a lump-sum tax is assessed on abortion clinics and raises their minimum average cost by 10%? Use a figure to illustrate your answer.

b. By how much would the market price of abortions and the number of abortions change if a lump-sum tax is assessed on abortion clinics that raises their minimum average cost by 10%? Use a figure to illustrate your answer.

9

Applying the Competitive Model

No more good must be attempted than the public can bear. —Thomas Jefferson

Challenge

"Big Dry" Water Restrictions

Between 1996 and 2010, Australia suffered from the worst drought in its history, the "Big Dry," which dramatically reduced the amount of water in storage throughout much of southeastern Australia. Heavy rains over much of central and northeastern Australia in 2010 brought limited relief there, but many areas, including the major

farming zone, still suffer from drought today. To reduce overall water consumption, Australian state governments and water utilities banned using water outdoors starting in 2002. At least 75% of Australians faced mandatory water restrictions in 2008, and most of Australia still had water restrictions in 2013.

Nature forced the government to reduce water consumption. However, is restricting outdoor water use a better way to reduce overall water consumption than allowing the price of water to rise to clear the market? Which consumers benefit and which ones lose from using restrictions?

In this chapter, we illustrate how to use the competitive market model to answer these types of questions. One of the major strengths of the competitive model is that it can predict how changes in government policies such as those concerning rationing and trade, and other shocks such as global warming and major cost-saving discoveries, affect consumers and producers.

We start this chapter by addressing how much competitive firms make in the long run, and who captures unusually high profit. Then we introduce the measure that economists commonly use to determine whether consumers or firms gain or lose when the equilibrium of a competitive market changes. Using such a measure, we can predict whether a policy change benefits the winners more than it harms the losers. To decide whether to adopt a particular policy, policymakers can combine these predictions with their normative views (values), such as whether they are more interested in helping the group that gains or the group that loses.

To most people, the term *welfare* refers to the government's payments to poor people. No such meaning is implied when economists employ the term. Economists use *welfare* to refer to the well-being of various groups such as consumers and producers. They call an analysis of the impact of a change on various groups' well-being a study of *welfare economics*.

9.1 Zero Profit for Competitive Firms in the Long Run

Competitive firms earn zero profit in the long run whether or not entry is completely free. Consequently, competitive firms must maximize profit.

Zero Long-Run Profit with Free Entry

The long-run supply curve is horizontal if firms are free to enter the market, firms have identical cost, and input prices are constant. All firms in the market are operating at minimum long-run average cost. That is, they are indifferent between shutting down or not because they are earning zero profit.

One implication of the shutdown rule (Chapter 8) is that the firm is willing to operate in the long run even if it is making zero *economic* profit, which is revenue minus opportunity cost. Because opportunity cost includes the value of the next best investment, at a zero long-run economic profit, the firm is earning the normal business profit that it could earn by investing elsewhere in the economy.

For example, if a firm's owner had not built the plant the firm uses to produce, the owner could have spent that money on another business or put the money in a bank. The opportunity cost of the current plant, then, is the forgone profit from what the owner could have earned by investing the money elsewhere.

The five-year after-tax accounting return on capital across all firms was 10.5%, indicating that the typical firm earned a business profit of 10.5¢ for every dollar it invested in capital (*Forbes*). These firms were earning roughly zero economic profit but positive business profit. Because business cost does not include all opportunity costs, business profit is larger than economic profit. Thus, a profit-maximizing firm may stay in business if it earns zero long-run economic profit but shuts down if it earns zero long-run business profit.

Zero Long-Run Profit When Entry Is Limited

In some markets, firms cannot enter in response to long-run profit opportunities. One reason for the limited number of firms is that the supply of an input is limited: only so much land is suitable for mining uranium; only a few people have the superior skills needed to play professional basketball.

One might think that firms could make positive long-run economic profits in such markets; however, that's not true. The reason why firms earn zero economic profits is that firms bidding for the scarce input drive its price up until the firms' profits are zero.

Suppose that the number of acres suitable for growing tomatoes is limited. Figure 9.1 shows a typical farm's average cost curve if the rental cost of land is zero (the average cost curve includes only the farm's costs of labor, capital, materials, and energy—not land). At the market price p^*, the firm produces q^* bushels of tomatoes and makes a profit of π^*, the shaded rectangle in the figure.

Thus, if the owner of the land does not charge rent, the farmer makes a profit. Unfortunately for the farmer, the landowner rents the land for π^*, so the farmer actually earns zero profit. Why does the landowner charge that much? The reason is that π^* is the opportunity cost of the land: The land is worth π^* to other potential farmers. These farmers will bid against each other to rent this land until the rent is driven up to π^*.

This rent is a fixed cost to the farmer because it doesn't vary with the amount of output. Thus, the rent affects the farm's average cost curve but not its marginal cost curve.

Figure 9.1 Rent

If it did not have to pay rent for its land, a farm with high-quality land would earn a positive long-run profit of π^*. Due to competitive bidding for this land, however, the rent equals π^*, so the landlord reaps all the benefits of the superior land and the farmer earns a zero long-run economic profit.

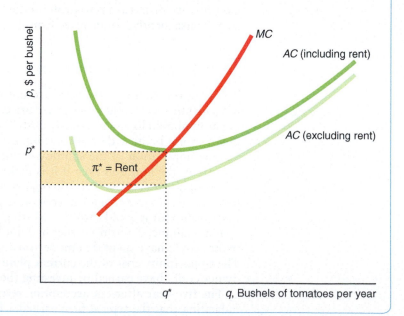

As a result, if the farm produces at all, it produces q^*, where its marginal cost equals the market price, no matter what rent is charged. The higher average cost curve in the figure includes a rent equal to π^*. The minimum point of this average cost curve is p^* at q^* bushels of tomatoes, so the farmer earns zero economic profit.

If the demand curve shifts to the left so that the market price falls, the farmer suffers short-run losses. In the long run, the rental price of the land will fall enough that once again each farm earns zero economic profit.

Does it make a difference whether farmers own or rent the land? Not really. The opportunity cost to a farmer who owns superior land is the amount for which that land could be rented in a competitive land market. Thus, the economic profit of both owned and rented land is zero at the long-run equilibrium.

Good-quality land is not the only scarce resource. The price of any fixed factor will be bid up in a similar fashion until economic profit for the firm is zero in the long run. Similarly, the government may require that a firm have a license to operate and then limit the number of licenses available. The price of the license gets bid up by potential entrants, driving profit to zero. For example, the license fee is more than half a million dollars a year for a hot dog stand next to the steps of the Metropolitan Museum of Art in New York City.[1]

rent
a payment to the owner of an input beyond the minimum necessary for the factor to be supplied

A scarce input, such as a person with high ability or land, earns an extra opportunity value. This extra value is called a **rent**: a payment to the owner of an input beyond the minimum necessary for the factor to be supplied.

Bonnie manages a store for the salary of $40,000, the amount paid to a typical manager. In this highly competitive retail market, firms typically earn zero economic profit. However, because Bonnie's an outstanding manager, her firm earns an economic profit of $50,000 a year. Other firms, seeing what a good job Bonnie is doing, offer her a higher salary. The bidding for her services drives her salary up to $90,000: her $40,000 base salary plus the $50,000 rent. After paying this rent to Bonnie, the store that employs her makes zero economic profit, just like the other firms in the market.

To summarize, if some firms in a market make short-run economic profits due to a scarce input, the other firms in the market bid for that input. This bidding drives up the price of the factor until all firms earn zero long-run profits. In such a market, the supply curve is flat because all firms have the same minimum long-run average cost.

People with unusual abilities can earn staggering incomes.[2] Though no law stops anyone from trying to become a professional entertainer or athlete, most of us do not have enough talent that others will pay to watch us perform. According to

---

[1]The auction value for this license hit $643,000 in 2009, but has fallen since then because disabled veterans are allowed to compete without paying a fee. (In the hot dog stand photo, I'm the fellow in the blue shirt with the dopey expression.) As of 2013, the highest fee in New York City is $1.39 million a year to operate a hot dog cart outside the former Tavern on the Green restaurant in Central Park.

[2]However, the estates of major celebrities continue to collect rents even after they die. In 2011, Elizabeth Taylor earned $210 million. In 2012, Michael Jackson earned $160 million, Elvis Presley $55 million, and Peanuts cartoonist Charles Schulz $37 million. Even Albert Einstein raked in $10 million from use of his image for products such as in Disney's Baby Einstein learning tools. (**Forbes.com**, October 24, 2012 and October 23, 2013.)

Forbes.com (August 26, 2013), in 2012, Madonna earned $125 million, topping other celebrities and film producers. Others earning large amounts include Steven Spielberg at $100, and Simon Cowell at $95 million. To put these receipts in perspective, these amounts exceed some small nations' gross domestic product (the value of the country's total output) such as the $38 million for Tuvalu with 10,698 people (CIA.gov, 2013).

Application

Tiger Woods' Rent

Tiger Woods was leading a charmed life as the world's greatest golfer and an advertising star—earning $100 million a year in endorsements—when he and much of his endorsement career came to a crashing halt as he smashed his car in front of his home at about 2:30 A.M. on November 27, 2009. A series of revelations about his personal life that followed over the next few days further damaged his pristine public reputation, and several endorsers either suspended using him in their advertisements or dropped him altogether.

Knittel and Stango (forthcoming) assessed the financial damage to these firms' shareholders using an event study approach in which they compared the stock prices of firms using Mr. Woods in their promotions relative to the stock market prices as a whole and those of close competitor firms. They examined the period between the crash and when Mr. Woods announced on December 11 that he was taking an "indefinite" leave from golf. Their results tell us about the rents that he was receiving.

They estimated that shareholders of companies endorsed by Mr. Woods lost $5 to $12 billion in wealth, which reflects stock investors' estimates of the damage from the end of effective endorsements over future years. Mr. Woods' five major sponsors—Accenture, Electronic Arts, Gatorade (PepsiCo), Gillette, and Nike—collectively lost 5.3% of their aggregate market value within 15 days after the accident.

The losses were higher for his main sports-related sponsors Electronic Arts, Gatorade, and Nike. As Knittel and Stango point out, sponsorship from firms that are not sports-related, such as Accenture ("a global management consulting, technology services, and outsourcing company"), probably does not increase the overall value of the Tiger brand. Presumably, when Mr. Woods negotiated his original deal with Accenture, he captured all the excess profit generated for Accenture as a rent of about $20 million a year. Consequently, we would not expect Accenture to lose much from the end of their relationship with Mr. Woods, as Knittel and Stango's estimates show.

In contrast, partnering with sports-related firms such as Nike presumably increased the value of both the Nike and Tiger brands and created other financial opportunities for Mr. Woods. If so, Nike would likely have captured some of the profit generated by partnering with Tiger Woods above and beyond the $20 to $30 million Nike paid him annually. Consequently, the sports-related firms' shareholders suffered a sizable loss from Mr. Woods' fall from grace. (However, when Mr. Woods started playing better in 2012–2013, some of his endorsements returned, and his annual earnings rose to $78 million—still substantially less than his pre-accident earnings.)

The Need to Maximize Profit

The worst crime against working people is a company which fails to operate at a profit.   —Samuel Gompers, first president of the American Federation of Labor

In a competitive market with identical firms and free entry, if most firms are profit-maximizing, profits are driven to zero at the long-run equilibrium. Any firm that does not maximize profit—that is, any firm that sets its output so that its marginal cost exceeds the market price or that fails to use the most cost-efficient methods of production—will lose money. Thus, *to survive in a competitive market, a firm must maximize its profit.*

9.2 Consumer Welfare

Economists and policymakers want to know how much consumers benefit from or are harmed by shocks that affect the equilibrium price and quantity. To what extent are consumers harmed if a local government imposes a sales tax to raise additional revenues? To answer such a question, we need some way to measure consumers' welfare. Economists use measures of welfare based on consumer theory (Chapters 4 and 5).

If we knew a consumer's utility function, we could directly answer the question of how an event affects a consumer's welfare. If the price of beef increases, the budget line facing someone who eats beef rotates inward, so the consumer is on a lower indifference curve at the new equilibrium. If we knew the levels of utility associated with the original indifference curve and the new one, we could measure the impact of a new tax in terms of the change in the utility level.

This approach is not practical for a couple of reasons. First, we rarely, if ever, know individuals' utility functions. Second, even if we had utility measures for various consumers, we would have no obvious way to compare them. One person might say that he got 1,000 utils (units of utility) from the same bundle that another consumer says gives her 872 utils of pleasure. The first person is not necessarily happier—he may just be using a different scale.

As a result, *we measure consumer welfare in terms of dollars*. Instead of asking the rather silly question "How many utils would you lose if your daily commute increased by 15 minutes?" we could ask "How much would you pay to avoid having your daily commute grow a quarter of an hour longer?" or "How much would it cost you in forgone earnings if your daily commute were 15 minutes longer?" It is easier to compare dollars across people than utils.

We first present the most widely used method of measuring consumer welfare. Then we show how it can be used to measure the effect of a change in price on consumer welfare.

Measuring Consumer Welfare Using a Demand Curve

Consumer welfare from a good is the benefit a consumer gets from consuming that good minus what the consumer paid to buy the good. How much pleasure do you get from a good above and beyond its price? If you buy a good for exactly what it's worth to you, you are indifferent between making that transaction and not. Frequently, however, you buy things that are worth more to you than what they cost. Imagine that you've played tennis in the hot sun and are very thirsty. You can buy a soft drink from a vending machine for $1, but you'd be willing to pay much more because you are so thirsty. As a result, you're much better off making this purchase than not.

If we can measure how much more you'd be willing to pay than you did pay, we'd know how much you gained from this transaction. Luckily for us, the demand curve contains the information we need to make this measurement.

Marginal Willingness to Pay To develop a welfare measure based on the demand curve, we need to know what information is contained in a demand curve. The demand curve reflects a consumer's *marginal willingness to pay*: the maximum amount a consumer will spend for an extra unit. The consumer's marginal willingness to pay is the *marginal value* the consumer places on the last unit of output.

David's demand curve for magazines per week, panel a of Figure 9.2, indicates his marginal willingness to buy various numbers of magazines. David places a marginal value of $5 on the first magazine. As a result, if the price of a magazine is $5, David

Figure 9.2 Consumer Surplus

(a) David's demand curve for magazines has a steplike shape. When the price is $3, he buys three magazines, point *c*. David's marginal value for the first magazine is $5, area $CS_1 + E_1$, and his expenditure is $3, area E_1, so his consumer surplus is $CS_1 = $2. His consumer surplus is $1 for the second magazine, area CS_2, and is $0 (and hence not labeled) for the third, CS_3—he is indifferent between buying and not buying it. Thus, his total consumer surplus is the shaded area $CS_1 + CS_2 + CS_3 = $3. (b) Steven's willingness to pay for trading cards is the height of his smooth demand curve. At price p_1, Steven's expenditure is E ($= p_1 q_1$), his consumer surplus is CS, and the total value he places on consuming q_1 trading cards per year is $CS + E$.

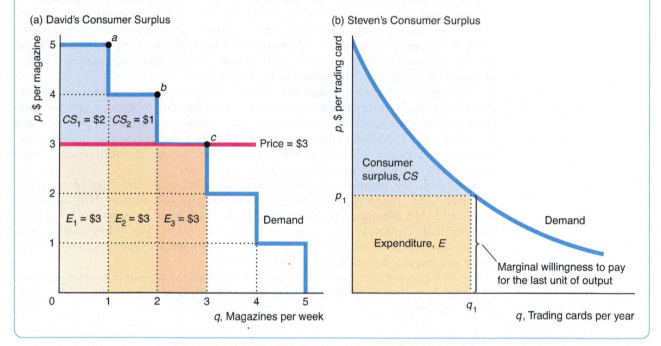

(a) David's Consumer Surplus

(b) Steven's Consumer Surplus

buys one magazine, point *a* on the demand curve. His marginal willingness to buy a second magazine is $4, so if the price falls to $4, he buys two magazines, *b*. His marginal willingness to buy three magazines is $3, so if the price of magazines is $3, he buys three magazines, *c*.

Consumer Surplus The monetary difference between what a consumer is willing to pay for the quantity of the good purchased and what the good actually costs is called **consumer surplus** (*CS*). Consumer surplus is a dollar-value measure of the extra pleasure the consumer receives from the transaction beyond its price.

David's consumer surplus from each additional magazine is his marginal willingness to pay minus what he pays to obtain the magazine.

His marginal willingness to pay for the first magazine, $5, is area $CS_1 + E_1$ in Figure 9.2. If the price is $3, his expenditure on the first magazine is area $E_1 = $3 \times 1 = 3. Thus, his consumer surplus on the first magazine is his marginal willingness to pay for that magazine, CS_1, minus his expenditure, E_1, which is area $CS_1 = (CS_1 + E_1) - E_1 = $5 - $3 = 2. Because his marginal willingness to pay for the second magazine is $4, his consumer surplus for the second magazine is the smaller area $CS_2 = $1. His marginal willingness to pay for the third magazine is $3, which equals what he must pay to obtain it, so his consumer surplus is zero, $CS_3 = $0 (and hence not shown as an area in the figure). He is indifferent between buying and not buying the third magazine.

consumer surplus (CS)
the monetary difference between what a consumer is willing to pay for the quantity of the good purchased and what the good actually costs

At a price of $3, David buys three magazines. His total consumer surplus from the three magazines he buys is the sum of the consumer surplus he gets from each of these magazines: $CS_1 + CS_2 + CS_3 = \$2 + \$1 + \$0 = \$3$. This total consumer surplus of $3 is the extra amount that David is willing to spend for the right to buy three magazines at $3 each. Thus, *an individual's consumer surplus is the area under the demand curve and above the market price up to the quantity the consumer buys*.

David is unwilling to buy a fourth magazine unless the price drops to $2 or less. If David's mother gives him a fourth magazine as a gift, the marginal value that David puts on that fourth magazine, $2, is less than what it cost his mother, $3.

We can determine consumer surplus for smooth demand curves in the same way as with David's unusual stairlike demand curve. Steven has a smooth demand curve for baseball trading cards, panel b of Figure 9.2. The height of this demand curve measures his willingness to pay for one more card. This willingness varies with the number of cards he buys in a year. The total value he places on obtaining q_1 cards per year is the area under the demand curve up to q_1, the areas *CS* and *E*. Area *E* is his actual expenditure on q_1 cards. Because the price is p_1, his expenditure is $p_1 q_1$. Steven's consumer surplus from consuming q_1 trading cards is the value of consuming those cards, areas *CS* and *E*, minus his actual expenditures, *E*, to obtain them, or *CS*. Thus, his consumer surplus, *CS*, is the area under the demand curve and above the horizontal line at the price p_1 up to the quantity he buys, q_1.

Just as we measure the consumer surplus for an individual using that individual's demand curve, we measure the consumer surplus of all consumers in a market using the market demand curve. *Market consumer surplus is the area under the market demand curve above the market price up to the quantity consumers buy*.

To summarize, consumer surplus is a practical and convenient measure of consumer welfare. There are two advantages to using consumer surplus rather than utility to discuss the welfare of consumers. First, the dollar-denominated consumer surplus of several individuals can be easily compared or combined, whereas the utility of various individuals cannot be easily compared or combined. Second, it is relatively easy to measure consumer surplus, whereas it is difficult to get a meaningful measure of utility directly. To calculate consumer surplus, all we have to do is measure the area under a demand curve.

Application

Willingness to Pay and Consumer Surplus on eBay

People differ in their willingness to pay for a given item. We can determine individuals' willingness to pay for an A.D. 238 Roman coin—a sesterce (originally equivalent in value to two and a half asses) with the image of Emperor Balbinus—by how much they bid in an eBay auction. On its Web site, eBay correctly argues (as we show in Chapter 14) that an individual's best strategy is to bid his or her *willingness to pay*: the maximum value that the bidder places on the item. From what eBay reports, we know the maximum bid of each person except the winner: eBay uses a *second-price auction*, where the winner pays the second-highest amount bid plus an increment. (The increment depends on the size of the bid. For example, the increment is $1 for bids between $25 and $100 and $25 for bids between $1,000 and $2,499.99.)

In the figure, the bids for the coin are arranged from highest to lowest. Because each bar on the graph indicates the bid for one coin, the figure shows how many units could have been sold to this group of bidders at various prices. That is, it is the market inverse demand curve.

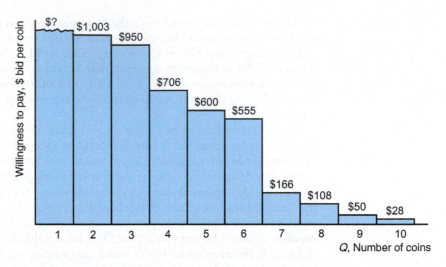

Bapna et al. (2008) set up a Web site (which is no longer active) that automatically bid on eBay at the last moment—a process called *sniping*. To use the site, individuals had to specify the maximum that they were willing to pay, so that the authors knew the top bidder's willingness to pay. Bapna et al. found that the median consumer had a maximum willingness to pay for goods that was $4 higher than the average cost of $14. They estimated the *CS* and the expenditures, *E*, for all eBay buyers and calculated that $CS/E = 30\%$. That is, bidders' consumer surplus gain is 30% of their expenditures.

Effect of a Price Change on Consumer Surplus

If the supply curve shifts upward or a government imposes a new sales tax, the equilibrium price rises, reducing consumer surplus. We illustrate the effect of a price increase on market consumer surplus using estimated supply and demand curves for sweetheart and hybrid tea roses sold in the United States.[3] We then discuss which markets are likely to have the greatest loss of consumer surplus due to a price increase.

Suppose that the introduction of a new tax causes the (wholesale) price of roses to rise from the original equilibrium price of 30¢ to 32¢ per rose stem, a shift along the demand curve in Figure 9.3. The consumer surplus is area $A + B + C = \$173.74$ million per year at a price of 30¢, and it is only area $A = \$149.64$ million at a price of 32¢.[4] Thus, the loss in consumer surplus from the increase in the price is $B + C = \$24.1$ million per year.

In general, as the price increases, consumer surplus falls more (1) the greater the initial revenues spent on the good and (2) the less elastic the demand curve (Appendix 9A). More is spent on a good when its demand curve is farther to the right so that areas like *A*, *B*, and *C* in Figure 9.3 are larger. The larger $B + C$ is, the greater is the drop in consumer surplus from a given percentage increase in price. Similarly, the less

---

[3] I estimated this model using data from the *Statistical Abstract of the United States, Floriculture Crops, Floriculture and Environmental Horticulture Products*, and **usda.mannlib.cornell.edu**. The prices are in real 1991 dollars.

[4] The height of triangle *A* is 25.8¢ = 57.8¢ − 32¢ per stem and the base is 1.16 billion stems per year, so its area is $\frac{1}{2} \times \$0.258 \times 1.16$ billion = $149.64 million per year. Rectangle *B* is $\$0.02 \times 1.16$ billion = \$23.2 million. Triangle *C* is $\frac{1}{2} \times \$0.02 \times 0.09$ billion = \$0.9 million.

Figure 9.3 Fall in Consumer Surplus from Roses as Price Rises

As the price of roses rises 2¢ per stem from 30¢ per stem, the quantity demanded decreases from 1.25 to 1.16 billion stems per year. The loss in consumer surplus from the higher price, areas *B* and *C*, is $24.1 million per year.

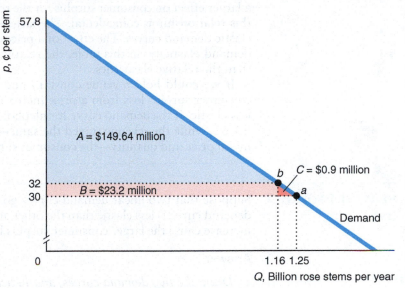

elastic a demand curve is (the closer it is to being vertical), the less willing consumers are to give up the good, so consumers do not cut their consumption much as the price increases, with the result of greater consumer surplus losses.

Higher prices cause greater consumer surplus loss in some markets than in others. Consumers would benefit if policymakers, before imposing a tax, considered in which market the tax is likely to harm consumers the most.

Application

Goods with a Large Consumer Surplus Loss from Price Increases

We can use estimates of demand curves to predict for which good a price increase causes the greatest loss of consumer surplus. The table shows the change in consumer surplus (ΔCS) in billions of 2012 dollars from a 10% increase in the price of various goods. As we would expect, the table shows that the larger the revenue (price times quantity) that is spent on a good, the larger the loss in consumer surplus.[5] A 10% increase in price causes a much greater loss of consumer surplus if it is imposed on medical services, $176 billion, than if it is imposed on alcohol and tobacco, $21 billion, because much more is spent on medical services.

	2012 Revenue	Estimated Elasticity of Demand, ε	Change in Consumer Surplus, ΔCS
Medical	1,818	−0.604	−176
Housing	1,623	−0.633	−157
Food	829	−0.245	−82
Clothing	366	−0.405	−36
Transportation	312	−0.461	−30
Utilities	307	−0.448	−30
Alcohol and tobacco	208	−0.162	−21

[5]Appendix 9A shows how to calculate ΔCS.

At first glance, the relationship between elasticities of demand and the loss in consumer surplus in the table looks backward: A given percent change in prices has a larger effect on consumer surplus for the relatively elastic demand curves. However, this relationship is coincidental: The large revenue goods happen to have relatively elastic demand curves. The effect of a price change depends on both revenue and the demand elasticity. In this table, the relative size of the revenues is more important than the relative elasticities.

If we could hold revenue constant and vary the elasticity, we would find that consumer surplus loss from a price increase is larger as the demand curve becomes less elastic. If the demand curve for alcohol and tobacco were 10 times more elastic, -1.62, while the revenue stayed the same—the demand curve became flatter at the initial price and quantity—the consumer surplus loss would be about $2 million less.

Solved Problem 9.1

Suppose that two linear demand curves go through the initial equilibrium, e_1. One demand curve is less elastic than the other at e_1. For which demand curve will a price increase cause the larger consumer surplus loss?

Answer

1. *Draw the two demand curves, and indicate which one is less elastic at the initial equilibrium.* Two demand curves cross at e_1 in the diagram. The steeper demand curve is less elastic at e_1.[6]

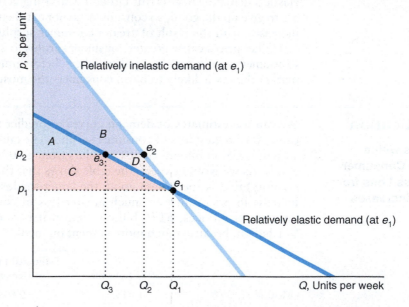

	Relatively Elastic Demand Curve	Relatively Inelastic Demand Curve
Consumer Surplus at p_1	$A + C$	$A + B + C + D$
Consumer Surplus at p_2	A	$A + B$
Consumer Surplus Loss	$-C$	$-C - D$

---

[6]As we discussed in Chapter 3, the price elasticity of demand, $\varepsilon = (\Delta Q/\Delta p)(p/Q)$, is 1 over the slope of the demand curve, $\Delta p/\Delta Q$, times the ratio of the price to the quantity. At the point of intersection where both demand curves have the same price, p_1, and quantity, Q_1, the steeper the demand curve, the lower the elasticity of demand.

2. *Illustrate that a price increase causes a larger consumer surplus loss with the less elastic demand curve.* If the price rises from p_1 to p_2, the consumer surplus falls by only $-C$ with the relatively elastic demand curve and by $-C - D$ with the relatively inelastic demand curve.

9.3 Producer Welfare

producer surplus (PS)
the difference between the amount for which a good sells and the minimum amount necessary for the seller to be willing to produce the good

A supplier's gain from participating in the market is measured by its **producer surplus** (*PS*), which is the difference between the amount for which a good sells and the minimum amount necessary for the seller to be willing to produce the good. The minimum amount a seller must receive to be willing to produce is the firm's avoidable production cost (the shutdown rule in Chapter 8).

Measuring Producer Surplus Using a Supply Curve

To determine a competitive firm's producer surplus, we use its supply curve: its marginal cost curve above its minimum average variable cost (Chapter 8). The firm's supply curve in panel a of Figure 9.4 looks like a staircase. The marginal cost of producing the first unit is $MC_1 = \$1$, which is the area under the marginal cost curve between 0 and 1. The marginal cost of producing the second unit is $MC_2 = \$2$, and so on. The variable cost, *VC*, of producing four units is the sum of the marginal costs for the first four units:

$$VC = MC_1 + MC_2 + MC_3 + MC_4 = \$1 + \$2 + \$3 + \$4 = \$10.$$

If the market price, p, is \$4, the firm's revenue from the sale of the first unit exceeds its cost by $PS_1 = p - MC_1 = \$4 - \$1 = \$3$, which is its producer surplus on the first unit. The firm's producer surplus is \$2 on the second unit and \$1 on the third unit. On the fourth unit, the price equals marginal cost, so the firm just breaks even. As a result, the firm's total producer surplus, *PS*, from selling four units at \$4 each is the sum of its producer surplus on these four units:

$$PS = PS_1 + PS_2 + PS_3 + PS_4 = \$3 + \$2 + \$1 + \$0 = \$6.$$

Graphically, the total producer surplus is the area above the supply curve and below the market price up to the quantity actually produced. This same reasoning holds when the firm's supply curve is smooth.

The producer surplus is closely related to profit. Producer surplus is revenue, *R*, minus variable cost, *VC*:

$$PS = R - VC.$$

In panel a of Figure 9.4, revenue is $\$4 \times 4 = \$16$ and variable cost is \$10, so producer surplus is \$6. Profit is revenue minus total cost, *C*, which equals variable cost plus fixed cost, F: $\pi = R - C = R - VC - F$. Thus, the difference between producer surplus and profit,

$$PS - \pi = (R - VC) - (R - VC - F) = F,$$

is the fixed cost. If the fixed cost is zero (as often occurs in the long run), producer surplus equals profit.[7]

---

[7]Even though each competitive firm makes zero profit in the long run, owners of scarce resources used in that market may earn rents. Thus, owners of scarce resources may receive positive producer surplus in the long run.

Figure 9.4 Producer Surplus

(a) The firm's producer surplus, $6, is the area below the market price, $4, and above the marginal cost (supply curve) up to the quantity sold, 4. The area under the marginal cost curve up to the number of units actually produced is the variable cost of production. (b) The market producer surplus is the area above the supply curve and below the line at the market price, p^*, up to the quantity produced, Q^*. The area below the supply curve and to the left of the quantity produced by the market, Q^*, is the variable cost of producing that level of output.

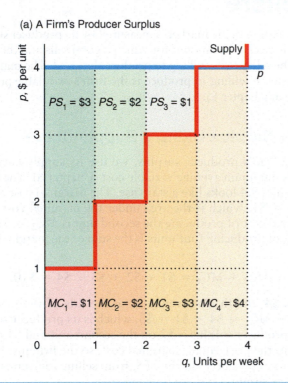

(a) A Firm's Producer Surplus

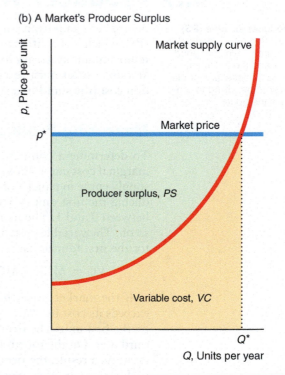

(b) A Market's Producer Surplus

Another interpretation of producer surplus is as a gain to trade. In the short run, if the firm produces and sells its good—trades—it earns a profit of $R - VC - F$. If the firm shuts down—does not trade—it loses its fixed cost of $-F$. Thus, producer surplus equals the profit from trade minus the profit (loss) from not trading of

$$(R - VC - F) - (-F) = R - VC = PS.$$

Using Producer Surplus

Even in the short run, we can use producer surplus to study the effects of any shock that does not affect the fixed cost of firms, such as a change in the price of a substitute or an input. Such shocks change profit by exactly the same amount as they change producer surplus because fixed costs do not change.

A major advantage of producer surplus is that we can use it to measure the effect of a shock on *all* the firms in a market without having to measure the profit of each firm in the market separately. We can calculate market producer surplus using the market supply curve in the same way as we calculate a firm's producer surplus using its supply curve. The market producer surplus in panel b of Figure 9.4 is the area above the supply curve and below the market price, p^*, up to the quantity sold, Q^*. The market supply curve is the horizontal sum of the marginal cost curves of each of the firms (Chapter 8). As a result, the variable cost for all the firms in the market of producing Q is the area under the supply curve between 0 and the market output, Q.

Solved Problem 9.2

If the estimated supply curve for roses is linear, how much producer surplus is lost when the price of roses falls from 30¢ to 21¢ per stem (so that the quantity sold falls from 1.25 billion to 1.16 billion rose stems per year)?

Answer

1. *Draw the supply curve, and show the change in producer surplus caused by the price change.* The figure shows the estimated supply curve for roses. Point a indicates the quantity supplied at the original price, 30¢, and point b reflects the quantity supplied at the lower price, 21¢. The loss in producer surplus is the sum of rectangle D and triangle E.

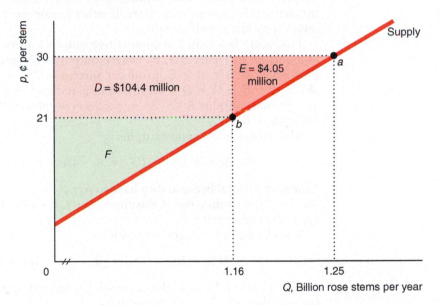

	Original Price, 30¢	Lower Price, 21¢	Change ($ millions)
Producer Surplus	$D + E + F$	F	$-(D + E) = -108.45$

2. *Calculate the lost producer surplus by adding the areas of rectangle D and triangle E.* The height of rectangle D is the difference between the original and the new price, 9¢, and its base is 1.16 billion stems per year, so the area of D (not all of which is shown in the figure because of the break in the quantity axis) is $0.09 per stem × 1.16 billion stems per year = $104.4 million per year. The height of triangle E is also 9¢, and its length is 90 million stems per year, so its area is $\frac{1}{2}$ × $0.09 per stem × 90 million stems per year = $4.05 million per year. Thus, the loss in producer surplus from the drop in price is $108.45 million per year.

9.4   Competition Maximizes Welfare

How should we measure society's welfare? People have proposed many reasonable welfare measures. One commonly used measure of the welfare of society, W, is the sum of consumer surplus plus producer surplus:

$$W = CS + PS.$$

This measure implicitly weights the well-being of consumers and producers equally. By using this measure, we are making a value judgment that the well-being of consumers and that of producers are equally important.

Not everyone agrees that society should try to maximize this measure of welfare. Groups of producers argue for legislation that helps them even if it hurts consumers by more than the producers gain—as though only producer surplus matters. Similarly, some consumer advocates argue that we should care only about consumers, so social welfare should include only consumer surplus.

We use the consumer surplus plus producer surplus measure of welfare in this chapter (and postpone a further discussion of other welfare concepts until the next chapter). One of the most striking results in economics is that competitive markets maximize this measure of welfare. If either less or more output than the competitive level is produced, welfare falls.

Producing less than the competitive output lowers welfare. At the competitive equilibrium in Figure 9.5, e_1, where output is Q_1 and price is p_1, consumer surplus is $CS_1 = A + B + C$, producer surplus is $PS_1 = D + E$, and total welfare is $W_1 = A + B + C + D + E$. If output is reduced to Q_2 so that price rises to p_2 at e_2, consumer surplus is $CS_2 = A$, producer surplus is $PS_2 = B + D$, and welfare is $W_2 = A + B + D$.

The change in consumer surplus is

$$\Delta CS = CS_2 - CS_1 = A - (A + B + C) = -B - C.$$

Consumers lose B because they have to pay $p_2 - p_1$ more than the competitive price for the Q_2 units they buy. Consumers lose C because they buy only Q_2 rather than Q_1 at the higher price.

The change in producer surplus is

$$\Delta PS = PS_2 - PS_1 = (B + D) - (D + E) = B - E.$$

Producers gain B because they now sell Q_2 units at p_2 rather than at p_1. They lose E because they sell $Q_2 - Q_1$ fewer units.

The change in welfare, $\Delta W = W_2 - W_1$, is[8]

$$\Delta W = \Delta CS + \Delta PS = (-B - C) + (B - E) = -C - E.$$

deadweight loss (DWL) the net reduction in welfare from a loss of surplus by one group that is not offset by a gain to another group from an action that alters a market equilibrium

The area B is a transfer from consumers to producers—the extra amount consumers pay for the Q_2 units goes to the sellers—so it does not affect welfare. Welfare drops because the consumer loss of C and the producer loss of E benefit no one. This drop in welfare, $\Delta W = -C - E$, is a **deadweight loss** (*DWL*): the net reduction in welfare from a loss of surplus by one group that is not offset by a gain to another group from an action that alters a market equilibrium.

---

[8]The change in welfare is $\Delta W = W_2 - W_1 = (CS_2 + PS_2) - (CS_1 + PS_1) = (CS_2 - CS_1) + (PS_2 - PS_1) = \Delta CS + \Delta PS$.

Figure 9.5 Why Reducing Output from the Competitive Level Lowers Welfare

Reducing output from the competitive level, Q_1, to Q_2 causes price to increase from p_1 to p_2. Consumers suffer: Consumer surplus is now A, a fall of $\Delta CS = -B - C$. Producers may gain or lose: Producer surplus is now $B + D$, a change of $\Delta PS = B - E$. Overall, welfare falls by $\Delta W = -C - E$, which is a deadweight loss (DWL) to society.

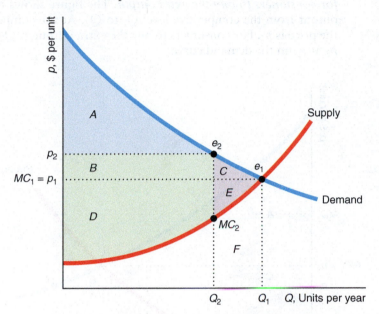

	Competitive Output, Q_1 (1)	Smaller Output, Q_2 (2)	Change (2) – (1)
Consumer Surplus, CS	$A + B + C$	A	$-B - C = \Delta CS$
Producer Surplus, PS	$D + E$	$B + D$	$B - E = \Delta PS$
Welfare, $W = CS + PS$	$A + B + C + D + E$	$A + B + D$	$-C - E = \Delta W = DWL$

The deadweight loss results because consumers value extra output by more than the marginal cost of producing it. At each output between Q_2 and Q_1, consumers' marginal willingness to pay for another unit—the height of the demand curve—is greater than the marginal cost of producing the next unit—the height of the supply curve. For example, at e_2, consumers value the next unit of output at p_2, which is much greater than the marginal cost, MC_2, of producing it. Increasing output from Q_2 to Q_1 raises firms' variable cost by area F, the area under the marginal cost (supply) curve between Q_2 and Q_1. Consumers value this extra output by the area under the demand curve between Q_2 and Q_1, area $C + E + F$. Thus, consumers value the extra output by $C + E$ more than it costs to produce it.

Society would be better off producing and consuming extra units of this good than spending this amount on other goods. In short, *the deadweight loss is the opportunity cost of giving up some of this good to buy more of another good*. Deadweight loss reflects a **market failure**—inefficient production or consumption—and is often due to the price not equaling the marginal cost.

market failure
inefficient production or consumption, often because a price exceeds marginal cost

Solved Problem 9.3

Show that increasing output beyond the competitive level decreases welfare because the cost of producing this extra output exceeds the value consumers place on it.

Answer

1. *Illustrate that setting output above the competitive level requires the price to fall for consumers to buy the extra output.* The figure shows the effect of increasing output from the competitive level Q_1 to Q_2. At the competitive equilibrium, e_1, the price is p_1. For consumers to buy the extra output at Q_2, the price must fall to p_2 at e_2 on the demand curve.

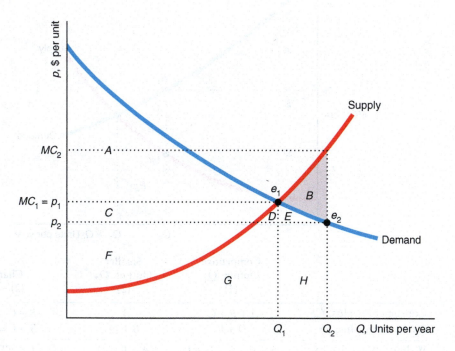

	Competitive Output, Q_1	Larger Output, Q_2	Change
Consumer Surplus, CS	A	$A + C + D + E$	$C + D + E = \Delta CS$
Producer Surplus, PS	$C + F$	$F - B - D - E$	$-B - C - D - E = \Delta PS$
Welfare, $W = CS + PS$	$A + C + F$	$A + C + F - B$	$-B = \Delta W = DWL$

2. *Show how the consumer surplus and producer surplus change when the output level increases.* Because the price falls from p_1 to p_2, consumer surplus rises by $\Delta CS = C + D + E$, which is the area between p_2 and p_1 to the left of the demand curve. At the original price, p_1, producer surplus was $C + F$. The cost of producing the larger output is the area under the supply curve up to Q_2, $B + D + E + G + H$. The firms sell this quantity for only $p_2 Q_2$, area $F + G + H$. Thus, the new producer surplus is $F - B - D - E$. As a result, the increase in output causes producer surplus to fall by $\Delta PS = -B - C - D - E$.

3. *Determine how welfare changes by adding the change in consumer surplus and producer surplus.* Because producers lose more than consumers gain, the deadweight loss is

$$DWL = \Delta W = \Delta CS + \Delta PS = (C + D + E) + (-B - C - D - E) = -B.$$

4. *Explain why welfare changes due to setting the price different than the marginal cost.* The new price, p_2, is less than the marginal cost, MC_2, of producing Q_2. Too much is being produced. A net loss occurs because consumers value the $Q_2 - Q_1$ extra output by only $E + H$, which is less than the extra cost, $B + E + H$, of producing it. The reason that competition maximizes welfare is that price equals marginal cost at the competitive equilibrium. At the competitive equilibrium, demand equals supply, which ensures that price equals marginal cost. When price equals marginal cost, consumers value the last unit of output by exactly the amount that it costs to produce it. If consumers value the last unit by more than the marginal cost of production, welfare rises if more is produced. Similarly, if consumers value the last unit by less than its marginal cost, welfare is higher at a lower level of production.

Application

Deadweight Loss of Christmas Presents

Just how much did you enjoy the expensive lime green woolen socks with the dancing purple teddy bears that your Aunt Fern gave you? Often the cost of a gift exceeds the value that a recipient places on it.

Until the advent of gift cards, only 10% to 15% of holiday gifts were monetary. A gift of cash typically gives at least as much pleasure to the recipient as a gift that costs the same but can't be exchanged for cash. (So what if giving cash is tacky?) Of course, it's possible that a gift can give more pleasure to the recipient than it cost the giver—but how often does that happen to you?

An *efficient gift* is one that the recipient values as much as the gift costs the giver, or more. The difference between the price of the gift and its value to the recipient is a deadweight loss to society. Joel Waldfogel (1993, 2009) asked Yale undergraduates just how large this deadweight loss is. He estimated that the deadweight loss is between 10% and 33% of the value of gifts. Waldfogel (2005) found that consumers value their own purchases at 10% to 18% more, per dollar spent, than items received as gifts.[9] Indeed, only 65% of holiday shoppers said they didn't return a single gift after the holidays in 2010.

Waldfogel found that gifts from friends and "significant others" are most efficient, while noncash gifts from members of the extended family are least efficient (one-third of the value is lost).[10] Luckily,

---

[9]Gift recipients may exhibit an endowment effect (Chapter 4), in which their willingness to pay (WTP) for the gift is less than what they would have to be offered to give up the gift, their willingness to accept (WTA). Bauer and Schmidt (2008) asked students at the Ruhr University in Germany their WTP and WTA for three recently received Christmas gifts. On average over all students and gifts, the average WTP was 11% percent below the market price and the WTA was 18% above the market price.

grandparents, aunts, and uncles are most likely to give cash.

Given holiday expenditures of about $66 billion in 2007 in the United States, Waldfogel concluded that a conservative estimate of the deadweight loss of Christmas, Hanukkah, and other holidays with gift-giving rituals is about $12 billion. (And that's not counting about 2.8 billion hours spent shopping.)

The question remains why people don't give cash instead of presents. Indeed, 61% of Americans gave a gift card as a holiday present. (A gift card is the equivalent of cash, though some can only be used in a particular store.) More than $110 billion in gift cards were purchased in 2012 in the United States. If the reason others don't give cash or gift cards is that they get pleasure from picking the "perfect" gift, the deadweight loss that adjusts for the pleasure of the giver is lower than these calculations suggest. (Bah, humbug!)

9.5 Policies That Shift Supply and Demand Curves

I don't make jokes. I just watch the government and report the facts. —Will Rogers

One of the main reasons that economists developed welfare tools was to predict the impact of government programs that alter a competitive equilibrium. Virtually all government actions affect a competitive equilibrium in one of two ways. Some government policies shift the demand curve or the supply curve, such as a limit on the number of firms in a market. Others, such as sales taxes, create a wedge or gap between price and marginal cost so that they are not equal, even though they were in the original competitive equilibrium.

These government interventions move us from an unconstrained competitive equilibrium to a new, constrained competitive equilibrium. Because welfare was maximized at the initial competitive equilibrium, the examples of government-induced changes that we consider here lower welfare. In later chapters, we examine markets in which government intervention may raise welfare because welfare was not maximized initially.[11]

During World War II, most of the nations involved limited the sales of consumer goods so that the nations' resources could be used for the war effort. Similarly, a

---

[10]People may deal with a disappointing present by *regifting* it. Some families have been passing the same fruitcake among family members for decades. According to one survey, 33% of women and 19% of men admitted that they pass on an unwanted gift (and 28% of respondents said that they would not admit it if asked whether they had done so).

[11]Welfare falls when governments restrict the consumption of competitive products that we all agree are *goods*, such as food and medical services. In contrast, if most of society wants to discourage the use of certain products, such as hallucinogenic drugs and cigarettes, policies that restrict consumption may increase some measures of society's welfare.

government may cause a supply curve to shift to the left by restricting the number of firms in a market, such as by licensing taxicabs.

In the Challenge Solution (later in this chapter), we examine a policy that affects demand curves. In this section, we concentrate on policies that affect supply curves. Governments, other organizations, and social pressures limit the number of firms in at least three ways. The number of firms is restricted explicitly in some markets, such as the one for taxi service. In other markets, some members of society are barred from owning firms or performing certain jobs or services. In yet other markets, the number of firms is controlled indirectly by raising the cost of entry or exit.

Restricting the Number of Firms

A limit on the number of firms causes a shift of the supply curve to the left, which raises the equilibrium price and reduces the equilibrium quantity. Consumers are harmed: They don't buy as much as they would at lower prices. Firms that are in the market when the limits are first imposed benefit from higher profits.

To illustrate these results, we examine the regulation of taxicabs. Countries throughout the world limit the number of taxicabs. To operate a cab in these cities legally, you must possess a city-issued permit, which may be a piece of paper or a medallion.

Two explanations are given for such regulation. First, using permits to limit the number of cabs raises the earnings of permit owners—usually taxi fleet owners—who lobby city officials for such restrictions. Second, some city officials contend that limiting cabs allows for better regulation of cabbies' behavior and protection of consumers. (However, it would seem possible that cities could directly regulate behavior and not restrict the number of cabs.)

Whatever the justification for such regulation, the limit on the number of cabs raises the market prices. If the city doesn't limit entry, a virtually unlimited number of potential taxi drivers with identical costs can enter freely.

Panel a of Figure 9.6 shows a typical taxi owner's marginal cost curve, MC, and average cost curve, AC^1. The MC curve slopes upward because a typical cabbie's opportunity cost of working more hours increases as the cabbie works longer hours (drives more customers). An outward shift of the demand curve is met by new firms entering, so the long-run supply curve of taxi rides, S^1 in panel b, is horizontal at the minimum of AC^1 (Chapter 8). For the market demand curve in the figure, the equilibrium is E_1, where the equilibrium price, p_1, equals the minimum of AC^1 of a typical cab. The total number of rides is $Q_1 = n_1 q_1$, where n_1 is the equilibrium number of cabs and q_1 is the number of rides per month provided by a typical cab.

Consumer surplus, $A + B + C$, is the area under the market demand curve above p_1 up to Q_1. Producer surplus is zero because the supply curve is horizontal at the market price, which equals marginal and average cost. Thus, welfare is the same as consumer surplus.

Legislation limits the number of permits to operate cabs to $n_2 < n_1$. The market supply curve, S^2, is the horizontal sum of the marginal cost curves above minimum average cost of the n_2 firms in the market. For the market to produce more than $n_2 q_1$ rides, the price must rise to induce the n_2 firms to supply more.

With the same demand curve as before, the equilibrium market price rises to p_2. At this higher price, each licensed cab firm produces more than before by operating longer hours, $q_2 > q_1$, but the total number of rides, $Q_2 = n_2 q_2$, falls because the number of cabs, n_2, drops. Consumer surplus is A, producer surplus is B, and welfare is $A + B$.

Figure 9.6 Effects of a Restriction on the Number of Cabs

A restriction on the number of cabs causes the supply curve to shift from S^1 to S^2 in the short run and the equilibrium to change from E_1 to E_2. The resulting lost surplus, C, is a deadweight loss to society. In the long run, the unusual profit, π, created by the restriction becomes a rent to the owner of the license. As the license owner increases the charge for using the license, the average cost curve rises to AC^2, so the cab driver earns a zero long-run profit. That is, the producer surplus goes to the permit holder, not to the cab driver.

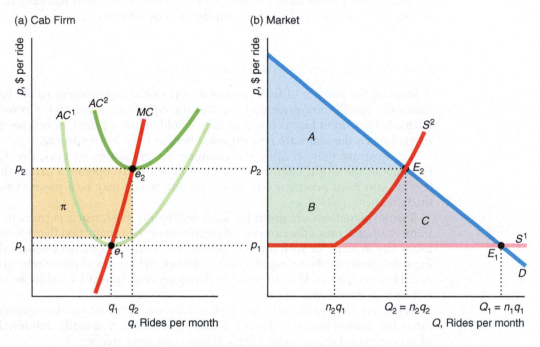

	No Restrictions	Restrictions	Change
Consumer Surplus, CS	$A + B + C$	A	$-B - C = \Delta CS$
Producer Surplus, PS	0	B	$B = \Delta PS$
Welfare, $W = CS + PS$	$A + B + C$	$A + B$	$-C = \Delta W = DWL$

Thus, because of the higher fares (prices) under a permit system, consumer surplus falls by

$$\Delta CS = -B - C.$$

The producer surplus of the lucky permit owners rises by

$$\Delta PS = B.$$

As a result, total welfare falls:

$$\Delta W = \Delta CS + \Delta PS = (-B - C) + B = -C,$$

which is a deadweight loss.

By preventing other potential cab firms from entering the market, limiting cab permits creates economic profit, the area labeled π in panel a, for permit owners. In many cities, these permits can be sold or rented, so the owner of the scarce resource, the permit, can capture the unusual profit, or rent. The rent for the permit or the implicit rent paid by the owner of a permit causes the cab driver's average cost to rise to AC^2. Because the rent allows the use of the cab for a certain period of time, it is a fixed cost that is unrelated to output. As a result, it does not affect the marginal cost.

Cab drivers earn zero economic profits because the market price, p_2, equals their average cost, the minimum of AC^2. The producer surplus, B, created by the limits on entry go to the original owners of the permits rather than to the current cab drivers. Thus, the permit owners are the *only* ones who benefit from the restrictions, and their gains are less than the losses to others. If the government collected the rents each year in the form of an annual license, then these rents could be distributed to all citizens instead of to just a few lucky permit owners.

In many cities, the rents and welfare effects that result from these laws are large. The size of the loss to consumers and the benefit to permit holders depend on how severely a city limits the number of cabs.

Application

Licensing Cabs

Too bad the only people who know how to run the country are busy driving cabs and cutting hair. —George Burns

Cities around the world—including most major U.S., Canadian, and European cities—license and limit the number of taxicabs. Some cities regulate the number of cabs much more strictly than others. Tokyo has five times as many cabs as New York City, which has fewer licenses today than when licensing started in 1937. San Francisco, which severely limits cabs, has only a tenth as many cabs as Washington, D.C., which has fewer people but does not restrict the number of cabs. How restrictive the licensing is varies across cities: The number of residents per cab is 757 in Detroit, 748 in San Francisco, 538 in Dallas, 533 in Baltimore, 350 in Boston, 301 in New Orleans, and 203 in Honolulu.

Where cabs are strictly limited, like in New York City, the owner of a taxi license earns an unusually high operating profit. Moreover, owners of a license—called a medallion—can sell them for large sums of money. In 2012, the owner of a New York City cab medallion sold it for over \$1.3 million.[12] The value of all New York City taxi licenses is over \$19.5 billion, which is more than seven times greater than the \$2.6 billion insured value of the World Trade Center in 2001.

Abelson (2010) estimated that people living in Sydney, Australia, would gain \$265 million annually by removing taxi restrictions, and most of that, \$221 million, would go to consumers. Movements toward liberalizing entry into taxi markets started in the United States in the 1980s and in Sweden, Ireland, the Netherlands, and the United Kingdom in the 1990s, but tight regulation remains common throughout the world.

---

[12]In 2013, New York City added a new class of taxi licenses and announced it would sell an additional 2,000 medallions (bringing the number of medallions to 15,000), which may lower the value of a medallion. The City estimated that the medallion sale would raise \$1 billion dollars, which implies a value of \$500,000 per medallion. However, soon after the extra medallions were approved, medallions were being offered for sale at slightly over a million dollars each.

Raising Entry and Exit Costs

Instead of directly restricting the number of firms that may enter a market, governments and other organizations may raise the cost of entering, thereby indirectly restricting that number. Similarly, raising the cost of exiting a market discourages some firms from entering.

Entry Barrier A government may also cause the supply curve to shift to the left by raising the cost of entry. If its cost will be greater than that of firms already in the market, a potential firm might not enter a market even if existing firms are making a profit. Any cost that falls only on potential entrants and not on current firms discourages entry. A long-run **barrier to entry** is an explicit restriction or a cost that applies only to potential new firms—existing firms are not subject to the restriction or do not bear the cost.

At the time they entered, incumbent firms had to pay many of the costs of entering a market that new entrants incur, such as the fixed costs of building plants, buying equipment, and advertising a new product. For example, the fixed cost to McDonald's and other fast-food chains of opening a new fast-food restaurant is about $2 million. These fixed costs are *costs of entry* but are *not* barriers to entry because they apply equally to incumbents and entrants. Costs incurred by both incumbents and entrants do not discourage potential firms from entering a market if existing firms are making money. Potential entrants know that they will do as well as existing firms once they begin operations, so they are willing to enter as long as profit opportunities exist.

Large sunk costs can be barriers to entry under two conditions. First, if capital markets do not work efficiently so that new firms have difficulty raising money, new firms may be unable to enter profitable markets. Second, if a firm must incur a large *sunk* cost, which increases the loss if it exits, the firm may be reluctant to enter a market in which it is uncertain of success.

Exit Restriction U.S., European, and other governments have laws that delay how quickly some (typically large) firms can go out of business so as to give workers warnings about layoffs. Although these restrictions keep the number of firms in a market relatively high in the short run, they may reduce the number of firms in a market in the long run.

Why do exit restrictions limit the number of firms in a market? Suppose that you are considering starting a construction firm with no capital or other fixed factors. The firm's only input is labor. You know that there is relatively little demand for construction during business downturns and in the winter. To avoid paying workers when business is slack, you plan to shut down during those periods. Because you can avoid losses by shutting down during low-demand periods, you enter this market if your expected economic profits during good periods are zero or positive.

A law that requires a firm to give its workers six months' warning before laying them off prevents it from shutting down quickly. The owners of the firm know that it will regularly suffer losses during business downturns because it will have to pay its workers for up to six months during those periods when it has nothing for them to do. Knowing that the firm will incur these regular losses, the owners are less inclined to enter the market. Unless the economic profits during good periods are much higher than zero—high enough to offset your losses—the owners will not choose to enter the market. If exit barriers limit the number of firms, the same analysis that we used to examine entry barriers applies. Thus, exit barriers may raise prices, lower consumer surplus, and reduce welfare.

---

barrier to entry
an explicit restriction or a cost that applies only to potential new firms—existing firms are not subject to the restriction or do not bear the cost

9.6 Policies That Create a Wedge Between Supply and Demand

The most common government policies that create a wedge between supply and demand curves are sales taxes (or subsidies) and price controls. Because these policies create a gap between marginal cost and price, either too little or too much is produced. For example, a tax causes price to exceed marginal cost—consumers value the good more than it costs to produce it—with the result that consumer surplus, producer surplus, and welfare fall.

Welfare Effects of a Sales Tax

A new sales tax causes the price consumers pay to rise (Chapter 3), resulting in a loss of consumer surplus, $\Delta CS < 0$, and a fall in the price firms receive, resulting in a drop in producer surplus, $\Delta PS < 0$. However, the new tax provides the government with new tax revenue, $\Delta T = T > 0$ (if tax revenue was zero before this new tax).

Assuming that the government does something useful with the tax revenue, we should include tax revenue in our definition of welfare: $W = CS + PS + T$. As a result, the change in welfare is

$$\Delta W = \Delta CS + \Delta PS + \Delta T.$$

Even when we include tax revenue in our welfare measure, a specific tax must lower welfare in a competitive market. We show the welfare loss from a specific tax of $t = 11¢$ per rose stem in Figure 9.7.

Without the tax, the intersection of the demand curve, D, and the supply curve, S, determines the competitive equilibrium, e_1, at a price of 30¢ per stem and a quantity of 1.25 billion rose stems per year. Consumer surplus is $A + B + C$, producer surplus is $D + E + F$, tax revenue is zero, and deadweight loss is zero.

The specific tax shifts the effective supply curve up by 11¢, creating an 11¢ wedge (Chapter 3) between the price consumers pay, 32¢, and the price producers receive, $32¢ - t = 21¢$. Equilibrium output falls from 1.25 to 1.16 billion stems per year.

The extra 2¢ per stem that buyers pay causes consumer surplus to fall by $B + C = \$24.1$ million per year, as we showed earlier. Due to the 9¢ drop in the price firms receive, they lose producer surplus of $D + E = \$108.45$ million per year (Solved Problem 9.2). The government gains tax revenue of $tQ = 11¢$ per stem $\times$ 1.16 billion stems per year $= \$127.6$ million per year, area $B + D$.

The combined loss of consumer surplus and producer surplus is only partially offset by the government's gain in tax revenue, so that welfare drops:

$$\Delta W = \Delta CS + \Delta PS + \Delta T = -\$24.1 - \$108.45 + \$127.6$$
$$= -\$4.95 \text{ million per year.}$$

This deadweight loss is area $C + E$.

Why does society suffer a deadweight loss? The reason is that the tax lowers output from the competitive level where welfare is maximized. An equivalent explanation for this inefficiency or loss to society is that the tax puts a wedge between price and marginal cost. At the new equilibrium, buyers are willing to pay 32¢ for one more rose, while the marginal cost to firms is only 21¢ (= the price minus t). Shouldn't at least one more rose be produced if consumers are willing to pay nearly a third more than the cost of producing it? That's what our welfare study indicates.

Figure 9.7 Effects of a Specific Tax on Roses

The $t = 11¢$ specific tax on roses creates an 11¢ per stem wedge between the price customers pay, 32¢, and the price producers receive, 21¢. Tax revenue is $T = tQ = \$127.6$ million per year. The deadweight loss to society is $C + E = \$4.95$ million per year.

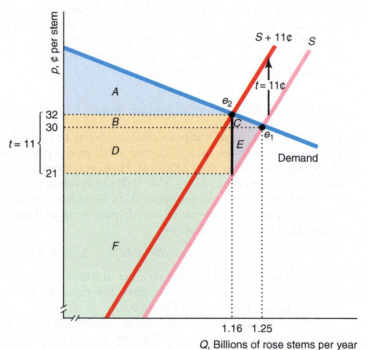

	No Tax	Specific Tax	Change ($ millions)
Consumer Surplus, CS	$A + B + C$	A	$-B - C = -24.1 = \Delta CS$
Producer Surplus, PS	$D + E + F$	F	$-D - E = -108.45 = \Delta PS$
Tax Revenue, $T = tQ$	0	$B + D$	$B + D = 127.6 = \Delta T$
Welfare, $W = CS + PS + T$	$A + B + C + D + E + F$	$A + B + D + F$	$-C - E = -4.95 = DWL$

Application

The Deadweight Cost of Raising Gasoline Tax Revenue

The social cost of collecting tax revenue is the deadweight loss that the tax causes. Blundell et al. (2012) found that the deadweight loss per dollar of gasoline tax revenue raised is 4.3% for high-income, 9.2% for middle-income, and 3.9% for low-income U.S. consumers.[13]

Why is a gasoline tax more distorting for middle-income consumers? Part of the explanation is that middle-income U.S. and Canadian consumers are much more responsive to changes in gasoline prices than low-income and high-income consumers. That is, middle-income consumers have a more elastic demand curve. Typically, the more that the quantity demanded falls in response to the tax, the wider is the deadweight loss triangle and the larger is the ratio of deadweight loss to tax revenue, as the next Solved Problem illustrates.

---

[13]The U.S. low-income group consists of the 25% lowest earners and has a median income of $42,500 per year. The middle-income group has a median income of $57,500. The median income of the high-income group is $72,500.

Solved Problem 9.4

Two linear demand curves go through the initial equilibrium, e_1. One demand curve is less elastic than the other at e_1. The original horizontal supply curve also goes through e_1. For which demand curve is the deadweight loss from a specific tax t greater? For which is the ratio of the deadweight loss (DWL) to the tax revenue (T) greater?

Answer

1. *Draw a horizontal supply curve and add two demand curves with different slopes that intersect at the initial equilibrium, e_1, on the supply curve.* In the figure, the original supply curve and the demand curves intersect at e_1, where the equilibrium quantity is Q_1 and the price is p_1. The flatter demand curve is relatively more elastic as Solved Problem 9.1 explains.

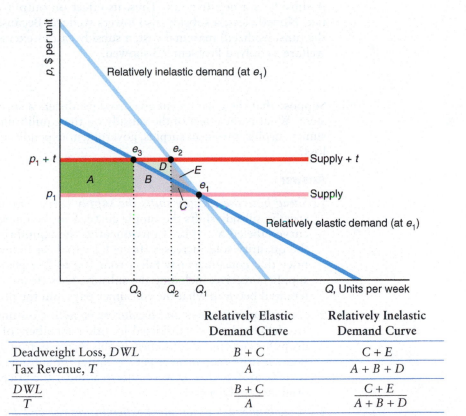

	Relatively Elastic Demand Curve	Relatively Inelastic Demand Curve
Deadweight Loss, DWL	$B + C$	$C + E$
Tax Revenue, T	A	$A + B + D$
$\dfrac{DWL}{T}$	$\dfrac{B + C}{A}$	$\dfrac{C + E}{A + B + D}$

2. *Show how the specific tax shifts the supply curve and determine the new equilibria for the two demand curves.* A specific tax of t shifts up the supply curve by t everywhere (Chapter 3). The relatively inelastic demand curve intersects this new supply curve at e_2, where the new equilibrium quantity is Q_2 and the new equilibrium price is $p_1 + t$. The relatively elastic demand curve intersects the new supply curve at e_3, where the equilibrium quantity is Q_3 and the price is again $p_1 + t$.

3. *Determine the DWL for the two demand curves.* The DWL is the area below the demand curve and above the supply curve between the new equilibrium quantity and Q_1. Thus, the DWL is area $C + E$ with the relatively inelastic demand curve and $B + C$ with the relatively elastic demand curve. Given that $B > E$, the DWL is greater with the more elastic demand curve.

4. *Determine the DWL/T for the two demand curves.* The tax revenue is t times the equilibrium quantity. Thus, T is the rectangle that lies between the two supply curves, which differ by t, between 0 and the equilibrium quantity. The tax revenue is area A with the relatively elastic demand curve and $A + B + D$ for the relatively inelastic demand curve. Thus, DWL/T is $(B + C)/A$ for the relatively elastic demand curve and $(C + E)/(A + B + D)$ for the relatively inelastic demand curve. Because the DWL is greater and T is smaller for the relatively elastic demand curve, DWL/T must be larger for the relatively elastic demand curve.

Welfare Effects of a Subsidy

A subsidy is a negative tax. Thus, its effect on output is the opposite of that of a tax. Nonetheless, a subsidy also lowers welfare. Because the new price is less than the (unsubsidized) marginal cost, a subsidy causes excess production, which lowers welfare as Solved Problem 9.3 showed.

Solved Problem 9.5

Suppose that the government gives rose producers a specific subsidy of $s = 11¢$ per stem. What is the effect of the subsidy on the equilibrium prices and quantity, consumer surplus, producer surplus, government expenditures, welfare, and deadweight loss?

Answer

1. *Show how the subsidy shifts the supply curve and affects the equilibrium.* The specific subsidy shifts the supply curve, S in the figure, down by $s = 11¢$, to the curve labeled $S - 11¢$. Consequently, the equilibrium shifts from e_1 to e_2, so the quantity sold increases (from 1.25 to 1.34 billion rose stems per year), the price that consumers pay falls (from 30¢ to 28¢ per stem), and the amount that suppliers receive, including the subsidy, rises (from 30¢ to 39¢), so that the differential between what the consumer pays and the producers receive is 11¢.

2. *Show that consumers and producers benefit.* Consumers and producers of roses are delighted to be subsidized by other members of society. Because the price drops for customers, consumer surplus increases from $A + B$ to $A + B + D + E$. Because firms receive more per stem after the subsidy, producer surplus rises from $D + G$ to $B + C + D + G$ (the area under the price they receive and above the original supply curve).

3. *Show how much government expenditures rise and determine the effect on welfare.* Because the government pays a subsidy of 11¢ per stem for each stem sold, the government's expenditures go from zero to the rectangle $B + C + D + E + F$. Thus, the new welfare is the sum of the new consumer surplus and producer surplus minus the government's expenses. As the table under the figure shows, welfare falls from $A + B + D + G$ to $A + B + D + G - F$. The deadweight loss, this drop in welfare, $\Delta W = -F$, results from producing too much: The marginal cost to producers of the last stem, 39¢, exceeds the marginal benefit to consumers, 28¢.

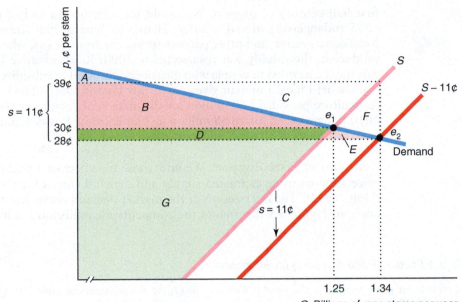

	No Subsidy	Subsidy	Change ($ millions)
Consumer Surplus, CS	$A + B$	$A + B + D + E$	$D + E = 116.55 = \Delta CS$
Producer Surplus, PS	$D + G$	$B + C + D + G$	$B + C = 25.9 = \Delta PS$
Government Expense, X	0	$-B - C - D - E - F$	$-B - C - D - E - F = -147.4 = \Delta X$
Welfare, $W = CS + PS - X$	$A + B + D + G$	$A + B + D + G - F$	$-F = -4.95 = DWL$

Welfare Effects of a Price Floor

No matter what your religion, you should try to become a government
program, for then you will have everlasting life.
—Lynn Martin (former U.S. Representative)

In some markets, the government sets a *price floor*, or minimum price, which is the lowest price a consumer can pay legally for the good. For example, in most countries the government creates price floors under at least some agricultural prices to guarantee producers that they will receive at least a price of $\underline{p}$ for their good. If the market price is above $\underline{p}$, the support program is irrelevant. If the market price would be below $\underline{p}$, however, the government buys as much output as necessary to drive the price up to $\underline{p}$. Since 1929 (the start of the Great Depression), the U.S. government has used price floors or similar programs to keep prices of many agricultural products above the price that competition would determine in unregulated markets.

My favorite program is the wool and mohair subsidy. The U.S. government instituted wool price supports after the Korean War to ensure "strategic supplies" for uniforms. Congress later added mohair subsidies, though mohair has no military use. In some years, the mohair subsidy exceeded the amount consumers paid for mohair, and the subsidies on wool and mohair reached a fifth of a billion dollars over the first half-century of support. No doubt the Clinton-era end of these subsidies in 1995 endangered national security. Thanks to Senator Phil Gramm, a well-known fiscal conservative, and other patriots (primarily from Texas, where much mohair is produced), the subsidy was resurrected in 2000! Representative Lamar Smith took vehement exception to people who questioned the need to subsidize mohair: "Mohair is popular! I have a mohair sweater! It's my favorite one!" The U.S. Department of Agriculture provided $60 million for the upkeep of Angora goats in 1990, and the 2010 budget called for an $8 million mohair subsidy. It was defunded the following year, but remains on the book waiting to be revived.

Agricultural Price Support We now show the effect of a traditional agricultural price support using estimated supply and demand curves for the soybean market (Holt, 1992). The intersection of the market demand curve and the market supply curve in Figure 9.8 determines the competitive equilibrium, e, in the absence of a

Figure 9.8 Effects of Price Supports on Soybeans

Without government price supports, the equilibrium is e, where $p_1 = \$4.59$ per bushel and $Q_1 = 2.1$ billion bushels of soybeans per year (based on estimates in Holt, 1992). With the price support at $\underline{p} = \$5.00$ per bushel, output sold increases to Q_s and consumer purchases fall to Q_d, so the government must buy $Q_g = Q_s - Q_d$ at a cost of 1.283 billion per year. The deadweight loss is $C + F + G = \$1.226$ billion per year, not counting storage and administrative costs.

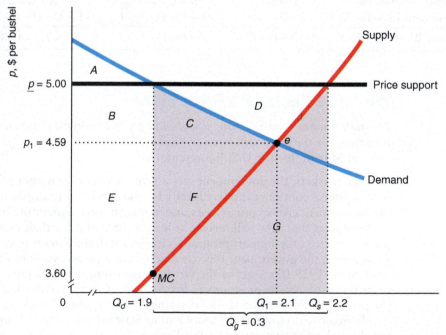

	No Price Support	Price Support	Change ($ millions)
Consumer Surplus, CS	$A + B + C$	A	$-B - C = -864 = \Delta CS$
Producer Surplus, PS	$E + F$	$B + C + D + E + F$	$B + C + D = 921 = \Delta PS$
Government Expense, $-X$	0	$-C - D - F - G$	$-C - D - F - G = -1{,}283 = \Delta X$
Welfare, $W = CS + PS - X$	$A + B + C + E + F$	$A + B + E - G$	$-C - F - G = -1{,}226 = \Delta W = DWL$

price support program, where the equilibrium price is $p_1 = \$4.59$ per bushel and the equilibrium quantity is $Q_1 = 2.1$ billion bushels per year.

With a price support on soybeans of $\underline{p} = \$5.00$ per bushel and the government's pledge to buy as much output as farmers want to sell, quantity sold is $Q_s = 2.2$ billion bushels.[14] At $\underline{p}$, consumers buy less output, $Q_d = 1.9$ billion bushels, than the Q_1 they would have bought at the market-determined price p_1. As a result, consumer surplus falls by $B + C = \$864$ million. The government buys $Q_g = Q_s - Q_d \approx 0.3$ billion bushels per year, which is the excess supply, at a cost of $T = \underline{p} \times Q_g = C + D + F + G = \$1.283$ billion.

The government cannot resell the output domestically because if it tried to do so, it would succeed only in driving down the price consumers pay. The government stores the output or sends it abroad.

Although farmers gain producer surplus of $B + C + D = \$921$ million, this program is an inefficient way to transfer money to them. Assuming that the government's purchases have no alternative use, the change in welfare is $\Delta W = \Delta CS + \Delta PS - T = -C - F - G = -\$1.226$ billion per year.[15] This deadweight loss reflects two distortions in this market:

- **Excess production.** More output is produced than is consumed, so Q_g is stored, destroyed, or shipped abroad.
- **Inefficiency in consumption.** At the quantity they actually buy, Q_d, consumers are willing to pay $\$5$ for the last bushel of soybeans, which is more than the marginal cost, $MC = \$3.60$, of producing that bushel.

Alternative Price Support Because of price supports, the government was buying and storing large quantities of food, much of which was allowed to spoil. As a consequence, the government started limiting the amount farmers could produce. Because the government is uncertain about how much farmers will produce, it sets quotas or limits on the amount of land farmers may use, so as to restrict their output. Today, the government uses an alternative subsidy program. The government sets a support price, $\underline{p}$. Farmers decide how much to grow and sell all of their produce to consumers at the price, p, that clears the market. The government then gives the farmers a *deficiency* payment equal to the difference between the support and actual prices, $\underline{p} - p$, for every unit sold, so that farmers receive the support price on their entire crop.

Solved Problem 9.6

What are the effects in the soybean market of a $\$5$-per-bushel price support using a deficiency payment on the equilibrium price and quantity, consumer surplus, producer surplus, and deadweight loss?

Answer

1. *Describe how the program affects the equilibrium price and quantity.* Without a price support, the equilibrium is e_1 in the figure, where the price is $p_1 = \$4.59$ and the quantity is 2.1 billion bushels per year. With a support price of $\$5$ per bushel, the new equilibrium is e_2. Farmers produce at the quantity where the price

---

[14]For most of the last several decades, the soybean price support was around $\$5$ per bushel; however, it rose to $\$6$ in 2013.

[15]This measure of deadweight loss underestimates the true loss. The government also pays storage and administration costs. The U.S. Department of Agriculture, which runs farm support programs, had about 105,000 employees in 2010, or one worker for every eight farms that received assistance (although many U.S.D.A. employees have other job responsibilities, such as administering the food stamp program).

support line hits their supply curve at 2.2 billion bushels. The equilibrium price is the height of the demand curve at 2.2 billion bushels, or approximately $4.39 per bushel. Thus, the equilibrium price falls and the quantity increases.

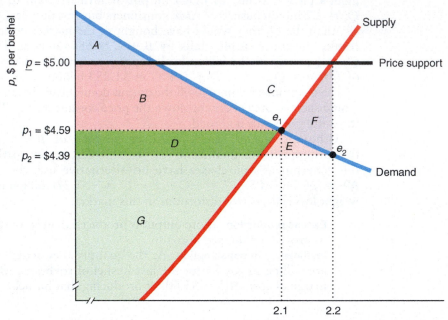

	No Price Support	Price Support	Change
Consumer Surplus, CS	$A + B$	$A + B + D + E$	$D + E = \Delta CS$
Producer Surplus, PS	$D + G$	$B + C + D + G$	$B + C = \Delta PS$
Government Expense, $-X$	0	$-B - C - D - E - F$	$-B - C - D - E - F = \Delta X$
Welfare, $W = CS + PS - X$	$A + B + D + G$	$A + B + D + G - F$	$-F = \Delta W = DWL$

2. *Show the welfare effects.* Because the price consumers pay drops from p_1 to p_2, consumer surplus rises by area $D + E$. Producers now receive $\underline{p}$ instead of p_1, so their producer surplus rises by $B + C$. Government payments are the difference between the support price, $\underline{p} = \$5$, and the price consumers pay, $p_2 = \$4.39$, times the number of units sold, 2.2 billion bushels per year, or the rectangle $B + C + D + E + F$. Because government expenditures exceed the gains to consumers and producers, welfare falls by the deadweight loss triangle F.[16]

Application

How Big Are Farm Subsidies and Who Gets Them?

Amount the EU paid to businessmen in Serbia–Montenegro for sugar subsidies before realizing that there was no sugar industry there: $1.2 million. —Harper's Index, 2004

Virtually every country in the world showers its farmers with subsidies. Although government support to farmers has fallen in developed countries over the last decade, support remains high. Farmers in developed countries received $252 billion in direct agricultural producer support payments (subsidies) in 2011, including $74 billion

---

[16]Compared to the soybean price support program in Figure 9.8, the deficiency payment approach results in a smaller deadweight loss (less than a tenth of the original one) and lower government expenditures (though the expenditures need not be smaller in general).

in the European Union, $31 billion in the United States, $7 billion in Canada, and $5 billion in Japan.

These payments were a large percentage of actual farm sales in many countries, averaging 19% in developed countries. They ranged from 58% in Norway, 54% in Switzerland, 52% in Japan, 18% in the European Union, 14% in Canada, 8% in the United States, 1.5% in Australia, to only 1% in New Zealand.

Total U.S. agricultural support payments were $147 billion, or 1% of the U.S. gross domestic product. Each adult in the United States pays $650 a year to support agriculture. Did you get full value for your money?

The lion's share of U.S. farm subsidies goes to large agricultural corporations, not to poor farmers. According to the Environmental Working Group in 2013, three-quarters of the payments go to the largest and wealthiest 10% of farm operations and landlords, while nearly two-thirds of farmers receive no direct payments. Indeed, 23 members of Congress receive payments, and $394 million went to absentee landlords who live in big cities.

Welfare Effects of a Price Ceiling

In some markets, the government sets a *price ceiling*: the highest price that a firm can legally charge. If the government sets the ceiling below the precontrol competitive price, consumers demand more than the precontrol equilibrium quantity and firms supply less than that quantity (Chapter 2). Producer surplus must fall because firms receive a lower price and sell fewer units.

As a result of the price ceiling, consumers buy the good at a lower price but are limited by sellers as to how much they can buy. Because less is sold than at the precontrol equilibrium, society suffers a deadweight loss: Consumers value the good more than the marginal cost of producing extra units.

This measure of the deadweight loss may *underestimate* the true loss for two reasons. First, because consumers want to buy more units than are sold, they may spend additional time searching for a store with units for sale. This (often unsuccessful) search activity is wasteful and thus an additional deadweight loss to society. Deacon and Sonstelie (1989) calculated that for every $1 consumers saved from lower prices due to U.S. gasoline price controls in 1973, they lost $1.16 in waiting time and other factors.[17]

Second, when a price ceiling creates excess demand, the customers who are lucky enough to buy the good may not be the consumers who value it most. In a market without a price ceiling, all consumers who value the good more than the market price buy it, and those who value it less do not, so that those consumers who value it most buy the good. In contrast with a price control where the good is sold on a first-come, first-served basis, the consumers who reach the store first may not be the consumers with the highest willingness to pay. With a price control, if a lucky customer who buys a unit of the good has a willingness to pay of p_1, while someone who cannot buy it has a willingness to pay of $p_2 > p_1$, then the *allocative cost* to society of this unit being sold to the "wrong" consumer is $p_2 - p_1$.[18]

---

[17]Perversely, this type of wasteful search does not occur if the good is efficiently but inequitably distributed to people according to a discriminatory criteria such as race, gender, or attractiveness, because people who are suffering discrimination know it is pointless to search.

[18]This allocative cost will be reduced or eliminated if a resale market exists where consumers who place a high value on the good can buy it from consumers who place a lower value on the good but were lucky enough to be able to buy it initially.

Solved Problem 9.7

What is the effect on the equilibrium, consumer surplus, producer surplus, and welfare if the government sets a price ceiling, $\bar{p}$, below the unregulated competitive equilibrium price?

Answer

1. *Show the initial unregulated equilibrium.* The intersection of the demand curve and the supply curve determines the unregulated, competitive equilibrium, e_1, where the equilibrium quantity is Q_1.

2. *Show how the equilibrium changes with the price ceiling.* Because the price ceiling, $\bar{p}$, is set below the equilibrium price of p_1, the ceiling binds (reduces the price that consumers pay). At this lower price, consumer demand increases to Q_d while the quantity firms are willing to supply falls to Q_s, so only $Q_s = Q_2$ units are sold at the new equilibrium, e_2. Thus, the price control causes the equilibrium quantity and price to fall, but consumers have excess demand of $Q_d - Q_s$.

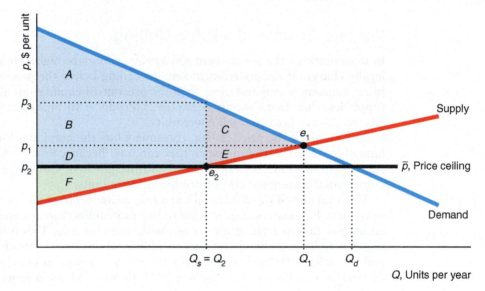

	No Ceiling	Price Ceiling	Change
Consumer Surplus, CS	$A + B + C$	$A + B + D$	$D - C = \Delta CS$
Producer Surplus, PS	$D + E + F$	F	$-D - E = \Delta PS$
Welfare, $W = CS + PS$	$A + B + C + D + E + F$	$A + B + D + F$	$-C - E = \Delta W = DWL$

3. *Describe the welfare effects.* Because consumers are able to buy Q_s units at a lower price than before the controls, they gain area D. Consumers lose consumer surplus of C, however, because they can purchase only Q_s instead of Q_1 units of output. Thus, consumers gain net consumer surplus of $D - C$. Because they sell fewer units at a lower price, firms lose producer surplus $-D - E$. Part of this loss, D, is transferred to consumers in the form of lower prices, but the rest, E, is a loss to society. The deadweight loss to society is at least $\Delta W = \Delta CS + \Delta PS = -C - E$.

Application

The Social Cost of a Natural Gas Price Ceiling

From 1954 through 1989, U.S. federal law imposed a price ceiling on interstate sales of natural gas. The law did not apply to sales within states in the Southwest that produced the gas—primarily Louisiana, Oklahoma, New Mexico, and Texas. Consequently, consumers in the Midwest and Northeast, where most of the gas was used, were less likely to be able to buy as much natural gas as they wanted, unlike consumers in the Southwest. Because they could not buy natural gas, some consumers who would have otherwise done so did not install natural gas heating. As heating systems last for years, even today, many homes use dirtier fuels such as heating oil due to this decades-old price control.

By comparing consumer behavior before and after the control period, Davis and Kilian (2011) estimated that demand for natural gas exceeded observed sales of natural gas by an average of 19.4% from 1950 through 2000. They calculated that the allocative cost averaged $3.6 billion annually during this half century. This additional loss is nearly half of the estimated annual deadweight loss from the price control of $10.5 billion (MacAvoy, 2000). The total loss is $14.1 (= $10.5 + $3.6) billion.[19]

9.7 Comparing Both Types of Policies: Imports

We've examined examples of government policies that shift supply or demand curves and policies that create a wedge between supply and demand. Governments use both types of policies to control international trade.

Allowing imports of foreign goods benefits the importing country. If a government reduces imports of a good, the domestic price rises; the profits of domestic firms that produce the good increase, but domestic consumers are hurt. Our analysis will show that the loss to consumers exceeds the gain to producers.

The government of the (potentially) importing country can use one of four import policies:

- **Allow free trade.** Any firm can sell in this country without restrictions.
- **Ban all imports.** The government sets a quota of zero on imports.
- **Set a positive quota.** The government limits imports to $\overline{Q}$.
- **Set a tariff.** The government imposes a tax called a **tariff** (or a *duty*) on only imported goods.

tariff (*duty*)
a tax on only imported goods

We compare welfare under free trade to welfare under bans and quotas, which change the supply curve, and to welfare under tariffs, which create a wedge between supply and demand.

To illustrate the differences in welfare under these various policies, we examine the U.S. market for crude oil. We make two assumptions for the sake of simplicity: We assume that transportation costs are zero and the supply curve of the potentially

---

[19]Consumers' share of the deadweight loss, area *C* in the figure in Solved Problem 9.7, is $9.3 billion annually; the sellers' share, area *E*, is $1.2 billion; so the entire deadweight loss is $10.5 billion. Consumers who are lucky enough to buy the gas gain area *D* = $6.9 billion from paying a lower price, which represents a transfer from sellers. Thus, altogether consumers lose $7.0 (= $9.3 + $4.6 − $6.9) billion and firms lose $8.1 (=$1.2 + $6.9) billion.

imported good is horizontal at the world price p^*. Given these assumptions, the importing country, the United States, can buy as much of this good as it wants at p^* per unit: It is a price taker in the world market because its demand is too small to influence the world price.

Free Trade Versus a Ban on Imports

No nation was ever ruined by trade.   —Benjamin Franklin

Preventing imports into the domestic market raises the price, as we illustrated in Chapter 2 for the Japanese rice market. In Figure 9.9, the estimated U.S. domestic supply curve, S^a, is upward sloping, and the foreign supply curve is horizontal at the world

Figure 9.9 Loss from Eliminating Free Trade

Because the world supply curve is horizontal at the world price of $93, the total U.S. supply curve of crude oil is S^1 without free trade. The free-trade equilibrium is e_1. With a ban on imports, the equilibrium e_2 occurs where the domestic supply curve, $S^a = S^2$, intersects D. The ban increases producer surplus by $B \approx \$1.09$ billion per day and decreases consumer surplus by $B + C \approx \$1.58$ billion per day, so the deadweight loss is $C = \$481$ million per day or $176 billion per year.

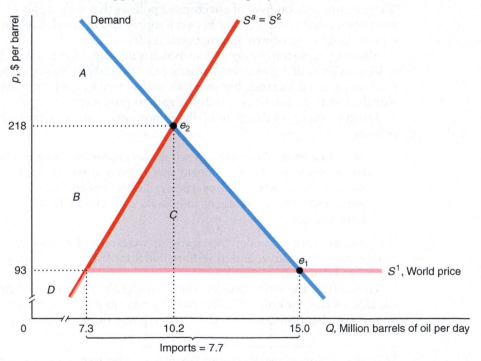

U.S.	Free Trade	U.S. Import Ban	Change ($ billions)
Consumer Surplus, CS	$A + B + C$	A	$-B - C = \Delta CS = -1.58$
Producer Surplus, PS	D	$B + D$	$B = \Delta PS = 1.09$
Welfare, $W = CS + PS$	$A + B + C + D$	$A + B + D$	$-C = \Delta W = DWL = -0.48$

price, which averaged $93 per barrel during the week of April 26, 2013.[20] The total U.S. supply curve, S^1, is the horizontal sum of the domestic supply curve and the foreign supply curve. Thus, S^1 is the same as the upward-sloping domestic supply curve for prices below $93 and is horizontal at $93. With free trade, the United States imports crude oil if its domestic price in the absence of imports would exceed the world price.

The free-trade equilibrium, e_1, is determined by the intersection of S^1 and the demand curve, where the U.S. price equals the world price, $93, and the quantity is 15 million barrels per day. At the equilibrium price, domestic supply is 7.3, so imports are 7.7 ($= 15 - 7.3$). U.S. consumer surplus is $A + B + C$, U.S. producer surplus is D, and the U.S. total surplus is $A + B + C + D$. Throughout our discussion of trade, we ignore welfare effects in other countries.

If imports are banned, the total U.S. supply curve, S^2, is the American domestic supply curve, S^a. The equilibrium is at e_2, where S^2 intersects the demand curve. The new equilibrium price is $218, and the new equilibrium quantity, 10.2 million barrels per day, is produced domestically. Consumer surplus is A, producer surplus is $B + D$, and total surplus is $A + B + D$.

Does the ban help the United States? No. The ban helps U.S. crude oil producers but harms U.S. consumers by more. Because of the higher price, domestic firms gain producer surplus of $\Delta PS = B \approx \$1.09$ billion per day. The change in consumers' surplus is $\Delta CS = -B - C \approx -\$1.58$ billion per day. That is, consumers lose $1.45 ($= 1.58/1.09$) for every $1 that producers gain from a ban. The U.S. deadweight loss is the change in welfare, ΔW: the sum of the gain to producers and the loss to consumers, $\Delta W = \Delta PS + \Delta CS \approx -\$481$ million per day or $-\$176$ billion per year. This deadweight loss is 44% ($= 0.481/1.09$) of the gain to producers.

Free Trade Versus a Tariff

TARIFF, n. A scale of taxes on imports, designed to protect the domestic producer against the greed of his customers. —Ambrose Bierce

Governments use *specific tariffs*—t dollars per unit—and *ad valorem tariffs*—α percent of the sales price. In recent years, tariffs have been applied throughout the world, most commonly to agricultural products.[21] American policymakers have frequently debated the optimal tariff on crude oil as a way to raise revenue or to reduce "dependence" on foreign oil.

You may be asking yourself, "Why should we study tariffs if we've already looked at taxes? Isn't a tariff just another tax?" Good point! Tariffs are just taxes. If the only goods sold were imported, the effect of a tariff in the importing country is the same as we showed for a sales tax. We study tariffs separately because a tariff is applied only to imported goods, so it affects domestic and foreign producers differently.

Because tariffs are applied to only imported goods, all else the same, they do not raise as much tax revenue or affect equilibrium quantities as much as taxes applied to all goods in a market. De Melo and Tarr (1992) calculated that almost five times more tax revenue would be generated by a 15% additional ad valorem tax on petroleum products than by a 25% additional import tariff on oil and gas.

---

[20]I derived these linear demand and supply curves using data for the week of April 26, 2013, and supply and demand elasticity estimates from Baumeister and Peersman (forthcoming).

[21]After World War II, most trading nations signed the General Agreement on Tariffs and Trade (GATT), which limited their ability to subsidize exports or limit imports using quotas and tariffs. The rules prohibited most export subsidies and import quotas, except when imports threatened "market disruption" (the term that was, unfortunately, not defined). The GATT also required that any new tariff be offset by a reduction in other tariffs to compensate the exporting country. Modifications of the GATT and agreements negotiated by its successor, the World Trade Organization, have reduced or eliminated many tariffs.

To illustrate the effect of a tariff, suppose that the government imposes a specific tariff of $t = \$40$ per barrel of crude oil. Given this tariff, firms will not import oil into the United States unless the U.S. price is at least $40 above the world price, $93. The tariff creates a wedge between the world price and the U.S. price. This tariff causes the total supply curve to shift from S^1 to S^3 in Figure 9.10. As the world

Figure 9.10 Effects of a Tariff (or Quota)

A tariff of $t = \$40$ per barrel of oil imported or a quota of 5.2 million barrels per day drives the U.S. price of crude oil to $133, which is $40 more than the world price. Under the tariff, the equilibrium, e_3, is determined by the intersection of the S_3 total U.S. supply curve and the D demand curve. Under the quota, e_3 is determined by a quantity wedge of 5.2 million barrels per day between the quantity demanded, 13.3 million barrels per day, and the quantity supplied by domestic firms, 8.1 million barrels per day, at a price of $133 per barrel. Compared to free trade, producers gain area B and consumers lose areas $B + C + D + E$ from either a tariff or a quota. If the government gives the quota rights to foreign producers, the deadweight loss is $C + D + E$. With a tariff, the government's tariff revenue increases by D, so the deadweight loss is only $C + E$.

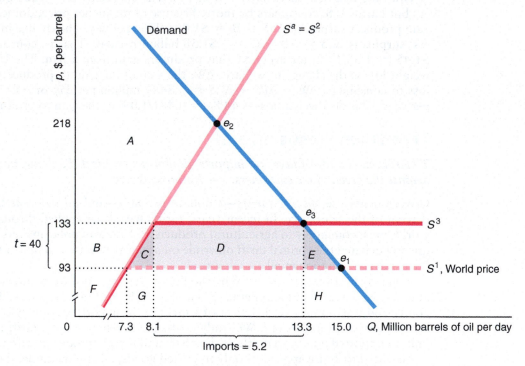

U.S.	Free Trade	U.S. Tariff or Quota	Change ($ millions)
Consumer Surplus, CS	$A + B + C + D + E$	A	$-B - C - D - E = -566$
Producer Surplus, PS	F	$B + F$	$B = 308$
Tariff Revenues, T	0	D (tariff)	$D = 208$ (tariff)
		0 (quota)	0 (quota)
Welfare from a Tariff, $W = CS + PS + T$	$A + B + C + D + E + F$	$A + B + D + F$	$-C - E = DWL = -50$
Welfare from a Quota, $W = CS + PS$	$A + B + C + D + E + F$	$A + B + F$	$-C - D - E = DWL = -258$

supply curve for oil is horizontal at a price of $93, adding a $40 tariff shifts this supply curve upward so that it is horizontal at $133. That is, the rest of the world will supply an unlimited amount of oil at $133 inclusive of the tariff. As a result, the total U.S. supply curve with the tariff, S^3, equals the domestic supply curve for prices below $133 and is horizontal at $133.

The new equilibrium, e_3, occurs where S^3 intersects the demand curve. At this equilibrium, price is $133 and quantity is 13.3 million barrels of oil per day. At this higher price, domestic firms supply 8.1 million barrels of oil per day, so imports are 5.2 (= 13.3 − 8.1) million barrels of oil per day.

The tariff *protects* U.S. producers from foreign competition. The larger the tariff, the less crude oil that is imported, hence the higher the price that domestic firms can charge. (With a large enough tariff, nothing is imported, and the price rises to the no-trade level, $218.) With a tariff of $40, domestic firms' producer surplus increases by area $B \approx$ $308 million per day.

Because of the $40 price increase, consumer surplus falls by $B + C + D + E \approx$ $566 million per day. The government receives tariff revenues, T, equal to area $D \approx$ $208 million per day.

The deadweight loss is $C + E =$ $50 million per day, or $18.3 billion per year.[22] Because the tariff doesn't completely eliminate imports, the loss of total surplus is smaller than it is if all imports are banned.

We can interpret the two components of this deadweight loss. First, C is the loss from domestic firms producing 8.1 million barrels per day instead of 7.3 million barrels per day. Domestic firms produce this extra output because the tariff drives up the price from $93 to $133. The cost of producing this extra 0.8 million barrels of oil per day domestically is $C + G$. Had Americans bought this oil at the world price, the cost would have been only G. Thus, C is the extra cost from producing the additional 0.8 million barrels of oil per day domestically instead of importing it.

Second, E is a *consumption distortion loss* from U.S. consumers buying too little oil, 13.3 instead of 15 million barrels per day, because of the tariff-induced price increase. U.S. consumers value this extra output as $E + H$, the area under their demand curve between 13.3 and 15, whereas the value in international markets is only H. Thus, E is the difference between the value at world prices and the value U.S. consumers place on this extra 1.7 million barrels per day.

Free Trade Versus a Quota

The effect on imports of a quota is similar to that of a tariff. In Figure 9.10, if the government limits imports to 5.2 million barrels per day, the quota is binding because 7.7 million barrels per day were imported under free trade. If the price equals $133, the gap between the quantity demanded, 13.3 million barrels per day, and the quantity supplied by domestic firms, 8.1 million barrels per day, is 5.2 million barrels per day. Thus, a quota on imports of 5.2 million barrels per day leads to the same equilibrium, e_3, as a tariff of $40.

With a quota, the gain to domestic producers, B, and the loss to consumers, $C + E$, are the same as with a tariff. The key difference between a tariff and a quota concerns who gets D. With a tariff, the government receives tariff revenue equal to area D.

When a quota is used, who receives D depends on how the quota is allocated. Most governments use one of three methods to allocate quotas: the quota may be

---

[22]If the foreign supply is horizontal, welfare in the importing country *must* fall. However, if the foreign supply is upward sloping, welfare in the importing country may rise.

(1) sold or auctioned, (2) given to domestic importing firms, or (3) given to foreign exporting firms.

If the government charges $40 per barrel (or auctions the quota raising the same amount), it captures area D, so the effect of the quota and the tariff are the same. However, governments rarely set a fee or auction a quota.

If the government gives the quota to domestic importing firms, they capture D. Thus, domestic welfare is the same with a tariff and a quota, but importers rather than the government capture the gains with the quota.

Finally, if the government gives the quota to foreign producers, they earn an extra arbitrage profit of D because they buy the oil quota, 5.2 million barrels per day, at the world price, $93, but sell it for $133. As a result, the deadweight loss is $C + E = \$50$ million per day with a tariff but $C + D + E = \$258$ million per day with a quota. Thus, the importing country fares better using a tariff than setting a quota that reduces imports by the same amount if the quota rights are given to foreigners.

Application

The Chicken Tax Trade War

When is a van not a van? Give up? The answer is "When there's a chicken tax." Still unclear? Welcome to the Alice-in-Wonderland world of trade wars.

Several times a month, Ford Motor Co. ships brand new, shiny Transit Connect wagons from its factory in Turkey to the United States, where virtually all are delivered to a brick warehouse. There, 65 workers rip out rear windows, rear seats, and rear seatbelts and send the fabric, steel parts, and glass to be recycled.

Why? Because by shipping light trucks with seats, Ford can tell U.S. Customs that it is importing *wagons*, which primarily transport people, instead of *commercial vans*, which primarily transport goods. The reason Ford cares about the definition is that the import tariff on a van is 25%, but it is only 2.5% on a wagon. Thus, by adding and then removing seats and windows at a cost of hundreds of dollars per van, Ford saves thousands in tariffs.

Ford is legally circumventing a half-century-old tariff that arose during a trade dispute. In the early 1960s, after European countries placed high tariffs on chickens imported from the United States to protect domestic producers, the United States retaliated with an import tax on foreign-made trucks and commercial vans that is still in effect. That is, tariffs can lead to social losses above and beyond their direct harms. Ironically, in contrast to the U.S.-based Ford's sneaky import strategy, the Japanese-based firms Toyota, Nissan, and Honda avoid the tariff by assembling their vans in the United States.

Rent Seeking

Given that tariffs and quotas hurt the importing country, why do the Japanese, U.S., and other governments impose tariffs, quotas, or other trade barriers? The reason is that domestic producers stand to make large gains from such government actions; hence, it pays for them to organize and lobby the government to enact these trade policies. Although consumers as a whole suffer large losses, most individual consumers face a negligible loss. Moreover, consumers rarely organize to lobby the government about trade issues. Thus, in most countries, producers are often able to convince (cajole, influence, or bribe) legislators or government officials to aid them, even though consumers suffer more-than-offsetting losses.

If domestic producers can talk the government into a tariff, quota, or other policy that reduces imports, they gain extra producer surplus (rents), such as area B in Figures 9.9 and 9.10. Economists call efforts and expenditures to gain a rent or a

rent seeking
efforts and expenditures to gain a rent or a profit from government actions

profit from government actions **rent seeking**. If producers or other interest groups bribe legislators to influence policy, the bribe is a transfer of income and hence does not increase deadweight loss (except to the degree that a harmful policy is chosen). However, if this rent-seeking behavior—such as hiring lobbyists and engaging in advertising to influence legislators—uses up resources, the deadweight loss from tariffs and quotas understates the true loss to society. The domestic producers may spend up to the gain in producer surplus to influence the government.[23]

Indeed, some economists argue that the government revenues from tariffs are completely offset by administrative costs and rent-seeking behavior. If so (and if the tariffs and quotas do not affect world prices), the loss to society from tariffs and quotas is all of the change in consumer surplus, such as areas $B + C$ in Figure 9.9 and areas $B + C + D + E$ in Figure 9.10.

Lopez and Pagoulatos (1994) estimated the deadweight loss and the additional losses due to rent-seeking activities in the United States in food and tobacco products. They estimated that the deadweight loss (in 2013 dollars) was $17.8 billion, which was 2.6% of the domestic consumption of these products. The largest deadweight losses were in milk products and sugar manufacturing, which primarily used import quotas to raise domestic prices. The gain in producer surplus was $64.4 billion, or 9.5% of domestic consumption, while the loss to consumers was $84.8 billion, or 12.5% of domestic consumption. The government obtained $2.6 billion in tariff revenues, or 0.4% of consumption. If all of producer surplus were expended in rent-seeking behavior, the total loss would be $82.3 billion, or 12.1% of consumption, which is 4.6 times larger than the deadweight loss alone. Thus, depending on the amount of rent seeking, the loss to society is somewhere between the deadweight loss of $17.8 billion and $82.3 billion.

Challenge Solution **"Big Dry" Water Restrictions**	We can use welfare analysis to answer the Challenge questions posed at the beginning of the chapter concerning Australia's major drought, the Big Dry. Is society better off—is welfare higher—if it reduces overall water usage by restricting outdoor water use or by raising the price of water for all uses? Who wins and who loses? We use the figure to compare the welfare effects of the two policies. The light-blue demand curve is for indoor use of water, such as for drinking, bathing, and cleaning. Not shown is the demand curve for outdoor use (such as watering lawns), which, for simplicity, we assume is a constant quantity $\overline{Q}$ at any price up to p_3. The dark-blue total demand curve is the horizontal sum of the indoor and outdoor demand curves. The drought has caused the short-run, vertical supply curve to shift to the left from its usual position. It is vertical at Q_1, which is the number of gigaliters of water that are available. If the government allows the price to clear the market, the equilibrium price is p_2, where the supply curve intersects the total demand curve. Instead, to keep the price down, the government forbids the use of water outdoors, so the market clears at p_1, where the supply curve intersects the indoor demand curve. With the water restriction, the water authority sells the water for p_1 and collects revenue of $p_1 \times Q_1$, which equals the area of the rectangle C. Consumer surplus is area $A + B$, which is the area under the indoor demand curve above p_1. Thus, society's total welfare is $A + B + C$. In contrast, if water use is not restricted, the price is p_2. The water authority collects revenue equal to $B + C + D$. The consumer surplus is $A + E$, which is the area under the total demand curve above p_2. If, as in the figure, $E > B$, then

---

[23]This argument is made in Tullock (1967) and Posner (1975). Fisher (1985) and Varian (1989) argue that the expenditure is typically less than the producer surplus.

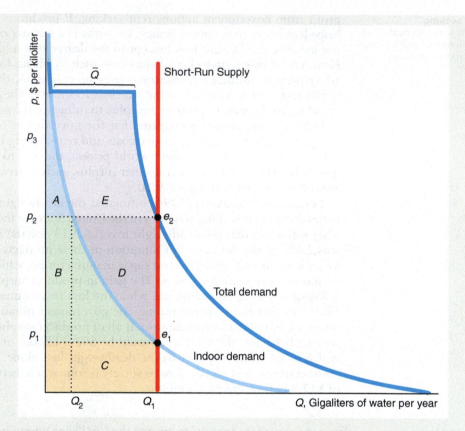

the consumer surplus is greater without the restriction. Society's total welfare is $A + B + C + D + E$. Thus, removing the restriction raises welfare by $D + E$, which is the deadweight loss from the restriction.

If the government allowed the price to rise to p_2, consumers would allocate the available Q_1 gigaliters of water between indoor and outdoor use as they saw fit, using Q_2 indoors and $Q_1 - Q_2$ outdoors. If outdoor use is prohibited, some consumers who value outdoor use by more than p_2 would be willing to pay p_2 to buy $Q_1 - Q_2$ gigaliters of water for outdoor use, while some other consumers who value that quantity of water for indoor use between p_1 and p_2 would be willing to sell it for p_2. Thus, were such trades feasible, society would benefit from these trades between consumers. By allowing the price to rise to p_2, we get the same water usage as we would from allowing such consumer trades.

Restrictions harm those people who want to water outside. The alternative policy of raising the price from p_1 to p_2 harms consumers of indoor water—particularly poor people—unless they receive compensating financial help. The government could use its extra revenue from charging the higher price to compensate poor consumers.

Grafton and Ward (2008) compared the consumer surplus loss from restricting outdoor water use in Australia rather than allowing the price to rise so as to clear the market. To achieve the same reduction in the water demanded on the original demand curve, the price would have had to more than double from $p_1 = \$1.01$ per kiloliter (kL) to $p_2 = \$2.35$ per kL. They estimated that the loss in consumer surplus from using mandatory water restrictions rather than price adjustments was $235 million annually, or about $150 per household, which was slightly less than half the average Sydney household's water bill. In addition, society incurs an allocation cost because some consumers are willing to pay more than others are paying.

Summary

1. **Zero Profit for Competitive Firms in the Long Run.** Although competitive firms may make profits or losses in the short run, they earn zero economic profit in the long run. If necessary, the prices of scarce inputs adjust to ensure that competitive firms make zero long-run profit. Because profit-maximizing firms just break even in the long run, firms that do not try to maximize profits will lose money. Competitive firms must maximize profit to survive.

2. **Consumer Welfare.** The pleasure a consumer receives from a good in excess of its cost is called *consumer surplus*. Consumer surplus equals the area under the consumer's demand curve above the market price up to the quantity that the consumer buys. How much consumers are harmed by an increase in price is measured by the change in consumer surplus.

3. **Producer Welfare.** A firm's gain from trading is measured by its producer surplus. Producer surplus is the largest amount of money that could be taken from a firm's revenue and still leave the firm willing to produce. That is, the producer surplus is the amount the firm is paid minus its variable cost of production, which is profit in the long run. It is the area below the price and above the supply curve up to the quantity that the firm sells. The effect of a change in a price on a supplier is measured by the change in producer surplus.

4. **Competition Maximizes Welfare.** One standard measure of welfare is the sum of consumer surplus and producer surplus. The more price is above marginal cost, the lower this measure of welfare. In the competitive equilibrium, in which price equals marginal cost, welfare is maximized.

5. **Policies That Shift Supply and Demand Curves.** Governments frequently limit the number of firms in a market directly, by licensing them, or indirectly, by raising the costs of entry to new firms or raising the cost of exiting. A reduction in the number of firms in a competitive market raises price, hurts consumers, helps producing firms, and lowers the standard measure of welfare. This reduction in welfare is a deadweight loss: The gain to producers is less than the loss to consumers.

6. **Policies That Create a Wedge Between Supply and Demand.** Taxes, price ceilings, and price floors create a gap between the price consumers pay and the price firms receive. These policies force price above marginal cost, which raises the price to consumers and lowers the amount consumed. The wedge between price and marginal cost results in a deadweight loss: The loss of consumer surplus and producer surplus is not offset by increased taxes or by benefits to other groups.

7. **Comparing Both Types of Policies: Imports.** A government may use either a quantity restriction such as a quota, which shifts the supply curve, or a tariff, which creates a wedge, to reduce imports or achieve other goals. These policies may have different welfare implications. A tariff that reduces imports by the same amount as a quota has the same harms—a larger loss of consumer surplus than increased domestic producer surplus—but has a partially offsetting benefit—increased tariff revenues for the government. Rent-seeking activities are attempts by firms or individuals to influence a government to adopt a policy that favors them. By using resources, rent seeking exacerbates the welfare loss beyond the deadweight loss caused by the policy itself. In a perfectly competitive market, government policies frequently lower welfare. However, as we show in later chapters, government policies may increase welfare in markets that are not perfectly competitive.

Questions

All questions are available on MyEconLab; * = *answer appears at the back of this book;* **A** = *algebra problem.*

1. Zero Profit for Competitive Firms in the Long Run

1.1 Only a limited amount of high-quality wine-growing land is available. The firms that farm the land are identical. Because the demand curve hits the market supply curve in its upward-sloping section, the firms initially earn positive profit.

a. The owners of the land charge a higher rent so as to capture the profit. Show how the market supply curve changes (if at all).

b. Suppose some firms own the land and some rent. Do these firms behave differently in terms of their shutdown decision or in any other way?

1.2 Explain the reasoning in the Application "Tiger Woods' Rent" as to why Tiger Woods was able to capture essentially all the rents from some companies but not from others.

1.3 The reputations of some of the world's most prestigious museums have been damaged by accusations that they obtained antiquities that were looted or stolen in violation of international laws and treaties aimed at halting illicit trade in art and antiquities. A new wariness among private and public collectors to buy works whose provenance has not been rigorously established threatens the business of even established dealers. Conversely, this fear has increased the value of antiquities that have a solid ownership history. Many of the world's most powerful dealers of antiquities, such as the Aboutaam brothers, backed an international ban on trade in excavated antiquities (Ron Stodghill, "Do You Know Where That Art Has Been?" *New York Times*, March 18, 2007; Daniel Grant, "Is It Possible to 'Collect' Antiquities These Days?" *Huffington Post*, April 5, 2011).

   a. What would be the effect of the ban on the current stock of antiquities for sale in the United States and Europe?

   b. Why would established dealers back such a ban?

   c. Would such a ban differentially affect established dealers and new dealers?

   d. Discuss the implications of a ban using the concept of an economic rent.

2. Consumer Welfare

*2.1 If the inverse demand function for toasters is $p = 60 - Q$, what is the consumer surplus if price is 30? **A**

2.2 If the inverse demand function for radios is $p = a - bQ$, what is the consumer surplus if price is $a/2$? **A**

2.3 Use the numbers for the alcohol and tobacco category from the table in the Application "Goods with a Large Consumer Surplus Loss from Price Increases" to draw a figure that illustrates the role that the revenue and the elasticity of demand play in determining the loss of consumer surplus due to an increase in price. Indicate how the various areas of your figure correspond to the equation derived in Appendix 9A and the discussion in this chapter about how a more elastic demand curve would affect consumer surplus. (*Hint*: See Solved Problem 9.1.) **A**

2.4 The U.S. Department of Agriculture's (USDA's) minimum general recommendation is five servings of fruits and vegetables a day. Jetter et al. (2004) estimated that, if consumers followed that advice, the equilibrium price and quantity of most fruits and vegetables would increase substantially. For example, the price of salad would rise 7.2%, output would increase 3.5%, and growers' revenues would jump 7.3% (presumably, health benefits would occur too). Use a diagram to illustrate as many of these effects as possible and to show how consumer surplus and producer surplus change. Discuss how to calculate the consumer surplus (given that the USDA's recommendation shifts consumers' tastes or behavior so that the demand curve shifts right or becomes less elastic at the equilibrium). (*Hint*: See Solved Problem 9.1.)

3. Producer Welfare

3.1 For a firm, how does the concept of *producer surplus* differ from that of *profit* if it has no fixed cost?

3.2 If the supply function is $Q = 10 + p$, what is the producer surplus if price is 20? (*Hint*: See Solved Problem 9.2.) **A**

4. Competition Maximizes Welfare

4.1 If society cared only about the well-being of consumers so that it wanted to maximize consumer surplus, would a competitive market achieve that goal given that the government cannot force or bribe firms to produce more than the competitive level of output? How would your answer change if society cared only about maximizing producer surplus? (*Hint*: See the discussion of Figure 9.5 and Solved Problem 9.3.)

4.2 Use an indifference curve diagram (gifts on one axis and all other goods on the other) to illustrate that one is better off receiving cash than a gift. (*Hint*: See the discussion of gifts in this chapter and the discussion of food stamps in Chapter 4.) Relate your analysis to the "Deadweight Loss of Christmas Presents" Application.

5. Policies That Shift Supply and Demand Curves

5.1 In 2002, Los Angeles imposed a ban on new billboards, which was upheld by the courts in 2009, and new digital billboards were shut down by court order in 2013. Owners of existing billboards did not oppose the initial ban. Why? What are the implications of the ban for producer surplus, consumer surplus, and welfare? Who are the producers and consumers in your analysis? How else does the ban affect welfare in Los Angeles?

5.2 A city may limit the number of cabs in many ways. The most common method is an explicit quota using a medallion that is kept forever and can be resold. One alternative is to charge a high license fee each year, which is equivalent to the city's issuing a medallion or license that lasts only a year. A third option is to charge a daily tax on taxicabs. Using figures, compare and contrast the equilibrium under each of these approaches. Discuss who wins and who loses from each plan, considering consumers, drivers, the city, and (if relevant) medallion owners. (*Hint*: See the "Licensing Cabs" Application and the discussion of Figure 9.6.)

5.3 In 2012, two Oakland City Council members called for slashing the annual fees the city charges for taxi medallions from $1,019 a year to $510 (Matthai Kuruvila, "Cheaper Oakland Taxi Medallions Proposed," *San Francisco Chronicle*, December 17, 2012). They say that they want to help cab drivers. Cab companies own and pay for the medallions. These companies charge drivers $500 a week to use the cabs. Would cutting the annual medallion fee help drivers? Explain.

5.4 Although 23 states barred the self-service sale of gasoline in 1968, most removed the bans by the mid-1970s. By 1992, self-service outlets sold nearly 80% of all U.S. gas. By 2013, only New Jersey and Oregon continued to ban self-service sales. Using predicted values for self-service sales for New Jersey and Oregon, Johnson and Romeo (2000) estimated that the ban in those two states raised the price by approximately 3¢ to 5¢ per gallon. Why did the ban affect the price? Illustrate using a figure and explain. Show the welfare effects in your figure. Use a table to show who gains or loses.

6. Policies That Create a Wedge Between Supply and Demand

6.1 If the inverse demand function for books is $p = 60 - Q$ and the supply function is $Q = p$, what is the initial equilibrium? What is the welfare effect of a specific tax of $t = \$2$? **A**

6.2 Suppose that the demand curve for wheat is $Q = 100 - 10p$ and the supply curve is $Q = 10p$. The government imposes a specific tax of $t = 1$ per unit.

a. How do the equilibrium price and quantity change?

b. What effect does this tax have on consumer

surplus, producer surplus, government revenue, welfare, and deadweight loss? **A**

6.3 What is the welfare effect of an ad valorem sales tax, α, assessed on each competitive firm in a market?

6.4 How would the analysis in Solved Problem 9.4 change if the supply curve were upward-sloping instead of horizontal?

6.5 In Solved Problem 9.4, what is the relationship between lost consumer surplus due to the tax, deadweight loss, and tax revenue? Discuss and reconcile the different results in Solved Problems 9.1 and 9.4.

*6.6 What is the welfare effect of a lump-sum tax, L, assessed on each competitive firm in a market? (*Hint*: See Chapter 8.)

*6.7 What is the long-run welfare effect of a profit tax (the government collects a specified percentage of a firm's profit) assessed on each competitive firm in a market?

6.8 The government wants to drive the price of soybeans above the equilibrium price, p_1, to p_2. It offers growers a lump-sum payment of x to reduce their output from Q_1 (the equilibrium level) to Q_2, which is the quantity demanded by consumers at p_2. Use a figure to show how large x must be (an area in the figure) for growers to reduce output to this level. What are the effects of this program on consumers, farmers, and total welfare? Compare this approach to (a) offering a price support of p_2, (b) offering a price support and a quota set at Q_1, and (c) offering a price support and a quota set at Q_2.

6.9 Suppose that the demand curve for wheat is $Q = 100 - 10p$ and the supply curve is $Q = 10p$. The government provides producers with a specific subsidy of $s = 1$ per unit.

a. How do the equilibrium price and quantity change?

b. What effect does this tax have on consumer surplus, producer surplus, government revenue, welfare, and deadweight loss? (*Hint*: See Solved Problem 9.5.) **A**

6.10 Use diagrams to compare the welfare implications of the traditional agricultural price support program and the deficiency payment program if both set the same price floor, p. Under what circumstances would farmers, consumers, or taxpayers prefer one program to the other? (*Hint*: See Solved Problem 9.6.)

*6.11 Suppose that the demand curve for wheat is $Q = 100 - 10p$ and the supply curve is $Q = 10p$. The government imposes a price support at $\underline{p} = 6$ using a deficiency payment program.

   a. What are the quantity supplied, the price that clears the market, and the deficiency payment?

   b. What effect does this program have on consumer surplus, producer surplus, welfare, and deadweight loss? (*Hint*: See Solved Problem 9.7.) **A**

6.12 The government sets a minimum wage above the current equilibrium wage. What effect does the minimum wage have on the market equilibrium? What are its effects on consumer surplus, producer surplus, and total surplus? Who are the consumers and who are the producers? (*Hint*: See the treatment of a ceiling in Solved Problem 9.7.)

6.13 A mayor wants to help renters in her city. She considers two policies that will benefit renters equally. One policy is *rent control*, which places a price ceiling, $\bar{p}$, on rents. The other is a government housing subsidy of s dollars per month that lowers the amount renters pay (to $\bar{p}$). Who benefits and who loses from these policies? Compare the two policies' effects on the quantity of housing consumed, consumer surplus, producer surplus, government expenditure, and deadweight loss. Does the comparison of deadweight loss depend on the elasticities of supply and demand? (*Hint*: Consider extreme cases.) If so, how? (*Hint*: See Solved Problem 9.7.)

6.14 Suppose that the demand curve is $Q = 100 - 10p$ and the supply curve is $Q = 10p$. The government imposes a price ceiling of $p = 3$.

   a. Describe how the equilibrium changes.

   b. What effect does this ceiling have on consumer surplus, producer surplus, and deadweight loss? (*Hint*: See Solved Problem 9.7.) **A**

7. Comparing Both Types of Policies: Imports

7.1 Show that if the importing country faces an upward-sloping foreign supply curve (excess supply curve), a tariff may raise welfare in the importing country.

7.2 Given that the world supply curve is horizontal at the world price for a given good, can a subsidy on imports raise welfare in the importing country? Explain your answer.

7.3 In 2013, the United States accused India, China, and three other Asian countries of dumping shrimp in the United States at prices below their costs, and proposed duties (tariffs) as high as 62.74% (Uttara Choudhury, "U.S. Sets Preliminary Anti-dumping Duties on Indian Shrimp," *FirstPost Business*, June 4, 2013). Suppose that these countries were subsidizing their shrimp fishers. Show in a diagram who gains and who loses in the United States (compared to the equilibrium in which those nations do not subsidize their shrimp fishers). Now use your diagram to show how the large tariff would affect the welfare of consumers and producers and government revenues.

7.4 In the first quarter of 2013, the world price for raw sugar, 23¢ per pound, was about 79% of the domestic price, 29¢ per pound, because of quotas and tariffs on sugar imports. Consequently, U.S.-made corn sweeteners can be profitably sold domestically. A decade ago, the U.S. Commerce Department estimated that the quotas and price support reduce U.S. welfare by about $3 billion a year, so each dollar of Archer Daniels Midland's profit from selling U.S. sugar costs Americans about $10. Model the effects of a quota on sugar in both the sugar and corn sweetener markets.

7.5 A government is considering a quota or a tariff, both of which will reduce imports by the same amount. Which does the government prefer, and why? Explain how your answer depends on the way that the quota is allocated.

7.6 During the Napoleonic Wars, Britain blockaded North America, seizing U.S. vessels and cargo and impressing sailors. At President Thomas Jefferson's request, Congress imposed a nearly complete—perhaps 80%—embargo on international commerce from December 1807 to March 1809. Just before the embargo, exports were about 13% of gross national product (GNP). Due to the embargo, U.S. consumers could not find good substitutes for manufactured goods from Europe, and producers could not sell farm produce and other goods for as much as in Europe. According to Irwin (2005), the welfare cost of the embargo was at least 8% of the U.S. GNP in 1807. Use graphs to show the effects of the embargo on a market for an exported good and for an imported good. Show the change in equilibria and the welfare effects on consumers and firms (assuming an upward-sloping import supply curve).

7.7 After Mexico signed the North American Free Trade Agreement (NAFTA) with the United States in 1994, corn imports from the United States doubled within a year, and, in some recent years, U.S. imports have approached half of the amount of corn consumed in Mexico. According to Oxfam (2003), the price of Mexican corn fell more than 70% in the first decade after NAFTA took effect. Part of the reason for this flow south of our border is that the U.S. government subsidizes corn production to the tune of $10 billion a year. According to Oxfam, the 2002 U.S. cost of production was $3.08 per bushel, but the export price was $2.69 per bushel, with the difference reflecting an export subsidy of 39¢ per bushel. The U.S. exported 5.3 metric tons. Use graphs to show the effect of such a subsidy on the welfare of various groups and on government expenditures in the United States and Mexico.

7.8 Canada has 20% of the world's known freshwater resources, yet many Canadians believe that the country has little or none to spare. Over the years, U.S. and Canadian firms have struck deals to export bulk shipments of water to drought-afflicted U.S. cities and towns. Provincial leaders have blocked these deals in British Columbia and Ontario. Use graphs to show the likely outcome of such barriers to exports on the price and quantity of water used in Canada and in the United States if markets for water are competitive. Show the effects on consumer and producer surplus in both countries.

7.9 The U.S. Supreme Court ruled in May 2005 that people can buy wine directly from out-of-state vineyards. Previously, some states had laws that required people to buy directly from wine retailers located in the state.

a. Suppose the market for wine in New York is perfectly competitive both before and after the Supreme Court decision. Use the analysis in Section 9.7 to evaluate the effect of the Court's decision on the price of wine in New York.

b. Evaluate the increase in New York consumer surplus.

c. How does the increase in consumer surplus depend on the price elasticity of supply and demand?

8. Challenge

8.1 The U.S. National Park Service wants to restrict the number of visitors to Yosemite National Park to Q^*, which is fewer than the current volume. It considers two policies: (a) raising the price of admissions and (b) setting a quota that limits the number of visits by in-state residents. Compare the effects of these two policies on consumer surplus and welfare. Use a graph to show which policy is superior by your criterion.

10

General Equilibrium and Economic Welfare

Let the good of the people be the supreme law. —Cicero

After a disaster strikes, prices tend to rise. The average U.S. gasoline price increased by 46¢ per gallon after Hurricane Katrina in 2005 damaged most Gulf Coast oil refineries. Many state governments enforce anti-price gouging laws to prevent prices from rising, while prices may be free to adjust in neighboring states. For example, Louisiana's anti-price gouging law went into effect when Governor Bobby Jindal declared a state of emergency in response to the 2010 BP oil spill that endangered Louisiana's coast.

On average, gasoline prices rose by a few cents immediately after Superstorm Sandy in October 2012; however, some stations increased the retail markup over the wholesale prices by up to 135%. New York Attorney General Eric Schneiderman's office received over 500 consumer complaints about price gouging within a week of the storm. The Attorney General sued 4 gasoline stations and settled price gouging claims with 25 other stations by May 2013.

As of 2013, the District of Columbia and 34 states have anti-price gouging laws. Arkansas, California, Maine, New Jersey, Oklahoma, Oregon, and West Virginia set a "percentage increase cap limit" on how much price may be increased after a disaster, ranging from 10% to 25% of the price before the emergency. Sixteen states prohibit "unconscionable" price increases. Connecticut, Georgia, Hawaii, Kentucky, Louisiana, Mississippi, and Utah have outright bans on price increases during an emergency.

Most of these laws were passed after natural disasters. California passed its law in 1994 after the Northridge earthquake. Georgia enacted its anti-price gouging statute after a 500-year flood in 1994. Consequently, often one state—hit by a recent disaster—has such a law while a neighboring one does not.

Governments pass anti-price gouging laws because they're popular. After the post-Katrina gas price increases, an ABC News/Washington Post poll found that only 16% of respondents thought that the price increase was "justified," 72.7% thought that "oil companies and gas dealers are taking unfair advantage," 7.4% said both views were true, and the rest held another or no opinion.

In Chapter 2, we showed that a national price control causes shortages. However, does a binding price control that affects one state, but not a neighboring state, cause shortages? How does it affect prices and quantities sold in the two states? Which consumers benefit from these laws?

In addition to natural disasters, a change in government policies or other shocks often affect equilibrium price and quantity in more than one market. To determine the effects of such a change, we examine the interrelationships among markets. In this chapter, we extend our analysis of equilibrium in a single market to equilibrium in all markets.

We then examine how a society decides whether a particular equilibrium (or change in equilibrium) in all markets is desirable. To do so, society must answer two questions: "Is the equilibrium efficient?" and "Is the equilibrium equitable?"

For the equilibrium to be efficient, both consumption and production must be efficient. Production is efficient only if it is impossible to produce more output at current cost given current knowledge (Chapter 7). Consumption is efficient only if goods cannot be reallocated across people so that at least someone is better off and no one is harmed. In this chapter, we show how to determine whether consumption is efficient.

Whether the equilibrium is efficient is a scientific question. It is possible that all members of society could agree on how to answer scientific questions concerning efficiency.

To answer the equity question, society must make a value judgment as to whether each member of society has his or her "fair" or "just" share of all the goods and services. A common view in individualistic cultures is that each person is the best—and possibly only legitimate—judge of his or her own welfare. Nonetheless, to make social choices about events that affect more than one person, we have to make interpersonal comparisons, through which we decide whether one person's gain is more or less important than another person's loss. For example, in Chapter 9 we argued that a price ceiling lowers a measure of total welfare given the value judgment that the well-being of consumers (consumer surplus) and the well-being of the owners of firms (producer surplus) should be weighted equally. People of goodwill—and others—may disagree greatly about equity issues.

As a first step in studying welfare issues, many economists use a narrow value criterion, called the *Pareto principle* (after an Italian economist, Vilfredo Pareto), to rank different allocations of goods and services for which no interpersonal comparisons need to be made. According to this principle, a change that makes one person better off without harming anyone else is desirable. An allocation is **Pareto efficient** if any possible reallocation would harm at least one person.

Pareto efficient describing an allocation of goods or services such that any reallocation harms at least one person

Presumably, you agree that any government policy that makes all members of society better off is desirable. Do you also agree that a policy that makes some members better off without harming others is desirable? What about a policy that helps one group more than it hurts another group? What about a policy that hurts another group more than it helps your group? It is very unlikely that all members of society will agree on how to answer these questions—much less on the answers.

The efficiency and equity questions arise even in small societies, such as your family. Suppose that your family has gathered together in November and everyone wants pumpkin pie. How much pie you get will depend on the answer to efficiency and equity questions: "How can we make the pie as large as possible with available resources?" and "How should we divide the pie?" It is probably easier to get agreement about how to make the largest possible pie than about how to divide it equitably.

Economists primarily use economic theory to answer scientific efficiency questions because they can do so without making value judgments. To examine equity questions, they must make value judgments, as we did in Chapter 9's welfare analysis. (Strangely, most members of our society seem to believe that economists are no better at making value judgments than anyone else.) In this chapter, we examine various views on equity.

In this chapter, we examine five main topics	1. **General Equilibrium.** The effects of a new government policy or other shock differ if the shock affects several markets rather than just one.
	2. **Trading Between Two People.** Where two people have goods but cannot produce more goods, both parties benefit from mutually agreed trades.
	3. **Competitive Exchange.** The competitive equilibrium has two desirable properties: Any competitive equilibrium is Pareto efficient, and any Pareto-efficient allocation can be obtained by using competition, given an appropriate income distribution.
	4. **Production and Trading.** The benefits from trade continue to hold when production is introduced.
	5. **Efficiency and Equity.** A society uses its views about equity to choose among the Pareto-efficient allocations.

10.1 General Equilibrium

partial-equilibrium analysis
an examination of equilibrium and changes in equilibrium in one market in isolation

So far we have used a **partial-equilibrium analysis**: an examination of equilibrium and changes in equilibrium in one market in isolation. In a partial-equilibrium analysis in which we hold the prices and quantities of other goods fixed, we implicitly ignore the possibility that events in this market affect other markets' equilibrium prices and quantities.

When stated this baldly, partial-equilibrium analysis sounds foolish. However, it needn't be. Suppose that the government puts a tax on hula hoops. If the tax is sizable, it will dramatically affect the sales of hula hoops. Even a very large tax on hula hoops is unlikely to affect the markets for automobiles, doctor services, or orange juice. Indeed, it is unlikely to affect the demand for other toys greatly. Thus, a partial-equilibrium analysis of the effect of such a tax should serve us well. Studying all markets simultaneously to analyze this tax would be unnecessary at best and confusing at worst.

general-equilibrium analysis
the study of how equilibrium is determined in all markets simultaneously

Sometimes, however, we need to use a **general-equilibrium analysis**: the study of how equilibrium is determined in all markets simultaneously. For example, the discovery of a major oil deposit in a small country raises the income of its citizens, and the increased income affects all that country's markets. Sometimes economists model many markets in an economy and solve for the general equilibrium in all of them simultaneously, using computer models.

Frequently, economists look at equilibrium in several—but not all—markets simultaneously. We would expect a tax on comic books to affect the price of comic books, which in turn would affect the price of video games because video games are substitutes for comics for some people. But we would not expect a tax on comics to have a measurable effect on the demand for washing machines. Therefore, it is reasonable to conduct a multimarket analysis of the effects of a tax on comics by looking only at the markets for comics, video games, and a few other closely related markets such as those for movies and trading cards. That is, a multimarket equilibrium analysis covers the relevant markets, but not all markets, as a general equilibrium analysis would.

Markets are closely related if an increase in the price in one market causes the demand or supply curve in another market to shift measurably. Suppose that a tax on coffee causes the price of coffee to increase. The rise in the price of coffee causes the demand curve for tea to shift outward (more is demanded at any given price of tea) because tea and coffee are substitutes. The coffee price increase also causes the demand curve for cream to shift inward because coffee and cream are complements.

Similarly, supply curves in different markets may be related. If a farmer produces corn and soybeans, an increase in the price of corn will affect the relative amounts of both crops the farmer chooses to produce.

Markets may also be linked if the output of one market is an input in another market. A shock that raises the price of computer chips will also raise the price of computers.

Thus, an event in one market may have a spillover effect on other related markets for various reasons. Indeed, a single event may initiate a chain reaction of spillover effects that reverberates back and forth between markets.

Feedback Between Competitive Markets

To illustrate the feedback of spillover effects between markets, we examine the corn and soybean markets using supply and demand curves estimated by Holt (1992). Consumers and producers substitute between corn and soybeans, so the supply and demand curves in these two markets are related. The quantity of corn demanded and the quantity of soybeans demanded both depend on the price of corn, the price of soybeans, and other variables. Similarly, the quantities of corn and soybeans supplied depend on their relative prices.

We can demonstrate the effect of a shock in one market on both markets by tracing the sequence of events in the two markets. Whether these steps occur nearly instantaneously or take some time depends on how quickly consumers and producers react.

The initial supply and demand curves for corn, S_0^c and D_0^c, intersect at the initial equilibrium for corn, e_0^c, in panel a of Figure 10.1.[1] The price of corn is $2.15 per bushel, and the quantity of corn is 8.44 billion bushels per year. The initial supply and demand curves for soybeans, S_0^s and D_0^s, intersect at e_0^s in panel b, where price is $4.12 per bushel and quantity is 2.07 billion bushels per year. The first row of Table 10.1 shows the initial equilibrium prices and quantities in these two markets.

Now suppose that the foreign demand for U.S. corn decreases, causing the export of corn to fall by 10% and the total U.S. demand for corn to shift from D_0^c to D_1^c in panel a. The new equilibrium is at e_1^c, where D_1^c intersects S_0^c. The price of corn falls by nearly 11% to $1.9171 per bushel, and the quantity falls 2.5% to 8.227 billion bushels per year, as the Step 1 row of the table shows.

If we were conducting a partial-equilibrium analysis, we would stop here. In a general-equilibrium analysis, however, we next consider how this shock to the corn market affects the soybean market. Because this shock initially causes the price of corn to fall relative to the price of soybeans (which stays constant), consumers substitute toward corn and away from soybeans: The demand curve for soybeans shifts to the left from D_0^s to D_2^s in panel b.

In addition, because the price of corn falls relative to the price of soybeans, farmers produce more soybeans at any given price of soybeans: The supply curve for soybeans shifts outward to S_2^s. The new soybean demand curve, D_2^s, intersects the new soybean supply curve, S_2^s, at the new equilibrium e_2^s, where price is $3.8325 per bushel, a fall of 7%, and quantity is 2.0514 billion bushels per year, a drop of less than 1% (Step 2 row).

As it turns out, this fall in the price of soybeans relative to the price of corn causes essentially no shift in the demand curve for corn (panel a shows no shift) but shifts the supply curve of corn, S_3^c, to the right. The new equilibrium is e_3^c, where S_3^c and

---

[1]Until recently, the corn and soybean markets were subject to price controls (Chapter 9). However, we use the estimated supply and demand curves to ask what would happen in these markets in the absence of price controls.

Figure 10.1 Relationship Between the Corn and Soybean Markets

Supply and demand curves in the corn and soybean markets (as estimated by Holt, 1992) are related.

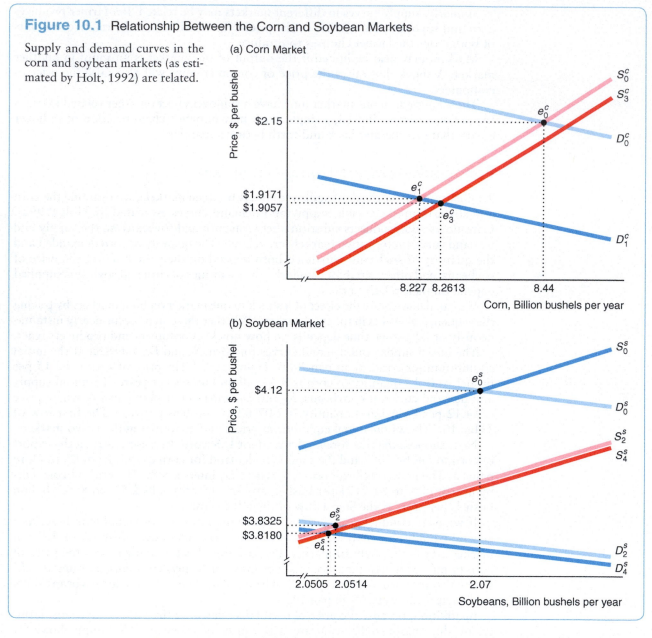

D_1^c intersect. Price falls to $1.9057 per bushel of corn and quantity to 8.2613 billion bushels per year (Step 3 row).

This new fall in the relative price of corn causes the soybean demand curve, D_4^s, to shift farther to the left and the supply curve, S_4^s, to shift farther to the right in panel b. At the new equilibrium at e_4^s, where D_4^s and S_4^s intersect, the price and quantity of soybeans fall slightly to $3.818 per bushel and 2.0505 billion bushels per year, respectively (Step 4 row).

These reverberations between the markets continue, with additional smaller shifts of the supply and demand curves. Eventually, a final equilibrium is reached at which none of the supply and demand curves will shift further. The final equilibria in these two markets (last row of Table 10.1) are virtually the same as e_3^c in panel a and e_4^s in panel b.

Table 10.1 Adjustment in the Corn and Soybean Markets

| | Corn | | Soybeans | |
Step	Price	Quantity	Price	Quantity
Initial (0)	2.15	8.44	4.12	2.07
1	1.9171	8.227		
2			3.8325	2.0514
3	1.9057	8.2613		
4			3.818	2.0505
5	1.90508	8.26308		
6			3.81728	2.05043
.	.	.	.	.
.	.	.	.	.
.	.	.	.	.
Final	1.90505	8.26318	3.81724	2.05043

If we were interested only in the effect of the shift in the foreign demand curve on the corn market, would we rely on a partial-equilibrium analysis? According to the partial-equilibrium analysis, the price of corn falls 10.8% to $1.9171. In contrast, in the general-equilibrium analysis, the price falls 11.4% to $1.905, which is 1.2¢ less per bushel. Thus, the partial-equilibrium analysis underestimates the price effect by 0.6 percentage point. Similarly, the fall in quantity is 2.5% according to the partial-equilibrium analysis and only 2.1% according to the general-equilibrium analysis. In this market, then, the biases from using a partial-equilibrium analysis are small.[2]

Solved Problem 10.1

Because many consumers choose between coffee and tea, the coffee and tea demand functions depend on both prices. Suppose the demand curves for coffee and tea are

$$Q_c = 120 - 2p_c + p_t,$$
$$Q_t = 90 - 2p_t + p_c,$$

where Q_c is the quantity of coffee, Q_t is the quantity of tea, p_c is the price of coffee, and p_t is the price of tea. These crops are grown in separate parts of the world, so their supply curves are not interrelated. We assume that the short-run, inelastic supply curves for coffee and tea are $Q_c = 45$ and $Q_t = 30$. Solve for the equilibrium prices and quantities. Now suppose that a freeze shifts the short-run supply curve of coffee to $Q_c = 30$. How does the freeze affect the prices and quantities?

Answer

1. *Equate the quantity demanded and supplied for both markets.* Equating the right sides of the coffee demand and supply functions, we obtain $120 - 2p_c + p_t = 45$, or $p_t = 2p_c - 75$. For the tea market, $90 - 2p_t + p_c = 30$, or $p_c = 2p_t - 60$. That leaves us with two equations and two unknowns, p_t and p_c.

---

[2]For an example where the bias from using a partial-equilibrium analysis instead of a general-equilibrium analysis is large, see MyEconLab, Chapter 10, "Sin Taxes."

2. *Substitute the expression for p_t from the coffee equation into the tea equation and solve for the price of coffee, then use that result to obtain p_t.* By substituting $p_t = 2p_c - 75$ into $p_c = 2p_t - 60$, we find that $p_c = 4p_c - 150 - 60$. Solving this expression for p_c, we find that $p_c = 70$. Substituting $p_c = 70$ into the coffee equation, we learn that $p_t = 2p_c - 75 = 140 - 75 = 65$. Substituting these prices into the demand equations, we confirm that the equilibrium quantities equal the fixed supplies: $Q_c = 45$ and $Q_t = 30$.

3. *Repeat the analysis for $Q_c = 30$.* The new quantity changes the coffee market equilibrium condition to $120 - 2p_c + p_t = 30$, or $p_t = 2p_c - 90$. Substituting this expression into the tea equilibrium condition, we find that $p_c = 4p_c - 180 - 60$, so $p_c = 240/3 = 80$, and hence $p_t = 2p_c - 90 = 70$. Thus, the price of coffee rises by 10 and the price of tea by 5 in response to the coffee freeze, which reduces Q_c by 15 while leaving Q_t unaffected.

Minimum Wages with Incomplete Coverage

We used a partial-equilibrium analysis in Chapter 2 to examine the effects of a minimum wage law that holds throughout the entire labor market. The minimum wage causes the quantity of labor demanded to be less than the quantity of labor supplied. Workers who lose their jobs cannot find work elsewhere, so they become unemployed.

However, the story changes substantially if the minimum wage law covers workers in only some sectors of the economy, as we show using a general-equilibrium analysis. Historically, the U.S. minimum wage law has not covered workers in all sectors of the economy.

When a minimum wage is applied to a covered sector of the economy, the increase in the wage causes the quantity of labor demanded in that sector to fall. Workers who are displaced from jobs in the covered sector move to the uncovered sector, driving down the wage in that sector. When the U.S. minimum wage law was first passed in 1938, some economists joked that its purpose was to maintain family farms. The law drove workers out of manufacturing and other covered industries into agriculture, which the law did not cover.

Figure 10.2 shows the effect of a minimum wage law when coverage is incomplete. The total demand curve, D in panel c, is the horizontal sum of the demand curve for labor services in the covered sector, D^c in panel a, and the demand curve in the uncovered sector, D^u in panel b. In the absence of a minimum wage law, the wage in both sectors is w_1, which is determined by the intersection of the total demand curve, D, and the total supply curve, S. At that wage, L_c^1 annual hours of work are hired in the covered sector, L_u^1 annual hours in the uncovered sector, and $L_1 = L_c^1 + L_u^1$ total annual hours of work.

If a minimum wage of $\underline{w}$ is set in only the covered sector, employment in that sector falls to L_c^2. To determine the wage and level of employment in the uncovered sector, we first need to determine how much labor service is available to that sector.

Anyone who can't find work in the covered sector goes to the uncovered sector. The supply curve of labor to the uncovered sector in panel b is a residual supply curve: the quantity the market supplies that is not met by demanders in other sectors at any given wage (Chapter 8). With a binding minimum wage in the covered sector, the residual supply function in the uncovered sector is[3]

$$S^u(w) = S(w) - D^c(\underline{w}).$$

---

[3]Without a minimum wage, the residual supply curve for the uncovered sector is $S^u(w) = S(w) - D^c(w)$.

Figure 10.2 Minimum Wage with Incomplete Coverage

In the absence of a minimum wage, the equilibrium wage is w_1. Applying a minimum wage, $\underline{w}$, to only one sector causes the quantity of labor services demanded in the covered sector to fall. The extra labor moves to the uncovered sector, driving the uncovered sector wage down to w_2.

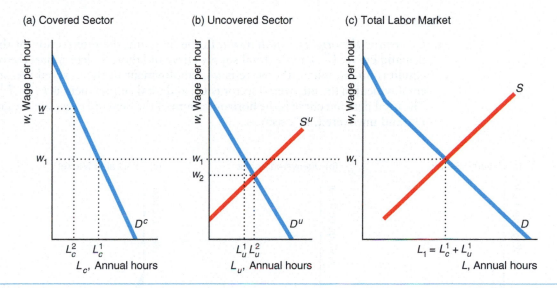

(a) Covered Sector (b) Uncovered Sector (c) Total Labor Market

Thus, the residual supply to the uncovered sector, $S^u(w)$, is the total supply, $S(w)$, at any given wage w minus the amount of labor used in the covered sector, $L_c^2 = D^c(\underline{w})$.

The intersection of D^u and S^u determines w_2, the new wage in the uncovered sector, and L_u^2, the new level of employment.[4] This general-equilibrium analysis shows that a minimum wage causes employment to drop in the covered sector, employment to rise (by a smaller amount) in the uncovered sector, and the wage in the uncovered sector to fall below the original competitive level. Thus, a minimum wage law with only partial coverage affects wage levels and employment levels in various sectors but need not create unemployment.

When the U.S. minimum wage was first passed in 1938, only 56% of workers were employed in covered firms (see MyEconLab, Chapter 10, "U.S. Minimum Wage Laws and Teenagers"). Today, many state minimum wages provide incomplete coverage.

More than 145 U.S. cities and counties now have living-wage laws, a new type of minimum wage legislation where the minimum is high enough to allow a fully employed person to live above the poverty level in a given locale. Living-wage laws provide incomplete coverage, typically extending only to the employees of a government or to firms that contract with that government.

---

[4]This analysis is incomplete if the minimum wage causes the price of goods in the covered sector to rise relative to those in the uncovered sector, which in turn causes the demands for labor in those two sectors, D^c and D^u, to shift. Ignoring that possibility is reasonable if labor costs are a small fraction of total costs (hence the effect of the minimum wage is minimal on total costs) or if the demands for the final goods are relatively price insensitive.

Solved Problem 10.2

After the government starts taxing the cost of labor by t per hour in a covered sector only, the wage that workers in both sectors receive is w, but the wage paid by firms in the covered sector is $w + t$. What effect does the subsidy have on the wages, total employment, and employment in the covered and uncovered sectors of the economy?

Answer

1. *Determine the original equilibrium.* In the diagram, the intersection of the total demand curve, D^1, and the total supply curve of labor, S, determines the original equilibrium, e_1, where the wage is w_1, employment in the covered sector is L_c^1, employment in the uncovered sector is L_u^1, and total employment is $L_1 = L_c^1 + L_u^1$. The total demand curve is the horizontal sum of the demand curves in the covered, D_1^c, and uncovered, D^u, sectors.

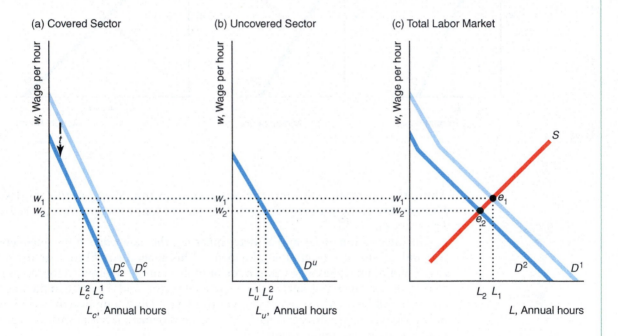

(a) Covered Sector   (b) Uncovered Sector   (c) Total Labor Market

2. *Show the shift in the demand for labor in the covered sector and the resulting shift in the total demand curve.* The tax causes the demand curve for labor in the covered sector to shift downward from D_1^c to D_2^c. As a result, the total demand curve shifts inward to D^2.

3. *Determine the equilibrium wage using the total supply and demand curves, and then determine employment in the two sectors.* Workers shift between sectors until the new wage is equal in both sectors at w_2, which is determined by the intersection of the new total demand curve, D^2, and the total supply curve, S. Employment in the covered sector is L_c^2, and employment in the uncovered sector L_u^2.

4. *Compare the equilibria.* The tax causes the wage, total employment, and employment in the covered sector to fall and employment in the uncovered sector to rise.

Application

Urban Flight

Philadelphia and some other cities tax wages, while suburban areas do not (or they set much lower rates). Philadelphia collects a wage tax from residents whether or not they work in the city and from nonresidents who work in the city. Unfortunately, this situation drives people and jobs from Philadelphia to the suburbs. To offset such job losses, the city has enacted a gradual wage tax reduction program. During the program, the wage tax on Philadelphia's workers declined slowly over time from a high of 4.96% in 1983 through 1995 to 3.924% for residents and 3.495% for nonresidents in 2013.

A study conducted for Philadelphia estimated that if the city were to lower the wage tax by 0.4175 percentage points, 30,500 more people would work in the city. Local wage tax cuts are more effective than a federal cut because generally employees will not leave the country to avoid taxes, but they will consider moving to the burbs. Indeed, growth has been greater on the suburban side of City Line Avenue, which runs along Philadelphia's border, than on the side within city limits.

10.2 Trading Between Two People

Tariffs, quotas, and other restrictions on trade usually harm both importing and exporting nations (Chapter 9). The reason is that both parties to a voluntary trade benefit from that trade or else they would not have traded. Using a general-equilibrium model, we will show that free trade is Pareto efficient: After all voluntary trades have occurred, we cannot reallocate goods so as to make one person better off without harming another person. We first demonstrate that trade between two people has this Pareto property. We then show that the same property holds when many people trade using a competitive market.

Endowments

Suppose that Jane and Denise live near each other in the wilds of Massachusetts. A nasty snowstorm hits, isolating them. They must either trade with each other or consume only what they have at hand.

endowment
an initial allocation of goods

Collectively, they have 50 cords of firewood and 80 bars of candy and no way of producing more of either good. Jane's **endowment**—her initial allocation of goods—is 30 cords of firewood and 20 candy bars. Denise's endowment is 20 (= 50 − 30) cords of firewood and 60 (= 80 − 20) candy bars. So Jane has relatively more wood, and Denise has relatively more candy.

We show these endowments in Figure 10.3. Panels a and b are typical indifference curve diagrams (Chapters 4 and 5) in which we measure cords of firewood on the vertical axis and candy bars on the horizontal axis. Jane's endowment is e_j (30 cords of firewood and 20 candy bars) in panel a, and Denise's endowment is e_d in panel b. Both panels show the indifference curve through the endowment.

If we take Denise's diagram, rotate it, and put it on Jane's diagram, we obtain the box in panel c. This type of figure, called an Edgeworth box (after an English economist, Francis Ysidro Edgeworth), illustrates trade between two people with fixed endowments of two goods. We use this Edgeworth box to illustrate a general-equilibrium model in which we examine simultaneous trade in firewood and in candy.

Figure 10.3 Endowments in an Edgeworth Box

(a) Jane's endowment is e_j; she has 20 candy bars and 30 cords of firewood. She is indifferent between that bundle and the others that lie on her indifference curve I_j^1. (b) Denise is indifferent between her endowment, e_d (60 candy bars and 20 cords of wood), and the other bundles on I_d^1. (c) Their endowments are at e in the Edgeworth box formed by combining panels a and b. Jane prefers bundles in A and B to e. Denise prefers bundles in B and C to e. Thus, both prefer any bundle in area B to e.

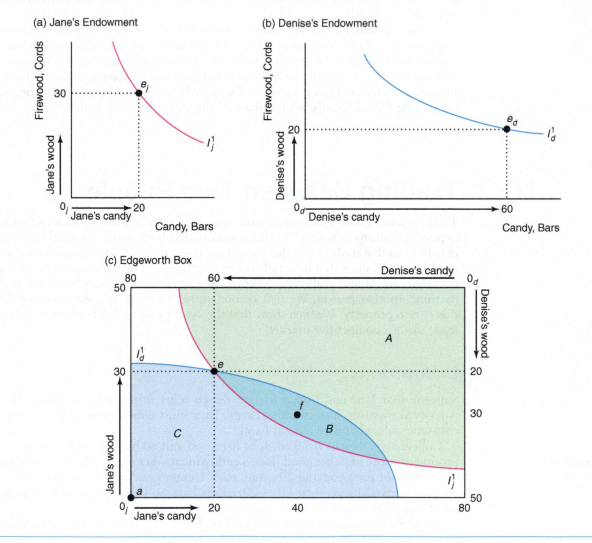

The height of the Edgeworth box represents 50 cords of firewood, and the length represents 80 candy bars, which are the combined endowments of Jane and Denise. Bundle e shows both endowments. Measuring from Jane's origin, 0_j, at the lower left of the diagram, we see that Jane has 30 cords of firewood and 20 candy bars at endowment e. Similarly, measuring from Denise's origin, 0_d, at the upper-right corner, we see that Denise has 60 bars of candy and 20 cords of firewood at e.

Mutually Beneficial Trades

Should Jane and Denise trade? The answer depends on their tastes, which are summarized by their indifference curves. We make four assumptions about their tastes and behavior:

- **Utility maximization.** Each person *maximizes* her *utility*.
- **Usual-shaped indifference curves.** Each person's indifference curves have the usual convex shape.
- **Nonsatiation.** Each person has strictly positive *marginal utility* for each good, so each person wants as much of the good as possible (neither person is ever satiated).
- **No interdependence.** Neither person's utility depends on the other's consumption (neither person gets pleasure or displeasure from the other's consumption), and neither person's consumption harms the other (one person's consumption of firewood does not cause smoke pollution that bothers the other person).

Figure 10.3 reflects these assumptions. In panel a, Jane's indifference curve, I_j^1, through her endowment point, e_j, is convex to her origin, 0_j. Jane is indifferent between e_j and any other bundle on I_j^1. She prefers bundles that lie above I_j^1 to e_j and prefers e_j to points that lie below I_j^1. Panel c also shows her indifference curve, I_j^1. The bundles that Jane prefers to her endowment are in the shaded areas A and B, which lie above her indifference curve, I_j^1.

Similarly, Denise's indifference curve, I_d^1, through her endowment is convex to her origin, 0_d, in the lower left of panel b. This indifference curve, I_d^1, is still convex to 0_d in panel c, but 0_d is in the upper right of the Edgeworth box. (It may help to turn this book around when viewing Denise's indifference curves in an Edgeworth box. Then again, possibly many points will be clearer if the book is held upside down.) The bundles Denise prefers to her endowment are in shaded areas B and C, which lie on the other side of her indifference curve I_d^1 from her origin 0_d (above I_d^1 if you turn the book upside down).

At endowment e in panel c, Jane and Denise can both benefit from a trade. Jane prefers bundles in A and B to e, and Denise prefers bundles in B and C to e, so both prefer bundles in area B to their endowment at e.

Suppose that they trade, reallocating goods from Bundle e to f. Jane gives up 10 cords of firewood for 20 more candy bars, and Denise gives up 20 candy bars for 10 more cords of wood. As Figure 10.4 illustrates, both gain from such a trade. Jane's indifference curve I_j^2 through allocation f lies above her indifference curve I_j^1 through allocation e, so she is better off at f than at e. Similarly, Denise's indifference curve I_d^2 through f lies above (if you hold the book upside down) her indifference curve I_d^1 through e, so she also benefits from the trade.

Now that they've traded to Bundle f, do Jane and Denise want to make further trades? To answer this question, we can repeat our analysis. Jane prefers all bundles above I_j^2, her indifference curve through f. Denise prefers all bundles above (when the book is held upside down) I_d^2 to f. However, they do not both prefer any other bundle because I_j^2 and I_d^2 are tangent at f. Neither Jane nor Denise wants to trade from f to a bundle such as e, which is below both of their indifference curves. Jane would love to trade from f to c, which is on her higher indifference curve I_j^3, but such a trade would make Denise worse off because this bundle is on a lower indifference curve, I_d^1. Similarly, Denise prefers b to f, but Jane does not. Thus, any move from f harms at least one of them.

The reason no further trade is possible at a bundle like f is that Jane's marginal rate of substitution (the slope of her indifference curve), MRS_j, between wood and

Figure 10.4   Contract Curve

The contract curve contains all the Pareto-efficient allocations. Any bundle for which Jane's indifference curve is tangent to Denise's indifference curve lies on the contract curve. At such a bundle, because no further trade is possible, and we can't reallocate goods to make one of them better off without harming the other. Starting at an endowment of *e*, Jane and Denise will trade to a bundle on the contract curve in area *B*: bundles between *b* and *c*. The table shows how they would trade to Bundle *f*.

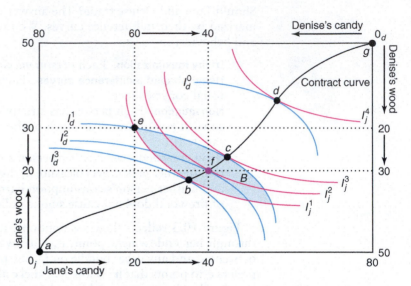

	Endowment, *e*		Trade		New Allocation, *f*	
	Wood	Candy	Wood	Candy	Wood	Candy
Jane	30	20	−10	+20	20	40
Denise	20	60	+10	−20	30	40

candy equals Denise's marginal rate of substitution, MRS_d. Jane's MRS_j is $-\frac{1}{2}$: She is willing to trade one cord of wood for two candy bars. Because Denise's indifference curve is tangent to Jane's, Denise's MRS_d must also be $-\frac{1}{2}$. When they both want to trade wood for candy at the same rate, they can't agree on further trades.

In contrast, at a bundle such as *e* where their indifference curves are not tangent, MRS_j does not equal MRS_d. Denise's MRS_d is $-\frac{1}{3}$, and Jane's MRS_j is -2. Denise is willing to give up one cord of wood for three more candy bars or to sacrifice three candy bars for one more cord of wood. If Denise offers Jane three candy bars for one cord of wood, Jane will accept because she is willing to give up two cords of wood for one candy bar. This example illustrates that trades are possible where indifference curves intersect because marginal rates of substitution are unequal.

To summarize, we can make four equivalent statements about allocation *f*:

1. The indifference curves of the two parties are tangent at *f*.
2. The parties' marginal rates of substitution are equal at *f*.
3. No further mutually beneficial trades are possible at *f*.
4. The allocation at *f* is Pareto efficient: One party cannot be made better off without harming the other.

Indifference curves are also tangent at Bundles *b*, *c*, and *d*, so these allocations, like *f*, are Pareto efficient. By connecting all such bundles, we draw the **contract curve**: the set of all Pareto-efficient bundles. The reason for this name is that only at these points are the parties unwilling to engage in further trades or contracts—these allocations are the final contracts. A move from any bundle on the contract curve would harm at least one person.

contract curve
the set of all Pareto-efficient bundles

Solved Problem 10.3

Are allocations a and g in Figure 10.4 part of the contract curve?

Answer

By showing that no mutually beneficial trades are possible at those points, demonstrate that those bundles are Pareto efficient. The allocation at which Jane has everything, allocation g, is on the contract curve because no mutually beneficial trade is possible: Denise has no goods to trade with Jane. As a consequence, we cannot make Denise better off without taking goods from Jane. Similarly, when Denise has everything, a, we can make Jane better off only by taking wood or candy from Denise and giving it to Jane.

Bargaining Ability

For every allocation off the contract curve, the contract curve has allocations that benefit at least one person. If they start at endowment e, Jane and Denise should trade until they reach a point on the contract curve between Bundles b and c in Figure 10.4. All the allocations in area B are beneficial. However, if they trade to any allocation in B that is not on the contract curve, further beneficial trades are possible because their indifference curves intersect at that allocation.

Where will they end up on the contract curve between b and c? That depends on who is better at bargaining. Suppose that Jane is much better at bargaining. Jane knows that the more she gets, the worse off Denise will be and that Denise will not agree to any trade that makes her worse off than she is at e. Thus, the best trade Jane can make is one that leaves Denise only as well off as at e, which are the bundles on I_d^1. If Jane could pick any point she wanted along I_d^1, she'd choose the bundle on her highest possible indifference curve, which is Bundle c, where I_j^3 is just tangent to I_d^1. After this trade, Denise is no better off than before, but Jane is much happier. By similar reasoning, if Denise is sufficiently better at bargaining, the final allocation will be at b.

10.3 Competitive Exchange

Most trading throughout the world occurs without one-on-one bargaining between people. When you go to the store to buy a bottle of shampoo, you read its posted price and then decide whether to buy it or not. You've probably never tried to bargain with the store's clerk over the price of shampoo: You're a price taker in the shampoo market.

If we don't know much about how Jane and Denise bargain, all we can say is that they will trade to some allocation on the contract curve. If we know the exact trading process they use, however, we can apply that process to determine the final allocation. In particular, we can examine the competitive trading process to determine the competitive equilibrium in a pure exchange economy.

In Chapter 9, we used a partial-equilibrium approach to show that one measure of welfare, W, is maximized in a competitive market in which many voluntary trades occur. We now use a general-equilibrium model to show that a competitive market has two desirable properties (which hold under fairly weak conditions):

- **The First Theorem of Welfare Economics:** *The competitive equilibrium is efficient.* Competition results in a Pareto-efficient allocation—no one can be made better off without making someone worse off—in all markets.
- **The Second Theorem of Welfare Economics:** *Any efficient allocations can be achieved by competition.* All possible efficient allocations can be obtained by competitive exchange, given an appropriate initial allocation of goods.

Competitive Equilibrium

When two people trade, they are unlikely to view themselves as price takers. However, if the market has a large number of people with tastes and endowments like Jane's and a large number of people with tastes and endowments like Denise's, each person is a price taker in the two goods. We can use an Edgeworth box to examine how such price takers would trade.

Because they can trade only two goods, each person needs to consider only the relative price of the two goods when deciding whether to trade. If the price of a cord of wood, p_w, is $2, and the price of a candy bar, p_c, is $1, then a candy bar costs half as much as a cord of wood: $p_c/p_w = \frac{1}{2}$. An individual can sell one cord of wood and use that money to buy two candy bars.

At the initial allocation, e, Jane has goods worth $80 = ($2 per cord × 30 cords of firewood) + ($1 per candy bar × 20 candy bars). At these prices, Jane could keep her endowment or trade to an allocation with 40 cords of firewood and no candy, 80 bars of candy and no firewood, or any combination in between as the price line (budget line) in panel a of Figure 10.5 shows. The price line is all the combinations of goods Jane could get by trading, given her endowment. The price line goes through point e and has a slope of $-p_c/p_w = -\frac{1}{2}$.

Given the price line, what bundle of goods will Jane choose? She wants to maximize her utility by picking the bundle where one of her indifference curves, I_j^2, is tangent to her budget or price line. Denise wants to maximize her utility by choosing a bundle in the same way.

In a competitive market, prices adjust until the quantity supplied equals the quantity demanded. An auctioneer could help determine the equilibrium. The auctioneer could call out relative prices and ask how much is demanded and how much is offered for sale at those prices. If demand does not equal supply, the auctioneer calls out

---

Figure 10.5 Competitive Equilibrium

The initial endowment is e. (a) If, along the price line facing Jane and Denise, $p_w = 2 and $p_c = 1, they trade to point f, where Jane's indifference curve, I_j^2, is tangent to the price line and to Denise's indifference curve, I_d^2. (b) No other price line results in an equilibrium. If $p_w = 1.33 and $p_c = 1, Denise wants to buy 12 (= 32 − 20) cords of firewood at these prices, but Jane wants to sell only 8 (= 30 − 22) cords. Similarly, Jane wants to buy 10 (= 30 − 20) candy bars, but Denise wants to sell 17 (= 60 − 43). Thus, these prices are not consistent with a competitive equilibrium.

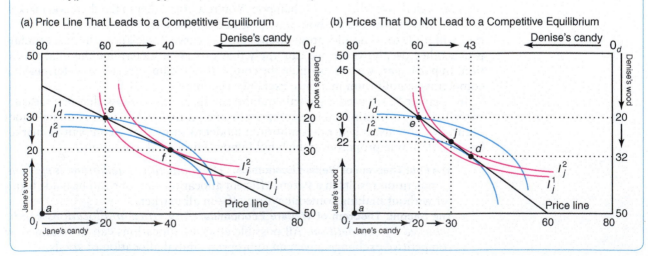

(a) Price Line That Leads to a Competitive Equilibrium

(b) Prices That Do Not Lead to a Competitive Equilibrium

another relative price. When demand equals supply, the transactions actually occur and the auction stops. At some ports, fishing boats sell their catch to fish wholesalers at a daily auction run in this manner.

Panel a shows that when candy costs half as much as wood, the quantity demanded of each good equals the quantity supplied. Jane (and every person like her) wants to sell 10 cords of firewood and use that money to buy 20 additional candy bars. Similarly, Denise (and everyone like her) wants to sell 20 candy bars and buy 10 cords of wood. Thus, the quantity of wood sold equals the quantity bought, and the quantity of candy demanded equals that supplied. We can see in the figure that the quantities demanded equal the quantities supplied because the optimal bundle for both types of consumers is the same, Bundle f.

At any other price ratio, the quantity demanded of each good would not equal the quantity supplied. For example, if the price of candy remained constant at $p_c = \$1$ per bar but the price of wood fell to $p_w = \$1.33$ per cord, the price line would be steeper, with a slope of $-p_c/p_w = -1/1.33 = -\frac{3}{4}$ in panel b. At these prices, Jane wants to trade to Bundle j and Denise wants to trade to Bundle d. Because Jane wants to buy 10 extra candy bars but Denise wants to sell 17 extra candy bars, the quantity supplied does not equal the quantity demanded, so this price ratio does not result in a competitive equilibrium when the endowment is e.

The Efficiency of Competition

In a competitive equilibrium, the indifference curves of both types of consumers are tangent at the same bundle on the price line. As a result, the slope (MRS) of each person's indifference curve equals the slope of the price line, so the slopes of the indifference curves are equal:

$$MRS_j = -\frac{p_c}{p_w} = MRS_d. \tag{10.1}$$

The marginal rates of substitution are equal across consumers in the competitive equilibrium, so the competitive equilibrium must lie on the contract curve. Thus, we have demonstrated the

First Theorem of Welfare Economics: *Any competitive equilibrium is Pareto efficient.*

The intuition for this result is that people (who face the same prices) make all the voluntary trades they want in a competitive market. Because no additional voluntary trades can occur, we cannot make someone better off without harming someone else. (If an involuntary trade occurs, at least one person is made worse off. A person who steals goods from another person—an involuntary exchange—gains at the expense of the victim.)

Obtaining Any Efficient Allocation Using Competition

Of the many possible Pareto-efficient allocations, the government may want to choose one. Can it achieve that allocation using the competitive market mechanism?

Our previous example illustrates that the competitive equilibrium depends on the endowment: the initial distribution of wealth. For example, if the initial endowment were a in panel a of Figure 10.5—where Denise has everything and Jane has nothing—the competitive equilibrium would be a because no trades would be possible.

Thus, for competition to lead to a particular allocation—say, *f*—the trading must start at an appropriate endowment. If the consumers' endowment is *f*, a Pareto-efficient point, their indifference curves are tangent at *f*, so no further trades occur. That is, *f* is a competitive equilibrium.

Many other endowments will also result in a competitive equilibrium at *f*. Panel a shows that the resulting competitive equilibrium is *f* if the endowment is *e*. In that figure, a price line goes through both *e* and *f*. If the endowment is any bundle along this price line—not just *e* or *f*—the competitive equilibrium is *f*, because only at *f* are the indifference curves tangent.

To summarize, any Pareto-efficient bundle *x* can be obtained as a competitive equilibrium if the initial endowment is *x*. That allocation can also be obtained as a competitive equilibrium if the endowment lies on a price line through *x*, where the slope of the price line equals the marginal rate of substitution of the indifference curves that are tangent at *x*. Thus, we've demonstrated the

> **Second Theorem of Welfare Economics:** *Any Pareto-efficient equilibrium can be obtained by competition, given an appropriate endowment.*

The first welfare theorem tells us that society can achieve efficiency by allowing competition. The second welfare theorem adds that society can obtain the particular efficient allocation it prefers based on its value judgments about equity by appropriately redistributing endowments.

10.4 Production and Trading

So far our discussion has been based on a pure exchange economy with no production. We now examine an economy in which a fixed amount of a single input can be used to produce two different goods.

Comparative Advantage

Jane and Denise can produce candy or chop firewood using their own labor. They differ, however, in how much of each good they produce from a day's work.

Production Possibility Frontier   Jane can produce either 3 candy bars or 6 cords of firewood in a day. By splitting her time between the two activities, she can produce various combinations of the two goods. If α is the fraction of a day she spends making candy and $1 - \alpha$ is the fraction cutting wood, she produces 3α candy bars and $6(1 - \alpha)$ cords of wood.

By varying α between 0 and 1, we trace out the line in panel a of Figure 10.6. This line is Jane's production possibility frontier, PPF_j, which shows the maximum combinations of wood and candy that she can produce from a given amount of input (Chapter 7). If Jane works all day using the best available technology (such as a sharp ax), she achieves efficiency in production and produces combinations of goods on PPF_j. If she sits around part of the day or does not use the best technology, she produces an inefficient combination of wood and candy inside PPF_j.

Marginal Rate of Transformation   The slope of the production possibility frontier is the *marginal rate of transformation (MRT)*.[5] The marginal rate of transformation

---

[5]In the standard consumer model (Chapter 4), the slope of a consumer's budget line is the marginal rate of transformation. That is, for a price-taking consumer who obtains goods by buying them, the budget line plays the same role as the production possibility frontier for someone who produces the two goods.

Figure 10.6 Comparative Advantage and Production Possibility Frontiers

(a) Jane's production possibility frontier, PPF_j, shows that in a day, she can produce 6 cords of firewood or 3 candy bars or any combination of the two. Her marginal rate of transformation (MRT) is -2. (b) Denise's production possibility frontier, PPF_d, has an MRT of $-\frac{1}{2}$. (c) Their joint production possibility frontier, PPF, has a kink at 6 cords of firewood (produced by Jane) and 6 candy bars (produced by Denise) and is concave to the origin.

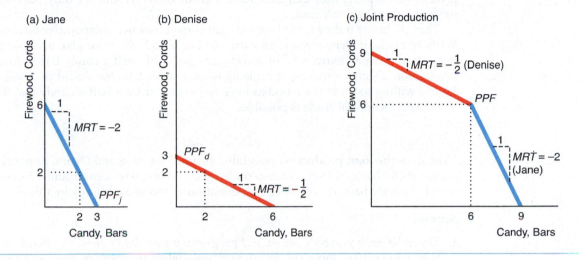

tells us how much more wood can be produced if the production of candy is reduced by one bar. Because Jane's PPF_j is a straight line with a slope of -2, her MRT is -2 at every allocation.

Denise can produce up to 3 cords of wood or 6 candy bars in a day. Panel b shows her production possibility function, PPF_d, with an $MRT = -\frac{1}{2}$. Thus, with a day's work, Denise can produce relatively more candy, and Jane can produce relatively more wood, as reflected by their differing marginal rates of transformation.

The marginal rate of transformation shows how much it costs to produce one good in terms of the forgone production of the other good. Someone with the ability to produce a good at a lower opportunity cost than someone else has a **comparative advantage** in producing that good. Denise has a comparative advantage in producing candy (she forgoes less in wood production to produce a given amount of candy), and Jane has a comparative advantage in producing wood.

By combining their outputs, they have the joint production possibility frontier PPF in panel c. If Denise and Jane spend all their time producing wood, Denise produces 3 cords and Jane produces 6 cords for a total of 9, which is where the joint PPF hits the wood axis. Similarly, if they both produce candy, they can jointly produce 9 bars. If Denise specializes in making candy and Jane specializes in cutting wood, they produce 6 candy bars and 6 cords of wood, a combination that appears at the kink in the PPF.

If they choose to produce a relatively large quantity of candy and a relatively small amount of wood, Denise produces only candy and Jane produces some candy and some wood. Jane chops the wood because that's her comparative advantage. The marginal rate of transformation in the lower portion of the PPF is Jane's, -2, because only she produces both candy and wood.

Similarly, if they produce little candy, Jane produces only wood and Denise produces some wood and some candy, so the marginal rate of transformation in the higher portion of the PPF is Denise's, $-\frac{1}{2}$. In short, the PPF has a kink at 6 cords of wood and 6 candy bars and is concave (bowed away from the origin).

comparative advantage
the ability to produce a good at a lower opportunity cost than someone else

Benefits of Trade Because of the difference in their marginal rates of transformation, Jane and Denise can benefit from a trade. Suppose that Jane and Denise like to consume wood and candy in equal proportions. If they do not trade, each produces 2 candy bars and 2 cords of wood in a day. If they agree to trade, Denise, who excels at making candy, spends all day producing 6 candy bars. Similarly, Jane, who has a comparative advantage at chopping, produces 6 cords of wood. If they split this production equally, they can each have 3 cords of wood and 3 candy bars—50% more than if they don't trade.

They do better if they trade because each person uses her comparative advantage. Without trade, if Denise wants an extra cord of wood, she must give up two candy bars. Producing extra cord of wood costs Jane only half a candy bar in forgone production. Denise is willing to trade up to two candy bars for a cord of wood, and Jane is willing to trade the wood as long as she gets at least half a candy bar. Thus, a mutually beneficial trade is possible.

Solved Problem 10.4

How does the joint production possibility frontier for Jane and Denise in panel c of Figure 10.6 change if they can also trade with Harvey, who can produce 5 cords of wood, 5 candy bars, or any linear combination of wood and candy in a day?

Answer

1. *Describe each person's individual production possibility frontier.* Panels a and b of Figure 10.6 show the production possibility frontiers of Jane and Denise. Harvey's production possibility frontier is a straight line that hits the firewood axis at 5 cords and the candy axis at 5 candy bars (not shown in Figure 10.6).

2. *Draw the joint PPF, by starting at the quantity on the horizontal axis that is produced if everyone specializes in candy and then connecting the individual production possibility frontiers in order of comparative advantage in chopping wood.* If all three produce candy, they make 14 candy bars in the figure. Jane has a comparative advantage at chopping wood over Harvey and Denise, and Harvey has a comparative advantage over Denise. Thus, Jane's production possibility frontier is

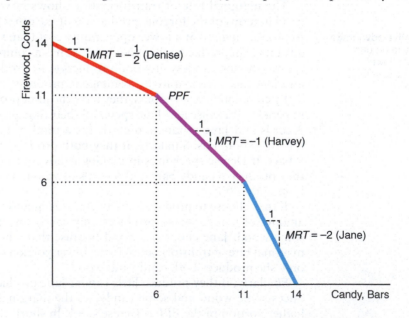

the first one (starting at the lower right), then comes Harvey's, and then Denise's. The resulting *PPF* is concave to the origin. (If we change the order of the individual frontiers, the resulting kinked line lies inside the *PPF*. Thus, the new line cannot be the joint production possibility frontier, which shows the maximum possible production from the available labor inputs.)

The Number of Producers If the only two ways of producing wood and candy are Denise's and Jane's methods with different marginal rates of transformation, the joint production possibility frontier has a single kink (panel c of Figure 10.6). If another method of production with a different marginal rate of transformation—Harvey's—is added, the joint production possibility frontier has two kinks (as in the figure in Solved Problem 10.4).

If many firms can produce candy and firewood with different marginal rates of transformation, the joint production possibility frontier has even more kinks. As the number of firms becomes very large, the *PPF* becomes a smooth curve that is concave to the origin, as in Figure 10.7.

Because the *PPF* is concave, the marginal rate of transformation decreases (in absolute value) as we move up the *PPF*. The *PPF* has a flatter slope at a, where the $MRT = -\frac{1}{2}$, than at b, where the $MRT = -1$. At a, giving up a candy bar leads to half a cord more wood production. In contrast, at b, where relatively more candy is produced, giving up producing a candy bar frees enough resources that an additional cord of wood can be produced.

The marginal rate of transformation along this smooth *PPF* tells us about the marginal cost of producing one good relative to the marginal cost of producing the

Figure 10.7 Optimal Product Mix

The optimal product mix, a, could be determined by maximizing an individual's utility by picking the allocation for which an indifference curve is tangent to the production possibility frontier. It could also be determined by picking the allocation where the relative competitive price, p_c/p_f, equals the slope of the *PPF*.

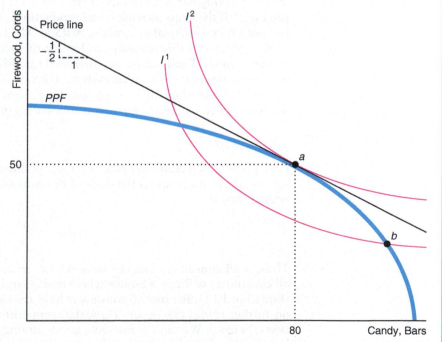

other good. The marginal rate of transformation is the negative of the ratio of the marginal cost of producing candy, MC_c, and wood, MC_w:

$$MRT = -\frac{MC_c}{MC_w}. \tag{10.2}$$

Suppose that at point a in Figure 10.7, a firm's marginal cost of producing an extra candy bar is \$1 and its marginal cost of producing an additional cord of firewood is \$2. As a result, the firm can produce one extra candy bar or half a cord of wood at a cost of \$1. The marginal rate of transformation is the negative of the ratio of the marginal costs, $-(\$1/\$2) = -\frac{1}{2}$. To produce one more candy bar, the firm must give up producing half a cord of wood.

Efficient Product Mix

Which combination of products along the *PPF* does society choose? If a single person were to decide on the product mix, that person would pick the allocation of wood and candy along the *PPF* that maximized his or her utility. A person with the indifference curves in Figure 10.7 would pick Allocation a, which is the point where the *PPF* touches indifference curve I^2.

Because I^2 is tangent to the *PPF* at a, that person's marginal rate of substitution (the slope of indifference curve I^2) equals the marginal rate of transformation (the slope of the *PPF*). The marginal rate of substitution, *MRS*, tells us how much a consumer is willing to give up of one good to get another. The marginal rate of transformation, *MRT*, tells us how much of one good we need to give up to produce more of another good.

If the *MRS* doesn't equal the *MRT*, the consumer will be happier with a different product mix. At Allocation b, the indifference curve I^1 intersects the *PPF*, so the *MRS* does not equal the *MRT*. At b, the consumer is willing to give up one candy bar to get a third of a cord of wood ($MRS = -\frac{1}{3}$), but firms can produce one cord of wood for every candy bar not produced ($MRT = -1$). Thus, at b, too little wood is being produced. If the firms increase wood production, the *MRS* will fall and the *MRT* will rise until they are equal at a, where $MRS = MRT = -\frac{1}{2}$.

We can extend this reasoning to look at the product mix choice of all consumers simultaneously. Each consumer's marginal rate of substitution must equal the economy's marginal rate of transformation, $MRS = MRT$, if the economy is to produce the optimal mix of goods for each consumer. How can we ensure that this condition holds for all consumers? One way is to use the competitive market.

Competition

Each price-taking consumer picks a bundle of goods so that the consumer's marginal rate of substitution equals the slope of the consumer's price line (the negative of the relative prices):

$$MRS = -\frac{p_c}{p_w}. \tag{10.3}$$

Thus, if all consumers face the same relative prices, in the competitive equilibrium, all consumers will buy a bundle where their marginal rates of substitution are equal (Equation 10.1). Because all consumers have the same marginal rates of substitution, no further trades can occur. Thus, the competitive equilibrium achieves *consumption efficiency*: We can't redistribute goods among consumers to make one consumer better off without harming another one. That is, the competitive equilibrium lies on the contract curve.

If candy and wood are sold by competitive firms, each firm sells a quantity of a candy for which its price equals its marginal cost,

$$p_c = MC_c, \tag{10.4}$$

and a quantity of wood for which its price and marginal cost are equal,

$$p_w = MC_w. \tag{10.5}$$

Taking the ratio of Equations 10.4 and 10.5, we find that in competition, $p_c/p_w = MC_c/MC_w$. From Equation 10.2, we know that the marginal rate of transformation equals $-MC_c/MC_w$, so

$$MRT = -\frac{p_c}{p_w}. \tag{10.6}$$

We can illustrate why firms want to produce where Equation 10.6 holds. Suppose that a firm were producing at b in Figure 10.7, where its MRT is -1, and that $p_c = \$1$ and $p_w = \$2$, so $-p_c/p_w = -\frac{1}{2}$. If the firm reduces its output by one candy bar, it loses $\$1$ in candy sales but makes $\$2$ more from selling the extra cord of wood, for a net gain of $\$1$. Thus, at b, where the $MRT < -p_c/p_w$, the firm should reduce its output of candy and increase its output of wood. In contrast, if the firm is producing at a, where the $MRT = -p_c/p_w = -\frac{1}{2}$, it has no incentive to change its behavior: The gain from producing a little more wood exactly offsets the loss from producing a little less candy.

Combining Equations 10.3 and 10.6, we find that in the competitive equilibrium, the MRS equals the relative prices, which equals the MRT:

$$MRS = -\frac{p_c}{p_w} = MRT.$$

Because competition ensures that the MRS equals the MRT, a competitive equilibrium achieves an *efficient product mix*: The rate at which firms can transform one good into another equals the rate at which consumers are willing to substitute between the goods, as reflected by their willingness to pay for the two goods.

By combining the production possibility frontier and an Edgeworth box, we can show the competitive equilibrium in both production and consumption. Suppose that firms produce 50 cords of firewood and 80 candy bars at a in Figure 10.8. The size of the Edgeworth box—the maximum amount of wood and candy available to consumers—is determined by point a on the *PPF*.

The prices consumers pay must equal the prices producers receive, so the price lines consumers and producers face must have the same slope of $-p_c/p_w$. In equilibrium, the price lines are tangent to each consumer's indifference curve at f and to the *PPF* at a.

In this competitive equilibrium, supply equals demand in all markets. The consumers buy the mix of goods at f. Consumers like Jane, whose origin, 0_j, is at the lower left, consume 20 cords of firewood and 40 candy bars. Consumers like Denise, whose origin is a at the upper right of the Edgeworth box, consume 30 ($= 50 - 20$) cords of firewood and 40 ($= 80 - 40$) candy bars.

The two key results concerning competition still hold in an economy with production. First, a competitive equilibrium is Pareto efficient, achieving efficiency in consumption and in output mix.[6] Second, any particular Pareto-efficient allocation

---

[6]Although we have not shown it here, competitive firms choose factor combinations so that their marginal rates of technical substitution between inputs equal the negative of the ratios of the relative factor prices (see Chapter 7). That is, competition also results in *efficiency in production*: We could not produce more of one good without producing less of another good.

Figure 10.8 Competitive Equilibrium

At the competitive equilibrium, the relative prices firms and consumers face are the same (the price lines are parallel), so the $MRS = -p_c/p_w = MRT$.

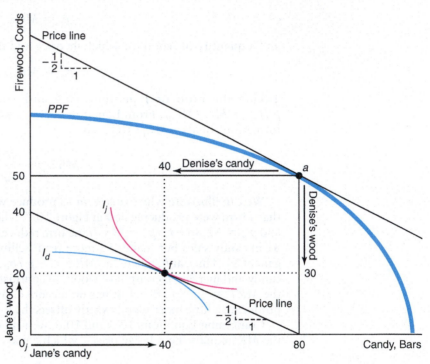

between consumers can be obtained through competition, given that the government chooses an appropriate endowment.

10.5 Efficiency and Equity

How well various members of society live depends on how society deals with efficiency (the size of the pie) and equity (how the pie is divided). The actual outcome depends on choices by individuals and on government actions.

Role of the Government

By altering the efficiency with which goods are produced and distributed and the endowment of resources, governments help determine how much is produced and how goods are allocated. By redistributing endowments or by refusing to do so, governments, at least implicitly, are making value judgments about which members of society should get relatively more of society's goodies.

Virtually every government program, tax, or action redistributes wealth. Proceeds from a British lottery, played mostly by lower-income people, support the "rich toffs" who attend the Royal Opera House at Covent Garden. Agricultural price support programs (Chapter 9) redistribute wealth to farmers from other taxpayers. Income taxes (Chapter 5) and food stamp programs (Chapter 4) redistribute income from the rich to the poor.

Application

The Wealth and Income of the 1%

In most countries, the richest people control a very large share of the wealth, but the degree of inequality varies substantially across the world. The richest 1% of adults—most of whom live in Europe and the United States—own 40% of global wealth, the richest 2% own 51%, the richest 5% have 71%, and the richest 10% account for 85% (Davies et al., 2007). In stark contrast, the bottom half of the world's adults own barely 1% of global assets.

Since the United States was founded, changes in the economy have altered the share of the nation's wealth held by the richest 1% of Americans (see the figure). An array of social changes—sometimes occurring during or after wars and often codified into new laws—have greatly affected the distribution of wealth. For example, the emancipation of slaves in 1863 transferred vast wealth—the labor of the former slaves—from rich Southern landowners to the poor freed slaves.

The share of wealth—the total assets owned—held by the richest 1% generally increased until the Great Depression, declined through the mid-1970s, and has increased substantially since then. Thus, greatest wealth concentration occurred in 1929 during the Great Depression and today, following the Great Recession. A key cause of the recent increased concentration of wealth is that the top income tax rate fell from 70% to less than 30% at the beginning of the Reagan administration, shifting more of the tax burden to the middle class.

In 2007, U.S. wealth was roughly equally divided among the wealthiest 1% of people (33.8%), the next 9% (37.7%), and the bottom 90% (31.5%). The poorest half owned only 2.5% of the wealth. However, just three years later, in 2010, the distribution was even more substantially skewed: the wealthiest 1% had 34.5% of the wealth, the next 9% had 40%, the bottom 90% owned 25.5%, and the bottom half had only 1.1%. Indeed, one in four households had a zero or negative net worth. The wealthiest 1% of U.S. households had a net worth that was 225 times greater than the median or typical household's net worth in 2009—the greatest ratio in history. According to Edward Wolff, the top 1% have $9 million or more in wealth.[7]

If income were equally distributed, the ratio of the share of income held by the "richest" 10% to that of the "poorest" 10% would equal 1. Instead, according to U.N. statistics for 2008, the top 10% had 168 times the income of the bottom 10% in Bolivia, 72 times as much in Haiti, 25 times in Mexico, 16 times in the United States, 14 times in the United Kingdom, 9 times in Canada, and 5 times in Japan.

Over the last 30 years, the share of income—current earnings—of the top 1% doubled in the United States and many other English-speaking countries, but went up by less in France, Germany, and Japan (Alvaredo et al., 2013). The U.S. income distribution is highly skewed, but less than the wealth distribution. In 2011, the top 1% of U.S. earners (who made over $367,000 per year) made 19.8% of total earnings, while the next 9% had 28.4%, so the top 10% of earners (over $111,000 per year) captured 48.2% of total income (Saez, 2013).[8] In 2012, a typical S&P 500 chief executive officer (CEO) earned 354 times that of the average U.S. worker. That is, the CEO earns almost as much on the first day of the year as a typical worker earns for the entire year.

---

[7]According to *Forbes*, the wealth of Bill Gates, the wealthiest American (and the second wealthiest person in the world), was $67 billion in 2013 (down from $85 billion in 1999). Mexican Carlos Slim Helu and his family's wealth was $73 billion—the highest in the world.

[8]The U.S. federal government transfers 5% of total national household income from the rich to the poor: 2% using cash assistance such as general welfare programs and 3% using in-kind transfers such as food stamps and school lunch programs. Poor households receive 26% of their income from cash assistance and 18% from in-kind assistance. The U.S. government gives only 0.1% of its gross national product to poor nations. In contrast, Britain gives 0.26% and the Netherlands transfers 0.8%.

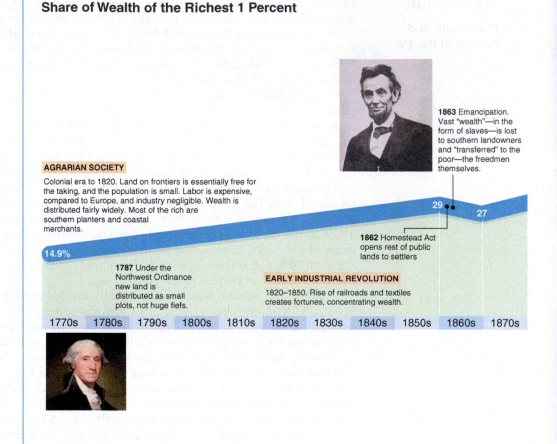

Share of Wealth of the Richest 1 Percent

AGRARIAN SOCIETY

Colonial era to 1820. Land on frontiers is essentially free for the taking, and the population is small. Labor is expensive, compared to Europe, and industry negligible. Wealth is distributed fairly widely. Most of the rich are southern planters and coastal merchants.

14.9%

1863 Emancipation. Vast "wealth"—in the form of slaves—is lost to southern landowners and "transferred" to the poor—the freedmen themselves.

29

27

1862 Homestead Act opens rest of public lands to settlers

1787 Under the Northwest Ordinance new land is distributed as small plots, not huge fiefs.

EARLY INDUSTRIAL REVOLUTION

1820–1850. Rise of railroads and textiles creates fortunes, concentrating wealth.

| 1770s | 1780s | 1790s | 1800s | 1810s | 1820s | 1830s | 1840s | 1850s | 1860s | 1870s |

Efficiency

Many economists and political leaders make the value judgment that governments *should* use the Pareto principle and prefer allocations by which someone is made better off if no one else is harmed. That is, governments should allow voluntary trades, encourage competition, and otherwise try to prevent problems that reduce efficiency.

We can use the Pareto principle to rank allocations or government policies that alter allocations. The Pareto criterion ranks allocation x over allocation y if some people are better off at x and no one else is harmed. If that condition is met, we say that x is Pareto superior to y.

The Pareto principle cannot always be used to compare allocations. If society is faced with many possible Pareto-efficient allocations, it must make a value judgment based on interpersonal comparisons to choose between them. Issues of interpersonal comparisons often arise when we evaluate various government policies. If both

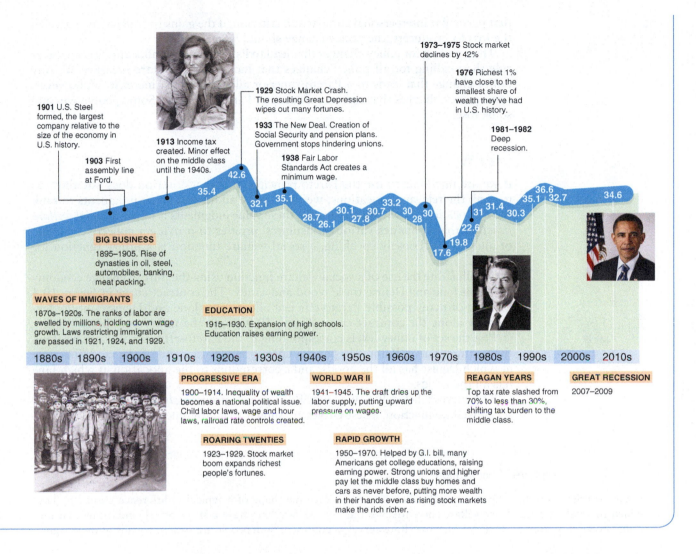

1901 U.S. Steel formed, the largest company relative to the size of the economy in U.S. history.

1903 First assembly line at Ford.

1913 Income tax created. Minor effect on the middle class until the 1940s.

1929 Stock Market Crash. The resulting Great Depression wipes out many fortunes.

1933 The New Deal. Creation of Social Security and pension plans. Government stops hindering unions.

1938 Fair Labor Standards Act creates a minimum wage.

1973–1975 Stock market declines by 42%

1976 Richest 1% have close to the smallest share of wealth they've had in U.S. history.

1981–1982 Deep recession.

42.6
35.4
32.1   35.1
28.7   30.1   30.7   33.2   30   30
26.1   27.8   30   28   19.8
31   31.4   35.1   32.7
22.6   30.3
17.6   36.6   34.6

BIG BUSINESS
1895–1905. Rise of dynasties in oil, steel, automobiles, banking, meat packing.

WAVES OF IMMIGRANTS
1870s–1920s. The ranks of labor are swelled by millions, holding down wage growth. Laws restricting immigration are passed in 1921, 1924, and 1929.

EDUCATION
1915–1930. Expansion of high schools. Education raises earning power.

| 1880s | 1890s | 1900s | 1910s | 1920s | 1930s | 1940s | 1950s | 1960s | 1970s | 1980s | 1990s | 2000s | 2010s |

PROGRESSIVE ERA
1900–1914. Inequality of wealth becomes a national political issue. Child labor laws, wage and hour laws, railroad rate controls created.

ROARING TWENTIES
1923–1929. Stock market boom expands richest people's fortunes.

WORLD WAR II
1941–1945. The draft dries up the labor supply, putting upward pressure on wages.

RAPID GROWTH
1950–1970. Helped by G.I. bill, many Americans get college educations, raising earning power. Strong unions and higher pay let the middle class buy homes and cars as never before, putting more wealth in their hands even as rising stock markets make the rich richer.

REAGAN YEARS
Top tax rate slashed from 70% to less than 30%, shifting tax burden to the middle class.

GREAT RECESSION
2007–2009

allocation *x* and allocation *y* are Pareto efficient, we cannot use this criterion to rank them. For example, if Denise has all the goods in *x* and Jane has all of them in *y*, we cannot rank these allocations using the Pareto rule.

Suppose that when a country ends a ban on imports and allows free trade, domestic consumers benefit by many times more than domestic producers suffer. Nonetheless, this policy change does not meet the Pareto efficiency criterion that someone is made better off without anyone suffering. However, the government could adopt a more complex policy that meets the Pareto criterion. Because consumers benefit by more than producers suffer, the government could take enough of the gains from free trade from consumers to compensate the producers so that no one is harmed and some or all people benefit.

The government rarely uses policies by which winners subsidize losers, however. If such subsidization does not occur, additional value judgments involving interpersonal comparisons must be made before deciding whether to adopt the policy.

We've been using a welfare measure, W = consumer surplus + producer surplus, that weights benefits and losses to consumers and producers equally. On the basis of that particular interpersonal comparison criterion, if the gains to consumers outweigh the loss to producers, the policy change should be made.

Thus, calling for policy changes that lead to Pareto-superior allocations is a weaker rule than calling for all policy changes that increase the welfare measure W. Any policy change that leads to a Pareto-superior allocation must increase W; however, some policy changes that increase W are not Pareto superior: Some people win and some lose.

Equity

If we are unwilling to use the Pareto principle or if that criterion does not allow us to rank the relevant allocations, we must make additional value judgments to rank these allocations. A way to summarize these value judgments is to use a *social welfare function* that combines various consumers' utilities to provide a collective ranking of allocations. Loosely speaking, a social welfare function is a utility function for society.

We illustrate the use of a social welfare function using the pure exchange economy in which Jane and Denise trade wood and candy. The contract curve in Figure 10.4 consists of many possible Pareto-efficient allocations. Jane and Denise's utility levels vary along the contract curve. Figure 10.9 shows the utility possibility frontier (*UPF*): the set of utility levels corresponding to the Pareto-efficient allocations along the contract curve. Point *a* in panel a corresponds to the end of the contract curve at which Denise has all the goods, and *c* corresponds to the allocation at which Jane has all the goods.

The curves labeled W^1, W^2, and W^3 in panel a are *isowelfare curves* based on the social welfare function. These curves are similar to indifference curves for individuals.

Figure 10.9 Welfare Maximization

Society maximizes welfare by choosing the allocation for which the highest possible isowelfare curve touches the utility possibility frontier, *UPF*. (a) The isowelfare curves have the shape of a typical indifference curve. (b) The isowelfare lines have a slope of −1, indicating that the utilities of both people are treated equally at the margin.

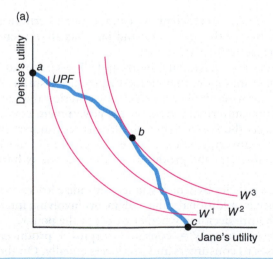

(a)

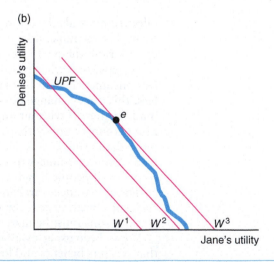

(b)

They summarize all the allocations with identical levels of welfare. Society maximizes its welfare at point *b*.

Who decides on the welfare function? In most countries, government leaders make decisions about which allocations are most desirable. These officials may believe that transferring money from wealthy people to poor people raises welfare, or vice versa. When government officials choose a particular allocation, they are implicitly or explicitly judging which consumers are relatively deserving and hence should receive more goods than others.

Voting In a democracy, important government policies that determine the allocation of goods are made by voting. Such democratic decision making is often difficult because people fundamentally disagree on how issues should be resolved and which groups of people should be favored.

In Chapter 4, we assumed that consumers could order all bundles of goods in terms of their preferences (completeness) and that their rank over goods was transitive.[9] Suppose now that consumers have preferences over allocations of goods across consumers. One possibility, as we assumed earlier, is that individuals care only about how many goods they receive—they don't care about how much others have. Another possibility is that because of envy, charity, pity, love, or other interpersonal feelings, individuals do care about how much everyone has.[10]

Let *a* be a particular allocation of goods that describes how much of each good an individual has. Each person can rank this allocation relative to Allocation *b*. For instance, individuals know whether they prefer an allocation by which everyone has equal amounts of all goods to another allocation by which people who work hard—or those of a particular skin color or religion—have relatively more goods than others.

Through voting, individuals express their rankings. One possible voting system requires that before the vote is taken, everyone agrees to be bound by the outcome in the sense that if a majority of people prefer Allocation *a* to Allocation *b*, then *a* is socially preferred to *b*.

Using majority voting to determine which allocations are preferred by society sounds reasonable, doesn't it? Such a system might work well. For example, if all individuals have the same transitive preferences, the social ordering has the same transitive ranking as that of each individual.

Unfortunately, sometimes voting does not work well, and the resulting social ordering of allocations is not transitive. To illustrate this possibility, suppose that three people have the individually transitive preferences in Table 10.2. Individual 1 prefers Allocation *a* to Allocation *b* to Allocation *c*. The other two individuals have different preferred orderings. Two out of three of these individuals prefer *a* to *b*; two out of three prefer *b* to *c*; and two out of three prefer *c* to *a*. Thus, voting leads to nontransitive social preferences, even though the preferences of each individual are transitive. As a result, voting does not produce a clearly defined socially preferred outcome. A majority of people prefers some other allocation to any particular allocation. Compared to Allocation *a*, a majority prefers *c*. Similarly, a majority prefers *b* over *c*, and a majority prefers *a* over *b*.

---

[9]The transitivity (or *rationality*) assumption is that a consumer's preference over bundles is consistent in the sense that if the consumer weakly prefers Bundle *a* to Bundle *b* and weakly prefers Bundle *b* to Bundle *c*, the consumer weakly prefers Bundle *a* to Bundle *c*.

[10]To an economist, love is nothing more than interdependent utility functions. Thus, it's a mystery how each successive generation of economists is produced.

Table 10.2 Preferences over Allocations of Three People

	Individual 1	Individual 2	Individual 3
First choice	*a*	*b*	*c*
Second choice	*b*	*c*	*a*
Third choice	*c*	*a*	*b*

If people have this type of ranking of allocations, the chosen allocation will depend crucially on the order in which the vote is taken. Suppose that these three people first vote on whether they prefer *a* or *b* and then compare the winner to *c*. Because a majority prefers *a* to *b* in the first vote, they will compare *a* to *c* in the second vote, and *c* will be chosen. If instead they first compared *c* to *a* and the winner to *b*, then *b* will be chosen. Thus, the outcome depends on the political skill of various factions in determining the order of voting.

Similar problems arise with other types of voting schemes. Kenneth Arrow (1951), who received a Nobel Prize in Economics in part for his work on social decision making, proved a startling and depressing result about democratic voting. This result is often referred to as Arrow's Impossibility Theorem. Arrow suggested that a socially desirable decision-making system, or social welfare function, should satisfy the following criteria:

■ Social preferences should be complete (Chapter 4) and transitive, like individual preferences.

■ If everyone prefers Allocation *a* to Allocation *b*, *a* should be socially preferred to *b*.

■ Society's ranking of *a* and *b* should depend only on individuals' ordering of these two allocations, not on how they rank other alternatives.

■ Dictatorship is not allowed; social preferences must not reflect the preferences of only a single individual.

Although each of these criteria seems reasonable—indeed, innocuous—Arrow proved that it is impossible to find a social decision-making rule that always satisfies all of these criteria. His result indicates that democratic decision making may fail—not that democracy must fail. After all, if everyone agrees on a ranking, these four criteria are satisfied.

If society is willing to give up one of these criteria, a democratic decision-making rule can guarantee that the other three criteria are met. For example, if we give up the third criterion, often referred to as the independence of irrelevant alternatives, certain complicated voting schemes in which individuals rank their preferences can meet the other criteria.

Application

How You Vote Matters

The 15 members of a city council must decide whether to build a new road (*R*), repair the high school (*H*), or install new street lights (*L*). Each councilor lists the options in order of preference. Six favor *L* to *H* to *R*; five prefer *R* to *H* to *L*; and four want *H* over *R* over *L*.

One of the proponents of street lights suggests a plurality vote where everyone would cast a single vote for his or her favorite project. Plurality voting would result in six votes for *L*, five for *R*, and four for *H*, so that lights would win.

"Not so fast," responds a council member who favors roads. Given that *H* was the least favorite first choice, he suggests a run-off between *L* and *R*. Since the four members whose first choice was *H* prefer *R* to *L*, roads would win by nine votes to six.

A supporter of schools is horrified by these self-serving approaches to voting. She calls for pairwise comparisons. A majority of 10 would choose *H* over *R*, and 9 would prefer *H* to *L*. Consequently, although the high school gets the least number of first-place votes, it has the broadest appeal in pairwise comparisons.

Finally, suppose the council uses a voting method developed by Jean-Charles de Borda in 1770 (to elect members to the Academy of Sciences in Paris), where, in an *n*-person race, a person's first choice gets *n* votes, the second choice gets *n* − 1, and so forth. Here, *H* gets 34 votes, *R* receives 29, and *L* trails with 27, and so the high school project is backed. Thus, the outcome of an election or other vote may depend on the voting procedures used.

Methods like Borda's are called *instant runoff* voting. This method of voting is used at many educational institutions such as Arizona State University, the College of William and Mary, Harvard, Southern Illinois University at Carbondale, the University of California Los Angeles, University of Michigan, University of Missouri, and Wheaton College. Instant runoffs are used to elect members of the Australian House of Representatives, the President of India, and the President of Ireland. Instant runoff voting is used in many U.S. cities and counties such as Cambridge, Massachusetts; Davis, California; Oakland, California; Minneapolis, Minnesota; Pierce County, Washington; and San Francisco, California. It is also used to elect mayors in London and Wellington, New Zealand.

In the last few years, President Obama, Senator John McCain, consumer advocate Ralph Nader, and others have called for some form of ranked voting. In 2011, at U.K. Prime Minister Gordon Brown's impetus, a national referendum on instant runoffs was held (but lost). However, an instant runoff vote was used to elect the leader of the Liberal Party of Canada in 2013.

Social Welfare Functions How would you rank various allocations if you were asked to vote? Philosophers, economists, newspaper columnists, politicians, radio talk show hosts, and other deep thinkers have suggested various rules that society might use to decide which allocations are better than others. Basically, all these systems answer the question of which individuals' preferences should be given more weight in society's decision making. Determining how much weight to give to the preferences of various members of society is usually the key step in determining a social welfare function.

Probably the simplest and most egalitarian rule is that every member of society is given exactly the same bundle of goods. If no further trading is allowed, this rule results in complete equality in the allocation of goods.

Jeremy Bentham (1748–1832) and his followers (including John Stuart Mill), the utilitarian philosophers, suggested that society should maximize the sum of the utilities of all members of society. Their social welfare function is the sum of the utilities of every member of society. The utilities of all people in society are given equal weight.[11] If U_i is the utility of Individual *i* and *n* is the number of people, the utilitarian welfare function is

$$W = U_1 + U_2 + \cdots + U_n.$$

---

[11]It is difficult to compare utilities across individuals because the scaling of utilities across individuals is arbitrary (Chapters 4 and 9). A rule that avoids this utility comparison is to maximize a welfare measure that equally weights consumer surplus and producer surplus, which are denominated in dollars.

This social welfare function may not lead to an egalitarian distribution of goods. Indeed, under this system, an allocation is judged superior, all else the same, if people who get the most pleasure from consuming certain goods are given more of those goods.

Panel b of Figure 10.9 shows some isowelfare lines corresponding to the utilitarian welfare function. These lines have a slope of −1 because the utilities of both parties are weighted equally. In the figure, welfare is maximized at *e*.

A generalization of the utilitarian approach assigns different weights to various individuals' utilities. If the weight assigned to Individual *i* is α_i, this generalized utilitarian welfare function is

$$W = \alpha_1 U_1 + \alpha_2 U_2 + \cdots + \alpha_n U_n.$$

Society could give greater weight to adults, hardworking people, or those who meet other criteria. Under South Africa's former apartheid system, the utilities of people with white skin were given more weight than those of people with other skin colors.

John Rawls (1971), a philosopher at Harvard, believed that society should maximize the well-being of the worst-off member of society, who is the person with the lowest level of utility. In the social welfare function, all the weight should be placed on the utility of the person with the lowest utility level. The Rawlsian welfare function is

$$W = \min\{U_1, U_2, \cdots, U_n\}.$$

Rawls' rule leads to a relatively egalitarian distribution of goods.

One final rule, which is frequently espoused by various members of Congress and by wealthy landowners in less-developed countries, is to maintain the status quo. Exponents of this rule believe that the current allocation is the best possible allocation. They argue against any reallocation of resources from one individual to another. Under this rule, the final allocation is likely to be very unequal. Why else would the wealthy want it?

All of these rules or social welfare functions reflect value judgments in which interpersonal comparisons are made. Because each reflects value judgments, we cannot compare them on scientific grounds.

Efficiency Versus Equity

Given a particular social welfare function, *society might prefer an inefficient allocation to an efficient one*. We can show this result by comparing two allocations. In Allocation *a*, you have everything and everyone else has nothing. This allocation is Pareto efficient: We can't make others better off without harming you. In Allocation *b*, everyone has an equal amount of all goods. Allocation *b* is not Pareto efficient: I would be willing to trade all my zucchini for just about anything else. Despite Allocation *b*'s inefficiency, most people probably prefer *b* to *a*.

Although society might prefer an inefficient Allocation *b* to an efficient Allocation *a*, according to most social welfare functions, society would prefer some efficient allocation to *b*. Suppose that Allocation *c* is the competitive equilibrium that would be obtained if people were allowed to trade starting from Endowment *b*, in which everyone has an equal share of all goods. By the utilitarian social welfare functions, Allocation *b* might be socially preferred to Allocation *a*, but Allocation *c* is certainly socially preferred to *b*. After all, if everyone is as well off or better off in Allocation *c* than in *b*, *c* must be better than *b* regardless of weights on individuals' utilities. According to the egalitarian rule, however, *b* is preferred to *c* because only strict equality matters. Thus, by most—but not all—of the well-known social welfare functions, society has an efficient allocation that is socially preferred to an inefficient allocation.

Competitive equilibrium may not be very equitable even though it is Pareto efficient. Consequently, societies that believe in equity may tax the rich to give to the poor. If the money taken from the rich is given directly to the poor, society moves from one Pareto-efficient allocation to another.

Sometimes, however, in an attempt to achieve greater equity, efficiency is reduced. For example, advocates for the poor argue that providing public housing to the destitute leads to an allocation that is superior to the original competitive equilibrium. This reallocation isn't efficient: The poor view themselves as better off receiving an amount of money equal to what the government spends on public housing. They could spend the money on the type of housing they like—rather than the type the government provides—or they could spend some of the money on food or other goods.[12]

Unfortunately, conflicts between a society's goal of efficiency and its goal of achieving an equitable allocation frequently occur. Even when the government redistributes money from one group to another, it incurs significant redistribution costs. If tax collectors and other government bureaucrats could be put to work producing rather than redistributing, total output would increase. Similarly, income taxes discourage people from working as hard as they otherwise would (Chapter 5). Nonetheless, probably few people believe that the status quo is optimal and that the government should engage in no redistribution at all (though some members of Congress seem to believe that we should redistribute from the poor to the rich).

Challenge Solution

Anti-Price Gouging Laws

We can use a multimarket model to analyze the Challenge questions about the effects of a binding price ceiling that applies to some states but not to others. The figure shows what happens if a binding price ceiling is imposed in the covered sector—those states that have anti-price gouging laws—and not in the uncovered sector—the other states.

We first consider what happens in the absence of the anti-price gouging laws. The demand curve for the entire market, D^1 in panel c, is the horizontal sum of the demand curve in the covered sector, D^c in panel a, and the demand curve in the uncovered sector, D^u in panel b. In panel c, the national supply curve S intersects the national demand curve D^1 at e_1 where the equilibrium price is p and the quantity is Q_1.

When the covered sector imposes a price ceiling at $\bar{p}$, which is less than p, it chops off the top part of the D^c above $\bar{p}$. Consequently, the new national demand curve, D^2, equals the uncovered sector's demand curve D^u above $\bar{p}$, is horizontal at $\bar{p}$, and is the same as D^1 below $\bar{p}$. The supply curve S intersects the new demand curve in the horizontal section at e_2, where the quantity is Q_2.[13] However, at a price of $\bar{p}$, national demand is Q, so the shortage is $Q - Q_2$.

---

[12]Letting the poor decide how to spend their income is efficient by our definition, even if they spend it on "sin goods" such as cigarettes, liquor, or illicit drugs. We made a similar argument about food stamps in Chapter 4.

[13]If $\bar{p}$ were low enough that the supply curve hit D_2 is the downward-sloping section, suppliers would sell in only the uncovered sector. For example, in 2009 when West Virginia imposed anti-price gouging laws after flooding occurred in some parts of the state, Marathon Oil halted sales to independent gasoline retailers there and sold its gasoline in other states. Similarly, until price controls in Zimbabwe were lifted in 2009 (see the Chapter 2 Application "Price Controls Kill"), many Zimbabwean firms had stopped selling goods in their own country and instead sold them in neighboring countries.

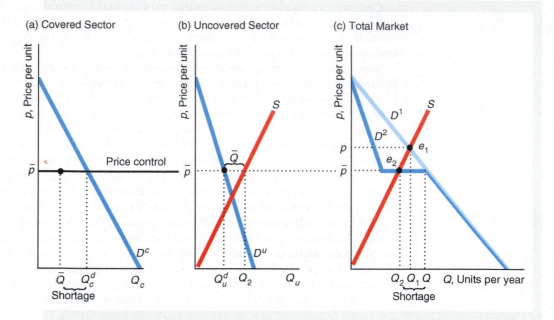

(a) Covered Sector (b) Uncovered Sector (c) Total Market

How the available supply Q_2 is allocated between customers in the covered and uncovered sectors determines in which sector the shortage occurs. If some of the customers in the uncovered sector cannot buy as much as they want at $\bar{p}$, they can offer to pay a slightly higher price to obtain extra supplies. Because of the price control, customers in the covered sector cannot match a higher price. Consequently, customers in the uncovered sector can buy as much as they want, Q_u^d, at $\bar{p}$, as panel b shows.

For convenience, panel b also shows the national supply curve. At $\bar{p}$, the gap between the quantity demanded in the uncovered sector, Q_u^d, and the quantity that firms are willing to sell, Q_2, is $\overline{Q}$. Firms sell this extra amount, $\overline{Q}$, in the covered sector. That quantity is less than the amount demanded, Q_c^d, so the shortage in the covered sector is $Q_c^d - \overline{Q} \; (= Q - Q_2)$.

In conclusion, the anti-price gouging law lowers the price in both sectors to $\bar{p}$, which is less than the price p that would otherwise be charged. The consumers in the uncovered states do not suffer from a shortage in contrast to consumers in the covered sector. Thus, anti-gouging laws benefit residents of neighboring jurisdictions who can buy as much as they want at a lower price. Residents of jurisdictions with anti-gouging laws who can buy the good at a lower price benefit, but those who cannot buy the good are harmed.

Summary

1. **General Equilibrium.** A shock to one market may have a spillover effect in another market. A general-equilibrium analysis takes account of the direct effects of a shock in a market and the spillover effects in other markets. In contrast, a partial-equilibrium analysis (such as we used in earlier chapters) looks only at one market and ignores the spillover effects in other markets. The partial-equilibrium and general-equilibrium effects can differ.

2. **Trading Between Two People.** If people make all the trades they want, the resulting equilibrium will be Pareto efficient: By moving from this equilibrium, we cannot make one person better off without harming another person. At a Pareto-efficient equilibrium, the marginal rates of substitution between people are equal because their indifference curves are tangent.

3. **Competitive Exchange.** Competition, in which all traders are price takers, leads to an allocation in which the ratio of relative prices equals the marginal rates of substitution of each person. Thus, *every competitive equilibrium is Pareto efficient.* Moreover, *any Pareto-efficient equilibrium can be obtained by competition, given an appropriate endowment.*

4. **Production and Trading.** When one person can produce more of one good and another person can produce more of another good using the same inputs, trading can result in greater combined production.

5. **Efficiency and Equity.** The Pareto efficiency criterion reflects a value judgment that a change from one allocation to another is desirable if it makes someone better off without harming anyone else. This criterion does not allow all allocations to be ranked, because some people may be better off with one allocation and others may be better off with another. Majority voting may not result in a consensus nor produce a transitive ordering of allocations. Economists, philosophers, and others have proposed many criteria for ranking allocations, as summarized in welfare functions. Society may use such a welfare function to choose among Pareto-efficient (or other) allocations.

Questions

*All questions are available on MyEconLab; * = answer appears at the back of this book; **A** = algebra problem.*

1. General Equilibrium

1.1 The demand functions for the only two goods in the economy are $Q_1 = 10 - 2p_1 + p_2$ and $Q_2 = 10 - 2p_2 + p_1$. Five units of each good are available for sale. Solve for the equilibrium: $p_1, p_2, Q_1,$ and Q_2. What is the general equilibrium? (*Hint*: See Solved Problem 10.1.) **A**

1.2 The demand functions for each of two goods depend on the prices of the goods, p_1 and p_2: $Q_1 = 15 - 3p_1 + p_2$ and $Q_2 = 6 - 2p_2 + p_1$. However, each supply curve depends on only its own price: $Q_1 = 2 + p_1$ and $Q_2 = 1 + p_2$. Solve for the equilibrium: $p_1, p_2, Q_1,$ and Q_2. (*Hint*: See Solved Problem 10.1.) **A**

1.3 A central city imposes a rent control law that places a binding ceiling on the rent that can be charged for an apartment. The suburbs of this city do not have a rent control law. What happens to the rental prices in the suburbs and to the equilibrium number of apartments in the total metropolitan area, in the city, and in the suburbs? For simplicity, assume that people are indifferent as to whether they live in the city or the suburbs. (*Hint*: See Solved Problem 10.2.)

*1.4 What is the effect of a subsidy of s per hour on labor in only one sector of the economy on the equilibrium wage, total employment, and employment in the covered and uncovered sectors? (*Hint*: See Solved Problem 10.2.)

1.5 Initially, all workers are paid a wage of w_1 per hour. The government taxes the cost of labor by t per hour only in the "covered" sector of the economy (if the wage received by workers in the covered sector is w_2 per hour, firms pay $w_2 + t$ per hour). Show how the wages in the covered and uncovered sectors are determined in the post-tax equilibrium. Compared to the pre-tax equilibrium, what happens to total employment, L, employment in the covered sector, L_c, and employment in the uncovered sector, L_u? (*Hint*: See Solved Problem 10.2.)

1.6 Suppose that the government gives a fixed subsidy of T per firm in one sector of the economy to encourage firms to hire more workers. What is the effect on the equilibrium wage, total employment, and employment in the covered and uncovered sectors? (*Hint*: See Solved Problem 10.2.)

1.7 Competitive firms located in Africa sell their output only in Europe and the United States (which do not produce the good themselves). The industry's supply curve is upward sloping. Europe puts a tariff of t per unit on the good but the United States does not. What is the effect of the tariff on total quantity of the good sold, the quantity sold in Europe and in the United States, and equilibrium price(s)? (*Hint*: See Solved Problem 10.2.)

1.8 A competitive industry with an upward-sloping supply curve sells Q_h of its product in its home country and Q_f in a foreign country, so the total quantity it sells is $Q = Q_h + Q_f$. No one else produces this product. Shipping is costless. Determine the equilibrium price and quantity in each country. Now the foreign government imposes a binding quota, Q ($< Q_f$ at the original price). What happens to prices and quantities in both the home and the foreign markets? (*Hint*: See Solved Problem 10.2.)

1.9 The demand curve in Sector 1 of the labor market is $L_1 = a - bw$. The demand curve in Sector 2 is $L_2 = c - dw$. The supply curve of labor for the entire market is $L = e + fw$. In equilibrium, $L_1 + L_2 = L$.

a. Solve for the equilibrium with no minimum wage.

b. Solve for the equilibrium at which the minimum wage is $\underline{w}$ in Sector 1 ("the covered sector") only. (*Hint*: See Solved Problem 10.2.)

c. Solve for the equilibrium at which the minimum wage $\underline{w}$ applies to the entire labor market.

1.10 Philadelphia collects an ad valorem tax on its residents' earnings (see the Application "Urban Flight"), unlike the surrounding areas. Show the effect of this tax on the equilibrium wage, total employment, employment in Philadelphia, and employment in the surrounding areas. (*Hint*: See Solved Problem 10.2.)

1.11 For years, Buffalo wings, barbequed chicken wings, have been popular at bars and restaurants, especially during football season. Now, restaurants across the country are selling *boneless wings*, a small chunk of chicken breast that is fried and smothered in sauce. Part of the reason for this substitution is that wholesale chicken prices have turned upside down. The once-lowly wing now sells for more than the former star of poultry parts, the skinless, boneless chicken breast (William Neuman, "'Boneless' Wings, the Cheaper Bite," *New York Times*, October 13, 2009). Use multimarket supply-and-demand diagrams to explain why prices have changed in the chicken breast and wings "markets." Note that the relationship between wings and breasts is fixed (at least, I hope so).

2. Trading Between Two People

2.1 Initially, Michael has 10 candy bars and 5 cookies, and Tony has 5 candy bars and 10 cookies. After trading, Michael has 12 candy bars and 3 cookies. In an Edgeworth box, label the initial Allocation *A* and the new Allocation *B*. Draw some indifference curves that are consistent with this trade being optimal for both Michael and Tony.

2.2 Two people in a pure exchange economy have identical utility functions. Will they ever want to trade?

2.3 Two people trade two goods that they cannot produce. Suppose that one consumer's indifference curves are bowed away from the origin—the usual type of curves—but the other's are concave to the origin. In an Edgeworth box, show that a point of tangency between the two consumers' indifference curves is not a Pareto-efficient bundle. (*Hint*: Identify another allocation that is Pareto superior.)

*2.4 In a pure exchange economy with two goods, G and H, the two traders have Cobb-Douglas utility functions. Amos' utility is $U_a = (G_a)^\alpha (H_a)^{1-\alpha}$ and Elise's is $U_e = (G_e)^\beta (H_e)^{1-\beta}$. What are their marginal rates of substitution? Between them, Amos and Elise own 100 units of G and 50 units of H. Thus, if Amos has G_a and H_a, Elise has $G_e = 100 - G_a$ and $H_e = 50 - H_a$. Solve for their contract curve.

2.5 Adrienne and Sarah consume pizza, Z, and cola, C. Adrienne's utility function is $U_A = Z_A C_A$, and Sarah's is $Z_D^{0.5} C_D^{0.5}$. Adrienne's marginal utility of pizza is $MU_Z^A = C_A$. Similarly, $MU_C^A = Z_A$, $MU_Z^D = \frac{1}{2} Z_D^{-0.5} C_D^{0.5}$, and $MU_C^D = \frac{1}{2} Z_D^{0.5} C_D^{-0.5}$. Their endowments are $Z_A = 10$, $C_A = 20$, $Z_D = 20$, $C_D = 10$.

a. What are the marginal rates of substitution for each person?

b. What is the formula for the contract curve? Draw an Edgeworth box and indicate the contract curve. **A**

2.6 Explain why point *e* in Figure 10.4 is not on the contract curve. (*Hint*: See Solved Problem 10.3.)

3. Competitive Exchange

3.1 In an Edgeworth box, illustrate that a Pareto-efficient equilibrium, point *a*, can be obtained by competition, given an appropriate endowment. Do so by identifying an initial endowment point, *b*, located somewhere other than at point *a*, such that the competitive equilibrium (resulting from competitive exchange) is *a*. Explain.

4. Production and Trading

*4.1 In panel c of Figure 10.6, the joint production possibility frontier is concave to the origin. When the two individual production possibility frontiers are combined, however, the resulting *PPF* could have been drawn so that it was convex to the origin. How do we know which of these two ways of drawing the *PPF* to use?

4.2 Suppose that Britain can produce 10 units of cloth or 5 units of food per day (or any linear combination) with available resources and Greece can produce 2 units of food per day or 1 unit of cloth (or any combination). Britain has an *absolute advantage* over Greece in producing both goods. Does it still make sense for these countries to trade?

*4.3 Pat and Chris can spend their nonleisure time working either in the marketplace or at home (preparing dinner, taking care of children, doing repairs). In the marketplace, Pat earns a higher wage, $w_p = \$20$, than Chris, $w_c = \$10$. Discuss how living together is likely to affect how much each of them works in the marketplace. In particular, discuss what effect the marriage has on their individual and combined budget constraint (Chapters 4 and 5) and their labor-leisure choice (Section 5.5, "Deriving Labor Supply Curves"). In your discussion, take into account the theory of comparative advantage.

4.4 If Jane and Denise have identical, linear production possibility frontiers, can they benefit by trading? Why? (*Hint*: See Solved Problem 10.4.)

4.5 Modify Solved Problem 10.4 to show that the *PPF* more closely approximates a quarter of a circle with five people. One of these new people, Bill, can produce five cords of wood, or four candy bars, or any linear combination. The other, Helen, can produce four cords of wood, or five candy bars, or any linear combination.

4.6 Mexico and the United States can both produce food and toys. Mexico has 100 workers and the United States has 300 workers. If they do not trade, the United States consumes 10 units of food and 10 toys, and Mexico consumes 5 units of food and 1 toy. The following table shows how many workers are necessary to produce each good:

	Mexico	United States
Workers per unit of food	10	10
Workers per toy	50	20

    a. In the absence of trade, how many units of food and toys can the United States produce? How many can Mexico produce?

b. Which country has a comparative advantage in producing food? In producing toys?

c. Draw the production possibility frontier for each country and show where the two produce without trade. Label the axes accurately.

d. Draw the production possibility frontier with trade.

e. Show that both countries can benefit from trade. (*Hint*: See Solved Problem 10.4.) **A**

5. Efficiency and Equity

5.1 A society consists of two people with utilities U_1 and U_2, and the social welfare function is $W = \alpha_1 U_1 + \alpha_1 U_2$. Draw a utility possibility frontier similar to the ones in Figure 10.9. When social welfare is maximized, show that as α_1/α_2 increases, Person 1 benefits and Person 2 is harmed. **A**

5.2 Give an example of a social welfare function that leads to the egalitarian allocation that everyone should be given exactly the same bundle of goods.

5.3 Suppose that society used the "opposite" of a Rawlsian welfare function: It tried to maximize the well-being of the best-off member of society. Write this welfare function. What allocation maximizes welfare in this society?

6. Challenge

6.1 Modify the figure in the Challenge Solution to show how much would be sold in both sectors in the absence of anti-price gouging laws. Discuss how these quantities differ from those that result from implementing such laws.

6.2 Peaches are sold in a competitive market to two types of demanders: consumers who eat fresh peaches and firms that can them. If the government places a binding price ceiling on only peaches sold directly to consumers, what happens to prices and quantities sold for each use?

11 Monopoly

Monopoly: one parrot.

A firm that creates a new drug may receive a patent that gives it the right to be the monopoly or sole producer of the drug for up to 20 years. As a result, the firm can charge a price much greater than its marginal cost of production. For example, one of the world's best-selling drugs, the heart medication Plavix, sold for about $7 per pill though it costs about 3¢ per pill to produce. Prices for drugs used to treat rare diseases are often very high. Soliris, a drug used to treat a rare blood disorder, costs over $400,000 per year.

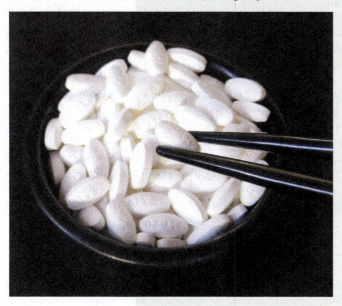

Recently, firms have increased their prices substantially for specialty drugs in response to perceived changes in willingness to pay by consumers and their insurance companies. Once, H.P. Acthar Gel, an anti-inflammatory, was used to treat relatively common ailments such as gout and sold for $50 a vial. Now it is a crucial anti-seizure drug, which is used to treat children with a rare and severe form of epilepsy. In 2007, its price increased from $1,600 to $23,000 per vial. The price reached $28,000 by 2013. Steve Cartt, an executive at the drug's manufacturer, Questcor, said that this price increase was based on a review of the prices of other specialty drugs and estimates of how much of the price insurers and employers would be willing to bear. Two courses of Acthar treatment for a severely ill 3-year-old girl, Reegan Schwartz, cost her father's health plan about $226,000. Acthar earned $126 million in revenue in the first quarter of 2013.

In 2013, 107 U.S. drug patents expired, including major products such as Cymbalta and OxyContin. When a patent for a highly profitable drug expires, many firms enter the market and sell generic (equivalent) versions of the brand-name drug.[1] Generics account for nearly 70% of all U.S. prescriptions and half of Canadian prescriptions.

---

[1]Under the 1984 Hatch-Waxman Act, the U.S. government allows a firm to sell a generic product after a brand-name drug's patent expires if the generic-drug firm can prove that its product delivers the same amount of active ingredient or drug to the body in the same way as the brand-name product. Sometimes the same firm manufactures both a brand-name drug and an identical generic drug, so the two have identical ingredients. Generics produced by other firms usually differ in appearance and name from the original product and may have different nonactive ingredients but the same active ingredients.

The U.S. Congress, when it originally passed a law permitting generic drugs to quickly enter a market after a patent expires, expected that patent expiration would subsequently lead to sharp declines in drug prices. If consumers view the generic product and the brand-name product as perfect substitutes, both goods will sell for the same price, and entry by many firms will drive the price down to the competitive level. Even if consumers view the goods as imperfect substitutes, one might expect the price of the brand-name drug to fall.

However, the prices of many brand-name drugs have increased after their patents expired and generics entered the market. The generic drugs are relatively inexpensive, but the brand-name drugs often continue to enjoy a significant market share and sell for high prices. Regan (2008), who studied the effects of generic entry on post-patent price competition for 18 prescription drugs, found an average 2% increase in brand-name prices. Studies based on older data have found up to a 7% average increase. Why do some brand-name prices rise after the entry of generic drugs?

monopoly
the only supplier of a good that has no close substitute

A **monopoly** is the only supplier of a good that has no close substitute. Monopolies have been common since ancient times. In the fifth century B.C., the Greek philosopher Thales gained control of most of the olive presses during a year of exceptionally productive harvests. Similarly, the ancient Egyptian pharaohs controlled the sale of food. In England, until Parliament limited the practice in 1624, kings granted monopoly rights called royal charters or patents to court favorites. Today, nearly every country grants a *patent*—an exclusive right to sell that lasts for a limited period of time—to an inventor of a new product, process, substance, or design. Until 1999, the U.S. government gave one company the right to be the sole registrar of Internet domain names. When first introduced, Apple's iPod had a virtual monopoly in the hard-disk, music player market, and Apple's iPad had a near monopoly in the tablet market.

A monopoly can *set* its price—it is not a price taker like a competitive firm. A monopoly's output is the market output, and the demand curve a monopoly faces is the market demand curve. Because the market demand curve is downward sloping, the monopoly (unlike a competitive firm) doesn't lose all its sales if it raises its price. As a consequence, the monopoly sets its price above marginal cost to maximize its profit. Consumers buy less at this high monopoly price than they would at the competitive price, which equals marginal cost.

In this chapter, we examine six main topics

1. **Monopoly Profit Maximization.** Like all firms, a monopoly maximizes its profit by setting its price or output so that its marginal revenue equals its marginal cost.

2. **Market Power.** How much the monopoly's price is above its marginal cost depends on the shape of the demand curve it faces.

3. **Market Failure Due to Monopoly Pricing.** By setting its price above marginal cost, a monopoly creates a deadweight loss.

4. **Causes of Monopoly.** Two important causes of monopoly are cost factors and government actions that restrict entry, such as patents.

5. **Government Actions That Reduce Market Power.** The welfare loss of a monopoly can be reduced or eliminated if the government regulates the price the monopoly charges or allows other firms to enter the market.

6. **Networks, Dynamics, and Behavioral Economics.** If its current sales affect a monopoly's future demand curve, a monopoly that maximizes its long-run profit may choose not to maximize its short-run profit.

11.1 Monopoly Profit Maximization

All firms, including competitive firms and monopolies, maximize their profits by setting *marginal revenue equal to marginal cost* (Chapter 8). We already know how to derive the marginal cost curve of a monopoly from its cost curve (Chapter 7). We now derive the monopoly's marginal revenue curve and then use the marginal revenue and marginal cost curves to examine the monopoly's profit-maximizing behavior.

Marginal Revenue

A firm's marginal revenue curve depends on its demand curve. We will show that a monopoly's marginal revenue curve lies below its demand curve at any positive quantity because its demand curve is downward sloping.

Marginal Revenue and Price A firm's demand curve shows the price, p, it receives for selling a given quantity, q. The price is the *average revenue* the firm receives, so a firm's revenue is $R = pq$.

A firm's *marginal revenue*, MR, is the change in its revenue from selling one more unit. A firm that earns ΔR more revenue when it sells Δq extra units of output has a marginal revenue (Chapter 8) of

$$MR = \Delta R / \Delta q.$$

If the firm sells exactly one more unit, $\Delta q = 1$, its marginal revenue is $MR = \Delta R$.

Although the marginal revenue curve is horizontal for a competitive firm, it is downward sloping for a monopoly. The competitive firm in panel a of Figure 11.1 faces a horizontal demand curve at the market price, p_1. Because its demand curve is horizontal, the competitive firm can sell another unit of output without dropping its price. As a result, the marginal revenue it receives from selling the last unit of output is the market price.

Initially, the competitive firm sells q units of output at the market price of p_1, so its revenue, R_1, is area A, which is a rectangle that is $p_1 \times q$. If the firm sells one more unit, its revenue is $R_2 = A + B$, where area B is $p_1 \times 1 = p_1$. The competitive firm's marginal revenue equals the market price:

$$\Delta R = R_2 - R_1 = (A + B) - A = B = p_1.$$

A monopoly faces a downward-sloping market demand curve, as in panel b of Figure 11.1. (We've called the number of units of output a firm sells q and the output of all the firms in a market, or market output, Q. Because a monopoly is the only firm in the market, q and Q do not differ, so we use Q to describe both the firm's and the market's output.) The monopoly, which is initially selling Q units at p_1, can sell one extra unit only if the price falls to p_2.

The monopoly's initial revenue, $p_1 \times Q$, is $R_1 = A + C$. When it sells the extra unit, its revenue, $p_2 \times (Q + 1)$, is $R_2 = A + B$. Thus, its marginal revenue is

$$\Delta R = R_2 - R_1 = (A + B) - (A + C) = B - C.$$

The monopoly sells the extra unit of output at the new price, p_2, so its extra revenue is $B = p_2 \times 1 = p_2$. The monopoly loses the difference between the new price and the original price, $\Delta p = (p_2 - p_1)$, on the Q units it originally sold: $C = \Delta p \times Q$. Thus, the monopoly's marginal revenue, $B - C = p_2 - C$, is less than the price it charges by an amount equal to area C.

Figure 11.1 Average and Marginal Revenue

The demand curve shows the average revenue or price per unit of output sold. (a) The competitive firm's marginal revenue, area B, equals the market price, p_1. (b) The monopoly's marginal revenue is less than the price p_2 by area C (the revenue lost due to a lower price on the Q units originally sold).

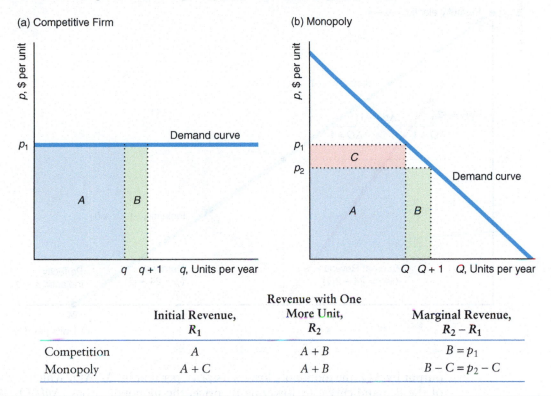

(a) Competitive Firm   (b) Monopoly

	Initial Revenue, R_1	Revenue with One More Unit, R_2	Marginal Revenue, $R_2 - R_1$
Competition	A	$A + B$	$B = p_1$
Monopoly	$A + C$	$A + B$	$B - C = p_2 - C$

The competitive firm in panel a does not lose an area C from selling an extra unit because its demand curve is horizontal. It is the downward slope of the monopoly's demand curve that causes its marginal revenue to be less than its price.

Marginal Revenue Curve Thus, *the monopoly's marginal revenue curve lies below the demand curve* at every positive quantity. In general, the relationship between the marginal revenue and demand curves depends on the shape of the demand curve.

For all *linear* demand curves, the relationship between the marginal revenue and demand curve is the same. The marginal revenue curve is a straight line that starts at the same point on the vertical (price) axis as the demand curve but has twice the slope of the demand curve, so the marginal revenue curve hits the horizontal (quantity) axis at half the quantity as the demand curve (see Appendix 11A). In Figure 11.2, the demand curve has a slope of −1 and hits the horizontal axis at 24 units, while the marginal revenue curve has a slope of −2 and hits the horizontal axis at 12 units.

Deriving the Marginal Revenue Curve To derive the monopoly's marginal revenue curve, we write an equation summarizing the relationship between price and marginal revenue that panel b of Figure 11.1 illustrates. (Because we want this equation to hold at all prices, we drop the subscripts from the prices.) For a monopoly to increase its

Figure 11.2   Elasticity of Demand and Total, Average, and Marginal Revenue

The demand curve (or average revenue curve), $p = 24 - Q$, lies above the marginal revenue curve, $MR = 24 - 2Q$. Where the marginal revenue equals zero, $Q = 12$, the elasticity of demand is $\varepsilon = -1$.

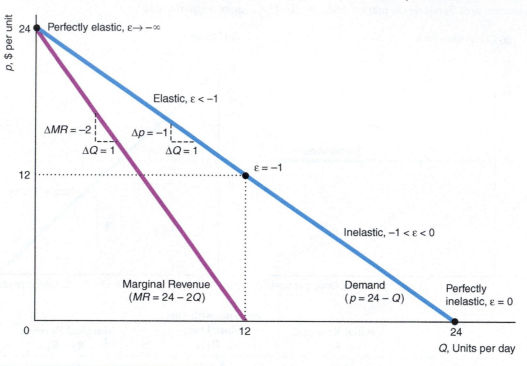

output by ΔQ, the monopoly lowers its price per unit by $\Delta p/\Delta Q$, which is the slope of the demand curve. By lowering its price, the monopoly loses $(\Delta p/\Delta Q) \times Q$ on the units it originally sold at the higher price (area C), but it earns an additional p on the extra output it now sells (area B). Thus, the monopoly's marginal revenue is[2]

$$MR = p + \frac{\Delta p}{\Delta Q} Q. \tag{11.1}$$

Because the slope of the monopoly's inverse demand curve, $\Delta p/\Delta Q$, is negative, the last term in Equation 11.1, $(\Delta p/\Delta Q)Q$, is negative. Equation 11.1 confirms that the price is greater than the marginal revenue, which equals p plus a negative term.

Solved Problem 11.1   Derive the marginal revenue curve when the monopoly faces the linear inverse demand function,

$$p = 24 - Q, \tag{11.2}$$

in Figure 11.2. How does the slope of the marginal revenue curve compare to the slope of the inverse demand curve?

---

[2]Revenue is $R(Q) = p(Q)Q$, where $p(Q)$, the inverse demand function, shows how price changes as quantity increases along the demand curve. Differentiating, we find that the marginal revenue is $MR = dR(Q)/dQ = p(Q) + [dp(Q)/dQ]Q$.

Answer

1. *Use the demand curve to calculate how much the price consumers are willing to pay falls if quantity increases by one unit.* According to the inverse demand function, Equation 11.2, the price consumers are willing to pay falls by 1 if quantity increases by one unit, so the slope of the inverse demand curve is $\Delta p/\Delta Q = -1$ (Chapter 2).[3]

2. *Use Equations 11.1 and 11.2 and the slope of the inverse demand curve to derive the marginal revenue function.* We obtain the marginal revenue function for this monopoly by substituting into Equation 11.1 the slope of the inverse demand function, $\Delta p/\Delta Q = -1$, and replacing p with $24 - Q$ (using Equation 11.2):

$$MR = p + \frac{\Delta p}{\Delta Q}Q = (24 - Q) + (-1)Q = 24 - 2Q. \qquad (11.3)$$

The MR curve in Figure 11.2 is a plot of Equation 11.3.

3. *Use Equation 11.3 to determine the slope of the marginal revenue curve.* Using the same type of calculation as in Step 1, we can use Equation 11.3 to show that the slope of this marginal revenue curve is $\Delta MR/\Delta Q = -2$, so the marginal revenue curve is twice as steeply sloped as is the demand curve.

Marginal Revenue and Price Elasticity of Demand The marginal revenue at any given quantity depends on the demand curve's height (the price) and shape. The shape of the demand curve at a particular quantity is described by the price elasticity of demand (Chapter 3), $\varepsilon = (\Delta Q/Q)/(\Delta p/p) < 0$, which is the percentage by which quantity demanded falls as the price increases by 1%.

At a given quantity, the marginal revenue equals the price times a term involving the elasticity of demand:[4]

$$MR = p\left(1 + \frac{1}{\varepsilon}\right). \qquad (11.4)$$

According to Equation 11.4, marginal revenue is closer to price as demand becomes more elastic. Where the demand curve hits the price axis ($Q = 0$), the demand curve is perfectly elastic, so the marginal revenue equals price: $MR = p$.[5] Where the demand elasticity is unitary, $\varepsilon = -1$, marginal revenue is zero: $MR = p[1 + 1/(-1)] = 0$. Marginal revenue is negative where the demand curve is inelastic, $-1 < \varepsilon \le 0$.

---

[3]In general, if the linear inverse demand curve is $p = a - bQ$ and the quantity increases from Q to $Q + \Delta Q$, then the new price is $p^* = a - b(Q + \Delta Q) = a - bQ - b\Delta Q = p - b\Delta Q$, so $\Delta p = p^* - p = -b\Delta Q$. By dividing both sides of this expression by ΔQ, we find that the slope of the demand curve is $\Delta p/\Delta Q = -b$. Here, $b = 1$, so $\Delta p/\Delta Q = -1$. Equivalently, we can use calculus to determine that the slope of the general linear demand curve is $dp/dQ = -b$.

[4]By multiplying the last term in Equation 11.1 by $p/p \,(= 1)$ and using algebra, we can rewrite the expression as

$$MR = p + p\frac{\Delta p}{\Delta Q}\frac{Q}{p} = p\left[1 + \frac{1}{(\Delta Q/\Delta p)(p/Q)}\right].$$

The last term in this expression is $1/\varepsilon$, because $\varepsilon = (\Delta Q/\Delta p)(p/Q)$.

[5]As ε approaches $-\infty$ (perfectly elastic demand), the $1/\varepsilon$ term approaches zero, so $MR = p(1 + 1/\varepsilon)$ approaches p.

With the demand function in Equation 11.2, $\Delta Q/\Delta p = -1$, so the elasticity of demand is $\varepsilon = (\Delta Q/\Delta p)(p/Q) = -p/Q$. Table 11.1 shows the relationship among quantity, price, marginal revenue, and elasticity of demand for this linear example. As Q approaches 24, ε approaches 0, and marginal revenue is negative. As Q approaches zero, the demand becomes increasingly elastic, and marginal revenue approaches the price.

Choosing Price or Quantity

Any firm maximizes its profit by operating where its marginal revenue equals its marginal cost. Unlike a competitive firm, a monopoly can adjust its price, so it has a choice of setting its price *or* its quantity to maximize its profit. (A competitive firm sets its quantity to maximize profit because it cannot affect market price.)

The monopoly is constrained by the market demand curve. Because the demand curve slopes down, the monopoly faces a trade-off between a higher price and a lower quantity or a lower price and a higher quantity. The monopoly chooses the point on the demand curve that maximizes its profit. Unfortunately for the monopoly, it cannot set both its quantity and its price. If it could do so, the monopoly would choose an extremely high price and an extremely high output level—above its demand curve—and would become exceedingly wealthy.

If the monopoly sets its price, the demand curve determines how much output it sells. If the monopoly picks an output level, the demand curve determines the price. Because the monopoly wants to operate at the price and output at which its profit is maximized, it chooses the same profit-maximizing solution whether it sets the price or output. In the rest of this chapter, we assume that the monopoly sets quantity.

Table 11.1 Quantity, Price, Marginal Revenue, and Elasticity for the Linear Inverse Demand Curve $p = 24 - Q$

Quantity, Q	Price, p	Marginal Revenue, MR	Elasticity of Demand, $\varepsilon = -p/Q$	
0	24	24	$-\infty$	▲
1	23	22	−23	
2	22	20	−11	
3	21	18	−7	
4	20	16	−5	more elastic
5	19	14	−3.8	
6	18	12	−3	
7	17	10	−2.43	
8	16	8	−2	
9	15	6	−1.67	
10	14	4	−1.4	
11	13	2	−1.18	
12	12	0	−1	less elastic
13	11	−2	−0.85	
...	...	...	...	
23	1	−22	−0.043	
24	0	−24	0	▼

Graphical Approach

All firms, including monopolies, use a two-step analysis to determine the output level that maximizes their profit (Chapter 8). First, the firm determines the output, Q^*, at which it makes the highest possible profit—the output at which its marginal revenue equals its marginal cost. Second, the firm decides whether to produce Q^* or shut down.

Profit-Maximizing Output   To illustrate how a monopoly chooses its output to maximize its profit, we continue to use the same linear demand and marginal revenue curves but add a linear marginal cost curve in panel a of Figure 11.3. Panel b shows the corresponding profit curve. The profit curve reaches its maximum at 6 units of output, where marginal profit—the slope of the profit curve—is zero. Because *marginal profit is marginal revenue minus marginal cost* (Chapter 8), marginal profit is zero where marginal revenue equals marginal cost. In panel a, marginal revenue equals marginal cost at 6 units. The price on the demand curve at that quantity is 18. Thus, the monopoly maximizes its profit at point *e*, where it sells 6 units per day at a price of 18 per unit.

Why does the monopoly maximize its profit by producing where its marginal revenue equals its marginal cost? At smaller quantities, the monopoly's marginal revenue is greater

Figure 11.3 Maximizing Profit

(a) At $Q = 6$, where marginal revenue, MR, equals marginal cost, MC, profit is maximized. The rectangle shows that the profit is $60, where the height of the rectangle is the average profit per unit, $p - AC = \$18 - \$8 = \$10$, and the length is the number of units, 6. (b) Profit is maximized at $Q = 6$ (where marginal revenue equals marginal cost).

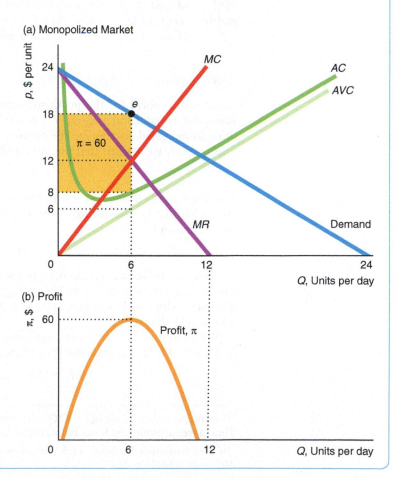

than its marginal cost, so its marginal profit is positive—the profit curve is upward sloping. By increasing its output, the monopoly raises its profit. Similarly, at quantities greater than 6 units, the monopoly's marginal cost is greater than its marginal revenue, so its marginal profit is negative, and the monopoly can increase its profit by reducing its output.

As Figure 11.2 illustrates, the marginal revenue curve is positive where the elasticity of demand is elastic, is zero at the quantity where the demand curve has a unitary elasticity, and is negative at larger quantities where the demand curve is inelastic. Because the marginal cost curve is never negative, the marginal revenue curve can only intersect the marginal cost curve where the marginal revenue curve is positive, in the range in which the demand curve is elastic. That is, *a monopoly's profit is maximized in the elastic portion of the demand curve.* (In our example, profit is maximized at $Q = 6$, where the elasticity of demand is -3.) *A profit-maximizing monopoly never operates in the inelastic portion of its demand curve.*

Shutdown Decision   A monopoly shuts down to avoid making a loss in the short run if its price is below its average variable cost at its profit-maximizing (or loss-minimizing) quantity (Chapter 8). In the long run, the monopoly shuts down if the price is less than its average cost.

In the short-run example in Figure 11.3, the average variable cost, $AVC = 6$, is less than the price, $p = 18$, at the profit-maximizing output, $Q = 6$, so the firm chooses to produce. Price is also above average cost at $Q = 6$, so the monopoly makes a positive profit.[6] At the profit-maximizing quantity of 6 units, the price is $p(6) = 18$ and the average cost is $AC(6) = 8$. As a result, the profit, $\pi = 60$, is the golden rectangle with a height equal to the average profit per unit, $p(6) - AC(6) = 18 - 8 = 10$, and a width of 6 units.

Mathematical Approach

We can also solve for the profit-maximizing quantity mathematically. We already know the demand and marginal revenue functions for this monopoly. We need to determine its marginal cost curve. The monopoly's cost is a function of its output, $C(Q)$. In Figure 11.3, we assume that the monopoly faces a short-run cost function of

$$C(Q) = Q^2 + 12, \tag{11.5}$$

where Q^2 is the monopoly's variable cost as a function of output and 12 is its fixed cost (Chapter 7). Given this cost function, Equation 11.5, the monopoly's marginal cost function is[7]

$$MC = 2Q. \tag{11.6}$$

This marginal cost curve is a straight line through the origin with a slope of 2 in panel a. The average variable cost is $AVC = Q^2/Q = Q$, so it is a straight line through the origin with a slope of 1. The average cost is $AC = C/Q = (Q^2 + 12)/Q = Q + 12/Q$, which is U-shaped.

We determine the profit-maximizing output by equating the marginal revenue (Equation 11.3) and marginal cost (Equation 11.6) functions:

$$MR = 24 - 2Q = 2Q = MC.$$

---

[6]Because profit is $\pi = p(Q)Q - C(Q)$, average profit is $\pi/Q = p(Q) - C(Q)/Q = p(Q) - AC$. Thus, average profit (and hence profit) is positive only if price is above average cost.

[7]By differentiating Equation 11.5 with respect to output, we find that the marginal cost is $MC = dC(Q)/dQ = 2Q$.

Solving for Q, we find that $Q = 6$. Substituting $Q = 6$ into the inverse demand function (Equation 11.2), we learn that the profit-maximizing price is

$$p = 24 - Q = 24 - 6 = 18.$$

At that quantity, the average variable cost is $AVC = 6$, which is less than the price, so the firm does not shut down. The average cost is $AC = 6 + 12/6 = 8$, which is less than the price, so the firm makes a profit.

Application

Apple's iPad

Apple started selling the iPad on April 3, 2010. The iPad was not the first tablet. (Indeed, it wasn't Apple's first tablet. Apple sold another tablet, the Newton, from 1993–1998.) But it was the most elegant one, and the first one that large numbers of consumers wanted to own. The iPad was a pioneer in a multi-touch, finger-sensitive touchscreen (rather than a pressure-triggered stylus) and a virtual onscreen keyboard. Most importantly, the iPad offered an intuitive interface and was very well integrated with Apple's iTunes, eBooks, and various application programs.

People loved the original iPad. Even at $499 for the basic model, Apple had a virtual monopoly in its first year. According to the research firm IDC, Apple's share of the 2010 tablet market was 87%. Moreover, the other tablets available in 2010 were not viewed by most consumers as close substitutes. Apple reported that it sold 25 million iPads worldwide in its first full year, 2010–2011. According to one estimate, the basic iPad's marginal cost was $MC = \$220$.

Unfortunately for Apple, its monopoly was short lived. Within a year of the iPad's introduction, over a hundred iPad want-to-be tablets were launched. To maintain its market dominance, Apple replaced the original iPad with the feature-rich iPad 2 in 2011. It added the enhanced iPad 3 and the iPad 4 with a Retina screen in 2012. In 2013, before the release of the iPad 5, Apple was selling an iPad 4 for the same $499 price. However, because its marginal cost, $316, was higher for the more advanced model, its profit per unit fell by about $100.

Solved Problem 11.2

When the iPad was introduced, Apple's constant marginal cost of producing this iPad was about $220. We estimate that its average cost was about $AC = 220 + 2{,}000/Q$, and that Apple's inverse demand function for the iPad was $p = 770 - 11Q$, where Q is measured in millions of iPads purchased.[8] What was Apple's marginal revenue function? What were its profit-maximizing price and quantity? What was its profit?

Answer

1. *Derive Apple's marginal revenue function using the information about its demand function.* Given that Apple's inverse demand function was linear, $p = 770 - 11Q$, its marginal revenue function has the same intercept and twice the slope: $MR = 770 - 22Q$.[9]

---

[8]See the Sources for the "Apple's iPad" Application for details on these estimates.

[9]We can use calculus to derive the marginal revenue curve. We multiply the inverse demand function by Q to obtain Apple's revenue function, $R = 770Q - 11Q^2$. The marginal revenue function is the derivative of the revenue with respect to quantity: $MR = dR/dQ = 770 - 22Q$.

2. *Derive Apple's profit-maximizing quantity and price by equating the marginal revenue and marginal cost functions and solving.* Apple maximized its profit where $MR = MC$:

$$770 - 22Q = 220.$$

Solving this equation for the profit-maximizing output, we find that $Q = 25$ million iPads, as the figure illustrates. By substituting this quantity into the inverse demand equation, we determine that the profit-maximizing price was $p = \$500$ per unit.

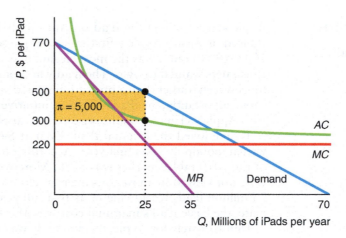

3. *Calculate Apple's profit using the profit-maximizing price and quantity and the average cost.* The firm's profit was $\pi = (p - AC)Q = [500 - (220 + 2,000/25)]25 = \$5,000$ million ($5 billion). The figure shows the profit rectangle has a height of $(p - AC) = 200$ and a length of $Q = 25$.

Effects of a Shift of the Demand Curve

Shifts in the demand curve or marginal cost curve affect the monopoly optimum and can have a wider variety of effects in a monopolized market than in a competitive market. In a competitive market, the effect of a shift in demand on a competitive firm's output depends only on the shape of the marginal cost curve (Chapter 8). In contrast, the effect of a shift in demand on a monopoly's output depends on the shapes of both the marginal cost curve and the demand curve.

As we saw in Chapter 8, a competitive firm's marginal cost curve tells us everything we need to know about the amount that firm will supply at any given market price. The competitive firm's supply curve is its upward-sloping marginal cost curve (above its minimum average variable cost). A competitive firm's supply behavior does not depend on the shape of the market demand curve because it always faces a horizontal demand curve at the market price. Thus, if you know a competitive firm's marginal cost curve, you can predict how much that firm will produce at any given market price.

In contrast, a monopoly's output decision depends on the shapes of its marginal cost curve and its demand curve. Unlike a competitive firm, *a monopoly does not have a supply curve.* Knowing the monopoly's marginal cost curve is not enough for us to predict how much a monopoly will sell at any given price.

Figure 11.4 illustrates that the relationship between price and quantity is unique in a competitive market but not in a monopoly market. If the market is competitive,

Figure 11.4 Effects of a Shift of the Demand Curve

(a) A shift of the demand curve from D^1 to D^2 causes the competitive equilibrium to move from e_1 to e_2 along the supply curve (the horizontal sum of the marginal cost curves of all the competitive firms). Because the competitive equilibrium lies on the supply curve, each quantity corresponds to only one possible equilibrium price. (b) With a monopoly, this same shift of demand causes the monopoly optimum to change from E_1 to E_2. The monopoly quantity stays the same, but the monopoly price rises. Thus, a shift in demand does not map out a unique relationship between price and quantity in a monopolized market: The same quantity, $Q_1 = Q_2$, is associated with two different prices, p_1 and p_2.

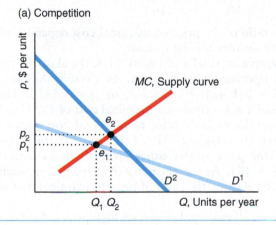

(a) Competition

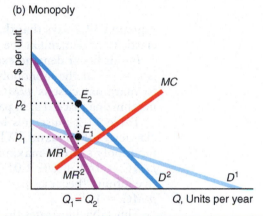

(b) Monopoly

the initial equilibrium is e_1 in panel a, where the original demand curve D^1 intersects the supply curve, MC, which is the sum of the marginal cost curves of a large number of competitive firms. When the demand curve shifts to D^2, the new competitive equilibrium, e_2, has a higher price and quantity. A shift of the demand curve maps out competitive equilibria along the marginal cost curve, so every equilibrium quantity has a single corresponding equilibrium price.

Now consider the monopoly example in panel b. As the demand curve shifts from D^1 to D^2, the monopoly optimum shifts from E_1 to E_2, so the price rises but the quantity stays constant, $Q_1 = Q_2$. Thus, *a given quantity can correspond to more than one monopoly-optimal price.* A shift in the demand curve may cause the monopoly-optimal price to stay constant and the quantity to change or both price and quantity to change.

11.2 Market Power

market power
the ability of a firm to charge a price above marginal cost and earn a positive profit

A monopoly has **market power**: the ability of a firm to charge a price above marginal cost and earn a positive profit. We now examine the factors that determine how much above its marginal cost a monopoly sets its price.

Market Power and the Shape of the Demand Curve

The degree to which the monopoly raises its price above its marginal cost depends on the shape of the demand curve at the profit-maximizing quantity. If the monopoly faces a highly elastic—nearly flat—demand curve at the profit-maximizing quantity, it would lose substantial sales if it raised its price by even a small amount. Conversely, if the demand curve is not very elastic (relatively steep) at that quantity, the monopoly would lose fewer sales from raising its price by the same amount.

We can derive the relationship between market power and the elasticity of demand at the profit-maximizing quantity using the expression for marginal revenue in Equation 11.4 and the firm's profit-maximizing condition that marginal revenue equals marginal cost:

$$MR = p\left(1 + \frac{1}{\varepsilon}\right) = MC. \tag{11.7}$$

By rearranging terms, we can rewrite Equation 11.7 as

$$\frac{p}{MC} = \frac{1}{1 + (1/\varepsilon)}. \tag{11.8}$$

Equation 11.8 says that the ratio of the price to marginal cost depends *only* on the elasticity of demand at the profit-maximizing quantity.

In our linear demand example in panel a of Figure 11.3, the elasticity of demand is $\varepsilon = -3$ at the monopoly optimum where $Q = 6$. As a result, the ratio of price to marginal cost is $p/MC = 1/[1 + 1/(-3)] = 1.5$, or $p = 1.5MC$. The profit-maximizing price, 18, in panel a is 1.5 times the marginal cost of 12.

Table 11.2 illustrates how the ratio of price to marginal cost varies with the elasticity of demand. When the elasticity is -1.01, only slightly elastic, the monopoly's profit-maximizing price is 101 times larger than its marginal cost: $p/MC = 1/[1 + 1/(-1.01)] \approx 101$. As the elasticity of demand approaches negative infinity (becomes perfectly elastic), the ratio of price to marginal cost shrinks to $p/MC = 1$.[10]

This table illustrates that not all monopolies can set high prices. A monopoly that faces a horizontal, perfectly elastic demand curve sets its price equal to its marginal cost—just like a price-taking, competitive firm. If this monopoly were to raise its price, it would lose all its sales, so it maximizes its profit by setting its price equal to its marginal cost.

The more elastic the demand curve at the optimum, the less a monopoly can raise its price without losing sales. All else the same, the more close substitutes for the monopoly's good, the more elastic is the demand curve at the optimum. For example, the publisher Pearson has the monopoly right to produce and sell this textbook. However, many other publishers have the rights to produce and sell similar

Table 11.2 Elasticity of Demand, Price, and Marginal Cost

Elasticity of Demand, ε	Price/Marginal Cost Ratio, $p/MC = 1/[1 + (1/\varepsilon)]$	Lerner Index, $(p - MC)/p = -1/\varepsilon$
-1.01	101	0.99
-1.1	11	0.91
-2	2	0.5
-3	1.5	0.33
-5	1.25	0.2
-10	1.11	0.1
-100	1.01	0.01
$-\infty$	1	0

(left margin: ↑ less elastic   ↓ more elastic)

---

[10]As the elasticity approaches negative infinity, $1/\varepsilon$ approaches zero, so $1/(1 + 1/\varepsilon)$ approaches $1/1 = 1$.

microeconomics texts (though you wouldn't like them as much). The demand curve that Pearson faces is much more elastic than it would be if no substitutes were available. If you think this textbook is expensive, imagine the cost if no substitutes were published!

Application

Cable Cars and Profit Maximization

Since San Francisco's cable car system started operating in 1873, it has been one of the city's main tourist attractions. In 2005, the cash-strapped Municipal Railway raised the one-way fare by two-thirds from $3 to $5. Not surprisingly, the number of riders dropped substantially, and many in the city called for a rate reduction.

The rate increase prompted many locals to switch to buses or other forms of transportation, but most tourists have a relatively inelastic demand curve for cable car rides. Frank Bernstein of Arizona, who visited San Francisco with his wife, two children, and mother-in-law, said that they would not visit San Francisco without riding a cable car: "That's what you do when you're here." But the round-trip $50 cost for his family to ride a cable car from the Powell Street turnaround to Fisherman's Wharf and back "is a lot of money for our family. We'll do it once, but we won't do it again."

If the city ran the cable car system like a profit-maximizing monopoly, the decision to raise fares would be clear. The 67% rate hike resulted in a 23% increase in revenue to $9,045,792 in the 2005–2006 fiscal year. Given that the revenue increased when the price rose, the city must have been operating in the inelastic portion of its demand curve ($\varepsilon > -1$), where $MR = p(1 + 1/\varepsilon) < 0$ prior to the fare increase.[11] With fewer riders, costs stayed constant (they would have fallen if the city had decided to run fewer than its traditional 40 cars), so the city's profit increased given the increase in revenue. Presumably the profit-maximizing price is even higher in the elastic portion of the demand curve.

However, the city may not be interested in maximizing its profit on the cable cars. At the time, then-Mayor Gavin Newsom said that having fewer riders "was my biggest fear when we raised the fare. I think we're right at the cusp of losing visitors who come to San Francisco and want to enjoy a ride on a cable car." The mayor said that he believed keeping the price of a cable car ride relatively low helps attract tourists to the city, thereby benefiting many local businesses. Newsom observed, "Cable cars are so fundamental to the lifeblood of the city, and they represent so much more than the revenue they bring in." The mayor decided to continue to run the cable cars at a price below the profit-maximizing level. The fare stayed at $5 for six years, then rose to $6 in 2011 and has stayed at $6 through at least 2013.

---

[11]The marginal revenue is the slope of the revenue function. Thus, if a reduction in quantity causes the revenue to increase, the marginal revenue must be negative. As Figure 9.2 illustrates, marginal revenue is negative in the inelastic portion of the demand curve.

Lerner Index

Lerner Index
the ratio of the difference between price and marginal cost to the price: $(p - MC)/p$

Another way to show how the elasticity of demand affects a monopoly's price relative to its marginal cost is to look at the firm's **Lerner Index** (or *price markup*): the ratio of the difference between price and marginal cost to the price: $(p - MC)/p$. This measure is zero for a competitive firm because a competitive firm cannot raise its price above its marginal cost. The greater the difference between price and marginal cost, the larger the Lerner Index and the greater the monopoly's ability to set price above marginal cost.

If the firm is maximizing its profit, we can express the Lerner Index in terms of the elasticity of demand by rearranging Equation 11.8:

$$\frac{p - MC}{p} = -\frac{1}{\varepsilon}. \tag{11.9}$$

Because $MC \geq 0$ and $p \geq MC$, $0 \leq p - MC \leq p$, so the Lerner Index ranges from 0 to 1 for a profit-maximizing firm.[12] Equation 11.9 confirms that a competitive firm has a Lerner Index of zero because its demand curve is perfectly elastic.[13] As Table 11.2 illustrates, the Lerner Index for a monopoly increases as the demand becomes less elastic at the monopoly optimum. If $\varepsilon = -5$, the monopoly's markup (Lerner Index) is $1/5 = 0.2$; if $\varepsilon = -2$, the markup is $1/2 = 0.5$; and if $\varepsilon = -1.01$, the markup is 0.99. Monopolies that face demand curves that are only slightly elastic set prices that are multiples of their marginal cost and have Lerner Indexes close to 1.

Solved Problem 11.3

Initially, Apple sold its iPad for $500 and its marginal cost was approximately $220 (see Solved Problem 11.2). What was its Lerner Index? If it was operating at the short-run profit-maximizing level, what was the elasticity of demand for the iPad?

Answer

1. *Calculate the Lerner Index by substituting the iPad's price and marginal cost into the definition.* Apple's Lerner Index for the iPad was $(p - MC)/p = (500 - 220)/500 = 0.56$.

2. *Determine the elasticity by substituting the iPad's Lerner Index into Equation 11.9.* According to Equation 11.9, a profit-maximizing monopoly operates where $(p - MC)/p = -1/\varepsilon$. Thus, if the Apple iPad was sold at the profit-maximizing price, $0.56 = -1/\varepsilon$, so $\varepsilon = -1/0.56 \approx -1.79$.

Sources of Market Power

When will a monopoly face a relatively elastic demand curve and hence have little market power? Ultimately, the elasticity of demand of the market demand curve depends on consumers' tastes and options. The more consumers want a good—the more willing they are to pay "virtually anything" for it—the less elastic is the demand curve.

All else the same, the demand curve a firm (not necessarily a monopoly) faces becomes more elastic as (1) *better substitutes* for the firm's product are introduced, (2) *more firms* enter the market selling the same product, or (3) firms that provide the same service

---

[12]For the Lerner Index to be above 1, ε would have to be a negative fraction, indicating that the demand curve was inelastic at the monopoly optimum. However, a profit-maximizing monopoly never operates in the inelastic portion of its demand curve.

[13]As the elasticity of demand approaches negative infinity, the Lerner Index, $-1/\varepsilon$, approaches zero.

locate closer to this firm. The demand curves for Xerox, the U.S. Postal Service, and McDonald's have become more elastic in recent decades for these three reasons.

When Xerox started selling its plain-paper copier, no other firm sold a close substitute. Other companies' machines produced copies on special slimy paper that yellowed quickly. As other firms developed plain-paper copiers, the demand curve that Xerox faced became more elastic.

In the past, the U.S. Postal Service (USPS) had a monopoly in overnight delivery services. Now FedEx, United Parcel Service, and many other firms compete with the USPS in providing overnight deliveries. Because of these increases in competition, the USPS's share of business and personal correspondence fell from 77% in 1988 to 59% in 1996. Its total mail volume fell 40% from 2006 to 2010. Its share of the ground shipping market fell to 16% by 2012 (FedEx has about a third and UPS about half of the market).[14] Compared to when it was a monopoly, the USPS's demand curves for first-class mail and package delivery have shifted downward and become more elastic.

As you drive down a highway, you may notice that McDonald's restaurants are located miles apart. The purpose of this spacing is to reduce the likelihood that two McDonald's outlets will compete for the same customer. Although McDonald's can prevent its own restaurants from competing with each other, it cannot prevent Wendy's or Burger King from locating near its restaurants. As other fast-food restaurants open near a McDonald's, that restaurant faces a more elastic demand. What happens as a profit-maximizing monopoly faces more elastic demand? It has to lower its price.

market failure
inefficient production or consumption, often because a price exceeds marginal cost

11.3 Market Failure Due to Monopoly Pricing

Of course you could get it done for less if I weren't the only plumber in town.

Unlike perfect competition, which achieves *economic efficiency* by maximizing welfare, W ($=$ consumer surplus $+$ producer surplus $= CS + PS$), a profit-maximizing monopoly is economically inefficient because it wastes potential surplus, resulting in a deadweight loss, DWL. The inefficiency of monopoly pricing is an example of a **market failure**: inefficient production or consumption, often because a price exceeds marginal cost (Chapter 9). The market failure from a monopoly occurs because its price is greater than its marginal cost. This economic inefficiency creates a rationale for governments to intervene.

We illustrate this loss using our continuing example. If the monopoly were to act like a competitive market and operate where its inverse demand curve, Equation 11.2, intersects its marginal cost (supply) curve, Equation 11.6,

$$p = 24 - Q = 2Q = MC,$$

---

[14]Peter Passell, "Battered by Its Rivals," *New York Times*, May 15, 1997, C1; Grace Wyler, "11 Things You Should Know about the U.S. Postal Service Before It Goes Bankrupt," *Business Insider*, May 31, 2011; "The U.S. Postal Service Nears Collapse," *Bloomberg Businessweek*, May 26, 2011; **www.economicfreedom.org/2012/12/12/stamping-out-waste**.

it would sell $Q_c = 8$ units of output at a price of 16, as in Figure 11.5. At this competitive price, consumer surplus is area $A + B + C$ and producer surplus is $D + E$.

If the firm acts like a monopoly and operates where its marginal revenue equals its marginal cost, only 6 units are sold at the monopoly price of 18, and consumer surplus is only A. Part of the lost consumer surplus, B, goes to the monopoly, but the rest, C, is lost.

By charging the monopoly price of 18 instead of the competitive price of 16, the monopoly receives 2 more per unit and earns an extra profit of area $B = 12$ on the $Q_m = 6$ units it sells. The monopoly loses area E, however, because it sells less than the competitive output. Consequently, the monopoly's producer surplus increases by $B - E$ over the competitive level. We know that its producer surplus increases, $B - E > 0$, because the monopoly had the option of producing at the competitive level and chose not to do so.

Welfare under monopoly is lower than with competition. The deadweight loss of monopoly is $-C - E$, which is the consumer surplus and producer surplus that is

Figure 11.5 Deadweight Loss of Monopoly

A competitive market would produce $Q_c = 8$ at $p_c = 16$, where the demand curve intersects the marginal cost (supply) curve. A monopoly produces only $Q_m = 6$ at $p_m = 18$, where the marginal revenue curve intersects the marginal cost curve. Under monopoly, consumer surplus is A, producer surplus is $B + D$, and the lost welfare or deadweight loss of monopoly is $-C - E$.

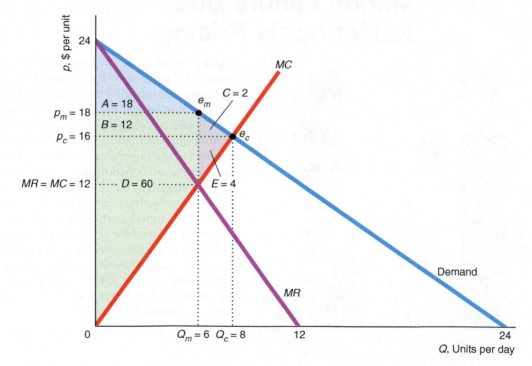

	Competition	Monopoly	Change
Consumer Surplus, CS	$A + B + C$	A	$-B - C = \Delta CS$
Producer Surplus, PS	$D + E$	$B + D$	$B - E = \Delta PS$
Welfare, $W = CS + PS$	$A + B + C + D + E$	$A + B + D$	$-C - E = \Delta W = DWL$

lost because less than the competitive output is produced. As in the tax analysis of a competitive market in Chapter 9, the deadweight loss is due to the gap between price and marginal cost at the monopoly output. At $Q_m = 6$, the price, 18, is above the marginal cost, 12, so consumers are willing to pay more for the last unit of output than it costs to produce it.

Solved Problem 11.4

In the linear example in panel a of Figure 11.3, how does charging the monopoly a specific tax of $t = 8$ per unit affect the monopoly optimum and the welfare of consumers, the monopoly, and society (where society's welfare includes the tax revenue)? What is the incidence of the tax on consumers?

Answer

1. *Determine how imposing the tax affects the monopoly optimum.* In the accompanying graph, the intersection of the marginal revenue curve, *MR*, and the before-tax marginal cost curve, MC^1, determines the monopoly optimum quantity, $Q_1 = 6$. At the before-tax optimum, e_1, the price is $p_1 = 18$. The specific tax causes the monopoly's before-tax marginal cost curve, $MC^1 = 2Q$, to shift

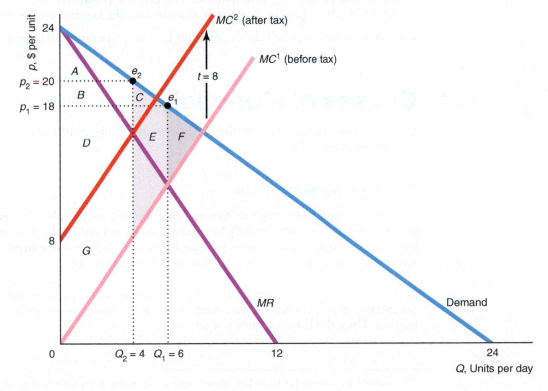

	Monopoly Before Tax	Monopoly After Tax	Change
Consumer Surplus, *CS*	$A + B + C$	A	$-B - C = \Delta CS$
Producer Surplus, *PS*	$D + E + G$	$B + D$	$B - E - G = \Delta PS$
Tax Revenues, $T = tQ$	0	G	$G = \Delta T$
Welfare, $W = CS + PS + T$	$A + B + C + D + E + G$	$A + B + D + G$	$-C - E = \Delta W$
Deadweight Loss, *DWL*	$-F$	$-C - E - F$	$-C - E = \Delta DWL$

upward by 8 to $MC^2 = MC^1 + 8 = 2Q + 8$. After the tax is applied, the monopoly operates where $MR = 24 - 2Q = 2Q + 8 = MC^2$. In the after-tax monopoly optimum, e_2, the quantity is $Q_2 = 4$ and the price is $p_2 = 20$. Thus, output falls by $\Delta Q = 6 - 4 = 2$ units and the price increases by $\Delta p = 20 - 18 = 2$.

2. *Calculate the change in the various welfare measures.* The graph shows how the welfare measures change. Area G is the tax revenue collected by the government, $tQ = 32$, because its height is the distance between the two marginal cost curves, $t = 8$, and its width is the output the monopoly produces after the tax is imposed, $Q_2 = 4$. The tax reduces consumer and producer surplus and increases the deadweight loss. We know that producer surplus falls because (a) the monopoly could have produced this reduced output level in the absence of the tax but did not because it was not the profit-maximizing output, so its before-tax profit falls, and (b) the monopoly must now pay taxes. The before-tax deadweight loss from monopoly is $-F$. The after-tax deadweight loss is $-C - E - F$, so the increase in deadweight loss due to the tax is $-C - E$. The table below the graph shows that consumer surplus changes by $-B - C$ and producer surplus by $B - E - G$.

3. *Calculate the incidence of the tax.* Because the tax goes from 0 to 8, the change in the tax is $\Delta t = 8$. The incidence of the tax (Chapter 3) on consumers is $\Delta p/\Delta t = 2/8 = \frac{1}{4}$. (The monopoly absorbs 6 of the tax and passes on only 2.)[15]

Comment: A tax increases the deadweight loss in a monopolized market.

11.4 Causes of Monopoly

Why are some markets monopolized? The two most important reasons involve costs and government actions.[16]

Cost-Based Monopoly

Certain cost structures may facilitate the creation of a monopoly. One possibility is that a firm may have substantially lower costs than potential rivals. A second possibility is that the firms in an industry have cost functions such that one firm can produce any given output at a lower cost than two or more firms can.

Cost Advantages If a low-cost firm profitably sells at a price so low that other potential competitors with higher costs would lose money, no other firms enter the market. Thus, the low-cost firm is a monopoly.

[15]In contrast to a competitive market, when a monopoly is taxed, the incidence of the tax on consumers can exceed 100%, as Appendix 11B demonstrates. "Welfare Effects of Ad Valorem Versus Specific Taxes" in MyEconLab, Chapter 11, proves that a government raises more tax revenue with an ad valorem tax applied to a monopoly than with a specific tax when the tax rates are set so that the after-tax output is the same with either tax.

[16]In later chapters, we discuss three other means by which monopolies are created. One method is the merger of several firms into a single firm (Chapter 13). This merger creates a monopoly if new firms fail to enter the market. A second method is for firms to coordinate their activities and set their prices as a monopoly would (Chapter 13). Firms that act collectively in this way are called a *cartel*. A third method is for a monopoly to use strategies that discourage other firms from entering the market (Chapter 14).

A firm can have a cost advantage over potential rivals for several reasons. It may have a superior technology or a better way of organizing production.[17] For example, Henry Ford's methods of organizing production using assembly lines and standardization allowed him to produce cars at substantially lower cost than rival firms until they copied his organizational techniques.

Another example is that the firm controls an *essential facility*: a scarce resource that a rival needs to use to survive. A firm that owns the only quarry in a region is the only firm that can profitably sell gravel to local construction firms.

Natural Monopoly   A market has a **natural monopoly** if one firm can produce the total output of the market at lower cost than several firms could. A firm can be a natural monopoly even if it does not have a cost advantage over rivals because average cost is lower if only one firm operates. Given that $C(q)$ is the cost for any firm to produce q, the condition for a natural monopoly is

natural monopoly situation in which one firm can produce the total output of the market at lower cost than several firms could

$$C(Q) < C(q_1) + C(q_2) + \cdots + C(q_n), \qquad (11.10)$$

where $Q = q_1 + q_2 + \ldots + q_n$ is the sum of the output of any $n \geq 2$ firms.

If a firm has economies of scale (Chapter 7) at all levels of output, its average cost curve falls as output increases for any observed level of output. If all potential firms have the same strictly declining average cost curve, this market is a natural monopoly, as we now illustrate.[18]

A company that supplies water to homes incurs a high fixed cost, F, to build a plant and connect houses to the plant. The firm's marginal cost, m, of supplying water is constant, so its marginal cost curve is horizontal and its average cost, $AC = m + F/Q$, declines as output rises. (An example is the iPad in Solved Problem 11.2.)

Figure 11.6 shows such marginal and average cost curves where $m = 10$ and $F = 60$. If the market output is 12 units per day, one firm produces that output at an average cost of 15, or a total cost of 180 ($= 15 \times 12$). If two firms each produce 6 units, the average cost is 20 and the cost of producing the market output is 240 ($= 20 \times 12$), which is greater than the cost with a single firm.

If the two firms divided total production in any other way, their cost of production would still exceed the cost of a single firm (as the following Solved Problem shows). The reason is that the marginal cost per unit is the same no matter how many firms produce, but each additional firm adds a fixed cost, which raises the cost of producing a given quantity. If only one firm provides water, the cost of building a second plant and a second set of pipes is avoided.

In an industry with a natural monopoly cost structure, having only one firm produce is the lowest cost way to produce any given output level.[19] Believing that they

---

[17]When a firm develops a better production method that provides it with a cost advantage, it is important for the firm to either keep the information secret or obtain a patent, so that the government protects it from having its innovation imitated. Thus, both secrecy and patents facilitate cost-based monopolies.

[18]A firm may be a natural monopoly even if its cost curve does not fall at all levels of output. If a U-shaped average cost curve reaches its minimum at 100 units of output, it may be less costly for only one firm to produce an output of slightly more than 100 units (such as 101 or 102) even though average cost is rising at that output. Thus, a cost function with economies of scale everywhere is a sufficient but not a necessary condition for a natural monopoly.

[19]However, society's welfare may be greater with more than one firm in the industry producing at higher cost, because competition drives down the price from the monopoly level. A solution that allows society to maximize welfare is to have only one firm produce, but the government regulates that firm to charge a price equal to marginal cost (as we discuss later in this chapter).

Figure 11.6 Natural Monopoly

This natural monopoly has a strictly declining average cost.

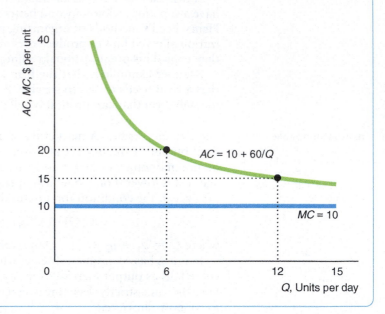

are natural monopolies, governments frequently grant monopoly rights to *public utilities* to provide essential goods or services such as water, gas, electric power, or mail delivery.

Solved Problem 11.5

A firm that delivers Q units of water to households has a total cost of $C(Q) = mQ + F$. If any entrant would have the same cost, does this market have a natural monopoly?

Answer

Determine whether costs rise if two firms produce a given quantity. Let q_1 be the output of Firm 1 and q_2 be the output of Firm 2. The combined cost of these two firms producing $Q = q_1 + q_2$ is

$$C(q_1) + C(q_2) = (mq_1 + F) + (mq_2 + F) = m(q_1 + q_2) + 2F = mQ + 2F.$$

If a single firm produces Q, its cost is $C(Q) = mQ + F$. Thus, the cost of producing any given Q is greater with two firms than with one firm (the condition in Equation 11.10), so this market has a natural monopoly.

Government Creation of a Monopoly

By preventing other firms from entering a market, governments create monopolies. We start by discussing common barriers to entry the governments erect and then concentrate on patents.

Barriers to Entry Sometimes governments own and manage monopolies, forbidding other firms from entering. In the United States, as in most countries, the postal service is a government monopoly. Several countries, such as China, maintain a tobacco monopoly. Many local governments own and operate public utility monopolies that provide garbage collection, electricity, water, gas, phone services, and other utilities.

Governments around the world have privatized many state-owned monopolies in the past several decades. By selling its monopolies to private firms, a government can capture the value of future monopoly earnings today. However, for political or other reasons, governments frequently sell at a lower price that does not capture all future profits.

In other markets, governments give or auction monopoly rights—a license to operate—to a private firm. For example, many cities let a single, private firm provide cable television services. Many government-owned airports auction off the rights for a single firm to provide a particular service, such as selling luggage. By auctioning a monopoly to a private firm, a government can capture the future value of monopoly earnings.[20]

Patents If a firm cannot prevent imitation by keeping its discovery secret, it may obtain government protection to prevent other firms from duplicating its discovery and entering the market. Virtually all countries provide such protection through a **patent**: an exclusive right granted to the inventor to sell a new and useful product, process, substance, or design for a fixed period of time. The length of a patent varies across countries, although it is now 20 years in the United States and in most other countries.

patent
an exclusive right granted to the inventor to sell a new and useful product, process, substance, or design for a fixed period of time

This right allows the patent holder to be the exclusive seller or user of the new invention.[21] Patents often give rise to monopoly, but not always. For example, although a patent may grant a firm the exclusive right to use a particular process in producing a product, other firms may be able to produce the same product using different processes.

A firm with a patent monopoly sets a high price that results in deadweight loss. Why, then, do governments grant patent monopolies? The main reason is to encourage inventive activity—less innovation would occur if successful inventors did not receive a patent monopoly. The costs of developing a new drug or new computer chip are often hundreds of millions or even billions of dollars. If anyone could copy a new drug or chip and compete with the inventor, few individuals or firms would undertake costly research. Thus, the government is explicitly trading off the long-run benefits of additional inventions against the shorter-term harms of monopoly pricing during the period of patent protection.

An alternative to using patents to spur research is for the government to provide research grants or offer prizes for important inventions. However, doing so is costly, so most governments rely primarily on patents.

---

[20]Alternatively, a government could auction the rights to the firm that offers to charge the lowest price, so as to maximize welfare. Oakland, California, tried to do that once with cable television service.

[21]Owners of patents may sell or license the right to other firms to use a patented process or produce a patented product.

Application

Botox Patent Monopoly

Ophthalmologist Dr. Alan Scott turned the deadly poison botulinum toxin into a miracle drug to treat two eye conditions: strabismus, a condition in which the eyes are not properly aligned, and blepharospasm, an uncontrollable closure of the eyes. Strabismus affects about 4% of children and blepharospasm left about 25,000 Americans functionally blind before Scott's discovery. His patented drug, Botox, is sold by Allergan, Inc.

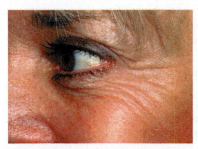

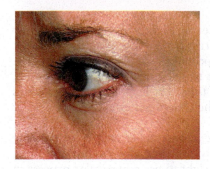

Dr. Scott has been amused to see several of the unintended beneficiaries of his research at the annual Academy Awards. Even before it was explicitly approved for cosmetic use, many doctors were injecting Botox into the facial muscles of actors, models, and others to smooth out their wrinkles. (The drug paralyzes the muscles, so those injected with it also lose their ability to frown or smile—and, some would say, act.) The treatment is only temporary, lasting up to 120 days, so repeated injections are necessary.

Allergan has a near-monopoly in the treatment of wrinkles, although plastic surgery and collagen, Restylane, hyaluronic acids, and other filler injections provide limited competition. Between 2002 and 2004, the number of facelifts dropped 3% to about 114,000 according to the American Society of Plastic Surgeons, while the number of Botox injections skyrocketed 166% to nearly 3 million. Allergan had Botox sales of $800 million in 2004 and about $1.8 billion in 2012. Indeed, Botox's value may increase. In 2013, the FDA approved its use for treating migraine headaches.

Dr. Scott can produce a vial of Botox in his lab for about $25. Allergan sells the potion to doctors for about $400. Assuming that the firm is setting its price to maximize its short-run profit, we can rearrange Equation 11.9 to determine the elasticity of demand for Botox:

$$\varepsilon = -\frac{p}{p - MC} = -\frac{400}{400 - 25} \approx -1.067.$$

Thus, the demand that Allergan faces is only slightly elastic: A 1% increase in price causes quantity to fall by slightly more than 1%.

If we assume that the demand curve is linear and given that the elasticity of demand is −1.067 at the monopoly optimum, e_m (1 million vials sold at $400 each, producing revenue of $400 million in 2002), then Allergan's inverse demand function was[22]

$$p = 775 - 375Q.$$

This demand curve (see the graph) has a slope of −375 and hits the price axis at $775 and the quantity axis at about 2.07 million vials per year. The corresponding marginal revenue curve,

$$MR = 775 - 750Q,$$

strikes the price axis at $775 and has twice the slope, −750, of the demand curve.

The intersection of the marginal revenue and marginal cost curves,

$$MR = 775 - 750Q = 25 = MC,$$

---

[22]The graph shows an inverse linear demand curve: $p = a - bQ$. The elasticity of demand for such a linear demand curve is $\varepsilon = -(1/b)(p/Q)$. Using Equation 11.9 and the data for the application, the elasticity of demand at the optimum is $-400/375 = -(1/b)(400/1)$, where Q is measured in millions of vials. Thus, $b = 375$. Solving $p = 400 = a - (375 \times 1)$, we find that $a = 775$. Solving $p = 400 = a - 375 \times 1$, we find that $a = 775$.

determines the monopoly equilibrium at the profit-maximizing quantity of 1 million vials per year and at a price of $400 per vial.

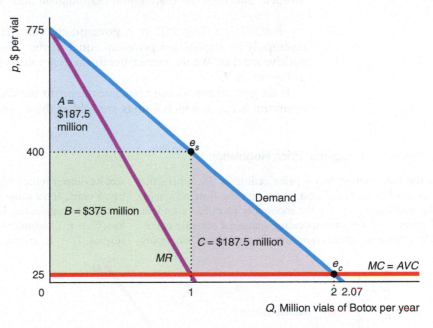

Were the company to sell Botox at a price equal to its marginal cost of $25 (as a competitive industry would), consumer surplus would equal area $A + B + C$. The height of triangle $A + B + C$ is $750 = $775 − $25, and its length is 2 million vials, so its area is $750 ($= \frac{1}{2} \times 750 \times 2$) million. At the higher monopoly price of $400, the consumer surplus is $A = $187.5 million. Compared to the competitive solution, e_c, buyers lose consumer surplus of $B + C = $562.5 million per year. Part of this loss, $B = $375 million per year, is transferred from consumers to Allergan. The rest, $C = $187.5 million per year, is the deadweight loss from monopoly pricing. Allergan's profit is its producer surplus, B, minus its fixed costs.

11.5 Government Actions That Reduce Market Power

Some governments act to reduce or eliminate monopolies' market power. Many governments directly regulate monopolies, especially those created by the government, such as public utilities. Most Western countries have designed laws to prevent a firm from driving other firms out of the market so as to monopolize it. A government may destroy a monopoly by breaking it up into smaller, independent firms (as the government did with Alcoa, the former aluminum monopoly).

Regulating Monopolies

Governments limit monopolies' market power in various ways. For example, most utilities are subject to direct regulation. Today, the most commonly used approach to regulating monopoly pricing is to impose a price ceiling, called a *price cap*. Price cap regulation is used for telecommunications monopolies in 33 U.S. states and in many countries, including Australia, Canada, Denmark, France, Germany, Mexico, Sweden, and the United Kingdom (Sappington and Weisman, 2010).

Optimal Price Regulation A government can eliminate the deadweight loss of monopoly by imposing a price cap equal to the price that would prevail in a competitive market. We use our earlier linear example to illustrate this type of regulation in Figure 11.7.

If the government doesn't regulate the profit-maximizing monopoly, the monopoly optimum is e_m, at which 6 units are sold at the monopoly price of 18. Suppose that

---

Figure 11.7 Optimal Price Regulation

If the government sets a price ceiling at 16, where the monopoly's marginal cost curve hits the demand curve, the new demand curve the monopoly faces has a kink at 8 units, and the corresponding marginal revenue curve, MR^r, "jumps" at that quantity. The regulated monopoly

sets its output where $MR^r = MC$, selling the same quantity, 8 units, at the same price, 16, as a competitive industry would. The regulation eliminates the monopoly deadweight loss, $C + E$. Consumer surplus, $A + B + C$, and producer surplus, $D + E$, are the same as under competition.

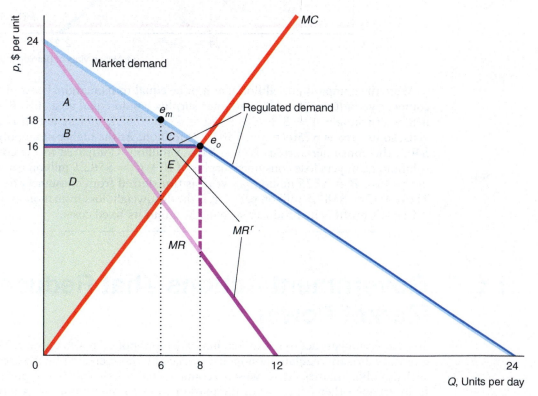

	Monopoly Without Regulation	Monopoly with Optimal Regulation	Change
Consumer Surplus, CS	A	$A + B + C$	$B + C = \Delta CS$
Producer Surplus, PS	$B + D$	$D + E$	$E - B = \Delta PS$
Welfare, $W = CS + PS$	$A + B + D$	$A + B + C + D + E$	$C + E = \Delta W$
Deadweight Loss, DWL	$-C - E$	0	$C + E = \Delta DWL$

the government sets a ceiling price of $16, the price at which the marginal cost curve intersects the market demand curve. Because the monopoly cannot charge more than 16 per unit, the monopoly's regulated demand curve is horizontal at 16 (up to 8 units) and is the same as the market demand curve at lower prices. The marginal revenue curve MR^r, which corresponds to the regulated demand curve, is horizontal where the regulated demand curve is horizontal (up to 8 units) and equals the marginal revenue curve MR, which corresponds to the market demand curve at larger quantities.

The regulated monopoly sets its output at 8 units, where MR^r equals its marginal cost, MC, and charges the maximum permitted price, 16. The regulated firm still makes a profit, because its average cost is less than 16 at 8 units. The optimally regulated monopoly optimum, e_o, is the same as the competitive equilibrium, where marginal cost (supply) equals the market demand curve.[23] Thus, setting a price ceiling where the MC curve and market demand curve intersect eliminates the deadweight loss of monopoly.

How do we know that this regulation is optimal? The answer is that this regulated outcome is the same as would occur if this market were competitive, where welfare is maximized (Chapter 9). As the table accompanying Figure 11.7 shows, the deadweight loss of monopoly, $C + E$, is eliminated by this optimal regulation.

Problems in Regulating   Governments often fail to regulate monopolies optimally for at least three reasons. First, due to limited information about the demand and marginal cost curves, governments may set a price ceiling above or below the competitive level.

Second, regulation may be ineffective when regulators are *captured*: influenced by the firms they regulate. Typically, this influence is more subtle than an outright bribe. Many American regulators worked in the industry before they became regulators and hence are sympathetic to those firms. For many other regulators, the reverse is true: They aspire to obtain good jobs in the industry eventually, so they do not want to offend potential employers. And some regulators, relying on industry experts for their information, may be misled or at least heavily influenced by the industry. For example, the California Public Utilities Commission urged telephone and cable companies to negotiate among themselves about how they wanted to open local phone markets to competition. Arguing that these influences are inherent, some economists contend that price and other types of regulation are unlikely to result in efficiency.

Third, because regulators generally cannot subsidize the monopoly, they may be unable to set the price as low as they want because the firm may shut down. In a natural monopoly where the average cost curve is strictly above the marginal cost curve, if the regulator sets the price equal to the marginal cost so as to eliminate deadweight loss, the firm cannot afford to operate. If the regulators cannot subsidize the firm, they must raise the price to a level where the firm at least breaks even.

Nonoptimal Price Regulation   If the government sets the price ceiling at a nonoptimal level, a deadweight loss results. Suppose that the government sets the regulated price below the optimal level, which is 16 in Figure 11.7. If it sets the price below the firm's minimum average cost, the firm shuts down, so the deadweight loss equals the sum of the consumer plus producer surplus under optimal regulation, $A + B + C + D + E$.

---

[23] The monopoly produces at e_o only if the regulated price is greater than its average variable cost. Here the regulated price, $16, exceeds the average variable cost at 8 units of $8. Indeed, the firm makes a profit because the average cost at 8 units is $9.50.

If the government sets the price ceiling below the optimally regulated price but high enough that the firm does not shut down, consumers who are lucky enough to buy the good benefit because they can buy it at a lower price than they could with optimal regulation. As we show in the following Solved Problem, society suffers a deadweight loss because less output is sold than with optimal regulation.

Solved Problem 11.6

Suppose that the government sets a price, p_2, that is below the socially optimal level, p_1, but above the monopoly's minimum average cost. How do the price, the quantity sold, the quantity demanded, and welfare under this regulation compare to those under optimal regulation?

Answer

1. *Describe the optimally regulated outcome.* With optimal regulation, e_1, the price is set at p_1, where the market demand curve intersects the monopoly's marginal cost curve on the accompanying graph. The optimally regulated monopoly sells Q_1 units.

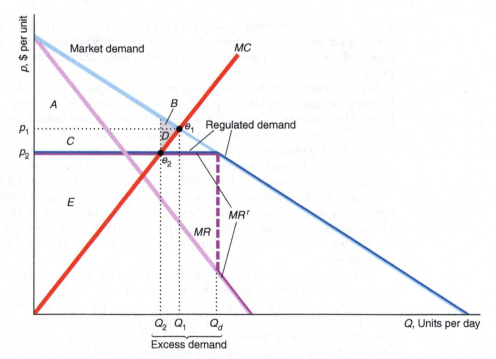

	Monopoly with Optimal Regulation	Monopoly with a Low Regulated Price	Change
Consumer Surplus, CS	$A + B$	$A + C$	$C - B = \Delta CS$
Producer Surplus, PS	$C + D + E$	E	$-C - D = \Delta PS$
Welfare, $W = CS + PS$	$A + B + C + D + E$	$A + C + E$	$-B - D = \Delta W = DWL$

2. *Describe the outcome when the government regulates the price at p_2.* Where the market demand is above p_2, the regulated demand curve for the monopoly is horizontal at p_2 (up to Q_d). The corresponding marginal revenue curve, MR^r,

is kinked. It is horizontal where the regulated demand curve is horizontal. The MR^r curve is the same as the marginal revenue curve corresponding to the market demand curve, MR, where the regulated demand curve is downward sloping. The monopoly maximizes its profit by selling Q_2 units at p_2. The new regulated monopoly optimum is e_2, where MR^r intersects MC. The firm does not shut down when regulated as long as its average variable cost at Q_2 is less than p_2.

3. *Compare the outcomes.* The quantity that the monopoly sells falls from Q_1 to Q_2 when the government lowers its price ceiling from p_1 to p_2. At that low price consumers want to buy Q_d, resulting in excess demand of $Q_d - Q_2$. Compared to optimal regulation, welfare is lower by at least $B + D$.

Comment: The welfare loss is greater if unlucky consumers waste time trying to buy the good unsuccessfully or if goods are not allocated optimally among consumers. A consumer who values the good at only p_2 may be lucky enough to buy it, while a consumer who values the good at p_1 or more may not be able to obtain it (Chapter 9).

Application

Natural Gas Regulation

Because U.S. natural gas monopolies usually have significant economies of scale and regulators generally cannot subsidize them, the regulated price is set above marginal cost, creating a deadweight loss. The figure is based on the estimates of Davis and Muehlegger (2010).[24] If unregulated, this monopoly would sell 12.1 trillion cubic feet of natural gas per year, which is determined by the intersection of its marginal revenue and marginal cost curves. It would charge the corresponding price on the demand curve at point a. Its profit is the rectangle labeled π, with a length equal to the quantity, 12.1 trillion cubic feet, and a height equal to the difference between the price at a and the corresponding average cost.

To eliminate deadweight loss, the government should set the price ceiling equal to the marginal cost of $5.78 per thousand cubic feet of natural gas so that the monopoly behaves like a price taker. The price ceiling or marginal cost curve hits the demand curve at c, where the quantity is 24.2 trillion cubic feet per year—double the unregulated quantity. At that quantity, the regulated utility would lose money. The average cost at that quantity is $7.78, which is 10¢ less than the average cost of $7.88 at a quantity of 23 trillion cubic feet. The regulated price, $5.78, is less than the average cost at that quantity of $7.78, so it would lose $2 on each thousand cubic feet it sells, or $48.4 billion in total. Thus, it would be willing to sell this quantity at this price only if the government subsidizes it.

Typically, it is politically infeasible for a government regulatory agency to subsidize a monopoly. On average, the natural gas regulatory agencies set the price at $7.88 per thousand cubic feet, where the demand curve intersects the average cost curve and the monopoly breaks even, point b. The monopoly sells 23 trillion cubic feet per year. The corresponding price, $7.88, is 36% above marginal cost, $5.78. Consequently, society incurs a deadweight loss of $1.26 billion annually, which is the gray triangle in the figure. This deadweight loss is much smaller than it would be if the monopoly were unregulated.

---

[24]We use their most conservative estimate: the one that produces the smallest deadweight loss. We approximate their demand curve with a linear one that has the same price elasticity of demand of -0.2 at point b. This figure represents the aggregation of state-level monopolies to the national level.

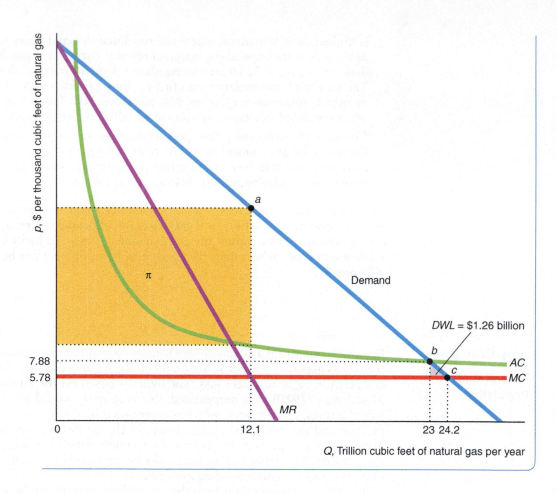

Increasing Competition

Encouraging competition is an alternative to regulation as a means of reducing the harms of monopoly. When a government has created a monopoly by preventing entry, it can quickly reduce the monopoly's market power by allowing other firms to enter. As new firms enter the market, the former monopoly must lower its price to compete, so welfare rises. Many governments are actively encouraging entry into telephone, electricity, and other utility markets that were formerly monopolized.

Similarly, a government may end a ban on imports so that a domestic monopoly faces competition from foreign firms. With many foreign firms with the same costs as the domestic firm, the former monopoly becomes just one of many competitive firms. As the market becomes competitive, consumers pay the competitive price, and the deadweight loss of monopoly is eliminated.

Governments around the world are increasing competition in formerly monopolized markets. For example, many U.S. and European governments are forcing former telephone and energy monopolies to compete.

Similarly, under pressure from the World Trade Organization, many countries are reducing or eliminating barriers that protected domestic monopolies. The entry of foreign competitive firms into a market can create a new, more competitive market structure.

Application

Generic Competition for Apple's iPod

Although not the first hard-drive music player, Apple's iPod became a virtual monopoly producer when it was introduced in 2001. Equipped with a tiny hard drive, it was about a quarter the size of its competitors, was the only player to use a high-speed FireWire interface to transfer files, held a thousand songs, offered an intuitive interface, and was very attractive. The iPod had 96% of the hard-drive player market in 2004 and over 90% in 2005.

Eventually, however, other firms produced products that at least some consumers were willing to buy instead of the iPod. Most consumers viewed its rivals' products as generic, me-too players. None of its competitors had a large share—the iPod's closest rival, Microsoft's Zune, had only 2% of the market in 2009, and exited the market in 2011. The iPod's market share is still over 70% in 2012. Apple, the industry's *dominant firm*, faces a *competitive fringe* made up of small, price-taking firms.

Apple has been able to produce the iPod at lower cost than its competitors. Due to its large size, Apple has formed strategic partnerships with other companies to buy large supplies of components, securing a lower price from suppliers than its competitors. According to Piper Jaffray in 2005, the cost of Apple's 30GB iPod was $10 per gigabyte compared to Creative's ZEN Vision:M at $11 per gigabyte, while Samsung and iRiver's costs were between $15–$25 per gigabyte. According to iSuppli (now IHS) in 2010, Apple's sixth-generation iPod nano's marginal cost was about $45, while its price was about $150. No other company could come close to matching Apple's cost.

Solved Problem 11.7

How did the presence of me-too rival products produced by firms with higher marginal costs affect Apple's iPod pricing in more recent years? Assume that Apple has a constant marginal cost MC. The large number of identical, higher-cost rivals—the competitive fringe—act like (competitive) price takers so that their collective supply curve is horizontal at $p_2 = MC + x$.

Answer

1. *Show how Apple priced the iPod when it was a monopoly by equating its marginal revenue and marginal cost.* The figure shows Apple's original (market) demand curve for its iPod as a light-blue line. The light-purple line is the corresponding marginal revenue curve. Its profit-maximizing outcome was e_1 when Apple set its quantity, Q_1, where its MR curve hit its MC curve, and the corresponding price was p_1.

2. *Show how the competitive supply curve alters the demand curve facing Apple.* The competitive supply curve acts like a government price ceiling. Now, Apple cannot charge more than $p_2 = MC + x$. Thus, its dark-blue residual demand curve is flat at $MC + x$ and the same as the original downward-sloping demand curve at lower prices. (That is, the residual demand curve for the iPod is similar to that of the regulated monopoly in Figure 11.7.)

3. *Determine Apple's new optimal outcome by equating its new marginal revenue with its marginal cost.* Apple acts like a monopoly with respect to its residual demand curve (rather than to its original demand curve). Corresponding to Apple's residual demand curve in the figure is a dark-purple, kinked marginal

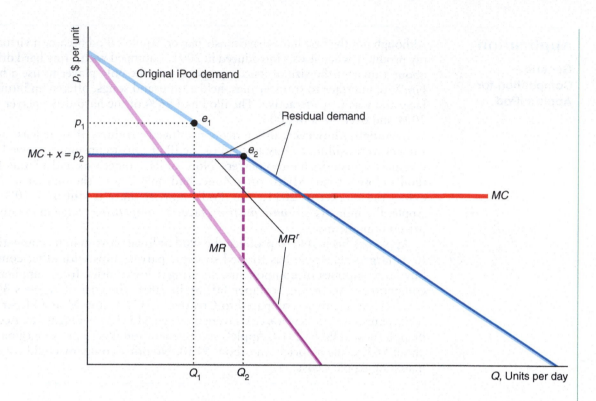

revenue curve, MR^r, that crosses Apple's marginal cost line at Q_2.[25] Apple maximizes its profit by selling Q_2 units for p_2 at e_2. That is, Apple sells more iPods at a lower price than before the other firms entered the market. Given that this figure captures reality, the fringe sells virtually nothing.

11.6 Networks, Dynamics, and Behavioral Economics

We have examined how a monopoly behaves in the current period, ignoring the future. For many markets, such an analysis is appropriate. However, in some markets, decisions today affect demand or cost in a future period, creating a need for a *dynamic* analysis, in which firms explicitly consider relationships between periods.

In such markets, the monopoly may maximize its long-run profit by making a decision today that does not maximize its short-run profit. For example, frequently a firm introduces a new product—such as a new type of candy bar—by initially charging a low price or giving away free samples to generate word-of-mouth publicity or to let customers learn about its quality in hopes of getting their future business. We now consider an important reason why consumers' demand in the future may depend on a monopoly's actions in the present.

---

[25]If MC crossed MR^r in the downward-sloping section, Apple would be a monopoly because its monopoly price would be less than $MC + x$.

Network Externalities

network externality
the situation where one person's demand for a good depends on the consumption of the good by others

The number of customers a firm has today may affect the demand curve it faces in the future. A good has a **network externality** if one person's demand depends on the consumption of a good by others.[26] If a good has a *positive* network externality, its value to a consumer grows as the number of units sold increases.

When a firm introduces a new good with a network externality, it faces a chicken-and-egg problem: It can't get Max to buy the good unless Sofia will buy it, but it can't get Sofia to buy it unless Max will. The firm wants its customers to coordinate or to make their purchase decisions simultaneously.

The telephone provides a classic example of a positive network externality. When the phone was introduced, potential adopters had no reason to get phone service unless their family and friends did. Why buy a phone if there's no one to call? For Bell's phone network to succeed, it had to achieve a *critical mass* of users—enough adopters that others wanted to join. Had it failed to achieve this critical mass, demand would have withered and the network would have died. Similarly, the market for fax machines grew very slowly until a critical mass was achieved where many firms had them.

Direct Size Effect Many industries exhibit positive network externalities where the customer gets a *direct* benefit from a larger network. The larger an automated teller machine (ATM) network such as the Plus network, the greater the odds that you will find an ATM when you want one, so the more likely it is that you will want to use that network. The more people who use a particular computer program, the more attractive it is to someone who wants to exchange files with other users.

Indirect Effects In some markets, positive network externalities are indirect and stem from complementary goods that are offered when a product has a critical mass of users. The more applications (apps) available for a smart phone, the more people want to buy that smart phone. However, many of these extra apps will be written only if a critical mass of customers buys the smart phone. Similarly, the more people who drive diesel-powered cars, the more likely it is that gas stations will sell diesel fuel; and the more stations that sell the fuel, the more likely it is that someone will want to drive a diesel car. Likewise, once a critical mass of customers had broadband Internet access, more services provided downloadable music and movies and high-definition Web pages. Once those popular apps appeared, more people signed up for broadband service.

Network Externalities and Behavioral Economics

The direct effect of network externalities depends on the size of the network, because customers want to interact with each other. However, sometimes consumers' behavior depends on beliefs or tastes that can be explained by psychological and sociological theories, which economists study in *behavioral economics* (Chapter 4).

One such explanation for a direct network externality effect is based on consumer attitudes toward other consumers. Harvey Leibenstein (1950) suggested

---

[26]In Chapter 18, we discuss the more general case of an *externality*, which occurs when a person's well-being or a firm's production capability is directly affected by the actions of other consumers or firms rather than indirectly through changes in prices. The following discussion on network externalities is based on Leibenstein (1950), Rohlfs (1974), Katz and Shapiro (1994), Economides (1996), Shapiro and Varian (1999), and Rohlfs (2001).

bandwagon effect
the situation in which a person places greater value on a good as more and more other people possess it

snob effect
the situation in which a person places greater value on a good as fewer and fewer other people possess it

that consumers sometimes want a good because "everyone else has it." A fad or other popularity-based explanation for a positive network externality is called a **bandwagon effect**: A person places greater value on a good as more and more other people possess it.[27] The success of the iPad today may be partially due to its early popularity. Ugg boots seem to be another example of a bandwagon effect.

The opposite, negative network externality is called a **snob effect**: A person places greater value on a good as fewer and fewer other people possess it. Some people prefer an original painting by an unknown artist to a lithograph by a star because no one else can possess that painting. (As Yogi Berra said, "Nobody goes there anymore; it's too crowded.")

Network Externalities as an Explanation for Monopolies

Because of the need for a critical mass of customers in a market with a positive network externality, we frequently see only one large firm surviving. Visa's ad campaign tells consumers that Visa cards are accepted "everywhere you want to be," including places that "don't take American Express." One could view its ad campaign as an attempt to convince consumers that its card has a critical mass and therefore that everyone should switch to it.

The Windows operating system largely dominates the market—not because it is technically superior to Apple's operating system or Linux—but because it has a critical mass of users. Consequently, a developer can earn more producing software that works with Windows than with other operating systems, and the larger number of software programs makes Windows increasingly attractive to users. Similarly, Engström and Forsell (2013) found that a 10 percentile increase in the displayed number of downloads of Android apps on Google Play increases downloads by about 20%.

But having obtained a monopoly, a firm does not necessarily keep it. History is filled with examples where one product knocks off another: "The king is dead; long live the king." Google replaced Yahoo! as the predominant search engine. Explorer displaced Netscape as the big-dog browser, and then was replaced by Chrome (2012–2013). Levi Strauss is no longer the fashion leader among the jeans set.

Application

Critical Mass and eBay

In recent years, many people have argued that natural monopolies emerge after brief periods of Internet competition. A typical Web business requires a large up-front fixed cost—primarily for development and promotion—but has a relatively low marginal cost. Thus, Internet start-ups typically have downward-sloping average cost-per-user curves. Which of the actual or potential firms with decreasing average costs will dominate and become a natural monopoly?[28]

---

[27]*Jargon alert*: Some economists use *bandwagon effect* to refer to any positive network externality—not just those that are based on popularity.

[28]If Internet sites provide differentiated products (see Chapter 13), then several sites may coexist even though average costs are strictly decreasing. In 2007, commentators were predicting the emergence of natural monopolies in social networks such as MySpace, but it was replaced as the dominant social network by Facebook within two years. However, whether a single social network can dominate for long is debatable given frequent innovations. By 2013, Facebook was losing traffic while MySpace was attempting a comeback and new models, such as Twitter, were poised to take over.

In the early years, eBay's online auction site, which started in 1995, faced competition from a variety of other Internet sites including the then mighty Yahoo!, which created an auction site in 1998. At the time, many commentators correctly predicted that whichever auction site first achieved a critical mass of users would drive the other sites out of business. Indeed, most of these alternative sites died or faded into obscurity. For example, Yahoo! Auctions closed its U.S. and Canada sections of the site in 2007, and its Singapore section in 2008 (although its Hong Kong, Taiwanese, and Japanese sites continue to operate in 2013).

Apparently the convenience of having one site where virtually all buyers and sellers congregate—which lowers buyers' search cost—and creating valuable reputations by having a feedback system (Brown and Morgan, 2006), more than compensates sellers for the lack of competition in sellers' fees. Brown and Morgan (2009) found that, prior to the demise of the U.S. Yahoo! Auction site, the same type of items attracted an average of two additional bidders on eBay and, consequently, the prices on eBay were consistently 20% to 70% percent higher than Yahoo! prices.

A Two-Period Monopoly Model

A monopoly may be able to solve the chicken-and-egg problem of getting a critical mass for its product by initially selling the product at a low introductory price. By doing so, the firm maximizes its long-run profit but not its short-run profit.

Suppose that a monopoly sells its good—say, root-beer-scented jeans—for only two periods (after that, the demand goes to zero as a new craze hits the market). If the monopoly sells less than a critical quantity of output, Q, in the first period, its second-period demand curve lies close to the price axis. However, if the good is a success in the first period—at least Q units are sold—the second-period demand curve shifts substantially to the right.

If the monopoly maximizes its short-run profit in the first period, it charges p^* and sells Q^* units, which is fewer than Q. To sell Q units, it would have to lower its first-period price to $\underline{p} < p^*$, which would reduce its first-period profit from π^* to $\underline{\pi}$.

In the second period, the monopoly maximizes its profit given its second-period demand curve. If the monopoly sold only Q^* units in the first period, it earns a relatively low second-period profit of π_l. However, if it sells Q units in the first period, it makes a relatively high second-period profit, π_h.

Should the monopoly charge a low introductory price in the first period? Its objective is to maximize its long-run profit: the sum of its profit in the two periods.[29] If the firm has a critical mass in the second period, its extra profit is $\pi_h - \pi_l$. To obtain this critical mass by charging a low introductory price in the first period, it lowers its first period profit by $\pi^* - \underline{\pi}$. Thus, the firm chooses to charge a low introductory period in the first period if its first period loss is less than its extra profit in the second period. This policy must be profitable for some firms: A 2013 Google search for "introductory price" found 13.2 million Web pages.

---

[29]In Chapter 16, we discuss why firms place lower value on profit in the future than profit today. However, for simplicity in this analysis, we assume that the monopoly places equal value on profit in either period.

When generic drugs enter the market after the patent on a brand-name drug expires, the demand curve facing the brand-name firm shifts to the left. Why do many brand-name drug companies raise their prices after generic rivals enter the market? The reason is that the demand curve not only shifts to the left but it rotates so that it is less elastic at the original price.

The price the brand-name firm sets depends on the elasticity of demand. When the firm has a patent monopoly, it faces the linear demand curve D^1 in the figure. Its monopoly optimum, e_1, is determined by the intersection of the corresponding marginal revenue curve MR^1 and the marginal cost curve. (Because it is twice as steeply sloped as the demand curve, MR^1 intersects the MC curve at Q_1, while the demand curve D^1 intersects the MC curve at $2Q_1$.) The monopoly sells the Q_1 units at a price of p_1.

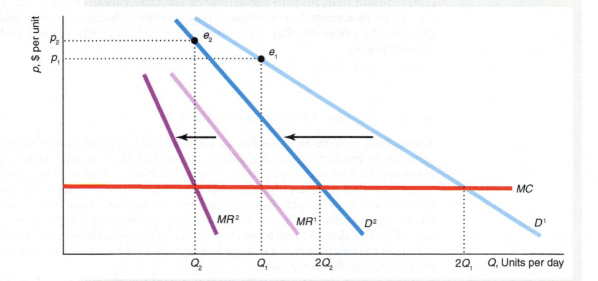

After the generic drugs enter the market, the linear demand curve facing the original patent holder shifts left to D^2 and becomes steeper and less elastic at the original price. The firm now maximizes its profit at e_2, where the quantity, Q_2, is smaller than Q_1 because D^2 lies to the left of D^1. However, the new price, p_2, is higher than the initial price, p_1, because the D^2 demand curve is less elastic at the new optimum quantity Q_2 than is the D^1 curve at Q_1.

Why might the demand curve rotate and become less elastic at the initial price? One explanation is that the brand-name firm has two types of consumers with different elasticities of demand who differ in their willingness to switch to a generic. One group of consumers is relatively price-sensitive and switches to the lower-priced generics. However, the brand-name drug remains the monopoly supplier to the remaining brand-loyal customers whose demand is less elastic than that of the price-sensitive consumers. These loyal customers prefer the brand-name drug because they are more comfortable with a familiar product, worry that new products may be substandard, or fear that differences in the inactive ingredients might affect them.

Older customers are less likely to switch brands than younger people. A survey by the American Association of Retired Persons found that people aged 65 and older were 15% less likely than people aged 45 to 64 to request generic versions of a drug from their doctor or pharmacist. Similarly, patients with generous insurance plans may be more likely to pay for expensive drugs (if their insurer permits) than customers with more limited insurance policies.

Summary

1. **Monopoly Profit Maximization.** Like any firm, a monopoly—a single seller—maximizes its profit by setting its output so that its marginal revenue equals its marginal cost. The monopoly makes a positive profit if its average cost is less than the price at the profit-maximizing output.

2. **Market Power.** Market power is the ability of a firm to charge a price above marginal cost and earn a positive profit. The more elastic the demand the monopoly faces at the quantity at which it maximizes its profit, the closer its price to its marginal cost and the closer the Lerner Index or price markup, $(p - MC)/p$, to zero, the competitive level.

3. **Market Failure Due to Monopoly Pricing.** Because a monopoly's price is above its marginal cost, too little output is produced, and society suffers a deadweight loss. The monopoly makes higher profit than it would if it acted as a price taker. Consumers are worse off, buying less output at a higher price.

4. **Causes of Monopoly.** A firm may be a monopoly if it has lower operating costs than rivals such as from superior knowledge or control of a key input. A market may also have a *natural monopoly* if one firm can produce the market output at lower average cost than can a larger number of firms (even if all firms have the same cost function). Many, if not most, monopolies are created by governments, which prevent other firms from entering the markets. One important barrier to entry is a patent, which gives the inventor of a new product or process the exclusive right to sell the product or use the process for 20 years in most countries.

5. **Government Actions That Reduce Market Power.** A government can eliminate the welfare harm of a monopoly by forcing the firm to set its price at the competitive level. If the government sets the price at a different level or otherwise regulates nonoptimally, welfare at the regulated monopoly optimum is lower than in the competitive equilibrium. A government can eliminate or reduce the harms of monopoly by allowing or facilitating entry.

6. **Networks, Dynamics, and Behavioral Economics.** If a good has a positive network externality so that its value to a consumer grows as the number of units sold increases, then current sales affect a monopoly's future demand curve. A monopoly may maximize its long-run profit—its profit over time—by setting a low introductory price in the first period that it sells the good and then later raising its price as its product's popularity ensures large future sales at a higher price. Consequently, the monopoly is not maximizing its short-run profit in the first period but is maximizing the sum of its profits over all periods. Behavioral economics provides an explanation for some network externalities, such as bandwagon effects and snob effects.

Questions

All questions are available on MyEconLab; * = *answer appears at the back of this book;* **A** = *algebra problem;* **C** = *calculus problem.*

1. Monopoly Profit Maximization

1.1 If the linear inverse demand function is $p = 100 - 2Q$, what is the marginal revenue function? Draw the demand and marginal revenue curves. (*Hint:* See Solved Problem 11.1) **A**

1.2 If the inverse demand curve a monopoly faces is $p = 10Q^{-0.5}$, what is the firm's marginal revenue curve? (*Hint:* See Solved Problem 11.1.) **C**

1.3 A demand curve $Q = A/p$, where A is a positive constant, has the property that the elasticity of demand is $\varepsilon = -1$. Accurately draw this demand curve. Now pick two different prices and show the associated revenue for each. (Draw a line from a given price on the vertical axis horizontally to the demand curve, then draw a vertical line that hits the horizontal axis. The resulting rectangle is the revenue: its height is price and its length is quantity, so the area is $p \times q = R$.) How do the two rectangles compare in size? Now do the same exercise with a linear demand curve and compare the size of the rectangles at two different prices.

1.4 The demand curve $Q = A/p$, where A is a positive constant, has the property that the elasticity of demand is $\varepsilon = -1$ everywhere.

a. Use math to show that the revenue is the same at any given point on the constant elasticity of demand curve. **C**

b. Show that, for any point on the constant elasticity of demand curve, the corresponding marginal revenue is zero. **C**

1.5 The demand curve $Q = A/p$, where A is a positive constant, has the property that the elasticity of demand is $\varepsilon = -1$. If a monopoly faces this demand curve, where would it set its price or quantity if it has a positive marginal cost? Explain. Is this situation plausible?

1.6 Does a monopoly's profit differ if it chooses price or quantity (assuming it chooses them optimally)? Why can't a monopoly choose both price and quantity?

*1.7 If the inverse demand function is $p = 500 - 10Q$, what is the elasticity of demand and revenue at $Q = 10$?

1.8 Under what conditions is a monopoly unlikely to be profitable in the long run? (*Hint*: Discuss the relationship between market demand and average cost.)

1.9 AT&T Inc., the large U.S. phone company and the one-time monopoly, left the payphone business at the beginning of 2009 because people were switching to wireless phones. U.S. consumers owning cellphones reached 80% by 2007 and 86% by 2012 according to the Pew Research Center (2013). The number of payphones fell from 2.6 million at the peak in 1998 to 1 million in 2006 (Crayton Harrison, "AT&T to Disconnect Pay-Phone Business After 129 Years," **Bloomberg.com**, December 3, 2007). (Where will Clark Kent go to change into Superman now?) Use graphs to explain why a monopoly exits a market when its demand curve shifts to the left.

1.10 Show why a monopoly may operate in the upward- or downward-sloping section of its long-run average cost curve but a competitive firm will operate only in the upward-sloping section.

1.11 The inverse demand curve a monopoly faces is $p = 100 - Q$. The firm's cost curve is $C(Q) = 10 + 5Q$ (so $MC = 5$). What is the profit-maximizing solution? How does your answer change if $C(Q) = 100 + 5Q$? (*Hint*: See Solved Problem 11.2.) **A**

1.12 The inverse demand curve a monopoly faces is $p = 10Q^{-0.5}$. The firm's cost curve is $C(Q) = 5Q$. What is the profit-maximizing solution? (*Hint*: See Solved Problem 11.2.) **C**

1.13 A monopoly manufactures its product in two factories with marginal cost functions $MC_1(Q_1)$ and $MC_2(Q_2)$, where Q_1 is the quantity produced in the first factory and Q_2 is the quantity manufactured in the second factory. The monopoly's total output is $Q = Q_1 + Q_2$. Use a graph or math to determine how much total output the monopoly produces and how much it produces at each factory. (*Hint*: Consider the cases where the factories have constant marginal costs—not necessarily equal—and where they have upward-sloping marginal cost curves.) **A**

1.14 Show that after a shift in the demand curve, a monopoly's price may remain constant but its output may rise.

1.15 In 2013, the Oakland A's were one of the hottest teams in baseball. They were regularly drawing "sellout" crowds, with many more fans wanting tickets. However, the A's do not sell all of the 56,000 seats. The A's have removed or put tarps over roughly 20,000 seats in most of the third deck and the outfield stands. The A's management says that the reason is to create a more intimate feeling for the fans. What's another explanation?

2. Market Power

2.1 Are major-league baseball clubs profit-maximizing monopolies? Some observers of this market have contended that baseball club owners want to maximize attendance or revenue. Alexander (2001) says that one test of whether a firm is a profit-maximizing monopoly is to check whether the firm is operating in the elastic portion of its demand curve (which he finds is true). Why is that a relevant test? What would the elasticity be if a baseball club were maximizing revenue?

2.2 Why is the ratio of the monopoly's price to its marginal cost, p/MC, smaller, the less elastic the demand curve at the optimum quantity? Can the demand curve be inelastic at that quantity?

2.3 When will a monopoly set its price equal to its marginal cost?

2.4 Draw an example of a monopoly with a linear demand curve and a constant marginal cost curve.

   a. Show the profit-maximizing price and output, p^* and Q^*, and identify the areas of consumer surplus, producer surplus, and deadweight loss. Also show the quantity, Q_c, that would be produced if the monopoly were to act like a price taker.

   b. Now suppose that the demand curve is a smooth concave-to-the-origin curve (whose ends hit the axes) that is tangent to the original demand curve at the point (Q^*, p^*). Explain why the monopoly equilibrium will be the same as with the linear demand curve. Show how much output the firm would produce if it acted like a price taker. Show how the welfare areas change.

c. Repeat the exercises in part b if the demand curve is a smooth convex-to-the-origin curve (whose ends hit the axes) that is tangent to the original demand curve at the point (Q^*, p^*).

2.5 Suppose that the inverse demand for San Francisco cable car rides is $p = 10 - Q/1,000$, where p is the price per ride and Q is the number of rides per day, and that the objective of San Francisco's Municipal Authority (the cable car operator) is to maximize its revenues. What is the revenue-maximizing price? Suppose that San Francisco calculates that the city's businesses benefit from tourists and residents riding on the city's cable cars at $4 per ride. If the city's objective is to maximize the sum of the cable car revenues and the economic impact, what is the optimal price? **C**

2.6 Using the information in Solved Problem 11.2, calculate the elasticity of demand for the iPad at the profit-maximizing solution using its inverse demand curve. Compare that answer to the one we obtained in Solved Problem 11.3 using the Lerner Index formula.

2.7 In 2009, the price of Amazon's Kindle 2 was $359, while iSuppli (HIS) estimated that its marginal cost was $159. What was Amazon's Lerner Index? What elasticity of demand did it face if it was engaging in short-run profit maximization? (*Hint*: See Solved Problem 11.3.)

2.8 According to iSuppli (HIS) in 2010, its sixth-generation iPod nano's marginal cost is about $45, while its price is about $150. What is Apple's price/marginal cost ratio? What is its Lerner Index? If we assume (possibly incorrectly) that Apple acts like a short-run profit-maximizing monopoly in pricing its iPod Shuffle, what elasticity of demand does Apple believe it faces? (*Hint*: See Solved Problem 11.3.) **A**

2.9 According to one estimate, the parts for a Segway Human Transporter—which has five gyroscopes, two tilt sensors, dual redundant motors, ten microprocessors, and can travel up to 12.5 mph—cost at least $1,500 (Eric A. Taub, "Segway Transporter Slow to Catch On," *San Francisco Chronicle*, August 11, 2003, E4). Suppose that Segway's marginal cost is $2,000. Given that the Segway's price is $5,000, calculate the firm's price/marginal cost ratio, its Lerner Index, and the elasticity of demand it believes it faces (assuming that it is trying to maximize its short-run profit). (*Hint*: See Solved Problem 11.3.) **A**

*2.10 The U.S. Postal Service (USPS) has a constitutionally guaranteed monopoly on first-class mail.

In 2012, it charged 44¢ for a stamp, which was not the profit-maximizing price—the USPS's goal, allegedly, is to break even rather than to turn a profit. Following the postal services in Australia, Britain, Canada, Switzerland, and Ireland, the USPS allowed Stamps.com to sell a sheet of twenty 44¢ stamps with a photo of your dog, your mommy, or whatever image you want for $18.99 (that's 94.95¢ per stamp, or a 216% markup). Stamps.com keeps the extra beyond the 44¢ it pays the USPS. What is the firm's Lerner Index? If Stamps.com is a profit-maximizing monopoly, what elasticity of demand does it face for a customized stamp? (*Hint*: See Solved Problem 11.3.) **A**

3. Market Failure Due to Monopoly Pricing

3.1 A monopoly has a constant marginal cost of production of $1 per unit and a fixed cost of $10. Draw the firm's MC, AVC, and AC curves. Add a downward-sloping demand curve, and show the profit-maximizing quantity and price. Indicate the profit as an area on your diagram. Show the deadweight loss. (*Hint*: See Solved Problem 11.4.)

3.2 What is the effect of a franchise (lump-sum) tax on a monopoly? (*Hint*: Consider the possibility that the firm may shut down.) (*Hint*: See Solved Problem 11.4.)

*3.3 Only Native American Indian tribes can run casinos in California. These casinos are spread around the state so that each is a monopoly in its local community. Then California Governor Arnold Schwarzenegger negotiated with the state's tribes, getting them to agree to transfer 10% of their profits to the state in exchange for concessions. How does a profit tax affect a monopoly's output and price? How would a monopoly change its behavior if the profit tax were 25% rather than 10%? (*Hint*: You may assume that the profit tax refers to the tribe's economic profit.) (*Hint*: See Solved Problem 11.4.)

3.4 If the inverse demand curve is $p = 120 - Q$ and the marginal cost is constant at 10, how does charging the monopoly a specific tax of $t = 10$ per unit affect the monopoly optimum and the welfare of consumers, the monopoly, and society (where society's welfare includes the tax revenue)? What is the incidence of the tax on consumers? (*Hint*: See Solved Problem 11.4.) **A**

*3.5 Show mathematically that a monopoly may raise the price to consumers by more than the specific tax t imposed on it. (*Hints*: Consider a monopoly facing a constant-elasticity demand curve and a constant marginal cost, m. See Solved Problem 11.4.) **C**

3.6 Show that a monopoly will not necessarily lower its price by the same percentage as its constant marginal cost drops. (*Hint*: See Solved Problem 11.4.)

3.7 If the inverse demand function facing a monopoly is $p(Q)$ and its cost function is $C(Q)$, show the effect of a specific tax, t, on its profit-maximizing output. How does imposing t affect its profit? (*Hint*: See Solved Problem 11.4.) **C**

3.8 A monopoly with a constant marginal cost m has a profit-maximizing price of p_1. It faces a constant elasticity demand curve with elasticity ε. After the government applies a specific tax of $1, its price is p_2. What is the price change $p_2 - p_1$ in terms of ε? How much does the price rise if the demand elasticity is -2? (*Hint*: Use Equation 11.9.) **C**

3.9 In 1996, Florida voted on and rejected a 1¢-per-pound excise tax on refined cane sugar in the Florida Everglades Agricultural Area. Swinton and Thomas (2001) used estimated linear supply and demand curves to calculate the incidence from this tax given that the market is competitive. Their inverse demand curve was $p = 1.787 - 0.0004641Q$, and their inverse supply curve was $p = -0.4896 + 0.00020165Q$, where p is measured in dollars. Calculate the incidence of the tax that falls on consumers (Chapter 3) for a competitive market. If producers joined together to form a monopoly, and the supply curve is actually the monopoly's marginal cost curve, what is the incidence of the tax? (*Hints*: The incidence that falls on consumers is the difference between the equilibrium price with and without the tax divided by the tax. You should find that the incidence is 70% in a competitive market and 41% with a monopoly. See Solved Problem 11.4.) **A**

4. Causes of Monopoly

*4.1 Can a firm be a natural monopoly if it has a U-shaped average cost curve? Why or why not? (*Hint*: See Solved Problem 11.5.)

4.2 Can a firm operating in the upward-sloping portion of its average cost curve be a natural monopoly? Explain. (*Hint*: See Solved Problem 11.5.)

4.3 In the "Botox Patent Monopoly" Application, consumer surplus, triangle A, equals the deadweight loss, triangle C. Show that this equality is a result of the linear demand and constant marginal cost assumptions. **A**

4.4 Based on the information in the Botox Application, what would happen to the equilibrium price and quantity if the government had collected a specific tax of $75 per vial of Botox? What welfare effects would such a tax have? **A**

4.5 A monopoly sells music CDs. It has a constant marginal and average cost of 20. It faces two groups of potential customers: honest and dishonest people. The dishonest and the honest consumers' demand functions are the same: $p = 120 - Q$.

a. If it is not possible for the dishonest customers to steal the music, what are the monopoly's profit-maximizing price and quantity? What is its profit? What are the consumer surplus, producer surplus, and welfare?

b. Answer the same questions as in the previous part if the dishonest customers can pirate the music.

c. How do consumer surplus, producer surplus, and welfare change if piracy occurs? **A**

5. Government Actions That Reduce Market Power

5.1 Describe the effects on output and welfare if the government regulates a monopoly so that it may not charge a price above $\bar{p}$, which lies between the unregulated monopoly price and the optimally regulated price (determined by the intersection of the firm's marginal cost and the market demand curve).

5.2 A monopoly drug company produces a lifesaving medicine at a constant cost of $10 per dose. The demand for this medicine is perfectly inelastic at prices less than or equal to the $100 (per day) income of the 100 patients who need to take this drug daily. At a higher price, nothing is bought. Show the equilibrium price and quantity and the consumer and producer surplus in a graph. Now the government imposes a price ceiling of $30. Show how the equilibrium, consumer surplus, and producer surplus change. What is the deadweight loss, if any, from this price control?

5.3 Based on the information in the "Botox Patent Monopoly" Application, what would happen to the equilibrium price and quantity if the government had set a price ceiling of $200 per vial of Botox? What welfare effects would such a restriction have? (*Hint*: See Solved Problem 11.6.) **A**

5.4 Bleyer Industries Inc., the only U.S. manufacturer of plastic Easter eggs, manufactured 250 million eggs each year. However, imports from China cut into its business. In 2005, Bleyer filed for bankruptcy because the Chinese firms could produce the eggs at much lower costs ("U.S. Plastic Egg Industry a Shell of Its Former Self," *San Francisco*

Chronicle, January 14, 2005), though a shrunken version of the firm still exists today. Use graphs to show how a competitive import industry could drive a monopoly out of business. (*Hint*: Look at Solved Problem 11.7.)

5.5 Malaysia's monopoly auto manufacturer produces the Proton, which is protected from imports by a specific tariff, t, on imported goods. The monopoly's profit-maximizing price is p^*. The world price of the good (comparable autos) is p_w, which is less than p^*. Because the price of imported goods with the tariff is $p_w + t$, no foreign goods are imported. Under WTO pressure the government removes the tariff so that the supply of foreign goods to the country's consumers is horizontal at p_w. Show how much the former monopoly produces and what price it charges. Show who gains and who loses from removing the tariff. (*Hint*: Look at Solved Problem 11.7.)

6. Networks, Dynamics, and Behavioral Economics

6.1 A monopoly chocolate manufacturer faces two types of consumers. The larger group, the hoi polloi, loves desserts and has a relatively flat, linear demand curve for chocolate. The smaller group, the snobs, is interested in buying chocolate only if the hoi polloi do not buy it. Given that the hoi polloi do not buy the chocolate, the snobs have a relatively steep, linear demand curve. Show the monopoly's possible outcomes—high price, low quantity, low price, high quantity—and explain the condition under which the monopoly chooses to cater to the snobs rather than to the hoi polloi.

*6.2 A monopoly produces a good with a network externality at a constant marginal and average cost of 2. In the first period, its inverse demand curve is $p = 10 - Q$. In the second period, its demand is $p = 10 - Q$ unless it sells at least $Q = 8$ units in the first period. If it meets or exceeds this target, then the demand curve rotates out by α (it sells α times as many units for any given price), so that its inverse demand curve is $p = 10 - Q/\alpha$. The monopoly knows that it can sell no output after the second period. The monopoly's objective is to maximize the sum of its profits over the two periods. In the first period, should the monopoly set the output that maximizes its profit in that period? How does your answer depend on α? (*Hint*: See the discussion of the two-period monopoly model in Section 11.7.) **A**

7. Challenge

7.1 Under what circumstances will a drug company charge more for its drug after its patent expires?

7.2 Does the Challenge Solution change if the entry of the generic causes a parallel shift to the left of the patent monopoly's linear demand curve?

7.3 Proposals to reduce patent length for drugs are sometimes made, but some critics argue that such a change would result in even higher prices during the patent period as companies would need to recover drug development costs more quickly. Is this argument valid if drug companies maximize profit?

12

Pricing and Advertising

Everything is worth what its purchaser will pay for it. —Publilius Syrus (first century B.C.)

Because many firms use *sales*—temporarily setting the price below the usual price—some customers pay lower prices than others over time. Grocery stores are particularly likely to put products on sale frequently. In large U.S. supermarkets, a soft drink brand is on sale 94% of the time. Either Coke or Pepsi is on sale half the weeks in a year.

Heinz Ketchup controls up to 60% of the U.S. ketchup market, 70% of the Canadian market, and 78% of the U.K. market. In 2012, Heinz sold over 650 million bottles of ketchup in more than 140 countries and had annual sales of more than $1.5 billion. When Heinz goes on sale, *switchers*—ketchup customers who normally buy whichever brand is least expensive—purchase Heinz rather than the low-price generic ketchup. How can Heinz design a pattern of sales that maximizes Heinz's profit by obtaining extra sales from switchers without losing substantial sums by selling to its loyal customers at a discount price? Under what conditions does it pay for Heinz to have a policy of periodic sales?

Sales are not the only means that firms use to charge customers different prices. Why are airline fares often substantially less if you book in advance? Why do the spiritualists who live at the Wonewoc Spiritualist Camp give readings for $45 for half an hour, but charge seniors only $40 on Wednesdays?[1] Why are some goods, including computers and software, combined and sold as a bundle? To answer these questions, we need to examine how monopolies and other noncompetitive firms set prices.

In Chapter 11, we examined how a monopoly chooses a single price when it uses **uniform pricing**: charging the same price for every unit sold of a particular good. However, a monopoly can increase its profit if it can use **nonuniform pricing**, where a firm charges consumers different prices for the same product or charges a single customer a price that depends on the number of units the customer buys. In this chapter, we analyze nonuniform pricing for monopolies, but similar principles apply to any firm with market power.

uniform pricing
charging the same price for every unit sold of a particular good

nonuniform pricing
charging consumers different prices for the same product or charging a single customer a price that depends on the number of units the customer buys

---

[1] www.campwonewoc.com (viewed September 12, 2013).

As we saw in Chapter 11, a monopoly that sets a uniform price sells only to customers who value the good enough to buy it at the monopoly price, and those customers receive some consumer surplus. The monopoly does not sell the good to other customers who value the good at less than the single price, even if those consumers would be willing to pay more than the marginal cost of production. These lost sales cause *deadweight loss*, which is the forgone value of these potential sales in excess of the cost of producing the good.

A firm with market power can earn a higher profit using nonuniform pricing than by setting a uniform price for two reasons. First, the firm captures some or all of the single-price consumer surplus. Second, the firm converts at least some of the single-price deadweight loss into profit by charging a price below the uniform price to some customers who would not purchase at the single-price level. A monopoly that uses nonuniform pricing can lower the price to these otherwise excluded consumers without lowering the price to consumers who are willing to pay higher prices.

We examine several types of nonuniform pricing including price discrimination, two-part pricing, and tie-in sales. The most common form of nonuniform pricing is **price discrimination**: charging consumers different prices for the same good based on individual characteristics of consumers, membership in an identifiable subgroup of consumers, or on the quantity purchased by the consumers. For example, for a full-year combination print and online subscription, the *Wall Street Journal* charges $99.95 to students, who are price sensitive, and $155 to other subscribers, who are less price sensitive.

price discrimination
practice in which a firm charges consumers different prices for the same good

Some firms with market power use other forms of nonuniform pricing to increase profits. A firm may use *two-part pricing*, where it charges a customer one fee for the right to buy the good and an additional fee for each unit purchased. For example, members of health or golf clubs typically pay an annual fee to belong to the club and then pay an additional amount each time they use the facilities. Similarly, cable television companies often charge a monthly fee for basic service and an additional fee for recent movies.

Another type of nonuniform pricing is called *bundling*, where several products are sold together as a package. For example, many restaurants provide full-course dinners for a fixed price that is less than the sum of the prices charged if the items (appetizer, main dish, and dessert) are ordered separately (à la carte).

A monopoly may also increase its profit by advertising. A monopoly may advertise to shift its demand curve so as to raise its profit, taking into account the cost of advertising.

In this chapter, we examine seven main topics

1. **Conditions for Price Discrimination.** A firm can increase its profit using price discrimination if it has market power, if customers differ in their willingness to pay, if the firm can identify which customers are more price sensitive than others, and if it can prevent customers who pay low prices from reselling to those who pay high prices.

2. **Perfect Price Discrimination.** If a monopoly can charge the maximum each customer is willing to pay for each unit of output, the monopoly captures all potential consumer surplus, and the efficient (competitive) level of output is sold.

3. **Group Price Discrimination.** A firm that lacks the ability to charge each individual a different price may be able to charge different prices to various groups of customers that differ in their willingness to pay for the good.

4. **Nonlinear Price Discrimination.** A firm may set different prices for large purchases than for small ones, discriminating among consumers by inducing them to self-select the effective price they pay based on the quantity they buy.

5. **Two-Part Pricing.** By charging consumers a fee for the right to buy a good and then allowing them to purchase as much as they wish at an additional per-unit fee, a firm earns a higher profit than with uniform pricing.

6. **Tie-In Sales.** By selling a combination of different products in a package or bundle, a firm earns a higher profit than by selling the goods or services separately.

7. **Advertising.** A monopoly advertises to shift its demand curve and to increase its profit.

12.1 Conditions for Price Discrimination

The prince travels through the forest for many hours and comes upon an inn, where he is recognized immediately. He orders a light meal of fried eggs. When he finishes, the prince asks the innkeeper, "How much do I owe you for the eggs?" The innkeeper replies, "Twenty-five rubles." "Why such an exorbitant price?" asks the prince. "Does this area have a shortage of eggs?" The innkeeper says, "We don't have a shortage of eggs, but we have a shortage of princes."[2]

We start by studying the most common form of nonuniform pricing, *price discrimination*, where a firm charges various consumers different prices for a good.[3]

Why Price Discrimination Pays

For almost any good or service, some consumers are willing to pay more than others. A firm that sets a single price faces a trade-off between charging consumers who really want the good as much as they are willing to pay and charging a low enough price that the firm doesn't lose sales to less enthusiastic customers. As a result, the firm usually sets an intermediate price. A price-discriminating firm that varies its prices across customers avoids this trade-off.

As with any kind of nonuniform pricing, price discrimination increases profit above the uniform pricing level through two channels. First, a price-discriminating firm charges a higher price to customers who are willing to pay more than the uniform price, capturing some or all of their consumer surplus—the difference between what a good is worth to a consumer and what the consumer paid—under uniform pricing. Second, a price-discriminating firm sells to some people who were not willing to pay as much as the uniform price.

We use a pair of extreme examples to illustrate the two benefits of price discrimination to firms—capturing more of the consumer surplus and selling to more customers. These examples are extreme in the sense that the firm sets a uniform price at the price the most enthusiastic consumers are willing to pay or at the price the least enthusiastic consumers are willing to pay, rather than at an intermediate level.

Suppose that the only movie theater in town has two types of patrons: college students and senior citizens. The college students will see the Saturday night movie if the price is $10 or less, and the senior citizens will attend if the price is $5 or less. For simplicity, we assume that the theater incurs no cost to show the movie, so profit is the same as revenue. The theater is large enough to hold all potential customers, so the marginal cost of admitting one more customer is zero. Table 12.1 shows how pricing affects the theater's profit.

---

[2]Thanks to Steve Salop.

[3]Price discrimination is legal in the United States unless it harms competition between firms, as specified in the Robinson-Patman Act.

Table 12.1 A Theater's Profit Based on the Pricing Method Used

(a) No Extra Customers from Price Discrimination

Pricing	Profit from 10 College Students	Profit from 20 Senior Citizens	Total Profit
Uniform, $5	$50	$100	$150
Uniform, $10	$100	$0	$100
Price discrimination*	$100	$100	$200

(b) Extra Customers from Price Discrimination

Pricing	Profit from 10 College Students	Profit from 5 Senior Citizens	Total Profit
Uniform, $5	$50	$25	$75
Uniform, $10	$100	$0	$100
Price discrimination*	$100	$25	$125

*The theater price discriminates by charging college students $10 and senior citizens $5.

Notes: College students go to the theater if they are charged no more than $10. Senior citizens are willing to pay at most $5. The theater's marginal cost for an extra customer is zero.

Panel a has 10 college students and 20 senior citizens. If the theater charges everyone $5, its profit is $150 = $5 × (10 college students + 20 senior citizens). If it charges $10, the senior citizens do not go to the movie, so the theater makes only $100. Thus, if the theater is going to charge everyone the same price, it maximizes its profit by setting the price at $5. Charging less than $5 makes no sense because the same number of people go to the movie as go when $5 is charged. Charging between $5 and $10 is less profitable than charging $10 because no extra seniors go and the college students are willing to pay $10. Charging more than $10 results in no customers.

At a price of $5, the seniors have no consumer surplus: They pay exactly what seeing the movie is worth to them. Seeing the movie is worth $10 to the college students, but they have to pay only $5, so each has a consumer surplus of $5, and their total consumer surplus is $50.

If the theater can price discriminate by charging senior citizens $5 and college students $10, its profit increases to $200. Its profit rises because the theater makes as much from the seniors as before but gets an extra $50 from the college students. By price discriminating, the theater sells the same number of seats but makes more money from the college students, capturing all the consumer surplus they had under uniform pricing. Neither group of customers has any consumer surplus if the theater price discriminates.

Panel b has 10 college students and 5 senior citizens. If the theater must charge a single price, it charges $10. Only college students see the movie, so the theater's profit is $100. (If it charges $5, both students and seniors go to the theater, but its profit is only $75.) If the theater can price discriminate and charge seniors $5 and college students $10, its profit increases to $125. Here the gain from price discrimination comes from selling extra tickets to seniors (not from making more money on the same number of tickets, as in panel a). The theater earns as much from the students as before and makes more from the seniors, and neither group enjoys consumer surplus. Leslie (1997) found that Broadway theaters in New York increase their profits 5% by price discriminating rather than using uniform prices.

These examples illustrate the two channels through which price discrimination can increase profit: charging some existing customers more or selling extra units. The movie theater's ability to increase its profits by price discrimination arises from its ability to segment the market into two groups, students and senior citizens, with different levels of willingness to pay.

Application

Disneyland Pricing

Disneyland, in Southern California, is a well-run operation that rarely misses a trick when it comes to increasing its profit.[4] In 2012, Disneyland charged out-of-state adults $199 for a 3-day park hopper ticket, which admits one to Disneyland and Disney's California Adventure Park, but charged residents of Southern California only $154.

This policy of charging locals a discounted price makes sense if visitors are willing to pay more than locals and if Disneyland can prevent locals from selling discounted tickets to nonlocals. Imagine a Midwesterner who's never been to Disneyland and wants to visit. Travel accounts for most of the trip's cost, so an extra few dollars for entrance to the park makes little percentage difference in the total cost of the visit and hence does not greatly affect that person's decision whether to go. In contrast, for a local who has been to Disneyland many times and for whom the entrance price is a larger share of the total cost, a slightly higher entrance fee might prevent a visit.[5]

Charging both groups the same price is not in Disney's best interest. If Disney were to charge the higher price to everyone, many locals wouldn't visit the park. If Disney were to use the lower price for everyone, it would be charging nonresidents much less than they are willing to pay. Thus, price discrimination increases Disney's profit.

Which Firms Can Price Discriminate

Not all firms can price discriminate. For a firm to price discriminate successfully, three conditions must be met.

First, a firm must have market power. Without market power, a firm cannot charge any consumer more than the competitive price. A monopoly, an oligopoly firm, or a monopolistically competitive firm might be able to price discriminate. However, a perfectly competitive firm cannot price discriminate because it must sell its product at the market price.

Second, for a firm to profitably discriminate, groups of consumers or individual consumers must have demand curves that differ, and the firm must be able to

---

[4]According to **www.babycenter.com**, it costs $411,214 to raise a child from cradle through college. Parents can cut that total in half, however: They don't *have* to take their kids to Disneyland.

[5]In 2012, a Southern Californian couple, Jeff Reitz and Tonya Mickesh, were out of work, so they decided to cheer themselves up by using their annual passes to visit Disneyland 366 days that year (a leap year).

identify how its consumers' demand curves differ. The movie theater knows that college students and senior citizens differ in their willingness to pay for a ticket, and Disneyland knows that tourists and local residents differ in their willingness to pay for admission. In both cases, the firms can identify members of these two groups by using driver's licenses or other forms of identification. Similarly, if a firm knows that each individual's demand curve slopes downward, it may charge each customer a higher price for the first unit of a good than for subsequent units.

Third, a firm must be able to prevent or limit resale. The price-discriminating firm must be able to prevent consumers who buy the good at low prices from reselling the good to customers who would otherwise pay high prices. Price discrimination doesn't work if resale is easy because the firm would be able to make only low-price sales. Disneyland and movie theaters can charge different prices for different groups of customers because those customers normally enter as soon as they buy their tickets, and therefore they do not have time to resell them. For events that sell tickets in advance, other methods can be used to prevent resale, such as having different colors for children's tickets and adults' tickets.

The first two conditions—market power and the ability to identify groups with different price sensitivities—are present in many markets. Usually, the biggest obstacle to price discrimination is a firm's inability to prevent resale.

Preventing Resale

In some industries, preventing resale is easier than in others. In industries where resale is initially easy, firms can act to make resale more difficult.

Resale is difficult or impossible for most *services* and when *transaction costs are high*. If a plumber charges you less than your neighbor for clearing a pipe, you cannot make a deal with your neighbor to resell this service. The higher the transaction costs a consumer must incur to resell a good, the less likely that resale will occur. Suppose that you are able to buy a jar of pickles for $1 less than the usual price. Could you practically find and sell this jar to someone else, or would the transaction costs be prohibitive? The more valuable a product or the more widely consumed it is, the more likely it is that transaction costs are low enough that resale occur.

Some firms act to raise transaction costs or otherwise make resale difficult. If your college requires that someone with a student ticket must show a student identification card with a picture on it before being admitted to a sporting event, you'll find it difficult to resell your low-price tickets to nonstudents who pay higher prices. When students at some universities buy computers at lower-than-usual prices, they must sign a contract that forbids them to resell the computer.

Similarly, a firm can prevent resale by *vertically integrating*: participating in more than one successive stage of the production and distribution chain for a good or service. Alcoa, the former aluminum monopoly, wanted to sell aluminum ingots to producers of aluminum wire at a lower price than was set for producers of aluminum aircraft parts. If Alcoa did so, however, the wire producers could easily resell their ingots. By starting its own wire production firm, Alcoa prevented such resale and was able to charge high prices to firms that manufactured aircraft parts (Perry, 1980).

Governments frequently aid price discrimination by preventing resale. State and federal governments require that milk producers, under penalty of law, price discriminate by selling milk at a higher price for fresh use than for processing (cheese, ice cream) and forbid resale. Government *tariffs* (taxes on imports) limit resale by making it expensive to buy goods in a low-price country and resell them in a high-price country. In some cases, laws prevent such reselling explicitly. Under U.S. trade laws, certain brand-name perfumes may not be sold in the United States except by their manufacturers.

Application

Preventing Resale of Designer Bags

During the holiday season, stores often limit how many of the hottest items—such as this year's best-selling toy—a customer can buy. But it may surprise you that Web sites of luxury-goods retailers such as Saks Fifth Avenue, Neiman Marcus, and Bergdorf Goodman limit how many designer handbags one can buy: "Due to popular demand, a customer may order no more than three units of this item every 30 days."

Why wouldn't manufacturers and stores want to sell as many units as possible? How many customers can even afford more than three Prada Visone Hobo handbags at $4,950 each? The simple explanation is that the restriction has nothing to do with "popular demand." Instead, it's designed to prevent resale so as to enable manufacturers to price discriminate internationally. The handbag manufacturers pressure the U.S. retailers to limit sales to prevent anyone from buying large numbers of bags and reselling them in Europe or Asia where the same items in Prada and Gucci stores often cost 20% to 40% more.

For example, in 2013, the Prada clutch sells for $1,350 in the United Sates, but sells for $1,420 on Prada's Swiss Web site. By purchasing from Prada's U.S. online site, one must agree that the purchase is solely for private household use, that commercial resale or sale outside of the United States is not authorized, and that the company reserves the right to reject orders and to limit order quantities.

Not All Price Differences Are Price Discrimination

Not every seller who charges consumers different prices is price discriminating. Hotels charge newlyweds more for bridal suites. Is that price discrimination? Some hotel managers say no. They contend that honeymooners, unlike other customers, always steal mementos, so the price differential reflects an actual cost differential.

The 2013 price for 51 weekly issues of the *Economist* magazine for a year is $356 if you buy it at the newsstand, $160 for a standard print subscription, and $96 for a college student subscription. The difference between the newsstand cost and the standard subscription cost reflects, at least in part, the higher cost of selling magazines at a newsstand versus mailing them directly to customers, so this price difference does not reflect pure price discrimination. In contrast, the price difference between the standard subscription rate and the college student rate does reflect pure price discrimination because the two subscriptions are identical in every respect except the price.

Types of Price Discrimination

Traditionally, economists focus on three types of price discrimination: perfect price discrimination, group price discrimination, and nonlinear price discrimination. With **perfect price discrimination** (also called *first-degree price discrimination*), a firm sells each unit at the maximum amount any customer is willing to pay for it. Under perfect price discrimination, price differs across consumers, and a given consumer may pay higher prices for some units than for others.

With **group price discrimination** (also called *third-degree price discrimination*), a firm charges each group of customers a different price, but it does not charge different prices within the group. The price that a firm charges a consumer depends on that consumer's membership in a particular group. Thus, not all customers pay different prices—the firm sets different prices only for a few groups of customers. Because group price discrimination is the most common type of price discrimination, the phrase *price discrimination* is often used to mean *group price discrimination*.

perfect price discrimination (*first-degree price discrimination*)
a firm sells each unit at the maximum amount any customer is willing to pay for it, so prices differ across customers and a given customer may pay more for some units than for others

group price discrimination (*third-degree price discrimination*)
a firm charges each group of customers a different price, but it does not charge different prices within the group

nonlinear price discrimination (*second-degree price discrimination*)
a firm charges a different price for large quantities than for small quantities but all customers who buy a given quantity pay the same price

A firm engages in **nonlinear price discrimination** (also called *second-degree price discrimination*) when it charges a different price for large purchases than for small quantities, so that the price paid varies according to the quantity purchased. With pure nonlinear price discrimination, all customers who buy a given quantity pay the same price; however, firms can combine nonlinear price discrimination with group price discrimination, setting different nonlinear price schedules for different groups of consumers.

12.2 Perfect Price Discrimination

If a firm with market power knows exactly how much each customer is willing to pay for each unit of its good and it can prevent resale, the firm charges each person his or her **reservation price**: the maximum amount a person would be willing to pay for a unit of output. Such an all-knowing firm *perfectly price discriminates*. By selling each unit of its output to the customer who values it the most at the maximum price that person is willing to pay, the perfectly price-discriminating monopoly captures all possible consumer surplus. For example, the managers of the Suez Canal set tolls on an individual basis, taking into account many factors such as weather and each ship's alternative routes.

reservation price
the maximum amount a person would be willing to pay for a unit of output

Perfect price discrimination is rare because firms do not have perfect information about their customers. Nevertheless, it is useful to examine perfect price discrimination because it is the most efficient form of price discrimination and provides a benchmark against which we can compare other types of nonuniform pricing.

We now show how a firm with full information about consumer reservation prices can use that information to perfectly price discriminate. Next, we compare the market outcomes (price, quantity, surplus) of a perfectly price-discriminating monopoly to those of perfectly competitive and uniform-price monopoly firms. Finally, we discuss how firms obtain the information they need to perfectly price discriminate.

How a Firm Perfectly Price Discriminates

A firm with market power that can prevent resale and has full information about each customer's reservation price—the maximum amount that a customer is willing to pay—can price discriminate by selling each unit at its reservation price. We use the demand curve facing a monopoly in Figure 12.1 to illustrate how a perfectly price-discriminating firm maximizes its profit (see Appendix 12A for a mathematical treatment).

The maximum price for any unit of output equals the height of the demand curve at that output level. The figure shows that a perfectly price-discriminating firm sells its first unit of output for $6. Having sold the first unit, the firm can get at most $5 for its second unit. The firm must drop its price by $1 for each successive unit it sells.

A perfectly price-discriminating monopoly's marginal revenue is the same as its price. As the figure shows, the firm's marginal revenue is $MR_1 = \$6$ on the first unit, $MR_2 = \$5$ on the second unit, and $MR_3 = \$4$ on the third unit. As a result, *the firm's marginal revenue curve is its demand curve*.

This firm has a constant marginal cost of $3 per unit. It pays for the firm to produce the first unit because the firm sells that unit for $6, so its marginal revenue exceeds its marginal cost by $3. Similarly, the firm sells the second unit for $5 and the third unit for $4. The firm breaks even when it sells the fourth unit for $3. The firm is unwilling to sell more than four units because its marginal cost would exceed

Figure 12.1 Perfect Price Discrimination

The monopoly can charge $6 for the first unit, $5 for the second, and $4 for the third, as the demand curve shows. Its marginal revenue is $MR_1 = \$6$ for the first unit, $MR_2 = \$5$ for the second unit, and $MR_3 = \$4$ for the third unit. Thus, the demand curve is also the marginal revenue curve. Because the firm's marginal and average cost is $3 per unit, it is unwilling to sell at a price below $3, so it sells 4 units, point *e*, and breaks even on the last unit.

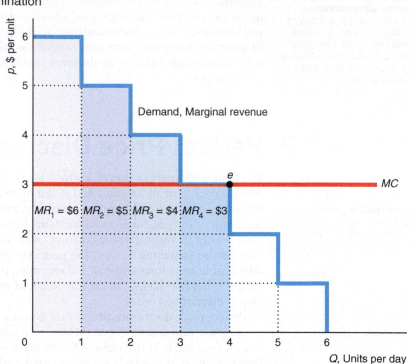

its marginal revenue on all successive units. Thus, like any profit-maximizing firm, a perfectly price-discriminating firm produces at point *e*, where its marginal revenue curve intersects its marginal cost curve.

This perfectly price-discriminating firm earns revenues of $MR_1 + MR_2 + MR_3 + MR_4 = \$6 + \$5 + \$4 + \$3 = \$18$, which is the area under its marginal revenue curve up to the number of units, four, it sells. If the firm has no fixed cost, its cost of producing four units is $\$12 = \$3 \times 4$, so its profit is $6.

Application

Google Uses Bidding for Ads to Price Discriminate

When you search using Google, paid advertising appears next to your results. The ads that appear vary according to your search term. By making searches for unusual topics easy and fast, Google helps firms reach difficult-to-find potential customers with targeted ads. For example, a lawyer specializing in toxic mold lawsuits can place an ad that is seen only by people who search for "toxic mold lawyer." Such focused advertising has a higher payoff per view than traditional print and broadcast ads that reach much larger, nontargeted groups ("wasted eyeballs") and avoids the problem of finding addresses for direct mailing.

Google uses auctions to price these ads. Advertisers are willing to bid higher to be listed first on Google's result pages. Goldfarb and Tucker (2011) found that how much lawyers will pay for context-based ads depends on the difficulty of making a match. Lawyers will pay more to advertise when fewer potential customers are self identified—fewer people searching for a particular phrase.

Some states have anti-ambulance-chaser regulations, which prohibit personal injury lawyers from directly contacting potential clients by snail mail, phone, or email for a few months after an accident. In those states, the extra amount bid for ads linked to personal injury keywords rather than for other keywords such as "tax lawyer" is $1.01 (11%) more than in unregulated states. We're talking big bucks here: Trial lawyers earned $40 billion in 2004, which is 50% more than Microsoft or Intel and twice that of Coca-Cola.

By taking advantage of advertisers' desire to reach small, difficult-to-find segments of the population and varying the price according to advertisers' willingness to pay, Google is essentially perfectly price discriminating.

Perfect Price Discrimination Is Efficient but Harms Some Consumers

Perfect price discrimination is efficient: It maximizes the sum of consumer surplus and producer surplus. Therefore, both perfect competition and perfect price discrimination maximize total surplus. However, *with perfect price discrimination, the entire surplus goes to the firm, whereas the surplus is shared under competition.*

If the market in Figure 12.2 is competitive, the intersection of the demand curve and the marginal cost curve, MC, determines the competitive equilibrium at e_c, where price is p_c and quantity is Q_c. Consumer surplus is $A + B + C$, producer surplus is $D + E$, and society has no deadweight loss. The market is efficient because the price, p_c, equals the marginal cost, MC_c.

With a single-price monopoly (which charges all its customers the same price because it cannot distinguish among them), the intersection of the MC curve and the single-price monopoly's marginal revenue curve, MR^s, determines the output, Q_s.[6] The monopoly operates at e_s, where it charges p_s. The deadweight loss from monopoly is $C + E$. This efficiency loss is due to the monopoly's charging a price, p_s, that's above its marginal cost, MC_s, so less is sold than in a competitive market.

The quantity, Q_d, that the perfectly price-discriminating firm produces is determined by the intersection of the marginal cost curve, MC, and the demand curve or marginal revenue curve, MR^d. A perfectly price-discriminating firm's producer surplus from selling Q_d units is the area below its demand curve and above its marginal cost curve, $A + B + C + D + E$. Its profit is the producer surplus minus its fixed cost, if any. Consumers receive no consumer surplus because each consumer pays his or her reservation price. The perfectly price-discriminating firm's profit-maximizing solution has *no deadweight loss* because the last unit is sold at a price, p_c, that equals the marginal cost, MC_c, as in a competitive market. Thus, both a perfect price discrimination outcome and a competitive equilibrium are efficient.

The perfect price discrimination solution differs from the competitive equilibrium in two important ways. First, in the competitive equilibrium, everyone is charged a price equal to the equilibrium marginal cost, $p_c = MC_c$; however, in the perfect price discrimination equilibrium, only the last unit is sold at that price. The other units are sold at customers' reservation prices, which are greater than p_c. Second, consumers receive some net benefit (consumer surplus, $A + B + C$) in a competitive market, whereas a perfectly price-discriminating monopoly captures all the surplus or potential gains from trade. Thus, perfect price discrimination does not reduce efficiency—both output and total surplus are the same as under competition—but it does redistribute income away from consumers. Consumers are much better off under competition.

---

[6]We assume that if we convert a monopoly into a competitive industry, the industry's marginal cost curve—the lowest cost at which an additional unit can be produced by any firm—is the same as the monopoly MC curve. The industry MC curve is the industry supply curve (Chapter 8).

Figure 12.2 Competitive, Single-Price, and Perfect Price Discrimination Equilibria

In the competitive market equilibrium, e_c, price is p_c, quantity is Q_c, consumer surplus is $A + B + C$, producer surplus is $D + E$, and society has no deadweight loss. In the single-price monopoly equilibrium, e_s, price is p_s, quantity is Q_s, consumer surplus falls to A, producer surplus is $B + D$, and deadweight loss is $C + E$. In the perfect price discrimination equilibrium, the monopoly sells each unit at the customer's reservation price on the demand curve, which is also its marginal revenue curve, MR^d. It sells $Q_d\ (= Q_c)$ units, where the demand curve intersects the marginal cost curve, so that the last unit is sold at its marginal cost. Customers have no consumer surplus, but society suffers no deadweight loss.

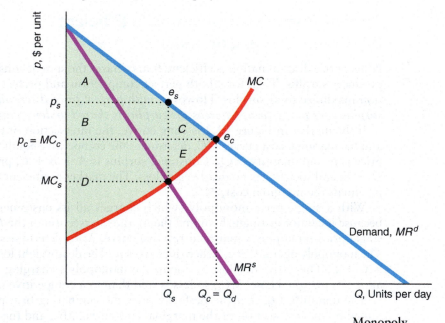

	Competition	Monopoly	
		Single Price	Perfect Price Discrimination
Consumer Surplus, CS	$A + B + C$	A	0
Producer Surplus, PS	$D + E$	$B + D$	$A + B + C + D + E$
Welfare, $W = CS + PS$	$A + B + C + D + E$	$A + B + D$	$A + B + C + D + E$
Deadweight Loss, DWL	0	$C + E$	0

Is a single-price or perfectly price-discriminating monopoly better for consumers? The perfect price discrimination equilibrium is more efficient than the single-price monopoly equilibrium because more output is produced. However, a single-price monopoly takes less consumer surplus from consumers than a perfectly price-discriminating monopoly. Consumers who put a very high value on the good are better off under single-price monopoly, where they have consumer surplus, than with perfect price discrimination, where they have none. Consumers with lower reservation prices who purchase from the perfectly price-discriminating monopoly but not from the single-price monopoly have no consumer surplus in either case. All the social gain from the extra output goes to the perfectly price-discriminating firm. Consumer surplus is greatest with competition, lower with single-price monopoly, and eliminated by perfect price discrimination.

Application

Botox Revisited

To show how perfect price discrimination differs from competition and single-price monopoly, we revisit the Application on Allergan's Botox from Chapter 11. The graph shows our estimated linear demand curve for Botox and a constant marginal cost (and average variable cost) of $25 per vial. If the market had been competitive (so that price equals marginal cost at e_c), consumer surplus would have been triangle $A + B + C = \$750$ million per year, and producer surplus and deadweight loss would be zero. In the single-price monopoly equilibrium, e_s, the Botox vials sell for $400, and one million vials are sold. The corresponding consumer surplus is triangle $A = \$187.5$ million per year, producer surplus is rectangle $B = \$375$ million, and the deadweight loss is triangle $C = \$187.5$ million.

If Allergan could perfectly price discriminate, its producer surplus would double to $A + B + C = \$750$ million per year, and consumers would obtain no consumer surplus. The marginal consumer would pay the marginal cost of $25, the same as in a competitive market.

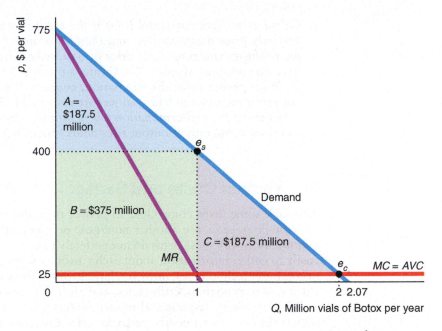

		Monopoly	
	Competition	Single Price	Perfect Price Discrimination
Consumer Surplus, *CS*	$A + B + C$	A	0
Producer Surplus, *PS*	0	B	$A + B + C$
Welfare, $W = CS + PS$	$A + B + C$	$A + B$	$A + B + C$
Deadweight Loss, *DWL*	0	C	0

Allergan's inability to perfectly price discriminate costs the company and society dearly. The profit of the single-price monopoly, $B = \$375$ million per year, is lower than what it could earn if it could use perfect price discrimination, $A + B + C = \$750$ million per year. Similarly, society's welfare under single-price monopoly is lower than from perfect price discrimination by the deadweight loss, C, of $187.5 million per year.

Solved Problem 12.1

How does welfare change if the movie theater described in Table 12.1 goes from charging a single price to perfectly price discriminating?

Answer

1. *Calculate welfare for panel a (a) if the theater sets a single price and (b) if it perfectly price discriminates, and then (c) compare them.* (a) If the theater sets the profit-maximizing single price of $5, it sells 30 tickets and makes a profit of $150. The 20 senior citizen customers are paying their reservation price, so they have no consumer surplus. The 10 college students have reservation prices of $10, so their consumer surplus is $50. Thus, welfare is $200: the sum of the profit, $150, and the consumer surplus, $50. (b) If the theater perfectly price discriminates, it charges seniors $5 and college students $10. Because the theater is charging all customers their reservation prices, they have no consumer surplus. The firm's profit rises to $200. (c) Thus, *welfare is the same under both pricing systems where output stays the same.*

2. *Calculate welfare for panel b (a) if the theater sets a single price and (b) if it perfectly price discriminates, and then (c) compare them.* (a) If the theater sets the profit-maximizing single price of $10, only college students attend and they have no consumer surplus. The theater's profit is $100, so total welfare is $100. (b) With perfect price discrimination, consumers receive no consumer surplus, but profit increases to $125, so welfare rises to $125. (c) Thus, *welfare is greater with perfect price discrimination where output increases.* (The result that welfare increases if and only if output rises holds generally.)

Transaction Costs and Perfect Price Discrimination

Although some firms come close to perfect price discrimination, many more firms set a single price or use another nonlinear pricing method. Transaction costs are a major reason why these firms do not perfectly price discriminate: It is too difficult or costly to gather information about each customer's price sensitivity. Recent advances in computer technologies, however, have lowered these costs, causing hotels, car and truck rental companies, cruise lines, and airlines to price discriminate more often.

Private colleges request and receive financial information from students, which allows the schools to nearly perfectly price discriminate. The schools give partial scholarships as a means of reducing tuition for relatively poor students.

Many other firms believe that, taking the transaction costs into account, it pays to use group price discrimination, or nonlinear price discrimination rather than try to perfectly price discriminate. We now turn to these alternative approaches.

12.3 Group Price Discrimination

Most firms have no practical way to estimate the reservation price for each of their customers. However, many of these firms know which groups of customers are likely to have higher reservation prices on average than others. A firm engages in *group price discrimination* by dividing potential customers into two or more groups and setting different prices for each group. Consumer groups may differ by age (such as adults and children), by location (such as by country), or in other ways. All units of the good sold to customers within a group are sold at a single price. As with individual price discrimination, to engage in group price discrimination, a firm must have market power, be able to identify groups with different reservation prices, and prevent resale.

For example, movie theaters with market power charge senior citizens a lower price than they charge younger adults because senior citizens are not willing to pay as much as others to see a movie. By admitting people as soon as they demonstrate their age and buy tickets, the theater prevents resale.

Application

Warner Brothers Sets Prices for a *Harry Potter* DVD

A copyright gives Warner Brothers the legal monopoly to produce and sell the *Harry Potter and the Deathly Hallows, Part 2* DVD. Warner sells the movie in the United States, the United Kingdom, and other countries. Because the U.S. and U.K. DVD formats differ, Warner can charge different prices in the two countries without worrying about resale.

The DVD was released during the holiday season of 2011–2012 and sold $Q_A = 5.8$ million copies to American consumers at $p_A = \$29$ and $Q_B = 2.0$ million copies to British consumers at $p_B = \$39$ (£25). Thus, Warner engaged in group price discrimination by charging different prices in various countries.

Group Price Discrimination with Two Groups

How does a monopoly price discriminate between two groups of consumers?[7] In particular, how should Warner have set its prices p_A and p_B—or equivalently Q_A and Q_B—so that it maximized its combined profit in the two countries?

Solving for the Group Price Discrimination Optimum To answer this question, we use our understanding of a single-price monopoly's behavior. Because Warner's marginal and average cost, m, is constant and identical in both countries, Warner maximized its total profit by maximizing its profit from each country separately. Warner's total profit, π, was the sum of its American and British profits, π_A and π_B:

$$\pi = \pi_A + \pi_B = (p_A Q_A - m Q_A) + (p_B Q_B - m Q_B),$$

where $p_A Q_A$ was the U.S. revenue, $m Q_A$ was the U.S. cost, $p_B Q_B$ was the U.K. revenue, and $m Q_B$ was the U.K. cost.

Figure 12.3 shows our estimates of the linear demand curves in the two countries. We estimate that Warner had a constant marginal cost of $m = \$1$ in both countries.

In panel a, Warner maximized its U.S. profit by selling $Q_A = 5.8$ million DVDs, where its marginal revenue equals its marginal cost $MR^A = m = 1$ (Chapter 11), and charged $p_A = \$29$. Similarly in panel b, Warner maximized its U.K. profit by selling $Q_B = 2.0$ million DVDS where $MR^B = m = \$1$, and charged $p_B = \$39$.

This price-setting rule must be profit maximizing if the firm does not want to change its price for either group. Would the monopoly want to lower its price and sell more output in the United States? If it did, its marginal revenue would be below its marginal cost, so this change would reduce its profit. Similarly, if the monopoly sold less output in the United States, its marginal revenue would be above its marginal cost, which would reduce its profit. The same arguments can be made about its pricing in Britain.

---

[7]See Appendix 12B for a calculus analysis.

Figure 12.3 Group Pricing of the *Harry Potter* DVD

Warner Brothers, the monopoly producer of the *Harry Potter and the Deathly Hallows, Part 2* DVD, charges more in the United Kingdom, $p_B = \$39$ (£25), than in the United States, $p_A = \$29$, because demand is more elastic in the United States. Warner Brothers sets the quantity independently in each country, where its relevant marginal revenue equals its common, constant marginal cost, $m = \$1$. As a result, it maximizes its profit by equating the two marginal revenues: $MR^A = 1 = MR^B$.

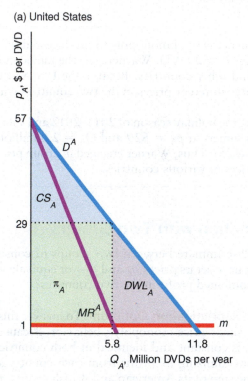

(a) United States

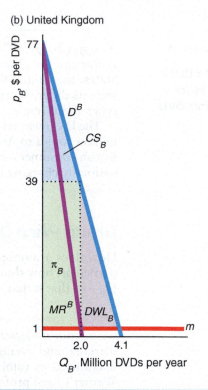

(b) United Kingdom

Thus, the price-discriminating monopoly maximizes its profit by operating where its marginal revenue for each country equals its common marginal cost. Because the monopoly equates the marginal revenue for each group to its common marginal cost, $MC = m$, the marginal revenues for the two countries are equal:

$$MR^A = m = MR^B. \qquad (12.1)$$

Solved Problem 12.2

We estimate that Warner faced inverse demand functions for its *Harry Potter and the Deathly Hallows, Part 2* DVD of $p_A = 57 - 4.8Q_A$ in the United States and $p_B = 77 - 19Q_B$ in the United Kingdom. Given that the marginal cost is 1 in both countries, solve for Warner's optimal prices and quantities in each country.

Answer

1. *Determine the marginal revenue functions.* The marginal revenue curve corresponding to a linear inverse demand curve has twice as steep a slope and the same price intercept (Chapter 11, Solved Problem 11.1). Thus, the marginal revenue function is $MR^A = 57 - 9.6Q_A$ in the United States and $MR^B = 77 - 38Q_B$ in the United Kingdom.

2. *Solve for Warner's optimal monopoly prices and quantities in each country separately.* Warner's optimal monopoly quantity is determined by equating the marginal revenue and marginal cost. The U.S. monopoly optimum condition is $57 - 9.6Q_A = 1$, so $Q_A = 56/9.6 \approx 5.833$. Using the inverse demand function, we learn that the corresponding price is $p \approx 29$. In the United Kingdom, the condition for an optimum is $77 - 38Q_B = 1$, so $Q_B = 76/38 = 2$, and $p_B = 39$.

Prices and Elasticities We can use Equation 12.1, $MR^A = m = MR^B$, to determine how the prices for the two groups vary with the price elasticities of demand at the profit-maximizing outputs. The marginal revenue for each group is a function of the corresponding price and the price elasticity of demand (as Chapter 11 showed in Equation 11.4). The U.S. marginal revenue is $MR^A = p_A(1 + 1/\varepsilon_A)$, where ε_A is the price elasticity of demand for U.S. consumers, and the U.K. marginal revenue is $MR^B = p_B(1 + 1/\varepsilon_B)$, where ε_B is the price elasticity of demand for British consumers.

Rewriting Equation 12.1 using these expressions for marginal revenue, we find that

$$MR^A = p_A\left(1 + \frac{1}{\varepsilon_A}\right) = m = p_B\left(1 + \frac{1}{\varepsilon_B}\right) = MR^B. \tag{12.2}$$

Given that $m = \$1$, $p_A = \$29$, and $p_B = \$39$ in Equation 12.2, Warner must have believed that $\varepsilon_A = p_A/[m - p_A] = 29/[-28] \approx -1.0357$ and $\varepsilon_B = p_B/[m - p_B] = 39/[-38] \approx -1.0263$.[8] By rearranging Equation 12.2, we learn that the ratio of prices in the two countries depends only on demand elasticities in those countries:

$$\frac{p_B}{p_A} = \frac{1 + 1/\varepsilon_A}{1 + 1/\varepsilon_B}. \tag{12.3}$$

Substituting the prices and elasticities into Equation 12.3, we determine that

$$\frac{p_B}{p_A} = \frac{\$39}{\$29} \approx 1.345 \approx \frac{1 + 1/(-1.0357)}{1 + 1/(-1.0263)} = \frac{1 + 1/\varepsilon_A}{1 + 1/\varepsilon_B}.$$

Thus, Warner Brothers apparently believed that the British demand curve was less elastic at its profit-maximizing prices than the U.S. demand curve, as $\varepsilon_B \approx -1.0263$ is closer to zero than is $\varepsilon_A \approx -1.0357$. Consequently, Warner charged British consumers 34% more than U.S. customers.

By mid-2012 as demand for the DVD fell, Amazon dropped the price for this DVD at its sites around the world, but maintained its price differentials. Amazon's U.S. price fell to $7, while its U.K. price dropped to $9.50, which still reflected about the same British markup: 36%.

Application

Reselling Textbooks

When Supap Kirtsaeng, a Thai math student, was an undergraduate at Cornell University and then a Ph.D. student at the University of Southern California, he found a way to pay for his education. He had his friends and relatives ship him textbooks that they bought in Thailand, which he resold to U.S. college students on eBay and elsewhere, netting hundreds of thousands of dollars.

---

[8]We obtain the expression $\varepsilon_i = p_i/(m - p_i)$, $i = A$ or B, by rearranging $p_i(1 + 1/\varepsilon_i) = m$ (Equation 11.4).

Why was reselling these books profitable? U.S. textbooks sell at much lower prices in foreign markets. Many of these books differ from their U.S. versions only by having a soft cover with an "international edition" label.

John Wiley & Sons, a publisher, sued Mr. Kirtsaeng for copyright infringement. The company claimed that by importing and selling its books, Mr. Kirtsaeng infringed the company's copyright. It asserted that the *first-sale* doctrine—which allows people who buy something to use or resell it however they want—did not apply to goods produced specifically for sale overseas.

The U.S. Court of Appeals for the 2nd Circuit in New York agreed with Wiley and upheld a $600,000 judgment against Mr. Kirtsaeng. However, in 2013, the U.S. Supreme Court reversed that ruling by a six-to-three vote, concluding that the first-sale rule holds generally. This decision applies to records, movies, art, software, and other goods as well as books that are covered under copyright law.[9]

Thus, unless Congress changes the copyright law, publishers will find it more difficult to maintain price differentials across countries. A possible consequence of this ruling is that poor foreign students will no longer be able to afford textbooks because the foreign price will rise. The U.S. and foreign price will differ by only the transaction cost of reselling the books. If those transaction costs are negligible, a single price will be charged throughout the world.

Alternatively, publishers may prevent resale. One possibility is that they will differentiate U.S. and foreign textbooks substantially to prevent reselling; however, doing so is expensive and time-consuming. Once electronic textbooks become common, students will rent the books for the term and be unable to resell them.

Solved Problem 12.3

A monopoly book publisher with a constant marginal cost (and average cost) of $MC = 1$ sells a novel in only two countries and faces a linear inverse demand curve of $p_1 = 6 - \frac{1}{2}Q_1$ in Country 1 and $p_2 = 9 - Q_2$ in Country 2. What price would a profit-maximizing monopoly charge in each country with and without a ban against shipments between the countries?

Answer

If resale across borders is banned so that price discrimination is possible:

1. *Determine the profit-maximizing price that the monopoly sets in each country by setting the relevant marginal revenue equal to the marginal cost.* If the monopoly can price discriminate, it sets a monopoly price (Section 11.1) independently in each country. By rearranging the demand function for Country 1, we find that the inverse demand function is $p_1 = 6 - \frac{1}{2}Q_1$ for quantities less than 6, and zero otherwise, as panel a in the figure shows. The marginal revenue curve is twice as steeply sloped as is the linear inverse demand curve (Chapter 11): $MR^1 = 6 - Q_1$. The monopoly maximizes its profit where its marginal revenue equals its marginal cost,

$$MR^1 = 6 - Q_1 = 1 = MC.$$

---

[9]However, the Supreme Court held in 2010 that Omega could prevent Costco from selling its watches produced outside the United States, citing a tiny trademark on each watch, so that they came under the jurisdiction of trademark laws, which provide owners more protection than do copyright laws.

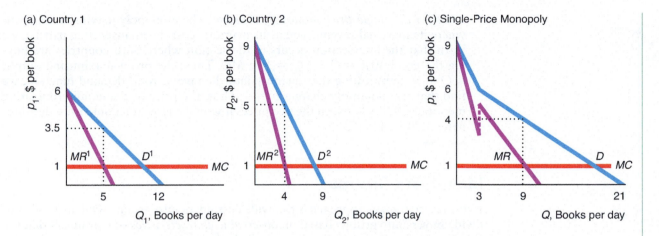

(a) Country 1

(b) Country 2

(c) Single-Price Monopoly

Solving, we find that its profit-maximizing output is $Q_1 = 5$. Substituting this expression back into the monopoly's inverse demand curve, we learn that its profit-maximizing price is $p_1 = 3.5$, as panel a illustrates. In Country 2, the inverse demand curve is $p_2 = 9 - Q_2$, so the monopoly chooses Q_2 such that $MR^2 = 9 - 2Q_2 = 1 = MC$. Thus, it maximizes its profit in Country 2 where $Q_2 = 4$ and $p_2 = 5$, as panel b shows.

If imports are permitted so that price discrimination is impossible:

2. *Derive the total demand curve.* If the monopoly cannot price discriminate, it charges the same price, p, in both countries. The monopoly faces the total demand curve in panel c, which is the horizontal sum of the demand curves for each of the two countries in panels a and b (Chapter 2). If the price is between 6 and 9, the quantity demanded is positive in only Country 2, so the total demand curve (panel c) is the same as Country 2's demand curve (panel b). If the price is less than 6 where both countries demand a positive quantity, the total demand curve (panel c) is the horizontal sum of the two individual countries' demand curves (panels a and b).[10] As panel c shows, the total demand curve has a kink at $p = 6$, because the quantity demanded in Country 1 is positive only below this price.

3. *Determine the marginal revenue curve corresponding to the total demand curve.* Because the total demand curve has a kink at $p = 6$, the corresponding marginal revenue curve has two sections. At prices above 6, the marginal revenue curve is the same as that of Country 2 in panel b. At prices below 6, where the total demand curve is the horizontal sum of the two countries' demand curves, the marginal revenue curve has twice the slope of the linear total inverse demand curve. The inverse total demand function is $p = 7 - \frac{1}{3}Q$, and the marginal revenue function is $MR = 7 - \frac{2}{3}Q$.[11] Panel c shows that the marginal revenue curve *jumps*—is discontinuous—at the quantity where the total demand curve has a kink.

---

[10]Rearranging the inverse demand functions, we find that the Country 1 demand function is $Q_1 = 12 - p_1$ and the Country 2 demand function is $Q_2 = 9 - p_2$. As a result for prices below 6, the total demand function is $Q = (12 - 2p) + (9 - p) = 21 - 3p$, where $Q = Q_1 + Q_2$ is the total quantity that the monopoly sells in both countries.

[11]From the previous footnote, we know that the total demand function for prices less than 6 is $Q = 21 - 3p$. Rearranging this expression, we find that the inverse demand function is $p = 7 - \frac{1}{3}Q$. Because the marginal revenue function has twice as steep a slope, it is $MR = 7 - \frac{2}{3}Q$.

4. *Solve for the single-price monopoly solution.* The monopoly maximizes its profit where its marginal revenue equals its marginal cost. From inspecting panel c, we learn that the intersection occurs in the section where both countries are buying the good: $MR = 7 - \frac{2}{3}Q = 1 = MC$. Thus, the profit-maximizing output is $Q = 9$. Substituting that quantity into the inverse total demand function, we find that the monopoly charges $p = 4$. Thus, the price of the nondiscriminating monopoly, 4, lies between the two prices it would charge if it could price discriminate: $3.50 < 4 < 5$.

Identifying Groups

Firms use two main approaches to divide customers into groups. One method is to divide buyers into groups based on *observable characteristics* of consumers that the firm believes are associated with unusually high or low reservation prices or demand elasticities. For example, movie theaters price discriminate using the age of customers, charging higher prices for adults than for children.

Similarly, some firms charge customers in one country higher prices than those in another country. In 2012, the Windows 8 Pro upgrade sold for $95 in the United States, £97 ($125) in the United Kingdom, C$160 ($156) in Canada, €54 ($70) in France, and ¥7,290 ($77) in Japan. Most of these differences are much greater than can be explained by shipping costs and reflect group price discrimination.

Another approach is to identify and divide consumers on the basis of their *actions*: The firm allows consumers to self-select the group to which they belong. For example, customers may be identified by their willingness to spend time to buy a good at a lower price or to order goods and services in advance of delivery.

Firms use differences in the value customers place on their time to discriminate by using queues (making people wait in line) and other time-intensive methods of selling goods. Store managers who believe that high-wage people are unwilling to "waste their time shopping" may run sales by which consumers who visit the store and pick up the good themselves get a low price while consumers who order over the phone or by mail pay a higher price. This type of price discrimination increases profit if people who put a high value on their time also have less elastic demands for the good.

Early adopters of a new product are often very enthusiastic and will pay premium prices. Firms can take advantage of early adopters by charging a high initial price for a new product and then lowering the price after the initial sales are made.

Application

Buying Discounts

Firms use various approaches to induce consumers to indicate whether they have relatively high or low elasticities of demand. For each of these methods, consumers must incur some cost, such as their time, to receive a discount. Otherwise, all consumers would get the discount. By spending extra time to obtain a discount, price-sensitive consumers are able to differentiate themselves.

Coupons. Many firms use discount coupons to group price discriminate. Through this device, firms divide customers into two groups, charging coupon clippers less than nonclippers. Offering coupons makes sense if the people who do not clip coupons are less price sensitive on average than those who do. People who are willing to spend their time clipping coupons buy cereals and other goods at lower prices than those who value their time more. A 2009 study by the Promotion Marketing Association Coupon Council found that consumers who spend 20 minutes per week clipping and

You've got to prove you really want a discount!

organizing coupons could save up to $1,000 on an average annual grocery bill of $5,000 or more. More than three-quarters of U.S. consumers redeem coupons at least occasionally. In 2012, coupons with a face value of $310 billion were distributed by consumer package goods marketers to U.S. consumers. Of these, 3.0 billion coupons were redeemed for $2.9 billion.

The introduction of digital coupons (for example, **EverSave.com** and **zavers.com**) has made it easier for firms to target appropriate groups, but has lowered consumers' costs of using coupons, which means that a larger share of people use them. According to eMarketer, 47% of U.S. adults used online coupons in 2012. Digital coupons are more likely to be redeemed (15%–20%) than are paper coupons (less than 1%).

Airline Tickets. By choosing between two different types of tickets, airline customers indicate whether they are likely to be business travelers or vacationers. Airlines give customers a choice between high-price tickets with no strings attached and low-price fares that must be purchased long in advance.

Airlines know that many business travelers have little advance warning before they book a flight and have relatively inelastic demand curves. In contrast, vacation travelers can usually plan in advance and have relatively high elasticities of demand for air travel. The airlines' rules ensure that vacationers with relatively elastic demand obtain low fares while most business travelers with relatively inelastic demand buy high-price tickets (often more than four times higher than the plan-ahead rate).

Reverse Auctions. Priceline.com and other online merchants use a name-your-own-price or "reverse" auction to identify price-sensitive customers. A customer enters a relatively low-price bid for a good or service, such as an airline ticket. Merchants decide whether or not to accept that bid. To prevent their less price-sensitive customers from using these methods, airlines force successful Priceline bidders to be flexible: to fly at off hours, to make one or more connections, and to accept any type of aircraft. Similarly, when bidding on groceries, a customer must list "one or two brands you like." As Jay Walker, Priceline's founder explained, "The manufacturers would rather not give you a discount, of course, but if you prove that you're willing to switch brands, they're willing to pay to keep you."

Rebates. Why do many firms offer a rebate of, say, $5 instead of reducing the price on their product by $5? The reason is that a consumer must incur an extra, time-consuming step to receive the rebate. Thus, only those consumers who are very price sensitive and place a low value on their time will actually apply for the rebate. According to a *Consumer Reports* survey, 47% of customers always or often apply for a rebate, 23% sometimes apply, 25% never apply, and 5% responded that the question was not applicable to them.

Welfare Effects of Group Price Discrimination

Group price discrimination results in inefficient production and consumption. As a result, welfare under group price discrimination is lower than that under competition or perfect price discrimination. However, welfare may be lower or higher with group price discrimination than with a single-price monopoly.

Group Price Discrimination Versus Competition Consumer surplus is greater and more output is produced with perfect competition than with group price discrimination. In Figure 12.3, consumer surplus with group price discrimination is CS_A for American consumers, shown in panel a, and CS_B for British consumers, shown in panel b. Under competition, consumer surplus is the area below the demand curve and above the marginal cost curve: $CS_A + \pi_A + DWL_A$ in panel a and $CS_B + \pi_B + DWL_B$ in panel b.

Thus, group price discrimination transfers some of the competitive consumer surplus, π_A and π_B, to the monopoly as additional profit and causes the deadweight loss, DWL_A and DWL_B, which is reduced consumer surplus that is simply lost or wasted. The deadweight loss is due to the group-price-discriminating monopoly charging prices above marginal cost, which results in reduced production from the optimal competitive level.

Group Price Discrimination Versus Single-Price Monopoly From theory alone, we can't tell whether welfare is higher if the monopoly uses group price discrimination or if it sets a single price. Both types of monopolies set price above marginal cost, so too little is produced relative to competition. Output may rise as the firm starts discriminating if groups that did not buy when the firm charged a single price start buying. In the movie theater example in panel b of Table 12.1, welfare is higher with discrimination than with single-price monopoly because more tickets are sold when the monopoly discriminates (see Solved Problem 12.1).

The closer the group-price-discriminating monopoly comes to perfectly price discriminating (by, for example, dividing its customers into many groups rather than just two), the more output it produces, which reduces the production inefficiency. However, total surplus falls if the firm switches to group price discrimination and total output falls.[12]

12.4 Nonlinear Price Discrimination

Many firms are unable to determine which customers have the highest reservation prices. However, such firms may know that most customers are willing to pay more for the first unit than for successive units. That is, a typical customer's demand curve is downward sloping. Such a firm can price discriminate by letting the price each customer pays vary with the number of units the customer buys. That is, the firm uses *nonlinear pricing*, which is also called *second-degree price discrimination* or *quantity discrimination*.

Here, the price varies with quantity but each customer faces the same nonlinear pricing schedule.[13] To use nonlinear pricing, a firm must have market power and be able to prevent customers who buy at a low price from reselling to those who would otherwise pay a high price.

A 64-ounce bottle of V8 vegetable juice sells for $4.39 or 6.8¢ an ounce, while a 12-ounce bottle sells for $2.79 or 23¢ an ounce. This difference in the price per ounce reflects nonlinear price discrimination unless the price difference is due to cost

---

[12]An additional source of inefficiency is time spent by consumers trying to resell the product to high-willingness-to-pay customers or searching for low prices. These activities do not occur if everyone knows the firm sets a uniform price.

[13]The term *nonlinear* is used because a consumer's expenditure is a nonlinear function of the quantity purchased. A consumer's expenditure, E, is a linear function of quantity, q, only if the price, p, is constant: $E = pq$. If the price varies with quantity, then the expenditure is not linear in quantity.

differences. This quantity discount results in customers who make large purchases paying less per ounce than those who make small purchases.[14]

Another nonlinear pricing strategy is *block pricing*. Many utilities use block pricing schedules, by which they charge one price per unit for the first few units (a *block*) purchased and a different price per unit for subsequent blocks. Both declining-block and increasing-block pricing are commonly used by gas, electric, water, and other utility companies.

The block-pricing utility monopoly in Figure 12.4 faces a linear demand curve for each (identical) customer. The demand curve hits the vertical axis at $90 and the

Figure 12.4 Block Pricing

If this monopoly engages in block pricing with quantity discounting, it makes a larger profit (producer surplus) than it does if it sets a single price, and welfare is greater. (a) With block pricing, its profit is $B = \$1,200$, welfare is $A + B + C = \$1,600$, and the deadweight loss is $D = \$200$. (b) If the monopoly sets a single price (so that its marginal revenue equals its marginal cost), the monopoly's profit is $F = \$900$, welfare is $E + F = \$1,350$, and the deadweight loss is $G = \$450$.

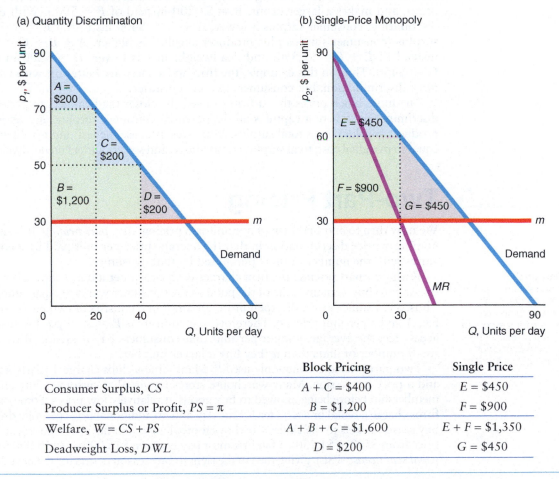

	Block Pricing	Single Price
Consumer Surplus, CS	$A + C = \$400$	$E = \$450$
Producer Surplus or Profit, $PS = \pi$	$B = \$1,200$	$F = \$900$
Welfare, $W = CS + PS$	$A + B + C = \$1,600$	$E + F = \$1,350$
Deadweight Loss, DWL	$D = \$200$	$G = \$450$

---

[14]Not all quantity discounts are a form of price discrimination. Some reflect the reduction in a firm's cost with large-quantity sales. For example, the cost per ounce of selling a soft drink in a large cup is less than that of selling it in a smaller cup; the cost of cups varies little with size, and the cost of pouring and serving is the same. A restaurant offering quantity discounts on drinks may be passing on actual cost savings to larger purchasers rather than price discriminating.

horizontal axis at 90 units. The monopoly has a constant marginal and average cost of $m = \$30$. Panel a shows how this monopoly maximizes its profit if it can quantity discriminate by setting two prices (and both prices lie on the demand curve).

The firm uses declining-block prices to maximize its profit. The monopoly charges a price of $70 on any quantity between 1 and 20—the first block—and $50 on any units beyond the first 20—the second block. The points that determine the blocks, $70 and 20 units and $50 and 40 units, lie on the demand curve. (See Appendix 12C for a mathematical analysis.)

Given each consumer's demand curve, a consumer decides to buy 40 units and pays $1,400 (= $70 × 20) for the first block and $1,000 (= $50 × 20) for the second block. The consumer gains consumer surplus equal to A on the first block and C on the second block, for a total of A + C. The quantity-discriminating monopoly's profit or producer surplus is area B. Society suffers a deadweight loss of D because price, $50, is above marginal cost, $30, on the last unit, 40, purchased.

In panel b, the firm can set only a single price. It produces where its marginal revenue equals its marginal cost, and sells 30 units at $60 per unit. By using nonlinear price discrimination instead of setting a single price, the utility sells more units, 40 instead of 30, and makes a larger profit, B = $1,200 instead of F = $900. With quantity discounting, consumer surplus is lower, A + C = $400 instead of E = $450; total surplus (consumer surplus plus producer surplus) is higher, A + B + C = $1,600 instead of E + F = $1,350; and deadweight loss is lower, D = $200 instead of G = $450. Thus, in this example, the firm and society are better off with nonlinear price discrimination, but consumers as a group suffer.

The more block prices that a firm can set, the closer the firm gets to perfect price discrimination, where it captures all the potential consumer surplus, and its profit or producer surplus equals total surplus. Moreover, because the last unit is sold at a price equal to marginal cost, total surplus is maximized and society suffers no deadweight loss.

12.5 Two-Part Pricing

We now turn to another form of nonuniform pricing, *two-part pricing*. It is similar to nonlinear price discrimination in that the average price per unit paid by a consumer varies with the number of units purchased by that consumer.

two-part pricing
a pricing system in which the firm charges each consumer a lump-sum *access fee* for the right to buy as many units of the good as the consumer wants at a per-unit *price*

With **two-part pricing**, the firm charges each consumer a lump-sum *access fee* for the right to buy as many units of the good as the consumer wants at a per-unit *price*.[15] Thus, a consumer's overall expenditure for amount q consists of two parts: an access fee, A and a per-unit price, p. Therefore, expenditure is $E = A + pq$. Because of the access fee, the average amount per unit that consumers pay is greater if they buy a small number of units than if they buy a larger number.

Two-part pricing is commonly used.[16] Many fitness clubs charge a yearly access fee and a price per session. Many warehouse stores require that customers buy an annual membership before being allowed to buy goods at relatively low prices. Some car rental firms charge a rental or access fee for the day and an additional price per mile driven. To buy season tickets to the Dallas Cowboys football games in the lower seating areas (at a price from $590 to $1,250), a fan first must pay between $16,000 to $150,000 for a *personal seat license* (PSL), giving the fan the right to buy season tickets for the next 30 years.

---

[15]The prices used in two-part pricing are often referred to as *two-part tariffs*.

[16]For example, *venting* stores are springing up in shopping malls in China. A customer pays to enter, and then pays for each second-hand mobile phone, television set, or other product that the customer smashes. (**english.people.com.cn/90001/90782/90872/6915069.html**, viewed April 17, 2013.)

To profit from two-part pricing, a firm must have market power, know how demand differs across customers or with the quantity that a single customer buys, and successfully prevent resale. We start by examining a firm's two-part pricing problem in the extreme case in which all customers have the same demand curve. We then consider what happens when the demand curves of individual customers differ.

Two-Part Pricing with Identical Customers

If all its customers are identical, a monopoly that knows its customers' demand curve can set a two-part price that possesses the same two important properties as perfect price discrimination. First, the efficient quantity is sold because the price of the last unit equals marginal cost. Second, all potential consumer surplus is transferred from consumers to the firm.

To illustrate these points we consider a monopoly that has a constant marginal cost of $MC = 10$ and no fixed cost, so its average cost is also constant at 10. All of the monopoly's customers have the same demand curve, $Q = 80 - p$. Panel a of Figure 12.5 shows the demand curve, D^1, of one such customer, Valerie.

However, if the firm also charges an access fee of 2,450, it captures this 2,450 as its producer surplus or its profit per customer, and leaves Valerie with no consumer surplus. The firm's total profit is 2,450 times the number of identical customers.

The firm maximizes its profit by setting its price equal to its marginal cost and charging an access fee that captures the entire potential consumer surplus. If the firm were to charge a price above its marginal cost of 10, it would sell fewer units and make a smaller profit.

Figure 12.5 Two-Part Pricing with Identical Consumers

(a) Because all customers have the same individual demand curve as Valerie, D^1, the monopoly captures the entire potential consumer surplus using two-part pricing. The monopoly charges a per-unit fee price, p, equal to the marginal cost of 10, and a lump-sum access fee, $A = 2,450$, which is the blue triangle under the demand curve and above the per-unit price of $p = 10$. (b) Were the monopoly to set a price at 20, which is above its marginal cost, it would earn less. It makes a profit of $B_1 = 600$ from the 10 it earns on the 60 units that Valerie buys at this higher price. However, the largest access fee the firm can make now is $A_1 = 1,800$, so its total profit is 2,400, which is less than the 2,450 it makes if it sets its price equal to marginal cost. The difference is a deadweight loss of $C_1 = 50$, which is due to fewer units being sold at the higher price.

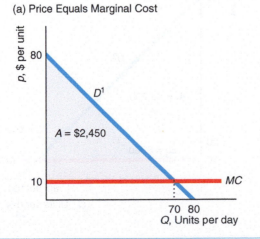

(a) Price Equals Marginal Cost

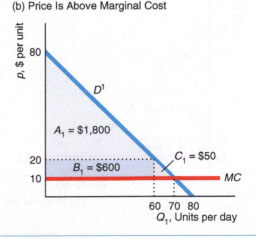

(b) Price Is Above Marginal Cost

In panel b of Figure 12.5, the firm charges $p = 20$. At that higher price, Valerie buys only 60 units, which is less than the 70 units that she buys at a price of 10 in panel a. The firm's profit from selling these 60 units is $B_1 = (20 - 10) \times 60 = 600$.

For Valerie to agree to buy any units, the monopoly has to lower its access fee to 1,800 $(= \frac{1}{2} \times 60 \times 60)$, the new potential consumer surplus, area A_1. The firm's total profit from Valerie is $A_1 + B_1 = 1,800 + 600 = 2,400$. This amount is less than the 2,450 $(= A$ in panel a) profit the firm earns if it sets price equal to marginal cost, 10, and charges the higher access fee. Area A in panel a equals $A_1 + B_1 + C_1$ in panel b. By charging a price above marginal cost, the firm loses C_1, which is the deadweight loss due to selling fewer units.

Similarly, if the firm were to charge a price below its marginal cost, it would also earn less profit. It would sell too many units and make a loss on each unit that it could not fully recapture by a higher access fee.

Two-Part Pricing with Nonidentical Consumers

Two-part pricing is more complex if consumers have different demand curves.[17] Suppose that the monopoly has two customers, Valerie, Consumer 1, and Neal, Consumer 2. Valerie's demand curve, $Q_1 = 80 - p$, is D^1 in panel a of Figure 12.6 (which is the same as panel b of Figure 12.5), and Neal's demand curve, $Q_2 = 100 - p$, is D^2 in panel b. The monopoly's marginal cost, MC, and average cost are constant at 10 per unit.

Figure 12.6 Two-Part Pricing with Different Consumers

The monopoly faces two consumers. Valerie's demand curve is D^1 in panel a, and Neal's demand curve is D^2 in panel b. If the monopoly can set different prices and access fees for its two customers, it charges both a per-unit price of $p = 10$, which equals its marginal cost, and it charges an access fee of 2,450 $(= A_1 + B_1 + C_1)$ to Valerie and 4,050 $(= A_2 + B_2 + C_2)$ to Neal. If the monopoly cannot charge its customers different prices, it sets its per-unit price at $p = 20$, where Valerie purchases 60 and Neal buys 80 units. The firm charges both the same access fee of 1,800 $= A_1$, which is Valerie's potential consumer surplus. The highest access fee that the firm could charge and have Neal buy is 3,200, but at that level, Valerie would not buy. By charging a price above its marginal cost, the firm captures $B_1 = 600$ from Valerie and $B_2 = 800$ from Neal. Thus, its total profit is 5,000 $(= [2 \times 1,800] + 600 + 800)$, which is less than the 6,500 $(= 2,450 + 4,050)$ it makes if it can charge separate access fees to each customer.

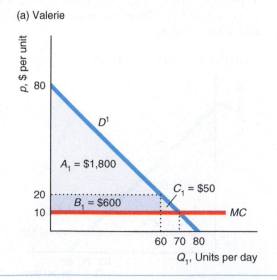

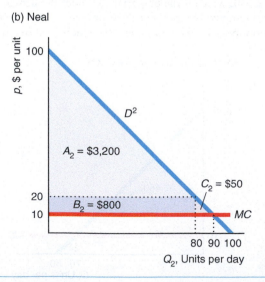

---

[17]See Appendix 12D for a calculus analysis.

If the firm knows each customer's demand curve, can prevent resale, and can charge its customers different prices and access fees, it can capture the entire potential consumer surplus. The monopoly sets its price for both customers at $p = MC = 10$ and sets its access fee equal to each customer's potential consumer surplus. At $p = 10$, Valerie buys 70 units (panel a), and Neal buys 90 units (panel b). If no access fees were charged, Valerie's consumer surplus would equal the triangle below her demand curve and above the 10 price line, $A_1 + B_1 + C_1$, which is 2,450 ($= \frac{1}{2} \times 70 \times 70$). Similarly, Neal's consumer surplus would be 4,050 ($= \frac{1}{2} \times 90 \times 90$), which is the triangle $A_2 + B_2 + C_2$. Thus, the monopoly charges an access fee of 2,450 to Valerie and 4,050 to Neal, so that the customers receive no consumer surplus. The firm's total profit is $2,450 + 4,050 = 6,500$. The monopoly maximizes its total profit by capturing the maximum potential consumer surplus from both customers.

Now suppose that the firm cannot charge its customers different prices or access fees. The firm maximizes its profit by setting a price of 20, which exceeds its marginal cost, and collecting an access fee equal to Valerie's potential consumer surplus, $A_1 = 1,800$. Although this access fee captures all of Valerie's potential consumer surplus, it is less than Neal's potential consumer surplus, $3,200 = A_2$. Were the firm to charge an access fee of 3,200, it would sell only to Neal and make less money.

At $p = 20$, Valerie buys 60 units, and Neal buys 80 units. Because the firm's average cost is 10, the firm makes $20 - 10 = 10$ per unit, so it earns $B_1 = 600$ ($= 10 \times 60$) from Valerie and $B_2 = 800$ ($= 10 \times 80$) from Neal for a total $= 1,400$. Adding that to what it makes from the access fees, 3,600, the monopoly's total profit is 5,000 ($= [2 \times 1,800] + 600 + 800$). Valerie receives no consumer surplus, but Neal enjoys a consumer surplus of 1,400 ($= 3,200 - 1,800$).

This 5,000 profit obtained from pure two-part pricing is less than the 6,500 that it could obtain if it could set different access fees for each customer. On the other hand, its profit from pure two-part pricing exceeds the 3,200 profit that the firm could earn from uniform monopoly pricing.[18]

Why does the firm charge a price above marginal cost when using two-part pricing in this case? By raising the price, the firm lowers the amount it can earn from the access fee but increases the amount it can earn from the per-unit price. The amount the firm earns from Valerie because of the higher price is less than the amount it loses from her reduced access fee. However, the situation with Neal is reversed. The gain the firm gets from charging Neal the higher price exceeds the loss from Neal's smaller access fee. Further, the net gain the firm obtains from Neal exceeds the net loss it takes on Valerie, so its total profit increases.[19] Thus, a price above marginal cost increases profit in this case.

---

[18]A single-price monopoly faces an aggregate demand function of the sum of the two individual demand functions: $Q = q_1 + q_2 = (80 - p) + (100 - p)$ or $Q = 180 - 2p$, for p less than 80, where both consumers demand a positive quantity. Its inverse demand function is $p(Q) = 90 - \frac{1}{2}Q$. Its revenue function is $R(Q) = p(Q) \times Q = 90Q - \frac{1}{2}Q^2$, so its marginal revenue function is $MR = dR(Q)/dQ = 90 - Q$. To maximize its profit given that it sets a uniform price, the monopoly equates its MR and its MC, so that $90 - Q = 10$, or $Q = 80$. At that quantity, the price is $p = 90 - (80/2) = 50$. The firm's profit is $\pi = (p - AC)Q = (50 - 10) \times 80 = 3,200$.

[19]If the monopoly lowers its price from 20 to the marginal cost of 10, it loses B_1 from Valerie, but it can raise its access fee from A_1 to $A_1 + B_1 + C_1$, so its total profit from Valerie increases by $C_1 = 50$. The access fee it collects from Neal also rises by $B_1 + C_1 = 650$, but its profit from unit sales falls by $B_2 = 800$, so its total profit decreases by 150. The loss from Neal, -150, more than offsets the gain from Valerie, 50. Thus, the monopoly makes 100 more by charging a price of 20 rather than 10.

Application

iTunes for a Song

Prior to 2009, Apple's iTunes music store, the giant of music downloading, used *uniform pricing*, where it sold songs at 99¢ each. However, some of its competitors, such as Amazon MP3, did not use uniform pricing. Some record labels told Apple that they would not renew their contracts if Apple continued to use uniform pricing. Apparently responding to this pressure and the success of some of its competitors, Apple switched in 2009 to selling each song at one of three prices.

Did Apple's one-price-for-all-songs policy cost it substantial potential profit? How do consumer surplus and deadweight loss vary with pricing methods such as a single price, song-specific prices, price discrimination, and two-part pricing? To answer such questions, Shiller and Waldfogel (2011) surveyed nearly 1,000 students and determined each person's willingness to pay for each of 50 popular songs. Then they used this information to calculate optimal pricing under various pricing schemes.

First, under uniform pricing, the same price is charged for every song. Second, under variable pricing, each song sells at its individual profit-maximizing price. Third, Apple could use two-part pricing, charging a monthly or annual fee for access and then a fixed price for each download.

If we know the demand curve and the marginal cost, we can determine the producer surplus (*PS*) or profit, the consumer surplus (*CS*), and the deadweight loss (*DWL*) from each pricing regime. By dividing each of these surplus measures by the total available surplus—the area under the demand curve and above the marginal cost curve—we can determine the shares of *PS, CS,* and *DWL*. The following table shows Shiller and Waldfogel's estimates of the percentage shares of *CS, PS,* and *DWL* under each of the three pricing methods:

Pricing	PS	CS	DWL
Uniform	28	42	29
Variable	29	45	26
Two-part pricing	37	43	20

If these students have tastes similar to those of the general market, then Apple raised its profit by switching from uniform pricing to variable pricing (see the *PS* column in the table). However, these results suggest that it could do even better using two-part pricing. Deadweight loss decreases under both of the alternatives to uniform pricing. Consumers do best with variable pricing, but two-part pricing is also better for consumers than uniform pricing.

12.6 Tie-In Sales

tie-in sale
a type of nonlinear pricing in which customers can buy one product only if they agree to buy another product as well

Another type of nonlinear pricing is a **tie-in sale**, in which customers can buy one product only if they agree to purchase another product as well. The two forms of tie-in sales are a *requirement tie-in sale* and *bundling*.

Requirement Tie-In Sale

requirement tie-in sale
a tie-in sale in which customers who buy one product from a firm are required to make all their purchases of another product from that firm

With a **requirement tie-in sale**, customers who buy one product from a firm are required to make all their purchases of another product from that firm. Some firms sell durable machines such as copiers under the condition that customers buy copier services and supplies from them in the future. This requirement allows the firm to identify heavier users and charge them more per unit. For example, if a printer manufacturer can require that consumers buy their ink cartridges only from the manufacturer, then that firm can capture most of the consumers' surplus. Heavy users of the printer, who presumably have a less elastic demand for it, pay the firm more than light users because of the high cost of the ink cartridges.

Application **Ties That Bind**	Unfortunately for printer manufacturers, the Magnuson-Moss Warranty Improvement Act of 1975 forbids a manufacturer from using such tie-in provisions as a condition of warranty. To get around this Act, printer firms such as Brother, Canon, Epson, and Hewlett-Packard (HP) write their warranties to strongly encourage consumers to use only their cartridges and not to refill them. The warranty for an HP inkjet printer says that it does not apply if printer failure or damage is attributable to a non-HP or refilled cartridge. Is this warning sufficient to induce most consumers to buy cartridges only from HP? Apparently so. HP sells its Deskjet 1000 printer for only \$34.99. That is, HP is virtually giving away an impressive machine that will print up to 4800 × 1200 optimized dots per inch in color. However, HP charges \$20.99 for its color cartridge (rated for 165 pages) and \$14.99 for its black cartridge (rated for 180 pages). If most customers bought inexpensive cartridges or refills from other firms, HP would not sell its printer at a rock-bottom price. Thus, HP has achieved the benefits of requirement tie-in sales through a carefully worded warranty.

Bundling

bundling (*package tie-in sale*)
selling multiple goods or services for a single price

A firm engages in **bundling** (or a *package tie-in sale*) by selling multiple goods or services for a single price. Indeed, most goods are bundles of many separate parts. Cars come assembled. Left and right shoes are sold together as a pair and include laces.

Usually goods are bundled for efficiency because combining goods in a bundle reduces the transaction costs incurred by consumers or the production costs associated with the product. For example, we buy shirts with buttons already attached. Rather than buying shirts without buttons, and then buying buttons, consumers prefer to buy assembled shirts, eliminating the need to make two separate purchases and then sew on buttons.

However, firms sometimes bundle even when they gain no production advantages and transaction costs are small. Bundling allows firms to increase their profit by charging different prices to different consumers based on the consumers' willingness to pay. For example, a computer firm may sell a package including a computer and a printer for a single price even if it has no cost savings from selling these products together.

A firm that sells two or more goods may sell the goods together in a *bundle* to raise its profit. In *pure bundling*, the goods are not sold separately but are sold only together. For example, a restaurant may offer a soup and sandwich special but not allow customers to purchase the soup or the sandwich separately. In *mixed bundling*, the firm offers consumers the choice of buying the goods separately or as a bundle. A restaurant may offer the soup and sandwich special as well as sell each item separately.

Bundling allows firms that can't directly price discriminate to charge customers different prices. Whether either type of bundling is profitable depends on customers' tastes and the ability to prevent resale.

Pure bundling is very common. An example of a pure bundle is Microsoft Works. The primary components of this software bundle are a word processing program and a spreadsheet program. These programs have fewer features than Microsoft's flagship Word and Excel programs and are not sold individually but only as a bundle.

Table 12.2 Negatively Correlated Reservation Prices

	Word Processor	*Spreadsheet*	*Bundle*
Alisha	$120	$50	$170
Bob	$90	$70	$160
Profit-maximizing price	$90	$50	$160
Units sold	2	2	2

Whether it pays for Microsoft to sell a bundle or sell the programs separately depends on how reservation prices for the components vary across customers. We use an example of a firm selling word processing and spreadsheet programs to illustrate two cases, one in which pure bundling produces a higher profit than selling the components separately, and one in which pure bundling is not profitable.

The firm has two customers, Alisha and Bob. The first two columns of Table 12.2 show the reservation prices for each consumer for the two products. Alisha's reservation price for the word processing program, $120, is greater than Bob's, $90. However, Alisha's reservation price for the spreadsheet program, $50, is less than Bob's, $70. The reservation prices are *negatively correlated*: The customer who has the higher reservation price for one product has the lower reservation price for the other product. The third column of the table shows each consumer's reservation price for the bundle, which is the sum of the reservation prices for the two underlying products.

If the firm sells the two products separately, it maximizes its profit by charging $90 for the word processor and selling to both consumers, so that its profit is $180, rather than charging $120 and selling only to Alisha. If it charges between $90 and $120, it still only sells to Alisha and earns less than if it charges $120. Similarly, the firm maximizes its profit by selling the spreadsheet program for $50 to both consumers, earning $100, rather than charging $70 and selling to only Bob. The firm's total profit from selling the programs separately is $280 (= $180 + $100).

If the firm sells the two products in a bundle, it maximizes its profit by charging $160, selling to both customers, and earning $320. This is a better outcome than charging $170 and selling only to Alisha. Pure bundling is more profitable for the firm because it earns $320 from selling the bundle and only $280 from selling the programs separately.

Pure bundling is more profitable because the firm captures more of the consumers' potential consumer surplus—their reservation prices. With separate prices, Alisha has consumer surplus of $30 (= $120 − $90) from the word processing program and none from the spreadsheet program. Bob receives no consumer surplus from the word processing program and $20 from the spreadsheet program. Thus, the total consumer surplus is $50. With pure bundling, Alisha gets $10 of consumer surplus and Bob gets none, so the total is only $10. Thus, the pure bundling approach captures $40 more potential consumer surplus than does pricing separately.

Whether pure bundling increases the firm's profit depends on the reservation prices. Table 12.3 shows the reservation prices for two different consumers, Carol and Dmitri. Carol has higher reservation prices for both products than does Dmitri.

Table 12.3 Positively Correlated Reservation Prices

	Word Processor	*Spreadsheet*	*Bundle*
Carol	$100	$90	$190
Dmitri	$90	$40	$130
Profit-maximizing price	$90	$90	$130
Units sold	2	1	2

These reservation prices are *positively correlated*: A higher reservation price for one product is associated with a higher reservation price for the other product.

If the programs are sold separately, the firm charges $90 for the word processor, sells to both consumers, and earns $180. However, it makes more charging $90 for the spreadsheet program and selling only to Carol, than it does charging $40 for the spreadsheet, selling to both consumers, and earning $80. The firm's total profit if it prices separately is $270 (= $180 + $90).

If the firm uses pure bundling, it maximizes its profit by charging $130 for the bundle, selling to both customers, and making $260. Because the firm earns more selling the programs separately, $270, than when it bundles them, $260, pure bundling is not profitable in this example. Even if Dmitri placed a higher value on the spreadsheet, as long as reservation prices are positively correlated, pure bundling cannot increase the profit.

Solved Problem 12.4

A firm that sells word processing and spreadsheet programs has four potential customers with the following reservation prices:

	Word Processor	Spreadsheet	Bundle
Aaron	$120	$30	$150
Brigitte	$110	$90	$200
Charles	$90	$110	$200
Dorothy	$30	$120	$150

The firm's cost of production is zero, so maximizing its profit is equivalent to maximizing its revenue. To maximize its profit, should the firm charge separate prices for each product, engage in pure bundling, or use mixed bundling?

Answer

1. *Calculate the profit-maximizing separate service prices and the resulting profit.* If the firm prices each program separately, it maximizes its profit by charging $90 for each product and selling each to three out of the four potential customers. It sells the word processing program to Aaron, Brigitte, and Charles. It sells the spreadsheet program to Brigitte, Charles, and Dorothy. Thus, it makes $270 (= 3 × $90) from each program or $540 total, which exceeds what it could earn by setting any other price per program.[20]

2. *Calculate the profit-maximizing pure bundle price and the resulting profit.* The firm can charge $150 for the bundle, sell to all four consumers, and make a profit of $600, $60 more than the $540 it makes from selling the programs separately.

3. *Determine how the firm maximizes its profit by using mixed bundling.* With mixed bundling, the firm charges $200 for the bundle and $120 for each product separately. The firm earns $400 from Brigitte and Charles, who buy the bundle. Aaron buys only the word processing program for $120, and Dorothy buys only the spreadsheet for another $120, so that the firm makes $240 from its individual program sales. Thus, its profit is $640 (= $400 + $240) from mixed bundling, which exceeds the $600 from pure bundling, and the $540 from individual sales.

---

[20]If it sets a price of a program as low as $30, it sells both programs to all four customers, but makes only $240. If it charges $110 it sells each program to two customers and earns $440. If it charges $120, it makes a single sale of each program, so it earns $240.

12.7 Advertising

The man who stops advertising to save money is like the man who stops the clock to save time.

In addition to setting prices or quantities, choosing investments, and lobbying governments, firms engage in many other strategic actions to boost their profits. One of the most important is advertising. By advertising, a monopoly can shift its demand curve, which may allow it to sell more units at a higher price. In contrast, a competitive firm has no incentive to advertise as it can sell as many units as it wants at the going price without advertising.

Advertising is only one way to promote a product. Other promotional activities include providing free samples and using sales agents. Some promotional tactics are subtle. For example, grocery stores place sugary breakfast cereals on lower shelves so that they are at children's eye level. According to a survey of 27 supermarkets nationwide by the Center for Science in the Public Interest, the average position of 10 child-appealing brands (44% sugar) was on the next-to-bottom shelf, while the average position of 10 adult brands (10% sugar) was on the next-to-top shelf.

A monopoly advertises to raise its profit. A successful advertising campaign shifts the market demand curve by changing consumers' tastes or informing them about new products. The monopoly may be able to change the tastes of some consumers by telling them that a famous athlete or performer uses the product. Children and teenagers are frequently the targets of such advertising. If the advertising convinces some consumers that they can't live without the product, the monopoly's demand curve may shift outward and become less elastic at the new equilibrium, at which the firm charges a higher price for its product (see Chapter 11).

If a firm informs potential consumers about a new use for the product, the demand curve shifts to the right. For example, a 1927 Heinz advertisement suggested that putting its baked beans on toast was a good way to eat beans for breakfast as well as dinner. By so doing, it created a British national dish and shifted the demand curve for its product to the right.

The Decision Whether to Advertise

Even if advertising succeeds in shifting demand, it may not pay for the firm to advertise. If advertising shifts demand outward or makes it less elastic, the firm's *gross profit*, ignoring the cost of advertising, must rise. The firm undertakes this advertising campaign, however, only if it expects its *net profit* (gross profit minus the cost of advertising) to increase.

If the monopoly does not advertise, it faces the demand curve D^1 in Figure 12.7. If it advertises, its demand curve shifts from D^1 to D^2.

The monopoly's marginal cost, MC, is constant and equals its average cost, AC. Before advertising, the monopoly chooses its output, Q_1, where its marginal cost hits its marginal revenue curve, MR^1, which corresponds to the demand curve, D^1. The profit-maximizing equilibrium is e_1, and the monopoly charges a price of p_1. The monopoly's profit, π_1, is a box whose height is the difference between the price and the average cost and whose length is the quantity, Q_1.

After its advertising campaign shifts its demand curve to D^2, the monopoly chooses a higher quantity, $Q_2(> Q_1)$, where the MR^2 and MC curves intersect. In this new equilibrium, e_2, the monopoly charges p_2. Despite this higher price, the monopoly sells more units after advertising because of the outward shift of its demand curve.

As a consequence, the monopoly's gross profit rises. Its new gross profit is the rectangle $\pi_1 + B$, where the height of the rectangle is the new price minus the average

Figure 12.7 Advertising

If the monopoly does not advertise, its demand curve is D^1. At its actual level of advertising, its demand curve is D^2. Advertising increases the monopoly's gross profit (ignoring the cost of advertising) from π_1 to $\pi_2 = \pi_1 + B$.

Thus, if the cost of advertising is less than the benefits from advertising, B, the monopoly's net profit (gross profit minus the cost of advertising) rises.

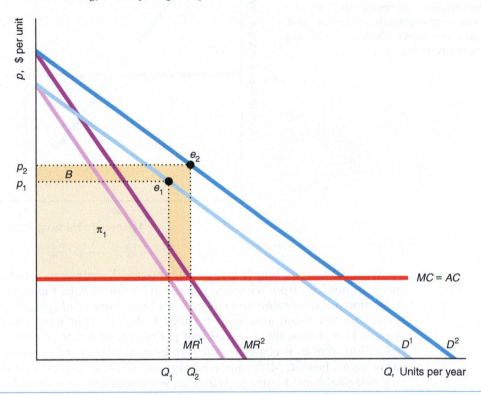

cost, and the length is the quantity, Q_2. Thus, the benefit, B, to the monopoly from advertising at this level is the increase in its gross profit. If its cost of advertising is less than B, its net profit rises, and it pays for the monopoly to advertise at this level rather than not to advertise at all.

How Much to Advertise

How much should a monopoly advertise to maximize its net profit? To answer this question, we consider what happens if the monopoly raises or lowers its advertising expenditures by $1, which is its marginal cost of an additional unit of advertising. If a monopoly spends one more dollar on advertising and its gross profit rises by more than $1, its net profit rises, so the extra advertising pays. In contrast, the monopoly should reduce its advertising if the last dollar of advertising raises its gross profit by less than $1, so its net profit falls. Thus, the monopoly's level of advertising maximizes its net profit if the last dollar of advertising increases its gross profit by $1 (see Appendix 12E for an analysis using calculus). In short, the rule for setting the profit-maximizing amount of advertising is the same as that for setting the profit-maximizing amount of output: Set advertising or quantity where the marginal benefit (the extra gross profit from one more unit of advertising or the marginal revenue from one more unit of output) equals its marginal cost.

Figure 12.8 Shift in the Marginal Benefit of Advertising

If the marginal benefit of advertising curve is MB^1, a firm purchases A_1 minutes of infomercials, where MB^1 intersects the marginal cost per minute of broadcast time curve, MC. If a special event causes regular viewers to watch another show instead of infomercials so that the marginal benefit curve shifts to the left to MB^2, only A_2 minutes of advertising time is sold.

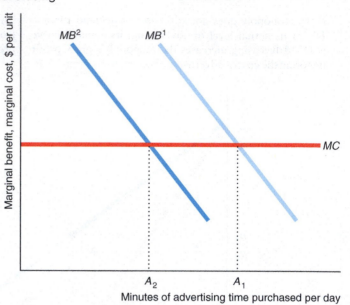

We can illustrate how firms use such marginal analysis to determine how much time to purchase from television stations for infomercials, those interminably long television advertisements sometimes featuring unique (and typically bizarre) plastic products: "Isn't that amazing?! It slices! It dices! ... But wait! That's not all!" As Figure 12.8 shows, the marginal cost per minute of broadcast time, MC, on small television stations is constant. The firm buys A_1 minutes of advertising time, where its marginal benefit, MB^1, equals its marginal cost. If an event occurs that shifts down the marginal benefit curve to MB^2 (e.g., some regular viewers watch the Super Bowl or the World Cup instead of infomercials), the amount of advertising falls to A_2.

Application

Super Bowl Commercials

Super Bowl commercials are the most expensive commercials on U.S. television. A 30-second spot during the Super Bowl averaged over $3.8 million in 2013. A high price for these commercials is not surprising because the cost of commercials generally increases with the number of viewers (*eyeballs* in industry jargon), and the Super Bowl is the most widely watched show, with over 108 million viewers in 2013. What is surprising is that Super Bowl advertising costs 2.5 times as much per viewer as other TV commercials.

However, a Super Bowl commercial is much more likely to influence viewers than commercials on other shows. The Super Bowl is not only a premier sports event; it showcases the most memorable commercials of the year, such as Apple's classic 1984 Macintosh ad, which is still discussed and rebroadcast annually. Indeed, many Super Bowl viewers are not even football fans—they watch to see these superior ads. Moreover, Super Bowl commercials receive extra exposure because these ads often *go viral* on the Internet.

Given that Super Bowl ads are more likely to be remembered by viewers, are these commercials worth the extra price? Obviously many advertisers believe so, as their demand for these ads has bid up the price. Kim (2011) found that immediately after a Super Bowl commercial airs, the advertising firm's stock value rises. Thus, investors apparently believe that Super Bowl commercials raise a firm's profits despite the high cost of the commercial. Ho et al. (2009) found that, for the typical movie with a substantial advertising budget, a Super Bowl commercial advertising the movie raises theater revenues by more than the same expenditure on other television advertising. They concluded that movie firms' advertising during the Super Bowl was at (or close to) the profit-maximizing amount.

Challenge Solution

Sale Prices

By putting Heinz Ketchup on sale periodically, Heinz can price discriminate. How often should Heinz put its ketchup on sale? Under what conditions does it pay for Heinz to have sales?

To answer these questions, we study a simplified market in which Heinz competes with one other ketchup brand, which we refer to as generic ketchup.[21] Every n days, the typical consumer buys either Heinz or generic ketchup. (The number of days between purchases is determined by the storage space in consumers' homes and how frequently they use ketchup.)

Switchers are price sensitive and buy the least expensive ketchup. They pay attention to price information and always know when Heinz is on sale.

Heinz considers holding periodic sales to capture switchers' purchases. The generic is sold at a competitive price equal to its marginal cost of production of $2.01 per unit. Suppose that Heinz's marginal cost is $MC = \$1$ per unit (due to its large scale) and that, if it only sold to its loyal customers, it would charge a monopoly price of $p = \$3$. Heinz faces a trade-off. If Heinz is infrequently on sale for less than the generic price, Heinz sells little to switchers. On the other hand, if Heinz is frequently on sale, it loses money on its sales to loyal customers.

We start by supposing that Heinz decides to charge a low sales price, $2, once every n days. For the other $n-1$ days, Heinz sells at the regular, nonsale (monopoly) price of $3, which is the monopoly price given the demand curve of the loyal customers. During a sale, the switchers buy enough Heinz to last them for n days until it's on sale again. Consequently, the switchers never buy the generic product. (Some other customers are loyal to the generic, so they buy it even when Heinz is on sale.)

If the loyal customers find that Heinz is on sale, which happens $1/n$ of all days, they buy n days' worth at the sale price. Otherwise, they pay the regular (monopoly) price. If the other loyal customers were aware of this promotion pattern, they could get on a schedule such that they always bought on sale too, thereby making this strategy nonprofit maximizing. However, their shopping schedules are determined independently: They buy many goods and are not willing to distort their shopping patterns solely to buy this one good on sale.[22]

Could Heinz make more money by altering its promotion pattern? It does not want to place its good on sale more frequently because it would earn less from its loyal customers without making more sales to switchers. If it pays to hold sales at

---

[21]The rest of the U.S. market consists primarily of Hunt's Ketchup (15%) and generic or house brands (22%). In the following discussion, we assume that customers who are loyal to Hunt's or generic ketchup are unaffected by Heinz sales, and hence ignore those customers.

[22]We make this assumption for simplicity. In the real world, firms achieve a similar result by having random sales or by placing ads announcing sales where the ads are seen by primarily the switchers.

all, it does not want to have a sale less frequently because it would sell fewer units to switchers. During a promotion, Heinz wants to charge the highest price it can and yet still attract switchers, which is $2. If it sets a lower price, the quantity sold is unchanged, so its profit falls. If Heinz sets a sale price higher than $2, it loses all switchers.

Does it pay for Heinz to have sales? Whether it pays depends on the number of switchers, S, relative to the number of brand-loyal customers, B. If each customer buys one unit per day, then Heinz's profit per day if it sells only to loyals is $\pi = (p - MC)B = (3 - 1)B = 2B$, where $p = 3$ is Heinz's regular price and $MC = 1$ is its marginal and average cost. If Heinz uses the sale pricing scheme, its average profit per day is

$$\pi^* = 2B(n - 1)/n + (B + S)/n,$$

where the first term is the profit it makes, $2 per unit, selling B units to loyal customers for the fraction of days that Heinz is not on sale, $(n - 1)/n$, and the second term is the profit it makes, $1 per unit, selling B units to the loyal customers and S units to switchers for the fraction of days that it is on sale, $1/n$.

Thus, it pays to put Heinz on sale if $\pi < \pi^*$, or $2B < 2B(n - 1)/n + (B + S)(1/n)$. Using algebra, we can simplify this expression to $B < S$. Thus, if switchers outnumber loyal customers, then having sales is more profitable than selling at a uniform price to only loyal customers.

Summary

1. **Conditions for Price Discrimination.** A firm can price discriminate if it has market power, knows which customers will pay more for each unit of output, and can prevent customers who pay low prices from reselling to those who pay high prices. A firm earns a higher profit from price discrimination than from uniform pricing because (a) the firm captures some or all of the consumer surplus of customers who are willing to pay more than the uniform price and (b) the firm sells to some people who would not buy at the uniform price.

2. **Perfect Price Discrimination.** To perfectly price discriminate, a firm must know the maximum amount each customer is willing to pay for each unit of output. If a firm charges customers the maximum each is willing to pay for each unit of output, the monopoly captures all potential consumer surplus and sells the efficient (competitive) level of output. Compared to competition, total welfare is the same, consumers are worse off, and firms are better off under perfect price discrimination.

3. **Group Price Discrimination.** A firm that does not have enough information to perfectly price discriminate may know the relative elasticities of demand of various groups of its customers. Such a profit-maximizing firm charges groups of consumers prices in proportion to their elasticities of demand, the group

of consumers with the least elastic demand paying the highest price. Welfare is less under group price discrimination than under competition or perfect price discrimination but may be greater or less than that under single-price monopoly.

4. **Nonlinear Price Discrimination.** Some firms charge customers different prices depending on how many units they purchase. A common example involves quantity discounts, so that the per-unit price for consumers who buy larger quantities is less than the per-unit price for consumers who buy smaller quantities.

5. **Two-Part Pricing.** By charging consumers an access fee for the right to buy a good and a separate price per unit, firms may earn higher profits than from using uniform pricing. If a firm knew all its customers' demand curves and could charge a different access fee to every customer, it could use two-part pricing to capture all potential consumer surplus. Even a firm that does not know each customer's demand curve or that cannot vary the access fee across customers can still use two-part pricing to earn a higher profit than it could earn using uniform pricing.

6. **Tie-In Sales.** A firm may increase its profit by using a tie-in sale that allows customers to buy one product only if they also purchase another one. In a

requirement tie-in sale, customers who buy one good must make all of their purchases of another good or service from that firm. Some firms use pure bundling, in which only the bundle is offered for sale. Others use mixed bundling, in which both the bundle and the individual goods are offered for sale. Bundling is likely to be a profitable pricing strategy when consumers have reservation prices that are negatively correlated—when consumers who have a relatively high willingness to pay for one good have a relatively low willingness to pay for the other good.

7. **Advertising.** A monopoly advertises or engages in other promotional activity to shift its demand curve to the right or make it less elastic so as to raise its profit net of its advertising expenses.

Questions

All questions are available on MyEconLab; * = *answer appears at the back of this book;* **A** = *algebra problem;* **C** = *calculus problem.*

1. Conditions for Price Discrimination

1.1 In the examples in Table 12.1, if the movie theater does not price discriminate, it charges either the highest price the college students are willing to pay or the one that the senior citizens are willing to pay. Why doesn't it charge an intermediate price? (*Hint*: Discuss how the demand curves of these two groups are unusual.)

*1.2 Many colleges provide students from low-income families with scholarships, subsidized loans, and other programs so that they pay lower tuitions than students from high-income families. Explain why universities behave this way.

1.3 The pharmaceutical companies Abbott Laboratories, AstraZeneca, Bristol-Myers Squibb Company, Eli Lilly, GlaxoSmithKline, Janssen, Johnson & Johnson, Novartis, Pfizer, and Sanofi-Aventis Pharmaceuticals provide low-income, elderly people with a card guaranteeing them discounts on many prescription medicines. Why would these firms do that?

1.4 Alexx's monopoly currently sells its product at a single price. What conditions must be met so that he can profitably price discriminate?

1.5 College students could once buy a computer at a substantial discount through a campus buying program. The discounts largely disappeared in the late 1990s, when PC companies dropped their prices. "The industry's margins just got too thin to allow for those [college discounts]," said the president of Educause, a group that promotes and surveys using technology on campus (David LaGesse, "A PC Choice: Dorm or Quad?" *U.S. News & World Report*, May 5, 2003, 64). Using the concepts and terminology discussed in this chapter, explain why shrinking profit margins are associated with the reduction or elimination of student discounts.

1.6 The 2002 production run of 25,000 new Thunderbirds included only 2,000 cars for Canada. Yet potential buyers besieged Ford dealers there. Many buyers hoped to make a quick profit by reselling the cars in the United States. Reselling was relatively easy, and shipping costs were comparatively low. When the Thunderbird with the optional hardtop first became available at the end of 2001, Canadians paid C$56,550 for the vehicle, while U.S. customers spent up to C$73,000 in the United States. Why? Why would a Canadian want to ship a T-Bird south? Why did Ford require that Canadian dealers sign an agreement with Ford that prohibited moving vehicles to the United States?

1.7 Disneyland price discriminates by charging lower entry fees for children than adults and for local residents than for other visitors. Why does it not have a resale problem?

1.8 On July 12, 2012, Hertz charged $126.12 to rent a Nissan Altima for one day in New York City, but only $55.49 a day in Miami. Is Hertz necessarily engaging in price discrimination? Explain.

2. Perfect Price Discrimination

2.1 Using the information in the "Botox Revisited" Application, determine how much Allergan loses by being a single-price monopoly rather than a perfectly price-discriminating monopoly. Explain your answer.

2.2 A firm is a natural monopoly (Chapter 11). Its marginal cost curve is flat, and its average cost curve is downward sloping (because it has a fixed cost). The firm can perfectly price discriminate.

a. In a graph, show how much the monopoly produces, Q^*. Will it produce to where price equals its marginal cost?

b. Show graphically (and explain) what its profit is.

2.3 Can Table 12.1 be modified so that the movie theater in Solved Problem 12.1 does not earn more by perfectly price discriminating than from charging a single price? What changes to the table would increase the extra profit from perfectly price discriminating?

2.4 How would the answers to Solved Problem 12.1 and Table 12.1 change if seniors' reservation price was $2.50?

2.5 Ticketmaster Corp. uses an Internet auction to sell tickets. Is it engaging in price discrimination? If so, what type?

*2.6 If a monopoly faces an inverse demand curve of $p = 90 - Q$, has a constant marginal and average cost of 30, and can perfectly price discriminate, what is its profit? What are the consumer surplus, welfare, and deadweight loss? How would these results change if the firm were a single-price monopoly? **A**

2.7 To promote her platinum-selling CD *Feels Like Home* in 2005, singer Norah Jones toured the country for live performances. However, she sold an average of only two-thirds of the tickets available for each show, T^* (Robert Levine, "The Trick of Making a Hot Ticket Pay," *New York Times*, June 6, 2005, C1, C4).

   a. Suppose that the local promoter is the monopoly provider of each concert. Each concert hall has a fixed number of seats. Assume that the promoter's cost is independent of the number of people who attend the concert (Ms. Jones received a guaranteed payment). Graph the promoter's marginal cost curve for the concert hall, where the number of tickets sold is on the horizontal axis (be sure to show T^*).

   b. If the monopoly can charge a single market price, does the concert's failure to sell out prove that the monopoly set too high a price? Explain.

   c. Would your answer in part b be the same if the monopoly can perfectly price discriminate? Use a graph to explain.

3. Group Price Discrimination

3.1 A firm charges different prices to two groups. Would the firm ever operate where it was suffering a loss from its sales to the low-price group? Explain.

3.2 A monopoly has a marginal cost of zero and faces two groups of consumers. At first, the monopoly could not prevent resale, so it maximized its profit by charging everyone the same price, $p = \$5$. No one from the first group chose to purchase. Now the monopoly can prevent resale, so it decides to price discriminate. Will total output necessarily expand? Why or why not? What happens to profit and consumer surplus?

3.3 Does a monopoly's ability to price discriminate between two groups of consumers depend on its marginal cost curve? Why or why not? Consider two cases: (a) the marginal cost is so high that the monopoly is uninterested in selling to one group, and (b) the marginal cost is low enough that the monopoly wants to sell to both groups.

3.4 Grocery stores often set consumer-specific prices by issuing frequent-buyer cards to willing customers and collecting information on their purchases. Grocery chains can use that data to offer customized discount coupons to individuals.

   a. Are grocery stores engaging in perfect or group price discrimination, or some other type of pricing?

   b. How should a grocery store use past-purchase data to set individualized prices to maximize its profit? (*Hint*: Refer to a customer's price elasticity of demand.)

*3.5 A patent gave Sony a legal monopoly to produce a robot dog called Aibo ("eye-BO"). The Chihuahua-size pooch robot can sit, beg, chase balls, dance, and play an electronic tune. When Sony started selling the toy, it announced that it would sell 3,000 Aibo robots in Japan for about $2,000 each and a limited litter of 2,000 in the United States for $2,500 each. Suppose that Sony's marginal cost of producing Aibos is $500. Its inverse demand curve is $p_J = 3,500 - \frac{1}{2}Q_J$ in Japan and $p_A = 4,500 - 4,500Q_A$ in the United States. Solve for the equilibrium prices and quantities (assuming that U.S. customers cannot buy robots from Japan). Show how the profit-maximizing price ratio depends on the elasticities of demand in the two countries. What are the deadweight losses in each country, and in which is the loss from monopoly pricing greater? **A**

*3.6 A monopoly sells its good in the U.S. and Japanese markets. The American inverse demand function is $p_A = 100 - Q_A$, and the Japanese inverse demand function is $p_J = 80 - 2Q_J$, where both prices, p_A and p_J, are measured in dollars. The firm's marginal cost of production is $m = 20$ in both countries. If the firm can prevent resale, what price will it charge in both markets? (*Hint*: The monopoly determines its optimal (monopoly) price in each country separately because customers cannot resell the good.) **A**

3.7 Warner Home Entertainment sold the *Harry Potter and the Prisoner of Azkaban* two-DVD movie set around the world. Warner charged 33% more in Canada and 66% more in Japan than in the United States, where it charged $15. Given that Warner's marginal cost was $1, determine what the elasticities of demand must have been in the United States, Canada, and Japan if Warner was profit maximizing. **A**

*3.8 Warner Home Entertainment sold the *Harry Potter and the Prisoner of Azkaban* two-DVD movie set in China for about $3, which was only one-fifth the U.S. price, and sold nearly 100,000 units. The price is extremely low in China because Chinese consumers are less wealthy than those in the other countries and because (lower-quality) pirated versions were available in China for 72¢–1.20 (Jin Baicheng, "Powerful Ally Joins Government in War on Piracy," *China Daily*, March 11, 2005, 13). Assuming a marginal cost of $1, what was the Chinese elasticity of demand? Derive the demand function for China and illustrate Warner's policy in China using a figure similar to panel a in Figure 12.3. **A**

*3.9 A copyright gave Universal Studios the legal monopoly to produce and sell the *Mama Mia!* DVD. The DVD sold for $20 in the United States and $36 (£22) in the United Kingdom. I estimate that the inverse demand functions for the United States and the United Kingdom were $p_A = 39 - 3Q_A$ and $p_B = 71 - 7Q_B$, respectively. The marginal cost in both countries was $m = 1$. Solve for Universal's optimal quantities and prices. (*Hint*: See Solved Problem 12.2.) **A**

3.10 A monopoly sells in two countries, and resale between the countries is impossible. The demand curves in the two countries are $p_1 = 100 - Q_1$ and $p_2 = 120 - 2Q_2$. The monopoly's marginal cost is $m = 30$. Solve for the equilibrium price in each country. (*Hint*: See Solved Problem 12.2.) **A**

3.11 A monopoly sells its good in the United States, where the elasticity of demand is –2, and in Japan, where the elasticity of demand is –5. Its marginal cost is $10. At what price does the monopoly sell its good in each country if resale is impossible? **A**

*3.12 In Solved Problem 12.3, calculate the firm's profit with and without a ban against shipments between the two countries.

3.13 How would the analysis in Solved Problem 12.3 change if $m = 7$ or if $m = 4$? (*Hint*: Where $m = 4$, the marginal cost curve crosses the *MR* curve three times—if we include the vertical section. The single-price monopoly will choose one of these three points where its profit is maximized.)

*3.14 Spenser's Superior Stoves advertises a one-day sale on electric stoves. The ad specifies that no phone orders are accepted and that the purchaser must transport the stove. Why does the firm include these restrictions?

3.15 According to a report from the Foundation for Taxpayer and Consumer Rights, gasoline costs twice as much in Europe as in the United States because taxes are higher in Europe. However, the amount per gallon net of taxes that U.S. consumers pay is higher than that paid by Europeans. The report argued that U.S. motorists effectively subsidize Europeans, who pay higher taxes but substantially less to oil companies. Given that oil companies have market power and can price discriminate across countries, is it reasonable to conclude that U.S. consumers are subsidizing Europeans? Explain your answer.

4. Nonlinear Pricing

4.1 Are all the customers of a monopoly that engages in nonlinear pricing (quantity discrimination) in panel a of Figure 12.4 worse off than they would be if the firm set a single price (panel b)?

4.2 The quantity-discriminating monopoly in panel a of Figure 12.4 sets three prices that depend on the quantity a consumer purchases. The firm's profit is
$$\pi = p_1 Q_1 + p_2(Q_2 - Q_1) + p_3(Q_3 - Q_2) - mQ_3,$$
where p_1 is the high price charged on the first Q_1 units (first block), p_2 is a lower price charged on the next $Q_2 - Q_1$ units, p_3 is the lowest price charged on the $Q_3 - Q_2$ remaining units, Q_3 is the total number of units actually purchased, and $m = \$30$ is the firm's constant marginal and average cost. Use calculus to determine the profit-maximizing $p_1, p_2,$ and p_3. **C**

*4.3 In our discussion of Figure 12.4, we assumed that the monopoly engaged in block-pricing by setting both block prices so that they were on the demand curve. However, suppose the monopoly sets the first block at 20 units but can choose a first-block price that is greater than $70. It then allows consumers to buy as many additional units as they want at $30 per unit. Can the monopoly choose a price for the first block such that consumers are willing to buy 60 units, the monopoly captures the entire potential surplus, and society does not suffer a deadweight loss? If so, what is the first-block price?

5. Two-Part Pricing

5.1 Using math, show why two-part pricing causes customers who purchase relatively few units to pay more per unit than customers who buy more units. **C**

5.2 Knoebels Amusement Park in Elysburg, Pennsylvania, charges an access fee, A, to enter its Crystal Pool. It also charges p per trip down the pool's water slides. Suppose that 400 teenagers visit the park, each of whom has a demand function of $q_1 = 5 - p$, and that 400 seniors also visit, each of whom has a demand function of $q_2 = 4 - p$. Knoebels' objective is to set A and p so as to maximize its profit given that it has no (nonsunk) cost and must charge both groups the same prices. What are the optimal A and p? **A**

*5.3 Joe has just moved to a small town with only one golf course, the Northlands Golf Club. His inverse demand function is $p = 120 - 2q$, where q is the number of rounds of golf that he plays per year. The manager of the Northlands Club negotiates separately with each person who joins the club and can therefore charge individual prices. This manager has a good idea of what Joe's demand curve is and offers Joe a special deal, where Joe pays an annual membership fee and can play as many rounds as he wants at $20, which is the marginal cost his round imposes on the Club. What membership fee would maximize profit for the Club? The manager could have charged Joe a single price per round. How much extra profit does the club earn by using two-part pricing? **A**

5.4 As described in the Application "iTunes for a Song," Shiller and Waldfogel (2011) estimated that if iTunes used two-part pricing charging an annual access fee and a low price per song, it would raise its profit by about 30% relative to what it would earn using uniform or variable pricing. Assume that iTunes uses two-part pricing and assume that the marginal cost of an additional download is zero. How should iTunes set its profit-maximizing price per song if all consumers are identical? Illustrate profit-maximizing two-part pricing in a diagram for the identical consumer case. Explain why the actual profit-maximizing price per song is positive.

5.5 Explain why charging a higher or lower price than $p = 10$ reduces the monopoly's profit in Figure 12.5. Show the monopoly's profit if $p = 20$ and compare it to its profit if $p = 10$.

6. Tie-In Sales

6.1 Why do Honda service departments emphasize to customers the importance of using "genuine Honda parts" when servicing and tuning Honda cars and motorcycles? Is Honda likely to be as successful as Hewlett-Packard in the Application "Ties That Bind"?

6.2 A monopoly sells two products, of which consumers want only one. Assuming that it can prevent resale, can the monopoly increase its profit by bundling them, forcing consumers to buy both goods?

6.3 Explain why in Table 12.2 the firm does not use mixed bundling.

*6.4 A computer hardware firm sells both laptop computers and printers. It has a large inventory of laptops and printers that it wants to sell, so it has no variable production cost. Through the magic of focus groups, their pricing team determines that they have an equal number of three types of customers, and that these customers' reservation prices are

	Laptop	Printer	Bundle
Customer Type A	$800	$100	$900
Customer Type B	$1,000	$50	$1,050
Customer Type C	$600	$150	$750

a. If the firm were to charge only individual prices (not use the bundle price), what prices should it set for its laptops and printers to maximize profit? Assuming for simplicity that the firm has only one customer of each type, how much does it earn in total?

b. After conducting a costly study, an outside consultant suggests that the company could make more money from its customers if it sold laptops and printers together as a bundle instead of separately. Is the consultant right? Assuming again that the firm has one customer of each type, how much does the firm earn in total from pure bundling?

c. Why does bundling pay or not pay? (*Hint*: See Solved Problem 12.4.) **A**

7. Advertising

7.1 Using a graph similar to Figure 12.7, explain why a firm might not want to spend A on advertising, even though it shifts the firm's demand curve to the right. (*Hint*: Discuss what happens to the elasticity of demand or the price at the monopoly optimum.)

7.2 Various services such as **Hulu.com** that provide television shows and movies over the Internet subject customers to customized commercials, as the firms learn more about their viewing habits. How does this customization affect the marginal benefit curve for an advertiser, and why?

*7.3 O. J. Simpson's 1995 trial for murder was broadcast by many television and radio stations. Viewership and sales sagged as viewers skipped program-length product pitches to watch trial coverage on weekday mornings. Estimates of average infomercial sales declines due to the Simpson trial ranged from 10% to 60% across cities (Stuart Elliott, "Advertising: The 'O. J. Factor' Takes a Toll on Producers of Infomercials," *New York Times*, March 24, 1995:C4).

a. Use a graph similar to Figure 12.8 to explain why.

b. Before the O. J. Simpson trial, when a firm spent $1,000 on commercial television time at 12:30 P.M. in Charlotte, North Carolina, its sales rose by $2,190. If the firm bought $1,000 of advertising time during the trial, was it advertising optimally? If not, should it have increased or decreased the amount it spent on advertising?

*7.4 A monopoly's inverse demand function is $p = 800 - 4Q + 0.2A^{0.5}$, where Q is its quantity, p is its price, and A is the level of advertising. Its marginal cost of production is 2, and its cost for a unit of advertising is 1. What are the firm's profit-maximizing price, quantity, and level of advertising? (*Hint*: See Appendix 12E.) **C**

7.5 Use a diagram to illustrate the effect of social media on the demand for Super Bowl commercials. (*Hint*: See the "Super Bowl Commercials" Application.)

8. Challenge

8.1 Each week, a department store places a different item of clothing on sale. Give an explanation based on price discrimination for why the store conducts such regular sales.

13

Oligopoly and Monopolistic Competition

Three can keep a secret, if two of them are dead. —Benjamin Franklin

Challenge

Government Aircraft Subsidies

Aircraft manufacturers lobby their governments for subsidies, which they use to better compete with rival firms. Airbus SAS, based in Europe, and the Boeing Co., based in the United States, are the only two major manufacturers of large commercial jet aircraft. France, Germany, Spain, and the United Kingdom subsidize Airbus, which competes in the wide-body aircraft market with Boeing. The U.S. government decries the European subsidies to Airbus despite giving lucrative military contracts to Boeing, which the Europeans view as implicit subsidies.

This government largess does not magically appear. Managers at both Boeing and Airbus lobby strenuously for this support. For example, in 2012, Boeing spent $15.64 million on lobbying and was represented by 115 lobbyists, including 2 former congressmen.

Washington and the European Union have repeatedly charged each other before the World Trade Organization (WTO) with improperly subsidizing their respective aircraft manufacturers. In 2010, the WTO ruled that Airbus received improper subsidies for its A380 superjumbo jet and several other aircraft, hurting Boeing, as the United States charged in 2005. In 2012, the WTO ruled that Boeing and Airbus both received improper subsidies. Yet the cycle of subsidies, charges, agreements, and new subsidies continues. . . .

If only one government subsidizes its firm, how does the firm use the subsidy to gain a competitive advantage? What happens if both governments subsidize their firms? Should Boeing and Airbus lobby for government subsidies that result in a subsidy war?

The major airlines within a country compete with relatively few other firms. Consequently, each firm's profit depends on the actions it and its rivals take. Similarly, three firms—Nintendo, Microsoft, and Sony—dominate the video game market, and each firm's profit depends on how its price stacks up to those of its rivals and whether its product has better features.

oligopoly
a small group of firms in a market with substantial barriers to entry

The airline and video game markets are each an **oligopoly**: a market with only a few firms and with substantial barriers to entry. Because relatively few firms compete in such a market, each can influence the price, and hence each affects rival firms. The need to consider the behavior of rival firms makes an oligopolistic firm's profit-maximization decision more difficult than that of a monopoly or a competitive firm.

A monopoly has no rivals, and a competitive firm ignores the behavior of individual rivals—it considers only the market price and its own costs in choosing its profit-maximizing output.

An oligopolistic firm that ignores or inaccurately predicts its rivals' behavior is likely to suffer a loss of profit. For example, as its rivals produce more cars, the price Ford can get for its cars falls. If Ford underestimates how many cars its rivals will produce, Ford may produce too many automobiles and lose money.

Oligopolistic firms may act independently or may coordinate their actions. A group of firms that explicitly agree (collude) to coordinate their activities is called a **cartel**. These firms may agree on how much each firm will sell or on a common price. By cooperating and behaving like a monopoly, the members of a cartel collectively earn the monopoly profit—the maximum possible profit. In most developed countries, cartels are generally illegal.

cartel
a group of firms that explicitly agree to coordinate their activities

If oligopolistic firms do not collude, they earn lower profits. However, because oligopolies consist of relatively few firms, oligopolistic firms that act independently may earn positive economic profits in the long run, unlike competitive firms.

In an oligopolistic market, one or more barriers to entry keep the number of firms small. In a market with no barriers to entry, firms enter the market until profits are driven to zero. In perfectly competitive markets, enough entry occurs that firms face a horizontal demand curve and are price takers. However, in other markets, even after entry has driven profits to zero, each firm faces a downward-sloping demand curve. Because of this slope, the firm can charge a price above its marginal cost, creating a market failure due to inefficient (too little) consumption (Chapter 9). **Monopolistic competition** is a market structure in which firms have market power (the ability to raise price profitably above marginal cost) but no additional firm can enter and earn positive profits.

monopolistic competition
a market structure in which firms have market power but no additional firm can enter and earn positive profits

In this chapter, we examine cartelized, oligopolistic, and monopolistically competitive markets in which firms set quantities or prices. As noted in Chapter 11, the monopoly equilibrium is the same whether a monopoly sets price or quantity. Similarly, if colluding oligopolies sell identical products, the cartel equilibrium is the same whether they set quantity or price. The oligopolistic and monopolistically competitive equilibria differ, however, if firms set prices instead of quantities.

In this chapter, we examine six main topics

1. **Market Structures.** The number of firms, price, profits, and other properties of markets vary, depending on whether the market is monopolistic, oligopolistic, monopolistically competitive, or competitive.

2. **Cartels.** If firms successfully coordinate their actions, they can collectively behave like a monopoly.

3. **Cournot Oligopoly.** In a Cournot oligopoly, firms choose their output levels without colluding and the market output, price, and firms' profits lie between the competitive and monopoly levels.

4. **Stackelberg Oligopoly.** In a Stackelberg oligopoly, in which a leader firm chooses its output level before its identical-cost rivals, market output is greater than if all firms choose their output simultaneously, and the leader makes a higher profit than the other firms.

5. **Bertrand Oligopoly.** In a Bertrand oligopoly, in which firms choose prices, the equilibrium differs from the quantity-setting equilibrium and depends on the degree of product differentiation.

6. **Monopolistic Competition.** When firms can freely enter the market but, in equilibrium, face downward-sloping demand curves, firms charge prices above marginal cost but make no profit.

13.1 Market Structures

Markets differ according to the number of firms in the market, the ease with which firms may enter and leave the market, and the ability of firms in a market to differentiate their products from those of their rivals. Table 13.1 lists characteristics and properties of the four major market structures: monopoly, oligopoly, monopolistic competition, and perfect competition. In the table, we assume that the firms face many price-taking buyers.

The first row describes the number of firms in each market structure. A monopoly is a single (*mono*) firm in a market. An *oligopoly* usually has a small number (*oligo*) of firms. A *monopolistically competitive* market may have a few or many firms, though typically few. A *perfectly competitive* market has many firms.

The reason why a monopoly and an oligopoly have few firms is because the markets have insurmountable barriers, such as government licenses or patents, that restrict entry (row 2). In contrast, in monopolistically and perfectly competitive markets, entry occurs until no new firm can profitably enter, so that long-run economic profit is zero (row 3). Monopolistic and oligopolistic firms can earn positive long-run profits.

Perfectly competitive firms face horizontal demand curves so they are price takers. Monopolistically competitive markets have fewer firms than perfectly competitive markets do. Because they have relatively few rivals they are large relative to the market, so each monopolistically competitive firm faces a downward-sloping demand curve as do monopolistic and oligopolistic firms. Thus, noncompetitive firms are price setters (row 4). That is, all but perfectly competitive firms have some degree of market power—the ability to set price above marginal cost—so a market failure occurs in each of these noncompetitive market structures because the price is above marginal cost. Typically, the fewer the firms in a market, the higher is the price (row 5).

Oligopolistic and monopolistically competitive firms pay attention to rival firms' behavior, in contrast to monopolistic or perfectly competitive firms (row 6). A monopoly has no rivals. A perfectly competitive firm ignores the behavior of

Table 13.1 Properties of Monopoly, Oligopoly, Monopolistic Competition, and Perfect Competition

	Monopoly	Oligopoly	Monopolistic Competition	Perfect Competition
1. Number of firms	1	Few	Few or many	Many
2. Entry conditions	No entry	Limited entry	Free entry	Free entry
3. Long-run profit	≥ 0	≥ 0	0	0
4. Ability to set price	Price setter	Price setter	Price setter	Price taker
5. Price level	Very high	High	High	Low
6. Strategy dependent on individual rival firms' behavior	No (has no rivals)	Yes	Yes	No (cares about market price only)
7. Products	Single product	May be differentiated	May be differentiated	Undifferentiated
8. Example	Local natural gas utility	Automobile manufacturers	Plumbers in a small town	Apple farmers

individual rivals in choosing its output because the market price tells the firm everything it needs to know about its competitors.

Oligopolistic and monopolistically competitive firms may produce differentiated products (row 7). For example, oligopolistic car manufacturers produce automobiles that differ in size, weight, and various other dimensions. In contrast, perfectly competitive apple farmers sell undifferentiated (homogeneous) products.

13.2 Cartels

People of the same trade seldom meet together, even for merriment and diversion, but the conversation ends in a conspiracy against the public, or some contrivance to raise prices. —Adam Smith, 1776

Oligopolistic firms have an incentive to form cartels in which they collude in setting prices or quantities so as to increase their profits. The Organization of Petroleum Exporting Countries (OPEC) is a well-known example of an international cartel; however, many cartels operate within a single country.

Typically, each member of a cartel agrees to produce less output than it would if it acted independently. As a result, the market price rises and the firms earn higher profits. If the firms reduce market output to the monopoly level, they achieve the highest possible collective profit.

Luckily for consumers, cartels often fail because of government policies that forbid cartels or because members of the cartel "cheat" on the agreement. Each member has an incentive to cheat because it can raise its profit if it increases its output while other cartel members stick to the agreement.

Why Cartels Form

A cartel forms if members of the cartel believe that they can raise their profits by coordinating their actions. But if a firm maximizes its profit when acting independently, why should joining a cartel increase its profit? The answer involves a subtle argument. When a firm acts independently, it considers how increasing its output affects its own profit only. The firm does not care that when it increases its output, it lowers the profits of other firms. A cartel, in contrast, takes into account how changes in any one firm's output affect the profits of all members of the cartel. Therefore, the aggregate profit of a cartel can exceed the combined profits of the same firms acting independently.

Although cartels are most common in oligopolistic markets, occasionally we see cartels formed in what would otherwise be highly competitive markets, such as in markets of professionals. If a competitive firm lowers its output, it raises the market price very slightly—so slightly that the firm ignores the effect not only on other firms' profits but also on its own. If all the identical competitive firms in an industry lower their output by this same amount, however, the market price will change noticeably. Recognizing this effect of collective action, a cartel chooses to produce a smaller market output than is produced by a competitive market.

Figure 13.1 illustrates this difference between a competitive market and a cartel. This oligopolistic market has *n* firms, and no further entry is possible. Panel a shows the marginal and average cost curves of a typical perfectly competitive firm. If all firms are price takers, the market supply curve, *S* in panel b, is the horizontal sum of the individual marginal cost curves above minimum average cost. At the competitive

Figure 13.1 Competition Versus Cartel

(a) The marginal cost and average cost of one of the n firms in the market are shown. A competitive firm produces q_c units of output, whereas a cartel member produces $q_m < q_c$. At the cartel price, p_m, each cartel member has an incentive to increase its output from q_m to q^* (where the dotted line at p_m intersects the MC curve). (b) The competitive equilibrium, e_c, has more output and a lower price than the cartel equilibrium, e_m.

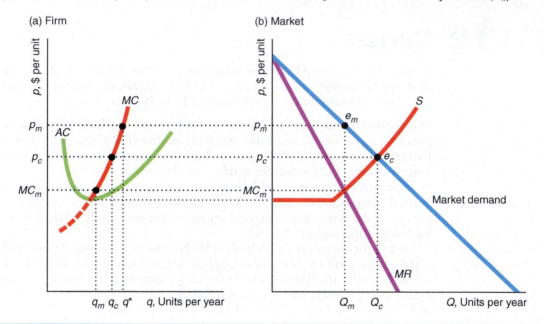

(a) Firm   (b) Market

price, p_c, each price-taking firm produces q_c units of output (which is determined by the intersection in panel a of MC and the dotted line at p_c).[1] The market output is $Q_c = nq_c$ (where S intersects the market demand curve in panel b).

Now suppose that the firms form a cartel. Should they reduce their output? At the competitive output, the cartel's marginal cost (which is the competitive industry supply curve, S in panel b) is greater than its marginal revenue, so the cartel's profit rises if it reduces output. The cartel's collective profit rises until output is reduced by enough that its marginal revenue equals its marginal cost at Q_m, the monopoly output. If the profit of the cartel increases, the profit of each of the n members of the cartel also increases. To achieve the cartel output level, each firm must reduce its output to $q_m = Q_m/n$, as panel a shows.

Why must the firms form a cartel to achieve these higher profits? A competitive firm produces q_c, where its marginal cost equals the market price. If only one firm reduces its output, it loses profit because it sells fewer units at essentially the same price. By getting all the firms to lower their output together, the cartel raises the market price and hence individual firms' profits. The less elastic the market demand the potential cartel faces, all else the same, the higher the price the cartel sets and the greater the benefit from cartelizing. If the penalty for forming an illegal cartel is relatively low, some unscrupulous businesspeople may succumb to the lure of extra profits and join.

---

[1]In the figure, the competitive price exceeds the minimum average cost. These competitive firms earn a profit because the number of firms is fixed.

Laws Against Cartels

In the late nineteenth century, cartels (or, as they were called then, *trusts*) were legal and common in the United States. Oil, railroad, sugar, and tobacco trusts raised prices substantially above competitive levels.[2]

We can't legally discuss price. However, look at how many sugar cubes I can stack!

In response to the trusts' high prices, the U.S. Congress passed the Sherman Antitrust Act in 1890 and the Federal Trade Commission Act of 1914, which prohibit firms from *explicitly* agreeing to take actions that reduce competition.[3] In particular, cartels that are formed for the purpose of jointly setting price are strictly prohibited. In legal jargon, price-fixing is a *per se* violation: It is strictly against the law and firms have no possible mitigating justifications. By imposing penalties on firms caught colluding, government agencies seek to discourage cartels from forming.

The Antitrust Division of the Department of Justice (DOJ) and the Federal Trade Commission (FTC) divide the responsibility for U.S. antitrust policy. The U.S. Department of Justice, quoting the Supreme Court that collusion was the "supreme evil of antitrust," stated that prosecuting cartels was its "top enforcement priority." The FTC's objective is "to prevent unfair methods of competition in commerce" and "to administer . . . other consumer protection laws."

Both U.S. agencies can use criminal and civil law to attack cartels, price-fixing, and other anticompetitive actions.

However, cartels persist despite these laws for three reasons. First, international cartels and cartels within certain countries operate legally. Some international cartels organized by countries rather than firms operate legally. An example is the OPEC cartel, which was formed in 1960 by five major oil-exporting countries: Iran, Iraq, Kuwait, Saudi Arabia, and Venezuela.[4] In 1971, OPEC members agreed to take an active role in setting oil prices.

Second, some illegal cartels operate believing that they can avoid detection or, if caught, that the punishment will be insignificant. At least until recently, they were often correct. For example, in a cartel case involving the $9 billion U.S. carpet industry, a firm with $150 million in annual sales agreed with the DOJ to plead guilty and pay a fine of $150,000. It is difficult to imagine that a fine one-tenth of 1% of annual sales significantly deters cartel behavior.

---

[2]Nineteenth century and early twentieth century robber barons who made fortunes due to these cartels include John Jacob Astor (real estate, fur), Andrew Carnegie (railroads, steel), Henry Clay Frick (steel), Jay Gould (finance, railroads), Mark Hopkins (railroads), J. P. Morgan (banking), John D. Rockefeller (oil), Leland Stanford (railroads), and Cornelius Vanderbilt (railroads, shipping).

[3]Some cartels are not prohibited by U.S. laws. A bizarre Supreme Court decision largely exempted Major League Baseball from antitrust laws (**www.slate.com/id/2068290**). Unions are explicitly exempt from antitrust laws. Workers are allowed to act collectively to raise wages. A historical justification for exempting labor unions was that the workers faced employers that could exercise monopsony power (Chapter 15). As long as they do not discuss such issues as prices and quantities, firms are allowed to coordinate R&D efforts or technical standards.

[4]As of 2013, OPEC had 12 member countries, including the 5 original members.

Even larger fines fail to discourage repeated collusion. In 1996, Archer Daniels Midland (ADM) paid to settle three civil price-fixing-related cases: $35 million in a case involving citric acid (used in many consumer products), $30 million to shareholders as compensation for lost stock value after the citric acid price-fixing scandal became public, and $25 million in a lysine (an animal feed additive) case. ADM paid a $100 million fine in a federal criminal case for fixing the price of lysine and citric acid in 1996, but only eight years later, ADM settled a fructose corn syrup price-fixing case for $400 million.

Third, some firms are able to coordinate their activities without explicitly colluding and thereby running afoul of competition laws. To determine guilt, U.S. antitrust laws use evidence of conspiracy—explicit agreements—rather than the economic effect of the suspected cartel. Charging monopoly-level prices is not necessarily illegal—only the "bad behavior" of explicitly agreeing to raise prices is against the law. As a result, some groups of firms charge monopoly-level prices without violating competition laws. These firms may *tacitly collude* without meeting by signaling to each other through their actions. If one firm raises its price and keeps it high only if other firms follow its lead, it is not necessarily violating the law if the firms did not explicitly communicate.

For example, shortly before Thanksgiving in 2012, United Airlines announced a fare increase. However, when rivals failed to match this increase, United rolled back its fares the next day. Shortly thereafter, the president of US Airways observed that if Southwest Airlines, the firm that carries the most passengers, fails to match an increase by other airlines, rivals cancel the increase.[5]

Canada is normally credited with the modern world's first antitrust statute, enacted in 1889, one year before the U.S. Sherman Act. Canada's current Competition Act regulates most business conduct. It contains both criminal and civil provisions that are designed to prevent anticompetitive practices. As under U.S. law, price-fixing cartels are *per se* illegal and are subject to civil and criminal punishment. Australia and New Zealand have laws on cartels that are similar to those in Canada and the United States.

In the past, the German, Japanese, and British governments permitted some cartels to operate because these governments felt doing so would promote economic efficiency. However, in recent years, most developed countries have followed Canada and the United States in strictly prohibiting cartels. The European Union's competition policy under the Treaty of the European Community (EC Treaty or Treaty of Rome) in 1957 gives the European Union and member states substantial civil powers to prevent actions that hinder competition, including formation of cartels. Again, price-fixing is *per se* illegal.

The DOJ, the FTC, the Canadian Competition Bureau, and the European Union authorities have become increasingly aggressive, prosecuting many more cases and increasing fines dramatically. Following the lead of the United States, which imposes both civil and criminal penalties, the British government introduced legislation in 2002 to criminalize certain cartel-related conduct. In 2004, Japan started pursuing antitrust cases more aggressively.

In 1993, the DOJ introduced the Corporate Leniency Program, guaranteeing that cartel whistle-blowers will receive immunity from federal prosecution. As a consequence, the DOJ has caught, prosecuted, and fined several gigantic cartels. In 2002, European authorities adopted a similar policy.

---

[5]Charisse Jones, "United Airlines Hikes Fares; Will Rivals Follow?" *USA Today*, October 11, 2012; "US Airways President Talks about Southwest Fares," *Businessweek*, October 24, 2012.

In addition to making price-fixing strictly illegal, these competition laws restrict mergers between firms and ban abusive behavior by firms that dominate a market. In addition, such laws limit various vertical relationships between firms (relationships governing how firms deal with their suppliers and their customers in the supply chain).[6]

Increasingly, antitrust authorities from around the world are cooperating. Cooperation agreements exist between authorities in Canada, Mexico, Europe, Australia, New Zealand, and the United States, among others. Such cooperation is critical given the increasingly global scope of the firms engaged in collusion and other anticompetitive activities.

Application

Catwalk Cartel

Being thin, rich, and beautiful doesn't make you immune to exploitation. In 2004, some of the world's most successful models charged 10 of New York's top modeling agencies—including Wilhelmina, Ford, Next, IMG, and Elite—with operating a cartel that cut their commissions by millions of dollars. Such collusion between firms is illegal under U.S. law.

Carolyn Fears—a 5'11″ redheaded former model who had earned up to $200,000 a year—initiated the suit when she learned that her agency not only charged her a 20% commission every time she was booked, but also extracted a 20% commission from her employers. Her class-action lawsuit (a lawsuit representing a group of people—here, models) alleged that the agencies collectively fixed commissions for Claudia Schiffer, Heidi Klum, Gisele Bundchen, and thousands of other models over many years.

The agencies had formed an industry group, International Model Managers Association, Inc. (IMMA), which held repeated meetings. Monique Pillard, an executive at Elite Model Management, fired off a memo concerning one IMMA meeting, in which she "made a point . . . that we are all committing suicide, if we do not stick together. Pauline's agreed with me but as usual, Bill Weinberg [of Wilhelmina] cautioned me about price fixing. . . . Ha! Ha! Ha! . . . the usual (expletive)." As the trial judge, Harold Baer, Jr., observed, while "Wilhelmina objects to the outward discussion of price fixing, it is plausible from Pillard's reaction that Wilhelmina's objection was to the dissemination of information, not to the underlying price-fixing agreement."

The models argued that the association was little more than a front for helping agency heads keep track of each other's pricing policies. Documents show that, shortly after association meetings, the agencies uniformly raised their commission rates from 10% to 15% and then to 20%. For example, at a meeting before the last increase, an Elite executive gave his competitors a heads-up—but had not informed his clients—that Elite planned to raise its commissions to 20%. He said that at Elite, "we were also favorable to letting everyone know as much as possible about our pricing policies."

In 2007, the models won their court case, having sued successfully under U.S. laws that prohibit price-fixing cartels. They received payments from the firms. For example, IMG paid the models $11 million. In 2011, the Competition Commission of Singapore fined a cartel consisting of 10 modeling agencies for price-fixing in a case remarkably similar to the U.S. case.

---

[6]The FTC has a broader range of other responsibilities that include *consumer protection*, such as preventing misleading advertising, which we do not discuss here.

Why Cartels Fail

A thing worth having is a thing worth cheating for.   —W. C. Fields

Many cartels fail even without legal intervention. *Cartels fail if noncartel members can supply consumers with large quantities of goods.* For example, copper producers formed an international cartel that controlled only about a third of the world's copper production and faced additional competition from firms that recycle copper from scrap materials. Because of this competition from noncartel members, the cartel was not successful in setting and maintaining a cartel price.

In addition, *each member of a cartel has an incentive to cheat on the cartel agreement.* The owner of a firm may reason, "I joined the cartel to encourage others to reduce their output and increase profits for everyone. I can make more, however, if I cheat on the cartel agreement by producing extra output. I can get away with cheating if the other firms can't tell who's producing the extra output because I'm just one of many firms and because I'll hardly affect the market price." By this reasoning, it is in each firm's best interest for all *other* firms to honor the cartel agreement—thus driving up the market price—while it ignores the agreement and makes extra, profitable sales at the high price.

Figure 13.1 illustrates why firms want to cheat. At the cartel output, q_m in panel a, each cartel member's marginal cost is MC_m. The marginal revenue of a firm that violates the agreement is p_m because it is acting like a price taker with respect to the market price. Because the firm's marginal revenue (price) is above its marginal cost, the firm wants to increase its output. If the firm decides to violate the cartel agreement, it maximizes its profit by increasing its output to q^*, where its marginal cost equals p_m.

As more and more firms leave the cartel, the cartel price falls. The colluding firms act like a dominant firm facing a competitive fringe (Chapter 11). Eventually, if enough firms quit, the cartel collapses.

Maintaining Cartels

To keep firms from violating the cartel agreement, the cartel must be able to detect cheating and punish violators. Further, the members of the cartel must keep their illegal behavior hidden from customers and government agencies.

Detection and Enforcement   Cartels use various techniques to detect cheating. Some cartels, for example, give members the right to inspect each other's accounts. Cartels may also divide the market by region or by customers, making it more likely that a firm that steals another firm's customers is detected, as in the case of a two-country mercury cartel (1928–1972) that allocated the Americas to Spain and Europe to Italy. Another option is for a cartel to turn to industry organizations that collect data on market share by firm. A cheating cartel's market share would rise, tipping off the other firms that it cheated.

You perhaps have seen "low price" ads in which local retail stores guarantee to meet or beat the prices of any competitors. These ads may in fact be a way for the firm to induce its customers to report cheating by other firms on an explicit or implicit cartel agreement (Salop, 1986).

Various methods are used to enforce cartel agreements. For example, GE and Westinghouse, the two major sellers of large steam-turbine generators, included "most-favored-customer" clauses in their contracts. These contracts stated that the seller would not offer a lower price to any other current or future buyer without offering the same price decrease to the firms that signed these contracts. This type of rebate clause creates a penalty for cheating on the cartel: If either company cheats by cutting prices, it has to lower prices to all previous buyers as well. Threats of violence are another means of enforcing a cartel agreement.[7]

Government Support Sometimes governments help create and enforce cartels, exempting them from antitrust and competition laws. By successfully lobbying the U.S. Congress for a special exemption, professional baseball teams have not been subject to most U.S. antitrust laws since 1922. As a result, they can use the courts to help enforce certain aspects of their cartel agreement.

The international airline market provides an example where governments first created a cartel and then later acted to end it. In 1944, 52 countries signed the Convention on International Civil Aviation, which established rules ("freedoms") that enabled airlines to fly between countries. International airfares were negotiated through bilateral governmental agreements rather than determined by the market, and airlines were given exemption from cartel laws, which allowed them to discuss prices through the International Air Transport Association (IATA). In the late 1970s, the United States deregulated its airline industry. Soon thereafter, European countries started to deregulate, allowing nongovernment-owned airlines to enter the market. Countries negotiated bilateral *open skies* agreements that weakened IATA's price-fixing role.[8]

Barriers to Entry Barriers to entry that limit the number of firms help the cartel detect and punish cheating and keep prices high. The fewer the firms in a market, the more likely it is that other firms will know if a given firm cheats and the easier it is to impose costs on that firm. Cartels with a large number of firms are relatively rare, except those involving professional associations. Hay and Kelley (1974) examined Department of Justice price-fixing cases from 1963 to 1972 and found that only 6.5% involved 50 or more conspirators, the average number of firms was 7.25, and nearly half the cases (48%) involved 6 or fewer firms.

When new firms enter their market, cartels frequently fail. For example, when only Italy and Spain sold mercury, they were able to establish and maintain a stable cartel. When a larger group of countries joined them, their attempts to cartelize the world mercury market repeatedly failed (MacKie-Mason and Pindyck, 1986).

Application

Casket Entry

You might think that anyone with some nails and a few pieces of board can make a casket and sell it. That's what the Benedictine monks of the century-old St. Joseph Abbey in Covington, Louisiana, thought. They tried to start a small business on All Souls' Day (the Day of the Dead) in 2007 to sell the simple wooden caskets that they have made for generations.

They hadn't reckoned with the full majesty of the Louisiana State Board of Funeral Directors. Before the brothers had sold their first casket, the Board, responding to a complaint from a government-licensed funeral director, shut them down. It is a crime in Louisiana to sell caskets without a license. (Are they worried that a substandard coffin will hurt a corpse?) To get a license, the monks would have had to turn their monastery into a funeral home complete with an embalming room, and at least one of the monks would have had to leave the order to spend years becoming a licensed funeral director.

[7]See the Application "Bad Bakers" in MyEconLab, Chapter 11.

[8]The European Court of Justice struck down the central provisions of aviation treaties among the United States and eight other countries in 2002.

The monks petitioned state legislators in 2008 and 2010, but they were no match for the funeral-industry lobby. So they turned to the federal courts. In 2013, the U.S. Fifth Circuit Court of Appeals struck down the Louisiana law. It held that the Constitution prohibits laws that are "naked transfers of wealth" to industry cartels. However, in another case, the U.S. Tenth Circuit Court of Appeals upheld a similar Oklahoma law. That court observed that "dishing out special economic benefits to certain in-state industries remains the favored pastime of state and local governments." Now we have to wait to see if the U.S. Supreme Court reviews this case to resolve whether state governments may create such barriers to entry with impunity.

Mergers

If antitrust or competition laws prevent firms from colluding, firms could try to achieve the same end by merging to form a monopoly. To prevent this potential problem, most antitrust and competition laws restrict the ability of firms to merge if the net effect is to harm society.

Proposed U.S. mergers beyond a certain size must be reported to U.S. authorities and may be evaluated by either the DOJ or the FTC. These agencies block mergers that they believe harm society. However, firms can appeal this decision to the federal courts. Most other developed countries also have similar merger review procedures.

Similarly, in recent years, the European Commission has been active in reviewing and, when it felt it was necessary, blocking mergers. Virtually none of the commission's decisions have been rejected by the courts. One reason why governments limit mergers is that all the firms in a market could combine and form a monopoly.

Would banning any possible merger increase economic efficiency? No, because some mergers reduce production costs substantially. Formerly separate firms may become more efficient because of greater scale, the sharing of trade secrets, or the closure of duplicative retail outlets. For example, when Chase and Chemical banks merged, they closed or combined seven Manhattan branches that were located within two blocks of other branches.

Whether a merger helps or harms society depends on which of its two offsetting effects—reducing competition and increasing efficiency—is larger. Consider two extreme cases. In one, the merger of the only two firms in the market does not lower costs, but it increases monopoly power, so the newly merged firm substantially raises prices to consumers. Here, the merger hurts society. At the other extreme, two of a large number of firms in the market merge, with substantial cost savings, but with no noticeable increase in market power or market price. Here, the merger benefits society.

The contentious cases lie in the middle, where market power increases significantly *and* costs decrease. However, if the price falls after the merger because the cost reduction effect dominates the increased market power effect, the merger is desirable.

Application

Hospital Mergers: Market Power Versus Efficiency

Since the 1990s, the hospital market has consolidated substantially through mergers, with an average of nearly 60 mergers per year in major metropolitan areas. When two hospitals merge, eliminating duplication can produce substantial efficiency gains, which may result in lower prices. However, the merger may reduce competition and raise price. Which effect dominates is an empirical question.

Using a sample of U.S. hospitals, Dafny (2009) found that local hospital prices rise by about 40% on average after a merger, with the (apparently large) cost savings going to the hospitals rather than to the patients. However, the price effects of hospital mergers vary substantially across hospitals. Haas-Wilson and Garmon (2011) studied a merger of two hospitals in Evanston, Illinois, and found that one hospital raised its prices by 20% but the other's prices remained constant. Tenn (2011) examined the Summit-Sutter mergers in Berkeley and Oakland, California, and found that Summit's prices increased between 28% and 44%. Gowrisankaran et al. (2013) looked very carefully at one proposed hospital merger in Virginia and argued that it would raise prices by 3.1%.

13.3 Cournot Oligopoly

How do oligopolistic firms behave if they do not collude? Although economists have only one model of competition and one model of monopoly, they have many models of noncooperative oligopolistic behavior with many possible equilibrium prices and quantities.

Which model is appropriate to use depends on the type of *actions* firms take—such as setting quantity or price—and whether firms act simultaneously or sequentially. We examine the three best-known oligopoly models in turn. In the *Cournot model*, firms simultaneously choose quantities without colluding. In the *Stackelberg model*, a leader firm chooses its quantity and then the other follower firms independently choose their quantities. In the *Bertrand model*, firms simultaneously and independently choose prices.

To illustrate these models as simply and clearly as possible, we start by making three restrictive assumptions, which we later relax. First, we initially assume that all firms are identical in the sense that they have the same cost functions and produce identical, *undifferentiated* products. We show how the market outcomes change if costs differ or if consumers believe that the products differ across firms.

duopoly
an oligopoly with two firms

Second, we initially illustrate each of these oligopoly models for a **duopoly**: an oligopoly with two (*duo*) firms. Each of these models can be applied to markets with many firms. The Cournot and Stackelberg outcomes vary, whereas the Bertrand market outcome with undifferentiated goods does not vary as the number of firms increases.

Third, we assume that the market lasts for only one period. Consequently, each firm chooses its quantity or price only once. In Chapter 14, we examine markets that last for more than one period.

To compare market outcomes under the various models, we need to be able to characterize the oligopoly equilibrium. In Chapter 2, we defined an *equilibrium* as a situation in which no one wants to change his or her behavior. For a competitive market to be in equilibrium, no firm wants to change its output level given what the other firms are producing. As oligopolistic firms may take many possible actions—such as setting price or quantity, or choosing a level of advertising—the oligopoly equilibrium rule needs to refer to their behavior more generally than just setting output.

John Nash, a Nobel Prize-winning economist and mathematician, defined an equilibrium concept that has wide applicability including to oligopoly models (Nash, 1951). We will give a general definition of a Nash equilibrium in Chapter 14. In this chapter we use a special case of that definition that is appropriate for the single-period oligopoly models where the only action that a firm can take is to set either its quantity or its price: A set of actions taken by the firms is a *Nash equilibrium* if, holding the actions of all other firms constant, no firm can obtain a higher profit by choosing a different action.

The Duopoly Nash-Cournot Equilibrium

The French economist and mathematician Antoine-Augustin Cournot introduced the first formal model of oligopoly in 1838. Cournot explained how oligopolistic firms behave if they simultaneously choose how much they produce. The firms act independently and have imperfect information about their rivals. Each firm must choose its output level before knowing what the other firms will choose. The quantity one firm produces directly affects the profit of the other firms because the market price depends on total output. Thus, in choosing its strategy to maximize its profit, each firm takes into account its beliefs about the output its rivals will sell. Cournot introduced an equilibrium concept that is the same as the Nash definition where the action that firms take is to choose quantities.

We look at equilibrium in a market that lasts for only one period. Initially, we make four assumptions:

1. The market has a small number of firms, and no other firms can enter.
2. The firms set their quantities independently and simultaneously.
3. The firms have identical costs.
4. The firms sell identical products.

Later, we relax each of these assumptions and examine how the equilibrium changes.

An Airlines Market Example

To illustrate the basic idea of the Cournot model, we turn to an actual market where American Airlines and United Airlines compete for customers on flights between Chicago and Los Angeles.[9] The total number of passengers flown by these two firms, Q, is the sum of the number of passengers flown on American, q_A, and those flown on United, q_U. We assume that no other companies can enter, perhaps because they cannot obtain landing rights at both airports.[10]

How many passengers does each airline choose to carry? To answer this question, we determine the Nash equilibrium for this model. This Nash equilibrium, in which firms choose quantities, is also called a **Cournot equilibrium** or **Nash-Cournot equilibrium** (or *Nash-in-quantities equilibrium*): a set of quantities chosen by firms such that, holding the quantities of all other firms constant, no firm can obtain a higher profit by choosing a different quantity.

To determine the Nash-Cournot equilibrium, we need to establish how each firm chooses its quantity. We start by using the total demand curve for the Chicago–Los Angeles route and a firm's belief about how much its rival will sell to determine its *residual demand curve*: the market demand that is not met by other sellers at any given price (Chapter 8). Next, we examine how a firm uses its residual demand curve to determine its best response: the output level that maximizes its profit, given its belief about how much its rival will produce. Finally, we use the information contained in the firms' best-response functions to determine the Nash-Cournot equilibrium quantities.

Cournot equilibrium (Nash-Cournot equilibrium)
a set of quantities chosen by firms such that, holding the quantities of all other firms constant, no firm can obtain a higher profit by choosing a different quantity

---

[9]This example is based on Brander and Zhang (1990). In calculating the profits, we assume that Brander and Zhang's estimate of the firms' constant marginal cost is the same as the firms' relevant long-run average cost.

[10]With the end of deregulation, existing firms were given the right to buy, sell, or rent landing slots. However, by controlling landing slots, existing firms can make entry difficult.

Graphical Approach The strategy that each firm uses depends on the demand curve it faces and its marginal cost. American Airlines' profit-maximizing output depends on how many passengers it believes United will fly. Figure 13.2 illustrates two possibilities.

If American were a monopoly, it wouldn't have to worry about United's strategy. American's demand would be the market demand curve, *D* in panel a. To maximize its profit, American would set its output so that its marginal revenue curve, *MR*, intersected its marginal cost curve, *MC*, which is constant at $147 per passenger. Panel a shows that the monopoly output is 96 units (thousands of passengers) per quarter and the monopoly price is $243 per passenger (one way).

Because American competes with United, American must take account of United's behavior when choosing its profit-maximizing output. American's demand is not the entire market demand. Rather, American is concerned with its *residual demand curve*: the market demand that is not met by other sellers at any given price. (This concept is analogous to the *residual supply curve* discussed in Chapter 8.) In general, if the market demand function is $D(p)$, and the supply of other firms is $S^o(p)$, then the residual demand function, $D^r(p)$, is

$$D^r(p) = D(p) - S^o(p).$$

Thus, if United flies q_U passengers regardless of the price, American transports only the residual demand, $Q = D(p)$, minus the q_U passengers, so $q_A = Q - q_U$.

Suppose that American believes that United will fly $q_U = 64$. Panel b shows that American's residual demand curve, D^r, is the market demand curve, D, moved to the left by $q_U = 64$. For example, if the price is $211, the total number of passengers who want to fly is $Q = 128$. If United transports $q_U = 64$, American flies $Q - q_U = 128 - 64 = 64 = q_A$.

Figure 13.2 American Airlines' Profit-Maximizing Output

(a) If American is a monopoly, it picks its profit-maximizing output, $q_A = 96$ units (thousand passengers) per quarter, so that its marginal revenue, *MR*, equals its marginal cost, *MC*. (b) If American believes that United will fly $q_U = 64$ units per quarter, its residual demand curve, D^r, is the market demand curve, D, minus q_U. American maximizes its profit at $q_A = 64$, where its marginal revenue, MR^r, equals *MC*.

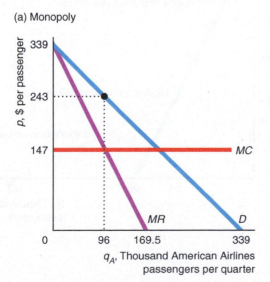

(a) Monopoly

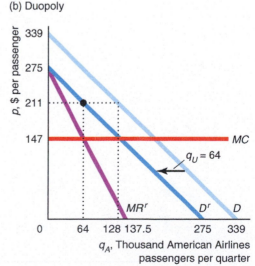

(b) Duopoly

What is American's best-response, profit-maximizing output if its managers believe that United will fly q_U passengers? American can think of itself as having a monopoly with respect to the people who don't fly on United, which its residual demand curve, D^r, shows. To maximize its profit, American sets its output so that its marginal revenue corresponding to this residual demand, MR^r, equals its marginal cost. Panel b shows that if $q_U = 64$, American's best response is $q_A = 64$.

By shifting its residual demand curve appropriately, American can calculate its best response to any given q_U using this type of analysis. Figure 13.3 plots American Airlines' best-response curve, which shows how many tickets American sells for each possible q_U.[11] As this curve shows, American will sell the monopoly number of tickets, 96, if American thinks United will fly no passengers, $q_U = 0$. The negative slope of the best-response curve shows that American sells fewer tickets the more people American thinks that United will fly. American sells $q_A = 64$ if it thinks q_U will be 64. American shuts down, $q_A = 0$, if it thinks q_U will be 192 or more, because operating wouldn't be profitable.

Similarly, United's best-response curve shows how many tickets United sells if it thinks American will sell q_A. For example, United sells $q_U = 0$ if it thinks American will sell $q_A = 192$, $q_U = 48$ if $q_A = 96$, $q_U = 64$ if $q_A = 64$, and $q_U = 96$ if $q_A = 0$.

A firm wants to change its behavior if it is selling a quantity that is not on its best-response curve. In a Nash-Cournot equilibrium, neither firm wants to change its behavior. Thus, in a Nash-Cournot equilibrium, each firm is on its best-response curve: Each firm is maximizing its profit, given its correct belief about its rival's output.

These firms' best-response curves intersect at $q_A = q_U = 64$. If American expects United to sell $q_U = 64$, American wants to sell $q_A = 64$. Because this point is on its

Figure 13.3 American's and United's Best-Response Curves

The best-response curves show the output each firm picks to maximize its profit, given its belief about its rival's output. The Nash-Cournot equilibrium occurs at the intersection of the best-response curves.

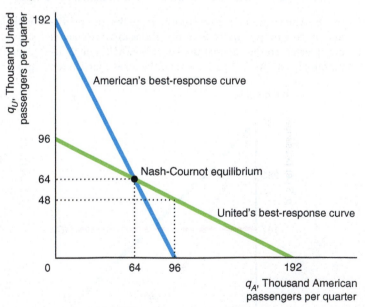

best-response curve, American doesn't want to change its output from 64. Similarly, if United expects American to sell $q_A = 64$, United doesn't want to change q_U from 64. Thus, this pair of outputs is a Cournot (Nash) equilibrium: Given its correct belief about its rival's output, each firm is maximizing its profit, and neither firm wants to change its output.

Any pair of outputs other than the pair at an intersection of the best-response functions is *not* a Nash-Cournot equilibrium. If either firm is not on its best-response curve, it changes its output to increase its profit. For example, the output pair $q_A = 96$ and $q_U = 0$ is not a Nash-Cournot equilibrium. American is perfectly happy producing the monopoly output if United doesn't operate at all: American is on its best-response curve. United, however, would not be happy with this outcome because it is not on United's best-response curve. As its best-response curve shows, if it knows that American will sell $q_A = 96$, United wants to sell $q_U = 48$. Only at $q_A = q_U = 64$ does neither firm want to change its behavior.

Algebraic Approach We can also use algebra to solve for the Nash-Cournot equilibrium for these two airlines. (See Appendix 13A for a more general analysis.) We use estimates of the market demand and firms' marginal costs to determine the equilibrium.

Our estimate of the market demand function is

$$Q = 339 - p, \tag{13.1}$$

where price, p, is the dollar cost of a one-way flight, and total quantity of the two airlines combined, Q, is measured in thousands of passengers flying one way per quarter. Panels a and b of Figure 13.2 show that this market demand curve, D, is a straight line that hits the price axis at $339 and the quantity axis at 339 units (thousands of passengers) per quarter. Each airline has a constant marginal cost, MC, and average cost, AC, of $147 per passenger per flight. Using only this information and our economic model, we can find the Nash-Cournot equilibrium for the two airlines.

If American believes that United will fly q_U passengers, American expects to fly only the total market demand minus q_U passengers. At a price of p, the total number of passengers, $Q(p)$, is given by the market demand function, Equation 13.1. Thus, the residual demand American faces is

$$q_A = Q(p) - q_U = (339 - p) - q_U.$$

Using algebra, we can rewrite this inverse residual demand function as

$$p = 339 - q_A - q_U. \tag{13.2}$$

In panel b, the linear residual demand, D^r, is parallel to the market demand, D, and lies to the left of D by $q_U = 64$.

If a demand curve is linear, the corresponding marginal revenue curve is twice as steep (Chapter 11). The slope of the residual demand curve, Equation 13.2, is $\Delta p / \Delta q_A = -1$, so the slope of the corresponding marginal revenue curve, MR^r in panel b in Figure 13.2, is -2. Therefore, the marginal revenue function is[12]

$$MR^r = 339 - 2q_A - q_U. \tag{13.3}$$

---

[12]American's revenue is $R = pq_A = (339 - q_A - q_U)q_A$. If American treats q_U as a constant and differentiates R with respect to its output, it finds that its marginal revenue is $MR = \partial R / \partial q_A = 339 - 2q_A - q_U$.

American Airlines' best response—its profit-maximizing output, given q_U—is the output that equates its marginal revenue, Equation 13.3, and its marginal cost:

$$MR^r = 339 - 2q_A - q_U = 147 = MC. \tag{13.4}$$

By rearranging Equation 13.4, we can write American's best-response output, q_A, as a function of q_U:

$$q_A = 96 - \tfrac{1}{2}q_U. \tag{13.5}$$

Figure 13.3 shows American's best-response function, Equation 13.5. According to this best-response function, $q_A = 96$ if $q_U = 0$ and $q_A = 64$ if $q_U = 64$. By the same reasoning, United's best-response function is

$$q_U = 96 - \tfrac{1}{2}q_A. \tag{13.6}$$

A Nash-Cournot equilibrium is a pair of quantities, q_A and q_U, such that Equations 13.5 and 13.6 both hold: Each firm is on its best-response curve. This statement is equivalent to saying that the Nash-Cournot equilibrium is a point at which the best-response curves cross.

One way to determine the Nash-Cournot equilibrium is to substitute Equation 13.6 into Equation 13.5,

$$q_A = 96 - \tfrac{1}{2}(96 - \tfrac{1}{2}q_A),$$

and solve for q_A. Doing so, we find that $q_A = 64$ is the Nash-Cournot equilibrium quantity for American. Substituting $q_A = 64$ into Equation 13.6, we find that $q_U = 64$ is the Nash-Cournot equilibrium quantity for United. As a result, the total output in the Nash-Cournot equilibrium is $Q = q_A + q_U = 128$. Setting $Q = 128$ in the market demand Equation 13.1, we learn that the Nash-Cournot equilibrium price is $211.

Equilibrium, Elasticity, and the Number of Firms

Our airlines example illustrates that, if two Cournot firms set output independently, the price to consumers is lower than the monopoly (or cartel) price. The price to consumers is even lower if more than two Cournot firms produce independently, as we now show.

Each Cournot firm maximizes its profit by operating where its marginal revenue equals its marginal cost. A firm's marginal revenue depends on the price and the elasticity of demand it faces where it maximizes its profit (Chapter 11). The marginal revenue for a typical Cournot firm is $MR = p(1 + 1/\varepsilon_r)$, where ε_r is the elasticity of the residual demand curve the firm faces. Appendix 13A shows that $\varepsilon_r = n\varepsilon$, where ε is the market elasticity of demand and n is the number of firms with identical costs. Thus, we can write a typical Cournot firm's profit-maximizing condition as

$$MR = p\left(1 + \frac{1}{n\varepsilon}\right) = MC. \tag{13.7}$$

If $n = 1$, the Cournot firm is a monopoly, and Equation 13.7 is the same as the profit-maximizing monopoly condition, Equation 11.7. The more firms, the larger the residual demand elasticity, $n\varepsilon$, that a single firm faces. As n grows very large, the residual demand elasticity approaches negative infinity $(-\infty)$, and Equation 13.7 becomes $p = MC$, which is the profit-maximizing condition of a price-taking competitive firm.

The Lerner Index, $(p - MC)/p$, is a measure of market power: the firm's ability to raise price above marginal cost. By rearranging the terms in Equation 13.7, we find that a Cournot firm's Lerner Index depends on the elasticity the firm faces:

$$\frac{p - MC}{p} = -\frac{1}{n\varepsilon}. \tag{13.8}$$

Thus, a Cournot firm's Lerner Index equals the monopoly level, $-1/\varepsilon$, with only one firm: Setting $n = 1$ in Equation 13.8, we obtain the monopoly expression (Equation 11.9). Again, as the number of firms grows large, the residual demand elasticity a firm faces approaches $-\infty$, so the Lerner Index approaches zero, which is the same as with price-taking, competitive firms.

We can illustrate these results using our airlines example. Suppose that other airlines with identical marginal cost, $MC = \$147$, were to fly between Chicago and Los Angeles. Table 13.2 shows how the Nash-Cournot equilibrium price and the Lerner Index vary with the number of firms.[13]

As we already know, one "Cournot" firm would produce the monopoly quantity, 96, at the monopoly price, $243. We also know that each duopoly firm's output is 64, so market output is 128 and price is $211. The duopoly market elasticity is $\varepsilon = 1.65$, so the residual demand elasticity each firm faces is twice as large as the market elasticity, $2\varepsilon = -3.3$.

As the number of firms increases, each firm's output falls toward zero, but total output approaches 192, the quantity on the market demand curve where price equals the marginal cost of $147. Although the market elasticity of demand falls as the number of firms grows, the residual demand curve for each firm becomes increasingly horizontal (perfectly elastic). As a result, the price approaches the marginal cost, $147. Similarly, as the number of firms increases, the Lerner Index approaches the price-taking level of zero.[14]

Table 13.2 Nash-Cournot Equilibrium Varies with the Number of Firms

Number of Firms, n	Firm Output, q	Market Output, Q	Price, p	Market Elasticity, ε	Residual Demand Elasticity, $n\varepsilon$	Lerner Index, $(p - m)/p = -1/(n\varepsilon)$
1	96	96	243	−2.53	−2.53	0.40
2	64	128	211	−1.65	−3.30	0.30
3	48	144	195	−1.35	−4.06	0.25
4	38.4	154	185.40	−1.21	−4.83	0.21
5	32	160	179	−1.12	−5.59	0.18
10	17.5	175	164.45	−0.94	−9.42	0.11
50	3.8	188	150.76	−0.80	−40.05	0.02
100	1.9	190	148.90	−0.78	−78.33	0.01

[13]In Appendix 13A, we derive the Nash-Cournot equilibrium quantity and price for a general linear demand. Given our particular demand curve, Equation 13.1, and marginal cost, $147, each firm's Nash-Cournot equilibrium output is $q = (339 - 147)/(n + 1) = 192/(n + 1)$ and the Cournot market price is $p = (339 + 147n)/(n + 1)$.

[14]As the number of firms goes to infinity, the Nash-Cournot equilibrium goes to perfect competition only if average cost is nondecreasing (Ruffin, 1971).

The table shows that having extra firms in the market benefits consumers. When the number of firms rises from 1 to 4, the price falls by a quarter and the Lerner Index is cut nearly in half. At ten firms, the price is one-third less than the monopoly level, and the Lerner Index is a quarter of the monopoly level.

Application

Mobile Number Portability

When cell phones were first introduced in most European countries, a single firm provided the service. After the market was opened to new entrants, customers were slow to switch firms because of large switching costs such as having to obtain a new phone number and get new handsets. Preventing customers from transferring their phone number if they switch carriers makes the demand curve facing a given firm less elastic.

To reduce switching costs and increase competition by new firms, many governments require Mobile Number Portability (MNP), which allows consumers to move their phone number to another mobile phone carrier.[15] Cho et al. (2013) estimated that the introduction of MNP in European countries decreased phone service prices by 7.9% and increased consumer surplus by 2.86€ ($3.86) per person per quarter.

Nonidentical Firms

We initially assumed that the firms were identical in the sense that they faced the same cost functions and produced identical products. However, costs often vary across firms, and firms often differentiate the products they produce from those of their rivals.

Unequal Costs   In the Cournot model, the firm sets its output so as to equate its marginal revenue to its marginal cost, which determines its best-response function. If the firms' marginal costs vary, then the firms' best-response functions will as well. In the resulting Nash-Cournot equilibrium, the relatively low-cost firm produces more. As long as the products are not differentiated, they both charge the same price.

We can illustrate the effect of unequal costs using our duopoly airlines example. Suppose that American Airlines' marginal cost remains at $147, but United's marginal cost drops to $99. The Cournot model still applies, but we have relaxed the assumption that the firms have identical costs. How does the Nash-Cournot equilibrium change? Your intuition probably tells you that United's output increases relative to that of American, as we now show.

Nothing changes for American, so its best-response function is unchanged. United's best response to any given American output is the output at which its marginal revenue corresponding to its residual demand, MR^r, equals its new, lower marginal cost. Because United's marginal cost curve fell, United wants to produce more than before for any given level of American's output.

Panel a of Figure 13.4 illustrates this reasoning. United's MR^r curve is unaffected, but its marginal cost curve shifts down from MC^1 to MC^2. Suppose we fix American's output at 64 units. Consequently, United's residual demand, D^r, lies 64 units to the left of the market demand, D. United's corresponding MR^r curve intersects its original marginal cost curve, $MC^1 = \$147$, at 64 and its new marginal cost, $MC^2 = \$99$, at 88. Thus, if we hold American's output constant at 64, United produces more as its marginal cost falls.

---

[15]The United States has required wireless local number portability nationwide since 2003, and Canada since 2007. In 2002, the European Commission mandated that MNP be enacted in each European Community country. At least 63 countries have MNP.

Figure 13.4 Effect of a Drop in One Firm's Marginal Cost on a Duopoly Nash-Cournot Equilibrium

(a) United's marginal cost falls from $MC^1 = \$147$ to $MC^2 = \$99$. If American produces $q_a = 64$, United's best response is to increase its output from $q_U = 64$ to 88 given its lower marginal cost. (b) If both airlines' marginal cost is $147, the Nash-Cournot equilibrium is e_1. After

United's marginal cost falls to $99, its best-response function shifts outward. It now sells more tickets in response to any given American output than previously. At the new Nash-Cournot equilibrium, e_2, United sells $q_U = 96$, while American sells only $q_A = 48$.

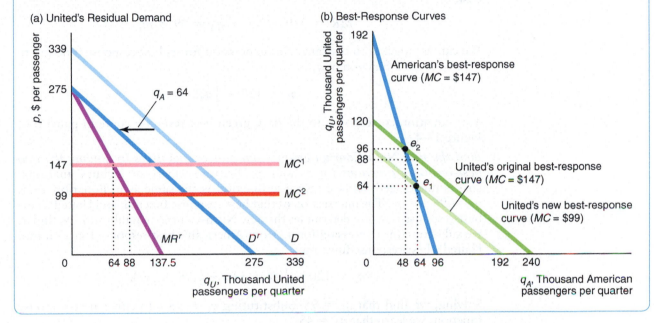

Because this reasoning applies for any level of output American picks, United's best-response function in panel b shifts outward as its marginal cost falls. United's best response to any given quantity that American sells is to sell more than at its previous, higher cost. As a result, the Nash-Cournot equilibrium shifts from e_1, at which both firms sold 64, to e_2, at which United sells 96 and American sells 48.

Using the market demand curve, Equation 13.1, we find that the market price falls from $211 to $195, benefiting consumers. United's profit increases from $4.1 million to $9.2 million, while American's profit falls to $2.3 million.[16] Thus, United and consumers gain and American loses from the fall in United's marginal cost.

Solved Problem 13.1

Derive United Airlines' best-response function if its marginal cost falls to $99 per unit. Given that American's marginal cost does not change, what is the new Nash-Cournot equilibrium?[17]

Answer

1. *Determine United's subsidized marginal revenue function corresponding to its residual demand curve.* Luckily, we already know that. The shift in its marginal

---

[16]Each firm's profit per passenger is price minus average cost, $p - AC$, so the firm's profit is $\pi = (p - AC)q$, where q is the number of passengers the firm flies. The Cournot price is $211 and the average cost is $147, so the Cournot profit per firm is $\pi = (211 - 147) \times 64$ units per quarter = $4.1 million per quarter in the original symmetric case.

[17]See Appendix 13A for a mathematical approach to a more general case.

cost curve does not affect United's residual demand curve, hence its marginal revenue function is the same as before: $MR^r = 339 - 2q_U - q_A$. (The same expression as American's marginal revenue function in Equation 13.3, where the A and U subscripts are reversed.)

2. *Equate United's subsidized marginal revenue function and its marginal cost to determine its best-response function.* For a given level of American's output, q_A, United chooses its output, q_U, to equate its marginal revenue and its marginal cost, m:

$$MR^r = 339 - 2q_U - q_A = 99 = m.$$

We can use algebra to rearrange this expression for its best-response function to express q_U as a function of q_a:

$$q_U = 120 - \tfrac{1}{2}q_A.$$

This equation corresponds to the dark green best-response curve in panel b of Figure 13.4.

3. *Find the new Nash-Cournot equilibrium pair of quantities by solving the two best-response functions for q_A and q_U.* Because American Airlines' marginal cost is unchanged, its best-response function is the same as in Equation 13.5, $q_A = 96 - \tfrac{1}{2}q_U$. The intersection of that best-response function and United's new best-response function determines the new Nash-Cournot equilibrium. To find it, we substitute the expression for q_A from American's best-response function into United's best-response function:

$$q_U = 120 - \tfrac{1}{2}q_A = 120 - \tfrac{1}{2}(96 - \tfrac{1}{2}q_U).$$

Solving, we find that $q_U = 96$. Substituting $q_U = 96$ into either best-response function, we learn that $q_A = 48$.

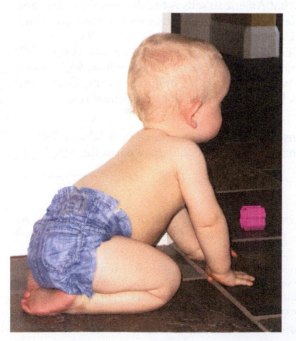

Differentiated Products By differentiating its product from those of a rival, an oligopolistic firm can shift its demand curve to the right and make it less elastic. The less elastic the demand curve, the more the firm can charge. Loosely speaking, consumers are willing to pay more for a product that they perceive as being superior.

One way to differentiate a product is to give it unique, "desirable" attributes, such as the Lexus car that parks itself. In 2010, Kimberly-Clark introduced a new Huggies disposable diaper with a printed denim pattern, including seams and back pockets, which sent their sales up 15%. A firm can differentiate its product by advertising, using colorful labels, and engaging in other promotional activities to convince consumers that its product is superior in some (possibly unspecified) way even though it is virtually identical to its rivals physically or chemically. Economists call this practice *spurious differentiation*. Bayer charges more for its chemically identical aspirin than other brands because Bayer has convinced consumers that its product is safer or superior in some other way. Clorox's bottle may be superior, but the bleach inside is chemically identical to that from rival brands costing much less.

Because differentiation makes demand curves less elastic, price markups over marginal cost are usually higher when products are differentiated than when they're identical. We know that consumer surplus falls as the gap between price and marginal cost rises for a given good. Does it follow that differentiating products lowers total surplus? Not necessarily. Although differentiation leads to higher prices, which harms consumers, differentiation is desirable in its own right. Consumers value having a choice, and some may greatly prefer a new brand to existing ones.

If consumers think products differ, the Cournot quantities and prices will differ across firms. Each firm faces a different inverse demand function and hence charges a different price. For example, suppose that Firm 1's inverse demand function is $p_1 = a - b_1q_1 - b_2q_2$, where $b_1 > b_2$ if consumers believe that Good 1 is different from Good 2 and $b_1 = b_2 = b$ if the goods are identical. Given that consumers view the products as differentiated and Firm 2 faces a similar inverse demand function, we replace the single market demand with these individual demand functions in the Cournot model. Solved Problem 13.2 shows how to solve for the Nash-Cournot equilibrium in an actual market with differentiated products.

Solved Problem 13.2

Intel and Advanced Micro Devices (AMD) are the only two firms that produce central processing units (CPUs)—the brains—for personal computers. Both because the products differ physically and because Intel's advertising "Intel Inside" campaign has convinced some consumers of its superiority, consumers view their CPUs as imperfect substitutes. Consequently, the two firms' estimated inverse demand functions differ:

$$p_A = 197 - 15.1q_A - 0.3q_I, \tag{13.9}$$

$$p_I = 490 - 10q_I - 6q_A, \tag{13.10}$$

where price is dollars per CPU, quantity is in millions of CPUs, the subscript I indicates Intel, and the subscript A represents AMD.[18] Each firm faces a constant marginal cost of $m = \$40$ per unit. (For simplicity, we assume that firms have no fixed costs.) Solve for the Nash-Cournot equilibrium quantities and prices.

Answer

1. *Using our rules for determining the marginal revenue for linear demand functions, calculate each firm's marginal revenue function.* For a linear demand curve, we know that the marginal revenue curve is twice as steeply sloped as is the demand curve. Thus, the marginal revenue functions that correspond to the inverse demand Equations 13.9 and 13.10 are[19]

$$MR^A = 197 - 30.2q_A - 0.3q_I, \tag{13.11}$$

$$MR^I = 490 - 20q_I - 6q_A. \tag{13.12}$$

---

[18]I thank Hugo Salgado for estimating these inverse demand functions for me and for providing evidence that this market is well described by a Nash-Cournot equilibrium.

[19]We can use calculus to derive these marginal revenue functions. For example, by multiplying both sides of AMD's inverse demand function (Equation 13.9) by q_A, we learn that its revenue function is $R_A = p_Aq_A = 197q_A - 15.2(q_A)^2 - 0.3q_Iq_A$. Holding q_I constant and differentiating with respect to q_A, we obtain $MR^A = dR_A/dq_A = 197 - 30.2q_A - 0.3q_I$.

2. *Equate the marginal revenue functions to the marginal cost to determine the best-response functions.* We determine AMD's best-response function by equating MR^A from Equation 13.11 to its marginal cost of $m = \$40$,

$$MR^A = 197 - 30.2q_A - 0.3q_I = 40 = m,$$

and solving for q_A to obtain AMD's best-response function:

$$q_A = \frac{157 - 0.3 \, q_I}{30.2}. \tag{13.13}$$

Similarly, Intel's best-response function is

$$q_I = \frac{450 - 6q_A}{20}. \tag{13.14}$$

3. *Use the best-response functions to solve for the Nash-Cournot equilibrium.* By simultaneously solving the system of best-response functions 13.13 and 13.14, we find that the Nash-Cournot equilibrium quantities are $q_A = 15,025/3,011 \approx 5$ million CPUs, and $q_I = 63,240/3,011 \approx 21$ million CPUs. Substituting these values into the inverse demand functions in Equations 13.9 and 13.10, we obtain the corresponding prices: $p_A = \$115.20$ and $p_I = \$250$ per CPU.

Application

Bottled Water

Bottled water is the most dramatic recent example of *spurious product differentiation*, where the products do not significantly differ physically. Firms convince consumers that their products differ through marketing.

Why are U.S. consumers willing to buy single-serving containers of water at an average per ounce cost that's nearly 2,000 times the cost of tap water and up to twice the cost of a gallon of regular gasoline? Fear. In a poll of U.S. consumers' top environmental fears, 53% of respondents said their greatest fear was that their drinking water isn't safe. Perhaps that helps to explain why the typical American consumed more than 30.8 gallons of bottled water in 2012.

If safety is their reason to buy bottled water, these consumers are being foolish. Not only does the U.S. Environmental Protection Agency set a stricter standard for tap water than the standard set by the Federal Drug Administration on bottled water (70% of bottled water is not federally regulated), but a quarter of all bottled water is tap water according to the Natural Resources Defense Council.

Both Coke and Pepsi have successfully differentiated their brands through marketing. Pepsico's top-selling bottled water, Aquafina, has a colorful blue label and a logo showing the sun rising over the mountains. From that logo, consumers may infer that the water comes from some bubbling spring high in an unspoiled wilderness. If so, they're wrong. Pepsi's best-selling bottled water comes from the same place as tap water: public-water sources. Pepsi also claims that it adds value by filtering the water using a state-of-the-art "HydRO-7 purification system," implying that such filtering (which removes natural minerals) is desirable. Similarly, Coke's marketing distinguishes its Dasani bottled water, even though it too is basically bottled public water.

In a recent "blind" taste test reported in *Slate*, no one could distinguish between Aquafina and Dasani, and both are equally clean and safe. However, many consumers, responding to perceived differences created by marketing, strongly prefer one or the other of these brands and pay a premium for that brand.

13.4 Stackelberg Oligopoly

In the Cournot model, both firms make their output decisions at the same time. Suppose, however, that one of the firms, called the *leader*, can set its output before its rival, the *follower*, sets its output. Having one firm act before another arises naturally if one firm enters the market first. Examples of leaders include IBM in the mainframe computer market, General Electric in the turbine generator industry, and General Foods among coffee roasters.

Would the firm that got to act first have an advantage? Heinrich von Stackelberg showed how to modify the Cournot model to answer this question.

How does the leader decide to set its output? The leader realizes that once it sets its output, the rival firm will use its Cournot best-response curve to pick a best-response output. Thus, the leader predicts what the follower will do before the follower acts. Using this knowledge, the leader manipulates the follower, thereby benefiting at the follower's expense.

We illustrate this model graphically using our airlines market example (Appendix 13B analyzes the model mathematically). Although it is difficult to imagine that either American Airlines or United Airlines actually has an advantage that would allow it to act before its rival, we assume (arbitrarily) that American Airlines can act before United Airlines.

Graphical Model

Given that American Airlines chooses its output first, how does American decide on its optimal policy? American uses its residual demand curve to determine its profit-maximizing output. American knows that when it sets q_A, United will use its Cournot best-response function to pick its best-response q_U. Thus, American's residual demand curve, D^r (panel a of Figure 13.5), is the market demand curve, D (panel a), minus the output United will produce, as summarized by United's best-response curve (panel b). For example, if American sets $q_A = 192$, United's best response is $q_U = 0$ (as United's best-response curve in panel b shows). As a result, the residual demand curve and the market demand curve are identical at $q_A = 192$ (panel a).

Similarly, if American set $q_A = 0$, United would choose $q_U = 96$, so the residual demand at $q_A = 0$ is 96 less than demand. The residual demand curve hits the vertical axis, where $q_A = 0$, at $p = \$243$, which is 96 units to the left of demand at that price. When $q_A = 96$, $q_U = 48$, so the residual demand at $q_A = 96$ is 48 units to the left of the demand curve where $p = \$195$.

The marginal revenue curve, MR^r, that corresponds to this residual demand curve hits the vertical axis at the same price, $243, as the residual demand curve, and has twice as steep a slope.

American chooses its profit-maximizing output, $q_A = 96$, where its marginal revenue curve, MR^r, equals its marginal cost, $147. At $q_A = 96$, the price, which is

Figure 13.5 Nash-Stackelberg Equilibrium

(a) The residual demand the Stackelberg leader faces is the market demand minus the quantity produced by the follower, q_U, given the leader's quantity, q_A. The leader chooses $q_A = 96$ so that its marginal revenue, MR^r, equals its marginal cost. The total output, $Q = 144$, is the sum of the output of the two firms. (b) The quantity the follower produces is its best response to the leader's output, as given by its Cournot best-response curve.

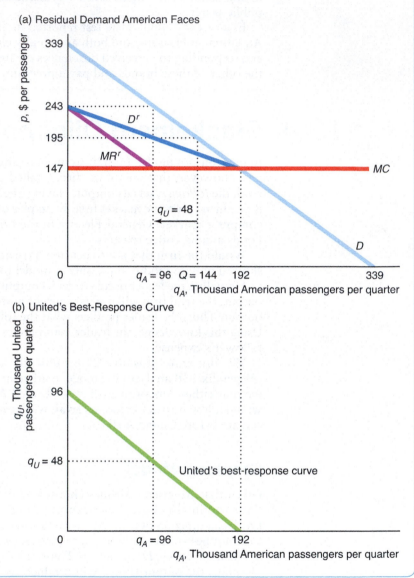

(a) Residual Demand American Faces

(b) United's Best-Response Curve

the height of the residual demand curve, is $195. Total demand at $195 is $Q = 144$. At that price, United produces $q_U = Q - q_A = 48$, its best response to American's output of $q_A = 96$.

Thus, in this Nash-Stackelberg equilibrium, the leader produces twice as much as the follower, as Figure 13.5 shows.[20] The total Stackelberg output, 144, is greater than

---

[20]Here the leader produces the same quantity as a monopoly would, and the follower produces the same quantity as it would in the cartel equilibrium. These relationships are due to the linear demand curve and the constant marginal cost—they do not hold more generally.

the total Cournot, 128, output. As a result, the Stackelberg price, $195, is less than the Cournot price, $211. Thus, consumers prefer the Nash-Stackelberg equilibrium to the Nash-Cournot equilibrium.

The Stackelberg leader earns $4.6 million, which is more than it could earn in a Nash-Cournot equilibrium, $4.1 million. Total Stackelberg profit is less than total Cournot profit because the Stackelberg follower, earning $2.3 million, is much worse off than in the Nash-Cournot equilibrium.

Solved Problem 13.3

Use algebra to solve for the Nash-Stackelberg equilibrium quantities and market price if American Airlines were a Stackelberg leader and United Airlines were a follower. (*Hint*: As the graphical analysis shows, American Airlines, the Stackelberg leader, maximizes its profit as though it were a monopoly facing a residual demand function.)

Answer

1. *Determine the inverse residual demand function facing American Airlines.* The residual demand function facing American Airlines is the market demand function (Equation 13.1), $Q = 330 - p$, minus the best-response function of United Airlines (Equation 13.6), $q_U = 96 - \frac{1}{2}q_A$:

$$q_A(p) = Q(p) - q_U(q_A) = 339 - p - [96 - \tfrac{1}{2}q_A] = 243 - p - \tfrac{1}{2}q_A. \quad (13.15)$$

Using algebra, we can rewrite Equation 13.15 as the inverse residual demand function (which is the D^r line in panel a of Figure 13.5):

$$p = 243 - \tfrac{1}{2}q_A. \quad (13.16)$$

2. *Solve for American Airlines' profit-maximizing output by equating its marginal revenue and marginal cost.* American Airlines, the Stackelberg leader, acts like a monopoly with respect to its residual demand. From Chapter 11, we know that its marginal revenue function is the same as its inverse residual demand function, Equation 13.16, except it has twice the slope: $MR_A = 243 - q_A$ (which is the MR^r line in panel a of Figure 13.5). To maximize its profit, American Airlines picks its output so as to equate its marginal revenue to its marginal cost:

$$MR_A = 243 - q_A = 147 = MC. \quad (13.17)$$

Solving Equation 13.17 for American Airlines' output, we find that $q_A = 96$.

3. *Use United Airlines' best-response function to solve for its quantity and the total output.* Substituting $q_A = 96$ into United Airlines' best-response function, Equation 13.6, we learn that United Airlines sells half as many seats as American Airlines: $q_U = 96 - \frac{1}{2}q_A = 48$. Thus, total output is

$$Q = q_A + q_U = 96 + 48 = 144.$$

4. *Use the market demand function to solve for the market price.* Substituting $Q = 144$, total output, into the market demand function, we determine that the market price is $195.

Comment: See Appendix 13B for the solution to a more general case.

Why Moving Sequentially Is Essential

Why don't we get the Nash-Stackelberg equilibrium when both firms move simultaneously? Why doesn't one firm—say, American—announce that it will produce the Stackelberg leader output to induce United to produce the Stackelberg follower output level? The answer is that when the firms move simultaneously, United doesn't view American's warning that it will produce a large quantity as a *credible threat*.

If United believed that threat, it would indeed produce the Stackelberg follower output level. But United doesn't believe the threat because it is not in American's best interest to produce that large a quantity of output. If American were to produce the leader level of output and United produced the Cournot level, American's profit would be lower than if it too produced the Cournot level. Because American cannot be sure that United will believe its threat and reduce its output, American produces the Cournot output level.

Indeed, each firm may make the same threat and announce that it wants to be the leader. Because neither firm can be sure that the other will be intimidated and produce the smaller quantity, both produce the Cournot output level. In contrast, when one firm moves first, its threat to produce a large quantity is credible because it has already *committed* to producing the larger quantity, thereby carrying out its threat.

Comparison of Competitive, Stackelberg, Cournot, and Collusive Equilibria

The Nash-Cournot and Nash-Stackelberg equilibrium quantities, prices, consumer surplus, and profits lie between those for the competitive (price-taking) and collusive equilibria, as Table 13.3 and Figure 13.6 show for our airline duopoly.

If the firms were to act as price takers, they would each produce where their residual demand curve intersects their marginal cost curve, so price would equal the marginal cost of \$147. The price-taking equilibrium is $q_A = q_U = 96$.

If American and United were to collude, they would maximize joint profits by producing the monopoly output, $q_A + q_U = 96$. Colluding airlines could split the monopoly quantity in many ways. American could act as a monopoly and serve all the passengers, $q_A = 96$ and $q_U = 0$, and give United some of the profits. Or they could reverse roles so that United served everyone: $q_A = 0$ and $q_U = 96$. Or the two airlines could share the passengers in any combination such that the sum of the airlines' passengers equals the monopoly quantity, or, equivalently,

$$q_U = 96 - q_A. \tag{13.18}$$

Figure 13.6 plots Equation 13.18, the set of possible collusive outcomes, which it labels the *Contract curve*. In the figure, we assume that the collusive firms split the market equally so that $q_A = q_U = 48$.

Table 13.3 Comparison of the Duopoly Airline Competitive, Stackelberg, Cournot, and Collusive Equilibria

	Competition	Stackelberg	Cournot	Collusion
Total output, Q (thousands)	192	144	128	96
Price, p (\$)	147	195	211	243
Consumer Surplus (\$ million)	18.4	10.4	8.2	4.6
Profit, π (\$ million)	0	6.9	8.2	9.2

Figure 13.6 Duopoly Equilibria

The intersection of the best-response curves determines the Nash-Cournot equilibrium, where each firm produces 64. The possible cartel equilibria lie on the contract curve: $q_U = 96 - q_A$. The figure shows the symmetric cartel case where each firm produces 48. If the firms act as price takers, each firm produces where its residual demand equals its marginal cost, 96. In the Nash-Stackelberg equilibrium, the leader produces more, 96, than the follower, 48.

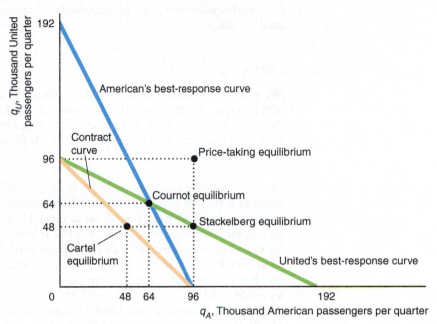

The table shows that the quantity, price, consumer surplus, and profit for the Nash-Stackelberg and Nash-Cournot equilibria lie between competition and collusion, with the Nash-Stackelberg equilibrium closer to competition and the Nash-Cournot equilibrium closer to collusion.

We showed that the Nash-Cournot equilibrium approaches the competitive, price-taking equilibrium as the number of firms grows. Similarly, we can show that the Nash-Stackelberg equilibrium approaches the price-taking equilibrium as the number of Stackelberg followers grows. As a result, the differences between the Cournot, Stackelberg, and price-taking market structures shrink as the number of firms grows.

13.5 Bertrand Oligopoly

We have examined how oligopolies set quantities to try to maximize their profits. However, many oligopolistic firms set prices instead of quantities and allow consumers to decide how much to buy. The market equilibrium is different if firms set prices rather than quantities.

In monopolistic and competitive markets, the issue of whether firms set quantities or prices does not arise. Competitive firms have no choice: They cannot affect price and hence can choose only quantity (Chapter 8). The monopoly equilibrium is the same whether the monopoly sets price or quantity (Chapter 11).

Bertrand equilibrium (Nash-Bertrand equilibrium)
a *Nash equilibrium* in prices; a set of prices such that no firm can obtain a higher profit by choosing a different price if the other firms continue to charge these prices

In 1883, Joseph Bertrand argued that oligopolies set prices and then consumers decide how many units to buy. The resulting Nash equilibrium is called a **Bertrand equilibrium** or **Nash-Bertrand equilibrium** (or Nash-in-prices equilibrium): a set of prices such that no firm can obtain a higher profit by choosing a different price if the other firms continue to charge these prices.

We will show that the price and quantity in a Nash-Bertrand equilibrium are different from those in a Nash-Cournot equilibrium. We will also show that a Nash-Bertrand equilibrium depends on whether firms are producing identical or differentiated products.

Identical Products

We start by examining a price-setting oligopoly in which firms have identical costs and produce identical goods. The resulting Nash-Bertrand equilibrium price equals the marginal cost, as in the price-taking equilibrium. To show this result, we use best-response curves to determine the Nash-Bertrand equilibrium, as we did in the Cournot model.

Best-Response Curves Suppose that each of the two price-setting oligopolistic firms in a market produces an identical product and faces a constant marginal and average cost of $5 per unit. What is Firm 1's best response—what price should it set—if Firm 2 sets a price of $p_2 = \$10$? If Firm 1 charges more than $10, it makes no sales because consumers will buy from Firm 2. Firm 1 makes a profit of $5 on each unit it sells if it also charges $10 per unit. If the market demand is 200 units and both firms charge the same price, we'd expect Firm 1 to make half the sales, so its profit is $500.

Suppose, however, that Firm 1 slightly undercuts its rival's price by charging $9.99. Because the products are identical, Firm 1 captures the entire market. Firm 1 makes a profit of $4.99 per unit and a total profit of $998. Thus, Firm 1's profit is higher if it slightly undercuts its rival's price. By similar reasoning, if Firm 2 charges $8, Firm 1 also charges slightly less than Firm 2.

Now imagine that Firm 2 charges $p_2 = \$5$. If Firm 1 charges more than $5, it makes no sales. The firms split the market and make zero profit if Firm 1 charges $5. If Firm 1 undercuts its rival, it captures the entire market, but it makes a loss on each unit. Therefore, Firm 1 will undercut only if its rival's price is higher than Firm 1's marginal and average cost of $5. By similar reasoning, if Firm 2 charges less than $5, Firm 1 chooses not to produce.

Figure 13.7 shows that Firm 1's best response is to produce nothing if Firm 2 charges less than $5. Firm 1's best response is $5 if Firm 2 charges $5. If Firm 2 charges prices above $5, Firm 1's best response is to undercut Firm 2's price slightly. Above $5, Firm 1's best-response curve is above the 45° line by the smallest amount possible. (The distance of the best-response curve from the 45° line is exaggerated in the figure for clarity.) By the same reasoning, Firm 2's best-response curve starts at $5 and lies slightly below the 45° line.

The two best-response functions intersect only at *e*, where each firm charges $5. It does not pay for either firm to change its price as long as the other charges $5, so *e* is the Nash-Bertrand equilibrium. In this equilibrium, each firm makes zero profit. Thus, *the Nash-Bertrand equilibrium when firms produce identical products is the same as the price-taking, competitive equilibrium.*

Bertrand Versus Cournot This Nash-Bertrand equilibrium differs substantially from the Nash-Cournot equilibrium. When firms produce identical products and have a constant marginal cost, firms receive positive profits and the price is above marginal cost in the Nash-Cournot equilibrium, whereas firms earn zero profits and price equals marginal cost in the Nash-Bertrand equilibrium.

When firms' products are identical, the Cournot model seems more realistic than the Bertrand model. The Bertrand model appears inconsistent with actual oligopolistic

Figure 13.7 Nash-Bertrand Equilibrium with Identical Products

With identical products and constant marginal and average costs of $5, Firm 1's best-response curve starts at $5 and then lies slightly above the 45° line. That is, Firm 1 undercuts its rival's price as long as its price remains above $5. The best-response curves intersect at e, the Nash-Bertrand equilibrium, where both firms charge $5.

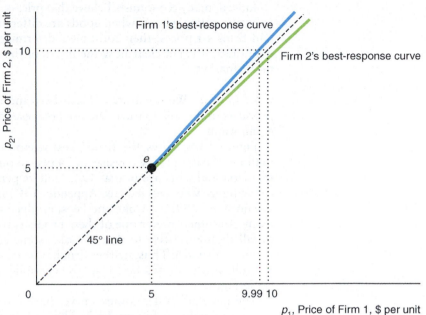

p_2, Price of Firm 2, $ per unit

Firm 1's best-response curve

Firm 2's best-response curve

10

5

e

45° line

0   5   9.99 10

p_1, Price of Firm 1, $ per unit

markets in at least two ways. First, the Bertrand model's "competitive" equilibrium price is implausible. In a market with few firms, why would the firms compete so vigorously that they would make no profit, as in the Nash-Bertrand equilibrium? In contrast, the Nash-Cournot equilibrium price with a small number of firms lies between the competitive price and the monopoly price. Because oligopolies typically charge a higher price than competitive firms, the Nash-Cournot equilibrium is more plausible.

Second, the Nash-Bertrand equilibrium price, which depends only on cost, is insensitive to demand conditions and the number of firms. In contrast, the Nash-Cournot equilibrium price depends on demand conditions and the number of firms as well as on cost. Consequently, economists are much more likely to use the Cournot model than the Bertrand model to study homogeneous goods markets.

Differentiated Products

If firms in most markets produced homogeneous goods, the Bertrand model would probably have been forgotten. However, markets with differentiated goods—automobiles, stereos, computers, toothpastes, and spaghetti sauces—are extremely common, as is price setting by firms in such markets. In differentiated-goods markets, the Nash-Bertrand equilibrium is plausible because the two "problems" of the homogeneous-goods model disappear:

Firms set prices above marginal cost, and prices are sensitive to demand conditions and the number of firms.

Indeed, many economists believe that price-setting models are more plausible than quantity-setting models when goods are differentiated. If products are differentiated and firms set prices, then consumers determine quantities. In contrast, if firms set quantities, it is not clear how the prices of the differentiated goods are determined in the market.

Cola Market   We illustrate a Nash-Bertrand equilibrium with the differentiated products in the cola market. We use best-response curves in a figure to solve for the equilibrium.

Figure 13.8 shows the firms' best-response curves. Quantities are in tens of millions of cases (a case consists of 24 twelve-ounce cans) per quarter, and prices (to retailers) and costs are in real 1982 dollars per 10 cases. The best-response curves in the figure were derived (see Appendix 13C) from demand functions estimated by Gasmi et al. (1992).[21] Coke and Pepsi produce similar but not identical products, so many consumers prefer one of these products to the other. If the price of Pepsi were to fall slightly relative to that of Coke, some consumers who prefer Coke to Pepsi would not switch. Thus, neither firm has to exactly match a price cut by its rival. As a result, neither firm's best-response curve lies along a 45° line through the origin (as in Figure 13.7).

The Bertrand best-response curves have different slopes than the Cournot best-response curves in Figure 13.3. The Cournot curves—which plot relationships between quantities—slope downward, showing that a firm produces less the more its rival produces. In Figure 13.8, the Bertrand best-response curves—which plot

---

Figure 13.8 Nash-Bertrand Equilibrium with Differentiated Products

Both Coke and Pepsi, which set prices, have upward-sloping best-response curves. These best-response curves of Coke and Pepsi intersect at e, the Nash-Bertrand equilibrium, where each sets a price of $13 per unit.

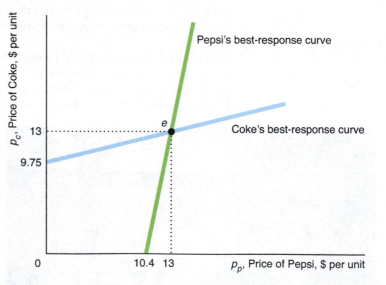

---

[21]Their estimated model allows the firms to set both prices and advertising. We assume that the firms' advertising is held constant. The Coke equations are the authors' estimates (with slight rounding). The Pepsi equation is rescaled so that the equilibrium prices of Coke and Pepsi are equal.

relationships between prices—slope upward, indicating that a firm charges a higher price the higher the price its rival charges.

The Nash-Bertrand equilibrium, *e* in Figure 13.8, occurs where each firm's price is $13 per unit. In this Nash-Bertrand equilibrium, each firm sets its best-response price *given the price the other firm is charging*. Neither firm wants to change its price because neither firm can increase its profit by doing so.

Product Differentiation and Welfare Because differentiation makes demand curves less elastic, prices are likely to be higher when products are differentiated than when they're identical. We also know that welfare falls as the gap between price and marginal cost rises. Does it follow that differentiating products lowers welfare? Not necessarily. Although differentiation leads to higher prices, which harm consumers, differentiation is desirable in its own right. Consumers value having a choice, and some may greatly prefer a new brand to existing ones.

One way to illustrate the importance of this second effect is to consider what the value is of introducing a new, differentiated product. This value reflects how much extra income consumers would require to be as well off without the good as with it.

Application	An article in the *Economist* asked, "Why does it cost more to wipe your bottom

Application

Welfare Gain from More Toilet Paper

An article in the *Economist* asked, "Why does it cost more to wipe your bottom in Britain than in any other country in the European Union?" The answer given was that British consumers are "extremely fussy" in demanding a soft, luxurious texture—in contrast to barbarians elsewhere. As a consequence, they pay twice as much for toilet paper as the Germans and French, and nearly 2.5 times as much as Americans.[22]

Probably completely uninfluenced by this important cross-country research, Hausman and Leonard (2002) used U.S. data to measure the price effect and the extra consumer surplus from greater variety resulting from Kimberly-Clark's introduction of Kleenex Bath Tissue (KBT). Bath tissue products are divided into premium, economy, and private labels, with premium receiving more than 70% of revenue. Before KBT's entry, the major premium brands were Angel Soft, Charmin, Cottonelle, and Northern. ScotTissue was the leading economy brand.

Firms incur a sizable fixed cost from capital investments. The marginal cost depends primarily on the price of wood pulp, which varies cyclically. Because KBT was rolled out in various cities at different times, Hausman and Leonard could compare the effects of entry at various times and control for variations in cost and other factors.

The prices of all rival brands fell after KBT entered; the price of the leading brand, Charmin, dropped by 3.5%, while Cottonelle's price plummeted 8.2%. In contrast, the price of ScotTissue, an economy brand, decreased by only 0.6%.

Hausman and Leonard calculated that the additional consumer surplus due to extra variety was $33.4 million, or 3.5% of sales. When they included the gains due to lower prices, the total consumer surplus increase was $69.2 million, or 7.3% of sales. Thus, the gains to consumers were roughly equally divided between the price effect and the benefit from extra variety.

---

[22]Indeed, British supermarkets reported that the share of luxury toilet paper sales spiked around Christmas 2009. Apparently during a major recession, Brits viewed luxury toilet paper as an appropriate present.

13.6 Monopolistic Competition

We now turn to monopolistic competition, which is a market structure that has the price setting characteristics of monopoly or oligopoly and the free entry characteristic of perfect competition. Monopolistically competitive firms have market power because they face downward-sloping demand curves, as do oligopolistic firms. However, in contrast to oligopolistic markets in which entry is very difficult, firms can freely enter a monopolistically competitive market, so firms earn zero economic profit, as do perfectly competitive firms.

If both competitive and monopolistically competitive firms make zero profits, what distinguishes these two market structures? In contrast to competitive firms (which face horizontal residual demand curves and charge prices equal to marginal cost), monopolistically competitive firms face downward-sloping residual demand curves, so they charge prices above marginal cost.

Monopolistically competitive firms face downward-sloping demand curves because the market is small or because the firms differentiate their products. Even if the firms produce identical products, if the market demand curve is close to the origin, the market may be able to support only a few firms, so the residual demand curve facing a single firm is downward sloping. For example, in a small town the market may be large enough to support only a few plumbing firms, each of which provides a similar service. If firms differentiate their products, each firm can retain those customers who particularly like that firm's product even if its price is higher than those of its rivals.

Application

Monopolistically Competitive Food Truck Market

One of the hottest food phenomena in the United States is gourmet food trucks, which started in major West Coast cities such as Los Angeles, Portland, and Seattle. Gourmet food trucks serve differentiated food in monopolistically competitive markets. Now, flocks of food trucks ply their business in previously underserved areas of town in cities across the country.

Nouveau food trucks like Chairman Bao, Curry Up Now, and Liba Falafel sell high-quality lunches in San Francisco's blighted mid-Market area, which has few traditional, high-quality lunch restaurants. Because some customers prefer Chinese food to Indian food, Chairman Bao could raise its price without losing all its customers to Curry Up Now. As a consequence, each of these trucks faces a downward-sloping demand curve.

The mobile restaurant business has been exploding. As William Bender, a food service consultant in Santa Clara, California, said, "The limited menu approach, high quality, and low operating costs have opened up an entirely new sector." Even top restaurant chefs have entered this business. Celebrity Los Angeles chef Ludovic Lefebvre created LudoTruck, a mobile fried chicken outlet. San Francisco's Chez Spencer has a "French takeaway," Spencer on the Go, which serves bistro food such as foie gras torchon and toast for $12.

The cost of entry is very low, ranging from $50,000 to lease the equipment and pay ancillary expenses, to $250,000 or more for a deluxe truck and top-of-the-line cooking and refrigeration facilities. Potential entrants can learn about the business at **mobilefoodnews.com**, which reports on local laws, where to buy equipment and obtain insurance, and a host of other topics.

Opening a new brick-and-mortar restaurant is very risky. If demand is less than anticipated, the firm loses its (large) fixed cost. However, if the manger of a food truck's first guess as to where to locate is wrong, it is easy to drive to another neighborhood.

How do firms identify profit opportunities? "Lunch is our consistent bread-and-butter market," said Matthew Cohen, proprietor of Off the Grid, a food truck promoter and location finder in the San Francisco Bay Area. When lines in front of his trucks grow longer at lunch time, he sets up additional trucks. Having started with about a dozen trucks in June 2010, Cohen had over 100 vendors in 2013.

Equilibrium

To examine the monopolistically competitive equilibrium, we initially assume that firms have identical cost functions and produce identical products. Two conditions hold in a long-run monopolistically competitive equilibrium: *marginal revenue equals marginal cost* because firms set output to maximize profit, and *price equals average cost*—that is, profit is zero—because firms enter until no further profitable entry is possible.

Figure 13.9 shows a monopolistically competitive market equilibrium. A typical monopolistically competitive firm faces a residual demand curve D^r. To maximize its profit, the firm sets its output, q, where its marginal revenue curve corresponding to the residual demand curve intersects its marginal cost curve: $MR^r = MC$. At that quantity, the firm's average cost curve, AC, is tangent to its residual demand curve. Because the height of the residual demand curve is the price, at the point of tangency, price equals average cost, $p = AC$, and the firm makes zero profit.

minimum efficient scale (full capacity) the smallest quantity at which the average cost curve reaches its minimum

The smallest quantity at which the average cost curve reaches its minimum is referred to as *full capacity* or **minimum efficient scale**. The firm's full capacity or minimum efficient scale is the quantity at which the firm no longer benefits from economies of scale. Because a monopolistically competitive equilibrium occurs in the downward-sloping section of the average cost curve (where the average cost curve is tangent to the downward-sloping demand curve), a monopolistically competitive firm operates at less than full capacity in the long run.

The fewer monopolistically competitive firms, the less elastic the residual demand curve each firm faces. As we saw, the elasticity of demand for an individual Cournot firm is $n\varepsilon$, where n is the number of firms and ε is the market elasticity. Thus, the fewer the firms in a market, the less elastic the residual demand curve and the higher the price. Similarly, the more differentiated are firms' products, the less elastic the residual demand curve and the higher the price.

Figure 13.9 Monopolistically Competitive Equilibrium

A monopolistically competitive firm, facing residual demand curve D^r, sets its output where its marginal revenue equals its marginal cost: $MR^r = MC$. Because firms can enter this market, the profit of the firm is driven to zero, so price equals the firm's average cost: $p = AC$.

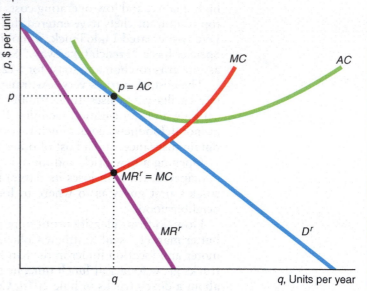

Fast-food restaurants are an example of such a monopolistically competitive industry. These restaurants differentiate their food, so each may face a downward-sloping demand curve. However, restaurants can easily enter and exit the market, so the marginal firm earns zero economic profit. Most restaurants have empty seats much of the time and hence are operating at less than full capacity. The following Solved Problem provides an explanation for this phenomenon.

Solved Problem 13.4

Show that a monopolistically competitive firm maximizes its profit where it is operating at less than *full capacity* or *minimum efficient scale*, which is the smallest quantity at which the average cost curve reaches its minimum (the bottom of a U-shaped average cost curve). The firm's minimum efficient scale is the quantity at which the firm no longer benefits from economies of scale.

Answer

Use the properties of the demand curve to show that a monopolistically competitive firm operates in the increasing-returns to scale section of its average cost curve (the downward-sloping section) in the long-run equilibrium. In the long-run equilibrium, a monopolistically competitive firm operates where its downward-sloping demand curve is tangent to its average cost curve, as Figure 13.9 illustrates. Because its demand curve is downward sloping, its average cost curve must also be downward sloping in the equilibrium. Thus, the firm chooses to operate at less than full capacity in equilibrium.

Fixed Costs and the Number of Firms

The number of firms in a monopolistically competitive equilibrium depends on firms' costs. The larger each firm's fixed cost, the smaller the number of monopolistically competitive firms in the market equilibrium.

Although entry is free, if the fixed costs are high, few firms may enter. In the automobile industry, just to develop a new fender costs $8 to $10 million. Developing a new pharmaceutical drug may cost $350 million or more.

We can illustrate this relationship using the airlines example, in which we modify our assumptions about entry and fixed costs. American and United are the only airlines providing service on the Chicago–Los Angeles route. Until now, we have assumed that a barrier to entry—such as an inability to obtain landing rights at both airports—prevented entry and that the firms had no fixed costs. If fixed cost is zero and marginal cost is constant at $147 per passenger, average cost is also constant at $147 per passenger. As we showed earlier, each firm in this oligopolistic market flies $q = 64$ per quarter at a price of $p = \$211$ and makes a profit of $4.1 million per quarter.

Now suppose that the market has no barriers to entry, but each airline incurs a fixed cost to enter of F due to airport fees, capital expenditure, or other factors. Each firm's marginal cost remains $147 per passenger, but its average cost,

$$AC = 147 + \frac{F}{q},$$

falls as the number of passengers rises, as panels a and b of Figure 13.10 illustrate for $F = \$2.3$ million.

If the monopolistically competitive market has only two firms, what must the fixed costs be so that the two firms earn zero profit? We know that these firms receive a profit of $4.1 million per firm in the absence of fixed costs. As a result, the fixed cost must be $4.1 million per firm for the firms to earn zero profit. With this fixed cost, the monopolistically competitive price and quantity are the same as in

---

Figure 13.10 Monopolistic Competition Among Airlines

(a) In a market with two identical airlines that each incurs a fixed cost of $2.3 million, each firm flies $q = 64$ units (thousands of passengers) per quarter at a price of $p = \$211$ per passenger and makes a profit of $1.8 million. This profit attracts entry. (b) After a third firm enters, the residual demand curve shifts, so each firm flies $q = 48$ units at $p = \$195$ and makes zero profit, which is the monopolistically competitive equilibrium.

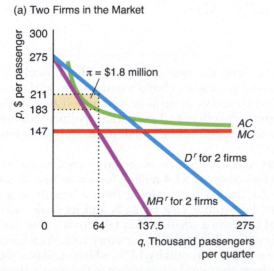

(a) Two Firms in the Market

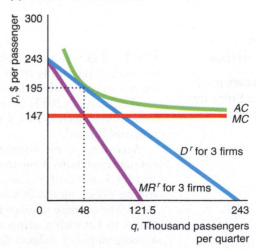

(b) Three Firms in the Market

the oligopolistic equilibrium, $q = 64$ and $p = \$211$, and the number of firms is the same, but now each firm's profit is zero.

If the fixed cost is only $2.3 million and the market has only two firms, each firm makes a profit, as panel a shows. Each duopoly firm faces a residual demand curve (labeled "D^r for 2 firms"), which is the market demand minus its rival's Nash-Cournot equilibrium quantity, $q = 64$. Given this residual demand, each firm produces $q = 64$, which equates its marginal revenue, MR^r, and its marginal cost, MC. At $q = 64$, the firm's average cost is $AC = \$147 + (\$2.3 \text{ million})/(64 \text{ units}) \approx \$183$, so each firm makes a profit of $\pi = (p - AC)q \approx (\$211 - \$183) \times 64$ units per quarter $\approx \$1.8$ million per quarter.

This substantial economic profit attracts an entrant. The entry of a third firm causes the residual demand for any one firm to shift to the left in panel b. In the new equilibrium, each firm sets $q = 48$ and charges $p = \$195$. At this quantity, each firm's average cost is $195, so the firms break even. No other firms enter because if one did, the residual demand curve would shift even farther to the left and all the firms would lose money. Thus, if fixed cost is $2.3 million, the market has three firms in the monopolistically competitive equilibrium. This example illustrates a general result: *The lower the fixed costs, the more firms in the monopolistically competitive equilibrium.*

Solved Problem 13.5	What is the monopolistically competitive airline equilibrium if each firm has a fixed cost of $3 million?

Answer

1. *Determine the number of firms.* We already know that the monopolistically competitive equilibrium has two firms if the fixed cost is $4.1 million and three firms if the fixed cost is $2.3 million. With a fixed cost of $3 million and two firms in the market, each firm makes a profit of $1.1 (= $4.1 − 3) million. If another firm enters, though, each firm's loss equals −$0.7 (= 2.3 − 3) million. Thus, the monopolistically competitive equilibrium has two firms, each of which earns a positive profit that is too small to attract another firm. This outcome is a monopolistically competitive equilibrium because no other firm wants to enter.

2. *Determine the equilibrium quantities and prices.* Because each duopoly firm produces $q = 64$, $Q = 128$ and $p = \$211$.

Application **Zoning Laws as a Barrier to Entry by Hotel Chains**	U.S. local governments restrict land use through zoning. The difficulty of getting permission (generally from many agencies) to build a new commercial structure is a barrier to entry, which limits the number of firms in a monopolistically competitive market. Suzuki (2013) examined the effect of Texas municipalities' zoning laws on chain hotels, such as Best Western, Comfort Inn, Holiday Inn, La Quinta Inn, Quality Inn, and Ramada.

According to his estimates, construction costs are large even in the absence of zoning regulations. Construction costs are $2.4 million for a new Best Western hotel and $4.5 million for a new La Quinta hotel. Going from a lenient to a stringent zoning policy increases a hotel's variable cost by 21% and its sunk entry cost by 19%. The average number of hotels in a small market falls from 2.3 under a lenient policy to 1.9 with a stringent policy due to the higher entry cost. As a consequence, a stringent policy reduces the number of rooms by 15%, which increases the revenue per room by 7%. The change from the most lenient policy to the most stringent policy decreases producer surplus by $1.5 million and consumer surplus by $1 million. Thus, more stringent zoning laws raise entry costs and thereby reduce the number of hotels and rooms, which causes the price to rise and lowers total surplus.

Therefore, owners of existing hotels often strongly support making zoning laws more stringent. These oligopolistic firms want to continue to earn positive economic profits, rather than see these profits driven to zero in a monopolistically competitive market with free entry.

Challenge Solution

Government Aircraft Subsidies

If only one government subsidizes its aircraft manufacturing firm, how does the firm use the subsidy to gain a competitive advantage? What happens if both firms are government subsidized? Should Boeing and Airbus lobby for government subsidies that result in a subsidy war?

To keep our answers to these questions as simple as possible, we use a Cournot model in which Airbus and Boeing produce identical products with identical costs and face a linear demand curve.[23] A government per-unit subsidy to only one firm would cause its marginal cost to be lower than its rival's.

To maximize profit, a firm in a Cournot market should respond by increasing its output for any expected output level by its rival. That is, its best-response curve shifts out. In panel a of Figure 13.4, we saw how the equilibrium changes if United Airline's marginal cost falls while American's stays constant. As its marginal cost drops, United wants to produce more for any given output of its rival, so that its best-response function shifts out, away from the origin in panel b.

The market equilibrium shifts from e_1 to e_2 in panel b, so that United's Nash-Cournot equilibrium output increases and American's falls. Because total output rises, the equilibrium price falls. United benefits at the expense of American. Indeed, United's profit rises by $5.1 million, which exceeds the actual cost saving of $4.6 million. That is, United's managers used the cost savings to gain a competitive advantage.

The same analysis applies to the aircraft market. If Airbus is subsidized and Boeing is not, Airbus should produce more given any expected output from Boeing. Its equilibrium quantity and profit rise while Boeing's quantity and profit fall.

How much should the government subsidize Airbus? The answer depends on the government's objective. A plausible objective is that the government wants to maximize the sum of its firm's profit including the subsidy minus the cost of the subsidy, which is the firm's profit.[24] With this objective, the government wants to give a subsidy that leads to the Stackelberg outcome, which maximizes the firm's profit.

If both governments give identical subsidies that lower each firm's marginal cost, then both firms' best-response curves shift out as the figure on the next page shows. The original, unsubsidized equilibrium, e_1, is determined by the intersection of the original best-response curves. The new, subsidized equilibrium, e_2, occurs where the new best-response curves intersect. Both firms produce more in the new equilibrium than in the original: $q_2 > q_1$.

---

[23]We would reach the same conclusions if we used a Cournot or Bertrand model with differentiated products.

[24]The subsidy is a transfer from some citizens (taxpayers) to others (the owners of Airbus), so the government may not be concerned about the size of the subsidy. The government doesn't care about consumers if they live in another country.

Unlike the situation in which only one government subsidizes its firm, each subsidized firm increases its equilibrium output by the same amount so that the price falls.[25] Each government is essentially subsidizing final consumers in other countries without giving its own firm a strategic advantage over its rival.

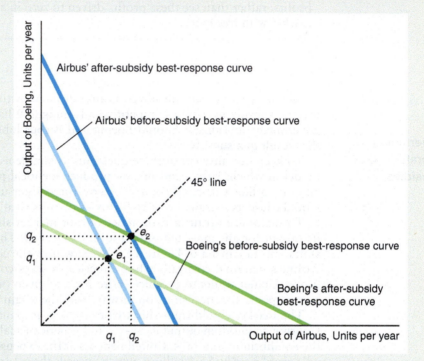

Each government's welfare is the sum of its firm's profit including the subsidy minus the cost of the subsidy, which is the firm's profit ignoring the subsidy. Because the firms produce more than in the Nash-Cournot equilibrium, both firms earn less (ignoring the subsidies) so both countries are harmed. It would be in both countries' best interests not to engage in a subsidy war. Nonetheless, both firms benefit from its subsidy, so both firms strongly lobby their governments for subsidies.

Summary

1. **Market Structures.** Prices, profits, and quantities in a market equilibrium depend on the market's structure. Because profit-maximizing firms set marginal revenue equal to marginal cost, price is above marginal revenue—and hence marginal cost—only if firms face downward-sloping demand curves. In monopolistic, oligopolistic, and monopolistically competitive markets, firms face downward-sloping demand curves, in contrast to firms in a perfectly competitive market. When entry is blocked, as with a monopoly or an oligopoly, firms may earn positive profits; however, when entry is free, as in perfect competition or

---

[25]In 1992, the relevant governments signed a U.S.–EU agreement on trade in civil aircraft that limits government subsidies, including a maximum direct subsidy limit of 33% of development costs and various limits on variable costs. Irwin and Pavcnik (2004) found that aircraft prices increased by about 3.7% after the 1992 agreement. This price hike is consistent with ending a subsidy that was 5% of the firms' marginal costs.

monopolistic competition, profits are driven toward zero. Noncooperative oligopolistic and monopolistically competitive firms, in contrast to competitive and monopolistic firms, must pay attention to their rivals.

2. **Cartels.** If firms successfully collude, they produce the monopoly output and collectively earn the monopoly level of profit. Although their collective profits rise if all firms collude, each individual firm has an incentive to cheat on a cartel arrangement so as to raise its own profit even higher. For cartel prices to remain high, cartel members must be able to detect and prevent cheating, and noncartel firms must not be able to supply very much output. When antitrust laws or competition policies prevent firms from colluding, firms may try to merge if permitted by law.

3. **Cournot Oligopoly.** If oligopolistic firms act independently, market output and the firms' profits lie between the competitive and monopoly levels. In a Cournot model, each oligopolistic firm sets its output at the same time. In the Cournot (Nash) equilibrium, each firm produces its best-response output—the output that maximizes its profit—given the output its rival produces. As the number of Cournot firms increases, the Nash-Cournot equilibrium price, quantity, and profits approach the price-taking levels.

4. **Stackelberg Oligopoly.** If one firm, the Stackelberg leader, chooses its output before its rivals, the Stackelberg followers, the leader produces more and earns a higher profit than each identical-cost follower firm.

A government may subsidize a domestic oligopolistic firm so that it produces the Stackelberg leader quantity, which it sells in an international market. For a given number of firms, the Nash-Stackelberg equilibrium output exceeds that of the Nash-Cournot equilibrium, which exceeds that of the collusive equilibrium (which is the same as a monopoly produces). Correspondingly, the Stackelberg price is less than the Cournot price, which is less than the collusive or monopoly price.

5. **Bertrand Oligopoly.** In many oligopolistic or monopolistically competitive markets, firms set prices instead of quantities. If the product is homogeneous and firms set prices, the Nash-Bertrand equilibrium price equals marginal cost (which is lower than the Nash-Cournot quantity-setting equilibrium price). If the products are differentiated, the Nash-Bertrand equilibrium price is above marginal cost. Typically, the markup of price over marginal cost is greater the more the goods are differentiated.

6. **Monopolistic Competition.** In monopolistically competitive markets, after all profitable entry occurs, the market has few enough firms that each firm faces a downward-sloping demand curve. Consequently, the firms charge prices above marginal cost. These markets are not perfectly competitive due to the relatively small number of firms. The number of firms may be small because of high fixed costs, economies of scale that are large relative to market demand, or because the firms sell differentiated products.

Questions

All questions are available on MyEconLab; * = *answer appears at the back of this book;* **A** = *algebra problem;* **C** = *calculus problem.*

1. Market Structures

1.1 Which market structure best describes (a) airplane manufacturing, (b) electricians in a small town, (c) farms that grow tomatoes, and (d) cable television in a city? Why?

2. Cartels

2.1 At each Organization of Petroleum Exporting Countries (OPEC) meeting, Saudi Arabia, the largest oil producer, argues that the cartel should cut production. The Saudis complain that most OPEC member countries, including Saudi Arabia, produce more oil than they are allotted under their cartel agreement. Use a graph and words to explain why cartel members would produce more than the allotted amount given that they know that overproduction will drive down the price of their product.

2.2 Holding the number of firms in the market fixed, what happens to the price as the number of noncartel members rises? Why?

2.3 What are the main factors that increase the likelihood of a cartel being successful?

*2.4 Many retail stores offer to match or beat the price offered by a rival store. Explain why firms that belong to a cartel might make this offer.

2.5 The Federation of Quebec Maple Syrup Producers supplies up to 78% of the world's maple syrup (Ian Austen, "In $18 Million Theft, Victim Was a Canadian Maple Syrup Cartel," *New York*

Times, December 19, 2012; **www.siropderable.ca/ Afficher.aspx?page=3&langue=en**). Under government rules, the member firms jointly market their syrup through the federation, which sets quotas on how much each firm can produce. Show this cartel's price determination process using a graph similar to Figure 13.1.

2.6 In 2012, the U.S. government sued to block the world's biggest beer maker, Anheuser-Busch InBev, from buying Mexico's Grupo Modelo (which manufactures Corona and other beers) for $20 billion (Brent Kendall and Valerie Bauerlein, "U.S. Sues to Block Big Beer Merger," *Wall Street Journal*, January 31, 2013). Currently, Anheuser-Busch InBev has 39% of the U.S. beer market, MillerCoors has 26%, and Grupo Modelo has 7%. When the suit was announced, both firms' stock prices dropped sharply. Why?

*2.7 A market has an inverse demand curve $p = 100 - 2Q$ and four firms, each of which has a constant marginal cost of $MC = 20$. If the firms form a profit-maximizing cartel and agree to operate subject to the constraint that each firm will produce the same output level, how much does each firm produce? (*Hint*: See Chapter 11's treatment of monopoly.) **A**

2.8 In 2013, a federal judge ruled that Apple colluded with five major U.S. publishers to artificially drive up the prices of e-books (which could be read on Apple's iPad). Apple collects a 30% commission on the price of a book from the publisher. Why would Apple want to help publishers raise their price? Given Apple's commission, what price would a book cartel want to set? (*Hint*: The marginal cost of an e-book is virtually zero.)

2.9 In 2013, the number two and number three office supply companies, OfficeMax Inc. and Office Depot, Inc., were discussing merging (Anupreeta Das et al., "OfficeMax, Office Depot in Talks to Merge," *Wall Street Journal*, February 18, 2013). Office Depot's market value was $1.3 billion and OfficeMax's was $933 million. Purportedly, the efficiency gains from merging would save the new company between $400 and $500 million. The U.S. Federal Trade Commission (FTC) blocked an earlier attempt by Staples, the largest office supply company, to merge with Office Depot. Why might the FTC block the earlier merger attempt but not this one?

3. Cournot Oligopoly

3.1 The state of Connecticut sets a maximum fee that bail-bond businesses can charge for posting

a given-size bond (Ayres and Waldfogel, 1994). The bail-bond fee is set at virtually the maximum amount allowed by law in cities with only one active firm (Plainville, 99% of the maximum; Stamford, 99%; and Wallingford, 99%). The price is as high in cities with a duopoly (Ansonia, 99.6%; Meriden, 98%; and New London, 98%). However, in cities with 3 or more firms, the price falls well below the maximum permitted price. The fees are only 54% of the maximum in Norwalk with 3 firms, 64% in New Haven with 8 firms, and 78% in Bridgeport with 10 firms. Give possible explanations based on the Cournot model for this pattern.

*3.2 What is the duopoly Nash-Cournot equilibrium if the market demand function is $Q = 1,000 - 1,000p$, and each firm's marginal cost is $0.28 per unit? **A**

3.3 Duopoly quantity-setting firms face the market demand $p = 150 - q_1 - q_2$. Each firm has a marginal cost of $60 per unit. What is the Nash-Cournot equilibrium? **A**

*3.4 The viatical settlement industry enables terminally ill consumers, typically HIV patients, to borrow against equity in their existing life insurance contracts to finance their consumption and medical expenses. The introduction and dissemination of effective anti-HIV medication in 1996 reduced AIDS mortality, extending patients' lives and hence delaying when the viatical settlement industry would receive the insurance payments. However, viatical settlement payments (what patients can borrow) fell more than can be explained by greater life expectancy. The number of viatical settlement firms dropped from 44 in 1995 to 24 in 2001. Sood et al. (2005) found that an increase in market power of viatical settlement firms reduced the value of life insurance holdings of HIV-positive persons by about $1.0 billion. When marginal cost rises and the number of firms falls, what happens to Nash-Cournot equilibrium price? Use graphs or math to illustrate your answer. (*Hint*: If you use math, it may be helpful to assume that the market demand curve has a constant elasticity throughout.) **A**

3.5 Show how the Nash-Cournot equilibrium for *n* firms given in Appendix 13A changes if each firm faces a fixed cost of *F* as well as a constant marginal cost per unit. (*Hint*: Very little, if any, formal math is needed, though it can be used.) **A**

3.6 Lee et al. (2010) estimated that a 2009 tax of 10 New Taiwan Dollars ($0.30) per pack of cigarettes reduced Taiwanese cigarette consumption by 13.19%. Assuming that the market consists of two cigarette firms, show how this specific tax affects the Nash-Cournot equilibrium. (*Hint*: Show how the tax affects the firms' marginal costs and hence their best-response functions.)

3.7 How would the airlines' Nash-Cournot equilibrium (Figure 13.3) change if United's marginal cost was $100 and American's was $200? (*Hint*: See Solved Problem 13.1.) **A**

3.8 In 2012, Southwest Airlines reported that its "cost per available seat mile" was 13.0¢ compared to 13.8¢ for United Airlines. Assuming that Southwest and United compete on a single route, use a graph to show that their equilibrium quantities differ. (*Hint*: See Solved Problem 13.1.)

*3.9 If the inverse market demand function facing a duopoly is $p = a - bQ$, what are the Nash-Cournot equilibrium quantities if the marginal cost of Firm 1 is m and that of Firm 2 is $m + x$, where $x > 0$? Which firm produces more and which has the higher profit? **A**

*3.10 Why do prices increase if oligopolistic firms differentiate their products?

3.11 How would the Intel-AMD equilibrium in Solved Problem 13.2 change if AMD faced the same demand function as Intel, Equation 13.10? **A**

3.12 Firms 1 and 2 produce differentiated goods. Firm 1's inverse demand function is $p_1 = 260 - 2q_1 - q_2$, while Firm 2's inverse demand function is $p_2 = 260 - 2q_2 - q_1$. Each firm has a constant marginal cost of 20. What is the Nash-Cournot equilibrium in this market? (*Hint*: See Solved Problem 13.2.) **A**

3.13 Draw a figure to illustrate the Intel-AMD Nash-Cournot equilibrium in Solved Problem 13.2. At what quantities do the best-response functions hit the axes?

3.14 In a Nash-Cournot equilibrium, does an oligopolistic firm produce at less than full capacity, full capacity, or more than full capacity? Explain.

4. Stackelberg Oligopoly

*4.1 Duopoly quantity-setting firms face the market demand $p = 150 - Q$. Each firm has a marginal cost of $60 per unit.
   a. What is the Nash-Cournot equilibrium?
   b. What is the Nash-Stackelberg equilibrium when Firm 1 moves first? **A**

4.2 Determine the Nash-Stackelberg equilibrium with one leader firm and two follower firms if the market demand curve is linear and each firm faces a

constant marginal cost, m, and no fixed cost. (*Hint*: See Appendix 13B for the Stackelberg model with one follower or use calculus.) **C**

4.3 If two quantity-setting firms act simultaneously, is the Stackelberg outcome likely? Why or why not?

*4.4 Your college is considering renting space in the student union to one or two commercial textbook stores. The rent the college can charge per square foot of space depends on the profit (before rent) of the firms and hence on whether the market has a monopoly or a duopoly. Which number of stores is better for the college in terms of rent? Which is better for students? Why?

*4.5 The market demand function is $Q = 1{,}000 - 1{,}000p$. Each firm has a marginal cost of $m = 0.28$ (28¢ per unit). Firm 1, the leader, acts before Firm 2, the follower. Solve for the Nash-Stackelberg equilibrium quantities, prices, and profits. (*Hint*: See Appendix 13B and Solved Problem 13.3.) Compare your solution to the Nash-Cournot equilibrium (Question 3.2). **C**

*4.6 To examine the trade-off between efficiency and market power from a merger, consider a market with two firms that sell identical products. Firm 1 has a constant marginal cost of 1, and Firm 2 has a constant marginal cost of 2. The market demand is $Q = 15 - p$.
   a. Solve for the Nash-Cournot equilibrium price, quantities, profits, consumer surplus, and deadweight loss.
   b. If the firms merge and produce at the lower marginal cost, how do the equilibrium values change?
   c. Discuss the change in efficiency (average cost of producing the output) and welfare—consumer surplus, producer surplus (or profit), and deadweight loss—if the firms merge. **A**

4.7 Zipcar invented the business of renting cars by the hour and is still the industry leader with half a million U.S. members and 9,000 vehicles. However, Hertz and Enterprise have more recently entered the market. Enterprise claims it has 58,000 car-sharing members and the second largest fleet of cars ("Zipcar Now Sees Enterprise in Rear Window," *Businessweek*, June 5, 2012). Zipcar's large network of members and cars may allow it to be a Stackelberg leader. Use graphs to show how the entry of rivals affects Zipcar. Discuss the difference between a market with a Stackelberg leader and one follower versus a market with two followers.

5. Bertrand Oligopoly

5.1 What happens to the homogeneous-good Nash-Bertrand equilibrium price if the number of firms increases? Why?

*5.2 Will the price be lower if duopoly firms set price or if they set quantity? Under what conditions can you give a definitive answer to this question?

5.3 In the Coke and Pepsi example, what is the effect of a specific tax, t, on the equilibrium prices? (*Hint:* What does the tax do to the firm's marginal cost? You do not have to use math to answer this problem.)

5.4 In the initial Nash-Bertrand equilibrium, two firms with differentiated products charge the same equilibrium prices. A consumer testing agency praises the product of one firm, causing its demand curve to shift to the right as new customers start buying the product. (The demand curve of the other product is not substantially affected.) Use a graph to illustrate how this new information affects the Nash-Bertrand equilibrium. What happens to the equilibrium prices of the two firms?

*5.5 Suppose that identical duopoly firms have constant marginal costs of $10 per unit. Firm 1 faces a demand function of $q_1 = 100 - 2p_1 + p_2$, where q_1 is Firm 1's output, p_1 is Firm 1's price, and p_2 is Firm 2's price. Similarly, the demand Firm 2 faces is $q_2 = 100 - 2p_2 + p_1$. Solve for the Nash-Bertrand equilibrium. **C**

5.6 Solve for the Nash-Bertrand equilibrium for the firms described in Question 5.5 if both firms have a marginal cost of $0 per unit. **A**

5.7 Solve for the Nash-Bertrand equilibrium for the firms described in Question 5.5 if Firm 1's marginal cost is $30 per unit and Firm 2's marginal cost is $10 per unit. **A**

5.8 Two pizza parlors are located within a few feet of each other on the Avenue of the Americas in New York City. Both were selling a slice of pizza for $1 (Matt Flegenheimer, "$1 Pizza Slice Is Back After a Sidewalk Showdown Ends Two Parlors' Price War," *New York Times*, September 5, 2012). Then, Bombay Fast Food/6th Ave. Pizza lowered its price to 79¢. The next morning, 2 Bros. Pizza dropped its price to 75¢, which Bombay quickly matched. These price cuts led to long lines of customers. However, both firms claimed that they were losing money. The two proprietors had a meeting on the sidewalk in front of their restaurants. According

to one, they reached an agreement and raised their prices back to a dollar. Can the identical-goods, Bertrand, or cartel models be used to explain this series of events? Why or why not?

6. Monopolistic Competition

6.1 Solved Problem 13.4 shows that a monopolistically competitive firm maximizes its profit where it is operating at less than full capacity. Does this result depend upon whether firms produce identical or differentiated products? Why?

6.2 In 2010 and 2011, the government gave incentives to new businesses. A new firm could write off $10,000 in startup costs, they could write off new capital investment, investors who invested in startups and small businesses would be exempt from capital gains tax if they sold their stakes for a profit, and the Small Business Administration increased the size of loans it would guarantee to $5 million. What effect would these incentives have on monopolistically competitive markets? Explain.

6.3 In the monopolistically competitive airlines model, what is the equilibrium if firms face no fixed costs?

6.4 Does an oligopolistic or a monopolistically competitive firm have a supply curve? Why or why not? (*Hint:* See the discussion in Chapter 11 of whether a monopoly has a supply curve.)

6.5 In a monopolistically competitive market, the government applies a specific tax of $1 per unit of output. What happens to the profit of a typical firm in this market? Does the number of firms in the market change? Why? (*Hint:* See Solved Problem 13.5.)

*6.6 An incumbent firm, Firm 1, faces a potential entrant, Firm 2, with a lower marginal cost. The market demand curve is $p = 120 - q_1 - q_2$. Firm 1 has a constant marginal cost of $20, while Firm 2's is $10.

a. What are the Nash-Cournot equilibrium price, quantities, and profits if the government does not intervene?

b. To block entry, the incumbent appeals to the government to require that the entrant incur extra costs. What happens to the Nash-Cournot equilibrium if the legal requirement causes the marginal cost of the second firm to rise to that of the first firm, $20?

c. Now suppose that the barrier leaves the marginal cost alone but imposes a fixed cost.

What is the minimal fixed cost that will prevent entry? (*Hint*: See Solved Problem 13.5.) **A**

7. Challenge

*7.1 Using our duopoly airlines example, (falsely) assume that the corporation that owns United Airlines is located in one country and American's is located in another.

    a. If only United's government provides a $48 per passenger subsidy, determine the equilibrium prices, quantities, and profits.

    b. Now suppose that both American and United receive a subsidy of $48 per passenger. Discuss how this equilibrium differs from the one in which only one firm is subsidized. **A**

7.2 Two firms, each in a different country, sell homogeneous output in a third country. Government 1 subsidizes its domestic firm by s per unit. The other government does not react. In the absence of government intervention, the market has a Nash-Cournot equilibrium. Suppose demand is linear, $p = 1 - q_1 - q_2$, and each firm's marginal and average costs of production are constant at m. Government 1 maximizes net national income (it does not care about transfers between the government and the firm, so it maximizes the firm's profit net of the transfers). Show that Government 1's optimal s results in its firm producing the Stackelberg leader quantity and the other firm producing the Stackelberg follower quantity in equilibrium. **C**

14 Game Theory

A camper awakens to the growl of a hungry bear and sees his friend putting on a pair of running shoes. "You can't outrun a bear," scoffs the camper. His friend coolly replies, "I don't have to. I only have to outrun you!"

Challenge

Competing E-book Standards

Amazon's Kindle was the first successful entrant into the e-book reader market, but it now has a variety of competitors. Not all e-book readers use the same format for books.[1] The current best-selling product, Amazon's Kindle, uses Amazon's proprietary AZW format. Amazon does not support the open-standard EPUB format, which is used by the Kindle's competitors such as Barnes & Noble's NOOK, Sony's Reader, and Apple's iPad. Amazon provides applications that allow consumers to read AZW books on the iPhone (and slightly less successfully on the iPad) as well as on Windows PCs.

If e-book readers' formats differ, e-book publishers must incur additional expenses in producing books for the various formats or sell books that can be read on only some readers, which affects consumers' costs and the practicality of using a given reader. What role did Amazon's early entry play in determining the standards used? How might the outcome have been different if the firms had chosen standards simultaneously?

When a small number of people or firms—such as e-book reader manufacturers—interact, they know that their actions significantly affect each other's welfare or profit, so they consider those actions carefully. Firms compete on many fronts beyond setting quantity or price. To gain an edge over rivals, a firm makes many decisions, such as which e-book standard to use, how much to advertise, whether to act to discourage a new firm from entering its market, how to differentiate its product, and whether to invest in new equipment.

---

[1] However, all readers can display Adobe PDF files, which are used for documents and books in the public domain.

An oligopolistic firm that ignores or inaccurately predicts the behavior of rivals is unlikely to do well. If Ford underestimates how many cars Toyota and Honda will produce, Ford may produce too many vehicles and lose money. These firms are aware of this strategic interdependence, recognizing that the plans and decisions of any one firm might significantly affect the profits of the other firms.

In this chapter, we use game theory (von Neumann and Morgenstern, 1944) to examine how a small number of firms or individuals interact. **Game theory** is a set of tools that economists, political scientists, military analysts, and others use to analyze players' strategic decision making. This chapter introduces the basic concepts of game theory.[2]

Game theory has many practical applications. It is particularly useful for analyzing how oligopolistic firms set prices, quantities, and advertising levels. In addition, economists use game theory to analyze bargaining between unions and management or between the buyer and seller of a car, interactions between polluters and those harmed by pollution, transactions between the buyers and sellers of homes, negotiations between parties with different amounts of information (such as between car owners and auto mechanics), bidding in auctions, and many other economic interactions. Game theory is also used by political scientists and military planners to avoid or fight wars, by biologists to analyze evolutionary biology and ecology, and by philosophers, computer scientists, and many others.

In this chapter, we concentrate on how oligopolistic firms interact within a *game*. A **game** is an interaction between players (such as individuals or firms) in which players use strategies. A **strategy** is a battle plan that specifies the *actions* that a player will make. An **action** is a move that a player makes at a specified stage of a game, such as how much output a firm produces in the current period.

For example, a firm may use a simple business strategy where it produces 100 units of output regardless of what any rival does. Here, the strategy consists of a single action—producing 100 units of output. However, some strategies consist of a combination of actions or moves, possibly contingent on what a rival does. For example, a firm might decide to produce a small quantity as long as its rival produced a small amount in the previous period, and a large quantity otherwise.

The **payoffs** of a game are the benefits received by players from the game's outcome, such as profits for firms, or incomes or utilities for individuals. A *payoff function* specifies each player's payoff as a function of the strategies chosen by all players. We normally assume that players seek to maximize their payoffs. In essence, this assumption simply defines what we mean by payoffs. Payoffs include all relevant benefits experienced by the players. Therefore, rational players should try to obtain the highest payoffs they can.

The **rules of the game** include the *timing* of players' moves (such as whether one player moves first), the various actions that are possible at a particular point in the game, and possibly other specific aspects of how the game is played. A full description of a game normally includes a statement of the players, the rules of the game (including the possible actions or strategies), and the payoff function, along with a statement regarding the information available to the players.

When analyzing a game, we usually have three objectives: to accurately describe and understand the game, to predict the likely outcome of the game, and to offer advice to managers as to how best to play the game.

In analyzing a game, it is crucial that we know how much information participants have. We start by assuming that all the relevant information is *common knowledge*

game theory
a set of tools that economists and others use to analyze decision making by players who use strategies

game
any competition between players (firms) in which strategic behavior plays a major role

strategy
a battle plan that specifies the action that a player will make conditional on the information available at each move and for any possible contingency

action
a move that a player makes at a specified stage of a game, such as how much output a firm produces in the current period

payoffs
benefits received by players from the game's outcome, such as profits for firms, or incomes or utilities for individuals

rules of the game
regulations that include the timing of players' moves, the various actions that a player may make at each stage of the game, and other aspects of how the game is played

---

[2]For more details, see, for example, Fudenberg and Tirole (1991) or Gibbons (1992). For an interesting, brief history, see **www.econ.canterbury.ac.nz/personal_pages/paul_walker/gt/hist.htm**.

common knowledge a piece of information known by all players, that is known to be known by all players, and so forth

to the players and then we relax that assumption. **Common knowledge** is a piece of information known by all players, and it is known by all players to be known by all players, and it is known to be known to be known, and so forth. In particular, we initially assume that players have **complete information**, a situation in which the strategies and payoffs of the game are *common knowledge*.

complete information a situation in which the strategies and payoffs of the game are common knowledge

The information possessed by firms affects the outcome of a game. The outcome of a game in which a particular piece of information is known by all firms may differ from the outcome when some firms are uninformed. A firm may suffer a worse outcome if it does not know the potential payoffs of other firms. Similarly, a firm may do worse if it has limited ability to make calculations, as when its cost of making many calculations is prohibitively high or its managers have limited analytical abilities. We address nonrational behavior at the end of the chapter.

In this chapter, we examine five main topics

1. **Static Games.** A static game is played once by players who act simultaneously and hence do not know how other players will act at the time they must make a decision.

2. **Repeated Dynamic Games.** If a static game is repeated over many periods, firms may use more complex strategies than in the static one-period game because a firm's action in one period may affect its rivals' actions in subsequent periods.

3. **Sequential Dynamic Games.** If one firm acts before its rival, it may gain an advantage by converting what would be an empty threat to its rival into a credible, observable action.

4. **Auctions.** An auction is a game where bidders have incomplete information about the value that other bidders place on the auctioned good or service.

5. **Behavioral Game Theory.** Some people make biased decisions based on psychological factors rather than using a rational strategy.

14.1 Static Games

static games games in which each player acts only once and the players act simultaneously

We start by examining **static games**, in which each player acts only once and the players act simultaneously (or, at least, each player acts without knowing rivals' actions). In these games, firms have complete information about the payoff functions but imperfect information about rivals' moves.

Examples include two rival firms making simultaneous one-time-only decisions on where to locate its new factory, teenagers' game of chicken in cars, the duel between Aaron Burr and Alexander Hamilton in 1804, an employer's hiring negotiations with a potential employee, street vendors' choice of locations and prices outside a Super Bowl or World Cup game, and the Cournot and Bertrand models (Chapter 13). In this section, we show how to represent these static games in a table and how to predict their outcomes.

Normal-Form Games

normal form a representation of a static game with complete information specifying the players, their possible strategies, and their payoffs for each combination of strategies

A **normal-form** representation of a static game with complete information specifies the players in the game, their possible strategies, and the payoff function that identifies the players' payoffs for each combination of strategies. We start with an example of two firms that can each take one of only two possible actions and play each other only once. Our example is a simplified version of the real-world competition (as estimated by Brander and Zhang, 1990) between United and American Airlines, which we described in Chapter 13.

In this game, the two *players* or firms are United and American Airlines. They play a *static game*—they compete only once. The *rules* of the game specify the possible actions or strategies that the firms can take and when they can take them. Each firm has only two possible *actions*: Each can fly either 48 thousand or 64 thousand passengers per quarter between Chicago and Los Angeles. Other than announcing their output levels, the firms cannot communicate, so that they cannot make side-deals or otherwise coordinate their actions. Each firm's *strategy* is to take one of the two actions, choosing either a low output (48 thousand passengers per quarter) or a high output (64 thousand). The firms announce their actions or strategies *simultaneously*. The firms have *complete information*: they know all the possible strategies and the corresponding payoff (profit) to each firm. However, their information is imperfect in one important respect: Because they choose their output levels simultaneously, neither airline knows what action its rival will take when it makes its output decision.

We summarize this static game using its normal-form representation, which is the *payoff matrix* or *profit matrix* in Table 14.1. This payoff matrix shows the profits for each of the four possible combinations of the strategies that the firms may choose. For example, if American chooses a large quantity, $q_A = 64$ units per quarter, and United chooses a small quantity, $q_U = 48$ units per quarter, the firms' profits are in the cell in the lower-left corner of the profit matrix. That cell shows that American's profit (upper-right number) is $5.1 million per quarter, and United's profit (bottom-left number) is $3.8 million per quarter. We now have a full description of the game, including a statement of the players, the rules, a list of the allowable strategies, the payoffs, and the available information.

Predicting a Game's Outcome

When you have eliminated the impossible, whatever remains, however improbable, must be the truth. —Sherlock Holmes (Sir Arthur Conan Doyle)

We can predict the outcome of some games by using the insight that rational players will avoid strategies that are *dominated* by other strategies. However, for many other games, this approach alone does not allow us to precisely predict the outcome. A broader class of games can be precisely predicted based on each player's choosing a *best response* to the other players' actions—the response that produces the largest possible payoff.

dominant strategy
a strategy that produces a higher payoff than any other strategy the player can use for every possible combination of its rivals' strategies

Dominant Strategies We can precisely predict the outcome of any game in which every player has a **dominant strategy**: a strategy that produces a higher payoff than any other strategy the player can use for every possible combination of its

Table 14.1 Dominant Strategies in a Quantity Setting, Prisoners' Dilemma Game

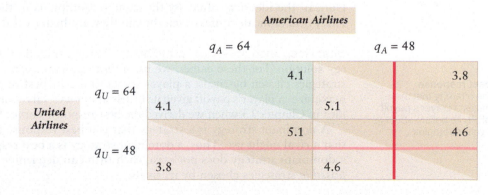

rivals' strategies. When a firm has a dominant strategy, a firm can hold no belief about its rivals' choice of strategies that would cause it to choose one of its other, strictly dominated strategies.

Although firms do not always have dominant strategies, they have them in our airline game. American's managers can determine its dominant strategy using the following reasoning:

- *If United chooses the high-output strategy* ($q_U = 64$), *American's high-output strategy maximizes its profit*: Given United's strategy, American's profit is $4.1 million (top-right number in the upper-left cell) with its high-output strategy ($q_A = 64$) and only $3.8 million (top-right number in the upper-right cell) with its low-output strategy ($q_A = 48$). Thus, American is better off using a high-output strategy if United chooses its high-output strategy.

- *If United chooses the low-output strategy* ($q_U = 48$), *American's high-output strategy maximizes its profit*: Given United's strategy, American's profit is $5.1 million with its high-output strategy and only $4.6 million with its low-output strategy.

- *Thus, the high-output strategy is American's dominant strategy*: Whichever strategy United uses, American's profit is higher if it uses its high-output strategy. We show that American won't use its low-output strategy (because that strategy is dominated by the high-output strategy) by drawing a vertical, dark-red line through American's low-output cells in Table 14.1.

By the same type of reasoning, United's high-output strategy is also a dominant strategy. We draw a horizontal, light-red line through United's low-output strategy. Because the high-output strategy is a dominant strategy for both firms, we can predict that the outcome of this game is the pair of high-output strategies, $q_A = q_U = 64$. We show the resulting outcome—the cell in Table 14.1 where both firms use high-output strategies—by coloring that cell green.

A striking feature of this game is that the players choose strategies that do not maximize their joint profit. Each firm earns $4.6 million if $q_A = q_U = 48$ rather than the $4.1 million they actually earn by setting $q_A = q_U = 64$. In this type of game—called a **prisoners' dilemma** game—all players have dominant strategies that lead to a profit (or another payoff) that is inferior to what they could achieve if they cooperated and pursued alternative strategies.

The prisoners' dilemma crops up in virtually every cops-and-robbers show. The cops arrest Larry and Duncan and put them in separate rooms so that they cannot talk to each other. An assistant district attorney tells Larry, "We have enough evidence to convict you both of a relatively minor crime for which you'll serve a year in prison. If you'll squeal on your partner and he stays silent, we can convict him of a major crime for which he'll serve five years and you'll go free. If you both confess, you'll each get two years." Meanwhile, another assistant district attorney is making Duncan the identical offer. By the same reasoning as in the airline example, both Larry and Duncan confess even though they are better off if they both keep quiet.

prisoners' dilemma
a game in which all players have dominant strategies that result in profits (or other payoffs) that are inferior to what they could achieve if they used cooperative strategies

Best Response and Nash Equilibrium Many games do not have a dominant strategy solution. For these games, we use a more general approach. For any given set of strategies chosen by rivals, a player wants to use its **best response**—the strategy that maximizes a player's payoff given its beliefs about its rivals' strategies. We illustrated this idea in Chapter 13 when we derived the best-response curves for an oligopolistic firm.

A dominant strategy is a strategy that is a best response to *all possible* strategies that a rival might use. Thus, a dominant strategy is a best response. However, even if a dominant strategy does not exist, each firm can determine its best response to *any possible* strategies chosen by its rivals.

best response
the strategy that maximizes a player's payoff given its beliefs about its rivals' strategies

The idea that players use best responses is the basis for the Nash equilibrium, a solution concept for games formally introduced by John Nash (1951). A set of strategies is a **Nash equilibrium** if, when all other players use these strategies, no player can obtain a higher payoff by choosing a different strategy.[3] An appealing property of the Nash equilibrium is that it is self-enforcing. If the other players use a Nash equilibrium strategy, then no player wants to switch to another strategy. Each player believes that "Given the strategies chosen by my rivals, I made the best possible choice—I chose my best response."

The Nash equilibrium is the primary solution concept used by economists in analyzing games. It allows us to find solutions to more games than just those with a dominant strategy solution. If a game has a dominant strategy solution, then that solution must also be a Nash equilibrium. However, a Nash equilibrium can be found for many games that do not have dominant strategy solutions.

To illustrate these points, we examine a more complex simultaneous-move game in which American and United can each produce an output of 48, 64, or 96 (thousand passengers per quarter). This game has nine possible output combinations, as the 3×3 profit matrix in Table 14.2 shows. Neither American nor United has a single, dominant strategy, but we can find a Nash equilibrium by using a two-step procedure. First, we determine each firm's best response to any given strategy of the other firm. Second, we check whether any pairs of strategies (cells in the profit matrix) are best responses for both firms. Each such pair of strategies is a Nash equilibrium.

We start by determining American's best response for each one of United's possible actions. If United chooses $q_U = 96$ (thousand passengers per quarter), the first row of the table, then American's profit is $0 if it sets $q_A = 96$ (the first column), $2.0 (million) if it chooses $q_A = 64$ (the second column), and $2.3 if it selects $q_A = 48$ (third column). Thus, American's best-response if United sets $q_U = 96$ is to select $q_A = 48$. We indicate American's best response by coloring the upper triangle in the last (third column) cell in this row dark green. Similarly, if United sets $q_U = 64$

Nash equilibrium
a set of strategies such that, when all other players use these strategies, no player can obtain a higher payoff by choosing a different strategy

Table 14.2 Best Responses in a Quantity Setting Game

		American Airlines		
		$q_A = 96$	$q_A = 64$	$q_A = 48$
United Airlines	$q_U = 96$	0 / 0	2.0 / 3.1	2.3 / 4.6
	$q_U = 64$	3.1 / 2.0	4.1 / 4.1	3.8 / 5.1
	$q_U = 48$	4.6 / 2.3	5.1 / 3.8	4.6 / 4.6

[3]In Chapter 13, we used a special case of this definition of a Nash equilibrium in which we referred to actions instead of strategies. An action and a strategy are the same if the players can move only once; however, later in this chapter, we will consider games that last for many periods and hence need a definition based on strategies.

(second row), American's best response is to set $q_A = 64$, where it earns \$4.1 million, so we color the upper triangle in the middle cell (second column) of the second row dark green. Finally, if United sets $q_U = 48$ (third row), American's best response is $q_A = 64$, where it earns \$5.1 million, so we color the upper triangle in the middle cell of the third row dark green.

We can use the same type of reasoning to determine United's best responses to each of American's strategies. If American chooses $q_A = 96$ (first column), then United maximizes its profit at \$2.3 million by setting $q_U = 48$, which we indicate by coloring the lower triangle light green in the lower left cell of the table. Similarly, we show that United's best response is $q_U = 64$, if American sets $q_A = 64$ or 48, which we show by coloring the relevant lower left triangles light green.

We now look for a Nash equilibrium, which is a pair of strategies where both firms are using a best-response strategy so that neither firm would want to change its strategy. In only one cell are both the upper and lower triangles green: $q_A = q_U = 64$. Given that its rival uses this strategy, neither firm wants to deviate from its strategy. For example, if United continued to set $q_U = 64$, but American raised its quantity to 96, American's profit would fall from \$4.1 to \$3.8. Or, if American lowered its quantity to 48, its profit would fall to \$3.1. Thus, American does not want to change its strategy.

Because no other cell has a pair of strategies that are best responses (green lower and upper triangles), at least one of the firms would want to change its strategy in each of these other cells. For example, at $q_A = q_U = 48$, either firm could raise its profit from \$4.6 to \$5.1 million by increasing its output to 64. At $q_A = 48$ and $q_U = 64$, American can raise its profit from \$3.8 to \$4.1 million by increasing its quantity to $q_A = 64$. Similarly, United would want to increase its output when $q_A = 64$ and $q_U = 48$. None of the other strategy combinations is a Nash equilibrium because at least one firm would want to deviate. Thus, we were able to find the single Nash equilibrium to this game by determining each firm's best responses.

In these airline examples, we have assumed that the firms can pick only between a small number of output levels. However, we can use game theory to find the Nash equilibrium in games in which the firms can choose any output level. We showed such a generalization for the airline example in Chapter 13. In Figure 13.3, we determined the best-response curves for each of these airlines, found that these best-response curves intersected only once, and identified the set of outputs at that intersection as the Nash-Cournot equilibrium. Indeed, that equilibrium is the same as the equilibria in Tables 14.1 and 14.2.

Multiple Nash Equilibria, No Nash Equilibrium, and Mixed Strategies

pure strategy
each player chooses an action with certainty

mixed strategy
a firm (player) chooses among possible actions according to probabilities it assigns

Each of the games that we have considered so far has only one Nash equilibrium, and each firm uses a **pure strategy**: Each player chooses a single action. In this section, we use a simultaneous-decision entry game to show that some games have more than one Nash equilibrium and that a firm may employ a **mixed strategy** in which the player chooses among possible actions according to probabilities it assigns. A pure strategy assigns a probability of 1 to a single action, whereas a mixed strategy is a probability distribution over actions. That is, a pure strategy is a rule telling the player what action to take, whereas a mixed strategy is a rule telling the player which dice to throw, coin to flip, or other device to use to choose an action.

The simultaneous-decision entry game in Table 14.3 has both pure and mixed-strategy Nash equilibria. Two firms are considering opening gas stations at a highway rest stop that has no gas stations. There's enough physical space for at most two gas stations. The profit matrix, Table 14.3, shows that only one station can operate profitably. If both firms enter, each loses 1 (say, \$100,000). If only one firm enters, it

Table 14.3 Nash Equilibria in an Entry Game

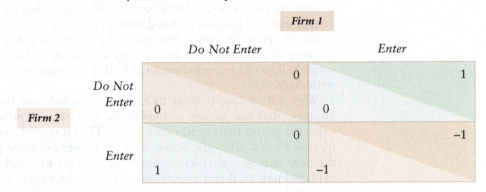

earns 1. Neither firm has a dominant strategy. Each firm's best action depends on what the other firm does.

Multiple Nash Equilibria This game has two Nash equilibria in pure strategies: Firm 1 *enters* and Firm 2 *does not enter*, or Firm 2 *enters* and Firm 1 *does not enter*. We can show this result by using a best-response analysis.

If Firm 1's strategy is not to enter, Firm 2's best response is to enter, which we show by the light-green triangle in the lower-left cell. If Firm 1's strategy is to enter, then Firm 2's best response is to stay out, which we show by the light-green triangle in the upper-right cell. Similarly, Firm 1's best responses are indicated by the dark-green triangles in the same cells.

Two of the four cells have both triangles shaded green. Each of these pairs of strategies is a Nash equilibrium because both players are using their best response to the other's strategy. The pair of strategies for which only Firm 1 enters is a Nash equilibrium because neither firm wants to change its behavior. Similarly, the pair of strategies for which only Firm 2 enters is a Nash equilibrium.

How do the players know which outcome will occur? They *don't* know. It is difficult to see how the firms choose strategies unless they collude and can enforce their agreement. For example, the firm that enters could pay the other firm to stay out of the market. Without an enforceable collusive agreement, even discussions between the firms before decisions are made are unlikely to help. These pure Nash equilibria are unappealing because they call for identical firms to use different strategies.

Mixed Strategies However, in this entry game, both firms may use the same mixed strategy. When both firms enter with a probability of one-half—say, if a flipped coin comes up heads—the outcome is a Nash equilibrium in mixed strategies because neither firm wants to change its strategy, given that the other firm uses its Nash equilibrium mixed strategy.

If both firms use this mixed strategy, each of the four outcomes in the payoff matrix in Table 14.3 is equally likely, as we will show. The probability that the outcome in a particular cell of the matrix occurs is the product of the probabilities that each firm chooses the relevant action because their actions are independent. The probability that a player chooses a given action is $\frac{1}{2}$, so the probability that both players will choose a given pair of actions (a cell) is $\frac{1}{2} \times \frac{1}{2} = \frac{1}{4}$. Firm 1 has a one-fourth chance of earning 1 (upper-right cell), a one-fourth chance of losing 1 (lower-right cell), and a one-half chance of earning 0 (upper-left and lower-left cells). Thus, Firm 1's expected profit—the firm's profit in each possible outcome times the probability of that outcome—is

$$(1 \times \tfrac{1}{4}) + (-1 \times \tfrac{1}{4}) + (0 \times \tfrac{1}{2}) = 0.$$

The key concept behind a mixed strategy is that a firm chooses its mixed strategy so that its rival is indifferent between picking either of its strategies. Given that Firm 1 uses the proposed mixed strategy, Firm 2 cannot achieve a higher expected profit by using one pure strategy rather than the other. If Firm 2 uses the pure strategy of entering with probability 1, it earns 1 half the time and loses 1 the other half, so its expected profit is 0. If it stays out with certainty, Firm 2 earns 0 with certainty.

Why does the firm want its rival to be indifferent between its two strategies? Suppose that one of the actions in the equilibrium mixed strategy had a higher expected payoff than some other action. Then it would pay to increase the probability that Firm 2 takes the action with the higher expected payoff. However, if all of the pure strategies that have positive probability in a mixed strategy have the same expected payoff, then the expected payoff of the mixed strategy must also have that expected payoff. Thus, Firm 2 is indifferent as to whether it uses any of these pure strategies or any mixed strategy over these pure strategies.

How did we calculate that each firm's mixed strategy is to enter with the probability of one-half? For Firm 2 to use a mixed strategy, it must be indifferent between entering or not entering if Firm 1 enters with probability θ. Firm 2's payoff from entering is $[\theta \times (-1)] + [(1 - \theta) \times 1] = 1 - 2\theta$. Its payoff from not entering is $[\theta \times 0] + [(1 - \theta) \times 0] = 0$. Equating these two expected profits, $1 - 2\theta = 0$, and solving, we find that $\theta = \frac{1}{2}$. Given the symmetry of the payoff matrix, a similar calculation shows that Firm 2's mixed strategy is also to enter with probability one-half. Thus, in the mixed-strategy Nash equilibrium, both firms use a mixed strategy where they enter with a probability of one-half.

To summarize, this game has two pure-strategy Nash equilibria—one firm employing the pure strategy of entering and the other firm pursuing the pure strategy of not entering—and a mixed-strategy Nash equilibrium. If Firm 1 decides to *enter* with a probability of one-half, Firm 2 is indifferent between choosing to enter with probability of 1 (the pure strategy of *enter*), 0 (the pure strategy of *do not enter*), or any fraction in between these extremes. However, for the firms' strategies to constitute a mixed-strategy Nash equilibrium, both firms must choose to enter with a probability of one-half.

How business decisions are made.

One important reason for introducing the concept of a mixed strategy is that some games have no pure-strategy Nash equilibria (see Solved Problem 14.1). However, Nash (1950) proved that every static game with a finite number of players and a finite number of actions has at least one Nash equilibrium, which may involve mixed strategies.

Some game theorists argue that mixed strategies are implausible because firms do not flip coins to choose strategies. One response is that firms may only appear to be unpredictable. In this game with no dominant strategies, neither firm has a strong reason to believe that the other will choose a pure strategy. It may think about its rival's behavior as random. However, in actual games, a firm may use some information or reasoning that its rival does not observe in choosing a pure strategy. Another response is that a mixed strategy may be appealing in some games, such as the entry game or the similar game of chicken, where a random strategy and symmetry between players are plausible.

Application

Tough Love

We can use game theory to explain many interactions between parents and their kids. In the United States, the term *boomerang generation* refers to young adults who return home after college, a first job, or the military to live with their parents. (In Japan, they're called *parasite singles*.)

The recent recession hit young people particularly hard. The U.S. unemployment rate for 20- to 24-year olds went from 8.5% in 2007 to 10.6% in 2008, then rose to 15.6% in 2009, and has stayed above 13% through 2012.

As a result, more adult children moved back into their parents' homes after college. The share of 25- to 34-year-olds living in multigenerational households rose from 11% in 1980 to 20% in 2008 and 26% in 2010 (the highest it has been since the 1950s).[4] In the European Union, nearly half (46%) of young adults aged 18–34 lived with their parents in 2008.

In many parents' minds, the question arises whether by supporting their kids, they discourage them from working. Rather than unconditionally supporting their children, would they help their kids more by engaging in tough love: kicking their kids out and making them support themselves? The next Solved Problem addresses this question.

Solved Problem 14.1

Mimi wants to support her son Jeff if he looks for work but not otherwise. Jeff (unlike most young people) wants to try to find a job only if his mother will not support his life of indolence. Their payoff matrix is

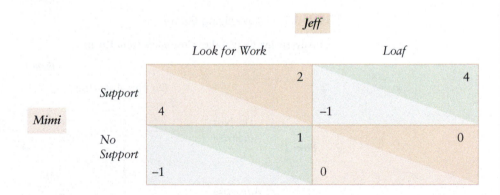

If Jeff and Mimi choose actions simultaneously, what are the pure- or mixed-strategy equilibria?

Answer

1. *Use a best-response analysis to determine whether any of the four possible pairs of pure strategies is a Nash equilibrium.* We start by determining each player's best responses. If Jeff loafs, Mimi's best response is to cut off support because her payoff is 0 without support and −1 with support. We show her best response by a light-green triangle in the lower left of the no support/loaf cell. Similarly, her best response if he works is to support him (the payoff is 4 with support and −1

---

[4]A 2011 survey found that 59% of U.S. parents provide financial support to their adult children who are no longer in school. A 2012 British study reported that 80% of young adults received parental financial support.

with no support), so we shade the lower-left triangle in the support/look cell. Jeff's best responses are the dark-green triangles in the upper right of the support/loaf and no support/look cells. In none of the four cells are both the triangles shaded. That is, none of these pairs of pure strategies is a Nash equilibrium because one or the other player would want to change his or her strategy.

2. *By equating expected payoffs, determine the mixed-strategy equilibrium.* If Mimi provides support with probability θ_M, Jeff's expected payoff from looking for work is $2\theta_M + [1 \times (1 - \theta_M)] = 1 + \theta_M$, and his expected payoff from loafing is $4\theta_M + [0 \times (1 - \theta_M)] = 4\theta_M$. Thus, his expected payoffs are equal if $1 + \theta_M = 4\theta_M$, or $\theta_M = \frac{1}{3}$. Similarly, if Jeff looks for work with probability θ_J, then Mimi's expected payoff from supporting him is $4\theta_J + [(-1) \times (1 - \theta_J)] = 5\theta_J - 1$, and her expected payoff from not supporting him is $-\theta_J + [0 \times (1 - \theta_J)] = -\theta_J$. By equating her expected payoffs, $5\theta_J - 1 = -\theta_J$, we determine that his mixed-strategy probability is $\theta_J = \frac{1}{6}$.

Comment: Although this game has no pure-strategy Nash equilibria, it has a mixed-strategy Nash equilibrium.

Cooperation

Whether players cooperate in a static game depends on the payoff function. Table 14.4 shows an advertising game in which each firm can choose to advertise or not, with two possible payoff functions. The unique Nash equilibrium maximizes the collective

Table 14.4 Advertising Game

(a) Advertising Only Takes Customers from Rivals

		Firm 1	
		Do Not Advertise	Advertise
Firm 2	Do Not Advertise	2 2	3 0
	Advertise	0 3	1 1

(b) Advertising Attracts New Customers to the Market

		Firm 1	
		Do Not Advertise	Advertise
Firm 2	Do Not Advertise	2 2	4 3
	Advertise	3 4	5 5

payoff to the players in the second game, but the unique Nash equilibrium in the first game is not the cooperative outcome.

The game in panel a is a prisoners' dilemma game similar to the airline game in Table 14.1. Each firm has a dominant strategy: to advertise. In this Nash equilibrium, each firm earns $1 million, which is less than the $2 million it would make if neither firm advertised. Thus, *the sum of the firms' profits is not maximized in this simultaneous-choice one-period game.*

Many people are surprised the first time they hear this result. Why don't the firms cooperate and use the individually and jointly more profitable low-output strategies, by which each earns a profit of $2 million instead of the $1 million in the Nash equilibrium?

The reason they don't cooperate is a lack of trust. Each firm uses the no-advertising strategy only if the firms have a binding (enforceable) agreement. The reason they do not trust each other is that each firm knows it is in the other firm's best interest to deviate from the actions that would maximize joint profits.

Suppose the two firms meet in advance and agree not to advertise. If the firms are going to engage in this game only once, each has an incentive to cheat on the agreement. If Firm 1 believes that Firm 2 will stick to the agreement and not advertise, Firm 1 can increase its profit from $2 million to $3 million by violating the agreement and advertising. Moreover, if Firm 1 thinks that Firm 2 will cheat on the agreement by advertising, Firm 1 wants to advertise (so that it will earn $1 million rather than $0). By this reasoning, each firm has a substantial profit incentive to cheat on the agreement. In this game, all else the same, if one firm advertises, its sales increase so that its profit rises, but its rival loses customers and hence the rival's profit falls.

In contrast, in panel b, when either firm advertises, the promotion attracts new customers to both firms. If neither firm advertises, both earn $2 (million). If only one firm advertises, its profit rises to $4, which is more than the $3 that the other firm makes. If both advertise, they are better off than if only one advertises or neither advertises. Again, advertising is a dominant strategy for both firms. In the Nash equilibrium, both firms advertise.

Both firms advertise in the games in panel a and panel b. The distinction is that the Nash equilibrium in which both advertise is the same as the collusive equilibrium in panel b where advertising increases the market size, but it is not the collusive equilibrium in panel a. When advertising cannibalizes the sales of other firms in the market in panel a, the payoffs are lower in the equilibrium in which they advertise.

Application

Strategic Advertising

Oligopolies often advertise.[5] Oligopolistic firms consider the likely actions of their rivals when deciding how much to advertise. How much a firm should spend on advertising depends critically on whether the advertising helps or harms its rival.

For example, when a firm advertises to inform consumers about a new use for its product, its advertising may cause the quantity demanded for its own *and* rival brands to rise, as happened with toothpaste ads. Before World War I, only 26% of Americans brushed their teeth. By 1926, in part because of ads like those in Ipana's "pink toothbrush" campaign, which detailed the perils of bleeding gums, the share

---

[5]In 2012, the largest U.S. advertiser, Procter & Gamble, the producer of Crest toothpaste, Pampers diapers, and many other household products, spent $9.3 billion on worldwide advertising. The next largest U.S. advertisers are General Motors, Verizon, Comcast, and AT&T. The largest advertisers based outside the United States are Unilever (United Kingdom, packaged household goods including Dove soap and Lipton foods), L'Oreal (France, cosmetics), Nestlé (Switzerland, foods), and Toyota (Japan, motor vehicles).

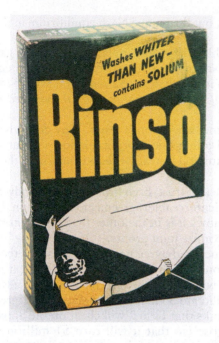

of Americans who brushed rose to 40%. Ipana's advertising helped all manufacturers of toothbrushes and toothpaste.

Alternatively, a firm's advertising might increase demand for its product by taking customers away from other firms. A firm can raise its profit if it can convince consumers that its product is superior to other brands. Historically, firms have implied that their products were superior because they contain secret ingredients. Dial soap boasted that it contained AT-7. Rinso detergent had solium, Comet included Chlorinol, and Bufferin had di-alminate. Among the toothpastes, Colgate had Gardol, Gleem had GL-70, Crest had fluoristan, and Ipana had hexachlorophene and Durenamel. More recently, natural ingredients have played this role.

Empirical evidence indicates that the impact of a firm's advertising on other firms varies across industries. The cola market is an example of the extreme case in which a firm's advertising brings few new customers into the market and primarily serves to steal business from rivals. Gasmi et al. (1992) reported that Coke or Pepsi's gain from advertising comes at the expense of its rivals; however, cola advertising has almost no effect on total market demand, as in panel a of Table 14.4. Similarly, celebrity endorsements (an important form of advertising) increase the sales of endorsed books but reduce sales of other books (Garthwaite, 2012). At the other extreme is cigarette advertising. Roberts and Samuelson (1988) found that cigarette advertising increases the size of the market but does not change market shares substantially, as in panel b.[6] Intermediate results include Canadian fast-foods, where advertising primarily increases general demand and only slightly affects market share (Richards and Padilla, 2009).

If these empirical results are correct, cola firms would be delighted to have the government ban their advertising, but cigarette firms wouldn't want an advertising ban. In a more general model in which firms set the amount of advertising (rather than just decide whether to advertise or not), the amount of advertising depends on whether advertising increases the market size or only steals customers from rivals.

14.2 Repeated Dynamic Games

So far, we have examined *static* games, in which firms make simultaneous decisions and in which each firm has just a single action to take, such as producing a particular output level, charging a particular price, or choosing a particular level of advertising. However, interactions between firms often are *dynamic* in the sense that firms act at different times. In a **dynamic game**, players move either repeatedly or sequentially. That is, dynamic games may be repeated games or sequential games.

dynamic games
games in which players move either sequentially or repeatedly

In a *repeated game*, a basic static *constituent* game might be played just once; repeated a finite, specified number of times; or repeated indefinitely (the end period is unknown to the players). Firms choose from the same set of possible actions again and again. An example of a repeated game is a static constituent Cournot oligopoly game (Chapter 13) that is played period after period.

---

[6]However, the Centers for Disease Control and Prevention's evidence suggests that advertising may shift the brand loyalty of youths.

In a *sequential game*, one player moves before another moves, possibly making alternating moves, as in chess or tic-tac-toe. A game is also sequential if players have a sequence of different decisions to make, even if moves are made simultaneously with a rival. For example, two firms might play a game in which they initially simultaneously choose how much capital to invest and then later simultaneously decide how much output to produce.

Strategies and Actions in Dynamic Games

A major difference between static and dynamic games is that dynamic games require us to distinguish between strategies and actions. An *action* is a single move that a player makes at a specified time, such as choosing an output level or a price. A *strategy* is a battle plan that specifies the full set of actions that a player will make throughout the game and may involve actions that are conditional on prior actions of other players or on additional information available at a given time.

In a static game, an action and a strategy are identical. The game lasts for only one period, so the action taken in that period represents the full battle plan or strategy. In contrast, in a repeated or sequential game, actions and strategies differ. If a static game in which the firms choose either a high price or a low price is played repeatedly period after period, a firm's strategy determines its action in each period. One possible strategy is for the firm to set the low price in each period. However, it could use a more complex strategy, such as one in which its action in a given period depends on its rival's actions in previous periods. For example, a firm could set a high price in the first period and then, in subsequent periods, it could set its price at the same level that its rival chose in the previous period.

Cooperation in a Repeated Prisoner's Dilemma Game

To illustrate the difference between a static game and a repeated game, we consider a repeated prisoners' dilemma game. Each period has a single stage in which both players move simultaneously. However, these are dynamic games because Player 1's move in period t precedes Player 2's move in period $t + 1$; hence, the earlier action may affect the later one. The players know all the moves from previous periods, but they do not know each other's moves within this period because they will act simultaneously.

In Table 14.1 in which American and United Airlines engage in a single-period prisoners' dilemma game, we showed that the two firms produce more than they would if they colluded. This result is surprising because we know that some real-world firms collude (Chapter 13). Why does our analysis differ from reality? The problem does not lie with the logic behind our analysis of the prisoners' dilemma game. Rather, the explanation is that we have been assuming that the game is played only once. In real-world markets, interactions between firms are often repeated. We now show that the cooperative or cartel outcome is more likely if the airlines' single-period prisoners' dilemma game in Table 14.1 is repeated indefinitely, quarter after quarter.

In a single-period game, each firm must choose its action *before* observing the rival's action. Therefore, a firm's choice cannot be influenced by its rival's action. It chooses its best response given what it *expects* the rival to do. When the same game is played repeatedly, United may use a strategy in which its action in the current period depends on American's observed actions in previous periods. American may use a similar strategy.

In a repeated game, a firm can influence its rival's behavior by *threatening to punish* in later periods by producing a high level of output if its rival produces a high level of output in an early period. In particular, suppose that American tells United that it will produce the smaller collusive or cooperative quantity in the first period, but that it will use the following two-part strategy to determine its output in subsequent periods:

- If United produces the smaller, cooperative quantity in all periods through period t, then American will produce the smaller, cooperative quantity in period $t + 1$.
- However, following the first period t in which United produces the larger quantity, American will produce the larger quantity in period $t + 1$ and in all subsequent periods.

If United believes that American will follow this strategy, United knows that it will make $4.6 million each period if it produces the smaller quantity. If United produces the large quantity its profit in that period rises to $5.1 million, but it lowers its potential profit to $4.1 million in each following period even if it continues to produce the high quantity. Thus, United gains half a million dollars relative to the cooperative payoff ($0.5 = $5.1 - $4.6) in the period when it first defects from the cooperative output, but it loses half a million dollars relative to cooperation (-$0.5 = $4.1 - $4.6) in each subsequent period. After only two punishment periods, the loss would be much larger in magnitude than the initial gain.[7]

Thus, if United believes that American will follow its announced strategy, it should produce the lower output level (unless it only cares about current profit). But should United believe American? While United cannot be certain of American's future strategy, it is at least reasonable for United to take this threat by American seriously because American's best response is to produce the larger quantity if it believes it can't trust United to produce the smaller quantity. Thus, if firms play the same game *indefinitely*, they should find it easier to reach the lower (and more profitable) output level.

American's strategy is an example of a *trigger strategy*, a strategy in which a rival's defection from a collusive outcome triggers a punishment. In this case, the trigger strategy is extreme because a single defection calls for a firm to permanently punish its rival by producing the high output in all subsequent periods. However, if both firms adopt this trigger strategy, the outcome is a Nash equilibrium in which both firms choose the low output and obtain the collusive profit in every period: Defection and punishment need not occur. Less extreme trigger strategies can also be used. For example, a strategy that involved just two periods of punishment for a defection would still be likely to make defection unattractive in this example.

When antitrust laws make a firm hesitant to directly contact its rival, it may try to influence its rival's behavior by *signaling*. For example, American could use a low-quantity strategy for a couple of periods to signal United that it desires that the two firms cooperate and produce that low quantity in the future. If United does not respond by lowering its output in future periods, then American suffers lower profits for only a couple of periods. However, if United responds to this signal and lowers its quantity, both firms can profitably produce at the low quantity thereafter.

If the low-output strategy is so lucrative for everyone, why don't firms always cooperate when engaging in such indefinitely repeated games? One reason is that the cooperative outcome is not the only possible Nash equilibrium. This game has another Nash equilibrium in which each firm chooses the high output every period. If United believes that American will produce the high output in every period, then

---

[7]Presumably a firm discounts future gains or losses (Chapter 16) because a dollar today is worth more than a dollar in the future. However, the effect of such discounting over a period as short as a few quarters is small.

its best response is to produce the high output every period. This same reasoning also applies to American. Each firm's belief about its rival will be confirmed by experience and neither firm will have an incentive to change its strategy.

Solved Problem 14.2

Show that if American and United Airlines know that they will play the game just described repeatedly for exactly T periods that the firms are unlikely to cooperate.

Answer

Start with the last period and work backward. In the last period, T, the firms know that they're not going to play again, so they know they can cheat—produce a large quantity—without fear of punishment. As a result, the last period is like a single-period game, and both firms produce the large quantity. That makes the $T - 1$ period the last interesting period. By the same reasoning, the firms will cheat in $T - 1$ because they know that they will both cheat in the last period and hence no additional punishment can be imposed. Continuing this type of argument, we conclude that maintaining an agreement to produce the small quantity will be difficult if the game has a known stopping point.

Comment: Playing the same game many times does not necessarily help the firms cooperate. With a known end period, cooperating is difficult. However, if the players know that the game will end but aren't sure when, cheating is less likely to occur. Cooperation is therefore more likely in a game that will continue forever or will end at an unknown period than in a game with a known final period.

14.3 Sequential Dynamic Games

We now turn to sequential dynamic games, in which one firm moves before another. We show how to represent these games diagrammatically and predict their outcomes.

Game Tree

extensive form
specifies the players, the sequence in which they move, the actions they can take, the information they have about other players' previous moves, and the payoffs over all possible strategies

Rather than use the normal form, economists analyze sequential dynamic games in their **extensive form**, which specifies the n players, the sequence in which they make their moves, the actions they can take at each move, the information that each player has about players' previous moves, and the payoff function over all possible strategies. We illustrate a sequential-move, two-stage game using the Stackelberg airline model (Chapter 13), where American chooses its output level before United does. For simplicity, we assume that American and United Airlines can choose only output levels of 96, 64, and 48 million passengers per quarter.

The normal-form representation of this game, Table 14.2, does not capture the sequential nature of the firms' moves. To demonstrate the role of sequential moves, we use an *extensive-form diagram* or *game tree*, Figure 14.1, which shows the order of the firms' moves, each firm's possible actions at the time of its move, and the resulting profits at the end of the game.

In the figure, each box is a point of decision by one of the firms, called a *decision node*. The name in the decision node box indicates that it is that player's turn to move. The lines or *branches* extending out of the box represent a complete list of the possible actions that the player can make at that point of the game. On the left side

Figure 14.1 Stackelberg Game Tree

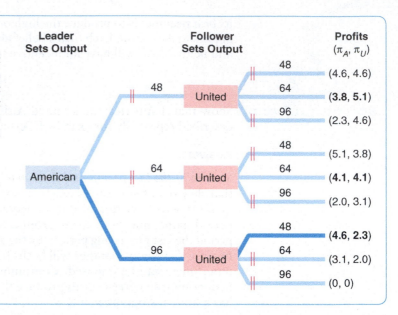

American, the leader firm, chooses its output level first. Given American's choice, United, the follower, picks an output level. The right side of the figure shows the firms' profits that result from these decisions. Two red lines through an action line indicate that the firm rejects that action.

of the figure, American, the leader, starts by picking one of the three output levels. In the middle of the figure, United, the follower, chooses one of the three quantities after learning the output level American chose. The right side of the figure shows the profits that American and United earn, given that they sequentially took the actions to reach this final branch. For instance, if American selects 64 and then United chooses 96, American earns $2.0 million profit per quarter and United earns $3.1 million.

subgame
all the subsequent decisions that players may make given the actions already taken and corresponding payoffs

Within this game are *subgames*. At a given stage, a **subgame** consists of all the subsequent decisions that players may make given the actions already taken and corresponding payoffs. The second stage, where United makes a choice, has three possible subgames. In Figure 14.1, if in the first stage American chooses $q_A = 48$, the relevant subgame is the top node in the second stage and its three branches. This game has four subgames. The second stage has three subgames in which United makes a decision given each of American's three possible first-stage actions. The fourth subgame is the entire game at the time of the first-stage decision.

Subgame Perfect Nash Equilibrium

In solving a problem of this sort, the grand thing is to be able to reason backward. —Sherlock Holmes (Sir Arthur Conan Doyle)

subgame perfect Nash equilibrium
players' strategies are a Nash equilibrium in every subgame

To predict the outcome of this sequential game, we introduce a stronger version of the Nash equilibrium concept. A set of strategies forms a **subgame perfect Nash equilibrium** if the players' strategies are a Nash equilibrium in every subgame. As the entire dynamic game is a subgame, a subgame perfect Nash equilibrium is also a Nash equilibrium. In contrast, in a simultaneous-move game such as the static prisoners' dilemma, the only subgame is the game itself, so the Nash equilibrium and the subgame perfect Nash equilibrium are the same.

Table 14.2 shows the normal-form representation of this game in which the Nash equilibrium for the simultaneous-move game is for each firm to choose 64. However, if the firms move sequentially, the subgame perfect Nash equilibrium results in a different outcome.

backward induction
first determine the best response by the last player to move, next determine the best response for the player who made the next-to-last move, then repeat the process back to the move at the beginning of the game

We can solve for the subgame perfect Nash equilibrium using **backward induction**, where we first determine the best response by the last player to move, next determine the best response for the player who made the next-to-last move, and then repeat the process until we reach the move at the beginning of the game. In our example, we work backward from the decision by the follower, United, to the decision by the leader, American, moving from the right to the left side of the game tree.

How should American, the leader, select its output in the first stage? For each possible quantity it can produce, American predicts what United will do and picks the output level that maximizes its own profit. Thus, to predict American's action in the first stage, American determines what United, the follower, will do in the second stage, given each possible output choice by American in the first stage. Using its conclusions about United's second-stage reaction, American makes its first-stage decision.

United, the follower, does not have a dominant strategy. The amount it chooses to produce depends on the quantity that American chose. If American chose 96, United's profit is $2.3 million if its output is 48, $2.0 million if it produces 64, and $0 if it picks a quantity of 96. Thus, if American chose 96, United's best response is 48. The double lines through the other two action lines show that United will not choose those actions.

Using the same reasoning, American determines how United will respond to each of American's possible actions, as the right side of the figure illustrates. American predicts that

- If American chooses 48, United will sell 64, so American's profit will be $3.8 million.
- If American chooses 64, United will sell 64, so American's profit will be $4.1 million.
- If American chooses 96, United will sell 48, so American's profit will be $4.6 million.

Thus, to maximize its profit, American chooses 96 in the first stage. United's strategy is to make its best response to American's first-stage action: United selects 64 if American chooses 48 or 64, and United picks 48 if American chooses 96. Thus, United responds in the second stage by selecting 48. In this subgame perfect Nash equilibrium, neither firm wants to change its strategy. Given that American Airlines sets its output at 96, United is using a strategy that maximizes its profit, $q_U = 48$, so it doesn't want to change. Similarly, given how United will respond to each possible American output level, American cannot make more profit than if it sells 96.

The subgame perfect Nash equilibrium requires players to believe that their opponents will act optimally—in their own best interests. No player has an incentive to deviate from the equilibrium strategies. The reason for adding the requirement of subgame perfection is that we want to explain what will happen if a player does not follow the equilibrium path. For example, if American does not choose its equilibrium output in the first stage, subgame perfection requires that United will still follow the strategy that maximizes its profit in the second stage conditional on American's actual output choice.

Not all Nash equilibria are subgame perfect Nash equilibria. For example, suppose that American's strategy is to pick 96 in the first stage, and United's strategy is to choose 96 if American selects 48 or 64, and 48 if American chooses 96. The outcome is the same as the subgame perfect Nash equilibrium we just derived because American selects 96, United chooses 48, and neither firm wants to deviate.[8] Thus, this set of

---

[8]Given United's strategy, American does not have any incentive to deviate. If American chooses 48 it will get $2.3 million and if it chooses 64 it will get $2.0 million, both of which are less than the $4.6 million if it chooses 96. And given American's strategy, no change in United's strategy would raise its profit.

strategies is a Nash equilibrium. However, this set of strategies is not a subgame perfect Nash equilibrium. Although this Nash equilibrium has the same equilibrium path as the subgame perfect Nash equilibrium, United's strategy differs from the equilibrium path. If American had selected 48 (or 64), United's strategy would not result in a Nash equilibrium. United would receive a higher profit if it produced 64 rather than the 96 that this strategy requires. Therefore, this Nash equilibrium is not subgame perfect.

This subgame perfect Nash equilibrium, or Stackelberg equilibrium, differs from the simultaneous-move, Nash-Cournot equilibrium. American, the Stackelberg leader, sells 50% more than the Cournot quantity, 64, and earns $4.6 million, which is 15% more than the Cournot level of profit, $4.1 million. United, the Stackelberg follower, sells a quantity, 48, and earns a profit, $2.3 million, both of which are less than the Cournot levels. Thus, although United has more information in the Stackelberg equilibrium than it does in the Cournot model—it knows American's output level—it is worse off than if both firms chose their actions simultaneously.

Come here! Don't make me run after you!

credible threat
an announcement that a firm will use a strategy that will harm its rival and that the rival believes because the firm benefits from using that strategy

Credibility

Why do the simultaneous-move and sequential-move games have different outcomes? Given the option to act first, American chooses a large output, 96, so that United's profit-maximizing action is to pick a relatively small output, 48. American benefits from moving first and choosing the Stackelberg leader quantity.

In the simultaneous-move game, why doesn't American announce that it will produce the Stackelberg leader's output to induce United to produce the Stackelberg follower's output level? The answer is that when the firms move simultaneously, United doesn't believe American's warning that it will produce a large quantity, because it is not in American's best interest to produce that large a quantity of output. For a firm's announced strategy to be a **credible threat**, rivals must believe that the firm's strategy is rational in the sense that it is in the firm's best interest to use it.[9] If American produced the leader's level of output and United produced the Cournot level, American's profit would be lower than if it too produced the Cournot level. Because American cannot be sure that United will believe its threat and reduce its output in the simultaneous-move game, American produces the Cournot output level. In contrast, in the sequential-move game, because American moves first, its commitment to produce a large quantity is credible.

The intuition for why commitment makes a threat credible is that of "burning bridges." If the general burns the bridge behind the army so that the troops can only

---

[9]No doubt you've been in a restaurant and listened to an exasperated father trying to control his brat with such extreme threats as "If you don't behave, you'll have to sit in the car while we eat dinner" or "If you don't behave, you'll never see television again." The kid, of course, does not view such threats as credible and continues to terrorize the restaurant—proving that the kid is a better game theorist than the father.

advance and not retreat, the army becomes a more fearsome foe—like a cornered animal. Similarly, by limiting its future options, a firm makes itself stronger.[10]

Not all firms can make credible threats, however, because not all firms can make commitments. Typically, for a threat to succeed, a firm must have an advantage that allows it to harm the other firm before that firm can retaliate. Identical firms that act simultaneously cannot credibly threaten each other. However, a firm may be able to make its threatened behavior believable if firms differ. An important difference is the ability of one firm to act before the other. For example, an incumbent firm could lobby for the passage of a law that forbids further entry.

Dynamic Entry Game

The Stackelberg game demonstrates that the leader firm can benefit from moving before the follower firm. In some markets, by moving first, a manager can act strategically to prevent potential rivals from entering the market. How can an *incumbent*, monopoly firm deter a (potential) *rival* from entering that market? Does it pay for the incumbent to take the actions that will deter entry?

The incumbent may prevent entry if it can make a creditable threat by acting first. However, a manager cannot deter entry merely by telling a potential rival, "Don't enter! This market ain't big enough for the two of us." The potential rival would merely laugh and suggest that the manager's firm exit if it doesn't want to share the market.

Exclusion Contracts We consider an example where the incumbent can pay a third-party to prevent entry. A mall has a single shoe store, the incumbent firm. If the incumbent pays the mall's owner b, a clause is added to their rental agreement that guarantees the incumbent the *exclusive right* to be the only shoe store in the mall. If this payment is made, the landlord agrees to rent the remaining space only to a restaurant, a toy store, or some other business that does not sell shoes. Should the shoe store pay?

The game tree in Figure 14.2 shows the two stages of the game involving the incumbent and its potential rival, another shoe store. In the first stage, the incumbent decides whether to pay b to prevent entry. In the second stage, the potential rival decides whether to enter. If it enters, it incurs a fixed fee of F to build its store in the mall.

The right side of the figure shows the incumbent's and the potential rival's profits (π_i, π_r) for each of the three possible outcomes. The outcome at the top of the figure shows that if the incumbent does not buy exclusivity and the potential rival does not enter, the incumbent earns the "monopoly" profit of $\pi_i = 10$ ($10 thousand) per month and its potential rival earns nothing, $\pi_r = 0$. The middle outcome shows that if the incumbent does not pay the exclusivity fee and the potential rival enters, the incumbent earns a duopoly profit of $\pi_i = 4$ and the rival earns the duopoly profit less its fixed cost, F, of entering, $\pi_r = 4 - F$. In the bottom outcome, the incumbent pays b for the exclusivity right so that it earns the monopoly profit less the exclusivity fee, $\pi_i = 10 - b$, and its potential rival earns nothing, $\pi_r = 0$.

To solve for the subgame perfect Nash equilibrium, we work backward, starting with the last decision, the potential rival's entry decision. The top portion of the game

---

[10]Some psychologists use the idea of commitment to treat behavioral problems. A psychologist may advise an author with writer's block to set up an irreversible procedure whereby if the author's book is not finished by a certain date, the author's check for $10,000 will be sent to the group the author hates most in the world—be it the Nazi Party, the Ku Klux Klan, or the National Save the Skeets Foundation. Such an irreversible commitment helps the author get the project done by raising the cost of failure. (We can imagine the author playing a game against the author's own better self.)

Figure 14.2 Game Tree: Whether an Incumbent Pays to Prevent Entry

If the potential rival stays out of the market, it makes no profit, $\pi_r = 0$, and the incumbent firm makes the monopoly profit, $\pi_i = 10$. If the potential rival enters, the incumbent earns the duopoly profit of 4 and the rival makes $4 - F$, where F is its fixed cost of entry. If the duopoly profit, 4, is less than F, entry does not occur. Otherwise, entry occurs unless the incumbent acts to deter entry by paying for exclusive rights to be the only shoe store in the mall. The incumbent pays the landlord only if $10 - b > 4$.

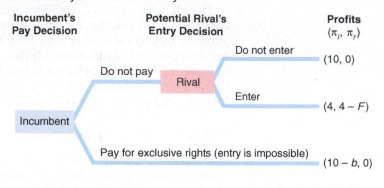

tree shows what happens if the incumbent does not pay the landlord to prevent entry. The potential rival enters if it earns more from entering, $\pi_r = 4 - F$, than if it stays out of the market, $\pi_r = 0$. That is, the potential rival enters if $F \leq 4$. In the bottom portion of the game tree, where the incumbent pays b for an exclusive contract that prevents entry, the potential rival has no possible action.

Which of the three possible outcomes occurs depends on the incumbent's exclusivity fee, b, and the potential rival's fixed cost of entering the market, F:

- **Blockaded entry** ($F > 4$): The potential rival chooses not to enter even if the incumbent does not pay to have an exclusive contract, so $\pi_r = 0$. The incumbent avoids spending b and still earns the monopoly profit, $\pi_i = 10$.
- **Deterred entry** ($F \leq 4, b \leq 6$): Because $F \leq 4$, entry will occur unless the incumbent pays the exclusivity fee. The incumbent chooses to pay the exclusivity fee, b, because its profit from doing so, $\pi_i = 10 - b \geq 4$, is at least as large as what it earns if it permits entry and earns the duopoly profit, $\pi_i = 4$. Because the rival does not enter, it earns nothing: $\pi_r = 0$.
- **Accommodated entry** ($F \leq 4, b > 6$): Entry will occur unless the incumbent pays the fee because the rival's fixed costs are less than or equal to 4. The incumbent does not pay for an exclusive contract. The exclusivity fee is so high that the incumbent earns more by allowing entry, $\pi_i = 4$, than it earns if it pays for exclusivity, $\pi_i = 10 - b < 4$. Thus, the incumbent earns the duopoly profit, $\pi_i = 4$, and the rival makes $\pi_r = 4 - F$.

In short, the incumbent does not pay for an exclusive contract if the potential rival's cost of entry is prohibitively high ($F > 4$) or if the cost of the exclusive contract is too high ($b > 6$).

Application

Dominant Airlines

Airlines that were early entrants at busy airports often control most boarding gates and slots—the right to take off or land at a particular time—through long-term leases. According to a 2012 U.S. Government Accountability Office report, "Generally, once airlines have been allocated slots . . ., so long as they comply with the rules, they may keep them indefinitely. . . ." That makes it difficult for new firms to be able to enter and fly many routes out of that airport.

It pays for airlines to buy up gates and slots to prevent rivals from entering. The markup of price over marginal cost is much greater on routes in which one airline carries most of the passengers than on other routes (Weiher et al., 2002). Unfortunately, a single firm is the only carrier or the dominant carrier on 58% of all U.S. domestic routes. A monopoly serves 18% of all routes. Duopolies control 19% of the routes.

Although nearly two-thirds of all routes have three or more carriers, one or two firms dominate virtually all routes in part because of their gate and slotting rights. We call a carrier a *dominant firm* if it has at least 60% of ticket sales by value but is not a monopoly. We call two carriers a *dominant pair* if they collectively have at least 60% of the market but neither firm is a dominant firm and three or more firms fly this route. All but 0.1% of routes have a monopoly (18%), a dominant firm (40%), or a dominant pair (42%).

The price is 3.3 times marginal cost for monopolies and 3.1 times marginal cost for dominant firms. In contrast, over the sample period, the average price is only 1.2 times marginal cost for dominant pairs. On average across all U.S. routes and market structures, price is slightly more than double (2.1 times) marginal cost.

limit pricing
a firm sets its price (or its output) so that another firm cannot enter the market profitably

Limit Pricing A firm is **limit pricing** if it sets its price (or, equivalently, its output) so that another firm cannot enter the market profitably. For example, the incumbent could set a price below the potential rival's marginal cost so entry would be unprofitable. Or the incumbent could produce so much output that the price is very low and too few customers remain for the potential rival to make a profit. However, to successfully limit price, a firm has to have an advantage over its rivals, as the following example illustrates.

An incumbent firm is making a large, monopoly profit, which attracts the interest of a potential rival. The incumbent could threaten that it will limit price if entry occurs. It could announce that, after entry, it will charge a price so low that the other firm will make a loss. This threat will only work if the threat is credible. It is not credible if the two firms have identical costs and market demand is adequate to support both firms. Once entry occurs, it is in the incumbent's best interest to charge the duopoly price and make a profit rather than charge such a low price that everyone loses money. Realizing that the incumbent won't actually limit price, the potential rival ignores the threat and enters.

For the threat of limit pricing to be credible, the incumbent must have an advantage over its rival. For example, if the incumbent's costs are lower than those of the potential rival, the incumbent can charge a price so low that the rival would lose money while the incumbent earns a higher profit than if it allows entry.

Another example is an extreme form of the Stackelberg oligopoly example. The Stackelberg leader acts first and produces a large quantity so that the follower produces a smaller quantity. Depending on the demand curve and the firms' costs, it may be even more profitable for the leader to produce such a large quantity that the follower cannot earn a profit. That is, the leader makes limit pricing credible by committing to provide a very large output level.

Solved Problem 14.3

In the first stage of a game between an incumbent and a potential rival, the incumbent builds its plant using either an inflexible technology that allows it to produce only a (large) fixed quantity, or a flexible technology that allows it to produce small or large quantities. In the second stage, the potential rival decides whether to enter. With the inflexible technology, the incumbent makes so much output that its threat to limit price is credible, as the following game tree illustrates. What strategy (technology) maximizes the incumbent's profit?

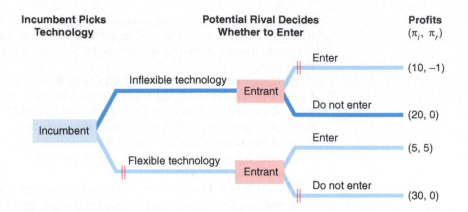

| Incumbent Picks Technology | Potential Rival Decides Whether to Enter | Profits (π_i, π_r) |

Answer

1. *Work backward by determining the potential rival's best strategy conditional on each possible action by the incumbent.* This game has two proper subgames. The upper right subgame shows the profits if the potential rival enters or if it does not enter given that the incumbent uses the inflexible technology. The potential rival loses money ($\pi_r = -1$) if it enters, but breaks even ($\pi_r = 0$) if it doesn't, so it does not enter. In the lower right subgame, the potential rival decides whether to enter given that the incumbent is using the flexible technology. Here, the potential rival prefers to enter and earn a profit of $\pi_r = 5$ rather than stay out and earn nothing.

2. *Given the responses by the potential rival to each of the incumbent's strategies, determine the incumbent's best strategy.* If the incumbent uses the flexible technology, entry occurs, and the incumbent earns $\pi_i = 5$. However, if the incumbent uses the inflexible technology, the other firm does not enter, and the incumbent's profit is $\pi_i = 20$. Thus, the incumbent chooses the inflexible technology.

Comment: The incumbent would earn even a higher profit with the flexible technology if no entry occurs. However, if the incumbent chooses the flexible technology, its rival will enter, so the incumbent is better off committing to the inflexible technology. The inflexible technology serves as a credible threat that the incumbent will limit price.

14.4 Auctions

To this point, we have examined games in which players have complete information about payoff functions. We now turn to an important game, the *auction*, in which players devise bidding strategies without knowing other players' payoff functions.

auction
a sale in which property or a service is sold to the highest bidder

An **auction** is a sale in which a good or service is sold to the highest bidder. A substantial amount of exchange takes place through auctions. Government contracts are typically awarded using procurement auctions. In recent years, governments have auctioned portions of the airwaves for radio stations, mobile phones, and wireless Internet access and have used auctions to set up electricity and transport markets. Other goods commonly sold at auction are natural resources such as timber, as well as houses, cars, agricultural produce, horses, antiques, and art. In this section, we first consider the various types of auctions and then investigate how the rules of the auction influence buyers' strategies.

Elements of Auctions

Before deciding what strategy to use when bidding in an auction, one needs to know the rules of the game. Auctions have three key components: the number of units being sold, the format of the bidding, and the value that potential bidders place on the good.

Number of Units Auctions can be used to sell one or many units of a good. In 2004, Google auctioned its initial public offering of many identical shares of stock at one time. In many other auctions, a single good—such as an original painting—is sold. For simplicity in this discussion, we concentrate on auctions where a single, indivisible item is sold.

Format of Bidding How auctions are conducted varies greatly. However, most approaches are variants of the *English auction*, the *Dutch auction*, or the *sealed-bid auction*.

- **English auction.** In the United States and Britain, almost everyone has seen an *English* or *ascending-bid auction*, at least in the movies. The auctioneer starts the bidding at the lowest price that is acceptable to the seller and then repeatedly encourages potential buyers to bid more than the previous highest bidder. The auction ends when no one is willing to bid more than the current highest bid: "Going, going, gone!" The good is sold to the last bidder for the highest bid. Sotheby's and Christie's use English auctions to sell art and antiques.
- **Dutch auction.** A *Dutch auction* or *descending-bid auction* ends dramatically with the first "bid." The seller starts by asking if anyone wants to buy at a relatively high price. The seller reduces the price by given increments until someone accepts the offered price and buys at that price. Variants of Dutch auctions are often used to sell multiple goods at once, such as in Google's initial public offering auction and the U.S. Treasury's sales of Treasury bills.
- **Sealed-bid auction.** In a *sealed-bid auction*, everyone submits a bid simultaneously without seeing anyone else's bid (for example, by submitting each bid in a sealed envelope), and the highest bidder wins. The price the winner pays depends on whether it is a first-price auction or a second-price auction. In a *first-price auction*, the winner pays its own, highest bid. Governments often use this type of auction. In a *second-price auction*, the winner pays the amount bid by the second-highest bidder. Many computer auction houses use a variant of the second-price auction.

For example, you bid on eBay by specifying the maximum amount you are willing to bid. If your maximum is greater than the maximum bid of other participants, eBay's computer places a bid on your behalf that is a small increment above the maximum bid of the second-highest bidder. This system differs from the traditional sealed-bid auction in that people can continue to bid until the official end-time of the auction, and potential bidders know the current bid price (but not the maximum that the highest bidder is willing to pay). Thus, eBay has some of the characteristics of an English auction.

Value Auctioned goods are normally described as having a *private value* or a *common value*. Typically, this distinction turns on whether the good is unique.

- **Private value.** If each potential bidder places a different personal value on the good, we say that the good has a *private value*. Individual bidders know how much the good is worth to them but not how much other bidders value it. The archetypical example is an original work of art about which people differ greatly as to how much they value it.

■ **Common value.** Many auctions involve a good that has the same fundamental value to everyone, but no buyer knows exactly what that *common value* is. For example, in a timber auction, firms bid on all the trees in a given area. All firms know what the current price of lumber is; however, they do not know exactly how many board feet of lumber are contained in the trees.

In many actual auctions, goods have both private value and common value. For example, in the tree auction, bidding firms may differ not only in their estimates of the amount of lumber in the trees (common value), but also in their costs of harvesting (private value).

Bidding Strategies in Private-Value Auctions

A potential buyer's optimal strategy depends on the number of units, the format, and the type of values in an auction. For specificity, we examine auctions in which each bidder places a different private value on a single, indivisible good.

Second-Price Auction Strategies According to eBay, if you choose to bid on an item in its second-price auction, you should "enter the maximum amount you are willing to pay for the item" (**pages.ebay.com/education/gettingstarted/bidding.html**). Is eBay's advice correct?

In a traditional sealed-bid, second-price auction, bidding your highest value *weakly dominates* all other bidding strategies: The strategy of bidding your maximum value leaves you *as well off* as, or *better off* than, bidding any other value. The amount that you bid affects whether you win, but it does not affect how much you pay if you win, which equals the second-highest bid.

Suppose that you value a folk art carving at $100. If the highest amount that any other participant is willing to bid is $85 and you place a bid greater than $85, you will buy the carving for $85 and receive $15 (= $100 − $85) of consumer surplus. Other bidders pay nothing and gain no consumer surplus.

Should you ever bid more than your value? Suppose that you bid $120. You face three possibilities. First, if the highest bid of your rivals is greater than $120, then you do not buy the good and receive no consumer surplus. This outcome is the same as what you would have received if you had bid $100, so bidding higher than $100 does not benefit you.

Second, if the highest alternative bid is less than $100, then you win and receive the same consumer surplus that you would have received had you bid $100. Again, bidding higher does not affect the outcome.

Third, if the highest bid by a rival were an amount between $100 and $120— say, $110—then bidding more than your maximum value causes you to win, but you purchase the good for more than you value it, so you receive negative consumer surplus: −$10 (= $100 − $110). In contrast, if you had bid your maximum value, you would not have won, and your consumer surplus would have been zero—which is better than losing $10. Thus, bidding more than your maximum value can never make you better off than bidding your maximum value and you may suffer.

Should you ever bid less than your maximum value, say, $90? No, because you only lower the odds of winning without affecting the price that you pay if you do win. If the highest alternative bid is less than $90 or greater than your value, you receive the same consumer surplus by bidding $90 as you would by bidding $100. However, if the highest alternative bid lies between $90 and $100, you will lose the auction and give up positive consumer surplus by underbidding.

Thus, you do as well or better by bidding your value than by over- or underbidding. This argument does not turn on whether or not you know other bidders' valuation. If you know your own value but not other bidders' values, bidding your value is your best strategy. If everyone follows this strategy, the person who places the highest value on the good will win and will pay the second-highest value.

English Auction Strategy Suppose instead that the seller uses an English auction to sell the carving to bidders with various private values. Your best strategy is to raise the current highest bid as long as your bid is less than the value you place on the good, $100. If the current bid is $85, you should increase your bid by the smallest permitted amount, say, $86, which is less than your value. If no one raises the bid further, you win and receive a positive surplus of $14. By the same reasoning, it always pays to increase your bid up to $100, where you receive zero surplus if you win.

However, it never pays to bid more than $100. The best outcome that you can hope for is to lose and receive zero surplus. Were you to win, you would have negative surplus.

If all participants bid up to their value, the winner will pay slightly more than the value of the second-highest bidder. Thus, the outcome is essentially the same as in the sealed-bid, second-price auction.

Equivalence of Auction Outcomes For Dutch or first-price sealed-bid auctions, one can show that participants will shave their bids to less than their value. The basic intuition is that you do not know the values of the other bidders. Reducing your bid reduces the probability that you win but increases your consumer surplus if you win. Your optimal bid, which balances these two effects, is lower than your actual value. Your bid depends on your beliefs about the strategies of your rivals. It can be shown that the best strategy is to bid an amount that is equal to or slightly greater than what you expect will be the second-highest bid, given that your value is the highest.

Thus, the expected outcome is the same under each format for private-value auctions: The winner is the person with the highest value, and the winner pays roughly the second-highest value. According to the Revenue Equivalence Theorem (Klemperer, 2004), under certain plausible conditions we would expect the same revenue from any auction in which the winner is the person who places the highest value on the good.

Winner's Curse

A phenomenon occurs in common-value auctions that does not occur in private-value auctions. The **winner's curse** is that the auction winner's bid exceeds the item's common value. The overbidding occurs when bidders are uncertain about the true value of the good.

When the government auctions off timber on a plot of land, potential bidders may differ in their estimates of how many board feet of lumber are available on that land. The higher one's estimate, the more likely that one will make the winning bid. If the average bid is accurate, then the high bid is probably excessive. Thus, the winner's curse is paying too much.

I can minimize the likelihood of falling prey to the winner's curse by shading my bid: reducing the bid below my estimate. I know that if I win, I am probably overestimating the value of the good. The amount by which I should shade my bid depends on the number of other bidders, because the more bidders, the more likely that the winning bid is an overestimate.

winner's curse
auction winner's bid
exceeds an item's
common value

Because intelligent bidders shade their bids, sellers can do better with an English auction than with a sealed-bid auction. In an English auction, bidders revise their views about the object's value as they watch others bid.

Application **Bidder's Curse**	What's the maximum you would bid for an item that you know that you can buy for a fixed price of p? No matter how much you value the good, it doesn't make sense to bid more than p. Yet, people commonly do that on eBay. Lee and Malmendier (2011) call bidding more than what should be one's valuation—here, the fixed price—the *bidder's curse*.

They examined eBay auctions of a board game, Cashflow 101, a game that is supposed to help people better understand their finances. A search on eBay for Cashflow 101 not only listed the auctions but also the availability of the game for a fixed price. During the period studied, the game was continuously available for a fixed price on the eBay site (with identical or better quality and seller reputation and lower shipping cost).

Even if only a few buyers overbid, they affect the auction price and who wins. The auction price exceeded the fixed price in 42% of the auctions. The average overpayment was 10% of the fixed price. This overbidding was caused by a small number of bidders—only 17% bid above the fixed price. However, people who bid too much are disproportionately likely to win the auction and, hence, determine the winning price.

One possible behavioral economics explanation is that bidders paid limited attention to the fixed-price option. Lee and Malmendier found that overbidding was less likely the closer the fixed price appeared on the same screen to the auction and hence the more likely that bidders would notice the fixed-price listing.

Another explanation is lack of bidding experience. Garratt et al. (2012) conducted an experimental sealed-bid, second-price auction under "laboratory" settings. They found that inexperienced bidders—college students—were more likely to overbid than underbid. In contrast, experienced eBay bidders did not exhibit a systematic bias: They were just as likely to underbid as to overbid. That is, although experienced bidders occasionally make random mistakes, they do not systematically overbid unlike inexperienced people.

14.5 Behavioral Game Theory

We normally assume that people are rational in the sense that they optimize using all available information. However, they may be subject to psychological biases and may have limited powers of calculation that causes them to act irrationally, as described in the Application "Bidder's Curse." Such possibilities are the domain of behavioral economics (Chapters 4 and 11), which seeks to augment the rational economic model so as to better understand and predict economic decision making.

Another example of nonoptimal strategies occurs in *ultimatum games*. People often face an *ultimatum*, where one person (the *proposer*) makes a "take it or leave it" offer to another (the *responder*). No matter how long the parties have negotiated, once an ultimatum is issued, the responder has to accept or reject the offer with no opportunity to make a counter-offer. An ultimatum can be viewed as a sequential game in which the proposer moves first and the responder moves second.

Application

GM's Ultimatum

In 2009, General Motors (GM) was struggling financially and planned to shut down about one-fourth of its dealerships in the United States and Canada.[11] Because GM was concerned that dealer opposition could cause delays and impose other costs, it offered dealers slated for closure an ultimatum. They would receive a (small) payment from GM if they did not oppose the restructuring plan.

Dealers could accept the ultimatum and get something, or they could reject the offer, oppose the reorganization, and receive nothing. Although it was irrational, some dealers rejected the ultimatum and loudly complained that GM was "high-handed, oppressive, and patently unfair." In 2011, some terminated Canadian dealerships filed a class-action suit against GM of Canada. The case was still moving forward at a glacial pace in 2013, using up resources as it proceeded.

An Experiment The possibility that someone might turn down an offer even at some personal cost is important in business and personal negotiations. To gain insight into real decisions, Camerer (2004) conducted an ultimatum experiment.

A group of student participants meets in a computer lab. Each person is designated as either a proposer or a responder. Using the computers, each proposer is matched (anonymously) with one responder. The game is based on dividing $10. Each proposer makes an ultimatum offer to the responder of a particular amount. A responder who accepts receives the amount offered and the proposer gets the rest of the $10. If the responder rejects the offer, both players get nothing.

To find the rational, subgame perfect solution, we use backward induction. In the second stage, the responder should accept if the offer x is positive. Thus in the first stage, the proposer should offer the lowest possible positive amount.

However, such rational behavior is not a good predictor of actual outcomes. The lowest possible offer is rarely made and, when it is, it is usually rejected. Thus, a proposer who makes the mistake of expecting the responder to be fully rational is likely to receive nothing. The most common range for offers is between $3 and $4—far more than the "rational" minimum offer. Offers less than $2 are relatively rare and, when they do occur, are turned down about half the time.

One concern about such experiments is that the payoffs are small enough that not all participants take the game seriously. However, when the total amount to be divided was increased to $100, the results were essentially unchanged: The typical offer remained between 30% and 40% of the total. If anything, responders are even more likely to turn down lowball offers when the stakes are higher.

Reciprocity Some responders who reject lowball offers feel the proposer is being greedy and would prefer to make a small sacrifice rather than reward such behavior. Some responders are angered by low offers, some feel insulted, and some feel that they should oppose "unfair" behavior. Most proposers anticipate such feelings and offer a significant amount to the responder, but almost always less than 50%.

Apparently, most people accept that the advantage of moving first should provide some extra benefit to proposers, but not too much. Moreover, they believe in *reciprocity*. If others treat us well, we want to return the favor. If they treat us badly, we want to "get even" and will retaliate if the cost does not seem excessive. Thus, if a proposer makes a low offer, many responders are willing to give up something to punish the proposer, using "an eye for an eye" philosophy.

---

[11]Robert Schoenberger, "GM Sends Ultimatums to All Its 6000 US dealers," *Cleveland Plain Dealer*, June 2, 2009; and "GM Dealers Sue to Keep Doors Open," *Toronto Star*, November 27, 2009.

Eckel and Grossman (1996) found that men are more likely than women to punish if the personal cost is high in an ultimatum game. They speculate that this difference may explain gender patterns in wages and unemployment during downturns, where men are more likely to rigidly insist on a given wage than are women, who are more flexible.

Challenge Solution

Competing E-book Standards

We can use all the methods that we've covered in this chapter to analyze the Challenge questions posed at the beginning of the chapter about a game where e-book reader manufacturers choose e-book standards. We'll start by answering the question about the outcome if firms had engaged in a simultaneous-move game, where firms may use pure or mixed strategies. We'll then address the question about the outcome given that Amazon entered the market first so it chose its standard before other firms using a sequential-move game, where we'll solve for the subgame perfect Nash equilibrium.

Consider a simplified simultaneous-move game with two players, Amazon and the group of all other firms (Other group), that choose between two standards, Amazon's AZW and the open-source EPUB. Depending on the payoffs in the normal-form game, it is possible that only one standard and one group of firms survives in the Nash equilibrium (similar to the simultaneous-entry game in Table 14.3). Another possibility is that the firms adopt a single standard (like the universally used MP3 standard for digital music players). Suppose that the payoff matrix is

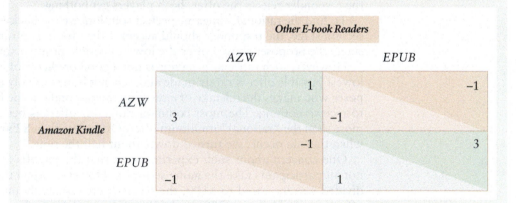

If the firms move simultaneously and can choose either standard, is a pure-strategy equilibrium possible? In the table, we add light-green triangles for Amazon and dark-green triangles for the Other group to the relevant cells in the payoff matrix to indicate the best responses to its rival's strategy. The game has two Nash equilibria in which Amazon and the other manufacturers choose the same standard. If both choose the AZW standard, neither Amazon nor the Other group would change its strategy if it knew that its rival was using the AZW standard. The Other group's profit falls from 1 to −1 if it changes its strategy from the AZW to the EPUB standard, whereas Amazon's profit falls from 3 to −1 if it makes that change. Similarly, no firm would change its strategy from the EPUB standard if it believed that the Other group would use the EPUB standard.[12]

What are the mixed-strategy equilibria? If the Other group chooses the AZW standard with a probability of θ_O, Amazon's expected profit is

---

[12]This game is of the same form as the game called *the battle of the sexes*. In that game, the husband likes to go to the mountains on vacation, and the wife prefers the ocean, but they both prefer to take their vacations together.

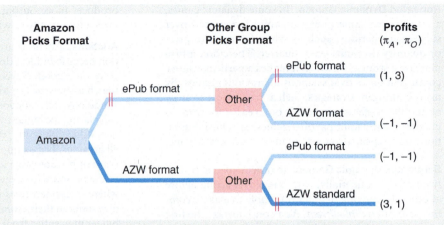

$(3 \times \theta_O) + (-1 \times [1 - \theta_O]) = 4\theta_O - 1$ if it chooses the AZW standard and $(-1 \times \theta_O) + (1 \times [1 - \theta_O]) = 1 - 2\theta_O$ if it chooses the EPUB standard. For Amazon to be indifferent between these two actions, its expected profits must be equal: $4\theta_O - 1 = 1 - 2\theta_O$. That is, if $\theta_O = \frac{1}{3}$, Amazon is indifferent between choosing either standard. Similarly, if Amazon selects the AZW standard with a probability of $\theta_A = \frac{2}{3}$, the Other group is indifferent between choosing either of the two standards.

Finally, we consider what happens if Amazon acts first (which is what actually happened). The figure shows the extensive-form diagram given that Amazon moved first and then the Other group moved. The figure assumes that the Other group could choose to adopt either the AZW or EPUB format. If Amazon initially chose the AZW standard, then the Other group would choose the AZW standard because its profit, π_0, would be higher (1) than if it chose EPUB (−1). Similarly, if Amazon initially chose the EPUB standard, so would the Other group. Because Amazon's profit, π_A, would be greater if it chose the AZW standard (3) than if it chose the EPUB standard (1), it prefers the AZW standard. Thus, with a first-mover advantage, Amazon chose the AZW standard, which the Other group would accept.

However, this analysis does not fully correspond to reality. We have assumed that other firms could use the AZW standard if they wanted. So far, Amazon has only been willing to let its AZW standard be used on Apple iPhones and iPads. Given its head start, Amazon may hope that it can drive the other e-reader firms out of business by not allowing them to use the AZW standard.

Summary

The set of tools that economists use to analyze conflict and cooperation among players (such as firms) is called game theory. Each player adopts a strategy or battle plan to compete with other firms. Economists typically assume that players have *common knowledge* about the rules of the game, the payoff functions, and other players' knowledge about these issues. In many games, players have *complete information* about how payoffs depend on the strategies of all players. In some games, players have *perfect information* about players' previous moves.

1. **Static Games.** In a static game, such as in the Cournot model or the prisoners' dilemma game, players each make one move simultaneously. Economists

use a normal-form representation or payoff matrix to analyze a static game. Typically, economists study static games in which players have complete information about the payoff function—the payoff to any player conditional on the actions all players take—but imperfect information about how their rivals behave because they act simultaneously. The set of players' strategies is a Nash equilibrium if, given that all other players use these strategies, no player can obtain a higher payoff by choosing a different strategy. A given game may have multiple Nash equilibria including pure-strategy and mixed-strategy Nash equilibria. A Nash equilibria in static games does not necessarily maximize the joint payoffs of all the players.

2. **Repeated Dynamic Games.** In some dynamic games, a constituent game (a static game) is repeated over subsequent periods, such as when firms make price or quantity decisions every quarter. Therefore, a firm may use a strategy in which it makes a particular move contingent on its rival's actions in previous periods. By using contingent strategies, such as a tit-for-tat strategy or another trigger strategy, it is often easier for firms to maximize their joint payoff—achieve a collusive solution—in a repeated game than in a single-period game.

3. **Sequential Dynamic Games.** In other dynamic games, firms move sequentially, with one player acting before another. By moving first, a firm is able to make a *commitment* or *credible threat*. As a consequence, the first mover may receive a higher profit than if the firms act simultaneously. For example, in the Stackelberg oligopoly model, one firm is a *leader* in a sequential game and therefore chooses its output level before rival firms (followers) choose theirs. Applying backward induction, the leader anticipates a follower's reaction and chooses its best output accordingly in the first stage. This first-stage output is a commitment that allows the leader to gain a first-mover advantage. The leader produces more output and earns higher profits than does a follower firm with the same costs.

4. **Auctions.** Auctions are games of incomplete information because bidders do not know the valuation others place on a good. Buyers' optimal strategies depend on the characteristics of an auction. Under fairly general conditions, if the auction rules result in a win by the person placing the highest value on a good that various bidders value differently, the expected price is the same in all auctions. For example, the expected price in various types of private-value auctions is the value of the good to the person who values it second highest. In auctions where everyone values the good the same, though they may differ in their estimates of that value, the successful bidder may suffer from the winner's curse—paying too much—unless bidders shade their bids to compensate for their overoptimistic estimation of the good's value.

5. **Behavioral Game Theory.** People may not use rational strategies because of psychological bias, lack of reasoning ability, or their belief that other managers will not use rational strategies. The ultimatum game illustrates that irrational strategies are commonly used in certain circumstances.

Questions

All questions are available on MyEconLab; * = *answer appears at the back of this book;* **A** = *algebra problem;* **C** = *calculus problem.*

1. Static Games

*1.1 Show the payoff matrix and explain the reasoning in the prisoners' dilemma example where Larry and Duncan, possible criminals, will get one year in prison if neither talks; if one talks, one goes free and the other gets five years; and if both talk, both get two years. (*Note:* The payoffs are negative because they represent years in jail, which is a bad.)

1.2 Two firms compete by advertising. Given the payoff matrix to this advertising game, identify each firm's best response to its rival's possible actions. Does either firm have a dominant strategy? What is the Nash equilibrium?

		Firm 1	
		Do Not Advertise	Advertise
Firm 2	Do Not Advertise	1 / 2	0 / 0
	Advertise	2 / 4	1 / 3

1.3 Two firms face the following profit matrix:

		Firm 1	
		Low Price	High Price
Firm 2	Low Price	0 / 2	2 / 1
	High Price	6 / 0	7 / 6

Is it true that, given this profit matrix, Firm 2 wants to match Firm 1's price, but Firm 1 does not want to match Firm 2's price? Does either firm have a dominant strategy? What is the Nash equilibrium in this game? Explain.

*1.4 Suppose that Toyota and GM are considering entering a new market for electric automobiles and that their profits (in millions of dollars) from entering or staying out of the market are

GM

Toyota		Enter	Do Not Enter
		−40	0
Enter			
		10	250
		200	0
Do Not Enter			
		0	0

If the firms make their decisions simultaneously, do either or both firms enter? How would your answer change if the U.S. government committed to paying GM a lump-sum subsidy of $50 million on the condition that it would produce this new type of car?

1.5 Two stars—the 100-meter gold medalist and the 200-meter gold medalist—agree to a 150-meter duel. Before the race, each athlete decides whether to improve his performance by taking anabolic steroids. If one athlete takes steroids and the other doesn't, the first athlete will win. Each athlete's utility payoff is 20 from winning the race, 10 from tying, and 0 from losing. Each athlete's utility of taking steroids is −6. Model this scenario as a game in which the players simultaneously decide whether to take steroids.

a. What is the Nash equilibrium? Is the game a prisoners' dilemma? Explain.

b. Suppose that one athlete's utility of taking steroids is −12, while the other's remains −6. What is the Nash equilibrium? Is the game a prisoners' dilemma?

1.6 Suppose Procter & Gamble (PG) and Johnson & Johnson (JNJ) are simultaneously considering new advertising campaigns. Each firm may choose a high, medium, or low level of advertising. What are each firm's best responses to its rival's strategies? Does either firm have a dominant strategy? What is the Nash equilibrium in this game?

PG

JNJ		High	Medium	Low
		1	2	3
High				
		1	3	5
		3	4	5
Medium				
		2	4	6
		5	6	5
Low				
		3	5	7

1.7 Firm 1 and Firm 2 manufacture blankets. They compete in quality. Given their payoff matrix, identify each firm's best response to its rival's actions. What is the Nash equilibrium?

Firm 1

Firm 2		Low	Medium	High
		1	2	3
Low				
		1	2	5
		3	4	8
Medium				
		3	4	3
		6	6	5
High				
		2	5	4

1.8 Modify the previous question so that if Firm 1 chooses High and Firm 2 chooses Low (the upper right corner), Firm 1 receives 1 rather than 3. How does that change your answer?

1.9 In their study of cigarette advertising, Roberts and Samuelson (1988) found that the advertising of a particular brand affects overall market demand for cigarettes but does not affect the brand's share of market sales. Suppose the demand for brand i is $q_i = a + b(A_i + A_j)^{0.5}$, where A_i is brand i's advertising expenditure. Brand i's profit function is $\pi_i = p_i(a + b(A_i + A_j)^{0.5}) - A_i$.

a. Does brand B's advertising expenditure affect A's market share, $q_A/(q_A + q_B)$?

b. In terms of a and b, what are the Nash equilibrium advertising expenditures? How does an increase in b affect the equilibrium expenditures? **C**

1.10 Takashi Hashiyama, president of the Japanese electronics firm Maspro Denkoh Corporation, was torn between having Christie's or Sotheby's auction the company's $20 million art collection, which included a van Gogh, a Cézanne, and an early Picasso (Carol Vogel, "Rock, Paper, Payoff," *New York Times*, April 29, 2005, A1, A24). He resolved the issue by having the two auction houses' representatives compete in the playground game of rock-paper-scissors. A rock (fist) breaks scissors (two fingers sticking out), scissors cut paper (flat hand), and paper smothers rock. At stake were several million dollars in commissions. Christie's won: scissors beat paper.

a. Show the profit or payoff matrix for this rock-paper-scissors game where the payoff is −1 if you lose, 0 if you tie, and 1 if you win.

b. Sotheby's expert in Impressionist and modern art said, "[T]his is a game of chance, so we didn't really give it much thought. We had no strategy in mind." In contrast, the president of Christie's in Japan researched the psychology of the game and consulted with the 11-year-old twin daughters of the director of the Impressionist and modern art department. One of these girls said, "Everybody knows you always start with scissors. Rock is way too obvious, and scissors beats paper." The other opined, "Since they were beginners, scissors was definitely the safest." Evaluate these comments on strategy. What strategy would you recommend if you knew that your rival was consulting with 11-year-old girls? In general, what pure or mixed strategy would you have recommended, and why?

1.11 Suppose that you and a friend play a "matching pennies" game in which each of you uncovers a penny. If both pennies show heads or both show tails, you keep both. If one shows heads and the other shows tails, your friend keeps them. Show the payoff matrix. What, if any, is the pure-strategy Nash equilibrium to this game? Is there a mixed-strategy Nash equilibrium? If so, what is it? **A**

*1.12 Two firms face the following payoff matrix:

Firm 1

	Low Price	High Price
Low Price	0 / 2	2 / 1
High Price	7 / 0	6 / 6

(Firm 2 labels the rows; cell entries show Firm 2 payoff (lower-left) and Firm 1 payoff (upper-right).)

Given these profits, Firm 2 wants to match Firm 1's price, but Firm 1 does not want to match Firm 2's price. Does either firm have a dominant strategy? Does this game have a unique, pure-strategy Nash equilibrium? Identify all pure- and mixed-strategy Nash equilibria. (*Hint*: See Solved Problem 14.1.) **A**

1.13 Two guys suffering from testosterone poisoning drive toward each other in the middle of a road. As they approach the impact point, each has the option of continuing to drive down the middle of the road or to swerve. Both believe that if only one driver swerves, that driver loses face (payoff = 0) and the other gains in self-esteem (payoff = 2). If neither swerves, they are maimed or killed (payoff = −10). If both swerve, no harm is done to either (payoff = 1). Show the payoff matrix for the two drivers engaged in this game of chicken. Determine the Nash equilibria for this game. (*Hint*: See Solved Problem 14.1.) **A**

1.14 Modify the payoff matrix in the game of chicken in the previous question so that the payoff is −2 if neither driver swerves. How does the equilibrium change? (*Hint*: See Solved Problem 14.1.) **A**

1.15 Lori employs Max. She wants him to work hard rather than to loaf. She considers offering him a bonus or not giving him one. All else the same, Max prefers to loaf.

Max

	Work	Loaf
Bonus	1 / 2	−1 / 3
No Bonus	3 / −1	0 / 0

(Lori labels the rows; in each cell Lori's payoff is lower-left, Max's payoff is upper-right.)

If they choose actions simultaneously, what are their strategies? Why does this game have a different type of equilibrium than the game in Solved Problem 14.1? **A**

1.16 Show that advertising is a dominant strategy for both firms in both panels of Table 14.4. Explain why that set of strategies is a Nash equilibrium.

2. Repeated Dynamic Games

2.1 In a repeated game, how does the outcome differ if firms know that the game will be (a) repeated indefinitely, (b) repeated a known, finite number of times, and (c) repeated a finite number of times but the firms are always unsure whether the current period will be the last? (*Hint*: See Solved Problem 14.2.)

*2.2 In the repeated-game airline example in Solved Problem 14.2, what happens if the players know the game will last only five periods? What happens if the game is played forever but the managers of one or both firms care only about current profit?

3. Sequential Dynamic Games

*3.1 Two firms are planning to sell 10 or 20 units of their goods and face the following profit matrix:

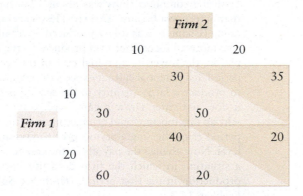

Firm 2

		10	20
Firm 1	**10**	30 / 30	35 / 50
	20	40 / 60	20 / 20

a. What is the Nash equilibrium if both firms make their decisions simultaneously?

b. Draw the game tree if Firm 1 can decide first. What is the outcome? Why?

c. Draw the game tree if Firm 2 can decide first. What is the outcome? Why?

3.2 How does your analysis in the previous question change if the government imposes a lump-sum franchise tax of 40 on each firm (that is, the payoffs in the matrix are all reduced by 40). Now explain how your analysis would change if the firms have an additional option of shutting down and avoiding the lump-sum tax rather than producing 10 or 20 units and paying the tax.

3.3 Solve for the Stackelberg subgame perfect Nash equilibrium for the following game tree. What is the joint-profit maximizing outcome? Why is that not the outcome of this game?

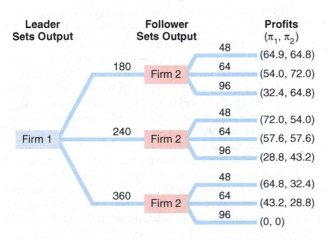

Leader Sets Output	Follower Sets Output		Profits (π_1, π_2)
		48	(64.9, 64.8)
	180 — Firm 2	64	(54.0, 72.0)
		96	(32.4, 64.8)
		48	(72.0, 54.0)
Firm 1	240 — Firm 2	64	(57.6, 57.6)
		96	(28.8, 43.2)
		48	(64.8, 32.4)
	360 — Firm 2	64	(43.2, 28.8)
		96	(0, 0)

3.4 In Solved Problem 14.1, suppose that Mimi can move first. What are the equilibria, and why

(use an extensive-form diagram)? Now repeat your analysis if Jeff can move first.

3.5 Suppose that Question 1.4 were modified so that GM has no subsidy but does have a head start over Toyota and can move first. What is the Nash equilibrium? Explain.

3.6 Levi Strauss and Wrangler are planning new-generation jeans and must decide on the colors for their products. The possible colors are white, black, and violet. The payoff to each firm depends on the color it chooses and the color chosen by its rival, as the profit matrix shows:

Levi Strauss

		White	Black	Violet
Wrangler	**White**	10 / 10	30 / 20	40 / 30
	Black	20 / 30	0 / 0	35 / 15
	Violet	15 / 40	20 / 35	0 / 0

a. Given that the firms move simultaneously, identify any dominant strategies in this game and find any Nash equilibria.

b. Now suppose the firms move sequentially, with Wrangler moving first. Draw a game tree and identify any subgame perfect Nash equilibria in this sequential-move game.

3.7 Suppose that Panasonic and Zenith are the only two firms that can produce a new type of 3D high-definition television. The following matrix shows the payoffs (in millions of dollars) from entering this product market:

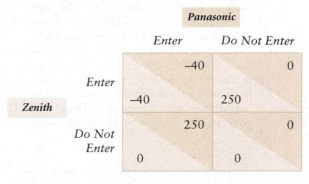

Panasonic

		Enter	Do Not Enter
Zenith	**Enter**	−40 / −40	0 / 250
	Do Not Enter	250 / 0	0 / 0

a. If both firms move simultaneously, does either firm have a dominant strategy? Explain.

b. What are the Nash equilibria given that both firms move simultaneously?

c. The U.S. government commits to paying Zenith a lump-sum subsidy of $50 million if it enters this market. What is the Nash equilibrium?

d. If Zenith does not receive a subsidy but has a head start over Panasonic, what is the Nash equilibrium?

3.8 A thug wants the contents of a safe and is threatening the owner, the only person who knows the code, to open the safe. "I will kill you if you don't open the safe, and let you live if you do." Should the information holder believe the threat and open the safe? The table shows the value that each person places on the various possible outcomes.

	Thug	Safe's Owner
Open the safe, thug does not kill	4	3
Open the safe, thug kills	2	1
Do not open, thug kills	1	2
Do not open, thug does not kill	3	4

Such a game appears in many films, including *Die Hard*, *Crimson Tide*, and *The Maltese Falcon*.

a. Draw the game tree. Who moves first?

b. What is the equilibrium?

c. Does the safe's owner believe the thug's threat?

d. Does the safe's owner open the safe?

3.9 In 2007, Italy announced that an Italian journalist, Daniel Mastrogiacomo, who had been held hostage for 15 days by the Taliban in Afghanistan, had been ransomed for 5 Taliban prisoners. Governments in many nations denounced the act as a bad idea because it rewarded terrorism and encouraged more abductions. Consequently, the Afghanistan government announced that it would no longer make such trades ("Afghanistan: Government Pledges End to Hostage Deals," Radio Free Europe, April 16, 2007). Use an extensive-form game tree to analyze the basic arguments. Can you draw any hard-and-fast conclusions about whether the Italians' actions were a good or bad idea? (*Hint*: Does your answer depend on the relative weight one

puts on future costs and benefits relative to those today?)

3.10 Salgado (2008) found that AMD's cost of manufacturing computer chips was about 12% higher than Intel's cost because AMD had less learning by doing (Chapter 7) as it had produced fewer units. The more an incumbent firm produces in the first period, the lower its marginal cost in the second period. If a potential entrant expects the incumbent to produce a large quantity in the second period, it does not enter. Draw a game tree to illustrate why an incumbent would produce more in the first period than the single-period profit-maximizing level. Now change the payoffs in the tree to show a situation in which the firm does not increase production in the first period. (*Hint*: See Solved Problem 14.3.)

*3.11 A monopoly manufacturing plant currently uses many workers to pack its product into boxes. It can replace these workers with an expensive set of robotic arms. Although the robotic arms raise the monopoly's fixed cost substantially, they lower its marginal cost because it no longer has to hire as many workers. Buying the robotic arms raises its total cost: The monopoly can't sell enough boxes to make the machine pay for itself, given the market demand curve. Suppose the incumbent does not invest. If its rival does not enter, it earns $0 and the incumbent earns $900. If the rival enters, it earns $300 and the incumbent earns $400. Alternatively, the incumbent invests. If the rival does not enter, it earns $0 and the incumbent earns $500. If the rival enters, the rival loses $36 and the incumbent makes $132. Show the game tree. Should the monopoly buy the machine anyway? (*Hint*: See Solved Problem 14.3.)

*3.12 Suppose that an incumbent can commit to producing a large quantity of output before the potential entrant decides whether to enter. The incumbent chooses whether to commit to produce a small quantity, q_i, or a large quantity. The rival then decides whether to enter. If the incumbent commits to the small output level and if the rival does not enter, the rival makes $0 and the incumbent makes $900. If it does enter, the rival makes $125 and the incumbent earns $450. If the incumbent commits to producing the large quantity, and the potential entrant stays out of the market, the potential entrant makes $0 and the incumbent makes $800. If the rival enters, the best the entrant can make is $0, the same amount it would earn if it didn't enter, but the incumbent earns only $400. Show the game tree. What is the subgame perfect Nash equilibrium? (*Hint*: See Solved Problem 14.3.)

*3.13 Before entry, the incumbent earns a monopoly profit of $\pi_m = \$10$ (million). If entry occurs, the incumbent and entrant each earn the duopoly profit, $\pi_d = \$3$. Suppose that the incumbent can induce the government to require all firms to install pollution-control devices that cost each firm $4. Show the game tree. Should the incumbent urge the government to require pollution-control devices? Why or why not?

3.14 A gas station at a rest stop along the highway can pay the owner of the rest stop $40,000 to prevent a second station from opening. Without entry, the incumbent gas station's profit is $\pi_i = \$100,000$. With entry, its duopoly profit would be $45,000 and the entrant would earn a profit of $30,000. Will the incumbent pay for exclusivity? Will entry occur? Use a game-tree diagram to answer these questions.

3.15 Show an example of an extensive-form game where a player who moves second has a higher payoff than one who moves first in the subgame perfect Nash equilibrium.

4. Auctions

4.1 Charity events often use silent auctions. A donated item, such as a date with a movie star (Colin Firth and Scarlett Johansson in 2008) or a former president (Bill Clinton in 2013), is put up for bid. In a silent auction, bidders write down bids and submit them. Some silent auctions use secret bids, which are submitted in sealed envelopes and kept confidential. Other silent auctions are open: the bidder writes down a bid on a bulletin board that everyone present can see. Which kind of auction would you expect to raise more revenue for the charity?

4.2 At the end of performances of his Broadway play "Cyrano de Bergerac," Kevin Kline, who starred as Cyrano, the cavalier poet with a huge nose, auctioned his prosthetic proboscis, which he and his costar, Jennifer Garner, autographed (Dan Mitchell, "This Time, Santa Has Been Too Naughty," *New York Times*, December 9, 2007) to benefit Broadway Cares in its fight against AIDS. An English auction was used. One night, a television producer

grabbed the nose for $1,400, while the next night it fetched $1,600. On other nights it sold for $3,000 and $900. Why did the value fluctuate substantially from night to night? Which bidder's bid determined the sales price? How was the auction price affected by the audience's knowledge that the proceeds would go to charity?

4.3 Suppose that Firm 1, Firm 2, and Firm 3 are the only three firms interested in the lot at the corner of First Street and Glendon Way. The lot is being auctioned by a second-price sealed-bid auction. Suppose Firm 1 values the lot at $v_1 = \$20,000$, Firm 2 at $18,500, and Firm 3 at $16,800. Each bidding firm's surplus is $v_i - p$ if it wins the auction and 0 if it loses. The values are private. What is each bidder's optimal bid? Which firm wins the auction, and what price does that firm pay?

5. Behavioral Game Theory

5.1 Draw a game tree that represents the ultimatum game in which the proposer is a first mover who decides how much to offer a responder and the responder then decides to accept or reject the offer. The total amount available is $50 if agreement is reached, but both players get nothing if the responder rejects the offer. Offers must be in whole dollars. What is the subgame perfect Nash equilibrium? What would you expect to happen in practice?

5.2 A prisoners' dilemma game is played for a fixed number of periods. The fully rational solution is for each player to defect in each period. However, in experiments with students, players often cooperate for a significant number of periods if the total number of repetitions is fairly large (such as 10 or 20). Why? (*Hint*: Consider reciprocity and players' limited reasoning ability.)

6. Challenge

6.1 Create an example to illustrate the Nash equilibria for the battle of the sexes game described in footnote 13. Discuss whether this game and equilibrium concept make sense for analyzing a couple's decisions. How might you change the game's rules so that it makes more sense? (*Hint*: In this game, the individuals pick a vacation spot simultaneously without consulting each other.)

*6.2 How would the analysis in the Challenge Solution change if the Other firms could have picked their standard before Amazon chose?

6.3 Most major electric car manufacturers are split into two rival camps. Each group uses one of two incompatible technologies to charge their cars at recharging stations (similar to gas stations). Both technologies use direct current to charge car batteries to 80% of capacity in less than 20 minutes. The Japanese auto manufacturers (Honda, Mazda, Mitsubishi, Nissan, Subaru, and Toyota) and PSA Peugeot Citroen back the CHAdeMO technology. Most German and U.S. auto makers (Audi, BMW, Chrysler, Daimler, Ford, General Motors, Porsche, and Volkswagen) back the Combo technology. The CHAdeMO technology was introduced first and is in much wider use (Julia Pyper, "Charger Standards Fight Confuses Electric Vehicle Buyers, Puts Car Company Investments at Risk," **www.eenews .net**, July 24, 2013). Relabel the extensive-form diagram in the Challenge Solution (keeping the current payoffs) to illustrate the decision making of these firms. Now, change your analysis. Some industry analysts believe that the Combo standard was introduced to slow sales of the Nissan Leaf so that rival manufacturers could catch up. Change the payoffs to illustrate why the German-American group might choose that standard even though the Japanese-Peugeot group acted first.

Factor Markets

15

The laborer is worthy of his reward.   —Timothy 5:18

In what baseball team owners think fondly of as the "good old days," teams successfully colluded to keep athletes' salaries low. The "reserve clause" in standard player contracts stated that even after the contract expired, the player could only negotiate with his current team. Through a series of court cases and collective bargaining, this clause became ineffective starting in 1976.

Since then, top players' salaries have skyrocketed.[1] With free agency—where star players can negotiate with any team—the average real salary rose from $208,000 (in 2013 dollars) in 1976 to $3.4 million in 2013 (the average salary for the Yankees was $7.2 million).

In 1999, the Los Angeles Dodgers announced that they had re-signed their star pitcher Kevin Brown to a new seven-year $105 million contract, making Brown the first $100 million player in baseball history. When Mr. Brown was asked what effect his contract would have on ticket prices, he responded, "I have never believed that players' salaries are directly related to ticket prices." The reporters snickered. Several of these newspaper pundits wrote that Mr. Brown's salary hike would drive up ticket prices to cover the expense.

Since then, salaries continued to rise. Alex Rodriguez inked a 2008–2018 contract with the New York Yankees worth $275 million. His 2013 salary of $29 million exceeded the $18 million of the Astros' entire payroll. Indeed, twenty-four major leaguers earned over $22 million in 2013.

After each such signing, a debate rings out about the effect of salaries on price. For example, a *St. Louis Today* columnist confidently predicted that the St. Louis Cardinals would raise ticket prices if the team re-signed Albert Pujols to a Rodriguez-like salary in 2012, and a *Washington Examiner* columnist blamed skyrocketing prices over the last couple of decades on free spending on players by owners such as George Steinbrenner. Yet some writers in the *Wall Street Journal* and other newspapers now accept Mr. Brown's argument—that no link exists between salaries and ticket prices.

---

[1]A similar pattern has been followed in other sports, including Canadian and U.S. football and hockey teams and especially European football (soccer) teams.

In Chapter 8, we showed that if both marginal and average cost curves shift up, the competitive market price rises. Does it follow that when a team re-signs a star athlete to a higher salary that it will raise ticket prices? If not, how does the sports example differ from the case where both marginal and average cost curves rise?

monopsony
the only buyer of a good in a given market

Sports teams, like other firms, hire labor and buy other inputs or factors, which they use to produce their outputs (goods and services). In this chapter, we show that a factor's market equilibrium price depends on the structure of factor markets and the output market. We first look at competitive factor and output markets, derive a competitive firm's demand curves for inputs, and determine the market equilibrium. Then, we examine the effect of a monopoly in either or both markets. Next, we consider markets in which a firm is a **monopsony**: the only buyer of a good in a market. A monopsony is the mirror image of a monopoly. Whereas a monopoly sells at a price higher than a competitive industry would charge, a monopsony buys at a lower price than a competitive industry would.

In this chapter, we examine three main topics

1. **Competitive Factor Market.** The intersection of the factor supply curve and factor demand curve (which depends on firms' production functions and the market price for output) determines the equilibrium in a competitive factor market.

2. **Effects of Monopolies on Factor Markets.** If firms exercise market power in either factor or output markets, the quantities of inputs and outputs sold fall.

3. **Monopsony.** A monopsony maximizes its profit by paying a price below the competitive level, which creates a deadweight loss for society.

15.1 Competitive Factor Market

Virtually all firms rely on factor markets for at least some inputs. The firms that buy factors may be competitive price takers or noncompetitive price setters, such as a monopsony. Perfectly competitive, monopolistically competitive, oligopolistic, and monopolistic firms sell factors. Here we examine factor markets in which buying and selling firms are competitive price takers. In the next section, we consider noncompetitive factor markets.

Factor markets with many small buyers and sellers are competitive. The FloraHolland flower auction in Amsterdam (Chapter 8) with 7,000 suppliers and 4,500 buyers typifies such a competitive market. The sellers supply inputs (flowers in bulk) to buyers, who sell outputs (trimmed flowers in vases, wrapped bouquets) at retail to final customers.

Chapter 5 derives the supply curve of labor by examining how individuals' choices between labor and leisure depend on tastes and the wage rate. The standard derivation of a competitive supply curve in output markets applies to factor markets as well. Chapter 8 determines the competitive supply curves of firms in general, including those that produce factors for other firms. Given that we know the supply curve, all we need to do to analyze a competitive factor market is to determine the factor's demand curve.

Short-Run Factor Demand of a Firm

A profit-maximizing firm's demand for a factor of production is downward sloping: The higher the price of an input, the less the firm wants to buy. To understand what is behind a firm's factor demand, we examine a firm that uses capital and labor to produce output from factors. Using the theory of how firms behave (Chapters 6 and 7), we show how the amount of an input the firm demands depends on the prices of the factors and the price of the final output.

We start by considering the short-run factor demand for labor of a firm that can vary labor but not capital. Then we examine long-run factor demands when both inputs are variable.

In the short run, a firm has a fixed amount of capital, $\overline{K}$, and can vary the number of workers, L, it employs. Will the firm's profit rise if it hires one more worker? The answer depends on whether its revenue or labor costs rise more when output expands.

An extra worker per hour raises the firm's output per hour, q, by the marginal product of labor, $MP_L = \Delta q / \Delta L$ (Chapter 6). How much is that extra output worth to the firm? The extra revenue, R, from the last unit of output is the firm's marginal revenue, $MR = \Delta R / \Delta q$. As a result, the **marginal revenue product of labor** (MRP_L), the extra revenue from hiring one more worker, is[2]

marginal revenue product of labor (MRP_L)
the extra revenue from hiring one more worker

$$MRP_L = MR \times MP_L.$$

For a firm that is a competitive employer of labor, the marginal cost of hiring one more worker per hour is the wage, w. Hiring an extra worker raises the firm's profit if the marginal benefit—the marginal revenue product of labor—is greater than the marginal cost—the wage—from one more worker: $MRP_L > w$. If the marginal revenue product of labor is less than the wage, $MRP_L < w$, the firm can raise its profit by reducing the number of workers it employs. Thus, *the firm maximizes its profit by hiring workers until the marginal revenue product of the last worker exactly equals the marginal cost of employing that worker, which is the wage*:

$$MRP_L = w.$$

For now, we restrict our attention to competitive firms. A competitive firm faces an infinitely elastic demand for its output at the market price, p, so its marginal revenue is p (Chapter 8), and its marginal revenue product of labor is

$$MRP_L = p \times MP_L.$$

A competitive firm's *marginal revenue product* for any input is also called the *value of the marginal product* because it equals the market price times the marginal product of labor: the market value of the extra output.

The competitive firm hires labor to the point at which its marginal revenue product of labor equals the wage:

$$MRP_L = p \times MP_L = w. \tag{15.1}$$

Table 15.1 illustrates the relationship in Equation 15.1. If the firm hires $L = 3$ workers per hour, the marginal product from the third worker is 5 units of output

---

[2]In the short run, output is a function of only labor, $q(L)$. The price the firm receives from selling q units of output is given by its demand function, $p(q)$. Thus, the revenue that the firm receives is $R(L) = p[q(L)]q(L)$. The extra revenue that the firm obtains from using an extra amount of labor services is derived using the chain rule of differentiation:

$$MRP_L \equiv \frac{dR}{dL} = \frac{dR}{dq} \times \frac{dq}{dL} \equiv MR \times MP_L.$$

Table 15.1 Marginal Product of Labor, Marginal Revenue Product of Labor, and Marginal Cost

Labor, L	Marginal Product of Labor, MP_L	Marginal Revenue Product of Labor, $MRP_L = 3MP_L$	Output, q	Marginal Cost, $MC = 12/MP_L$
2	6	$18	13	$2
3	5	$15	18	$2.4
4	4	$12	22	$3
5	3	$9	25	$4
6	2	$6	27	$6

Notes: Wage, w, is $12 per hour of work. Price, p, is $3 per unit of output. Labor is variable, and capital is fixed.

per hour. Because the firm can sell the output at the market price $p = $3 per unit, the extra revenue from hiring the third worker is $MRP_L = p \times MP_L = $3 \times 5 = 15. By hiring this worker, the firm increases its profit because the wage of this worker is only $w = $12. If the firm hires a fourth worker, the marginal product of labor from this last worker falls to 4, and the marginal revenue product of labor falls to $12. Thus, the extra revenue from the last worker exactly equals that worker's wage, so the firm's profit is unchanged. Were the firm to hire a fifth worker, the $MRP_L = $9 is less than the wage of $12, so its profit would fall.

Panel a of Figure 15.1 shows the same relationship. The wage line, $w = $12, intersects the MRP_L curve at $L = 4$ workers per hour. *The wage line is the supply of labor the firm faces.* As a competitive buyer of labor services, the firm can hire as many workers as it wants at a constant wage of $12. *The marginal revenue product*

Figure 15.1 The Relationship Between Labor Market and Output Market Equilibria

(a) The firm's profit is maximized at $L = 4$ workers per hour where the wage line, $w = $12, crosses the marginal revenue product of labor, MRP_L, curve, which is also the demand curve for labor. (b) The firm's profit is maximized at 22 units of output (produced by 4 workers), for which its marginal cost, $MC = w/MP_L$, curve equals the market price, $p = $3.

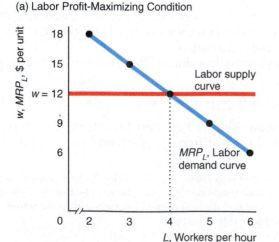

(a) Labor Profit-Maximizing Condition

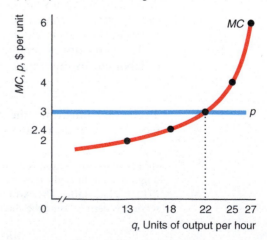

(b) Output Profit-Maximizing Condition

of labor curve, MRP_L, *is the firm's demand curve for labor* when other inputs are fixed. It shows the maximum wage a firm is willing to pay to hire a given number of workers. Thus, the intersection of the supply curve of labor facing the firm and the firm's demand curve for labor, Equation 15.1, determines the profit-maximizing number of workers.

A firm's labor demand curve is usually downward sloping because of the law of diminishing marginal returns (Chapter 6). The marginal product from extra workers, MP_L, of a firm with fixed capital eventually falls as the firm increases the amount of labor it uses. Table 15.1 illustrates that the marginal product of labor falls from 6 for the second worker to 2 for the sixth worker. Because the marginal product of labor declines as more workers are hired, the marginal revenue product of labor (which equals a constant price times the marginal product of labor) or demand curve must slope downward as well.

Solved Problem 15.1

A paper firm's short-run Cobb-Douglas production function is $q = AL^\alpha \overline{K}^\beta$, where $\overline{K}$ is the fixed amount of capital. What is its short-run labor demand function? The estimated Cobb-Douglas production function for the paper firm is[3]

$$q = L^{0.6}\overline{K}^{0.2}. \tag{15.2}$$

That is, $A = 1$, $\alpha = 0.6$, and $\beta = 0.2$. In the short-run, the firm's capital is fixed at $\overline{K} = 32$. The price of a unit of paper is $p = 50$. What is the paper firm's short-run production function and labor demand function? How many workers does the firm hire if the wage is $w = 15$?

Answer

1. *Multiply the short-run marginal product of labor by price to determine the marginal product of labor.* The marginal product of labor of the Cobb-Douglas production function is $MP_L = \alpha AL^{\alpha-1}\overline{K}^\beta$ (Appendix 6C). Thus, the short-run marginal revenue product of labor (or the labor demand function) is $MRP_L = p\alpha AL^{\alpha-1}\overline{K}^\beta$.

2. *Determine the paper firm's short-run production function by substituting $\overline{K}$ into Equation 15.2.* Setting $\overline{K} = 32$ in Equation 15.2, we find that $q = L^{0.6}32^{0.2} = 2L^{0.6}$.

3. *Calculate the short-run marginal revenue product of labor by substituting the paper firm's estimated parameters, $\overline{K} = 32$ and $p = 50$, into the general Cobb-Douglas result in part 1.* Making these substitutions, we find that the $MRP_L = p\alpha AL^{\alpha-1}\overline{K}^\beta = 50 \times 0.6L^{-0.4}32^{0.2} = 60L^{-0.4}$.

4. *Determine the number of workers per hour that the firm hires using Equation 15.1.* According to Equation 15.1, $MRP_L = w$, so for the paper firm, $60L^{-0.4} = 15$, or $L = 32$.

Profit Maximization Using Labor or Output Chapter 8 presents another profit-maximization condition: A competitive firm maximizes its profit by operating where the market price, p, equals the marginal cost of an extra unit of output, MC: $p = MC$.

---

[3]This production function is based on the estimates of Hossain et al. (2012) for a Bangladesh paper firm. I chose the units of output so that the constant multiplier A in the general Cobb-Douglas, $q = AL^\alpha K^\beta$, equals 1.

This output profit-maximizing condition is equivalent to the labor profit-maximizing condition in Equation 15.1. Dividing Equation 15.1 by MP_L, we find that

$$p = \frac{w}{MP_L} = MC.$$

As Chapter 7 shows, the marginal cost equals the wage, w, times 1 over the marginal product of labor, which is the extra labor, $\Delta L / \Delta q$, necessary to produce one more unit of output. The marginal cost is the cost of the extra labor, $w\Delta L$, needed to produce the extra output, Δq.

Table 15.1 illustrates this relationship. The fourth column shows how the amount of output produced varies with the number of workers. Because 3 workers produce 18 units of output and 4 workers produce 22 units of output, the marginal product of the fourth worker is 4 units of output. With a wage of $12, the marginal cost for the last unit of output is $MC = w/MP_L = \$12/4 = \$3$. The market price is also $3, so the firm maximizes its profit by producing 22 units of output, as panel b of Figure 15.1 illustrates.

In summary, the two profit-maximizing equilibria in Figure 15.1 give the same answer: The firm maximizes its profit by hiring 4 workers to produce 22 units of output. Panel a shows that the firm maximizes its profit by hiring 4 workers, for which the marginal benefit or marginal revenue product from the last worker, MRP_L, equals the marginal cost of that worker, w. Panel b shows that the firm maximizes its profit by producing 22 units of output, for which the marginal benefit or marginal revenue from the last unit of output, $p = \$3$, equals the marginal cost of the last unit of output, MC.

How Changes in Wages and Prices Affect Factor Demand   The number of workers a firm hires depends on the wage and the price of the final good, as Equation 15.1 shows. Suppose that the supply of labor shifts so that the wage falls from $w_1 = \$12$ to $w_2 = \$6$ while the market price remains constant at $3. The firm hires more workers because the cost of more labor falls while the incremental revenue from additional output is unchanged. Figure 15.2 shows that a drop in the wage due to a downward shift of the labor supply curve from S^1 to S^2 causes a shift along the labor demand curve D^1 from point a, where the firm hires 4 workers, to point b, where the firm hires 6 workers per hour.

If the market price falls from $3 to $2, the demand curve for labor shifts downward from D^1 to D^2. Demand D^2 is only $\frac{2}{3} = (2MP_L)/(3MP_L)$ as high as D^1 at any given quantity of labor. If the wage stays constant at $w_1 = \$12$, the firm reduces its demand for workers from 4, point a, to 2, point c. Thus, a shift in either the market wage or the market price affects the amount of labor that a firm employs.

Solved Problem 15.2

How does a competitive firm adjust its demand for labor when the government imposes a specific tax of t on each unit of output?

Answer

1. *Give intuition.* The specific tax lowers the price per unit the firm receives, so we can apply the same type of analysis we just used for a fall in the market price.

2. *Show how the tax affects the marginal revenue product of labor.* The marginal revenue product of labor for a competitive firm is the price the firm receives for the good times the marginal product of labor. The tax reduces the price the firm receives. The tax does not affect the relative prices of labor and capital, so it does not affect the marginal product of labor for a given amount of labor, $MP_L(L)$.

For a given amount of labor, the marginal revenue product of labor falls from $p \times MP_L(L)$ to $(p - t) \times MP_L(L)$. The marginal revenue product of labor curve—the labor demand curve—shifts downward until it is only $(p - t)/p$ as high as the original labor demand curve at any quantity of labor.

Figure 15.2 Shift of and Movement Along the Labor Demand Curve

If the market price is \$3, the firm's labor demand curve is D^1. A fall in the wage causes a *shift of the supply curve* from S^1 to S^2 and a *movement along the demand curve for labor*. If the wage is $w_1 = \$12$, the firm hires 4 workers per hour, equilibrium point a. If the wage falls to $w_2 = \$6$, the firm hires 6 workers, point b. A fall in the market price to \$2 causes a *shift of the firm's demand curve for labor* from D^1 to D^2. If the market wage stays constant at $w_1 = \$12$, the fall in the market price causes a *movement along the supply curve* S^1: The number of workers the firm hires falls from 4, point a on D^1 and S^1, to 2, point c on D^2 and S^1.

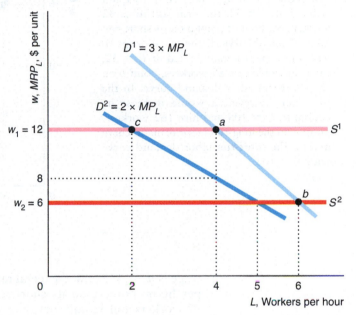

Long-Run Factor Demand

In the long run, the firm may vary all of its inputs. Now if the wage of labor rises, the firm adjusts both labor and capital. As a result, the short-run marginal revenue product of labor curve that holds capital fixed is not the firm's long-run labor demand curve. The long-run labor demand curve takes account of changes in the firm's use of capital as the wage rises.

In both the short run and the long run, the labor demand curve is the marginal revenue product curve of labor. In the short run, the firm cannot vary capital, so the short-run MP_L curve and hence the short-run MRP_L curve are relatively steep. In the long run, when the firm can vary all inputs, its long-run MP_L curve and MRP_L curves are flatter.

Figure 15.3 shows the relationship between the long-run and short-run labor demand curves for the paper firm.[4] In the short run, capital is fixed at $\overline{K} = 32$, the

---

[4]Appendix 15A formally shows that the long-run labor demand and capital demand functions for a Cobb-Douglas production function are functions of the market price, p; the wage rate, w; and the rental rate of capital, r. Substituting the parameters for the paper firm, $\alpha = 0.6$, $\beta = 0.2$, and $A = 1$, into Equation 15A.4, we find that the firm's long-run labor demand curve is

$$L = (0.6/w)^4(0.2/r)p^5.$$

Its long-run capital demand curve, Equation 15A.5, is

$$K = (0.6/w)^3(0.2/r)^2p^5.$$

Figure 15.3 Labor Demand of a Paper Firm

If the long-run market price is $50 per unit, the rental rate of capital services is $r = \$5$, and the wage is $w = \$15$ per hour, a paper firm hires 32 workers (and uses 32 units of capital) at point *a* on its long-run labor demand curve. In the short run, if capital is fixed at $\overline{K} = 32$, the firm still hires 32 workers per hour at point *a* on its short-run labor demand curve. If the wage drops to $10 and capital remains fixed at $\overline{K} = 32$, the firm would hire 88 workers, point *b* on the short-run labor demand curve. In the long run, however, it would increase its capital to $K = 108$ and hire 162 workers, point *c* on the long-run labor demand curve and on the short-run labor demand curve with $K = 108$.

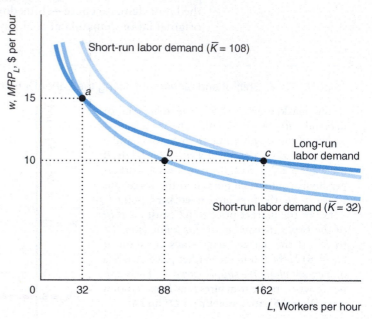

wage is $w = \$15$, and the rental rate of capital is $r = \$5$. The firm hires 32 workers per hour, point *a* on its short-run labor demand curve, where $\overline{K} = 32$. Using 32 workers and 32 units of capital is profit maximizing in the long run, so point *a* is also on the firm's long-run labor demand curve.

In the short run, if the wage fell to $10, the firm could not increase its capital, so it would hire 88 workers, point *b* on the short-run labor demand curve, where $\overline{K} = 32$. In the long run, however, the firm would employ more capital and even more labor (because it can sell as much output as it wants at the market price). It would hire 162 workers and use 108 units of capital, which is point *c* on both the long-run labor demand curve and the short-run labor demand curve for $K = 108$.

Factor Market Demand

A factor market demand curve is the sum of the factor demand curves of the various firms that use the input. Determining a factor market demand curve is more difficult than deriving consumers' market demand for a final good. In a single market, we derive the market demand curve by horizontally summing the demand curves for individual consumers (Chapter 2). However, inputs such as labor and capital are used in many output markets. Thus, to derive the labor market demand curve, we first determine the labor demand curve for each output market and then sum across output markets to obtain the factor market demand curve.

The Marginal Revenue Product Approach Earlier we derived the factor demand of a competitive firm that took the output market price as given. The problem we face here is that the output market price depends on the factor's price. As the factor's price falls, each firm, taking the original market price as given, uses more of the factor to produce more output. This extra production by all the firms in the market causes the market price to fall. As the market price falls, each firm reduces its output and hence its demand for the input. Thus, a fall in an input price causes less of an increase in factor demand than would occur if the market price remained constant, as Figure 15.4 illustrates.

At the initial output market price of $9 per unit, the competitive firm's labor demand curve (panel a) is $MRP_L(p = 9) = 9 \times MP_L$. When the wage is $25 per hour, the firm hires 50 workers: point a. The 10 firms in the market (panel b) demand 500 hours of work: point A on the demand curve $D(p = 9) = 100 \times 9 \times MP_L$. If the wage falls to $10 while the market price remains fixed at $9, each firm hires 90 workers, point c, and all the firms in the market would hire 900 workers, point C. However, the extra output drives the price down to $7, so each firm hires 70 workers, point b, and the firms collectively demand 700 workers, point B. The market labor demand curve for this output market that takes price adjustments into account, D (price varies), goes through points A and B. Thus, the market's demand for labor is steeper than it would be if output prices were fixed.

An Alternative Approach For certain types of production functions, it is easier to determine the market demand curve by using the output profit-maximizing equation rather than the marginal revenue product approach. Suppose that calculator

---

Figure 15.4 Firm and Market Demand for Labor

When the output price is $p = \$9$, the individual competitive firm's labor demand curve is $MRP_L(p = 9)$. If $w = \$25$ per hour, the firm hires 50 workers, point a in panel a, and the 10 firms in the market demand 500 workers, point A on the labor demand curve $D(p = 9)$ in panel b. If the wage falls to $10, each firm would hire 90 workers, point c, if the market price stayed fixed at $9. The extra output, however, drives the price down to $7, so each firm hires 70 workers, point b. The market's demand for labor that takes price adjustments into account, D(price varies), goes through points A and B.

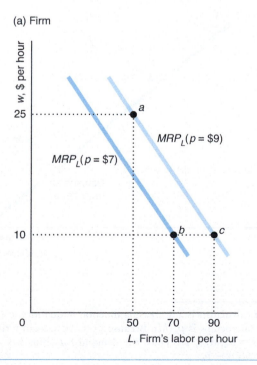

(a) Firm

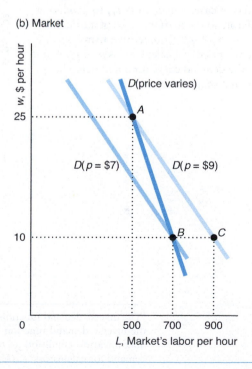

(b) Market

manufacturers are competitive and use a fixed-proportions production function, producing each calculator using one microchip and one plastic case. Each plastic case costs p_p, and each microchip costs p_m. What is the calculator market's demand for microchips?

Figure 15.5 shows the demand both for calculators, Q, and microchips, M. Because the numbers of chips and calculators are equal, $Q = M$, the horizontal axes for chips and calculators are the same.

Because each calculator requires one chip and one case, the marginal cost of producing a calculator is $MC = p_p + p_m$. Each competitive firm operates where the market price equals the marginal cost: $p = p_p + p_m = MC$. As a result, the most that any firm would pay for a silicon chip is $p_m = p - p_p$, the amount left over from selling a calculator after paying for the plastic case. Thus, the calculator market's demand curve for microchips lies p_p below the demand curve for calculators, as the figure shows.[5]

Competitive Factor Market Equilibrium

The intersection of the factor market demand curve and the factor market supply curve determines the competitive factor market equilibrium. We've just derived the factor market demand. The long-run factor supply curve for each firm is its marginal cost curve above the minimum of its average cost curve, and the factor market supply curve is the horizontal sum of the firms' supply curves (Chapter 8). As we've already analyzed competitive market equilibria for markets in general in Chapters 2, 3, 8, and 9, we won't repeat the analysis. (Been there. Done that.)

Figure 15.5 Demand for Microchips in Calculators

It takes one microchip, which costs p_m, and one plastic case, which costs p_p, to produce a calculator, so the marginal cost of a calculator is $MC = p_m + p_p$. Competitive firms operate where the price of a calculator is $p = p_m + p_p$. Thus, the demand curve for a microchip lies p_p below that of a calculator.

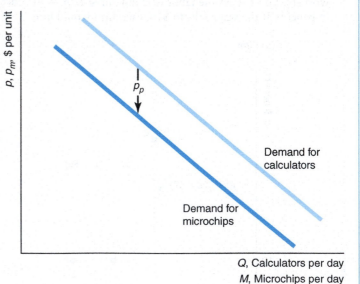

---

[5]The inverse demand function for calculators is a decreasing function of quantity, $p(Q)$. Similarly, the inverse demand function for microchips is $p_m(M)$. Because $Q = M$, we can write the profit-maximization condition as $p(Q) = p_m(M) + p_p$. Thus, the demand for chips lies p_p below the demand for calculators: $p_m(M) = p(Q) - p_p$.

Factor prices are equalized across markets (Chapter 10). For example, if wages were higher in one industry than in another, workers would shift from the low-wage industry to the high-wage industry until the wages were equalized.

15.2 Effects of Monopolies on Factor Markets

Having examined the factor market equilibrium where competitive firms sell a factor to a competitive output market, we now survey the effects of market power on factor market equilibrium. If firms in the output market *or* the factor market exercise market power by setting price above marginal cost, fewer factors are sold than would be sold if all firms were competitive.

Market Structure and Factor Demands

Factor demand curves vary with market power. As we saw in Chapters 11 and 12, the marginal revenue of a profit-maximizing firm, $MR = p(1 + 1/\varepsilon)$, is a function of the elasticity, ε, of its output demand curve and the market price, p. Thus, the firm's marginal revenue product of labor function is

$$MRP_L = p\left(1 + \frac{1}{\varepsilon}\right)MP_L.$$

The labor demand curve is $p \times MP_L$ for a competitive firm because it faces an infinitely elastic demand at the market price, so its marginal revenue equals the market price.

The marginal revenue product of labor or labor demand curve for a competitive market is above that of a monopoly or oligopoly firm. Figure 15.6 shows the short-run market factor demand for a paper firm if it is a competitive firm, one of two identical Cournot quantity-setting firms, or a monopoly.[6]

A monopoly operates in the elastic section of its downward-sloping demand curve (Chapter 11), so its demand elasticity is less than −1 and finite: $-\infty < \varepsilon \le -1$. As a result, at any given price, the monopoly's labor demand, $p(1 + 1/\varepsilon)MP_L$, lies below the labor demand curve, pMP_L, of a competitive firm with an identical marginal product of labor curve.

The elasticity of demand a Cournot firm faces is $n\varepsilon$, where n is the number of identical firms and ε is the market elasticity of demand (Chapter 13). Given that they have the same market demand curve, a duopoly Cournot firm faces twice as elastic a demand curve as a monopoly faces. Consequently, a Cournot duopoly firm's labor demand curve, $p[1 + 1/(2\varepsilon)]MP_L$, lies above that of a monopoly but below that of a competitive firm. From now on, we concentrate on the competitive and monopoly equilibria because the oligopoly and monopolistically competitive equilibria lie between these polar cases.

---

[6]In the short run, the paper firm's marginal product function is $MP_L = 1.2L^{-0.4}$. The labor demand is $p \times 1.2L^{-0.4}$ for a competitive firm, $p[1 + 1/(2\varepsilon)] \times 1.2L^{-0.4}$ for one of two identical Cournot duopoly firms, and $p(1 + 1/\varepsilon) \times 1.2L^{-0.4}$ for a monopoly.

Figure 15.6 How Paper Firm Labor Demand Varies with Market Structure

For all profit-maximizing firms, the labor demand curve is the marginal revenue product of labor: $MRP_L = MR \times MP_L$. Because marginal revenue differs with market structure, so does the MRP_L. At a given wage, a competitive paper firm demands more workers than a Cournot duopoly firm, which demands more workers than a monopoly.

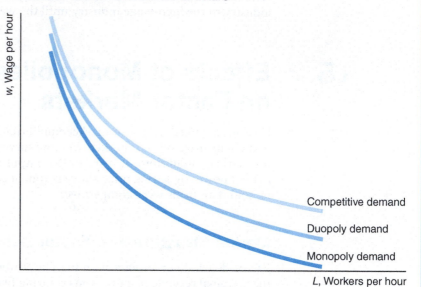

A Model of Market Power in Input and Output Markets

When a firm with market power in either the factor or the output market raises its price, the price to final consumers rises. As a result, consumers buy fewer units, so fewer units of the input are demanded. We use a linear example to illustrate how monopolies affect factor market equilibrium. The inverse demand, $p(Q)$, for the final good is

$$p = 80 - Q. \tag{15.3}$$

Figure 15.7 plots this demand curve. An unlimited number of workers can be hired at $20 an hour. Each unit of output, Q, requires one unit of labor, L, and no other factor, so the marginal product of labor is 1.

As a benchmark, we start our analysis with competitive factor and output markets. Then we ask how the factor market equilibrium changes if the output market is monopolized. Next, we examine a monopolized factor market and a competitive output market. Finally, we investigate the effect of market power in both markets.

Competitive Factor and Output Markets The intersection of the relevant supply and demand curves determines the competitive equilibria in both input and output markets in Figure 15.7. Because $Q = L$, the figure measures both output and labor on the same horizontal axis.

The marginal product of labor is 1 because one extra worker produces one more unit of output. Thus, the competitive market's demand for labor, $MRP_L = p \times MP_L = p$, is identical to the output demand curve. The labor demand function is the same as the output demand function, where we replace p with w and Q with L:

$$w = 80 - L. \tag{15.4}$$

The competitive supply of labor is a horizontal line at $20. Given a competitive output market, the intersection of this supply curve of labor and the competitive

Figure 15.7 Effect of Output Market Structure on Labor Market Equilibrium

Because one unit of output is produced with one unit of labor, the marginal product of labor is 1, so the competitive labor demand curve is the same as the output demand curve. If both markets are competitive, the labor market equilibrium is e_1. A monopoly's labor demand curve is identical to its marginal revenue curve. An output monopoly charges final consumers a higher price, so it buys less labor. The new labor equilibrium is e_2. With a labor monopoly (union), the equilibrium is e_3.

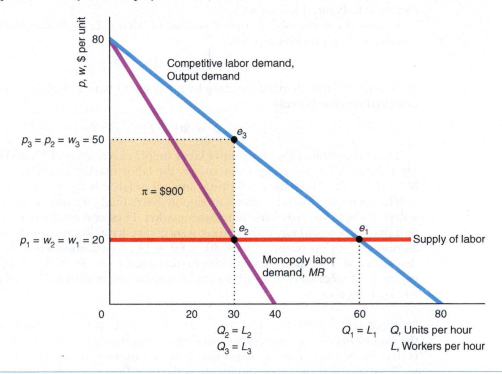

demand for labor (Equation 15.4) determines the labor market equilibrium, e_1, where $20 = 80 - L$. Thus, the competitive equilibrium amount of labor services is $L_1 = 60$, and the equilibrium wage is $w_1 = \$20$.

The cost of producing a unit of output equals the wage, so the supply curve of output is also horizontal at \$20. The intersection of this output supply curve and the output demand curve, Equation 15.3, occurs at $Q_1 = 60$ and $p_1 = \$20$. A competitive firm's average cost, w_1, exactly equals the price at which it sells its good, p_1, so the competitive firm breaks even.

Competitive Factor Market and Monopolized Output Market Because a monopoly in the output market charges a higher price than a competitive market would, it sells fewer units of output and hires fewer workers. The monopoly faces a competitive labor supply curve that is horizontal at the wage $w_2 = \$20$. Thus, the output monopoly's marginal cost is \$20 per unit.

The monopoly's marginal revenue curve is twice as steep as the linear output demand curve it faces (Chapter 11):

$$MR_Q = 80 - 2Q.$$

The monopoly maximizes its profit where its marginal revenue equals its marginal cost:

$$MR_Q = 80 - 2Q = 20 = MC.$$

Thus, the equilibrium quantity is $Q_2 = 30$. Substituting this quantity into the output demand, Equation 15.3, we find that the equilibrium price is $50. The monopoly makes $p_2 - w_2 = \$50 - \$20 = \$30$ per unit. Its profit is $\pi = \$900$, as the shaded rectangle in Figure 15.7 shows.

Because the monopoly's marginal product of labor is 1, its demand curve for labor equals its marginal revenue curve:

$$MRP_L = MR_Q \times MP_L = MR_Q.$$

We obtain its labor demand function by replacing Q with L and MR_Q with w in its marginal revenue function:

$$w = 80 - 2L.$$

The intersection of the competitive labor supply curve, $w_2 = \$20$, and the monopoly's demand for labor curve determines the labor market equilibrium, e_2, where $80 - 2L = 20$. Thus, the equilibrium amount of labor is $L_2 = 30$.

This example illustrates that a monopoly hurts final consumers and drives some sellers of the factor (workers) out of this market. Final consumers pay $30 more per unit than they would pay if the market were competitive. Because of the higher price, consumers buy less output, $Q_2 = 30 < 60 = Q_1$. As a consequence, the monopoly demands less labor than a competitive market does: $L_2 = 30 < 60 = L_1$. If the supply curve of labor were upward sloping, this reduction in demand would also reduce workers' wages.

Monopolized Factor Market and Competitive Output Market Now suppose that the output market is competitive and that a labor monopoly exists. One possibility is that the workers form a union that acts as a monopoly. Instead, for simplicity, we'll assume that the labor monopoly is the only firm that can supply the workers employed in the output market.[7]

The labor monopoly sets its marginal revenue equal to its marginal cost, which is $20. Because the competitive output market's labor demand curve is the same as the output demand curve, the marginal revenue curve this labor monopoly faces is the same as the marginal revenue curve of an output monopoly, where we replace Q with L:

$$MR_L = 80 - 2L.$$

The labor monopoly operates at e_3 in Figure 15.7, where its marginal revenue equals its marginal cost of $20:

$$80 - 2L = 20.$$

The labor monopoly sells $L_3 = 30$ hours of labor services. Substituting this quantity into the labor demand curve, Equation 15.4, we find that the monopoly wage is $w_3 = \$50$. Because the labor monopoly makes $w_3 - \$20 = \$30$ per hour of labor services and it sells 30 hours, its profit is $\pi = \$900$.

---

[7]Many markets have firms that only supply labor to other firms. Manpower, Kelly Services, and Accountemps provide temporary office workers and other employees. Many construction firms supply only skilled craftspeople. Still other firms specialize in providing computer programmers.

The competitive supply to the output market is horizontal at $w_3 = \$50$. The output equilibrium occurs where this supply curve hits the output demand curve, Equation 15.3: $50 = 80 - Q$. Thus, the equilibrium quantity is $Q_3 = 30$. The equilibrium price is the same as the wage, $p_3 = w_3 = \$50$. As a result, the output firms break even.

In our example, in which one unit of labor produces one unit of output, consumers fare the same whether the labor market or the output market is monopolized. Consumers pay $p_2 = p_3 = \$50$ and buy $Q_2 = Q_3 = 30$ units of output. The labor market equilibria are different: The wage is higher if the monopoly is in the labor market rather than the output market. The profit goes to the monopoly regardless of which market is monopolized.

Application

Unions and Profits

Workers acting collectively within a union can raise the wage much in the same manner as any other monopoly. A union's success in raising the wage depends on the elasticity of demand it faces, members' ability to act collectively, laws, and the share of the labor market that is unionized.

In the United States, if the majority of workers in a firm vote to unionize, all workers will be covered by a union contract. Through the union's negotiations with the firm, workers' wages may rise. Consequently, following unionization, the value of the stock of that firm—which reflects the profitability of the firm—may fall. Lee and Mas (2012) estimated that the average decrease in the value of a unionized firm is $40,500 (in $1998) per worker eligible to vote, or about a 10% drop in the value of the firm.

Lee and Mas noted that this drop in value following unionization is due to workers capturing some of the firm's former profit through higher wages and the rest results from inefficiency because the firm cannot use the optimal mix of labor and capital. Based on estimates from other studies, Lee and Mas calculated that 8% of the loss in value is due to higher wages and 2% stems from inefficiency.

Monopoly in Successive Markets   If the labor and output markets are both monopolized, consumers get hit with a double monopoly markup. The labor monopoly raises the wage, in turn raising the cost of producing the final output. The output monopoly then increases the final price even further.[8]

Figure 15.8 illustrates this double markup. The output monopoly's marginal revenue curve, $MR_Q = 80 - 2Q$, is the same as its labor demand curve, $w = 80 - 2L$. Because the labor demand curve is linear, the labor monopoly's marginal revenue curve is twice as steeply sloped:

$$MR_L = 80 - 4L.$$

The labor monopoly maximizes its profit by setting its marginal revenue equal to its marginal cost: $80 - 4L = 20$. Thus, at the labor market equilibrium, e_4, the labor monopoly provides $L_4 = 15$ workers. Substituting this quantity into the labor demand curve, $w = 80 - 2L$, we find that the labor monopoly's equilibrium wage

---

[8]In our example, the labor monopoly has a constant marginal cost of $m = \$20$. It operates where its marginal cost equals its marginal revenue, $w(1 + 1/\varepsilon_L)$, where ε_L is the elasticity of labor demand. Thus, the wage is greater than marginal cost: $w = m\mu_L$, where $\mu_L = 1/(1 + 1/\varepsilon_L) > 1$ is the multiplicative labor monopoly markup. The wage is the output monopoly's marginal cost. The output monopoly further marks up the price: $p = w\mu_Q = m\mu_L\mu_Q$, where $\mu_Q = 1/(1 + 1/\varepsilon_Q) > 1$ is the multiplicative output monopoly markup and ε_Q is the output demand elasticity.

Figure 15.8 Double Monopoly Markup

If a market has two successive monopolies, consumers are hit with a double monopoly markup. The labor market equilibrium is e_4, where the wage, w_4, is $30 above the labor market's marginal and average cost of $20. The product market monopoly's price, p_4, is $15 above its marginal cost, w_4. If the labor monopoly integrates vertically, consumers gain ($p_3 < p_4$), and total profit increases from $A + B$ to $B + C$.

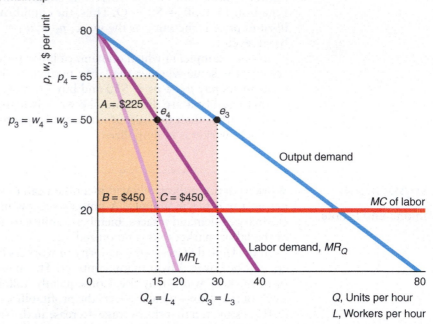

is $w_4 = \$50$. Thus, the labor monopoly marks up its wage $30 above its marginal cost. Its profit is area $B = \$30 \times 15 = \$450$ in the figure.

To maximize its profit, the output monopoly sets its marginal revenue, $MR_Q = 80 - 2Q$, equal to its marginal cost, $w_4 = \$50$. It sells $Q_4 = 15$ units of output. Substituting this quantity into the output demand curve, we learn that the output monopoly's equilibrium price is $p_4 = \$65$. The output monopoly's markup is $15 above its marginal cost. Its profit is area $A = \$225$.

This double markup harms consumers. They pay a higher price—$65 rather than $50—than they would pay if a monopoly was in just one market or the other.

Solved Problem 15.3

How are consumers affected and how do profits change in the example if the labor monopoly buys the monopoly producer, which is called *vertical integration*?[9]

Answer

1. *Solve for the postmerger equilibrium.* The new merged monopoly's output demand is the market demand, and its marginal revenue from extra output is $MR_Q = 80 - 2Q$, as Figure 15.8 shows. Now that the firms are one, the former labor monopoly no longer marks up the labor to its production unit. Its marginal cost of an extra unit of output is $20. The monopoly maximizes its profit by setting its marginal cost equal to MR_Q. The resulting output equilibrium is the same

---

[9]See the Supplemental Material "Vertical Integration" in MyEconLab, Chapter 15, for more details on vertical integration.

as it would be with a single labor monopoly. Equilibrium output is $Q_3 = 30$ and $p_3 = \$50$. The integrated monopoly's profit is $\$30 \times 30 = \$900$, area $B + C$.

2. *Compare the premerger and postmerger equilibria.* Consumers benefit from this merger. Because the price they pay falls from $p_4 = \$65$ to $p_3 = \$50$, they buy 15 extra units of output. The firms also benefit. The combined profit with two monopolies is areas $A + B = \$675$, which is less than the profit of the integrated firm, areas $B + C = \$900$. The labor monopoly can offer the output monopoly more than it earns as a separate firm and still increase its own profit: The firms can split the extra $\$225$. Thus, everyone may gain from a vertical merger that eliminates one of the two monopoly markups.

Comment: The potential of a double markup occurs in many markets. For example, for the first five years after the Apple iPhone was introduced, it was sold only through AT&T in the United States. Apparently, Apple and AT&T worked together to avoid a double markup by *quasi-integrating*: signing a contract to share the profit and to set the price at the joint profit-maximizing level.

15.3 Monopsony

In Chapter 11, we saw that a *monopoly*, a single *seller*, picks a point—a price and a quantity combination—on the market *demand curve* that maximizes its profit. A *monopsony*, a single *buyer* in a market, chooses a price-quantity combination from the industry *supply curve* that maximizes its profit. A monopsony is the mirror image of a monopoly, and it exercises its market power by buying at a price *below* the price that competitive buyers would pay.

A U.S. manufacturer of state-of-the-art weapon systems can legally sell only to the federal government. U.S. professional football teams, which act collectively, are the only U.S. firms that hire professional football players.[10] Many fisheries have only one buyer of fish (or at most a small number of buyers, an *oligopsony*).

Monopsony Profit Maximization

Suppose that a firm is the sole employer in town—a monopsony in the local labor market. The firm uses only one factor, labor (L), to produce a final good. The value the firm places on the last worker it hires is the marginal revenue product of that worker—the value of the extra output the worker produces—which is the height of the firm's labor demand curve for the number of workers the firm employs.

The firm has a downward-sloping demand curve in panel a of Figure 15.9. The firm faces an upward-sloping supply curve of labor: The higher its daily wage, w, the more people want to work for the firm. The firm's *marginal expenditure*—the additional cost of hiring one more worker—depends on the shape of the supply curve.

The supply curve shows the average expenditure, or wage, the monopsony pays to hire a certain number of workers. For example, the monopsony's average expenditure or wage is $w_m = \$20$ if it hires $L = 20$ workers per day. If the monopsony wants to obtain one more worker, it must raise its wage because the supply curve is upward sloping. Because it pays all workers the same wage, the monopsony must also pay more to each worker it was already employing. Thus, the monopsony's marginal

---

[10]Football players belong to a union that acts collectively, like a monopoly, in an attempt to offset the monopsony market power of the football teams.

Figure 15.9 Monopsony

(a) The marginal expenditure curve—the monopsony's marginal cost of buying one more unit—lies above the upward-sloping market supply curve. The monopsony equilibrium, e_m, occurs where the marginal expenditure curve intersects the monopsony's demand curve. The monopsony buys fewer units at a lower price, $w_m = \$20$, than a competitive market, $w_c = \$30$, would. (b) The supply curve is more elastic at the optimum than in (a), so the value that the monopsony places on the last unit (which equals the marginal expenditure of $40) exceeds the price the monopsony pays, $w_m = \$30$, by less than in (a).

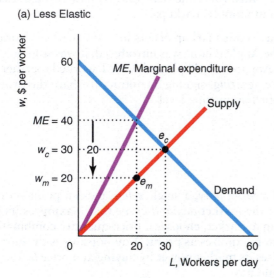

(a) Less Elastic

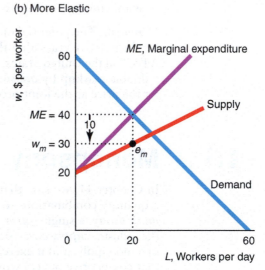

(b) More Elastic

expenditure on the last worker is greater than that worker's wage.[11] The marginal expenditure curve in the figure has twice as steep a slope as the linear supply curve.[12]

In contrast, if the firm were a competitive price taker in the labor market, it would face a supply curve that was horizontal at the market wage. Consequently, such a competitive firm's marginal expenditure to hire one more worker would be the market wage.

Any buyer—including a monopsony (Appendix 15B) or a competitive firm—*buys labor services up to the point at which the marginal value of the last unit of a factor equals the firm's marginal expenditure.* If the last unit is worth more to the buyer than its marginal expenditure, the buyer purchases another unit. Similarly, if the last unit is less valuable than its marginal expenditure, the buyer purchases one less unit.

The monopsony buys 20 units of the factor. The intersection of its marginal expenditure curve and the demand curve determines the monopsony equilibrium, e_m. The monopsony values the labor services of the last worker at $40 (height of its demand curve), and its marginal expenditure on that unit (height of its marginal expenditure

---

[11]The monopsony's total expenditure is $E = w(L)L$, where $w(L)$ is the wage given by the supply curve. Its marginal expenditure is $ME = dE/dL = w(L) + L[dw(L)/dL]$, where $w(L)$ is the wage paid the last worker and $L[dw(L)/dL]$ is the extra amount the monopsony pays the workers it was already employing. Because the supply curve is upward sloping, $dw(L)/dL > 0$, the marginal expenditure, ME, is greater than the average expenditure, $w(L)$.

[12]Appendix 15B shows that the ME curve is twice as steep as the labor supply curve for any linear labor supply curve.

curve) is $40. It pays only $20 (height of the supply curve). In other words, the monopsony values the last unit at $20 more than it actually has to pay.

If the market in Figure 15.9 were competitive, the intersection of the market demand curve and the market supply curve would determine the competitive equilibrium at e_c, where buyers purchase 30 units at $w_c = \$30$ per unit. Thus, the monopsony hires fewer workers, 20 versus 30, than a competitive market would hire and pays a lower wage, $20 versus $30.

Monopsony power is the ability of a single buyer to pay less than the competitive price profitably. The size of the gap between the value the monopsony places on the last worker (the height of its demand curve) and the wage it pays (the height of the supply curve) depends on the elasticity of supply at the monopsony optimum. The markup of the marginal expenditure (which equals the value to the monopsony) over the wage is inversely proportional to the elasticity of supply at the optimum (Appendix 15B):

$$\frac{ME - w}{w} = \frac{1}{\eta}.$$

By comparing panels a and b in Figure 15.9, we see that the less elastic the supply curve is at the optimum, the greater the gap between marginal expenditure and the wage. At the monopsony optimum, the supply curve in panel b is more elastic than the supply curve in panel a.[13] The gap between marginal expenditure and wage is greater in panel a, $ME - w = \$20$, than in panel b, $ME - w = \$10$. Similarly, the markup in panel a, $(ME - w)/w = 20/20 = 1$, is much greater than that in panel b, $(ME - w)/w = 10/30 = \frac{1}{3}$.

Application

Walmart's Monopsony Power

Does Walmart have monopsony power? This debate has been spirited. Walmart, the largest retailer in the world, employed 1.3 million people in the United States in 2013. More importantly, it is often the major employer of low-skilled workers in small towns.

Walmart is rarely a pure monopsony—the only employer in town—but it may be a *dominant-firm monopsony*. This concept is analogous to the dominant-firm monopoly model of Apple's iPod in Chapter 11. Walmart's relatively small, competitive rivals—the *fringe employers*—hire as many workers as they want and Walmart, the *dominant employer*, has monopsony power over the residual supply of workers. If the fringe is relatively large in a major metropolitan area, Walmart has no monopsony power because it faces a horizontal residual supply curve. However, in a small town, it may face an upward-sloping residual supply curve and hence can exercise monopsony power. (This example presumes that workers cannot easily move from small towns to cities to avoid this monopsony power.)

---

[13]The supply curve in panel a is $w = L$, while that in panel b is $w = 20 + \frac{1}{2}L$. The elasticity of supply, $\eta = (dL/dw)(w/L)$, at the optimum is $w/L = 20/20 = 1$ in panel a and $2w/L = 2 \times 30/20 = 3$ in panel b. Consequently, the supply curve at the optimum is three times as elastic in panel b as in panel a.

A recent study, Bonanno and Lopez (2012), estimates Walmart's residual supply curve and concludes that it has the potential to lower its wage below the competitive level by between 2.1% and 2.8% on average across the United States. It has negligible power in the northeastern states. However, they estimate that Walmart could lower wages by at least 5% in the non-metropolitan counties of Kansas, Kentucky, Louisiana, Utah, and Virginia.

Welfare Effects of Monopsony

By creating a wedge between the value to the monopsony and the value to the suppliers, the monopsony causes a welfare loss in comparison to a competitive market. In Figure 15.10, sellers lose producer surplus, $D + E$, because the monopsony price, p_m, for a good is below the competitive price, p_c. Area D is a transfer from the sellers to the monopsony and represents the savings of $p_c - p_m$ on the Q_m units the monopsony buys. The monopsony loses C because suppliers sell it less output, Q_m instead of Q_c, at the low price. Thus, the deadweight loss of monopsony is area $C + E$. This loss is due to the wedge between the value the monopsony places on the Q_m units, the monopoly expenditure ME in the figure, and the price it pays, p_m. The greater the difference between Q_c and Q_m and the larger the gap between ME and p_m, the greater the deadweight loss.

Figure 15.10 Welfare Effects of Monopsony

By setting a price, p_m, below the competitive level, p_c, a monopsony causes too little to be sold by the supplying market, thereby reducing welfare.

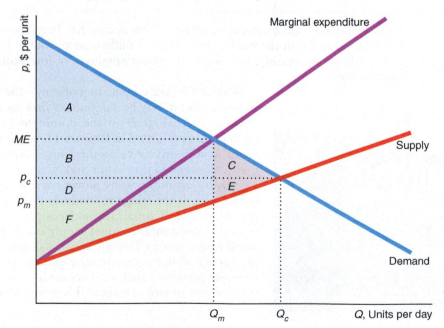

	Competition	Monopsony	Change
Consumer Surplus, CS	$A + B + C$	$A + B + D$	$D - C = \Delta CS$
Producer Surplus, PS	$D + E + F$	F	$- D - E = \Delta PS$
Welfare, W = CS + PS	$A + B + C + D + E + F$	$A + B + D + F$	$- C - E = \Delta W = DWL$

Solved Problem 15.4

How does the equilibrium in a labor market with a monopsony employer change if a minimum wage is set at the competitive level?

Answer

1. *Determine the original monopsony equilibrium.* Given the supply curve in the graph, the marginal expenditure curve is ME^1. The intersection of ME^1 and the demand curve determines the monopsony equilibrium, e_1. The monopsony hires L_1 workers at a wage of w_1.

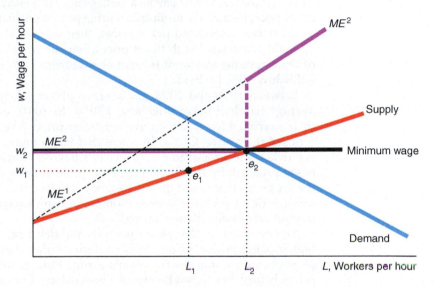

2. *Determine the effect of the minimum wage on the marginal expenditure curve.* The minimum wage makes the supply curve, as viewed by the monopsony, flat in the range where the minimum wage is above the original supply curve (fewer than L_2 workers). The new marginal expenditure curve, ME^2, is flat where the supply curve is flat. Where the supply curve is upward sloping, ME^2 is the same as ME^1.

3. *Determine the post-minimum-wage equilibrium.* The monopsony operates where its new marginal expenditure curve, ME^2, intersects the demand curve. With the minimum wage, the demand curve crosses the ME^2 curve at the end of the flat section. Thus, at the new equilibrium, e_2, the monopsony pays the minimum wage, w_2, and employs L_2 workers.

4. *Compare the equilibria.* The post-minimum-wage equilibrium is the same as the competitive equilibrium determined by the intersection of the supply and demand curves. Workers receive a higher wage, and more are employed than in the monopsony equilibrium. The minimum wage helps workers and hurts the monopsony.

Challenge Solution

Athletes' Salaries and Ticket Prices

In the Challenge at the beginning of the chapter, we asked whether, when a baseball team re-signs its star player at a much higher salary, it would raise the ticket price as a result. We've seen that an increase in the wage does lead to a higher competitive market price. Is the sports example different than the competitive market, and if so, why?

When a sports team re-signs a star player at a higher salary, it does not raise its ticket price. The sports case differs in two major ways. First, a sports team can set prices—it is a local monopoly (or at least a member of an oligopoly). Second, the player is paid a fixed salary for the year, which does not vary with the number of fans in the stadium.

A monopolistic baseball club's ticket price is determined by the intersection of its marginal revenue curve and its marginal cost curve. When a team raises a star player's salary, it increases its fixed cost but not its marginal cost. The player's salary doesn't affect the cost of bringing one more fan to the stadium. Indeed, if a stadium has unfilled seats, the marginal cost of the last fan is essentially zero.

Thus, to maximize its profit, the firm should set its price to maximize its revenue. That is, if the team starts paying a higher salary to a current player it should not raise its ticket price, because the profit-maximizing price is unchanged by a shift in a fixed cost.[14]

If salaries determined ticket prices, then we would expect changes in salaries to be highly correlated with ticket prices, but the correlation is not strong. The share of team revenue that went to salaries rose from 25% in 1976 to 54% in 2006, but fell below 40% by 2012.

Between 1990 and 2005, the average player salary increased 100%, while the average baseball ticket price rose 120%. In 2010, of the 14 teams that reduced their payroll, 4 lowered their average ticket price, 7 kept their price unchanged, and 3 raised their price. Of the 16 teams that had a higher payroll, 2 lowered the average ticket price (for example, the Tiger's payroll increased by 6.8%, but its average ticket price fell by 14.2%), 6 kept their price unchanged, and 8 raised the price. Of the six teams that raised their prices, one had its payroll fall—the Rangers raised the average ticket price 6.4% even though the team's payroll fell 19%—and another's payroll was essentially unchanged.

The main reason that player payrolls and ticket prices are correlated at all is that higher ticket prices "cause" higher salaries rather than the other way around. Star players capture some of the team's profit. Indeed, the Dodgers raised their ticket prices before they signed Brown to a high salary. Teams in cities where they can earn the highest revenues tend to pay the highest salaries. The New York Yankees' YES cable television network pays them about $350 million in revenue per year (plus the team owns a third of the company), which more than covers the Yankee's payroll ($229 million in 2013) before a single fan entered Yankee Stadium. The five other highest payrolls are paid by teams with new, large stadiums that double as virtual cash registers and provide funds to hire players.

Summary

1. **Competitive Factor Market.** Any firm maximizes its profit by choosing the quantity of a factor such that the marginal revenue product (MRP) of that factor— the marginal revenue times the marginal product of the factor—equals the factor price. The MRP is the firm's factor demand. A competitive firm's marginal revenue is the market price, so its MRP is the market price times the marginal product. The firm's long-run factor demand is usually flatter than its short-run demand because it can adjust more factors, thus giving it more flexibility. The market demand for a factor reflects how changes in factor prices affect output prices and hence output levels in product markets.

2. **Effects of Monopolies on Factor Markets.** If firms exercise market power to raise price above marginal cost in an output market or factor market, the quantity demanded by consumers falls. Because the quantity of

---

[14]In contrast, if by hiring a new star player (rather than re-signing one) the team attracts more fans, the demand curve it faces may shift so that it pays for the team to raise ticket prices. However, the team raises its price due to the shift in the demand curve rather than for cost reasons.

output and the quantity of inputs are closely related, a reduction in the quantity of an input reduces output, and a reduction in output reduces the demand for inputs.

3. **Monopsony.** A profit-maximizing monopsony—a single buyer—sets its price so that the marginal value to the monopsony equals its marginal expenditure. Because the monopsony pays a price below the competitive level, fewer units are sold than in a competitive market, producers of factors are worse off, the monopsony earns higher profits than it would if it were a price taker, and society suffers a deadweight loss. A monopsony may also price discriminate.

Questions

All questions are available on MyEconLab; * = *answer appears at the back of this book;* **A** = *algebra problem;* **C** = *calculus problem.*

1. Competitive Factor Market

1.1 What does a competitive firm's labor demand curve look like at quantities of labor such that the marginal product of labor is negative? Why?

*1.2 A firm's production function is Cobb-Douglas: $q = AL^{\alpha}K^{\beta}$. What is the firm's marginal revenue product of labor? (*Hint*: Use Appendix 6C and see Solved Problem 15.1.) **A**

1.3 The Cobb-Douglas production function for a U.S. tobacco products firm is $q = L^{0.2}K^{0.3}$ ("Returns to Scale in Various Industries" Application, Chapter 6). Derive the marginal revenue product of labor for this firm. (*Hint*: Use Appendix 6C and see Solved Problem 15.1.) **A**

*1.4 A competitive firm's production function is $q = 2LK$. What is its marginal revenue product of labor? (*Hint*: $MP_L = 2K$ and see Solved Problem 15.1.) **A**

*1.5 What effect does an ad valorem tax of α on the revenue of a competitive firm have on that firm's demand for labor? (*Hint*: See Solved Problem 15.2.)

1.6 How does a fall in the rental price of capital affect a firm's demand for labor in the long run?

1.7 If the firm uses a fixed-proportion production process where one unit of labor and one unit of capital produce one unit of output, what is the marginal revenue product of labor?

1.8 Suppose that a modern plague (AIDS, SARS, Ebola virus, avian flu) wipes out or incapacitates a major share of a small country's work force. If this country's labor market is competitive, what effect will this disaster have on wages in this country?

1.9 Oil companies, prompted by improvements in technology and increases in oil prices, are drilling in deeper and deeper water. Using a marginal revenue product and marginal cost diagram of drilling in deep water, show how improvements in drilling technology and increases in oil prices result in more deep-water drilling.

1.10 Suppose that a firm's production function is $q = L + K$. Can it be a competitive firm? Explain. **A**

2. Effects of Monopolies on Factor Markets

2.1 How does a monopoly's demand for labor shift if a second firm enters its output market and the result is a Cournot duopoly equilibrium?

2.2 Does a shift in the supply curve of labor have a greater effect on wages if the output market is competitive or if it is monopolistic?

2.3 If a monopoly has a Cobb-Douglas production function, $Q = L^{\alpha}K^{\beta}$, and faces an inverse demand function of $p = Q^{-b}$, what is its marginal revenue product of labor? (*Hint*: Use Appendix 6C, and note that the monopoly's marginal revenue function is $MR = [1 - b]Q^{-b} = [1 - b]p$.) **A**

2.4 What is a monopoly's demand for labor if it uses a fixed-proportions production function in which each unit of output takes one unit of labor and one of capital?

2.5 In 1998, four television networks (including ESPN) agreed to pay $17.6 billion for eight years of National Football League broadcast rights. In three of the deals, the price was more than double that of the previous contracts. What effect would you expect this deal to have on advertising rates and the number of commercials, and why?

2.6 Many grocery stores charge manufacturers a *slotting fee*: a one-time fee to place a given good on the shelf. Although stores sometimes claim that these fees are to cover their transaction costs of relabeling shelves and updating their computer files, the fees are too large—$50,000 or more—for that to be the only reason. Suppose that both the manufacturer and the grocery stores were monopolies.

What is the effect of a slotting fee on the manufacturer's wholesale price, the final price in the store, the number of units sold, and the two firms' profits?

2.7 Can a merger of an upstream and a downstream monopoly help consumers? Explain. (*Hint*: See Solved Problem 15.3.)

2.8 For the first five years after the iPhone was introduced, Apple sold it in the United States with the requirement that it be used only on the AT&T cell phone network. Indeed, Apple took a series of steps to prevent customers from "unlocking" the phone so that it could be used on other networks. The Orange network in France began selling the first iPhone for €399 ($588) with a two-year subscription. Unlike in the United States, one could get an unlocked iPhone in France from the vendor. Orange would unlock an iPhone for an additional €100 ($144) if the customer chose an iPhone service plan, €150 if the customer stayed with the carrier and had a non-iPhone plan (which didn't allow one to use the iPhone's special features), and €250 if the customer didn't have a plan with Orange (Stan Beer, "Orange iPhone Unlock Starts Demise of Exclusive Carrier Model," *ITWire*, November 28, 2007). Give plausible explanations why Apple chose to have an exclusive deal with AT&T, why AT&T wanted Apple to enforce exclusivity, and why Orange was being more flexible. Was Apple or the phone service "extending monopoly power?"

2.9 Apple sold its iPhone to AT&T, which in turn sold it to the final consumers. Suppose that the consumers' constant elasticity demand function for the iPhone was $Q = Ap^{-\varepsilon}$, Apple's marginal cost of production was m, and AT&T's marginal cost of reselling the phone was c. If both Apple and AT&T were monopolies and set prices independently, what price would they set? If they were to have merged, what price would they have set? (*Hint*: See Solved Problem 15.3.) **C**

2.10 The U.S. Department of Justice (DOJ) accused Apple and five publishers of colluding to fix e-book prices, which Apple wanted to sell for viewing on its iPad. The publishers settled with the DOJ and Apple was found guilty in 2013. Apple's standard arrangement with book publishers and others who sell apps for the iPad is that Apple keeps 30% of the revenue. Compare the equilibria if the publishers act as a cartel and sell directly to final consumers to one in which Apple sells to consumers and keeps 30% of the revenue. (*Hint*: The marginal cost of an e-book is essentially zero.)

3. Monopsony

3.1 Can a monopsony exercise monopsony power—profitably setting its price below the competitive level—if the supply curve it faces is horizontal?

3.2 A monopsony faces a supply curve of $p = 10 + Q$. What is its marginal expenditure curve? **A**

3.3 Suppose that the original labor supply curve, S^1, for a monopsony shifts to the right to S^2 if the firm spends $1,000 in advertising. Under what condition should the monopsony engage in this advertising? (*Hint*: See the monopoly advertising analysis in Chapter 12.)

3.4 Firms are taxed to pay for workers' medical care. How is the incidence of a specific tax per worker shared between competitive firms and workers? How does your answer change if the firm is a monopsony?

3.5 Suppose that a modern plague (AIDS, SARS, Ebola virus, avian flu) wipes out or incapacitates a major share of a small country's work force. If this country's labor market is monopsonistic, what effect will this disaster have on wages in this country? Compare your answer to that in Question 1.8.

3.6 A firm is a monopoly in the output market and a monopsony in the input market. Its only input is the finished good, which it buys from a competitive market with an upward-sloping supply curve. The firm sells the same good to competitive buyers in the output market. Determine its profit-maximizing output. What price does it charge in the output market? What price does it pay to its suppliers?

3.7 Compare the equilibrium in a market in which a firm is both a monopoly and a monopsony (as in the previous question) to the competitive equilibrium.

3.8 Compare the equilibrium quantity and price in two markets: one in which a firm is both a monopsony and a monopoly (as in Question 3.6) and one in which the firm buys inputs competitively but has a monopoly in the output market.

3.9 If the monopsony faces a supply curve of $p = 10 + Q$ and has a demand curve of $p = 50 - Q$, what are the equilibrium quantity and price? How does this equilibrium differ from the competitive equilibrium? **A**

3.10 Compare welfare in a market where a firm is both a monopsony and a monopoly (as in Question 3.6) to welfare in markets in which the firm has a monopsony in the input market but acts as a price taker in the output market.

3.11 What happens to the monopsony equilibrium if the minimum wage is set slightly above or below the competitive wage? (*Hint*: See Solved Problem 15.4.)

3.12 What effect does a price support have on a monopsony? In particular, describe the equilibrium if the price support is set at the price where the supply curve intersects the demand curve. (*Hint*: See Solved Problem 15.4.)

3.13 In 2012, the U.S. Department of Justice (DOJ) alleged that eBay and Intuit had an agreement that "barred either firm from soliciting each other's employees, and for over a year barred at least eBay from hiring any employees from Intuit at all" (**www.justice.gov/atr/public/press_releases/ 2012/288865.htm**). (In an earlier case, the DOJ made similar allegations about Adobe, Apple, Google, Intel, Intuit, and Pixar, which these firms settled by agreeing not to engage in such activities in the future.) If true, what would be the purpose of such an agreement? What type of market structure would these firms be trying to achieve?

4. Challenge

4.1 The Challenge points out that if a ball club raises a player's salary, it increases its fixed cost but not its variable cost. Use a figure to show what effect such an increase has if (a) the firm is competitive or (b) the firm is a monopoly.

16

Interest Rates, Investments, and Capital Markets

I'd gladly pay you Tuesday for a hamburger today. —Wimpy

Challenge

Should You Go to College?

For most of your childhood, your parents, teachers, or other adults urged you to go to college. However, a survey of Americans find that those who think college is a good investment has plummeted from 81% in 2008 to just half the population in 2013.

In the fall of 2012, 66% percent of high school graduates were enrolled in colleges or universities. Yet only four out of ten young people earn two- or four-year college degrees now. Three out of ten adults over 25 years old have a bachelor's degree.

Going to college is expensive. In the 2011–2012 school year, half of all 18- to 24-year-old undergraduate students borrowed money to pay for college. Is going to college worth it?

This chapter continues the treatment of factor markets in Chapter 15 by focusing on capital markets and examining which investments pay. People invest in capital and other durable goods: products that are usable for years. Firms use durable goods—such as manufacturing plants, machines, and trucks—to produce and distribute goods and services. Consumers spend one in every eight of their dollars on durable goods such as houses, cars, and refrigerators. Just as a firm considers whether or not to invest in physical capital, individuals decide whether to invest in their own *human capital*. Where a firm chooses the durability of a piece of equipment, some people invest in lengthening their expected life spans by exercising or purchasing medical care. Where a firm buys machinery and other capital to produce more output and increase its future profits, individuals invest in education to raise their productivity and their future earnings.

Until now, we have examined the choices between nondurable goods and services, which are consumed when they are purchased or soon thereafter. You eat an ice-cream cone or see a movie in a theater once after paying for it.

If a firm rents a durable good by the week, it faces a decision similar to buying a nondurable good or service. A firm demands workers' services (or other nondurable input) up to the point at which its *current* marginal cost (the wage) equals its *current* marginal benefit (the marginal revenue product of the workers' services). A firm that rents a durable good, such as a truck, by the month can use the same rule to decide how many trucks to employ per month. The firm rents trucks up to the point at which the *current* marginal rental cost equals its *current* marginal benefit—the marginal revenue product of the trucks.

If the capital good must be bought or built rather than rented, the firm cannot apply this rule on the basis of current costs and benefits alone. (Many types of capital, such as factories or specialized pieces of equipment, *cannot* be rented.) In deciding whether to build a long-lived factory, a firm must compare the *current* cost of the capital to the *future* higher profits it will make from using the plant.

stock
a quantity or value that is measured independently of time

Often such comparisons involve *stocks* and *flows*. A **stock** is a quantity or value that is measured independently of time. Because a durable good lasts for many periods, its stock is discussed without reference to its use within a particular time period. We say that a firm owns "an apartment building *this* year" (not "an apartment building *per* year"). If a firm buys the apartment house for $500,000, we say that it has a capital stock worth $500,000 today.

flow
a quantity or value that is measured per unit of time

A **flow** is a quantity or value that is measured per unit of time. The consumption of nondurable goods, such as the number of ice-cream cones you eat per week, is a flow. Similarly, the stock of a durable good provides a flow of services. A firm's apartment house—its capital stock—provides a flow of housing services (apartments rented per month or year) to tenants. In exchange for these housing services, the firm receives a flow of rental payments from the tenants.

Does it pay for the firm to buy the apartment house? To answer this question, we need to extend our analysis in two ways. First, we must develop a method of comparing a flow of dollars in the future to a dollar today, as we do in this chapter. Second, we need to consider the role of uncertainty about the future (can the firm rent all the apartments each month?), a subject that we discuss in Chapter 17.

In this chapter, we examine four main topics

1. **Comparing Money Today to Money in the Future.** Interest rates tell us how much more money is worth today than in the future.

2. **Choices over Time.** Investing money in a project pays if the return from that investment is greater than that on the best alternative when both returns are expressed on a comparable basis.

3. **Exhaustible Resources.** Scarcity, rising costs of extraction, and positive interest rates may cause the price of exhaustible resources like coal and gold to rise exponentially over time.

4. **Capital Markets, Interest Rates, and Investments.** Supply and demand in capital markets determine the market rate of interest, which affects how much people invest.

16.1 Comparing Money Today to Money in the Future

Even without inflation—so a bundle of goods would sell for the same price today, next year, and 100 years from now—most people would still value receiving a dollar today more than a dollar to be received tomorrow. Wouldn't you rather eat a dollar's worth of chocolate today than wait ten years to eat that same amount of chocolate?

Interest Rates

Because virtually everyone values having a dollar today more than having a dollar in the future, getting someone to loan you a dollar today requires agreeing to pay back more than a dollar in the future. You may have borrowed money to pay for

interest rate
the percentage more that must be repaid to borrow money for a fixed period of time

your college education in exchange for a credible promise to repay a greater amount after you graduate. How much more you must pay in the future is specified by an **interest rate**: the percentage more that must be repaid to borrow money for a fixed period of time.[1]

If you put money in a savings account, you are lending the bank your money, which it may in turn loan to someone who wants to buy a car or a house. For the use of your deposited funds for one year, the bank agrees to pay you an interest rate, i, of, say, 4%. That is, the bank promises to return to you $1.04 $(= 1 + i)$ one year from now for every dollar you loan it. If you put $100 in your savings account, you will have your $100 plus interest of $100 \times 0.04 = \$4$ for a total of $104 at the end of the year. (See MyEconLab, Chapter 16, "Usury," for a discussion of ancient people's opposition to paying interest, and current restrictions on Islamic banks.)

Discount Rate   You may value future consumption more or less than do other members of society. If you knew you had two years to live, you would place less value on payments three or more years in the future than most other people do. We call an individual's personal "interest" rate that person's **discount rate**: a rate reflecting the relative value an individual places on future consumption compared to current consumption.

discount rate
a rate reflecting the relative value an individual places on future consumption compared to current consumption

A person's willingness to borrow or lend depends on whether his or her discount rate is greater or less than the market interest rate. If your discount rate is nearly zero—you view current and future consumption as equally desirable—you would gladly loan money in exchange for a positive interest rate. Similarly, if your discount rate is high—current consumption is much more valuable to you than future consumption—you would be willing to borrow at a lower interest rate. In the following discussion, we assume for simplicity that an individual's discount rate is the same as the market interest rate unless we explicitly state otherwise.

Compounding   If you place $100 in a bank account that pays 4%, at the end of a year, you can take out the interest payment of $4 and leave your $100 in the bank to earn more interest in the future. If you leave your $100 in the bank indefinitely and the interest rate remains constant over time, you will receive a payment of $4 each year. In this way, you can convert your $100 stock into a flow of $4-a-year payments forever.

In contrast, if you leave both your $100 and your $4 interest in the bank, the bank must pay you interest on $104 at end of the second year. The bank owes you interest of $4 on your original deposit of $100 and interest of $4 \times 0.04 = \$0.16$ on your interest from the first year, for a total of $4.16.

Thus, at the end of Year 1, your account contains

$$\$104.00 = \$100 \times 1.04 = \$100 \times 1.04^1.$$

By the end of Year 2, you have

$$\$108.16 = \$104 \times 1.04 = \$100 \times 1.04^2.$$

At the end of Year 3, your account has

$$\$112.49 \approx \$108.16 \times 1.04 = \$100 \times 1.04^3.$$

---

[1]For simplicity, we refer to *the* interest rate throughout this chapter, but most economies have many interest rates. For example, a bank charges a higher interest rate to loan you money than it pays you to borrow your money.

If we extend this reasoning, by the end of Year t, you have

$$\$100 \times 1.04^t.$$

In general, if you let your interest accumulate in your account, for every dollar you loan the bank, it owes you $1 + i$ dollars after one year, $(1 + i) \times (1 + i) = (1 + i)^2$ dollars after two years, $(1 + i) \times (1 + i) \times (1 + i) = (1 + i)^3$ after three years, and $(1 + i)^t$ dollars at the end of t years. This accumulation of interest on interest is called *compounding*.

Frequency of Compounding To get the highest return on your savings account, you need to check both the interest rate and the frequency of compounding. We have assumed that interest is paid only at the end of the year. However, many banks pay interest more frequently than once a year. If you leave your interest in the bank for the entire year, you receive compounded interest—interest on the interest.

If a bank's annual interest rate is $i = 4\%$, but it pays interest two times a year, the bank pays you half a year's interest, $i/2 = 2\%$, after six months. For every dollar in your account, the bank pays you $(1 + i/2) = 1.02$ dollars after six months. If you leave the interest in the bank, at the end of the year, the bank must pay you interest on your original dollar and on the interest you received at the end of the first six months. At the end of the year, the bank owes you $(1 + i/2) \times (1 + i/2) = (1 + i/2)^2 = (1.02)^2 = \$1.0404$, which is your original \$1 plus 4.04¢ in interest.

If the bank were to compound your money more frequently, you would earn even more interest. Some banks offer continuous compounding, paying interest at every instant. Such compounding is only slightly better for you than daily compounding. Table 16.1 shows you that the amount you would earn after one year of investing \$10,000 at a 4% or at an 18% annual rate of interest depends on the frequency of compounding.

Because most people cannot easily perform such calculations, the 1968 U.S. Truth-in-Lending Act requires lenders to tell borrowers the equivalent noncompounded annual percentage rate (APR) of interest. As the table shows, twice-a-year compounding at 4% has an APR of 4.04%. That is, over a year, an account with a noncompounded interest rate of 4.04% pays you the same interest as a 4% account that was compounded twice during the year.

Thus, when considering various loans or interest rates, you should compare the APRs; comparing rates that are compounded at different frequencies can be misleading. If you use credit cards to borrow money, it's particularly important that you compare APRs across accounts because credit card interest rates are usually high. If the interest rate on your card is 18%, a continuously compounded rate has an APR of over 19.7%. If you borrow \$10,000 for a year, you'll owe \$1,972.17 with continuous compounding, which is 9.6% more than the \$1,800 you'd owe with annual compounding. From now on, we assume that compounding takes place annually.

Table 16.1 Interest and the Frequency of Compounding

Frequency of Compounding	Interest Payments on a $10,000 Investment at the End of 1 Year, $	
	4%	**18%**
Once a year	400.00	1,800.00
Twice a year	404.00	1,881.00
Four times a year	406.04	1,925.19
Daily	408.08	1,971.64
Continuous	408.11	1,972.17

Using Interest Rates to Connect the Present and Future

Interest rates connect the value of the money you put in the bank today, the *present value* (PV), and the *future value* (FV) that you are later repaid, which is the present value plus interest. Understanding this relationship allows us to evaluate the attractiveness of investments involving payments today for profits in the future and of purchases made today but paid for later. Knowing the interest rate and the present value allows us to calculate the future value. Similarly, we can determine the present value if we know the future value and the interest rate.

Future Value If you deposit PV dollars in the bank today and allow the interest to compound for *t* years, how much money will you have at the end? The future value, FV, is the present value times a term that reflects the compounding of the interest payments:

$$FV = PV \times (1 + i)^t. \tag{16.1}$$

Table 16.2 shows how much $1 put in the bank today will be worth in the future at various annually compounded interest rates. For example, $1 left in the bank for 50 years will be worth only $1.64 at a 1% interest rate. However, that same investment is worth $7.11 at a 4% interest rate, $117.39 at a 10% rate, and $9,100.44 at a 20% rate.

Application	*One thousand dollars left to earn interest at 8% a year will grow to $43 quadrillion in 400 years, but the first 100 years are the hardest.*

Power of Compounding

—Sidney Homer, Salomon Brothers analyst

No doubt you've read that the Dutch got a good deal buying Manhattan from the original inhabitants in 1626 for about $24 worth of beads and trinkets. However, that conclusion may be wrong. If these native Americans had had the opportunity to sell the beads and invest in tax-free bonds with an APR of 7%, the bond would be worth $6 trillion in 2014, which is much more than the assessed value of Manhattan Island. On the other hand, if the United States had taken the $7.2 million it paid for the purchase of Alaska from Russia in 1867 and invested in the same type of bonds, that money would now be worth only $150 billion, which is much less than Alaska's current value.

Present Value Instead of asking how much a dollar today is worth in the future, we can ask how much a dollar in the future is worth today, given the market interest rate. For example, we may want to know how much money, PV, we have to put in the

Table 16.2 Future Value, *FV*, to Which $1 Grows by the End of Year *t* at Various Interest Rates, *i*, Compounded Annually, $

t, Years	1%	4%	5%	10%	20%
1	1.01	1.04	1.05	1.10	1.20
5	1.05	1.22	1.28	1.61	2.49
10	1.10	1.48	1.63	2.59	6.19
25	1.28	2.67	3.39	10.83	95.40
50	1.64	7.11	11.47	117.39	9,100.44

Note: $FV = (1 + i)^t$, where *FV* is the future value of $1 invested for *t* years at an annual interest rate of *i*.

bank today at an interest rate i to get a specific amount of money, FV, in the future. If we want to have $FV = \$100$ at the end of a year and the interest rate is $i = 4\%$, then from Equation 16.1 we know that $PV \times 1.04 = \$100$. Dividing both sides of this expression by 1.04, we learn that we need to put $PV = \$100/1.04 = \$96.15$ in the bank today to have $100 next year.

A more general formula relating money t periods in the future to money today is obtained by dividing both sides of Equation 16.1 by $(1 + i)^t$ to obtain

$$PV = \frac{FV}{(1 + i)^t}. \tag{16.2}$$

This equation tells us what FV dollars in year t are worth today at an interest i compounded annually. Table 16.3 and Figure 16.1 show what $1 in the future is worth today at various interest rates. At high interest rates, money in the future is virtually

Table 16.3 Present Value, *PV*, of a Payment of $1 at the End of Year *t* at Various Interest Rates, *i*, Compounded Annually, $

t, Years	1%	4%	5%	10%	20%
1	0.99	0.96	0.95	0.91	0.83
5	0.95	0.82	0.78	0.62	0.40
10	0.91	0.68	0.61	0.39	0.16
25	0.78	0.38	0.30	0.09	0.01
50	0.61	0.14	0.09	0.009	0.00011

Note: $PV = 1/(1 + i)^t$, where PV is the present value of $1 at the end of year t at an annual interest rate of i.

Figure 16.1 Present Value of a Dollar in the Future

The present value of a dollar is lower the farther in the future it is paid. At a given time in the future, the present value is lower when the interest rate is higher.

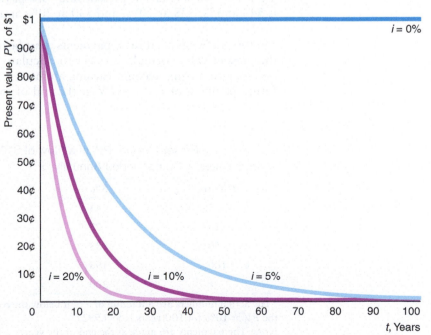

worthless today: A dollar paid to you in 25 years is worth only 1¢ today at a 20% interest rate.

Stream of Payments

Sometimes we need to deal with payments per period, which are flow measures, rather than a present value or future value, which are stock measures. Often a firm pays for a new factory or an individual pays for a house by making monthly mortgage payments. In deciding whether to purchase the factory or house, the decision maker compares the value of the stock (factory or home) to a flow of payments over time.

Present Value of Payments over Time   One way to make such an evaluation is to use our knowledge of the relationship between present and future value to determine the present value of the stream of payments. To do so, we calculate the present value of each future payment and sum them.

Payments for a Finite Number of Years   We start with a specific example. Suppose that you agree to pay $10 at the end of each year for three years to repay a debt. If the interest rate is 10%, the present value of this series of payments is

$$PV = \frac{\$10}{1.1} + \frac{\$10}{1.1^2} + \frac{\$10}{1.1^3} \approx \$24.87.$$

More generally, if you make a *future payment* of f per year for t years at an interest rate of i, the present value (stock) of this flow of payments is

$$PV = f\left[\frac{1}{(1 + i)^1} + \frac{1}{(1 + i)^2} + \cdots + \frac{1}{(1 + i)^t}\right]. \tag{16.3}$$

Table 16.4 shows that the present value of a payment of $f = \$10$ a year for five years is $43 at 5%, $38 at 10%, and $30 at 20% annual interest.

Payments Forever   If these payments must be made at the end of each year forever, the present value formula is easier to calculate than Equation 16.3. If you put PV dollars into a bank account earning an interest rate of i, you can get an interest or future payment of $f = i \times PV$ at the end of the year. Dividing both sides of this

Table 16.4 Present Value, *PV*, of a Flow of $10 a Year for *t* Years at Various Interest Rates, *i*, Compounded Annually, $

t, Years	5%	10%	20%
5	43	38	30
10	77	61	42
50	183	99	50*
100	198	100*	50*
∞	200	100	50

*The actual numbers are a fraction of a cent below the rounded numbers in the table. For example, the *PV* at 10% for 100 years is $99.9927.

Note: The payments are made at the end of the year.

expression by i, we find that to get a payment of f each year forever, you'd have to put

$$PV = \frac{f}{i} \qquad (16.4)$$

in the bank. Thus, you'd have to deposit $10/i$ in the bank to ensure a future payment of $f = \$10$ forever. (See Appendix 16A for a mathematical derivation.) Using this formula, we determine that the present value of $10 a year forever is $200 at 5%, $100 at 10%, and $50 at 20%.[2]

Solved Problem 16.1

Melody Toyota advertises that it will sell you a Corolla for $14,000 or lease it to you. To lease it, you must make a down payment of $1,650 and agree to pay $1,800 at the end of each of the next two years. After the last lease payment, you may buy the car for $12,000. If you plan to keep the car until it falls apart (at least a decade) and the interest rate is 10%, which approach has a lower present value of costs?

Answer

1. *Calculate the present value of leasing.* The present value of leasing the car and then buying it is the sum of the down payment of $1,650, the present value of paying $f = \$1,800$ at the end of each year for $t = 2$ years, and the present value of purchasing the car for $FV = \$12,000$ in $t = 2$ years. Using Equation 16.2, we find that the present value of buying the car at the end of the lease period is

$$PV = \frac{f}{i^2} = \frac{\$12,000}{1.1^2} \approx \$9,917.$$

Thus, the present value of leasing the car and then buying it is approximately

$$\$1,650 + \$3,124 + \$9,917 = \$14,691.$$

2. *Compare leasing to buying the car.* The present value of buying the car is $14,000, which is $691 less than the present value of leasing it.

Future Value of Payments over Time We just calculated the present value of a stream of payments. This type of computation can help you decide whether to buy something today that you'll pay for over time. Sometimes, however, we want to know about the future value of a stream of payments.

For example, suppose that you want to know how much you'll have in your savings account, FV, at some future time if you save f each year. The first year, you place f dollars in your account. The second year, you add another f and you have the first year's payment plus its accumulated interest, $f(1 + i)^1$. Thus, at the end of the second year, your account has $f[1 + (1 + i)^1]$. In the third year, you have

---

[2]This payment-in-perpetuity formula, Equation 16.4, provides a good approximation of a payment for a large but finite number of years. As Table 16.4 shows, at a 5% interest rate, the present value of a payment of $10 a year for 100 years, $198, is close to the present value of a permanent stream of payments, $200. At higher interest rates, this approximation is nearly perfect. At 10%, the present value of payments for 100 years is $99.9927 compared to $100 for perpetual payments. The reason this approximation works better at high rates is that a dollar paid more than 50 or 100 years from now is essentially worthless today, as Table 16.3 shows.

the third year's payment, f, plus the current value of the second year's payment, $f(1 + i)$, plus the current value of the first year's payment, $f(1 + i)^2$, for a total of $f[1 + (1 + i) + (1 + i)^2]$. Continuing in this way, we see that, at the end of t years, the account has[3]

$$FV = f[1 + (1 + i)^1 + (1 + i)^2 + \cdots + (1 + i)^{t-1}]. \qquad (16.5)$$

Application

Saving for Retirement

If all goes well, you'll live long enough to retire. Will you live like royalty off your savings, or will you depend on Social Security to provide enough income that you can avoid having to eat dog food to stay alive? (When I retire, I'm going to be a Velcro farmer.)

You almost certainly don't want to hear this, but it isn't too early to think about saving for retirement. Thanks to the power of compounding, if you start saving when you're young, you don't have to save as much per year as you would if you start saving when you're middle-aged.

Suppose that you plan to work full time from age 22 until you retire at 70 and that you can earn 7% on your retirement savings account. Let's consider two approaches to savings:

- **Early bird.** You save $3,000 a year for the first 15 years of your working life and then let your savings accumulate interest until you retire.
- **Late bloomer.** After not saving for the first 15 years, you save $3,000 a year for the next 33 years until retirement.

Which scenario leads to a bigger retirement nest egg? To answer this question, we calculate the future value at retirement of each of these streams of investments.

The early bird adds $3,000 each year for 15 years into a retirement account. Using Equation 16.5, we calculate that the account has

$$\$3,000(1 + 1.07^1 + 1.07^2 + \ldots + 1.07^{14}) = \$75,387$$

at the end of 15 years. This amount then grows as the interest compounds for the next 33 years. Using Equation 16.1, we determine that the fund grows about 9.3 times to

$$\$75,387.07 \times 1.07^{33} = \$703,010$$

by retirement.

The late bloomer makes no investments for 15 years and then invests $3,000 a year until retirement. Again using Equation 16.5, we calculate that the funds at retirement are

$$\$3,000(1 + 1.07 + 1.07^2 + \ldots + 1.07^{32}) = \$356,800.$$

Thus, even though the late bloomer contributes to the account for more than twice as long as the early bird, the late bloomer has saved only about half as much at retirement. Indeed, to have roughly the same amount at retirement as the early bird, the late bloomer would have to save nearly $6,000 a year for the 33 years. (By the way, someone who saved $3,000 each year for all 48 years would have $703,010 + $356,800 = $1,059,810 salted away by retirement.)

---

[3]This equation can also be written as $FV = f[(1 + i)^0 + (1 + i)^1 + (1 + i)^2 + \cdots + (1 + i)^{t-1}]$ because $(1 + i)^0 = 1$.

Inflation and Discounting

So far, we've ignored inflation (implicitly assumed an inflation rate of zero). Now we suppose that general inflation occurs so that *nominal prices*—actual prices that are not adjusted for inflation—rise at a constant rate over time. By adjusting for this rate of inflation (Chapter 5), we can convert nominal prices to *real prices*, which are constant prices that are independent of inflation. To calculate the real present value of future payments, we adjust for inflation and use interest rates to discount future real payments.

To illustrate this process, we calculate the real present value of a payment made next year. First, we adjust for inflation so as to convert next year's nominal payment to a real amount. Then we determine the real interest rate. Finally, we use the real interest rate to convert the real future payment to a real present value.

Adjusting for Inflation   Suppose that the rate of inflation is γ ("gamma") and the nominal amount you pay next year is $\tilde{f}$. This future debt in today's dollars—the real amount you owe—is $f = \tilde{f}/(1 + \gamma)$. If the rate of inflation is $\gamma = 10\%$, a nominal payment of $\tilde{f}$ next year is $\tilde{f}/1.1 \approx 0.909\tilde{f}$ in today's dollars.

Nominal and Real Rates of Interest   To calculate the present value of this future real payment, we discount using an interest rate. Just as we converted the future payments into real values by adjusting for inflation, we convert a nominal interest rate into a real interest rate by adjusting for inflation.

Without inflation, a dollar today is worth $1 + i$ next year, where i is the real interest rate. With an inflation rate of γ, a dollar today is worth $(1 + i)(1 + \gamma)$ nominal dollars tomorrow. If $i = 5\%$ and $\gamma = 10\%$, a dollar today is worth $1.05 \times 1.1 = 1.155$ nominal dollars next year.

Banks pay a nominal interest rate, $\tilde{i}$, rather than a real one. If they're going to get people whose real discount rate is i to save, banks' nominal interest rate must be such that a dollar pays $(1 + i)(1 + \gamma)$ dollars next year. Because $1 + \tilde{i} = (1 + i)(1 + \gamma)$ $= 1 + i + i\gamma + \gamma$, the nominal rate is

$$\tilde{i} = i + i\gamma + \gamma.$$

By rearranging this equation, we see that the real rate of interest depends on the nominal rate of interest and the rate of inflation:

$$i = \frac{\tilde{i} - \gamma}{1 + \gamma}. \tag{16.6}$$

Equation 16.6 shows that the real rate of interest is less than the nominal rate in the presence of inflation.

If the inflation rate is small, the denominator of Equation 16.6, $1 + \gamma$, is close to 1. As a result, many people approximate the real rate of interest as the nominal rate of interest minus the rate of inflation:

$$\tilde{i} - \gamma.$$

If the nominal rate of interest is 15.5% and the rate of inflation is 10%, the real rate of interest is $(15.5\% - 10\%)/1.1 = 5\%$. The approximation to the real rate, $15.5\% - 10\% = 5.5\%$, is above the true rate by half a percentage point. The lower the rate of inflation, the closer the approximation is to the real rate of interest. If the inflation rate falls to $\gamma = 2\%$ while the nominal rate remains 15.5%, the approximation to the real rate, 13.5%, is above the real rate, 13.24%, by only slightly more than a quarter of a percentage point.

Real Present Value To obtain the real present value of a payment one year from now, we discount the future real payment of $f = \tilde{f}/(1 + \gamma)$ using the real interest rate:

$$PV = \frac{f}{1 + i} = \frac{\tilde{f}}{(1 + \gamma)(1 + i)}.$$

Thus, the real present value is obtained by adjusting for inflation and by discounting using the real interest rate.

Suppose that you sign a contract with a store to pay $100 next year for a DVD player you get today. The rate of inflation is $\gamma = 10\%$, and the real rate of interest is $i = 5\%$. We calculate the real present value by converting the future payment into real dollars and by using the real interest rate to discount. Next year's nominal payment of $100 is only $100/1.1 \approx $90.91 in real dollars. Discounting by the real rate of interest, we find that the real present value of that payment is $90.91/1.05 \approx $86.58.

If everyone anticipates a particular inflation rate, γ, the nominal interest is roughly $i + \gamma$. Suppose, however, that the inflation rate turns out to be higher than the anticipated rate of γ. Such unanticipated inflation helps debtors because it lowers the real cost of future payments that are set in nominal rather than real terms.

Suppose that when you buy the DVD player, no one expects inflation ($\gamma = 0$), so both you and the store's owner believe that the present value of your future payment is $100/1.05 \approx $95.24. Immediately after you make the deal, the inflation rate suddenly increases to $\gamma = 10\%$, so the actual present value is only $86.58. Thus, because of the unexpected inflation, the present value of what you owe is less than either you or the store owner initially expected.

Application **Winning the Lottery**	Gloria C. Mackenzie won a 2013 Powerball lottery jackpot.[4] She chose a lump-sum cash payout of $370.8 million, before taxes, instead of $590.5 million in 30 annual payments. By offering these options, the lottery was implicitly acknowledging that money in the future is worth less than money today.[5] Several states boast that their lottery pays a winner $1 million. This claim is misleading (translation: They lie through their teeth). Typically, a lottery winner gets $50,000 a year for 20 years, which means that the winner receives $20 \times $50,000 = 1 million nominal dollars over time. However, after adjustment for inflation and discounting, the real present value of these prize payments over time is much less than $1 million. What is a payment of $50,000 for 20 years worth today? If the first payment is made today, its real present value is $50,000, regardless of the inflation and interest rates. The later payments need to be adjusted for inflation and discounted to the present to be comparable to this year's payment.

---

[4]This discussion of lottery prizes is not intended to encourage you to play the lottery. The important thing to remember about a lottery is that the probability of winning if you buy a ticket (about 1 in 175.2 million) is almost exactly the same as the probability of winning if you don't buy a ticket: zero.

[5]Sheila Botelho was asked why she chose the single payment option after winning Rhode Island's Multi-State Powerball lottery. Mrs. Botelho and her husband responded, "At our age, we don't even buy green bananas."

If the rate of inflation is 5% and the real rate of interest is 4%, a $50,000 payment next year is worth only $45,788 ≈ $50,000/(1.05 × 1.04) this year. Generalizing, we determine that the real present value of a dollar t years from now is

$$\frac{1}{(1.05)^t(1.04)^t}.$$

The $(1.05)^t$ term in the denominator adjusts for inflation between now and the year t: It expresses the payment in the future in terms of today's dollars. The $(1.04)^t$ term in the denominator converts the payment in year t to a present value.

At these rates, the real present value of the 20 payments is less than half of the alleged value: $491,396. Without inflation ($\gamma = 0$), the real present value would be $706,697. With 5% inflation and a real interest rate of 10%, the present value of the prize is only $351,708.

16.2 Choices over Time

Earlier chapters discuss how consumers and firms make choices that do not involve time. Often, however, such decisions involve comparisons over time. Individuals and firms must choose between two or more options—such as investments and contracts—that have different present and future values. A land speculator decides whether to sell a plot of land today for $100,000 or next year for $200,000. Margi decides among putting $1,000 into a bank account, buying $1,000 worth of stocks, paying $1,000 for a course in computer programming, and consuming the $1,000 now. MGM, a conglomerate, decides whether to produce a movie that stars a muscle-bound hero who solves the pollution problem by beating up an evil capitalist, to build a new hotel in Reno, to buy a television studio, or to put money in a long-term savings account.

One way to make a choice involving time is to *pick the option with the highest present value*. By borrowing or lending at the market interest rate, we can shift wealth from one period to another. Thus, if we choose the option that has the highest present value, we can shift our wealth between periods so that we have more money in every period than we'd have if we made a less attractive choice.

Investing

Investment decisions may be made by comparing present values. *A firm makes an investment if the expected return from the investment is greater than the opportunity cost* (Chapter 7). The opportunity cost is the best alternative use of its money, which is what it would earn in the next best use of the money.

Thus, to decide whether to make an investment, the firm needs to compare the potential outlay of money to the firm's best alternative. One possibility is that its best alternative is to put the money that it would otherwise spend on this investment in an interest-bearing bank account. We consider two methods for making this comparison: the *net present value* approach and the *internal rate of return* approach.

Net Present Value Approach A firm has to decide whether to buy a truck for $20,000. Because the opportunity cost is $20,000, the firm should make the investment only if the present value of expected future returns from the truck is greater than $20,000.

More generally, *a firm should make an investment only if the present value of the expected return exceeds the present value of the costs*. If R is the present value of the expected returns to an investment and C is the present value of the costs of the investment, the firm should make the investment if $R > C$.[6]

This rule is often restated in terms of the net present value, $NPV = R - C$, which is the difference between the present value of the returns, R, and the present value of the costs, C. *A firm should make an investment only if the net present value is positive*:

$$NPV = R - C > 0.$$

Assume that the initial year is $t = 0$, the firm's revenue in year t is R_t, and its cost in year t is C_t. If the last year in which either revenue or cost is nonzero is T, the net present value rule holds that the firm should invest if

$$NPV = R - C$$

$$= \left[R_0 + \frac{R_1}{(1 + i)^1} + \frac{R_2}{(1 + i)^2} + \cdots + \frac{R_T}{(1 + i)^T} \right]$$

$$- \left[C_0 + \frac{C_1}{(1 + i)^1} + \frac{C_2}{(1 + i)^2} + \cdots + \frac{C_T}{(1 + i)^T} \right] > 0.$$

Instead of comparing the present values of the returns and costs, we can examine whether the present value of the *cash flow* in each year (loosely, the annual *profit*), $\pi_t = R_t - C_t$, is positive. By rearranging the terms in the previous expression, we can rewrite the net present value rule as

$$NPV = (R_0 - C_0) + \frac{R_1 - C_1}{(1 + i)^1} + \frac{R_2 - C_2}{(1 + i)^2} + \cdots + \frac{R_T - C_T}{(1 + i)^T}$$

$$= \pi_0 + \frac{\pi_1}{(1 + i)^1} + \frac{\pi_2}{(1 + i)^2} + \cdots + \frac{\pi_T}{(1 + i)^T} > 0. \qquad (16.7)$$

This rule does not restrict the firm to making investments only where its cash flow is positive each year. For example, a firm buys a piece of equipment for $100 and spends the first year learning how to use it, so it makes no revenues from the machine and has a negative cash flow that year: $\pi_0 = -100$. The next year, its revenue is $350 and the machine's maintenance cost is $50, so its second year's cash flow is $\pi_1 = \$300$. At the end of that year, the machine wears out, so the annual cash flow from this investment is zero thereafter. Setting the interest rate at 5% in Equation 16.7, we learn that the firm's net present value is

$$NPV = -100 + 300/1.05 \approx \$185.71.$$

Because this net present value is positive, the firm makes the investment.

---

[6]This rule holds when future costs and returns are known with certainty and investments can be reversed but cannot be delayed (Dixit and Pindyck, 1994).

Solved Problem 16.2

Peter Guber and Joe Lacob bought the Golden State Warriors basketball team for $450 million in 2010. *Forbes* magazine estimated that the team's net income for 2009 was $11.9 million. If the new owners believed that they would continue to earn this annual profit (after adjusting for inflation), $f = \$11.9$ million, forever, was this investment more lucrative than putting the $450 million in a savings account that pays a real interest rate of $i = 2\%$ or $i = 3\%$?

Answer

Determine the net present value of the team. The net present value of buying the Warriors is positive given a real interest rate of 2% if the present value of the stream of income, $11.9 million/0.02 = $595 million, minus the present value of the cost, which is the purchase price of $450 million, is positive:

$$NPV = \$595 \text{ million} - \$450 \text{ million} = \$145 \text{ million} > 0.$$

Thus, it paid for the investors to buy the Warriors if their best alternative investment paid 2%. However, if the interest rate were 3%, then the present value of the income stream is only $11.9 million/0.03 ≈ $397 million, so the investment would not pay: $397 − $450 = −53 million < 0.

Internal Rate of Return Approach Whether the net present value of an investment is positive depends on the interest rate, as Solved Problem 16.2 shows. At what discount rate (rate of return) is a firm indifferent between making an investment and not? The **internal rate of return** (*irr*) is the discount rate such that the net present value of an investment is zero. Replacing the interest rate, i, in Equation 16.7 with *irr* and setting the *NPV* equal to zero, we implicitly determine the internal rate of return by solving

internal rate of return (*irr*)
the discount rate that results in a net present value of an investment of zero

$$NPV = \pi_0 + \frac{\pi_1}{1 + irr} + \frac{\pi_2}{(1 + irr)^2} + \cdots + \frac{\pi_T}{(1 + irr)^T} = 0$$

for *irr*.

It is easier to calculate *irr* when the investment pays a steady stream of profit, f, forever and the cost of the investment is *PV*. The investment's rate of return is found by rearranging Equation 16.4 and replacing i with *irr*:

$$irr = \frac{f}{PV}. \tag{16.8}$$

Instead of using the net present value rule, we can decide whether to invest by comparing the internal rate of return to the interest rate. If the firm is borrowing money to make the investment, *it pays for the firm to borrow to make the investment if the internal rate of return on that investment exceeds that of the next best alternative* (which we assume is the interest rate):[7]

$$irr > i.$$

---

[7] The net present value approach always works. The internal rate of return method is inapplicable if *irr* is not unique. In Solved Problem 16.3, *irr* is unique, and using this approach gives the same answer as the net present value approach.

Solved Problem 16.3

Peter Guber and Joe Lacob can buy the Golden State Warriors basketball team for $450 million, and they expect an annual real flow of payments (profits) of $f = \$11.9$ million forever. Using the internal rate of return approach, should they buy the team if the real interest rate is 2%?

Answer

Determine the internal rate of return to this investment and compare it to the interest rate. Using Equation 16.8, we calculate that the internal rate of return from buying the Warriors is

$$irr = \frac{f}{PV} = \frac{\$11.9 \text{ million}}{\$450 \text{ million}} \approx 2.6\%.$$

Because this internal rate of return, 2.6%, is greater than the real interest rate, 2%, they buy the team.

Rate of Return on Bonds

Instead of investing in capital or putting their money in a bank, firms or individuals may invest in a *bond*, a piece of paper issued by a government or a corporation that promises to repay the borrower with a payment stream. The amount borrowed is called the *face value* of the bond. Some bonds have a number of *coupons*. Each year, the holder of the bond clips one coupon, returns it to the issuer, and receives a payment of a fixed amount of money. At the *maturity date* shown on the bond—when no coupons remain—the borrower redeems the bond by returning the face value, the amount borrowed.

Some bonds, *perpetuities*, have no maturity date and the face value is never returned. Instead, the bondholder receives annual payments forever.

For example, last year Jerome paid $PV = \$2,000$ to buy a government-issued bond that guarantees the holder a payment of $f = \$100$ a year forever. According to Equation 16.8, the rate of return on Jerome's bond was 5% = $100/$2,000. At the time, banks were paying 5% on comparable accounts and were expected to do so in the future. As a result, Jerome was indifferent between buying a bond and keeping his money in a bank account.

This year, however, because of *unanticipated* inflation, the nominal interest rate that banks paid *unexpectedly* rose to 10%, and everyone expects this new interest rate to persist. If the bonds were to continue to sell for $2,000, the rate of return would remain 5%, so everyone would prefer to keep their money in the bank. Thus, if Jerome wants to sell his bond, he must lower the price until the rate of return on the bond reaches 10%. As a result, the present value of Jerome's bond falls to $1,000 = $100/0.1 this year, according to Equation 16.4. In general, a bond's selling price falls from the face value of the bond if the nominal interest rate rises over time (and the price rises if the interest rate falls).

Similarly, the real return to a bond that pays a nominal rate of return varies with the inflation rate. During the high-inflation 1970s and early 1980s, holders of U.S. bonds lost much of their wealth for this reason. Following Canada, Britain, and other countries, the United States in 1997 started offering bonds that adjust for the inflation rate. These bonds are supposed to provide a constant, real rate of return.

★Behavioral Economics: Time-Varying Discounting

Tomorrow: One of the greatest labor saving devices of today.

People want immediate gratification.[8] We want rewards now and costs delayed until later: "Rain, rain, go away; Come again some other day; We want to go outside and play; Come again some other day."

Time Consistency So far in this chapter, we have explained such impatience by assuming that people discount future costs or benefits by using *exponential discounting*, as in Equation 16.2: The present value is the future value divided by $(1 + i)^t$, where t is the exponent and the discount rate, i, is constant over time. If people use this approach, their preferences are *time consistent*: They will discount an event that occurs a decade from the time they're asked by the same amount today as they will one year from now.

However, many of us indulge in immediate gratification in a manner that is inconsistent with our long-term preferences: Our "long-run self" disapproves of the lack of discipline of our "short-run self." Even though we plan today not to overeat tomorrow, tomorrow we may overindulge. We have *present-biased preferences*: When considering the trade-off between two future moments, we put more weight on the earlier moment as it gets closer. For example, if you are offered $100 in 10 years or $200 in 10 years and a day, you will almost certainly choose the larger amount one day later. After all, what's the cost of waiting one extra day a decade from now? However, if you are offered $100 today or $200 tomorrow, you may choose the smaller amount today because an extra day is an appreciable delay when your planning horizon is short.

One explanation that behavioral economists (see Chapter 4) use for procrastination and other time-inconsistent behavior is that people's personal discount rates are smaller in the far future than in the near future. For example, suppose that you know that you can mow your lawn today in two hours, but if you wait until next week, it will take you two-and-a-quarter hours because the grass will be longer. Your displeasure (negative utility) from spending 2 hours mowing is −20 and from spending 2.25 hours mowing is −22.5. The present value of mowing next week is $-22.5/(1 + i)$, where i is your personal discount rate for a week. If today your discount rate is $i = 0.25$, then your present value of mowing in a week is $-22.5/1.25 = -18$, which is not as bad as −20, so you delay mowing. However, if you were asked six months in advance, your discount rate might be much smaller, say $i = 0.1$. At that interest rate, the present value is $-22.5/1.1 \approx -20.45$, which is worse than −20, so you would plan to mow on the first of the two dates. Thus, falling discount rates may explain this type of time-inconsistent behavior.

Falling Discount Rates and the Environment A social discount rate that declines over time may be useful in planning for global warming or other future environmental disasters (Karp, 2005). Suppose that the harmful effects of greenhouse gases will not be felt for a century and that society used traditional, exponential discounting. We would be willing to invest at most 37¢ today to avoid a dollar's worth of damages in a century if society's constant discount rate is 1%, and only 1.8¢ if the discount rate is 4%. Thus, even a modest discount rate makes us callous toward our distant descendants: We are unwilling to incur even moderate costs today to avoid large damages far in the future.

---

[8]This section draws heavily on Rabin (1998), O'Donoghue and Rabin (1999), and Karp (2005).

One alternative is for society to use a declining discount rate, although doing so will make our decisions time inconsistent. Parents today may care more about their existing children than their (not yet seen) grandchildren, and therefore may be willing to significantly discount the welfare of their grandchildren relative to that of their children. They probably have a smaller difference in their relative emotional attachment to the tenth future generation relative to the eleventh generation. If society agrees with such reasoning, our future social discount rate should be lower than our current rate. By reducing the discount rate over time, we are saying that the weights we place on the welfare of any two successive generations in the distant future are more similar than the weights on two successive generations in the near future.

Application

Falling Discount Rates and Self-Control

If people's discount rates fall over time, they have a *present bias* or a *self-control problem*, which means that they prefer immediate gratification to delayed gratification.[9] Several recent studies argue that governments should help people with this bias by providing self-control policies.

Shapiro (2004) finds that food stamp recipients' caloric intake declines by 10% to 15% over the food stamp month, implying that they prefer immediate consumption. With a constant discount rate, they would be more likely to spread their consumption evenly over the month. Governments can help people with a present bias by delivering food stamps at two-week intervals instead of once a month, as several states do with welfare payments.

Cigarette smokers often have inconsistent preferences with respect to smoking. Individuals with declining discount rates lack self-control and perpetually postpone quitting smoking. According to a 2011 Gallup survey, 78% of U.S. smokers would like to quit. Consequently, a smoker who wants to quit may support the government's impositions of control devices. Based on a survey in Taiwan, Kan (2007) found that a smoker who intends to quit is more likely to support a smoking ban and a cigarette tax increase. In 2012, most (59%) New Zealand smokers supported more government action on tobacco, and nearly half (46%) supported banning sales of cigarettes in 10 years, provided effective nicotine substitutes were available.

In 2009, President Obama—who at the time smoked, but wanted to quit—signed a law bringing tobacco products under federal law for the first time. He said that this law, aimed at stopping children from starting to smoke, would have prevented him from taking up smoking. Perhaps the most striking evidence of smokers' mixed feelings is that Gruber and Mullainathan (2005) found that cigarette taxes make people with a propensity to smoke happier in both the United States and Canada.

16.3 Exhaustible Resources

The meek shall inherit the earth, but not the mineral rights.   —J. Paul Getty

Discounting plays an important role in decision making about how fast to consume oil, gold, copper, uranium, and other **exhaustible resources**: nonrenewable natural assets that cannot be increased, only depleted. An owner of an exhaustible resource decides when to extract and sell it so as to maximize the present value of the resource.

exhaustible resources nonrenewable natural assets that cannot be increased, only depleted

---

[9]In the famous marshmallow test, small children are offered one marshmallow now or a second one if they wait. See an excellent reenactment at **www.youtube.com/watch?v=QX_oy9614HQ**. Children who could delay gratification reportedly did better later in life (**www.newyorker.com/reporting/2009/05/18/090518fa_fact_lehrer**), though this result is now disputed.

Scarcity of the resource, mining costs, and market structure affect whether the price of such a resource rises or falls over time.

When to Sell an Exhaustible Resource

Suppose that you own a coal mine. In what year do you mine the coal, and in what year do you sell it to maximize the present value of your coal? To illustrate how to answer these questions, we assume that you can sell the coal only this year or next in a competitive market, that the interest rate is i, and that the cost of mining each pound of coal, m, stays constant over time.

Given the last two of these assumptions, the present value of mining a pound of coal is m if you mine it this year and $m/(1 + i)$ if you mine it next year. As a result, if you're going to sell the coal next year, you're better off mining it next year because you postpone incurring the cost of mining. You mine the coal this year only if you plan to sell it this year.

Now that you have a rule that tells you when to mine the coal—at the last possible moment—your remaining problem is when to sell it. That decision depends on how the price of a pound of coal changes from one year to the next. Suppose that you know that the price of coal will increase from p_1 this year to p_2 next year.

To decide in which year to sell, you compare the present value of selling today to that of selling next year. The present value of your profit per pound of coal is $p_1 - m$ if you sell your coal this year and $(p_2 - m)/(1 + i)$ if you sell it next year. Thus, to maximize the present value from selling your coal:

- *You sell all the coal this year* if the present value of selling this year is greater than the present value of selling next year: $p_1 - m > (p_2 - m)/(1 + i)$.
- *You sell all the coal next year* if $p_1 - m < (p_2 - m)/(1 + i)$.
- *You sell the coal in either year* if $p_1 - m = (p_2 - m)/(1 + i)$.

The intuition behind these rules is that storing coal in the ground is like keeping money in the bank. You can sell a pound of coal today, netting $p_1 - m$, invest the money in the bank, and have $(p_1 - m)(1 + i)$ next year. Alternatively, you can keep the coal in the ground for a year and then sell it. If the amount you'll get next year, $p_2 - m$, is less than what you can earn from selling now and keeping the money in a bank account, you sell the coal now. In contrast, if the price of coal is rising so rapidly that the coal will be worth more in the future than wealth left in a bank, you leave your wealth in the mine.

Price of a Scarce Exhaustible Resource

This two-period analysis generalizes to many time periods (Hotelling, 1931). We use a multiperiod analysis to show how the price of an exhaustible resource changes over time.

The resource is sold both this year, year t, and next year, $t + 1$, only if the present value of a pound sold now is the same as the present value of a pound sold next year: $p_t - m = (p_{t+1} - m)/(1 + i)$, where the price is p_t in year t and p_{t+1} in the following year. Using algebra to rearrange this equation, we obtain an expression that tells us how price changes from one year to the next:

$$p_{t+1} = p_t + i(p_t - m). \tag{16.9}$$

If you're willing to sell the coal in both years, the price next year must exceed the price this year by $i(p_t - m)$, which is the interest payment you'd receive if you sold a pound of coal this year and put the profit in a bank that paid interest at rate i.

Figure 16.2 Price of an Exhaustible Resource

The price of an exhaustible resource in year $t + 1$ is higher than the price in year t by the interest rate times the difference between the price in year t and the marginal cost of mining, $i(p_t - m)$. Thus, the gap between the price line and the marginal cost line, $p_t - m$, grows exponentially with the interest rate.

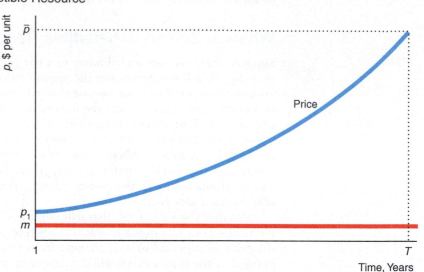

The gap between the price and the constant marginal cost of mining grows over time, as Figure 16.2 shows. To see why, we subtract p_t from both sides of Equation 16.9 to obtain an expression for the change in the price from one year to the next:

$$\Delta p = p_{t+1} - p_t = i(p_t - m).$$

This equation shows that the gap between this year's price and next year's price widens as your cash flow this year, $p_t - m$, increases. Thus, the price rises over time, and the gap between the price line and the flat marginal cost of mining line grows, as the figure illustrates.

Although we now understand how price changes over time, we need more information to determine the price in the first year and hence in each subsequent year. Suppose that mine owners know that the government will ban the use of coal in year T (or that a superior substitute will become available that year). They want to price the coal so that all of it is sold by the year T, because any resource that is unsold by then is worthless. The restriction that all the coal is used up by T and Equation 16.9 determine the price in the first year and the increase in the price thereafter.

Price in a Two-Period Example To illustrate how the price is determined in each year, we assume that the market has many identical competitive mines, no more coal will be sold after the second year because of a government ban, and the marginal cost of mining is zero in each period. Setting $m = 0$ in Equation 16.9, we learn that the price in the second year equals the price in the first year plus the interest rate times the first-year price:

$$p_2 = p_1 + (i \times p_1) = p_1(1 + i). \qquad (16.10)$$

Thus, the price increases with the interest rate from the first year to the second year.

The mine owners face a resource constraint: They can't sell more coal than they have in their mines. The coal they sell in the first year, Q_1, plus the coal they sell in the second year, Q_2, equals the total amount of coal in the mines, Q. The mine owners want to sell all their coal within these two years because any coal they don't sell does them no good.

Suppose that the demand curve for coal is $Q_t = 200 - p_t$ in each year t. If the amount of coal in the ground is less than would be demanded at a zero price, the sum of the amount demanded in both years equals the total amount of coal in the ground:

$$Q_1 + Q_2 = (200 - p_1) + (200 - p_2) = Q.$$

Substituting the expression for p_2 from Equation 16.10 into this resource constraint to obtain $(200 - p_1) + [200 - p_1(1 + i)] = Q$ and rearranging terms, we find that

$$p_1 = (400 - Q)/(2 + i). \tag{16.11}$$

Thus, the first-year price depends on the amount of coal in the ground and the interest rate.

If the mines initially contain $Q = 169$ pounds of coal, p_1 is $110 at a 10% interest rate and only $105 at a 20% interest rate, as Table 16.5 shows. At the lower interest rate, the difference between the first- and second-year price is smaller ($11 versus $21), so relatively more of the original stock of coal is sold in the second year (47% versus 44%).

Rents If coal is a scarce good, its competitive price is above the marginal cost of mining the coal ($m = 0$ in our example). How can we reconcile this result with our earlier finding that price equals marginal cost in a competitive market? The answer is that when coal is scarce, it earns a *rent*: a payment to the owner of an input beyond the minimum necessary for the factor to be supplied (Chapter 9).

The owner of the coal need not be the same person who mines the coal. A miner could pay the owner for the right to take the coal out of the mine. After incurring the marginal cost of mining the coal, m, the miner earns $p_1 - m$. The owner of the mine, however, charges that amount in rent for the right to mine this scarce resource rather than giving any of this profit to the miner. Even if the owner of the coal and the miner are the same person, the amount beyond the marginal mining cost is a rent to scarcity.

If the coal were not scarce, no rent would be paid, and the price would equal the marginal cost of mining. Given the demand curve in the example, the most coal anyone would buy in a year is 200 pounds, which is the amount demanded at a price of zero. If the initial stock of coal in the group is 400 pounds—enough to provide 200 pounds in each year—coal is not scarce, so the price of coal in both years is zero (the

Table 16.5 Price and Quantity of Coal Reflecting the Amount of Coal and the Interest Rate

	Q = 169		Q = 400
	$i = 10\%$	$i = 20\%$	Any i
$p_1 = (400 - Q)/(2 + i)$	$110	$105	$0
$p_2 = p_1(1 + i)$	$121	$126	$0
$\Delta p \equiv p_2 - p_1 = i \times p_1$	11	21	0
$Q_1 = 200 - p_1$	90	95	200
$Q_2 = 200 - p_2$	79	74	200
Share sold in Year 2	47%	44%	50%

Figure 16.3 First-Year Price in a Two-Period Model

In a two-period model, the price of coal in the first year, p_1, falls as the amount of coal in the ground initially, Q, increases. This figure is based on an interest rate of 10%.

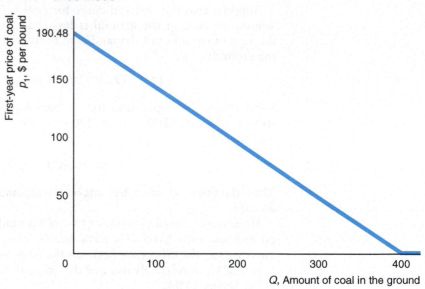

marginal mining cost), as Table 16.5 shows.[10] As Figure 16.3 illustrates, the less coal in the ground initially, Q, the higher the initial price of coal.

Rising Prices Thus, according to our theory, the price of an exhaustible resource rises if the resource (1) is scarce, (2) can be mined at a marginal cost that remains constant over time, and (3) is sold in a competitive market. The price of old-growth redwood trees rose as predicted by this theory.

Application

Redwood Trees

Many of the majestic old-growth redwood trees in America's western forests are several hundred to several thousand years old. If a mature redwood is cut, young redwoods will not grow to a comparable size within our lifetime. Thus, an old-growth redwood forest, like fossil fuels, is effectively a nonrenewable resource, even though new redwoods are being created and grow very slowly. In contrast, many other types of trees, such as those grown as Christmas trees, are quickly replenished and therefore are renewable resources like fish.

The exponential trend line on the graph shows that the real price of redwoods rose from 1953 to 1983 at an average rate of 8% a year. By the end of this period, virtually no redwood trees were available for sale. The trees either had been harvested or

---

[10]Equation 16.11 holds only where coal is scarce: $Q \leq 400$. According to this equation, $p_1 = 0$ when $Q = 400$. If the quantity of coal in the ground is even greater, $Q > 400$, coal is not scarce—people don't want all the coal even if the price is zero—so the price in the first year equals the marginal mining cost of zero. That is, the price is not negative, as Equation 16.11 would imply if it held for quantities greater than 400.

were growing in protected forests. The last remaining privately owned stand was purchased by the U.S. government and the state of California from the Maxxam Corporation in 1996.

The unusually high prices observed in the late 1960s through the 1970s are in large part due to actions of the federal government, which used its power of eminent domain to buy a considerable fraction of all remaining old-growth redwoods for the Redwood National Park at the market price. The government bought 1.7 million million-board feet (MBF) in 1968 and 1.4 million MBF in 1978. The latter purchase represented about two and a quarter years of cutting at previous rates. These two government purchases combined equaled 43% of private holdings in 1978 of about 7.3 million MBF. Thus, the government purchases were so large that they moved up the time of exhaustion of privately held redwoods by several years, causing the price to jump to the level it would have reached several years later.

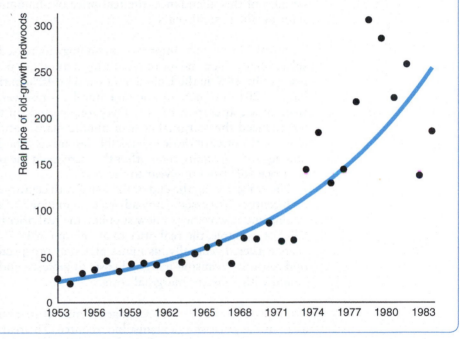

Why Price May Be Constant or Fall

If any one of the three conditions we've been assuming—*scarcity*, *constant marginal mining costs*, and *competition*—is not met, the price of an exhaustible resource may remain steady or fall.[11] Most exhaustible resources, such as aluminum, coal, lead, natural gas, silver, and zinc, have had decades-long periods of falling or constant real prices. Indeed, the real price of each major mineral, each metal, and oil was lower in 1998 than in 1980.

---

[11]The following discussion of why prices of exhaustible resources may not rise and the accompanying examples are based on Berck and Roberts (1996) and additional data supplied by these authors. Their paper also shows that pollution and other environmental controls can keep resource prices from rising. Additional data are from Brown and Wolk (2000).

Abundance As we've already seen, the initial price is set at essentially the marginal cost of mining if the exhaustible resource is not scarce. The gap between the price and the marginal cost grows with the interest rate. If the good is so abundant that the initial gap is zero, the gap does not grow and the price stays constant at the marginal cost. Further, if the gap is initially very small, it has to grow for a long time before the increase becomes noticeable.

Because of abundance, the real prices for many exhaustible resources have remained relatively constant for decades. Moreover, the price falls when the discovery of a large deposit of the resource is announced.

The amount of a resource that can be profitably recovered using current technology is called a *reserve*. Known reserves of some resources are enormous; others are more limited.[12] The world has enough silicon (from sand) and magnesium to last virtually forever at 2012 rates of extraction. Known reserves of zinc will last 19 years; lead, 17 years; gold, 19 years; and silver, 23 years. Known reserves of aluminum (bauxite) will last 106 years, and additional reserves are constantly being discovered. Because of this abundance, the real price of aluminum has remained virtually constant for the past 50 years.

Technical Progress Improved technology increased potential natural gas reserves substantially. New means of recovering natural gas from shale increased estimates of reserves by 38% in the United States and by 48% in the rest of the world.[13] According to a 2013 estimate of known natural gas reserves, the world has enough for 56 years of use at current rates.[14] Over long periods of time, steady technical progress has reduced the marginal cost of mining many natural resources and has thereby lowered the price of those exhaustible resources. A large enough drop in the marginal mining cost may more than offset the increase in the price due to the interest rate, so the price falls from one year to the next.[15]

The era spanning the end of the nineteenth century and the beginning of the twentieth century witnessed many advances in mining. As a result of technical progress in mining and discoveries of new supplies, the real prices of many exhaustible resources fell. For example, the real price of aluminum in 1945 was only 12% of the price 50 years earlier. Eventually, as mines play out, prospectors have to dig ever deeper to find resources, causing marginal costs to increase and prices to rise faster than they would with constant marginal costs.

Changing Market Power Changes in market structure can result in either a rise or a fall in the price of an exhaustible resource. The real price of oil remained virtually constant from 1880 through 1972. But when the Organization of Petroleum Exporting Countries (OPEC) started to act as a cartel in 1973, the price of oil climbed rapidly. At its peak in 1981, the real price of oil was nearly five times higher than its nearly constant level during the period 1880–1972. When Iran and Iraq went to

---

[12]Data are from **minerals.usgs.gov/minerals/pubs/mcs/2013/mcs2013.pdf**.

[13]**www.eia.gov/analysis/studies/worldshalegas**.

[14]**www.reuters.com/article/2013/06/12/bp-reserves-idUSL5N0EO1I720130612**.

[15]When the marginal cost of mining is constant at m, Equation 16.9 shows that $p_{t+1} = p_t + i(p_t - m)$, so p_{t+1} must be more than p_t. If we allow mining costs to vary from year to year, then

$$p_{t+1} = p_t + i(p_t - m_t) + (m_{t+1} - m_t).$$

Thus, if the drop in the mining costs, $m_{t+1} - m_t$, is greater than $i(p_t - m)$, the price p_{t+1} is less than p_t.

war in 1980, the OPEC cartel began to fall apart and the real price of oil sank to traditional levels, where it remained through the 1990s. In the first decade of the new millennium, the price increased substantially, in large part due to worldwide increases in demand. In the last few years, the price has fluctuated due in large part to political uncertainty.

16.4 Capital Markets, Interest Rates, and Investments

We've seen that an individual's decision about whether to make an investment depends on the market interest rate. The interest rate is determined in the capital market, where the interest rate is the price, the quantity supplied is the amount of funds loaned, and the quantity demanded is the amount of funds borrowed.

Because the capital market is competitive, the interest rate and the quantity of funds loaned and borrowed is determined by the intersection of the supply curve for funds and the demand curve for funds, as in Figure 16.4. Funds are demanded by individuals buying homes or paying for a college education, governments borrowing money to build roads or wage wars, and firms investing in new plants or equipment. The demand curve, D, is downward sloping because more is borrowed as the interest rate falls.

The supply curve reflects loans made by individuals and firms. Many people, when their earnings are relatively high, save money in bank accounts and buy bonds (which they convert back to money for consumption when they retire or during lean times). Firms that have no alternative investments with higher returns may also loan money to banks or others. Higher interest rates induce greater savings by both groups, so the initial supply curve, S^1, is upward sloping.

The initial equilibrium is e_1, with an equilibrium rate of interest of i_1 and an equilibrium quantity of funds loaned and borrowed of Q_1. As usual, this equilibrium changes if any of the variables—such as tastes and government regulations—that affect supply and demand shifts.

Figure 16.4 Capital Market Equilibrium

The initial equilibrium, e_1, is determined by the intersection of the demand curve for loans, D, and the initial supply curve, S^1. Changes in laws induce more people to save, shifting the supply curve to S^2. The interest rate, i_2, at the new equilibrium, e_2, is lower than the original interest rate, i_1. More funds are loaned than originally: $Q_2 > Q_1$.

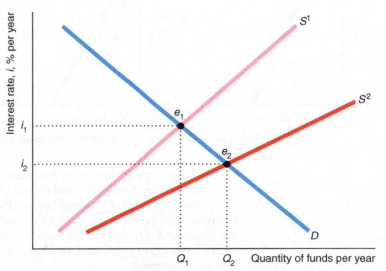

The supply curve of funds may shift to the right for many reasons. The government may remove a restriction on investment by foreigners. Or the government may make Individual Retirement Accounts (IRAs) tax exempt until retirement, a policy that induces additional savings at any given interest rate.

Such a change causes the supply curve to shift to the right to S^2 in Figure 16.4. The new equilibrium is e_2, with a lower interest rate, i_2. At the lower interest rate, firms and others undertake investment projects with lower rates of return than before the shift. They borrow more funds, so the new equilibrium is at $Q_2 > Q_1$.

Solved Problem 16.4

Suppose the government needs to borrow money to pay for fighting a war in a foreign land. Show that increased borrowing by the government—an increase in the government's demand for money at any given interest rate—raises the equilibrium interest rate, which discourages or *crowds out* private investment.

Answer

Using three side-by-side graphs, show how an outward shift of the government's demand curve affects the equilibrium interest rate and thereby reduces private investment. In the figure, panel a shows the private sector demand curve for funds, D_p, which are funds that private firms and individuals borrow to make investments. Panel b shows that the government sector demand curve shifts to the right from D_g^1 to D_g^2. As a result, in panel c, the total demand curve—the horizontal sum of the private and government demand curves—shifts from D^1 to D^2. Panel c also shows the supply curve of money, S.

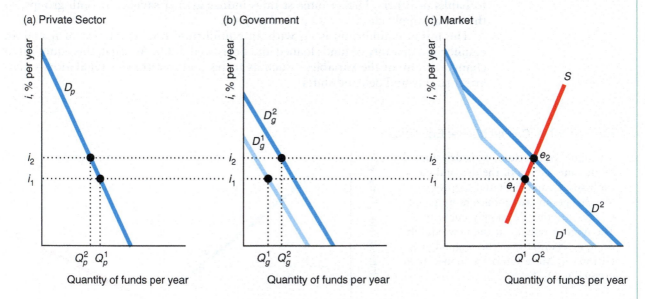

(a) Private Sector (b) Government (c) Market

The initial equilibrium, e_1 in panel c, is determined by the intersection of the initial total demand for funds, D^1, and the supply curve, S, where the interest rate is i_1 and the quantity of funds borrowed is Q_1. After the government demand curve shifts out, the new equilibrium is e_2, where the interest rate is higher, $i_2 > i_1$, and more funds are borrowed, $Q_2 > Q_1$. The higher market interest rate causes private investment to fall from Q_p^1 to Q_p^2 (panel a). That is, the government borrowing crowds out some private investment.

Challenge Solution

Should You Go to College?

I have often thought that if there had been a good rap group around in those days, I would have chosen a career in music instead of politics.   —Richard Nixon

Probably the most important human capital decision you've had to make was whether to attend college. If you opted to go to college solely for the purpose of increasing your lifetime earnings, have you made a good investment?

Let's look back at your last year of high school. During that year, you have to decide whether to invest in a college education or go directly into the job market. If you go straight into the job market, we assume that you work full time (35 hours or more a week) from age 18 until you retire at age 70.

If your motivation for attending college is to increase your lifetime earnings, you should start college upon finishing high school so that you can earn a higher salary for as long as possible. To keep the analysis relatively simple, we'll assume that you graduate from college in four years, during which time you do not work and you spend $20,000 a year on tuition and other schooling expenses such as books and fees, which is what a typical student paid for a year of college in 2012. When you graduate from college, you work full time from age 22 to 70. Thus, the opportunity cost of a college education includes the tuition payments plus the four years of forgone earnings for someone with a high school diploma. The expected benefit is the stream of higher earnings in the future.

The figure shows how much the typical person earns with a high school diploma and with a college degree at each age.[16] At age 22, a typical college grad earns $29,335, and those with only a high school diploma earn $25,009. The college grad's earnings peak at 51 years of age, at $77,865. A high school grad's earnings also reach a maximum at 51 years, at $42,707.

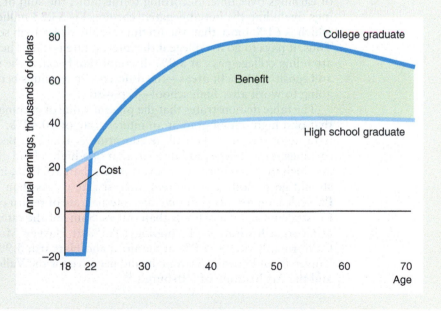

---

[16]The statistical analysis controls for age, education, and demographic characteristics but not innate ability. See Sources for information about the data. I thank Yann Panassie, a former student in my intermediate microeconomics course, for estimating this model. We assumed that wages increase at the same rate as inflation, so real earnings are constant over time. No adjustment is made for the greater incidence of unemployment among high school graduates, which was more than twice that of college graduates in 2012.

If one stream of earnings is higher than the other at every age, we would pick the higher stream. Because these streams of earnings cross at age 22, we cannot use that simple approach to answer the question. One way to decide whether investing in a college education pays is to compare the present values at age 18 of the two earnings streams. The present values depend on the interest rate used, as the table shows.

Discount Rate, %	Present Value, Thousands of 2009 Dollars	
	High School	College
0	2,007	3,225
2	1,196	1,823
4	779	1,103
6	547	708
8	410	476
10	323	332
10.42	309	309
12	264	238
14	223	174

If potential college students can borrow money at an interest rate of 0%, money in the future is worth as much as money today, so the present value equals the sum of earnings over time. According to the table, the sum of a college graduate's earnings (including the initial negative earnings) is $3.23 million (first row of the table), which is 61% more than the lifetime earnings of a high school grad, $2.01 million. Thus, it pays to go to college if the interest rate is 0%. The figure also illustrates that attending college pays at a 0% discount rate because the sum of the (negative) cost and (positive) benefit areas—the difference in earnings between going to college and going to work after high school—is positive.

The table demonstrates that the present value of earnings for a college grad equals that of a high school grad at an interest rate of 10.42%. That is, the average internal rate of return to the college education is 10.42%. Because the present value of earnings for a college grad exceeds that of a high school grad if the real interest rate at which they can borrow or invest is less than 10.42%, income-maximizing people should go to college if the real interest rate is less than that rate.[17] According to **Payscale.com** for 2013, the average internal rate of return of going to college is higher for students at some schools than others. Some of the rates (without aid) are 10.0% at Georgia Institute of Technology; 8.3% at Harvey Mudd and the University of California, Berkeley; 6.9% at Stanford and Harvard; 5.9% at Drexel; 4.8% for the University of Phoenix, Savannah; and negative for the Valley Forge Christian College and the Art Institute of Pittsburgh.[18]

---

[17]The government-subsidized nominal interest rate on federal Stafford loans was 3.4% in 2011–2013. Some poor people who cannot borrow to pay for college at all—effectively, they face extremely high interest rates—do not go to college, unlike wealthier people with comparable abilities.

[18]For more schools, see **www.payscale.com/college-education-value-2013**. The Payscale's calculations, though similar to the one used in this Challenge Solution, differ in not controlling for individual characteristics and in several other ways.

The decision whether to go to college is more complex for people for whom education has a consumption component. Somebody who loves school may want to go to college even if alternative investments pay more. Someone who hates going to school invests in a college education only if the financial rewards are much higher than those for alternative investments.

Summary

1. **Comparing Money Today to Money in the Future.** Inflation aside, most people value money in the future less than money today. An interest rate reflects how much more people value a dollar today than a dollar in the future. To compare a payment made in the future to one made today, we can express the future payment in terms of current dollars by adjusting it using the interest rate. Similarly, a flow of payments over time is related to the present or future value of these payments by the interest rate.

2. **Choices over Time.** An individual or a firm may choose between two options with different cash flows over time by picking the one with the higher present value. Similarly, a firm invests in a project if its net present value is positive or its internal rate of return is greater than the interest rate. If people have a decreasing discount rate over time, they are not consistent in their behavior over time: They lack self-control and procrastinate.

3. **Exhaustible Resources.** Nonrenewable resources such as coal, gold, and oil are used up over time and cannot be replenished. If these resources are scarce, the marginal cost of mining them is constant or increasing, and the market structure remains unchanged, their prices rise rapidly over time because of positive interest rates. However, if the resources are abundant, the marginal cost of mining falls over time, or the market becomes more competitive, nonrenewable resource prices may remain constant or fall over time.

4. **Capital Markets, Interest Rates, and Investments.** Supply and demand in capital markets determine the market rate of interest. A shock that shifts the supply curve to the left or the demand curve to the right raises the interest rate. As the interest rate increases, firms want to make fewer investments.

Questions

All questions are available on MyEconLab; * = *answer appears at the back of this book;* **A** = *algebra problem.*

1. Comparing Money Today to Money in the Future

1.1 Some past and current civilizations, believing that interest should not be charged, passed usury laws forbidding it. What are the private and social benefits or costs of allowing interest to be charged?

1.2 What is the effect of a usury law that limits the market rate of interest if some potential lenders, hoping that the authorities do not catch them, are still willing to loan money at illegally high rates?

1.3 The Web site **www.timetravelfund.com** discusses investing $1 at 5% interest, which it says will be worth $39,323,261,827.22 in 500 years. Is its calculation correct, and, if so, for what frequency of

compounding? If you wish, you may also discuss how good an investment you think this site provides. **A**

1.4 Many retirement funds charge an administrative fee equal to 0.25% on managed assets. Suppose that Alexx and Spenser each invest $5,000 in the same stock this year. Alexx invests directly and earns 5% a year. Spenser uses a retirement fund and earns 4.75%. After 30 years, how much more will Alexx have than Spenser? **A**

*1.5 How does an individual with a zero discount rate weight current and future consumption? How does your answer change if the discount rate is infinite?

1.6 Discussing the $350 price of a ticket for one of her concerts, Barbra Streisand said, "If you amortize the money over 28 years, it's $12.50 a year. So is it worth $12.50 a year to see me sing? To hear me sing live?"[19] Under what condition is it useful for an individual to apply Ms. Streisand's rule to decide whether to go to the concert? What do we know about the discount rate of a person who made such a purchase?

1.7 If you buy a car for $100 down and $100 a year for two more years, what is the present value of these payments at a 5% rate of interest? **A**

1.8 What is the present value of $100 paid a year from now and another $100 paid two years from now if the interest rate is i? **A**

1.9 Dell Computer makes its suppliers wait 37 days on average to be paid for their goods; however, Dell is paid by its customers immediately. Thus, Dell earns interest on this *float*, the money that it is implicitly borrowing. If Dell can earn an annual interest rate of 4%, what is this float worth to Dell per dollar spent on inputs? **A**

1.10 What is the present value of a stream of payments of f per year for t years that starts T years from now if the interest rate is i? **A**

1.11 How much money do you have to put into a bank account that pays 10% interest compounded annually to receive annual payments of $200 forever? **A**

1.12 Horizon Ford advertises that it will sell you a Taurus for $24,000 or lease it to you. To lease it, you must make a down payment of $3,000 and agree to pay $3,000 at the end of each of the next two years. After the last lease payment, you may buy the car for $20,000. If you plan to keep the car until it falls apart (at least a decade) and the interest rate is 10%, which approach has a lower present value of costs? (*Hint*: See Solved Problem 16.1.) **A**

*1.13 How much money do you have to put into a bank account that pays 10% interest compounded annually to receive perpetual annual payments of $200 in today's dollars if the rate of inflation is 5%? **A**

*1.14 You rent an apartment for two years. You owe a payment of $\tilde{f}$ today and another equal nominal payment next year. If the inflation rate is γ and the real interest rate is i, what is the present value of these rental payments? **A**

2. Choices over Time

*2.1 Two different teams offer a professional basketball player contracts for playing this year. Both contracts are guaranteed, and payments will be made even if the athlete is injured and cannot play. Team A's contract would pay him $1 million today. Team B's contract would pay him $500,000 today and $2 million ten years from now. In the absence of inflation, our pro is concerned only about which contract has the highest present value. If his personal discount rate (interest rate) is 5%, which contract does he accept? Does the answer change if his discount rate is 20%? **A**

2.2 At a 10% interest rate, do you prefer to buy a phone for $100 or to rent the same phone for $10 a year? Does your answer depend on how long you think the phone will last?

2.3 Pacific Gas & Electric sent its customers a comparison showing that a person could save $80 per year in gas, water, and detergent expenses by replacing a traditional clothes washer with a new tumble-action washer. Suppose that the interest rate is 5%. You expect your current washer to die in five years. If the cost of a new tumble-action washer is $800, should you replace your washer now or in five years? **A**

2.4 You plan to buy a used refrigerator this year for $200 and to sell it when you graduate in two years. Assuming no inflation, you sell the refrigerator for $100 at graduation, and the interest rate is 5%, what is the true cost (your current outlay minus the resale value in current terms) of the refrigerator to you? **A**

2.5 You want to buy a room air conditioner. The price of one machine is $200. It costs $20 a year to operate. The price of the other air conditioner is $300, but it costs only $10 a year to operate. Assuming that both machines last 10 years, which is a better deal? (Do you need to do extensive calculations to answer this question?) **A**

2.6 With the end of the Cold War, the U.S. government decided to "downsize" the military. Along with a pink slip, the government offered ex-military personnel their choice of $8,000 a year for 30 years or a lump-sum payment of $50,000 immediately. The lump-sum option was chosen by 92% of enlisted personnel and 51% of officers (Warner and Pleeter, 2001). What is the break-even personal discount

---

[19]"In Other Words . . ." *San Francisco Chronicle*, January 1, 1995, Sunday Section, p. 3. She divided the $350 ticket price by 28 years to get $12.50 as the payment per year.

rate at which someone would be indifferent between the two options? What can you conclude about the personal discount rates of the enlisted personnel and officers? **A**

2.7 Firms are increasingly offering retiring employees a choice of whether to take a lump-sum payment now or receive monthly payments for the rest of their lives (**www.fidelity.com/viewpoints/personal-finance/lump-sum-or-monthly-pension**). Discuss the benefits and drawbacks of accepting the lump-sum payment taking into account discounting, inflation, and uncertainty.

*2.8 Your gas-guzzling car gets only ten miles to the gallon and has no resale value, but you are sure that it will last five years. You know that you can always buy a used car for $8,000 that gets 20 miles to the gallon. A gallon of gas costs $2.00 and you drive 6,000 miles a year. If the interest rate is 5% and you are interested only in saving money, should you buy a new car now rather than wait until your current car dies? Would you make the same decision if you faced a 10% interest rate? **A**

2.9 You are buying a new $20,000 car and have the option to pay for the car with a 0% loan or to receive $500 cash back at the time of the purchase. With the loan, you pay $5,000 down when you purchase the car and then make three $5,000 payments, one at the end of each year of the loan. You currently have $50,000 in your savings account.

   a. The rate of interest on your savings account is 4% and will remain so for the next three years. Which payment method should you choose?

   b. What interest rate, i, makes you indifferent between the two payment methods? **A**

2.10 As a resident of New York City, you are considering purchasing a new Toyota Prius. The Prius sells for $20,000. Your annual expense of owning and driving the car is $3,000 (most of which is the cost of parking the car in a Manhattan garage). If you do not purchase the car, you will spend $5,000 per year on public transportation and rental cars. The interest rate is 4%. What is the smallest number of years that you must own the car so that the discounted cost of owning the car is less than the discounted cost of the alternative? **A**

2.11 An economic consultant explaining the effect on labor demand of increasing health care costs, interviewed for the *Wall Street Journal*'s Capital column (David Wessel, "Health-Care Costs Blamed for Hiring Gap," March 11, 2004, A2), states, "Medical costs are rising more rapidly than anything else in the economy—more than prices, wages or profits.

It isn't only current medical costs, but also the present value of the stream of endlessly high cost increases that retards hiring."

   a. Why does the present value of the stream of health care costs, and not just the current health care costs, affect a firm's decision whether to create a new position?

   b. Why should an employer discount the future health care costs in its decision whether to create a new position? **A**

2.12 Lewis Wolff and his investment group bought the Oakland A's baseball team for $180 million in 2005. *Forbes* magazine estimated that the team's net income for that year was $5.9 million. If the new owners believed that they would continue to earn this annual profit (after adjusting for inflation) forever, was this investment more lucrative than putting the $180 million into a savings account that paid a real interest rate of 3%? (*Hint*: See Solved Problems 16.2 and 16.3.) **A**

2.13 As discussed in the previous question, Lewis Wolff and his investment group bought the Oakland A's baseball team for $180 million in 2005. Reportedly, Hall-of-Famer Reggie Jackson offered $25 million more but was rebuffed (*Forbes*, 2005). How would the calculations in Solved Problem 16.3 change if the sales price had been $205 million? **A**

2.14 To virtually everyone's surprise, the new Washington Nationals baseball team earned a pre-tax profit of $20 million in 2005, compared to a $10 million loss when the team was the Montreal Expos in 2004 (Thomas Heath, "Nationals' Expected '05 Profit Is $20 Million," *Washington Post*, June 21, 2005, A1). Major League Baseball, which bought the franchise for $120 million in 2002, sold the team for $450 million in 2006 (**washington.nationals.mlb.com**). If the Nationals are expected to earn $20 million each year in the future, what is the internal rate of return on a $400 million investment for this club? (*Hint*: See Solved Problem 16.3.) **A**

2.15 According to *Forbes*, a typical National Basketball Association (NBA) franchise would sell for $372 million—though the Knicks were worth $600 million in 2007. NBA teams posted average earnings (before interest, taxes, depreciation, and amortization) of $9.8 million. Assuming that the team can maintain this earnings flow indefinitely, does it pay for a profit-maximizing investor to buy such a franchise if the real interest rate is 3%? Answer using the methods in Solved Problems 16.2 and 16.3. **A**

2.16 A group that includes former Lakers star Magic Johnson bought the Los Angeles Dodgers for $2.15 billion in 2012. The Dodgers reported earnings of $11.3 million (John Gittelsohn and Nadja Brandt, "Dodgers Costing $2.15 Billion Hinges on Property Return," **businessweek.com**, April 4, 2012). Financial experts, puzzled by the high price, speculated that the new owners expect to make additional earnings from the surrounding land they purchased. If the real rate of interest is 2%, how much do they have to earn annually for this purchase to make sense? (*Hint*: See Solved Problems 16.2 and 16.3.) **A**

2.17 A firm's profit is π = revenue − labor costs − capital costs. Its capital cost can be stated as its internal rate of return on capital, *irr*, times the value of its capital, $p_K K$, where p_K is the price of a unit of capital and K is the number of units of capital. What is the firm's implicit rate of return on its capital? (*Hint*: Set profit equal to zero and solve for the *irr*.) **A**

*2.18 A firm is considering an investment where its cash flow is π_1 = $1 (million), π_2 = −$12, π_3 = $20, and π_t = 0 for all other t. The interest rate is 7%. Use the net present value rule to determine whether the firm should make the investment. Can the firm use the internal rate of return rule to make this decision? **A**

3. Exhaustible Resources

3.1 You have a barrel of oil that you can sell today for p dollars. Assuming no inflation and no storage cost, how high would the price have to be next year for you to sell the oil next year rather than now? **A**

3.2 Trees, wine, and cattle become more valuable over time and then possibly decrease in value. Draw a figure with present value on the vertical axis and years (age) on the horizontal axis and show this relationship. Show in what year the owner should "harvest" such a good assuming that the cost to harvesting is zero. (*Hint*: If the good's present value is P_0 and we take that money and invest it at interest rate i [a small number such as 2% or 4%], then its value in year t is $P_0(1 + i)^t$; or if we allow continuous compounding, $P_0 e^{it}$. Such a curve increases exponentially over time and looks like the curve labeled *Price* in Figure 16.2. Draw curves with different possible present values. Use those curves to choose the optimal harvest time.) How would your answer change if the interest rate were zero? Show in a figure. **A**

3.3 If all the coal in the ground, Q, is to be consumed in two years and the demand for coal is $Q_t = A(p_t)^{-\varepsilon}$

in each year t where ε is a constant demand elasticity, what is the price of coal each year? **A**

4. Capital Markets, Interest Rates, and Investments

4.1 If the government bars foreign lenders from loaning money to its citizens, how does the capital market equilibrium change?

4.2 In the figure in Solved Problem 16.4, suppose that the government's demand curve remains constant at D_g^1 but the government starts to tax private earnings, collecting 1% of all interest earnings. How does the capital market equilibrium change? What is the effect on private borrowers? (*Hint*: See Solved Problem 16.4.)

5. Challenge

5.1 If the interest rate is near zero, should an individual go to college, given the information in the Challenge Solution figure? State a simple rule for determining whether this individual should go to college in terms of the areas labeled *Benefit* and *Cost* in the figure.

5.2 At current interest rates, it pays for Bob to go to college if he graduates in four years. If it takes an extra year to graduate from college, does going to college still pay? Show how the figure in the Challenge Solution changes. Illustrate how the present value calculation changes using a formula and variables. **A**

5.3 Which is worth more to you: (a) a $10,000 payment today or (b) a $1,000-per-year higher salary for as long as you work? At what interest rate would (a) be worth more to you than (b)? Does your answer depend on how many years you expect to work? **A**

5.4 In 2012, the Clarkson Community Schools in Clarkson, Michigan, paid starting teachers $38,087 if they had a bachelor's degree and $41,802 if they had a master's degree. (For simplicity, assume that these salaries stay constant and do not increase with experience.) Suppose you know that you want to work for this school district and want to maximize your life-time earnings. To get a master's degree takes one extra year of schooling and costs $20,000. Should you get the master's if you cannot work during that year? Should you get your master's degree if you can work while studying? In your calculations, assume that you'll work for 40 years and then retire and consider interest rates of 3% and 10%. (*Hint*: You can get a reasonable approximation to the answer by assuming that you work forever and use Equation 16.4.) **A**

Uncertainty 17

Lottery: A tax on people who are bad at math.

On April 20, 2010, a massive explosion occurred on the Transocean Deepwater Horizon oil rig, which was leased by the oil company BP. The explosion killed 11 workers and seriously injured 17 others. In addition, many of the 90,000 workers who participated in the cleanup suffered significant health problems from exposure to various toxins. Safeguards in the well to automatically cap the oil in case of an accident did not work as expected.

Consequently, a massive spill of roughly 200 million gallons of oil polluted the Gulf of Mexico before the well was finally capped. This catastrophic oil spill inflicted gigantic costs for cleaning up Louisiana and other Gulf states and inflicted very large losses on the Gulf fishing and tourism industries.

A bad outcome does necessarily imply that bad decisions were made. BP could have taken reasonable safety precautions and merely been unlucky. However, government agencies concluded that the explosion and the resulting massive oil leak were largely due to a failure to take appropriate safety and other precautions by BP and its subcontractors. In 2012, BP pled guilty to 11 counts of seaman's manslaughter and was fined a record $4 billion in penalties. In addition, BP was liable for much more due to cleanup costs, civil lawsuits, and other fines and penalties.

BP may have ignored or underestimated the chance of these expensive calamities, improperly reasoning that such major disasters had not happened to them before and would therefore never happen in the future (or at least that the chances were miniscule). However, a more likely explanation for BP's behavior is that it did not expect to bear the full cost if a catastrophe occurred. In 1990, Congress passed a law that limited liability beyond cleanup costs at $75 million for a rig spill, a tiny fraction of the harm in this case.

However, in the face of international condemnation for the massive Gulf spill, BP agreed to waive this cap and estimated that it would ultimately pay $42 billion for the cleanup and fines. (Based on court decisions in 2013, it may owe substantially more.) These losses are substantial compared to its profit of $9 billion and shareholders' equity of $73 billion in 2012.

BP made a calculated choice about the risks that a catastrophic oil spill would happen, presumably taking the $75 million cap on liability into account in making their decisions. How does a cap on liability affect a firm's willingness to make a risky investment or to invest less than the optimal amount in safety? How does a cap affect the amount of risk that the firm and others in society bear? How does a cap affect the amount of insurance against the costs of an oil spill that a firm buys?

Life's a series of gambles. Will you get a good summer job? Will you avoid disasters such as air crashes, disease, earthquakes, and fire? Will you receive Social Security when you retire? Will you win the lottery tomorrow? Will your stock increase in value?

In this chapter, we extend the model of decision making by individuals and firms to include uncertainty. We look at how uncertainty affects consumption decisions made by individuals and business decisions made by firms.

When making decisions about investments and other matters, consumers and firms consider the possible *outcomes* under various circumstances, or *states of nature*. For example, a pharmaceutical firm's drug may either be approved or rejected by a regulatory authority, so the two states of nature are *approve* or *reject*. Associated with each of these states of nature is an outcome: the value of the pharmaceutical firm's stock will be $100 per share if the drug is approved and only $75 if the drug is rejected.

Although we cannot know with certainty what the future outcome will be, we may know that some outcomes are more likely than others. Often an uncertain situation—one in which no single outcome is certain to occur—can be quantified in the sense that we can assign a probability to each possible outcome. For example, if we toss a coin, we can assign a probability of 50% to each of the two possible outcomes: heads or tails. When uncertainty can be quantified, it is sometimes called **risk**: The likelihood of each possible outcome is known or can be estimated, and no single possible outcome is certain to occur. However, because many people do not distinguish between the terms risk and *uncertainty*, we use these terms interchangeably. All the examples in this chapter concern quantifiable uncertainty.[1]

risk
situation in which the likelihood of each possible outcome is known or can be estimated and no single possible outcome is certain to occur

Consumers and firms modify their decisions about consumption and investment as the degree of risk varies. Indeed, most people are willing to spend money to reduce risk by buying insurance or taking preventive measures. Moreover, most people will choose a riskier investment over a less risky one only if they expect a higher return from the riskier investment.

In this chapter, we examine five main topics

1. **Assessing Risk.** Probability, expected value, and variance are important concepts that are used to assess the degree of risk and the likely profit from a risky undertaking.

2. **Attitudes Toward Risk.** Whether managers or consumers choose a risky option over a nonrisky alternative depends on their attitudes toward risk and on the expected payoffs of each option.

---

[1]Uncertainty is unquantifiable when we do not know enough to assign meaningful probabilities to different outcomes or if we do not even know what the possible outcomes are. If asked "Who will be the U.S. president in 15 years?" most of us do not even know the likely contenders, let alone the probabilities.

3. **Reducing Risk.** People try to reduce their overall risk by choosing safe rather than risky options, taking actions to reduce the likelihood of bad outcomes, obtaining insurance, pooling risks by combining offsetting risks, and in other ways.

4. **Investing Under Uncertainty.** Whether people make an investment depends on the riskiness of the payoff, the expected return, attitudes toward risk, the interest rate, and whether it is profitable to alter the likelihood of a good outcome.

5. **Behavioral Economics of Uncertainty.** Because some people do not choose among risky options the way that traditional economic theory predicts, some researchers have switched to new models that incorporate psychological factors.

17.1 Assessing Risk

In America, anyone can be president. That's one of the risks you take.
—Adlai Stevenson

Gregg is considering whether to schedule an outdoor concert on July 4th. Booking the concert is a gamble: He stands to make a tidy profit if the weather is good, but he'll lose a substantial amount if it rains.

To analyze this decision Gregg needs a way to describe and quantify risk. A particular *event*—such as holding an outdoor concert—has a number of possible *outcomes*—here, either it rains or it does not rain. When deciding whether to schedule the concert, Gregg quantifies how risky each outcome is using a *probability* and then uses these probabilities to determine what he can expect to earn.

Probability

A *probability* is a number between 0 and 1 that indicates the likelihood that a particular outcome will occur. If an outcome cannot occur, it has a probability of 0. If the outcome is sure to happen, it has a probability of 1. If it rains one time in four on July 4th, the probability of rain is $\frac{1}{4}$ or 25%.

How can Gregg estimate the probability of rain on July 4th? Usually the best approach is to use the *frequency*, which tells us how often an uncertain event occurred in the past. Otherwise, one has to use a *subjective probability*, which is an estimate of the probability that may be based on other information, such as informal "best guesses" of experienced weather forecasters.

Frequency   The probability is the actual chance that an outcome will occur. Gregg does not know the true probability so he has to estimate it. Because Gregg (or the weather department) knows how often it rained on July 4th over many years, he can use that information to estimate the probability that it will rain this year.

He calculates θ (theta), the frequency that it rained, by dividing n, the number of years that it rained on July 4th, by N, the total number of years for which he has data:

$$\theta = \frac{n}{N}.$$

For example, if it rained 20 times on July 4th in the last 40 years, $n = 20$, $N = 40$, and $\theta = 20/40 = 0.5$. Gregg then uses θ, the frequency, as his estimate of the true probability that it will rain this year.

Subjective Probability Unfortunately, we often lack a history of repeated events that allows us to calculate frequencies. For example, the disastrous magnitude-9 earthquake that struck Japan in 2011, with an accompanying tsunami and nuclear reactor crisis, was unprecedented in modern history.

Where events occur very infrequently, we cannot use a frequency calculation to predict a probability. We use whatever information we have to form a *subjective probability*, which is a best estimate of the likelihood that the outcome will occur— that is, our best, informed guess.

The subjective probability can combine frequencies and all other available information—even information that is not based on scientific observation. If Gregg is planning a concert months in advance, his best estimate of the probability of rain is based on the frequency of rain in the past. However, as the event approaches, a weather forecaster can give him a better estimate that takes into account atmospheric conditions and other information in addition to the historical frequency. Because the forecaster's probability estimate uses personal judgment in addition to an observed frequency, it is a subjective probability.

Probability Distribution A *probability distribution* relates the probability of occurrence to each possible outcome. Panel a of Figure 17.1 shows a probability distribution over five possible outcomes: zero to four days of rain per month in a relatively dry city. The probability that it rains no days during the month is 10%, as is the probability of exactly four days of rain. The chance of two rainy days is 40%, and the chance of one or three rainy days is 20% each. The probability that it rains five or more days a month is 0%.

Figure 17.1 Probability Distributions

The probability distribution shows the probability of occurrence for each of the mutually exclusive outcomes. Panel a shows five possible mutually exclusive outcomes. The probability that it rains exactly two days per month is 40%. The probability that it rains five or more days per month is 0%. The probability distributions in panels a and b have the same mean. The variance is smaller in panel b, where the probability distribution is more concentrated around the mean than the distribution in panel a.

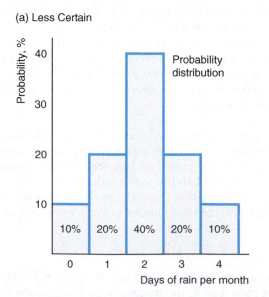

(a) Less Certain

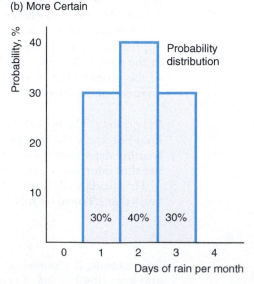

(b) More Certain

These weather outcomes are *mutually exclusive*—only one of these outcomes can occur at a given time—and *exhaustive*—no other outcomes than those listed are possible. Where outcomes are mutually exclusive and exhaustive, exactly one of these outcomes will occur with certainty, and the probabilities must add up to 100%. For simplicity, we concentrate on situations with only two possible outcomes.

Expected Value

One of the common denominators I have found is that expectations rise above that which is expected. —George W. Bush

Gregg, a promoter, schedules an outdoor concert for tomorrow.[2] How much money he'll make depends on the weather. If it doesn't rain, his profit or value from the concert is $V = 15$. (If it will make you happier—and it will certainly make Gregg happier—you can think of the profits in this example as $15,000 instead of $15.) If it rains, he'll have to cancel the concert and he'll lose $V = -5$, which he must pay the band. Although Gregg does not know what the weather will be with certainty, he knows that the weather department forecasts a 50% chance of rain.

Gregg may use the *mean* or the *average* of the values from both outcomes as a summary statistic of the likely payoff from booking this concert. The mean or average value is called his *expected value* (here, his *expected profit*). The expected value, EV, is the value of each possible outcome times the probability of that outcome:[3]

$$EV = [Pr(\text{no rain}) \times \text{Value(no rain)}] + [Pr(\text{rain}) \times \text{Value(rain)}]$$
$$= [\tfrac{1}{2} \times 15] + [\tfrac{1}{2} \times (-5)] = 5,$$

where Pr is the probability of an outcome, so $Pr(\text{rain})$ is the "probability that rain occurs."

The expected value is the amount Gregg would earn on average if the event were repeated many times. If he puts on such concerts many times over the years and the weather follows historical patterns, he will earn 15 at half of the concerts without rain, and he will get soaked for −5 at the other half of the concerts, at which it rains. Thus, he'll earn an average of 5 per concert over a long period of time.

Solved Problem 17.1

Suppose that Gregg could obtain perfect information so that he can accurately predict whether it will rain far enough before the concert that he could book the band only if needed. How much would he expect to earn, knowing that he will eventually have this perfect information? How much does he gain by having this perfect information?

Answer

1. *Determine how much Gregg would earn if he had perfect information in each state of nature.* If Gregg knew with certainty that it would rain at the time of the concert, he would not book the band, so he would make no loss or profit: $V = 0$. If Gregg knew that it would not rain, he would hold the concert and make 15.

---

[2]My brother Gregg, a successful concert promoter, wants me to inform you that the hero of the following story is some other Gregg who is a concert promoter.

[3]With n possible outcomes, the value of outcome i is V_i, and the probability of that outcome is Pr_i, the expected value is $EV = Pr_1 V_1 + Pr_2 V_2 + \ldots + Pr_n V_n$.

2. *Determine how much Gregg would expect to earn before he learns with certainty what the weather will be.* Gregg knows that he'll make 15 with a 50% probability $(= \frac{1}{2})$ and 0 with a 50% probability, so his expected value, given that he'll receive perfect information in time to act on it, is $EV = (\frac{1}{2} \times 15) + (\frac{1}{2} \times 0) = 7.5$.

3. *Calculate his gain from perfect information as the difference between his expected earnings with perfect information and his expected earnings with imperfect information.* Gregg's gain from perfect information is the difference between the expected earnings with perfect information, 7.5, and the expected earnings without perfect information, 5. Thus, Gregg expects to earn 2.5 $(= 7.5 - 5)$ more with perfect information than with imperfect information.[4]

Comment: Having information has no value if it doesn't alter behavior. This information is valuable to Gregg because he avoids hiring the band if he knows that it will rain.

Variance and Standard Deviation

From the expected value, Gregg knows how much he is likely to earn on average if he books many similar concerts. However, he cannot tell from the expected value how risky the concert is.

If Gregg's earnings are the same whether it rains or not, he faces no risk and the actual return he receives is the expected value. If the possible outcomes differ from one another, he faces risk.

We can measure the risk Gregg faces in various ways. The most common approach is to use a measure based on how much the values of the possible outcomes differ from the expected value, EV. If it does not rain, the *difference* between Gregg's actual earnings, 15, and his expected earnings, 5, is 10. The difference if it does rain is $-5 - 5 = -10$. It is convenient to combine the two differences—one difference for each state of nature (possible outcome)—into a single measure of risk.

One such measure of risk is the *variance*, which measures the spread of the probability distribution. For example, the variance in panel a of Figure 17.1, where the probability distribution ranges from zero to four days of rain per month, is greater than the variance in panel b, where the probability distribution ranges from one to three days of rain per month.

Formally, the variance is the probability-weighted average of the squares of the differences between the observed outcome and the expected value.[5] The variance of the value Gregg obtains from the outdoor concert is

$$\text{Variance} = [Pr(\text{no rain}) \times (\text{Value(no rain)} - EV)^2]$$

$$+ [Pr(\text{rain}) \times (\text{Value(rain)} - EV)^2]$$

$$= [\tfrac{1}{2} \times (15 - 5)^2] + [\tfrac{1}{2} \times (-5 - 5)^2]$$

$$= [\tfrac{1}{2} \times (10)^2] + [\tfrac{1}{2} \times (-10)^2] = 100.$$

---

[4]This answer can be reached directly. The value of this information is his expected savings from not hiring the band when it rains: $\frac{1}{2} \times 5 = 2.5$.

[5]With n possible outcomes, an expected value of EV, a value of V_i for each outcome i, and Pr_i probability of each outcome i, the variance is

$$Pr_1(V_1 - EV)^2 + Pr_2(V_2 - EV)^2 + \cdots + Pr_n(V_n - EV)^2.$$

The variance puts more weight on large deviations from the expected value than on smaller ones.

Table 17.1 Variance and Standard Deviation: Measures of Risk

Outcome	Probability	Value	Deviation	Deviation^2	Deviation^2 × Probability
No rain	$\frac{1}{2}$	15	10	100	50
Rain	$\frac{1}{2}$	−5	−10	100	50
				Variance	100
				Standard Deviation	10

Note: Deviation = Value − EV = Value − 5.

Table 17.1 shows how to calculate the variance of the profit from this concert step by step. The first column lists the two outcomes: rain and no rain. The next column gives the probability. The third column shows the value or profit of each outcome. The next column calculates the difference between the values in the third column and the expected value, $EV = \$5$. The fifth column squares these differences, and the last column multiplies these squared differences by the probabilities in the second column. The sum of these probability weighted differences, $100, is the variance.

Instead of describing risk using the variance, economists and businesspeople often report the *standard deviation*, which is the square root of the variance. The usual symbol for the standard deviation is σ (sigma), so the symbol for variance is σ^2. For the outdoor concert, the variance is $\sigma^2 = \$100$ and the standard deviation is $\sigma = \$10$.

17.2 Attitudes Toward Risk

Given the risks Gregg faces if he schedules a concert, will Gregg stage the concert? To answer this question, we need to know Gregg's attitude toward risk.

Expected Utility

If Gregg did not care about risk, then he would decide whether to promote the concert based on its expected value (profit) regardless of any difference in the risk. However, most people care about risk as well as expected value. Indeed, most people are *risk averse*—they dislike risk. They will choose a riskier option over a less risky option only if the expected value of the riskier option is sufficiently higher than that of the less risky one.

We need a formal means to judge the trade-off between expected value and risk—to determine if the expected value of a riskier option is sufficiently higher to justify the greater risk. The most commonly used method is to extend the model of utility maximization. In Chapter 4, we noted that one can describe an individual's preferences over various bundles of goods by using a utility function. John von Neumann and Oskar Morgenstern (1944) extended the standard utility-maximizing model to include risk.[6] This approach can be used to show how people's taste for risk affects

[6]This approach to handling choice under uncertainty is the most commonly used method. Schoemaker (1982) discusses the logic underlying this approach, the evidence for it, and several variants. Machina (1989) discusses a number of alternative methods. Here we treat utility as a cardinal measure rather than an ordinal measure.

their choices among options that differ in both expected value and risk, such as career choices, the types of contracts to accept, where to build plants, whether to buy insurance, and which stocks to buy.

In this reformulation, we assume that the individual knows the value of each possible outcome and the probability that it will occur. A rational person maximizes *expected utility*. Expected utility is the probability-weighted average of the utility from each possible outcome. For example, Gregg's expected utility, EU, from promoting the concert is

$$EU = [Pr(\text{no rain}) \times U(\text{Value(no rain)})] + [Pr(\text{rain}) \times U(\text{Value(rain)})]$$
$$= [\tfrac{1}{2} \times U(15)] + [\tfrac{1}{2} \times U(-5)],$$

where his utility function, U, is a function of his earnings. For example, $U(15)$ is the amount of utility Gregg gets from earnings or wealth of 15.[7]

In short, the expected utility calculation is similar to the expected value calculation. Both are weighted averages in which the weights are the probabilities that correspond to the various possible outcomes. The mathematical difference is that the expected value is the probability-weighted average of the monetary value, whereas the expected utility is the probability-weighted average of the utility from the monetary value. The key economic difference is that the expected utility captures the trade-off between risk and value, whereas the expected value considers only value.

If we know how an individual's utility increases with wealth, we can determine how that person reacts to risky situations. We refer to a risky situation as a *bet*. Thus, for example, if Gregg schedules his concert outdoors, he is betting that it will not rain. We can classify people in terms of their willingness to make a **fair bet**: a wager with an expected value of zero. An example of a fair bet is one in which you pay a dollar if a flipped coin comes up heads and receive a dollar if it comes up tails. Because you expect to win half the time and lose half the time, the expected value of this bet is zero:

$$[\tfrac{1}{2} \times (-1)] + [\tfrac{1}{2} \times 1] = 0.$$

In contrast, a bet in which you pay 2 if you lose the coin flip and receive 4 if you win is an unfair bet that favors you, with an expected value of

$$[\tfrac{1}{2} \times (-2)] + [\tfrac{1}{2} \times 4] = 1.$$

Someone who is unwilling to make a fair bet is **risk averse**. A person who is indifferent about making a fair bet is **risk neutral**. A person who is **risk preferring** will make a fair bet.[8]

Risk Aversion

Most people are risk averse. We can use our expected utility model to examine how Irma, who is risk averse, makes a choice under uncertainty. Figure 17.2 shows Irma's utility function. The utility function is concave to the wealth axis, indicating that

fair bet
a wager with an expected value of zero

risk averse
unwilling to make a fair bet

risk neutral
indifferent about making a fair bet

risk preferring
willing to make a fair bet

---

[7]People have preferences over the goods they consume. However, for simplicity, we'll say that a person receives utility from earnings or wealth, which can be spent on consumption goods.

[8]*Jargon alert*: The terms *risk loving* and *risk seeking* are common synonyms for risk preferring.

Figure 17.2 Risk Aversion

Initially, Irma's wealth is 40, so her utility is $U(40) = 120$, at point d. If she buys the stock and it's worth 70, her utility is $U(70) = 140$ at point c. If she buys the stock and it's worth only 10, she is at point a, where $U(10) = 70$. If her subjective probability that the stock will be worth 70 is 50%, the expected value of the stock is $40 = (0.5 \times 10) + (0.5 \times 70)$ and her expected utility from buying the stock is $0.5U(10) + 0.5U(70) = 105$, at point b, which is the midpoint of the line between the good outcome, point c, and the bad outcome, point a. Thus, her expected utility from buying the stock, 105, is less than her utility from having a certain wealth of 40, $U(40) = 120$, so she does not buy the stock. In contrast, if Irma's subjective probability that the stock will be worth 70 is 90%, her expected utility from buying the stock is $0.1U(10) + 0.9U(70) = 133$, point f, which is more than her utility with a certain wealth of 40, $U(40) = 120$, at d, so she buys the stock.

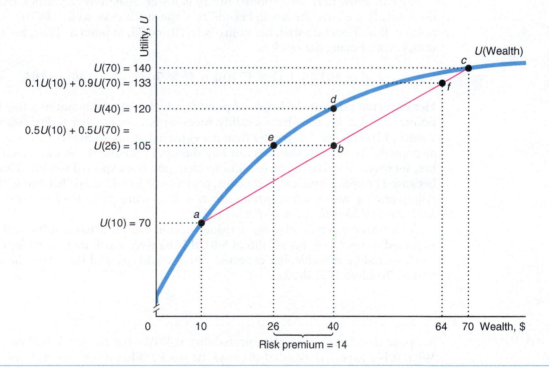

Irma's utility rises with wealth but at a diminishing rate.[9] She has *diminishing marginal utility of wealth*: The extra pleasure from each extra dollar of wealth is smaller than the pleasure from the previous dollar. An individual whose utility function is concave to the wealth axis is risk averse, as we now illustrate.

Unwillingness to Take a Fair Bet Suppose that Irma has an initial wealth of 40 and can choose between two options. One option is to do nothing and keep the 40, so that her utility is $U(40) = 120$ (the height of point d in Figure 17.2) with certainty. Her other option is to buy a share (a unit of stock) in a start-up company. Her wealth will

---

[9]Irma's utility from W wealth is $U(W)$. She has positive marginal utility from extra wealth, $\mathrm{d}U(W)/\mathrm{d}W > 0$; however, her utility increases with wealth at a diminishing rate, $\mathrm{d}^2U(W)/\mathrm{d}W^2 < 0$.

be 70 if the start-up is a big success and 10 otherwise. Irma's subjective probability is 50% that the firm will be a big success. Her expected value of wealth remains

$$40 = (\tfrac{1}{2} \times 10) + (\tfrac{1}{2} \times 70).$$

Thus, buying the stock is a fair bet because she has the same expected wealth whether she purchases the stock or not.

If Irma were risk neutral so that she only cared about her expected value and didn't care about risk, she would be indifferent between buying the stock or not. However, because Irma is risk averse, Irma prefers not buying the stock because both options have the same expected wealth and buying the stock carries more risk.

We can show that her expected utility is lower if she buys the stock than if she does not. If she buys the stock, her utility if the stock does well is $U(70) = 140$, at point c. If it doesn't do well, her utility is $U(10) = 70$, at point a. Thus, her expected utility from buying the stock is

$$[\tfrac{1}{2} \times U(10)] + [\tfrac{1}{2} \times U(70)] = [\tfrac{1}{2} \times 70] + [\tfrac{1}{2} \times 140] = 105.$$

Her expected utility is the height of point b, which is the midpoint of a line between points a and c. Because Irma's utility function is concave, her utility from certain wealth, 120 at point d, is greater than her expected utility from the risky activity, 105 at point b. As a result, she does not buy the stock. Buying the stock, which is a fair bet, increases the risk she faces without changing her expected wealth. Thus, Irma, because her utility function is concave, prefers not to take a fair bet and is therefore risk averse. *A person whose utility function is concave picks the less risky choice if both choices have the same expected value.*

A risk-averse person chooses a riskier option only if it has a sufficiently higher expected value. Given her wealth of $40, if Irma were much more confident that the stock would be valuable, her expected value would rise and she'd buy the stock, as Solved Problem 17.2 shows.

Solved Problem 17.2

Suppose that Irma's subjective probability is 90% that the stock will be valuable. What is her expected wealth if she buys the stock? What is her expected utility? Does she buy the stock?

Answer

1. *Calculate Irma's expected wealth.* Her expected value or wealth is 10% times her wealth if the stock bombs plus 90% times her wealth if the stock does well:

$$(0.1 \times 10) + (0.9 \times 70) = 64.$$

In Figure 17.2, 64 is the distance along the wealth axis corresponding to point f.

2. *Calculate Irma's expected utility.* Her expected utility is the probability-weighted average of her utility under the two outcomes:

$$[0.1 \times U(10)] + [0.9 \times U(70)] = [0.1 \times 70] + [0.9 \times 140] = 133.$$

Her expected utility is the height on the utility axis of point f. Point f is nine-tenths of the distance along the line connecting point a to point c.

3. *Compare Irma's expected utility to her certain utility if she does not buy the stock.* Irma's expected utility from buying the stock, 133 (at point *f*), is greater than her certain utility, 120 (at point *d*), if she does not. Thus, if Irma is this confident that the stock will do well, she buys it. Although the risk is greater from buying than from not buying, her expected wealth is sufficiently higher (64 instead of 40) that it's worth it to her to take the chance.

risk premium
the amount that a risk-averse person would pay to avoid taking a risk

The Risk Premium The **risk premium** is the maximum amount that a decision maker would pay to avoid taking a risk. Equivalently, the risk premium is the minimum extra compensation (premium) that a decision maker would require to willingly incur a risk.

We can use Figure 17.2, where Irma owns the stock that has a 50% chance of being worth 70 and a 50% chance of being worth 10, to determine her risk premium. The risk premium is the difference between her expected wealth from the risky stock and the amount of wealth, called the *certainty equivalent*, that if held with certainty, would yield the same utility as this uncertain prospect.

Irma's expected wealth from holding the stock is 40, and the corresponding expected utility is 105. The certainty equivalent income is 26, because Irma's utility is 105 if she has 26 with certainty: $U(26) = 105$, which is the same as her expected utility from owning the stock. Thus, she would be indifferent between keeping the stock or selling it for a price of 26. Thus her risk premium, the difference between the expected value of the uncertain prospect and the certainty equivalent, is $40 - 26 = 14$, as the figure shows.

Application

Stocks' Risk Premium

Usually, stock values are more variable over time than are bond values. Because stocks are riskier than bonds, for both to be sold in the market to risk-averse investors, the rates of return on investing in stocks must exceed those on bonds over the period that the investor plans to hold these investments. This greater return is an investor's risk premium for stocks.

For example, a U.S. government bond is essentially free of any risk that the U.S. government will default. As Figure 17.2 illustrates, an investor will buy a stock only if it provides a risk premium over a risk-free U.S. government bond. That is, the investor buys the stock only if the amount by which the expected return on the stock exceeds the rate of return on the bond.

In 2012, the stocks in the Standard and Poor's index of 500 leading stocks, the S&P 500, had a return of 15.8%, which substantially exceeded the 3.0% return on 10-year U.S. treasury bonds. However, stocks do not always outperform safe government bonds. In some years, such as 2011, stocks have performed worse than bonds.

Nonetheless, stocks have had a higher rate of return over longer periods. For the 50-year period 1963–2012, the average annual return was 11.1% for S&P 500 stocks and 7.2% on long-term bonds.[10]

---

[10]Adjusting for inflation, which averaged 4.2% per year over this period, the average annual real rates of return were 6.9% on the S&P 500 and 3.0% on long-term U.S. government bonds.

Risk Neutrality

Someone who is risk neutral is indifferent about taking a fair bet. Such a person has a constant marginal utility of wealth: Each extra dollar of wealth raises utility by the same amount as the previous dollar. With a constant marginal utility of wealth, the utility function is a straight line in a graph of utility against wealth. As a consequence, a risk-neutral person's utility depends only on wealth and not on risk.

Suppose that Irma is risk neutral and has the straight-line utility function in panel *a* of Figure 17.3. She would be indifferent between buying the stock and receiving 40 with certainty if her subjective probability is 50% that it will do well. Her expected utility from buying the stock is the average of her utility at points *a* (10) and *c* (70):

$$[\tfrac{1}{2} \times U(10)] + [\tfrac{1}{2} \times U(70)] = [\tfrac{1}{2} \times 70] + [\tfrac{1}{2} \times 140] = 105.$$

Her expected utility exactly equals her utility with certain wealth of 40 (at point *b*) because the line connecting points *a* and *c* lies on the utility function and point *b* is the midpoint of that line.

Here Irma is indifferent between buying and receiving 40 with certainty, a fair bet, because she doesn't care how much risk she faces. Because the expected wealth from both options is 40, she is indifferent between them.

In general, *a risk-neutral person chooses the option with the highest expected value, because maximizing expected value maximizes utility.* A risk-neutral person chooses the riskier option if it has even a slightly higher expected value than the less risky option. Equivalently, the risk premium for a risk-neutral person is zero.

Figure 17.3 Risk Neutrality and Risk Preference

(a) If Irma's utility function can be graphed as a straight line, she is risk neutral and is indifferent as to whether or not to make a fair bet. Her expected utility from buying the stock, 105 at *b*, is the same as from a certain wealth of 40 at *b*. (b) If the plot of Irma's utility function is convex to the horizontal axis, Irma has increasing marginal utility of wealth and is risk preferring. She buys the stock because her expected utility from buying the stock, 105 at *b*, is higher than her utility from a certain wealth of 40, 82 at *d*.

(a) Risk-Neutral Individual

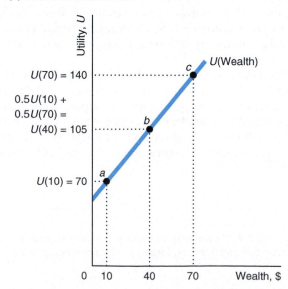

(b) Risk-Preferring Individual

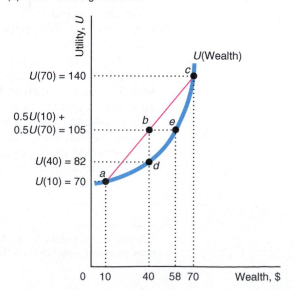

Risk Preference

An individual with an increasing marginal utility of wealth is risk preferring and is therefore happy to take a fair bet. If Irma has the utility function in panel b of Figure 17.3, she is risk preferring. Her expected utility from buying the stock, 105 at *b*, is higher than her certain utility if she does not buy the stock, 82 at *d*. Therefore, she buys the stock.

A risk-preferring person is willing to pay for the right to make a fair bet (a negative risk premium). As the figure shows, Irma's expected utility from buying the stock is the same as the utility from a certain wealth of 58. Given her initial wealth of 40, if you offer her the opportunity to buy the stock or offer to give her 18, she is indifferent. With any payment smaller than 18, she prefers to buy the stock.

Application **Gambling**	Most people say that they don't like bearing risk. Consistent with such statements, most consumers purchase car, homeowner's, medical, and other forms of insurance that reduce the risks they face. But many of these same people gamble. The American Gaming Association reported that consumers gambled over $37 billion at U.S. casinos in 2012. According to MarketLine, the global market for casinos and gaming was $382 billion in 2010 and was expected to reach $513 billion by 2015. Christiansen Capital Advisors estimated that global Internet gambling was $24.5 billion in 2010.

Over half of the countries in the world have lotteries. Global lottery sales were $275 billion in 2012, according to La Fleur's 2013 *World Lottery Almanac*.

Not only do many people gamble, but they make unfair bets, in which the expected value of the gamble is negative. That is, if they play the game repeatedly, they are likely to lose money in the long run. For example, the British government keeps half of the total amount bet on its lottery. Americans lose at least $50 billion or 7% of all legal bets.

Why do people take unfair bets? One explanation concerns tastes. Some people gamble because they are risk preferring or because they have a compulsion to gamble.[11] However, neither of these observations is likely to explain noncompulsive gambling by most people who exhibit risk-averse behavior in the other aspects of their lives (such as buying insurance). Risk-averse people may make unfair bets because they get pleasure from participating in the game or because they falsely believe that the gamble favors them.

Gambling provides entertainment as well as risk. Risk-averse people insure their property, such as their homes, because they do not want to bear the risk of theft, flooding, and fire. However, these same people may play poker or bet on horse races because they get enough pleasure from playing those games to put up with the financial risk and the expected loss.

---

[11]Friedman and Savage (1948) suggest that some gamblers are risk averse with respect to small gambles but risk preferring for large ones, such as a lottery.

People definitely like games of chance. One survey found that 65% of Americans say that they engage in games of chance, even when the games involve no money or only trivial sums (Brunk, 1981). That is, they play because they enjoy the games.[12]

Instead or in addition, people may gamble because they make mistakes.[13] Either people do not know the true probabilities or cannot properly calculate expected values, so they do not realize that they are participating in an unfair bet. And some gamblers are simply overconfident: they overestimate their likelihood of winning.

17.3 Reducing Risk

If most accidents occur at home, why not move away?

Risk-averse people want to eliminate or reduce the risks they face. Risk-neutral people avoid unfair bets that are stacked against them, and even risk-preferring people avoid very unfair bets. Individuals can avoid optional risky activities, but often they can't escape risk altogether. Property owners, for instance, always face the possibility that their property will be damaged, stolen, or burnt. They may be able to reduce the probability that bad states of nature occur, however.

The simplest way to avoid risk is to abstain from optional risky activities. No one forces you to bet on the lottery, go into a high-risk occupation, or buy stock in a start-up biotech firm. If one brand of a product you use comes with a warranty and an otherwise comparable brand does not, you lower your risk by buying the guaranteed product.

Even when you can't avoid risk altogether, you can take precautions to reduce the probability of bad states of nature or the magnitude of any loss that might occur. For example, you can maintain your car as the manufacturer recommends to reduce the probability that it will break down. By locking your apartment door, you lower the chance that your television will be stolen. Getting rid of your twelve-year-old collection of newspapers lessens the likelihood that your house will burn. Not only do these actions reduce your risk, but they also raise the expected value of your asset.

In this section, we look at the three most common actions that people and firms take to avoid or limit the risks they face: obtain information, diversify, and buy insurance.

---

[12]When I was an undergraduate at the University of Chicago, I lived in a dorm and saw overwhelming evidence that the "love of the game" is a powerful force. As the neighborhood provided few forms of entertainment, the dorm's denizens regularly watched the man from the vending company refill the candy machine with fresh candy. He took the old, stale, unpopular bars that remained in the machine and placed them in the "mystery candy" bin. Thanks to our careful study of stocking techniques, we all knew that buying the mystery candy was not a fair bet—who would want unpopular, stale candy bars at the same price as a fresh, popular bar? Nonetheless, one of the dorm dwellers always bought the mystery candy. When asked why, he responded, "I love the excitement of not knowing what'll come out." Life was very boring indeed on the South Side of Chicago.

[13]Economists, who know how to calculate expected values and derive most of their excitement from economic models, are apparently less likely to gamble than are other people. A number of years ago, an association of economists met in Reno, Nevada. Reno hotels charge low room rates on the assumption that they'll make plenty from guests' gambling losses. However, the economists gambled so little that they were asked pointedly not to return.

Obtain Information

Collecting accurate information before acting is one of the most important ways in which people can reduce risk and increase expected value and expected utility, as Solved Problem 17.1 illustrated. Armed with information, you may avoid a risky choice or you may be able to take actions that reduce the probability of a disaster or the size of the loss.

Before buying a car or refrigerator, many people read *Consumer Reports* to determine how frequently a particular brand is likely to need repairs. Similarly, before deciding where to locate a new plant, a prudent manager collects information about various locations concerning local crime rates, fire risks, and other potential hazards.

Diversify

Although it may sound paradoxical, individuals and firms often reduce their overall risk by making many risky investments instead of only one. This practice is called *risk pooling* or *diversification*. As your grandparents may have advised, "Don't put all your eggs in one basket."

Correlation and Diversification The extent to which diversification reduces risk depends on the degree to which the payoffs of various investments are correlated or move in the same direction.[14] If two investments are positively correlated, one performs well when the other performs well. If two investments are negatively correlated, when one performs well, the other performs badly. If the performances of two investments move *independently*—do not move together in a predictable way—their payoffs are uncorrelated.

Diversification can eliminate risk if the returns to two investments are perfectly negatively correlated. Suppose that two firms are competing for a government contract and have an equal chance of winning it. Because only one firm can win, if one wins the other must lose. You can buy a share of stock in either firm for $20. The stock of the firm that wins the contract will be worth $40, whereas the stock of the loser will be worth $10. Investments in these stocks have a perfect negative correlation. If one stock turns out to have the high value, 40, the other must have the low value, 10, and vice versa.

If you buy two shares of the same company, your shares are going to be worth either 80 or 20 after the contract is awarded. Thus, their expected value is

$$EV = (\tfrac{1}{2} \times 80) + (\tfrac{1}{2} \times 20) = 50$$

with a variance of

$$\sigma^2 = [\tfrac{1}{2} \times (80 - 50)^2] + [\tfrac{1}{2} \times (20 - 50)^2] = 900.$$

---

[14]A measure of the *correlation* between two random variables x and y is

$$\rho = E\left(\frac{x - \bar{x}}{\sigma_x} \frac{y - \bar{y}}{\sigma_y}\right),$$

where the $E(\cdot)$ means "take the expectation" of the term in parentheses, $\bar{x}$ and $\bar{y}$ are the means (expected values), and σ_x and σ_y are the standard deviations of x and y. This correlation can vary between -1 and 1. If $\rho = 1$, these random variables are perfectly positively correlated; if $\rho = -1$, they have a perfect negative correlation; and if $\rho = 0$, they are uncorrelated.

However, if you buy one share of each, your two shares will be worth $50 no matter which firm wins, and the variance is zero—the risk has been completely eliminated by investing in these negatively correlated stocks.

For diversification to reduce risk, it is not necessary for the investments to have a perfect negative correlation. Indeed, it is not even necessary for the investments to have a negative correlation. Diversification reduces risk even if the two investments are uncorrelated or imperfectly positively correlated, although the risk reduction is not as dramatic as in the case of perfect negative correlation, where the risk can be completely eliminated.

Suppose, for example, that each of the two firms has a 50% chance of getting a government contract, but whether one firm gets a contract does *not* affect whether the other firm wins one. Thus, the stock values of the two firms are uncorrelated and each firm's stock price has an equal probability of being 40 or 10. The probability that both firms win contracts and have a stock price of 40 is $\frac{1}{4}$, the chance that one is worth 40 and the other is worth 10 is $\frac{1}{2}$, and the chance that each is worth 10 is $\frac{1}{4}$. If you buy one share of each firm, the expected value of these two shares is

$$\mathrm{EV} = (\tfrac{1}{4} \times 80) + (\tfrac{1}{2} \times 50) + (\tfrac{1}{4} \times 20) = 50,$$

and the variance is

$$\sigma^2 = [\tfrac{1}{4} \times (80 - 50)^2] + [\tfrac{1}{2} \times (50 - 50)^2] + [\tfrac{1}{4} \times (20 - 50)^2] = 450.$$

This expected value is the same as from buying two shares of one firm, but the variance is only half as large. Thus, diversification lowers risk when the values are uncorrelated.

Diversification can reduce risk even if the investments are positively correlated provided that the correlation is not perfect. *Diversification does not reduce risk if two investments have a perfect positive correlation.* For example, if the government awards contracts only to both firms or to neither firm, the risks are perfectly positively correlated. The expected value of the stocks and the variance are the same whether you buy two shares of one firm or one share of each firm.

Diversification Through Mutual Funds Given that the value of the stock of most firms is not perfectly positively correlated with the value of other stocks, buying stock in several companies reduces risk compared to buying stock in only one company. One way that investors can effectively own shares in a number of companies at once is by buying shares in a *mutual fund* of stocks. A mutual fund share is issued by a company that buys stocks in many other companies.

Several mutual funds are based on the *Standard & Poor's Composite Index of 500 Stocks* (S&P 500), which is a market value-weighted average of 500 large firms' stocks. The S&P 500 companies constitute only about 7% of all the publicly traded firms in the United States, but they represent approximately 80% of the total value of the U.S. stock market. A number of mutual funds cover even more stocks. The *Wilshire 5000 Index Portfolio* initially covered 5,000 stocks but now includes many more, as Wilshire seeks to include nearly all U.S. publicly traded stocks and adds new stocks as they are issued. Other mutual funds are based on bonds or on a mixture of stocks, bonds, and other types of investments.

Mutual funds allow investors to reduce the risk associated with uncorrelated price movements across stocks through diversification. However, a stock mutual fund has a *market-wide risk*—a risk that is common to the overall market—which arises because the prices of almost all stocks tend to rise when the economy is expanding and to fall when the economy is contracting. Buying a diversified stock mutual fund does not protect you against the systematic risks associated with shifts in the economy that have a similar effect on most stocks.

Application

Diversifying Retirement Funds

To reduce risk, managers and other employees can diversify their own retirement funds and other savings. However, many managers fail to properly diversify their own portfolios by keeping a large portion of their wealth tied up in their employer's stock. One reason for this large share is that many managers receive company stock from their employers as bonuses or to match their pension contributions. In addition, some managers invest voluntarily in company stock as a sign of loyalty.

An important example is the investment firm Bear Stearns, where employees owned one-third of the company's stock. The firm faced bankruptcy in early 2008. Claiming that the firm was too big to be allowed to fail, the U.S. government bailed it out. Under the rescue plan, JPMorgan Chase offered $10 a share to buy Bear Stearns in 2008, which was only a tenth of the stock's value in December 2007. Consequently, not only did many Bear Stearns employees face losing their livelihoods, they also had lost most of their wealth.

In 2007, at the beginning of the recent financial crisis, nearly two of every five employees participating in 401(k) retirement plans in large firms held 20% or more of their money in employer stock.[15] About one-sixth of participants invested 50% or more. On average, these funds held 16% in company stock.

It is very risky for workers to hold such a high percentage of their employer's stock. If a Bear Stearns employee's 401(k) retirement fund invested $100,000 in a Standard & Poor's 500-stock index fund at the end of 2007, its value would have fallen to $90,760 by the end of the first quarter of 2008. However, if that employee shifted 16% into Bear Stearns stock, the investment would have fallen to slightly less than $77,838. Even worse, if all the funds had been in Bear Stearns stock, the 401(k) would only have been worth $10,000.

Many investment advisors recommend investing no more than 5% in employer stock. However, many employees have failed to learn the lesson of Bear Sterns and do not follow this advice. For example, in 2011 Morgan Stanley employees held 24% of their retirement assets in company stock at the beginning of the year. The stock price dropped 44% in 2011, imposing a loss of $570 million on these retirement funds. Even by 2013, the average share of 401(k) funds invested in company stock was still over 13%. As managers and other employees are at risk of losing their jobs if their employer does poorly, they should consider diversifying their risk by making investments that are independent of their employer.

Buy Insurance

I detest life-insurance agents; they always argue that I shall some day die, which is not so. —Stephen Leacock

Individuals and organizations can also avoid or reduce risk by purchasing insurance. As we've already seen, a risk-averse person is willing to pay money—a risk premium—to avoid risk. The demand for risk reduction is met by insurance companies, which bear the risk for anyone who buys an insurance policy. Many risk-averse individuals and firms buy insurance, leading to an industry of enormous size: Global insurance revenues exceeded $4.613 trillion in 2012, over 6% of world GDP.[16]

---

[15]A 401(k) plan is a retirement program run by a firm for its employees under Section 401 (paragraph k) of the Internal Revenue Code. Employees defer paying taxes on investment returns from such plans provided they do not start withdrawing income until after age $59\frac{1}{2}$.

[16]Based on **www.insurancejournal.com/news/international/2013/06/26/296846.htm** and **www.plunkettresearch.com/insurance-risk-management-market-research/industry-overview.**

Determining the Amount of Insurance to Buy   Many individuals and firms buy insurance to shift some or all of the risk they face to an insurance company. A risk-averse person or firm pays a premium to the insurance company, and the insurance company transfers money to the policyholder if a bad outcome occurs, such as becoming ill, having an accident, or suffering a property loss due to theft or fire.

Because Scott is risk averse, he wants to insure his store, which is worth 500. The probability that his store will burn next year is 20%. If a fire occurs, the store will be worth nothing.

With no insurance, the expected value of his store is

$$EV = (0.2 \times 0) + (0.8 \times 500) = 400.$$

Scott faces a good deal of risk. The variance of the value of his store is

$$\sigma^2 = [0.2 \times (0 - 400)^2] + [0.8 \times (500 - 400)^2] = 40,000.$$

fair insurance
a bet between an insurer and a policyholder in which the value of the bet to the policyholder is zero

Suppose that an insurance company offers **fair insurance**: a contract between an insurer and a policyholder in which the expected value of the contract to the policyholder is zero. That is, the insurance is a fair bet. With fair insurance, for every 1 dollar that Scott pays the insurance company, the *insurance premium*, the company will pay Scott 5 dollars to cover the damage if the fire occurs, so that he has 1 dollar less if the fire does not occur, but 4 (= 5 − 1) dollars more if it does occur.[17]

Because Scott is risk averse and the insurance is fair, he wants to *fully insure* by buying enough insurance to eliminate his risk altogether. That is, he wants to buy the amount of fair insurance that will leave him equally well off in both states of nature. He pays a premium of x so that he has 500 − x if the fire does not occur, and has 4x if the fire occurs, such that 500 − x = 4x, or x = 100.[18] If a fire does not occur, he pays a premium of 100 and has a store worth 500 for a net value of 400. If a fire does occur, Scott pays 100 but receives 500 from the insurance company for a net value of 400. Thus, Scott's wealth is 400 in either case.

Although Scott's expected value with full and fair insurance is the same as his expected value without insurance, the variance he faces drops from 40,000 without insurance to 0 with insurance. Scott is better off with full fair insurance because he has the same expected value and faces no risk. A risk-averse person always wants full insurance if the insurance is fair.

Sometimes insurance companies put limits on the amount of insurance offered. For example, the insurance company could offer Scott fair insurance but only up to a maximum gross payment of, for example, 400 rather than 500. Given this limit, Scott would buy the maximum amount of fair insurance that he could.

**Solved Problem
17.3**

The local government collects a property tax of 20 on Scott's store. If the tax is collected whether or not the store burns, how much fair insurance does Scott buy? If the tax is collected only if the store does not burn, how much fair insurance does Scott buy?

---

[17]Following standard practice in the insurance industry, we use the term *insurance premium* (or just *premium*) in this section to refer to the amount *actually paid* for insurance. The *insurance premium* is different from a *risk premium*, which is a person's *willingness to pay* to avoid risk.

[18]The expected value of Scott's insurance contract is [0.8 × (−100)] + [0.2 × 400] = 0, which shows that the insurance is fair.

Answer

1. *Determine the after-tax expected value of the store without insurance.* If the tax is always collected, the store is worth $480 = 500 - 20$ if it does not burn and -20 if it does burn. Thus, the expected value of the store is

$$380 = [0.2 \times (-20)] + [0.8 \times 480].$$

   If the tax is collected only if the fire does not occur, the expected value of the store is

$$384 = [0.2 \times 0] + [0.8 \times 480].$$

2. *Calculate the amount of fair insurance Scott buys if the tax is always collected.* Because Scott is risk averse, he wants to be fully insured so that the after-tax value of his store is the same in both states of nature. If the tax is always collected, Scott pays the insurance company 100. If no fire occurs, his net wealth is $500 - 100 - 20 = 380$. If a fire occurs, the insurance company pays 500, or a net payment of 400 above the cost of the insurance, and Scott pays 20 in taxes, leaving him with 380 once again. That is, he buys the same amount of insurance as he would without any taxes. The tax has no effect on his insurance decision because he owes the tax regardless of the state of nature.

3. *Calculate the amount of fair insurance Scott buys if the tax is collected only if no fire occurs.* If the tax is collected only if no fire occurs, Scott pays the insurance company 96 and receives 480 if a fire occurs. With no fire, Scott's wealth is $500 - 96 - 20 = 384$. If a fire occurs, the insurance company pays 480, so Scott's wealth is $480 - 96 = 384$. Thus, he has the same after-tax wealth in both states of nature.

Comment: Because the tax system is partially insuring Scott by dropping the tax in the bad state of nature, he purchases less private insurance, 480, than the 500 he buys if the tax is collected in both states of nature.

Fairness and Insurance When fair insurance is offered, risk-averse people fully insure. If insurance companies charge more than the fair-insurance price, individuals buy less insurance.[19]

   Because insurance companies do not offer fair insurance, most people do not fully insure. An insurance company could not stay in business if it offered fair insurance. With fair insurance, the insurance company's expected payments would equal the amount the insurance company collects. Because the insurance company has operating expenses—costs of maintaining offices, printing forms, hiring sales agents, and so forth—an insurance firm providing fair insurance would lose money. Insurance companies' rates must be high enough to cover their operating expenses, so the insurance is less than fair to policyholders.

   How much can insurance companies charge for insurance? A monopoly insurance company could charge an amount up to the risk premium a person is willing to pay to avoid risk. For example, in Figure 17.2, Irma's risk premium is 14. She would be willing to pay up to $14 for an insurance policy that would compensate her if her stock did not perform well. The more risk averse an individual is, the more a

---

[19]As Solved Problem 17.3 shows, tax laws may act to offset this problem, so that some insurance may be fair or more than fair after tax.

monopoly insurance company can charge. If many insurance companies compete for business, the price of an insurance policy is less than the maximum that risk-averse individuals are willing to pay—but still high enough that the firms can cover their operating expenses.

Application

Flight Insurance

If flying is so safe, why do they call the airport the terminal?

Many folks fear flying. Many companies such as Travel Guard (TG) offer accidental death insurance for individual flights. If, just before I take my next regularly scheduled commercial flight, I buy a TG insurance policy for $23 and I die on that flight, TG will pay my family $200,000. (Although TG offers much larger amounts of insurance, it seems a bad idea to make myself worth more to my family dead than alive.)

What are the chances of a given flight crashing? Given that probability, should I buy TG flight insurance for my next flight?

If θ is my probability of dying on a flight, my family's expected value from this bet with TG is $200,000\theta - 23$. For this insurance to be fair, this expected value must be zero, which is true if $\theta = 0.000115$. That is, one in every 8,696 passengers dies.

But dear! Flying is safer than driving.

How great *is* the danger of being in a fatal commercial airline crash? According to the National Transportation Safety Board, scheduled U.S. commercial airline flights had no fatalities in 1993, 1998, 2002, 2007, 2008, 2010, 2011, and 2012 (and none through July of 2013).

In 2001, the probability was much higher than any other year because of the 525 on-board deaths caused by the terrorist hijacking and crashes on September 11 and the subsequent sharp reduction in the number of flights. However, even in 2001, the probability was 0.00000077, or 1 in 1.4 million fliers—still much lower than the probability that makes TG's insurance a fair bet. For the decade 2002–2011, the probability was 0.00000002, or 1 fatality per 51 million fliers.

Suppose that the probability of a fatal accident per flight (rather than per passenger) is 0.00000088, the probability from 2002 through 2011. If I randomly choose a flight each day for 10 years, the probability of avoiding a fatal crash is 99.7%. After 100 years of flying every day, the probability drops to only 96.8%. Indeed, only by flying every day for about 2,150 years would the probability of a fatal accident reach 50%. (For most people, the greatest risk of an airplane trip is the drive to and from the airport. Twice as many people are killed in vehicle-deer collisions than in plane crashes.)

Given that my chance of dying in a fatal crash is $\theta = 0.00000002$ (the rate for the decade 2002–2011), the fair rate to pay for $200,000 of flight insurance is about 0.4¢. TG is offering to charge me 5,750 times more than the fair rate for this insurance.

I would have to be incredibly risk averse to be tempted by their kind offer. Even if I were that risk averse, I would be much better off buying general life insurance, which is much less expensive than flight insurance and covers accidental death from all types of accidents and diseases.

Insurance Only for Diversifiable Risks Why is an insurance company willing to sell policies and take on risk? By pooling the risks of many people, the insurance company can lower its risk much below that of any individual. If the probability that one car is stolen is independent of whether other cars are stolen, the risk to an insurance company of insuring one person against theft is much greater than the average risk of insuring many people.

An insurance company sells policies only for risks that it can diversify. If the risks from disasters to its policyholders are highly positively correlated, an insurance company is not well diversified by holding many policies. A war affects all policyholders, so the outcomes that they face are perfectly correlated. Because wars are *nondiversifiable risks*, insurance companies do not offer policies insuring against wars.

Application **Limited Insurance for Natural Disasters**	Losses from natural catastrophes have increased significantly in recent years (Kunreuther and Heal, 2012). As more homes have been built in areas where damage from storms or earthquakes is likely, the size of the potential losses to insurers from nondiversifiable risks has grown.

Insurers paid out $12.5 billion in claims to residential homeowners after the 1994 Los Angeles earthquake. Farmers Insurance Group reported that it paid out three times more for the Los Angeles earthquake than it had collected in earthquake premiums over the previous 30 years.

According to some estimates, Hurricane Katrina in 2005 caused $100 to $200 billion worth of damage and major loss of life. Private insurers paid out $41 billion, or between 20.5% and 41% of the total damages.

Japan's 2011 magnitude-9 earthquake and the associated tsunami was the most costly in history, with estimated damages of more than $200 billion (with some estimates as high as $350 billion). However, the insurance industry paid only $35 billion, or about 17%, because of Japan's low levels of earthquake insurance protection.

The United States suffered 90% of the $160 billion of global natural disaster damages in 2012, compared to 65% in a typical year. Much of the 2012 U.S. loses were due to drought damage to Midwestern crops and Superstorm Sandy, a massive Atlantic storm that flooded shorelines in the Northeast and even parts of New York City, causing an estimated $50 billion of losses.

Insurance companies now refuse to offer hurricane or earthquake insurance in many parts of the world for these relatively nondiversifiable risks. When Nationwide Insurance Company announced that it was sharply curtailing sales of new policies along the Gulf of Mexico and the eastern seaboard from Texas to Maine, a company official explained, "Prudence requires us to diligently manage our exposure to catastrophic losses."

The U.S. government has stepped in to partially replace private insurers. Since 2008, the Flood Insurance and Mitigation Administration, which is part of the Federal Emergency Management Agency, has provided flood insurance under the National Flood Insurance Program. It has insured over 5.6 million Americans against floods associated with hurricanes, tropical storms, heavy rains, and other conditions. Congress has not provided consistent funding for this program, which lapsed at least four times in 2010 alone. In 2012 after extensive debate, Congress passed an act that extended the flood insurance program for five years, but does not guarantee that adequate funding will be available. Thus, consumers may not be able to count on federal flood insurance.[20]

---

[20]The major argument against programs that subsidize insurance is that they provide incentives to engage in excessively risky behavior, such as building or buying homes in areas that have a high probability of being flooded.

In some high-risk areas, state-run insurance pools—such as the Florida Joint Underwriting Association and the California Earthquake Authority—provide households with insurance. However, not only do these policies provide less protection, but their rates are often three times more expensive than previously available commercial insurance, and they provide compensation only for damages beyond a specified level, called the *deductible*.

17.4 Investing Under Uncertainty

Attitudes toward risk affect people's willingness to invest. In some case, investors can pay to alter their probabilities of success.

In the following examples, the owner of a monopoly decides whether to open a new retail outlet. Because the firm is a monopoly, the return from the investment—the profit from the new store—does not depend on the actions of other firms. As a result, the owner of the monopoly faces no strategic considerations. The owner knows the cost of the investment but is unsure about how many people will patronize the new store; hence, the store's future profit is uncertain. Because the investment has an uncertain payoff, the owner must take risk into account when deciding to invest in the new store.

We first consider the decision of Chris, a risk-neutral owner. Because she is risk neutral, she invests if the expected value of the firm rises due to the investment. Any action that increases her expected value must also increase her expected utility because she is indifferent to risk. In contrast, in the next example, Ken is risk averse, so he might not make an investment that increases his firm's expected value if the investment is very risky. That is, maximizing expected value does not necessarily maximize his expected utility.

Risk-Neutral Investing

Chris, the risk-neutral owner of the monopoly, uses a *decision tree* (panel a of Figure 17.4) to decide whether to invest. The rectangle, called a *decision node*, indicates that she must make a decision about whether to invest or not. The circle, a *chance node*, denotes that a random process determines the outcome (consistent with the given probabilities).

If Chris does not open the new store, she makes $0. If she does open the new store, she expects to make $200 (thousand) with 80% probability and to lose $100 (thousand) with 20% probability. The expected value from a new store (see the circle in panel a) is

$$EV = [0.2 \times (-100)] + [0.8 \times 200] = 140.$$

Because Chris is risk neutral, she prefers an expected value of 140 to a certain one of 0, so she invests. Thus, her expected value in the rectangle is 140.

Risk-Averse Investing

Let's compare Chris' decision-making process to that of Ken's, a risk-averse owner of a monopoly who faces the same investment decision. Ken invests in the new store if his expected utility from investing is greater than his certain utility from not investing. Panel b of Figure 17.4 shows his decision tree, which is based on a particular

Figure 17.4 Investment Decision Trees

Chris and Ken, each the owner of a monopoly, must decide whether to invest in a new store. (a) The expected value of the investment is 140, so it pays for Chris, who is risk neutral, to invest. (b) Ken is so risk averse that he does not invest even though the expected value of the investment is positive. His expected utility falls if he makes this risky investment.

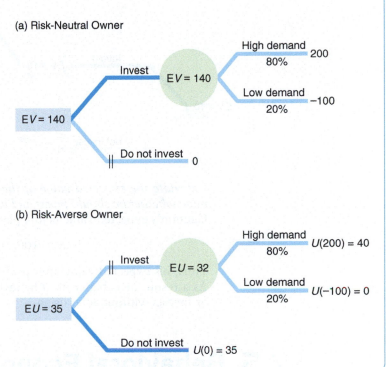

(a) Risk-Neutral Owner

(b) Risk-Averse Owner

risk-averse utility function. The circle shows that Ken's expected utility from the investment is

$$EU = [0.2 \times U(-100)] + [0.8 \times U(200)]$$
$$= (0.2 \times 0) + (0.8 \times 40) = 32.$$

Ken's certain utility from not investing is $U(0) = 35$, which is greater than 32. Thus, Ken does not invest. As a result, his expected utility in the rectangle is 35, his certain utility from not investing.

Solved Problem 17.4

We have been assuming that nature dictates the probabilities of various possible events. However, sometimes an investor can pay to alter the probabilities. Gautam, who is risk neutral, is considering whether to invest in a new store, as the figure shows. After investing, he can increase the probability that demand will be high at the new store by advertising at a cost of 50 ($50,000). If he makes the investment but does not advertise, he has a 40% probability of making 100 and a 60% probability of losing 100. Should he invest in the new store?

Answer

1. *Calculate the expected value of the investment if Gautam does not advertise.* If Gautam makes the investment but does not advertise, the expected value of his investment is

$$[0.4 \times 100] + [0.6 \times (-100)] = -20.$$

Thus, if he does not advertise, he expects to lose money if he makes this investment.

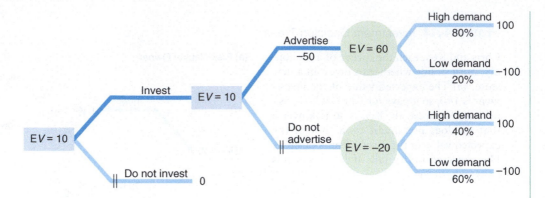

2. *Calculate the expected value of the investment if Gautam advertises and determine whether he should invest and whether he should advertise.* With advertising, Gautam's expected value before paying for the advertisements is

$$[0.8 \times 100] + [0.2 \times (-100)] = 60.$$

Thus, his expected value after paying for the advertisements is 10 (= 60 − 50). As a result, he is better off if he invests *and* advertises than if he does not invest or invests without advertising.

17.5 Behavioral Economics of Uncertainty

Many individuals make choices under uncertainty that are inconsistent with the predictions of expected utility theory. Economists and psychologists explain some of these departures from the predictions of the expected utility model using *behavioral economics*: the use of insights from psychology and research on human cognition and emotional biases to augment the rational economic model in an attempt to better predict economic decision making. (We discussed other applications of behavioral economics in Chapters 4, 11, and 14.)

Biased Assessment of Probabilities

People often have mistaken beliefs about the probability that an event will occur. These biases in estimating probabilities come from several sources, including false beliefs about causality and overconfidence.

Gambler's Fallacy One common confusion, the *gambler's fallacy*, arises from the false belief that past events affect current, independent outcomes.[21] For example, suppose that you flip a fair coin and it comes up heads six times in a row. What are the odds that you'll get a tail on the next flip? Because past flips do not affect this one, the chance of a tail remains 50%, yet many people believe that a head is much more likely because they're on a "run." Others hold the opposite but equally false view that the chance of a tail is high because a tail is "due."

---

[21]The false belief that one event affects another independent event is captured by the joke about a man who brings a bomb on board a plane whenever he flies because he believes that "The chance of having one bomb on a plane are very small, so the chance of having two bombs on a plane is near zero!"

Suppose that you have an urn containing three black balls and two red ones. If you draw a ball without looking, your probability of getting a black ball is $\frac{3}{5} = 60\%$. If you replace the ball and draw again, the chance of picking a black ball remains the same. However, if you draw a black ball and do not replace it, the probability of drawing a black ball again falls to $\frac{2}{4} = 50\%$. Thus, the belief that a tail is due after several heads are tossed in a row is analogous to falsely believing that you are drawing without replacement when you are actually drawing with replacement.

Overconfidence   Another common explanation for why some people make bets that the rest of us avoid is that these gamblers are overconfident. For example, Golec and Tamarkin (1995) found that football bettors tend to make low-probability bets because they greatly overestimate their probabilities of winning certain types of exotic football bets (an *exotic bet* depends on the outcome of more than one game). In one survey, gamblers estimated their chance of winning a particular bet at 45% when the objective probability was 20%.

Few groups exhibit more overconfidence than male high school athletes. Many U.S. high school basketball and football players believe they will get an athletic scholarship to attend college, but less than 5% receive one. Of this elite group, about 25% expect to become professional athletes, but only about 1.5% succeed.[22]

Application

Biased Estimates

Do newspaper stories, television, and movies cause people to overestimate relatively rare events and underestimate relatively common ones? Newspapers are more likely to publish "man bites dog" stories than the more common "dog bites man" reports.[23]

If you have seen the movie *Jaws*, you can't help but think about sharks before wading into the ocean. In 2013, French authorities on the Indian Ocean island of Réunion have announced a plan to kill 90 sharks along its coastline in response (revenge?) to five human deaths from shark attacks since 2011. Do you worry about shark attacks? You really shouldn't.

Only seven people died in unprovoked shark attacks worldwide in 2012. Only 8 people were killed by sharks in U.S. waters from 2003 through 2012: an average of 0.8 a year. U.S. beachgoers on East and West Coast beaches face a 1 in 2 million chance of dying from drowning and other causes, a 1 in 11.5 million chance of being attacked by a shark, and less than a 1 in 264 million chance of dying from a shark bite. The chance of dying from other causes is much higher: 1 in 80 thousand from lightning, 1 in 14 thousand from sun or heat exposure, 1 in 218 from a fall, 1 in 84 from a car accident, 1 in 63 from flu, 1 in 38 from hospital infection, 1 in 24 from a stroke, 1 in 7 from cancer, and 1 in 5 from a heart attack.

Benjamin et al. (2001) reported that, when asked to estimate the frequency of deaths from various causes for the entire population, people overestimate the number of deaths from infrequent causes and underestimate those from more common causes. In contrast, if they are asked to estimate the number of deaths among their own age group from a variety of causes, their estimates are almost completely unbiased. That is not to say that people know the true probabilities—only that their mistakes are not systematic. (However, you should know that, despite the widespread warnings issued every Christmas season, poinsettias are not poisonous.)

---

[22]See www.ncaa.org/wps/wcm/connect/public/NCAA/Resources/Research/Probability+of+Going+Pro and Rossi and Armstrong (1989).

[23]For example, Indian papers reported on a man bites snake story, noting that Neeranjan Bhaskar has eaten more than 4,000 snakes (*Calcutta Telegraph*, August 1, 2005) and the even stranger "Cobra Dies after Biting Priest of Snake Temple!" (*Express India*, July 11, 2005).

Violations of Expected Utility Theory

Economists and psychologists have shown that some people's choices violate the basic assumptions of expected utility theory. One important class of violations arises because people change their choices in response to inessential changes in how choices are described or *framed*, even when the underlying probabilities and events do not change. Another class of violations arises because of a bias toward *certainty*.

Framing   Many people reverse their preferences when a problem is presented or *framed* in different but equivalent ways. Tversky and Kahneman (1981) posed the problem that the United States expects an unusual disease (e.g., avian flu) to kill 600 people. The government is considering two alternative programs to combat the disease. The "exact scientific estimates" of the consequences of these programs are:

- If Program A is adopted, 200 out of 600 people will be saved.
- If Program B is adopted, the probabilities are $\frac{1}{3}$ that 600 people will be saved and $\frac{2}{3}$ that no one will be saved.

When college students were asked to choose, 72% opted for the certain gains of Program A over the possibly larger but riskier gains of Program B.

A second group of students was asked to choose between an alternative pair of programs, and were told:

- If Program C is adopted, 400 out of 600 people will die.
- If Program D is adopted, the probabilities are $\frac{1}{3}$ that no one will die, and $\frac{2}{3}$ that 600 people will die.

When faced with this choice, 78% chose the potentially larger but uncertain losses of Program D over the certain losses of Program C. These results are surprising if people maximize their expected utility: Program A is identical to Program C and Program B is the same as Program D in the sense that these pairs have identical expected outcomes. Expected utility theory predicts consistent choices for the two pairs of programs, but many people make inconsistent choices, preferring Programs A and D. (Even after rereading the options and having the inconsistency problem explained, most of us still feel drawn toward Programs A and D.)

In many similar experiments, researchers have repeatedly observed this pattern, called the *reflection effect*: attitudes toward risk are reversed (reflected) for gains versus losses. People are often risk averse when making choices involving gains, but they are often risk preferring when making choices involving losses.

The Certainty Effect   Many people put excessive weight on outcomes that they consider to be certain relative to risky outcomes. This *certainty effect* (or *Allais effect*, after the French economist who first noticed it) can be illustrated using another example from Kahneman and Tversky (1979). First, a group of subjects was asked to choose between two options:

- **Option A.** You receive $4,000 with probability 80% and $0 with probability 20%.
- **Option B.** You receive $3,000 with certainty.

The vast majority, 80%, chose the certain outcome, B.

Then, the subjects were given another set of options:

- **Option C.** You receive $4,000 with probability 20% and $0 with probability 80%.
- **Option D.** You receive $3,000 with probability 25% and $0 with probability 75%.

Now, 65% prefer C.

Kahneman and Tversky found that over half the respondents violated expected utility theory by choosing B in the first experiment and C in the second one. If $U(0) = 0$, then choosing B over A implies that the expected utility from B is greater than the expected utility from A, so that $U(3,000) > 0.8U(4,000)$, or $U(3,000)/U(4,000) > 0.8$. Choosing C over D implies that $0.2U(4,000) > 0.25U(3,000)$, or $U(3,000)/U(4,000) < 0.8 (= 0.2/0.25)$. Thus, these choices are inconsistent with each other, and hence inconsistent with expected utility theory. The certainty of B seems to give it extra attractiveness over and above what is implied by expected utility theory.

Expected utility theory is based on gambles with known probabilities, whereas most real-world situations involve unknown or subjective probabilities. Ellsberg (1961) pointed out that expected utility theory cannot account for an ambiguous situation in which many people are reluctant to put substantial decision weight on any outcome. He illustrated the problem in a "paradox." Each of two urns contains 100 balls that are either red or black. You know with certainty that the first urn has 50 red and 50 black balls. You do not know the ratio of red to black balls in the second urn. Most of us would agree that the known probability of drawing a red from the first urn, 50%, equals the subjective probability of drawing a red from the second urn. That is, not knowing how many red and black balls are in the second urn, we have no reason to believe that the probability of drawing a red is greater or less than 50%. Yet, most people would prefer to bet that a red ball will be drawn from the first urn rather than from the second urn.

Prospect Theory

Kahneman and Tversky's (1979) *prospect theory* is an alternative theory of decision making under uncertainty that can explain some of the choices people make that are inconsistent with expected utility theory. According to *prospect theory*, people are concerned about gains and losses—the changes in wealth—rather than the level of wealth, as in expected utility theory. People start with a reference point—a base level of wealth—and think about alternative outcomes as gains or losses relative to that reference level.

Comparing Expected Utility and Prospect Theories   We can illustrate the differences in the two theories by comparing how people would act under the two theories when facing the same situation. Both Muzhe and Rui have initial wealth W. They may choose a gamble where they get A dollars with probability θ or B dollars with probability $1 - \theta$. For example, A might be negative, reflecting a loss, and B might be a positive, indicating a gain.

Muzhe wants to maximize his expected utility. If he does not gamble, his utility is $U(W)$. To calculate his expected utility if he gambles, Muzhe uses the probabilities θ and $1 - \theta$ to weight the utilities from the two possible outcomes:

$$EU = \theta U(W + A) + (1 - \theta)U(W + B),$$

where $U(W + A)$ is the utility he gets from his after-gambling wealth if A occurs and $U(W + B)$ is the utility if he receives B. He chooses to gamble if his expected utility from gambling exceeds his certain utility from his initial wealth: $EU > U(W)$.

In contrast, Rui's decisions are consistent with prospect theory. Rui compares the gamble to her current reference point, which is her initial situation where she has W with certainty. The value she places on her reference point is $V(0)$, where 0 indicates that she has neither a gain nor a loss with this certain outcome. The (negative) value that she places on losing is $V(A)$, and the value from winning is $V(B)$.

To determine the value from taking the gamble, Rui does not calculate the expectation using the probabilities θ and $1 - \theta$, as she would with expected utility theory. Rather, she uses *decision weights* $w(\theta)$ and $w(1 - \theta)$, where the w function assigns different weights than the original probabilities. If people assign disproportionately high weights to rare events (see the Application "Biased Estimates"), the weight $w(\theta)$ exceeds θ for low values of θ and is less for high values of θ.

Rui gambles if the value from not gambling, $V(0)$, is less than her evaluation of the gamble, which is the weighted average of her values in the two cases:

$$V(0) < [w(\theta) \times V(A)] + [w(1 - \theta) \times V(B)].$$

Thus, prospect theory differs from expected utility theory in both the valuation of outcomes and how they are weighted.

Properties of Prospect Theory

To resolve various choice mysteries, the prospect theory value function, V, has an S-shape, as in Figure 17.5. This curve has three properties. First, the curve passes through the reference point at the origin, because gains and losses are determined relative to the initial situation.

Second, both sections of the curve are concave to the horizontal, outcome axis. Because of this curvature, Rui is less sensitive to a given change in the outcome for large gains or losses than for small ones. For example, she cares more about whether she has a loss of $1 rather than $2 than she does about a loss of $1,001 rather than $1,002.

Third, the curve is asymmetric with respect to gains and losses. People treat gains and losses differently, in contrast to the predictions of expected utility theory. The S-curve in the figure shows a bigger impact to a loss than to a comparable size gain. That is, the value function reflects *loss aversion*: people hate making losses more than they like making gains.

Figure 17.5 Prospect Theory Value Function

The prospect theory value function has an S-shape. It passes through the reference point at the origin, because gains and losses are measured relative to the initial condition. Because both sections of the curve are concave to the outcome axis, decision makers are less sensitive to a given change in the outcome for large gains or losses than for small ones. Because the curve is asymmetric with respect to gains and losses, people treat gains and losses differently. This S-curve shows a bigger impact to a loss than to a comparable size gain, reflecting loss aversion.

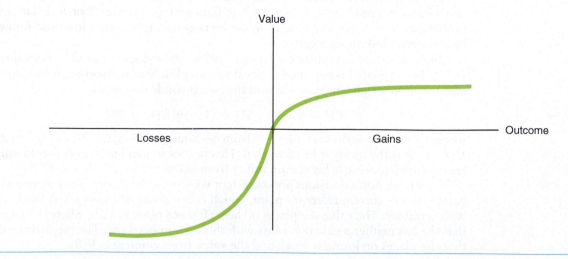

Given the subjective weights, valuations based on gains and losses, and the shape of the value curve, prospect theory can resolve some of the behavioral mysteries. Because prospect theory uses different weights than expected utility theory, prospect theory provides an explanation as to why some people engage in unfair lotteries: They put heavier weight on rare events than the true probability used in expected utility theory.

Similarly, we could use a weighting function to resolve the Ellsberg paradox. For example, with the urn containing an unknown ratio of black and red balls, an individual might put 40% on getting a black ball, 40% on getting a red ball, and leave 20% to capture an unwillingness to take a gamble when faced with substantial ambiguity. Doing so reduces the expected value of the gamble relative to that of the initial, certain situation where one does not gamble.

The S-shaped curve shows that people treat gains and losses differently. As such, it can explain the reflection effect in the disease experiment described earlier in this section.

Challenge Solution

BP and Limited Liability

We now address the three questions raised in the Challenge: How does a cap on liability affect a firm's willingness to make a risky investment or to invest less than the optimal amount in safety? How does a cap affect the amount of risk borne by the firm and by the rest of society? How does a cap affect the amount of insurance that a firm buys?

To illustrate the basic ideas, suppose that an oil rig firm expects to earn $1 billion in the absence of a spill on its new rig and to lose $39 billion if a spill occurs. The probability of a spill is θ. We start by considering whether the firm invests in a new rig (the analysis would be similar if it were deciding to invest in a given safety feature for a rig).

If the firm is risk neutral, then it invests in the new rig only if the expected return is positive, $[(1 - \theta) \times 1] + [\theta \times (-39)] > 0$, or if $\theta < 1/40 = 2.5\%$.[24] If the firm is risk averse, this *threshold probability*—the highest probability at which the firm is willing to invest—is less than 2.5%.

Now suppose that the firm's liability is capped at $19 billion. If the firm is risk neutral, it invests in the new rig if $[(1 - \theta) \times 1] + [\theta \times (-19)] > 0$, or if $\theta < 1/20 = 5\%$. Similarly, if the firm is risk averse, the threshold probability is higher than it would be without the limit on liability.

A limit on liability increases society's total risk if it encourages the drilling company to drill when it would not otherwise. If the drilling company is risk neutral, the probability of a spill is $\theta = 3\%$, and the firm bears the full liability for the damages from a spill, then the company's expected earnings are $[0.97 \times 1] + [0.03 \times (-39)] = -0.2 < 0$, so it would not drill. However, if its liability is capped at $19 billion, then its expected gain from drilling is $[0.97 \times 1] + [0.03 \times (-19)] = 0.4 > 0$, so it would drill. Because the firm is more likely to drill because of the liability cap, the cap causes the rest of society's total risk to increase. Moreover, the rest of society bears the risk from the $20 billion ($39 billion − $19 billion) for which it is now responsible if a spill occurs.

If the firm is risk averse, it wants to buy fair insurance to cover its risk. To illustrate the effect of the cap on its decision as to how much insurance the firm buys, we now assume that the probability of a disaster is $\theta = 1\%$. Without either a liability cap or

---

[24]The firm compares the expected return to that of the second-best investment opportunity, which we assume is zero for simplicity.

insurance, the firm's expected gain is $[0.99 \times 1] + [0.01 \times (-39)] = \$0.6$ billion. If an insurance company would provide fair insurance, the drilling firm could buy $100 of insurance for each $1 spent. Given that the drilling company is risk averse, it fully insures, so that if a spill occurs, the insurance company pays $39 billion. To buy this much insurance, the drilling company pays $0.39 billion, so that the expected value of the insurance contract is $-0.39 + [0.01 \times 39] = \$0$. With the insurance, the company earns $[0.99 \times 1] - 0.39 = \$0.6$ billion whether or not a spill occurs.

If the drilling company's liability is capped at $19 billion, it buys $19 billion worth of insurance for $0.19 billion, so that its expected gain in either state of nature is $1 - 0.19 = \$0.81$ billion. That is, the drilling company's expected profit increases by $0.2 billion due to the limit on its liability. This amount is a transfer from the rest of society to the firm, because society will be responsible for the extra $20 billion in damages if the spill occurs.

Summary

1. **Assessing Risk.** A probability measures the likelihood that a particular state of nature occurs. People may use historical frequencies, if available, to calculate probabilities. Lacking detailed information, people may form subjective estimates of a probability on the basis of available information. The expected value is the probability-weighted average of the values in each state of nature. One widely used measure of risk is the variance (or the standard deviation, which is the square root of the variance). The variance is the probability-weighted average of the squared difference between the value in each state of nature and the expected value.

2. **Attitudes Toward Risk.** Whether people choose a risky option over a nonrisky one depends on their attitudes toward risk and the expected payoffs of the various options. Most people are *risk averse* and will choose a riskier option only if its expected value is sufficiently higher than that of a less risky option. *Risk-neutral* people choose whichever option has the higher rate of return because they do not care about risk. *Risk-preferring* people may choose the riskier option even if it has a lower rate of return because they like risk and are willing to give up some expected return to take on more risk. An individual's utility function reflects that person's attitude toward risk. Expected utility is the probability-weighted average of the utility from the outcomes in the various states of nature. According to expected utility theory, decision makers choose the option that provides the highest expected utility.

3. **Reducing Risk.** People try to reduce the risk they face in several ways. They avoid some risks altogether and, when risks cannot be completely avoided, take actions that lower the probabilities of bad events or reduce the harm from bad events when they do occur. By collecting information before acting, investors can make better choices. People can reduce risk by diversifying over a range of investments unless the various investments are perfectly positively correlated. Insurance companies offer policies for risks that they can diversify by pooling risks across many individuals. Insurance is called fair if the expected return to the policyholder is zero: the expected payout equals the premium paid. Risk-averse people fully insure if they are offered fair insurance. Because insurance companies must earn enough income to cover their full operating costs, they offer insurance that is less than fair. Although risk-averse people may buy unfair insurance, they buy less than with full insurance.

4. **Investing Under Uncertainty.** Whether a person makes an investment depends on the uncertainty of the payoff, the expected return, the individual's attitudes toward risk, the interest rate, and the cost of altering the probabilities of various outcomes. For a risk-neutral person, an investment pays if the expected value is positive. A risk-averse person invests only if that person's expected utility is higher after investing. Thus, risk-averse people make risky investments if the investments pay sufficiently higher rates of return than do safer investments. People pay to alter the probabilities of various outcomes from an investment if doing so raises their expected utility.

5. **Behavioral Economics of Uncertainty.** Economists and psychologists have identified behavior under uncertainty that is inconsistent with expected utility theory. These choices may be due to biased estimates of probabilities or different objectives than expected

utility. For example, some people care more about losses than about gains. One alternative theory that is consistent with many of these puzzling choices is prospect theory, which allows people to treat gains and losses asymmetrically and to weight outcomes differently than with the probabilities used in expected utility theory.

Questions

*All questions are available on MyEconLab; * = answer appears at the back of this book; A = algebra problem; C = calculus problem.*

1. Assessing Risk

1.1 In a neighborhood with 1,000 houses, 5 catch fire, 7 are damaged by high winds, and the rest are unharmed during a one-year period. What do you estimate is the probability that a house is harmed by fire or high winds? **A**

*1.2 Asa buys a painting. The probability that the artist will become famous and the painting will be worth $1,000 is 20%. The probability that the painting will be destroyed by fire or some other disaster is 10%. If the painting is not destroyed and the artist does not become famous, it will be worth $500. What is the expected value of the painting? **A**

*1.3 By next year, the stock you own has a 25% chance of being worth $400 and a 75% probability of being worth $200. What are the expected value and the variance? **A**

1.4 Tiffany plans to sell pies that she will buy this evening at a street fair tomorrow. If the weather is nice, she will earn $200; however, if it rains, she will lose $60, the amount she would pay for the pies that she won't be able to sell. The weather forecast says that the chance of rain is 25%. What does she expect to earn? How much more would she expect to earn if she had perfect information about the probability of rain far enough before the street fair that she would only buy the pies she could sell? (*Hint*: See Solved Problem 17.1.) **A**

1.5 The EZ Construction Company is offered a $20,000 contract to build a new deck for a house. The company's profit if it does not have to sink piers (vertical supports) down to bedrock will be $4,000. However, if it does have to sink the piers, it will lose $1,000. The probability it will have to put in the piers is 25%. What is the expected value of this contract? Now, EZ learns that it can obtain a seismic study of the property that would specify whether piers have to be sunk before EZ must accept or reject this contract. By how much would the seismic study increase EZ's expected value? What is the most that it will pay for such a study? (*Hint*: See Solved Problem 17.1.)

2. Attitudes Toward Risk

2.1 Ryan offers to bet Kristin that if a six-sided die comes up with one or two dots showing, he will pay her $3, but if it comes up with any other number of dots, she'll owe him $2. Is that a fair bet for Kristin? **A**

2.2 Suppose that Maoyong's utility function with respect to wealth is $U(W) = \ln W$ (where "ln W" means the natural logarithm of W). Plot this utility function and illustrate in your figure why Maoyong is risk averse.

2.3 Jen's utility function with respect to wealth is $U(W) = \sqrt{W}$. Plot this utility function and illustrate in your figure why Jen is risk averse.

2.4 Suppose that Laura's utility function is $U(W) = W^{0.5}$, where W is wealth. Is she risk averse? Show mathematically. **C**

*2.5 Given the information in Solved Problem 17.2, Irma prefers to buy the stock. Show graphically how high her certain income would have to be for her to choose not to buy the stock. (*Hint*: See Solved Problem 17.2.)

2.6 Suppose that an individual is risk averse and has to choose between $100 with certainty and a risky option with two equally likely outcomes: $100 - x$ and $100 + x$. Use a graph (or math) to show that this person's risk premium is smaller, the smaller x is (the less variable the gamble is). (*Hint*: See Solved Problem 17.2.)

2.7 Suppose that Laura has a utility function of $U(W) = W^{0.5}$ and an initial wealth of $W = 100. How much of a risk premium would she want to participate in a gamble that has a 50% probability of raising her wealth to $120 and a 50% probability of lowering her wealth to $80? (*Hint*: See Solved Problem 17.2.) **A**

2.8 What is the risk premium if, in Question 2.7, Laura's utility function were ln W? (*Hint*: See Solved Problem 17.2.) **A**

*2.9 Hugo has a concave utility function of $U(W) = W^{0.5}$. His only asset is shares in an Internet start-up company. Tomorrow he will learn the stock's value. He believes that it is worth $144 with probability $\frac{2}{3}$ and $225 with probability $\frac{1}{3}$. What is his expected utility? What risk premium would he pay to avoid bearing this risk? (*Hint*: See Solved Problem 17.2.) **A**

2.10 Joanna is considering three possible jobs. The following table shows the possible incomes she might get in each job.

	Outcome A		Outcome B	
	Probability	Earnings	Probability	Earnings
Job 1	0.5	20	0.5	40
Job 2	0.3	15	0.7	45
Job 3	1	30		

For each job, calculate the expected value, the variance, and the standard deviation. If Joanna is averse to risk (as measured by variance), what can you predict about her job choice? What if she is risk neutral?

2.11 Lisa just inherited a vineyard from a distant relative. In good years (without rain or frost during the harvest season), she earns $100,000 from the sale of grapes from the vineyard. If the weather is poor, she loses $20,000. Lisa's estimate of the probability of good weather is 60%.

a. Calculate the expected value and the variance of Lisa's income from the vineyard.

b. Lisa is risk averse. Ethan, a grape buyer, offers Lisa a guaranteed payment of $70,000 each year in exchange for her entire harvest. Will Lisa accept this offer? Explain.

c. Why might Ethan make such an offer? Give three reasons, and explain each. One of these reasons should refer to his attitude toward risk. Illustrate this reason using a diagram that shows the general shape of Ethan's utility function over income. **A**

2.12 Farrell et al. (2000) estimated that the elasticity of demand for lottery tickets is about −1. If the U.K. National Lottery is running its game to make money (it gets a percentage of the total revenues), is it running the lottery optimally? Explain your answer. **A**

3. Reducing Risk

3.1 Lori, who is risk averse, has two pieces of jewelry, each worth $1,000. She wants to send them to her sister in Thailand, but she is concerned about the safety of shipping them. She believes that the probability that the jewelry won't arrive is θ. Is her expected utility higher if she sends the articles together or in two separate shipments? Explain.

3.2 Lucy, the manager of the medical test firm, Dubrow Labs, worries about being sued for botched results from blood tests. The firm expects to earn a profit of 100 if it is not sued, but only 10 if it is successfully sued. Lucy believes the probability of a successful suit is 5%. If fair insurance is available and Lucy is risk averse, how much insurance will she buy? **A**

*3.3 Consider a household that possesses $160,000 worth of valuables such as jewelry. This household faces a 0.2 probability of burglary, in which case it loses $70,000 worth of the valuables. Suppose it can buy an insurance policy for $15,000 that would fully reimburse the amount of loss from burglary. The household's utility is given by $U(X) = 4X^{0.5}$.

a. Should the household buy this insurance policy?

b. What is the fair price for the insurance policy?

c. What is the most the household is willing to pay for this insurance policy that fully covers it against the loss? **A**

3.4 Would risk-neutral people ever buy insurance that was not fair (that was biased against them)? Explain. (*Hint*: See Solved Problem 17.3.)

3.5 After Superstorm Sandy in 2012, the government offered subsidies to people whose houses were destroyed. How do these subsidies affect the probability that these people will buy insurance and the amount they buy? (*Hint*: Use a utility curve for a risk-averse person to illustrate your answer. See Solved Problem 17.3.)

3.6 Using information from the Application "Flight Insurance," calculate the price of fair insurance if the probability were as high as 0.00000077, the frequency in 2001 when many people died in the 9/11 disasters. **A**

4. Investing Under Uncertainty

4.1 What is the difference—if any—between an individual's gambling at a casino and buying a stock? What is the difference for society?

*4.2 Andy and Kim live together. Andy may invest $10,000 (possibly by taking on an extra job to earn the additional money) in Kim's education this year. This investment will raise Kim's future earnings by $24,000 (in present value terms—see Chapter 16). If they stay together, they will share the benefit from the additional earnings. However, the probability is $\frac{1}{2}$ that they will split up in the future. If they were married and then split, Andy would get half of Kim's additional earnings. If they were living together without any legal ties and they split, then Andy would get nothing. Suppose that Andy is risk neutral. Will Andy invest in Kim's education? Does your answer depend on the couple's legal status? **A**

4.3 Use a decision tree to illustrate how a risk-neutral plaintiff in a lawsuit decides whether to settle a claim or go to trial. The defendants offer $50,000 to settle now. If the plaintiff does not settle, the plaintiff believes that the probability of winning at trial is 60%. If the plaintiff wins, the amount awarded is X. How large can X be before the plaintiff refuses to settle? How does the plaintiff's attitude toward risk affect this decision? **A**

4.4 Use a decision tree to illustrate how a kidney patient would make a decision about whether to have a transplant operation. The patient currently uses a dialysis machine, which lowers her utility. If the operation is successful, her utility will return to its level before the onset of her kidney problems. However, if she has the operation, the probability that she will die is 5%. (If it will help, make up utility numbers to illustrate your answer.)

*4.5 To discourage people from breaking the traffic laws, society can increase the probability that someone exceeding the speed limit will be caught and punished, or it can increase the size of the fine for speeding. Explain why either method can be used to discourage speeding. Which approach is a government likely to prefer, and why? (*Hint*: See Solved Problem 17.3.)

4.6 In Solved Problem 17.4, advertising increases the probability of high demand to 80%. If all the other information in the Solved Problem stays the same, what is the minimum probability of high demand resulting from advertising such that Gautam decides to invest and advertise?

4.7 During the Great Recession, many homeowners around the world owed more on their houses than they were worth. Often, U.S. borrowers who cannot meet their mortgage payments can give their houses to the banks that hold their mortgage without declaring bankruptcy or being held accountable for any unpaid balance. However, Europeans, who face tougher bankruptcy laws, are responsible for unpaid mortgage balances even after losing their homes (Gabriele Steinhauser and Matthew Dalton, "Lingering Bad Debts Stifle Europe Recovery," *Wall Street Journal*, January 31, 2013). Using a decision tree, show that Americans are more likely to buy houses than Europeans, all else the same.

5. Behavioral Economics of Uncertainty

5.1 First answer the following two questions about your preferences:

a. You are given $5,000 and offered a choice between receiving an extra $2,500 with certainty or flipping a coin and getting $5,000 more if heads or $0 if tails. Which option do you prefer?

b. You are given $10,000 if you will make the following choice: return $2,500 or flip a coin and return $5,000 if heads and $0 if tails. Which option do you prefer?

Most people choose the sure $2,500 in the first case but flip the coin in the second. Explain why this behavior is not consistent. What do you conclude about how people make decisions concerning uncertain events? **A**

5.2 Evan is risk seeking with respect to gains and risk averse with respect to losses. Louisa is risk seeking with respect to losses and risk averse with respect to gains. Illustrate both utility functions. Which person's attitudes toward risk are consistent with prospect theory? Which of these people would you expect to be susceptible to framing effects?

5.3 Draw a person's utility curve and illustrate that the person is risk averse with respect to a loss but risk preferring with respect to a gain.

*5.4 Joe has lost a substantial amount gambling at a racetrack today. On the last race of the day, he decides to make a large enough bet on a longshot so that, if he wins, he will make up for his earlier losses and break even on the day. His friend Sue, who won more than she lost on the day, makes just a small final bet so that she will end up ahead for the day even if she loses the last race. This is typical race track behavior for winners and losers. Would you explain this behavior using overconfidence bias, prospect theory, or some other principle of behavioral economics?

6. Challenge

6.1 Global Gas International offers to subcontract the Halidurton Heavy Construction Corporation to build an oil pipeline from Canada to New Orleans for $500 million. The probability that the oil pipeline will leak causing environmental damage is θ. If so, the legal liabilities will be $600 million.

a. If Halidurton is risk neutral and liable for the damages from a leak, what is the θ such that it is indifferent between accepting and rejecting the contract?

b. If Halidurton is risk averse and fair insurance is offered, how much insurance would it buy?

c. If Global Gas International will partially indemnify Halidurton so that the largest damages that Halidurton would have to pay is $200 million, what is the θ that leaves Halidurton indifferent about accepting the contract?

d. If partially indemnified, how much fair insurance will Halidurton buy?

Externalities, Open-Access, and Public Goods

18

I shot an arrow in the air and it stuck.

Does free trade among nations exacerbate pollution problems? The World Trade Organization (WTO)—an organization that promotes free trade among its 159 member countries—requires that its members not impose domestic policies that unreasonably block trade, including environmental policies. For years, protesters have made it very difficult for the WTO to hold meetings. Many of these protesters

argue that rich countries with relatively strict pollution controls export manufacturing to poor countries without controls so that world pollution rises. The flip side of this argument is that if a country does not regulate pollution, then allowing international trade raises pollution in that country. Does free trade benefit a country that does not optimally limit domestic pollution?

In this chapter, we show that if a **property right**—an exclusive privilege to use an asset—is not clearly assigned, a market failure is likely. By owning this book, you have a property right to read it and to stop others from reading or taking it. But many goods have incomplete or unclear property rights.

property right
the exclusive privilege to use an asset

Unclearly defined property rights may cause *externalities*, which occur when someone's consumption or production activities help or harm someone else outside of a market. A harmful externality occurs when a manufacturing plant spews pollution, injuring neighboring firms and individuals. When people lack a property right to clean air, factories, drivers, and others pollute the air rather than incur the cost of reducing their pollution.

Indeed, if no one holds a property right for a good or a bad (like pollution), it is unlikely to have a price. If you had a property right to be free from noise pollution, you could use the courts to stop your neighbor from playing loud music. Or you could sell your right, permitting your neighbor to play the music. If you did not have this property right, no one would be willing to pay you a positive price for it.

We start our analysis by examining pollution. Some of the most important bad externalities arise as a by-product of production (such as water pollution from manufacturing) and consumption (such as congestion or air pollution from driving). A competitive market produces more pollution than a market that is optimally regulated by the government, but a monopoly may not create as much of a pollution problem as a competitive market. Clearly defined property rights help reduce externality problems.

Next we show that market failures due to externalities also occur if a good lacks exclusion. A good has *exclusion* if its owner has clearly defined property rights and can prevent others from consuming it. You have a legal right to stop anyone from eating your apple. However, a country's national defense cannot protect some citizens without protecting all citizens.

Market failures may also occur if a good lacks *rivalry*, where only one person can consume it, such as an apple. National defense lacks rivalry because my consumption does not prevent you from consuming it.

We look at three types of markets that lack exclusion or rivalry or both. An *open-access common property* is a resource, such as an ocean fishery, where *exclusion* of potential users is impossible. A *club good*, such as a swimming pool, is a good or service that allows for exclusion but is *nonrival:* One person's consumption does not use up the good, and others can also consume it (at least until capacity is reached). A *public good*, such as national defense and clean air, is both nonexclusive and nonrival. Public goods may not have a market or the market undersupplies these goods.

When such market failures arise, government intervention may raise welfare. A government may regulate an externality such as pollution directly, or indirectly control an externality through taxation or laws that make polluters liable for the damage they cause. Similarly, a government may provide a public good.

<table>
<tr><td>In this chapter, we examine six main topics</td><td>

1. **Externalities.** By-products of consumption and production may benefit or harm other people.

2. **The Inefficiency of Competition with Externalities.** A competitive market produces too much of a harmful externality.

3. **Regulating Externalities.** Overproduction of pollution and other externalities can be prevented through taxation or regulation.

4. **Market Structure and Externalities.** With a harmful externality, a noncompetitive market equilibrium may be closer to the socially optimal level than that of a competitive equilibrium.

5. **Allocating Property Rights to Reduce Externalities.** Clearly assigning property rights allows exchanges that reduce or eliminate externality problems.

6. **Rivalry and Exclusion.** If goods lack rivalry or exclusion, competitive markets suffer from a market failure.

</td></tr>
</table>

18.1 Externalities

externality
the direct effect of the actions of a person or firm on another person's well-being or a firm's production capability rather than an indirect effect through changes in prices

An **externality** occurs when a person's well-being or a firm's production capability is directly affected by the actions of other consumers or firms rather than indirectly through changes in prices. A firm whose production process lets off fumes that harm its neighbors is creating an externality, which is not traded in a market. In contrast, the firm is not causing an externality when it harms a rival by selling extra output that lowers the market price.

Externalities may either help or harm others. An externality that harms someone is called a *negative externality.* You are harmed if your neighbors keep you awake by screaming at each other late at night. A chemical plant spoils a lake's beauty when it dumps its waste product into the water and in so doing also harms a firm that rents boats for use on that waterway. Government officials in Sydney, Australia, used loud Barry Manilow music to drive away late-night revelers from a suburban park—and in the process drove local residents out of their minds.[1]

A *positive externality* benefits others. By installing attractive shrubs and outdoor sculpture around its plant, a firm provides a positive externality to its neighbors.

A single action may confer positive externalities on some people and negative externalities on others. The smell of pipe smoke pleases some people and annoys others. Some people think that their wind chimes please their neighbors, whereas anyone with an ounce of sense would realize that those chimes are annoying! It was reported that efforts to clean the air in Los Angeles, while helping people breathe more easily, caused radiation levels to increase far more rapidly than if the air had remained dirty.

Application

Negative Externalities from Spam

Spam—unsolicited bulk e-mail messages—inflicts a major negative externality on businesses and individuals around the world. A spammer targets people who might be interested in the information provided in the spam message. This target group is relatively small compared to the vast majority of recipients who do not want the message and who incur the costs of reading and removing it. Moreover, many spam messages are scams.

In 2012, 30 billion spam messages were sent daily, constituting 69% of global email traffic according to Symantec. The share rose to 71.1% by June 2013.

Firms incur large costs to delete spam by installing spam filters and using employees' labor. A study at a German university found that the working time losses caused by spam were approximately 1,200 minutes or 2½ days per employee per year (Caliendo et al., 2012). The worldwide cost of spam is enormous. Various estimates of the cost range from $20 billion to $50 billion per year.

18.2 The Inefficiency of Competition with Externalities

Competitive firms and consumers do not have to pay for the harms of their negative externalities, so they create excessive amounts. Similarly, because producers are not compensated for the benefits of a positive externality, too little of such externalities is produced.

To illustrate why externalities lead to nonoptimal production, we examine a (hypothetical) competitive market in which firms produce paper and by-products of the production process—such as air and water pollution—that harm people who live near paper mills. We'll call the pollution *gunk*. Each ton of paper that is produced increases the amount of gunk by one unit. The only way to decrease the volume of gunk is to reduce the amount of paper manufactured. No less-polluting technologies are available, and it is not possible to locate plants where the gunk bothers no one.

private cost
the cost of production only, not including *externalities*

Paper firms do not have to pay for the harm from the pollution they cause. As a result, each firm's **private cost**—the cost of production only, not including externalities—includes its direct costs of labor, energy, and wood pulp but not the indirect

---

[1]"Manilow Tunes Annoy Residents," **cnn.com**, July 17, 2006.

social cost
the private cost plus the
cost of the harms from
externalities

costs of the harm from gunk. The true **social cost** is the private cost plus the cost of the harms from externalities.

The paper industry is the major industrial source of water pollution. We use a supply-and-demand diagram for the paper market in Figure 18.1 to illustrate that *a competitive market produces excessive pollution because the firms' private cost is less than their social cost.*[2] In the competitive equilibrium, the firms consider only their private costs in making decisions and ignore the harms of the pollution externality

---

Figure 18.1 Welfare Effects of Pollution in a Competitive Market

The competitive equilibrium, e_c, is determined by the intersection of the demand curve and the competitive supply or private marginal cost curve, MC^p, which ignores the cost of pollution. The social optimum, e_s, is at the intersection of the demand curve and the social marginal cost curve, $MC^s = MC^p + MC^g$, where MC^g is the marginal cost of the pollution (gunk). Private producer surplus is based on the MC^p curve, and social producer surplus is based on the MC^s curve.

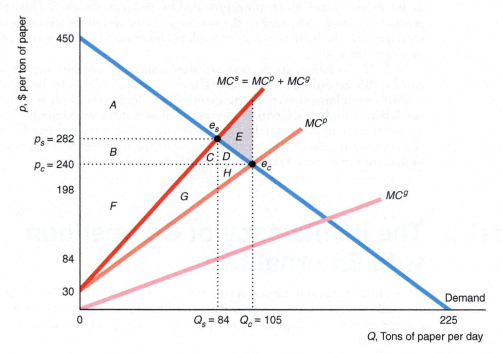

	Social Optimum	Private	Change
Consumer Surplus, CS	A	$A + B + C + D$	$B + C + D$
Private Producer Surplus, PS_p	$B + C + F + G$	$F + G + H$	$H - B - C$
Externality Cost, C_g	$C + G$	$C + D + E + G + H$	$D + E + H$
Social Producer Surplus, $PS_s = PS_p - C_g$	$B + F$	$F - C - D - E$	$-B - C - D - E$
Welfare, $W = CS + PS_s$	$A + B + F$	$A + B + F - E$	$-E = DWL$

---

[2]Appendix 18A uses algebra to analyze this model and derives the numbers in the figure. These numbers are not based on actual estimates.

they inflict on others. The market supply curve is the aggregate *private marginal cost* curve, MC^p, which is the horizontal sum of the private marginal cost curves of each of the paper manufacturing plants.

The competitive equilibrium, e_c, is determined by the intersection of the market supply curve and the market demand curve for paper. The competitive equilibrium quantity is $Q_c = 105$ tons per day, and the competitive equilibrium price is $p_c = \$240$ per ton.

The firms' *private producer surplus* is the producer surplus of the paper mills based on their *private marginal cost* curve: the area, $F + G + H$, below the market price and above MC^p up to the competitive equilibrium quantity, 105. The competitive equilibrium maximizes the sum of consumer surplus and private producer surplus (Chapter 9). If the market had no externality, the sum of consumer surplus and private producer surplus would equal welfare, so competition would maximize welfare.

Because of the pollution, however, the competitive equilibrium does *not* maximize welfare. Competitive firms produce too much gunk because they do not have to pay for the harm from the gunk. This *market failure* (Chapter 9) results from competitive forces that equalize the price and *private marginal cost* rather than *social marginal cost*, which includes both the private costs of production and the externality damage.

For a given amount of paper production, the full cost of one more ton of paper to society, the *social marginal cost* (MC^s), is the cost of manufacturing one more ton of paper to the paper firms plus the additional externality damage to people in the community from producing this last ton of paper. Thus, the height of the social marginal cost curve, MC^s, at any given quantity equals the vertical sum of the height of the MC^p curve (the private marginal cost of producing another ton of paper) plus the height of the MC^g curve (the marginal externality damage) at that quantity.

The social marginal cost curve intersects the demand curve at the socially optimal quantity, $Q_s = 84$. At smaller quantities, the price—the value consumers place on the last unit of the good sold—is higher than the full social marginal cost. The gain to consumers of paper exceeds the cost of producing an extra unit of output (and hence an extra unit of gunk). At larger quantities, the price is below the social marginal cost, so the gain to consumers is less than the cost of producing an extra unit.

Welfare is the sum of consumer surplus and *social producer surplus*, which is based on the *social marginal cost* curve rather than the *private marginal cost* curve. *Welfare is maximized where price equals social marginal cost*. At the social optimum, e_s, welfare equals $A + B + F$: the area between the demand curve and the MC^s curve up to the optimal quantity, 84 tons of paper.

Welfare at the competitive equilibrium, e_c, is lower: $A + B + F - E$, the areas between the demand curve and the MC^s curve up to 105 tons of paper. The area between these curves from 84 to 105, $-E$, is a deadweight loss because the social cost exceeds the value that consumers place on these last 21 tons of paper. *A deadweight loss results because the competitive market equates price with private marginal cost instead of with social marginal cost.*

Welfare is higher at the social optimum than at the competitive equilibrium because the gain from reducing pollution from the competitive to the socially optimal level more than offsets the loss to consumers and producers of the paper. The cost of the pollution to people who live near the factories is the area under the MC^g curve between zero and the quantity produced. By construction, this area is the same as the area between the MC^p and the MC^s curves. The total damage from the gunk is $-C - D - E - G - H$ at the competitive equilibrium and only $-C - G$ at the social optimum. Consequently, the extra pollution damage from producing the competitive output rather than the socially optimal quantity is $-D - E - H$.

The main beneficiaries from producing at the competitive output level rather than at the socially optimal level are the paper buyers, who pay \$240 rather than \$282

Good news. Production's up 13%!

for a ton of paper. Their consumer surplus rises from A to $A + B + C + D$. The corresponding change in private producer surplus is $H − B − C$, which is negative in this figure.

The figure illustrates two main results with respect to negative externalities. First, *a competitive market produces excessive negative externalities.* Because the price of the pollution to the firms is zero, which is less than the marginal cost that the last unit of pollution imposes on society, an unregulated competitive market produces more pollution than is socially optimal.

Second, *the optimal amount of pollution is greater than zero.* Even though pollution is harmful and we'd like to have none of it, we cannot wipe it out without eliminating virtually all production and consumption. Making paper, dishwashers, and televisions creates air and water pollution. Fertilizers used in farming pollute the water supply. Delivery people pollute the air by driving to your home.

18.3 Regulating Externalities

Because competitive markets produce too many negative externalities, government intervention may provide a social gain. In 1952, London suffered from unusually thick "peasouper" fog—pollution so dense that people had trouble finding their way home—that killed an estimated 4,000 to 12,000 people. Those dark days prompted the British government to pass its first Clean Air Act, in 1956.[3] The United States and Canada passed Clean Air Acts in 1970.

Now virtually the entire world is concerned about pollution. Carbon dioxide (CO_2), which is primarily produced by burning fossil fuels, is a major contributor to global warming, damages marine life, and causes additional harm. China and the United States are by far the largest producers of CO_2 from industrial production, as Table 18.1 shows. China produces 26% of the world's CO_2 and the United States spews out 18%, so together they're responsible for nearly half. The amount of CO_2 per person is extremely high in Australia, the United States, Canada, and Russia, while China and Russia have a very high ratio of pollution to gross domestic product (GDP). The last column of the table shows that China and India substantially increased their production of CO_2 since 1990, while a few countries—such as Russia, Germany, the United Kingdom, and France—reduced their CO_2 production.

Developing countries spend little on controlling pollution, while many developing countries' public expenditures have fallen in recent years. In response, various protests have erupted. China and India now face regular pollution protests.

Nonetheless, politicians around the world disagree about how and whether to control pollution. In 2012 at the United Nations (UN) Rio+20 meeting, 120 heads of state and 50,000 environmentalists, social activists, and business leaders met to encourage sustainable, green growth in poor countries. After many discussions and

---

[3]King Edward I established an air pollution commission in 1286 to reduce London's smog. The commission recommended banning burning coal in the city. However, little was done until 1956. www.eenews.net/climatewire/2013/04/05/1.

Table 18.1 Industrial CO_2 Emissions, 2010

	CO_2, Million Metric Tons	CO_2 Tons per Capita	CO_2 kg per $100 GDP	Percentage Change in CO_2 Since 1990
China	8,287	6.2	91	237
United States	5,433	17.5	42	14
India	2,009	1.6	53	191
Russian Federation	1,741	12.2	86	−54
Japan	1,171	9.3	30	7
Germany	745	9.1	27	−20
Canada	499	14.7	42	11
United Kingdom	494	8.0	24	−13
Mexico	444	3.9	31	41
Australia	373	16.8	49	30
France	361	5.8	19	−10

Source: **mdgs.un.org/unsd/mdg/Data.aspx**, CDIAC (viewed August 7, 2013).

arguments, they accomplished little. Most U.S. Congressional Democrats favor stiffer pollution controls but many Republicans call for removing such regulations. Similar fights occur in Britain and many European nations. Since British Columbia, Canada, passed the first carbon tax in North America in 2008, their political parties have fought over whether to increase the tax or eliminate it.[4] Clearly, pollution control will be a major bone of contention throughout the world for the foreseeable future.

Suppose that a government wants to regulate pollution, and it has full knowledge about the marginal damage from pollution, the demand curve, costs, and the production technology. The government could optimally control pollution directly by restricting the amount of pollution that firms may produce or by taxing them for the pollution they create. A limit on the amount of air or water pollution that may be released is an *emissions standard*. A tax on air pollution is an *emissions fee*, and a tax on discharges into the air or waterways is an *effluent charge*.

Frequently, however, a government controls pollution indirectly, through quantity restrictions or taxes on outputs or inputs. Whether the government restricts or taxes outputs or inputs may depend on the nature of the production process. It is generally better to regulate pollution directly rather than to regulate output. Direct regulation of pollution encourages firms to adopt efficient new technologies to control pollution (a possibility we ignore in our paper mill example).

Emissions Standard We use the paper mill example in Figure 18.1 to illustrate how a government may use an *emissions standard* to reduce pollution. Here the government can achieve the social optimum by forcing the paper mills to produce no more than 84 units of paper per day. (Because output and pollution move together in this example, regulating either reduces pollution in the same way.)

---

[4]The tax had substantial effects. A study by the environmental think tank Sustainable Prosperity concluded that British Columbia's fuel consumption declined 17.4% per capita (and 18.8% compared with the rest of Canada) from 2008 to 2012. **www.eenews.net/climatewire/2013/07/30/stories/1059985278.**

Unfortunately, the government usually does not know enough to regulate optimally. For example, to set quantity restrictions on output optimally, the government must know how the marginal social cost curve, the demand for paper curve, and pollution vary with output. The ease with which the government can monitor output and pollution may determine whether it sets an output restriction or a pollution standard.

Even if the government knows enough to set the optimal regulation, it must enforce this regulation to achieve the desired outcome. The U.S. Environmental Protection Agency (EPA) tightened its ozone standard to 0.075 parts per million in 2008. As of 2012, 36 areas were marginally out of compliance with this rule, three moderately, three severely, and two extremely (the Los Angeles-South Coast Air Basin and the San Joaquin Valley, California).[5]

Application

Pulp and Paper Mill Pollution and Regulation

Pulp and paper mills are major sources of air and water pollution. For simplicity in our example, we assumed that pollution is emitted in fixed ratio to output and controlled by reducing output. However, firms can also choose less-polluting technologies, use additional pollution-controlling capital, and take other actions to lower the amount of pollution per ton of paper (Gray and Shimshack, 2011).

These regulations reduce pollution. For example, a 10% increase in pollution-reducing capital in U.S. paper plants reduced air pollution per unit of paper by 6.9% (Shadbegian and Gray, 2003). Each dollar spent on extra capital stock provided an annual return of about 75¢ in pollution reduction benefits. In the year following an additional fine for not meeting pollution standards at a paper plant, water pollution discharges fell by 7% (Shimshack and Ward, 2005).

Emissions Fee   The government may impose costs on polluters by taxing their output or the amount of pollution produced. (Similarly, a law could make a polluter liable for damages in court.) In our paper mill example, taxing output works as well as taxing the pollution directly because the relationship between output and pollution is fixed. However, if firms can vary the output-pollution relationship by varying inputs or adding pollution-control devices, then the government should tax pollution.

In our example, if the government knows the marginal cost of the gunk, MC^g, it can set the output tax equal to this marginal cost curve: $T(Q) = MC^g$. We write this tax as $T(Q)$ to show that it varies with output, Q. Figure 18.2 illustrates the manufacturers' after-tax marginal cost, $MC^s = MC^p + T(Q)$.

internalize the externality
to bear the cost of the harm that one inflicts on others (or to capture the benefit that one provides to others)

The output tax causes a manufacturer to **internalize the externality**: to bear the cost of the harm that one inflicts on others (or to capture the benefit that one provides to others). The after-tax private marginal cost or supply curve is the same as the social marginal cost curve. As a result, the after-tax competitive equilibrium is the social optimum.

---

[5]See **www.epa.gov/epahome/commsearch.htm** or **www.scorecard.org** for details on the environmental risks in your area.

Figure 18.2 Taxes to Control Pollution

Placing a tax on the firms equal to the harm from the gunk, $T(Q) = MC^g$, causes them to internalize the externality, so their private marginal cost is the same as the social marginal cost, MC^s. As a result, the competitive after-tax equilibrium is the same as the social optimum, e_s. Alternatively, applying a specific tax of $t = 84$ per ton of paper, which is the marginal harm from the gunk at $Q_s = 84$, also results in the social optimum.

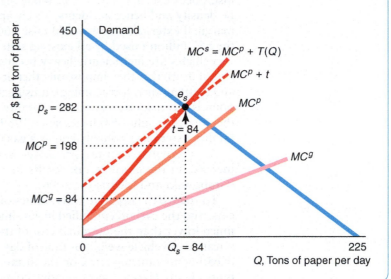

Usually, the government sets a specific tax rather than a tax that varies with the amount of pollution, as MC^g does. As Solved Problem 18.1 shows, applying an appropriate specific tax results in the socially optimal level of production.

Solved Problem 18.1

For the market with pollution in Figure 18.1, what constant, specific tax, t, on output could the government set to maximize welfare?

Answer

Set the specific tax equal to the marginal harm of pollution at the socially optimal quantity. At the socially optimal quantity, $Q_s = 84$, the marginal harm from the gunk is $84, as Figure 18.2 shows. If the specific tax is $t = 84, the after-tax private marginal cost (after-tax competitive supply curve), $MC^p + t$, equals the social marginal cost at the socially optimal quantity. As a consequence, the after-tax competitive supply curve intersects the demand curve at the socially optimal quantity. By paying this specific tax, the firms internalize the cost of the externality at the social optimum. All that is required for optimal production is that the tax equals the marginal cost of pollution at the optimum quantity; it need not equal the marginal cost of pollution at other quantities.

Application

Why Tax Drivers

Driving causes many externalities including pollution, congestion, and accidents. Taking account of pollution from producing fuel and driving, Hill et al. (2009) estimated that burning one gallon of gasoline (including all downstream effects) causes a carbon dioxide-related climate change cost of 37¢ and a health-related cost of conventional pollutants associated with fine particulate matter of 34¢.

A driver imposes delays on other drivers during congested periods. Parry et al. (2007) estimated that this cost is $1.05 per gallon of gas on average across the United States.

Edlin and Karaca-Mandic (2006) measured the accident externality from additional cars by the increase in the cost of insurance. These externalities are big in states with a high concentration of traffic but not in states with low densities. In California, with many cars per mile of road, an extra driver raises the total statewide insurance costs of other drivers by between $1,725 and $3,239 per year. A 1% increase in driving raises insurance costs 3.3% to 5.4%. While the state could build more roads to lower traffic density and hence accidents, it's cheaper to tax the externality. A tax equal to the marginal externality cost would raise $66 billion annually in California—more than the $57 billion raised by all existing state taxes—and over $220 billion nationally.

Vehicles are inefficiently heavy because owners of heavier cars ignore the greater risk of death that they impose on other drivers and pedestrians in accidents (Anderson and Auffhammer, forthcoming). Raising the weight of a vehicle that hits you by 1,000 pounds increases the chance of a fatality by 47%. The higher externality risk due to the greater weight of vehicles since 1989 is 27¢ per gallon of gasoline and the total fatality externality roughly equals a gas tax of $1.08 per gallon.

An alternative to a tax per driver is a tax per mile or gallon of gas. Each 10% increase in the gasoline tax results in a 0.6% decrease in the traffic fatality rate (Grabowski and Morrissey, 2006).

To reduce the negative externalities of driving, governments have taxed gasoline, cars, and the carbon embodied in gasoline. However, such taxes have generally been much lower than the marginal cost of the externality and have not been adequately sensitive to vehicle weight or time of day. The United States and the Netherlands are debating introducing a tax on the distance driven (a pay-as-you-drive tax), which is more clearly targeted at preventing congestion, accidents, and pollution.

Benefits Versus Costs from Controlling Pollution

The U.S. Clean Air Act of 1970 and the Clean Air Act Amendments of 1990 cleansed U.S. air. Between 1980 and 2010, the national average of sulfur dioxide (SO_2) plummeted 83%, carbon monoxide (CO) fell 82%, nitrogen dioxide (NO_2) tumbled 52%, and ozone dropped 28%. From 1990 to 2010, particulate matter (PM10) in the air decreased 38%.[6]

The EPA believes that the Clean Air Act saves over 160,000 lives a year, avoids more than 100,000 hospital visits, prevents millions of cases of respiratory problems, and saves 13 million lost workdays. The EPA (2011) estimated the costs of complying with the Clean Air Act were $53 billion, but the benefits were $1.3 trillion in 2010. Thus, the benefits outweighed costs by nearly 25 to 1.

Application

Protecting Babies

Some policy changes raise benefits and *lower* costs. E-ZPass reduces congestion and pollution and improves babies' health. The E-ZPass, an electronic toll collection system on toll ways in New Jersey, Pennsylvania, and 13 other states, allows vehicles to pay a toll without stopping at a toll booth. It lowers the cost of collecting tolls.

Idling cars waiting to pay a toll create extra pollution and waste drivers' time. E-ZPass reduces delays at toll plazas by 85% and lowers NO_2 emissions from traffic by about 6.8%. Introducing E-ZPass reduced premature births by 11% and led to 12% fewer low birth-weight babies of mothers who lived within 2 kilometers (km) of a toll plaza relative to those who lived 2 to 10 km from a toll plaza (Currie and Walker, 2011). Knittel et al. (2011) found that lowering the amount of particulate matter by one unit (during their sample period, the average was 29 micrograms per cubic meter of air) saves 18 lives per 100,000 births: a decrease in the infant mortality rate of about 6%. Thus, using E-ZPass cuts government costs, saves commuters' time, and saves lives.

---

[6]According to **www.epa.gov/air/airtrends** (viewed August 1, 2013).

18.4 Market Structure and Externalities

Two of our main results concerning competitive markets and negative externalities—that too much pollution is produced and that a tax equal to the marginal social cost of the externality solves the problem—do not hold for other market structures. Although a competitive market always produces too many negative externalities, a noncompetitive market may produce more or less than the optimal level of output and pollution. If a tax is set so that firms internalize the externalities, a competitive market produces the social optimum, whereas a noncompetitive market does not.

Monopoly and Externalities

We use the paper-gunk example to illustrate these results. In Figure 18.3, the monopoly equilibrium, e_m, is determined by the intersection of the marginal revenue, MR, and private marginal cost, MC^p, curves. Like the competitive firms, the monopoly ignores the harm its pollution causes, so it considers just its direct, private costs in making decisions.

Figure 18.3 Monopoly, Competition, and Social Optimum with Pollution

At the competitive equilibrium, e_c, more is produced than at the social optimum, e_s. As a result, the deadweight loss in the competitive market is D. The monopoly equilibrium, e_m, is determined by the intersection of the marginal revenue and the private marginal cost, MC^p, curves. The social welfare (based on the marginal social cost, MC^s, curve) under monopoly is $A + B$. Here the deadweight loss of monopoly, C, is less than the deadweight loss under competition, D.

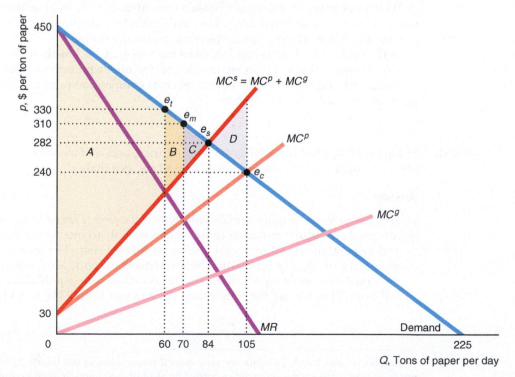

Output is only 70 tons in the monopoly equilibrium, e_m, which is less than the 84 tons at the social optimum, e_s. Thus, this figure illustrates that *the monopoly outcome may be less than the social optimum even with an externality.*

Although the competitive market with an externality always produces more output than the social optimum, a monopoly may produce more than, the same as, or less than the social optimum. The reason that a monopoly may produce too little or too much is that it faces two offsetting effects: The monopoly tends to produce too little output because it sets its price above its marginal cost, but the monopoly tends to produce too much output because its decisions depend on its private marginal cost instead of the social marginal cost.

Which effect dominates depends on the elasticity of demand for the output and on the extent of the marginal damage the pollution causes. If the demand curve is very elastic, the monopoly markup is small. As a result, the monopoly equilibrium is close to the competitive equilibrium, e_c, and greater than the social optimum, e_s. If extra pollution causes little additional harm—MC^g is close to zero at the equilibrium—the social marginal cost essentially equals the private marginal cost, and the monopoly produces less than the social optimum.

Monopoly Versus Competitive Welfare with Externalities

In the absence of externalities, welfare is greater under competition than under an unregulated monopoly (Chapter 11). However, with an externality, welfare may be greater with monopoly than with competition.[7]

If both monopoly and competitive outputs are greater than the social optimum, welfare must be greater under monopoly because the competitive output is larger than the monopoly output. If the monopoly produces less than the social optimum, we need to check which distortion is greater: the monopoly's producing too little or the competitive market's producing too much.

Welfare is lower at monopoly equilibrium, area $A + B$, than at the social optimum, $A + B + C$, in Figure 18.3. The deadweight loss of monopoly, C, results from the monopoly's producing less output than is socially optimal.

In the figure, the deadweight loss from monopoly, C, is less than the deadweight loss from competition, D, so welfare is greater under monopoly. The monopoly produces only slightly too little output, whereas competition produces excessive output—and hence far too much gunk.

Solved Problem 18.2	In Figure 18.3, what is the effect on output, price, and welfare of taxing the monopoly an amount equal to the marginal harm of the externality?

Answer

1. *Show how the monopoly equilibrium shifts if the firm is taxed.* A tax equal to the marginal cost of the pollution causes the monopoly to internalize the externality and to view the social marginal cost as its private cost. The intersection of the marginal revenue, MR, curve and the social marginal cost, MC^s, curve determines the taxed-monopoly equilibrium, e_t. The tax causes the equilibrium quantity to fall from 70 to 60 and the equilibrium price to rise from \$310 to \$330.

---

[7]Pennsylvania and North Carolina use state-owned monopolies to sell liquor. By charging high prices, they may reduce the externalities created by alcohol consumption, such as drunk driving.

2. *Determine how this shift affects the deadweight loss of monopoly.* The sum of consumer and producer surplus is only *A* after the tax, compared to *A* + *B* before the tax. Thus, welfare falls. The difference between *A* and welfare at the social optimum, *A* + *B* + *C*, is −(*B* + *C*), which is the deadweight loss from the taxed monopoly. The tax exacerbates the monopoly's tendency to produce too little output. The deadweight loss increases from *C* to *B* + *C*. The monopoly produced too little before the tax; the taxed monopoly produces even less.

Taxing Externalities in Noncompetitive Markets

Many people recommend that the government tax firms an amount equal to the marginal harm of pollution because such a tax achieves the social optimum in a competitive market. Solved Problem 18.2 shows that such a tax may lower welfare if applied to a monopoly. The tax definitely lowers welfare if the untaxed monopoly was producing less than the social optimum. If the untaxed monopoly was originally producing more than the social optimum, a tax may cause welfare to increase.

If the government has enough information to determine the social optimum, it can force either a monopolized or a competitive market to produce it. If the social optimum is greater than the unregulated monopoly output, however, the government has to subsidize (rather than tax) the monopoly to get it to produce as much output as is desired.

In short, trying to solve a negative externality problem is more complex in a noncompetitive market than in a competitive market. To achieve a social optimum in a competitive market, the government only has to reduce the externality, possibly by decreasing output. In a noncompetitive market, the government must eliminate problems arising from both externalities *and* the exercise of market power. Thus, the government needs more information to regulate a noncompetitive market optimally and may require more tools, such as a subsidy. To the degree that the problems arising from market power and pollution are offsetting, however, the failure to regulate a noncompetitive market is less harmful than the failure to regulate a competitive market.

18.5 Allocating Property Rights to Reduce Externalities

Instead of controlling externalities directly through emissions fees and emissions standards, the government may take an indirect approach by assigning a *property right*: an exclusive privilege to use an asset. If no one holds a property right for a good or a bad, the good or bad is unlikely to have a price. If you had a property right that assured you of the right to be free from air pollution, you could go to court to stop a nearby factory from polluting the air. Or you could sell your right, permitting the factory to pollute. If you did not have this property right, no one would be willing to pay you a positive price for it. Because of this lack of a price, a polluter's private marginal cost of production is less than the full social marginal cost.

Coase Theorem

According to the Coase Theorem (Coase, 1960), a polluter and its victim can achieve the optimal levels of pollution if property rights are clearly defined and they can practically bargain. Coase's Theorem is not a practical solution to most pollution problems. Rather, it demonstrates that a lack of clearly defined property rights is the root of the externality problem.

To illustrate the Coase Theorem, we consider two adjacent firms, Alice's Auto Body Shop and Theodore's Tea House. The noise from the auto body shop hurts the tea house's business, as Table 18.2 illustrates. As the auto body shop works on more cars per hour, its profit increases, but the resulting extra noise reduces the tea house's profit. The last column shows the total profit of the two firms. Having the auto body shop work on one car at a time maximizes their joint profit: the socially optimal solution.

Initially, rights are not clearly defined. Alice won't negotiate with Theodore. After all, why would she reduce her output and the associated noise, if Theodore has no legal right to be free of noise? Why would Theodore pay Alice to reduce the noise if he harbors the hope that the courts will eventually declare that he has a right to be free from noise pollution? Thus, Alice's shop works on two cars per hour, which maximizes her profit at 400. The resulting excessive pollution drives Theodore out of business, so their joint profit is 400.

Now, suppose that the courts grant Theodore the right to silence. He can force Alice to shut down, so that he makes 400 and their joint profit is 400. However, if Alice works on one car, her gain is 300, while Theodore's loss is 200. They should be able to reach an agreement where she pays him between 200 and 300 for the right to work on one car. As a result, they maximize their joint profit at 500.

Why doesn't Alice buy the rights to work on two cars instead of one? Her gain of 100 from working on the second car is less than Theodore's loss of 200, so they cannot reach a deal to let her work on the second car.

Alternatively, suppose that the court says that Alice has the right to make as much noise as she wants. Unless Theodore pays her to reduce the noise, he has to shut down. The gain to Theodore of 200 from Alice working on one rather than two cars is greater than the 100 loss to Alice. They should be able to reach a deal in which Theodore pays Alice between 100 and 200, she works on only one car, and they maximize their joint profit at 500.

This example illustrates the three key results of the Coase Theorem:

1. If property rights are not clearly assigned, one firm pollutes excessively and joint profit is not maximized.
2. Clearly assigning property rights results in the social optimum, maximizing joint profit, regardless of who gets the rights.
3. However, who gets the property rights affects how they split the joint profit. Because the property rights are valuable, the party with the property rights is compensated by the other party.

To achieve the socially optimal outcome, the two sides must bargain successfully with each other. However, the parties may not be able to bargain successfully for at least three important reasons.

First, if transaction costs are very high, it might not pay for the two sides to meet. For example, if a manufacturing plant pollutes the air, thousands or even millions of people may be affected. The cost of getting all of them together to bargain is prohibitive.

Table 18.2 Daily Profits Vary with Production and Noise

Auto Body Shop's Output, Cars per Hour	Profit, $		
	Auto Body Shop	Tea House	Total
0	0	400	400
1	300	200	500
2	400	0	400

Second, if firms engage in strategic bargaining behavior, an agreement may not be reached. For instance, if one party says, "Give me everything I want" and will not budge, reaching an agreement may be impossible.

Third, if either side lacks information about the costs or benefits of reducing pollution, the outcome is likely not to be optimal. It is difficult to know how much to offer the other party and to reach an agreement if you do not know how the polluting activity affects the other party.

For these reasons, Coasian bargaining is likely to occur in relatively few situations. Where bargaining cannot occur, the allocation of property rights affects the amount of pollution.

Application

Buying a Town

When the Environmental Protection Agency (EPA) stated that James Gavin American Electric Power was violating the Clean Air Act by polluting Cheshire, Ohio, the EPA effectively gave the residents the right to be free from pollution. To avoid the higher cost of litigation, installing new equipment, and other actions to reduce pollution at its plant, the company bought the town for $20 million, inducing the residents to pack up and leave. Thus, once clear property rights are established, a firm may find it less expensive to purchase those rights from others rather than incur endless litigation and pollution-reduction costs.

Markets for Pollution

If high transaction costs preclude bargaining, society may be able to overcome this problem by using a market, which facilitates exchanges between individuals. Starting in the early 1980s, the U.S. federal government, some state governments, and many governments around the world introduced cap-and-trade systems. Under a *cap-and-trade* system, the government distributes a fixed number of permits that allow firms to produce a specified amount of pollution. These permits not only create a property right to pollute, but they also limit or cap the total amount of pollution. These permits can then be traded in a market, often by means of an auction. Firms that do not use all their permits sell them to other firms that want to pollute more—much as sinners bought indulgences in the Middle Ages.

Firms whose products are worth a lot relative to the harm from pollution they create buy rights from firms that make less valuable products. Suppose that the cost in terms of forgone output from eliminating each ton of pollution is $200 at one firm and $300 at another. If the government reduces the permits it gives to each firm so that each must reduce its pollution by 1 ton, the total cost is $500. With tradable permits, the first firm can reduce its pollution by 2 tons and sell one permit to the second firm, so the total social cost is only $400. The trading maximizes the value of the output for a given amount of pollution damage, thus increasing efficiency.

If the government knew enough, it could assign the optimal amount of pollution to each firm, and trading would be unnecessary. By using a market, the government does not have to collect this type of detailed information to achieve efficiency. It only has to decide how much total pollution to allow.

Application

Acid Rain Program

The Acid Rain Program under the 1990 U.S. Clean Air Act was designed to reduce 10 million tons of sulfur dioxide (SO_2) and 2 million tons of nitrogen oxides (NO_x), the primary components of acid rain. It reduced the SO_2 in 2010 level to only 30% of that in 1990.

Under the law, the EPA issues SO_2 permits, each of which allows a firm to produce 1 ton of emissions of SO_2 annually, equal to the aggregate emissions cap. A firm that exceeds its pollution limit is fined $2,000 per ton of emissions above its allowance. At the end of a year, if a company's emissions are less than its allowance, it may sell the remaining allowance to another firm, thus providing the firm with an incentive to reduce emissions.

The EPA holds an annual spot auction for permits that may be used in the current year and an advanced auction for permits effective in seven years. Anyone can purchase allowances. Recently, environmental groups, such as the Acid Rain Retirement Fund, the University of Tampa Environmental Protection Coalition, University of Tampa Environmental Protection Coalition, and Bates College Environmental Economics classes purchased permits and withheld them from firms to reduce pollution further. (You can see the outcome of the 2013 auctions at **www.epa.gov/airmarkets/trading/2013/13summary.html**.)

According to some estimates, pollution reduction under this market program costs about a quarter to a third less than it would cost if permits were not tradable—a savings on the order of $225 to $375 million per year. Moreover, the EPA calculated the Acid Rain Program's annual benefits in 2010 at approximately $340 billion (in 2012 dollars), at an annual cost of about $8 billion, or a 40-to-1 benefit-to-cost ratio.

Markets for Positive Externalities

The harms from negative externalities cannot be solved by a market without regulation or government intervention to clearly define property rights. However, many positive externality problems are solved by markets without additional government intervention because property rights are usually clearly defined.

Bees pollinate oranges, almonds, avocados, and many other produce. If an orange orchard is located next to a commercial beekeeping firm, the beekeeper might not maintain enough bees to optimally pollinate the oranges because the beekeeper does not capture the full value from the bees. However, markets have formed to solve this problem. Beekeepers have a clearly defined property right to their bees. Consequently, orange farms hire beekeepers to bring hives to the farms during pollination season. This market transaction results in optimal pollination.

18.6 Rivalry and Exclusion

rival good
good that is used up as it is consumed

exclusion
others can be prevented from consuming a good

Until now, we've focused on *private goods*, which have the properties of rivalry and exclusion. A **rival good** is used up as it is consumed. If Jane eats an orange, that orange is gone so that no one else can consume it. **Exclusion** means that others can be prevented from consuming a good. If Jane owns an orange, she can easily prevent others from consuming that orange by locking it in her home. Thus, an orange is subject to rivalry and exclusion.

If a good lacks rivalry, everyone can consume the same good, such as clean air or national defense. If a market charges a positive price for that good, a market

Table 18.3 Rivalry and Exclusion

	Exclusion	*No Exclusion*
Rivalry	*Private good*: apple, pencil, computer, car	*Open-access common property*: fishery, freeway, park
No Rivalry	*Club good*: cable television, concert, tennis club	*Public good*: national defense, clean air, lighthouse

failure occurs because the marginal cost of providing the good to one more person is zero.

If the good lacks exclusion, such as clean air, no one can be stopped from consuming it because no one has an exclusive property right to the good. Consequently, a market failure may occur when people who don't have to pay for the good overexploit it, as when they pollute the air. If the market failure is severe—as it often is for open-access common resources and for public goods—governments may play an important role in provision or control of the good. For example, governments usually pay for streetlights.

We can classify goods by whether they exhibit rivalry and exclusion. Table 18.3 outlines the four possibilities: private good (which have rivalry and exclusion); open-access common property (rivalry, no exclusion); club good (no rivalry, exclusion); and public good (no rivalry, no exclusion).

Open-Access Common Property

open-access common property
a resource that is nonexclusive and rival

An **open-access common property** is a resource that is nonexclusive and rival. Everyone has free access and an equal right to exploit this resource.

Many fisheries are open-access common properties. Fish are rival. Anyone can fish in an open-access fishery. Each fisher wants to land a fish to gain the property right to that fish so as to exclude others. The lack of clearly defined property rights while the fish are in the water leads to overfishing. Fishers have an incentive to catch more fish than they would if the fishery were private property.

Like polluting manufacturers, fishing boat owners look at only their private costs. In calculating these costs, they include the cost of boats, other equipment, a crew, and supplies. They do not include the cost that they impose on future generations by decreasing the stock of fish today, which reduces the number of fish in the sea next year. The fewer fish, the harder it is to catch any, so reducing the population today raises the cost of catching fish for others, both now and in the future.

The social cost of catching a fish is the private cost plus the *externality cost* from reduced current and future populations of fish. Thus, the market failure arising from open-access common property is a negative externality.

In contrast, if each fisher owns a private pond, no externality occurs because the property rights are clearly defined. Each owner is careful not to overfish in any one year to maintain the stock (or number) of fish in the future.

Other important examples of open-access common property are petroleum, water, and other fluids and gases that are often extracted from a *common pool*. Owners of wells drawing from a common pool compete to remove the substance most rapidly, thereby gaining ownership of the good. This competition creates an externality by lowering fluid pressure, which makes further pumping more difficult. Iraq justified its invasion of Kuwait, which led to the Persian Gulf War in 1991, on the grounds that Kuwait was overexploiting common pools of oil underlying both countries. In 2011, the state of Alaska proposed leasing land next to the federal Alaska National

Wildlife Reserve (ANWR), which would allow the leasing companies to drill and potentially drain oil from ANWR.

If many people try to access a single Web site at one time, congestion may slow traffic to a crawl. In addition, email messages can be sent freely, even though they may impose handling costs on recipients, leading to excessive amounts of unwanted or junk email, a negative externality.

If you own a car, you have a property right to drive that car but public roads and freeways are common property. Because you lack an exclusive property right to the highway on which you drive, you cannot exclude others from driving on the highway and must share it with them. Each driver, however, claims a temporary property right in a portion of the highway by occupying it, thereby preventing others from occupying the same space. Competition for space on the highway leads to congestion, a negative externality that slows every driver.

To prevent overuse of a common resource, a government can clearly define property rights, restrict access, or tax users. Many developing countries over the past century have broken up open-access, common agricultural land into smaller private farms with clearly defined property rights. Governments frequently grant access to a resource on a first-come, first-served basis, such as at some popular national parks.

Alternatively, the government can impose a tax or fee to use the resource. Only those people who value the resource most gain access. Governments often charge an entrance fee to a park or a museum. Tolls are commonly used on highways and bridges. By applying a tax or fee equal to the externality harm that each individual imposes on others (such as the value of increased congestion on a highway), the government forces each person to internalize the externality.

Club Goods

club good
a good that is nonrival but is subject to exclusion

A **club good** is a good that is nonrival but is subject to exclusion. Some club goods are provided through true clubs, such as swimming clubs or golf clubs. These clubs exclude people who do not pay membership fees, but the services they provide, swimming or golfing, are nonrival: An extra person can swim or golf without reducing the enjoyment of others until these facilities become congested as capacity is reached.

However, the most significant club goods are not offered through actual clubs. An important example is cable television. The service lacks rivalry as adding one more viewer for a given channel in no way impairs the viewing experience of other viewers (and the marginal cost is virtually zero). However, people can be easily excluded. Only people who pay for the service receive the signal and can view the channel.

If a positive price is charged to view a channel, a market failure occurs because the price exceeds the marginal cost of providing the good. If some cable subscribers are willing to pay a positive amount for the channel, but less than the current price, then failure to provide the channel to those people is a deadweight loss to society.

Although club goods create a market failure, government intervention is rare because it is difficult for the government to help. As with regulation, an attempt to eliminate deadweight loss by forcing a cable television company to charge a price equal to its near-zero marginal cost would be self-defeating, as the service would not be produced and even more total surplus would be lost. A government could cap the cable TV price at average cost, which would reduce but not eliminate the deadweight loss.

Application

Piracy

One of the most important examples of a good that is not rival but does allow for exclusion is computer software, such as Microsoft Word. Software is nonrival. At almost no extra cost, Microsoft can provide a copy of the software program to another consumer. Because Microsoft charges a (high) positive price, a market failure results in which too few units are sold.

However, if Microsoft cannot enforce its property right by preventing *pirating* of its software (use of software without paying for it), an even greater market failure may result: It may stop producing the product altogether. In countries where the cost of excluding nonpaying users is high, computer software is pirated and widely shared, which reduces the profitability of producing and selling software. The Business Software Alliance (BSA) estimated that the share of software that was pirated in 2011 was over 90% in some developing countries such as Bangladesh, Georgia, and Zimbabwe; between 22% and 30% for most EU countries, Australia, Canada, Japan, and New Zealand; and 19% in the United States. In 2013, Microsoft reported that 45% of counterfeit software came from the Internet.

Public Goods

public good
a good that is nonrival and nonexclusive

A **public good** is nonrival and nonexclusive. Clean air is a public good. One person's enjoyment of clean air does not stop other people from enjoying clean air as well, so clean air is nonrival.

A public good is a special type of externality. If a firm reduces the amount of pollution it produces, thereby cleaning the air, it provides a nonpriced benefit to its neighbors: a positive externality.

free riding
benefiting from the actions of others without paying

Free Riding   Unfortunately, markets undersupply public goods due to a lack of clearly defined property rights. Because people who do not pay for the good cannot be excluded from consuming it, the provider of a public good cannot exercise property rights over the services provided by the public good. This problem is due to **free riding**: benefiting from the actions of others without paying. That is, free riders want to benefit from a positive externality. Consequently, it is very difficult for firms to profitably provide a public good because few people want to pay for the good no matter how valuable it is to them.

We illustrate the free rider problem using the example of a mall with two stores, an ice-cream parlor and a television store. Each store decides whether to pay for guard service to protect their merchandise. Guards patrolling the mall provide a service without rivalry: Both stores in the mall are simultaneously protected. The more guards, the more protection for both stores.

To show why public goods are underprovided by markets, we examine how the demand curve for a public good differs from that for a private good. The social marginal benefit of a private good is the same as the marginal benefit to the individual who consumes that good. The market demand or social marginal benefit curve for private goods is the *horizontal* sum of the demand curves of each individual (Chapter 2).

In contrast, the social marginal benefit of a public good is the sum of the marginal benefit to each person who consumes the good. Because a public good lacks rivalry, many people can get pleasure from the same unit of output. Consequently, the *social demand curve* or *willingness-to-pay curve* for a public good is the *vertical* sum of the demand curves of each individual.

We illustrate this vertical summing by deriving the demand for guard services by stores in a mall that want to discourage theft. Each store's demand for guards reflects its marginal benefit from a reduction in thefts due to the guards. The demand curve for the electronics store, which stands to lose a lot if thieves strike, is D^1 in Figure 18.4. The ice-cream parlor, which is at less risk from a theft, demands fewer guards at any given price, D^2.

Figure 18.4 Inadequate Provision of a Public Good

Security guards protect both tenants of the mall. If each guard costs $20 per hour, the television store, with demand D^1, is willing to hire four guards per hour. The ice-cream parlor, with demand D^2, is not willing to hire any guards. Thus, if everyone acts independently, the equilibrium is e_p. The social demand for this public good is the vertical sum of the individual demand curves, D. Thus, the social optimum is e_s, at which five guards are hired.

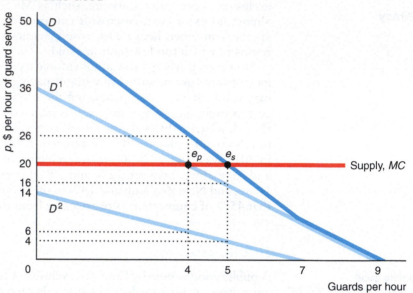

Because a guard patrolling the mall protects both stores at once, the marginal benefit to society of an additional guard is the sum of the benefit to each store. The social marginal benefit of a fifth guard, $20, is the sum of the marginal benefit to the television store, $16 (the height of D^1 at five guards per hour), and the marginal benefit to the ice-cream store, $4 (the height of D^2 at five guards per hour). Thus, the social demand is the vertical sum of the individual demand curves.

A competitive market supplies as many guards as the stores want at $20 per hour per guard. At that price, the ice-cream store would not hire any guards on its own. The television store would hire four. If the stores act independently, four guards are hired at the private equilibrium, e_p. The sum of the marginal benefit to the two stores from four guards is $26, which is greater than the $20 marginal cost of an additional guard. If a fifth guard is hired, the social marginal benefit, $20, equals the marginal cost of the last guard. Therefore, the social equilibrium, e_s, has five guards.

The ice-cream store can get guard services without paying because the guard service is a public good. Acting alone, the television store hires fewer guards than are socially optimal because it ignores the positive externality provided to the ice-cream store, which the television store does not capture. Thus, the competitive market for guard services provides too little of this public good.

In more extreme cases, no public good is provided because nonpurchasers cannot be stopped from consuming the good. Usually, if the government does not provide a nonexclusive public good, no one provides it.

Solved Problem 18.3

In a different mall, a stereo store and a television store each decide whether to hire one guard or none—extra guards provide no extra protection. A guard costs 20 per hour. The benefit to each store is 16 per hour. The stores play a game in which they act independently. The table shows their payoffs. What is the outcome of this game? What is the socially optimal solution?

Answer

1. *Use a best-response analysis (Chapter 14) to determine the Nash equilibrium to this game.* If the television store hires a guard, the stereo store's payoff is −4 if it hires a guard and 16 if it does not, so its best response is to not hire. The light-green triangle in the lower-left cell shows this choice. Similarly, if the television store does not hire a guard, the stereo store's payoff is −4 if it hires and 0 if it does not, so its best response is to not hire. Thus, the stereo store has a dominant strategy of not hiring. Using a similar analysis, the television store also has a dominant strategy of not hiring (as the dark-green triangles show). The only Nash equilibrium to this game is for neither store to hire.

2. *Calculate the benefits and costs of hiring a guard to determine the social optimum.* The cost of a guard is 20, but the payoff to the two stores combined is 32, so it pays to hire a guard.

		Television Store	
		Hire	**Do Not Hire**
Stereo Store	**Hire**	−4 / −4	−4 / 16
	Do Not Hire	16 / −4	0 / 0

Comment: Acting independently, the stores do not achieve the social optimum because each firm tries to free ride. This game is an example of the prisoners' dilemma (Chapter 14).

Application

Radiohead's "Public Good" Experiment

In 2007, the British rock band Radiohead sold its album *In Rainbows* by offering its fans a digital download without copy restriction software off the Internet at a price chosen by each fan for a three-month period. By so doing, the band faced a problem similar to that of society for a public good: Fans knew that the album could be theirs regardless of what they paid, so individuals were tempted to pay substantially less than their valuations of the album or the price of comparable albums.

The band did not release official figures about digital sales. According to comScore's estimates, 38% of fans paid an average of $6, while the rest paid nothing. Thus, many fans chose to free ride. After the initial three months, the band removed the digital version from the Internet and issued a traditional CD version with a list price of $13.98. The band chose not to repeat this experiment with their 2011 album, *The King of Limbs*.

Reducing Free Riding One solution to the free riding problem is for the government to provide the good. Governments provide public defense, roads, and many other public goods.

Alternatively, governmental or other collective actions can reduce free riding. Methods that may be used include social pressure, mergers, privatization, and compulsion.

Social pressure may reduce or eliminate free riding, especially for a small group. Such pressure may cause most firms in a mall to contribute "voluntarily" to hire security guards. The firms may cooperate in a repeated prisoners' dilemma game, especially if the market has relatively few firms.

A direct way to eliminate free riding by firms is for them to *merge* into a single firm and thereby internalize the positive externality. The sum of the benefit to the individual stores equals the benefit to the single firm, so an optimal decision is made to hire guards.

If the independent stores sign a contract that commits them to share the cost of the guards, they achieve the practical advantage from a merger. However, the question remains as to why they would agree to sign the contract, given the prisoners' dilemma problem (Chapter 14).

Privatization—exclusion—eliminates free riding. A good that would be a public good if anyone could use it becomes a private good if access to it is restricted. An example is clean water provided by water utilities, which can be monitored and priced using individual meters.

Another way to overcome free riding is through *mandates*. Some outside entity such as the government may mandate (dictate) a solution to a free-riding problem. For example, the management of a mall with many firms may require tenants to sign a rental contract committing them to pay fees to hire security guards that are determined through tenants' votes. If the majority votes to hire guards, all must share the cost. Although a firm might be unwilling to pay for the guard service if it has no guarantee that others will also pay, it may vote to assess everyone—including itself—to pay for the service.

Application

What's Their Beef?

Under U.S. federal law, agricultural producers can force all industry members to contribute to public goods if the majority of firms agrees. Under the Beef Promotion and Research Act, all beef producers must pay a $1-per-head fee on cattle sold in the United States. The $80 million raised by this fee annually finances research, educational programs on mad cow disease, and collective advertising such as its original "Beef: It's What's for Dinner" campaign and its 2013 campaign, "Stay Home. Grill Out." Supporters of this collective advertising estimate that producers receive $5.67 in additional marginal revenue for every dollar they contribute.

Valuing Public Goods To ensure that a nonexclusive public good is provided, a government usually produces it or compels others to do so. Issues faced by a government when it provides such a public good include whether to provide it at all and, if so, how much of the good to provide. When grappling with these questions, the government needs to know the cost—usually the easy part—and the value of the public good to many individuals—the hard part.

Through surveys or voting results, the government may try to determine the value that consumers place on the public good. A major problem with these methods is that most people do not know how much a public good is worth to them. How much would you pay to maintain the National Archives? How much does reducing air pollution improve your health? How much better do you sleep at night knowing that the armed forces stand ready to protect you?

Even if people know how much they value a public good, they have an incentive to lie on a survey. Those who highly value the good and want the government to provide it may exaggerate its value. Similarly, people who place a low value on it may report *too low* a value—possibly even a negative one—to discourage government action.

Rather than relying on surveys, a government may ask its citizens to vote on public goods. Suppose that a separate, majority-rule vote is held on whether to install a traffic signal—a public good—at each of several street corners. If a signal is installed, all voters are taxed equally to pay for it. An individual will vote to install a signal if the value of the signal to that voter is at least as much as the tax that each voter must pay for the signal.

Table 18.4 Voting on $300 Traffic Signals

Signal Location	Value to Each Voter, $			Value to Society, $	Outcome of Vote*
	Nancy	Hayley	Asa		
Corner A	50	100	150	300	Yes
Corner B	50	75	250	375	No
Corner C	50	100	110	260	Yes

*An individual votes to install a signal at a particular corner if and only if that person thinks that the signal is worth at least $100, the tax that individual must pay if the signal is installed.

Whether the majority votes for the signal depends on the preferences of the *median voter*: the voter with respect to whom half the populace values the project less and half values the project more. If the median voter wants to install a signal, then at least half the voters agree, so the vote carries. Similarly, if the median voter is against the project, at least half the voters are against it, so the vote fails.

It is *efficient* to install the signal if the value of the signal to society is at least as great as its cost. Does majority voting result in efficiency? The following examples illustrate that efficiency is not ensured.

Each signal costs $300 to install. Three people vote and will be taxed to pay for the signal if it is approved. Thus, each individual votes for the signal only if that person puts a value on the signal of at least $100, which is the share of the tax each person pays if the signal is installed. Table 18.4 shows the value that each voter places on installing a signal at each of three intersections.

For each of the proposed signals, Hayley is the median voter, so her views "determine" the outcome. If Hayley, the median voter, likes the signal, then she and Asa, a majority, vote for it. Otherwise, Nancy and Hayley vote against it. The majority favors installing a signal at corners *A* and *C* and is against doing so at corner *B*. It would be efficient to install the signal at corner *A*, where the social value is $300, and at corner *B*, where the social value is $375, because each value equals or exceeds the cost of $300.

At corner *A*, the citizens vote for the signal, and that outcome is efficient. The other two votes lead to inefficient outcomes. No signal is installed at corner *B*, where society values the signal at more than $300, but a signal is installed at corner *C*, where voters value the signal at less than $300.

The problem with yes-no votes is that they ignore the intensity of preferences. A voter indicates only whether or not the project is worth more or less than a certain amount. Thus, such majority voting fails to value the public good fully and hence does not guarantee that the public good is efficiently provided.[8]

Challenge Solution

Trade and Pollution

In the Challenge at the beginning of the chapter, we asked whether free trade benefits a country if it does not regulate its domestic pollution. This issue is increasingly important as nations move toward free trade and trade expands.

The United States has signed free-trade agreements (FTA) that eliminate or reduce tariffs and quotas and liberalize rules on foreign investment to increase trade with Australia, Bahrain, Canada, Chile, Costa Rica, El Salvador, Guatemala, Honduras,

---

[8]Although voting does not reveal how much a public good is worth, Tideman and Tullock (1976) and other economists have devised taxing methods that can sometimes induce people to reveal their true valuations. However, these methods are rarely used.

Israel, Jordan, Mexico, Morocco, Nicaragua, Peru, Singapore, South Korea, and other countries. As of May 2012, FTA countries accounted for 46% of U.S. exports and 35% of imports.

Liberalized trade has expanded trade. Trade was 28% of the U.S. gross domestic product (GDP) in 2008–2010, compared to only 10% in 1970. The GDP share of trade is even greater in many other countries: 30% in the European Union, 31% in Japan, 48% in India, 55% in China, 59% in Mexico and the United Kingdom, and 63% in Canada.

Everyone can gain from free trade if losers are compensated and if domestic markets are perfectly competitive and not distorted by taxes, tariffs, or pollution (Chapters 9 and 10). Business and jobs lost in one sector from free trade are more than offset by gains in other sectors. However, if an economy has at least two market distortions, correcting one of them may either increase or decrease welfare.[9] For example, if a country bars trade and has uncontrolled pollution, then allowing free trade without controlling pollution may not increase welfare.

What are the welfare effects of permitting trade if a country's polluting export industry is unregulated? To analyze this question, we couple the trade model from Chapter 9 with the pollution model from this chapter.

Suppose that the country's paper industry is a price taker on the world paper market. The world price is p_w. Panel a of the figure shows the gain to trade in a market without pollution (or optimally regulated pollution). The domestic supply curve, S, is upward sloping, and the home country can import as much as it wants at the world price, p_w. In the free-trade equilibrium, e_1, the equilibrium quantity is Q_1 and the equilibrium price is the world price, p_w. With a ban on imports, the equilibrium is e_2, quantity falls to Q_2, and price rises to p_2. Consequently, the deadweight loss from the ban is area D. (See the discussion of Figure 9.10 for a more thorough analysis.)

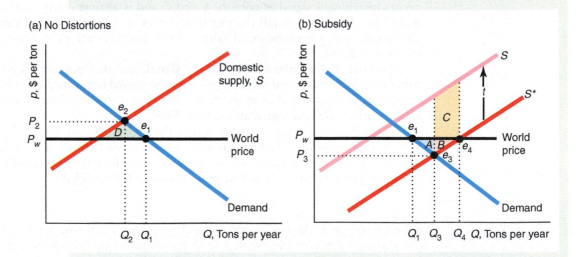

(a) No Distortions

(b) Subsidy

In panel b, we include pollution in the analysis. The supply curve S^* is the sum of the firms' private marginal cost curves where the firms do not bear the cost of the pollution (and similar to curve MC^p in Figure 18.1.) If the government imposes a specific tax, t, that equals the marginal cost of the pollution per ton of paper, then

---

[9]In the economics literature, this result is referred to as the *Theory of the Second Best*.

the firms internalize the cost of pollution, and the resulting supply curve is S (similar to MC^s in Figure 18.1).

If the government does not tax or otherwise regulate pollution, the private supply curve S^* lies below the social supply curve, which results in excess domestic production. If trade is banned, the equilibrium is e_3, with a larger quantity, Q_3, than in the original free-trade equilibrium and a lower consumer price, p_3. Deadweight loss results because the true marginal cost (the height of the S curve at Q_3) exceeds the consumer price.

If free trade is permitted, the Theory of the Second Best tells us that welfare does not necessarily rise, because the country still has the pollution distortion. The free-trade equilibrium is e_4. Firms sell all their quantity, Q_4, at the world price, with Q_1 going to domestic consumers and $Q_4 - Q_1$ to consumers elsewhere. The private gain to trade—ignoring the government's cost of providing the subsidy—is area $A + B$. However, the expansion of domestic output increases society's cost due to excess pollution from producing Q_4 rather than Q_3, which is area $B + C$. The height of this area is the distance between the two supply curves, which is the marginal and average costs of the pollution damage (t), and the length is the extra output sold ($Q_4 - Q_3$). Thus, if area C is greater than area A, trade causes a net welfare loss. As the diagram is drawn, C is greater than A, so allowing trade lowers welfare if pollution is not taxed.

Should the country prohibit free trade? No, the country should allow free trade and regulate pollution to maximize welfare.

Summary

1. **Externalities.** An externality occurs when a consumer's well-being or a firm's production capabilities are directly affected by the actions of other consumers or firms rather than indirectly affected through changes in prices. An externality that harms others is a negative externality, and one that helps others is a positive externality. Some externalities benefit one group while harming another.

2. **The Inefficiency of Competition with Externalities.** Because producers do not pay for a negative externality such as pollution, the private costs are less than the social costs. Consequently, competitive markets produce more negative externalities than are optimal. If the only way to cut externalities is to decrease output, the optimal solution is to set output where the marginal benefit from reducing the externality equals the marginal cost to consumers and producers from less output. It is usually optimal to have some negative externalities, because eliminating all of them requires eliminating desirable outputs and consumption activities as well. If the government has sufficient information about demand, production cost, and the harm from the externality, it can use taxes or quotas to force the competitive market to produce the social optimum. It may tax or limit the negative externality, or it may tax or limit output.

3. **Regulating Externalities.** Governments may use emissions fees (taxes) or emissions standards to control externalities. If the government has full knowledge, it can set a fee equal to the marginal harm of the externality that causes firms to internalize the externality and produce the socially optimal output. Similarly, the government can set a standard that achieves the social optimum. However, if the government lacks full information, whether it should use a tax or fee depends on a number of factors.

4. **Market Structure and Externalities.** Although a competitive market produces excessive output and negative externalities, a noncompetitive market may produce more or less than the optimal level. With a negative externality, a noncompetitive equilibrium may be closer than a competitive equilibrium to the social optimum. A tax equal to the marginal social harm of a negative externality—which results in the social optimum when applied to a competitive market—may lower welfare when applied to a noncompetitive market.

5. **Allocating Property Rights to Reduce Externalities.** Externalities arise because property rights are not clearly defined. According to the Coase Theorem, allocating property rights to *either* of two parties results in an efficient outcome if the parties can bargain. The assignment of the property rights, however, affects income distribution, as the rights are valuable. Unfortunately, bargaining is usually not practical, especially when many people are involved. In such cases, markets for permits to produce externalities may overcome the externality problem. Positive externality problems are often solved by markets because property rights are clearly defined.

6. **Rivalry and Exclusion.** Private goods are subject to rivalry—if one person consumes a unit of the good it cannot be consumed by others—and to exclusion—others can be stopped from consuming the good. Some goods lack one or both of these properties.

Open-access common property, such as a fishery, is nonexclusive, but is subject to rivalry. This lack of exclusion causes overfishing because users of the fishery do not take into account the costs they impose on others (forgone fish) when they go fishing. A club good is nonrival but exclusive. For example, a swimming club lacks rivalry up to capacity but can exclude nonmembers. A market failure occurs if a positive price is charged for a good that is produced with excess capacity, because the marginal cost of providing the good to one more person is zero, which is less than the price. A public good such as public defense is both nonrival and nonexclusive. The lack of exclusion causes a free rider problem in a market: People use the good without paying for it. Therefore, potential suppliers of such goods are not adequately compensated and underprovide the good. Because private markets tend to underprovide nonprivate goods, governments often produce or subsidize such goods.

Questions

*All questions are available on MyEconLab; * = answer appears at the back of this book; A = algebra problem; C = calculus problem.*

1. Externalities

1.1 According to a study in the *New England Journal of Medicine*, your friendships or "social networks" are more likely than your genes to make you obese (Jennifer Levitz, "Can Your Friends Make You Fat?" *Wall Street Journal*, July 26, 2007, D1). If it is true that people who have overweight friends are more likely to be overweight all else the same, is that an example of a negative externality? Why? (*Hints*: Is this relationship a causal one, or do heavier people choose heavier friends? Also remember that people with thinner friends may be thinner.)

1.2 According to the digital media company Captivate Network, employees viewing the 2012 Olympics instead of working caused a $1.38 billion loss in productivity for U.S. companies. Is this productivity loss an example of a negative externality? Explain.

1.3 Analyze the following statement. Is garbage a positive or negative externality? Why is a market solution practical here?

Since the turn of the twentieth century, hog farmers in New Jersey fed Philadelphia garbage to their pigs. Philadelphia saved $3 million a year and reduced its garbage mound by allowing New Jersey

farmers to pick up leftover food scraps for their porcine recyclers. The city paid $1.9 million to the New Jersey pig farmers for picking up the waste each year, which was about $79 a ton. Otherwise, the city would have had to pay $125 a ton for curbside recycling of the same food waste.

1.4 When a visiting sports team with a superstar athlete plays a home team, the home team benefits financially (such as from selling extra tickets). Do such positive externalities lower social welfare? If not, why not? If so, what could the teams do to solve that problem?

2. The Inefficiency of Competition with Externalities

2.1 Why is zero pollution not the best solution for society? Can there be too little pollution? Why or why not?

2.2 In 2009, when the world was worried about the danger of the H1N1 influenza virus (swine flu), Representative Rosa DeLauro and Senator Edward Kennedy proposed the Healthy Families Act in Congress to guarantee paid sick days to all workers. Although the Centers for Disease Control and Prevention urges ill people to stay home from work or school to keep from infecting others, many workers—especially those who do not receive paid sick days—ignore this advice. Evaluate the efficiency and welfare implications of the proposed law taking account of externalities.

2.3 Northern Victoria, Australia, imposed a vomit tax on pubs in the Greater Shepparton area that remain open between 3:00 A.M. and 6:00 A.M. The tax was to be used to pay for cleaning up the mess left by drunks who get sick in the street. Pub owners objected that politicians assume that their customers are responsible for the mess. Discuss the pros and cons of using such a tax to deal with this externality.

3. Regulating Externalities

3.1 Australia required that incandescent light bulbs be phased out by 2010 in favor of the more fuel-efficient compact fluorescent bulbs. Ireland's ban started in 2009, and the United States started phasing out incandescent bulbs in 2012. It is hoped that these restrictions will reduce carbon and global warming. What alternative approaches could be used to achieve the same goals? What are the advantages and disadvantages of a ban relative to the alternatives?

*3.2 In the paper market example in this chapter, what are the optimal emissions fee and the optimal tax on output (assuming that only a single, constant fee or tax is applied)? (*Hint*: See Solved Problem 18.1.)

3.3 In Figure 18.2, the government may optimally regulate the paper market using a tax on output. A technological change drives down the private marginal cost of production. Discuss the welfare implications if the output tax is unchanged. (*Hint*: See Solved Problem 18.1.)

3.4 In Figure 18.1, could the government use a price ceiling or a price floor to achieve the optimal level of production?

3.5 If global warming occurs, output of three of the major U.S. cash crops could decline by as much as 80% according to Roberts and Schenkler (2012). Crop yields increase on days when the temperature rises above 50°, but fall precipitously on days when it is above 86°. Given this relationship between agricultural output and temperature and that this agricultural effect is the only externality from global warming, what would be the government's optimal policy if it can predictably control pollution and hence temperature? Can you use either a tax or an emissions standard to achieve your optimal policy? How does your policy recommendation change if the government is uncertain about its ability to control pollution and temperature or there are other externalities?

*3.6 Using the numerical example in Appendix 18A, determine the social optimum if the marginal harm of gunk is $MC^g = 84$ (instead of Equation 18A.3). Is there a shortcut that would allow you to solve this problem without algebra? **A**

3.7 Markowitz et al. (2012) found that limiting the number of liquor stores reduces crime. To maximize welfare taking into account the harms associated with alcohol sales, how should a regulatory agency set the number of liquor licenses? Should the profit-maximizing owner of a liquor store lobby for or against tighter restrictions on licenses?

3.8 The National Highway Traffic Safety Administration distributed a film *Without Helmet Laws, We All Pay the Price*. Two reasons for this title are that some injured motorcyclists are treated at public expense (Medicaid) and that the dependents of those killed in accidents receive public assistance.

  a. Does the purchase of a motorcycle by an individual who does not wear a helmet create a negative externality? Explain.

  b. If so, how should government set a no-helmet tax that would lead to a socially desirable level of motorcycle sales?

3.9 Connecticut announced that commercial fleet operators would get a tax break if they converted vehicles from ozone-producing gasoline to what the state said were cleaner fuels such as natural gas and electricity. For every dollar spent on the conversion of their fleets or building alternative fueling stations, operators could deduct 50¢ from their corporate tax. Is this approach likely to be a cost-effective way to control pollution?

4. Market Structure and Externalities

4.1 Suppose that the only way to reduce pollution from paper production is to reduce output. The government imposes a tax equal to the marginal harm from the pollution on the monopoly producer. Show that the tax may raise welfare.

4.2 Suppose that the inverse demand curve for paper is $p = 200 - Q$, the private marginal cost (unregulated competitive market supply) is $MC^p = 80 + Q$, and the marginal harm from gunk is $MC^g = Q$.

  a. What is the unregulated competitive equilibrium?

  b. What is the social optimum? What specific tax (per unit of output or gunk) results in the social optimum?

  c. What is the unregulated monopoly equilibrium?

d. How would you optimally regulate the monopoly? What is the resulting equilibrium? (*Hint*: See Solved Problems 18.1 and 18.2.) **A**

5. Allocating Property Rights to Reduce Externalities

5.1 List three specific examples where Coasian bargaining may result in the social optimum.

*5.2 Suppose in the example in Table 18.2 that the two parties cannot negotiate. The government imposes a tax on the auto body shop equal to the marginal harm it does to the tea house. What is that tax schedule? Does it result in the welfare-maximizing outcome? How does the outcome change if the tax is imposed and they can bargain? (*Hint*: If Alice is paying the tax, then she has the right to produce at whatever level she wants.)

6. Rivalry and Exclusion

6.1 List three examples of goods that do not fit neatly into the categories in Table 18.3 because they are not strictly rival or exclusive.

6.2 Are heavily used bridges, such as the Brooklyn Bridge and the Golden Gate Bridge, common properties? If so, what can be done to mitigate externality problems?

6.3 Are broadcast television and cable television public goods? Is exclusion possible? If either is a public good, why is it privately provided?

6.4 Do publishers sell the optimal number of intermediate microeconomics textbooks? Discuss in terms of public goods, rivalry, and exclusion.

6.5 To prevent overfishing, could one set a tax on fish or on boats? Explain and illustrate with a graph.

6.6 Guards patrolling a mall protect the mall's two stores. The television store's demand curve for guards is strictly greater at all prices than that of the ice-cream parlor. The marginal cost of a guard is $10 per hour. Use a diagram to show the equilibrium, and compare that to the socially optimal equilibrium. Now suppose that the mall's owner will provide a $$s$ per hour subsidy per guard. Show in your graph the optimal s that leads to the socially optimal outcome for the two stores.

6.7 Two tenants of a mall are protected by the guard service, q. The number of guards per hour demanded by the television store is $q_1 = a_1 + b_1 p$, where p is the price of one hour of guard services. The ice-cream store's demand is $q_2 = a_2 + b_2 p$. What is the social demand for this service? **A**

6.8 Vaccinations help protect the unvaccinated from disease. Boulier et al. (2007) found that the marginal externality effect can be greater than one case of illness prevented among the unvaccinated. Is vaccination a public good? If so, what might the government do to protect society optimally?

6.9 You and your roommate have a stack of dirty dishes in the sink. Either of you would wash the dishes if the decision were up to you; however, neither will do it in the expectation (hope?) that the other will deal with the mess. Explain how this example illustrates the problem of public goods and free riding.

6.10 Anna and Bess are assigned to write a joint paper within a 24-hour period about the Pareto optimal provision of public goods. Let t_A denote the number of hours that Anna contributes to the project and t_B the number of hours that Bess contributes. The numeric grade that Anna and Bess earn is a function, $23 \ln (t_A + t_B)$, of the total number of hours that they contribute to the project. If Anna contributes t_A, then she has $(24 - t_A)$ hours in the day for leisure. Anna's utility function is $U_A = 23 \ln (t_A + t_B) + \ln(24 - t_A)$, and Bess' utility function is $U_B = 23 \ln (t_A + t_B) + \ln (24 - t_B)$. If they choose the hours to contribute simultaneously and independently, what is the Nash equilibrium number of hours that each will provide? What is the number of hours each should contribute to the project that maximizes the sum of their utilities? **C**

*6.11 Every dollar of collective advertising by the beef industry results in $5.67 in additional marginal revenue for producers (as discussed in the Application "What's Their Beef?"). Is the industry advertising optimally (see Chapter 12)? Explain your answer.

6.12 In Solved Problem 18.3, suppose that the firms will split the cost of a guard if they both vote to hire one. Show the new payoff matrix. Do they hire a guard?

7. Challenge

*7.1 Redraw panel b of the Challenge Solution figure to show that it is possible for trade to increase welfare even when pollution is not taxed or otherwise regulated.

*7.2 In the Challenge Solution, where there is no pollution as in panel a of the figure, how do we know that winners from trade can compensate losers and still have enough left over to benefit themselves?

Asymmetric Information

19

The buyer needs a hundred eyes, the seller not one. —George Herbert (1651)

Challenge

Dying to Work

In part because of the differing amounts that firms invest in safety, jobs in some firms are more dangerous than in others. In 2010, 11 workers died when BP's Deepwater Horizon oil rig exploded in the Gulf of Mexico, 29 coal miners died in a disaster at Massey Energy's West Virginia mine explosion, and 33 Chilean miners were trapped half a mile underground for 69 days in another mine disaster. In 2011, workers with inadequate protection were sent to deal with the nuclear crisis at Japan's Fukushima Daiichi power plant. (By 2013, 1,973 of these workers had radiation exposure levels that indicate they are at increased risk of thyroid and other cancers.) In China, 1,384 coal miners died in 2012. An apparel factory collapsed in Bangladesh killing at least 1,132 and injuring more than 2,500 garment workers in 2013.

Prospective employees often do not know the injury rates at individual firms but may know the *average* injury rate over an entire industry, in part because such data are reported by governments. Injury rates vary dramatically by industry. U.S. government statistics released in 2012 tell us that some occupations are particularly dangerous. Construction has 9.8 fatal injuries per 100,000 workers each year; police, 18.1; mining, 19.8; truck driving, 23.0; agriculture, 42.5; logging, 93.5; and fishing, 152.9. On the other hand, safe occupations include sales, 2.0; financial services, 1.3; and educational services, 0.9 (although students sometimes risk dying of boredom).[1]

If people are rational and fear danger, they agree to work in a dangerous job only if that job pays a sufficiently higher wage than less-risky alternative jobs. Economists have found that workers receive *compensating wage differentials* in industries and occupations that government statistics show are relatively risky.

However, if workers are unaware of the greater risks at certain firms within an industry, they may not receive compensating wage differentials from more dangerous employers within that industry.[2] Workers are likely to have a sense of the

---

[1] Government statistics also tell us that males have an accident rate, 6.0, that is an order of magnitude greater than females, 0.7. Some of this difference is due to different occupations and some to different attitudes toward risk. How many women are injured after saying, "Hey! Watch this!"?

[2] Of course, a few good employers may gain a positive reputation. In 2012, Redhook Brewery started selling a special beer in memory of an employee who was killed when a keg exploded, with the proceeds going to his family (**boston.cbslocal.com**, July 20, 2012).

risks associated with an industry: Everyone knows that mining is relatively risky—but they do not know which mining companies are particularly risky until a major accident occurs. For example, in the decade before Massey Energy was acquired by Alpha Natural Resources in 2011, 54 coal miners were killed in Massey mines, a much higher rate than at other mines, yet there's no evidence that these workers received higher pay than workers at other mining firms.[3]

Because workers do not know which firms are safer than others, each firm bears the full cost of its safety investments but does not get the full benefits. If workers are aware of the average risk in an industry, all firms benefit from one firm's safety investment because that investment improves the industry average. Thus, other firms share the benefit from one firm's investment in safety. Consequently, firms, when making the important strategic decision of how much they should invest in safety, take this spillover effect into account.

Does such a situation cause firms to underinvest in safety? Can government intervention overcome such safety problems?

In previous chapters, we focused on situations in which all firms and consumers have *symmetric information*: Everyone is equally knowledgeable or equally ignorant about prices, product quality, and other factors relevant to a transaction. In perfectly competitive markets, everyone knows all the relevant facts. Companies that sell insurance and the people who buy it may be equally uncertain about future events. In contrast, in this chapter, people have **asymmetric information**: One party to a transaction has relevant information that another party lacks. For example, the seller of a house knows its defects unlike the buyer.

We concentrate on two types of asymmetric information: *hidden characteristics* and *hidden actions*. A **hidden characteristic** is an attribute of a person or thing that is known to one party but unknown to others. For example, the owner of a property may possess extensive information about the mineral composition of the land that is unknown to a mining company that is considering buying the land.

A **hidden action** is an act by one party to a transaction that is not observed by the other party. An example is a firm's manager using a company jet for personal use without the owners' knowledge.

When both parties to a transaction have equal information or equally limited information, neither has an advantage over the other. In contrast, asymmetric information leads to **opportunistic behavior**, where one party takes economic advantage of another when circumstances permit. Such *opportunistic behavior* due to asymmetric information leads to market failures, and destroys many desirable properties of competitive markets.

Two problems of opportunistic behavior arise from asymmetric information. One—*adverse selection*—is due to hidden characteristics, while the other—*moral hazard*—is associated with hidden actions. The problem of **adverse selection** arises when one party to a transaction possesses information about a hidden characteristic

asymmetric information one party to a transaction has relevant information that another party lacks

hidden characteristic an attribute of a person or thing that is known to one party but unknown to others

hidden action an act by one party to a transaction that is not observed by the other party

opportunistic behavior one party takes economic advantage of another when circumstances permit

adverse selection occurs when one party to a transaction possesses information about a hidden characteristic that is unknown to other parties and takes economic advantage of this information

[3]The U.S. Mine Safety and Health Administration issued Massey 124 safety-related citations in 2010 prior to the April 2010 accident at Massey's Upper Big Branch mine in West Virginia that killed 29 workers. Massey had 515 violations in 2009. Mine Safety and Health Administration safety officials concluded in 2011 that the 2010 explosion that took 29 lives could have been prevented by Massey. The former head of security at the mine was prosecuted and convicted of two felonies and ultimately sentenced to 36 months in prison.

that is unknown to other parties and takes economic advantage of this information. For example, if a roadside vendor sells a box of oranges to a passing motorist and only the vendor knows that the oranges are of low quality, the vendor may allege that the oranges are of high quality and charge a premium price for them. That is, the seller seeks to benefit from an informational asymmetry due to a hidden characteristic, the quality of the oranges. If potential buyers worry about such opportunistic behavior, they may be willing to pay only low prices or may forgo purchasing the oranges entirely.

moral hazard
an informed party takes an action that the other party cannot observe and that harms the less-informed party

The primary problem arising from hidden action is **moral hazard**, which occurs when an informed party takes an action that the other party cannot observe and that harms the less-informed party. If you pay a mechanic by the hour to fix your car, and you do not actually watch the repairs, then the time spent by the mechanic on your car is a hidden action.[4] Moral hazard occurs if the mechanic bills you for excessive hours.

This chapter focuses on adverse selection and unobserved characteristics. Adverse selection often leads to markets in which some desirable transactions do not take place or even the market as a whole cannot exist. We also discuss how adverse selection problems can sometimes be solved. Chapter 20 concentrates on moral hazard problems due to unobserved actions and on the use of contracts to deal with them.

In this chapter, we examine five main topics

1. **Adverse Selection.** Adverse selection may prevent desirable transactions from occurring, possibly eliminating a market entirely.

2. **Reducing Adverse Selection.** To reduce the harms from adverse selection, government actions or contracts between involved parties may be used, or the information asymmetry may be reduced or eliminated.

3. **Price Discrimination Due to False Beliefs About Quality.** If some consumers incorrectly think that quality varies across identical products, a firm may price discriminate.

4. **Market Power from Price Ignorance.** Consumers' ignorance about the price that each firm charges gives firms market power.

5. **Problems Arising from Ignorance When Hiring.** Attempts to eliminate information asymmetries in hiring may raise or lower social welfare.

19.1 Adverse Selection

One of the most important problems associated with adverse selection is that consumers may not make purchases to avoid being exploited by better-informed sellers. As a result, not all desirable transactions occur, and potential consumer and producer surplus is lost. Indeed, in the extreme case, adverse selection may prevent a market from operating at all. We illustrate this idea using two important examples of adverse selection problems: insurance and products of varying quality.

---

[4]A lawyer dies in an accident and goes to heaven. A host of angels greet him with a banner that reads, "Welcome Oldest Man!" The lawyer is puzzled: "Why do you think I'm the oldest man who ever lived? I was only 47 when I died." One of the angels replied, "You can't fool us; you were at least 152 when you died. We saw how many hours you billed!"

Adverse Selection in Insurance Markets

Hidden characteristics and adverse selection are very important in the insurance industry. Were a health insurance company to provide fair insurance by charging everyone a rate for insurance equal to the average cost of health care for the entire population, the company would lose money due to adverse selection. Many unhealthy people—people who expect to incur health care costs that are higher than average—would view this insurance as a good deal and would buy it. In contrast, unless they were very risk averse, healthy people would not buy it because the premiums would exceed their expected health care costs. Given that a disproportionately large share of unhealthy people would buy the insurance, the market for health insurance would exhibit adverse selection, and the insurance company's average cost of medical care for covered people would exceed the population's average.

Adverse selection results in an inefficient market outcome because the sum of producer and consumer surplus is not maximized. The loss of potential surplus occurs because some potentially beneficial sales of insurance to relatively healthy individuals do not occur. These consumers would be willing to buy insurance at a lower rate that was closer to the fair rate for them given their superior health. The insurance company would be willing to offer such low rates only if it could be sure that these individuals were relatively healthy.

Products of Unknown Quality

Anagram for General Motors: or great lemons

Adverse selection often arises because sellers of a product have better information about the product's quality—a hidden characteristic—than do buyers. Used cars that appear to be identical on the outside often differ substantially in the number of repairs they will need. Some cars—*lemons*—are cursed. They have a variety of insidious problems that become apparent to the owner only after driving the car for a while. Thus, the owner knows from experience if a used car is a lemon, but a potential buyer does not.

If buyers have the same information as sellers, no adverse selection problem arises. However, when sellers have more information than buyers, adverse selection may drive high-quality products out of the market (Akerlof, 1970). Why? Used car buyers worry that a used car might be a lemon. As a result they will not pay as high a price as they would if they knew the car was of good quality. They will only buy if the price is low enough to reflect the possibility of getting a lemon. Given that sellers of

excellent used cars do not want to sell their cars for that low a price, they do not enter the market. Adverse selection has driven the high-quality cars out of the market, leaving only the lemons.

In the following example, we assume that sellers cannot alter the quality of their used cars and that the number of potential used car buyers is large. All potential buyers are willing to pay $4,000 for a lemon and $8,000 for a good used car: The demand curve for lemons, D^L, is horizontal at $4,000 in panel a of Figure 19.1, and the demand curve for good cars, D^G, is horizontal at $8,000 in panel b.

Although the number of potential buyers is virtually unlimited, only 1,000 owners of lemons and 1,000 owners of good cars are willing to sell. The *reservation price* of lemon owners—the lowest price at which they will sell their cars—is $3,000. Consequently, the supply curve for lemons, S^L in panel a, is horizontal at $3,000 up to 1,000 cars, where it becomes vertical (no more cars are for sale at any price).

Figure 19.1 Markets for Lemons and Good Cars

If everyone has full information, the equilibrium in the lemons market is e (1,000 cars sold for $4,000 each), and the equilibrium in the good-car market is E (1,000 cars sold for $8,000 each). If buyers can't tell quality before buying but assume that equal numbers of the two types of cars are for sale, their demand in both markets is D^*, which is horizontal at $6,000. If the good-car owners' reservation price is $5,000, the supply curve for good cars is S^1, and 1,000 good cars (point F) and 1,000 lemons (point f) sell for $6,000 each. If their reservation price is $7,000, the supply curve is S^2. No good cars are sold; 1,000 lemons sell for $4,000 each (point e).

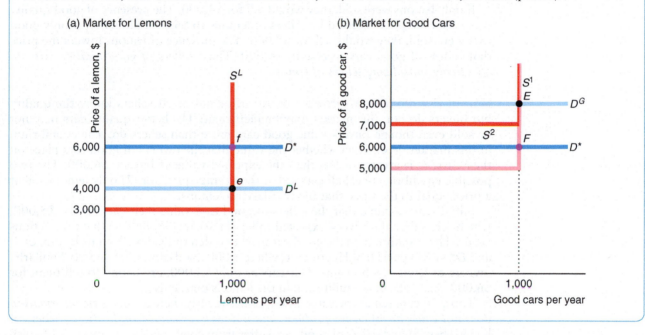

Market Equilibrium with Symmetric Information If both sellers and buyers know the quality of all the used cars before any sales take place—they have full, symmetric information—all 2,000 cars are sold, and the good cars sell for more than lemons. In panel a of Figure 19.1, the intersection of the lemons demand curve D^L and the lemons supply curve S^L determines the equilibrium at e in the lemons market, where 1,000 lemons sell for $4,000 each. Regardless of whether the supply curve for good cars is S^1 or S^2 in panel b, the equilibrium in the good-car market is E, where 1,000 good cars sell for $8,000 each.

The reservation price of owners of high-quality used cars is v, which is less than $8,000. Panel b shows two possible values of v. If $v = \$5,000$, the supply curve for good cars, S^1, is horizontal at $5,000 up to 1,000 cars and then becomes vertical. If $v = \$7,000$, the supply curve is S^2.

All the cars are sold if everyone has the same information. As a result, *this market is efficient because the goods go to the people who value them the most.* All current owners, who value the cars less than the potential buyers, sell their cars.

It does not matter whether all buyers and sellers have full information or all lack information—it's the equality (or symmetry) of information that matters. However, *the amount of information they have affects the price at which the cars sell.* With full information, good cars sell for $8,000 and lemons for $4,000.

If no one can tell a lemon from a good car at the time of purchase, both types of cars sell for the same price. Suppose that everyone is risk neutral (Chapter 17) and no one can identify the lemons: Buyers *and* sellers are equally ignorant. A buyer has an equal chance of buying a lemon or a good car. The expected value (Chapter 17) of a used car is

$$\$6,000 = (\tfrac{1}{2} \times \$4,000) + (\tfrac{1}{2} \times \$8,000).$$

A risk-neutral buyer would pay $6,000 for a car of unknown quality. Because sellers cannot distinguish between the cars either, sellers accept this amount and sell all the cars.[5] Thus, this market is efficient because the cars go to people who value them more than their original owners.

If only lemons were sold, they would sell for $4,000. The presence of good-quality cars raises the price received by sellers of lemons to $6,000. Similarly, if only good cars were sold, they would sell for $8,000. The presence of lemons lowers the price that sellers of good cars receive to $6,000. Thus, *sellers of good-quality cars are effectively subsidizing sellers of lemons.*

Market Equilibrium with Asymmetric Information If sellers know the quality but buyers do not, this market may be inefficient: The better-quality cars may not be sold even though buyers value good cars more than sellers do. The equilibrium in this market depends on whether the value that the owners of good cars place on their cars, v, is greater or less than the expected value of buyers, $6,000. The two possible equilibria are (1) all cars sell at the average price, or (2) only lemons sell at a price equal to the value that buyers place on lemons.

Initially, we assume that the sellers of good cars value their cars at $v = \$5,000$, which is less than the buyers' expected value of the cars ($6,000), so that transactions occur. The equilibrium in the good-car market is determined by the intersection of S^1 and D^* at F in panel b of Figure 19.1, where 1,000 good cars sell at $6,000. Similarly, owners of lemons, who value their cars at only $3,000, are happy to sell them for $6,000 each. The new equilibrium in the lemons market is f.

Thus, all cars sell at the same price. Consequently, here *asymmetric information does not cause an efficiency problem, but it does have equity implications.* Sellers of lemons benefit and sellers of good cars suffer from consumers' inability to distinguish quality. Consumers who buy the good cars get a bargain, and buyers of lemons are left with a sour taste in their mouths.

Now suppose that the sellers of good cars place a value of $v = \$7,000$ on their cars and thus are unwilling to sell them for $6,000. As a result, in this case, the *lemons drive good cars out of the market.* Buyers realize that they can buy only lemons at any price less than $7,000. Consequently, in equilibrium, the 1,000 lemons sell for the expected (and actual) price of $4,000, and no good cars change hands. *This equilibrium is inefficient* because high-quality cars remain in the hands of people who value them less than potential buyers do.

In summary, if buyers have less information about product quality than sellers do, the result might be a lemons problem in which high-quality cars do not sell even though potential buyers value the cars more than their current owners do. If so, the asymmetric information causes a competitive market to lose its desirable efficiency and welfare properties. The lemons problem does not occur if the information is symmetric. If buyers and sellers of used cars know the quality of the cars, each car sells for its true value in a perfectly competitive market. If, as with new cars, neither buyers nor sellers can identify lemons, both good cars and lemons sell at a price equal to the expected value rather than at their (unknown) true values.

---

[5]Risk-neutral sellers place an expected value of $(\tfrac{1}{2} \times \$3,000) + \tfrac{1}{2}v = \$1,500 + \tfrac{1}{2}v$ on a car of unknown quality. If $v = \$7,000$, this expected value is $1,500 + $3,500 = $5,000. If $v = \$5,000$, the expected value is only $4,000. In either case, sellers would be happy to sell their cars for $6,000.

Solved Problem 19.1

Suppose that everyone in our used car example is risk neutral, and potential car buyers value lemons at $4,000 and good used cars at $8,000. The reservation price of lemon owners is $3,000 and the reservation price of owners of high-quality used cars is $7,000. The share of current owners who have lemons is θ (in our previous example, the share was $\theta = \frac{1}{2}$). For what values of θ do all potential sellers sell their used cars? Describe the equilibrium.

Answer

1. *Determine how much buyers are willing to pay if all cars are sold.* Because buyers are risk neutral, if they believe that the probability of getting a lemon is θ, the most they are willing to pay for a car of unknown quality is the average price,

$$p = \$4,000\theta + (\$8,000 \times [1 - \theta]) = \$8,000 - \$4,000\theta. \qquad (19.1)$$

For example, $p = \$6,000$ if $\theta = \frac{1}{2}$, and $p = \$7,000$ if $\theta = \frac{1}{4}$.

2. *Solve for the values of θ such that all the cars are sold, and describe the equilibrium.* All owners will sell if the market price equals or exceeds the reservation price of good car owners, $7,000. Using Equation 19.1, we know that the market (equilibrium) price is $7,000 or more if a quarter or fewer of the used cars are lemons, $\theta \le \frac{1}{4}$. Thus, for $\theta \le \frac{1}{4}$, all the cars are sold at the price in Equation 19.1.

Varying Quality with Asymmetric Information Most firms can adjust their product's quality. If consumers cannot identify high-quality goods before purchase, they pay the same for all goods regardless of quality. Because the price that firms receive for top-quality goods is the same as they receive for low-quality items, they do not produce top-quality goods. Such an outcome is inefficient if consumers are willing to pay sufficiently more for top-quality goods.

This unwillingness to produce high-quality products is due to an externality (Chapter 18): *A firm does not completely capture the benefits from raising the quality of its product.* By selling a better product than what other firms offer, a seller raises the average quality in the market, so buyers are willing to pay more for all products. As a result, the high-quality seller shares the benefits from its high-quality product with sellers of low-quality products by raising the average price to all. *The social value of raising the quality*, as reflected by the increased revenues shared by all firms, *is greater than the private value*, which is only the higher revenue received by the firm with the good product.

Solved Problem 19.2

It costs $10 to produce a low-quality wallet and $20 to produce a high-quality wallet. Consumers cannot distinguish between the products before purchase, they do not make repeat purchases, and they value the wallets at the cost of production. The five firms in the market produce 100 wallets each. Each firm produces only high-quality or only low-quality wallets. Consumers pay the expected value of a wallet. Do any of the firms produce high-quality wallets?

Answer

1. *Calculate the expected value of wallet.* If all five firms make a low-quality wallet, consumers pay $10 per wallet. If one firm makes a high-quality wallet and all the

others make low-quality wallets, the probability that a consumer buys a high-quality wallet is $\frac{1}{5}$. Thus, the expected value per wallet to consumers is

$$(\$10 \times \tfrac{4}{5}) + (\$20 \times \tfrac{1}{5}) = \$12.$$

2. *Show that it does not pay for one firm to make high-quality wallets if the other firms make low-quality wallets due to asymmetric information.* If one firm raises the quality of its product, all firms benefit because the wallets sell for $12 instead of $10. The high-quality firm receives only a fraction of the total benefit from raising quality. It gets $2 extra per high-quality wallet sold, which is less than the extra $10 it costs to make the better wallet. The other $8 is shared by the other firms. The high-quality firm would incur all the expenses of raising quality, $10 extra per wallet, and reap only a fraction, $2, of the benefits. Therefore, due to asymmetric information, no firm produces high-quality goods even though consumers are willing to pay for the extra quality.

19.2 Reducing Adverse Selection

Because adverse selection results from one party exploiting asymmetric information about a hidden characteristic, the two main methods for solving adverse selection problems are to *restrict the ability of the informed party to take advantage of hidden information* and to *equalize information* among the parties. Responses to adverse selection problems increase welfare in some markets, but may do more harm than good in others.

Restricting Opportunistic Behavior

Which type of restriction works best to curb opportunistic behavior depends on the nature of the adverse selection problem. For insurance, adverse selection may be prevented by mandating universal insurance coverage. With varying product quality, laws to prevent opportunism are commonly used.

Universal Coverage Health insurance markets have adverse selection because low-risk consumers do not buy insurance at prices that reflect the average risk. Such adverse selection can be eliminated by providing insurance to everyone or by mandating that everyone buy insurance. Canada, the United Kingdom, and many other countries provide basic health insurance to all residents, financed by a combination of mandatory premiums and taxes. In 2012, the U.S. Supreme Court confirmed the constitutionality of the *individual mandate* in the 2010 Patient Protection and Affordable Care Act, which requires virtually all Americans to have health care coverage.

Similarly, firms often provide mandatory health insurance to all employees as a benefit, rather than paying a higher wage and letting employees decide whether to buy such insurance on their own. By doing so, firms reduce adverse selection problems for their insurance carriers: Both healthy and unhealthy people are covered. As a result, firms can buy medical insurance for their workers at a lower cost per person than workers could obtain on their own.

Laws to Prevent Opportunism Product quality and product safety are often hidden characteristics that are known to manufacturers but are not observed by consumers. Manufacturers have an incentive to behave opportunistically by selling low-quality products or unsafe products to consumers at excessive prices. However, product liability laws protect consumers from being stuck with nonfunctional or dangerous products.

Moreover, many U.S. state supreme courts have concluded that products are sold with an implicit understanding that they will safely perform their intended function. If they do not, consumers can sue the seller even in the absence of product liability laws. If consumers can rely on explicit or implicit product liability laws to force a manufacturer to make good on defective products, they need not worry about adverse selection. Similarly, truth-in-advertising laws and food labeling requirements are both efforts to discourage opportunistic behavior by preventing misleading claims about product characteristics.

Equalizing Information

Adverse selection problems can be reduced or eliminated by providing information to all parties. Either informed or uninformed parties can eliminate information asymmetries. Three methods for reducing informational asymmetries are:

screening
an action taken by an uninformed person to determine the information possessed by informed people

signaling
an action taken by an informed person to send information to an uninformed person

1. An uninformed party (such as an insurance company) can use **screening**: an action taken by an uninformed person to determine the information possessed by informed people.
2. An informed party (such as a person seeking to buy health insurance) can use **signaling**: an action taken by an informed person to send information to a less-informed person.
3. A *third party* (such as a firm or a government agency) not directly involved in the transaction may collect information and sell it or give it to the uninformed party.

Screening   Uninformed people may try to eliminate their disadvantage by screening to gather information on the hidden characteristics of informed people. Insurance companies reduce adverse selection problems by screening potential customers based on their health records or requiring them to undergo medical exams. A life insurance company uses such information to better estimate the probability that it will have to pay off on a policy. The firm can then decide not to insure high-risk individuals or can charge high-risk people higher premiums.

It is costly to collect information on the health of a person or whether that individual has dangerous habits such as smoking, drinking, or skydiving. As a result, insurance companies collect information only up to the point at which the marginal benefit from the extra information they gather equals the marginal cost of obtaining it. Over time, insurance companies have increasingly concluded that it pays to collect information about whether individuals exercise, have a family history of dying young, or engage in potentially life-threatening activities.

Consumers can use screening techniques too. For example, a potential customer can screen a used car by test-driving it, by having an objective, trustworthy mechanic examine the car, or by paying a company such as CARFAX to check the history of the repairs

Congratulations! You qualify for our auto insurance.

on the vehicle. As long as the consumers' costs of securing information are less than the private benefits, they obtain the information, transactions occur, and markets function smoothly.

In some markets, consumers can avoid the adverse selection problem by buying only from a firm that has a *reputation* for providing high-quality goods. For example, consumers know that a used car dealer that expects repeat purchases has a stronger incentive not to sell defective cars than does an individual.

Generally, in markets in which the same consumers and firms trade regularly, a reputation is easy to establish. In markets in which consumers buy a good only once, such as in tourist areas, firms cannot establish reputations as easily and we might expect adverse selection to be a more significant problem.

Application

Changing a Firm's Name

A firm's good name is one of its most valuable assets. If the firm has sold high-quality goods or provided superior service in the past, then its reputation serves as a signal to consumers that they can expect the same excellence in the future. Consequently, good managers work hard to maintain the firm's reputation so that its name remains a signal of quality.

What should a firm do if its good or service has been below par in the past so that it is poison to consumers? A manager of such a firm can spend a great deal of money trying to improve its reputation. However, a less expensive approach may be to change the firm's name, because having no reputation is better than having a bad one. In a more extreme case, the firm may exit the market. For example, Cabral and Hortacsu (2010) reported that sellers on eBay are likely to stop selling on the site after receiving their first negative feedback.

McDevitt (2011) found that the more complaints that the Better Business Bureau received about a plumbing firm in Illinois, the more likely that firm was to change its name or exit the industry.[6] Firms that extensively advertised were more likely to change their names than to exit. Finally, all else the same, firms in smaller cities outside of Chicago were 49% less likely to change their names than firms within metro Chicago. Presumably it is more difficult to shake a bad reputation just by changing names in a small town than in a large city.

Because shady operators can simply change the names of their businesses, some consumer advocates have called for making name changes more difficult. The U.S. Government Accountability Office found that at least 9% of motor coach carriers that were ordered "out of service" by the Federal Motor Carrier Safety Administration for violating safety standards merely changed their names, undermining the effectiveness of such regulatory bodies.

Signaling An informed party may signal the uninformed party to eliminate adverse selection. However, signals solve the adverse selection problem only when the recipients view them as credible. Smart consumers may place little confidence in a firm's unsubstantiated claims. Would you believe that a used car runs well just because an ad tells you so?

If only high-quality firms find it worthwhile to send a signal, then a signal is credible. Producers of high-quality goods often try to signal to consumers that their products are of better quality than those of their rivals. If consumers believe their signals, these firms can charge higher prices for their goods.

---

[6]Controlling for other factors, a firm with a record of complaints one standard deviation above the mean was 133% more likely to change its name or exit.

But if the signals are to be effective, they must be credible. A firm may, for example, distribute a favorable report on its product by an independent testing agency to try to convince buyers that its product is of high quality. If low-quality firms cannot obtain such a report from a reliable independent testing agency, consumers believe this signal.

A warranty may serve as both a signal and a guarantee. It is less expensive for the manufacturer of a reliable product to offer a warranty than it is for a firm that produces low-quality products. Consequently, if one firm offers a warranty and another does not, then a consumer may infer that the firm with the warranty produces a superior product. Of course, sleazy firms may try to imitate high-quality firms by offering a warranty that they do not intend to honor.

An applicant for life insurance could have a physical examination and then present an insurance company with a written statement from the doctor as a signal of good health. If only people who believe that they can show that they are better than others want to send a signal, insurance companies may rely upon it. However, an insurance company may not trust such a signal if it is easy for people to find unscrupulous doctors who will report falsely that they are in good health. Here screening by the insurance company using its own doctors may work better because the information is more credible.

Application

Adverse Selection on eBay Motors

Because consumers can't see a good before buying it over the Internet, it's easy for a shady seller to misrepresent its quality. In the worst-case lemons-market scenario, low-quality goods drive out high-quality goods. We'd expect adverse selection to be particularly bad on eBay Motors, the largest used car marketplace in the United States, where nearly 50,000 cars are sold each month. Three-quarters of the cars are sold to out-of-state buyers, so most people cannot examine the car before bidding.

Sellers' reputations and warranties are of limited help. Although eBay posts reviews from past customers, most sellers have limited records except for dealers, who sell only 30% of the cars. Usually only dealers offer warranties, and then on only some cars.

However, enforceable contracts and sellers' signals reduce adverse selection on eBay Motors. The disclosures on eBay's Web page create an enforceable contract. If the car doesn't live up to the claims, buyers can refuse to pay on delivery. In addition, outright lies are fraudulent and may be prosecuted. (In contrast, in most private sales between individuals, buyers do not have an enforceable contract.)

Each Web page contains some standard, mandatory information such as car make, model, and mileage. But most sellers signal by voluntarily disclosing additional information ("the car has no rust, scratches, or dents") and post photos, graphics, and videos. The typical Web page has 17 photos.

Sellers disclose more information for high-quality cars than for lemons. All else the same, a seller who posts 10 photos rather than 9 sells a car for 1.54% more, about $171 on average (Lewis, 2011).

Third-Party Information In some markets, consumer groups, nonprofit organizations, and government agencies provide buyers with information about the quality of different goods and services. If this information is credible, it can reduce adverse selection by enabling consumers to avoid buying low-quality goods or paying less for poorer quality products.

For an outside organization to provide believable information, it must convince consumers that it is trustworthy. Consumers Union, which publishes the product evaluation guide *Consumer Reports*, tries to establish its trustworthiness by refusing to accept advertising or other payments from firms.

Auditing is another important example of third-party assessment, in which an independent accounting firm assesses the financial statements of a firm or other organization. Sometimes a firm obtains an audit voluntarily to enhance its reputation (a signal). Sometimes audits are required as a condition of being listed on a particular exchange or of participating in a particular transaction, and sometimes audits are required by law (screening).

Many local governments require that home sellers disclose all important facts about the home to potential buyers such as the age of the home and any known defects in the electrical work or plumbing. By doing so, these governments protect buyers against adverse selection due to undisclosed defects.

Governments, consumer groups, industry groups, and others also provide information by establishing a **standard**: a metric or scale for evaluating the quality of a particular product. For example, the R-value of insulation—a standard—tells how effectively insulation works. Consumers learn of a brand's quality through **certification**: a report that a particular product meets or exceeds a given standard.

Many industry groups set their own standards and get an outside group or firm, such as Underwriters Laboratories (UL) or Factory Mutual Engineering Corporation (FMEC), to certify that their products meet specified standard levels. For example, by setting standards for the size of the thread on a screw, we ensure that screws work in products regardless of brand.

When standard and certification programs inexpensively and completely inform consumers about the relative quality of all goods in a market and do not restrict the goods available, the programs are socially desirable. However, some of these programs have harmful effects for two reasons.

First, standard and certification programs that provide imprecise information may mislead consumers. Some standards use only a high- versus low-quality rating even though quality varies continuously. Such standards encourage the manufacturing of products that have either the lowest possible quality (and cost of production) or the minimum quality level necessary to obtain the top rating.

Second, if standard and certification programs restrict salable goods and services to those that are certified, such programs may also have anticompetitive effects. For example, many governments license only professionals and craftspeople who meet some minimum standards. People without a license are not allowed to practice their profession or craft (See the Application "Occupational Licensing" in Chapter 2). The license drives up the price because the average quality of workers is higher and because competition by lower-skilled workers has been eliminated. As a result, welfare may go up or down, depending on whether the increased-quality effect or the higher-price effect dominates. Whether such restrictions can be set properly and cost-effectively by government agencies is widely debated.

standard
a metric or scale for evaluating the quality of a particular product

certification
a report that a particular product meets or exceeds a given standard

19.3 Price Discrimination Due to False Beliefs About Quality

We've seen that bad products can drive out good products if consumers cannot distinguish lemons from good-quality products at the time of purchase. The market outcome also changes if consumers falsely believe that identical products differ in quality. Consumers pay more for a product that they believe is of higher quality.

If some consumers know that two products are identical while others believe that they differ in quality, a firm can profitably price discriminate. The firm takes advantage of the less-informed customers by charging them a high price for the allegedly superior product. The firm does not want to charge informed customers this same high price. Doing so would reduce profit because the resulting fall in sales would be greater than the gain from the higher price on sales that are made.

Asymmetric information on the part of some, but not all, consumers makes price discrimination possible. However, if all customers are informed or all are uninformed about the quality of different products, firms charge a single price.

By intentionally increasing consumer uncertainty, a firm may be better able to exploit ignorant consumers and earn a higher profit (Salop, 1977). One way in which firms confuse consumers is to create *noise* by selling virtually the same product under various brand names. A *noisy monopoly* may be able to sell a product under its own brand name at a relatively high price and supply grocery or discount stores with a virtually identical product that is sold at a lower price under a *private-label* (house or store) brand. For example, a single firm produces Prego spaghetti sauce and similar house brands for various grocery stores.

If some consumers know that two products are identical while others believe that their qualities differ, a firm can engage in a special type of price discrimination (Chapter 12). For example, a food manufacturer may take advantage of less-informed customers by charging a higher price for the allegedly superior national brand while informed customers buy a less expensive but equally good private-label brand.

Brand proliferation pays if the cost of producing multiple brands is relatively low and the share of consumers who are willing to buy the higher-price product is relatively large. Otherwise, the firm makes a higher profit by selling a single product at a moderate price than by selling one brand at a low price and another at a high price.

Application

Reducing Consumers' Information

By selling the same product under more than one brand name, firms can charge ignorant consumers higher prices. For decades, outside firms have manufactured products that Sears, Roebuck & Company sells under its house brand names, Kenmore, Die-Hard, and Craftsman. Amana refrigerators are sold under their own brand name and under the Kenmore brand name. Similarly, Whirlpool sells its own washers and driers, but Sears also markets these products under the Kenmore name. Sears also places its label on Caloric, Frigidaire, GE, Gibson, Jenn-Air, and Toshiba products.[7]

Frequently, the Kenmore product is identical to or even superior to the brand-name product and costs less. Knowledgeable consumers realizing that the two brands are identical except for the label buy the Sears brand at the lower price. But customers who falsely believe that the name brand is better than the Kenmore product pay more for the name brand.

Over time, as consumers have become familiar with private-label brands and recognized their quality, private-label products have rapidly gained market share. According to the Private Label Manufacturers Association's 2012 *International Private Label Yearbook*, the private-label share of relevant products was 53% of the market in Switzerland, 49% in Spain, and over 40% in the United Kingdom and Germany. Private-label goods are not as popular in North America, but their share is growing and has reached 20% in both the United States and Canada. As a result of increased consumer knowledge about the quality of private-label brands, the advantage from maintaining multiple brands has diminished.

---

[7]Want to know which firm made the product you bought at Sears? Go to **www.applianceaid.com/searscodes.html**.

19.4 Market Power from Price Ignorance

We've just seen that consumer ignorance about quality can keep high-quality goods out of markets or lead to price discrimination. Consumer ignorance about how prices vary across firms has yet another effect: It gives firms market power. As a result, firms have an incentive to make it difficult for consumers to collect information about prices. For this reason, some stores won't quote prices over the phone, though the Internet has made hiding prices more difficult.

We now examine why asymmetric information about prices leads to noncompetitive pricing in a market that would otherwise be competitive. Suppose that many stores in a town sell the same good. If consumers have *full information* about prices, all stores charge the full-information competitive price, p^*. If one store were to raise its price above p^*, the store would lose all its business. Each store faces a residual demand curve that is horizontal at the going market price and has no market power.

In contrast, if consumers have *limited information* about the price that firms charge for a product, one store can charge more than others and not lose all its customers. Customers who do not know that the product is available for less elsewhere keep buying from the high-price store.[8] Thus, each store faces a downward-sloping residual demand curve and has some market power.

Tourist-Trap Model

We now show that, if the market has a single price, it is higher than p^*. You arrive in a small town near the site of the discovery of gold in California. Souvenir shops crowd the street. Wandering by one of these stores, you see that it sells the town's distinctive snowy: a plastic ball filled with water and imitation snow featuring a model of the Donner Party. You instantly decide that you must buy at least one of these tasteful mementos—perhaps more if the price is low enough. Your bus will leave very soon, so you can't check the price at each shop to find the lowest price. Moreover, determining which shop has the lowest price won't be useful to you in the future because you do not intend to return anytime soon.

Let's assume that you and the many other tourists have a guidebook that reports how many souvenir shops charge each possible price for the snowy, but the guidebook does not state the price at any particular shop.[9] You and the other tourists have identical demand functions.

It costs each tourist c in time and expenses to visit a shop to check the price or buy a snowy. Thus, if the price is p, the cost of buying a snowy at the first shop you visit is $p + c$. If you go to two souvenir shops before buying at the second shop, the cost of the snowy is $p + 2c$.

When Price Is Not Competitive Will all souvenir shops charge the same price? If so, what price will they charge? We start by considering whether each shop charges the full-information, competitive price, p^*.

---

[8]A grave example concerns the ripping-off of the dying and their relatives. A cremation arranged through a memorial society—which typically charges a nominal enrollment fee of $10 to $25—often costs half or less than the same service when it is arranged through a mortuary (**articles.moneycentral.msn.com/RetirementandWills/PlanYourEstate/HowToPlanAFuneral.aspx? page=all**, September 18, 2007). Consumers who know about memorial societies—which get competitive bids from mortuaries—can obtain a relatively low price.

[9]We make this assumption about the guidebook to keep the presentation as simple as possible. This assumption is not necessary to obtain the following result.

The full-information, competitive price is the equilibrium price only if no firm has an incentive to charge a different price. No firm would charge less than p^*, which equals marginal cost, because it would lose money on each sale.

However, a firm could gain by charging a higher price than p^*, so p^* is *not* an equilibrium price. If all other shops charge p^*, a firm can profitably charge $p_1 = p^* + \varepsilon$, where ε, a small positive number, is the shop's price markup. Suppose that you walk into this shop and learn that it sells the snowy for p_1. You know from your guidebook that all other souvenir shops charge only p^*. You say to yourself, "How unfortunate [or other words to that effect], I've wandered into the only expensive shop in town." Annoyed, you consider going elsewhere. Nonetheless, you do not go to another shop if this shop's markup, $\varepsilon = p_1 - p^*$, is less than c, the cost of going to another shop.

As a result, it pays for this shop to raise its price by an amount that is just slightly less than the cost of an additional search, thereby deviating from the proposed equilibrium where all other shops charge p^*. Thus, *if consumers have limited information about price, an equilibrium in which all firms charge the full-information, competitive price is impossible.*

Monopoly Price We've seen that the market price cannot be lower than or equal to the full-information, competitive price. Is an equilibrium in which all stores charge the same price and that price is higher than the competitive price possible? In particular, can we have an equilibrium when all shops charge $p_1 = p^* + \varepsilon$? No, shops would deviate from this proposed equilibrium for the same reason that they deviated from charging the competitive price. A shop can profitably raise its price to $p_2 = p_1 + \varepsilon = p^* + 2\varepsilon$. Again, it does not pay for a tourist who is unlucky enough to enter that shop to go to another shop as long as $\varepsilon < c$. Thus, p_1 is not the equilibrium price. By repeating this reasoning, we can reject other possible equilibrium prices that are above p^* and less than the monopoly price, p_m.

However, the monopoly price may be an equilibrium price. No firm wants to raise its price above the monopoly level because its profit would fall due to reduced sales. When tourists learn the price at a particular souvenir shop, they decide how many snowies to buy. If the price is set too high, the shop's lost sales more than offset the higher price, so its profit falls. Thus, although the shop can charge a higher price without losing all its sales, it chooses not to do so.

The only remaining question is whether a shop would like to charge a lower price than p_m if all other shops charge that price. If not, p_m is an equilibrium price.

Should a shop reduce its price below p_m by less than c? If it does so, it does not pay for consumers to search for this low-price firm. The shop makes less on each sale, so its profits must fall. Thus, a shop should not deviate by charging a price that is only slightly less than p_m.

Does it pay for a shop to drop its price below p_m by more than c? If the market has few stores, consumers may search for this low-price shop. Although the shop makes less per sale than the high-price shops, its profits may be higher because of greater sales volume. However, in a market with many stores, consumers do not search for the low-price shop because their chances of finding it are low. As a result, when the presence of a large number of shops makes searching for a low-price shop impractical, no firm lowers its price, so p_m is the equilibrium price. Thus, *when consumers have asymmetric information and when search costs and the number of firms are large, the only possible single-price equilibrium is at the monopoly price.*

If the single-price equilibrium at p_m can be broken by a firm charging a low price, no single-price equilibrium is possible. Either no equilibrium exists or the equilibrium has prices that vary across shops (see Stiglitz, 1979, or Carlton and Perloff, 2005). Multiple-price equilibria are common.

Solved Problem 19.3

Initially, the market has many souvenir shops, each of which charges p_m (because consumers do not know the shops' prices), and buyers' search costs are c. If the government pays for half of consumers' search costs, is a single-price equilibrium at a price less than p_m possible?

Answer

Show that the argument we used to reject a single-price equilibrium at any price except the monopoly price did not depend on the size of the search cost. If all other stores charge any single price p, where $p^* \leq p < p_m$, a firm profits from raising its price. As long as it raises its price by no more than $c/2$ (the new search cost to a consumer), unlucky consumers who stop at this deviant store do not search further. This profitable deviation shows that the proposed single-price equilibrium is not an equilibrium. Again, the only possible single-price equilibrium is at p_m.[10]

Advertising and Prices

The U.S. Federal Trade Commission (FTC), a consumer protection agency, opposes groups that want to forbid price advertising; the FTC argues that advertising about price benefits consumers. If a firm informs consumers about its unusually low price, it may be able to gain enough extra customers to more than offset its loss from the lower price. If low-price stores advertise their prices and attract many customers, they can break the monopoly-price equilibrium that occurs when consumers must search store by store for low prices. The more successful the advertising, the larger these stores grow and the lower the average price in the market. If enough consumers become informed, all stores may charge the low price. Thus, without advertising, no store may find it profitable to charge low prices, but with advertising, all stores may charge low prices. See MyEconLab, Chapter 19, "Advertising Lowers Prices."

19.5 Problems Arising from Ignorance When Hiring

Asymmetric information is frequently a problem in labor markets. Prospective employees may have less information about working conditions than firms do—a question we raised in the Challenge at the beginning of the chapter and address at the end. Conversely, firms may have less information about potential employees' abilities than the workers do.

Information asymmetries in labor markets lower welfare below the full-information level. Workers may signal and firms may screen to reduce the asymmetry in information about workers' abilities. In this section, we consider situations in which workers have more information about their ability than firms do. We look first at inexpensive signals sent by workers, then at expensive signals sent by workers, and finally at screening by firms.

---

[10]If the search cost is low enough, however, the single-price equilibrium at p_m can be broken profitably by charging a low price so that only a multiple-price equilibrium is possible. If the search cost falls to zero, consumers have full information, so the only possible equilibrium is at the full-information, competitive price.

Cheap Talk

Honesty is the best policy—when there is money in it. —Mark Twain

cheap talk
unsubstantiated claims
or statements

When an informed person voluntarily provides information to an uninformed person, the informed person engages in **cheap talk**: unsubstantiated claims or statements (see Farrell and Rabin, 1996). People use cheap talk to distinguish themselves or their attributes at low cost. Even though informed people may lie when it suits them, it is often in their and everyone else's best interest for them to tell the truth. Nothing stops me from advertising that I have a chimpanzee for sale, but doing so serves no purpose if I actually want to sell my DVD player. One advantage of cheap talk, if it is effective, is that it is a less expensive method of signaling ability to a potential employer than paying to have that ability tested.

Suppose that a firm plans to hire Cyndi to do one of two jobs. The demanding job requires someone with high ability. The undemanding job can be done better by someone of low ability because the job bores more able people, who then perform poorly.

Cyndi knows whether her ability level is high or low, but the firm is unsure. It initially thinks that either level is equally likely. Panel a of Table 19.1 shows the payoffs to Cyndi and the firm under various possibilities.[11] If Cyndi has high ability, she enjoys the demanding job: Her payoff is 3. If she has low ability, she finds the

Table 19.1 Employee–Employer Payoffs

(a) *When Cheap Talk Works*

		Job That the Firm Gives to Cyndi	
		Demanding	Undemanding
Cyndi's Ability	High	3 ⟍ 2	1 ⟍ 1
	Low	1 ⟍ 1	2 ⟍ 4

(b) *When Cheap Talk Fails*

		Job That the Firm Gives to Cyndi	
		Demanding	Undemanding
Cyndi's Ability	High	3 ⟍ 2	1 ⟍ 1
	Low	3 ⟍ 1	2 ⟍ 4

---

[11]Previously, we used a 2 × 2 matrix to show a simultaneous-move game in which both parties choose an action at the same time. Here only the firm can make a move. Cyndi does not take an action, because she cannot choose her ability level.

demanding job too stressful—her payoff is only 1—but she can handle the undemanding job. The payoff to the firm is greater if Cyndi is properly matched to the job: She is given the demanding job if she has high ability and the undemanding job if she has low ability.

We can view this example as a two-stage game. In the first stage, Cyndi tells the firm something. In the second stage, the firm decides which job she gets.

Cyndi could make many possible statements about her ability. For simplicity, we assume that she says either "My ability is high" or "My ability is low." This two-stage game has an equilibrium in which Cyndi tells the truth and the firm, believing her, assigns her to the appropriate job. If she claims to have high ability, the firm gives her the demanding job.

If the firm reacts to her cheap talk in this manner, Cyndi has no incentive to lie. If she did lie, the firm would make a mistake, and a mistake would be bad for both parties. Cyndi and the firm want the same outcomes, so cheap talk works.

However, in many other situations, cheap talk does not work. Given the payoffs in panel b, Cyndi and the firm do not want the same outcomes. The firm still wants Cyndi in the demanding job if she has high ability and in the undemanding job otherwise. But Cyndi wants the demanding job regardless of her ability. So she claims to have high ability regardless of the truth. Knowing her incentives, the firm views her statement as meaningless babbling—her statement does not change the firm's view that her ability is equally likely to be high or low.

Given that belief, the firm gives her the undemanding job, for which its expected payoff is higher. The firm's expected payoff is $(\frac{1}{2} \times 1) + (\frac{1}{2} \times 4) = 2.5$ if it gives her the undemanding job and $(\frac{1}{2} \times 2) + (\frac{1}{2} \times 1) = 1.5$ if it assigns her to the demanding job. Thus, given the firm's asymmetric information, the outcome is inefficient if Cyndi has high ability.

When the interests of the firm and the individual diverge, cheap talk does not provide a credible signal. Here an individual has to send a more expensive signal to be believed. We now examine such a signal.

Education as a Signal

No doubt you've been told that one good reason to go to college is to get a good job. Going to college may get you a better job because you obtain valuable training. Another possibility is that a college degree may land you a good job because it serves as a signal to employers about your ability. If high-ability people are more likely to go to college than low-ability people, schooling signals ability to employers (Spence, 1974).

To illustrate how such signaling works, we'll make the extreme assumptions that graduating from an appropriate school serves as the signal and that schooling provides no training that is useful to firms (Stiglitz, 1975). High-ability workers are θ share of the workforce, and low-ability workers are $1 - \theta$ share. The value of output that a high-ability worker produces for a firm is worth w_h, and that of a low-ability worker is w_l (over their careers). If competitive employers knew workers' ability levels, they would pay this value of the marginal product to each worker, so a high-ability worker receives w_h and a low-ability worker earns w_l.

We assume that employers cannot directly determine a worker's skill level. For example, when production is a group effort—such as in an assembly line—a firm cannot determine the productivity of a single employee.

Two types of equilibria are possible, depending on whether or not employers can distinguish high-ability workers from others. If employers have no way of telling

pooling equilibrium
an equilibrium in which dissimilar people are treated (paid) alike or behave alike

workers apart, the outcome is a **pooling equilibrium**: Dissimilar people are treated (paid) alike or behave alike. Employers pay all workers the average wage:

$$\overline{w} = \theta w_h + (1 - \theta)w_l. \tag{19.2}$$

Risk-neutral, competitive firms expect to break even because they underpay high-ability people by enough to offset the losses from overpaying low-ability workers.

We assume that high-ability individuals can get a degree by spending c to attend a school and that low-ability people cannot graduate from the school (or that the cost of doing so is prohibitively high). If high-ability people graduate and low-ability people do not, a degree is a signal of ability to employers. Given such a clear signal, the outcome is a **separating equilibrium**: One type of people takes actions (such as sending a signal) that allow them to be differentiated from other types of people. Here a successful signal causes high-ability workers to receive w_h and the others to receive w_l, so wages vary with ability.

separating equilibrium
an equilibrium in which one type of people takes actions (such as sending a signal) that allows them to be differentiated from other types of people

We now examine whether a pooling or a separating equilibrium is possible. We consider whether anyone would want to change behavior in an equilibrium. If no one wants to change, the equilibrium is feasible.

Separating Equilibrium In a separating equilibrium, high-ability people pay c to get a degree and are employed at a wage of w_h, while low-ability individuals do not get a degree and work for a wage of w_l. The low-ability people have no choice, as they can't get a degree. High-ability individuals have the option of not going to school. Without a degree, however, they are viewed as low ability once hired, and they receive w_l. If they go to school, their net earnings are $w_h - c$. Thus, it pays for a high-ability person to go to school if

$$w_h - c > w_l.$$

Rearranging terms in this expression, we find that a high-ability person chooses to get a degree if

$$w_h - w_l > c. \tag{19.3}$$

Equation 19.3 says that the benefit from graduating, the extra pay $w_h - w_l$, exceeds the cost of schooling, c. If Equation 19.3 holds, no worker wants to change behavior, so a separating equilibrium is feasible.

Suppose that $c = \$15,000$ and that high-ability workers are twice as productive as others: $w_h = \$40,000$ and $w_l = \$20,000$. Here the benefit to a high-ability worker from graduating, $w_h - w_l = \$20,000$, exceeds the cost by $5,000. Thus, no one wants to change behavior in this separating equilibrium.

Pooling Equilibrium In a pooling equilibrium, all workers are paid the average wage from Equation 19.2, $\overline{w}$. Again, because low-ability people cannot graduate, they have no choice. A high-ability person must choose whether or not to go to school. Without a degree, that individual is paid the average wage. With a degree, the worker is paid w_h. It does not pay for the high-ability person to graduate if the benefit from graduating, the extra pay $w_h - \overline{w}$, is less than the cost of schooling:

$$w_h - \overline{w} < c. \tag{19.4}$$

Thus, if Equation 19.4 holds, no worker wants to change behavior, so a pooling equilibrium persists.

For example, if $w_h = \$40{,}000$, $w_l = \$20{,}000$, and $\theta = \tfrac{1}{2}$, then

$$\overline{w} = (\tfrac{1}{2} \times \$40{,}000) + (\tfrac{1}{2} \times \$20{,}000) = \$30{,}000.$$

If the cost of going to school is $c = \$15{,}000$, the benefit to a high-ability person from graduating, $w_h - \overline{w} = \$10{,}000$, is less than the cost, so a high-ability individual does not want to go school. As a result, a pooling equilibrium occurs.

Solved Problem 19.4

For what values of θ is a pooling equilibrium possible in general? In particular, if $c = \$15{,}000$, $w_h = \$40{,}000$, and $w_l = \$20{,}000$, for what values of θ is a pooling equilibrium possible?

Answer

1. *Determine the values of θ for which it pays for a high-ability person to go to school.* From Equation 19.4, we know that a high-ability individual does not go to school if $w_h - \overline{w} < c$. Using Equation 19.2, we substitute for $\overline{w}$ in Equation 19.4 and rearrange terms to find that high-ability people do not go to school if $w_h - [\theta w_h + (1 - \theta)w_l] < c$, or

$$\theta > 1 - \frac{c}{w_h - w_l}. \tag{19.5}$$

If almost everyone has high ability, so θ is large, a high-ability person does not go to school. The intuition is that, as the share of high-ability workers, θ, gets large (close to 1), the average wage approaches w_h (Equation 19.2), so the benefit, $w_h - \overline{w}$, in going to school is small.

2. *Solve for the possible values of θ for the specific parameters.* If we substitute $c = \$15{,}000$, $w_h = \$40{,}000$, and $w_l = \$20{,}000$ into Equation 19.5, we find that high-ability people do not go to school—a pooling equilibrium is possible—if $\theta > \tfrac{1}{4}$.

Unique or Multiple Equilibria Depending on differences in abilities, the cost of schooling, and the share of high-ability workers, only one type of equilibrium may be possible or both may be possible. In the following examples, using Figure 19.2, $w_h = \$40{,}000$ and $w_l = \$20{,}000$.

Only a pooling equilibrium is possible if schooling is very costly: $c > w_h - w_l = \$20{,}000$, so Equation 19.3 does not hold. A horizontal line in Figure 19.2 shows where $c = w_h - w_l = \$20{,}000$. Only a pooling equilibrium is feasible above that line, $c > \$20{,}000$, because it does not pay for high-ability workers to go to school.

Equation 19.5 demonstrates that, with few high-ability people (relative to the cost and earnings differential), only a separating equilibrium is possible. The figure shows a sloped line where $\theta = 1 - c/(w_h - w_l)$. Below that line, where $\theta < 1 - c/(w_h - w_l)$, relatively few people have high ability, so the average wage, $\overline{w}$, is low. A pooling equilibrium is not possible because high-ability workers would want to signal. Thus, below this line, only a separating equilibrium is possible. Above this line, Equation 19.5 holds, so a pooling equilibrium is possible. (The answer to Solved Problem 19.4 shows that no one wants to change behavior in a pooling equilibrium if $c = \$15{,}000$ and $\theta > \tfrac{1}{4}$, which are points to the right of x in the figure, such as y.)

Figure 19.2 Pooling and Separating Equilibria

If firms know workers' abilities, high-ability workers are paid w_h = \$40,000 and low-ability workers get w_l = \$20,000. The type of equilibrium depends on the cost of schooling, c, and the share of high-ability workers, θ. If c > \$20,000, only a pooling equilibrium, in which everyone gets the average wage, is possible. If there are relatively few high-ability people, θ < 1 − c/\$20,000, only a separating equilibrium is possible. Between the horizontal and sloped lines, either type of equilibrium may occur.

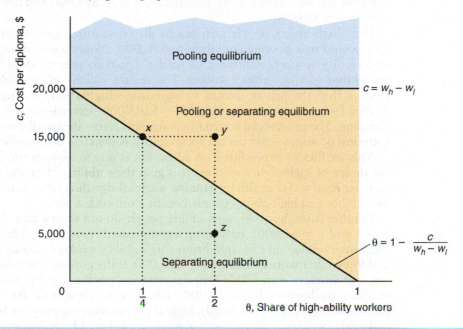

Below the horizontal line, where the cost of signaling is less than \$20,000 and above the sloped line, with relatively many high-ability workers, either equilibrium may occur. For example, where c = \$15,000 and $\theta = \frac{1}{2}$, Equations 19.3 and 19.4 (or equivalently, Equation 19.5) hold, so both a separating equilibrium and a pooling equilibrium are possible. In the pooling equilibrium, no one wants to change behavior, so this equilibrium is possible. Similarly, no one wants to change behavior in a separating equilibrium.

A government could ensure that one or the other of these equilibria occurs. It achieves a pooling equilibrium by banning schooling (and other possible signals). Alternatively, the government creates a separating equilibrium by subsidizing schooling for some high-ability people. Once some individuals start to signal, so that firms pay either a low or high wage (not a pooling wage), it pays for other high-ability people to signal.

Efficiency In our example of a separating equilibrium, high-ability people get an otherwise useless education solely to show that they differ from low-ability people. An education is privately useful to the high-ability workers if it serves as a signal that gets them higher net pay. In our extreme example, education is socially inefficient because it is costly and provides no useful training.

Signaling changes the distribution of wages: Instead of everyone getting the average wage, high-ability workers receive more pay than low-ability workers. Nonetheless, the total amount that firms pay is the same, so firms make zero expected profits in both equilibria.[12] Moreover, everyone is employed in both the pooling and the screening equilibrium, so total output is the same.

Nonetheless, everyone may be worse off in a separating equilibrium. At point y in Figure 19.2 ($w_h = \$40{,}000$, $w_l = \$20{,}000$, $c = \$15{,}000$, and $\theta = \frac{1}{2}$), either a pooling equilibrium or a separating equilibrium is possible. In the pooling equilibrium, each worker is paid $\overline{w} = \$30{,}000$ and no wasteful signaling occurs. In the separating equilibrium, high-ability workers make $w_h - c = \$25{,}000$ and low-ability workers make $w_l = \$20{,}000$.

Here high-ability people earn less in the separating equilibrium, $25{,}000$, than they would in a pooling equilibrium, $30{,}000$. Nonetheless, if anyone signals, all high-ability workers will want to send a signal to prevent their wage from falling to that of a low-ability worker. The reason socially undesirable signaling happens is that the private return to signaling—high-ability workers net an extra $\$5{,}000$ [$=(w_h - c) - w_l = \$25{,}000 - \$20{,}000$]—exceeds the net social return to signaling. The gross social return to the signal is zero—the signal changes only the distribution of wages—and the net social return is negative because the signal is costly.

This inefficient expenditure on education is due to asymmetric information and the desire of high-ability workers to signal their ability. Here the government can increase total social wealth by banning wasteful signaling (eliminate schooling). Both low-ability and high-ability people benefit from such a ban.

In other cases, however, high-ability people do not want a ban. At point z (where $\theta = \frac{1}{2}$ and $c = \$5{,}000$), only a separating equilibrium is possible without government intervention. In this equilibrium, high-ability workers earn $w_h - c = \$35{,}000$ and low-ability workers make $w_l = \$20{,}000$. If the government bans signaling, both types of workers earn $30{,}000$ in the resulting pooling equilibrium, so high-ability workers are harmed, losing $5{,}000$ each. So even though the ban raises efficiency (wasteful signaling is eliminated), high-ability workers oppose the ban.

In this example, efficiency can always be increased by banning signaling because signaling is unproductive. However, some signaling is socially efficient because it increases total output. Education may raise output because its signal results in a better matching of workers and jobs or because it provides useful training as well as serving as a signal. Education also may make people better citizens. In conclusion, *total social output falls with signaling if signaling is socially unproductive but may rise with signaling if signaling also raises productivity or serves some other desirable purpose.*

Empirical evidence on the importance of signaling is mixed. Tyler et al. (2000) found that, for the least-skilled high school dropouts, passing the General Educational Development (GED) equivalency credential (the equivalent of a high school diploma) increases white dropouts' earnings by 10% to 19% but has no statistically significant effect on minority dropouts.

Screening in Hiring

Firms screen prospective workers in many ways. An employer may base hiring on an individual's characteristic that the employer believes is correlated with ability, such as how a person dresses or speaks, or a firm may use a test. Further, some employers engage in *statistical discrimination*, believing that an individual's gender, race, religion, or ethnicity is a proxy for ability.

---

[12]Firms pay high-ability workers more than low-ability workers in a separating equilibrium, but the average amount they pay per worker is $\overline{w}$, the same as in a pooling equilibrium.

Most societies accept the use of interviews and tests by potential employers. Firms commonly use interviews and tests as screening devices to assess abilities. If such screening devices are accurate, the firm benefits by selecting superior workers and assigning them to appropriate tasks. However, as with signaling, these costly activities are inefficient if they do not increase output. In the United States, the use of hiring tests may be challenged and rejected by the courts if the employer cannot demonstrate that the tests accurately measure skills or abilities required on the job.

If employers think that people of a certain gender, race, religion, or ethnicity have higher ability on average than others, they may engage in *statistical discrimination* (Aigner and Cain, 1977) and hire only such people. Employers may engage in this practice even if they know that the correlation between these factors and ability is imperfect.

Figure 19.3 illustrates one employer's belief that members of Race 1 have, on average, lower ability than members of Race 2. The figure shows that the employer believes that some members of Race 1 have higher ability than some members of the second race: Part of the Race 1 curve lies to the right of part of the Race 2 curve. Still, because the employer believes that a group characteristic, race, is an (imperfect) indicator of individual ability, the employer hires only people of Race 2 if enough of them are available.

The employer may claim not to be prejudiced but to be concerned only with maximizing profit.[13] Nonetheless, this employer's actions harm members of Race 1 as much as they would if they were due to racial hatred.

It may be very difficult to eliminate statistical discrimination even though ability distributions are identical across races. If all employers share the belief that members

Figure 19.3 Statistical Discrimination

This figure shows the beliefs of an employer who thinks that people of Race 1 have less ability on average than people of Race 2. This employer hires only people of Race 2, even though the employer believes that some members of Race 1 have greater ability than some members of Race 2. Because this employer never employs members of Race 1, the employer may never learn that workers of both races have equal ability.

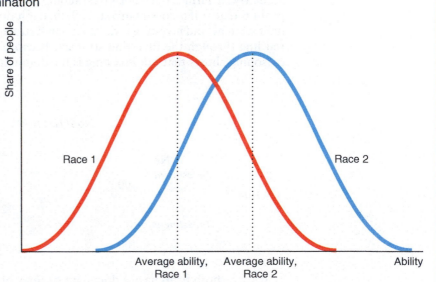

---

[13]Not all employment discrimination is due to statistical discrimination. Other common sources of discrimination are prejudice (Becker, 1971) and the exercise of monopsony power (Madden, 1973).

of Race 1 have such low ability that it is not worth hiring them, people of that race are never hired, so employers never learn that their beliefs are incorrect. Thus, false beliefs can persist indefinitely. Such discrimination lowers social output if it keeps skilled members of Race 1 from performing certain jobs.

However, statistical discrimination may be based on true differences between groups. For example, insurance companies offer lower auto insurance rates to young women than to young men because young men are more likely, *on average*, to have an accident. The companies report that this practice lowers their costs of providing insurance by reducing moral hazard. Nonetheless, this practice penalizes young men who are unusually safe drivers and benefits young women who are unusually reckless drivers.

Challenge Solution

Dying to Work

In the Challenge at the beginning of the chapter, we asked two questions: Does a firm underinvest in safety if it knows how dangerous a job is but potential employees do not? Can the government intervene to improve this situation?

Consider an industry with two firms that are simultaneously deciding whether to make costly safety investments such as sprinkler systems in a plant or escape tunnels in a mine. Unlike the firms, potential employees do not know how safe it is to work at each firm. They know only how risky it is to work in this industry. If only Firm 1 invests, workers in the industry do not know that safety has improved at only Firm 1's plant. Because the government's accident statistics for the industry fall, workers realize that it is safer to work in the industry, so both firms pay lower wages. Thus, one firm's safety investment provides an externality to the other firm.

A prisoners' dilemma game (Chapter 14) illustrates this result. The profit table shows how the firms' profits depend on their safety investments. Firm 1 has a dominant strategy. If Firm 2 invests (compare profits in the cells in the right column), Firm 1's *no investment* strategy has a higher profit, 250, than its *investment* strategy, 225. Similarly, if Firm 2 does not invest (compare the cells in the left column), Firm 1's profit is higher if it doesn't invest, 200, than if it does. Thus, not investing is the dominant strategy and investing is the dominated strategy, as is indicated by the horizontal red line through the investing strategy. Because the game is symmetric, the same reasoning shows that not investing is the dominant strategy for Firm 2 as well.

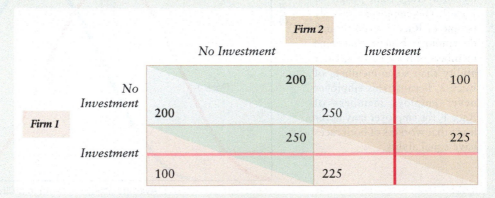

Because both firms have a dominant strategy of not investing, that combination of dominant strategies (the upper left cell) is the Nash equilibrium. Both firms receive an equilibrium profit of 200. If both firms invest in safety (the lower right cell), each earns 225, which is more than they earn in the Nash equilibrium. However, investment by both firms is not an equilibrium, because each firm can increase its profit from 225 to 250 by not investing if the other firm invests.

The firms underinvest in safety because each firm bears the full cost of its safety investments but derives only some of the benefits. In contrast, if workers knew how safe each firm is, only a firm that invests in safety would be able to pay a lower wage, which would change the profit table and increase the likelihood that the firms invest in safety.[14]

Thus, if the government or a union were to collect and provide workers with firm-specific safety information, the firms might invest. However, for the government or a union to provide this information, their cost of gathering the necessary information has to be relatively low.

Summary

Asymmetric information causes market failures when informed parties engage in opportunistic behavior at the expense of uninformed parties. Two types of problems arise from opportunism. Adverse selection occurs when someone with a characteristic that is hidden from other parties to a deal exploit this information to the detriment of the less informed. Moral hazard occurs when an informed party takes advantage of a less-informed party through a hidden action.

1. **Adverse Selection.** Adverse selection creates problems in insurance markets because people with low risk do not buy insurance, which drives up the price for high-risk people. Due to adverse selection not all desirable transactions take place. As a result, low-quality items tend to be overrepresented in transactions, as with the lemons problem associated with used cars and many other products. Bad products may drive good products out of the market.

2. **Reducing Adverse Selection.** Methods for dealing with adverse selection problems include laws limiting the ability of informed parties to exploit their private information, consumer screening (such as by using experts or relying on firms' reputations), signaling by firms (including establishing brand names and providing guarantees or warranties), and the provision of information by third parties such as government agencies or consumer groups.

3. **Price Discrimination Due to False Beliefs About Quality.** Firms may price discriminate if some consumers incorrectly think that quality varies across identical products. Because only some consumers collect information about quality, only those consumers know whether the quality differs between products in some markets. Firms can exploit ignorant consumers by creating noise: selling the same good under two different brand names at different prices.

4. **Market Power from Price Ignorance.** If consumers do not know how prices vary across firms, a firm can raise its price without losing all its customers. As a consequence, consumers' ignorance about price creates market power. In a market that would be competitive with full information, consumer ignorance about price may lead to a monopoly price or a distribution of prices.

5. **Problems Arising from Ignorance When Hiring.** Companies use signaling and screening to try to eliminate information asymmetries in hiring. Where prospective employees and firms share common interests—such as assigning the right worker to the right task—everyone benefits from eliminating the information asymmetry by having informed job candidates honestly tell the firms—through *cheap talk*—about their abilities. When the two parties do not share common interests, cheap talk does not work. Potential employees may inform employers about their abilities by using expensive signals such as a college degree. If these signals are unproductive (as when education serves only as a signal and provides no training), they may be privately beneficial but socially harmful. If the signals are productive (as when education provides training or leads to greater output due to more

---

[14]Because this information is a public good (Chapter 18), others may obtain this information if the firm provides it to employees. The cost to the firm of having others, such as government regulators (who fine firms for accidents and transgressions), obtain this information may exceed the lower-wage benefit from providing it to workers.

fitting job assignments), they may be both privately and socially beneficial. Firms may also screen. Job interviews, objective tests, and other screening devices that lead to a better matching of workers and jobs may be socially beneficial. Screening by statistical discrimination, however, is harmful to discriminated-against groups. Employers who discriminate on the basis of a particular group characteristic may never learn that their discrimination is based on false beliefs because they never test these beliefs.

Questions

*All questions are available on MyEconLab; * = answer appears at the back of this book;* **A** *= algebra problem.*

1. Adverse Selection

1.1 According to a 2007 study by the Federal Trade Commission, 4.8 million U.S. consumers were victims of weight-loss fraud, ranging from a tea that promised to help people shed pounds to fraudulent clinical trials and fat-dissolving injections. Do these frauds illustrate adverse selection or moral hazard?

1.2 Suppose that half the population is healthy and the other half is unhealthy. If an insured healthy person gets sick, the full cost to the insurance company is $1,000. If an insured unhealthy person gets sick, the cost to the insurance company is $10,000. In a given year, any one person (healthy or unhealthy) has a 40% chance of getting sick. People know whether they are healthy but the insurance company does not. The insurance company offers complete, actuarially fair insurance at the same price to everyone. The insurance company covers all medical expenses of its policyholders, and its expected profit is zero.

   a. If everyone purchases insurance, what is the price of the insurance?

   b. If only unhealthy people purchase insurance, what is the price of the insurance?

   c. If each person has the option of buying insurance, explain why adverse selection might be expected unless healthy people are highly risk averse. **A**

1.3 You want to determine whether the market for single-engine airplanes has a lemons problem. Can you use any of the following information to help answer this question? If so, how?

   a. Repair rates for original-owner planes versus planes that have been resold

   b. The fraction of planes resold in each year after purchase

1.4 If you buy a new car and try to sell it in the first year—indeed, in the first few days after you buy it—the price that you get is substantially less than the original price. Use the lemons model to give one explanation for why.

1.5 Use the lemons model to explain why restaurants that cater to tourists are likely to serve low-quality meals. Tourists will not return to this area, and they have no information about the relative quality of the food at various restaurants, but they can determine the relative price by looking at menus posted outside each restaurant.

1.6 What are the answers to Solved Problem 19.1 if customers are willing to pay $10,000 for a good used car?

*1.7 Many buyers value high-quality used cars at the full-information market price of p_1 and lemons at p_2. A limited number of potential sellers value high-quality cars at $v_1 \le p_1$ and lemons at $v_2 \le p_2$. Everyone is risk neutral. The share of lemons among all the used cars that might potentially be sold is θ. Under what conditions are all cars sold? When are only lemons sold? Under what conditions (if any) are no cars sold? (*Hint*: See Solved Problem 19.1.) **A**

1.8 Suppose that the buyers in the previous question incur a transaction cost of $800 to purchase a car. This transaction cost is the value of their time to find a car. What is the equilibrium? Is it possible that no cars are sold? (*Hint*: See Solved Problem 19.1.) **A**

1.9 In Solved Problem 19.2, show that, if all the other firms were producing a high-quality wallet, it would pay for one firm to start producing a low-quality wallet. **A**

1.10 In Solved Problem 19.2, would any of the firms produce high-quality wallets if the cost of producing a higher-quality wallet was only $11? Explain. **A**

1.11 It costs $12 to produce a low-quality electric stapler and $16 to produce a high-quality stapler. Consumers cannot distinguish good staplers from poor staplers when they make their purchases. Four firms produce staplers. Consumers value staplers at their cost of production and are risk neutral. Will any of the four firms be able to produce high-quality staplers without making losses? What happens if consumers are willing to pay $36 for high-quality staplers? (*Hint*: See Solved Problem 19.2.) **A**

1.12 In the world of French high cuisine, a three-star rating from the Michelin Red Guide is a widely accepted indicator of gastronomic excellence. French consumers consider Gault Milleau, another restaurant guide, not as authoritative as the Michelin guide because Gault Milleau, unlike Michelin, accepts advertising and its critics accept free meals (William Echikson, "Wish Upon a Star," *Wall Street Journal*, February 28, 2003, A8).

  a. Why are guides' ratings important to restaurant owners and chefs? Discuss the effect of a restaurant's rating on the demand for the restaurant.

  b. Why do advertising and free meals taint the credibility of Gault Milleau? Discuss the moral hazard problem of Gault Milleau's ratings.

  c. If advertising and free meals taint the credibility of Gault Milleau, why does the guide accept advertising and free meals?

2. Reducing Adverse Selection

2.1 Some states prohibit insurance companies from using car owners' home addresses to set auto insurance rates. Why do insurance companies use home addresses? What are the efficiency and equity implications of forbidding such practices?

*2.2 The state of California set up its own earthquake insurance program for homeowners. The rates vary by ZIP code, depending on the proximity of the nearest fault line. However, critics claim that the people who set the rates ignored soil type. Some houses rest on bedrock; others sit on unstable soil. What are the implications of such rate setting?

*2.3 A firm spends a great deal of money in advertising to inform consumers of the brand name of its mushrooms. Should consumers conclude that its mushrooms are likely to be of higher quality than unbranded mushrooms? Why or why not?

2.4 According to Edelman (2011), the widely used online "trust" authorities issue certifications without adequate verification, giving rise to adverse selection. Edelman finds that TRUSTe-certified sites are more than twice as likely to be untrustworthy as uncertified sites. Explain why.

3. Price Discrimination Due to False Beliefs About Quality

3.1 Explain how a monopoly firm can price discriminate by advertising sales in newspapers or magazines that only some of its customers see. Is it a noisy monopoly?

3.2 The "Reducing Consumers' Information" Application notes that a food manufacturer may sell a national brand product for more than an identical private-label product. Is the firm a noisy monopoly (or oligopoly)?

3.3 Sometimes a firm sells the same product under two brand names at different prices. For example, although the Chevy Tahoe and the GMC Yukon are virtually twins, the 2014 Yukon sells for $1,355 more than the 2014 Tahoe. Give an asymmetric information explanation as to why the firm might use pairs of brand names and why one product might sell for more than the other.

4. Market Power from Price Ignorance

*4.1 In Solved Problem 19.3, if the vast majority of all consumers know the true prices at all stores and only a few shoppers have to incur a search cost to learn the prices, would firms set a single-price equilibrium price at the monopoly level, p_m?

4.2 The Federal Trade Commission objected to the California Dental Association's prohibitions against its members engaging in advertising about prices, calling them restraints on trade. What effect should such restraints have on equilibrium prices?

5. Problems Arising from Ignorance When Hiring

5.1 Suppose that you are given w_h, w_l, and θ in the signaling model in the chapter. For what value of c are both a pooling equilibrium and a separating equilibrium possible? For what value of c are both types of equilibria possible and do high-ability workers have higher net earnings in a separating equilibrium than in a pooling equilibrium? (*Hint*: See Solved Problem 19.4.) **A**

5.2 Education is a continuous variable, where e_h is the years of schooling of a high-ability worker and e_l is the years of schooling of a lower-ability worker. The cost per period of education for these types of workers is c_h and c_l, respectively, where $c_l > c_h$. The wages they receive if employers can tell them apart are w_h and w_l. Under what conditions is a separating equilibrium possible? How much education will each type of worker get?

5.3 In Question 5.2, under what conditions is a pooling equilibrium possible? **A**

5.4 In Questions 5.2 and 5.3, describe the equilibrium if $c_l \leq c_h$. **A**

5.5 Certain universities do not give letter grades. One rationale is that eliminating the letter-grade system reduces the pressure on students, thus enabling them to do better in school. Why might this policy help or hurt students?

5.6 In the ability signaling model, suppose that firms can pay c^* to have a worker's ability determined through a test. Does it pay for a firm to make this expenditure?

5.7 When is statistical discrimination privately inefficient? When is it socially inefficient? Does it always harm members of the discriminated-against group?

5.8 Some firms are willing to hire only high school graduates. On the basis of past experience or statistical evidence, these companies believe that high school graduates perform better than nongraduates, on average. How does this hiring behavior compare to statistical discrimination by employers on the basis of race or gender? Discuss the equity and efficiency implications of this practice.

6. Challenge

6.1 Can you change the payoffs in the table in the Challenge Solution so that the firms choose to invest in safety? Explain. **A**

6.2 What is the minimum fine that the government could levy on firms that do not invest in safety that would lead to a Nash equilibrium in which both firms invest? **A**

Contracts and Moral Hazards

20

The contracts of at least 33 major league baseball players have incentive clauses providing a bonus if that player is named the Most Valuable Player in a Division Series. Unfortunately, no such award is given for a Division Series.[1]

A major cause of the 2007–2009 worldwide financial crisis (and its repercussions which still continue around the world today) was that managers and other employees of banks, insurance companies, and other firms took excessive risks. Looking back on the events that led to the financial meltdown, Goldman Sachs Chief Executive Lloyd Blankfein admitted that Wall Street firms, caught up in the pursuit of profits, had ignored risks, and that these firms needed to dramatically change compensation practices. As he said, "Decisions on compensation and other actions taken and not taken, particularly at banks that rapidly lost a lot of shareholder value, look self-serving and greedy in hindsight."

During the mortgage market meltdown that started in 2007, record numbers of mortgage holders defaulted on their loans and their homes went into foreclosure, where the lender took ownership. In the United States, foreclosures rose from 100,000 a month in the summer of 2006 to 250,000 in 2007, 300,000 in 2008, and 350,000 in 2009 and 2010, before falling to 225,000 in 2011, 200,000 in 2012, and 128,000 in June 2013.

Leading up to the crash, many banks and other mortgage-initiating firms started providing riskier mortgages in four ways. First, many mortgage-initiating firms stopped requiring down payments for *subprime* mortgage loans, which are loans made to people who are not prime—low-risk—borrowers. In the San Francisco Bay Area, 69% of families whose owner-occupied homes were in foreclosure had put down 0% at the time of purchase, and only 10% made the traditional 20% down payment in the first nine months of 2007.

Second, firms loaned to speculators who were more likely to walk away from a loan than would someone who lived in the mortgaged house. Speculators were a serious problem in Miami and Las Vegas. In Las Vegas during the first half of 2007, absentee investors owned 74% of single-family homes in foreclosure. (Nationwide, nonowner-occupied homes accounted for 13% of prime defaults and 11% of subprime defaults.)

We're now tying annual executive bonuses to performance. You owe us $100,000.

---

[1]Tom FitzGerald, "Top of the Sixth," *San Francisco Chronicle*, January 31, 1997, C6.

Third, mortgages used adjustable rates that started very low and increased rapidly over time. Because the implications of these escalator clauses were not made clear to borrowers, many poor people suddenly found themselves unable to make their mortgage payments.

Fourth, many mortgage-originating firms such as banks failed to check borrowers' creditworthiness properly. Of the properties repossessed in the San Francisco Bay Area, one in six was owned by people who had two or more previous foreclosures, and some had five or more.

Why did executives at these banks take these extra risks that resulted in major lost shareholder value? (We examine how a manager's incentives can lead to excessive risk taking in Solved Problem 20.1.) How can a firm compensate its corporate executives so as to prevent them from undertaking irresponsible and potentially devastating actions? In the Challenge Solution, we examine how a manager's incentives can be changed to reduce excessive risk taking.

A dentist caps a tooth, not because the patient needs it, but because the dentist wants a new flat-screen TV. An employee cruises the Internet for jokes instead of working when the boss is not watching. A driver of a rental car takes it off the highway, risking ruining the suspension. Each of these examples illustrates an inefficient use of resources due to a *moral hazard*, where an informed person takes advantage of a less-informed person, often through a *hidden action* (Chapter 19).

Insurance companies introduced the term *moral hazard* into common usage. Many types of insurance are highly vulnerable to hidden actions by insured parties that result in moral hazard problems. For example, Ralph, the owner of a clothing store, purchased a large quantity of designer jeans and stored the jeans in a warehouse. Following standard practice, he insured the merchandise for its original purchase price against such hazards as fire or theft. Unfortunately for Ralph, these jeans have become unfashionable and are not selling. Because he faces a significant financial loss, he burns down the warehouse and makes an insurance claim. The hidden action is that of setting the warehouse on fire. Because most people view such an action as unethical or *immoral* (as well as being illegal), we use the term *moral* hazard.

A somewhat less extreme example of moral hazard arises when medical insurance covers the expense of doctor visits. If insured people do not have to pay for visits to their doctors, some insured people make "excessive" visits to the doctor—more than if they had to pay for the visits themselves. For example, some people visit a doctor in part because they are hypochondriacs or are lonely and want some company. Such behavior is not illegal and may not seem unethical. However, because it is costly, insurance companies take actions to reduce the number of visits.

In this chapter, we concentrate on moral hazard problems that occur when a *principal* contracts with an *agent* to take an *action* that benefits the principal. For example, the principal may be an employer who hires an employee or agent to work in the principal's store. Until now, we have assumed that firms can produce efficiently. However, if the principal cannot practically monitor the agent all the time, the agent may steal, not work hard, or engage in other opportunistic behavior that lowers productivity. If so, the principal and the agent are collectively worse off than if both had full information so that opportunistic behavior were impossible.

After discussing the causes of these moral hazard problems, we address various means of preventing them. Key among these methods is designing contracts that *eliminate production inefficiencies* due to moral hazard problems *without shifting risk to people who hate bearing it* (Chapter 17)—or contracts that at least reach a good compromise between these two goals.

20.1 The Principal-Agent Problem

Moral hazard in a principal-agent relationship is referred to as a *principal-agent problem* or an *agency problem*. If information is symmetric so that actions cannot be hidden, principal-agent relationships do not give rise to a moral hazard problem. When a building contractor (the principal) subcontracts with a house painter (the agent) and both work on the same building site, the contractor can directly observe how hard and how well the painter is working. Due to this close monitoring, the painter cannot engage in any hidden action, such as taking an hour-long coffee break or running personal errands during work hours. Consequently, no inefficiency arises from this principal-agent relationship.

In contrast, when you contract with people whose actions you cannot observe or evaluate, they may take advantage of you. If you (the principal) pay an auto mechanic (the agent) by the hour to fix your car, you do not know whether that person worked all the hours billed. If you retain a lawyer to represent you in a suit arising from an accident, you do not know whether the settlement the lawyer recommends is in your best interest or the lawyer's.

To illustrate the principal-agent problem, we consider an example where the payoffs to the owner of a firm (the principal) and the manager (the agent) depend on the agent's actions and the *state of nature*, such as weather (which affects demand) or input prices (which affect costs). The principal and the agent care about how payoffs are allocated and how the risk is shared.

Paul, the principal, owns many ice cream parlors across North America. He contracts with Amy, the agent, to manage his Miami shop. Her duties include supervising workers, purchasing supplies, and performing other necessary actions.

The shop's daily earnings depend on the local demand conditions and on how hard Amy works. Demand for ice cream varies with the weather, and is high half the time, and low otherwise.

Amy puts forth either normal or extra effort. She views herself as an honest person and would never steal from Paul. She is always at the shop during regular business hours and puts in at least a normal amount of effort, even if Paul cannot check on her. She politely, but impersonally, asks everyone who enters the shop, "May I help you?"

Nonetheless, Amy might not be working as hard as possible. She could put forth extra effort by enthusiastically greeting regular customers by name, serving customers rapidly, spending extra hours checking with nearby businesses to see if they would be interested in joint promotions, and improving the appearance of the shop.

However, extra work is tiring and prevents Amy from spending time at the beach with friends, reading novels, watching "Dancing with the Stars," and engaging in other activities that she enjoys. She values her personal cost of this extra effort at 40 per day.

For any given level of demand, the shop sells more ice cream if Amy puts forth extra effort. The shop also sells more for a given level of Amy's effort if demand is high. The profit of the ice cream shop before Amy is paid—the combined payoff to Paul and Amy—for the four possible combinations of effort and demand are:

		Demand	
		Low	*High*
Amy's Effort	*Normal*	100	300
	Extra	300	500

If the demand is high and Amy puts forth normal effort, or if the demand is low and she works hard, the firm's daily profit is 300. The profit is 500 if the demand is high and Amy works hard but is only 100 if the demand is low and she applies only normal effort.

Efficiency

efficient contract
an agreement in which neither party can be made better off without harming the other party

Ideally, the principal, Paul, and the agent, Amy, agree to an **efficient contract**: an agreement in which neither party can be made better off without harming the other party. Using an efficient contract results in *efficiency in production* and *efficiency in risk sharing*.

efficiency in production
a situation in which the principal's and agent's combined value (profits, payoffs), π, is maximized

Efficiency in production requires that the principal's and agent's combined value (profits, payoffs) is maximized. In our example, moral hazard hurts the principal by more than it helps the agent, so achieving efficiency in production requires preventing the moral hazard.

efficiency in risk bearing
a situation in which risk sharing is optimal in that the person who least minds facing risk—the risk-neutral or less risk-averse person—bears more of the risk

Efficiency in risk bearing requires that risk sharing is optimal in that the person who least minds facing risk—the risk-neutral or less-risk-averse person—bears more of the risk. Risk-averse people are willing to pay a risk premium to avoid risk, whereas risk-neutral people do not care if they face fair risk or not (Chapter 17). In our example, Paul owns many ice cream parlors across North America, he can pool the returns from all these stores, and he is risk neutral. Amy, like most people, is risk averse. Thus, risk bearing is efficient if Paul bears all of the risk and Amy bears none of it.

Symmetric Information

Moral hazard is not a problem if Paul lives in Miami and can directly supervise Amy. They could agree to a contract that specifies Amy receives 200 per day if she works extra hard, but loses her job if she doesn't. Because Amy's cost of working extra hard is 40, she nets 160 (= 200 − 40) if she works hard, which is better than being fired and getting nothing. Even though the shop's profit varies with demand, Amy bears no risk: She receives 200 regardless of demand conditions.

Paul is the *residual claimant*: He receives the *residual profit*, which is the amount left over from the store's profit after Amy's wage is paid. Because Amy works hard (as she does not want to get fired), Paul's residual profit varies only with demand. If demand is low, the shop earns 300, he pays Amy 200, and retains 100. If demand is high, the shop earns 500, so Paul keeps 300 after paying Amy 200. Paul's expected profit is the probability of low demand, 50%, times 100 plus the probability of high demand, 50%, times 300, or

$$(\tfrac{1}{2} \times 100) + (\tfrac{1}{2} \times 300) = 200.$$

Under this contract, Paul bears all the risk from the shop's uncertain earnings. The variance of Paul's earnings is large relative to his expected profit: $\tfrac{1}{2}(100 - 200)^2 + \tfrac{1}{2}(300 - 200)^2 = 10,000.$[2]

This result is summarized in the first row of Table 20.1, which is labeled *perfect monitoring*. The last two columns show that this contract is efficient because Paul, the risk-neutral party, bears all the risk, and their combined earnings are as high as possible because Amy works extra hard.

Asymmetric Information

Paul grows tired of warm weather and moves from Miami to Toronto, Canada, where he can no longer observe Amy's effort. Because Amy's effort is now a hidden action to Paul, he faces a moral hazard problem.

Table 20.1 Ice Cream Shop Outcomes

| | Expected Payoffs | | | | Efficiency | |
Contract	Paul	Amy[a]	Paul + Amy	Amy's Variance	Risk Bearing[b]	Joint Payoff[c]
Symmetric Information						
Perfect monitoring	200	160	360	0	yes	yes
Asymmetric Information						
Fixed wage of 100	100	100	200	0	yes	no
Licensing fee of 200	200	160	360	10,000	no	yes
State-contingent fee of 100 or 300	200	160	360	0	yes	yes
50% profit share	200	160	360	2,500	no	yes
Wage and bonus of 200; Amy is risk neutral	200	160	360	10,000	yes	yes
Wage and bonus of 200; Amy is very risk averse	100	100	200	0	yes	no

[a]If Amy puts in extra work, her payoff is her earnings minus 40, which is the value she places on having to work harder.
[b]Because Amy is risk averse and Paul is risk neutral, risk bearing is efficient only if Paul bears all the risk, so that Amy's variance is zero.
[c]Production is efficient if Amy puts in extra work, so that the shop's expected payoff is 400 rather than 200.

---

[2]The variance (Chapter 17) is the probability of low demand, 50%, times the square of the difference between the payoff under low demand, 100, and the expected payoff, 200, plus the probability of high demand, 50%, times the square of the difference between the payoff under high demand, 300, and the expected payoff.

When Paul could monitor Amy's effort, he could make her wage contingent on hard work. Now, he pays her a wage that does not vary with her (hidden) effort. Initially, we assume that Paul and Amy's contract specifies that Paul pays Amy a *fixed wage* of 100 regardless of how much profit the shop earns. Such a contract is a special case of a *fixed-fee contract*, in which one party pays the other a constant payment or fee.

Because Amy receives the same amount no matter how hard she works, Amy chooses not to work hard, which is a moral hazard problem. If she works normally, she incurs no additional personal cost from extra effort and receives 100. On the other hand, if she provides extra effort, she receives a wage of 100 but incurs a personal cost of 40, so her net return is only 60.

Because Amy provides normal effort, the shop earns 100 with low demand, which is just enough to pay Amy with nothing left over for Paul, and the shop earns 300 with high demand, so Paul nets 200. Thus, Paul faces an uncertain profit with an expected value of $(\frac{1}{2} \times 0) + (\frac{1}{2} \times 200) = 100$. The variance of Paul's earnings remains high: $\frac{1}{2}(0 - 100)^2 + \frac{1}{2}(200 - 100)^2 = 10,000$.

The second row of Table 20.1 summarizes the effects of this fixed-wage contract. Paul bears all the risk, so risk bearing is again efficient. However, their expected combined earnings, 200, are less than in the previous example with symmetric information, 360. Amy now makes 100. Paul has an expected value of 100, which is all he cares about because he is risk neutral. Both were better off with symmetric information: Amy netted 160 and Paul expected to earn 200. Because the moral hazard substantially reduces the shop's expected earnings, having Paul pay Amy a fixed wage is not the best way to compensate her. In the next section, we examine how well-designed contracts can reduce inefficiency due to moral hazard.

Application

Selfless or Selfish Doctors?

Patients (principals) rely on doctors (agents) for good medical advice. Do doctors selflessly act only in their patient's best interests, or do they take advantage of their superior knowledge to exploit patients or the companies that insure them?

Lu (2014) conducted an experiment to investigate doctors' behavior at top Beijing hospitals, in which the doctors were unaware that they were part of an experiment. In the experiment, a doctor knew whether a patient had insurance or not. The doctor also knew if the patient planned to buy any prescribed drugs at the hospital, where the doctor received a share of the patient's payment for drugs, or at an outside drugstore, where the doctors received no compensation from the prescriptions. Many doctors were asked to recommend treatment for a particular patient under these four possibilities: insurance–buy at the hospital, insurance–buy elsewhere, no insurance–buy at the hospital, and no insurance–buy elsewhere.

If a doctor is concerned about a patient's overall well-being and takes the patient's ability to pay into account, the doctor may prescribe more for patients with insurance, even if the doctor does not receive compensation for extra prescriptions. *If the doctor is primarily interested in earning as much as possible*, the doctor is likely to prescribe excessively for patients who are insured and who buy the drugs at the hospital. This excessive prescribing is a hidden action that creates a moral hazard.

Lu found that doctors prescribed similarly whether or not a patient had insurance if the doctors received no compensation for prescriptions. However, if the doctors were compensated for prescriptions, they prescribed drugs that cost 43% more on average on insured patients than for uninsured patients. Moreover, many of these extra, very expensive drugs were unjustified by the patient's medical condition. Thus, many of these doctors appeared to be motivated largely by self-interest rather than purely out of concern for their patients.

Solved Problem 20.1

Traditionally the Las Vegas Home Bank made only *prime* loans—providing mortgages just to people who were very likely to repay the loans. However, Leonardo, a senior executive at the bank, is considering offering *subprime* loans—mortgages to speculators and other less creditworthy borrowers. If he makes only prime loans, the bank will earn $160 million. If he also makes subprime loans, the bank will make a very high profit, $800 million, if the economy is good so that few people default. However, if the economy is bad, the large number of defaults will cause the bank to lose $320 million.

The probability that the economy is bad is 75%. Leonardo will receive 1% of the bank's profit if it is positive. He believes that if the bank loses money, he can walk away from his job without repercussions but with no compensation. Leonardo and the bank's shareholders are risk neutral. Does Leonardo provide subprime loans if all he cares about is maximizing his personal expected earnings? What would the bank's stockholders prefer that Leonardo do (given that they know the risks involved)?

Answer

1. *Compare the bank's expected return on the two types of mortgages.* If the bank makes both prime and subprime loans, its expected return is $(0.25 \times 800) + (0.75 \times [-320]) = -40$ million dollars, an expected loss. That is substantially less than the certain profit of $160 million the bank makes if it provides only prime mortgages.

2. *Compare the manager's expected profits on the two investments.* Leonardo earns 1% of $160 million, or $1.6 million, if he provides only prime loans. If he makes prime and subprime loans, he earns 1% of $800 million, or $8 million, with a probability of 25%, and gets no compensation with a probability of 75%. Thus, he expects to earn $(0.25 \times 8) + (0.75 \times 0) = 2$ million dollars. Because Leonardo is risk neutral and does not care about the shareholders' returns, he makes both types of loans.

3. *Compare the shareholders' expected profits on the two types of mortgages.* If the bank provides only prime mortgages, the bank's shareholders earn 99% of the profit from the prime mortgages, or $0.99 \times \$160$ million $= \$158.4$ million. If the bank makes both prime and subprime loans, shareholders earn 99% of the $800 million, $792 million, if the economy is good. But in a bad economy, the shareholders bear the full loss, $320 million. The expected return to shareholders is $(0.25 \times 792) + (0.75 \times [-320]) = -42$ million dollars, an expected loss. Thus, the shareholders would prefer that the bank make only prime loans.

Comment: Given that Leonardo has the wrong incentives (and ignores his responsibility to shareholders), he takes a hidden action—choosing to provide subprime loans—that is not in the shareholders' best interest. One possible solution to the problem of managers' and shareholders' diverging interests is to change the manager's compensation scheme, as we discuss in the Challenge Solution.

20.2 Using Contracts to Reduce Moral Hazard

A skillfully designed contract that provides the agent with strong incentives to act so as to achieve production efficiency may reduce or eliminate moral hazard problems. In this section, we illustrate how several types of contracts increase efficiency in the Paul and Amy ice cream shop example. These contracts provide greater incentives for Amy, the agent, to work hard, but some require her to bear some risk even though she is more risk averse than Paul, the principal. Thus, some of these contracts create a trade-off: increasing production efficiency while reducing risk-bearing efficiency.

Fixed-Fee Contracts

We initially considered a fixed-fee contract in which Paul (the principal) pays Amy (the agent) a fixed wage, with the result that Paul bears all of the risk and Amy bears none. Alternatively, Amy could pay Paul a fixed amount so that she receives the residual profit: the profit left over after Paul has been paid his fixed return. Amy is, in effect, paying a *license fee* to operate Paul's ice cream shop. With such a contract, Paul bears no risk as he receives a fixed fee, while Amy bears all the risk.[3]

As Amy receives the residual profit under such a licensing contract, she receives all the increase in expected profit from her extra effort. She is therefore motivated to work hard.

To illustrate why, we suppose that Amy pays Paul a fixed licensing fee of 200 per day and keeps any residual profit. (Our analysis depends *only* on Amy paying Paul a fixed fee and *not* on the exact amount that she pays.) If she does not work hard, she makes 100 (= 300 − 200) with high demand, but suffers a loss, −100 (= 100 − 200), if demand is low. Her expected gain if she does not work hard is $0 = (\frac{1}{2} \times [-100]) + (\frac{1}{2} \times 100)$. If she works hard, she nets 60 (= 300 − 200 − 40) with low demand and 260 (= 500 − 200 − 40) with high demand, so that her expected gain from working hard is $160 = (\frac{1}{2} \times 60) + (\frac{1}{2} \times 260)$.

Her variance in earnings is $10,000 = \frac{1}{2}(-100 - 0)^2 + \frac{1}{2}(100 - 0)^2$ with low demand, which is the same as the variance with high demand, $10,000 = \frac{1}{2}(60 - 160)^2 + \frac{1}{2}(260 - 160)^2$. Thus, because her risk is the same with both levels of effort but her expected net earnings are higher if she puts forth high effort, it is in her best interest to work hard.

Consequently, Amy's and Paul's total expected earnings are higher if Amy pays a fixed fee to Paul than if Paul pays a fixed fee to Amy, because Amy works harder if she is the residual claimant and therefore reaps all the benefits of working harder. As the third row (*licensing fee*) of Table 20.1 shows, when Amy pays Paul a license fee, the shop's expected earnings are 400 because Amy works hard. Paul makes 200 with certainty, and Amy expects a net gain of 160 after deducting her cost, 40, of providing high effort. Therefore, the expected sum of their payoffs is 360. In contrast, if Paul pays Amy a fixed wage (second row), Amy earns 100 and Paul expects to earn 100 for an expected total payoff of 200.

Although Amy paying Paul rather than the other way around increases their total earnings, it makes the risk-averse person, Amy, bear all the risk, while Paul, the risk-neutral person, bears no risk. Therefore, although this contract maximizes combined expected earnings, it does not provide for efficient risk bearing.

Which contract is better depends on how risk averse Amy is. If Amy is nearly risk neutral, the fixed payment to Paul is superior, because both parties have higher expected earnings and Amy is not very concerned about the risk. However, if Amy is

---

[3]In some businesses, both types of fixed-fee contracts are used. For example, in some hair salons, hairdressers rent a chair from the owner for a fixed fee and bear all the risk associated with variations in demand, while other hairdressers are paid an hourly rate, with the owner getting the residual profit from their activities.

extremely risk averse, she may prefer receiving a fixed wage even if that means giving up significant expected earnings.[4]

Contingent Contracts

Many contracts specify that the parties receive payoffs that are contingent on some other variable, such as the action taken by the agent, the state of nature, or the firm's profit, output, or revenue. For example, when Paul could monitor Amy's effort, he offered her a contract that made her payoff contingent on her effort. She was paid only if she provided extra effort and lost her job otherwise. Such a contract would be efficient, but is not feasible if Paul cannot monitor Amy's effort. However, contingent contracts may be used even when monitoring is not feasible.

State-Contingent Contracts In a *state-contingent contract*, one party's payoff is contingent on *only* the state of nature. For example, suppose Amy pays Paul a license fee of 100 if demand is low and a license fee of 300 if demand is high and keeps any additional earnings. As the residual claimant, Amy has an incentive to provide high effort. With low demand the shop earns 300, Amy pays Paul 100, and Amy's residual profit is $160 = 300 - 100 - 40$, where 40 is the cost of her extra effort. With high demand, the shop earns 500, Amy pays Paul 300, and Amy's residual profit is $160 = 500 - 300 - 40$.

Paul's expected payoff is $200 = (\frac{1}{2} \times 100) + (\frac{1}{2} \times 300)$, as the fourth row of Table 20.1 shows. Because Amy earns 160 in both states of nature, she bears no risk, while Paul bears all the risk. This result is efficient because Paul is risk neutral and Amy is risk averse. This state-contingent contract is fully efficient even if Paul cannot monitor Amy's effort. However, it does require that both parties observe and agree on the state of nature, which may not be possible.

Solved Problem 20.2

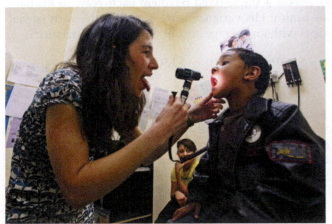

Gary's demand for doctor visits depends on his health. Half the time his health is good and his demand is D^1 in the figure. When his health is poor, his demand is D^2. Gary is risk averse. Without medical insurance, he pays $50 a visit. With full insurance, he pays a fixed fee at the beginning of the year, and the insurance company pays the full cost of any visit. Alternatively, with a contingent contract, Gary pays a smaller premium at the beginning of the year, and the insurance company covers only $20 per visit, with Gary paying the remaining $30. How likely is a moral hazard problem to occur with each of these contracts? What is Gary's risk (the variance of his medical costs) with no insurance and with each of the two types of insurance? Compare the contracts in terms of the trade-offs between risk and moral hazard.

---

[4]Amy might be more risk averse if, for example, she has no savings and would find it difficult to support herself during periods of low demand if she were the residual claimant.

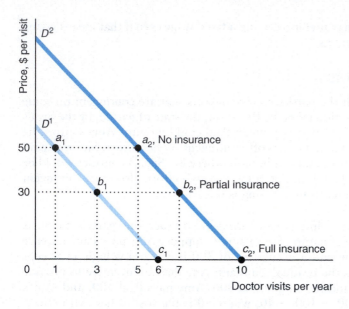

Answer

1. *Describe the moral hazard for each demand curve for each contract.* Given that Gary's health is good, if he does not have insurance, Gary pays the doctor $50 a visit and goes to the doctor once, at point a_1 in the figure. In contrast, with full insurance where he pays nothing per visit, he visits the doctor six times, at c_1. Similarly, if his health is poor, he goes to the doctor five times, a_2, without insurance, and 10 times, c_2, with full insurance. Thus, regardless of his health, he makes five extra visits a year with full insurance. These extra visits are the moral hazard.

   With a contingent contract, Gary pays $30 a visit. He makes three visits if his health is good (at point b_1)—only two more than at a_1. If his health is poor, he makes seven visits, once again two more than if he were paying the full fee (at point a_1). Thus, with a contingent contract, he makes only two extra visits, so the moral hazard problem is reduced.

2. *Calculate the variance of Gary's medical expenses for no insurance and for the two insurance contracts.* Without insurance, his average number of visits is $3 = (\frac{1}{2} \times 1) + (\frac{1}{2} \times 5)$, so his average annual medical cost is $150. Thus, the variance of his medical expenses without insurance is

$$\sigma_n^2 = \tfrac{1}{2}[(1 \times \$50) - \$150]^2 + \tfrac{1}{2}[(5 \times 50) - \$150]^2$$
$$= \tfrac{1}{2}(\$50 - \$150)^2 + \tfrac{1}{2}(\$250 - \$150)^2$$
$$= \$10,000.$$

If he has full insurance, he makes a single fixed payment each year, so his payments do not vary with his health: His variance is $\sigma_f^2 = 0$. Finally, with partial insurance, he averages 5 visits with an average cost of $150, so his variance is

$$\sigma_p^2 = \tfrac{1}{2}(\$90 - \$150)^2 + \tfrac{1}{2}(\$210 - \$150)^2 = \$3,600.$$

Thus, $\sigma_n^2 > \sigma_p^2 > \sigma_f^2$.

3. *Discuss the trade-offs.* Because Gary is risk averse, efficiency in risk bearing requires the insurance company to bear all the risk, as with full insurance. However, full insurance results in the largest moral hazard. Removing insurance eliminates the moral hazard, but forces Gary to bear all the risk. The contingent contract is a compromise in which both the moral hazard and the degree of risk lie between the extremes.

Profit-Sharing Contracts Even if the principal cannot observe the state of nature or the agent's actions, the principal may be able to design a contingent contract that reduces the moral hazard problem by making payments contingent on an outcome, such as profit or output. One common contingent contract is a *profit-sharing contract*, in which the payoff to each party is a fraction of the observable total profit.

Suppose that Paul and Amy agree to split the earnings of the ice cream shop equally. Does making Amy's pay contingent on the firm's earnings induce Amy to work hard?

If Amy works normally, the shop earns 100 if the demand is low and Amy receives half, or 50. If demand is high, the shop earns 300, so Amy's share is 150 ($= \frac{1}{2} \times 300$). Thus, Amy's expected value from normal effort is $100 = (\frac{1}{2} \times 50) + (\frac{1}{2} \times 150)$. The variance of her earnings is $2{,}500 = \frac{1}{2}(50 - 100)^2 + \frac{1}{2}(150 - 100)^2$.

If Amy provides extra effort, the shop earns 300 if the demand is low, and Amy receives 150, but she incurs a personal cost of 40 for providing high effort, so her net return is 110. If the demand is high, the shop's profit is 500, so that Amy nets 210 ($= 250 - 40$). Thus, her expected return from high effort is $160 = (\frac{1}{2} \times 110) + (\frac{1}{2} \times 210)$. The variance of her earnings is $2{,}500 = \frac{1}{2}(110 - 160)^2 + \frac{1}{2}(210 - 160)^2$, which is the same as with normal effort. Because extra effort provides Amy with higher expected earnings without increasing her risk, she provides extra effort.

Given that Amy works hard, Paul makes 150 ($= \frac{1}{2} \times 300$) if demand is low and 250 ($= \frac{1}{2} \times 500$) if demand is high. His expected profit is $200 = (\frac{1}{2} \times 150) + (\frac{1}{2} \times 250)$, as the profit-sharing row of Table 20.1 shows. Paul prefers this profit-sharing contract to a fixed-fee contract where he pays Amy a fixed wage of 100 and makes an expected profit of 100.

However, Amy chooses to work harder only if she gets a large enough share of the profit to offset her personal cost from doing the extra work. If Amy gets less than 20% of the profit, she chooses not to work hard and earns less than she would from the wage of 100.[5] Thus, profit sharing may reduce or eliminate the moral hazard problem, especially if the agent's share of the profit is large, but may not do so if the agent's share is small.

Solved Problem 20.3

Penny, the owner of a store, makes a deal with Arthur, her manager, that at the end of the year, she receives two-thirds of the store's profit and he gets one-third. If Arthur is interested in maximizing his earnings, will Arthur act in a manner that maximizes the store's total profit (which both Penny and Arthur can observe)? Answer using a graph.

Answer

1. *Draw a diagram showing the total profit curve and use it to derive Arthur's profit curve.* The figure shows that the total profit (π) curve is first increasing and then decreasing as output rises. At every output, Arthur's profit curve is one-third of the height of the profit curve, $\frac{1}{3}\pi$.

2. *Determine the quantity that maximizes Arthur's profit and check whether that quantity also maximizes total profit.* Because Arthur, the manager, gets a third of the total profit, $\frac{1}{3}\pi$, he sets output at q^*, which maximizes his share of the profit. Total profit and the owner's share of profit are also maximized at q^*. (Penny's share, $\frac{2}{3}\pi$—the vertical difference between the total profit curve and the agent's earnings at each output—is also maximized.)

---

[5] If θ is Amy's share, then her expected earnings with normal effort is $(\frac{1}{2} \times 100\theta) + (\frac{1}{2} \times 300\theta) = 200\theta$, and her expected net earnings from extra effort is $(\frac{1}{2} \times 300\theta) + (\frac{1}{2} \times 500\theta) - 40 = 400\theta - 40$. She chooses not to put in extra effort if what she expects to earn from normal effort exceeds that from extra effort: $200\theta > 400\theta - 40$, or $\theta < 20\%$.

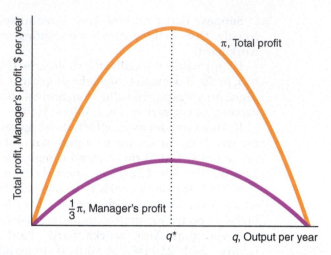

Comment: At the output where total profit is maximized, any fraction of total profit is also maximized.[6]

Bonuses and Options To induce an agent to work hard, a principal may offer the agent a *bonus*: an extra payment if a performance target is hit. For example, Paul could offer Amy a base wage of 100 and a bonus of 200 if the shop's earnings (before paying Amy) exceed 300.

If Amy provides normal effort, the shop does not earn enough to trigger the bonus, so Amy receives 100 in both states of nature. If Amy provides extra effort but the demand is low, the shop earns 300, so Amy receives her wage of 100 and incurs a cost of 40, so her net benefit is 60. However, if she works hard and the demand is high, the shop earns 500, the bonus is triggered, and Amy gets her wage of 100 plus the bonus of 200. After subtracting her cost of extra effort, 40, she nets 260. Thus, Amy's expected return with extra effort is $160 = (\frac{1}{2} \times 60) + (\frac{1}{2} \times 260)$, which exceeds the 100 she earns with normal effort.

However, the variance in her net earnings with extra effort is $10{,}000 = \frac{1}{2}(60 - 160)^2 + \frac{1}{2}(260 - 160)^2$. Thus, whether Amy chooses to work extra hard depends on how risk averse she is. If she is nearly risk neutral, she works extra hard. However, if she is very risk averse, she puts in only normal effort, receives a modest but predictable wage, and avoids the risk of sometimes earning very little.

The next to last row of Table 20.1 shows the outcome of a bonus contract if Amy is risk neutral. If Amy is risk neutral or nearly risk neutral, she chooses to work hard. If demand is low, the bonus is not triggered, so Paul pays Amy only her base salary of 100 and keeps the residual amount of 200. With high demand, Paul pays Amy 300—the base of 100 plus the bonus of 200 —and keeps the residual of $200 (= 500 - 300)$. Paul expects to earn $200 = (\frac{1}{2} \times 200) + (\frac{1}{2} \times 200)$. Indeed, he earns 200 regardless of demand conditions, so he bears no risk. Thus, if Amy is risk neutral, the bonus leads to efficient payoffs and efficient risk bearing even though

---

[6]To determine where profit is maximized using calculus, we differentiate the profit function, $\pi(q)$, with respect to output, q, and set that derivative, which is marginal profit, equal to zero: $d\pi(q)/dq = 0$. The quantity that maximizes the manager's share of profit, $\frac{1}{3}\pi(q)$, is determined by $\frac{1}{3}d\pi(q)/dq = \frac{1}{3}d\pi(q)/dq = 0$, or $d\pi(q)/dq = 0$. That is, the quantity at which the manager's share of profit reaches a maximum is determined by the same condition as the one that determines that total profit reaches a maximum.

Amy bears all the risk. (If Amy were nearly but not quite risk neutral, she would still choose to work hard, but would dislike bearing all the risk.)

The last row in Table 20.1 shows the outcome of a bonus contract if Amy is extremely risk averse. Now, she'd rather have 100 with certainty than take a chance on sometimes netting only 60 after incurring the cost of high effort, so she works only normal hours. Consequently, the total payoffs are low and hence not efficient, but risk is shared efficiently, with Paul bearing all the risk. Thus, this bonus may—but does not necessarily—induce Amy to work hard.

Many senior executives receive part of their salary in the form of an *option*, which is a type of bonus. An option gives the holder the right to buy up to a certain number of shares of the company at a given price (the *exercise price*) during a specified time interval. An option provides a benefit to the executive if the firm's stock price exceeds the exercise price and is therefore a bonus based on the stock price.

Piece Rates Another common type of contingent contract is a *piece-rate contract*, in which the agent receives a payment for each unit of output the agent produces. Under such a contract, Amy is paid for every serving of ice cream she sells rather than by the hour, which gives her an incentive to work hard, but she bears the risk from fluctuations in demand, which she does not control.

Owners often use piece rates if they can observe output but not labor. Piece rates are commonly used in agricultural field work, auto glass repair shops, and other firms where the employer wants to encourage employees to perform a repetitive job quickly.

Commissions Often, when at least one party cannot observe total profit, but both can observe revenue, they use a revenue-sharing contract: the agent receives a share of the revenue. For people who work in sales, such payments are called *commissions*. For example, a salesperson in a clothing store might receive a commission of 5% of the revenue for each item sold.

As with profit sharing, piece rates and commissions provide an incentive for agents to provide more effort than they would with a fixed-rate contract. However, as with a bonus, this incentive is not necessarily strong enough to offset the agent's cost of extra effort and the agent bears some risk.

Solved Problem 20.4

Peter, the owner of a firm, pays his salesperson, Ann, a commission on her sales (revenue). Thus, Ann has an incentive to maximize revenue. The graph shows how revenue and profit vary with output. Show that if she succeeds in maximizing revenue that she does not maximize the firm's profit.

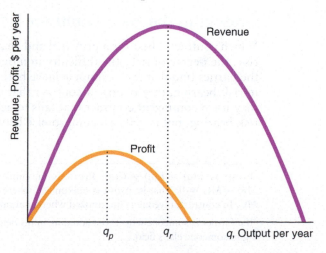

Answer

Show the quantities of output that maximize both curves and compare them. As the figure shows, Ann maximizes revenue by selling q_r units. Profit is maximized at a smaller quantity, q_p. Thus, if Ann works to maximize sales, she does not maximize profit.[7]

Application

Contracts and Productivity in Agriculture

In agriculture, landowners (principals) frequently contract with farmers (agents) to work their land. Farmers may work on their own land, work on land rented from a landowner (a fixed-fee rental contract), work as employees for a wage or a piece rate, or sharecrop. A sharecropper splits the output (crop) with the landowner at the end of the growing season.[8] Sharecropping is therefore a form of revenue sharing.

Our analysis tells us that farmers' willingness to work hard depends on the type of contract used. Farmers who keep all the marginal profit from additional work—those who own the land or rent it for a fixed fee—work hard and maximize (joint) profit. Sharecroppers, who bear the full marginal cost of working an extra hour and get only some fraction of the extra revenue, would put in too little effort. Hired farm workers who are paid by the hour may not work hard unless they are very carefully supervised.

Foster and Rosenzweig (1994) tested these predictions using data on Philippine farmers. Foster and Rosenzweig could not directly monitor farmers' work effort—any more than most landowners can. Rather, they ingeniously measured the effort indirectly. They contended that the harder people work, the more they eat and the more they use up body mass, holding calorie intake constant.

Foster and Rosenzweig estimated the effect of each compensation method on a measure of relative body mass (weight divided by height squared) and on consumption (after adjusting for gender, age, type of activity, and other factors). They found that people who work for themselves or are paid by the piece use up 10% more body mass, holding calorie consumption constant, than workers paid by the hour, and 13% more than sharecroppers. Foster and Rosenzweig also discovered that piece-rate workers consume 25% more calories per day and that people who work on their own farm consume 16% more than workers paid by the hour. Thus, these farm workers respond strongly to contractual incentives.

Choosing the Best Contract

Which contract is best for a principal and an agent depends on their attitudes toward risk, the degree of risk, the difficulty in monitoring, and other factors. Often when the parties find that they cannot achieve both efficiency in production and efficiency in risk bearing, they choose a contract that attains neither goal. For example, they may use a contingent contract that fails to achieve efficiency in either production or risk bearing, but it strikes a compromise between the two goals.

---

[7]Profit is $\pi(q) = R(q) - C(q)$. Profit is maximized where $d\pi(q)/dq = dR(q)/dq - dC(q)/dq = MR - MC = 0$. That is, profit is maximized where marginal revenue, MR, equals marginal cost, MC. In contrast, revenue is maximized where marginal revenue equals zero: $dR(q)/dq = MR = 0$.

[8]If a farmer is someone who is out standing in his field, a sharecropper is someone who is out standing in someone else's field.

The type of contract chosen depends on many factors. Someone who hires a lawyer and who cannot observe the lawyer's work effort or easily judge the quality of the lawyer's work, worries about moral hazard. Either party may be particularly concerned about risk bearing.

Lawyers usually work for a fixed fee only if the task or case is very simple, such as writing a will or handling an uncontested divorce. The client has some idea of whether the work is done satisfactorily, so monitoring is relatively easy and little risk is involved. However, a lawyer may not accept a fixed fee if the number of hours required for a more complex project is unknown.

In riskier situations, other types of contracts are more commonly used. When the lawyer is relatively risk averse or when the principal is very concerned that the lawyer works hard, an hourly wage may be used. However, unless the principal can observe the lawyer's effort, such contracts may result in the lawyer overbilling for hours.

contingent fee
a payment to a lawyer that is a share of the award in a court case (usually after legal expenses are deducted) if the client wins and nothing if the client loses

Alternatively, the parties may use a **contingent fee**: a payment to a lawyer that is a share of the award in a court case (usually after legal expenses are deducted) if the client wins and nothing if the client loses. Contingent fee arrangements are particularly common for plaintiffs' lawyers who specialize in auto accidents, medical malpractice, product liability, and other *torts*: wrongful acts in which a person's body, property, or reputation is harmed and for which the injured party is entitled to compensation. Because these plaintiffs' lawyers can typically pool risks across clients, they are less concerned than their clients about risk, and are willing to accept contingent fees. Moreover, accident victims often lack the resources to pay for a lawyer's time before winning at trial, so they often prefer contingent contracts.

Application

Music Contracts: Changing Their Tunes

Ice Cube, Jackson Browne, Jay-Z, the Eagles, Madonna, Pearl Jam, Prince, and Radiohead are no longer signing traditional contracts with major-label recording companies. Many have their own labels. Justin Timberlake's label dates back to 2007, while Justin Bieber started his in 2012.

Traditional contracts obligate the artist to deliver a specific number of albums. The record company gives a cash advance and retains the lion's share (often 90%) of the revenue. The artist receives a share of revenue (usually less than $2 a copy) only after the advance is paid back to the company. The recording company owns the master recordings of the music and pays to produce, promote, and distribute the album.

Now many stars are forgoing the upfront payments. Each artist bears the recording and promotional cost and retains ownership of the album, leaving only distribution to one of the major labels. The artist licenses the music to whichever major label offers the biggest share of sales instead of being contractually tied to one label. Consequently, the artist receives a larger share of revenue than in the past, but the artist incurs more of the costs, as well as much more of the risk.

Ice Cube chose to "bet on himself" and took the risk on his CD *Laugh Now, Cry Later*. EMI made and distributed the album, but Ice Cube paid for the recordings and, with his managers, oversaw most of the U.S. marketing. Pearl Jam sold its *Pearl Jam* album through a "partnership" agreement with Sony BMG's J Records, where the label received a percentage of sales for distribution and other services it provided.

When Jackson Browne's contract with Warner Music Group Corporation's Elektra Records expired, he financed an album, *Solo Acoustic Vol. 1*, and licensed it to a Warner unit that distributes for independent record companies. It sold more copies than his last studio album for Elektra. Mr. Browne earned 7 to 10 times as much per copy sold under the new arrangement than under his previous contract.

Jay-Z made *Magna Carta Holy Grail* available for free digital download by the first million Samsung customers who used his new Jay-Z Magna Carta app on July 4, 2013. Three days later, his companies Roc-A-Fella and Roc Nation started selling the album, which was distributed by Universal.

Thus, these new relationships between artists and record companies are changing production incentives and risk sharing. Because the artist bears more of the production and promotion costs and much more of the risk, only successful, wealthy artists are likely to use this new approach. However, as a consequence of using this new type of contract, some artists are releasing more albums because their incentives to produce have increased. And some of these artists are earning substantial returns for bearing the extra costs and risks.

20.3 Monitoring to Reduce Moral Hazard

A complex contract to prevent moral hazard problems may be unnecessary if the principal can monitor the agent's work. In addition, a principal who can observe the final product but not work effort may be able to avoid moral hazard by making payments contingent on the final product.

Employees who are paid a fixed salary have little incentive (except self respect) to work hard if the employer cannot observe them. That is, they may engage in **shirking**: a moral hazard in which agents do not provide all the services they are paid to provide. A firm can reduce such shirking by intensively supervising or monitoring its workers. Monitoring eliminates the asymmetric information problem: Both the employee and the employer know how hard the employee works. If the cost of monitoring workers is low enough, it pays to prevent shirking by carefully monitoring and firing employees who do not work hard.

Firms have experimented with various means of lowering the cost of monitoring. Requiring employees to punch a time clock and installing video cameras to record the work effort are examples of firms' attempts to use capital to monitor job performance. Similarly, by installing assembly lines that force employees to work at a pace dictated by the firm, employers can control employees' work rate.

According to a survey by the American Management Association, nearly two-thirds of employers record employees' voice mail, email, or phone calls; review computer files; or videotape workers. A quarter of the firms that use surveillance don't tell their employees. The most common types of surveillance are tallying phone numbers called and recording the duration of the calls (37%), videotaping employees' work (16%), storing and reviewing email (15%), storing and reviewing computer files (14%), and taping and reviewing phone conversations (10%). Monitoring and surveillance are most common in the financial sector, in which 81% of firms use these techniques. Rather than watching all employees all the time, companies usually monitor selected workers using spot checks.

For some jobs, however, monitoring is counterproductive or not cost effective. Monitoring may lower employees' morale, in turn reducing productivity. Several years ago, Northwest Airlines (now Delta Airlines) took the doors off bathroom stalls to prevent workers from slacking off there. When new management eliminated this policy (and made many other changes as well), productivity increased.

It is usually impractical for firms to monitor how hard salespeople work if they spend most of their time away from the main office. As telecommuting increases, monitoring workers may become increasingly difficult.

A firm's board of directors is supposed to represent shareholders (principals) by monitoring senior executives (agents) to ensure that executive decisions are made in the

shirking
a *moral hazard* in which agents do not provide all the services they are paid to provide

shareholders' interests. Bad executives may try to hide their actions from directors or select directors who won't "rat" on them. González et al. (2013) studied firms in which senior executives were engaging in illegal price-fixing, exposing the firm and its shareholders to significant legal liability. They found that senior executives in such firms were more inclined to recruit directors who were likely to be inattentive monitors.

When direct monitoring is very costly, firms may use various financial incentives, which we consider in the next section, to reduce the amount of monitoring that is necessary. Each of these incentives—bonding, deferred payments, and efficiency (unusually high) wages—acts as a *hostage* for good behavior (Williamson, 1983). Workers who are caught shirking or engaging in other undesirable acts not only lose their jobs but give up the hostage too. The more valuable the hostage, the less monitoring the firm needs to use to deter bad behavior.

Bonding

A direct approach to ensuring good behavior by agents is to require that they deposit funds guaranteeing their good behavior, just as a landlord requires tenants to post security deposits to ensure that they will not damage an apartment. An employer may require an employee to provide a performance *bond*, an amount of money that will be given to the principal if the agent fails to complete certain duties or achieve certain goals. Typically, the agent *posts* (leaves) this bond with the principal or another party, such as an insurance company, before starting the job.

Many couriers who transport valuable shipments (such as jewels) or guards who watch over them have to post bonds against theft and other moral hazards. Similarly, bonds may be used to keep employees from quitting immediately after receiving costly training (Salop and Salop, 1976). Academics who take a sabbatical—a leave of absence that is supposed to be devoted to training or other activities that increase their future productivity—must typically sign an agreement to pay the college or university a certain sum if they quit within a year after returning from their sabbatical. Most of the other approaches we will examine as strategies for controlling shirking can be viewed as forms of bonding.

Bonding to Prevent Shirking Some employers require a worker to post a bond that is forfeited if the employee is discovered shirking. For example, a professional athlete faces a specified fine (the equivalent of a bond) for skipping a meeting or game. The higher the bond, the less frequently the employer needs to monitor to prevent shirking.

Suppose that the value that a worker puts on the gain from taking it easy on the job is G dollars. If a worker's only potential punishment for shirking is dismissal if caught, some workers will shirk.

Suppose, however, that the worker must post a bond of B dollars that the worker forfeits if caught not working. Given the firm's level of monitoring, the probability that a worker is caught is θ. Thus, a worker who shirks expects to lose θB.[9] A risk-neutral worker chooses not to shirk if the certain gain from shirking, G, is less than or equal to the expected penalty, θB, from forfeiting the bond if caught: $G \leq \theta B$. Therefore, the minimum bond that discourages shirking is

$$B = \frac{G}{\theta}. \tag{20.1}$$

---

[9]The expected penalty is $\theta B + (1 - \theta)0 = \theta B$, where the first term on the left side is the probability of being caught times the fine of B and the second term is the probability of not being caught and facing no fine.

Equation 20.1 shows that the bond must be larger for the higher the value that the employee places on shirking and the lower the probability that the worker is caught.

Trade-Off Between Bonds and Monitoring Thus, the larger the bond, the less monitoring is necessary to prevent shirking. Suppose that a worker places a value of $G = \$1,000$ a year on shirking. A bond that is large enough to discourage shirking is $1,000 if the probability of being caught is 100%, $2,000 at 50%, $5,000 at 20%, $10,000 at 10%, and $20,000 if the probability of being caught is only 5%.

Solved Problem 20.5

Workers post bonds of B that are forfeited if they are caught stealing (but no other punishment is imposed). Each extra unit of monitoring, M, raises the probability that a firm catches a worker who steals, θ, by 5%. A unit of M costs $10. A worker can steal a piece of equipment and resell it for its full value of G dollars. What is the optimal M that the firm uses if it believes that workers are risk neutral? In particular, if $B = \$5,000$ and $G = \$500$, what is the optimal M?

Answer

1. *Determine how many units of monitoring are necessary to deter stealing.* The least amount of monitoring that deters stealing is the amount at which a worker's gain from stealing equals the worker's expected loss if caught. A worker is just deterred from stealing when the gain, G, equals the expected penalty, θB. Thus, the worker is deterred when the probability of being caught is $\theta = G/B$. The number of units of monitoring effort is $M = \theta/0.05$, because each extra unit of monitoring raises θ by 5%.

2. *Determine whether monitoring is cost effective.* It pays for the firm to pay for M units of monitoring only if the expected benefit to the firm is greater than the cost of monitoring, $\$10 \times M$. The expected benefit if stealing is prevented is G, so monitoring pays if $G > \$10 \times M$, or $G/M > \$10$.

3. *Solve for the optimal monitoring in the special case.* The optimal level of monitoring is

$$M = \frac{\theta}{0.05} = \frac{G/B}{0.05} = \frac{500/5{,}000}{0.05} = \frac{0.1}{0.05} = 2.$$

It pays to engage in this level of monitoring because $G/M = \$500/2 = \$250 > \$10$.

Problems with Bonding Employers like the bond-posting solution because it reduces the amount of employee monitoring necessary to discourage moral hazards such as shirking and thievery. Nonetheless, firms use explicit bonding only occasionally to prevent stealing, and they rarely use it to prevent shirking.

Two major problems are inherent in posting bonds. First, to capture a bond, an unscrupulous employer might falsely accuse an employee of stealing. An employee who fears such employer opportunism might be unwilling to post a bond. One possible solution to this problem is for the firm to develop a reputation for not behaving in this manner. Another possible approach is for the firm to make the grounds for forfeiture of the bond objective and thus verifiable by others.

A second problem with bonds is that workers may not have enough wealth to post them. In Solved Problem 20.5, if the worker could steal $10,000, and if the probability of being caught were only 5%, shirking would be deterred only if a risk-neutral worker were required to post a bond of at least $200,000.

Principals and agents use bonds when these two problems are avoidable. Bonds are more common in contracts between firms than in those between an employer and employees. Moreover, firms have fewer problems than typical employees do in raising funds to post bonds.

Construction contractors sometimes post bonds to guarantee that they will satisfactorily finish their work by a given date. Both parties can verify whether the contract has been completed on time, so the principal has relatively little chance to engage in opportunistic behavior.

Deferred Payments

Effectively, firms can post bonds for their employees through the use of deferred payments. For example, a firm pays new workers a low wage for some initial period of employment. Then, over time, workers who are caught shirking are fired, and those who remain get higher wages. In another form of deferred wages, the firm provides a pension that rewards only hard workers who stay with the firm until retirement. *Deferred payments serve the same function as bonds.* They raise the cost of being fired, so less monitoring is necessary to deter shirking.

Workers care about the present value (Chapter 16) of their earnings stream over their lifetime. A firm may offer its workers one of two wage payment schemes. In the first, the firm pays w per year for each year that the worker is employed by the firm. In the second arrangement, the starting wage is less than w but rises over the years to a wage that exceeds w.

If employees can borrow against future earnings, those who work for one company for their entire career are indifferent between the two wage payment schemes if those plans have identical present values. The firm, however, prefers the second payment method because employees work harder to avoid being fired and losing the high future earnings.

Reduced shirking leads to greater output. If the employer and employee share the extra output in the form of higher profit and lifetime earnings, both the firm and workers prefer the deferred-payment scheme that lowers incentives to shirk.

A drawback of the deferred-payment approach is that, like bond posting, it can encourage employers to engage in opportunistic behavior. For example, an employer might fire nonshirking senior workers to avoid paying their higher wages and replace them with less expensive junior workers. However, if the firm can establish a reputation for not firing senior workers unjustifiably, the deferred-payment system can help prevent shirking.

Efficiency Wages

efficiency wage
an unusually high wage that a firm pays workers as an incentive to avoid shirking

As we've seen, the use of bonds and deferred payments discourages shirking by raising an employee's cost of losing a job. An alternative is for the firm to pay an **efficiency wage**: an unusually high wage that a firm pays workers as an incentive to avoid shirking.[10] If a worker who is fired for shirking can immediately go to another firm and earn the same wage, the worker risks nothing by shirking. However, a high wage payment raises the cost of getting fired, so it discourages shirking.[11]

---

[10]The discussion of efficiency wages is based on Yellen (1984), Stiglitz (1987), and especially Shapiro and Stiglitz (1984).

[11]Economists have varying explanations for why efficiency wages lead to higher productivity. Some claim that employers in less-developed countries pay an efficiency wage—more than they need to hire workers—to ensure that workers can afford to eat well enough that they can work hard. Other economists (such as Akerlof, 1982) and management experts contend that the higher wage acts like a gift, making workers feel beholden or loyal to the firm, so that less (or no) monitoring is needed.

How Efficiency Wages Act like Bonds Suppose that a firm pays each worker an efficiency wage w, which is more than the *going wage* $\underline{w}$ that an employee would earn elsewhere after being fired for shirking. We now show that the less frequently the firm monitors workers, the greater the wage differential must be between w and $\underline{w}$ to prevent shirking.

A worker decides whether to shirk by comparing the expected loss of earnings from getting fired to the value, G, that the worker places on shirking. A shirking worker expects to lose $\theta(w - \underline{w})$, where θ is the probability that a shirking worker is caught and fired and the term in parentheses is the lost earnings from being fired. A risk-neutral worker does not shirk if the expected loss from being fired is greater than or equal to the gain from shirking (see Appendix 20A):

$$\theta(w - \underline{w}) \geq G. \tag{20.2}$$

The smallest amount by which w can exceed $\underline{w}$ and prevent shirking is determined where this expression holds with equality, $\theta(w - \underline{w}) = G$, or

$$w - \underline{w} = \frac{G}{\theta}. \tag{20.3}$$

The extra earnings, $w - \underline{w}$, in Equation 20.3 serve the same function as the bond, B, in Equation 20.1 in discouraging bad behavior.

Suppose that the worker gets $G = \$1,000$ pleasure a year from not working hard and $\underline{w}$ is $\$20,000$ a year. If the probability that a shirking worker is caught is $\theta = 20\%$, then the efficiency wage w must be at least $\$25,000$ to prevent shirking. With greater monitoring, so that θ is 50%, the minimum w that prevents shirking is $\$22,000$. From the possible pairs of monitoring levels and efficiency wages that deter shirking, the firm picks the combination that minimizes its labor cost.

Efficiency Wages and Unemployment We've argued that it is in a firm's best interest to pay more than the "going wage" to discourage shirking. The problem with this conclusion is that if it pays for one firm to raise its wage, it pays for all firms to do so. But if all firms raise their wages and pay the same amount, no one firm can discourage shirking by paying more than the others.

Nonetheless, the overall high wages do help prevent shirking. Because all firms are paying above the competitive wage, their labor demand falls, causing unemployment. Now if a worker is fired, the worker remains unemployed for a period of time while searching for a new job. Thus, the amount that the fired worker earns elsewhere, $\underline{w}$, is less than w because of this period of unemployment.[12] As a result, the (high) efficiency wages discourage shirking by creating unemployment.

One implication of this theory is that unemployment benefits provided by the government actually increase the unemployment rate. Such benefits raise $\underline{w}$, decrease the markup of w over $\underline{w}$, and thereby reduce the penalty of being fired. Thus, to discourage shirking, firms have to raise their efficiency wage even higher, and even more unemployment results.

Monitoring Outcomes

So far we've concentrated on monitoring by employers looking for bad behavior as it occurs. If shirking or other bad behavior is detected after the fact, the offending employee is fired or otherwise disciplined. This punishment discourages shirking in the future.

---

[12]If γ is the share of time that the fired worker remains unemployed, the worker's expected earnings are $\underline{w} = (1 - \gamma)w + \gamma 0 = (1 - \gamma)w$.

It is often very difficult to monitor bad behavior when it occurs but relatively easy to determine it after the fact. As long as a contract holds off payment until after the principal checks for bad behavior, after-the-fact monitoring discourages bad behavior. For example, an employer can check the quality of an employee's work. If it is substandard, the employer can force the employee to make it right.

Insurance companies frequently use this approach in contracts with their customers. Insurance firms try to avoid extreme moral hazard problems by offering contracts that do not cover spectacularly reckless, stupid, or malicious behavior. If an insurance company determines after the fact that a claim is based on reckless behavior rather than chance, the firm refuses to pay.

For example, an insurance company will not pay damages for a traffic accident if the insured driver is shown to have been drunk at the time. A house insurance company disallows claims due to an explosion that is found to result from an illegal activity such as making methamphetamines. It will certainly disallow claims by arsonists who torch their own homes or businesses. Life insurance companies may refuse to pay benefits to the family of someone who commits suicide (as in the play *Death of a Salesman*).

Finding out about moral hazards after they occur is too late if wrongdoers cannot be punished at that time. Indeed, it's pointless to monitor after the fact if punishment is then impossible or impractical. Although it's upsetting to find that you've been victimized, you can't do anything beyond trying to prevent the situation from happening again.

Application

Abusing Leased Cars

Because drivers of fleet automobiles such as rental cars do not own them, they do not bear all the cost from neglecting or abusing the vehicles, resulting in a moral hazard problem. These vehicles are driven harder and farther and depreciate faster than owner-operated vehicles. According to the Research and Innovative Technology Administration in 2013, new vehicle leases were 26% of new vehicle sales.

Using data from sales at used-car auctions, Dunham (2003) found that fleet vehicles (not including taxis or police cars) depreciate 10% to 13% faster than owner-driven vehicles, after controlling for mileage.[13] The difference between a nonfleet and a fleet car's average auction price for a typical car was 25% of the fleet car's price, which reflected the increased depreciation of fleet cars.

To deal with this moral hazard, an automobile-leasing firm commonly writes contracts—open-ended leases—in which the driver's final payment for the vehicle depends on the selling price of the car. Such a contract makes the leasing driver responsible for some of the wear and tear, which encourages the lessee to take greater care of the vehicle. However, given the difference in auction prices, such leases apparently are not the full solution to this moral hazard.

20.4 Checks on Principals

To this point, we have concentrated on situations in which the agent knows more than the principal. Sometimes, however, the principal may have asymmetric information and engage in opportunistic behavior.

---

[13]According to National Public Radio's *Car Talk*—one of the world's most reliable sources of information—police cars have very few miles on them, but their engines are quickly shot because cops spend untold hours sitting in their cruisers in front of donut shops with the engine running and the air conditioner on high.

Because employers (principals) often pay employees (agents) after work is completed, employers have many opportunities to exploit workers. For example, a dishonest employer can underpay after falsely claiming that a worker took time off or that some of the worker's output was substandard. The employer can decrease piece rates over time, after employees are committed to this payment system. Employers who provide bonuses can underreport the firm's output or profit. An employer can dock earnings, claim that an employee bond was forfeited, or refuse to make deferred payments such as pensions after dishonestly claiming that a monitored worker engaged in bad behavior. Efficient contracts prevent or reduce such moral hazard problems created by employers as well as those caused by employees.

Requiring that a firm post a bond can be an effective method of deterring the firm's opportunistic behavior. For example, a firm may post bonds to ensure that it has the means of paying current wages and future pensions.

Another strategy for preventing a firm from acting opportunistically is to eliminate asymmetric information by requiring the employer to reveal relevant information to employees. For example, an employer can provide access to such information by allowing employee representatives to sit on the company board—from which vantage point they can monitor the firm's behavior. To induce workers to agree to profit sharing, a firm may provide workers with information about the company's profit by allowing them (or an independent auditor) to check its accounts. Alternatively, the firm may argue that its stock closely mirrors its profit and suggest that the known stock price be used for incentive payments.

As another means of conveying information to employees, firms may seek to establish a good reputation. For instance, a firm may publicize that it does not make a practice of firing senior employees to avoid paying pensions. The better the firm's reputation, the more likely workers are to accept a deferred payment scheme, which deters shirking.

When firms find these approaches infeasible, they may use inefficient contracts that might, for example, stipulate payments to employees on the basis of easily observed revenues rather than less reliable profit reports. The following Application discusses a particularly damaging but common type of inefficient contract.

Application

Layoffs Versus Pay Cuts

During recessions and depressions, demand for most firms' products fall. Many firms respond by laying off workers and reducing production rather than by lowering wages and keeping everyone employed. From June 2002 through June 2013, the average real U.S. weekly earnings fluctuated in a narrow band from $333 to $356. In contrast, the U.S. unemployment rate over this period started at 5.8% in 2002, rose to 6.3% in 2003, dropped to 4.5% in 2007, rose to 9.6% in mid-2010, and then dropped to 8.2% in 2012 and 7.6% in June of 2013.

If both sides agreed to it, a wage reduction policy would benefit firms and workers alike. Workers would earn more than they would if they were laid off. Because the firm's costs would fall, it could sell more during the downturn than it otherwise could, so its profits would be higher than with layoffs. Firms that provide relatively low wages and then share profits with employees achieve this type of wage flexibility.

Why then are wage reductions less common than layoffs? A major explanation involves asymmetric information: Workers, unlike the firm, don't know whether the firm is actually facing a downturn, so they don't agree to wage cuts. In short, they don't trust the firm to tell them the truth. They fear that the firm will falsely claim that economic conditions are bad to justify a wage cut. If the firm has to lay off workers—an action that hurts the firm as well as the workers—the firm is more likely to be telling the truth about economic conditions.

We illustrate this reasoning in the following matrix, which shows the payoffs if wages are reduced during downturns. The value of output produced by each worker is $21 during good times and $15 during bad times. The lower left of each cell is the amount the firm pays workers. The firm pays employees $12 per hour if it reports that economic conditions are good and $8 if it says that conditions are bad. The amount the firm keeps is in the upper right of each cell. If economic conditions are bad, the firm earns more by reporting these bad conditions, $7, than it earns if it says that conditions are good, $3. Similarly, if conditions are good, the firm earns more if it claims that conditions are bad, $13, than if it says that they are good, $9. Thus, regardless of the true state, the firm always claims that conditions are bad.

Wage Cut

		Firm's Claim About Conditions	
		Bad	Good
Actual Conditions	Bad	8 7	12 3
	Good	8 13	12 9

To shield themselves from such systematic lying, employees may insist that the firm lay off workers whenever it says that conditions are bad. This requirement provides the firm with an incentive to report the true conditions. In the next matrix, the firm must lay off workers for half of each period if it announces that times are bad, causing the value of output to fall by one-third. Because they now work only half the time, workers earn only half as much, $6, as they earn during good times, $12. If conditions are bad, the firm makes more by telling the truth, $4, than by claiming that conditions are good, $3. In good times, the firm makes more by announcing that conditions are good, $9, than by claiming that they are bad, $8. Thus, the firm reports conditions truthfully.

Worker Layoff (for half of any period the firm claims is bad)

		Firm's Claim About Conditions	
		Bad	Good
Actual Conditions	Bad	6 4	12 3
	Good	6 8	12 9

With the wage-cut contract in which the firm always says that conditions are bad, workers earn $8 regardless of actual conditions. If economic conditions are good half the time, the firm earns an average of $10 = ($\frac{1}{2}$ × $7) + ($\frac{1}{2}$ × $13). Under the contract that requires layoffs, the workers earn an average of $9 = ($\frac{1}{2}$ × $6) + ($\frac{1}{2}$ × $12) and the firm earns an average of $6.50 = ($\frac{1}{2}$ × $4) + ($\frac{1}{2}$ × $9).

Therefore, the firm prefers the wage-cut contract and the workers favor the layoff contract. However, if the workers could observe actual conditions, both parties would prefer the wage-cut contract. Workers would earn an average of $10 = (\frac{1}{2} \times \$8) + (\frac{1}{2} \times \$12)$, and the firm would make $8 = (\frac{1}{2} \times \$7) + (\frac{1}{2} \times \$9)$. With the layoff contract, total payoffs are lower because of lost production. Thus, socially inefficient layoffs may be used because of the need to keep relatively well-informed firms honest.

20.5   Contract Choice

We have examined how to construct a single contract so as to prevent moral hazards. Often, however, a principal gives an agent a choice of contract. By observing the agent's choice, the principal obtains enough information to prevent agent opportunism.

Firms want to avoid hiring workers who will shirk. Employers know that not all workers shirk, even when given an opportunity to do so. So rather than focusing on stopping lazy workers from shirking, an employer may concentrate on hiring only industrious people. With this approach, the firm seeks to avoid *moral hazard* problems by preventing *adverse selection*, whereby lazy employees falsely assert that they are hardworking.

As discussed in Chapter 19, employees may *signal* to employers that they are productive. For example, if only nonshirking employees agree to work long hours, a commitment to work long hours serves as a reliable signal. In addition, employees can signal by developing a reputation as hard workers. To the degree that employers can rely on this reputation, sorting is achieved.

When workers cannot credibly signal, firms may try to *screen out* bad workers. One way firms can determine which prospective employees will work hard and which will shirk is to give them a choice of contracts. If job candidates who are hard workers select a contingent contract whereby their pay depends on how hard they work and if job applicants who are lazy workers choose a fixed-fee contract, the firm can tell the applicants apart by their choices.

Suppose that a firm wants to hire a salesperson who will run its Cleveland office and that the potential employees are risk neutral. A hardworking salesperson can sell $100,000 worth of goods a year, but a lazy one can sell only $60,000 worth (see Table 20.2). A hard worker can earn $30,000 from other firms, so the firm considers using a contingent contract that pays a salesperson a 30% commission on sales.

If the firm succeeds in hiring a hard worker, the salesperson makes $30,000 = \$100,000 \times 0.30$. The firm's share of sales is $70,000. The firm has no costs of production (for simplicity), but maintaining this branch office costs the firm $50,000 a year. The firm's profit is therefore $20,000. If the firm hires a lazy salesperson under the same contract, the salesperson makes $18,000, the firm's share of sales is $42,000, and the firm loses $8,000 after paying for the office.

Thus, the firm wants to hire only a hard worker. Unfortunately, the firm does not know in advance whether a potential employee is a hard worker. To acquire this information, the firm offers a potential employee a choice of contracts:

- **Contingent contract.** No salary and 30% of sales
- **Fixed-fee contract.** Annual salary of $25,000, regardless of sales

A prospective employee who doesn't mind hard work would earn $5,000 more by choosing the contingent contract. In contrast, a lazy candidate would make $7,000 more from a salary than from commissions. If an applicant chooses the fixed-fee

Table 20.2 Firm's Spreadsheet

	Contingent Contract (30% of Sales), $	Fixed-Fee Contract ($25,000 Salary), $
Hard Worker		
Sales	100,000	100,000
− Salesperson's pay	−30,000	−25,000
= Firm's net revenue	70,000	75,000
− Office expenses	−50,000	−50,000
= Firm's profit	20,000	25,000
Lazy Worker		
Sales	60,000	60,000
− Salesperson's pay	−18,000	−25,000
= Firm's net revenue	42,000	35,000
− Office expenses	−50,000	−50,000
= Firm's profit	−8,000	−15,000

contract, the firm knows that the person does not intend to work hard and decides not to hire that person.

The firm learns what it needs to know by offering this contract choice as long as the lazy applicant does not pretend to be a hard worker by choosing the contingent contract. Under the contingent contract, the lazy person makes only $18,000, but that offer may dominate others available in the market. If this pair of contracts fails to sort workers, the firm may try different pairs. If all these choices fail to sort, the firm must use other means to prevent shirking.

Challenge Solution

Changing Bankers' Incentives

In the aftermath of the financial crisis of 2007–2009, most economists and government officials concluded that banks and many other firms in the financial sector had taken on excessive risks. In Solved Problem 20.1, we answered the first question in our Challenge as to why bankers take on excessive risks by showing that they have an incentive to take a hidden, risky action if they're compensated for success and not substantially penalized for failure.

We now return to the second Challenge question: How can a firm compensate its corporate executives so as to prevent them from undertaking irresponsible and potentially damaging actions? One approach is to provide incentives that penalize them relatively more for failure.

We can illustrate this idea by modifying Solved Problem 20.1. As before, Leonardo, a senior executive at the Las Vegas Home Bank, either offers only low-risk prime mortgages or a combination of prime and riskier subprime mortgages. If he provides only prime mortgages, the bank's profit is $160 million with certainty. If he sells both prime and subprime mortgages, the bank earns $800 million with a 25% probability or loses $320 million with a 75% probability, because subprime loans carry a high risk of default.

Before, Leonardo received 1% of the bank's profit if it was positive and nothing if it was negative. Under his new contract, Leonardo receives a salary of $1.15 million a year and 0.25% of the bank's profit. If the bank suffers a loss, Leonardo is fired, so that he loses his salary and receives no bonus.

This new compensation scheme gives him the same earnings if he makes only prime loans. However, now he stands to lose his salary if he chooses to also make the riskier, subprime loans and the firm loses money.

Given Leonardo's original compensation scheme—1% of the bank's profit—he chooses the riskier approach: He has a 25% chance of earning $8 million, so that he expects to earn $2 million. Because that exceeds his earnings of $1.6 million if he sells only prime mortgages, he decides to provide subprime loans as well, so the firm has a negative expected profit (see Solved Problem 20.1).

With the new compensation plan of $1.15 million salary plus 0.25% of positive profits, if Leonardo provides only prime loans, he makes $1.6 million (= $1.15 million + [0.0025 × $180 million]), which is the same as he previously made. If he also makes subprime loans, he expects to earn nothing three-quarters of the time, and $3.15 million (= $1.15 million + [0.0025 × $800 million]) one-quarter of the time. As a result, his expected earnings are (0.75 × 0) + (0.25 × $3.15 million) = $0.7875 million. As he expects to earn more than twice as much from providing only prime loans, he no longer wants to offer subprime mortgages.

Thus, with this new compensation scheme, the bank shareholders avoid the original moral hazard problem. Leonardo's hidden action—whether he offers subprime loans—no longer exposes them to excessive risk.

Before the 2007–2009 financial crisis, contracts creating this excessive risk-taking moral hazard were very common, partly because the people designing the contracts—firms' senior executives—were the beneficiaries of the generous incentives. If shareholders had understood these contracts and had symmetric information, they would have objected, but few shareholders had the time, the ability, or sufficient information to scrutinize executive compensation contracts.

Summary

1. **The Principal-Agent Problem.** A moral hazard may occur if a principal contracts with an agent to perform an action and the principal cannot observe the agent's actions so that the agent takes advantage of the principal. For example, if the owner cannot observe how hard an employee works, the employee may shirk. This moral hazard reduces their joint profit. An efficient contract leads to efficiency in production (joint profit is maximized by eliminating moral hazards) and efficiency in risk bearing (the less-risk-averse party bears more of the risk). Whether efficiency in production is achieved depends on the contract that the principal and the agent use and the degree to which their information is asymmetric. Ideally, the contract or agreement between the parties is efficient, so that they maximize the total profit of the parties and share risk optimally.

2. **Using Contracts to Reduce Moral Hazard.** A principal and an agent may agree to a contract that eliminates a moral hazard or at least strikes a balance between reducing the moral hazard and allocating risk optimally. Contracts that eliminate moral hazards often require the agent to bear the risk. If the agent is more risk averse than the principal, the parties may trade off a reduction in production efficiency to lower risk for the agent.

3. **Monitoring to Reduce Moral Hazard.** Because of asymmetric information, an employer must normally monitor workers' efforts to prevent shirking. Less monitoring is necessary as the employee's interest in keeping the job increases. The employer may require the employee to post a large bond that is forfeited if the employee is caught shirking, stealing, or otherwise misbehaving. If an employee cannot afford to post a bond, the employer may use deferred payments or efficiency wages—unusually high wages—to make it worthwhile for the employee to keep the job. Employers may also be able to prevent shirking by engaging in after-the-fact monitoring. However, such monitoring works only if bad behavior can be punished after the fact.

4. **Checks on Principals.** Often both agents and principals can engage in opportunistic behavior. If a firm must reveal its actions to its employees, it is less likely to be able to take advantage of the employees. To convey information, an employer may let employees participate in decision-making meetings or audit the company's books. Alternatively, an employer may make commitments so that it is in the employer's best interest to tell employees the truth. These commitments, such as laying off workers rather than reducing wages during downturns, may reduce moral hazards but lead to nonoptimal production.

5. **Contract Choice.** A principal may be able to obtain valuable information from an agent by offering a choice of contracts. Employers avoid moral hazard problems by preventing adverse selection. For example, they may present potential employees with a choice of contracts, prompting hardworking job applicants to choose one contract and lazy candidates to choose another.

Questions

All questions are available on MyEconLab; * = *answer appears at the back of this book;* **A** = *algebra problem;* **C** = *calculus problem.*

1. The Principal-Agent Problem

*1.1 Sometimes a group of hungry students will go a restaurant and agree to share the bill at the end regardless of who orders what. What is the implication of this fee-sharing arrangement on the size of the overall bill? Why?

1.2 In 2012, a California environmental group found that 14 plum and ginger candies imported from Asia contained 4 to 96 times the level of lead allowed under California law (Stephanie M. Lee, "Lead Found in Asian Candies," *San Francisco Chronicle*, August 14, 2012). Some observers predicted that U.S. consumers would face significant price increases if U.S. law were changed to require third-party testing by manufacturers and sellers. Suppose instead that candies could be reliably labeled "tested" or "untested," and untested candy sold at a discount. Discuss reasons why consumers might buy cheaper, untested goods or would not because they fear a moral hazard problem.

*1.3 A promoter arranges for many different restaurants to set up booths to sell Cajun-Creole food at a fair. The promoter provides appropriate music and other entertainment. Customers can buy food using only "Cajun Cash," which is scrip with the same denominations as actual cash sold by the promoter at the fair. Why aren't the food booths allowed to sell food directly for cash?

1.4 California set up its own earthquake insurance program. Because the state agency in charge has few staff members, it pays private insurance carriers to handle claims for earthquake damage. These insurance firms receive 9% of each approved claim. Is this compensation scheme likely to lead to opportunistic behavior by insurance companies? If so, what would be a better way to handle the compensation?

*1.5 Some sellers offer to buy back a good later at some prespecified price. Why would a firm make such a commitment to deal with moral hazard concerns?

1.6 According to a flyer from one of the world's largest brokers, "Most personal investment managers base their fees on a percentage of assets managed. We believe this is in your best interest because your manager is paid for investment management, not solely on the basis of trading commissions charged to your account. You can be assured your manager's investment decisions are guided by one primary goal—increasing your assets." Is this policy in a customer's best interest? Why or why not?

1.7 A study by Jean Mitchell found that urologists in group practices that profit from tests for prostate cancer order more of them than doctors who send samples to independent laboratories. Doctors' groups that perform their own lab work bill Medicare for analyzing 72% more prostate tissue samples per biopsy and detect fewer cases of cancer than doctors who use outside labs (Christopher Weaver, "Prostate-Test Fees Challenged," *Wall Street Journal*, April 9, 2012). Explain these results. Do these results necessarily demonstrate moral hazard or can the results be explained in another way? (*Hint*: See the Application "Selfless or Selfish Doctors?".)

1.8 Sarah, the manager of a bank, can make one of two types of loans. She can loan money to local firms, and have a 75% probability of earning $100 million and a 25% probability of earning $80 million. Alternatively, she can loan money to oil speculators, and have a 25% probability of earning $400 million and a 75% probability of losing $160 million (due to loan defaults by the speculators). Sarah receives 1% of the bank's earnings.

She believes that if the bank loses money, she can walk away from her job without repercussions, although she will not receive any compensation. Sarah and the bank's shareholders are risk neutral. How does Sarah invest the bank's money if all she cares about is maximizing her personal expected earnings? How would the stockholders prefer that Sarah invest the bank's money? (*Hint*: See Solved Problem 20.1.) **A**

2. Using Contracts to Reduce Moral Hazard

2.1 Padma has the rights to any treasure on the sunken ship the *Golden Calf*. Aaron is a diver who specializes in marine salvage. If Padma is risk averse and Aaron is risk neutral, does paying Aaron a fixed fee result in efficiency in risk bearing and production? Does your answer turn on how predictable the value of the sunken treasure is? Would another compensation scheme be more efficient?

2.2 A health insurance company tries to prevent the moral hazard of "excessive" dentist visits by limiting the visits per person per year to a specific number. How does such a restriction affect moral hazard and risk bearing? Show these results in a graph. (*Hint*: See Solved Problem 20.2.)

2.3 Traditionally, doctors have been paid on a fee-for-service basis. Now doctors are increasingly paid on a capitated basis (they get paid for treating a patient for a year, regardless of how much treatment is required), though a patient may still have to pay a small fee each visit. In this arrangement, doctors form a group and sign a capitation contract whereby they take turns seeing a given patient. What are the implications of this change in compensation for moral hazards and for risk bearing?

*2.4 Priscilla hires Arnie to manage her store. Arnie's effort is given in the left column of the table. Each cell shows the net profit to Priscilla (ignoring Arnie's cost of effort).

	Low Demand	High Demand
Low Effort	20	40
Medium Effort	40	80
High Effort	80	100

Arnie's personal cost of effort is 0 at low effort, 10 at medium effort, and 30 at high effort. It is equally likely that demand will be low or high. Arnie and Priscilla are risk neutral.

They consider two possible contracts: (1) *fixed fee*: Arnie receives a fixed wage of 10; and (2) *profit*

sharing: Arnie receives 50% of the firm's net income but no wage.

a. What happens if they use the fixed fee contract?

b. What happens if they use the profit-sharing contract?

c. Which contract does each prefer? **A**

2.5 In the situation described in the previous question, how do your answers change if Arnie's first contract changes so that he receives a basic fixed wage of 10 and, in addition, a bonus equal to 80% of any net income?

2.6 Patrick, the owner, makes the same offer to the manager at each of his stores: "At the end of the year, pay me a lump-sum of $100,000, and you can keep any additional profit." Astrid, a manager at one of the stores, gladly agrees, knowing that the total profit at the store will substantially exceed $100,000 if it is well run. If she is interested in maximizing her earnings, will Astrid act in a manner that maximizes the store's total profit? (*Hint*: See Solved Problem 20.3.)

*2.7 Zhihua and Pu are partners in a store in which they do all the work. They split the store's *business profit* equally (ignoring the opportunity cost of their own time in calculating this profit). Does their business profit-sharing contract give them an incentive to maximize their joint economic profit if neither can force the other to work? (*Hint*: Imagine Zhihua's thought process late one Saturday night when he is alone in the store, debating whether to keep the store open a little later or to go out on the town, and see Solved Problem 20.4.)

2.8 In Solved Problem 20.4, does joint profit increase, decrease, or remain the same as the share of revenue going to Ann increases?

*2.9 Jack and Jill live in different cities. Regardless of which one chooses to fly to visit the other, they agree to split the cost of the flight equally. What is the implication of this fee-sharing arrangement? (*Hint*: See Solved Problem 20.4.)

2.10 In the National Basketball Association (NBA), the owners share revenue but not their costs. Suppose that one team, the L.A. Clippers, sells only general-admission seats to a home game with the visiting Philadelphia 76ers (Sixers). Suppose that the inverse demand for the Clippers-Sixers tickets is $p = 100 - 0.004Q$. The Clippers' cost function of selling Q tickets and running the franchise is $C(Q) = 10Q$.

a. Find the Clippers' profit-maximizing number of tickets sold and the price if the Clippers must give 50% of their revenue to the Sixers. At this maximum, what are the Clippers' profit and the Sixers' earnings?

b. Instead, suppose that the Sixers set the Clippers' ticket price based on the same revenue-sharing rule. What price will the Sixers set, how many tickets are sold, and what revenue payment will the Sixers receive? Explain why your answers to parts a and b differ.

c. Now suppose that the Clippers share their profit rather than their revenue. The Clippers keep 45% of their profit and the Sixers receive 55%. The Clippers set the price. Find the Clippers' profit-maximizing price and determine how many tickets the team sells and its share of the profit.

d. Compare your answers to parts a and c using marginal revenue and marginal cost in your explanation. (*Hint*: See Solved Problems 20.3 and 20.4.) **C**

2.11 Suppose that a textbook author is paid a royalty of α share of the revenue from sales where the revenue is $R = pq$, p is the competitive market price for textbooks, and q is the number of copies of this textbook (which is similar to others on the market) sold. The publisher's cost of printing and distributing the book is $C(q)$. Determine the equilibrium, and compare it to the outcome that maximizes the sum of the payment to the author plus the firm's profit. Answer using both math and a graph. Why do you think royalties are typically based on revenue rather than profit? **C**

2.12 Suppose now that the textbook publisher in the previous question faces a downward-sloping demand curve. The revenue is $R(Q)$, and the publisher's cost of printing and distributing the book is $C(Q)$. Compare the equilibria for the following compensation methods in which the author receives the same total compensation from each method:

a. The author is paid a lump sum, $\mathcal{L}$.

b. The author is paid α share of the revenue.

c. The author receives a lump-sum payment and a share of the revenue.

Why do you think that authors are usually paid a share of revenue? **C**

3. Monitoring to Reduce Moral Hazard

3.1 Many law firms consist of partners who share profits. On being made a partner, a lawyer must post a bond, a large payment to the firm that will be forfeited on bad behavior. Why?

*3.2 In Solved Problem 20.5, a firm calculated the optimal level of monitoring to prevent stealing. If $G = \$500$ and $\theta = 20\%$, what is the minimum bond that deters stealing? **A**

3.3 In the previous question, suppose that for each extra $1,000 of bonding that the firm requires a worker to post, the firm must pay that worker $10 more per period to get the worker to work for the firm. What is the minimum bond that deters stealing? (*Hint*: See Solved Problem 20.5.) **A**

3.4 Explain why full employment may be inconsistent with no shirking.

3.5 As of 2008, Medicare stopped covering the costs of a surgeon leaving an instrument in a patient, giving a patient transfusions of the wrong blood type, certain types of hospital-acquired infections, and other "preventable" mistakes (Liz Marlantes, "Medicare Won't Cover Hospital Mistakes: New Rules Aimed at Promoting Better Hospital Care and Safety," *ABC News*, August 19, 2007). Hospitals now have to cover these costs and cannot bill the patient. These changes were designed to provide hospitals with a stronger incentive to prevent such mistakes, particularly infections. The Centers for Disease Control and Prevention estimated that 2 million patients are annually infected in hospitals, costing society more than $27 billion. Nearly 100,000 of those infections are fatal. Many of these infections could be prevented if hospitals more rigorously follow basic infection control procedures, including having doctors and nurses wash their hands between every patient. Is Medicare's new policy designed to deal with adverse selection (Chapter 19) or moral hazard? Is it likely to help? Explain.

3.6 When rental cars are sold on the used car market, they are sold for lower prices than cars of the same model and year that were owned by individual owners. Does this price difference reflect adverse selection or moral hazard? Could car rental companies reduce this problem by carefully inspecting rental cars for damage when renters return such cars? Why do car companies normally perform only a cursory inspection?

4. Checks on Principals

4.1 List as many ways as possible that a principal can reassure an agent that it will avoid opportunistic behavior.

4.2 Fourteen states have laws that limit conditions under which a franchisor (such as McDonald's) can terminate a franchise agreement. Franchisees typically pay the franchisor a fixed fee or a share of revenues. What effects would such laws have on production efficiency and risk bearing? (*Hint*: See Solved Problems 20.3 and 20.4.)

5. Contract Choice

5.1 List some necessary conditions for a firm to be able to sort potential employees by providing them with a choice of contracts.

5.2 In the contract choice example in the chapter, what are the implications for risk bearing of the fixed-fee and contingent contract if the sales revenue varies with market conditions? Will a worker's attitude toward risk affect which contract the worker chooses?

6. Challenge

6.1 In the Challenge Solution, show that shareholders' expected earnings are higher with the new compensation scheme than with the original one.

6.2 In 2012, Hewlett-Packard Co. announced that its new chief executive, Meg Whitman, would receive a salary of $1 and about $16.1 million in stock options, which are valuable if the stock does well (**marketwatch.com**, February 3, 2012). How would you feel about this compensation package if you were a shareholder? What are the implications for moral hazard, efficiency, and risk sharing?

6.3 Adrienne, a manager of a large firm, must decide whether to launch a new product or make a minor change to an existing product. The new product has a 30% chance of being a big success and generating profits of $20 million, a 40% chance of being fairly successful and generating profits of $5 million, and a 30% chance of being a costly failure and losing $10 million. Making minor changes in the old product would generate profits of $10 million for sure. Adrienne's contract gives her a bonus of 10% of any profits above $8 million arising from this decision. If Adrienne is risk neutral and cares only about her own income, what is her decision? Should shareholders be happy with this compensation contract? Design a contract that would be better for both Adrienne and the shareholders. **A**

Chapter Appendixes

Appendix 2A: Regressions

An economist's guess is as likely to be as good as anyone else's. — Will Rogers

Economists use a *regression* to estimate economic relationships such as demand curves and supply curves. A regression analysis allows us to answer three types of questions:

- How can we best fit an economic relationship to actual data?
- How confident are we in our results?
- How can we determine the effect of a change in one variable on another if many other variables are changing at the same time?

Estimating Economic Relations

We use a demand curve example to illustrate how regressions can answer these questions. The points in Figure 2A.1 show eight years of data on Nancy's annual purchases of candy bars, q, and the prices, p, she paid.[1] For example, in the year when candy bars cost 20¢, Nancy bought q_2 candy bars.

Because we assume that Nancy's tastes and income did not change during this period, we write her demand for candy bars as a function of the price of candy bars and unobservable random effects. We believe that her demand curve is linear and want to estimate the demand function:

$$q = a + bp + e,$$

where a and b are coefficients we want to determine and e is an error term. This *error term* captures random effects that are not otherwise reflected in our function. For instance, in one year, Nancy broke up with her longtime boyfriend and ate more candy bars than usual, resulting in a relatively large positive error term for that year.

The data points in the figure exhibit a generally downward-sloping relationship between quantity and price, but the points do not lie strictly on a line because of the error terms. We could draw a line through these data points in many possible ways.

---

[1]We use a lowercase q for the quantity demanded for an individual instead of the uppercase Q that we use for a market. Notice that we violated the rule economists usually follow of putting quantity on the horizontal axis and price on the vertical axis. We are now looking at this relationship as statisticians who put the independent or explanatory variable, price, on the horizontal axis and the dependent variable, quantity, on the vertical axis.

Figure 2A.1 Regression

The circles show data on how many candy bars Nancy bought in a year at several different prices. The regression line minimizes the sum of the squared residuals, e_1 through e_8.

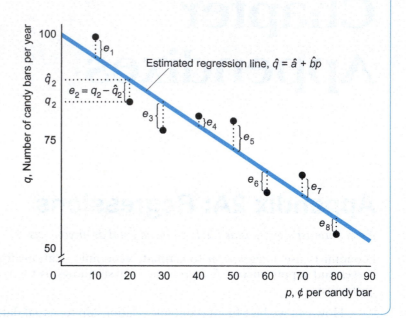

The way we fit the line in the figure is to use the standard criterion that our estimates *minimize the sum of squared residuals*, where a residual, $e = q - \hat{q}$, is the difference between an actual quantity, q, and the fitted or predicted quantity on the estimated line, $\hat{q}$. That is, we choose estimated coefficients $\hat{a}$ and $\hat{b}$ so that the estimated quantities from the regression line,

$$\hat{q} = \hat{a} + \hat{b}p,$$

make the sum of the squared residuals, $e_1^2 + e_2^2 + \cdots + e_8^2$, as small as possible. By summing the square of the residuals instead of the residuals themselves, we treat the effects of a positive or negative error symmetrically and give greater weight to large errors than to small ones.[2] In the figure, the regression line is

$$\hat{q} = 99.4 - 0.49p,$$

where $\hat{a} = 99.4$ is the intercept of the estimated line and $\hat{b} = -0.49$ is the slope of the line.

Confidence in Our Estimates

Because the data reflect random errors, so do the estimated coefficients. Our estimate of Nancy's demand curve depends on the *sample* of data we use. If we were to use data from a different set of years, our estimates, $\hat{a}$ and $\hat{b}$, of the true coefficients, a and b, would differ.

---

[2]Using calculus, we can derive the $\hat{a}$ and $\hat{b}$ that minimize the sum of squared residuals. The estimate of the slope coefficient is a weighted average of the observed quantities, $\hat{b} = \Sigma_i w_i q_i$, where $w_i = (p_i - \bar{p})/\Sigma_i(p_i - \bar{p})^2$, $\bar{p}$ is the average of the observed prices, and Σ_i indicates the sum over each observation i. The estimate of the intercept, $\hat{a}$, is the average of the observed quantities.

If we had many estimates of the true parameter based on many samples, the estimates would be distributed around the true coefficient. These estimates are *unbiased* in the sense that the average of the estimates would equal the true coefficients.

Computer programs that calculate regression lines report a *standard error* for each coefficient, which is an estimate of the dispersion of the estimated coefficients around the true coefficient. In our example, a computer program reports

$$\hat{q} = 99.4 - 0.49p,$$
$$(3.99) \quad (0.08)$$

where, below each estimated coefficient, its estimated standard error appears between parentheses.

The smaller the estimated standard error, the more precise the estimate, and the more likely it is to be close to the true value. As a rough rule of thumb, there is a 95% probability that the interval that is within two standard errors of the estimated coefficient contains the true coefficient.[3] Using this rule, the *confidence interval* for the slope coefficient, $\hat{b}$, ranges from

$$-0.49 - (2 \times 0.08) = -0.65 \text{ to } -0.49 + (2 \times 0.08) = -0.33.$$

If zero were to lie within the confidence interval for $\hat{b}$, we would conclude that we cannot reject the hypothesis that the price has no effect on the quantity demanded. In our case, however, the entire confidence interval contains negative values, so we are reasonably sure that the higher the price, the less Nancy demands.

Multiple Regression

We can also estimate relationships involving more than one explanatory variable using a *multiple regression*. For example, Moschini and Meilke (1992) estimate a pork demand function, Equation 2.2, in which the quantity demanded is a function of income, Y, and the prices of pork, p, beef, p_b, and chicken, p_c:

$$Q = 171 - 20p + 20p_b + 3p_c + 2Y.$$

The multiple regression is able to separate the effects of the various explanatory variables. The coefficient 20 on the p variable says that an increase in the price of pork by \$1 per kg lowers the quantity demanded by 20 million kg per year, holding the effects of the other prices and income constant.

Appendix 3A: Effects of a Specific Tax on Equilibrium

Given that the government collects a specific or unit tax, t, from sellers, sellers receive $p - t$ when consumers pay p. We can use this information to determine the effect of a new tax on the equilibrium. In the post-tax equilibrium, the price that consumers pay is determined by the equality between the demand function and the after-tax supply function,

$$D(p) - S(p - t) = 0. \tag{3A.1}$$

---

[3]The confidence interval is the coefficient plus or minus 1.96 times its standard error for large samples (at least hundreds of observations) in which the coefficients are normally distributed. For smaller samples, the confidence interval tends to be larger.

where the supply equals demand equation is written in implicit function form (the right side of the equation is zero). That is, this equation implicitly defines the price as a function of t: $p(t)$.

We determine the effect a small tax has on the price by differentiating Equation 3A.1 with respect to t:

$$\frac{dD}{dp}\frac{dp}{dt} - \frac{dS}{dp}\frac{d(p(t) - t)}{dt} = \frac{dD}{dp}\frac{dp}{dt} - \frac{dS}{dp}\left(\frac{dp}{dt} - 1\right) = 0.$$

Rearranging the terms, it follows that the change in the price that consumers pay with respect to the change in the tax is

$$\frac{dp}{dt} = \frac{\dfrac{dS}{dp}}{\dfrac{dS}{dp} - \dfrac{dD}{dp}}. \tag{3A.2}$$

We know that $dD/dp < 0$ from the Law of Demand. If the supply curve slopes upward so that $dS/dp > 0$, then $dp/dt > 0$. The higher the tax, the greater the price consumers pay. If $dS/dp < 0$, the direction of change is ambiguous: It depends on the relative slopes of the supply and demand curves (the denominator).

By multiplying both the numerator and denominator of the right side of Equation 3A.2 by p/Q, we can express this derivative in terms of elasticities,

$$\frac{dp}{dt} = \frac{\dfrac{dS}{dp}\dfrac{p}{Q}}{\dfrac{dS}{dp}\dfrac{p}{Q} - \dfrac{dD}{dp}\dfrac{p}{Q}} = \frac{\eta}{\eta - \varepsilon}, \tag{3A.3}$$

where the last equality follows because dS/dp and dD/dp are the changes in the quantities supplied and demanded as price changes, and the consumer and producer prices are identical when $t = 0$. That is, for small changes in the tax rate, Δt, the change in price, Δp, equals $[\eta/(\eta - \varepsilon)]\Delta t$.

To determine the effect on quantity, we can combine the price result from Equation 3A.3 with information from either the demand or the supply function. Differentiating the demand function with respect to t, we know that

$$\eta > 0. \frac{dD}{dp}\frac{dp}{dt} = \frac{dD}{dp}\frac{\eta}{\eta - \varepsilon},$$

which is negative if the supply curve is upward sloping so that $\eta = 0$.

Appendix 4A: Utility and Indifference Curves

We now use calculus to examine the relationship between utility and indifference curves and some properties of indifference curves. Suppose that Lisa's utility function is $U(B, Z)$, where B is the number of burritos and Z is the number of pizzas. Lisa's marginal utility for burritos, MU_B, is the amount of extra pleasure she would get from extra burritos, holding her consumption of pizza constant. Formally, her marginal utility for burritos, B, is the partial derivative of utility, $U(B, Z)$, with respect to B holding Z constant:

$$MU_B(B, Z) = \lim_{\Delta B \to 0} \frac{U(B + \Delta B, Z) - U(B, Z)}{\Delta B} = \frac{\partial U(B, Z)}{\partial B}.$$

By assumption, marginal utility is always nonnegative: A little more of a good makes you better off or at least doesn't harm you. The marginal utility depends on the current levels of B and Z.

Which combinations of B and Z leave Lisa with a given level of pleasure, say, $\overline{U}$? We can write those combinations as

$$\overline{U} = U(B, Z). \tag{4A.1}$$

Equation 4A.1 is the equation for an indifference curve with utility level $\overline{U}$.

We can express the slope of an indifference curve—the marginal rate of substitution, *MRS*—in terms of the marginal utilities. The slope of the indifference curve is found by determining the changes in B and P that leave utility unchanged. Totally differentiating Equation 4A.1, we find that

$$d\overline{U} = 0 = \frac{\partial U(B, Z)}{\partial B} dB + \frac{\partial U(B, Z)}{\partial Z} dZ \equiv MU_B dB + MU_Z dZ \tag{4A.2}$$

This equation says that a little extra utility, MU_B, times the change in B, dB, plus the extra utility, MU_Z, times the change in Z, dZ, must add to zero. If we increase one of the goods, we must decrease the other to hold utility constant so that we stay on the same indifference curve. In Equation 4A.2, $d\overline{U} = 0$ because we are holding utility constant so that we stay on the same indifference curve. Rearranging the terms in Equation 4A.2, we find that

$$\frac{dB}{dZ} = -\frac{MU_Z}{MU_B}.$$

The slope of the indifference curve is the negative of the ratio of the marginal utilities.

Suppose that Lisa has the following utility function, known as a *Cobb-Douglas utility function*:

$$U(B, Z) = AB^{\alpha}Z^{\beta}. \tag{4A.3}$$

Her marginal utility of burritos is

$$MU_B(B, Z) = \alpha AB^{\alpha-1}Z^{\beta} = \alpha \frac{U(B, Z)}{B},$$

and her marginal utility of pizza is

$$MU_Z(B, Z) = \beta AB^{\alpha}Z^{\beta-1} = \beta \frac{U(B, Z)}{Z}.$$

Suppose that $\alpha = \beta = \frac{1}{2}$ and $A = 20$. If $B = Z = 4$, then $U(4, 4) = 80$ and $MU_B(4, 4) = MU_Z(4, 4) = 10$. If $B = 1$ and $Z = 4$, however, $U(1, 4) = 40$, $MU_B(1, 4) = 20$, and $MU_Z(1, 4) = 5$. The extra pleasure that Lisa gets from an extra burrito is greater, the fewer burritos she initially has, all else the same.

The slope of her indifference curve is

$$MRS = \frac{dB}{dZ} = -\frac{MU_Z}{MU_B} = -\frac{\beta AB^\alpha Z^{\beta-1}}{\alpha AB^{\alpha-1}Z^\beta} = -\frac{\beta B}{\alpha Z}.$$

The slope of the indifference curve differs with the levels of B and Z. If $\alpha = \beta = \frac{1}{2}$, $B = 4$, and $Z = 1$, $MRS(4, 1) = -(\frac{1}{2} \times 4)/(\frac{1}{2} \times 1) = -4$. At $B = Z = 4$, $MRS(4, 4) = -1$.

Appendix 4B: Maximizing Utility

Lisa's objective is to maximize her utility, $U(B, Z)$, subject to (s.t.) a budget constraint:

$$\max_{B, Z} U(B, Z)$$
$$\text{s.t.} \quad Y = p_B B + p_Z Z, \tag{4B.1}$$

where B is the number of burritos she buys at price p_B, Z is the number of pizzas she buys at price p_Z, Y is her income, and $Y = p_B B + p_Z Z$ is her budget constraint (her spending on burritos and pizza can't exceed her income). The mathematical statement of her problem shows that her *control variables* (what she chooses) are B and Z, which appear under the "max" term in the equation. We assume that Lisa has no control over the prices she faces or her budget.

To solve this type of constrained maximization problem, we use the Lagrangian method:

$$\max_{B, Z, \lambda} \mathcal{L} = U(B, Z) - \lambda(p_B B + p_Z Z - Y), \tag{4B.2}$$

where λ is called the Lagrangian multiplier. With normal-shaped utility functions, the values of B, Z, and λ that are determined by the first-order conditions of this Lagrangian problem are the same as the values that maximize the original constrained problem. The first-order conditions of Equation 4B.2 with respect to the three control variables, B, Z, and λ, are:[4]

$$\frac{\partial \mathcal{L}}{\partial B} = MU_B(B, Z) - \lambda p_B = 0, \tag{4B.3}$$

$$\frac{\partial \mathcal{L}}{\partial Z} = MU_Z(B, Z) - \lambda p_Z = 0, \tag{4B.4}$$

$$\frac{\partial \mathcal{L}}{\partial \lambda} = Y - p_B B - p_Z Z = 0, \tag{4B.5}$$

where $MU_B(B, Z) \equiv \partial U(B, Z)/\partial B$ is the partial derivative of utility with respect to B (the marginal utility of B) and $MU_Z(B, Z)$ is the marginal utility of Z. Equation 4B.5 is the budget constraint. Equations 4B.3 and 4B.4 say that the marginal utility of each good equals its price times λ.

---

[4]For simplicity, we assume that we have an interior solution, B and Z are infinitely divisible, and $U(B, Z)$ is continuously differentiable at least twice (so that the second-order condition is well defined). The first-order conditions give us the necessary conditions for an interior solution in which positive quantities of both goods are consumed. We assume that the second-order (sufficient) conditions hold, which is true if the utility function is quasiconcave or if the indifference curves are convex to the origin. That is, Lisa is maximizing rather than minimizing her utility when she chooses the levels of B and Z given by the first-order conditions.

What is λ? If we equate Equations 4B.3 and 4B.4 and rearrange terms, we find that

$$\lambda = \frac{MU_B}{p_B} = \frac{MU_Z}{p_Z}. \tag{4B.6}$$

Because the Lagrangian multiplier, λ, equals the marginal utility of each good divided by its price, λ equals the extra pleasure one gets from one's last dollar of expenditures. Equivalently, λ is the value of loosening the budget constraint by one dollar.[5] Equation 4B.6 tells us that for Lisa to maximize her utility, she should pick a B and Z so that if she got one more dollar, spending that dollar on B or on Z would give her the same extra utility.

An alternative interpretation of this condition for maximizing utility. Using the ratio of Equations 4B.3 and 4B.4 (or rearranging 4B.6), we find that

$$\frac{MU_Z}{MU_B} = \frac{p_Z}{p_B}. \tag{4B.7}$$

The left side of Equation 4B.7 is the absolute value of the marginal rate of substitution, $MRS = -MU_Z/MU_B$, and the right side is the absolute value of the marginal rate of transformation, $MRT = -p_Z/p_B$. Thus, the calculus approach gives us the same condition for an optimum that we derived using graphs. The indifference curve should be tangent to the budget constraint: The slope of the indifference curve, MRS, should equal the slope of the budget constraint, MRT.

For example, suppose that the utility is Cobb-Douglas, as in Equation 4A.3: $U = AB^\alpha Z^\beta$. The first-order condition, Equation 4B.5, the budget constraint, stays the same, and Equations 4B.3 and 4B.4 become

$$\frac{\partial \mathcal{L}}{\partial B} = \alpha \frac{U(B, Z)}{B} - \lambda p_B = 0, \tag{4B.8}$$

$$\frac{\partial \mathcal{L}}{\partial Z} = \beta \frac{U(B, Z)}{Z} = \lambda p_Z = 0. \tag{4B.9}$$

Using Equations 4B.8 and 4B.9, we can write Equation 4B.6 as

$$\lambda = \alpha \frac{U(B, Z)}{p_B B} = \beta \frac{U(B, Z)}{p_Z Z}.$$

Taking the ratio of Equations 4B.8 and 4B.9 and rearranging terms, we find that

$$\beta p_B B = \alpha p_Z Z. \tag{4B.10}$$

---

[5]Differentiating utility with respect to Y, we find that

$$\frac{dU}{dY} = MU_B(B, Z)\frac{dB}{dY} + MU_Z(B, Z)\frac{dZ}{dY}.$$

Substituting from Equation 4B.6 into this expression, we obtain

$$\frac{dU}{dY} = \lambda p_B \frac{dB}{dY} + \lambda p_Z \frac{dZ}{dY} = \lambda \frac{p_B\,dB + p_Z\,dZ}{dY}.$$

Totally differentiating the budget constraint, we learn that

$$dY = p_B\,dB + p_Z\,dZ.$$

Substituting this expression into the previous expression gives us

$$\frac{dU}{dY} = \frac{\lambda p_B\,dB + \lambda p_Z\,dZ}{p_B\,dB + p_Z\,dZ} = \lambda.$$

Thus, λ equals the extra utility one gets from one more dollar of income.

Substituting $Y - p_B B$ for $p_Z Z$, using Equation 4B.5, into Equation 4B.10 and rearranging terms, we get

$$B = \frac{\alpha}{\alpha + \beta} \frac{Y}{p_B}. \tag{4B.11}$$

Similarly, by substituting Equation 4B.11 into Equation 4B.10, we find that

$$Z = \frac{\beta}{\alpha + \beta} \frac{Y}{p_Z}. \tag{4B.12}$$

Thus, knowing the utility function, we can solve the expression for the B and Z that maximize utility in terms of income and prices.

Equations 4B.11 and 4B.12 are the consumer's demand curves for B and Z, respectively. (We derive demand curves using graphs in Chapter 5.)

If $\alpha = \beta = \frac{1}{2}$, $A = 20$, $Y = 80$, and $p_Z = p_B = 10$, then $B = Z = 4$ and the value of loosening the budget constraint is $\lambda = MU_B/p_B = MU_Z/p_Z = 10/10 = 1$. If p_B rises to 40, then $Z = 4$, $B = 1$, and $\lambda = 20/40 = 5/10 = \frac{1}{2}$.

Appendix 5A: The Slutsky Equation

The total effect on the quantity demanded when the price of a good rises equals the sum of the substitution and income effects. The Slutsky equation (named after its discoverer, the Russian economist Eugene Slutsky) explicitly shows the relationship among the price elasticity of demand, ε, the pure substitution elasticity of demand, ε^*, and the income elasticity of demand, ξ:

$$\text{Total effect} = \text{substitution effect} + \text{income effect}$$
$$\varepsilon \quad = \quad \varepsilon^* \quad + \quad (-\theta\xi)$$

where θ is the budget share of this good: the amount spent on this good divided by the total budget.

We now sketch the derivation of the Slutsky equation (for a formal derivation, see a graduate microeconomics textbook such as Varian, 1992). The total effect, $\Delta q/\Delta p$, is the change in the quantity demanded, Δq, for a given change in the good's price, Δp. The substitution effect is the change in quantity demanded for a change in price, holding utility constant, which we label $(\Delta q/\Delta p)_{U\ constant}$.

A change in the price affects how much the consumer can buy and acts like a change in income. The income effect is the change in quantity as income changes times the change in income as price changes, $(\Delta q/\Delta Y)(\Delta Y/\Delta p)$, where ΔY is the change in income. The change in income from a change in price is $\Delta Y/\Delta p = -q$. For example, if price rises by \$1, income falls by the number of units purchased. From this last result, the income effect is $-q(\Delta q/\Delta Y)$.

Using these expressions, we write the identity that the total effect equals the substitution plus the income effect as

$$\Delta q/\Delta p = (\Delta q/\Delta p)_{U\ constant} - q(\Delta q/\Delta Y).$$

Multiplying this equation through by p/q, multiplying the last term by Y/Y, and rearranging terms, we obtain

$$\frac{\Delta q}{\Delta p} \frac{p}{q} = \left(\frac{\Delta q}{\Delta p}\right)_{U\ constant} \frac{p}{q} - \frac{\Delta q}{\Delta Y} \frac{Y}{q} \frac{pq}{Y}.$$

Substituting $\varepsilon = (\Delta q/\Delta p)(p/q)$, $\varepsilon^* = (\Delta q/\Delta p)_{U\,constant}(p/q)$, $\xi = (\Delta q/\Delta Y)(Y/q)$, and $\theta = pq/Y$ into this last expression, we have the Slutsky equation:

$$\varepsilon = \varepsilon^* - \theta\xi.$$

Appendix 5B: Labor-Leisure Model

Jackie's utility, U, is a function,

$$U = U(Y, N), \tag{5B.1}$$

of her leisure, N, and her income, Y, which she uses to buy all other goods and services. Jackie maximizes her utility, Equation 5B.1, subject to two constraints. The first, imposed by the clock, is that the number of hours she works, H, equals her total hours in a day minus her hours of leisure:

$$H = 24 - N. \tag{5B.2}$$

The second constraint is that her earned income (earnings), Y, equals her wage, w, times the hours she works:

$$Y = wH. \tag{5B.3}$$

For now, we assume that her unearned income is zero.

Although we can maximize Equation 5B.1 subject to Equations 5B.2 and 5B.3 using Lagrangian techniques, it is easier to do so by substitution. By substituting Equations 5B.2 and 5B.3 into Equation 5B.1, we can convert this constrained problem into an unconstrained maximization problem:

$$\max_{H} U = U(wH, 24 - H). \tag{5B.4}$$

By using the chain rule of differentiation, we find that the first-order condition for an interior maximum to the problem in Equation 5B.4 is

$$\frac{dU}{dH} = MU_Y w - MU_N = 0,$$

where MU_Y, the marginal utility of goods or income, is the partial derivative of utility with respect to income, $\partial U/\partial Y$, and MU_N, the marginal utility of leisure, is the partial derivative with respect to leisure, $\partial U/\partial N$.[6] This expression can be rewritten as $w = MU_N/MU_Y$.

To maximize her utility, Jackie must set her marginal rate of substitution of income for leisure, $MRS = -MU_N/MU_Y$, equal to her marginal rate of transformation of income for leisure, $MRT = -w$, in the market:

$$MRS = -\frac{MU_N}{MU_Y} = -w = MRT.$$

Suppose that Jackie's utility is

$$U = Y^\alpha N^{1-\alpha} = (wH)^\alpha (24 - H)^{1-\alpha},$$

which is a Cobb-Douglas utility function (Appendix 4A). Differentiating this utility function with respect to H, setting the derivative equal to zero, and rearranging terms,

---

[6]The second-order condition for an interior maximum is

$$\frac{d^2U}{dH^2} = \frac{\partial^2 U}{\partial Y^2}w^2 - 2\frac{\partial^2 U}{\partial Y \partial N}w + \frac{\partial^2 U}{\partial N^2} < 0.$$

we find that $H = 24\alpha$. With this particular utility function, an individual's hours of leisure and work are fixed regardless of the wage. If $\alpha = \frac{1}{2}$, the individual works 12 hours a day (and has 12 hours of leisure) whether the wage is 50¢ an hour or $500 an hour.

Appendix 6A: Properties of Marginal and Average Product Curves

We can use calculus to show that the MP_L curve crosses the AP_L curve at its peak. Because capital is fixed, we can write the production function solely in terms of labor: $q = f(L)$. In Figure 6.1, $MP_L = dq/dL = df/dL > 0$, $d^2f/dL^2 < 0$, and $AP_L = q/L = f(L)/L > 0$. A necessary condition to identify the amount of labor where the AP_L curve reaches a maximum is that the derivative of AP_L with respect to L equals zero:

$$\frac{dAP_L}{dL} = \left(\frac{dq}{dL} - \frac{q}{L}\right)\frac{1}{L} = 0.$$

(At the L determined by this first-order condition, AP_L is maximized if the second-order condition is negative: $d^2AP_L/dL^2 = d^2f/dL^2 < 0$.) By rearranging this first-order condition, $MP_L = dq/dL = q/L = AP_L$ at the peak of the AP_L curve.

Appendix 6B: The Slope of an Isoquant

We can use calculus to determine the slope at a point on an isoquant. We totally differentiate the isoquant, $\bar{q} = f(L, K)$, with respect to L and K. Along the isoquant, we can write capital as an implicit function of labor: $K(L)$. That is, for a given quantity of labor, the firm needs a certain level of capital to produce $\bar{q}$ units. Differentiating with respect to labor (and realizing that output does not change along the isoquant as we change labor), we have

$$\frac{d\bar{q}}{dL} = 0 = \frac{\partial f}{\partial L} + \frac{\partial f}{\partial K}\frac{dK}{dL} = MP_L + MP_K\frac{dK}{dL},$$

where $MP_K = \partial f/\partial K$ is the marginal product of capital. Rearranging this expression, we find that $-MP_L/MP_K = dK/dL = MRTS$.

Appendix 6C: Cobb-Douglas Production Function

The Cobb-Douglas production function is

$$q = AL^{\alpha}K^{\beta}. \tag{6C.1}$$

Economists use statistical means to estimate A, α, and β, which determine the exact shape of the production function. The larger A is, the more output the firm gets from a given amount of labor and capital.

The average product of labor is determined by dividing both sides of Equation 6C.1 by q:

$$AP_L = q/L = AL^\alpha K^\beta/L = AL^{\alpha-1}K^\beta. \qquad (6C.2)$$

The α term tells us the relationship between the average product of labor and the marginal product of labor. By differentiating the Cobb-Douglas production function with respect to L, holding K constant, we find that the marginal product of labor is

$$MP_L = \frac{\partial q}{\partial L} = \alpha AL^{\alpha-1}K^\beta = \alpha\frac{AL^\alpha K^\beta}{L} = \alpha\frac{q}{L}.$$

The marginal product of labor equals α times the average product of labor: $MP_L = \alpha AP_L$. Consequently, $\alpha = AP_L/MP_L$. Using similar reasoning, the marginal product of capital is $MP_K = \beta q/K$. As Equation 6.7 shows, the marginal rate of technical substitution is $MRTS = -MP_L/MP_K = -(\alpha q/L)/(\beta q/K) = -(\alpha/\beta)K/L$.

The change in the average product of labor as labor increases is $\partial AP_L/\partial L = (\alpha - 1)AL^{\alpha-2}K^\beta = (\alpha - 1)q/L^2$. If $\alpha - 1 < 0$ (that is, $\alpha < 1$), then the change in the average product of labor as the number of workers increases is negative.

Appendix 7A: Minimum of the Average Cost Curve

To determine the output level q where the average cost curve, $AC(q)$, reaches its minimum, we set the derivative of average cost with respect to q equal to zero:

$$\frac{dAC(q)}{dq} = \frac{d(C(q)/q)}{dq} = \left(\frac{dC(q)}{dq} - \frac{C(q)}{q}\right)\frac{1}{q} = 0.$$

This condition holds at the output q where $dC(q)/dq = C(q)/q$, or $MC = AC$. If the second-order condition holds at that q, the average cost curve reaches its minimum at that quantity. The second-order condition requires that the average cost curve be falling to the left of this q and rising to the right.

Appendix 7B: Japanese Beer Manufacturer's Short-Run Cost Curves

We can use math to derive the various short-run cost curves for a Japanese beer manufacturer. Based on the estimates of Flath (2011), its production function is

$$q = 1.52L^{0.6}K^{0.4},$$

where labor, L, is measured in hours, K is the number of units of capital, and q is the amount of output. (*Note:* The coefficient 1.52 was chosen to produce round numbers.)

In the short run, the firm's capital is fixed at $\overline{K} = 100$. If the rental rate of a unit of capital is $8, the fixed cost, F, is $800. The figure in Chapter 7's Application

"Short-Run Cost Curves for a Beer Manufacturer" shows that the average fixed cost, $AFC = F/q = 800/q$, falls as output increases.

We can use the production function to derive the variable cost. First, we determine how output and labor are related. Setting capital, K, at 100 units in the production function, we find that the output produced in the short run is solely a function of labor:

$$q = 1.52L^{0.6}100^{0.4} \approx 9.59L^{0.6}.$$

Rearranging this expression, we can write the number of workers per year, L, needed to produce q units of output, as a function solely of output:

$$L(q) = \left(\frac{q}{1.52 \times 100^{0.4}} \right)^{\frac{1}{0.6}} \approx 0.023q^{1.67}. \qquad (7B.1)$$

Now that we know how labor and output are related, we can calculate variable cost directly. The only variable input is labor, so if the wage is \$24, the firm's variable cost is $VC(q) = wL(q) = 24L(q)$. Substituting for $L(q)$ using Equation 7B.1, we see how variable cost varies with output:

$$VC(q) = 24L(q) = 24\left(\frac{q}{1.52 \times 100^{0.4}} \right)^{\frac{1}{0.6}} \approx 0.55q^{1.67}. \qquad (7B.2)$$

Using this expression for variable cost, we can construct the other cost measures.

We obtain the average variable cost as a function of output, $AVC(q)$, by dividing both sides of Equation 7B.2 by q:

$$AVC(q) = \frac{VC(q)}{q} = \frac{24L(q)}{q} \approx 24\left(\frac{0.023q^{1.67}}{q} \right) = 0.55q^{0.67}.$$

As the figure in the application shows, the average variable cost is strictly increasing.

To obtain the equation for marginal cost as a function of output, we differentiate the variable cost, $VC(q)$, with respect to output:

$$MC(q) = \frac{dVC(q)}{dq} \approx \frac{d(0.55q^{1.67})}{dq} = 1.67 \times 0.55q^{0.67} \approx 0.92q^{0.67}.$$

Thus, to construct all the cost measures of the beer manufacturer, we need only the production function and the prices of the inputs.

Appendix 7C: Minimizing Cost

We can use calculus to derive the cost minimization conditions, Equations 7.5 and 7.8, discussed in the chapter. The problem the firm faces in the long run is to choose the level of labor, L, and capital, K, that will minimize the cost of producing a particular level of output, $\bar{q}$, given a wage of w and a rental rate of capital of r.

The relationship between inputs and output is summarized in the firm's production function: $q = f(L, K)$. The marginal product of labor, which is the extra output the firm produces from a little more labor, holding capital constant, is $MP_L(L, K) = \partial f(L, K)/\partial L$, which is positive. This has diminishing marginal returns to labor, however, so the marginal product of labor falls as labor increases: $\partial MP_L(L, K)/\partial L = \partial^2 f(L, K)/\partial L^2 < 0$. The marginal product of capital has the same properties: $\partial f(L, K)/\partial K > 0$ and $\partial MP_K(L, K)/\partial K < 0$.

The firm's problem is to minimize its cost, C, of production, through its choice of labor and capital,

$$\min_{L, K} C = wL + rK,$$

subject to the constraint that a given amount of output, $\bar{q}$, is to be produced:

$$f(L, K) = \bar{q}. \tag{7C.1}$$

Equation 7C.1 is the $\bar{q}$ isoquant.

We can change this constrained minimization problem into an unconstrained problem by using the Lagrangian technique. The firm's unconstrained problem is to minimize the Lagrangian, $\mathcal{L}$, through its choice of labor, capital, and the Lagrangian multiplier, λ:

$$\min_{L, K, \lambda} \mathcal{L} = wL + rK - \lambda(f(L, K) - \bar{q}).$$

The necessary conditions for a minimum are obtained by differentiating $\mathcal{L}$ with respect to L, K, and λ and setting the derivatives equal to zero:

$$\partial\mathcal{L}/\partial L = w - \lambda MP_L(L, K) = 0, \tag{7C.2}$$

$$\partial\mathcal{L}/\partial K = r - \lambda MP_K(L, K) = 0, \tag{7C.3}$$

$$\partial\mathcal{L}/\partial\lambda = f(L, K) - \bar{q} = 0. \tag{7C.4}$$

We can rewrite Equations 7C.2 and 7C.3 as $w = \lambda MP_L(L, K)$ and $r = \lambda MP_K(L, K)$. Taking the ratio of these two expressions, we obtain

$$\frac{w}{r} = \frac{MP_L(L, K)}{MP_K(L, K)} = -MRTS, \tag{7C.5}$$

which is the same as Equation 7.5. This condition states that cost is minimized when the rate at which firms can exchange capital for labor in the market, w/r, is the same as the rate at which capital can be substituted for labor along an isoquant. That is, the isocost line is tangent to the isoquant.

We can rewrite Equation 7C.5 to obtain the expression

$$\frac{MP_L(L, K)}{w} = \frac{MP_K(L, K)}{r}.$$

This equation tells us that the last dollar spent on labor should produce as much extra output as the last dollar spent on capital; otherwise, the amount of factors used should be adjusted.

We can rearrange Equations 7C.2 and 7C.3 to obtain an expression for the Lagrangian multiplier:

$$\lambda = \frac{w}{MP_L(L, K)} = \frac{r}{MP_K(L, K)}. \tag{7C.6}$$

Equation 7C.6 says that the Lagrangian multiplier, λ, equals the ratio of the factor price to the marginal product for each factor. The marginal product for a factor is the extra amount of output one gets by increasing that factor slightly, so the reciprocal of the marginal product is the extra input it takes to produce an extra unit of output. By multiplying the reciprocal of the marginal product by the factor cost, we learn the extra cost of producing an extra unit of output by using more of this factor. Thus, the Lagrangian multiplier equals the marginal cost of production: It measures how much the cost increases if we produce one more unit of output.

If a firm has a Cobb-Douglas production function, $Q = AL^\alpha K^\beta$, the marginal product of capital is $MP_K = \beta q/K$ and the marginal product of labor is $MP_L = \alpha q/L$ (see Appendix 6C), so the *MRTS* is $\alpha K/(\beta L)$. Thus, the tangency condition, Equation 7C.5, requires that

$$\frac{w}{r} = \frac{\alpha K}{\beta L}. \tag{7C.7}$$

Using algebra, we can rewrite Equation 7C.7 as

$$K = \frac{\beta w}{\alpha r} L, \tag{7C.8}$$

which is the expansion path for a Cobb-Douglas production function given w and r. According to Equation 7C.8, the expansion path of a firm with a Cobb-Douglas production function is an upward-sloping straight line through the origin with a slope of $\beta w/(\alpha r)$.

Appendix 8A: The Elasticity of the Residual Demand Curve

Here we derive the expression for the elasticity of the residual demand curve given in Equation 8.2. Differentiating the residual demand (Equation 8.1),

$$D^r(p) = D(p) - S^o(p),$$

with respect to p, we obtain

$$\frac{dD^r}{dp} = \frac{dD}{dp} - \frac{dS^o}{dp}.$$

Because the firms are identical, the quantity produced by each is $q = Q/n$, and the total quantity produced by all the other firms is $Q_o = (n - 1)q$. Multiplying both sides of the expression by p/q and multiplying and dividing the first term on the right side by Q/Q and the second term by Q_o/Q_o, this expression may be rewritten as

$$\frac{dD^r}{dp}\frac{p}{q} = \frac{dD}{dp}\frac{p}{Q}\frac{Q}{q} - \frac{dS^o}{dp}\frac{p}{Q_o}\frac{Q_o}{q},$$

where $q = D^r(p)$, $Q = D(p)$, and $Q_o = S^o(p)$. This expression can in turn be rewritten as Equation 8.2,

$$\varepsilon_i = n\varepsilon - (n - 1)\eta_o,$$

by noting that $Q/q = n$, $Q_o/q = (n - 1)$, $(dD^r/dp)(p/q) = \varepsilon_i$, $(dD/dp)(p/Q) = \varepsilon$, and $(dS^o/dp)(p/Q_o) = \eta_o$.

Appendix 8B: Profit Maximization

In general, a firm maximizes its profit, $\pi(q) = R(q) - C(q)$, by its choice of output q. A *necessary condition* for a maximum at a positive level of output is found by differentiating profit with respect to q and setting the derivative equal to zero:

$$\frac{d\pi}{dq} = \frac{dR(q^*)}{dq} - \frac{dC(q^*)}{dq} = 0, \tag{8B.1}$$

where q^* is the profit-maximizing output. Because $dR(q)/dq$ is the marginal revenue, $MR(q)$, and $dC(q)/dq$ is the marginal cost, $MC(q)$, Equation 8B.1 says that marginal revenue equals marginal cost at q^*:

$$MR(q^*) = MC(q^*). \tag{8B.2}$$

A *sufficient condition* for profit to be maximized at $q^* > 0$ is that the second-order condition holds:

$$\frac{d^2\pi}{dq^2} = \frac{d^2R(q^*)}{dq^2} - \frac{d^2C(q^*)}{dq^2} = \frac{dMR(q^*)}{dq} - \frac{dMC(q^*)}{dq} < 0. \tag{8B.3}$$

Equation 8B.3 can be rewritten as

$$\frac{dMR(q^*)}{dq} < \frac{dMC(q^*)}{dq}. \tag{8B.4}$$

Thus, a sufficient condition for a maximum is that the slope of the marginal revenue curve is less than that of the marginal cost curve and that the MC curve cuts the MR curve from below at q^*.

For a competitive firm, $\pi(q) = pq - C(q)$, so the necessary condition for profit to be maximized, Equation 8B.1 or 8B.2, can be written as

$$p = MC(q^*). \tag{8B.5}$$

Equation 8B.5 says that a profit-maximizing, competitive firm sets its output at q^*, where its marginal cost equals its price.

Because a competitive firm's marginal revenue, p, is a constant, $dMR/dq = dp/dq = 0$. Thus, the sufficient condition for profit to be maximized, Equation 8B.4, can be rewritten as

$$0 < \frac{dMC(q^*)}{dq} \tag{8B.6}$$

for a competitive firm. Equation 8B.6 shows that a sufficient condition for a competitive firm to be maximizing its profit at q^* is that its marginal cost curve is upward sloping at the equilibrium quantity.

Appendix 9A: Demand Elasticities and Surplus

If the demand curve is linear, as in Figure 9.3, the lost consumer surplus, area $B + C$, equals the sum of the area of a rectangle, $Q\Delta p$, with length Q and height Δp, plus the area of a triangle, $\frac{1}{2}\Delta Q\Delta p$, of length ΔQ and height Δp. We can approximate any demand curve with a straight line, so that $\Delta CS = Q\Delta p + \frac{1}{2}\Delta Q\Delta p$ is a reasonable approximation to the true change in consumer surplus. We can rewrite this expression for ΔCS as

$$\Delta p(Q + \tfrac{1}{2}\Delta Q) = Q\Delta p\left[1 + \tfrac{1}{2}\left(\frac{\Delta Q}{Q}\frac{p}{\Delta p}\right)\frac{\Delta p}{p}\right]$$

$$= (pQ)\frac{\Delta p}{p}\left(1 + \tfrac{1}{2}\varepsilon\frac{\Delta p}{p}\right)$$

$$= Rx(1 + \tfrac{1}{2}\varepsilon x),$$

where $x = \Delta p/p$ is the percentage increase in the price, R ($= pQ$) is the total revenue from the sale of good Q, and ε is the elasticity of demand. (This equation is used to calculate the last column in the table in the Application "Goods with a Large Consumer Surplus Loss from Price Increases.")

Appendix 11A: Relationship Between a Linear Demand Curve and Its Marginal Revenue Curve

When the demand curve is linear, its marginal revenue curve is twice as steep and hits the horizontal axis at half the quantity of the demand curve. A linear demand curve can be written generally as $p = a - bQ$. The monopoly's revenues are quadratic, $R = pQ = aQ - bQ^2$. Differentiating revenue with respect to quantity, we find that the marginal revenue, $dR(Q)/dQ$ $dR(Q)/dQ$, is linear, $MR = a - 2bQ$. The demand and MR curves hit the price axis at a. The slope of the demand curve, $dp/dQ = -b$, is half (in absolute value) the slope of the marginal revenue curve, $dMR/dQ = -2b$. The MR curve hits the quantity axis at half the distance, $a/(2b)$, of the demand curve, a/b.

Appendix 11B: Incidence of a Specific Tax on a Monopoly

In a monopolized market, the incidence of a specific tax falling on consumers can exceed 100%: The price may rise by an amount greater than the tax. To demonstrate this possibility, we examine a market where the demand curve has a constant elasticity of ε and the marginal cost is constant at $MC = m$.

Suppose that the inverse demand curve the monopoly faces is

$$p = Q^{1/\varepsilon}. \tag{11B.1}$$

The monopoly's revenue is $R = pQ = Q^{1+1/\varepsilon}$. By differentiating, we learn that the monopoly's marginal revenue is $MR = (1 + 1/\varepsilon)Q^{1/\varepsilon}$.

To maximize its profit, the monopoly operates where its marginal revenue equals its marginal cost:

$$MR = (1 + 1/\varepsilon)Q^{1/\varepsilon} = m = MC.$$

Solving this equation for the profit-maximizing output, we find that $Q = [m/(1 + 1/\varepsilon)]^\varepsilon$. Substituting that value of Q into Equation 11B.1, we find that

$$p = m/(1 + 1/\varepsilon).$$

A specific tax of t per unit raises the marginal cost to $m + t$, so that the monopoly price increases to

$$p_t = (m + t)/(1 + 1/\varepsilon).$$

Consequently, the increase in price is $t/(1 + 1/\varepsilon)$. The incidence of the tax that falls on consumers is $\Delta p/\Delta t = [t/(1 + 1/\varepsilon)]/t = 1/(1 + 1/\varepsilon) > 1$, because $\varepsilon < -1$ (a monopoly never operates in the inelastic portion of its demand curve).

Appendix 12A: Perfect Price Discrimination

A perfectly price-discriminating monopoly charges each customer the reservation price $p = D(Q)$, where $D(Q)$ is the inverse demand function and Q is total output. The discriminating monopoly's revenue, R, is the area under the demand curve up to the quantity, Q, it sells:

$$R = \int_0^Q D(z)\,dz,$$

where z is a placeholder for quantity. The monopoly's objective is to maximize its profit through its choice of Q:

$$\max_Q \pi = \int_0^Q D(z)\,dz - C(Q). \tag{12A.1}$$

Its first-order condition for a maximum is found by differentiating Equation 12A.1 to obtain

$$\frac{d\pi}{dQ} = D(Q) - \frac{dC(Q)}{dQ} = 0. \tag{12A.2}$$

According to Equation 12A.2, the discriminating monopoly sells units up to the quantity, Q, where the reservation price for the last unit, $D(Q)$, equals its marginal cost, $dC(Q)/dQ$. (This quantity is $Q_c = Q_d$ in Figure 12.2.)

For this solution to maximize profits, the second-order condition must hold: $d^2\pi/dQ^2 = dD(Q)/dQ - d^2C(Q)/dQ^2 < 0$. Thus, the second-order condition holds if the marginal cost curve has a nonnegative slope (because the demand curve has a negative slope). More generally, the second-order condition holds if the demand curve has a greater (absolute) slope than the marginal cost curve.

The perfectly price-discriminating monopoly's profit is

$$\pi = \int_0^Q D(z)\,dz - C(Q).$$

For example, if $D(Q) = a - bQ$,

$$\pi = \int_0^Q (a - bz)dz - C(Q) = aQ - \frac{b}{2}Q^2 - C(Q). \qquad (12A.3)$$

The monopoly finds the output that maximizes the profit by setting the derivative of the profit in Equation 12A.3 equal to zero:

$$a - bQ - \frac{dC(Q)}{dQ} = 0.$$

By rearranging terms, we find that $D(Q) = a - bQ = dC(Q)/dQ = MC$, as in Equation 12A.2. Thus, the monopoly produces the quantity at which the demand curve hits the marginal cost curve.

Appendix 12B: Group Price Discrimination

Suppose that a monopoly can divide its customers into two groups, as in Figure 12.3. It sells Q_1 to the first group and earns revenues of $R_1(Q_1)$, and it sells Q_2 units to the second group and earns $R_2(Q_2)$. Its cost of producing total output $Q = Q_1 + Q_2$ units is $C(Q)$. The monopoly can maximize its profit through its choice of prices or quantities to each group. We examine its problem when it chooses quantities:

$$\max_{Q_1, Q_2} \pi = R_1(Q_1) + R_2(Q_2) - C(Q_1 + Q_2). \qquad (12C.1)$$

The first-order conditions corresponding to Equation 12C.1 are obtained by differentiating with respect to Q_1 and Q_2 and setting the partial derivative equal to zero:

$$\frac{\partial \pi}{\partial Q_1} = \frac{dR_1(Q_1)}{dQ_1} - \frac{dC(Q)}{dQ}\frac{\partial Q}{\partial Q_1} = 0, \qquad (12C.2)$$

$$\frac{\partial \pi}{\partial Q_2} = \frac{dR_2(Q_2)}{dQ_2} - \frac{dC(Q)}{dQ}\frac{\partial Q}{\partial Q_2} = 0. \qquad (12C.3)$$

Equation 12C.2 says that the marginal revenue from sales to the first group, $MR^1 = dR_1(Q_1)/dQ_1$, should equal the marginal cost of producing the last unit of total output, $MC = dC(Q)/dQ$, because $\partial Q/\partial Q_1 = 1$. Similarly, Equation 12C.3 says that the marginal revenue from the second group, MR^2, should also equal the marginal cost. By combining Equations 12C.2 and 12C.3, we find that the two marginal revenues are equal where the monopoly is profit maximizing:

$$MR^1 = MR^2 = MC.$$

Appendix 12C: Block Pricing

In the block-pricing utility monopoly example in the chapter, we assume that the utility monopoly faces an inverse demand curve and that its marginal and average cost is $m = 30$. Consequently, the quantity-discounting utility's profit is

$$\pi = p(Q_1)Q_1 + p(Q_2)(Q_2 - Q_1) - mQ_2$$
$$= (90 - Q_1)Q_1 + (90 - Q_2)(Q_2 - Q_1) - 30Q_2,$$

$p = 90 - Q$ where Q_1 is the largest quantity for which the first-block rate, $p_1 = 90 - Q_1$, is charged and Q_2 is the total quantity a consumer purchases. The utility chooses Q_1 and Q_2 to maximize its profit. It sets the derivative of profit with respect to Q_1 equal to zero, $Q_2 - 2Q_1 = 0$, and the derivative of profit with respect to Q_2 equal to zero, $Q_1 - 2Q_2 + 60 = 0$. By solving these two equations, the utility determines its profit-maximizing quantities, $Q_1 = 20$ and $Q_2 = 40$. The corresponding block prices are $p_1 = 90 - 20 = 70$ and $p_2 = 50$.

Appendix 12D: Two-Part Pricing

In the example of a two-part pricing with nonidentical consumers, the demand curves for Valerie, Consumer 1, and Neal, Consumer 2, are $q_1 = 80 - p$ and $q_2 = 100 - p$. The consumer surplus for Consumer 1 is $CS_1 = \frac{1}{2}(80 - p)q_1 = \frac{1}{2}(80 - p)^2$. Similarly, $CS_2 = \frac{1}{2}(100 - p)^2$. If the monopoly charges the lower fee, $\mathscr{L} = CS_1$, it sells to both consumers and its profit is

$$\pi = 2\mathscr{L} + (p - m)(q_1 + q_2) = (80 - p)^2 + (p - 10)(180 - 2p).$$

Setting the derivative of π with respect to p equal to zero, we find that the profit-maximizing price is $p = 20$. The monopoly charges a fee of $\mathscr{L} = CS_1 = \$1,800$ and makes a profit of $\$5,000$. If the monopoly charges the higher fee, $\mathscr{L} = CS_2$, it sells only to Consumer 2, and its profit is

$$\pi = \mathscr{L} + (p - m)q_2 = \frac{1}{2}(100 - p)^2 + (p - 10)(100 - p).$$

The monopoly's profit-maximizing price is $p = 10$, and its profit is $\mathscr{L} = CS_2 = \$4,050$. Thus, the monopoly makes more by setting $\mathscr{L} = CS_1$ and selling to both customers.

Appendix 12E: Profit-Maximizing Advertising and Production

To maximize its profit, a monopoly must optimally set its advertising, A, and quantity, Q. Suppose that advertising affects only current sales, so the demand curve the monopoly faces is $p = p(Q, A)$.

As a result, the firm's revenue is $R = p(Q, A)Q = R(Q, A)$. The firm's cost of production is the function $C(Q)$. Its cost of advertising is A, because each unit of advertising costs $\$1$ (we chose the units of measure appropriately). Thus, its total cost is $C(Q) + A$.

The monopoly maximizes its profit through its choice of quantity and advertising:

$$\max_{Q, A} \pi = R(Q, A) - C(Q) - A. \tag{12E.1}$$

Its necessary (first-order) conditions are found by differentiating the profit function in Equation 12E.1 with respect to Q and A in turn:

$$\frac{\partial \pi(Q, A)}{\partial Q} = \frac{\partial R(Q, A)}{\partial Q} - \frac{dC(Q)}{dQ} = 0, \tag{12E.2}$$

$$\frac{\partial \pi(Q, A)}{\partial A} = \frac{\partial R(Q, A)}{\partial A} - 1 = 0. \tag{12E.3}$$

The profit-maximizing output and advertising levels are the Q^* and A^* that simultaneously satisfy Equations 12E.2 and 12E.3. Equation 12E.2 shows that output should be chosen so that the marginal revenue, $\partial R(Q, A)/(\partial Q)$, equals the marginal cost, $dC(Q)/(dQ)$. According to Equation 12E.3, the monopoly advertises to the point where its marginal revenue from the last unit of advertising, $\partial R(Q, A)/(\partial A)$, equals the marginal cost of the last unit of advertising, \$1.

Appendix 13A: Nash-Cournot Equilibrium

Here we use calculus to determine the Nash-Cournot equilibrium for n identical oligopolistic firms. We first solve for the equilibrium using general demand and cost functions, which are identical for all firms. Then we apply this general solution to a linear example. Finally, using the linear example, we determine the equilibrium when two firms have different marginal costs.

General Model

Suppose that the market demand function is $p(Q)$ and that each firm's cost function is the same $C(q_i)$. To analyze a Cournot market of identical firms, we first examine the behavior of a representative firm. Firm 1 tries to maximize its profits through its choice of q_1:

$$\max_{q_1} \pi_1(q_1, q_2, \cdots, q_n) = q_1 p(q_1 + q_2 + \cdots + q_n) - C(q_1), \quad (13A.1)$$

where $q_1 + q_2 + \cdots + q_n = Q$, the total market output. Firm 1 takes the outputs of the other firms as fixed. If Firm 1 changes its output by a small amount, the price changes by $(dp(Q)/dQ)(dQ/dq_1) = dp(Q)/dQ$. Its necessary condition to maximize profit (first-order condition) is found by differentiating profit in Equation 13A.1 and setting the result equal to zero. After we rearrange terms, this necessary condition is

$$MR = p(Q) + q_1\frac{dp(Q)}{dQ} = \frac{dC(q_1)}{dq_1} = MC, \quad (13A.2)$$

or marginal revenue equals marginal cost. Equation 13A.2 specifies the firm's best-response function: the optimal q_1 for any given output of other firms.

The marginal revenue expression can be rewritten as $p[1 + (q_1/p)(dp/dQ)]$. Multiplying and dividing the last term by n, noting that $Q = nq_1$ (given that all firms are identical), and observing that ε, the market elasticity of demand, is $(dQ/dp)(p/Q)$, we can rewrite Equation 13A.2 as

$$p\left(1 + \frac{1}{n\varepsilon}\right) = \frac{dC(q_1)}{dq_1}. \quad (13A.3)$$

The left side of Equation 13A.3 expresses Firm 1's marginal revenue in terms of the elasticity of demand of its residual demand curve, $n\varepsilon$, which is the number of firms, n, times the market demand elasticity, ε. Holding ε constant, the more firms, the more elastic the residual demand curve, and hence the closer a firm's marginal revenue to the price.

We can rearrange Equation 13A.3 to obtain an expression for the Lerner Index, $(p - MC)/p$, in terms of the market demand elasticity and the number of firms:

$$\frac{p - MC}{p} = -\frac{1}{n\varepsilon}. \tag{13A.4}$$

The larger the Lerner Index, the greater the firm's market power. As Equation 13A.4 shows, if we hold the market elasticity constant and increase the number of firms, the Lerner Index falls. As n approaches ∞, the elasticity any one firm faces approaches $-\infty$, so the Lerner Index approaches 0 and the market is competitive.

Linear Example

Now suppose that the market demand is linear, $p = a - bQ$, and each firm's marginal cost is m, a constant, and it has no fixed cost. Firm 1, a typical firm, maximizes its profits through its choice of q_1:

$$\max_{q_1} \pi_1(q_1, q_2, \cdots, q_n) = q_1[a - b(q_1 + q_2 + \cdots + q_n)] - mq_1. \tag{13A.5}$$

Setting the derivative of profit with respect to q_1, holding the output levels of the other firms fixed, equal to zero, and rearranging terms, we find that the necessary condition for Firm 1 to maximize its profit is

$$MR = a - b(2q_1 + q_2 + \cdots + q_n) = m = MC. \tag{13A.6}$$

Because all firms have the same cost function, $q_2 = q_3 = \cdots = q_n \equiv q$ in equilibrium. Substituting this expression into Equation 13A.6, we find that the first firm's best-response function is

$$q_1 = R_1(q_2, \cdots, q_n) = \frac{a - m}{2b} - \frac{n - 1}{2}q. \tag{13A.7}$$

The other firms' best-response functions are derived similarly.

All these best-response functions must hold simultaneously. The intersection of the best-response functions determines the Nash-Cournot equilibrium. Setting $q_1 = q$ in Equation 13A.7 and solving for q, we find that the Nash-Cournot equilibrium output for each firm is

$$q = \frac{a - m}{(n + 1)b}. \tag{13A.8}$$

Total market output, $Q = nq$, equals $n(a - m)/[(n + 1)b]$. The corresponding price is obtained by substituting this expression for market output into the demand function:

$$p = \frac{a + nm}{n + 1}. \tag{13A.9}$$

Setting $n = 1$ in Equations 13A.8 and 13A.9 yields the monopoly quantity and price. As n becomes large, each firm's quantity approaches zero, total output approaches $(a - m)/b$, and price approaches m, which are the competitive levels. In Equation 13A.9, the Lerner Index is

$$\frac{p - MC}{p} = \frac{a - m}{a + nm}.$$

As n grows very large, the denominator goes to ∞, so the Lerner Index goes to 0, and the firm has no market power.

Different Costs

In the linear example with two firms, how does the equilibrium change if the firms have different marginal costs? The marginal cost of Firm 1 is m_1, and that of Firm 2 is m_2. Firm 1 chooses output to maximize its profit:

$$\max_{q_1} \pi_1(q_1, q_2) = q_1[a - b(q_1 + q_2)] - m_1 q_1. \tag{13A.10}$$

Setting the derivative of Firm 1's profit with respect to q_1, holding q_2 fixed, equal to zero, and rearranging terms, we find that the necessary condition for Firm 1 to maximize its profit is $MR_1 = a - b(2q_1 + q_2) = m_1 = MC$. Using algebra, we can rearrange this expression to obtain Firm 1's best-response function:

$$q_1 = \frac{a - m_1 - bq_2}{2b}. \tag{13A.11}$$

By similar reasoning, Firm 2's best-response function is

$$q_2 = \frac{a - m_2 - bq_1}{2b}. \tag{13A.12}$$

To determine the equilibrium, we solve Equations 13A.11 and 13A.12 simultaneously for q_1 and q_2:

$$q_1 = \frac{a - 2m_1 + m_2}{3b}, \tag{13A.13}$$

$$q_2 = \frac{a - 2m_2 + m_1}{3b}. \tag{13A.14}$$

By inspecting Equations 13A.13 and 13A.14, we find that the firm with the smaller marginal cost has the larger equilibrium output. Similarly, the low-cost firm has a higher profit. If m_1 is less than m_2, then

$$\pi_1 = \frac{(a + m_2 - 2m_1)^2}{9b} > \frac{(a + m_1 - 2m_2)^2}{9b} = \pi_2.$$

Appendix 13B: Nash-Stackelberg Equilibrium

We use calculus to derive the Nash-Stackelberg equilibrium for the linear example given in Appendix 13A with two firms that have the same marginal cost, m. Because Firm 1, the Stackelberg leader, chooses its output first, it knows that Firm 2, the follower, will choose its output using its best-response function, which is (see Equation 13A.7, where $n = 2$)

$$q_2 = R_2(q_1) = \frac{a - m}{2b} - \frac{1}{2}q_1. \tag{13B.1}$$

The Stackelberg leader's profit, $\pi_1(q_1 + q_2)$, can be written as $\pi_1(q_1 + R_2(q_1))$, where we've replaced the follower's output with its best-response function. The Stackelberg leader maximizes its profit by taking the best-response function as given:

$$\max_{q_1} \pi_1\,(q_1, R_2(q_1)) = q_1\left[a - b\left(q_1 + \frac{a-m}{2b} - \frac{1}{2}q_1 \right) \right] - mq_1. \quad (13B.2)$$

Setting the derivative of Firm 1's profit (in Equation 13B.2) with respect to q_1 equal to zero and solving for q_1, we find that the profit-maximizing output of the leader is

$$q_1 = \frac{a-m}{2b}. \quad (13B.3)$$

Substituting the expression for q_1 in Equation 13B.3 into Equation 13B.1, we obtain the equilibrium output of the follower:

$$q_2 = \frac{a-m}{4b}. \quad (13B.4)$$

Appendix 13C: Nash-Bertrand Equilibrium

We can use math to determine the cola market Nash-Bertrand equilibrium discussed in the chapter. First, we determine the best-response functions each firm faces. Then we equate the best-response functions to determine the equilibrium prices for the two firms.

Coke's best-response function tells us the price Coke charges that maximizes its profit as a function of the price Pepsi charges. We use the demand curve for Coke to derive the best-response function.

The reason Coke's price depends on Pepsi's price is that the quantity of Coke demanded, q_c, depends on the price of Coke, p_c, and the price of Pepsi, p_p. Coke's demand curve is

$$q_c = 58 - 4p_c + 2p_p. \quad (13C.1)$$

Partially differentiating Equation 13C.1 with respect to p_c (that is, holding the price of Pepsi fixed), we find that the change in quantity for every dollar change in price is $\partial q_c/\partial p_c = -4$, so a \$1-per-unit increase in the price of Coke causes the quantity of Coke demanded to fall by 4 units. Similarly, the demand for Coke rises by 2 units if the price of Pepsi rises by \$1, while the price of Coke remains constant: $\partial q_c/\partial p_p = 2$.

If Coke faces a constant marginal and average cost of m per unit, its profit is

$$\pi_c = (p_c - m)q_c = (p_c - m)(58 - 4p_c + 2p_p), \quad (13C.2)$$

where $p_c - m$ is Coke's profit per unit. To determine Coke's profit-maximizing price (holding Pepsi's price fixed), we set the partial derivative of the profit function, Equation 13C.2, with respect to the price of Coke equal to zero,

$$\frac{\partial \pi_c}{\partial p_c} = q_c + (p_c - m)\frac{\partial q_c}{\partial p_c} = q_c - 4(p_c - m) = 0, \quad (13C.3)$$

and solve for p_c as a function of p_p and m to find Coke's best-response function:

$$p_c = 7.25 + 0.25p_p + 0.5m. \quad (13C.4)$$

Equation 13C.4 shows that Coke's best-response price is 25¢ higher for every extra dollar that Pepsi charges and 50¢ higher for every extra dollar of Coke's marginal cost.

If Coke's average and marginal cost of production is \$5 per unit, its best-response function is

$$p_c = 9.75 + 0.25p_p, \tag{13C.5}$$

as Figure 13.8 shows. If $p_p = \$13$, then Coke's best response is to set $p_c = \$13$. Pepsi's demand curve is

$$q_p = 63.2 - 4p_p + 1.6p_c. \tag{13C.6}$$

Using the same approach, we find that Pepsi's best-response function (for $m = \$5$) is

$$p_p = 10.4 + 0.2p_c. \tag{13C.7}$$

The intersection of Coke's and Pepsi's best-response functions (Equations 13C.5 and 13C.7) determines the Nash equilibrium. By substituting Pepsi's best-response function, Equation 13C.7, for p_p in Coke's best-response function, Equation 13C.5, we find that $p_c = 9.75 + 0.25(10.4 + 0.2p_c)$. Solving this equation for p_c, we determine that the equilibrium price of Coke is \$13. Substituting $p_c = \$13$ into Equation 13C.6, we discover that the equilibrium price of Pepsi is also \$13.

Appendix 15A: Factor Demands

If a competitive firm hires L units of labor at a wage rate of w and K units of capital at a rental rate of r, it can produce $q = f(L, K)$ units of output. The firm sells its output at the market price of p. The firm picks L and K to maximize its profit:

$$\max_{L, K} \pi = pq - (wL + rK) = pf(L, K) - (wL + rK). \tag{15A.1}$$

Thus, the firm's revenue, pq, and cost both depend on L and K, so its profit depends on L and K.

Profit is maximized by setting the partial derivatives of profit (in Equation 15A.1) with respect to L and K equal to zero:

$$\frac{\partial \pi}{\partial L} = pMP_L - w = 0, \tag{15A.2}$$

$$\frac{\partial \pi}{\partial L} = pMP_K - r = 0, \tag{15A.3}$$

where $MP_L = \partial f(L, K)/\partial L$, the marginal product of labor, is the partial derivative of the production function with respect to L, and $MP_K = \partial f(L, K)/\partial K$ is the marginal product of capital. Solving Equations 15A.2 and 15A.3 simultaneously produces the factor demand equations.

Rearranging Equations 15A.2 and 15A.3, we can write these factor demand equations as

$$MRP_L \equiv pMP_L = w,$$
$$MRP_K \equiv pMP_K = r.$$

Thus, the firm maximizes its profit when it picks its inputs such that the marginal revenue product of labor equals the wage and the marginal revenue product of capital equals the rental rate of capital. For these conditions to produce a maximum, the second-order conditions must also hold. These second-order conditions say that the MRP_L and MRP_K curves slope downward.

If the production function is Cobb-Douglas, $q = AL^\alpha K^\beta$, then Equations 15A.2 and 15A.3 are

$$\frac{\partial \pi}{\partial L} = p\alpha AL^{\alpha-1}K^\beta - w = 0,$$

$$\frac{\partial \pi}{\partial K} = p\beta AL^\alpha K^{\beta-1} - r = 0.$$

Solving these equations for L and K, we find that the factor demand functions are

$$L = \left(\frac{\alpha}{w}\right)^{(1-\beta)/\delta}\left(\frac{\beta}{r}\right)^{\beta/\delta}(Ap)^{1/\delta}, \tag{15A.4}$$

$$K = \left(\frac{\alpha}{w}\right)^{\alpha/\delta}\left(\frac{\beta}{r}\right)^{(1-\alpha)/\delta}(Ap)^{1/\delta}, \tag{15A.5}$$

where $\delta = 1 - \alpha - \beta$. By differentiating Equations 15A.4 and 15A.5, we can show that the demand for each factor decreases with w or r and increases with p.

If the Cobb-Douglas production function has constant returns to scale, $\delta = 0$, then Equations 15A.4 and 15A.5 are not helpful. The problem is that with constant returns to scale, a competitive firm with a Cobb-Douglas production function does not care how much it produces (and hence how many inputs it uses) as long as the market price and input prices are consistent with zero profit.

A competitive firm with a Cobb-Douglas production function pays labor the value of its marginal product, $w = p \times MP_L = p \times \alpha AL^{\alpha-1}K^\beta = \alpha pQ/L$. As a result, the share of the firm's revenues that is paid to labor is $\omega_L = wL/(pQ) = \alpha$. Similarly, $\omega_K = rK/(pQ) = \beta$. Thus, with a Cobb-Douglas production function, the shares of labor and of capital are fixed and independent of prices.

Appendix 15B: Monopsony

If only one firm can hire labor in a town, the firm is a monopsony. It chooses how much labor to hire to maximize its profit,

$$\pi = p(Q(L))Q(L) - w(L)L,$$

where $Q(L)$ is the production function, the amount of output produced using L hours of labor, and $w(L)$ is the labor supply curve, which shows how the wage varies with the amount of labor the firm hires. The firm maximizes its profit by setting the derivative of profit with respect to labor equal to zero (if the second-order condition holds):

$$\left(p + Q(L)\frac{dp}{dQ}\right)\frac{dQ}{dL} - w(L) - \frac{dw}{dL}L = 0. \tag{15B.1}$$

Rearranging terms in Equation 15B.1, we find that the maximization condition is that the marginal revenue product of labor,

$$MRP_L = p \times MPL = \left(p + Q(L)\frac{dp}{dQ}\right)\frac{dQ}{dL} = p\left(1 + \frac{1}{\varepsilon}\right)\frac{dQ}{dL},$$

equals the marginal expenditure,

$$ME = w(L) + \frac{dw}{dL}L = w(L)\left(1 + \frac{w}{L}\frac{dw}{dL}\right) = w(L)\left(1 + \frac{1}{\eta}\right), \quad (15B.2)$$

where η is the supply elasticity of labor.

If the supply curve is linear, $w(L) = g + hL$, the monopsony's expenditure is $E = w(L)L = gL + hL^2$, and the monopsony's marginal expenditure is $ME = dE/dL = g + 2hL$. Thus, the slope of the marginal expenditure curve, $2h$, is twice as great as that of the supply curve, h.

By rearranging the terms in Equation 15B.2, we find that

$$\frac{ME - w}{w} = \frac{1}{\eta}.$$

Thus, the markup of the marginal expenditure (and the value to the monopsony) to the wage, $(ME - w)/w$, is inversely proportional to the elasticity of supply. If the firm is a price taker, so η is infinite, the wage equals the marginal expenditure.

Appendix 16A: Perpetuity

We derive Equation 16.4, $PV = f/i$, which gives the present value, PV, of a stream of payments f that lasts forever if the interest rate is i. Using Equation 16.3, where the number of periods is infinite, we know that the present value is

$$PV = \frac{f}{1 + i} + \frac{f}{(1 + i)^2} + \frac{f}{(1 + i)^3} + \cdots . \quad (16A.1)$$

Factoring Equation 16A.1, we can factor $1/(1 + i)$ out and rewrite the equation as

$$PV = \frac{1}{1 + i}\left[f + \frac{f}{1 + i} + \frac{f}{(1 + i)^2} + \frac{f}{(1 + i)^3} + \cdots \right]. \quad (16A.2)$$

The term in the brackets in Equation 16A.2 is $f + PV$ as given in Equation 16A.1. When we make this substitution, Equation 16A.2 becomes

$$PV = \frac{1}{1 + i}(f + PV). \quad (16A.3)$$

Rearranging terms in Equation 16A.3, we obtain Equation 16A.4:

$$PV = \frac{f}{i}. \quad (16A.4)$$

Appendix 18A: Welfare Effects of Pollution in a Competitive Market

We now show the welfare effects of a negative externality in a competitive market where demand and marginal costs are linear, as in Figure 18.1. The inverse demand curve is

$$p = a - bQ, \quad (18A.1)$$

where p is the price of the output and Q is the quantity. The private marginal cost is the competitive supply curve if pollution is an externality:

$$MC^p = c + dQ. \tag{18A.2}$$

The marginal cost to people exposed to the pollution (gunk) is

$$MC^g = eQ. \tag{18A.3}$$

Equation 18A.3 shows that no pollution harm occurs if output is zero and that the marginal harm increases linearly with output. The social marginal cost is the sum of the private marginal cost and the marginal cost of the externality:

$$MC^s = c + (d + e)Q. \tag{18A.4}$$

The intersection of the demand curve, Equation 18A.1, and the supply curve, Equation 18A.2, determines the competitive equilibrium where pollution is an externality:

$$p_c = a - bQ_c = c + dQ_c = MC^p. \tag{18A.5}$$

If we solve Equation 18A.5 for Q, the competitive equilibrium quantity is

$$Q_c = \frac{a - c}{b + d}.$$

Substituting this quantity into the demand curve, we find that the competitive price is $p_c = a - b(a - c)/(b + d)$.

If the externality is taxed at a rate equal to its marginal cost, so the externality is internalized, the market produces the social optimum. We find the social optimum by setting p in Equation 18A.1 equal to MC^s in Equation 18A.4 and solving for the resulting quantity:

$$Q_s = \frac{a - c}{b + d + e}.$$

The corresponding price is $p_s = a - b(a - c)/(b + d + e)$.

If output is sold only by a monopoly, the monopoly's revenue is found by multiplying both sides of Equation 18A.1 by quantity: $R = aQ - bQ^2$. Differentiating with respect to quantity, we find that the monopoly's marginal revenue is

$$MR = a - 2bQ. \tag{18A.6}$$

If the monopoly is unregulated, its equilibrium is found by setting MR, Equation 18A.6, equal to private marginal cost, Equation 18A.2, and solving for output:

$$Q_m = \frac{a - c}{2b + d}.$$

The corresponding price is $p_m = a - b(a - c)/(2b + d)$. If the monopoly internalizes the externality due to a tax equal to MC^g, the equilibrium quantity is

$$Q_m^* = \frac{a - c}{2b + d + e}.$$

The price is $p_m^* = a - b(a - c)/(2b + d + e)$.

In Figure 18.1, $a = 450$, $b = 2$, $c = 30$, $d = 2$, and $e = 1$. Substituting these values into the equations, we solve for the following equilibrium values:

	Quantity	Price
Competition	105	240
Social optimum (competition with a tax)	84	282
Monopoly	70	310
Monopoly with a tax	60	330

Appendix 20A: Nonshirking Condition

An efficiency wage acts like a bond to prevent shirking. An employee who never shirks is not fired and earns the efficiency wage, w. A fired worker goes elsewhere and earns the lower, going wage, $\underline{w}$. The expected value to a shirking employee is

$$\theta\underline{w} + (1 - \theta)w + G,$$

where the first term is the probability of being caught shirking, θ, times earnings elsewhere if caught and fired; the second term is the probability of not being caught times the efficiency wage; and the third term, G, is the value a worker derives from shirking. The worker chooses not to shirk if the certain high wage from not shirking exceeds the expected return from shirking:

$$w \geq (1 - \theta)w + \theta\underline{w} + G,$$

which simplifies to Equation 20.2, $\theta(w - \underline{w}) \geq G$. That is, a risk-neutral worker does not shirk if the expected loss from being fired is greater than or equal to the gain from shirking.

Answers to Selected Questions and Problems

I know the answer! The answer lies within the heart of all mankind! The answer is twelve? I think I'm in the wrong building.   —Charles Schultz

Chapter 2

1.1 Substituting the values for $p_b, p_c,$ and Y into the demand function, we find that $Q = 171 - 20p + 20p_b + 3p_c + 2Y = 171 - 20p + (20 \times 4) + (3 \times 3\frac{1}{3}) + (2 \times 12.5) = 286 - 20p$.

1.2 Because the demand curve for pork is $Q = 171 - 20p + 20p_b + 3p_c + 2Y$, a ΔY change in income causes the quantity demanded to change by $\Delta Q = 2\Delta Y$. That is, a $1,000 increase in income causes the quantity demanded to increase by 2 million kg per year, and a $100 increase in income causes the quantity demanded to increase by a tenth as much, 0.2 million kg per year. (*Hint:* See Solved Problem 2.1.)

1.7 $Q = Q_1 + Q_2 = (120 - p) + (60 - \frac{1}{2}p)$
$= 180 - 1.5p$.

2.1 The change in the supply curve is $-60\Delta p_h = -60 \times (3 - 1.50) = -90$. That is, the supply curve shifts to the left by 90 million kg per year.

3.1 The statement "Talk is cheap because supply exceeds demand" makes sense if we interpret it to mean that the *quantity supplied* of talk exceeds the *quantity demanded* at a price of zero. Imagine a downward-sloping demand curve that hits the horizontal, quantity axis to the left of where the upward-sloping supply curve hits the axis. (The correct aphorism is "Talk is cheap until you hire a lawyer.")

3.5 In equilibrium, the quantity demanded, $Q = a - bp$, equals the quantity supplied, $Q = c + ep$, so $a - bp = c + ep$. By solving this equation for p, we find that the equilibrium price is $p = (a - c)/(b + e)$. By substituting this expression for p into either the demand curve or the supply curve, we find that the equilibrium quantity is $Q = (ae + bc)/(b + e)$.

3.6 Equating the right sides of the supply and demand functions and using algebra, we find that $\ln(p) = 3.2 + 0.2 \ln(p_t)$. We then set $p_t = 110$, solve for $\ln(p)$, and exponentiate $\ln(p)$ to obtain the equilibrium price: $p \approx $61.62/ton$. Substituting p into the supply curve and exponentiating, we determine the equilibrium: $Q \approx 11.78$ million short tons/year.

5.2 A ban has no effect if foreigners supply nothing at the pre-ban, equilibrium price. Thus, if imports occur only at prices above those actually observed, a ban has no practical effect.

5.9 Such a law creates a price ceiling. Because the supply curve shifts substantially to the left during the emergency, the price control creates a shortage: A smaller quantity will be supplied at the ceiling price than will be demanded.

7.1 When Japan banned U.S. imports, the supply curve of beef in Japan shifted to the left from S^1 to S^2 in panel a of the figure. (The figure shows a parallel shift, for the sake of simplicity.) Presumably, the Japanese demand curve, D, was unaffected as Japanese consumers had no increased risk of consuming tainted meat. Thus, the shift of the supply curve caused the equilibrium to move along the demand curve from e_1 to e_2. The equilibrium price rose from p_1 to p_2 and the equilibrium quantity fell from Q_1 to Q_2. U.S. beef consumers' fear of mad cow disease caused their demand curve in panel b of the figure to shift slightly to the left from D^1 to D^2. In the short run, total U.S. production was essentially unchanged. Because of the ban on exports, beef that would have been sold in Japan and elsewhere was sold in the United States, causing the U.S. supply curve to shift to the right from S^1 to S^2. As a result, the U.S. equilibrium changed from e_1 (where S^1 intersects D^1) to e_2 (where S^2 intersects D^2). The U.S. price fell 15% from p_1 to $p_2 = 0.85p_1$, while the quantity rose

(a) Japanese Beef Market

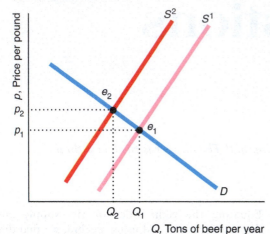

(b) U.S. Beef Market

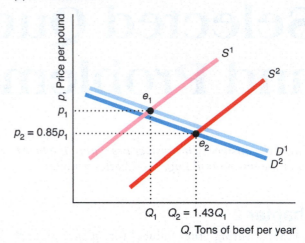

43% from Q_1 to $Q_2 = 1.43Q_1$. *Note:* Depending on exactly how the U.S. supply and demand curves had shifted, it would have been possible for the U.S. price and quantity to have both fallen. For example, if D^2 had shifted far enough left, it could have intersected S^2 to the left of Q_1, so that the equilibrium quantity would have fallen.

Chapter 3

2.2 According to Equation 3.1, the elasticity of demand is $\varepsilon =$ (percentage change in quantity demanded) ÷ (percentage change in price) $= -3.8\% \div 10\% = -0.38$, which is inelastic.

2.6 Differentiating the demand function as $Q = Ap^\varepsilon$ with respect to p, we find that $dQ/dp = \varepsilon Ap^{\varepsilon-1}$. To get the elasticity, we multiply dQ/dp by $p/Q = p/Ap^\varepsilon = 1/Ap^{\varepsilon-1}$. That is, the elasticity is $\varepsilon Ap^{\varepsilon-1} \times 1/Ap^{\varepsilon-1} = \varepsilon$. Because this result holds for any p, the elasticity is the same, ε, at every point along the demand curve.

2.14 The elasticity of demand is (slope) $\times (p/Q) = (\Delta Q/\Delta p)(p/Q) = (-9.5$ thousand metric tons per year per cent) $\times (45¢/1,275$ thousand metric tons per year) ≈ -0.34. That is, for every 1% fall in the price, a third of a percent more coconut oil is demanded. The cross-price elasticity of demand for coconut oil with respect to the price of palm oil is $(\Delta Q/\Delta p_p)(p_p/Q) = 16.2 \times (31/1,275) \approx 0.39$.

3.1 Because the linear supply function is $Q = g + hp$, a change in price of Δp causes a $\Delta Q = h\Delta p$ change in quantity. Thus, $\Delta Q/\Delta p = h$, and the elasticity of supply is $\eta = (\Delta Q/\Delta p)(p/Q) = hp/Q$. By substituting for Q using the supply function, we find that

$\eta = hp/(g + hp)$. By using the supply function to substitute for p, we learn that $\eta = (Q - g)/Q$.

3.3 If the quantity changes by 10.4% and the price elasticity of demand is -1.6, then we would expect the price to change by $-1.6 \times 10.4\% = -16.64\%$ (which is close to the 15% drop actually observed in the first month after the announcement).

4.6 By dividing both the numerator and the denominator of the right side of Equation 3.7 by η, we can rewrite that incidence equation as

$$\frac{\eta}{\eta - \varepsilon} = \frac{1}{1 - \varepsilon/\eta}.$$

As η goes to infinity, ε/η goes to zero, so the incidence approaches 1.

4.15 In a competitive market, the effect of a specific tax is the same whether it is placed on suppliers or demanders. Thus, if the market for milk is competitive, consumers will pay the same price in equilibrium regardless of whether the government taxes consumers or stores.

4.19 The incidence of the tax on consumers is zero if the demand curve is perfectly elastic or the supply curve is perfectly inelastic.

Chapter 4

1.5 If the neutral product is on the vertical axis, the indifference curves are parallel vertical lines.

1.7 Sofia's indifference curves are right angles (as in panel b of Figure 4.4). Her utility function is $U = \min(H, W)$, where *min* means the minimum of the two arguments, H is the number of units of hot dogs, and W is the number of units of whipped cream.

2.5 Because José Maria's utility is $U(B, Z) = AB^\alpha Z^\beta$, his marginal utility of B is $MU_B = \alpha AB^{\alpha-1}Z^\beta$, his marginal utility of Z is $MU_Z = \beta AB^\alpha Z^{\beta-1}$, and his marginal rate of substitution is $MRS = -MU_Z/MU_B = (\beta B)/(\alpha Z)$.

3.4 Suppose that Dale purchases two goods at prices p_1 and p_2. If her original income is Y, the intercept of the budget line on the Good 1 axis (where the consumer buys only Good 1) is Y/p_1. Similarly, the intercept is Y/p_2 on the Good 2 axis. A 50% income tax lowers income to half its original level, $Y/2$. As a result, the budget line shifts inward toward the origin. The intercepts on the Good 1 and Good 2 axes are $Y/(2p_1)$ and $Y/(2p_2)$, respectively. The opportunity set shrinks by the area between the original budget line and the new line.

4.5 Andy's marginal utility of apples divided by its price is $\frac{3}{2} = 1.5$. The marginal utility for kumquats is $\frac{5}{4} = 1.2$. That is, a dollar spent on apples gives him more extra utils than a dollar spent on kumquats. Thus, he maximizes his utility by spending all his money on apples and buying $40/2 = 20$ pounds of apples.

4.6 If we plot B on the vertical axis and Z on the horizontal axis, the slope of David's indifference curve is $-MU_Z/MU_B = -2$. The marginal utility from one extra unit of Z is twice that from one extra unit of B. Thus, if the price of Z is less than twice as much as that of B, David buys only Z (the optimal bundle is on the Z axis at Y/p_Z, where Y is his income and p_Z is the price of Z). If the price of Z is more than twice that of B, David buys only B. If the price of Z is exactly twice as much as that of B, he is indifferent between buying any bundle along his budget line.

4.9 Using Equations 4B.11 and 4B.12, we find that the necessary conditions for a utility maximum are $B = 100\alpha/[2(\alpha + \beta)]$ and $Z = 100\beta/(\alpha + \beta)$.

4.18 If a wealthy person spends more on food than a poor person before the subsidy, then the wealthy person is more likely to be spending more than the value of the food stamps prior to receiving them and hence is less likely to have a tangency at a point like f in Figure 4.12.

5.2 Consumers do not always notice taxes that are added at the register, so including the tax in the list price may discourage sales. This effect is less likely to be important for people buying a car because they are more likely to keep the tax in mind.

6.2 After West Virginia imposed a food tax, it was less expensive to buy food across the border for those people who lived close to the border. As the tax is raised, people who live further from the border start going to other states to buy their food. This effect can be illustrated using a diagram similar to that in the Challenge Solution or Solved Problem 4.4.

Chapter 5

1.2 Point E_1 corresponds to Bundle e_1 on indifference curve I^1, whereas E_2 corresponds to Bundle e_2 on indifference curve I^2, which is farther from the origin than I^1, so Mimi's utility is higher at E_2 than at E_1. Mimi is better off at E_2 than at E_1 because the price of beer is lower at E_2, so she can buy more goods with the same budget. This result generalizes: consumers are better off along the demand curve at lower prices.

2.4 An opera performance must be a normal good for Don because he views the only other good he buys as an inferior good. To show this result in a graph, draw a figure similar to Figure 5.3, but relabel the vertical "Housing" axis as "Opera performances." Don's equilibrium will be in the upper-left quadrant at a point like a in Figure 5.3.

2.5 The consumer's budget constraint is

$$p_1 q_1 + p_2 q_2 + \cdots + p_n q_n = Y,$$

where Y is income, and p_i is the price and q_i is the quantity of Good i. Differentiating with respect to Y, we find that

$$p_1 \frac{dp_1}{dY} + p_2 \frac{dq_2}{dY} + \cdots + p_n \frac{dq_n}{dY} = \frac{dY}{dY} = 1.$$

Multiplying and dividing each term by $q_i Y$, we rewrite this last equation as

$$\frac{p_1 q_1}{Y} \frac{dq_1}{dY} \frac{Y}{q_1} + \frac{p_2 q_2}{Y} \frac{dq_2}{dY} \frac{Y}{q_2} + \cdots$$
$$+ \frac{p_n q_n}{Y} \frac{dq_n}{dY} \frac{Y}{q_n} = 1,$$

or

$$\omega_1 \eta_1 + \omega_2 \eta_2 + \cdots + \omega_n \eta_n = 1,$$

where η_i, the income elasticity for each Good i, equals $(dq_i/dY)(Y/q_i)$, and the budget share of Good i is $\omega_i = p_i q_i/Y$. That is, the weighted sum of the income elasticities equals 1. For this equation to hold, at least one of the goods must have a positive income elasticity; hence, not all the goods can be inferior.

3.7 In the graph, L^f is the budget line at the factory store and L^o is the constraint at the outlet store. At the factory store, the consumer maximum occurs at e_f on indifference curve I^f. Suppose that we increase the income of a consumer who shops at the outlet store to Y^*, so that the resulting budget line L^* is tangent to the indifference curve I^f. The consumer would buy Bundle e^*. That is, the pure substitution effect (the movement from e_f to e^*) causes the consumer to buy relatively more firsts. The total effect (the movement from e_f to

e_o) reflects both the substitution effect (firsts are now relatively less expensive) and the income effect (the consumer is worse off after paying for shipping).

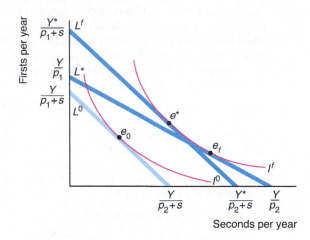

4.4 The CPI accurately reflects the true cost of living because Alix does not substitute between the goods as the relative prices change.

5.14 As the marginal tax rate on income increases, people substitute away from work due to the pure substitution effect. However, the income effect can be either positive or negative, so the net effect of a tax increase is ambiguous. Also, because wage rates differ across countries, the initial level of income differs, again adding to the theoretical ambiguity. If we know that people work less as the marginal tax rate increases, we can infer that the substitution effect and the income effect go in the same direction or the substitution effect is larger. However, Prescott's (2004) evidence alone about hours worked and marginal tax rates does not allow us to draw such an inference because U.S. and European workers may have different tastes and face different wages.

6.2 The government could give a smaller lump-sum subsidy that shifts the L^{LS} curve down so that it is parallel to the original curve but tangent to indifference curve I^2. This tangency point is to the left of e_2, so the parents would consume fewer hours of child care than with the original lump-sum payment.

6.3 Parents who do not receive subsidies prefer that poor parents receive lump-sum payments rather than a subsidized hourly rate for child care. If the supply curve for day-care services is upward sloping, by shifting the demand curve farther to the right, the price subsidy raises the price of day care for these other parents.

Chapter 6

2.3 No, it is not possible for $q = 10$, $L = 3$, and $K = 6$ to be a point on this production function. Holding output and other inputs fixed, a production function shows the minimum amount needed of a given factor. As only 5 units of capital are needed to produce 10 units of output given that 3 units of labor are used, using 6 units of capital would imply excess capital.

3.1 One worker produces one unit of output, two workers produce two units of output, and n workers produce n units of output. Thus, the product of labor equals the number of workers: $q = L$. The total product of labor curve is a straight line with a slope of 1. Because we are told that each extra worker produces one more unit of output, we know that the marginal product of labor, $\Delta q / \Delta L$, is 1. By dividing both sides of the production function, $q = L$, by L, we find that the average product of labor, q/L, is 1.

3.3 a. The average product of labor, holding capital fixed at $\overline{K}$, is $AP_L = q/L = L^{-0.25}\overline{K}^{0.25} = (\overline{K}/L)^{0.25}$.
   b. The marginal product of labor is $MP_L = dq/dL = \frac{3}{4}(\overline{K}/L)^{0.25}$.

4.7 Using Equation 6.3, we know that the marginal rate of technical substitution is $MRTS = -MP_L/MP_K = -\frac{2}{3}$.

4.8 The isoquant for $q = 10$ is a straight line that hits the B axis at 10 and the G axis at 20. The marginal product of B is 1 everywhere along the isoquant. The marginal rate of technical substitution is $-\frac{1}{2}$ if B is on the horizontal axis.

4.9 The isoquant looks like the "right angle" ones in panel b of Figure 6.3 because the firm cannot substitute between disks and machines but must use them in equal proportions: one disk and one hour of machine services.

5.5 This production function is a Cobb-Douglas: $Q = L^{0.23}K^{0.10}M^{0.66}$. Even though it has three inputs instead of two, the same logic applies. We can calculate the returns to scale as the sum of the exponents: $\gamma = 0.23 + 0.10 + 0.66 = 0.99$. Thus, it has (nearly) constant returns to scale.

6.2 The marginal product of labor of Firm 1 is only 90% of the marginal product of labor of Firm 2 for a particular level of inputs. Using calculus, we find that the MP_L of Firm 1 is $\partial q_1/\partial L = 0.9\partial f(L, K)/\partial L = 0.9\partial q_2/\partial L$.

7.2 Not enough information is given to fully answer this question. If we assume that Japanese and U.S. firms have identical production functions and produce using the same ratio of factors during good times, Japanese firms will have a lower average product of labor during recessions because they are less likely to lay off workers. However, it is not clear how Japanese and U.S. firms expand output during good times (do they hire the same number of extra workers?). As a result, we cannot predict which country has the higher average product of labor.

Chapter 7

1.3 If the plane cannot be resold, its purchase price is a sunk cost, which is unaffected by the number of times the plane is flown. Consequently, the average cost per flight falls with the number of flights, but the total cost of owning and operating the plane rises because of extra consumption of gasoline and maintenance. Thus, the more frequently someone has reason to fly, the more likely that flying one's own plane costs less per flight than a ticket on a commercial airline. However, by making extra ("unnecessary") trips, Mr. Agassi raises his total cost of owning and operating the airplane.

1.4 The sunk cost is $1 per pipe. The opportunity cost of each pipe is $9.

2.10 The total cost of building a 1-cubic-foot crate is $6. It costs four times as much to build an 8-cubic-foot crate, $24. In general, as the height of a cube increases, the total cost of building it rises with the square of the height, but the volume increases with the cube of the height. Thus, the cost per unit of volume falls.

3.2 You produce your output, exam points, using as inputs the time spent on Question 1, t_1, and the time spent on Question 2, t_2. If you have diminishing marginal returns to extra time on each problem, your isoquants have the usual shapes: They curve away from the origin. You face a constraint that you may spend no more than 60 minutes on the two questions: $60 = t_1 + t_2$. The slope of the 60-minute isocost curve is -1: For every extra minute you spend on Question 1, you have one less minute to spend on Question 2. To maximize your test score, given that you can spend no more than 60 minutes on the exam, you want to pick the highest isoquant that is tangent to your 60-minute isocost curve. At the tangency, the slope of your isocost curve, -1, equals the slope of your isoquant, $-MP_1/MP_2$. That is, your score on the exam is maximized when $MP_1 = MP_2$, where the last minute spent on Question 1 would increase your score by as much as spending it on Question 2 would. Therefore, you've allocated your time on the exam wisely if you are indifferent as to which question to work on during the last minute of the exam.

3.3 According to Equation 7.8, if the firm were minimizing its cost, the extra output it gets from the last dollar spent on labor, $MP_L/w = \frac{50}{200} = 0.25$, should equal the extra output it derives from the last dollar spent on capital, $MP_K/r = \frac{200}{1,000} = 0.2$. Thus, the firm is not minimizing its costs. It would do better if it used relatively less capital and more labor, from which it gets more extra output from the last dollar spent.

3.6 The firm chooses its optimal labor/capital ratio using Equation 7.8: $MP_L/w = MP_K/r$. That is, $\frac{1}{2}q/(wL) = \frac{1}{2}q/(rK)$, or $L/K = r/w$. Thus, in the United States where $w = r = 10$, the optimal $L/K = 1$, or $L = K$. Hence, the firm produces where $q = 100 = L^{0.5}K^{0.5} = K^{0.5}K^{0.5} = K$. Therefore, $K = 100 = L$. The cost is $C = wL + rK = (10 \times 100) + (10 \times 100) = 2,000$. At its Asian plant, the optimal input ratio is $L^*/K^* = 1.1r/(w/1.1) = 11/(10/1.1) = 1.21$. That is, $L^* = 1.21K^*$. Thus, $q = (1.21K^*)^{0.5}(K^*)^{0.5} = 1.1K^*$. Therefore, $K^* = 100/1.1$ and $L^* = 110$. The cost is $C^* = [(10/1.1) \times 110] + [11 \times (100/1.1)] = 2,000$. That is, the firm will use a different factor ratio in Asia, but the cost will be the same. If the firm could not substitute toward the less expensive input, its cost in Asia would be $C^{**} = [(10/1.1) \times 100] + [11 \times 100] = 2,009.09$.

3.7 From the information given and assuming no economies of scale in shipping baseballs, it appears that balls are produced using a constant returns to scale, fixed-proportion production function. The corresponding cost function is $C(q) = [w + s + m]q$, where w is the wage for the time period it takes to stitch one ball, s is the cost of shipping one ball, and m is the price of all material to produce a ball. As the cost of all inputs other than labor and transportation are the same everywhere, the cost difference between Georgia and Costa Rica depends on $w + s$ in both locations. As firms choose to produce in Costa Rica, the extra shipping cost must be less than the labor savings in Costa Rica.

3.12 Let w be the cost of a unit of L and r be the cost of a unit of K. Because the two inputs are perfect substitutes in the production process, the firm uses only the less expensive of the two inputs. Therefore, the long-run cost function is $C(q) = wq$ if $w \leq r$; otherwise, it is $C(q) = rq$.

4.2 The average cost of producing one unit is α (regardless of the value of β). If $\beta = 0$, the average cost does not change with volume. If learning by doing increases with volume, $\beta < 0$, so the average cost falls with volume. Here the average cost falls exponentially (a smooth curve that asymptotically approaches the quantity axis).

4.4 a. If $r = 0$, the average cost (AC) of producing one unit is $a + b$ (regardless of the value of N). This case doesn't have any learning by doing.

b. If $r > 0$, then average cost falls as N rises, so learning by doing does occur. As N gets very large, AC approaches a. Therefore, a is the lower limit for average cost—no matter how much learning is done, AC can never fall below a.

5.2 This firm has significant economies of scope, as producing gasoline and heating oil separately would cost approximately twice as much as producing them together. In this case, the measure of economies of scope, SC, is a positive number.

6.1 If $-w/r$ is the same as the slope of the line segment connecting the wafer-handling stepper and stepper technologies, then the isocost will lie on that line segment, and the firm will be indifferent between using either of the two technologies (or any combination of the two). In all the isocost lines in the figure, the cost of capital is the same, and the wage varies. The wage such that the firm is indifferent lies between the relatively high wage on the C^2 isocost line and the lower wage on the C^3 isocost line.

Chapter 8

2.5 The first-order condition to maximize profit is the derivative of the profit function with respect to q set equal to zero: $120 - 40 - 20q = 0$. Thus, profit is maximized where $q = 4$, so that $R(4) = 120 \times 4 = 480$, $VC(4) = (40 \times 4) + (10 \times 16) = 320$, $\pi(4) = R(4) - VC(4) - F = 480 - 320 - 200 = -40$. The firm should operate in the short run because its revenue exceeds its variable cost: $480 > 320$.

3.1 Suppose that a U-shaped marginal cost curve cuts a competitive firm's demand curve (price line) from above at q_1 and from below at q_2. By increasing output to $q_1 + 1$, the firm earns extra profit because the last unit sells for price p, which is greater than the marginal cost of that last unit. Indeed, the price exceeds the marginal cost of all units between q_1 and q_2, so it is more profitable to produce q_2 than q_1. Thus, the firm should either produce q_2 or shut down (if it is making a loss at q_2). We can also derive this result using calculus. The second-order condition, Equation 8B.3, for a competitive firm requires that marginal cost cut the demand line from below at q^*, the profit-maximizing quantity: $dMC(q^*)/dq > 0$.

3.3 The competitive firm's marginal cost function is found by differentiating its cost function with respect to quantity: $dC(q)/dq = b + 2cq + 3dq^2$. The firm's necessary profit-maximizing condition is $p = MC = b + 2cq + 3dq^2$. The firm solves this equation for q for a specific price to determine its profit-maximizing output.

3.14 Some farms did not pick apples so as to avoid incurring the variable cost of harvesting apples. These farmers left open the question of whether they will harvest in the future if the price rises above the shutdown level. Other more pessimistic farmers did not expect price to rise anytime soon, so they bulldozed their trees, leaving the market for good. (Most planted alternative apples such as Granny Smith and Gala that are more popular with the public and sell at a price above the minimum average variable cost.)

4.3 The shutdown notice reduces the firm's flexibility, which matters in an uncertain market. If conditions suddenly change, the firm may have to operate at a loss for six months before it can shut down. This potential extra expense of shutting down may discourage some firms from entering the market initially.

4.8 To derive the expression for the elasticity of the residual or excess supply curve in Equation 8.7, we differentiate the residual supply curve (Equation 8.6), $S^r(p) = S(p) - D^o(p)$, with respect to p to obtain

$$\frac{dS^r}{dp} = \frac{dS}{dp} - \frac{dD^o}{dp}.$$

Let $Q_r = S^r(p)$, $Q = S(p)$, and $Q_o = D(p)$. We multiply both sides of the differentiated expression by p/Q_r, and for convenience, we also multiply the second term by $Q/Q = 1$ and the last term by $Q_o/Q_o = 1$:

$$\frac{dS^r}{dp}\frac{p}{Q_r} = \frac{dS}{dp}\frac{p}{Q_r}\frac{Q}{Q} - \frac{dD^o}{dp}\frac{p}{Q_r}\frac{Q_o}{Q_o}.$$

We can rewrite this expression as Equation 8.7,

$$\eta_r = \frac{\eta}{\theta} - \frac{1-\theta}{\theta}\varepsilon_o,$$

where $\eta_r = (dS^t/dp)(p/Q_r)$ is the residual supply elasticity, $\eta = (dS/dp)(p/Q)$ is the market supply elasticity, $\varepsilon_o = (dD^o/dp)(p/Q_o)$ is the demand elasticity of the other countries, and $\theta = Q_r/Q$ is the residual country's share of the world's output (hence, $1 - \theta = Q_o/Q$ is the share of the rest of the world). *Note*: If n countries have equal outputs, then $1/\theta = n$, so this equation can be rewritten as $\eta_r = n\eta - (n-1)\varepsilon_o$.

4.9 See Equation 8.7 for details on the residual supply elasticity.

 a. The incidence of the federal specific tax is shared equally between consumers and firms, whereas the firms bear virtually none of the incidence of the state tax (they pass the tax on to consumers).

 b. From Chapter 3, we know that the incidence of a tax that falls on consumers in a competitive market is approximately $\eta/(\eta - \varepsilon)$. Although the national elasticity of supply may be a relatively small number, the residual supply elasticity facing a particular state is very large. Using the analysis about residual supply curves, we can infer that the supply curve to a particular state is likely to be nearly horizontal—nearly perfectly elastic. For example, if the price rises even slightly in Maine relative to Vermont, suppliers in Vermont will be willing to shift up to their entire supply to Maine. Thus, we expect the incidence on consumers to be nearly one from a state tax but less from a federal tax, consistent with the empirical evidence.

c. If all 50 states were identical, we could write the residual elasticity of supply equation as $\eta_r = 50\eta - 49\varepsilon_o$. Given this equation, the residual supply elasticity to one state is at least 50 times larger than the national elasticity of supply, $\eta_r \geq 50\eta$, because $\varepsilon_o < 0$, so the $-49\varepsilon_o$ term is positive and increases the residual supply elasticity.

5.4 a. Because the clinics are operating at minimum average cost, a lump-sum tax that caused the minimum average cost to rise by 10% would cause the market price of abortions to rise by 10%. (Show in a figure by shifting up the horizontal market supply curve by 10%.)

b. Based on the estimated price elasticity of −1.071, the number of abortions would fall by nearly 11%.

Chapter 9

2.1 The consumer surplus at a price of 30 is

$$450 = \tfrac{1}{2}(30 \times 30).$$

6.6 The Challenge Solution in Chapter 8 shows the long-run effect of a lump-sum tax in a competitive market. Consumer surplus falls by more than tax revenue increases, and producer surplus remains zero, so welfare falls.

6.7 If the tax is based on *economic* profit, the tax has no long-run effect because the firms make zero economic profit. If the tax is based on *business* profit and business profit is greater than economic profit, the profit tax raises firms' after-tax costs and results in fewer firms in the market. The exact effect of the tax depends on why business profit is less than economic profit. For example, if the government ignores opportunity labor cost but includes all capital cost in computing profit, firms will substitute toward labor and away from capital.

6.11 a. The initial equilibrium is determined by equating the quantity demanded to the quantity supplied: $100 - 10p = 10p$. That is, the equilibrium is $p = 5$ and $Q = 50$. At the support price, the quantity supplied is $Q_s = 60$. The market-clearing price is $p = 4$. The deficiency payment was $D = (p - p)Q_s = (6 - 4)60 = 120$.

b. Consumer surplus rises from

$$CS_1 = \tfrac{1}{2}(10 - 5)50 = 125 \text{ to}$$

$$CS_2 = \tfrac{1}{2}(10 - 4)60 = 180.$$

Producer surplus rises from

$$PS_1 = \tfrac{1}{2}(5 - 0)50 = 125 \text{ to}$$

$$PS_2 = \tfrac{1}{2}(6 - 0)60 = 180.$$

Welfare falls from

$$CS_1 + PS_1 = 125 + 125 = 250 \text{ to}$$

$$CS_2 + PS_2 - D = 180 + 180 - 120 = 240.$$

Thus, the deadweight loss is 10.

Chapter 10

1.4 A subsidy is a negative tax. Thus, we can use the same analysis as in Solved Problem 10.2 to answer this question (reversing the signs of the effects).

2.4 Amos' marginal rate of substitution is $MRS_a = [\alpha/(1 - \alpha)]H_a/G_a$, and Elise's is $MRS_e = [\beta/(1 - \beta)]H_e/G_e$. Along the contract curve, the two marginal rates of substitution are equal: $MRS_a = MRS_e$. Thus, to find the contract curve, we equate the right sides of the expressions for MRS_a and MRS_e. Using the information about the endowments and some algebra, we can write the (quadratic) formula for the contract curve as

$$(\beta - \alpha)G_aH_a + \beta(\alpha - 1)50G_a + \alpha(1 - \beta)100H_a = 0.$$

4.1 If you draw the convex production possibility frontier on panel c of Figure 10.6, you will see that it lies strictly inside the concave production possibility frontier. Thus, more output can be obtained if Jane and Denise use the concave frontier. That is, each should specialize in producing the good for which she has a comparative advantage.

4.3 As Chapter 5 shows, the slope of the budget constraint facing an individual equals the negative of that person's wage. Panel a of the figure illustrates that Pat's budget constraint is steeper than Chris' because Pat's wage is larger than Chris'. Panel b shows their combined budget constraint after they marry. Before they marry, each spends some time in the market earning money and other time at home cooking, cleaning, and consuming leisure. After they marry, one can specialize in earning money and the other at working at home. If they are both equally skilled at household work (or if Chris is better), then Pat has a comparative advantage (see Figure 10.6) in working in the market and Chris has a comparative advantage in working at home. Of course, if both enjoy consuming leisure, they may not fully specialize. As an example, suppose that before they lived together Chris and Pat each spent 10 hours a day in sleep and leisure activities, 5 hours

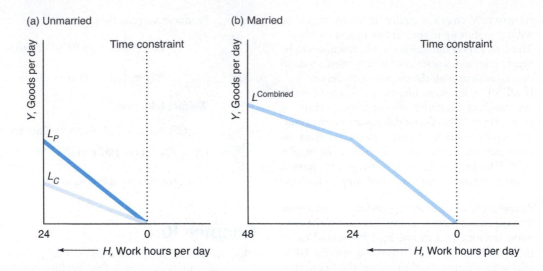

(a) Unmarried

Y, Goods per day

Time constraint

L_P

L_C

24   0

← *H*, Work hours per day

(b) Married

Y, Goods per day

Time constraint

L Combined

48   24   0

← *H*, Work hours per day

working in the marketplace, and 9 hours working at home. Because Chris earns $10 an hour and Pat earns $20, they collectively earned $150 a day and worked 18 hours a day at home. After they marry, they can benefit from specialization. If Chris works entirely at home and Pat works 10 hours in the market and the rest at home, they collectively earn $200 a day (a one-third increase) and still have 18 hours of work at home. If they do not need to spend as much time working at home because of economies of scale, one or both could work more hours in the marketplace, and they will have even greater disposable income.

Chapter 11

1.7   At $Q = 10$, $p = 500 - 10(10) = 400$. The elasticity is $\varepsilon = -0.1(400)/10 = -4$. Revenue $R = pQ = 10(400) = 4,000$.

2.10   The Lerner Index is $(p - MC)/p = (94.95 - 44)/94.95 \approx 0.54$. If **Stamp.com** is acting like a profit-maximizing monopoly, then, using Equation 11.9, $0.54 = -1/\varepsilon$, or $\varepsilon \approx -1.85$.

3.3   A profit tax (of less than 100%) has no effect on a firm's profit-maximizing behavior. If the government's share of the profit is γ, then the firm wants to maximize its after-tax profit, which is $(1 - \gamma)\pi$. However, the Q that maximizes π also maximizes $(1 - \gamma)\pi$ because $(1 - \gamma)$ is a constant. Consequently, the tribe's behavior is unaffected by a change in the share that the government receives. We can also answer this problem using calculus. The before-tax profit is $\pi_B = R(Q) - C(Q)$, and the after-tax profit is $\pi_A = (1 - \gamma)[R(Q) - C(Q)]$. For both, the first-order condition is marginal revenue equals marginal cost: $R'(Q) = C'(Q)$.

3.5   Suppose that the monopoly faces a constant-elasticity demand curve, with elasticity ε, has a

constant marginal cost, m, and that the government imposes a specific tax of t. The monopoly sets its price such that $p = (m + t)/(1 + 1/\varepsilon)$. Thus, $dp/dt = 1/(1 + 1/\varepsilon) > 1$.

4.1   Yes. For example, if the demand curve cuts the average cost curve only in its downward-sloping section, the average cost curve is strictly downward sloping in the relevant region.

6.2   If the demand curve is $p = 10 - Q$, its marginal revenue curve is $MR = 10 - 2Q$. Thus, the output that maximizes the monopoly's profit is determined by $MR = 10 - 2Q = 2 = MC$, or $Q^* = 4$. At that output level, its price is $p^* = 6$ and its profit is $\pi^* = 16$. If the monopoly chooses to sell 8 units in the first period (it has no incentive to sell more), its price is 2 and it makes no profit. Given that the firm sells 8 units in the first period, its demand curve in the second period is $p = 10 - Q/\alpha$, so its marginal revenue function is $MR = 10 - 2Q/\alpha$. The output that leads to its maximum profit is determined by $MR = 10 - 2Q/\alpha = 2 = MC$, or its output is 4α. Thus, its price is 6 and its profit is 16α. It pays for the firm to set a low price in the first period if the lost profit, 16, is less than the extra profit in the second period, which is $16(\alpha - 1)$. Thus, it pays to set a low price in the first period if $16 < 16(\alpha - 1)$, or $2 < \alpha$.

Chapter 12

1.2   The colleges may be providing scholarships as a form of charity, or they may be price discriminating by lowering the final price to less wealthy families (with presumably higher elasticities of demand).

2.6   Under perfect price discrimination, the firm's profit is the area below the demand curve and above marginal cost. This area is $0.5 \times 60 \times 60 = 1,800$. The consumer surplus is zero, as all consumer surplus is extracted by the monopoly. The total surplus is therefore 1,800. The deadweight loss is zero because the monopoly produces up to the point where marginal cost cuts the demand curve. For a single-price monopoly, the profit is 900, the consumer surplus is 450, the total surplus is 1,350, and the deadweight loss is 450.

2.8 See MyEconLab, Chapter 12, Supplemental Material, "Aibo," for more details about this robot. The two marginal revenue curves are $MR_J = 3,500 - Q_J$ and $MR_A = 4,500 - 2Q_A$. Equating the marginal revenues with the marginal cost of $500, we find that $Q_J = 3,000$ and $Q_A = 2,000$. Substituting these quantities into the inverse demand curves, we learn that $p_J = \$2,000$ and $p_A = \$2,500$. Rearranging Equation 11.9, we know that the elasticities of demand are $\varepsilon_J = p/(MC - p) = 2,000/(500 - 2,000) = -4/3$ and $\varepsilon_A = 2,500/(500 - 2,500) = -5/4$. Thus, using Equation 12.3, we find that

$$\frac{p_J}{p_A} = \frac{2,000}{2,500} = 0.8 = \frac{1 + 1/(-5/4)}{1 + 1/(-4/3)} = \frac{1 + 1/\varepsilon_A}{1 + 1/\varepsilon_J}.$$

The profit in Japan is $(p_J - m)Q_J = (\$2,000 - \$500) \times 3,000 = \$4.5$ million, and the U.S. profit is $4 million. The deadweight loss is greater in Japan, $2.25 million $(= \frac{1}{2} \times \$1,500 \times 3,000)$, than in the United States, $2 million $(= \frac{1}{2} \times \$2,000 \times 2,000)$.

3.6 The marginal revenue function corresponding to a linear inverse demand function has the same intercept and twice as steep a slope (see Chapter 11). Thus, the U.S. marginal revenue function is $MR_A = 100 - 2Q_A$, and the Japanese one is $MR_J = 80 - 4Q_J$. To determine how many units to sell in the United States, the monopoly sets its U.S. marginal revenue equal to its marginal cost, $MR_A = 100 - 2Q_A = 20$, and solves for the optimal quantity, $Q_A = 40$ units. Similarly, because $MR_J = 80 - 4Q_J = 20$, the optimal quantity is $Q_J = 15$ units in Japan. Substituting $Q_A = 40$ into the U.S. demand function, we find that $p_A = 100 - 40 = \$60$. Similarly, substituting $Q_J = 15$ units into the Japanese demand function, we learn that $p_J = 80 - (2 \times 15) = \$50$. Thus, the price-discriminating monopoly charges 20% more in the United States than in Japan. We can also show this result using elasticities. From Equation 3.3, we know that the elasticity of demand is $\varepsilon_A = -p_A/Q_A$ in the United States and $\varepsilon_J = -\frac{1}{2}p_J/Q_J$ in Japan. In the equilibrium, $\varepsilon_A = -60/40 = -3/2$ and $\varepsilon_J = -50/(2 \times 15) = -5/3$. As Equation 12.3 shows, the ratio of the prices depends on the relative elasticities of demand:

$$p_A/p_J = 60/50 = (1 + 1/\varepsilon_J)/(1 + 1/\varepsilon_A)$$
$$= (1 - 3/5)/(1 - 2/3) = 6/5.$$

3.8 From the problem, we know that the profit-maximizing Chinese price is $p = 3$ and the quantity is $Q = 0.1$ (million). The marginal cost is $m = 1$. The Lerner markup equation is $(p - MC)/p = -1/\varepsilon$ (Equation 11.9). Thus, $(p_C - m)/p_C = (3 - 1)/3 = -1/\varepsilon_C$, so $\varepsilon_C = -3/2$. If the Chinese inverse demand curve is $p = a - bQ$, then the corresponding marginal revenue curve is $MR = a - 2bQ$. Warner maximizes its profit where $MR = a - 2bQ = m = 1$, so its optimal $Q = (a - 1)/(2b)$. Substituting this expression into the inverse demand curve, we find that its optimal $p = (a + 1)/2 = 3$, or $a = 5$. Substituting that result into the output equation, we have $Q = (5 - 1)/(2b) = 0.1$ (million). Thus, $b = 20$, the inverse demand function is $p = 5 - 20Q$, and the marginal revenue function is $MR = 5 - 40Q$. Using this information, you can draw a figure similar to Figure 12.3.

3.9 Given that $p_A = 39 - 3Q_A$ and $p_B = 71 - 7Q_B$, the corresponding marginal revenue functions are $MR_A = 39 - 6Q_A$ and $MR_B = 71 - 14Q_B$. Setting MR_A equal to the marginal cost, 1, and solving, we find that $39 - 6Q_A = 1$, or $38 = 6Q_A$, or $Q_A = 38/6 \approx 6.33$. Substituting this quantity into the inverse demand function, we find that $p_A = 39 - 3(38/6) = 20$. Similarly, $Q_B = 5$ and $p_B = 36$.

3.12 With the ban, the monopoly's profit in each country is the output times the difference between the price and its constant average cost, 1. The monopoly's profit in Country 1 is $\pi_1 = (3.50 - 1)5 = 12.50$. Its profit in Country 2 is $\pi_2 = (5 - 1)4 = 16$. Thus, its total profit is $\pi = \pi_1 + \pi_2 = 12.50 + 16 = 28.50$. Without the ban, the monopoly's profits are $\pi_1 = (4 - 1)4 = 12$, $\pi_2 = (4 - 1)5 = 15$, and $\pi = 12 + 15 = 27$. Thus, the monopoly's profit falls from 28.50 to 27 if it loses the ability to price discriminate.

3.14 This policy allows the firm to maximize its profit by price discriminating if people who put a lower value on their time (are willing to drive to the store and move their purchases themselves) have a higher elasticity of demand than people who want to order over the phone and have the goods delivered.

4.3 If the monopoly sets the first-block price equal to $120, the cost to consumers of buying 60 units is $3,600, which equals their consumer surplus. Thus, consumers are willing to make this purchase, and the monopoly captures the entire potential surplus. This outcome is the same as perfect price discrimination.

5.3 Under two-part pricing, the club would charge a fee per round of $20 and Joe would purchase 50 rounds. In the absence of a membership fee his consumer surplus would be $2,500 (= 0.5 \times 100 \times 50)$. The club can charge this amount as an annual membership fee and thereby convert this consumer surplus to profit. Therefore, the profit-maximizing membership fee is $2,500. Under uniform monopoly pricing, the club would charge a price of $70 and Joe would purchase 25 rounds, generating a profit of only $1,250 for the club. Therefore, the club earns an additional $1,250 from using two-part pricing.

6.4 a. If the firm uses individual pricing, the best it can do is to charge $600 for the laptop and $100 for the printer. It sells laptops to all consumer types and sells printers to only *Type A* and *Type B* consumers. Assuming just one consumer of each type, the revenue (and profit) is $1,800 for laptops and $200 for printers, or $2,000 in total.

b. If the firm bundles the two products, it maximizes its profit by charging a bundle price of $750 and selling to all three customers for a profit of $2,250, which is $250 more than it earns from pricing the products individually.

c. Bundling pays because reservation prices are negatively correlated.

7.3 a. The reason for the sales slump was that the marginal benefit curve for infomercials shifted. For a given quantity ($1,000 worth of advertising time), the marginal benefit curve shifts down, similar to the shift from MB^1 to MB^2 in Figure 12.8. Because the marginal benefit curve shifted, a typical firm reduced the amount of advertising time it purchased from A_1 to A_2, where MB^2 intersects MC.

b. If the marginal benefit exceeds the marginal cost, the firm should buy more advertising.

7.4 The monopoly's profit is $\pi = (800-4Q + 0.2A^{0.5})Q -2Q - A = 798Q - 4Q^2 + 0.2A^{0.5}Q - A$. Setting the partial derivatives of the profit function with respect to Q and A equal to zero, we obtain the first-order conditions $\partial\pi/\partial Q = 798 - 8Q + 0.2A^{0.5} = 0$ and $\partial\pi/\partial A = 0.1A^{-0.5}Q - 1 = 0$. Rearranging the first of these conditions, we learn that $A^{0.5} = 0.1Q$. Substituting this expression into the second condition, we find that $798 - 8Q + 0.02Q = 0$, or $Q = 100$. Thus, $A^{0.5} = 0.1Q = 10$, so $A = 100$.

Chapter 13

2.4 Members of a cartel can use this technique to detect cheating on the cartel agreement by having customers report which firms are charging low prices.

2.7 The profit-maximizing cartel output is the monopoly output. Setting $MR = MC$ yields $100 - 4Q = 20$,

so $Q = 20$. Each of the four firms produces $q = 20/4 = 5$.

3.2 The inverse demand curve is $p = 1 - 0.001Q$. The first firm's profit is $\pi_1 = [1 - 0.001(q_1 + q_2)]q_1 - 0.28q_1$. Its first-order condition is $d\pi_1/dq_1 = 1 - 0.001(2q_1 + q_2) - 0.28 = 0$. If we rearrange the terms, the first firm's best-response function is $q_1 = 360 - \frac{1}{2}q_2$. Similarly, the second firm's best-response function is $q_2 = 360 - \frac{1}{2}q_1$. By substituting one of these best-response functions into the other, we learn that the Nash-Cournot equilibrium occurs at $q_1 = q_2 = 240$, so the equilibrium price is 52¢.

3.4 One approach is to show that the effect a rise in marginal cost or a fall in the number of firms tends to cause is the price to rise. The section titled "Equilibrium, Elasticity, and the Number of Firms" shows that as the number of firms falls, market power increases and the markup of price over marginal cost increases. The two effects reinforce each other. Suppose the market demand curve has a constant elasticity of ε. We can rewrite Equation 13.7 as $p = m/[1 + 1/(n\varepsilon)] = m\mu$, where $\mu = 1/[1 + 1/(n\varepsilon)]$ is the markup factor. Suppose that marginal cost increases to $(1 + \alpha)m$ and the drop in the number of firms causes the markup factor to rise to $(1 + \beta)\mu$. The resulting change in price is $[(1 + \alpha)m \times (1 + \beta)\mu] - m\mu = (\alpha + \beta + \alpha\beta)m\mu$. That is, price increases by the fractional increase in the marginal cost, α, plus the fractional increase in the markup factor, β, plus the interaction of the two, $\alpha\beta$.

3.9 Firm 1's profit is $\pi_1 = q_1[a - b(q_1 + q_2)] - mq_1$. Consequently, its best-response function is $q_1 = (a - m - bq_2)/(2b)$, where we replace m_1 with m in Equation 13A.11. (Alternatively, you can derive this result using calculus.) Firm 2's profit is $\pi_2 = q_2[a - b(q_1 + q_2)] - (m + x)q_2$. Simultaneously solving these best-response functions for q_1 and q_2, we get the equilibrium quantities in Equations 13A.13 and 13A.14, where we've substituted for the appropriate marginal costs:

$$q_1 = \frac{a - 2m + (m + x)}{3b} = \frac{a - m + x}{3b},$$

$$q_2 = \frac{a - 2(m + x) + m}{3b} = \frac{a - m - 2x}{3b}.$$

By inspection,

$$q_1 = [a - m + x]/[3b] > q_2$$
$$= [a - m - 2x]/[3b].$$

The low-cost firm, Firm 1, has the higher profit. The profits are $\pi_1 = (a + [m + x] - 2m)^2/[9b]$ and $\pi_2 = (a + m - 2[m + x])^2/[9b]$. Thus,

$$\pi_1 = \frac{(a - m + x)^2}{9b} > \frac{(a - m - 2x)^2}{9b} = \pi_2.$$

3.10 By differentiating its product, a firm makes the residual demand curve it faces less elastic everywhere. For example, no consumer will buy from that firm if its rival charges less and the goods are homogeneous. In contrast, some consumers who prefer this firm's product to that of its rival will still buy from this firm even if its rival charges less. As the chapter shows, a firm sets a higher price, the lower the elasticity of demand at the equilibrium.

4.1 To answer these questions, we use Appendixes 13A (Nash-Cournot) and 13B (Nash-Stackelberg).

 a. Using Equation 13A.8, the Nash-Cournot equilibrium quantity for each of the duopoly firms is $q = (a - m)/(3b) = (150 - 60)/3 = 30$. As a result, the Cournot price is $p = (a + 2m)/3 = (150 + 120)/3 = 90$ (using Equation 13A.9).

 b. From Equation 13B.3, we know that the Stackelberg leader's quantity is $q_1 = (a - m)/(2b) = (150 - 60)/2 = 45$. The follower's quantity, from Equation 13B.4, is $q_2 = (a - m)/(4b) = (150 - 60)/4 = 22.5$. Thus, the Nash-Stackelberg equilibrium price is $p = 150 - 45 - 22.5 = 82.5$.

4.4 The monopoly will make more profit than the duopoly will, so the monopoly is willing to pay the college more rent all else the same. Although granting monopoly rights may be attractive to the college in terms of higher rent, students will suffer (lose consumer surplus) due to the higher prices.

4.5 The inverse demand curve is $p = 1 - 0.001Q$. The first firm's profit is $\pi_1 = [1 - 0.001(q_1 + q_2)]q_1 - 0.28q_1$. Its first-order condition is $d\pi_1/dq_1 = 1 - 0.001(2q_1 + q_2) - 0.28 = 0$. If we rearrange the terms, the first firm's best-response function is $q_1 = 360 - \frac{1}{2}q_2$. Similarly, the second firm's best-response function is $q_2 = 360 - \frac{1}{2}q_1$. By substituting one of these best-response functions into the other, we learn that the Nash-Cournot equilibrium occurs at $q_1 = q_2 = 240$, and the equilibrium price is 52¢.

4.6 Appendix 13A shows the general formulas for the linear demand, constant marginal cost Cournot model.

 a. For the duopoly, $q_1 = (15 - 2 + 2)/3 = 5$, $q_2 = (15 - 4 + 1)/3 = 4$, $p_d = 6$, $\pi_1 = (6 - 1)5 = 25$, $\pi_2 = (6 - 2)4 = 16$. Total output is $Q_d = 5 + 4 = 9$. Total profit is $\pi_d = 25 + 16 = 41$. Consumer surplus is $CS_d = \frac{1}{2}(15 - 6)9$

$= 81/2 = 40.5$. At the efficient price (equal to a marginal cost of 1), the output is 14. The deadweight loss is $DWL_d = \frac{1}{2}(6 - 1)(14 - 9) = 25/2 = 12.5$.

 b. A monopoly equates its marginal revenue and marginal cost: $MR = 15 - 2Q_m = 1 = MC$. Thus, $Q_m = 7$, $p_m = 8$, $\pi_m = (8 - 1)7 = 49$. Consumer surplus is $CS_m = \frac{1}{2}(15 - 8)7 = 49/2 = 24.5$. The deadweight loss is $DWL_m = \frac{1}{2}(8 - 1)(14 - 7) = 49/2 = 24.5$.

 c. The average cost of production for the duopoly is $[(5 \times 1) + (4 \times 2)]/(5 + 4) = 1.44$, whereas the average cost of production for the monopoly is 1. The increase in market power effect swamps the efficiency gain so that consumer surplus falls while deadweight loss nearly doubles.

5.2 Given that the duopoly firms produce identical goods, the equilibrium price is lower if the duopolies set price rather than quantity. If the goods are heterogeneous, we cannot answer this question definitively.

5.5 Firm 1 wants to maximize its profit: $\pi_1 = (p_1 - 10)q_1 = (p_1 - 10)(100 - 2p_1 + p_2)$. Its first-order condition is $d\pi_1/dp_1 = 100 - 4p_1 + p_2 + 20 = 0$, so its best-response function is $p_1 = 30 + \frac{1}{4}p_2$. Similarly, Firm 2's best-response function is $p_2 = 30 + \frac{1}{4}p_1$. Solving, the Nash-Bertrand equilibrium prices are $p_1 = p_2 = 40$. Each firm produces 60 units.

6.6 a. The Nash-Cournot equilibrium in the absence of a government intervention is $q_1 = 30$, $q_2 = 40$, $p = 50$, $\pi_1 = 900$, and $\pi_2 = 1{,}600$.

 b. The Nash-Cournot equilibrium is now $q_1 = 33.3$, $q_2 = 33.3$, $p = 53.3$, $\pi_1 = 1{,}108.9$, and $\pi_2 = 1{,}108.9$.

 c. As Firm 2's profit was 1,600 in part a, a fixed cost slightly greater than 1,600 will prevent entry.

7.1 a. If neither government intervenes, we have our original Nash-Cournot equilibrium, in which each firm flies 64 thousand passengers per quarter and makes a profit of $4.096 million per quarter. Using Solved Problem 13.1, we know that if only United's government provides a $48 per passenger subsidy, United flies 96 thousand passengers and American flies only 48 thousand. United's profit is $9.216 million, which is $5.120 million more than it earned without the subsidy.

 b. If both governments provide their firms with a $48 per passenger subsidy, each firm's profit rises by only $3.824 million, which is less than the total subsidy that it receives from its government, $3.840 million.

Chapter 14

1.1 The payoff matrix in this prisoners' dilemma game is

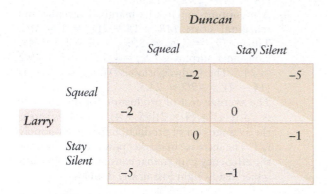

If Duncan stays silent, Larry gets 0 if he squeals and -1 (a year in jail) if he stays silent. If Duncan confesses, Larry gets -2 if he squeals and -5 if he does not. Thus, Larry is better off squealing in either case, so squealing is his dominant strategy. By the same reasoning, squealing is also Duncan's dominant strategy. As a result, the Nash equilibrium is for both to confess.

1.4 We start by checking for dominant strategies. Given the payoff matrix, Toyota always does at least as well by entering the market. If GM enters, Toyota earns 10 by entering and 0 by staying out of the market. If GM does not enter, Toyota earns 250 if it enters and 0 otherwise. Thus, entering is Toyota's dominant strategy. GM does not have a dominant strategy. It wants to enter if Toyota does not enter (earning 200 rather than 0), and it wants to stay out if Toyota enters (earning 0 rather than -40). Because GM knows that Toyota will enter (entering is Toyota's dominant strategy), GM stays out of the market. Toyota's entering and GM's not entering is a Nash equilibrium. Given the other firm's strategy, neither firm wants to change its strategy.

Next we examine how the subsidy affects the payoff matrix and dominant strategies. The subsidy does not affect Toyota's payoff, so Toyota still has a dominant strategy: It enters the market. With the subsidy, GM's payoffs if it enters increase by 50: GM earns 10 if both enter and 250 if it enters and Toyota does not. With the subsidy, entering is a dominant strategy for GM. Thus, both firms' entering is a Nash equilibrium.

1.12 Neither firm has a dominant strategy. The game does not have a pure-strategy Nash equilibrium. To determine the mixed-strategy equilibrium, we let the probability that a firm sets a low price be θ_1 for Firm

1 and θ_2 for Firm 2. Because the firms choose their prices independently, $\theta_1\theta_2$ is the probability that both set a low price, $(1 - \theta_1)(1 - \theta_2)$ is the probability that both set a high price, $\theta_1(1 - \theta_2)$ is the probability that Firm 1 prices low and Firm 2 prices high, and $(1 - \theta_1)\theta_2$ is the probability that Firm 1 prices high and Firm 2 prices low. Firm 2's expected payoff is

$$E(\pi_2) = 2\theta_1\theta_2 + (0)\theta_1(1 - \theta_2) + (1 - \theta_1)\theta_2$$
$$+ 6(1 - \theta_1)(1 - \theta_2)$$
$$= (6 - 6\theta_1) - (5 - 7\theta_1)\theta_2.$$

Similarly, Firm 1's expected payoff is

$$E(\pi_1) = (0)\theta_1\theta_2 + 7\theta_1(1 - \theta_2) + 2(1 - \theta_1)\theta_2$$
$$+ 6(1 - \theta_1)(1 - \theta_2)$$
$$= (6 - 4\theta_2) - (1 - 3\theta_2)\theta_1.$$

Firm 2 believes that Firm 1 believes Firm 2 will use a mixed strategy if Firm 1's belief about Firm 2 makes Firm 1 unpredictable. That is, Firm 1 uses a mixed strategy only if it is *indifferent* between setting a high or a low price. Given θ_2, Firm 1's profit if it uses its low-price strategy is $(6 - 4\theta_2) - (1 - 3\theta_2) = 5 - \theta_2$ and its profit if it uses its high-price strategy is $6 - 4\theta_2$. Equating these expected profits, $5 - \theta_2 = 6 - 4\theta_2$ and solving, we find that $\theta_2 = \frac{1}{3}$. By similar reasoning, Firm 2 will use a mixed strategy only if its belief is that Firm 1 chooses a low price with probability $\theta_2 = \frac{5}{7}$. Thus, the mixed-stategy Nash equilibrium is $\theta_1 = \frac{5}{7}$ and $\theta_2 = \frac{1}{3}$.

2.2 If the game is repeated a finite number of times, the outcome will yield the noncooperative solution if the players are fully rational. That is, $q_u = 64$ and $q_a = 64$ in each period. The same outcome occurs if both firms know that one firm cares only about current period profits.

3.1 a. The game has two pure-strategy Nash equilibria: Firm 1 sells 10 and Firm 2 sells 20, and Firm 1 sells 20 and Firm 2 sells 10.

   b. You can use a game tree and backward induction to show that if Firm 1 sells 10 then Firm 2 will choose 20 while if Firm 1 sells 20 then Firm 1 will sell 10. The first of these possibilities is better for Firm 1. Since Firm 1, the leader, chooses first, the subgame perfect Nash equilibrium is for Firm 1 to sell 10 and Firm 2 to sell 20.

   c. If Firm 2 is the leader, the subgame perfect Nash equilibrium is Firm 2 sells 10 and Firm 1 sells 20.

3.11 The game tree illustrates why the incumbent may install the robotic arms to discourage entry even though its total cost rises. If the incumbent fears that a rival is poised to enter, it invests to discourage entry. The incumbent can invest in equipment that lowers its marginal cost. With the lowered marginal cost, it is credible that the incumbent will produce larger quantities of output, which discourages entry. The incumbent's monopoly (no-entry) profit drops from $900 to $500 if it makes the investment because the investment raises its total cost. If the incumbent doesn't buy the robotic arms, the rival enters because it makes $300 by entering and nothing if it stays out of the market. With entry, the incumbent's profit is $400. With the investment, the rival loses $36 if it enters, so it stays out of the market, losing nothing. Because of the investment, the incumbent earns $500. Nonetheless, earning $500 is better than earning only $400, so the incumbent invests.

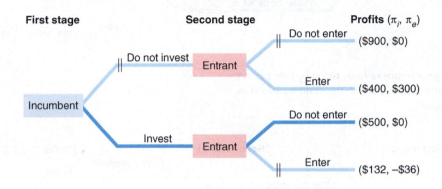

3.12 The incumbent firm has a *first-mover advantage*, as the game tree illustrates. Moving first allows the incumbent or leader firm to *commit* to producing a relatively large quantity. If the incumbent does not make a commitment before its rival enters, entry occurs and the incumbent earns a relatively low profit. By committing to produce such a large output level that the potential entrant decides not to enter because it cannot make a positive profit, the incumbent's commitment discourages entry. Moving backward in time (moving to the left in the diagram), we examine the incumbent's choice. If the incumbent commits to the small quantity, its rival enters and the incumbent earns $450. If the incumbent commits to the larger quantity, its rival does not enter and the incumbent earns $800. Clearly, the incumbent should commit to the larger quantity because it earns a larger profit and the potential entrant chooses to stay out of the market. Their chosen paths are identified by the darker blue in the figure.

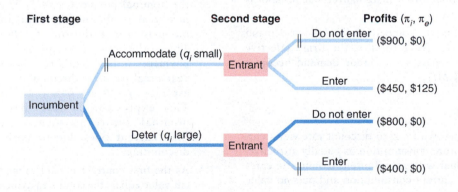

3.13 It is worth more to the monopoly to keep the potential entrant out than it is worth to the potential entrant to enter, as the figure shows. Before the pollution-control device requirement, the entrant would pay up to $3 to enter, whereas the incumbent would pay up to $\pi_m - \pi_d = \$7$ to exclude the potential entrant. The incumbent's profit is $6 if entry does not occur, and it loses $1 if entry occurs. Because the new firm would lose $1 if it enters, it does not enter. Thus, the incumbent has an incentive to raise costs by $4 to both firms. The incumbent's profit is $6 if it raises costs rather than $3 if it does not.

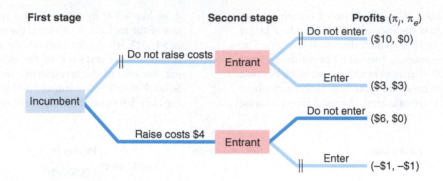

6.2 If the Other group moves first, the subgame perfect Nash equilibrium is to choose the ePub standard as the figure shows.

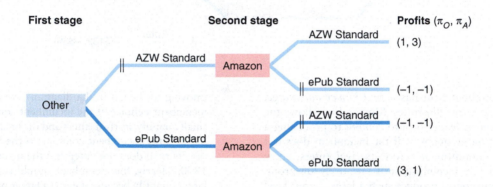

Chapter 15

1.2 The answer is given in Appendix 15A.

1.4 The competitive firm's marginal revenue of labor is $MRP_L = 2pK$.

1.5 Before the tax, the competitive firm's labor demand was $p \times MP_L$. After the tax, the firm's effective price is $(1 - \alpha)p$, so its labor demand becomes $(1 - \alpha)p \times MP_L$.

Chapter 16

1.5 An individual with a zero discount rate views current and future consumption as equally attractive. An individual with an infinite discount rate cares only about current consumption and puts no value on future consumption.

1.13 If the interest rate is set in real terms, putting $2,000 in the bank today results in an annual flow of $200 in real terms. If the interest rate is set in nominal terms, the real payment will shrink over time, so you cannot receive a real payment of $200 annually. (If the nominal rate were set at 15.5%, an initial $2,000 investment would ensure an annual flow of $200 in real terms.)

1.14 The real payment this year is the same as the nominal payment: $f = \tilde{f}$. The real payment next year is obtained by adjusting the nominal payment for inflation: $f = f/(1 + \tau) = \tilde{f}/1.1$. Thus, the real present value of the two payments is this year's real payment plus next year's real payment discounted by the real interest rate: $f + f/(1 + i) = \tilde{f} + \tilde{f}/[(1 + \gamma)(1 + i)]$. This expression is less than $2\tilde{f}$, because nominal future payments are worth less than current ones due to both inflation and discounting.

2.1 As the first contract is paid immediately, its present value equals the contract payment of $1 million. Our pro can use Equation 16.2 and a calculator to determine the present value of the second contract (or hire you to do the job for him). The present value of a $2 million payment 10 years from now is $2,000,000/(1.05)^{10} \approx \$1,227,827$ at 5% and $2,000,000/(1.2)^{10} \approx \$323,011$ at 20%. Consequently, the present values are:

	Present Value at 5%	Present Value Payment at 20%
$500,000 today	$50,000	$500,000
$2 million in 10 years	$1,227,827	$323,011
Total	$1,727,827	$823,011

Thus, at 5%, he should accept Contract B, with a present value of $1,727,827, which is much greater than the present value of Contract A, $1 million. At 20%, he should sign Contract A.

2.8 Currently, you are buying 600 gallons of gas at a cost of $1,200 per year. With a more gas-efficient car, you would spend only $600 per year, saving $600 per year in gas payments. If we assume that these payments are made at the end of each year, the present value of this savings for five years is $2,580 at a 5% annual interest rate and $2,280 at 10% (using Table 16.4). The present value of the amount you must spend to buy the car in five years is $6,240 at 5% and $4,960 at 10% (using Table 16.3). Thus, the present value of the additional cost of buying now rather than later is $1,760 (= $8,000 − $6,240) at 5% and $3,040 at 10%. The benefit from buying now is the present value of the reduced gas payments. The cost is the present value of the additional cost of buying the car sooner rather than later. At 5%, the benefit is $2,580 and the cost is $1,760, so you should buy now. However, at 10%, the benefit, $2,280, is less than the cost, $3,040, so you should buy later.

2.18 Solving for *irr*, we find that *irr* equals 1 or 9. This approach fails to give us a unique solution, so we should use the *NPV* approach instead.

Chapter 17

1.2 Assuming that the painting is not insured against fire, its expected value is $550 = (0.2 × $1,000) + (0.1 × $0) + (0.7 × $500).

1.3 The expected value of the stock is $(\frac{1}{4} \times 400) + (\frac{3}{4} \times 200) = 150$. The variance is $\frac{1}{4}(400 - 150)^2 + \frac{3}{4}(200 - 150)^2 = \frac{1}{4}(150)^2 + \frac{3}{4}(-50)^2 = 5,625 + 1,875 = 2,500$.

2.5 As the graph shows, Irma's expected utility of 133 at point *f* (where her expected wealth is $64) is the same as her utility from a certain wealth of Y.

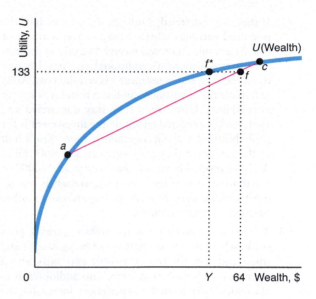

2.9 Hugo's expected wealth is $EW = (\frac{2}{3} \times 144) + (\frac{1}{3} \times 225) = 96 + 75 = 171$.

His expected utility is

$$EU = [\tfrac{2}{3} \times U(144)] + [\tfrac{1}{3} \times U(225)]$$
$$= [\tfrac{2}{3} \times \sqrt{144}] + [\tfrac{1}{3} \times \sqrt{225}]$$
$$= [\tfrac{2}{3} \times 12] + [\tfrac{1}{3} \times 15] = 13.$$

He would pay up to an amount P to avoid bearing the risk, where $U(EW - P)$ equals his expected utility from the risky stock, EU. That is, $U(EW - P) = U(171 - P) = \sqrt{171 - P} = 13 = EU$. Squaring both sides, we find that $171 - P = 169$, or $P = 2$. That is, Hugo would accept an offer for his stock today of $169 (or more), which reflects a risk premium of $2.

3.3 a. $EU(\text{No Insurance}) = 0.2U(90,000) + 0.8U(160,000) = 240 + 1,280 = 1,520. U(\text{Insurance}) = U(160,000 - 15,000) = 1,523.15$. Because $U(\text{Insurance}) > EU(\text{No Insurance})$, this household should buy the insurance.

b. The fair price is the expected value of the payout, which is $0.2 \times 70,000 = 14,000$.

c. The maximum the household would pay for this insurance is the price that would give it the same utility as not buying the insurance. If this price is p, then $U(160,000 - p) = EU(\text{No Insurance}) = 1,520$. Therefore, $4(160,000 - p)^{0.5} = 1,520$ or $160,000 - p = (1,520/4)^2 = 144,400$. It follows that $p = 15,600$.

4.2 If they were married, Andy would receive half the potential earnings whether they stayed married or not. As a result, Andy will receive $12,000 in present-value terms from Kim's additional earnings. Because the returns to the investment exceed the cost, Andy will make this investment (unless a better investment is available). However, if they stay unmarried and split, Andy's expected return on the investment is the probability of staying together, $\frac{1}{2}$, times Kim's half of the returns if they stay together, $12,000. Thus, Andy's expected return on the investment, $6,000, is less than the cost of the education, so Andy is unwilling to make that investment (regardless of other investment opportunities).

4.5 The expected punishment for violating traffic laws is θV, where θ is the probability of being caught and fined and V is the fine. If people care only about the expected punishment (there's no additional psychological pain from the experience), increasing the expected punishment by increasing θ or V works equally well in discouraging bad behavior. The government prefers to increase the fine, V, which is costless, rather than to raise θ, which is costly due to the extra police, district attorneys, and courts required.

Chapter 18

3.2 As Figure 18.2 shows, a specific tax of $84 per ton of output or per unit of emissions (gunk) leads to the social optimum.

3.6 Use the model in Appendix 18A to determine the equilibrium if the marginal harm of gunk is $MC^g = \$84$ (instead of Equation 18A.3). We care only about the marginal harm of gunk at the social optimum, which we know is $MC^g = \$84$ (because it is the same at every level of output). That is the same marginal cost as in the table at the end of Appendix 18A. Thus, the social optimum is the same as in that example (and no algebra is necessary). Using algebra, we set the demand curve equal to the new social marginal cost, $MC^2 = c + dQ + 84$, and we find that the socially optimal quantity is $Q_s = (a - c - 84)/(b + d) = (450 - 30 - 84)/(2 + 2) = 84$.

5.2 The government charges Alice's auto body shop a tax of $200 if it works on one car and $400 if it works on two cars per hour, which equals the marginal harm to the tea house. Alice makes $100 after tax if she works on one car and $0 if she works on two cars, so the social optimum is achieved. If they can bargain, the tea house offers Alice an amount between $100 and $200 to shut down, which maximizes their after-tax joint profits but not social

welfare. Thus, the "optimal" tax may not maximize social welfare if the parties can bargain.

6.11 No. The marginal benefit of advertising exceeds the marginal cost.

7.1 You can use several ways to demonstrate that welfare can go up despite the pollution. For example, you could redraw panel b with flatter supply curves so that area C became smaller than A (area A remains unchanged). Similarly, if the marginal pollution harm is very small, then we are very close to the no-distortion case, so that welfare will increase.

7.2 Going from no trade to free trade, consumers gain areas B and C, while domestic firms lose B. Thus, if consumers give firms an amount between B and $B + C$, both groups will be better off than with no trade.

Chapter 19

1.7 Because buyers are risk neutral, if they believe that the probability of getting a lemon is θ, the most they are willing to pay for a car of unknown quality is $p = p_1(1 - \theta) + p_2\theta$. If p is greater than both v_1 and v_2, all cars are sold. If $v_1 > p > v_2$, only lemons are sold. If p were less than both v_1 and v_2, no cars would be sold. However, we know that $v_2 < p_2$ and $p_2 < p$, so owners of lemons are certainly willing to sell them. (If sellers bear a transaction cost of c and $p < v_2 + c$, no cars are sold.)

2.2 Because insurance costs do not vary with soil type, buying insurance is unattractive for houses on good soil and relatively attractive for houses on bad soil. These incentives create a moral hazard problem: Relatively more homeowners with houses on poor soil buy insurance, so the state insurance agency will face disproportionately many bad outcomes in the next earthquake.

2.3 Brand names allow consumers to identify a particular company's product in the future. If a mushroom company expects to remain in business over time, it would be foolish to brand its product if its mushrooms are of inferior quality. (Just ask Babar's grandfather.) Thus, all else the same, we would expect branded mushrooms to be of higher quality than unbranded ones.

4.1 If almost all consumers know the true prices, and all but one firm charges the full-information competitive price, then it does not pay for a firm to set a high price. It gains a little from charging ignorant consumers the high price, but it sells to no informed customers. Thus, the full-information competitive price is charged in this market.

Chapter 20

1.1 Each member of the group may engage in moral hazard by ordering a more expensive meal than that student otherwise would, knowing that student will only pay for $1/n$ of the higher cost if the group has n students.

1.3 Presumably, the promoter collects a percentage of the revenue at each restaurant. If customers can pay cash, the restaurants may lie to the promoter as to the amount of food they sold. The scrip makes such opportunistic behavior difficult.

1.5 By making this commitment, the company may be trying to assure customers who cannot judge how quickly the product will deteriorate that the product is durable enough to maintain at least a certain value in the future. The firm is trying to eliminate asymmetric information to increase the demand for its product.

2.4 a. If Arnie is paid a fixed wage of 10, then Arnie provides low effort. Any additional effort would be costly to him and would not increase his wage and therefore be a net loss.

b. Given that they share profit equally, Arnie chooses medium effort. With medium effort the expected profit is $(0.5 \times 40) + (0.5 \times 80) = 60$. Arnie gets 50% or 30 and subtracts the cost of effort, 10, yielding a net gain of 20. With either low effort or high effort, Arnie's net gain is only 15.

c. Arnie receives 20 under the profit-sharing contract and 10 with a fixed wage, so he prefers the fixed wage. Priscilla has an expected value of $30 - 10 = 20$ with a fixed wage and $0.5(60) = 30$ under profit sharing, so she also prefers profit sharing.

2.7 A partner who works an extra hour bears the full opportunity cost of this extra hour but gets only half the marginal benefit from the extra business profit. The opportunity cost of extra time spent at the store is the partner's best alternative use of time. A partner could earn money working for someone else or use the time to have fun. Because a partner bears the full marginal cost but gets only half the marginal benefit (the extra business profit) from an extra hour of work, each partner works only up to the point at which the marginal cost equals half the marginal benefit. Thus, each has an incentive to put in less effort than the level that maximizes their joint profit, where the marginal cost equals the marginal benefit.

2.9 This agreement may lead to more trips than if each paid the entire amount when flying. Under the sharing plan, whichever of them most wants to visit the other more receives the full marginal benefit of one more visit while having to pay only half the marginal cost.

3.2 The minimum bond that deters stealing is $2,500 (= \$500/0.2)$.

Sources for Challenges and Applications

Chapter 1

Income Threshold Model and China: "Next in Line: Chinese Consumers," *Economist*, 326 (7795), January 23, 1993:66–67. Jeff Pelline, "U.S. Businesses Pour into China," *San Francisco Chronicle*, May 17, 1994:B1–B2. Keith Bradsher, "With First Car, a New Life in China," *New York Times*, April 24, 2008. "Foreign Direct Investment in China in 2010 Rises to Record $105.7 Billion," **bloomberg .com**, January 18, 2011. "China's Auto-Sales Growth Trails U.S. for First Time in at Least 14 Years," **bloomberg.com**, January 11, 2012. **www.worldometers.info/cars** (viewed May 6, 2012). Chris Woodyard, "Ford Investing $600 million in Chinese Car Factory," **content.usatoday.com/ communities/driveon/post/2012/04/ford-investing-600- million-in-chinese-car-factory/1**. *China Yearbook* (various years). **www.worldometers.info/cars** (viewed May 6, 2012).

Chapter 2

Quantities and Prices of Genetically Modified Foods: Dick Ahlstrom, "Use of GM Foods Inevitable in EU—Expert," *Irish Times*, July 18, 2008. Hong Van, "Genetically Modified Food Is Almost Everywhere," *The Saigon Times*, April 21, 2010. David Cronin, "Advantage GM in Europe," *Inter Press Service*, May 18, 2010. Stefanie Hundsdorfer, "Europe Takes Step Towards Ban on Genetically Modified Crops," **www .greenpeace.org**, viewed April 13, 2011. **www.guardian.co.uk/ environment/2012/feb/08/industry-claims-rise-gm-crops**, February 8, 2012. **www.ers.usda.gov/data-products/adoption- of-genetically-engineered-crops-in-the-us.aspx** (viewed May 8, 2013). **www.isaaa.org/resources/publications/briefs/44/ executivesummary** (viewed May 8, 2013).

Calorie Counting at Starbucks: Bollinger, Leslie, and Sorensen (2011). Lisa Baertlein, "U.S. McDonald's to Put Calorie Counts in Lights," **reuters.com**, September 12, 2012. Mary Clare Jalonick, "Menu Labeling Law: Calorie Counts Are a 'Thorny' Issue, FDA Head Says," **Huffingtonpost.com**, March 12, 2013. Duane D. Stanford, "Coca-Cola Expands Calorie Labels and Emphasizes No-Cals," **bloomberg.com**, May 8, 2013.

Aggregating Corn Demand Curves: McPhail and Babcock (2012). **www.ncga.com/worldofcorn** (viewed May 11, 2013).

Occupational Licensing: **www.ncbex.org/assets/media_ files/Bar-Examiner/articles/2013/8201132012statistics.pdf**, March 2013. **admissions.calbar.ca.gov/Examinations/ Statistics.aspx** (viewed May 23, 2013). Kleiner and Krueger (2013).

Price Controls Kill: Ivan Vera, "Zimbabwe: Forex Shortage Spurs Sugar Smuggling," *Harare*, November 10, 2000, **allafrica.com/stories/200011100299.html**. Kumbirai Mafunda, "Construction Industry Faces Bleak Future," *Zimbabwe Standard*, May 5, 2002. Ngoni Chanakira, "Makoni Admits Price Controls to Blame for Thriving Black Market," *The Daily News*, May 10, 2002. "Zim Slaps Price Control on Food," *News24*, June 4, 2005, **www .news24.com/Africa/Zimbabwe/Zim-slaps-price-control- on-food-20050406-2** (viewed February 27, 2010). Fanuel Jongwe, "Watchdog Unlikely to Get Teeth into Zimbabwe Inflation," *Mail & Guardian*, November 12, 2006, **mg.co.za/ article/2006-11-12-watchdog-unlikely-to-get-teeth-into-zim- inflation**. Kotchen and Burger (2007). "Zimbabwe Arrests over Price Curbs," *Al Jazeera*, July 9, 2007, **www.aljazeera .com/news/africa/2007/07/2008525132038645691.html**. "Robert Mugabe Zimbabwe Poll Ploy Strips White Firms," *The Australian*, March 11, 2008, **www.theaustralian.news .com.au/story/0,25197,23351335-2703,00.html**. "Zimbabwe Manufacturing Output Falls 27 Percent," *Harare*, July 24, 2008, **www.monstersandcritics.com/news/business/news/ printer_1419238.php**. Brian Latham, "Zimbabwe abandons price controls, promotes currency trading," January 29, 2009, **www.tradeafricablog.com/2009/01/zimbabwe- abandons-price-controls.html** (viewed July 8, 2012). Marawanyika, Godfrey, "Mugabe Defends Sale of Foreign Firms to Locals," **www.google.com/hostednews/afp/article/ ALeqM5jKPanDRNzEjTbmWRZ48AgI9KesNw**, February 27, 2010. Godfrey Marawanyika, "Zimbabwe Mining Companies Reject State Control, Document," **bloomberg .com**, May 20, 2013.

Chapter 3

Who Pays the Gasoline Tax?: Chouinard and Perloff (2007). Scott Horsley, "Obama Says Illinois' Gas Tax Holiday Didn't Work," NPR, May 9, 2008, **www.npr .org/templates/story/story.php?storyId=90309571**. Josh Voorhees, "Oberstar Proposes Future Gas Tax Hike," *E&ENews*, March 26, 2010, **www.eenews.net/ eenewspm/2010/03/26/2**. "Shuler Wants Gas Tax Break as Asheville Prices Rise," **citizen-times.com**, May 4, 2011. **www.iea.org/stats/surveys/mps.pdf**, April 2013.

www.api.org/oil-and-natural-gas-overview/industry-economics/fuel-taxes/gasoline-tax (viewed May 24, 2013). www.eia.gov/dnav/pet/pet_pnp_cap1_dcu_nus_a.htm (viewed May 29, 2013).

Do Farmers Benefit from a Major Drought?: National Corn Growers Association, *World of Corn Metrics*, 2013. www.ers.usda.gov/topics/in-the-news/us-drought-2012-farm-and-food-impacts.aspx (viewed June 1, 2013). usda.mannlib.cornell.edu (viewed June 1, 2013). John Eligon, "After Drought, Rains Plaguing Midwest Farms," *New York Times*, June 9, 2013. Tony C. Dreibus, "Bumper Crop Stalks Corn," *Wall Street Journal*, October 1, 2013.

Oil Drilling in the Arctic National Wildlife Refuge: United States Geological Survey, "Arctic National Wildlife Refuge, 1002 Area, Petroleum Assessment, 1998, Including Economic Analysis," pubs.usgs.gov/fs/fs-0028-01/fs-0028-01.pdf, April 2001. Energy Information Administration, "The Effects of Alaska Oil and Natural Gas Provisions of H.R. 4 and S. 1776 on U.S. Energy Markets," February 2002. Severin Borenstein, "ANWR Oil and the Price of Gasoline," U.C. Energy Institute, *Energy Notes*, 3(2), June 2005. Phil Taylor, "GOP Governors Urge Expanded Offshore Drilling, Opening ANWR," *E&E News PM*, August 22, 2012. tonto.eia.doe.gov (viewed May 11, 2013). www.eia.gov (viewed May 11, 2013).

Taxes to Prevent Obesity: Jacobson and Brownell (2000). Pierre Lemieux, "It's the Fat Police," *National Post*, April 6, 2002. Helen Tobler, "Call for Tax War on Obesity," *Australian IT*, August 16, 2002. "Soda Pop to Be Banned in L.A. Schools," CBSNEWS.com, August 28, 2002. Chouinard et al. (2007). "'Fat Tax' Proposed for Obese in Britain," sify.com/news/fat-tax-proposed-for-obese-in-britain-news-national-jegmLFabedd.html, February 25, 2008. Suzanne Daley, "Hungary Tries a Dash of Taxes to Promote Healthier Eating Habits," *New York Times*, March 2, 2013.

The Ethanol Subsidy: "Ethanol Subsidies Are $82 per Barrel of Replaced Gasoline, Says Incendiary Baker Institute Report," www.biofuelsdigest.com/blog2/2010/01/07/ethanol-subsidies-are-82-per-barrel-of-replaced-gasoline-says-incendiary-baker-institute-report July 1, 2010. Robert Pear, "After Three Decades, Tax Credit for Ethanol Expires," *New York Times*, January 1, 2012. McPhail and Babcock (2012). www.ers.usda.gov/topics/crops/corn/policy.aspx (viewed May 27, 2013).

Chapter 4

Why Americans Buy More E-Books Than Do Germans: Rüdiger Wischenbart et al., *The Global ebook Market*, O'Reilly: 2012. Biba, "Publishing Business Conference: International Trends in Ebook Consumption," www.teleread.com, March 20, 2012. Aaron Wiener, "We Read Best on Paper, Cultural Resistance Hobbles German E-Book Market," www.spiegel.de, April 13, 2012. Caroline Winter, "The Story Behind Germany's Scant E-Book Sales," *Bloomberg Businessweek*, April 19, 2012.

You Can't Have Too Much Money: *Businessweek*, February 28, 2005, p. 13. "Money Cannot Buy Happiness but It Helps," *Gulf Times*, May 30, 2010. "Annual Happiness Index Again Finds One-Third of Americans Very Happy," Harris Interactive, June 22, 2011, www.digitaljournal.com. Emily Alpert, "Happiness Tops in Denmark, Lowest in Togo, Study Says," *Los Angeles Times*, April 2, 2012. Helliwell et al. (2013). Stevenson and Wolfers (2013).

Indifference Curves Between Food and Clothing: Eastwood and Craven (1981).

Substituting Alcohol for Marijuana: Crost and Guerrero (2012).

Benefiting from Food Stamps: Whitmore (2002). "U.S. Converting Food Stamps into Debit-Card Benefits," *Chattanooga Times Free Press*, June 23, 2004. U.S. Department of Agriculture, *Characteristics of Food Stamp Households: Fiscal Year 2007*, September 2008. www.fns.usda.gov/snap/faqs.htm (viewed August 31, 2009). Hoynes and Schanzenbach (2009). "State Supplemental Nutrition Program Participation Rates in 2007," www.usda.gov/documents/2007SNAPparticipationreport.pdf, 2009. "New FRAC Report on 24 Cities Finds Only 67 Percent of Eligible Urban Households Participate in SNAP/Food Stamp Program," frac.org/urban-snapfood-stamp-report, September 9, 2009. Center on Budget and Policy Priorities, "Policy Basics: Introduction to the Supplemental Nutrition Assistance Program (SNAP)," March 28, 2013.

Opt In Versus Opt Out: Madrian and Shea (2001, 2002). Jesse J. Holland, "Pension Law Addresses Auto-Enrollment," Associated Press, October 22, 2007. Robert Powell, "Meet the Investments That Will Be Your Default 401(k) Choices," *MarketWatch*, October 31, 2007. AON, "Aon Hewitt Study Shows Record-High Participation in Defined Contribution Plans Driven by Automatic Enrollment," May 24, 2011, aon.mediaroom.com/index.php?s=43&item=2285. Ariel Investments, "401(k) Plans in Living Color," April 3, 2012, www.arielinvestments.com/401k-Study-2012. www.bls.gov/opub/btn/volume-1/retirement-costs-for-defined-benefit-plans-higher-than-for-defined-contribution-plans.htm, December 2012.

Unaware of Taxes: Chetty et al. (2009). Goldin and Homonoff (2013). Zheng et al. (2013).

Chapter 5

Per-Hour Versus Lump-Sum Child-Care Subsidies: Blau and Tekin (2001). Elena Cherney, "Giving Day-Care Cash to Stay-at-Home Parents Sounds Like Politics to Some Canadians," *Wall Street Journal*, July 3, 2006:A2. Tekin (2007). Currie and Gahvari (2008). nccic.acf.hhs.gov/categories/index.cfm?categoryId=2\# (viewed May 26, 2009). U.S. Department of Health Services, "Child Care and Development Fund," www.acf.hhs.gov/programs/ccb/ccdf/factsheet.htm (viewed May 26, 2012). www.hss.gov.yk.ca/pdf/childcaresubsidy_en.pdf, February 2012.

Smoking Versus Eating and Phoning: Busch et al. (2004). Labonne and Chase (2011). www.cdc.gov/tobacco/data_statistics/fact_sheets/fast_facts (viewed June 5, 2013). www.who.int/tobacco/mpower/tobacco_facts/en/index.html (viewed June 5, 2013). ash.org/cigtaxfacts.html (viewed June 5, 2013). Nikaj and Chaloupka (2013).

Fast-Food Engel Curve: Kim and Leigh (2011).

Shipping the Good Stuff Away: Hummels and Skiba (2004).

What's the Value of Using the Internet?: David Dean et al., *The Internet Economy in the G-20*, Boston Consulting Group, 2012, www.bcgperspectives.com/Images/Internet_Economy_G20_tcm80-100409.pdf. Sarah Kidner, "What Would you Give Up for the Net?" conversation.which.co.uk/technology/what-would-you-give-up-for-internet-chocolate-coffee-sex, March 22, 2012.

Paying Employees to Relocate: Barbara Worthington, "FYI: Relocation," www.hreonline.com/HRE/story.jsp?storyId=69921696, February 1, 2008. www.orcworldwide.com/news/080212.php (February 12, 2008). Grace W. Weinstein, "The Good and Bad of Moving Overseas," *Financial Times*, May 24, 2008. www.mercer.com/referencecontent.htm?idContent=1312800 (viewed July 21, 2008). Jane M. Von Bergen, "More U.S. Workers Getting Global Assignments," *Philadelphia Inquirer*, July 31, 2008. Herod (2008). www.mercer.com/summary.htm?idContent=1351425. "The Most Expensive and Richest Cities in the World," *City Mayors Economics*, August 18, 2011 (viewed July 14, 2012). "Cost of Living Comparison Between London (United Kingdom) and Seattle (United States)," Expatistan, 2012, www.expatistan.com/cost-of-living/comparison/seattle/london (viewed July 14, 2012). Mercer Worldwide Survey of International Assignment Policies and Practices Report, 2012, www.imercer.com/products/2012/WorldwideIAPP.aspx. mthink.mercer.com/commitment-to-global-mobility-remains-strong (viewed May 31, 2013). Mercer, "Global Mobility: The New Business Imperative," www.imercer.com/uploads/Europe/pdfs/global_mobility-the_new_business_imperative.pdf (viewed May 31, 2013). www.lib.umich.edu/govdocs/steccpi.html (viewed October 7, 2013).

Working After Winning the Lottery: Imbens et al. (2001). Highhouse et al. (2010). Kuhn et al. (2011). Hedenus (2012).

Chapter 6

Labor Productivity During Recessions: Flath (2011). The data files (viewed June 26, 2012) underlying Susan Fleck et al., "The Compensation-Productivity Gap: A Visual Essay," *Monthly Labor Review*, January 2011. www.nber.org/cycles.html (viewed June 15, 2013).

Chinese State-Owned Enterprises: Gao Xu, "State-Owned Enterprises in China: How Big Are They?" January 19, 2010, blogs.worldbank.org/eastasiapacific/state-owned-enterprises-in-china-how-big-are-they. China Statistical Database, doi 219.235.129.58 (viewed June 9, 2013).

Malthus and the Green Revolution: www.unep.org/aeo/251.htm.www.fao.org/NEWS/2000/000704-e.htm. Norman Borlaug, "Nobel Lecture," December 11, 1970, Nobelprize.org. Gregg Easterbrook, "Forgotten Benefactor of Humanity," *Atlantic Monthly*, February 1997. "Biotechnology and the Green Revolution: Interview with Norman Borlaug," November 2002, ActionBioscience.org. United Nations, *Millennium Development Goals Report*, New York, 2008. www.fao.org/economic/ess/ess-fs/ess-fadata/en (viewed February 3, 2013). www.ers.usda.gov/data-products.aspx (viewed June 11, 2013). www.wfp.org/hunger/stats (viewed June 11, 2013). National Corn Growers Association, *World of Corn Metrics*, 2013.

A Semiconductor Integrated Circuit Isoquant: Nile Hatch, personal communications. Roy Mallory, personal communications. "PC Processor War Rages On," Deutsche Presse-Agentur, September 1, 2002.

Returns to Scale in Various Industries: Hsieh (1995). Flath (2011). Fox and Smeets (2011). Devine et al. (2012). Hossain et al. (2012). Zhang et al. (2012).

A Good Boss Raises Productivity: Lazear et al. (2012).

Tato Nano's Technical and Organizational Innovations: "Engineering the Nano," *The Times of India*, January 11, 2008. John Hagel and John Seely Brown, "Learning from Tata's Nano," February 27, 2008, www.businessweek.com/print/innovate/content/feb2008/id20080227_377233.htm. Gerard J. Tellis, "A Lesson for Detroit—Tata Nano," *San Francisco Chronicle*, March 31, 2009:A15. Datamonitor staff writer, "Tata Nano: Not Only a Product Revolution, But Also a Breakthrough in Product Distribution," May 7, 2009, www.automotive-business-review.com/comment/tata_nano_not_only_a_product_revolution_but_also_a_breakthrough_in_product_distribution_070509?. "Tata Opens Plant for World's Cheapest Car on Demand, *San Francisco Chronicle*, June 2, 2010. Lijee Philip and Kala Vijayraghavan, "Smart Selling Helps Tata Nano Sales Drive Past 10k Units Mark in April," *The Economic Times*, May 10, 2011. Nachiket Kelkar, "LCVs, Nano Push Tata Motors May Sales Up 4%," *Money Control*, June 1, 2012, www.moneycontrol.com/news/business/lcvs-nano-push-tata-motors-may-sales4_712210.html. "Tata Nano in Jamaica for the Long Haul—Dealer," *The Gleanor*, May 17, 2013.

Chapter 7

Technology Choice at Home Versus Abroad: www.sia-online.org (June 2013).

The Opportunity Cost of an MBA: Peter Edmonston, "In Tough Times, M.B.A. Applications May Be an Economic Indicator," *New York Times*, October 7, 2008. www.gmac.com/gmac/NewsandEvents/DeansDigest/2008/August2008/08AppTrendsResult.htm (viewed October 17, 2008). Menachem Wecker, "Fewer 2012 MBA Applications May Mean More Competition in 2013," usnews.com, October 15, 2012. "Application Trends," www.gmac.com (viewed June 15, 2013).

Short-Run Cost Curves for a Beer Manufacturer: Flath (2011).

Economies of Scale in Nuclear Power Plants: Davis and Wolfram (2012).

Long-Run Cost Curves in Beer Manufacturing: Flath (2011).

Choosing an Inkjet or a Laser Printer: Various advertisements (2013).

Learning by Drilling: Kellogg (2011).

Economies of Scope: Ida and Kuwahara (2004). Cohen and Morrison Paul (2011). Meyer (2012). Gonçalves and Barros (2013).

Chapter 8

The Rising Cost of Keeping On Truckin': Nicholas Katers, "About Interstate Trucking Authority," eHow, www.ehow.com/about_4739672_interstate-trucking-authority.html (viewed June 16, 2013). "Rules & Regulations," U.S. Department of Transportation, www.fmcsa.dot.gov/rules-regulations/rules-regulations.htm (viewed June 26, 2013). "Unified Carrier Registration," www.dotauthority.com/ucr.htm?gclid=CKma5tebnqQCFSFZiAodN2bunA (viewed June 26, 2013). www.ucr.in.gov (viewed June 26, 2013).

Oil, Oil Sands, and Oil Shale Shutdowns: Agis Salpukas, "Low Prices Have Sapped Little Oil Producers," *New York Times*, April 3, 1999. Robert Collier, "Fueling America, Oil's Dirty Future," *San Francisco Chronicle*, May 22, 2005. Robert Collier, "Coaxing Oil from Huge U.S. Shale Deposits," *San Francisco Chronicle*, September 4, 2006. Jon Birger, "Oil Shale May Finally Have Its Moment," *Fortune*, November 1, 2007. Judith Kohler, "Energy Firms Cautious on Oil Shale," OCRegister, November 3, 2007, www.ocregister.com/news/oil-204519-shale-research.html. Ben Geman, "Canada Warns U.S. Against Using Energy Law to Bar Fuel from Oil Sands," Greenwire, February 28, 2008, groups.google.com/forum/#!msg/parklandsupdate/J_sCB8bxBpc/Uho5ZYVlpUUJ. Robert Kunzig, "Scraping Bottom," *National Geographic Magazine*, March 2009. Oil reserve data are from the BP Statistical Review at www.bp.com (viewed June 20, 2013).

The Size of Ethanol Processing Plants: "Statistics," Renewable Fuels Association, www.ethanolrfa.org/pages/statistics (viewed June 20, 2013). www.neo.ne.gov/statshtml/122.htm (viewed June 20, 2013).

Fast-Food Firms' Entry in Russia: Andrew E. Kramer, "Russia Becomes a Magnet for U.S. Fast-Food Chains," *New York Times*, August 3, 2011. Sasha Horne, "US Fast Food Chains Banking on Russian Bellies," *RIA Novosti*, February 25, 2013. pizza.com/news/russian-to-make-more-deliveries (viewed June 20, 2013).

Upward-Sloping Long-Run Supply Curve for Cotton: International Cotton Advisory Committee, *Survey of the Cost of Production of Raw Cotton*, September 1992:5. *Cotton: World Statistics*, April 1993:4–5. The figure shows the supply of the major producing countries for which we have cost information. The only large producers for whom cost data are missing are India and China.

Reformulated Gasoline Supply Curves: Borenstein et al. (2004). David R. Baker, "Rules Fuel Patchwork Quilt of Gas Blends Nationwide," *San Francisco Chronicle*, June 19, 2005:B1, B3. Brown et al. (2008). Ronald D. White, "Refinery Work Boosts Gasoline Prices in California," *Los Angeles Times*, September 9, 2009. David R. Baker, "Why Californians Are Paying Even More for Gas," *San Francisco Chronicle*, September 23, 2009, p. A1. Auffhammer and Kellogg (2011). www.eia.gov/dnav/pet/pet_pnp_cap1_dcu_nus_a.htm (viewed June 20, 2013).

Chapter 9

"Big Dry" Water Restrictions: Nick Bryant, "'Big Dry' Turns Farms into Deserts," BBC News, August 31, 2008. Grafton and Ward (2008). "Torrential Rains Can't Quench Australia's 'Big Dry,'" www.mysinchew.com/node/34104, January 18, 2010. "Australian floods help ease the 'Big Dry,'" www.france24.com/en/20100404-australian-floods-help-ease-big-dry, April 4, 2010. www.bom.gov.au/water/restrictions (viewed June 29, 2013).

Tiger Woods' Rent: Tiger Woods: A Timeline of the Golfer's Turmoil," www.guardian.co.uk/sport/2009/dec/15/tiger-woods-timeline-golf-turmoil. Richest Athletes, *Forbes*, June 5, 2013. Knittel and Stango (forthcoming).

Willingness to Pay and Consumer Surplus on eBay: Bapna et al. (2008). www.eBay.com.

Goods with a Large Consumer Surplus Loss from Price Increases: Revenues in 2012 from the U.S. National Income and Product Accounts, www.bea.gov and www.econstats.com (viewed June 28, 2013). Elasticities are based on Blanciforti (1982). Appendix 9A shows how ΔCS was calculated.

Deadweight Loss of Christmas Presents: Waldfogel (1993, 2005, 2009). Bauer and Schmidt (2008). Eve Mitchell, "Cashing In," *Oakland Tribune*, June 12, 2011, C1. Barbara Farfan, "2011 U.S. Christmas Holiday Retail Data, Statistics, Results, Numbers Roundup Complete U.S. Retail Industry Christmas Holiday Shopping Year-Over-Year Results," December 29, 2011. Miguel Helft, "Meet the Anti-Groupon," CNN Money, April 30, 2012. tech.fortune.cnn.com/2012/04/30/wrapp/. Matt Brownell, "Gift Cards," *Forbes*, December 12, 2012.

Licensing Cabs: Jonathan Marshall, "Cab Companies Hauled into Court," *San Francisco Chronicle*, July 1, 1993:A1, A11. Boroski and Mildner (1998). Edward Epstein, "S.F. Tax Deal Rejected by Board of Supervisors," *San Francisco Chronicle*, April 13, 1999:A16. Barrett (2003). Chris Berdik, "Fare Game," *Boston Globe*, 42(9) September 2004:98–105. Hansu Kim, "Taxi Medallions—Why Give S.F. Assets Away?" *San Francisco Chronicle*, March 29, 2005:B7. Schaller Consulting (2006). "Better than Gold," www.upi.com/Business_News/2009/08/06/Better-than-gold-A-cab-medallion/UPI-87711249585126/print/,

August 6, 2009. Abelson (2010). **Slate.com**, June 6, 2012. **blogs.reuters.com/felix-salmon/2011/10/21/why-taxi-medallions-cost-1-million** (viewed June 23, 2012). Jeff Horwitz and Chris Cumming, "Taken for a Ride," **www.nyc.gov/html/tlc/downloads/pdf/corporate_accessible.pdf** (viewed June 23, 2012).

The Deadweight Cost of Raising Gasoline Tax Revenue: Blundell et al. (2012).

How Big Are Farm Subsidies and Who Gets Them?: *Agricultural Policies Monitoring and Evaluations 2011*, Organization for Economic Cooperation and Development, **www.oecd.org** (viewed June 27, 2013). **farm.ewg.org** (viewed June 27, 2013).

The Social Cost of a Natural Gas Price Ceiling: MacAvoy (2000). Davis and Kilian (2011).

The Chicken Tax Trade War: "U.S. Files Complaint Over Chinese Chicken Tariffs," *The New York Times*, September 20, 2011. Justin Berkowitz, "Free-Trade Cars: Why a U.S.–Europe Free-Trade Agreement Is a Good Idea," *Car and Driver*, June 2013.

Chapter 10

Anti-Price Gouging Laws: Carden (2008). Davis (2008). Michael Giberson, "Predictable consequences of anti-price gouging laws," **knowledgeproblem.com/2009/06/01/predictable-consequences-of-anti-price-gouging-laws**, June 1, 2009. "Bill Allows Gas Price Increase in Emergency," **www.ajc.com**, March 22, 2010. "Price Gouging Law Goes into Effect Following State of Emergency Declaration," **www.neworleans.com**, April 29, 2010. Keith Goble, "Rhode Island Imposes Price-gouging Protections," **landlinemag.com**, June 25, 2012. Michael Giberson, "List of State Anti-Price Gouging Laws," **knowledgeproblem.com/2012/11/03/list-of-price-gouging-laws**, November 3, 2012. **www.ag.ny.gov/press-release/ag-schneiderman-cracks-down-gas-stations-engaged-hurricane-sandy-price-gouging**, May 2, 2013.

Urban Flight: Econsult (2003). Crawford et al. (2004). **www.bassman.com/01_06.html**, December 2007. **www.phila.gov/Revenue/businesses/taxes/Pages/WageTax.aspx** (viewed July 4, 2013).

The Wealth and Income of the 1%: Sylvia Nasar, "The Rich Get Richer, but Never the Same Way Twice," *New York Times*, August 16, 1992:3. Kennickell (2001, 2003, 2009, 2011). Davies et al. (2007). United Nations, *Human Development Reports*, **hdrstats.undp.org**, 2008. Ben Rooney, "Millions Are No Longer Millionaires," **money.cnn.com/2009/03/11/news/economy/millionaires_2008**. *America's Bailout Barons*, Institute for Policy Studies, 2009. Anderson et al. (2009). Bucks et al. (2009). Card (2009). Mishel and Sabadish (2012). **www.aflcio.org/Corporate-Watch/CEO-Pay-and-the-99/Trends-in-CEO-Pay** (viewed July 4, 2013). Saez (2013). Alvarado et al., 2013.

How You Vote Matters: "The Mathematics of Voting: Democratic Symmetry," *The Economist*, March 4, 2000:83. Nancy Vogel, "'Instant Runoff' Voting Touted,"

Los Angeles Times, December 25, 2006, **articles.latimes.com/2006/dec/25/local/me-voting25**. **www.sfelections.org/demo**, December 2007. Rob Richie, "Of Alternative Voting Methods, Instant Runoff Is Best," **minnesota.publicradio.org/display/web/2009/09/29/richie/**. "Our View: Charter Commission Should Split Decisions," *Portland Press Herald*, June 30, 2010. Rosemary Westwood, "Explainer: What Comes Next in the Liberal Vote," *Maclean's*, April 5, 2013.

Chapter 11

Brand-Name and Generic Drugs: "Thailand imports generic Plavix from India," PMLiVE Intelligence Online, August 24, 2007, **www.pmlive.com/pharma_news/thailand_imports_generic_plavix_from_india_8936**. Richard G. Frank, "The Ongoing Regulation of Generic Drugs," *New England Journal of Medicine*, November 15, 2007. Regan (2008). Milt Freudenheim, "Benefit Managers Profit by Specialty Drug Rights," *New York Times*, April 19, 2008. "Canada Generics Set for Double Digit Growth," EmailWire, August 26, 2009, **www.emailwire.com/release/printPR.php?prID=26411**. Ken MacQueen, "The Case for a National Drug Plan," *Maclean's*, June 8, 2011, **www2.macleans.ca/2011/06/08/the-case-for-a-national-drug-plan**. "Top 15 Patent Losses for 2013," **www.fiercepharma.com/special-reports/top-15-patent-expirations-2013**. Andrew Pollack, "Questcor Finds Profits, at $28,000 a Vial," *The New York Times*, December 29, 2012. **www.q1medicare.com/PartD-BrandNameDrugPatentExpirationsRX.php**. "Questcor: Near The Tipping Point," **seekingalpha.com**, July 8, 2013.

Apple's iPad: Chloe Albanesius, "iSuppli: iPad Could Produce Profits for Apple," *PC Magazine*, February 10, 2010. Arik Hesseldahl, "Apple iPad Components Cost At Least $259," *Businessweek*, April 7, 2010. Don Reisinger, "IDC: Apple iPad Secures 87 Percent Market Share," CNET News **cnet.com**, January 18, 2011. Don Reisinger, "Study: iPad Tallies 89 Percent of Tablet Traffic," CNET News **cnet.com**, January 24, 2011. Jenna Wortham, "So Far Rivals Can't Beat iPad's Price," *New York Times*, March 6, 2011. "iPad Remains Dominant in 1Q 2012 While Kindle Fire Fizzles," ABI Research, **www.abiresearch.com/press/3919-iPad+Remains+Dominant+in+1Q%E2%80%992012+While+Kindle+Fire+Fizzles**. Andrew Rassweiler, "New iPad 32GB + 4G Carries $364.35 Bill of Materials," **isuppli.com**, March 16, 2012. In Solved Problem 11.2, the marginal cost estimate (slightly rounded) is from iSuppli. We assumed that the company's gross profit margin for 2010 of about 40% (**forbes.com**) held for the iPad and used that to calculate the fixed cost. We derived the linear demand curve by assuming Apple maximizes short-run profit using the information on price, marginal cost, and quantity. Seth Fiegerman, "Apple Vs. Samsung: Everything You Need to Know About the (Patent) Trial of the Century," **www.businessinsider.com**, June 30, 2012. **store.apple.com** (viewed July 12, 2013).

Cable Cars and Profit Maximization: Rachel Gordon, "A Fare Too Steep?" *San Francisco Chronicle*, September 12,

2006:B-1. Rachel Gordon, "Cable Car Fares Rising a Buck to $6 on July 1," *San Francisco Chronicle*, June 7, 2011. "Cable Car Fares," *SFMTA*, 2012, **www.sfmta.com/cms/mfares/fareinfo.htm#cable** (viewed July 6, 2013).

Botox Patent Monopoly: Mike Weiss, "For S.F. Doctor, Drug Botox Becomes a Real Eye-Opener," *San Francisco Chronicle*, April 14, 2002:A1, A19. Reed Abelson, "F.D.A. Approves Allergan Drug for Fighting Wrinkles," *New York Times*, April 16:2002. Vita Reed, "Botox, Medical Cosmetics Boost Allergan's Profits," **www.ocbj.com/news/2010/may/09/botox-medical-cosmetics-boost-allergans-profits** (July 2010). "Nice News for Allergan—Analyst Blog," **community.nasdaq.com/News/2012-06/nice-news-for-allergan-analyst-blog.aspx?storyid=152408**, June 29, 2012. Deborah Knapp, "Botox Approved As Migraine Medicine, Spurs Headache Club," **kens5.com**, July 8, 2013.

Natural Gas Regulation: Davis and Muehlegger (2010): We used their most conservative estimate (the one that produced the smallest deadweight loss). We approximated their demand curve with a linear one that has the same price elasticity of demand at point *b*. This figure represents the aggregation of state-level monopolies to the national level.

Generic Competition for Apple's iPod: Brad Gibson, "First on TMO," **www.macobserver.com**, November 3, 2004, and May 4, 2005. Katie Marsal, "iPod Competitors Can't Compete with Apple," **appleinsider.com**, December 13, 2005. Phillip Cruz, "U.S. Top Selling Computer Hardware for January 2007," **www.bloomberg.com/apps/news?pid=conewsstory&refer=conews&tkr=AAPL:US&sid=ap0bqJw2VpwI**, 2008. Arik Hesseldahl, "Deconstructing Apple's Tiny iPod Shuffle," **businessweek.com**, April 13, 2009. Jessica Hodgson, "New Zune Undercuts Apple's iPod Prices," *Wall Street Journal*, August 14, 2009. Tim Nash, "2010 Will Be the Year of the iPod Touch," **lowendmac.com/nash/09tn/year-of-the-ipod-touch.html**. Darcy Travlos, "The iPad will Mirror the iPod's Market Dominance," **forbes.com**, July 13, 2012.

Critical Mass and eBay: Brown and Morgan (2006, 2009). John Barrett, "MySpace Is a Natural Monopoly," January 17, 2007, **www.ecommercetimes.com/story/55185.html?welcome=1218648444&wlc=1251740474**. Carol Xiaojuan Ou and Robert M. Davison, "Why eBay Lost to TaoBao in China: The Global Advantage," *Communications of the ACM*, 52(1), January 2009:145–148.

Chapter 12

Sale Prices: Karen Datko, "My Ketchup Taste Test: It's an Upset!" *MSN Money*, January 14, 2011, **money.msn.com/saving-money-tips/post.aspx?post=80c1a82a-df10-4e84-960b-30ed5ad96a33**. Rebecca Smithers, "Heinz Left Playing Tomato Catch-up after Ketchup Tasting Trouncing," *The Guardian*, May 26, 2011. Andrew Adam Newman, "Ketchup Moves Upmarket, With a Balsamic Tinge," *New York Times*, October 25, 2011. **www.heinz.com** (viewed July 15, 2013). **www.wikinvest.com/stock/H.J._Heinz_Company_%28HNZ%29** (viewed August 14, 2013).

Disneyland Pricing: "Couple Tries for Year of Daily Disneyland Visits," *San Francisco Chronicle*, July 3, 2012. **www.Disneyland.com** (viewed July 15, 2013).

Preventing Resale of Designer Bags: Eric Wilson, "Retailers Limit Purchases of Designer Handbags," *New York Times*, January 10, 2008. Various stores' Web sites, July 15, 2013.

Google Uses Bidding for Ads to Price Discriminate: Goldfarb and Tucker (2011).

BotoxRevisited: See Chapter 11, "Botox Patent Monopoly."

Warner Brothers Sets Prices for a *Harry Potter* DVD: amazon.com, amazon.co.uk, warnerbros.com, the UK Film Council, **www.the-numbers.com/dvd/charts/annual/2011.php**, and **www.bbc.co.uk/newsbeat/16444062**. In the analysis, we assumed that the demand curves in each country are linear.

Reselling Textbooks: Adam Liptak, Justices Weigh Case on Imported Textbooks, *New York Times*, October 29, 2012. Robert Barnes, "In copyright case, Supreme Court rules that goods made overseas can be resold here," *Washington Post*, March 19, 2013. Daniel Fisher, "Supreme Court Upholds Right To Sell Foreign-Published Books," *Forbes*, March 19, 2013. Ry Rivard, "Libraries Can Lend Foreign Books," *Inside Higher Ed*, March 20, 2013.

Buying Discounts: Borenstein and Rose (1994). Jenna Wortham, "Coupons You Don't Clip, Sent to Your Cellphone," *New York Times*, August 29, 2009. "Up Front," *Consumer Reports*, September 2009:7. Carmen Musick, "Computer Technology Fueling Coupon Trend," *Times News*, October 31, 2009. "Groupon and the Online Deal Revolution," eMarketer, June 7, 2011, **www.emarketer.com/Article.aspx?R=1008427**. "Coupon Trends," *JPS*, March 2, 2012, **www.santella.com/Trends.htm**. "NCH Annual Coupon Facts," NCH Marketing, 2012, **www.nchmarketing.com/** (viewed July 15, 2013). **www.inmar.com/Communications/Pages/2013%20Inmar%20Coupon%20Trends.pdf**.

iTunes for a Song: "iTunes Store Tops 10 Billion Songs Sold," **www.apple.com/pr/library/2010/02/25itunes.html**. Shiller and Waldfogel (2011).

Ties That Bind: hp.com (viewed July 15, 2013). **www.consumerchoice.info/warranty.htm** (viewed July 15, 2013). **www.mlmlaw.com/library/guides/ftc/warranties/undermag.htm** (viewed July 15, 2013).

Super Bowl Commercials: Ho et al. (2009). Kim (2011). Yinka Adegoke, "Super Bowl Advertisers Seek Buzz on Social Media," Reuters, January 29, 2012. Sharon Terlep and Suzanne Vranica, "GM to Forgo Pricey Super Bowl Ads," *Wall Street Journal*, May 18, 2012. Lisa de Moraes, "Super Bowl Commercial Prices Spike," *Washington Post*, February 1, 2013. Scott Collins, "TV Ratings Dip for Blackout-Plagued CBS Game," *Los Angeles Times*, February 4, 2013.

Chapter 13

Government Aircraft Subsidies: Irwin and Pavcnik (2004). John Heilpin, "WTO: Boeing Got $5B In Illegal Subsidies," March 12, 2012, **www .manufacturing.net/news/2012/03/wto-boeing-got-5b-in-illegal-subsidies. www.opensecrets.org/lobby/clientsum.php?id=D000000100&year=2012.**

Catwalk Cartel: William Sherman, "Catwalk Rocked by Legal Catfight," *Daily News*, March 14, 2004. *Carolyn Fears et al.* v. *Wilhelmina Model Agency, Inc., et al.*, 02 Civ. 4911 (HB), United States District Court for the Southern District of New York, 2004 U.S. Dist. Lexis 4502. 2004–1 Trade Cas. (CCH) P74,351, March 23, 2004. Warren St. John, "Behind the Catwalk, Suspicion and Suits," *New York Times*, April 18, 2004:sec. 9:1, 12. Neil Chandler, "Models in GBP 28m Wage Battle," *Daily Star*, June 6, 2004:8. **graphics8.nytimes.com/packages/pdf/national/20071126Fears.pdf** (viewed July 5, 2007). "Singapore—Competition Commission Fines Modelling Agencies for Price Fixing," Conventus Law, December 8, 2011, **conventuslaw.com/competition-commission-of-singapore-fines-modelling-agencies-for-price-fixing.**

Casket Entry: Chip Mellor and Jeff Rowes, "A Casket Cartel and the Louisiana Way of Death," *Wall Street Journal*, March 23, 2013:A11.

Hospital Mergers: Market Power Versus Efficiency: Town et al. (2006). Dafny (2009).

Mobile Number Portability: Cho et al. (2013).

Bottled Water: David Lazarus, "How Water Bottlers Tap Into All Sorts of Sources," *San Francisco Chronicle*, January 19, 2007. Vinnee Tong, "What's in that Bottle?" **suntimes.com**, July 28, 2007. Jennifer Alsever, "Bottled Water Sales Dry Up. Industry Asks 'Why?'" **www.msnbc .msn.com/id/34451973/ns/business-going_green**, December 18, 2009. "Top Environmental Concerns of the American Public: Selected Years, 1997–2008," **www.worldwater .org/data20082009/Table20.pdf** (viewed December 23, 2009). **money.cnn.com/galleries/2010/technology/1003/gallery.green_myths.fortune/index.html** (viewed July 2010). Julia Felsenthal, "Water, Water Everywhere: What's the best-tasting kind of water?" **slate.com**, October 12, 2011. Matthew Boesler, "You Are Paying 300 Times More for Bottled Water than Tap Water," **slate.com**, July 12, 2013.

Welfare Gain from More Toilet Paper: "Going Soft?" *The Economist*, March 4, 2000:59. Hausman and Leonard (2002). "Brits buying top-end TP for holidays," **www.upi.com/Odd_News/2009/12/21/Brits-buying-top-end-TP-for-holidays/UPI-84811261428817.**

Monopolistically Competitive Food Truck Market: Andrew S. Ross, "San Francisco Food Truck Empire Expanding," *San Francisco Chronicle*, February 18, 2011. **www.mobilefoodnews.com** (viewed June 17, 2012). **offthegridsf.com/about-3** (viewed March 29, 2013).

Zoning Laws as a Barrier to Entry by Hotel Chains: Suzuki (2013).

Chapter 14

Competing E-book Standards: "Sony Cuts E-reader Price to Stay on Same Page as iPad," **www.nzherald.co.nz**, July 8, 2010. Claire Cain Miller, "E-Books Top Hardcovers at Amazon," *New York Times*, July 19, 2010. Brian Enigma, "Migrating from Kindle to iPad: An Illustrated DRM Primer," netninja.com/2010/04/05/migrating-from-kindle-to-ipad-an-illustrated-drm-primer. en.wikipedia.org/wiki/E-book. ebook-reader-review.toptenreviews.com (viewed July 27, 2013).

Tough Love: Marta Choroszewicz and Pascal Wolff, "Population and Social Conditions," *Eurostat*, 50/2010. Jenna Goudreau, "Nearly 60% of Parents Provide Financial Support to Adult Children," forbes.com, May 20, 2011. Kevin Fagan, "Boomerang Kids Moving Back Home with Parents," San Francisco Chronicle, October 16, 2011. Kim Parker, "The Boomerang Generation," Pew Research Center, March 15, 2012. **www.britishinsurance.com/insurance-news/2nd-july—financial-support.aspx**, July 2, 2012.

Strategic Advertising: Roberts and Samuelson (1988). Slade (1995). Gasmi et al. (1992). Salgado (2008). Richards and Padilla (2009). "Leading Global Advertisers in 2010 by Estimated Revenue," **www.adbrands.net/top_global_advertisers.htm**, 2010. Garthwaite (2012). "Kantar Media Reports U.S. Advertising Expenditures Increased 0.8 Percent in 2011," Kantar Media, **www.kantarmedia.com/sites/default/files/press/Kantar_Media_2011__Q4_US_Ad_Spend .pdf**, March 12, 2012. Procter and Gamble 2012 Annual Report online, **annualreport.pg.com/annualreport2012/index.shtml.**

Dominant Airlines: Weiher (2002). U.S. Government Accountability Office, *Slot-Controlled Airports*, 2012.

Bidders' Curse: Lee and Malmendier (2011). Garratt et al. (2012).

GM's Ultimatum: Robert Schoenberger, "GM Sends Ultimatums to All Its 6000 US dealers," *Cleveland Plain Dealer*, June 2, 2009. Tony Van Alphen, "GM Dealers Sue to Keep Doors Open," *Toronto Star*, November 27, 2009. Janet Kurnovich, "GM Canada Sued For $750 Million By Former Dealers," May 17, 2011, **insurance-car.co/automotive-insurance/gm-canada-sued-for-750-million-by-former-dealers/.**

Chapter 15

Athletes' Salaries and Ticket Prices: Bill Shaikin, "Experts Say Demand, Not Higher Salaries, Drives Up Baseball Ticket Prices," *Los Angeles Times*, April 1, 1999. Jon Birger and Tim Arango, "The dismantling of the Yankee empire," **money.cnn.com/2007/08/01/news/companies/yes_sale.fortune/index.htm**. forbes.com (2010). Team Marketing Report, **teammarketing.com**, April 2010. Anthony Crupi, "RSNs Posted Across the Board Revenue Gains in '09," *MediaWeek*, June 16, 2010. Rick Snider, "Steinbrenner: Trailblazer to the Lavish, Diva Owner," *Washington Examiner*, **www.washingtonexaminer .com**, July 14, 2010. "Joe Strauss Live: Cardinals Chat

Q-&-A," www.stltoday.com/sports/baseball/professional/article_e8736348-9509-11df-bf07-00127992bc8b.html, July 21, 2010. www.cbssports.com/mlb/salaries/avgsalaries (viewed July 31, 2013). data.newsday.com/long-island/data/baseball/mlb-salaries-2013 (viewed July 31, 2013). www.usatoday.com/sports/fantasy/baseball/salaries/2013/all/team/all (viewed July 31, 2013). www.smallmarketball.com/2013/04/the-misleading-meandering-musings-of.html (viewed July 31, 2013). www.bloomberg.com/news/2012-11-20/news-corp-to-buy-49-of-yes-network-with-option-for-80-stake.html (viewed July 31, 2013).

Unions and Profits: Lee and Mas (2012).

Walmart's Monopsony Power: Bonanno and Lopez (2012). news.walmart.com (viewed August 1, 2013).

Chapter 16

Should You Go to College?: Richard Pérez-Peña, "U.S. Bachelor Degree Rate Passes Milestone," *New York Times*, February 23, 2012. Allison Linn, "Fewer People See College as Good Financial Investment," lifeinc.today.msnbc.msn.com, July 17, 2012. www.bls.gov/news.release/hsgec.nr0.htm, April 17, 2013. Juliette Fairley, "Why Half of Americans Don't Think College Is a Sound Investment," www.mainstreet.com, August 1, 2013. *How America Pays for College*, SallieMae, 2012. The statistical analysis is based on annual earnings (wages or self-employment) data from the 2009 U.S. *Current Population Survey* (Miriam King, Steven Ruggles, J. Trent Alexander, Sarah Flood, Katie Genadek, Matthew B. Schroeder, Brandon Trampe, and Rebecca Vick), and the *Integrated Public Use Microdata Series, Current Population Survey: Version 3.0*. Minneapolis: University of Minnesota, 2010).

Power of Compounding: Helen Huntley, Kim Norris, and Robert Trigaux, "An Early Lesson in Investing for the Long Term," *St. Petersburg Times*, March 14, 1994:Business 3, and the author's calculations.

Saving for Retirement: Author's calculations.

Winning the Lottery: Geetika Rudra, "Powerball Record Winner Is 84-Year-Old Woman Gloria Mackenzie," abcnews.go.com, June 5, 2013.

Falling Discount Rates and Self-Control: Shapiro (2004). Gruber and Mullainathan (2005). Kan (2007). Jeff Zeleny, "Occasional Smoker, 47, Signs Tobacco Bill," *New York Times*, June 23, 2009. aspire2025.org.nz/2012/05/22/article-support-for-a-tobacco-endgame, May 22, 2012.www.gallup.com/poll/1717/Tobacco-Smoking.aspx (viewed July 22, 2012).

Redwood Trees: Berck and Bentley (1997). Peter Berck, personal communications.

Chapter 17

BP and Limited Liability: Mark Long and Angel Gonzalez, "Transocean Seeks Limit on Liability," *Wall Street Journal*, May 13, 2010. David Leonhardt, "Spillonomics:

Underestimating Risk," *New York Times*, May 21, 2010. Andrew Ross Sorkin, "Imagining the Worst in BP's Future," *New York Times*, June 7, 2010. "BP Reports $4.9bn Annual Loss after Oil Spill Costs," BBC News, February 1, 2011, www.bbc.co.uk/news/business-12331804. Sabrina Canfield, "BP, Transocean Wrangle Over Insurance," Courthouse News Service, February 28, 2011, www.courthousenews.com/2011/02/28/34488.htm. Jef Feeley and Allen Johnson Jr., "BP Wins Final Approval of Guilty Plea Over Gulf Oil Spill," Bloomberg News, January 29, 2013, www.bloomberg.com/news/2013-01-29/bp-wins-final-approval-of-guilty-plea-over-gulf-oil-spill.html. Kathy Finn, "Gulf Oil Spill Payouts," www.huffingtonpost.com/2013/04/05/bp-gulf-oil-spill-payouts_n_3022877.html. www.bp.com/sectiongenericarticle800.do?categoryId=9048917&contentId=7082602 (viewed on April 12, 2013).

Stocks' Risk Premium: "The Cost of Looking," *Economist*, 328(7828), September 11, 1993:74. Leslie Eaton, "Assessing a Fund's Risk Is Part Math, Part Art," *New York Times*, April 2, 1995. Jagannathan et al. (2000). www.standardandpoors.com (viewed June 25, 2012). people.stern.nyu.edu/adamodar/New_Home_Page/datafile/histretSP.html (viewed April 8, 2013).

Gambling: Friedman and Savage (1948). Brunk (1981). Garrett (2001). Marsha Walton, "The Business of Gambling," CNN.com, July 6, 2005. grossannualwager.com/PrimaryNavigation/OnlineDataStore/internet_gambling_data.htm (viewed December 2009). www.americangaming.org/Industry/factsheets/statistics_detail.cfv?id=7 (viewed December 2009). www.reportlinker.com/p0157384-summary/Global-Online-Gaming-Report.html (viewed August 4, 2013). American Gaming Association, *2013 State of the States*, www.americangaming.org (viewed August 4, 2013). www.economist.com/blogs/graphicdetail/2013/05/daily-chart-16 (viewed August 4, 2013).

Diversifying Retirement Funds: Paul J. Lim, "Don't Paint Nest Eggs in Company Colors," *New York Times*, March 30, 2008. Jilian Mincer, "Company-Stock Ownership Down Amid Fears," August 9, 2010, financialadviserblog.dowjones.com/blog/stay-ahead-of-your-clients/company-stock-ownership-down-amid-fears. Michael J. Moore, "Wall Streeters Lose $2 Billion in 401(k) Bet on Own Firms," July 9, 2012, www.bloomberg.com/news/2012-07-09/wall-streeters-lose-2-billion-in-401-k-bet-on-own-firms.html.

Flight Insurance: www.worldtravelcenter.com (viewed July 26, 2012). www.ntsb.gov/data/table3_2012.html and www.ntsb.gov/data/table6_2012.html (viewed August 4, 2013).

Limited Insurance for Natural Disasters: Joseph B. Treaster, "Insurer Curbing Sales of Policies in Storm Areas," *New York Times*, October 10, 1996:A1, C4. Joseph B. Treaster, "Why Insurers Shrink from Earthquake Risk," *New York Times*, November 21, 1999:sec.3: 1, 13. Paul Vitello, "Home Insurers Canceling in East," *New York Times*, October 16, 2007. Pielke et al. (2008). "Tropical Storm Bonnie Dissipates. Still No Plan from Congress on Flood Insurance," insurancenewsnet.com/article.aspx?id=210913&type=newswires (July 28, 2010). Evan Lehmann, "U.S. Hit with 90% of the World's

Disaster Costs in 2012," *Climatewire*, **www.eenews.net/ stories/1059974314**, January 4, 2013.

Biased Estimates: Benjamin et al. (2001). Juliet Eilperin, "Shark Attacks Are Uncommon but Not Unheard Of," *Washington Post*, July 29, 2013. "What Should You Really Be Afraid Of? Mortality Risks," **www.questia .com/library/1G1-93135768/what-should-you-really-be-afraid-of-mortality-risks** (viewed August 4, 2013). "Shark Cull Announced By France Follows Second Fatal Attack Off Réunion Island This Year," **huffingtonpost.com**, August 4, 2013. **www.arthurhu.com/index/health/death .htm\#deathrank** (viewed August 4, 2013). International Shark Attack File, *Ichthyology*, **www.flmnh.ufl.edu/fish/ sharks/isaf/graphs.htm** (viewed August 4, 2013).

Chapter 18

Trade and Pollution: Tideman and Tullock (1976). **wto.org** (viewed August 7, 2013). **unctadstat.unctad .org** (viewed August 8, 2013). **www.trade.gov** (viewed August 8, 2013).

Negative Externalities from Spam: "Email Attacks: This Time It's Personal," **www.cisco.com/en/US/prod/collateral/ vpndevc/ps10128/ps10339/ps10354/targeted_attacks .pdf**, June 2011. Nicole Henderson, "Symantec Report Finds Spam Accounts for 73 Percent of June Email," *Web Host Industry Review*, June 28, 2011. Dino Grandoni, "Spam Costs You a Lot More Than You'd Think," **www .huffingtonpost.com/2012/08/08/cost-of-spam_n_1757726 .html**. Lance Whitney, "Targeted Cyberattacks Jump 42 Percent in 2012, Symantec Says," **news.cnet.com/8301-1009_3-57579847-83/targeted-cyberattacks-jump-42-percent-in-2012-symantec-says**. Caliendo et al. (2012). Rao and Reiley (2012). **www.kaspersky.com/about/news/ virus/2013/Spam_in_June_2013_Learn_the_secret_of_Steve_ Jobs_success** (viewed August 7, 2013).

Pulp and Paper Mill Pollution and Regulation: Shadbegian and Gray (2003). Shimshack and Ward (2005). Gray and Shimshack (2011).

Why Tax Drivers: Edlin and Karaca-Mandic (2006). Grabowski and Morrissey (2006). Hill et al. (2009). "Dutch Road Tax Inflames Debate in Neighboring Germany," *Deutsche Welle*, November 16, 2009, **www.dw-world.de/ dw/article/0,,4896686,00.html**. Bengt Halvorson, "Obama: Pay As You Drive, Instead of Gas Tax?" **thecarconnection .com**, May 5, 2011. Anderson and Auffhammer (forthcoming).

Protecting Babies: Currie and Walker (2011). Knittel et al. (2011).

Buying a Town: Katharine Q. Seelye, "Utility Buys Town It Choked, Lock, Stock and Blue Plume," *New York Times*, May 13, 2002. "Cheshire Ohio," Abandoned, **www .abandonedonline.net/neighborhoods/cheshire-ohio** (viewed August 7, 2013).

Acid Rain Program: Peter Passell, "For Utilities, New Clean-Air Plan," *New York Times*, November 18, 1994:C1, C6. Dallas Burtraw, "Trading Emissions to Clean the Air:

Exchanges Few but Savings Many," *Resources*, 122, Winter 1996:3–6. Peter Passell, "Economic Scene," *New York Times*, January 4, 1996:C2. Boyce Rensberger, "Clean Air Sale," *Washington Post*, August 8, 1999:W7. Schmalensee et al. (1998). EPA (2011). **www.epa.gov/airmarkets/ trading/2012/12spotbids.html**. **www.epa.gov/airtrends/ sulfur.html** (viewed August 1, 2012).

Piracy: "2011 Piracy Study," Business Software Alliance, **portal.bsa.org/globalpiracy2011/**. "Software Piracy Costs Billions in Time, Money for Consumers and Businesses," Microsoft.com, March 5, 2013.

Radiohead's "Public Good" Experiment: Jeff Leads, "Radiohead to Let Fans Decide What to Pay for Its New Album," *New York Times*, October 2, 2007. Eliot Van Buskirk, "Estimates: Radiohead Made Up To $10 Million on Initial Album Sales," **blog.wired.com/music/2007/10/ estimates-radio.html**, October 19, 2007. David Jenison, "Radiohead Fans Still Not Over the *Rainbow*," **www .eonline.com**, January 9, 2008. Andrew Perry, "Radiohead's King of Limbs Is Wet Weekend Mood Music," *The Telegraph*, February 25, 2011.

What's Their Beef?: Gina Holland, "Top Court Considers Challenge to Beef Ads," *San Francisco Chronicle*, December 9, 2004:C1, C4. **www.extension.iastate.edu/agdm/articles/ mceowen/McEowJuly05.htm**. **www.beefboard.org/ promotion/checpromotion.asp** (viewed December 2009 and August 2013).

Chapter 19

Dying to Work: Viscusi (1979). Dick Meister, "Safety First!" **www.truth-out.org/safety-first61799**, July 28, 2010. Kris Alingod, "Massey to Resume Operations in West Virginia Mine Despite Deaths," **allheadlinenews.com**, July 29, 2010. **osha.gov** (viewed August 2010). Tracie Mauriello and Len Boselovic, "Historic Fine Issued for Mine Disaster," *Pittsburgh Post-Gazette*, December 7, 2011, **www.post-gazette.com/pg/11341/1195085-455.stm**. Faith Aquino, "Nearly 2,000 Fukushima Daiichi Workers at Higher Risk of Thyroid Cancer," **japandailypress.com**, July 19, 2013. Emran Hossain, "Rana Plaza Collapse Victims Still Waiting For Compensation," *Huffington Post*, August 6, 2013.

Changing a Firm's Name: Cabral and Hortacsu (2010). McDevitt (2011).

Adverse Selection on eBay Motors: Lewis (2011). **pages .ebay.com/help/sell/motorfees.html** (viewed August 10, 2013).

Reducing Consumers' Information: Private Label Manufacturers Association's 2012 *International Private Label Yearbook*.

Chapter 20

Changing Bankers' Incentives: **www.realtytrac.com** (viewed August 2013).

Selfless or Selfish Doctors?: Lu (2012).

Contracts and Productivity in Agriculture: Foster and Rosenzweig (1994).

Music Contracts: Changing Their Tunes: Ethan Smith, "Bands on the Run," *Wall Street Journal*, July 14, 2006, p. W8. www.adweek.com/aw/magazine/article_display .jsp?vnu_content_id=1003686015, December 24, 2007. Marshall Brain, "How Recording Contracts Work," entertainment.howstuffworks.com/recording-contract .htm, 2008. "Leto Reached Out to De Havilland over EMI Lawsuit," www.contactmusic.com/news.nsf/story/leto-reached-out-to-de-havilland-over-emi-lawsuit_1124108 (November 30, 2009). Alistair Foster, "In the Pink, Zarif Is the Star Who Turned Down Simon Cowell, *London Evening Standard*, May 8, 2010. www.broadwayworld.com/printcolumn.php?id=156206 (July 2010). "Johnson Goes to Fans to Fund New Album," www.voxy.co.nz/entertainment/ johnson-goes-fans-fund-new-album/5/57692 (August 5, 2010). masterclasslady.com/2012/02/16/canadian-carly-rae-jepson-signed-by-justin-bieber, February 16, 2012. en .wikipedia.org/wiki/Magna_Carta..._Holy_Grail (viewed August 16, 2013).

Abusing Leased Cars: *Car Talk*, National Public Radio, May 1997. Dunham (2003). Peter Valdes-Dapena, "Car Leases Are Back: Should You Bite?" *CNN/Money*, May 26, 2005. Colin Bird, "Should I Pay Cash, Lease or Finance My New Car?" www.cars.com/go/advice/Story .jsp?section=fin&story=should-i-pay-cash&subject=loan-quick-start&referer=&aff=sacbee (April 27, 2009). www .rita.dot.gov (viewed August 16, 2013).

Layoffs Versus Pay Cuts: Hall and Lilien (1979). www .bls.gov (viewed August 2013).

References

Abelson, Peter, "The High Cost of Taxi Regulation, with Special Reference to Sydney," *Agenda*, 17(2), 2010:41–70.

Aigner, Dennis J., and Glen G. Cain, "Statistical Theories of Discrimination in Labor Markets," *Industrial and Labor Relations Review*, 30(2), January 1977:175–187.

Akerlof, George A., "The Market for 'Lemons': Quality Uncertainty and the Market Mechanism," *Quarterly Journal of Economics*, 84(3), August 1970:488–500.

Akerlof, George A., "Labor Contacts as Partial Gift Exchanges," *Quarterly Journal of Economics*, 97(4), November 1982:543–569.

Alexander, Donald L., "Major League Baseball," *Journal of Sports Economics*, 2(4), November 2001:341–355.

Altonji, Joseph G., and Ernesto Villanueva, "The Marginal Propensity to Spend on Adult Children," *B.E. Journal of Economic Analysis & Policy*, Advances, 7(1), 2007, Article 14.

Alvaredo, Facundo, Anthony B. Atkinson, Thomas Piketty, and Emmanuel Saez. 2013. "The Top 1 Percent in International and Historical Perspective" *Journal of Economic Perspectives*, 27(3), Summer, 2013:3–20.

Anderson, Keith B., and Michael R. Metzger, *Petroleum Tariffs as a Source of Government Revenues*. Washington, D.C.: Bureau of Economics, Federal Trade Commission, 1991.

Anderson, Michael, and Maximilian Auffhammer, "Pounds that Kill: The External Costs of Vehicle Weight," *Review of Economic Studies*, forthcoming.

Anderson, Sarah, John Cavanagh, Chuck Collins, and Sam Pizigati, *America's Bailout Barons*, Institute for Policy Studies, 2009.

Arrow, Kenneth, *Social Choice and Individual Values*. New York: Wiley, 1951.

Atalay, Enghin, "Materials Prices and Productivity," Center for Economic Studies, 2012.

Auffhammer, Maximilian, and Ryan Kellogg, "Clearing the Air? The Effects of Gasoline Content Regulation on Air Quality," *American Economic Review*, 101(6), October 2011:2, 687–2, 722.

Ayres, Ian, and Joel Waldfogel, "A Market Test for Race Discrimination in Bail Setting," *Stanford Law Review*, 46(5), May 1994:987–1047.

Bapna, Ravi, Wolfgang Jank, and Galit Shmueli, "Consumer Surplus in Online Auctions," *Information Systems Research*, 19(4), December 2008:400–416.

Barrett, Sean D., "Regulatory Capture, Property Rights and Taxi Deregulation: A Case Study, *Economic Affairs*, 23(4), 2003:34–40.

Basker, Emek, "Raising the Barcode Scanner: Technology and Productivity in the Retail Sector," NBER Working Paper 17825, 2012.

Battalio, Raymond, John H. Kagel, and Carl Kogut, "Experimental Confirmation of the Existence of a Giffen Good," *American Economic Review*, 81(3), September 1991:961–970.

Bauer, Thomas K., and Christoph M. Schmidt, "WTP vs. WTA: Christmas Presents and the Endowment Effect," Institute for the Study of Labor Working Paper, 2008.

Baumeister, Christiane, and Gert Peersman, "The Role of Time-Varying Price Elasticities in Accounting for Volatility Changes in the Crude Oil Market," *Journal of Applied Econometrics*, forthcoming.

Beatty and Tuttle, "Expenditure Response to Increases in In-Kind Transfers: Evidence from the Supplemental Nutrition Assistance Program," Working Paper, 2012.

Becker, Gary S., *The Economics of Discrimination*, 2nd ed. Chicago: University of Chicago Press, 1971.

Benjamin, Daniel K., William R. Dougan, and David Buschena, "Individuals' Estimates of the Risk of Death: Part II—New Evidence," *Journal of Risk and Uncertainty*, 22(1), January 2001:35–57.

Berck, Peter, and William R. Bentley, "Hotelling's Theory, Enhancement, and the Taking of the Redwood National Park," *American Journal of Agricultural Economics*, 79(2), May 1997:287–298.

Berck, Peter, and Michael Roberts, "Natural Resource Prices: Will They Ever Turn Up?" *Journal of Environmental Economics and Management*, 31(1), July 1996:65–78.

Bezmen, Trisha L., and Craig A. Depken II, "Influences on Software Piracy: Evidence from the Various United States," *Economic Letters*, 90(3), March 2006:356–361.

Blanciforti, Laura Ann, "The Almost Ideal Demand System Incorporating Habits: An Analysis of Expenditures on Food and Aggregate Commodity Groups." Doctoral thesis, University of California, Davis, 1982.

Blau, David, and Erdal Tekin, "The Determinants and Consequences of Child Care Subsidy Receipt by Low-Income Families," in Bruce Meyer and Greg Duncan, *The Incentives of Government Programs and the Well-Being of Families*, Joint Center for Poverty Research, 2001.

Blundell, Richard, Joel L. Horowitz, and Matthias Parey, "Measuring the Price Responsiveness of Gasoline Demand: Economic Shape Restrictions and Nonparametric Demand Estimation," *Quantitative Economics*, 3(1), March 2012:29–51.

Bollinger, Bryan, Phillip Leslie, and Alan Sorensen, "Calorie Posting in Chain Restaurants," *American Economic Journal: Economic Policy*, 3(1), February 2011: 91–128.

Bonanno, Alessandro, and Rigoberto A. Lopez, "Wal-Mart's Monopsony Power in Metro and Non-metro Labor Markets," *Regional Science and Urban Economics*, 42(4), July 2012:569–579.

Borenstein, Severin, James Bushnell, and Matthew Lewis, "Market Power in California's Gasoline Market," University of California Energy Institute, CSEM WP 132, May 2004, **www.ucei.berkeley.edu/PDF/csemwp132.pdf.**

Borenstein, Severin, and Nancy L. Rose, "Competition and Price Dispersion in the U.S. Airline Industry," *Journal of Political Economy*, 102(4), August 1994:653–683.

Borjas, George J., "The Labor Demand Curve Is Downward Sloping: Reexamining the Impact of Immigration on the Labor Market," *Quarterly Journal of Economics*, 118(4), November 2003:1335–1374.

Boroski, John W., and Gerard C. S. Mildner, "An Economic Analysis of Taxicab Regulation in Portland, Oregon," Cascade Policy Institute, **www.cascadepolicy.org**, 1998.

Boulier, Bryan L., Tejwant S. Datta, Robert S. Goldfarb, "Vaccination Externalities," *The B.E. Journal of Economic Analysis & Policy*, 7(1, Contributions), 2007: Article 23.

Bradbury, Hinton, and Karen Ross, "The Effects of Novelty and Choice Materials on the Intransitivity of Preferences of Children and Adults," *Annals of Operations Research*, 23(1–4), June 1990:141–159.

Brander, James A., and M. Scott Taylor, "The Simple Economics of Easter Island: A Ricardo-Malthus Model of Renewable Resource Use," *American Economic Review*, 88(1), March 1998:119–138.

Brander, James A., and Anming Zhang, "Market Conduct in the Airline Industry: An Empirical Investigation," *Rand Journal of Economics*, 21(4), Winter 1990:567–583.

Brown, Jennifer, Justine Hastings, Erin T. Mansur, and Sofia B. Villas-Boas, "Reformulating Competition: Gasoline Content Regulation and Wholesale Gasoline Prices," *Journal of Environmental Economics and Management*, 55(1), January 2008:1–19.

Brown, Jennifer, and John Morgan, "Reputation in Online Auctions: The Market for Trust," *California Management Review*, 49(1), Fall 2006:61–81.

Brown, Jennifer, and John Morgan, "How Much Is a Dollar Worth? Tipping versus Equilibrium Coexistence on Competing Online Auction Sites," *Journal of Political Economy*, 117(4), August 2009:668–700.

Brown, Stephen P. A., and Daniel Wolk, "Natural Resource Scarcity and Technological Change," *Economic and Financial Review* (Federal Reserve Bank of Dallas), First Quarter 2000:2–13.

Brownlee, Oswald, and George Perry, "The Effects of the 1965 Federal Excise Tax Reductions on Prices," *National Tax Journal*, 20(3), September 1967:235–249.

Brunk, Gregory G., "A Test of the Friedman-Savage Gambling Model," *Quarterly Journal of Economics*, 96(2), May 1981:341–348.

Bucks, Brian K., Arthur B. Kennickell, Traci L. Mach, and Kevin B. Moore, "Changes in U.S. Family Finances from 2004 to 2007: Evidence from the Survey of Consumer Finances," *Federal Reserve Bulletin*, 2009.

Busch, Susan H., Mireia Jofre-Bonet, Tracy Falba, and Jody Sindelar, "Burning a Hole in the Budget: Tobacco Spending and its Crowd-out of Other Goods," *Applied Health Economics and Policy*, 3(4), 2004:263–272.

Buschena, David E., and Jeffrey M. Perloff, "The Creation of Dominant Firm Market Power in the Coconut Oil Export Market," *American Journal of Agricultural Economics*, 73(4), November 1991:1000–1008.

Cabral, Luis, and Ali Hortacsu, "The Dynamics of Seller Reputation: Evidence from eBay," *Journal of Industrial Economics*, 58(1), March 2010:54–78.

Caliendo, Marco Michel Clement, Dominik Papies, and Sabine Scheel-Kopeinig, "The Cost Impact of Spam Filters: Measuring the Effect of Information System Technologies in Organizations," *Information Systems Research*, 2012:1068–1080.

Callison, Kevin, and Robert Kaestner, "Do Higher Tobacco Taxes Reduce Adult Smoking? New Evidence of the Effect of Recent Cigarette Tax Increases on Adult Smoking," NBER Working Paper, 2012.

Camerer, Colin F., George Lowenstein, and Matthew Rabin, eds., *Advances in Behavioral Economics*. New York: Russell Sage Foundation, 2004.

Card, David, "Immigration and Inequality," *American Economic Review*, 99(2), May 2009:1–21.

Card, David, and Alan B. Krueger, *Myth and Measurement: The New Economics of the Minimum Wage*. Princeton, NJ: Princeton University Press, 1995.

Carden, Art, "Beliefs, Bias, and Regime Uncertainty after Hurricane Katrina," *International Journal of Social Economics*, 35(7), 2008:531–545.

Carlton, Dennis W., and Jeffrey M. Perloff, *Modern Industrial Organization*, 4th ed. Reading, MA: Addison Wesley Longman, 2005.

Carman, Hoy F., "Offsetting Price Impacts from Imports with Generic Advertising and Promotion Programs: The Hass Avocado Promotion and Research Order," *Review of Agricultural Economics*, 28(4), January, 2006:463–481.

Chetty, Raj, Adam Looney, and Kory Kroft, "Salience and Taxation: Theory and Evidence," *American Economic Review*, 99(4), September 2009:1145–1177.

Cho, Daegon, Pedro Ferreira, and Rahul Telang, "The Impact of Mobile Number Portability on Switching Costs and Pricing Strategy," Carnegie-Mellon Working Paper, 2013.

Chou, Yen-Chun, Benjamin B. M. Shao, and Winston T. Lin, "Performance Evaluation of Production of IT Capital Goods Across OECD Countries: A Stochastic Frontier Approach to Malmquist Index, *Decision Support Systems*, 54(1), December 2012:173–184.

Chouinard, Hayley H., David E. Davis, Jeffrey T. LaFrance, and Jeffrey M. Perloff, "Fat Taxes: Big Money for Small Change," *Forum for Health Economics & Policy*, 10(2, 2), 2007.

Chouinard, Hayley, and Jeffrey M. Perloff, "Incidence of Federal and State Gasoline Taxes," *Economic Letters*, 83(1), April 2004:55–60.

Chouinard, Hayley H., and Jeffrey M. Perloff, "Gasoline Price Differences: Taxes, Pollution Regulations, Mergers, Market Power, and Market Conditions," *The B.E. Journal of Economic Analysis & Policy*, 7(1:8) (Contributions), 2007.

Clemens, Jeffrey, and Joshua D. Gottlieb, "Do Physicians' Financial Incentives Affect Medical Treatment and Patient Health?" Working Paper, 2013.

Coase, Ronald H., "The Problem of Social Cost," *Journal of Law and Economics*, 3, October 1960:1–44.

Cohen, Jeffrey P., and Catherine Morrison Paul, "Scale and Scope Economies for Drug Abuse Treatment Costs: Evidence for Washington State," *Applied Economics*, 43(30), 2011:4827–4834.

Cranfield, John, "Canadian Beef Demand Elasticity Study," University of Guelph Working Paper, 2012.

Crawford, David, John Del Roccili, and Richard Voith, "Comments on Proposed Tax Reforms," Econsult Corporation, June 9, 2004.

Crost, Benjamin, and Santiago Guerrero, The Effect of Alcohol Availability on Marijuana Use: Evidence from the Minimum Legal Drinking Age," *Journal of Health Economics*, 31(1), January 2012:112–121.

Currie, Janet, and Firouz Gahvari, "Transfers in Cash and In-Kind: Theory Meets the Data," *Journal of Economic Literature*, 46(2), June, 2008:333–383.

Currie, Janet, and Reed Walker, "Traffic Congestion and Infant Health: Evidence from E-ZPass." *American Economic Journal: Applied Economics*, 3(1), January 2011: 65–90.

Dafny, Leemore, "Estimation and Identification of Merger Effects: An Application to Hospital Mergers," *Journal of Law and Economics*, 52(3), August 2009:523–550.

Davies, James B., Susanna Sandström, Anthony Shorrocks, and Edward N. Wolff, "Estimating the Level and Distribution of Global Household Wealth," World Institute for Development Economic Research Working Paper, 2007.

Davis, Cale Wren, "An Analysis of the Enactment of Anti-Price Gouging Laws," Master of Science thesis, Montana State University, 2008.

Davis, Lucas W., and Lutz Kilian, "Estimating the Effect of a Gasoline Tax on Carbon Emissions," *Journal of Applied Econometrics*, 26(7), November 2011:1187–1214.

Davis, Lucas W., and Lutz Kilian, "The Allocative Cost of Price Ceilings in the U.S. Residential Market for Natural Gas," *Journal of Political Economics*, 119(2), April 2011:212–241.

Davis, Lucas W., and Erich Muehlegger, "Do Americans Consume Too Little Natural Gas? An Empirical Test of Marginal Cost Pricing," *RAND Journal of Economics*, 41(4), Winter 2010:791–810.

Davis, Lucas W., and Catherine Wolfram, "Deregulation, Consolidation, and Efficiency: Evidence from U.S. Nuclear Power," *American Economic Journal: Applied Economics*, 4(4), October 2012:194–225.

Deacon, Robert T., and Jon Sonstelie, "The Welfare Costs of Rationing by Waiting," *Economic Inquiry*, 27(2), April 1989:179–196.

de Melo, Jaime, and David Tarr, *A General Equilibrium Analysis of U.S. Foreign Trade Policy*. Cambridge, MA: MIT Press, 1992.

DellaVigna, Stefano, "Psychology and Economics: Evidence from the Field," *Journal of Economic Literature*, 47(2), June 2009:315–372.

Devine, Hilary, Tinh Doan, and Philip Stevens, "Explaining Productivity Distribution in New Zealand Industries: The Effects of Input Quality on Firm Productivity Differences," New Zealand Ministry of Economic Development, 2012.

Dixit, Avinash K., and Robert S. Pindyck, *Investment Under Uncertainty*. Princeton, NJ: Princeton University Press, 1994.

Duffy-Deno, Kevin T., "Business Demand for Broadband Access Capacity," *Journal of Regulatory Economics*, 24(3), 2003:359–372.

Dunham, Wayne R., "Moral Hazard and the Market for Used Automobiles," *Review of Industrial Organization*, 23(1), August 2003:65–83.

Eastwood, David B., and John A. Craven, "Food Demand and Savings in a Complete, Extended, Linear Expenditure System," *American Journal of Agricultural Economics*, 63(3), August 1981:544–549.

Economides, Nicholas, "The Economics of Networks," *International Journal of Industrial Organization*, 14(6), October 1996:673–699.

Econsult Corporation, *Choosing the Best Mix of Taxes for Philadelphia: An Econometric Analysis of the Impacts of Tax Rates on Tax Bases, Tax Revenue, and the Private Economy*, Report to the Philadelphia Tax Reform Commission, 2003.

Edelman, Benjamin, "Adverse Selection in Online 'Trust' Certifications and Search Results," *Electronic Commerce Research and Applications*, 10(1), January-February, 2011:17–25.

Edlin, Aaron S., and Pinar Karaca-Mandic, "The Accident Externality from Driving," *Journal of Political Economy*, 114(5), October 2006:931–955.

Einav, Liran, Dan Knoepfle, Jonathan D. Levin, and Neel Sundaresan, "Sales Taxes and Internet Commerce," NBER Working Paper, 2012.

Ellsberg, Daniel, "Risk, Ambiguity, and the Savage Axioms," *Quarterly Journal of Economics*, 75(4), November 1961:643–669.

Engström, Per, and Eskil Forsell, "Demand Effects of Consumers' Stated and Revealed Preferences," Uppsala University Working Paper, 2013.

Environmental Protection Agency, *The Benefits and Costs of the Clean Air Act from 1990 to 2020*, www.epa.gov/oar/sect812/feb11/fullreport.pdf, 2011.

Evers, Michiel, Ruud De Mooij, and Daniel Van Vuuren, "The Wage Elasticity of Labour Supply: A Synthesis of Empirical Estimates," *De Economist*, 156(1), March 2008:25–43.

Farrell, Joseph, and Matthew Rabin, "Cheap Talk," *Journal of Economic Perspectives*, 10(3), Summer 1996:103–118.

Farrell, Lisa, Roger Hartley, Gauthier Lanot, and Ian Walker, "The Demand for Lotto," *Journal of Business & Economic Statistics*, 18(2), April 2000:228–241.

Fisher, Franklin M., "The Social Cost of Monopoly and Regulation: Posner Reconsidered," *Journal of Political Economy*, 93(2), April 1985:410–416.

Flath, David, "Industrial Concentration, Price-Cost Margins, and Innovation," *Japan and the World Economy*, 23(2), March 2011:129–139.

Foster, Andrew D., and Mark R. Rosenzweig, "A Test for Moral Hazard in the Labor Market: Contractual Arrangements, Effort, and Health," *Review of Economics and Statistics*, 76(2), May 1994:213–227.

Fox, Jeremy T., and Valerie Smeets, "Does Input Quality Drive Measured Differences in Firm Productivity?" *International Economic Review*, 52(4), November 2011:961–989.

Friedman, Milton, and Leonard J. Savage, "The Utility Analysis of Choices Involving Risk," *Journal of Political Economy*, 56(4), August 1948:279–304.

Fudenberg, Drew, and Jean Tirole, *Game Theory*. Cambridge, MA: MIT Press, 1991.

Garratt, Rod, Mark Walker, and John Wooders, "Behavior in Second-Price Auctions by Highly Experienced eBay Buyers and Sellers," *Experimental Economics*, 15(1), March 2012:44–57.

Garrett, Thomas A., "An International Comparison and Analysis of Lotteries and the Distribution of Lottery Expenditures," *International Review of Applied Economics*, 15(20), April 2001:213–227.

Garthwaite, Craig L., "You Get a Book! Demand Spillovers, Combative Advertising, and Celebrity Endorsements," NBER Working Paper, 2012.

Gasmi, Farid, Jean-Jacques Laffont, and Quang H. Vuong, "Econometric Analysis of Collusive Behavior in a Soft-Drink Market," *Journal of Economics and Management Strategy*, 1(2), Summer 1992, 277–311.

Gowrisankaran, Gautam, Aviv Nevo and Robert Town, "Mergers When Prices Are Negotiated: Evidence from the Hospital Industry," Working Paper, 2013.

Gibbons, Robert, *Game Theory for Applied Economists*. Princeton, NJ: Princeton University Press, 1992.

Gillen, David, and Hamed Hasheminia, "Estimating the Demand Responses for Different Sizes of Air Passenger Groups," *Transportation Research Part B*, 49, 2013:24–38.

Goldfarb, Avi, and Catherine E. Tucker, "Search Engine Advertising: Channel Substitution When Pricing Ads to Context," *Management Science*, 57(3), March 2011:458–470.

Goldin, Jacob, and Tatiana Homonoff, "Smoke Gets in Your Eyes: Cigarette Tax Salience and Regressivity," *American Economic Journal: Economic Policy*, 5(1), February 2013:302–336.

Golec, Joseph, and Maurry Tamarkin, "Do Bettors Prefer Long Shots Because They Are Risk Lovers, or Are They Just Overconfident?" *Journal of Risk and Uncertainty*, 11(1), July 1995:51–64.

Gonçalves, Ricardo, and Pedro Pita Barros, "Economies of Scale and Scope in the Provision of Diagnostic Techniques and Therapeutic Services in Portuguese Hospitals," *Applied Economics*, 45(4), February 2013:415–433.

González, Tanja Markus Schmid, and David Yermack, "Smokescreen: How Managers Behave When They Have Something to Hide," NBER Working Paper, 2013.

Gowrisankaran, Gautam, et al., "Mergers When Prices Are Negotiated: Evidence from the Hospital Industry," NBER Working Paper, 2013.

Grabowski, David C., and Michael A. Morrissey, "Do Higher Gasoline Taxes Save Lives?" *Economics Letters*, 90(1), January 2006:51–55.

Grafton, R. Quentin, and Michael B. Ward, "Prices Versus Rationing: Marshallian Surplus and Mandatory Water Restrictions," *Economic Record*, 84(S1), September 2008:S57–S65.

Graham, Daniel J., and Stephen Glaister, "Road Traffic Demand Elasticities: A Review," *Transport Reviews*, 24(3), May 2004:261–274.

Gray, Wayne B., and Jay P. Shimshack, "The Effectiveness of Environmental Monitoring and Enforcement: A Review of the Empirical Evidence," *Review of Environmental Economics and Policy*, 5(1), Winter 2011:1–23.

Green, Richard, Richard Howitt, and Carlo Russo, "Estimation of Supply and Demand Elasticities of California Commodities," manuscript, May 2005.

Grossman, Michael, and Frank Chaloupka, "Demand for Cocaine by Young Adults: A Rational Addiction Approach," *Journal of Health Economics*, 17(4), August 1998:427–474.

Gruber, Jonathan H., and Sendhil Mullainathan, "Do Cigarette Taxes Make Smokers Happier," *Advances in Economic Analysis & Policy*, 5(1), 2005:article 4.

Guinnane, Timothy W., "The Historical Fertility Transition: A Guide for Economists," *Journal of Economic Literature*, 49(3), September 2011: 589–614.

Haas-Wilson, Deborah, and Christopher Garmon, "Hospital Mergers and Competitive Effects: Two Retrospective Analyses," *International Journal of the Economics of Business*, 18(1), February 2011:37–41.

Hall, Robert E., and David M. Lilien, "Efficient Wage Bargains Under Uncertain Supply and Demand," *American Economic Review*, 69(5), December 1979:868–879.

Haskel, Jonathan, and Raffaella Sadun, "Regulation and UK Retailing Productivity: Evidence from Micro Data," *Economica*, 79, July 2012:425–448.

Harkness, Joseph, and Sandra Newman, "The interactive effects of housing assistance and food stamps on food spending," *Journal of Housing Economics*, 12(3), September 2003:224–249.

Hausman, Jerry A., and Gregory K. Leonard, "The Competitive Effects of a New Product Introduction: A Case Study," *Journal of Industrial Economics*, 50(3), September 2002:237–263.

Hay, George A., and Daniel Kelley, "An Empirical Survey of Price-Fixing Conspiracies," *Journal of Law and Economics*, 17(1), April 1974:13–38.

Hedenus, Anna, "Who Wants to Work Less? Significance of Socio-Economic Status and Work Conditions for Work Commitment Among Swedish Lottery Winners," *Acta Sociologica*, 55(4), December 2012:335–350.

Helliwell, John, Richard Layard, and Jeffrey Sachs,, *World Happiness Report*, The Earth Institute, Columbia University, 2012, **www.earth.columbia.edu/articles/view/2960**.

Henderson, Jason, "FAQs about Mad Cow Disease and Its Impacts," *The Main Street Economist*, December 2003.

Herod, Roger, "Analyzing the Metrics of Global Mobility Programs," *International HR Journal*, Summer 2008:9–15.

Highhouse, Scott, Michael J. Zickar, and Maya Yankelevich, "Would You Work If You Won the Lottery? Tracking Changes in the American Work Ethic," *Journal of Applied Psychology*, 95(2), March 2010:349–357.

Hill, Jason, S. Polasky, E. Nelson, D. Tilman, H. Huo, L. Ludwig, J. Neumann, H. Zheng, and D. Bonta, "Climate Change and Health Costs of Air Emissions from Biofuels and Gasoline," *Proceedings of the National Academy of Sciences*, 106(6), February 2009:2077–2082.

Ho, Jason, Tirtha Dhar, and Charles Weinberg, "Playoff payoff: Super Bowl advertising for movies," *International Journal of Research in Marketing*, 26(3), September 2009:168–179.

Holt, Matthew, "A Multimarket Bounded Price Variation Model Under Rational Expectations: Corn and Soybeans in the United States," *American Journal of Agricultural Economics*, 74(1), February 1992:10–20.

Hossain, Md. Moyazzem Tapati Basak, and Ajit Kumar Majumder, "An Application of Non-Linear Cobb-Douglas Production Function to Selected Manufacturing Industries in Bangladesh," *Open Journal of Statistics*, 2, October 2012:460–468.

Hotelling, Harold, "The Economics of Exhaustible Resources," *Journal of Political Economy*, 39(2), April 1931:137–175.

Hoynes, Hilary W., and Diane Whitmore Schanzenbach, "Consumption Responses to In-Kind Transfers: Evidence from the Introduction of the Food Stamp Program," *American Economic Journal: Applied Economics*, 1(4), October 2009:109–139.

Hsieh, Wen-Jen, "Test of Variable Output and Scale Elasticities for 20 U.S. Manufacturing Industries," *Applied Economics Letters*, 2(8), August 1995:284–287.

Hummels, David, and Alexandre Skiba, "Shipping the Good Apples Out? An Empirical Confirmation of the Alchian-Allen Conjecture," *Journal of Political Economy*, 112(6), December 2004:1384–1402.

Ida, Takanori, and Tetsuya Kuwahara, "Yardstick Cost Comparison and Economies of Scale and Scope in Japan's Electric Power Industry," *Asian Economic Journal*, 18(4), December 2004:423–438.

Imbens, Guido W., Donald B. Rubin, and Bruce I. Sacerdote, "Estimating the Effect of Unearned Income on Labor Earnings, Savings, and Consumption: Evidence from a Survey of Lottery Players," *American Economic Review*, 91(4), September 2001:778–794.

Irwin, Douglas A., "The Welfare Cost of Autarky: Evidence from the Jeffersonian Trade Embargo, 1807–09," *Review of International Economics*, 13(4), September 2005:631–645.

Irwin, Douglas A., and Nina Pavcnik, "Airbus versus Boeing Revisited: International Competition in the Aircraft Market," *Journal of International Economics*, 64(2), December 2004:223–245.

Jacobson, Michael F., and Kelly D. Brownell, "Small Taxes on Soft Drinks and Snack Foods to Promote Health," *American Journal of Public Health*, 90(6), June 2000:854–857.

Jagannathan, Ravi, Ellen R. McGrattan, and Anna Scherbina, "The Declining U.S. Equity Premium," *Federal Reserve Bank of Minneapolis Quarterly Review*. 24(4), 2000:3–19.

Jensen, Robert T., and Nolan H. Miller, "Giffen Behavior and Subsistence Consumption," *American Economic Review*, 98(4), September 2008:1553–1577.

Jetter, Karen M., James A. Chalfant, and David A. Sumner, "Does 5-a-Day Pay?" *AIC Issues Brief*, No. 27, August 2004.

Johnson, Ronald N., and Charles J. Romeo, "The Impact of Self-Service Bans in the Retail Gasoline Market," *Review of Economics and Statistics*, 82(4), November 2000:625–633.

Kahneman, Daniel, Jack L. Knetsch, and Richard H. Thaler, "Experimental Tests of the Endowment Effect and the Coase Theorem," *Journal of Political Economy*, 98(6), December 1990:1325–1348.

Kahneman, Daniel, and Amos Tversky, "Prospect Theory: An Analysis of Decision under Risk," *Econometrica*, 47(2), March 1979:313–327.

Kan, Kamhon, "Cigarette Smoking and Self-Control," *Journal of Health Economics*, 26(1), January 2007:61–81.

Karp, Larry, "Global Warming and Hyperbolic Discounting," *Journal of Public Economics*, 89(2–3), February 2005:261–282.

Katz, Michael L., and Carl Shapiro, "Systems Competition and Network Effects," *Journal of Economic Perspectives*, 8(2), 1994:93–115.

Keane, Michael P., "Labor Supply and Taxes: A Survey," *Journal of Economic Literature*, 49(4), December 2011:961–1075.

Kellogg, Ryan, "Learning by Drilling: Inter-Firm Learning and Relationship Persistence in the Texas Oilpatch," *Quarterly Journal of Economics*, 126(4), 2011:1961–2004.

Kennickell, Arthur B., "An Examination of the Changes in the Distribution of Wealth from 1989 to 1998: Evidence from the Survey of Consumer Finances," Federal Reserve, 2001.

Kennickell, Arthur B., "A Rolling Tide: Changes in the Distribution of Wealth in the U.S., 1989–2001," Federal Reserve Board, 2003.

Kennickell, Arthur B., "Ponds and Streams: Wealth and Income in the U.S., 1989 to 2007," Federal Reserve Board, 2009.

Kennickell, Arthur B., "Tossed and Turned: Wealth Dynamics of U.S. Households 2007–2009," Federal Reserve Board, 2011.

Kim, DaeHwan, and J. Paul Leigh, "Are Meals at Full-Service and Fast-Food Restaurants Normal or Inferior?" *Population Health Management*, 14(6), December 2011: 307–315.

Kim, Jim-Yoo, *When Are Super Bowl Advertisings Super?* University of Texas at Arlington Ph.D. dissertation, 2011.

Kleiner, Morris M., and Alan B. Krueger, "Analyzing the Extent and Influence of Occupational Licensing on the Labor Market," *Journal of Labor Economics*, April 2013, 31(2):S173–S202.

Klemperer, Paul, *Auctions: Theory and Practice*. Princeton, NJ: Princeton University Press, 2004.

Knetsch, Jack L., "Preferences and Nonreversibility of Indifference Curves," *Journal of Economic Behavior and Organization*, 1992, 17(1):131–139.

Knittel, Christopher R., Douglas L. Miller, and Nicholas J. Sanders, "Caution, Drivers! Children Present: Traffic, Pollution, and Infant Health," NBER Working Paper, 2011.

Knittel, Christopher R., and Victor Stango, "Celebrity Endorsements, Firm Value and Reputation Risk: Evidence from the Tiger Woods Scandal," *Management Science*, forthcoming.

Kotchen, Matthew J., and Nicholas E. Burger, "Should We Drill in the Arctic National Wildlife Refuge? An Economic Perspective," *Energy Policy*, 35(9), September 2007:4720–4729.

Kuhn, Peter J., Peter Kooreman, Adriaan R. Soetevent, and Arie Kapteyn, "The Own and Social Effects of an Unexpected Income Shock: Evidence from the Dutch Postcode Lottery," *American Economic Review*, 101(5), August 2011: 2226–2247.

Kunreuther, Howard, and Geoffrey Heal, "Managing Catastrophic Risk," NBER Working Paper, 2012.

Kuroda, Sachiko, and Isamu Yamamoto, "Estimating Frisch Labor Supply Elasticity in Japan," *Journal of Japanese International Economies*, 22(4), December 2008:566–585.

Labonne, Julien, and Robert S. Chase, "So You Want to Quit Smoking: Have You Tried a Mobile Phone?" *Applied Economic Letters*, 18(2), 2011:103–106.

Lazear, Edward P., Kathryn L. Shaw, and Christopher T. Stanton, "The Value of Bosses," NBER Working Paper, 2012.

Lee, David, and Alexandre Mas, "Long-Run Impacts of Unions on Firms: New Evidence from Financial Markets, 1961–1999," *Quarterly Journal of Economics*, 127(1), February 2012:333–378.

Lee, J. M., M. G. Chen, T. C. Hwang, and C. Y. Yeh, "Effect of Cigarette Taxes on the Consumption of Cigarettes, Alcohol, Tea and Coffee in Taiwan," *Public Health*, 124(8), August 2010:429–436.

Lee, Young Han, and Ulrike Malmendier, "The Bidder's Curse," *American Economic Review*: 101(2), April 2011:749–787.

Leibenstein, Harvey, "Bandwagon, Snob, and Veblen Effects in the Theory of Consumers' Demand," *Quarterly Journal of Economics*, 64(2), May 1950:183–207.

Leslie, Phillip J., "A Structural Econometric Analysis of Price Discrimination in Broadway Theatre," Working Paper, University of California, Los Angeles, November 15, 1997.

Lewis, Gregory, "Asymmetric Information, Adverse Selection and Online Disclosure: The Case of eBay Motors," *American Economic Review*, 101(4), June 2011:1535–1546.

List, John A., "Does Market Experience Eliminate Market Anomalies?" *Quarterly Journal of Economics*, 118(1), February 2003:41–71.

Lopez, Rigoberto A., and Emilio Pagoulatos, "Rent Seeking and the Welfare Cost of Trade Barriers," *Public Choice*, 79(1–2), April 1994:149–160.

Lu, Fangwen, "Insurance Coverage and Agency Problems in Doctor Prescriptions: Evidence from a Field Experiment in China," *Journal of Development Economics*, 106(1), January 2014:156–167.

MacAvoy, Paul W., *The Natural Gas Market*. New Haven: Yale University Press, 2000.

MacCrimmon, Kenneth R., and M. Toda, "The Experimental Determination of Indifference Curves," *Review of Economic Studies*, 56(3), July 1969:433–451.

Machina, Mark, "Dynamic Consistency and Non-Expected Utility Models of Choice Under Uncertainty," *Journal of Economic Literature*, 27(4), December 1989:1622–1668.

MacKie-Mason, Jeffrey K., and Robert S. Pindyck, "Cartel Theory and Cartel Experience in International Minerals Markets," in R. L. Gordon, H. D. Jacoby, and M. B. Zimmerman, eds., *Energy: Markets and Regulation: Essays in Honor of M. A. Adelman*. Cambridge, MA: MIT Press, 1986.

Madden, Janice F., *The Economics of Sex Discrimination*. Lexington, MA: Heath, 1973.

Madrian, Brigitte C., and Dennis F. Shea, "The Power of Suggestion: Inertia in 401(k) Participation and Savings Behavior," *Quarterly Journal of Economics*, 116(4), November 2001:1149–1187.

Madrian, Brigitte C., and Dennis F. Shea, "The Power of Suggestion: Inertia in 401(k) Participation and Savings Behavior: Erratum," *Quarterly Journal of Economics*, 117(1), February 2002:377.

Markowitz, Sara Erik Nesson, Eileen Poe-Yamagata, Curtis Florence, Partha Deb, Tracy Andrews, Sarah Beth L. Barnett, "Estimating the Relationship Between Alcohol Policies and Criminal Violence and Victimization," NBER Working Paper, 2012.

McDevitt, Ryan C., "Names and Reputations: An Empirical Analysis," *American Economic Journal: Microeconomics*, 3(3), August 2011:193–209.

McPhail, Lihong Lu, and Bruce A. Babcock, "Impact of US Biofuel Policy on US Corn and Gasoline Price Variability," *Energy*, 37(1), February 2012:505–513.

Medoff, Marshall H., "Price, Restrictions and Abortion Demand," *Journal of Family and Economic Issues*, 28(4), December 2007:583–599.

Meyer, Roland, "Economies of Scope in Electricity Supply and the Costs of Vertical Separation for Different Unbundling Scenarios," *Journal of Regulatory Economics*, 42(1), August 2012:95–114.

Mishel, Lawrence, and Natalie Sabadish, "CEO Pay and the Top 1%," *EPI Issue Brief*, May 2, 2012.

Moschini, Giancarlo, and Karl D. Meilke, "Production Subsidy and Countervailing Duties in Vertically Related Markets: The Hog-Pork Case Between Canada and the United States," *American Journal of Agricultural Economics*, 74(4), November 1992:951–961.

Nash, John F., "Equilibrium Points in *n*-Person Games," *Proceedings of the National Academy of Sciences*, 36, 1950:48–49.

Nash, John F., "Non-Cooperative Games," *Annals of Mathematics*, 54(2), July 1951:286–295.

Nataraj, Shanthi, "Do Residential Water Consumers React to Price Increases? Evidence from a Natural Experiment in Santa Cruz," *Agricultural and Resource Economics Update*, 10(3), January/February 2007:9–11.

Nikaj, Silda, and Frank J. Chaloupka, "The Effect of Prices on Cigarette Use Among Youths in the Global Youth Tobacco Survey," *Nicotine and Tobacco Research*, 2013.

O'Donoghue, Ted, and Matthew Rabin, "Doing It Now or Later," *American Economic Review*, 89(1), March 1999:103–124.

Oxfam, "Dumping Without Borders," Oxfam Briefing Paper 50, 2003.

Panzar, John C., and Robert D. Willig, "Economies of Scale in Multi-Output Production," *Quarterly Journal of Economics*, 91(3), August 1977:481–493.

Panzar, John C., and Robert D. Willig, "Economies of Scope," *American Economic Review*, 71(2), May 1981:268–272.

Parry, Ian W. H., Margaret Walls, and Winston Harrington, "Automobile Externalities and Policies," *Journal of Economic Literature*, 45(2), June 2007:373–399.

Perry, Martin K., "Forward Integration by Alcoa: 1888–1930," *Journal of Industrial Economics*, 29(1), September 1980:37–53.

Pielke, Roger A., Jr., Joel Gratz, Christopher W. Landsea, Douglas Collins, Mark A. Saunders, and Rade Musulin, "Normalized Hurricane Damages in the United States: 1900–2005," *Natural Hazards Review*, 9(1), February 2008:29–42.

Plott, Charles R., and Kathryn Zeiler, "The Willingness to Pay—Willingness to Accept Gap, the 'Endowment Effect,' Subject Misconceptions, and Experimental Procedures for Eliciting Values," *American Economic Review*, 95(3), June 2005:530–545.

Posner, Richard A., "The Social Cost of Monopoly and Regulation," *Journal of Political Economy*, 83(4), August 1975:807–827.

Prescott, Edward C., "Why Do Americans Work So Much More Than Europeans?" *Federal Reserve Bank of Minneapolis Quarterly Review*, 28(1), July 2004:2–13.

Prince, Jeffrey T., "Repeat Purchase amid Rapid Quality Improvement: Structural Estimation of Demand for Personal Computers," *Journal of Economics & Management Strategy*, 17(1), Spring 2008:1–33.

Rabin, Matthew, "Psychology and Economics," *Journal of Economic Literature*, 36(1), March 1998:1–46.

Rao, Justin M., and David H. Reiley, "The Economics of Spam," *Journal of Economic Perspectives*, 26(3), Summer 2012:87–110.

Rawls, John, *A Theory of Justice*. New York: Oxford University Press, 1971.

Regan, Tracy L., "Generic Entry, Price Competition, and Market Segmentation in the Prescription Drug Market,"

International Journal of Industrial Organization, 26(4), July 2008:930–948.

Reinstein, David A., and Christopher M. Snyder, "The Influence of Expert Reviews on Consumer Demand for Experience Goods: A Case Study of Movie Critics," *Journal of Industrial Economics*, 53(1), March 2005:27–51.

Richards, Timothy J., and Luis Padilla, "Promotion and Fast Food Demand," *American Journal of Agricultural Economics*, 91(1), February 2009:168–183.

Roberts, Mark J., and Larry Samuelson, "An Empirical Analysis of Dynamic Nonprice Competition in an Oligopolistic Industry," *Rand Journal of Economics*, 19(2), Summer 1988:200–220.

Roberts, Michael J., and Wolfram Schlenker, "Is Agriculture Becoming More or Less Sensitive to Extreme Heat? Evidence from U.S. Corn and Soybean Yields." *The Design and Implementation of U.S. Climate Policy*, NBER, 2012.

Roberts, Michael J., and Wolfram Schlenker, "Identifying Supply and Demand Elasticities of Agricultural Commodities: Implications for the US Ethanol Mandate," *American Economic Review*, forthcoming.

Robidoux, Benoît, and John Lester, "Econometric Estimates of Scale Economies in Canadian Manufacturing," Working Paper No. 88-4, Canadian Dept. of Finance, 1988.

Robidoux, Benoît, and John Lester, "Econometric Estimates of Scale Economies in Canadian Manufacturing," *Applied Economics*, 24(1), January 1992:113–122.

Rohlfs, Jeffrey H., "A Theory of Interdependent Demand for a Communications Service," *Bell Journal of Economics and Management Science*, 5(1), Spring 1974:16–37.

Rohlfs, Jeffrey H., *Bandwagon Effects in High-Technology Industries*, Cambridge, MA: MIT Press, 2001.

Rosenberg, Howard R., "Many Fewer Steps for Pickers—A Leap for Harvestkind? Emerging Change in Strawberry Harvest Technology," *Choices*, 1st Quarter 2004:5–11.

Rossi, R. J., and T. Armstrong, Studies of intercollegiate athletics: Summary results from the 1987–88 National Study of Intercollegiate Athletes (Report No. 1), Palo Alto, CA: Center for the Study of Athletics, American Institutes for Research, 1989.

Rousseas, S. W., and A. G. Hart, "Experimental Verification of a Composite Indifference Map," *Journal of Political Economy*, 59(4), August 1951:288–318.

Ruffin, R. J., "Cournot Oligopoly and Competitive Behavior," *Review of Economic Studies*, 38(116), October 1971:493–502.

Saez, Emmanuel, "Striking It Richer: The Evolution of Top Incomes in the United States (Updated with 2011 Estimates)," University of California, Berkeley Working Paper, 2013.

Salgado, Hugo, "A Dynamic Duopoly Model under Learning-by-doing in the Computer CPU Industry," U.C. Berkeley Ph.D. dissertation chapter, 2008.

Salop, Joanne, and Steven C. Salop, "Self-Selection and Turnover in the Labor Market," *Quarterly Journal of Economics*, 90(4), November 1976:619–627.

Salop, Steven C., "The Noisy Monopolist: Imperfect Information, Price Dispersion, and Price Discrimination," *Review of Economic Studies*, 44(3), October 1977:393–406.

Salop, Steven C., "Practices That (Credibly) Facilitate Oligopoly Coordination," in Joseph E. Stiglitz and G. Frank Mathewson, eds., *New Developments in the Analysis of Market Structure*. Cambridge, MA: MIT Press, 1986.

Salvo, Alberto, and Christian Huse, "Build It, But Will They Come? Evidence from Consumer Choice Between Gasoline and Sugarcane Ethanol," *Journal of Environmental Economics and Management*, forthcoming.

Sappington, David E. M., and Dennis L. Weisman, "Price Cap Regulation: What Have We Learned from 25 Years of Experience in the Telecommunications Industry?" *Journal of Regulatory Economics*, 38(3), 2010:227–257.

Sato, Yoshihiro and Måns Söderbom, "Are Larger Firms More Productive Because of Scale Economies? Evidence from Swedish Register Data," in Yoshihiro Sato, *Dynamic Investment Models, Employment Generation and Productivity—Evidence from Swedish Data*, University of Gothenburg Ph.D. Dissertation, 2012.

Schaller Consulting, *New York City Taxicab Fact Book*, March 2006.

Scherer, F. M., "An Early Application of the Average Total Cost Concept," *Journal of Economic Literature*, 39(3), September 2001:897–901.

Schlenker, Wolfram, and Sofia B. Villas-Boas, "Consumer and Market Responses to Mad-Cow Disease," *American Economic Review*, 91(4), November 2009:1140–1152.

Schmalensee, Richard, Paul L. Joskow, A. Denny Ellerman, Juan Pablo Montero, and Elizabeth M. Bailey, "An Interim Evaluation of Sulfur Dioxide Emissions Trading," *Journal of Economic Perspectives*, 12(3), Summer 1998:53–68.

Schoemaker, Paul J. H., "The Expected Utility Model: Its Variants, Purposes, Evidence and Limitation," *Journal of Economic Literature*, 20(2), June 1982:529–563.

Sexton, Steven, "The Economics of Agricultural Biotechnology: Implications for Biofuel Sustainability," Working Paper, 2010.

Shadbegian, Ronald J., and Wayne B. Gray, "What Determines Environmental Performance at Paper Mills? The Roles of Abatement Spending, Regulation and Efficiency," Center for Economic Studies Working Paper CES 03–10, 2003.

Shapiro, Carl, and Joseph E. Stiglitz, "Equilibrium Unemployment as a Worker Discipline Device," *American Economic Review*, 74(3), June 1984:434–444.

Shapiro, Carl, and Hal R. Varian, *Information Rules: A Strategic Guide to the Network Economy*. Boston: Harvard Business School Press, 1999.

Shapiro, Jesse M., "Is There a Daily Discount Rate? Evidence from the Food Stamp Nutrition Cycle," *Journal of Public Economics*, 89(2–3), February 2004:303–325.

Shiller, Ben, and Joel Waldfogel, "Music for a Song: An Empirical Look at Uniform Pricing and Its Alternatives," *The Journal of Industrial Economics*, 59(4), December 2011:630–660.

Shimshack, Jay, and Michael B. Ward, "Regulator Reputation, Enforcement, and Environmental Compliance," *Journal of Environmental Economics and Management*, 50(3), November 2005:519–540.

Slade, Margaret E., "Product Rivalry with Multiple Strategic Weapons: An Analysis of Price and Advertising Competition," *Journal of Economics and Management Strategy*," 4(3), Fall 1995:224–276.

Sood, Neeraj, Abby Alpert, and Jay Bhattacharya, "Technology, Monopoly, and the Decline of the Viatical Settlements Industry," NBER Working Paper, 2005.

Spence, A. Michael, *Market Signaling*. Cambridge, MA: Harvard University Press, 1974.

Stevenson, Betsey, and Justin Wolfers, "Subjective Well-Being and Income: Is There Any Evidence of Satiation?" *American Economic Review*, 103(3), May 2013:598–604.

Stiglitz, Joseph E., "The Theory of 'Screening,' Education, and the Distribution of Income," *American Economic Review*, 65(3), June 1975:283–300.

Stiglitz, Joseph E., "Equilibrium in Product Markets with Imperfect Information," *American Economic Review*, 69(2), May 1979:339–345.

Stiglitz, Joseph E., "The Causes and Consequences of the Dependence of Quality on Price," *Journal of Economic Literature*, 25(1), March 1987:1–48.

Suzuki, Junichi, "Land Use Regulation as a Barrier to Entry: Evidence from the Texas Lodging Industry," *International Economic Review*, 54(2), 2013:495–523.

Swinton, John R., and Christopher R. Thomas, "Using Empirical Point Elasticities to Teach Tax Incidence," *Journal of Economic Education*, 32(4), Fall 2001:356–368.

Syverson, Chad, "Product Substitutability and Productivity Dispersion," *Review of Economics and Statistics*, 86(2), May 2004: 534–550.

Tekin, Erdal, "Single Mothers Working at Night: Standard Work and Child Care Subsidies," *Economic Inquiry*, 45(2), April 2007:233–250.

Tenn, Steven, "The Price Effects of Hospital Mergers: A Case Study of the Sutter–Summit Transaction," *International Journal of the Economics of Business*, 18(1), February, 2011:65–82.

Tideman, T. Nicholaus, and Gordon Tullock, "A New and Superior Process for Making Social Choices," *Journal of Political Economy*, 84(6), December 1976:1145–1159.

Tosun, Mehmet S., and Mark L. Skidmore, "Cross-Border Shopping and the Sales Tax: An Examination of Food Purchases in West Virginia," *The B.E. Journal of Economic Analysis & Policy*, 7(1), 2007:Article 63.Town, Robert, Douglas Wholey, Roger Feldman, and Lawton R. Burns, "The Welfare Consequences of Hospital Mergers," NBER Working Paper, 2006.

Trabandt, Mathias, and Harald Uhlig, "How Far Are We from the Slippery Slope? The Laffer Curve Revisited," NBER Working Paper, 2009, 2011.

Tullock, G., "The Welfare Cost of Tariffs, Monopolies, and Theft," *Western Economic Journal*, 5(3), June 1967:224–232.

Tversky, Amos, and Daniel Kahneman, "The Framing of Decisions and the Psychology of Choice," *Science*, 211(4481), January 1981:453–458.

Tyler, John H., Richard J. Murnane, and John B. Willett, "Estimating the Labor Market Signaling Value of the GED," *Quarterly Journal of Economics*, 115(2), May 2000:431–468.

Varian, Hal R., "Measuring the Deadweight Cost of DUP and Rent-Seeking Activities," *Economics and Politics*, 1(1), Spring 1989:81–95.

Varian, Hal R., *Microeconomic Analysis*, 3rd ed. New York: Norton, 1992.

Veracierto, Marcelo, "Firing Costs and Business Cycle Fluctuations," *International Economic Review*, 49(1), February 2008:1–39.

Viscusi, W. Kip, *Employment Hazards*. Cambridge, MA: Harvard University Press, 1979.

Von Neumann, John, and Oskar Morgenstern, *Theory of Games and Economic Behavior*. Princeton, NJ: Princeton University Press, 1944.

Waldfogel, Joel, "The Deadweight Loss of Christmas," *American Economic Review*, 83(5), December 1993:1328–1336.

Waldfogel, Joel, "Does Consumer Irrationality Trump Consumer Sovereignty?" *Review of Economics and Statistics*, 87(4), November 2005:691–696.

Waldfogel, Joel, *Scroogenomics*. Princeton, NJ: Princeton University Press, 2009.

Waldfogel, Joel, "Copyright Research in the Digital Age: Moving from Piracy to the Supply of New Products," *American Economic Review*, 102(3), May 2012:337–342.

Warner, John T., and Saul Pleeter, "The Personal Discount Rate: Evidence from Military Downsizing Programs," *American Economic Review*, 91(1), March 2001:33–53.

Weiher, Jesse C., Robin C. Sickles, and Jeffrey M. Perloff, "Market Power in the U.S. Airline Industry," D. J. Slottje, ed., *Economic Issues in Measuring Market Power, Contributions to Economic Analysis*, Volume 255. Amsterdam: Elsevier, 2002.

Weinstein, Arnold A., "Transitivity of Preferences: A Comparison Among Age Groups," *Journal of Political Economy*, 76(2), March/April 1968:307–311.

Whitmore, Diane, "What Are Food Stamps Worth?" Princeton University Working Paper #468, July 2002.

Williamson, Oliver E., "Credible Commitments: Using Hostages to Support Exchange," *American Economic Review*, 73(4), September 1983:519–540.

Yellen, Janet L., "Efficiency Wage Models of Unemployment," *American Economic Review*, 74(2), May 1984:200–205.

Zhang, Rui Kai Sun, Michael S. Delgado, and Subal C. Kumbhakar, "Productivity in China's High Technology Industry," *Technology Forecasting and Social Change*, 79(1), 2012:127–141.

Zheng, Yuqing, Edward W. McLaughlin, and Harry M. Kaiser, "Salience and Taxation: Salience Effect vs. Knowledge Effect," *Applied Economics Letters*, 20(5), 2013.

Definitions

I hate definitions. —Benjamin Disraeli

action: a move that a player makes at a specified stage of a game, such as how much output a firm produces in the current period. (14)[*]

adverse selection: occurs when one party to a transaction possesses information about a hidden characteristic that is unknown to other parties and takes economic advantage of this information. (19)

asymmetric information: one party to a transaction has relevant information that another party lacks. (19)

auction: a sale in which property or a service is sold to the highest bidder. (14)

average cost (*AC*): the total cost divided by the units of output produced: $AC = C/q$. (7)

average fixed cost (*AFC*): the fixed cost divided by the units of output produced: $AFC = F/q$. (7)

average product of labor (*AP*$_L$): the ratio of output, q, to the number of workers, L, used to produce that output: $AP_L = q/L$. (6)

average variable cost (*AVC*): the variable cost divided by the units of output produced: $AVC = VC/q$. (7)

backward induction: first determine the best response by the last player to move, next determine the best response for the player who made the next-to-last move, and then repeat the process back to the move at the beginning of the game. (14)

bad: something for which less is preferred to more, such as pollution. (4)

bandwagon effect: the situation in which a person places greater value on a good as more and more other people possess it. (11)

barrier to entry: an explicit restriction or a cost that applies only to potential new firms—existing firms are not subject to the restriction or do not bear the cost. (9)

behavioral economics: by adding insights from psychology and empirical research on human cognition and emotional biases to the rational economic model, economists try to better predict economic decision making. (4)

Bertrand equilibrium (*Nash-Bertrand equilibrium or Nash-in-prices equilibrium*): a *Nash equilibrium* in prices; a set of prices such that no firm can obtain a higher profit by choosing a different price if the other firms continue to charge these prices. (13)

best response: the strategy that maximizes a player's payoff given its beliefs about its rivals' strategies. (14)

bounded rationality: people have a limited capacity to anticipate, solve complex problems, or enumerate all options. (4)

budget line (or *budget constraint*): the bundles of goods that can be bought if the entire budget is spent on those goods at given prices. (4)

bundling (*package tie-in sale*): selling multiple goods or services for a single price. (12)

cartel: a group of firms that explicitly agrees to coordinate their activities. (13)

certification: a report that a particular product meets or exceeds a given standard. (19)

cheap talk: unsubstantiated claims or statements. (19)

club good: a good that is nonrival but is subject to exclusion. (18)

common knowledge (in a game): a piece of information that is known by all players, and it must be known by all players to be known by all players, and it must be known to be known to be known by all players, and so forth. (14)

(open-access) common property: a resource to which everyone has free access and an equal right to exploit. (18)

comparative advantage: the ability to produce a good at a lower opportunity cost than someone else. (10)

compensating variation (*CV*): the amount of money one would have to give a consumer to offset completely the harm from a price increase. (5)

complete information (in a game): the situation where the payoff function is common knowledge among all players. (14)

constant returns to scale (*CRS*): property of a production function whereby when all inputs are increased by a certain percentage, output increases by that same percentage. (6)

consumer surplus (*CS*): the monetary difference between what a consumer is willing to pay for the quantity of the good purchased and what the good actually costs. (9)

contract curve: the set of all Pareto-efficient bundles. (10)

cost (*total cost, C*): the sum of a firm's variable cost and fixed cost: $C = VC + F$. (7)

Cournot equilibrium (*Nash-Cournot equilibrium or Nash-in-prices equilibrium*): a set of quantities chosen by firms such that, holding the quantities of all other firms constant, no firm can obtain a higher profit by choosing a different quantity. (13)

credible threat: an announcement that a firm will use a strategy harmful to its rival and that the rival believes because the firm's strategy is rational in the sense that it is in the firm's best interest to use it. (14)

---

[*]The numbers in the parentheses refer to the chapter in which the term was defined.

cross-price elasticity of demand: the percentage change in the *quantity demanded* in response to a given percentage change in the price of another good. (3)

deadweight loss (*DWL*): the net reduction in welfare from a loss of surplus by one group that is not offset by a gain to another group from an action that alters a market equilibrium. (9)

decreasing returns to scale (*DRS*): property of a production function whereby output increases less than in proportion to an equal percentage increase in all inputs. (6)

demand curve: the *quantity demanded* at each possible price, holding constant the other factors that influence purchases. (2)

discount rate: a rate reflecting the relative value an individual places on future consumption compared to current consumption. (16)

diseconomies of scale: property of a cost function whereby the average cost of production rises when output increases. (7)

dominant strategy: a strategy that produces a higher payoff than any other strategy the player can use for every possible combination of its rivals' strategies. (14)

duopoly: an *oligopoly* with two firms. (13)

durable good: a product that is usable for years. (7)

dynamic game: a game in which players move either sequentially or repeatedly. (14)

economic cost (*opportunity cost*): the value of the best alternative use of a resource. (7)

economic profit: revenue minus *economic cost*. (8)

economically efficient: minimizing the cost of producing a specified amount of output. (7)

economies of scale: property of a cost function whereby the average cost of production falls as output expands. (7)

economies of scope: the situation in which it is less expensive to produce goods jointly than separately. (7)

efficiency in production: a situation in which the principal's and agent's combined value (profits, payoffs), π, is maximized. (20)

efficiency in risk bearing: a situation in which risk sharing is optimal in that the person who least minds facing risk— the risk-neutral or less risk-averse person— bears more of the risk. (20)

efficiency wage: an unusually high wage that a firm pays workers as an incentive to avoid shirking. (20)

efficient contract: an agreement in which neither party can be made better off without harming the other party. (20)

efficient production (*technological efficiency*): the situation in which the current level of output cannot be produced with fewer inputs, given existing knowledge about technology and the organization of production. (6)

elasticity: the percentage change in a variable in response to a given percentage change in another variable. (3)

elasticity of demand (or *price elasticity of demand*, ε): the percentage change in the *quantity demanded* in response to a given percentage change in the price. (3)

elasticity of supply (or *price elasticity of supply*, η): the percentage change in the *quantity supplied* in response to a given percentage change in the price. (3)

endowment: an initial allocation of goods. (10)

endowment effect: people place a higher value on a good if they own it than they do if they are considering buying it. (4)

Engel curve: the relationship between the quantity demanded of a single good and income, holding prices constant. (5)

equilibrium: a situation in which no one wants to change his or her behavior. (2)

equivalent variation (*EV*): the amount of money one would have to take from a consumer to harm the consumer by as much as the price increase. (5)

excess demand: the amount by which the *quantity demanded* exceeds the *quantity supplied* at a specified price. (2)

excess supply: the amount by which the *quantity supplied* is greater than the *quantity demanded* at a specified price. (2)

exclusion: others can be prevented from consuming a good. (18)

exhaustible resources: nonrenewable natural assets that cannot be increased, only depleted. (16)

expansion path: the cost-minimizing combination of labor and capital for each output level. (7)

extensive form (of a game): specifies the n players, the sequence in which they make their moves, the actions they can take at each move, the information that each player has about players' previous moves, and the payoff function over all possible strategies. (14)

externality: the direct effect of the actions of a person or firm on another person's well-being or a firm's production capability rather than an indirect effect through changes in prices. (18)

fair bet: a wager with an expected value of zero. (17)

fair insurance: a bet between an insurer and a policyholder in which the value of the bet to the policyholder is zero. (17)

firm: an organization that converts inputs such as labor, materials, energy, and capital into outputs, the goods and services that it sells. (6)

fixed cost (*F*): a production expense that does not vary with output. (7)

fixed input: a factor of production that cannot be varied practically in the short run. (6)

flow: a quantity or value that is measured per unit of time. (16)

free riding: benefiting from the actions of others without paying. (18)

game: any competition between players (firms) in which strategic behavior plays a major role. (14)

game theory: a set of tools that economists, political scientists, military analysts, and others use to analyze decision making by players who use strategies. (14)

general-equilibrium analysis: the study of how equilibrium is determined in all markets simultaneously. (10)

Giffen good: a commodity for which a decrease in its price causes the quantity demanded to fall. (5)

good: a commodity for which more is preferred to less, at least at some levels of consumption. (4)

group price discrimination (*third-degree price discrimination*): a situation in which a firm charges different groups of customers different prices but charges a given customer the same price for every unit of output sold. (12)

hidden action: an act by one party to a transaction that is not observed by the other party. (19)

hidden characteristic: an attribute of a person or thing that is known to one party but unknown to others. (19)

incidence of a tax on consumers: the share of the tax that falls on consumers. (3)

income effect: the change in the quantity of a good a consumer demands because of a change in income, holding prices constant. (5)

income elasticity of demand (or *income elasticity*): the percentage change in the *quantity demanded* in response to a given percentage change in income. (3)

increasing returns to scale (*IRS*): property of a production function whereby output rises more than in proportion to an equal increase in all inputs. (6)

indifference curve: the set of all bundles of goods that a consumer views as being equally desirable. (4)

indifference map (or *preference map*): a complete set of indifference curves that summarize a consumer's tastes or preferences. (4)

inferior good: a commodity of which less is demanded as income rises. (5)

interest rate: the percentage more that must be repaid to borrow money for a fixed period of time. (16)

internal rate of return (*irr*): the discount rate that results in a net present value of an investment of zero. (16)

internalize the externality: to bear the cost of the harm that one inflicts on others (or to capture the benefit that one provides to others). (18)

isocost line: all the combinations of inputs that require the same (*iso*) total expenditure (*cost*). (7)

isoquant: a curve that shows the efficient combinations of labor and capital that can produce a single (*iso*) level of output (*quant*ity). (6)

Law of Demand: consumers demand more of a good the lower its price, holding constant tastes, the prices of other goods, and other factors that influence consumption. (2)

learning by doing: the productive skills and knowledge that workers and managers gain from experience. (7)

learning curve: the relationship between average costs and cumulative output. (7)

Lerner Index: the ratio of the difference between price and marginal cost to the price: $(p - MC)/p$. (11)

limit pricing: a price (or, equivalently, an output level) that a firm sets its price so that another firm cannot enter the market profitably. (14)

limited liability: the condition whereby the personal assets of the owners of the corporation cannot be taken to pay a corporation's debts if it goes into bankruptcy. (6)

long run: a lengthy enough period of time that all inputs can be varied. (6)

marginal cost (*MC*): the amount by which a firm's cost changes if the firm produces one more unit of output. (7)

marginal product of labor (*MP_L*): the change in total output, Δq, resulting from using an extra unit of labor, ΔL, holding other factors constant: $MP_L = \Delta q/\Delta L$. (6)

marginal profit: the change in profit a firm gets from selling one more unit of output. (8)

marginal rate of substitution (*MRS*): the maximum amount of one good a consumer will sacrifice to obtain one more unit of another good. (4)

marginal rate of technical substitution (*MRTS*): the number of extra units of one input needed to replace one unit of another input that enables a firm to keep the amount of output it produces constant. (6)

marginal rate of transformation (*MRT*): the trade-off the market imposes on the consumer in terms of the amount of one good the consumer must give up to obtain more of the other good. (4)

marginal revenue (*MR*): the change in revenue a firm gets from selling one more unit of output. (8)

marginal revenue product of labor (*MRP_L*): the extra revenue from hiring one more worker. (15)

marginal utility: the extra utility that a consumer gets from consuming the last unit of a good. (4)

market: an exchange mechanism that allows buyers to trade with sellers. (1)

market failure: inefficient production or consumption, often because a price exceeds marginal cost. (9)

market power: the ability of a firm to charge a price above marginal cost and earn a positive profit. (11)

market structure: the number of firms in the market, the ease with which firms can enter and leave the market, and the ability of firms to differentiate their products from those of their rivals. (8)

microeconomics: the study of how individuals and firms make themselves as well off as possible in a world of scarcity and the consequences of those individual decisions for markets and the entire economy. (1)

minimum efficient scale (*full capacity*): the smallest quantity at which the average cost curve reaches its minimum. (13)

mixed strategy: a firm (player) chooses among possible actions according to probabilities it assigns. (14)

model: a description of the relationship between two or more economic variables. (1)

monopolistic competition: a market structure in which firms have market power but no additional firm can enter and earn positive profits. (13)

monopoly: the only supplier of a good that has no close substitute. (11)

monopsony: the only buyer of a good in a given market. (15)

moral hazard: an informed party takes an action that the other party cannot observe and that harms the less-informed party. (19)

Nash equilibrium: a set of strategies such that, if all other players use these strategies, no player can obtain a higher payoff by choosing a different strategy. (14)

Nash-Bertrand equilibrium (*Bertrand equilibrium or Nash-in-prices equilibrium*): a set of prices such that no firm can obtain a higher profit by choosing a different price if the other firms continue to charge these prices. (13)

Nash-Cournot equilibrium (*Cournot equilibrium or Nash-in-quantities equilibrium*): a set of quantities sold by firms such that, holding the quantities of all other firms constant, no firm can obtain a higher profit by choosing a different quantity. (13)

natural monopoly: the situation in which one firm can produce the total output of the market at lower cost than several firms could. (11)

network externality: the situation where one person's demand for a good depends on the consumption of the good by others. (11)

nonlinear price discrimination (*second-degree price discrimination*): the situation in which a firm charges a different price for large quantities than for small quantities, so that the price paid varies according to the quantity purchased. (12)

nonuniform pricing: charging consumers different prices for the same product or charging a customer a price that depends on the number of units the customer buys. (12)

normal form (of a game): a representation of a static game with complete information that specifies the players in the game, their possible strategies, and the payoff function that identifies the players' payoffs for each combination of strategies. (14)

normal good: a commodity of which as much or more is demanded as income rises. (5)

normative statement: a conclusion as to whether something is good or bad. (1)

oligopoly: a small group of firms in a market with substantial barriers to entry. (13)

open-access common property: a resource that is nonexclusive and rival. (18)

opportunistic behavior: one party takes economic advantage of another when circumstances permit. (19)

opportunity cost (*economic cost*): the value of the best alternative use of a resource. (7)

opportunity set: all the bundles a consumer can buy, including all the bundles inside the budget constraint and on the budget constraint. (4)

Pareto efficient: describing an allocation of goods or services such that any reallocation harms at least one person. (10)

partial-equilibrium analysis: an examination of equilibrium and changes in equilibrium in one market in isolation. (10)

patent: an exclusive right granted to the inventor to sell a new and useful product, process, substance, or design for a fixed period of time. (11)

payoffs (of a game): players' valuations of the outcome of the game, such as profits for firms or utilities for individuals. (14)

perfect complements: goods that a consumer is interested in consuming only in fixed proportions. (4)

perfect price discrimination (*first-degree price discrimination*): the situation in which a firm sells each unit at the maximum amount any customer is willing to pay for it, so prices differ across customers and a given customer may pay more for some units than for others. (12)

perfect substitutes: goods that a consumer is completely indifferent as to which to consume. (4)

pooling equilibrium: an equilibrium in which dissimilar people are treated (paid) alike or behave alike. (19)

positive statement: a testable hypothesis about cause and effect. (1)

price discrimination: practice in which a firm charges consumers different prices for the same good based on individual characteristics of consumers, membership in an identifiable subgroup of consumers, or on the quantity purchased by the consumers. (12)

price elasticity of demand (or *elasticity of demand*, ε): the percentage change in the *quantity demanded* in response to a given percentage change in the price. (3)

price elasticity of supply (or *elasticity of supply*, η): the percentage change in the *quantity supplied* in response to a given percentage change in the price. (3)

prisoners' dilemma: a game in which all players have dominant strategies that result in profits (or other payoffs) that are inferior to what they could achieve if they used cooperative strategies. (14)

private cost: the cost of production only, not including *externalities*. (18)

producer surplus (*PS*): the difference between the amount for which a good sells and the minimum amount necessary for the seller to be willing to produce the good. (9)

production function: the relationship between the quantities of inputs used and the maximum quantity of output that can be produced, given current knowledge about technology and organization. (6)

production possibility frontier: the maximum amount of outputs that can be produced from a fixed amount of input. (7)

profit (π): the difference between revenues, R, and costs, C: $\pi = R - C$. (6)

property right: the exclusive privilege to use an asset. (18)

public good: a good that is nonrival and nonexclusive. (18)

pure strategy: each player chooses an action with certainty. (14)

quantity demanded: the amount of a good that consumers are willing to buy at a given price, holding constant the other factors that influence purchases. (2)

quantity supplied: the amount of a good that firms *want* to sell at a given price, holding constant other factors that influence firms' supply decisions, such as costs and government actions. (2)

quota: the limit that a government sets on the quantity of a foreign-produced good that may be imported. (2)

rent: a payment to the owner of an input beyond the minimum necessary for the factor to be supplied. (9)

rent seeking: efforts and expenditures to gain a rent or a profit from government actions. (9)

requirement tie-in sale: a tie-in sale in which customers who buy one product from a firm are required to make all their purchases of another product from that firm. (12)

reservation price: the maximum amount a person would be willing to pay for a unit of output. (12)

residual demand curve: the market demand that is not met by other sellers at any given price. (8)

residual supply curve: the quantity that the market supplies that is not consumed by other demanders at any given price. (8)

risk: the situation in which the likelihood of each possible outcome is known or can be estimated and no single possible outcome is certain to occur. (17)

risk averse: unwilling to make a fair bet. (17)

risk neutral: indifferent about making a fair bet. (17)

risk preferring: willing to make a fair bet. (17)

risk premium: the amount that a risk-averse person would pay to avoid taking a risk. (17)

rival good: a good that is used up as it is consumed. (18)

rules of the game: regulations that determine the timing of players' moves and the actions that players can make at each move. (14)

screening: an action taken by an uninformed person to determine the information possessed by informed people. (19)

separating equilibrium: an equilibrium in which one type of people takes actions (such as sending a *signal*) that allows them to be differentiated from other types of people. (19)

shirking: a *moral hazard* in which agents do not provide all the services they are paid to provide. (20)

short run: a period of time so brief that at least one factor of production cannot be varied practically. (6)

shortage: a persistent excess demand. (2)

signaling: an action taken by an informed person to send information to an uninformed person. (19)

snob effect: the situation in which a person places greater value on a good as fewer and fewer other people possess it. (11)

social cost: the private cost plus the cost of the harms from *externalities*. (18)

standard: a metric or scale for evaluating the quality of a particular product. (19)

static game: a game in which each player acts only once and the players act simultaneously (or, at least, each player acts without knowing rivals' actions). (14)

stock: a quantity or value that is measured independently of time. (16)

strategy: a battle plan that specifies the action that a player will make conditional on the information available at each move and for any possible contingency. (14)

subgame: all the subsequent decisions that players may make given the actions already taken and corresponding payoffs. (14)

subgame perfect Nash equilibrium: players' strategies are a Nash equilibrium in every subgame. (14)

substitution effect: the change in the quantity of a good that a consumer demands when the good's price changes, holding other prices and the consumer's *utility* constant. (5)

sunk cost: a past expenditure that cannot be recovered. (7)

supply curve: the *quantity supplied* at each possible price, holding constant the other factors that influence firms' supply decisions. (2)

tariff (*duty*): a tax on only imported goods. (9)

technical progress: an advance in knowledge that allows more output to be produced with the same level of inputs. (6)

tie-in sale: a type of nonlinear pricing in which customers can buy one product only if they agree to buy another product as well. (12)

total cost (*C*): the sum of a firm's variable cost and fixed cost: $C = VC + F$. (7)

transaction costs: the expenses of finding a trading partner and making a trade for a good or service beyond the price paid for that good or service. (2)

two-part pricing: a pricing system in which the firm charges each consumer a lump-sum access fee for the right to buy as many units of the good as the consumer wants at a per-unit price. (12)

uniform pricing: charging the same price for every unit sold of a particular good. (12)

utility: a set of numerical values that reflect the relative rankings of various bundles of goods. (4)

utility function: the relationship between *utility* values and every possible bundle of goods. (4)

variable cost (*VC*): a production expense that changes with the quantity of output produced. (7)

variable input: a factor of production whose quantity can be changed readily by the firm during the relevant time period. (6)

winner's curse: auction winner's bid exceeds an item's common-value. (14)

Index

Credits

Symbols Used in This Book

α [alpha] = *ad valorem* tax (or tariff) rate, or an exponent in a Cobb-Douglass production function

Δ [capital delta] = change in the following variable (for example, the change in p between Periods 1 and 2 is $\Delta p = p_2 - p_1$, where p_2 is the value of p in Period 2 and p_1 is the value in Period 1)

ε [epsilon] = the price elasticity of demand

η [eta] = the price elasticity of supply

$\mathscr{L}$ = lump-sum tax

π [pi] = profit = revenue − total cost = $R - C$

ρ [rho] = profit tax rate

σ [sigma] = standard deviation

θ [theta] = probability or share

ω [omega] = share

ξ [xi] = the income elasticity of demand

Abbreviations, Variables, and Function Names

AFC = average fixed cost = fixed cost divided by output = F/q

AVC = average variable cost = variable cost divided by output = VC/q

AC = average cost = total cost divided by output = C/q

AP_Z = average product of input Z (for example, AP_L is the average product of labor)

C = total cost = variable cost + fixed cost = $VC + F$

CRS = constant returns to scale

CS = consumer surplus

CV = compensating variation

D = market demand curve

D_r = residual demand curve

DRS = decreasing returns to scale

DWL = deadweight loss

F = fixed cost

i = interest rate

I = indifference curve

IRS = increasing returns to scale

K = capital

L = labor

LR = long run

m = constant marginal cost

M = materials

MC = marginal cost = $\Delta C/\Delta q$

MP_Z = marginal (physical) product of input Z (for example, MP_L is the marginal product of labor)

MR = marginal revenue = $\Delta R/\Delta q$

MRS = marginal rate of substitution

$MRTS$ = marginal rate of technical substitution

MU_Z = marginal utility of good Z

n = number of firms in an industry

p = price

PPF = production possibility frontier

PS = producer surplus = revenues − variable costs = $R - VC$

Q = market (or monopoly) output

$\bar{Q}$ = output quota

q = firm output

R = revenue = pq

r = price of capital services

s = per-unit subsidy

S = market supply curve

S_o = supply curve of all the other firms in the market

SC = a market of economies of scope

SR = short run

t = specific or unit tax (or tariff)

T = tax revenue (αpQ, τQ, $\rho\pi$)

U = utility

VC = variable cost

w = wage

W = welfare

Y = income or budget

Featured Applications in This Book